OSBORNE
16-Bit
Microprocessor
Handbook

Adam Osborne
Gerry Kane

OSBORNE/McGraw-Hill
Berkeley, California

This book may be used to update the
Osborne 4 & 8-Bit Microprocessor Handbook
(formerly An Introduction to Microcomputers:
Volume 2 — Some Real Microprocessors)
or as a stand alone reference.

Published by
OSBORNE/McGraw-Hill
630 Bancroft Way
Berkeley, California 94710
U. S. A.

For information on translations and book distributors
outside of the U. S. A. , please write
OSBORNE/McGraw-Hill at the above address.

3456789   DODO   898765432
ISBN 0-931988-43-8
Cover design by Marc Miyashiro.

Contributing Authors

The following persons have contributed
to the writing of sections of this book
in addition to its principal authors.

Bob Abramovitz
Janice K. Enger
Curtis A. Ingraham
Susanna Jacobson
Patrick L. McGuire

Contents

1. **The National Semiconductor PACE and INS8900   1-1**
   PACE and INS8900 Microcomputer System Overviews   1-2
   INS8900 and PACE Timing and Instruction Execution   1-11
   The INS8900 and PACE Instruction Set   1-11
   The PACE DP8302 System Timing Element (STE)   1-35
   The PACE Bidirectional Transceiver Element (BTE)   1-36
   Using Other Microcomputer Support Devices with the PACE and INS8900   1-38
   Data Sheets   1-D1

2. **The General Instrument CP1600   2-1**
   CP1600 Instruction Timing and Execution   2-10
   The CP1600 Instruction Set   2-16
   Support Devices that may be used with the CP1600   2-27
   The CP1680 Input/Output Buffer (IOB)   2-30
   Data Sheets   2-D1

3. **The Texas Instruments TMS 9900, TMS 9980, and TMS 9440 Products   3-1**
   The TMS 9900 Microprocessor   3-2
   TMS 9900 Timing and Instruction Execution   3-15
   The TMS 9900 Instruction Set   3-35
   The TMS 9980A and the TMS 9981 Microprocessors   3-44
   The TMS 9940 Single-Chip Microcomputers   3-52
   The TIM 9904 Four-Phase Clock Generator/Driver   3-67
   The TMS 9901 Programmable System Interface (PSI)   3-70
   The TMS 9902 Asynchronous Communications Controller   3-82
   The TMS 9903 Synchronous Communications Controller   3-95
   Data Sheets   3-D1

4. **Single Chip Nova Minicomputer Central Processing Units   4-1**
   A Product Overview   4-2
   CPU Logic and Instruction Execution   4-18
   9440 Timing and Instruction Execution   4-24
   The MicroNova and 9440 Instruction Sets   4-35
   9440-Nova Bus Interface   4-77
   Data Sheets   4-D1

5. **The Intel 8086   5-1**
   The 8086 CPU   5-4
   8086 Timing and Instruction Execution   5-30
   The 8086 Instruction Set   5-47
   The 8088 CPU   5-87
   The Intel 8284 Clock Generator/Driver   5-91
   The Intel 8288 Bus Controller   5-98
   The 8282/8283 8-Bit Input/Output Latch   5-102
   The 8286/8287 8-Bit Bidirectional Bus Transceivers   5-104
   Some 8086 Microprocessor Bus Configurations   5-105
   Data Sheets   5-D1

6. **The Zilog Z8000 Series   6-1**
   The Z8001 and Z8002 CPUs   6-3
   Z8001 and Z8002 Timing and Instruction Execution   6-23
   The Z8000 Instruction Set   6-36
   Data Sheets   6-D1

7. The Motorola MC68000   7-1
MC68000 Pins and Signals   7-9
The MC68000 Instruction Set   7-38
Interfacing the MC68000 with 6800 Peripherals   7-44
Data Sheets   7-D1

8. 2900 Series Chip Slice Products   8-1
The 2901, 2901A, and 2901B Microprocessor Slice   8-2
The 2903 Microprocessor Slice   8-40
The 2902 Carry Look-Ahead Device   8-87
The 2909 and 2911 Microprogram Sequencers   8-92
The 2910 Microprogram Sequencer   8-110
The 2930 and 2932 Program Control Units   22-125
Data Sheets   8-D1

INTRODUCTION

This is one of two books that replace *An Introduction to Microcomputers: Volume 2 — Some Real Microprocessors*. That volume went through several printings and in 1978 was printed loose-leaf. Six bimonthly updates to the loose-leaf version were published in 1979 and early 1980 to provide information on newly introduced microcomputer devices. The loose-leaf version proved, however, to be quite unpopular with bookstores because of packaging and handling considerations. It also became more and more difficult to maintain a timely flow of the bimonthly updates. For these reasons, *Volume 2* is being replaced by two bound paperback books: the *Osborne 4 & 8-Bit Microprocessor Handbook* and the *Osborne 16-Bit Microprocessor Handbook*. Together these handbooks include all of the information that was contained in *Volume 2* and the six updates. All known errors have been corrected and new data sheets have been added to the two handbooks. We have divided *Volume 2* into two separate handbooks because the single-volume version would be over 1800 pages in length and rather difficult to bind. In addition, the devices lend themselves to this grouping since the 16-bit microprocessors are generally much more powerful than the four- and eight-bit microprocessors, and thus are directed toward different applications.

Volume 2 was part of a four-volume *Introduction to Microcomputers* series:

- *Volume 0 — The Beginner's Book* was written for readers who know nothing about computers.
- *Volume 1 — Basic Concepts* provides a detailed explanation of microprocessor concepts including number systems, addressing modes, typical instruction sets, input/output techniques, and so on. The device descriptions in the 4 & 8-Bit Microprocessor Handbook and the 16-Bit Microprocessor Handbook assume that you have a working knowledge of the general concepts presented in *Volume 1*, and we will occasionally make references to material presented in *Volume 1*.
- *Volume 2 — Some Real Microprocessors*, which is being replaced by these handbooks.
- *Volume 3 — Some Real Support Devices*, which describes general support devices that may be used with any microprocessor. Some dedicated support devices are the *4 & 8-Bit Microprocessor Handbook* and the *16-Bit Microprocessor Handbook*. We define a "dedicated" support device as one best used with its parent microprocessor. We define a "general" support device as one that can be used with any microprocessor. We will occasionally make reference in this book to some of the general support devices in *Volume 3*. When designing a system based on one of the microprocessors described in this handbook, you should not automatically assume that the dedicated support devices described in this book are the only ones or the best ones to use with a particular microprocessor: you should always check the functionally equivalent parts described in *Volume 3*.

In addition to this *Introduction to Microcomputers* series, we have begun publishing other individual handbooks. The first two handbooks of this series are: *The 8089 I/O Processor Handbook*, which includes the 8289 bus arbiter, and the *CRT Controller Handbook*, which describes five LSI CRT controller devices. This individual handbook approach will be used in the future to maintain a convenient flow of detailed, objective information on new microprocessors and related support devices.

SIGNAL CONVENTIONS

Signals may be active high, active low or active in two states. An active high signal is one which, in the high state, causes events to occur, while in the low state has no significance. A signal that is active low causes events to occur when in the low state, but has no significance in the high state. A signal that has two active states will cause two different types of events to occur, depending upon whether the signal is high or low; this signal has no inactive state. Within this book a signal that is active low has a bar placed over the signal name. For example, WR identifies a "write strobe" signal which is pulsed low when data is ready for external logic to receive. A signal that is active high or has two active states has no bar over the signal name.

TIMING DIAGRAM CONVENTIONS

Timing diagrams play an important part in the description of any microprocessor or support device. Timing diagrams are therefore used extensively in this book. All timing diagrams observe the following conventions:

1) A low signal level is equivalent to no voltage. A high signal level is equivalent to voltage present:

2) A single signal making a low-to-high transition like this:

3) A single signal making a high-to-low transition is illustrated like this:

4) When using two or more parallel signals exist, the notation:

states that one or more of the parallel signals change level, but the transition (high-to low or low-to-high) is unspecified).

5) A three-state single signal is shown floating thus:

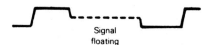

6) A three-state bus containing two or more signals is shown floating thus:

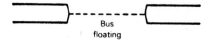

7) When one signal condition triggers other signal changes, an arrow indicates the relationship as follows:

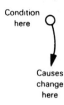

Thus a signal making a low-to-high transition would be illustrated triggering another signal making a high-to-low transition as follows:

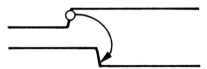

A signal making a high-to-low transition triggering a bus change of state would be illustrated as follows:

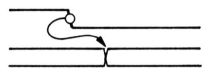

8) When two or more conditions must exist in order to trigger another logic event, the following illustration is used:

These conditions

cause
change
here

Thus a low-to-high transition of one signal occurring while another signal is low would be illustrated triggering a third event as follows:

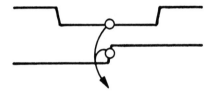

9) When a single triggering condition causes two or more events to occur, the following illustration is used:

This condition

causes
these
changes

Thus a low-to-high transition of one signal triggering changes in two other signal levels would be illustrated as follows:

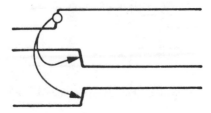

10) All signal level changes are shown as square waves. Thus rise and fall times are ignored. These times are given in the data sheets which appear at the end of every chapter.

INSTRUCTION SET CONVENTIONS

Every microcomputer instruction set is described with two tables. One table identifies the operations which occur when the instruction set is executed, while the second table defines object codes and instruction times.

Because of the wide differences that exist between one instruction set and another, we have elected not to use a single set of codes and symbols to describe the operations for all instructions in all instruction sets. We believe any type of universal convention is like to confuse rather than clarify; therefore each instruction set table is preceded by a list of symbols as used within the table alone.

A short benchmark program is given to illustrate each instruction set. Some comments regarding benchmark programs in general are, however, in order. We are not attempting to highlight strengths or weaknesses of different devices, nor does this book make any attempt to comparative analyses, since the criteria which make one microcomputer better than another are simply too dependent on the application.

Consider an application which requires relatively high speed processing. The only important criterion will be program execution speed, which may limit the choice to just one of the microcomputers we are describing.

> **COMPARATIVE ANALYSIS**

Execution speeds of all of the microcomputers may, on the other hand, be quite adequate for a second application; in this case, price may be the only overriding factor. In a third application, a manufacturer may have already invested in a great deal of engineering development expense, using one particular microcomputer that was available in quantity earlier than any others; the advantages or disadvantages of using a different microcomputer, based on minor cost of performance advantages, will likely be overwhelmed by the extra expense and time delays involved with switching in midstream.

And what about benchmark programs?

> **BENCHMARK PROGRAMS**

There have been a number of benchmark programs in the literature, purporting to show the strengths or weaknesses of one microcomputer versus another; individual manufacturers have added to the confusion by putting out their own competing benchmarks, aimed at showing their product to be superior to an immediate rival.

Benchmark programs are misleading, irrelevant and worthless for these reasons:

1) **In a majority of microcomputer applications, program execution speed, and minor variations in program length, are simply overwhelmed by pricing considerations.**

2) **Even assuming that for some specific application, program length and execution speed are important, trivial changes in the benchmark program definition can profoundly alter the results that are obtained. This is one point we will demonstrate in this book, while describing individual instruction sets.**

3) **Benchmark programs are invariable written by the smartest programmers in an organization, and they take an enormous amount of time to ensure programming accuracy and excellence. This is not the level at which any user should anticipate "run of the mill" programmers working; indeed, a far more realistic evaluation of a microcomputer's instruction set could be generated by giving an average programmer too little time in which to implement an incompletely defined benchmark. This will more closely approximate the working conditions under which real products are developed. Of course, defining the "average programmer," "too little time" and an "incomplete specification" are all sufficiently subjective that they defy resolution.**

We will demonstrate the capriciousness of benchmark programs via the following benchmark program:

Raw data has been input to a general purpose input buffer, beginning at IOBUF. This raw data is to be moved to a permanent table, which may be partially filled; the raw data is to be stored in the data table starting with the first unfilled byte. The benchmark may be illustrated as follows:

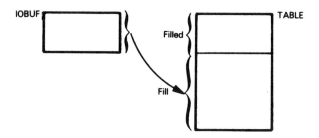

HOW THIS BOOK HAS BEEN PRINTED

Notice that text in this book has been printed in boldface type and lightface type. This has been done to help you skip those parts of the book that cover subject matter with which you are familiar. You can be sure that lightface type only expands on information presented in the previous boldface type. Therefore, only read boldface type until you reach a subject about which you want to know more, at which point start reading the lightface type.

Chapter 1
THE NATIONAL SEMICONDUCTOR
PACE AND INS8900

PACE was developed by National Semiconductor as a single-chip implementation of its multi-chip IMP-16. Since it was the first 16-bit, single-chip microprocessor, PACE is the first 16-bit microprocessor described in this book.

As might be expected of an early entry product, **PACE had a number of problems — both in design and fabrication technology** — which limited its acceptance. Therefore the INS8900 was recently introduced by National Semiconductor. **The INS8900 is a redesigned, NMOS PACE, with internal logic problems resolved.**

In this chapter we will describe both PACE and the INS8900. Specifically, we will identify the problems faced by a PACE user, which have been eliminated in the INS8900.

PACE and the INS8900 are 16-bit microprocessors because they handle data in 16-bit units. In many ways, however, the internal architecture of PACE and the INS8900 have an 8-bit orientation; this is something you should keep in mind while reading this chapter, because it does result in PACE and the INS8900 having program execution speeds that are comparable to, rather than being significantly faster than, the 8-bit microprocessors we have described in earlier chapters.

The only current manufacturer for PACE and the INS8900 is:

NATIONAL SEMICONDUCTOR, INC.
2900 Semiconductor Drive
Santa Clara, CA 95050

There are agreements between Rockwell International and National Semiconductor and between Signetics and National Semiconductor to exchange microcomputer technical information and to produce each other's products. At the present time, neither Signetics nor Rockwell International has elected to second source PACE or the INS8900, and it is extremely unlikely that they will since both PACE and the INS8900 are products with limited futures. The amount of support that National Semiconductor provides is rapidly declining as newer, more powerful 16-bit microprocessors enter the marketplace.

As shown in Figure 1-1, a typical PACE microcomputer will consist of a mixture of special-purpose PACE support devices and standard devices. The PACE microcomputer devices described in this chapter consist of:

- **The PACE CPU**
- **The System Timing Element (STE), which generates clock signals for PACE and the system.**
- **The Bidirectional Transceiver Element (BTE), which converts the MOS-level PACE signals to TTL-level signals for other devices. The BTE is 8 bits wide.**

The INS8900 needs a clock generator; a 2 MHz crystal and a 74C04 inverter are recommended. Otherwise, there are no special INS8900 support devices; in fact, **you can easily use any NMOS support devices described in Volume 3 with the INS8900.** Specifically, the STE and BTE devices cannot be used with the INS8900, because they provide MOS-to-TTL signal level conversions for PACE.

PACE requires +5V, +8V and -12V power supplies. The +8V is a substrate voltage requirement of the CPU and can be derived from the +5V power using a few discrete components. Therefore, a system can be implemented using only two primary power supplies: +5V and -12V. The INS8900 also uses three power supplies: +12V, +5V and -8V.

PACE/INS8900 POWER SUPPLY
EXECUTION SPEED

The INS8900 uses a 500 nanosecond clock to provide typical instruction execution times in the range of 8 to 20 microseconds. PACE (IPC-16A/520D) uses a 750 nanosecond clock to provide typical instruction execution times in the range of 12 to 30 microseconds.

Before making direct comparisons of these instruction execution times with those of other devices, however, note carefully that because of the 16-bit architecture of PACE and the INS8900, it may take many instructions on another microcomputer to perform the same operations as a single INS8900/PACE instruction.

MOS level signals are input and output by PACE. TTL level signals are input and output by the INS8900.

PACE/INS8900 LOGIC LEVEL

P-channel silicon gate, MOS/LSI technology is used with PACE. N-channel MOS technology is used by the INS8900.

PACE AND INS8900 MICROCOMPUTER SYSTEM OVERVIEWS

Figure 1-1 conceptually illustrates a PACE system. Figure 1-2 conceptually illustrates an INS8900 system.

As with any mini- or microcomputer system, the CPU outputs data, address, and control signals. In the case of PACE and the INS8900, the data and address signals use the same bus lines; therefore, they are said to be multiplexed.

Timing signals needed by PACE are generated by the System Timing Element (STE). PACE signals are all MOS level; the STE therefore generates two sets of timing signals; one set are MOS level for PACE, the other set are TTL level for external logic.

SYSTEM TIMING ELEMENT (STE)

Since PACE signals are MOS level, Bidirectional Transceiver Elements (BTEs) must be present to translate outgoing signals from MOS to TTL levels, and to translate incoming signals from TTL to MOS levels. BTEs are quite indiscriminating in the signals they translate; in either direction, any signal arriving at an input pin is faithfully reproduced at the corresponding output pin. Control signal options allow a BTE to operate bidirectionally, to drive output signals only, or to place both the MOS and TTL outputs in a high-impedance mode. Since the BTE is 8 bits wide, two BTEs operating bidirectionally provide buffering for the 16-bit Address/Data Bus. A third BTE, operating in the drive-only mode, provides buffering for the PACE control signals (NADS, ODS, IDS, and Flags).

BIDIRECTIONAL TRANSCEIVER ELEMENT (BTE)

A complete TTL level bus is created by combining BTE outputs with the TTL level timing signals output by the STE. Remember, though, that the 16 address/data lines are multiplexed. External logic that can demultiplex these lines and that can respond to the PACE timing and control signal logic can connect directly to the TTL level address/data lines. For example, National Semiconductor provides ROM and RAM devices with on-chip address latches; these devices can interface directly to the TTL level bus.

TTL LEVEL PACE BUS

If memory devices or I/O ports are used that cannot demultiplex the address/data lines, you must provide separate logic to perform this function. No special PACE family devices are available for this purpose; however, standard logic devices can be used. For example, two hex flip-flop devices and a quad flip-flop device would provide a latched 16-bit Address Bus. Two 8212 I/O ports could also be used to latch the 16 bits of address information. The PACE Address Data Strobe (NADS) signal can be used as the CLK input to the flip-flops or as the STB input to the 8212s. The PACE Address Data Strobe (NADS) signal can be used as the CLK input to the flip-flops. In many systems this is the most effective approach since a latched Address Bus allows you to use simpler address decoding techniques to generate memory chip enable and I/O port select signals.

ADDRESS LATCHES AND DECODERS

Figure 1-2 illustrates an INS8900 microcomputer system. Logic is quite elementary — and equivalent to that which you would expect with any other microcomputer. Control Bus, Data Bus, and Address Bus lines are buffered using INS8208 bidirectional buffers. These are National Semiconductor standard catalog devices, recommended by National Semiconductor and illustrated in their literature; however, any other buffer would do equally well. The Data/Address Bus is shown being demultiplexed by 8212s to create separate Data and Address Busses. This again is straightforward logic.

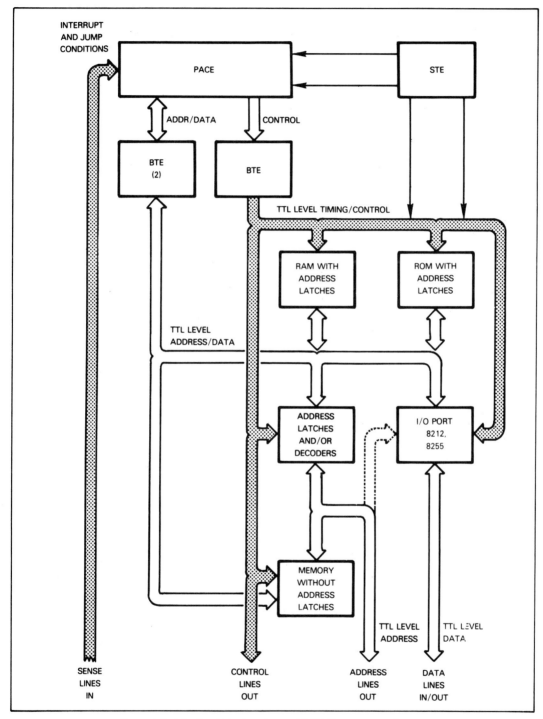

Figure 1-1. A National Semiconductor PACE Microcomputer System

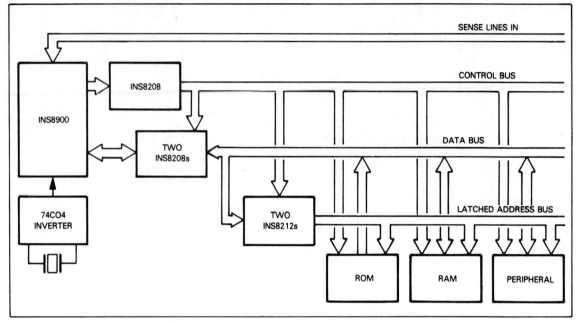

Figure 1-2. A National Semiconductor INS8900 Microcomputer System

INS8900 PROGRAMMABLE REGISTERS

The INS8900 (and PACE) has four 16-bit Accumulators and a 16-bit Program Counter; these registers may be illustrated as follows:

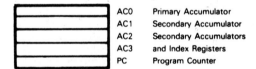

AC0	Primary Accumulator
AC1	Secondary Accumulator
AC2	Secondary Accumulators
AC3	and Index Registers
PC	Program Counter

Accumulator AC0 may be likened to a primary Accumulator as described for our hypothetical microcomputer in Volume 1.

Accumulator AC1 is a secondary Accumulator.

Accumulators AC2 and AC3 are equivalent to a combination of secondary Accumulators and Index registers.

Recall from Volume 1, Chapter 6 that an Index register differs from a Data Counter in that the Index register contents are added to a displacement (which is provided by a memory reference instruction) in order to determine the effective memory address.

The Program Counter serves the same function in an INS8900 system as it does in our hypothetical microcomputer described in Volume 1.

Figure 1-3 illustrates that part of our general microcomputer system logic which has been implemented in the INS8900 microprocessor.

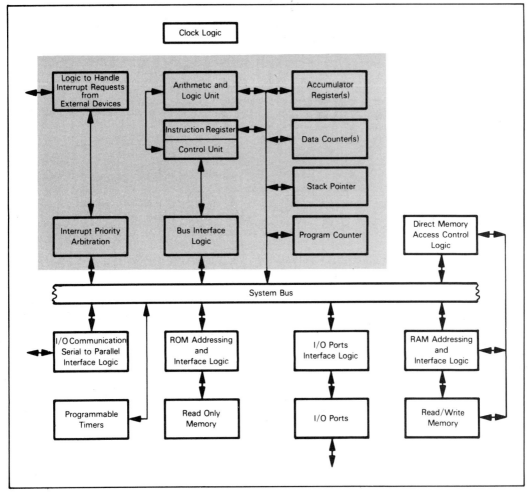

Figure 1-3. Logic of the INS8900 Microprocessor

INS8900 STACK

A Stack is provided on the INS8900 (and PACE) chip. The Stack is 16 bits wide and 10 words deep. The Stack is not a cascade stack, as described in Volume 1, Chapter 6; rather, chip logic maintains its own Stack Pointer to identify the next free Stack word. The Stack Pointer is automatically incremented and decremented in response to Push and Pull operations. Stack Push and Pull operations are initiated by CPU logic during execution of Jump-to-Subroutine (JSR) and Return-from-Subroutine (RTS) instructions, and during interrupt processing, to automatically save and restore the Program Counter.

In addition, **the Stack can be used for temporary storage of data or status information.** There are instructions which allow you to transfer words between the Stack and any Accumulator, or the Status and Control Flag register. This capability can significantly reduce the number of memory accesses required (thus increasing system speed) and can also reduce read/write memory requirements since intermediate values can be stored on the Stack.

Whenever the Stack becomes completely filled or emptied, an Interrupt Request is generated on the INS8900 chip. If you have enabled Stack Interrupts, program execution will be suspended, allowing you to deal with the situation. A Stack Full condition will indicate that it is time to dump data accumulated on the Stack out to read/write memory.

| INS8900 AND PACE STACK INTERRUPTS |

INS8900 AND PACE ADDRESSING MODES

Most INS8900 (and PACE) memory reference instructions use either direct or direct, indexed addressing. A few instructions also offer indirect addressing and pre-indexed, indirect addressing. Refer to Volume 1, Chapter 6 for a description of these addressing modes.

All memory reference instructions have the following object code format:

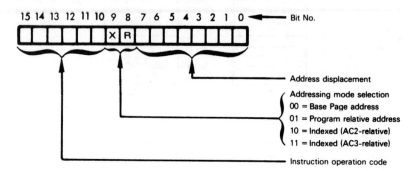

The 2-bit XR field lets you specify with each instruction the type of direct addressing you want used: base page, program relative or indexed (AC2- or AC3-relative). Since the address displacement is an 8-bit field in the instruction word, direct addresses are paged and each page consists of 256 words. Indexed and paged addressing variations have been described in Volume 1, Chapter 6.

In addition, **the INS8900 (and PACE) offers a variation of base page addressing, which is not described in Volume 1, Chapter 6. There is a control input signal (BPS) which allows the base page to be split between the top and bottom 128 words of memory,** as follows:

> **INS8900 AND PACE SPLIT BASE PAGE**

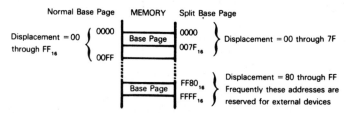

BPS high splits the base page; BPS low keeps the base page as the bottom 256 words of memory.

Depending on how an INS8900 system has been configured, the base page may be permanently defined as split or as normal; or the base page may be varied between the two options under program control. There are a number of output control flags (which are described next) that may be set or reset under program control. If one of these flags is connected to the base page select pin, then setting or resetting this flag determines which base page option will be in effect:

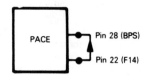

Splitting the base page between the top and bottom of memory is useful in an INS8900 microcomputer system because it simplifies external device addressing. If we reserve all memory addresses in the range $FF80_{16}$ - $FFFF_{16}$ for external devices, then external logic merely has to AND the top nine bits of an address and thus determine if an external device (rather than a memory location) is being addressed:

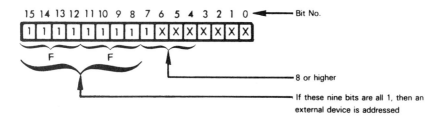

Splitting the base page also makes it easy to implement half of the base page in ROM, leaving the other half in RAM.

To a programmer, this scheme provides an easy way of generating 128 external device addresses. If the split base page option is in effect, then base page, direct addressing can be interpreted as external device addressing, so long as the high-order bit of the displacement is 1:

INS8900/PACE SPLIT BASE PAGE TO ADDRESS I/O

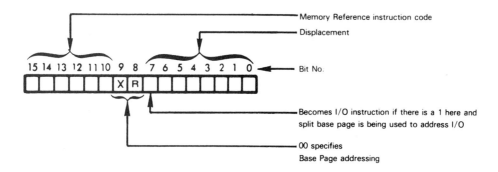

The base page and program relative options do not apply when the displacement is part of a direct, indexed address. **When indexed addressing is specified, the INS8900 adds the contents of the displacement, as a signed binary number, to the contents of the identified Index register (AC2 or AC3). The sum becomes the effective address.** Here are some examples:

INS8900/PACE DIRECT INDEXED ADDRESSING

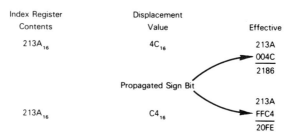

Observe that the high-order bit of the displacement, being a sign bit, is propagated through the missing high-order displacement byte.

Instructions that allow indirect addressing simply superimpose indirect addressing logic on the preceding direct address generation logic. For example, if indirect addressing without indexing is specified, then a base page or program relative direct, address will be computed in the normal way, but the effective address is contained in the memory location identified by the direct address.

This illustration shows base page, indirect addressing; arbitrary memory addresses are used to make the illustration easier to understand:

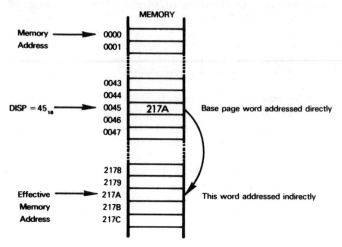

This illustration shows program relative, indirect addressing, again using arbitrary memory addresses:

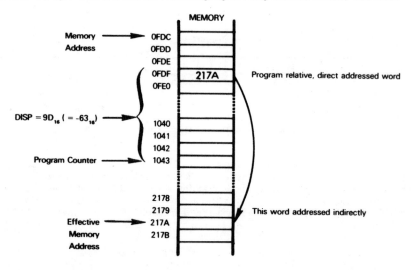

If indirect addressing with indexing is specified, then a direct address is first computed by adding the displacement, as a signed binary number, to the contents of the specified Index register; the direct indexed address thus computed provides the memory location where the indirect address will be found. This is illustrated as follows:

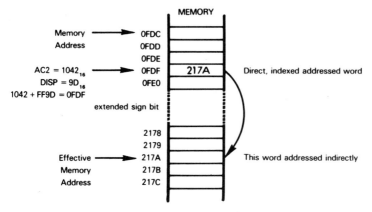

INS8900 AND PACE STATUS AND CONTROL FLAGS

The INS8900 has a 16-bit Status and Control Flag register. This register is on the CPU chip and is illustrated as follows:

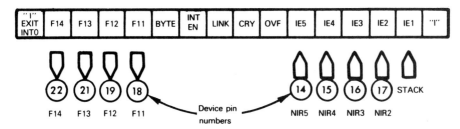

Fourteen of the 16 register bits are used. Three of the 14 bits are status flags as we define a status flag. These three flags are:

Overflow (OVF), which is a typical Overflow status.

Carry (CRY), which is set and reset by arithmetic operations, as described for a typical Carry status.

Link (LINK), which is set and reset by Shift and Rotate instructions, as described for the hypothetical microcomputer's Carry status in Volume 1, Chapter 7.

The separation of Carry into two statuses, one for shift and rotate operations, and the other for arithmetic operations, is a fairly common minicomputer feature; the advantage of separating these two statuses is that the results of arithmetic operations can be preserved across subsequent Shift and Rotate instructions.

BYTE causes data to be accessed in 8-bit lengths when this status is set to 1, or in 16-bit lengths when this status is set to 0.

Five bits (IE1 through IE5) are reserved for interrupt processing. These five bits selectively enable and disable five interrupt lines. One of these lines (IE1) is reserved for the Stack Overflow interrupt, the other four lines are available for external device interrupt requests. There is also a master interrupt enable and disable bit (INT EN).

Bits F11, F12, F13 and F14 are control flags which are output directly to INS8900 and PACE device pins; they can be used in any way to control external devices. One use, to select normal or split base page addressing, has already been described.

Only the three status flags OVF, CRY and LINK are automatically set or reset in the course of instruction execution. The remaining 11 bits of the Status and Control Flags register are set and reset by instructions or instruction sequences that read data into, or write data out of, the Status and Control Flags register.

INS8900 AND PACE CPU PINS AND SIGNALS

Pins and signals are illustrated in **Figure 1-4** for the INS8900 and PACE devices. **There are some small differences between the two sets of pin outs.** These differences are shaded in Figure 1-4. Within the shaded areas, the INS8900 signal is shown closest to the arrow. The PACE signal is shown in brackets further out. Here is a summary of pins that differ:

Pin Number	INS8900 Signal	PACE Signal
20	GND	V_{SS} (+5V)
23	V_{BB} (-8V)	V_{BB} (+8V)
24	CLKX	NCLK
25	V_{CC} (+5V)	CLK
29	V_{DD} (+12V)	V_{GG} (-12V)

The pin out differences between PACE and the INS8900 are not surprising. Since PACE uses P-channel MOS technology, while the INS8900 uses N-channel MOS technology, we would expect power supply differences. Also, the INS8900, being a newer product, requires just one clock signal input (CLKX), compared to the two required by PACE (CLK and NCLK).

Let us examine the pins and signals in detail.

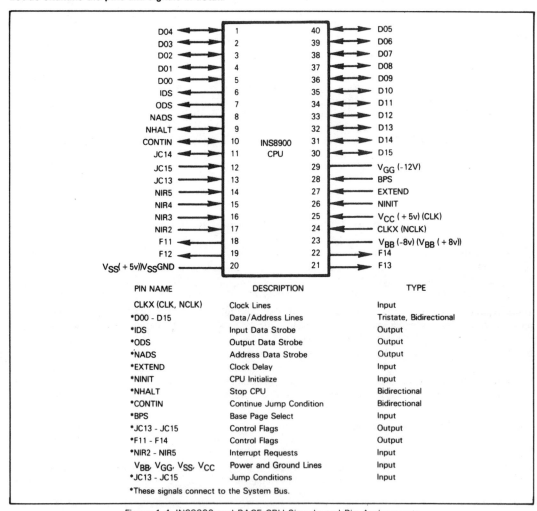

PIN NAME	DESCRIPTION	TYPE
CLKX (CLK, NCLK)	Clock Lines	Input
*D00 - D15	Data/Address Lines	Tristate, Bidirectional
*IDS	Input Data Strobe	Output
*ODS	Output Data Strobe	Output
*NADS	Address Data Strobe	Output
*EXTEND	Clock Delay	Input
*NINIT	CPU Initialize	Input
*NHALT	Stop CPU	Bidirectional
*CONTIN	Continue Jump Condition	Bidirectional
*BPS	Base Page Select	Input
*JC13 - JC15	Control Flags	Output
*F11 - F14	Control Flags	Output
*NIR2 - NIR5	Interrupt Requests	Input
V_{BB}, V_{GG}, V_{SS}, V_{CC}	Power and Ground Lines	Input
*JC13 - JC15	Jump Conditions	Input

*These signals connect to the System Bus.

Figure 1-4. INS8900 and PACE CPU Signals and Pin Assignments

1-10

There are 16 data and address lines (D0 - D15), which are multiplexed for data input, data output and address output. Two control lines, ODS and NADS, identify output on the data and address lines as either data (ODS) or addresses (NADS). A further control line, IDS, is used to strobe data input.

The EXTEND control input is used by slow memories or external devices to lengthen an instruction's execution time by increasing the duration of a data input/output cycle; this extends the time available for memories or external devices to capture data output, or to present input data.

The NINIT input control initializes PACE; the Program Counter is set to 0. The Stack Pointer, the Stack and the Status and Control Flags register are cleared.

BPS has already been described; it is used to select either normal or split base page, for base page direct addressing.

NHALT is a bidirectional control signal **used by interrupt and halt logic.** As an input, NHALT can induce a Halt state, or in conjunction with CONTIN, it can generate a level 0 (highest priority) interrupt request. When the CPU executes a Halt instruction, NHALT is output high to identify the Halt state. The various uses of NHALT and its interaction with CONTIN are described in detail later in this chapter.

The CONTIN signal is used to terminate a Halt condition and is also used as an output interrupt acknowledge signal. When CONTIN is properly sequenced with the NHALT signal, it initiates a high priority interrupt, as we mentioned in the preceding paragraph. **CONTIN can also be used as a Jump condition input** in the same way as JC13, 14 and 15, which are described next.

JC13, 14 and 15 provide an interesting capability found in very few microcomputers discussed in this book; the condition of these three **inputs can be tested by a Branch-on-Condition (BOC) instruction,** thus allowing external control signals to directly manipulate PACE program instruction sequences.

F11, 12, 13 and 14 are the outputs for the corresponding flag bits in the Status and Control Flags register.

NIR2, 3, 4 and 5 are the external interrupt request lines. Interrupt priority arbitration logic is included on the INS8900 (and PACE) chip. NIR2 has the highest priority of the external interrupt lines, and NIR5 has the lowest priority.

INS8900 AND PACE TIMING AND INSTRUCTION EXECUTION

PACE uses a combination of two clock signal inputs to time events internally within the microprocessor CPU. **The clock signals and the resultant internal clock phases can be illustrated as follows:**

> PACE
> CLOCK
> SIGNALS

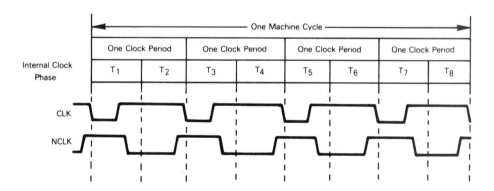

The INS8900 clock logic has been simplified. A single, uniform clock signal generates all timing as follows:

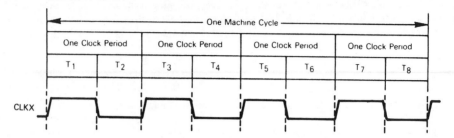

Several points should be noted regarding INS8900 and PACE timing. **The internal clock phases (T1 through T8) are meaningless to external logic since they are not accessible, nor are they needed for any external synchronization purposes.** We have shown them merely because they will simplify later discussions of data input/output operations. **Four clock periods constitute a single machine cycle.** Most instructions require between four and seven machine cycles for execution.

So far as external logic is concerned, there are only three types of machine cycles which can occur during execution of an instruction:

1) **A data input operation (read)** during which external logic must present a word of data to the CPU.

2) **A data output operation (write)** during which the CPU transmits a word of data to external logic.

3) **An internal operation** during which no CPU-initiated activity occurs on the System Bus.

All instructions include one or more data input machine cycles, and two or more internal operation machine cycles. Only a few instructions include data output machine cycles. The first machine cycle of any instruction's execution must, of course, be an instruction fetch operation — which to external logic is simply a data input cycle. **Let us therefore begin by examining the data input machine cycle.**

Figure 1-5 illustrates timing for a standard data input machine cycle. Notice that the address is only present on the data lines for the first portion of the machine cycle. The NADS signal is sent out approximately in the center of the time interval during which the address data is valid; therefore, either the leading edge or trailing edge of NADS can be used to clock the address data.

The IDS signal is sent out at about the same time as the address information is taken off the data lines — well before the time when input data is expected by the CPU. This gives external logic time to prepare the input data. The input data needs to be valid only for a short time interval later in the machine cycle. Exact timing is given in the data sheets at the end of this chapter.

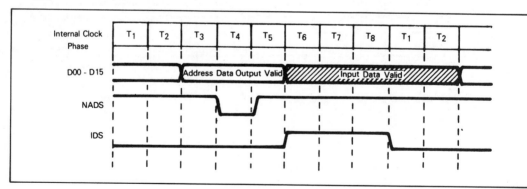

Figure 1-5. INS8900 and PACE Data Input Timing

Figure 1-6 illustrates timing for a standard data output cycle. The address-output portion of the cycle is identical to that of the data input cycle just described; the ODS signal is sent out at the same part of the cycle as IDS was. At approximately the same time that ODS is sent out, the output data word is placed on the data lines. The output data remains valid beyond the end of the ODS signal so that the trailing edge of ODS can be used as the clock for external data latches.

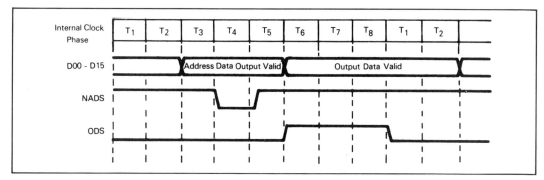

Figure 1-6. INS8900 and PACE Data Output Timing

The data input/output cycles just described allow approximately two clock periods for external logic to respond. If this time interval is too short, the EXTEND signal input to the CPU can be used to lengthen the I/O cycle by multiples of the clock period (one clock period equals two internal clock phases). **The EXTEND signal** can be placed high during address time or immediately after the start of IDS or ODS, but it **must be high before the end of internal clock phase 6 as shown in Figure 1-7.**

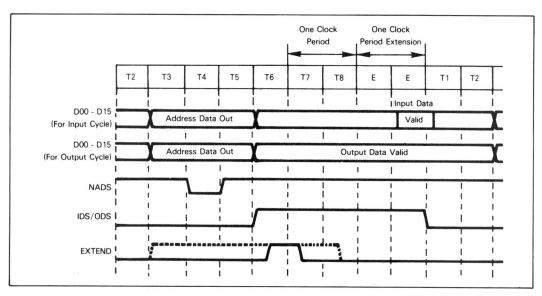

Figure 1-7. Using the EXTEND Signal to Lengthen I/O Cycles

The timing shown in Figure 1-7 provides the minimum I/O cycle extension of one clock period.

The maximum extension permitted by PACE is 2 microseconds; so with a clock period of 750 nanoseconds, this means that only two clock period extensions can be added to an input/output cycle. The second clock period extension is achieved by holding the EXTEND signal high for one additional clock period beyond the timing shown in Figure 1-7. The INS8900 has no maximum permitted extension.

Notice that the EXTEND signal does just what its name implies; it simply extends the duration of the data transfer portion of an I/O machine cycle. The trailing edge of the IDS or ODS signal is delayed and, for data input, the time until valid input data must be present is delayed. On data output cycles, the valid data is simply maintained on the data lines by the CPU for an extended period of time.

The EXTEND signal can also be used to suspend CPU input activity. This use of EXTEND will be described later under the heading of Direct Memory Access.

THE INITIALIZATION OPERATION

A NINIT low signal input to the CPU initializes the microprocessor. The NINIT signal is the equivalent of the Reset signal described for other microcomputers in this book. While NINIT is held low, CPU operations are suspended; IDS and ODS are reset low. NINIT must be held low for a minimum of eight clock periods to give the CPU time to respond. After NINIT goes high again, this is what happens:

1) The internal Stack Pointer is cleared.
2) All flags and interrupt enables are set low (except Level 0 Interrupt Enable which is set high).
3) The Accumulators contain arbitrary values.
4) The Program Counter is set to zero.
5) 16 to 24 clock periods after NINIT returns high, the NADS signal is output high. The first instruction is thus fetched from memory location zero (0000_{16}).

Figure 1-8 illustrates the timing for the initialization operation. Note that the NINIT signal is shown going low after power and clocks are both stable. The NINIT signal must be applied whenever the CPU is powered-up; if NINIT is held low before clocks and/or power have stabilized, the NADS and NHALT output signals may have undefined states for eight clock pulses after the trailing edge of NINIT.

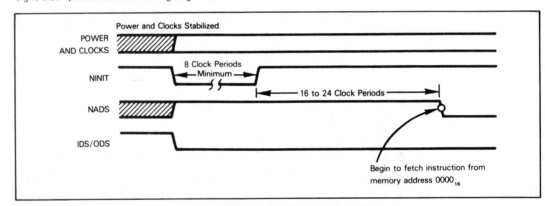

Figure 1-8. INS8900 and PACE Initialization Timing

THE HALT STATE AND PROCESSOR STALL OPERATIONS

Most microprocessors described in this book have a Hold state, which typically describes a CPU condition during which there is no CPU-initiated activity on the System Busses; external logic can then perform Direct Memory Access operations. The INS8900 and PACE CPUs have an equivalent state that can be initiated under program control or by external logic. **When this state is initiated under program control (by executing a Halt instruction) INS8900 and PACE literature calls it the Halt state; when initiated by external logic, it is called a Processor Stall.**

During normal program execution, the CPU NHALT control line provides a high output. When a Halt instruction is executed, the NHALT output is driven low to indicate that CPU activity is suspended. While in the Halt state, the NHALT output has a 7/8 duty cycle; that is, every eighth clock phase, the NHALT output goes high. If the NHALT output is merely used to drive an indicator on a

INS8900 AND THE PACE HALT STATE

control panel, this 7/8 duty cycle is of little concern; but, if the NHALT signal is used as a logic signal, the 7/8 duty cycle must be accounted for. **The Halt state is terminated by setting the CONTIN input signal high for a minimum of 16 clock cycles, and then resetting it low for at least four clock cycles, as shown in Figure 1-9 .** CPU operation then resumes by executing the next instruction, that is, the instruction that follows the Halt instruction.

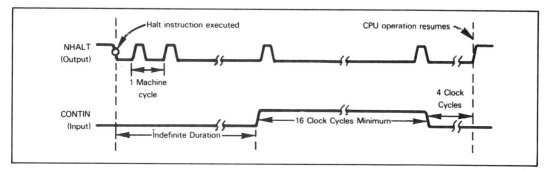

Figure 1-9. Terminating INS8900 or PACE Halt State

As we have just seen, **the PACE NHALT and CONTIN signals are interrelated.** We mentioned earlier that **these signals are also multifunctional.** We will describe separately each of the functions that can be implemented with NHALT and CONTIN. **Do not use these signals to implement more than one function unless your application absolutely requires the additional functions.** Critical and complicated timing relationships are required by the CPU to differentiate between various functions. For PACE, but not the INS8900, timing is further complicated by some circuit problems in the CPU's interrupt system, which we will describe later.

> NHALT AND CONTIN
> SIGNALS ARE
> MULTIFUNCTIONAL

The INS8900 and PACE CPU can be forced into the Halt state by external logic. INS8900 and PACE literature defines this operation as a Processor Stall. A Processor Stall uses both NHALT and CONTIN as control signal inputs. Figure 1-10 shows the timing sequence required. The NHALT input must be driven low by external logic to initiate the sequence. CPU operation is then suspended after execution of the current instruction is completed. The minimum

> INS8900
> AND PACE
> PROCESSOR
> STALL

response time is five clock cycles. The maximum response time is equal to the longest instruction execution time (refer to Table 1-2). There is no maximum time limit for a Processor Stall. The CPU simply remains in the Halt state until it is terminated by the CONTIN input signal, which must be properly sequenced with the removal of the NHALT input, as shown in Figure 1-10 .

Let us take another look at the beginning of the Processor Stall timing sequence. **Notice that when the CPU has completed the current instruction and recognized the stall request, the CONTIN output signal is briefly driven low by the CPU.** This pulse is referred to as ACK INT (Acknowledge Interrupt) and can be used to let external logic know that the

> PROCESSOR STALL
> AND LEVEL 0
> INTERRUPT
> SIMILARITIES

CPU is responding to the stall request. It may seem inappropriate for the CPU to provide an Acknowledge Interrupt response when we are initiating a Processor Stall. However, as we shall see later in this chapter, **a Level 0 Interrupt request begins with exactly the same timing sequence as a Processor Stall; in fact, the reaction of the CPU is the same for both operations until that point in the sequence where NHALT goes high.** Therefore, the initial response of ACK INT is always sent out after NHALT is driven low.

DIRECT MEMORY ACCESS OPERATIONS

At the beginning of our Halt state and Processor Stall discussion we mentioned that these are the equivalent of Hold states provided by other microprocessors. But **there are some significant differences between the INS8900 and PACE Halt state, and the Hold state described for other microprocessors in this book. Because of these differences, Direct Memory Access operations with PACE or the INS8900 are not straightforward.**

The INS8900 and PACE CPUs never float their Data or Control Busses. But remember that the design of any realistic INS8900 or PACE system is going to require buffer/drivers for the data lines and control signals. The BTE, which is part of the PACE microcomputer family, performs this buffering function.

> FLOATING
> INS8900
> AND PACE
> SYSTEM
> BUSSES

Any bidirectional three-state buffer can be used to float INS8900 bus lines. In Figure 1-2 , INS8208 devices are shown performing this function. Thus it is the control signals input to the BTE by PACE or to the INS8208 by the INS8900 that actually float bus lines at the proper time, in order to allow DMA operations.

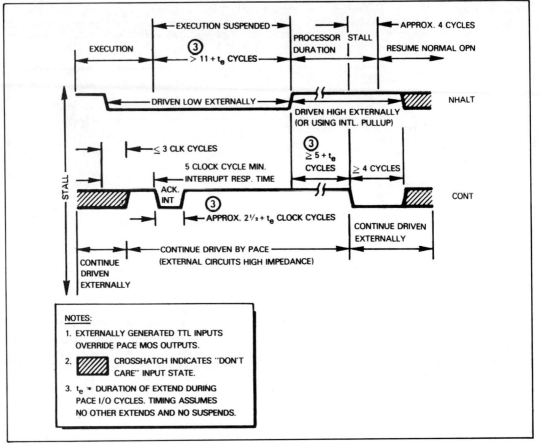

Figure 1-10. Timing Diagram for Processor Stall Using
NHALT and CONTIN Signals

But we must have a way of determining whether the CPU is going to be using the System Busses. There are several methods of making this determination; we will conceptually examine each of them within the context of three different DMA schemes:

1) DMA block data transfers initiated by the CPU
2) DMA block data transfers initiated by external logic
3) Cycle-stealing DMA transfers

From a hardware point of view, the simplest method of implementing DMA in a PACE or INS8900 system is to have the CPU initiate block transfers of data. Consider the following approach. The CPU will treat an external DMA controller as a peripheral device and will establish initial conditions such as starting address, word count, and direction (memory read or write). This information can be passed to the controller by treating its registers as memory

CPU INITIATED DMA BLOCK DATA TRANSFERS

locations and using Store instructions to write into the registers. When the required information has been passed, the CPU simply executes a Halt instruction. As we described earlier, **when a Halt instruction is executed, the NHALT control output line from the CPU is driven low (7/8 duty cycle). This signal could thus be used by the DMA controller as an indication that the CPU will not be using the System Bus and the DMA transfer can begin. When the transfer is completed, the DMA controller will use the CONTIN input to the CPU, as shown in Figure 1-9 , to terminate the Halt instruction. Normal CPU operation will then resume.**

Most microprocessors have a Bus Request input signal that can be used by external logic to request access to the System Busses. **In a PACE or INS8900 system, the NHALT input signal can be used to force the CPU into a Processor Stall, as described earlier, and thus free the System Busses for DMA operations. The Acknowledge Interrupt (ACK INT) pulse on the CONTIN output line shown in Figure 1-10 is then equivalent to a Bus Grant signal, and the DMA controller may begin the data transfer. When the transfer is complete, the CONTIN line is used as a control input line to the CPU to terminate the Processor Stall.**

DMA BLOCK DATA TRANSFERS INITIATED BY EXTERNAL LOGIC IN PACE AND INS8900 SYSTEMS

Cycle-stealing DMA operations typically transfer a single word via the System Busses during a brief interval when the CPU is not using the busses. With this method, CPU operations need not be stopped; instead, they are only slowed down slightly, or in some cases not affected at all. **In order to implement cycle-stealing DMA, external logic must have a way of detecting those time intervals when the CPU will not be using the System Busses.** There are two ways that this can be accomplished with the INS8900 or PACE CPU. The first method involves the use of the EXTEND input signal to the CPU to suppress or suspend input/output operations; the second method uses a special technique to sense when the CPU is beginning an internal (non-I/O) machine cycle.

CYCLE-STEALING DMA IN PACE AND INS8900 SYSTEMS

Earlier we described how to use the EXTEND input signal to lengthen the CPU input/output cycles. The EXTEND signal can also be used to prevent the CPU from beginning an I/O cycle, and thus ensure that the System Busses will be available to external devices for DMA operations.

Figure 1-11 illustrates both uses of the EXTEND signal. The CPU looks at the EXTEND input signal at internal clock phases T1 and T6. Notice that during I/O cycles the IDS or ODS signal goes high at the beginning of T6 and low at the beginning of T1. If EXTEND is high during T6, then extra clock cycles are inserted after T8; this is the method that would be used to lengthen an I/O cycle. If EXTEND is high during T1, then extra clock cycles are inserted between T3 and T4; this is the method we would use for DMA operations.

EXTEND USED TO SUSPEND INS8900 AND PACE I/O DURING DMA OPERATIONS

The trailing edge of IDS/ODS indicates that the CPU has just completed an I/O cycle and is therefore not using the System Busses at this instant. By setting EXTEND high at this time, we suppress the beginning of another I/O cycle while we use the busses for a DMA transfer.

Notice that we are merely lengthening the beginning of the machine cycle, and thus delaying that part of the machine cycle where the CPU might begin I/O activity. We do not know whether the current machine cycle will be an internal machine cycle or an I/O cycle, and we do not care. We have merely stolen the busses by slowing down the CPU.

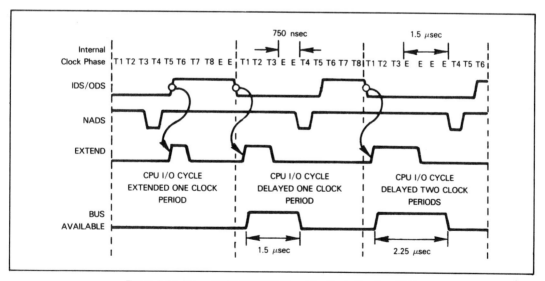

Figure 1-11. Using PACE EXTEND Signal for Cycle-Stealing DMA

There are two drawbacks inherent in the EXTEND method of cycle-stealing DMA. First, whenever we use the System Busses for a DMA transfer, we slow down the operation of the CPU. Second, we must wait until the CPU has just completed an input/output cycle before we can perform the cycle steal. Since only about one-third of the CPU machine cycles are used for I/O, this means that bus access for DMA will be quite limited. Both of these drawbacks can be eliminated if we can find some technique for determining when the CPU is performing an internal (non-I/O) machine cycle. **We could then use the System Busses any time that the CPU is not using them (which is more than 60% of the time) and we could perform the DMA transfer without slowing down CPU operations. We shall now describe just such a technique.**

We stated earlier in this chapter that the internal clock phases (T1 through T8) are not available to external logic. However, National Semiconductor data sheets include a figure that shows circuits for internal drivers and receivers. A detailed examination of this figure reveals a very interesting and useful fact: the JC13 (Jump Condition 13) pin on the CPU is intended as an input signal; but, because of the way in which the receiver for this signal is designed, it also produces an output pulse on the JC13 pin during every machine cycle. The output pulse occurs

CYCLE-STEALING DMA DURING INS8900 AND PACE INTERNAL MACHINE CYCLES

during T4 of each machine cycle, and we can use this fact to design a very efficient cycle-stealing DMA arrangement.

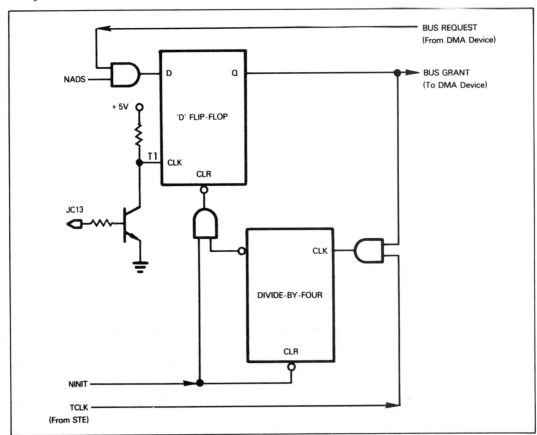

Figure 1-12. Idealized Circuit for Cycle-Stealing DMA During INS8900 and
PACE Internal Machine Cycles

Figure 1-12 shows a circuit that uses the output pulse provided by JC13 to implement cycle-stealing DMA. Recall that the CPU sends out a negative-going NADS pulse at T4 of every input/output cycle. This NADS signal is ANDed in our circuit with an external device's DMA Bus Request and applied to the D input of a flip-flop. The JC13 output pulse, which also occurs at T4, is inverted via a transistor and applied to the clock input of the flip-flop. Thus, if NADS is high at T4 (indicating that the current CPU machine cycle is not an I/O cycle) the flip-flop will be set if there is a Bus Request present. The output of this flip-flop is then used by external logic as a Bus Grant signal and the DMA transfer can be initiated. Since we do not know whether or not the next cycle will be a CPU I/O cycle, we must terminate DMA activity on the bus prior to the next T4 time. In Figure 1-12, this is accomplished using a divide-by-four counter.

The CLK input to the counter is a combination of the Bus Grant signal and the TCLK signal which is available from the PACE STE. This results in the timing shown in Figure 1-13. Notice that this scheme makes the bus available for about 7/8 of a machine cycle, or approximately 2.25 microseconds. If you refer back to Figure 14-10 you will notice that this is about the same length of time as was obtained by using the maximum duration of EXTEND. So, we have not increased the maximum time available for a DMA transfer. But, we have made two significant gains: DMA transfers can occur more frequently, and these transfers do not slow down CPU operations.

We must add a final note of caution to the description of this otherwise straightforward DMA technique. There are several critical timing paths in the idealized circuit shown in Figure 1-12. Both the JC13 pulse and the NADS signal occur at T4, although the trailing edge of NADS does occur slightly after the trailing edge of JC13. Therefore, the components used to provide CLK and D inputs to the flip-flop must be selected carefully to ensure that there is not a race condition. Additionally, we have shown the Bus Grant signal being reset at the end of T3. Since the leading edge of NADS occurs at T4, this timing relationship can be critical. However, if external devices such as address latches and decoders use the trailing edge of NADS, this timing should present no problems.

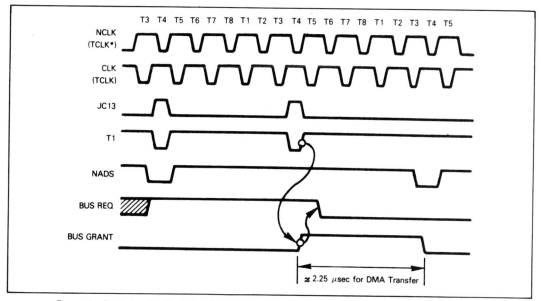

Figure 1-13. Timing for Cycle-Stealing DMA During INS8900 and PACE Internal Machine Cycle

THE INS8900 AND PACE INTERRUPT SYSTEM

The INS8900 and PACE CPUs have complete on-chip interrupt systems. Six separate levels of interrupts are provided: one internal and five external interrupt request inputs, including a non-maskable input. Priority logic is provided on the CPU, and all interrupts are vectored, thus eliminating any polling requirements. Because of the various ways in which interrupts can be initiated, and also because of a few problems that exist in the PACE interrupt system, we will divide our description of the system into three parts:

1) Low priority external interrupts
2) Internal (Stack) interrupts
3) Non-maskable (Level 0) interrupts

But first, let us take an overview of the INS8900 and PACE interrupt system.

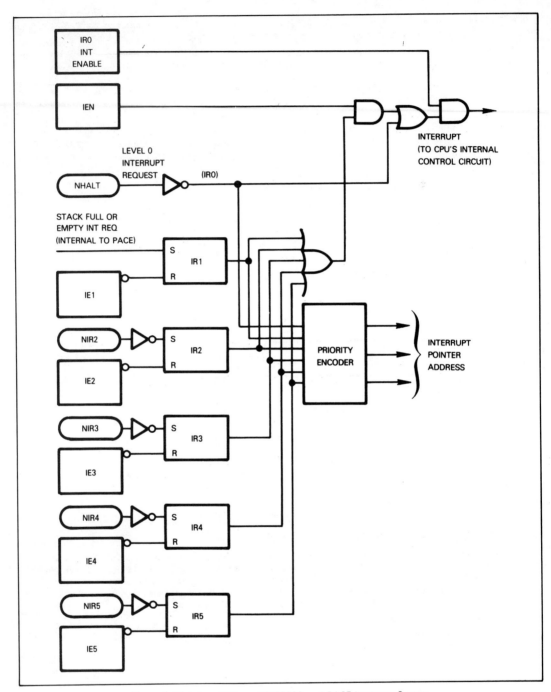

Figure 1-14. Internal View of INS8900 and PACE Interrupt System

Figure 1-14 depicts the interrupt logic that is contained on the CPU. **The highest priority interrupt request is the non-maskable Level 0 interrupt request, which is initiated using the NHALT control input to the CPU. The lowest priority interrupt request is NIR5.**

INS8900 AND PACE INTERRUPT PRIORITIES

The Stack Interrupt and each of the four lower-priority external interrupt requests can be individually enabled or disabled by setting or clearing associated bits (IE1 - IE5) in the Status and Control Flag register. Notice in Figure 1-14 that these bits are shown as providing the 'R' input to a latch. The 'S' input to each of these latches is the actual interrupt request line. The significance of this is rather subtle. It means that an interrupt request need not supply a continuous low level until it is acknowledged. Instead, any pulse exceeding one PACE clock period will set the associated interrupt request latch; this allows narrow timing or control pulses to be used as interrupt request inputs. Note, however, that the 'R' input to the latches overrides the 'S' input. Therefore, if the individual Interrupt Enable flag is reset, it not only prevents the latch from being set by interrupt requests, it will also clear a previously latched request that may or may not have been serviced. If this logic is not clear to you, you should study the characteristics of the RS flip-flop.

ENABLING AND DISABLING INS8900 AND PACE INTERRUPTS

A master interrupt enable (IEN) flag is also provided in the Status and Control Flag register. IEN must be set true to allow any of the latched interrupt requests to be recognized by the CPU.

The CPU checks for interrupts at the beginning of every instruction fetch. If an interrupt request is present (and enabled), the instruction fetch is aborted, the contents of the Program Counter are pushed onto the Stack, and the master interrupt enable (IEN) is set low. The CPU then loads the Program Counter with the address vector for your interrupt service routine and executes the instruction contained at that address. (We'll describe the address vectors in the next paragraph.) The interrupt request just described requires a total of 28 clock cycles from the time the interrupt is recognized by the CPU until the time when the first instruction of your interrupt service routine begins execution.

INS8900 AND PACE INTERRUPT RESPONSE

Memory locations 0002_{16} through 0008_{16} are used as pointer locations or address vectors. You load each of these locations with the starting address of the interrupt service routine for each interrupt as follows:

INS8900 AND PACE INTERRUPT POINTERS

MEMORY LOCATION	INTERRUPT POINTER FOR	
2	Stack Interrupt	
3	NIR2	
4	NIR3	
5	NIR4	
6	NIR5	
7	Level 0 Program Counter Pointer	Special
8	Level 0 Interrupt Origin	case

The level 0 interrupt is a special case which we will describe on its own. But first let us look at interrupts in general.

When the CPU responds to an interrupt, it loads the Program Counter with the contents of memory locations 2 through 6, depending on the specific level of interrupt that is being acknowledged. Control is thus vectored to the proper service routine. Suppose, for example, memory location 4 contains the value $2A30_{16}$. If an interrupt request occurring at pin NIR3 is acknowledged, then during the acknowledge process the contents of the Program Counter are saved on the Stack, following which the value $2A30_{16}$ is loaded into the Program Counter. Had the value 4728_{16} been in memory location 4, then 4728_{16} would have been loaded into the Program Counter instead of $2A30_{16}$. Thus, whatever memory address is stored in the memory location associated with the interrupt being acknowledged, this address will be loaded into the Program Counter, becoming the starting address for the specific interrupt service routine to be executed.

As part of the interrupt response we've just described, the CPU sends out a low-going pulse on the CONTIN line. Refer back to Figure 1-10 and associated text for a description of the ACK INT pulse. The last instruction executed by your interrupt service routine must be a Return-from-Interrupt (RTI) instruction. This instruction sets IEN high to re-enable interrupts, then pulls the top of the Stack into the Program Counter. This returns program control to the point where it was interrupted. The RTI instruction does not clear the internal Interrupt Request latch; therefore your interrupt service routine must reset the latch (using a Pulse Flag instruction), or the same interrupt request will still be present after the RTI instruction has been executed. Once the latch has been cleared, it can then be re-enabled for subsequent interrupt requests.

INS8900 AND PACE INTERRUPT ACKNOWLEDGE AND RETURN FROM INTERRUPT

The interrupt sequence does not save the contents of any registers except the Program Counter. If the program that was interrupted requires that the contents of CPU registers be saved and then restored, your interrupt service routine must perform these operations.

SAVING
INS8900 AND
PACE CPU
REGISTERS
DURING
INTERRUPTS

The CPU's response to a Stack interrupt is as described for external interrupts. However, the interrupt request is generated internally by the CPU chip; it can be caused either by a Stack Full or a Stack Empty condition. Remember that the 10-word Stack is part of the CPU chip. It consists of an internal RAM and a pointer that can address Stack words 0 through 9. A Stack Empty interrupt request is generated whenever the pointer is at 0 and a Pull instruction is executed. A Stack Full interrupt request occurs when the pointer is at 7 (eight entries on the Stack) and a Push instruction is executed to fill the ninth word. The tenth word of the Stack will then be used as part of the interrupt response to store the Program Counter contents. Unless you intend to extend the Stack out

INS8900 AND
PACE STACK
INTERRUPTS

into main memory, your application program will not require a Stack Empty or Full interrupt. These interrupts become error conditions and can be avoided by careful programming.

If your program is treating the Stack Empty and Stack Full interrupts as error conditions, then you can disable Stack interrupts, in which case the full ten words of the Stack are available for nested interrupts and subroutines. Of course, this means that a Stack Full or Empty condition, should it occur, will become an undetected error, with unpredictable consequences.

When using PACE, but not the INS8900, there is an additional reason for not using the Stack interrupt capability unless you really need it. **PACE has an internal circuit problem that can cause improper interrupt response. If a Stack interrupt request occurs at the same time as an NIR3 or NIR5 interrupt request, the Stack interrupt address vector will be incorrectly accessed from location 0 instead of location 2.** The solution recommended in PACE literature is to load

PACE
STACK
INTERRUPT
PROBLEMS

both of these locations with the Stack interrupt vector. This apparently straightforward solution is complicated by the fact that location 0 also happens to be the initialization address; whenever the CPU is initialized, the first instruction executed is the one that is contained in location 0. Thus, the word in location 0 must serve a dual purpose:

1) It serves as an instruction whenever the CPU is initialized.

2) It serves as an address vector if a Stack interrupt occurs at the same time as NIR3 or NIR4.

Here's an example. The object code for a Copy Flags to Register (CFR) instruction is 0400_{16}. So, if locations 0 and 2 both contain a value of 0400_{16} the problem is solved. Your Stack interrupt service routine would have to begin at memory address 0400_{16}, but you would be correctly vectored to that address regardless of whether or not the interrupt error we've just described occurs. On initialization, the first instruction executed would be the CFR instruction: this is not a very useful initialization instruction, but at least no damage is done.

For a fuller discussion of this interrupt problem and the solution, refer to PACE literature. Also keep in mind that the problem has been fixed in the INS8900.

The non-maskable (Level 0) interrupt cannot be disabled and differs from the other interrupt levels both in the way it is initiated and in the way the CPU responds to it.

The Level 0 interrupt request is initiated using the NHALT control input signal in combination with the CONTIN input line. Figure 1-15 shows the timing relationships between NHALT and CONTIN that are required to initiate the non-maskable interrupt. If you

INS8900
AND PACE
NON-MASKABLE
(LEVEL 0)
INTERRUPT

compare this figure with Figure 1-10 , you will notice that the Level 0 interrupt request and the Processor Stall begin in exactly the same way; NHALT is driven low by external logic and held low for some time after a low-going pulse (ACK INT) has been sent out on the CONTIN line. The only difference between the two operations is towards the end of the timing sequence. For a Processor Stall, NHALT is allowed to return high while CONTIN is still high; for a Level 0 interrupt, the CONTIN line must be driven low by external logic before the NHALT line is allowed to go high. This critical timing sequence is the only way that the CPU has to differentiate between a Processor Stall and a Level 0 interrupt. Notice that this Level 0 interrupt timing sequence never requires external logic to drive CONTIN high. Therefore, if you're using the CONTIN line for any of its other multiple functions (including the ACK INT output pulse) you can merely tie CONTIN to ground and use NHALT to initiate the Level 0 interrupt.

The response of the CPU to the Level 0 interrupt is subtly different from its response to other interrupts. These subtle differences are related to the slightly different purpose of a non-maskable interrupt versus a normal program interrupt request. A non-maskable interrupt is typically used only when there is a catastrophic error or failure (such as loss of power) or to implement a control panel for program development or debug purposes. Both of these uses require that

INS8900
AND PACE
LEVEL 0
INTERRUPT
RESPONSE

an asynchronous, unplanned program termination have a minimum effect upon system status; that is, you want to leave behind a picture of the system as it looked immediately before the program termination occurred.

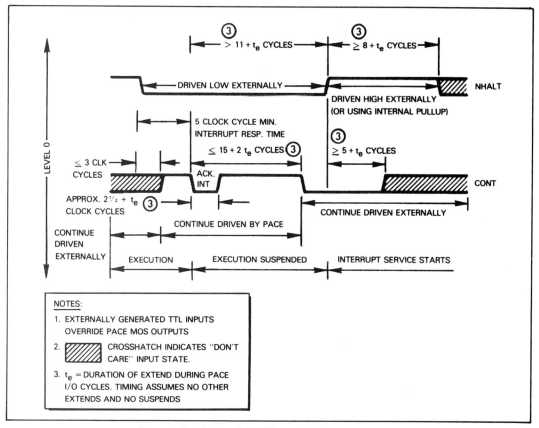

Figure 1-15. Initiating INS8900 and PACE Level 0 Interrupt
Using NHALT and CONTIN Signals

Remember that other levels of interrupts store the contents of the Program Counter or the Stack and reset the IEN flag in the Status and Control Flag register. This sequence obviously alters the "picture" of the CPU, since both Stack contents and Status and Control Flag register contents are changed. To avoid this, the Level 0 interrupt response by the CPU uses an external memory location to store the contents of the Program Counter. Memory location 0007_{16} holds the address of the memory word where the Program Counter will be stored. The contents of the Status and Control Flag register are unaltered. CPU internal circuitry resets an "IRO INT ENABLE flag to prevent another interrupt from being recognized (refer to Figure 1-16), but this is not discernible to you. After the Program Counter has been saved in the designated memory location, the instruction contained in memory location 0008_{16} is executed; this is the first instruction of your Level 0 interrupt service routine. Suppose, for example, that memory location 0007_{16} contains the value $FF00_{16}$. Following a Level 0 interrupt request, the Program Counter contents will be stored in location $FF00_{16}$. Following the Level 0 interrupt acknowledge, the actual instruction stored in memory location 0008_{16} is executed.

Note that the Level 0 interrupt acknowledge sequence has not altered anything within the CPU that is discernible to you or to a program; the Stack, Accumulators, and Status and Control Flag register are all unchanged. Additionally, avoiding use of the Stack ensures that there will not be a Stack overflow — and in consequence a Stack interrupt will not be generated by this interrupt response sequence.

The normal Return-from-Interrupt (RTI) instruction that must be executed at the end of your interrupt service routine causes the Program Counter to be restored from the Stack. **Since the Level 0 interrupt sequence does not utilize the Stack to store the Program Counter, a different technique must be used to return control to the interrupted program.** First you must execute a Set

RETURN FROM PACE LEVEL 0 INTERRUPT

Flag (SFLG) or Pulse Flag (PFLG) instruction, referencing bit 15 in the Status and Control Flag register. This bit always appears to be set to a '1', but must be referenced in this case to enable lower levels of interrupts. Next you must execute a Jump Indirect (JMP@) through the location pointed to by the contents of memory location 0007_{16} to restore the original Program Counter contents.

PACE, but not the INS8900, has some Level 0 interrupt circuit problems.

If a Level 0 interrupt occurs within the 12-clock-cycle period following the recognition of any other interrupt, PACE will either perform a Processor Stall (which we described earlier) or PACE will execute the Level 0 interrupt — but using the wrong pointer address. In short,

> **PACE
> LEVEL 0
> INTERRUPT
> PROBLEMS**

you don't know what might happen under these circumstances. There is a solution for this problem. It requires that external logic allow NHALT to be applied to the PACE CPU only while the NADS signal is present, provided no Acknowledge Interrupt (ACK INT) has occurred since the last NADS pulse. ACK INT is accompanied by a negative-going pulse on the CONTIN line. Sound complicated? It is.

The circuit shown in Figure 1-16 is reproduced from PACE literature and solves the problem we've just described. We won't attempt to describe here how this circuit solves the problem. Note that this circuit only takes care of Level 0 interrupt problems; if you also want to use NHALT and CONTIN to cause a Processor Stall, you must design additional external logic.

Once again, we must advise that these interrupt system problems exist in PACE CPU chips. The INS8900 has none of these problems.

THE INS8900 AND PACE INSTRUCTION SET

Table 1-1 summarizes the INS8900 and PACE instruction set.

The primary memory reference instructions have typical minicomputer addressing modes. These instructions will also be used as I/O instructions, since external devices are identified via selected memory addresses.

In Table 1-1 , "direct addressing options" means the instruction can reference memory using any of the direct or direct indexed addressing options described earlier.

> **INS8900
> AND PACE
> DIRECT
> ADDRESSING
> OPTIONS**

"Indirect addressing options" similarly specifies any of the indirect addressing options described earlier.

Both Branch and Skip instructions are provided, and each differs significantly from the philosophies described in Volume 1, Chapter 6.

There are 16 conditions that can cause a Branch, as shown in Table 1-3 . Notice that three of the conditions are determined by external inputs JC13, 14, and 15. If a Branch-on-Condition is true, then the displacement which is added to the Program Counter is an 8-bit signed binary number as described in Volume 1, Chapter 6.

There are three varieties of Skip-on-Condition instructions. SKNE, SKG and SKAZ compare the contents of an Accumulator to a memory location which is addressed using direct or direct indexed addressing. Based on the results of the comparison, the instruction following the Skip may or may not be executed. These three instructions are therefore combined Skip and Memory Reference instructions.

ISZ and DSZ identify a memory location using direct or direct indexed addressing; the contents of the addressed memory location are incremented (ISZ) or decremented (for DSZ); if after the increment or decrement operation the memory location contains a 0 value, then the Skip is performed.

The AISZ instruction adds an 8-bit, signed binary number to the contents of an Accumulator; if the result is 0, a Skip is performed.

These Skip instructions will be very familiar to minicomputer programmers, and on most microcomputers are equivalent to a secondary Memory Reference or Immediate Operate instruction, followed by a Branch-on-Condition instruction.

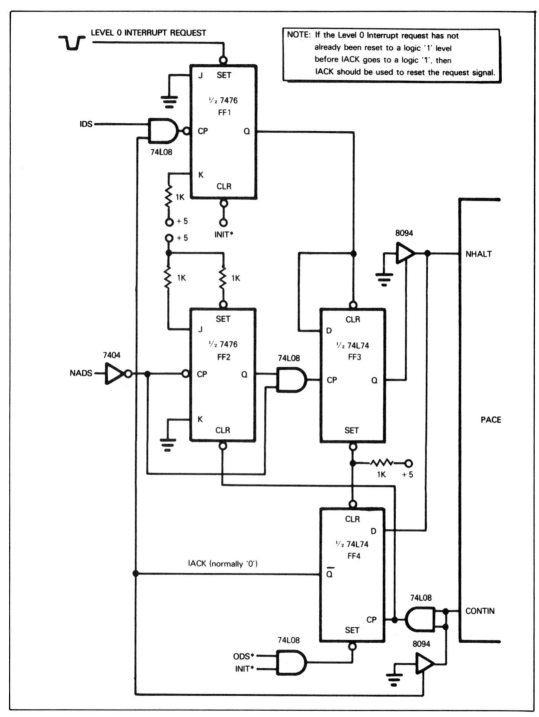

Figure 1-16. Circuit to Prevent Conflicts Between PACE Level 0
Interrupts and Lower Priority Interrupts

The following symbols are used in Table 1-1:

AC0	Accumulator 0
C	Carry status
CC	4-bit Condition Code described in Table 15-3
D	Any Destination register
DATA8	8 bit binary data unit
DISP(X)	Direct or indexed addressing operands as explained in the text.
@DISP(X)	Indirect addressing operands as explained in the text.
EA	The effective address generated by the specified operands.
f	4-bit quantity selecting a bit in the Flag Word.
FW	Flag Word described in the text.
IEN	Interrupt Enable status
I	A 1-bit unit determining whether LINK is included in the shift/rotate.
L	Link status
n	Seven bits determining how many single bit shift/rotates are performed.
O	Overflow status
PC	Program Counter
r	Any register of the Accumulator: AC0, AC1, AC2 or AC3
S	Any Source register
ST	Top word of on-chip Stack.
$x<y,z>$	Bits y through z of the quantity x. For example, $r<7,0>$ is the low-order byte of the specified register.
[ ]	Contents of location enclosed within brackets. If a register designation is enclosed within the brackets, then the designated register's contents are specified. If a memory address is enclosed within the brackets, then the contents of the addressed memory location are specified.
[[ ]]	Implied memory addressing; the contents of the memory location designated by the contents of a register.
Λ	Logical AND
V	Logical OR
$\forall$	Logical Exclusive-OR
$\leftarrow$	Data is transferred in the direction of the arrow.
$\longleftrightarrow$	Data is exchanged between the two locations designated on either side of the arrow.

Under the heading of STATUSES in Table 1-1 , an X indicates statuses which are modified in the course of the instruction's execution. If there is no X, it means that the status maintains the value it had before the instruction was executed.

Table 1-1. INS8900 and PACE Instruction Set Summary

TYPE	MNEMONIC	OPERAND(S)	BYTES	STATUSES			OPERATION PERFORMED
				C	O	L	
PRIMARY MEMORY REFERENCE AND I/O	LD	r,DISP(X)	2				[r]→[EA] Load any Accumulator, direct addressing options.
	LD	0,@DISP(X)	2				[AC0]→[EA] Load Primary Accumulator, indirect addressing options.
	ST	r,DISP(X)	2				[EA]→[r] Store any Accumulator, direct addressing options.
	ST	0,@DISP(X)	2				[EA]→[AC0] Store Primary Accumulator, indirect addressing options.
	LSEX	0,DISP(X)	2				[AC0]→[EA](sign extended) Load a signed byte into Primary Accumulator, extend sign bit into high order byte. Direct addressing options.
SECONDARY MEMORY REFERENCE (MEMORY OPERATE)	ADD	r,DISP(X)	2	X	X		[r]→[r]+[EA] Add to any Accumulator, direct addressing options.
	DECA	0,DISP(X)	2	X	X		[AC0]→[AC0]+[EA]+[C] Add decimal with Carry to any Accumulator, direct addressing options.
	SUBB	0,DISP(X)	2	X	X		[AC0]→[AC0]-[EA]+[C] Subtract from Primary Accumulator with borrow, direct addressing options.
	AND	0,DISP(X)	2				[AC0]→[AC0]∧[EA] AND with Primary Accumulator, direct addressing options.
	OR	0,DISP(X)	2				[AC0]→[AC0]∨[EA] OR with Primary Accumulator, direct addressing options.
IMMEDIATE	LI	r,DATA8	2				[r<7,0>]→DATA8 (sign extended) Load immediate into any Accumulator. DATA8 is an 8-bit signed binary value. The sign bit is propagated through 8 high order bits
	JMP	DISP(X)	2				[PC]→EA Jump by loading the effective direct address into the Program Counter.
	JMP	@DISP(X)	2				[PC]→EA Jump by loading the effective indirect address into the Program Counter.

Table 1-1. INS8900 and PACE Instruction Set Summary (Continued)

TYPE	MNEMONIC	OPERAND(S)	BYTES	STATUSES			OPERATION PERFORMED
				C	O	L	
IMMEDIATE (CONTINUED)	JSR	DISP(X)	2				[ST]←[PC] [PC]←EA Jump to subroutine direct. As JMP direct. but push old Program Counter contents onto Stack.
	JSR	@DISP(X)	2				[ST]←[PC] [PC]←EA Jump to subroutine indirect. As JMP indirect. but push old Program Counter contents onto Stack.
IMMEDIATE OPERATE	CAI	r,DATA8	2				[r]←[r]+DATA8 (sign extended) Complement contents of any register. then add immediate data.
BRANCH ON CONDITION	BOC	CC,DISP	2				If CC true: then [PC]←EA Branch on CC true. as defined in Table 14-3.
MEMORY REFERENCE AND SKIP (SEE TEXT)	SKNE	r,DISP(X)	2				If [r] ≠ [EA]: then [PC]←[PC]+1 Skip if any Accumulator not equal.
	SKG	0,DISP(X)	2				If [AC0] > [EA]: then [PC]←[PC]+1 **Skip if Primary Accumulator greater.**
	SKAZ	0,DISP(X)	2				If ([AC0] ∧ [EA]) = 0: then [PC]←[PC]+1 Skip if AND with Primary Accumulator is zero.

1-28

Table 1-1. INS8900 and PACE Instruction Set Summary (Continued)

TYPE	MNEMONIC	OPERAND(S)	BYTES	STATUSES C	STATUSES O	STATUSES L	OPERATION PERFORMED
MEMORY REFERENCE OPERATE AND SKIP	ISZ	DISP(X)	2				$[EA]\rightarrow[EA]+1$ If $[EA]=0$: then $[PC]\rightarrow[PC]+1$ Increment memory, skip if zero.
	DSZ	DISP(X)	2				$[EA]\rightarrow[EA]-1$ If $[EA]=0$: then $[PC]\rightarrow[PC]+1$ Decrement memory, skip if zero.
IMMEDIATE OPERATE AND SKIP	AISZ	r,DATA8	2				$[r]\rightarrow[r]+DATA8$ If $[r]=0$: then $[PC]\rightarrow[PC]+1$ Add immediate to any Accumulator. Skip if zero. DATA8 is an 8-bit signed binary immediate data value.
REGISTER-REGISTER MOVE	RCPY	S,D	2				$[D]\rightarrow[S]$ Move contents of any Accumulator (S) to any Accumulator (D).
	RXCH	S,D	2				$[D]\longleftrightarrow[S]$ Exchange contents of any Accumulators.
REGISTER-REGISTER OPERATE	RADD	S,D	2	X	X		$[D]\rightarrow[S]+[D]$ Binary add any Accumulator to any Accumulator.
	RADC	S,D	2	X	X		$[D]\rightarrow[S]+[D]+[C]$ Binary add with Carry any Accumulator to any Accumulator.
	RAND	S,D	2				$[D]\rightarrow[S]\wedge[D]$ AND any Accumulator with any Accumulator.
	RXOR	S,D	2				$[D]\rightarrow[S]\veebar[D]$ Exclusive-OR any Accumulator with any Accumulator.
REGISTER OPERATE	SHL	r,n,1	2			X	Shift any Accumulator left n bits. Simple if 1 = 0: through Link if 1 = 1.
	SHR	r,n,1	2			X	Shift any Accumulator left n bits. Simple if 1 = 0, through Link if 1 = 1.
	ROL	r,n,1	2			X	As SHL, but rotate.
	ROR	r,n,1	2			X	As SHR, but rotate.

Table 1-1. INS8900 and PACE Instruction Set Summary (Continued)

TYPE	MNEMONIC	OPERAND(S)	BYTES	STATUSES			OPERATION PERFORMED
				C	O	L	
STACK	PUSH	r	2				$[ST] \leftarrow [r]$ Push any Accumulator contents onto Stack.
	PUSHF		2				$[ST] \leftarrow [FW]$ Push flags onto Stack.
	PULL	r	2				$[r] \leftarrow [ST]$ Pull top of Stack into any Accumulator.
	PULLF		2	X	X	X	$[FW] \leftarrow [ST]$ Pull top of Stack into flags.
	XCHRS	r	2				$[ST] \leftrightarrow [r]$ Exchange contents of any Accumulator with top of Stack.
	RTS	DISP	2				$[PC] \leftarrow [ST] + DISP$ Return from subroutine. Move sum of DISP and top of Stack to PC. DISP is an 8-bit signed binary number.
INTERRUPT	RTI	DISP	2				$[PC] \leftarrow [ST] + DISP$ $[EN] \leftarrow 1$ Return from interrupt. Like RTS, but enable interrupts.
STATUS	CFR	r	2				$[r] \leftarrow [FW]$ Copy flags to any Accumulator.
	CRF	r	2	X	X	X	$[FW] \leftarrow [r]$ Move any Accumulator contents to flags.
	SFLG	f	2				$[FW<n>] \leftarrow 1$ Set flag f to 1. (f = 0 to 15).
	PFLG	f	2				$[FW<f>] \leftarrow 1$ for four clock periods Pulse flag f (invert flag status for four clock periods). (f = 0 to 15).
	HALT		2				Halt

The following symbols are used in Table 1-2:

aa	Two bits choosing the destination register.
bb	Two bits choosing the Index register
cccc	Four bits choosing the Condition Code. See Table 1-3.
ee	Two bits choosing the source register.
ffff	Four bits selecting a bit in the Flag Word
l	One bit determining whether Link is included in a shift or rotate.
nnnnnnn	Seven bits determining how many single bit shifts or rotates are performed.
PP	8-bit signed displacement
QQ	Eight bits of immediate data
x	A "don't care" bit
XX	A "don't care" byte

Table 1-2. INS8900 and PACE Instruction Set Object Codes

INSTRUCTION		OBJECT CODE	BYTES	MACHINE CYCLES			
				TOTAL	INTERNAL	INPUT	OUTPUT
ADD	r,DISP (X)	1110aabb PP	2	4	2	2	
AISZ	r,DATA8	011110aa QQ	2	5/6	4/5	1	
AND	0,DISP (X)	101010bb PP	2	4	2	2	
BOC	CC,DISP	0100cccc PP	2	5/6	4/5	1	
CAI	r,DATA8	011100aa QQ	2	5	4	1	
CFR	f	000001aa XX	2	4	3	1	
CRF	f	000010aa XX	2	4	3	1	
DECA	0,DISP (X)	100010bb PP	2	7	5	2	
DSZ	DISP (X)	101011bb PP	2	7/8	4/5	2	1
HALT		000000xx XX	2	-	-	1	
ISZ	DISP (X)	100011bb PP	2	7/8	4/5	2	1
JMP	DISP (X)	000110bb PP	2	4	3	1	
JMP	@DISP (X)	100110bb PP	2	4	2	2	
JSR	DISP (X)	000101bb PP	2	5	4	1	
JSR	@DISP (X)	100101bb PP	2	5	3	2	
LD	r,DISP (X)	1100aabb PP	2	4	2	2	
LD	0,@DISP (X)	101000bb PP	2	5	2	3	
LI	r,DATA8	010100aa QQ	2	4	3	1	
LSEX	0,DISP (X)	101111bb PP	2	4	2	2	
OR	0,DISP (X)	101001bb PP	2	4	2	2	

Table 1-2. INS8900 and PACE Instruction Set Object Codes (Continued)

INSTRUCTION		OBJECT CODE	BYTES	MACHINE CYCLES			
				TOTAL	INTERNAL	INPUT	OUTPUT
PFLG	f	0011ffff 0xxxxxxx	2	6	5	1	
PULL	r	011001aa XX	2	4	3	1	
PULLF		000100xx XX	2	4	3	1	
PUSH	r	011000aa XX	2	4	3	1	
PUSHF		000011xx XX	2	4	3	1	
RADC	S,D	0011101aa eexxxxxx	2	4	3	1	
RADD	S,D	011010aa eexxxxxx	2	4	3	1	
RAND	S,D	010101aa eexxxxxx	2	4	3	1	
RCPY	S,D	010111aa eexxxxxx	2	4	3	1	
ROL	r,n,l	001000aa nnnnnnnl	2	5 + 3n	4 + 3n	1	
ROR	r,n,l	001001aa nnnnnnnl	2	5 + 3n	4 + 3n	1	
RTI		011111xx PP	2	6	5	1	
RTS		100000xx PP	2	5	4	1	
RXCH	S,D	011011aa eexxxxxx	2	6	5	1	
RXOR	S,D	010110aa eexxxxxx	2	4	3	1	
SFLG	f	0011ffff 1xxxxxxx	2	5	4	1	
SHL	r,n,l	001010aa nnnnnnnl	2	5 + 3n	4 + 3n	1	
SHR	r,n,l	001011aa nnnnnnnl	2	5 + 3n	4 + 3n	1	
SKAZ	0,DISP (X)	101110bb PP	2	5/6	3/4	2	
SKG	0,DISP (X)	100111bb PP	2	7/8	5/6	2	
SKNE	r,DISP (X)	1111aabb PP	2	5/6	3/4	2	
ST	r,DISP (X)	1101aabb PP	2	4	2	1	1
ST	0,@DISP (X)	101100bb PP	2	4	1	2	1
SUBB	0,DISP (X)	100100bb PP	2	4	2	2	
XCHRS	r	000111aa XX	2	6	5	1	

*All instructions may take additional cycles if Extend Read and Extend Write are implemented.

Table 1-3. Branch Conditions for INS8900 and PACE BOC Instruction

Condition Code (CC)	Mnemonic	Condition
0000	STFL	Stack Full (contains nine or more words).
0001	REQ0	(AC0) equal to zero (see Note 1).
0010	PSIGN	(AC0) has positive sign (see Note 2).
0011	BIT0	Bit 0 of AC0 true.
0100	BIT1	Bit 1 of AC0 true.
0101	NREQ0	(AC0) is nonzero (see Note 1).
0110	BIT2	Bit 2 of AC0 is true.
0111	CONTIN	CONTIN (continue) input is true.
1000	LINK	LINK is true.
1001	IEN	IEN is true.
1010	CARRY	CARRY is true.
1011	NSIGN	(AC0) has negative sign (see Note 2).
1100	OVF	OVF is true.
1101	JC13	JC13 input is true (see Note 3).
1110	JC14	JC14 input is true.
1111	JC15	JC15 input is true.

NOTES:

1. If selected data length is 8 bits, only bits 0 through 7 of AC0 are tested.
2. Bit 7 is sign bit (instead of bit 15) if selected data length is 8 bits.
3. JC13 is used by INS8900 and PACE Microprocessor Development System and is not accessible during prototyping.

THE BENCHMARK PROGRAM

For PACE, our standard benchmark program adopts this modified form:

```
        LD      2,IOBUF     LOAD I/O BUFFER ADDRESS INTO AC2
        LD      0,@TABLE    LOAD ADDRESS OF FIRST FREE TABLE BYTE
        RCPY    0,3         MOVE TO AC3
LOOP    LD      0,0(2)      LOAD NEXT BYTE FROM I/O BUFFER
        ST      0,0(3)      STORE IN NEXT TABLE BYTE
        AISZ    2,1         INCREMENT AC2
        AISZ    3,1         INCREMENT AC3
        DSZ     IOCNT       DECREMENT I/O BUFFER LENGTH. SKIP IF ZERO
        JMP     LOOP        RETURN FOR MORE BYTES
        RCPY    3,0         MOVE AC3 CONTENTS TO AC0
        ST      0,@TABLE    RESTORE ADDRESS OF FIRST FREE TABLE BYTE
```

In order to take advantage of INS8900 and PACE indirect addressing, three memory locations are reserved on page 0 as follows:

IOBUF   holds the beginning address of the I/O buffer.

TABLE   holds the address of the first free byte in the permanent data table.

IOCNT   holds the number of data words in the I/O buffer.

Memory, as organized for the benchmark program will look like this:

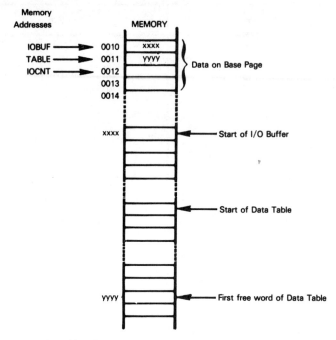

Suppose the benchmark program rules arbitrarily require that a displacement be stored in the first word of the data table, and that this displacement be added to the address of the first word of the data table in order to compute the address of the first free data table word:

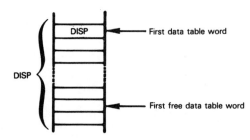

Now the instructions:

```
LD      0,@TABLE    LOAD ADDRESS OF FIRST FREE TABLE BYTE
RCPY    0,3         MOVE TO AC3
```

must be replaced by these instructions:

```
LD      3,TABLE     LOAD BEGINNING ADDRESS OF DATA TABLE
LD      0,0(3)      LOAD DISPLACEMENT TO FIRST FREE TABLE WORD
RADD    0,3         ADD DISPLACEMENT TO AC3
```

The new displacement must be restored to the first data table word. The instructions:

```
RCPY    3,0         MOVE AC3 CONTENTS TO AC0
ST      0,@TABLE    RESTORE ADDRESS OF FIRST FREE TABLE BYTE
```

must be replaced by these instructions:

```
LD     0,TABLE     LOAD BEGINNING ADDRESS OF DATA TABLE IN AC0
CAI    0,1         FORM TWOS COMPLEMENT
RADD   0,3         SUBTRACT AC0 FROM AC3 TO FORM DISPLACEMENT
RCPY   3,0         MOVE DISPLACEMENT TO AC0
LD     3,TABLE     LOAD BEGINNING ADDRESS OF DATA TABLE IN AC3
ST     0,0(3)      SAVE DISPLACEMENT IN FIRST FREE TABLE WORD
```

Forcing an INS8900/PACE programmer to conform to programming logic suited to some other microcomputer's instruction set only proves that the two microcomputers have different instruction sets.

THE PACE DP8302 SYSTEM TIMING ELEMENT (STE)

The STE is a very elementary clock device used with PACE, but not with the INS8900; it accepts inputs from an external crystal and generates the MOS clock signals for PACE, plus a pair of TTL-level clock outputs that can be used for synchronizing system operations. Figure 1-17 illustrates the pin assignments of the STE.

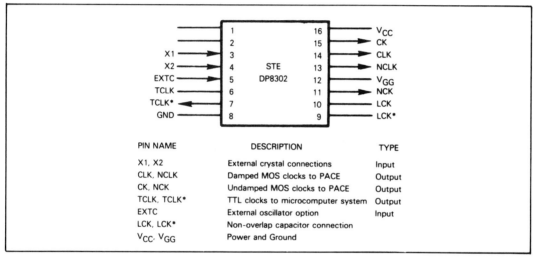

PIN NAME	DESCRIPTION	TYPE
X1, X2	External crystal connections	Input
CLK, NCLK	Damped MOS clocks to PACE	Output
CK, NCK	Undamped MOS clocks to PACE	Output
TCLK, TCLK*	TTL clocks to microcomputer system	Output
EXTC	External oscillator option	Input
LCK, LCK*	Non-overlap capacitor connection	
V_{CC}, V_{GG}	Power and Ground	

Figure 1-17. DP8302 System Timing Element (STE) Pins and Signals

The frequency of the MOS clocks output by the STE is one-half the input crystal frequency. The STE is designed to operate with a 2.6667 MHz crystal. The MOS clock frequency is thus 1.3333 MHz which results in a clock period (tp) of 750 nanoseconds (tp = 1/f); this is the optimal clock period for the PACE CPU. **STE CLOCK FREQUENCY**

Two pairs of MOS clock outputs are generated by the STE; NCLK/NCLK* and NCK/NCK*. The first pair of outputs contain a 25 Ω series of damping resistor; typically, these outputs will be used in circuit board layouts where the STE-to-PACE interconnect lines are less than two inches. The other MOS outputs, NCK and NCK*, are undamped, and you can select some other value of series damping resistors that might be better suited for your particular board layout.

In addition to the +5V and -12V power supplies typically needed with MOS devices, the PACE CPU has a third power supply requirement: a substrate bias voltage (V_{BB}) of +8V must be applied to the CPU chip. Since it is unlikely that any other devices in your microcomputer system would require this voltage level, the need for a third external system power source can be eliminated by providing a voltage converter circuit. **Figure 1-18 shows a circuit that generates the required V_{BB} voltage level;** the circuit requires only a few components and uses one of the STE's TTL clock outputs as a 'charge pump' for the circuit. **GENERATING THE PACE SUBSTRATE BIAS VOLTAGE**

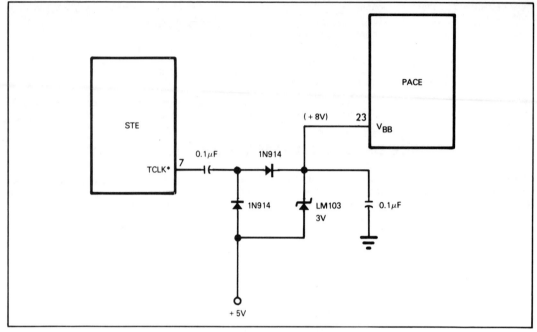

Figure 1-18. Circuit to Generate Substrate Bias Voltage (V_{BB}) for PACE CPU

THE PACE BIDIRECTIONAL TRANSCEIVER ELEMENT (BTE)

The DP8300 BTE is an 8-bit device that provides an interface between the PACE MOS-level signals and the TTL-level signals required by other devices in a microcomputer system (the BTE is not used in INS8900 systems). If you refer to Figure 1-1 at the beginning of this chapter, you will see that a typical PACE microcomputer system requires three BTEs: two are used to buffer the CPU's 16 address/data lines, and the third is used as a TTL driver for the CPU's control signal outputs (NADS, ODS, IDS, F11 - F14).

Figure 1-19 shows the pin assignments for the BTE.

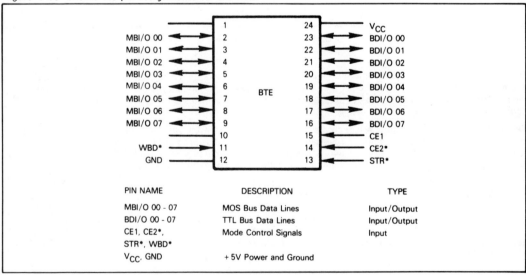

PIN NAME	DESCRIPTION	TYPE
MBI/O 00 - 07	MOS Bus Data Lines	Input/Output
BDI/O 00 - 07	TTL Bus Data Lines	Input/Output
CE1, CE2*, STR*, WBD*	Mode Control Signals	Input
V_{CC}, GND	+ 5V Power and Ground	

Figure 1-19   BTE Signals and Pin Assignments

1-36

Table 1-4 summarizes the operating modes of the BTE.

WBD* is the main mode control signal; when this signal is low, the other control signals are ignored and the BTE simply converts the MOS signals from the CPU into TTL-level output signals. The TTL outputs have a high fan-out capability and can service up to thirty 50 milliampere loads.

The BTE used to buffer the PACE control signals normally operates continuously in this 'drive-only' mode (Mode 1) and is kept in this mode by simply connecting the WBD* signal to ground.

The BTEs used to buffer bidirectional (address/data) lines must be switched back and forth between Modes 1 and 2; Mode 1 is used for CPU data output and Mode 2 for CPU data input. The simplest way of accomplishing this is to continuously enable the CE1, CE2*, and STR* controls by connecting them to appropriate logic levels (+5V or ground) and then use the WBD* signal for directional control. For example, in a PACE system, the IDS signal from the CPU could be used as the input to WBD*. During a PACE data input cycle, IDS will go high at the appropriate portion of the cycle and place the BTE in Mode 2; IDS is low at all other times and the BTE will operate in Mode 1.

Table 1-4. PACE BTE Truth Table

MODE #	CONTROL INPUTS				MODE DESCRIPTION
	CE1	CE2*	STR*	WBD*	
1	X	X	X	0	Receive MOS signals and drive TTL signals
2	1	0	0	1	Receive TTL signals and drive MOS signals
3	0	0	0	1	Outputs in high-impedance state
	0	1	0	1	
	1	1	0	1	
4	X	X	1	1	On positive-edge transition of STR*, latch into Mode 2 or 3 as determined by state of CE1 and CE2*

X = don't care

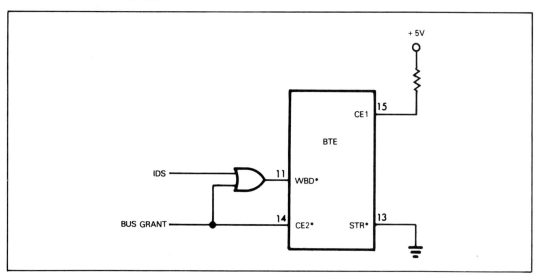

Figure 1-20. Signal Connections to Control BTE in a DMA System

1-37

In a DMA or multiprocessor we will need to use BTE Mode 3 to place the BTE outputs in a high-impedance state and thus free the System Busses for use by other devices. In such a system an externally generated Bus Grant signal could be used to place the BTE in Mode 3. Figure 1-20 illustrates one method of doing this: whenever the BUS GRANT signal is high, the BTE is in Mode 3. At other times the IDS signal operates as we've just described to switch the BTE back and forth between Modes 1 and 2.

The fourth BTE mode uses a negative-to-positive transition on the STR* input to latch the state of CE1 and CE2*, and then places the BTE in either Mode 2 or Mode 3. This latch mode function might be useful when the BTE is used as a simple input buffer. For example, in a system with multiplexed address/data lines (such as PACE), address outputs could be applied to CE1 and CE2*, and an address strobe signal (such as NADS) connected to STR*. Then, when the BTE is selected by the appropriate address bits, the trailing edge of the strobe signal will gate TTL data through the BTE and apply the data to the MOS lines of the CPU. When the BTE is not selected (addressed), its outputs will be in the high impedance state (Mode 3).

USING OTHER MICROCOMPUTER SUPPORT DEVICES
WITH THE PACE AND INS8900

The INS8900 CPU has numerous control signals which allow general purpose microcomputer support devices to be included in an INS8900 system.

Let us see how 8080A support devices might be used with the INS8900 CPU. First, we'll take an overview of the general CPU-to-device interface that all the 8080A family of devices expect.

All of the 8080A family devices require that address information (or enabling/select signals derived from the address lines) be valid during the data transfer (read/write) portion of an input/output cycle. Recall that the INS8900 data lines are multiplexed: at the beginning of an input/output cycle, the data lines are used to output address information; the address information is then removed and the data lines are used for the actual input or output of data during the latter portion of the I/O cycle.

Thus, the first thing we must do to interface the INS8900 to an 8080A family device is to demultiplex the INS8900 address/data lines. There are several different approaches that we can use to accomplish the required demultiplexing.

DEMULTIPLEXING THE INS8900 ADDRESS/DATA LINES

The most obvious way is to use D-type flip-flops or data registers with the INS8900 NADS signal as the clock pulse. Here are some of the standard 7400 family devices that might be used:

- 7475 Double 2-Bit Gated Latches with Q and Q Outputs
- 7477 Double 2-Bit Gated Latches with Q Output Only
- 74100 Double 4-Bit Gated Latches
- 74166 Dual 4-Bit Gated Latches with Clear
- 74174 Hex D-Type Flip-Flops with Common Clock and Clear
- 74175 Quad D-Type Flip-Flops with Common Clock and Clear

Some of these devices require that the NADS signal be inverted to provide the necessary clocking signal. Remember, though, that PACE address information is valid during both the leading edge (high-to-low transition) and trailing edge (low-to-high transition) of NADS; this generally simplifies the demultiplexing operation.

In many systems you will not need to latch all 16 bits of address information since it would be an unusual application that required all of the 64K of address space that this provides. There will usually be some tradeoff between system address requirements (how many system devices require a latched Address Bus) and the type and amount of address decoding required. When a fully latched Address Bus is provided, then simpler nonlatched address decoders can be used. In fact, often address bits can then be used directly as device select signals, or simple AND/OR gate combinations can perform the decoding.

The alternative method of demultiplexing the address/data lines is to use address decoding devices that are clocked by the NADS signal and provide latched outputs. These latched outputs can then be used as the device/chip select signals during I/O cycles.

Many systems will use some combination of a fully latched Address Bus and simple or latched address decoders. In the discussions that follow, we will not generally describe in detail the method used to obtain the required addressing or select/enabling signals, since the method used is so dependent on the particular system that you are designing.

Once the INS8900 address/data lines have been demultiplexed, the only major considerations we are left with are to ensure that the input/output control signals are of the proper polarity, and to verify that there are no timing problems. We will see that generally the INS8900 I/O control signals must be inverted to operate with the 8080A family of devices, although the 8212 offers us a choice of using the IDS and ODS signals, in either their original or inverted form.

INS8900 CONTROL SIGNAL POLARITY CONSIDERATIONS

Now we will provide a few specific examples of how devices from the 8080A family can be used with the INS8900 CPU.

In our first example the 8212 I/O Port is used as a simple input port by the INS8900 CPU. The interconnections required are shown in the following figure:

THE 8212 USED AS A SIMPLE INPUT PORT IN AN INS8900 SYSTEM

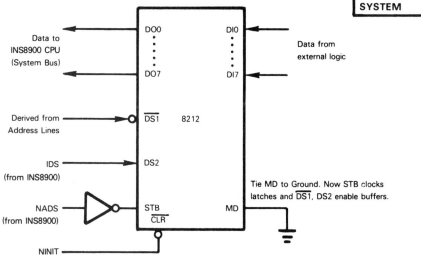

Here, the INS8900 Address Strobe signal (NADS) is inverted and used as the STB input to the 8212. Since MD is tied to ground, the STB signal clocks the data into the 8212: this will occur every time the INS8900 performs an input/output cycle, but the latched data will only be placed on the System Bus when the 8212 is selected. We accomplish device selection by applying a negative-true decoded address signal to the $\overline{DS1}$ input and then using the INS8900 IDS strobe signal as the DS2 input. Now, whenever the proper address is decoded, the IDS signal will cause the data that was previously latched by NADS to be placed on the System Bus for input to the INS8900. The timing would look like this:

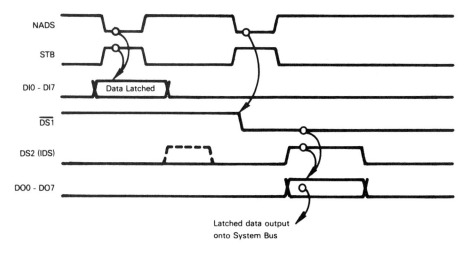

1-39

Notice that the data from external logic will be latched whenever NADS occurs. The actual selection of the 8212 and input of the latched data to the INS8900 might not occur for quite some time. Frequently, this arrangement will be completely acceptable. If not, then an input-with-handshaking arrangement, which we will describe next, might provide a better solution.

Before we proceed to our next example, let us make one more general comment about interfacing devices to the INS8900 CPU.

The INS8900 is a 16-bit microcomputer: it can transfer 16 bits of parallel data in a single input or output cycle. All of the other devices that we will be discussing are 8-bit devices. Frequently, you may not need the full width of the 16-bit Data Bus when transferring data between the CPU and external logic. In these cases, you can simply connect the data lines to/from the support device to the less significant data lines (D0 - D7) of the INS8900 System Bus, as we have shown in our first example. Masking of the unused, more significant data bits would then be handled under program control.

When you are going to utilize the full 16 bits of the Data Bus, you merely connect two 8-bit devices in parallel, as described in more detail for the CP1600 in Chapter 2. One device would be connected as we've already described; the data lines of the other device would then be connected to the more significant bits (D8 - D15) of the System Bus. All other connections to the two devices (device select signals, strobe signals, etc.) would be identical.

In this example, we will use the 8212 interrupt request signal INT to establish an input port with handshaking. The connection diagram is very similar to our first example:

THE 8212 USED IN AN INS8900 SYSTEM FOR INPUT WITH HANDSHAKING

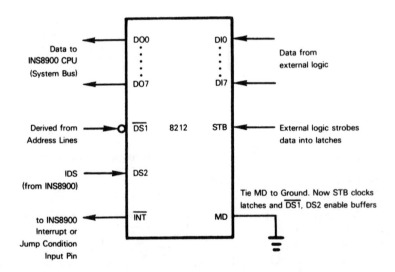

Here, the device select signals are the same as in our first example. However, instead of using the INS8900 NADS signal to clock data into the latches, we will require external logic to input the STB signal when it has data ready. When the data has been latched, the 8212 will output the INT signal, which will be used as the input to one of the INS8900 CPU interrupt request lines (NIR2 - NIR5) or Jump Condition inputs (JC13 - JC15). The CPU will then execute a service routine program that will include an instruction to read the data from the input port. This instruction will send out the input port's address, thus generating the DS1 signal, and then gate the latched data onto the System Bus when the IDS signal is generated. When the latched data is read out of the 8212, the INT signal returns high to complete the transaction. This sequence is summarized by the following timing diagram:

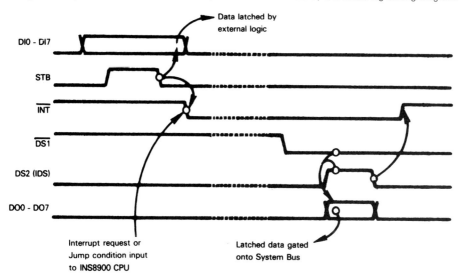

Using the 8212 as an output port in an INS8900 system requires a simple reversal of the connections we have described in the two preceding examples, and we will now use the ODS (Output Data Strobe) signal from the INS8900 instead of the IDS signal.

THE 8212 USED AS AN OUTPUT PORT IN AN INS8900 SYSTEM

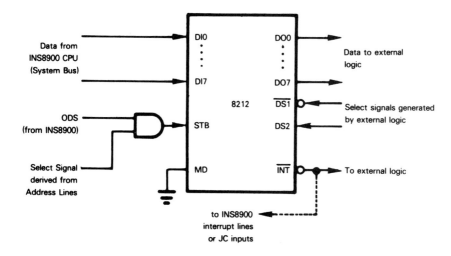

When the output port's address is sent out and decoded from the Address Bus, one input to the AND gate is enabled. The ODS signal then goes high to generate the STB signal and latch the contents of the system Data Bus into the 8212. This will cause the $\overline{INT}$ signal to go low and inform external logic that data has been loaded into the output port. The external logic will then generate the $\overline{DS1}$ and DS2 signals to gate the data out of the latches. When the data has been gated out, the $\overline{INT}$ signal will return high. This low-to-high transition could be used as an interrupt request or jump condition input to an INS8900 to enable output of new data. **Notice that if we continuously enable the 8212 outputs by tying $\overline{DS1}$ to ground and DS2 to +5V, then whenever the INS8900 loads a new data word into the latch, it will be immediately output to external logic.** This approach may be more advantageous in some applications.

Although the 8255 Programmable Peripheral Interface (PPI) is a more complicated device than the 8212, interfacing the 8255 to an INS8900 CPU is no more complicated (from a hardware point of view) than the INS8900-to-8212 interfaces we've described. This is due to the programmability of the 8255; mode control is performed by your program instead of by hardwired signals. Let us look at an example to illustrate this point:

8255 PPI DEVICES USED IN AN INS8900 SYSTEM

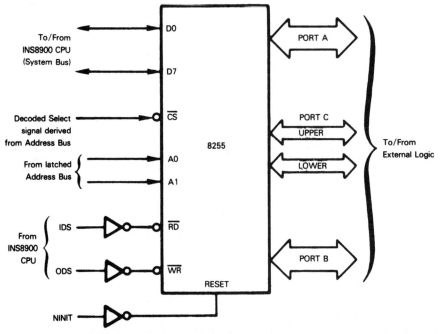

The $\overline{CS}$ signal selects the 8255 and this signal would typically be the output of an address decoder. The A0 and A1 inputs select one of the three I/O ports (A, B or C) or the 8255 Control registers. The $\overline{RD}$ and $\overline{WR}$ control signals are obtained by simply inverting the IDS and ODS signals from PACE. A generalized timing diagram for input/output operations would look like this:

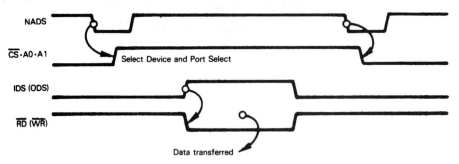

If two 8255s are used in parallel to provide 16-bit I/O ports, there is one special consideration beyond the general rules that we discussed earlier. Recall that mode control of the 8255 is accomplished by writing data into one 8-bit Control register within the device. When wired in parallel, one 8255 would be connected to bits 0 - 7 of the system Data Bus, and the other 8255 would be connected to bits 8 - 15. Therefore, when we send out a 16-bit control word from the INS8900 CPU to establish the desired mode of operation, the upper and lower bytes of the word must be identical.

From a hardware point of view, interfacing either of these devices to an INS8900 CPU is no different than interfacing an 8255 PPI to the INS8900. All we need to do is invert the IDS and ODS signals from the CPU to obtain $\overline{RD}$ and $\overline{WR}$ (or $\overline{IOR}$ and $\overline{IOW}$) signals, and provide chip select and latched address bits for input to the devices. All other interfacing and usage considerations are software functions and are described in Chapter 4. We will not describe them here since those portions of the device descriptions apply regardless of the CPU being used.

We will conclude our discussion of the use of 8080A devices in INS8900 systems by comparing INS8900 System Bus signals with those of 8080A systems. This comparison will be a useful guide for interfacing any 8080A device to an INS8900 system. Table 1-5 is a summary of INS8900 System Bus signals and the corresponding signals available in 8080A systems. Two separate columns are provided for 8080A signals: the first applies strictly to the 8080A CPU; the right-hand column refers to the signals present in a typical three-chip 8080A system consisting of the CPU, an 8228 System Controller, and an 8224 Clock Generator and Driver.

Since we have already discussed these signals in preceding paragraphs, we won't perform an item-by-item analysis of the table. Nonetheless, **there are a few signals in this table that do need additional explanation.**

We have included the INS8900 BPS signal in the I/O Control Signal group although it is not the type of signal you would normally classify within this group. However, you will recall that **when the BPS input is high, the INS8900 operates in a Base-Page-Split mode;** base page then consists of the top 128 words of memory and the bottom 128 words of memory. In our earlier discussion of the BPS signal, we described how **this mode can be used to simplify addressing of I/O devices.** If you refer back to that discussion, you will see that **by doing a little address decoding we can come up with a signal that will tell us when the INS8900 is addressing an I/O device** (as opposed to memory). Let us call this decoded signal 'I/O Device' (I/OD). Now, **we can combine this decoded signal with IDS and ODS as shown below to generate signals equivalent to the 8080A $\overline{I/OR}$ and $\overline{I/OW}$ signals.**

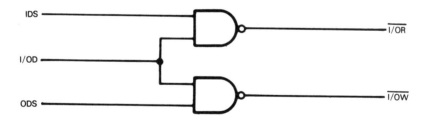

And if we invert the I/OD signal we can generate the 8080A $\overline{MEMR}$ and $\overline{MEMW}$ signals.

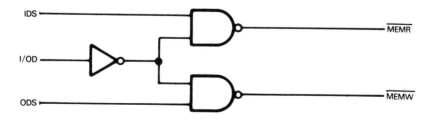

One other portion of Table 1-5 requires some explanation. **Notice that we have not drawn a line to separate the I/O control signals from the DMA-Related Signals. We've done this intentionally because there is some overlapping of functions with some of these signals.** For example, the INS8900 EXTEND signal can be used either to extend I/O cycles or to suspend I/O to allow DMA operations. We've also compared the INS8900 NHALT output signal to the 8080A WAIT signal. This comparison is valid if limited to the CPU Halt state initiated in either system by a Halt instruction. However, in 8080A systems the WAIT signal is also an acknowledgement to the READY or RDYIN input signals. There is no comparable EXTEND acknowledgement signal in PACE systems.

The 6800 family includes many devices that might be useful in INS8900 systems. Unfortunately, all of these devices have one common requirement which effectively makes them incompatible for use in an INS8900 system. That requirement is enabling input signal E which should more accurately be described as a synchronizing signal. In 6800 systems, E is usually generated by ANDing one of the primary system clock signals ($\Phi2$) with the Valid Memory Address signal (VMA) from the 6800 CPU. The clock period of the resulting E signal can be no less than one microsecond. The clock signals (CLK and NCLK) used in PACE systems, however, cannot have a clock period greater than 850 nanoseconds, and therefore cannot be used to simulate the 6800 $\Phi2$ signal. Therefore, we cannot recommend using 6800 family devices in an INS8900 system.

6800 SUPPORT DEVICES NOT COMPATIBLE WITH INS8900

Table 1-5. Comparing INS8900 System Busses to 8080A System Busses

SYSTEM BUS	INS8900 SYSTEM SIGNALS	8080A CPU SIGNALS	8080A SYSTEM (CPU, 8228, 8224) SIGNALS
Bidirectional Data Bus	D00 - D15 (16 Bits)	D0 - D7 (8 Bits)	DB0 - DB7 (8 Bits)
Address Bus	D00 - D15 Address information must be demultiplexed from Data Bus	A0 - A15	A0 - A15
Control Bus			
I/O Control Signals	NADS Strobe signal used by external logic to demultiplex address from Data Bus	—	—
	IDS	DBIN	$\overline{\text{MEMR}}$ and $\overline{\text{I/OR}}$
	ODS	$\overline{\text{WR}}$	$\overline{\text{MEMW}}$ and $\overline{\text{I/OW}}$
	BPS	—	—
	EXTEND	READY	RDYIN
	NHALT (output)	WAIT	WAIT
DMA-Related Signals	NHALT and CONTIN inputs	HOLD	HOLD
	CONTIN (ACK INT output)	HLDA	HLDA
	—	—	BUSEN
Interrupt Signals	NIR2 - NIR5	INT	INT
	CONTIN (ACK INT output)	D0 and SYNC	$\overline{\text{INTA}}$
	—	INTE	INTE
	Non-maskable Interrupt (CONTIN and NHALT inputs)	—	—
Initialize	NINIT	RESET	RESIN
Jump Condition Inputs	JC13 - JC15	—	—
Control Flag Outputs	F11 - F14	—	—

DATA SHEETS

This section contains specific electrical and timing data for the following devices:

PACE CPU
INS8900
PACE STE
PACE DTE

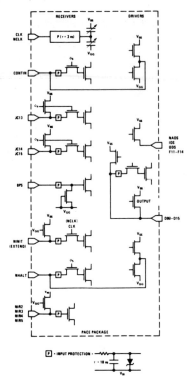

FIGURE 4. PACE Driver and Receiver Equivalent Circuits

external clock timing

PACE requires non-overlapping true and complemented clock inputs as shown in *Figure 5*. Refer to Electrical Characteristics for timing specifications.

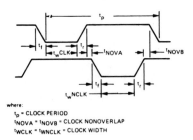

where:
t_p = CLOCK PERIOD
t_{NOVA} = t_{NOVB} = CLOCK NONOVERLAP
t_{WCLK} = t_{WNCLK} = CLOCK WIDTH

FIGURE 5. External Clock Timing

We reprint data sheets on pages 1-D2 through 1-D17 by permission of National Semiconductor Corporation.

For systems utilizing memories with access times greater than 2 clock periods it may be desirable to use the EXTEND input to lengthen the I/O cycle by multiples of the clock period. Timing for this is shown in *Figure 9*. In the case of either input or output operations, the extend· should be brought true prior to the end of internal phase 6. The timing shown in *Figure 9* will provide the minimum extend of one clock period. Holding EXTEND true for n additional clock periods longer will cause an extension of n + 1 clock periods.

In DMA or multiprocessor systems it may be desirable to prevent I/O operations by PACE when the bus is in use by another device. This may be done by using the EXTEND input immediately following an IDS or ODS as shown in *Figure 10*. Alternatively, the extend timing of *Figure 9* may be used, as the extend function occurs independent of whether there is an I/O operation, that is, whenever the internal clock phase 6 occurs.

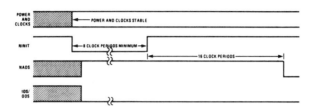

FIGURE 6. Initialization Timing

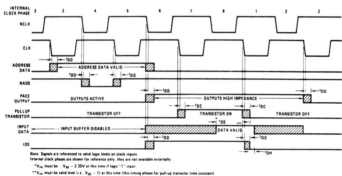

Figure 7. Address Output and Data Input Timing

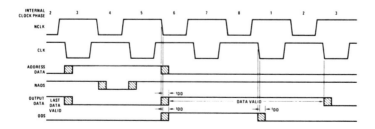

FIGURE 8. Data Output Timing

PACE CPU

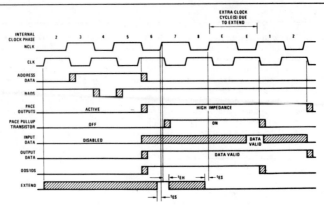

FIGURE 9. Extend I/O Signal Timing

absolute maximum ratings

All Input or Output Voltages with Respect to Most Positive Supply Voltage (V_{BB})	+0.3V to −21.5V	Storage Temperature Range	−65°C to +150°C
		Lead Temperature (Soldering, 10 seconds)	300°C
Operating Temperature Range	0°C to +70°C		

electrical characteristics (T_A = 0°C to +70°C, V_{SS} = +5V ±5%, V_{GG} = −12V ±5%, V_{BB} = V_{SS} + 3V ±0.5V)

PARAMETER	CONDITIONS	MIN	MAX	UNITS
OUTPUT SPECIFICATIONS				
D00−D15, F11−F14, ODS, IDS, NADS (These are open drain outputs which may be used to drive DS3608 sense amplifiers, or may be used with pull-down resistors to provide a voltage output.)				
Logic "1" Output Current (Except F11−F14)	V_{OUT} = 2.4V	−1.0	−5.0	mA
Logic "1" Output Current, F11−F14 (Note 7)	V_{OUT} = 2.4V	−0.7	−5.0	mA
Logic "0" Output Current	$V_{GG} \leqslant V_{OUT} \leqslant V_{SS}$		±10	µA
NHALT, CONTIN (Low Power TTL Output.)				
Logic "1" Output Voltage	I_{OUT} = −650µA	2.4		V
Logic "0" Output Voltage	I_{OUT} = 300µA		0.4	V
INPUT SPECIFICATIONS				
D00−D15, NIR2−NIR5, EXTEND, JC13−JC15, CONTIN, NINIT, NHALT (These are TTL compatible inputs.) (Note 2)				
Logic "1" Input Voltage		V_{SS}−1	V_{SS}+0.3	V
Logic "0" Input Voltage		V_{SS}−7	V_{SS}−4	V
Pullup Transistor "ON" Resistance (D00−D15) (Note 3)	$V_{IN} = V_{SS}$−1V		7	kΩ
Pullup Transistor "ON" Resistance (all others)	$V_{IN} = V_{SS}$−1V		5	kΩ
Logic "0" Input Current (D00−D15)	V_{IN} = 0.4		−1.8	mA
Logic "0" Input Current (NHALT, CONTIN)	V_{IN} = 0.4		−12	mA
Logic "0" Input Current (all others)	V_{IN} = 0.4		−3.6	mA
Capacitance, Input and Output (except clocks)	$V_{IN} = V_{SS}$, f_T = 500 kHz		20	pF
BPS (This is a MOS Level Input.) (Note 4)				
Logic "1" Input Voltage		V_{SS}−1	V_{SS}+0.3	V
Logic "0" Input Voltage		V_{GG}	V_{SS}−7	V
Logic "1" Input Current	$V_{IN} = V_{SS}$−1V		100	µA
CLK, NCLK (These are MOS Clock Inputs)				
Clock "1" Voltage (Note 5)		V_{SS}−1	V_{SS}+0.3	V
Clock "0" Voltage		V_{GG}	V_{GG}+1	V
Input Capacitance (Note 6)		30	150	pF
Bias Supply Current	$V_{BB} = V_{SS}$ +3.0V		100	µA
V_{GG} Supply Current	t_p = .65µs, T_A = 25°C		40	mA
V_{SS} Supply Current	t_p = .65µs, T_A = 25°C		85	mA

PACE CPU

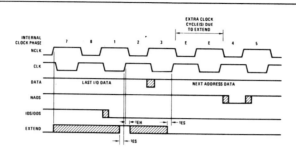

FIGURE 10. Suspend I/O Signal Timing

TIMING SPECIFICATIONS (See *Figures 5 to 10* for additional timing information.)

CLK, NCLK (See *Figure 5*) (Referenced to 10% and 90% Amplitude)				
Rise and Fall Time (t_r, t_f)		10	50	ns
Clock Width (t_W CLK, t_W NCLK)		300	375	ns
Clock Non-Overlap (t_{NOVA}, t_{NOVB})		5		ns
Clock Period (t_p)		.65	.8	μs
EXTEND				
Individual Extend Duration			2	μs
Extend Setup Time (t_{ES}) (Note 10)		100		ns
Extend Hold Time (t_{EH}) (Note 13)		20		ns
Propagation Delay (t_{DD})				
NHALT, CONTIN (Note 9)	C_L = 20 pF		200	ns
NADS, IDS, ODS, D00–D15 (Note 8)	V_{OUT} = 2.4V		100	ns
D00–D15				
Input Setup Time (t_{DS}) (Note 11)		200		ns
Hold Time (t_{DH}) (Note 12)		0		ns
Turn-on or Turn-off Time of Pullup Transistor (t_{DC}) (Note 13)		150		ns
F11–F14 Pulse Flag (PFLG) Pulse Width		$4t_p$ –300	$4t_p$ +300	ns
NINIT Initialization Pulse Width		8		clock periods
NIR2–NIR5 Input Pulse Width to Set Latch		1		clock periods

Note 1: Maximum ratings indicate limits beyond which permanent damage may occur. Continuous operation at these limits is not intended and should be limited to those conditions specified under dc electrical characteristics.
Note 2: Pullup transistor provided on chip (See *Figure 4*.)
Note 3: Pullup transistors on JC13, JC14, JC15 are turned on for one out of 8 clock intervals. Pullup transistors on D00–D15 are turned on during last clock period of Input Data Strobe (IDS). Other pullup transistors are on continuously when in data input mode.
Note 4: Pulldown transistor provided on chip.
Note 5: Clamp diodes and series damping resistors may be required to prevent clock overshoot.
Note 6: Capacitance is not constant and varies with clock voltage and internal state of processor.
Note 7: For $V_{SS} \geqslant V_{OUT} \geqslant 2.0V$ output current is a linear function of V_{OUT}.
Note 8: Delay measured from valid logic level on clock edge initiating change to valid current output level.
Note 9: Delay measured from valid logic level on clock edge initiating change to valid voltage output level.
Note 10: With respect to rising edge of NCLK. (See *Figure 9* and *10*.)
Note 11: With respect to falling edge of CLK. (See *Figure 7*.)
Note 12: With respect to the valid "0" level on the falling edge of Input Data Strobe (IDS). (See *Figure 7*.)
Note 13: With respect to valid logic level of appropriate clock.

Absolute Maximum Ratings

Voltage at Any Pin with Resepct to
Most Negative Supply (V_{BB}). . . . . −0.3 V to +20 V
Operating Temperature Range . . . . 0°C to +70°C
Storage Temperature Range. . . . . −65°C to +150°C
Lead Temperature (soldering, 10 seconds) . . . . +300°C

Electrical Characteristics

(T_A = 0°C to +70°C, V_{SS} = 0 V, V_{DD} = +12 V ± 5%, V_{CC} = +5 V ± 5%, V_{BB} = −8 V ± 5%)

Symbol	Parameter	Conditions	Min	Max	Units
OUTPUT SPECIFICATIONS					
	D00–D15, F11–F14, ODS, IDS, NADS (These are low-power Schottky-compatible push-pull outputs.)				
V_{OH}	Logic "1" Output Voltage	I_{OUT} = −500 μA	2.4		V
V_{OL}	Logic "0" Output Voltage	I_{OUT} = 900 μA		0.4	V
	NHALT, CONTIN (low-power Schottky outputs)				
V_{OH}	Logic "1" Output Voltage	I_{OUT} = −250 μA	2.4		V
V_{OL}	Logic "0" Output Voltage	I_{OUT} = 600 μA		0.4	V
INPUT SPECIFICATIONS					
	D00–D15, NIR2–NIR5, EXTEND, JC13–JC15, NINIT, CONTIN, NHALT (low-power Schottky inputs)				
V_{IH}	Logic "1" Input Voltage		2.4	V_{CC} + 1	V
V_{IL}	Logic "0" Input Voltage		−1.0	+0.8	V
I_L	Input Leakage Current (except NHALT, CONTIN, JC13–JC15)	$V_{SS} \leqslant V_{IN} \leqslant V_{CC}$ + 1		40	μA
I_{IL}	Logic "0" Input Current, NHALT, CONTIN (Note 2)	V_{IN} = 0.4 V		−7.0	mA
I_{IL}	Logic "0" Input Current, JC13–JC15 (Note 2)	V_{IN} = 0.4 V		−3.0	mA
	BPS (This is an MOS level input.)				
V_{IH}	Logic "1" Input Voltage		V_{DD} − 1	V_{DD} + 1	V
V_{IL}	Logic "0" Input Voltage		−1.0	+0.8	V
I_{IH}	Logic "1" Input Current (Note 3)	V_{IN} = 13.6 V		750	μA
	CLKX (This is an MOS level input.)				
V_{CIL}	Clock "0" Voltage		−1.0	+0.8	V
V_{CIH}	Clock "1" Voltage		V_{DD} − 1	V_{DD} + 1	V
C_{IN}	Input Capacitance			20	pF
I_{DD}	Average Supply Current (V_{DD}) (Note 4)	tp = 500 ns, T_A = 25°C		100	mA
I_{CC}	Average Supply Current (V_{CC}) (Note 4)	tp = 500 ns, T_A = 25°C		10	mA
I_{BB}	Average Supply Current (V_{BB})	V_{BB} = −8 V		−200	μA

Timing Specifications

Symbol	Parameter	Conditions	Min	Max	Units
	CLKX				
t_r, t_f	Rise and Fall Times (Note 5) (Referenced to 10% and 90% amplitude)		5	30	ns
t_P	Clock Period		500	650	ns
t_{CLK}, t_{NCLK}	Pulse Width (Referenced to 50% amplitude)		$t_P/2 - 5\%$	$t_P/2 + 5\%$	ns
	EXTEND				
	Individual Extend Duration			2	μs
t_{ES}	Extend Setup Time (Note 6)		70		ns
t_{EH}	Extend Hold Time (Note 6)		120		ns
	Propagation Delay				
t_{DD1}	NHALT, CONTIN (Note 7)	$C_L = 40\,pF$, 1 low-power Schottky load		200	ns
t_{DD2}	NADS, IDS, ODS, D00-D15 (Note 7)	$C_L = 40\,pF$, 1 INS8208 load		200	ns
	D00-D15				
t_{DS}	Input Setup Time (Note 6)		50		ns
t_{DH}	Hold Time (Note 8)		0		ns
t_{FW}	F11-F14 Pulse Flag (PFLG) Pulse Width		$4t_P - 300$	$4t_P + 300$	ns
t_{NW}	NINIT Initialization Pulse Width		8		t_P
t_{IRW}	NIR2-NIR5 Input Pulse Width to Set Latch		1		t_P

Note 1: Maximum ratings indicate limits beyond which permanent damage may occur. Continuous operation at these limits is not intended and should be limited to those conditions specified under DC electrical characteristics.

Note 2: NHALT, CONTIN, and JC13-JC15 logic "0" input currents specified when the internal chip loads are putting out a logic "1."

Note 3: Pull-down transistor provided on chip.

Note 4: Supply currents measured with 40 pF and INS8208 loads.

Note 5: Clamp diode and series damping resistor may be required to prevent clock overshoot.

Note 6: Measured with respect to appropriate valid logic level of CLKX.

Note 7: Delay measured from valid logic level on CLKX edge initiating change to valid output voltage level.

Note 8: With respect to the valid "0" level on the falling edge of Input Data Strobe (IDS).

Note 9: Typical load circuit:

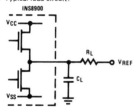

$R_L = 3.6k$ (3.3k for testing)
$C_L = 40\,pF$
$V_{REF} = 1.72\,V$

Note 10: Typical output delay versus load capacitance C_L for load circuit in Note 9:

Note 11: Typical V_{DD} supply current versus temperature.

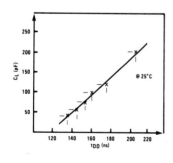

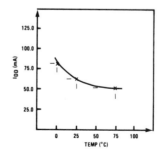

Timing Waveforms

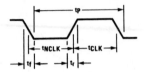

Figure 1. External Clock Timing (CLKX)

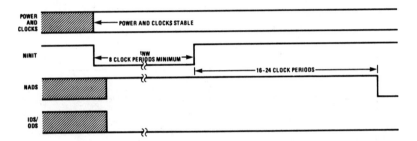

Figure 2. Initialization Timing

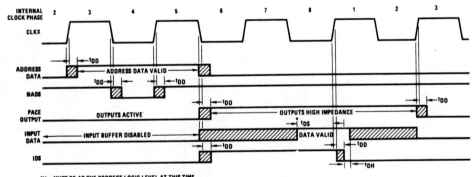

*V_IN MUST BE AT THE CORRECT LOGIC LEVEL AT THIS TIME.

NOTE: SIGNALS ARE REFERENCED TO VALID LOGIC LEVELS ON CLOCK INPUT. INTERNAL CLOCK PHASES ARE SHOWN FOR REFERENCE ONLY; THEY ARE NOT AVAILABLE EXTERNALLY.

Figure 3. Address Output and Data Input Timing

Timing Waveforms (continued)

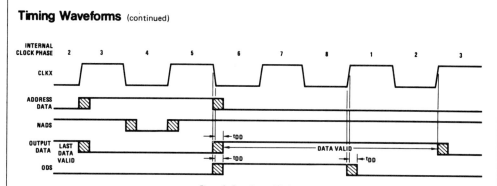

Figure 4. Data Output Timing

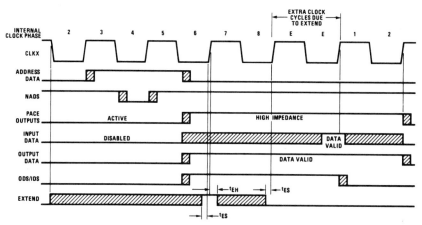

Figure 5. Extend I/O Signal Timing

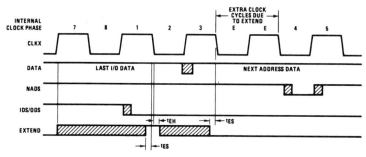

Figure 6. Suspend I/O Signal Timing

Timing Waveforms (continued)

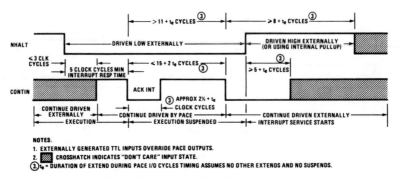

NOTES:
1. EXTERNALLY GENERATED TTL INPUTS OVERRIDE PACE OUTPUTS.
2. ▨ CROSSHATCH INDICATES "DON'T CARE" INPUT STATE.
③ t_e = DURATION OF EXTEND DURING PACE I/O CYCLES TIMING ASSUMES NO OTHER EXTENDS AND NO SUSPENDS.

Figure 7. Relative Timing for Level-0 Interrupt Generation

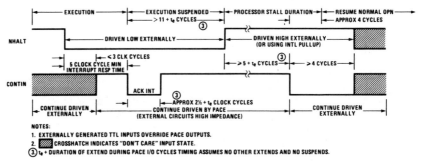

NOTES:
1. EXTERNALLY GENERATED TTL INPUTS OVERRIDE PACE OUTPUTS.
2. ▨ CROSSHATCH INDICATES "DON'T CARE" INPUT STATE.
③ t_e + DURATION OF EXTEND DURING PACE I/O CYCLES TIMING ASSUMES NO OTHER EXTENDS AND NO SUSPENDS.

Figure 8. Relative Timing for Processor Stall

The architecture of the INS8900 (shown in Figure 9) features a number of resources to minimize system program and read/write storage, increase throughput, and reduce the amount and cost of external support hardware. Principal resources that allow these efficiencies to be achieved include:

Four 16-bit general purpose working registers available to the user reduce the number of memory load and store operations associated with saving temporary and intermediate results in system memory.

An independent 16-bit status and control flag register automatically and continuously preserves system status. The user may operate on its contents as data, allowing masking, testing, and modification of several bit fields simultaneously.

A ten-word (16-bit) last-in, first-out (LIFO) stack inherently decreases response time to interrupts while eliminating both program and read/write system storage overhead associated with storing stack information outside the microprocessor chip.

Stack full/stack empty interrupts are provided to facilitate off-chip stack storage in those applications where additional stack capacity is desirable.

A six-level vectored priority interrupt system internal to the chip provides automatic interrupt identification, eliminating both program storage overhead and the time normally required to poll peripherals in order to identify the interrupting device.

Three sense inputs and four control flag outputs allow the user to respond directly to specific combinations of status present in the microprocessor-based system, thus eliminating costly hardware, program overhead, and throughput associated with implementing these functions over the system data bus.

A comprehensive set of input/output control signals provided by the internal control logic simplifies interfaces to memory and peripherals and allows flexible control of INS8900 operations.

Single-phase 2.0 MHz clock input is easily generated with a minimum of external components.

recommended crystal specifications

- AT-cut crystal

- 2.6667 MHz ± 0.1%, fundamental
  mode

- 5 mW maximum

- 150 Ω maximum series resistance

timing diagram

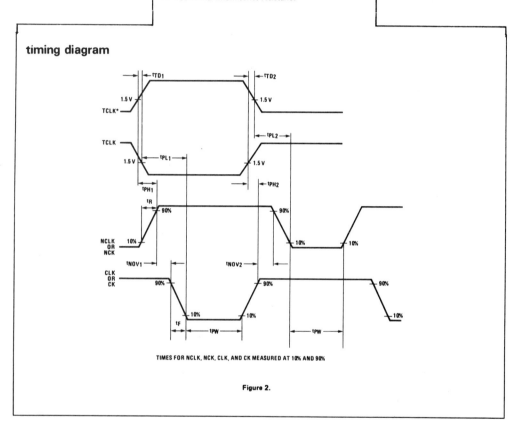

TIMES FOR NCLK, NCK, CLK, AND CK MEASURED AT 10% AND 90%

Figure 2.

absolute maximum ratings [1]

Supply Voltage (V_{CC}) . . . . 7.0 V
           (V_{GG}) . . . . −15.0 V
Input Voltage . . . . 5.5 V
Storage Temperature . . . . −65°C to +150°C
Lead Temperature (soldering, 10 seconds) . . . . . 300°C

operating conditions

	Min.	Max.	Units
Supply Voltage (V_{CC})	4.75	5.25	V
(V_{GG})	−11.40	−12.6	V
Temperature	0	+70	°C

dc electrical characteristics (Notes 2 and 3)

Parameter	Conditions		Min.	Typ.	Max.	Units
OUTPUT SPECIFICATIONS:						
T CLK, T CLK* (TTL Clocks)						
V_{OH} Logic "1" Output Voltage	V_{CC} = 4.75 V	I_{OH} = −1 mA	3.65	4.25		V
V_{OL} Logic "0" Output Voltage	V_{CC} = 4.75 V	I_{OL} = 32 mA		0.25	0.4	V
I_{OS} Output Short Circuit Current	(Note 4), V_{CC} = 5.25 V, V_O = 0		− 10	−33	−55	mA
CK, NCK, CLK, NCLK						
V_{OH} Logic "1" Output Voltage	I_{OH} = −100 μA			V_{CC} − 0.9	4.5	V
V_{OL} Logic "0" Output Voltage	V_{CC} = 4.75 V	I_{OL} = 100 μA		V_{GG} + 0.1	V_{GG} + 0.25	V
	V_{GG} = −11.4 V	I_{OL} = 5 mA		V_{GG} + 0.2	V_{GG} + 0.5	V
INPUT SPECIFICATIONS:						
EXTC						
V_{IH} Logic "1" Input Voltage			2.0			V
I_{IH} Logic "1" Input Current	V_{CC} = 5.25 V	V_{IN} = 2.4 V			40	μA
		V_{IN} = 5.5 V			1.0	mA
V_{IL} Logic "0" Input Voltage					0.8	V
I_{IL} Logic "0" Input Current	V_{CC} = 5.25 V	V_{IL} = 0.4 V		−0.9	−1.6	mA
V_{CLAMP} Input Clamp Diode	V_{CC} = 4.75 V	I_{IL} = −12 mA		−0.8	−1.5	V
POWER SUPPLY CURRENT						
I_{CC} Supply Current from V_{CC}	V_{CC} = 5.25 V			20	30	mA
I_{GG} Supply Current from V_{GG}	V_{GG} = −12.6 V			−40	−55	mA

ac electrical characteristics Crystal Frequency at 2.6667 MHz I_A = 0°C to +70°C, V_{CC} − V_{GG} = +17 V ± 5%

Symbol	Parameter	Limits			Units	Test Conditions
		Min.	Typ.	Max.		
t_{NOV1}, t_{NOV2}	Non-Overlap Time	5	12		ns	See Note 5
t_{PW}	MOS Clocks Pulse Width (NCLK, CLK, NCK, CK)	300	320		ns	See Note 5
t_R	MOS Clocks Rise Time (NCLK, CLK, NCK, CK)			40	ns	See Note 5
t_F	MOS Clocks Fall Time (NCLK, CLK, NCK, CK)			40	ns	See Note 5
t_{PH1}, t_{PH2}	TTL Clocks to MOS Clocks High Level Delay	−40		40	ns	See Note 5
t_{PL1}, t_{PL2}	TTL Clocks to MOS Clocks Low Level Delay			80	ns	See Note 5
t_{TD1}, t_{TD2}	TTL Clock to TTL Clock Delay	−25		25	ns	See Note 5
t_{START}	Time Delay from Last Power Applied to MOS Clocks Stabilized			100	ms	See Figure 7

Notes:
1. "Absolute Maximum Ratings" are those values beyond which the safety of the device cannot be guaranteed. They are not meant to imply that the devices should be operated at these limits. The table of "Electrical Characteristics" provides conditions for actual device operation.
2. Unless otherwise specified, min/max limits apply across the 0°C to +70°C temperature range and V_{CC} = 4.75 V to 5.25 V, V_{GG} = −11.4 V to −12.6 V power supply range. All typicals are given for V_{CC} = 5.0 V, V_{GG} = −12 V, and T_A = +25°C.
3. All currents into device pins are shown as positive; currents out of device pins are shown as negative. All voltages are references to ground unless otherwise noted.
4. Only one output at a time should be shorted.
5. The test conditions for measuring AC parameters are shown in Figures 2 and 3, with C_1 = C_2 = 60 pF, C_3 = 80 pF, C_{NOV} = 60 pF. Load conditions for MOS clocks and TTL clocks are shown in Figures 4 and 5. Including probe and jig capacitance, C_{L1} = 20 to 80 pF, and C_{L2} = 40 pF.

PACE STE

test conditions

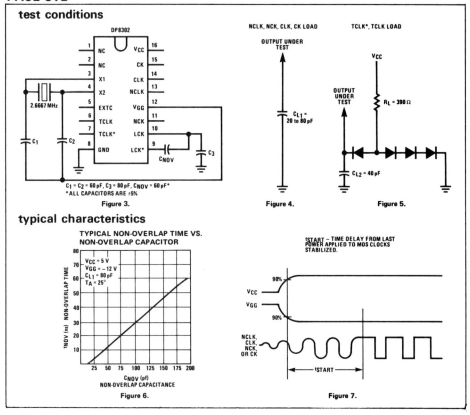

$C_1 = C_2 = 60\,pF$, $C_3 = 80\,pF$, $C_{NOV} = 60\,pF^*$
*ALL CAPACITORS ARE ±5%

Figure 3.

NCLK, NCK, CLK, CK LOAD

OUTPUT UNDER TEST

$C_{L1} = 20$ to $80\,pF$

Figure 4.

TCLK*, TCLK LOAD

V_{CC}

$R_L = 390\,\Omega$

OUTPUT UNDER TEST

$C_{L2} = 40\,pF$

Figure 5.

typical characteristics

TYPICAL NON-OVERLAP TIME VS. NON-OVERLAP CAPACITOR

$V_{CC} = 5\,V$
$V_{GG} = -12\,V$
$C_{L1} = 80\,pF$
$T_A = 25°$

t_{NOV} (ns) NON-OVERLAP TIME

C_{NOV} (pf) NON-OVERLAP CAPACITANCE

Figure 6.

t_{START} — TIME DELAY FROM LAST POWER APPLIED TO MOS CLOCKS STABILIZED.

V_{CC}

V_{GG}

90%

90%

NCLK, CLK, NCK, OR CK

t_{START}

Figure 7.

PACE BTE/8

absolute maximum ratings (Note 1)

Supply Voltage	7V
Input Voltage (All Inputs Except MBI/O Input Active)	5.5V
Output Voltage	5.5V
MOS Bus Input Current	±10 mA
Storage Temperature	−65°C to +150°C
Lead Temperature (Soldering, 10 seconds)	300°C

recommended operating conditions

	MIN	MAX	UNITS
Supply Voltage (V_{CC})	4.75	5.25	V
Temperature (T_A)	0	+70	°C

dc electrical characteristics (Notes 2 and 3)

PARAMETER		CONDITIONS		MIN	TYP	MAX	UNITS
TTL BUS PORT (BDI/O 00–07)							
V_{IH}	Logical "1" Input Voltage			2.0			V
V_{IL}	Logical "0" Input Voltage					0.8	V
V_{OH}	Logical "1" Output Voltage	$WBD^* = 0.8V$,	$I_{OH} = -1$ mA	$V_{CC}-1.1$	$V_{CC}-0.8$		V
		$MBI/O = 0.5$ mA	$I_{OH} = -5.2$ mA	2.4	3.7		V
V_{OL}	Logical "0" Output Voltage	$WBD^* = 0.8V$,	$I_{OL} = 20$ mA		0.25	0.4	V
		$MBI/O = 100\mu A$	$I_{OL} = 50$ mA		0.4	0.5	V
I_{OS}	Output Short Circuit Current	$WBD^* = 0.8V$, $MBI/O = 0.5$ mA, $V_{OUT} = 0V$, $V_{CC} = 5.25V$, (Note 4)		−10	−35	−75	mA
I_{IH}	Logical "1" Input Current	$WBD^* = 2V$, $V_{IH} = 2.4V$				80	μA
I_1	Input Current at Maximum Input Voltage	$WBD^* = 2V$, $V_{IH} = 5.5V$, $V_{CC} = 5.25V$				1	mA
I_{IL}	Logical "0" Input Current	$WBD^* = 2V$, $V_{IL} = 0.4V$			−10	−250	μA
V_{CLAMP}	Input Clamp Voltage	$WBD^* = 2V$, $I_{IN} = -12$ mA			−0.2	−1.5	V
I_{OD}	Output/Input Bus Disable Current	$WBD^* = STR^* = 2V$, $BDI/O = 0.4V$ to 4V, $V_{CC} = 5.25V$		−80		80	μA
MOS BUS PORT (MBI/O 00–07)							
I_0	Logical "0" Input Current	$WBD^* = 0.8V$, $I_{OL(TTL)} = 50$ mA, $V_{OL} \leq 0.5V$, (Note 5)		−5.0		0.10	mA
I_1	Logical "1" Input Current	$WBD^* = 0.8V$, $I_{OH(TTL)} = -1$ mA, $V_{OH} \geq V_{CC} - 1.1V$, (Notes 5 and 6)		0.50		5.0	mA
V_0	Logical "0" Input Voltage	$WBD^* = 0.8V$, $I_{OL(TTL)} = 50$ mA, $V_{OL} \leq 0.5V$				0.8	V
V_1	Logical "1" Input Voltage	$WBD^* = 0.8V$, $I_{OH(TTL)} = -1$ mA, $V_{OH} \geq V_{CC} - 1.1V$		2.0	1.5		V
V_{OH}	Logical "1" Output Voltage	$WBD^* = CE1 = BDI/O = 2V$, $I_{OH(MOS)} = -1$ mA, $CE2^* = STR^* = 0.8V$		2.4	3.3		V
V_{OL}	Logical "0" Output Voltage	$WBD^* = CE1 = 2V$, $I_{OL(MOS)} = 5$ mA, $CE2^* = STR^* = BDI/O = 0.8V$			0.28	0.5	V
I_{OS}	Output Short Circuit Current	$WBD^* = CE1 = BDI/O = 2V$, $V_{CC} = 5.25V$, $V_{OUT} = 0V$, $STR^* = CE2^* = 0.8V$, (Note 4)		−7	−15	−45	mA
V_{CLAMP}	Input Clamp Voltage	$I_{IN} = -12$ mA				−1.5	V
I_{OD}	Output/Input Bus Disable Current	$MBI/O = 0.4V$ to 4V, $V_{CC} = 5.25V$		−80		80	μA
CONTROL INPUTS (WBD*, CE1, CE2*, STR*)							
V_{IH}	Logical "1" Input Voltage			2.0			V
V_{IL}	Logical "0" Input Voltage					0.8	V
I_{IH}	Logical "1" Input Current	$V_{IN} = 2.4V$				20	μA
I_1	Input Current at Maximum Input Voltage	$V_{IN} = 5.5V$				1.0	mA

dc electrical characteristics (Continued) (Notes 2 and 3)

PARAMETER		CONDITIONS	MIN	TYP	MAX	UNITS
CONTROL INPUTS (WBD*, CE1, CE2*, STR*) (continued)						
I_{IL}	Logical "0" Input Current	$V_{IN} = 0.4V$		−250	−400	μA
V_{CLAMP}	Input Clamp Voltage	$I_{IN} = -12$ mA		−0.85	−1.5	V
POWER SUPPLY CURRENT						
I_{CC}	Power Supply Current	$V_{CC} = 5.25V$		70	110	mA

Note 1: "Absolute Maximum Ratings" are those values beyond which the safety of the device cannot be guaranteed. They are not meant to imply that the devices should be operated at these limits. The table of "Electrical Characteristics" provides conditions for actual device operation.

Note 2: Unless otherwise specified, min/max limits apply across the 0°C to +70°C temperature range and the 4.75V to 5.25V power supply range. All typicals are given for $V_{CC} = 5V$ and $T_A = 25^{\circ}$C.

Note 3: All currents into device pins are shown as positive, out of device pins are negative. All voltages are referenced to ground unless otherwise noted.

Note 4: Only one output at a time should be shorted.

Note 5: The MBI/O Input Characteristic Graph illustrates this parameter and defines the regions of guaranteed logical "0" and logical "1" outputs. See equivalent input structure for clarification. When the MBI/O input is loaded with a high impedance source (open), the TTL output will be in the logic "0" state.

Note 6: The maximum MOS bus positive input current specification is intended to define the upper limit on guaranteed input clamp operation. At higher input currents (up to the absolute maximum rating) clamp operation is not guaranteed but TTL bus logic state is valid and no device damage will occur.

Note 7: In most applications the MOS bus data lines are higher impedance and more sensitive to noise coupling than TTL bus lines. Conservative design practice would dictate routing MOS bus lines away from high speed, low impedance TTL lines and MOS clock lines or providing a ground shield when they are adjacent.

ac electrical characteristics $V_{CC} = 5V \pm 5\%$, $T_A = 0^{\circ}$C to +70°C

PARAMETER		CONDITIONS		MIN	TYP	MAX	UNITS
DATA TRANSFER SPECIFICATIONS							
Receiving Mode (BDI/O Bus to MBI/O Bus)		WBD* = 3V, C_L = 15 pF,	t_{pd0}		17	40	ns
		R_L = 1 kΩ, (Figures 4 and 6)	t_{pd1}		20	40	ns
	Driving Mode (MBI/O Bus to BDI/O Bus)	WBD* = CE1 = 0V, STR* = CE2* = 3V, C_L = 50 pF, R_L = 100 Ω, (Figures 3 and 5)	t_{pd0}		40	60	ns
			t_{pd1}		40	60	ns
TRANSCEIVER MODE SPECIFICATIONS							
Select Bus							
t_{DS}	Chip Enable Data Set-Up	(Figure 1)		45	23		ns
t_{DH}	Chip Enable Data Hold	(Figure 1)		0			ns
t_{ES}	Set-Up	(Figure 1)		0			ns
TTL Data Bus (BDI/O 00—07)							
$t_{BD\ OD}$	Bus Data Output Disable	C_L = 5 pF, R_L = 100 Ω, (Figure 1)		5	20	50	ns
$t_{BD\ OE}$	Bus Data Output Enable	C_L = 50 pF, R_L = 100 Ω, (Figure 1)			25	80	ns
$t_{BD\ IE}$	Bus Data Input Enable	(Figure 1)			30		ns
$t_{BD\ ID}$	Bus Data Input Disable	(Figure 1)			30		ns
MOS Data Bus (MBI/O 00—07)							
$t_{MB\ OD}$	MOS Bus Output Disable	C_L = 15 pF, R_L = 1 kΩ, (Figure 1)		15	50	100	ns
$t_{MB\ OE}$	MOS Bus Output Enable	C_L = 15 pF, R_L = 1 kΩ, (Figure 1)			50	100	ns
$t_{MB\ ID}$	MOS Bus Input Disable	(Figure 1)			55		ns
$t_{MB\ IE}$	MOS Bus Input Enable	(Figure 1)			20		ns
Select Bus							
t_{CLR}	Clear Previous Chip Enable	(Figure 2)			25	50	ns

switching time waveforms and ac test circuits

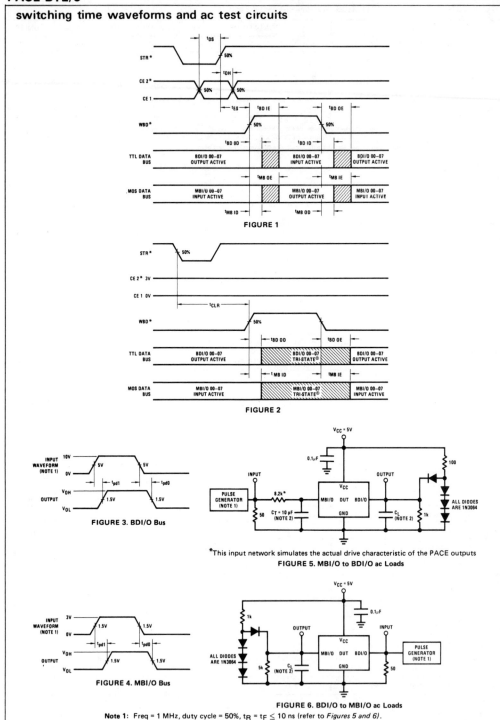

FIGURE 1

FIGURE 2

FIGURE 3. BDI/O Bus

*This input network simulates the actual drive characteristic of the PACE outputs

FIGURE 5. MBI/O to BDI/O ac Loads

FIGURE 4. MBI/O Bus

FIGURE 6. BDI/O to MBI/O ac Loads

Note 1: Freq = 1 MHz, duty cycle = 50%, t_R = $t_F \leq$ 10 ns (refer to *Figures 5 and 6*).

Note 2: All capacitance values include probe and jig capacitance (refer to *Figures 5 and 6*).

PACE BTE/8

typical performance characteristics

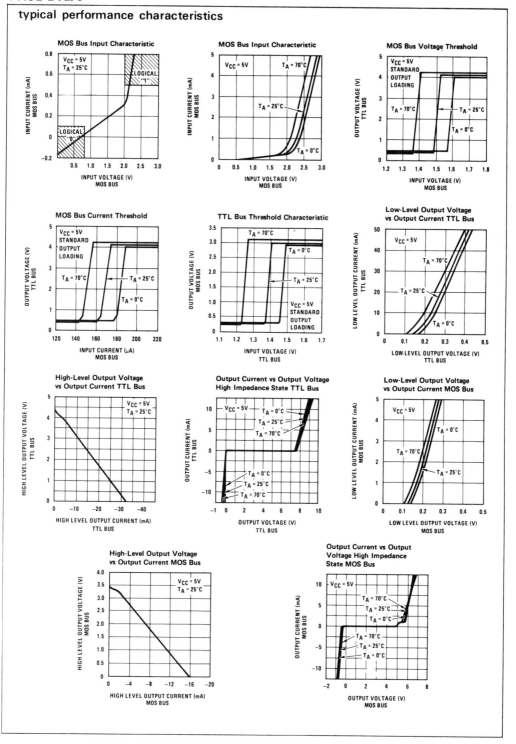

Chapter 2
THE GENERAL INSTRUMENT CP1600

The CP1600 and the TMS 9900 were the first two NMOS 16-bit microprocessors commercially available. Even a superficial inspection of the CP1600 shows it to be more powerful than the National Semiconductor PACE (or 8900), **yet the CP1600 is not widely used.** This is because General Instrument does not support the CP1600 to the extent that National Semiconductor originally supported PACE, or most manufacturers support their 8-bit microprocessors.

General Instrument's marketing philosophy has been to seek out very high-volume customers; General Instrument supports low-volume customers only to the extent that this support would not require substantial investment on the part of General Instrument.

From the viewpoint of the low-volume microprocessor user, General Instrument's marketing philosophy is unfortunate. The CP1600 is an ideal microprocessor for the more sophisticated video games that are appearing, and its rich instruction set and capable architecture make it an ideal choice for data processing terminals and home computer systems. However, due to its limited support, potential low-volume CP1600 customers are likely to choose another equally capable product.

Three CP1600 parts are available, differentiated only by the clock speeds for which they have been designed.

The CP1600 requires a 3.3 MHz, two-phase clock and generates a 600 nanosecond machine cycle time.

The CP1600 requires a 4 MHz, two-phase clock and generates a 500 nanosecond machine cycle time.

The CP1610 requires a 2 MHz, two-phase clock and generates a 1 microsecond cycle time.

In addition to the CP1600 microprocessors themselves, the CP1680 Input/Output Buffer (IOB) is described in this chapter. Additional support devices for the CP1600 may be found in <u>An Introduction to Microcomputers:</u> <u>Volume 3 — Some Real Support Devices</u>.

The sole source for the CP1600 is:

GENERAL INSTRUMENT
Microelectronics Division
600 West John Street
Hicksville, New York 11802

There is no second source for the CP1600. General Instrument has a policy of discouraging second sources for its product line.

The CP1600 is fabricated using NMOS ion implant LSI technology; the device is packaged as a 40-pin DIP.

Three power supplies are required: +12V, +5V and -3V.

THE CP1600 MICROCOMPUTER SYSTEM OVERVIEW

Logic of our general microcomputer system which has been implemented by the CP1600 CPU is illustrated in Figure 2-1.

Observe that the CP1600 requires external logic to create its various timing and clock signals.

Some bus interface logic is shown as absent because a number of devices must surround the CP1600; these include:

1) An address buffer, since data and addresses are multiplexed on a single 16-bit bus.

2) Buffer amplifiers to provide the power required by the type of memory and I/O devices that will normally be connected to a CP1600 CPU.

3) A one-of-eight decoder chip to create eight individual control signals out of three controls output by the CP1600.

4) A one-of-sixteen multiplex chip to funnel sixteen external status signals into the CP1600 if using external branches.

Were you to compare Figure 2-1 with an equivalent figure for a low-end microprocessor such as the SC/MP (which is described in Chapter 3 of the Osborne 4 & 8-Bit Microprocessor Handbook (Osborne/McGraw-Hill, 1980), the CP1600 might appear to offer fewer logic functions; but within the functions it does provide, the CP1600 provides considerably more logic and program execution capabilities. Where low-end microprocessors choose to condense, onto a single chip, simple implementations of different logic functions, high-end products such as the CP1600 choose to provide more devices — with greater capabilities on each device.

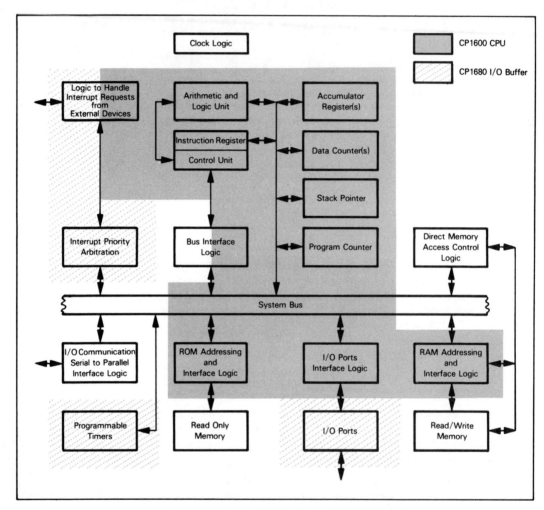

Figure 2 -1. Logic of the CP1600 CPU and CP1680 I/O Buffer

CP1600 PROGRAMMABLE REGISTERS

The CP1600 has eight 16-bit programmable registers, which may be illustrated as follows:

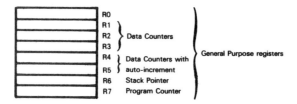

The way in which the registers illustrated above are used is unusual when compared to other microcomputers described in this book. All eight 16-bit registers can be addressed as though they were general purpose registers; however, only Register R0 has no other assigned function. We may therefore look upon Register R0 as the Primary Accumulator for this CPU.

Registers R1, R2, and R3 serve as general purpose registers, but may also be used as Data Counters.

In addition to serving as general purpose registers, R4 and R5 may be used as auto-incrementing Data Counters. Memory reference instructions that identify Register R4 or R5 as holding the implied memory address will cause the contents of Register R4 or R5 to be incremented — after the memory reference instructions have completed execution.

Registers R6 and R7, in addition to being accessible as general purpose registers, also serve as a Stack Pointer and a Program Counter, respectively.

Having the Stack Pointer accessible as a general purpose register makes it quite simple to maintain more than one Stack in external memory; also, you can easily address the Stack as data memory using the Stack Pointer as a Data Counter.

Having the Program Counter accessible as a general purpose register can be useful when executing various types of conditional branch logic.

While having the Stack Pointer and the Program Counter accessible as though they were general purpose registers may appear strange, this is a feature of the PDP-11 minicomputer — and is a very powerful programming tool.

CP1600 MEMORY ADDRESSING MODE

The CP1600 addresses memory and I/O devices within a single address space.

When referencing external memory, you can use direct addressing, implied addressing, or implied addressing with auto-increment.

Direct addressing instructions are all two or more words long, where the second or last word of the instruction object code provides a 16-bit direct address.

CP1600 DIRECT ADDRESSING

CP1600 direct addressing instructions are complicated by the fact that CP1600 program memory is frequently only 10 bits wide. That is to say, even though the CP1600 is a 16-bit microprocessor, its instruction object codes are only 10 bits wide. If program memory is only 10 bits wide, then direct addresses will only be 10 bits wide. A 10-bit direct address will access the first 1024 words of memory only.

Were you to implement a 16-bit wide program memory, then you could directly address up to 65,536 words of memory; however, six bits of the first object program word for every instruction in program memory would be wasted. This may be illustrated as follows:

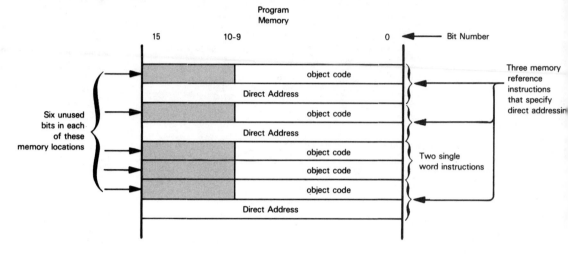

Instructions that reference memory using implied addressing identify general purpose Register R1, R2, or R3 as containing the implied address.

<table>
<tr><td>CP1600
IMPLIED
ADDRESSING</td></tr>
</table>

A memory reference instruction which identifies Register R4 or R5 as providing the external memory address will always cause Register R4 or R5 contents to be incremented following the memory access; thus you have implied memory addressing with auto-increment.

Memory reference instructions that specify implied memory addressing via Register 1, 2, 3, 4, or 5 can access 8-bit memory. An SDBD instruction executed directly before a valid memory reference instruction forces the memory reference instruction to access memory one byte at a time. If implied memory addressing via Register 1, 2, or 3 is specified, then the same byte of memory will be accessed twice. For an instruction that loads the contents of data memory into Register R0, this may be illustrated as follows:

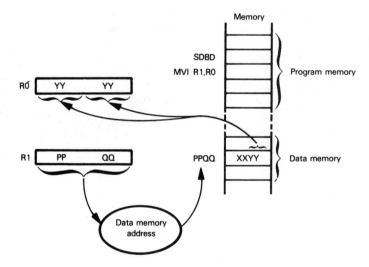

2-4

If Register R4 or R5 provides the implied memory address for the instruction which follows an SDBD instruction, then the implied memory address is incremented twice, and two sequential low-order bytes of data are accessed. For an instruction which loads data into Register R0, this may be illustrated as follows:

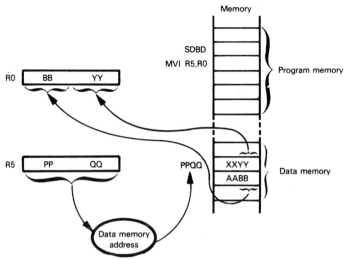

The SDBD instruction may also precede an immediate instruction. Now the immediate data will be fetched from the low-order byte of the next two sequential program memory locations. This may be illustrated as follows:

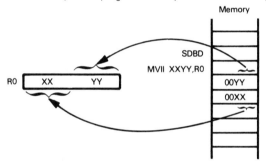

Without the preceding SDBD instruction, an immediate instruction will access the next single program memory word to find the required immediate data. Ten or more bits of immediate data will be accessed, depending on the width of program memory words.

The CP1600 has no Stack reference instructions such as a Push or Pull; rather, a variety of memory reference instructions can identify Register R6 as providing the implied address. When Register R6 provides the implied address, it is treated as an upward migrating Stack

```
CP1600
STACK
ADDRESSING
```

Pointer. When a memory write operation specifies Register R6 as providing the implied memory address, Register R6 contents will be incremented following the memory write. A memory read instruction that specifies Register R6 as providing the implied memory address will cause the contents of Register R6 to be decremented before the read operation occurs.

An unusual feature of the CP1600 is the fact that a variety of secondary memory reference instructions can also reference memory via the Stack Pointer. When these instructions are executed, Register R6 contents are decremented before the memory access occurs — as though a Pull operation from the Stack were being executed.

Logically, Register R6, the Stack Pointer, is being handled as though it were a Data Counter with post-increment and pre-decrement.

Jump instructions use direct memory addressing. Jump instructions are all three words long. The direct address is computed from the second and third memory words as follows:

AAAAAABBBBBBBBBB   Jump address (binary)
yy   are enable/disable bits for interrupts
xx   identify the register where the return address will be stored for JSR
xx   and yy are described in detail in Table 2-4.

You can enable or disable interrupts whenever you execute a Jump or Jump-to-Subroutine instruction.

The only difference between a Jump instruction and a Jump-to-Subroutine instruction is that the Jump-to-Subroutine instruction saves the Program Counter contents in Register 4, 5, or 6. The two high-order bits (xx) or the second Jump-to-Subroutine object code word specifies which of the three registers will be used to hold the return address.

Jump-to-Subroutine instructions, like the Jump instruction, allow direct memory addressing only.

CP1600 STATUS AND CONTROL FLAGS

The CP1600 CPU has four of the standard status flags; in addition, it has some unusual control signals.

These are the four standard status flags:

Sign (S). This status is set equal to the high-order bit of any arithmetic operation result.

Zero (Z). This status is set to 1 when any instruction's execution creates a zero result. The status is set to 0 for a nonzero result.

The Carry (C) and Overflow (O) statuses are standard carry and overflow, as described in Volume 1.

Four control signals (EBCA0 - EVCA3) are output during a Branch-on-External (BEXT) instruction. These four signals are output to reflect the low-order four bits of the BEXT instruction's object code. External logic receives these four signals and (depending on their state), may or may not return a high input via EBCI. If EBCI is returned high, then the BEXT instruction will perform a branch; if EBCI is returned low, then the BEXT instruction will cause the next sequential instruction to be executed. The four control signals EBCA0 - EBCA3 therefore provide the CP1600 with a means of testing 16 external conditions.

CP1600 CPU PINS AND SIGNALS

CP1600 CPU pins and signals are illustrated in Figure 2-2.

D0 - D15 is a multiplexed Address and Data Bus. Given a total of 40 pins in a package, CP1600 designers have been forced to share 16 pins between addresses and data. **Three control signals, BDIR, BC1, and BC2, identify the traffic on the Address/Data Bus. External logic (one MSI chip) must decode these three signals to create eight control signals, as summarized in Table 2-1.**

Remaining signals may be divided into four groups: timing, status/control, interrupt, and DMA.

Two timing clock signals are required: Φ1 and Φ2. These are complementary clock signals which may be illustrated as follows:

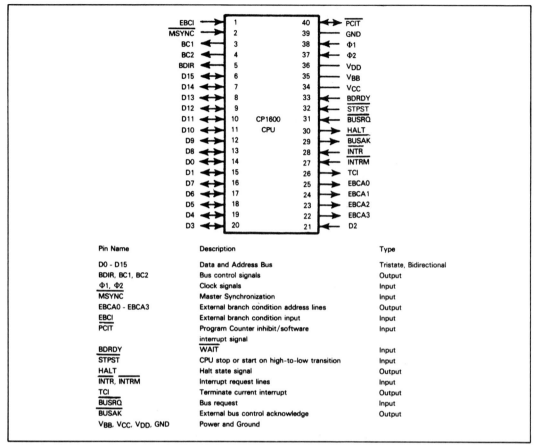

Pin Name	Description	Type
D0 - D15	Data and Address Bus	Tristate, Bidirectional
BDIR, BC1, BC2	Bus control signals	Output
Φ1, Φ2	Clock signals	Input
MSYNC	Master Synchronization	Input
EBCA0 - EBCA3	External branch condition address lines	Output
EBCI	External branch condition input	Input
PCIT	Program Counter inhibit/software interrupt signal	Input
BDRDY	WAIT	Input
STPST	CPU stop or start on high-to-low transition	Input
HALT	Halt state signal	Output
INTR, INTRM	Interrupt request lines	Input
TCI	Terminate current interrupt	Output
BUSRQ	Bus request	Input
BUSAK	External bus control acknowledge	Output
VBB, VCC, VDD, GND	Power and Ground	

Figure 2-2. CP1600 CPU Signals and Pin Assignments

MSYNC is a somewhat unusual signal, as compared to other microcomputer clock signals in this book. Following powerup, MSYNC must be held low for at least 10 milliseconds. On the subsequent rising edge of MSYNC, logic internal to the CP1600 CPU will synchronize the Φ1 and Φ2 clock signals to start a new machine cycle. Most of the CPU devices we have described in this book use a reset signal, or have internal powerup logic which performs this clock synchronization.

Now consider the status and control signals.

First of all, **there are the four control outputs** which we have already described: **EBCA0 - EBCA3. There is one conditional Branch instruction (BEXT) which will only branch if a high signal is input via EBCI.** When the BEXT instruction is executed, the low-order four BEXT instruction object code bits are output via EBCA0 - EBCA3. External logic is supposed to decode these four signals by whatever means are appropriate — and thence determine whether EBCI should be input high or low. A high input, as we have just stated, will result in a branch; a low input will cause the next sequential instruction to be executed.

In reality, there is no connection within CP1600 CPU logic between the EBCI input and the four EBCA0 - EBCA3 outputs. So far as external logic is concerned, the execution of a BEXT instruction is identified by signal levels output and maintained on the EBCA0 - EBCA3 outputs, while the EBCI input determines whether a branch will or will not occur. How external logic chooses to determine whether EBCI will be set high or low is entirely up to external logic. The only vital function served by EBCA0 - EBCA3 is to identify the instant at which a BEXT instruction is executed.

Another unusual control signal provided by the CP1600 is PCIT; this is a bidirectional signal. When input low, this signal prevents the Program Counter from being incremented following an instruction fetch. This signal is also output as a low pulse following execution of a software interrupt instruction. Instruction timing separates the active input and active output of this signal; providing external logic adheres to timing requirements, a conflict between input and output logic will never arise.

BDRDY is equivalent to the WAIT signal we have described for a number of other microcomputers. $\overline{BDRDY}$ is input low by any external logic which requires more time in order to respond to an I/O access. Recall that the CP1600 uses a single address space to reference memory or I/O devices. The $\overline{BDRDY}$ signal causes the CPU to enter a Wait state for as long as $\overline{BDRDY}$ is being input low; however, during the Wait state CPU logic is not refreshed. Thus a Wait state cannot last for more than 40 microseconds, or the contents of internal CPU locations will be lost.

STPST, a Halt/Reset input, is an edge-triggered signal. When external logic inputs a high-to-low transition via $\overline{STPST}$, the CPU will complete execution of any interrupt instruction, then will enter a Halt state and output HALT high. If a non-interruptable instruction is being executed, then the Halt state will not being until completion of next interruptable instruction's execution. The Halt state will last until external logic inputs another high-to-low $\overline{STPST}$ transition, at which time the Halt output will be returned low and normal programming execution will continue. Execution of the HLT instruction also causes the CP1600 to enter a Halt state, as described above.

Let us now look at interrupt signals.

The CP1600 has two interrupt request inputs — $\overline{INTR}$ and $\overline{INTRM}$. $\overline{INTR}$ has higher priority than $\overline{INTRM}$. $\overline{INTR}$ cannot be disabled. Typically, $\overline{INTR}$ will be used to trigger an interrupt upon power failure or other catastrophes.

The interrupt acknowledge signal is created by external logic which must decode the BC1, BC2, and BDIR signals, as shown in Table 2-1. Observe that there are, in fact, two interrupt acknowledge signals; the first (INTAK) acknowledges the interrupt itself, while the second (DAB) is used as a strobe for external logic to return an interrupt address vector. The interrupt sequence is described later in this chapter.

The CP1600 has two additional interrupt-related signals which are unusual when compared to other microcomputers described in this book.

TCI is output high when an End-of-Interrupt instruction is executed. This signal makes it easy for external logic to generate interrupt priorities which extend across the execution of an interrupt service routine.

Table 2-1. CP1600 Bus Control Signals

BC1	BC2	BDIR	SIGNAL	FUNCTION
0	0	0	NACT	The CPU is inactive and the Data/Address Bus is in a high impedance state.
0	0	1	BAR	A memory address must be input to the CPU via the Data/Address Bus.
0	1	0	IAB	Acknowledged external interrupt requesting logic must place the starting address for the interrupt service routine on the Address Bus.
0	1	1	DWS	Data write strobe for external memory.
1	0	0	ADAR	This signal identifies a time interval during which the Data/Address Bus is floated, while data input on the Data Bus is being interpreted as the effective memory address during a direct memory addressing operation.
1	0	1	DW	The CPU is writing data into external memory. DW will precede DWS by one machine cycle.
1	1	0	DTB	This is a read strobe which external memory or I/O logic can use in order to place data on the Data/Address Bus.
1	1	1	INTAK	This is an interrupt acknowledge signal. It is followed by IAD which is a strobe telling the external logic which is being acknowledged to identify itself by placing an address vector on the Data/Address Bus.

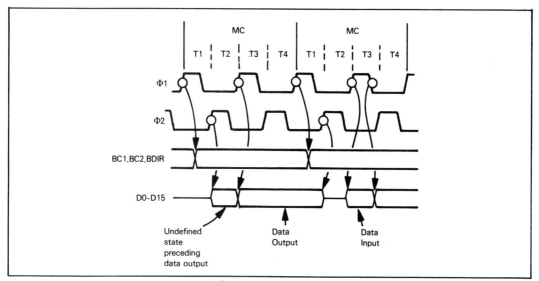

Figure 2-3. CP1600 Machine Cycles and Bus Timing

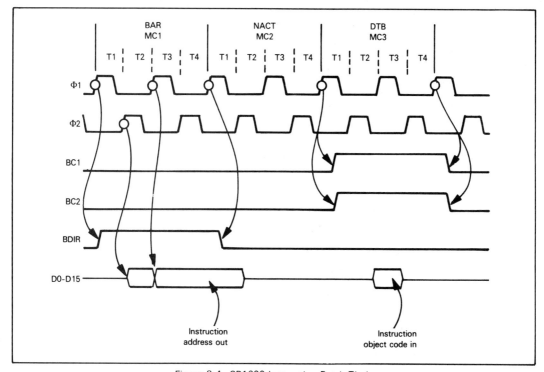

Figure 2-4. CP1600 Instruction Fetch Timing

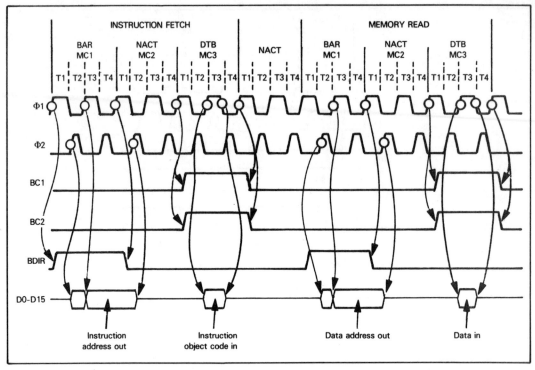

Figure 2-5. CP1600 Timing for Memory Read Instruction with Implied Memory Addressing

CP1600 INSTRUCTION TIMING AND EXECUTION

CP1600 instructions are executed as a sequence of machine cycles. Each machine cycle has four clock periods, as illustrated in Figure 2-3. Machine cycles are identified by their cycle number and by the levels of the BC1, BC2, and BDIR signals. Each of the eight level combinations is given a name, taken from Table 2-1. This name becomes the name of the machine cycle. Thus in Figure 2-4, and in subsequent instruction timing illustrations, **each machine cycle is identified by a signal name from Table 2-1.**

Figure 2-3 shows general case timing for data output or input on the Data/Address Bus. In between data input or output operations the bus is floated.

CP1600 MEMORY ACCESS TIMING

Figure 2-4 illustrates instruction fetch timing for a CP1600 instruction's execution. Three machine cycles are required. During the first machine cycle an address is output. Nothing happens during the second machine cycle; it is a "time spacing" machine cycle that routinely separates two CP1600 Bus access machine cycles. The object code for the accessed instruction is returned during the third machine cycle.

Figure 2-5 illustrates timing for the simplest memory read instruction's execution. In this case the data memory address is taken from one of the CPU registers. There is no difference between timing for the three machine cycles of an instruction fetch or a data memory read. As illustrated in Figure 2-5, a simple memory read instruction's execution consists of two three-machine cycle memory read operations, separated by a spacing no operation machine cycle.

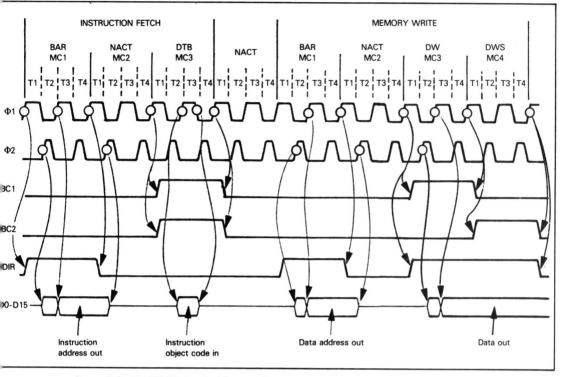

Figure 2-6. CP1600 Timing for Memory Write Instruction with Implied Memory Addressing

Figure 2-6 illustrates timing for a simple CP1600 memory write instruction execution. Data is output for two machine cycles, giving external logic ample time to respond to the data output. External logic uses the DWS machine cycle as a write strobe.

Any memory reference instruction that specifies direct memory addressing will require one three-clock-period machine cycle to fetch each word of the instruction object code; an NACT clock period will separate each machine cycle. After the first instruction fetch machine cycle, an ADAR-NACT clock period combination will be inserted in the second (and third, if present) instruction fetch machine cycle. During an ADAR clock period, BC1 is high, while BC2 and BDIR are low. No other control signals are active. Thus, **for a two-word memory read or memory write instruction that specifies direct addressing, the following clock periods and machine cycles will be required for instruction execution:**

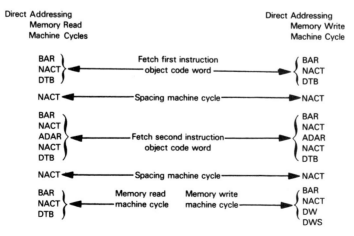

2-11

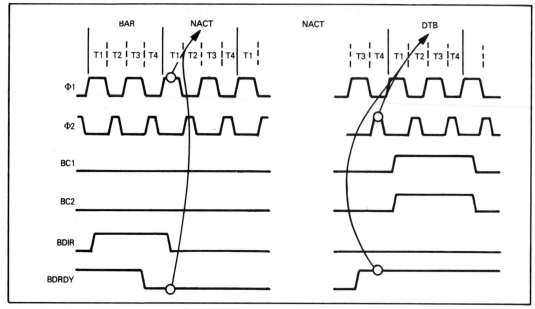

Figure 2-7. CP1600 Wait State Timing

THE CP1600 WAIT STATE

The CP1600 has a Wait state equivalent to those described for other microcomputers in this book. External logic that requires more time to respond to an access must input $\overline{BDRDY}$ low before the end of the BAR machine cycle, during which an address is output and the device is selected. **Timing is illustrated in Figure 2-7.**

If you examine Figures 2-4, 2-5 and 2-6, you will see that an address is output during a BAR machine cycle to initiate any external device access. The BAR machine cycle is always followed by an NACT machine cycle; in the middle of T1 during this NACT machine cycle, the CP1600 samples $\overline{BDRDY}$. If $\overline{BDRDY}$ is low, then a sequence of NACT machine cycles occurs. In the middle of T4 for every NACT machine cycle, the CP1600 samples $\overline{BDRDY}$ again. Upon detecting $\overline{BDRDY}$ high, the CP1600 resumes instruction execution with a DTB machine cycle.

A Wait state must last for less than 40 microseconds, since the CP1600 is a dynamic device.

THE CP1600 HALT STATE

The CP1600 has a Halt state which may follow execution of the Halt instruction, or may be initiated by external logic.

When the Halt instruction is executed, then, following the instruction fetch machine cycle, the HALT signal is output high and a sequence of NACT machine cycles is executed.

External logic initiates a Halt state by making the STPST input undergo a high-to-low transition. Following execution of the next interruptable instruction, a Halt state begins. The HALT signal is output high and a sequence of NACT machine cycles is executed.

A Halt state, whether it is initiated by execution of a Halt instruction or by a high-to-low transition of STPST, must be terminated by a high-to-low transition of STPST. This will cause the Halt state to end at the conclusion of the next NACT machine cycle. Timing for a Halt state which is initiated and terminated by STPST may be illustrated as follows:

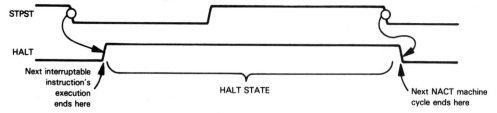

The $\overline{\text{PCIT}}$ signal as an input inhibits CP1600 Program Counter increment logic. Thus, external logic can input $\overline{\text{PCIT}}$ low — in which case the same instruction will be continuously re-executed until $\overline{\text{PCIT}}$ goes high again. However, $\overline{\text{PCIT}}$ should only change levels while the CPU has been halted. Thus, **$\overline{\text{PCIT}}$ and $\overline{\text{STPST}}$ should be used together as follows:**

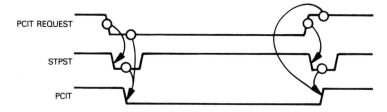

CP1600 INITIALIZATION SEQUENCE

The CP1600 is initialized by inputting the $\overline{\text{MSYNC}}$ signal low for a minimum of 10 milliseconds after power is first applied to the CPU.

$\overline{\text{MSYNC}}$ must make a low-to-high transition, marking the end of the initialization, on a rising edge of the $\Phi 1$ clock signal. On the next rising edge of $\Phi 1$, instruction execution will begin. This may be illustrated as follows:

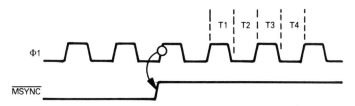

When instruction execution begins, interrupts are disabled. The following sequence of machine cycles is executed:

```
NACT
IAB  ◄──── Read Data/Address Bus and load into Program Counter
NACT
NACT
NACT
BAR  ◄──── Output Program Counter contents to fetch first instruction
NACT
DTB
etc
```

During the IAB machine cycle, external logic must supply a 16-bit address at D0 - D15. Your external logic must provide this address, which in the simplest case may be 0000 by grounding the bus, or FFFF_{16} by tying it to +5V following a startup.

The address which is input at IAB is output at BAR, initiating program execution.

CP1600 DMA LOGIC

CP1600 DMA logic is quite standard. When external logic wishes to transfer data under DMA control, it inputs $\overline{\text{BUSRQ}}$ low. At the conclusion of the next interruptable instruction's execution, the CPU floats the Data/Address Bus and enters a Wait state, during which a sequence of NACT machine cycles is executed. $\overline{\text{BUSAK}}$ is output low at the beginning of the first NACT machine cycle.

The NACT machine cycles that occur during a DMA operation refresh the CPU. NACT machine cycles that occur during a Wait state do not refresh the CPU. This means that any number of NACT machine cycles can occur during a DMA break, while a Wait state must be shorter than 40 microseconds.

The DMA break ends when external logic inputs $\overline{\text{BUSRQ}}$ high again. $\overline{\text{BUSRQ}}$ is sampled during T1 of every DMA NACT machine cycle. When $\overline{\text{BUSRQ}}$ is sampled high, two additional NACT machine cycles are executed, then $\overline{\text{BUSAK}}$ is output high and normal program execution resumes.

DMA timing is illustrated in Figure 2-8.

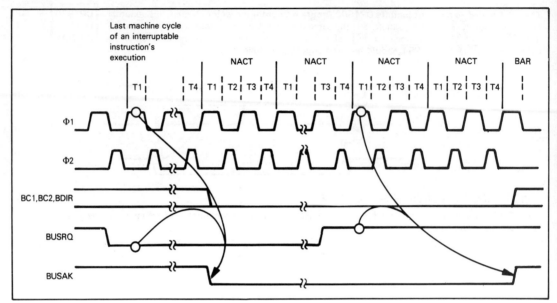

Figure 2-8. CP1600 DMA Timing

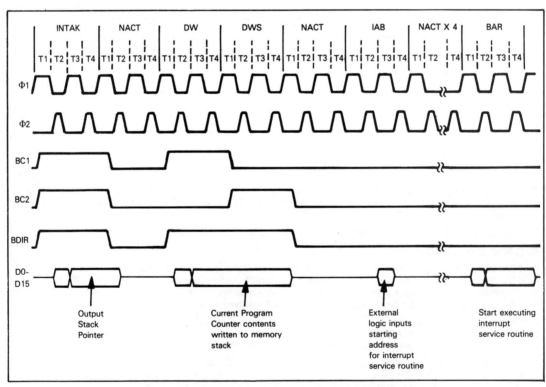

Figure 2-9. CP1600 Interrupt Service Routine Initialization

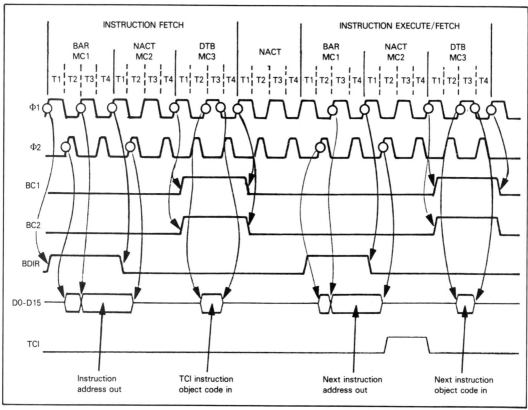

Figure 2-10. CP1600 Timing for TCI Instruction's Execution

THE CP1600 INTERRUPT LOGIC

The CP1600 uses a vectored interrupt processing system.

External logic requests an interrupt by inputting a low signal at either the $\overline{\text{INTR}}$ or $\overline{\text{INTRM}}$ pins.

Following the execution of the next interruptable instruction, the CP1600 acknowledges the interrupt by pushing Register R7 contents (the Program Counter) onto the Stack; then the CP1600 outputs 111, followed by 010 at BC1, BC2, and BDIR. External logic must respond by placing 16 bits of data on the Data/Address Bus. These 16 bits of data will be loaded into Register R7, the Program Counter, thus causing program execution to branch to an interrupt service routine dedicated to the interrupt. **Timing is illustrated in Figure 2-9.**

The $\overline{\text{PCIT}}$ signal is output low following execution of a software interrupt instruction (SIN). This is the only microcomputer described in this book which allows external logic to respond to a software interrupt in this fashion. Allowing external logic to respond to a software interrupt only makes sense when you anticipate your product being used in a minicomputer-like environment. Typically, the software interrupt will interface to logic of a front panel or console. When an SIN instruction is executed, a one-machine cycle low $\overline{\text{PCIT}}$ pulse is output.

You may, if you wish, end an interrupt service routine by executing a Terminate Current Interrupt (TCI) instruction, in which case the TCI signal will be output high.

Timing for TCI is given in Figure 2-10.

Following an interrupt acknowledge, the interrupt service routine must execute instructions in order to disable interrupts and save the contents of registers on the Stack. The exception is Register R7, the Program Counter, which is automatically pushed onto the Stack following an interrupt acknowledge.

External logic is entirely responsible for any type of interrupt priority arbitration which may occur, and for the generation of the interrupt vector address which must be input following an interrupt acknowledge.

It is quite easy to generate signals equivalent to other microcomputer system busses from the CP1600 System Bus. Therefore, you can use parts described in Volume 3 to handle CP1600 interrupt requirements.

THE CP1600 INSTRUCTION SET

The CP1600 instruction set is relatively straightforward. Addressing modes, which we have already described, are simple, and instructions are typical of those we have seen and described for other microcomputers. Unusual features relating to addressing modes available with **individual instructions are summarized in Table 2-2,** which describes the CP1600 instruction set.

If you have never programmed a PDP-11 minicomputer, then you should pay particular attention to programming techniques that result from the Stack Pointer and Program Counter being accessed as general purpose registers.

A wide variety of Register Operate instructions allow you to compute data and load the result directly into Register R7, the Program Counter. In effect, these become computed Jump instructions.

The ability to manipulate Register R6, the Stack Pointer, as though it were a general purpose register means that it is easy to maintain a number of different Stacks in external read/write memory.

The Jump-to-Subroutine instruction has a minicomputer flavor to it. Rather than saving the return address on the Stack, Register R7 contents are moved to General Purpose Register R4 or R5. A number of minicomputers will save a subroutine return address in a general purpose register in this fashion. The problem with this logic is that you must execute an additional instruction within the subroutine to save the return address on the Stack if you are going to use nesting subroutines. If you are passing subroutine parameters, however, this is an excellent arrangement, for the Jump-to-Subroutine instruction places the address of the parameter list directly in a Data Counter with auto-increment. We have described the concept of parameter passing in Volume 1, Chapter 7.

Note that the CP1600 instruction set lacks a logical OR.

In Tables 2-2 and 2-4, instruction length is given in terms of "words" rather than "bytes", as we have done in previous chapters. Since only the lower 10 bits of the CP1600 object code are presently used, system configurations need not have the full 16-bit word size. Hence a "word" may be 10 to 16 bits wide, depending on the implementation.

The following notation is used in Table 2-2:

ADDR	One word of direct address
cond	Condition on which a branch may be taken. Table 1-3 lists all 14 branch conditions.
DATA	One word of immediate data.
DISP	One word displacement. See Table 2-4 for location of sign bit.
E	External branch condition.
EBCA0-3	The external branch condition address lines: EBCA0, EBCA1, EBCA2, and EBCA3.
EBCI	The external branch condition input line.
LABEL	A 16-bit direct address, target of a Jump instruction. See Table 2-4 for the bit format.
$\overline{PCIT}$	The software interrupt output line.
RB	General Purpose Register R4, R5, or R6.
RD	One of the general purpose registers, used as a destination for operation results.
RM	One of the general purpose registers used as a Data Counter, R4 or R5, if specified, is auto-incremented after the memory access. R6 is incremented after a write, and decremented before a read.
RR	General Purpose Register R0, R1, R2, or R3.
RS	One of the general purpose registers, used as the source of an operand.

Statuses:

    S the Sign status
    C the Carry status
    Z the Zero status
    O the Overflow status
    The following symbols are used in the STATUSES column:
    X the status flag is affected by the operation
      a blank means the status flag is not affected
    0 the operation clears the status flag
    1 the operation sets the flag
    2 the Overflow flag is affected only on 2-bit shifts or rotates

SW   The Status Word, whose bits correspond to the condition of the status flags in the following way:

When the status word is copied into a register, it goes to the upper half of each byte:

When the status word is loaded from a register, it comes from the upper half of the lower byte:

x<y,z>   Bits y through z of the Register x. For example, R7<15,8> represents the upper byte of the Program
            Counter
(,2)   Indicates that the operand ",2" is optional
            A low pulse
[ ]   Contents of location enclosed within brackets. If a register designation is enclosed within the brackets,
            then the designated register's contents are specified. If a memory address is enclosed within the brackets,
            then the contents of the addressed memory location are specified.
[[ ]]   Implied memory addressing: the contents of the memory location designated by the contents of a register.
Λ   Logical AND
⩛   Logical Exclusive-OR
±   Addition or subtraction of a displacement, depending on the sign bit in the object code.
←   Data is transferred in the direction of the arrow.

Table 2-2. CP1600 Instruction Set Summary

TYPE	MNEMONIC	OPERAND(S)	WORDS	STATUSES S	Z	C	O	OPERATION PERFORMED
PRIMARY I/O AND MEMORY REFERENCE	MVI	ADDR,RD	2					[RD]←[ADDR] Load register from memory, using direct addressing.
	MVI@	RM,RD	1					[RD]←[[RM]] Load register from memory, using implied addressing.
	MVO	RS,ADDR	2					[ADDR]←[RS] Store register to memory, using direct addressing.
	MVO@	RS,RM	1					[[RM]]←[RS] Store register to memory, using implied addressing. If RS=R4, R5, R6 or R7, then RS=RM is not supported.
SECONDARY I/O AND MEMORY REFERENCE	ADD	ADDR,RD	2	X	X	X	X	[RD]←[RD]+[ADDR] Add memory contents to register, using direct addressing.
	ADD@	RM,RD	1	X	X	X	X	[RD]←[RD]+[[RM]] Add memory contents to register, using implied addressing.
	SUB	ADDR,RD	2	X	X	X	X	[RD]←[RD]-[ADDR] Subtract memory contents from register, using direct addressing.
	SUB@	RM,RD	1	X	X	X	X	[RD]←[RD]-[[RM]] Subtract memory contents from register, using implied addressing.
	CMP	ADDR,RS	2	X	X	X	X	[RS]-[ADDR] Compare memory contents with registers, using direct addressing. Only the status flags are affected.
	CMP@	RM,RS	1	X	X	X	X	[RS]-[[RM]] Compare memory contents with register's, using implied addressing. Only the status flags are affected.
	AND	ADDR,RD	2	X	X			[RD]←[RD]∧[ADDR] AND memory contents with those of register, using direct addressing.
	AND@	RM,RD	1	X	X			[RD]←[RD]∧[[RM]] AND memory contents with those of register, using implied addressing.
	XOR	ADDR,RD	2	X	X			[RD]←[RD]⊻[ADDR] Exclusive-OR memory contents with those of register, using direct addressing.
	XOR@	RM,RD	1	X	X			[RD]←[RD]⊻[[RM]] Exclusive-OR memory contents with those of register, using implied addressing.

Table 2-2. CP1600 Instruction Set Summary (Continued)

TYPE	MNEMONIC	OPERAND(S)	WORDS	STATUSES S	Z	C	O	OPERATION PERFORMED
IMMEDIATE	MVII	DATA,RD	2					[RD]←DATA Load immediate to specified register.
	MVOI	RS,DATA	2					[[R7]+1]←[RS] Store contents of specified register in immediate field of MVOI instruction. This is only possible if program memory is read/write memory (rather than ROM).
IMMEDIATE OPERATE	ADDI	DATA,RD	2	x	x	x	x	[RD]←[RD]+DATA Add immediate to specified register.
	SUBI	DATA,RD	2	x	x	x	x	[RD]←[RD]-DATA Subtract immediate data from specified register.
	CMPI	DATA,RS	2	x	x	x	x	[RD]-DATA Compare immediate data with contents of specified register. Only the status flags are affected.
	ANDI	DATA,RD	2	x	x			[RD]←[RD]∧DATA AND immediate data with contents of specified register.
	XORI	DATA,RD	2	x	x			[RD]←[RD]⊻DATA Exclusive-OR immediate data with contents of specified register.
JUMP	J	LABEL	3					[R7]←LABEL Jump to given address.
	JR	RS	1					[R7]←[RS] Jump to address contained in specified register.
	JSR	RB,LABEL	3					[RB]←[R7]: [R7]←LABEL Jump to given address, saving Program Counter in R4, R5, or R6.
	B	DISP	2					[R7]←[R7]+2±DISP Branch relative to Program Counter contents.
BRANCH ON CONDITION	Bcond	DISP	2					If cond is true, [R7]←[R7]+2±DISP Branch relative on given condition; otherwise, execute next sequential instruction. EBCA0-3 ← E;
	BEXT	DISP,E	2					If EBCi=1, [R7]←[R7]+2±DISP Branch relative if external condition is true.

2-19

Table 2-2. CP1600 Instruction Set Summary (Continued)

TYPE	MNEMONIC	OPERAND(S)	WORDS	STATUSES S	STATUSES Z	STATUSES C	STATUSES O	OPERATION PERFORMED
REGISTER-REGISTER MOVE AND OPERATE	MOVR	RS,RD	1	X	X			[RD]←[RS] Move contents of source register to destination register.
	ADDR	RS,RD	1	X	X	X	X	[RD]←[RS]+[RD] Add contents of specified registers.
	SUBR	RS,RD	1	X	X	X	X	[RD]←[RD]-[RS] Subtract contents of source register from those of destination register.
	CMPR	RS,RD	1	X	X	X	X	[RD]-[RS] Compare registers' contents. Only the status flags are affected.
	ANDR	RS,RD	1	X	X			[RD]←[RD]∧[RS] AND contents of specified registers.
	XORR	RS,RD	1	X	X			[RD]←[RD]⊻[RS] Exclusive-OR contents of specified registers.
REGISTER OPERATE	CLRR	RD	1	0	1			[RD]←[RD]∨[RD] Clear specified register.
	TSTR	RS	1	X	X			[RS]-[RS] Test contents of specified register.
	INCR	RD	1	X	X			[RD]←[RD]+1 Increment contents of specified register.
	DECR	RD	1	X	X			[RD]←[RD]-1 Decrement contents of specified register.
	COMR	RD	1	X	X			[RD]←[RD] Complement contents of specified register (ones complement).
	NEGR	RD	1	X	X	X	X	[RD]←[RD]+1 Negate contents of specified register (twos complement).
	ADCR	RD	1	X	X	X	X	[RD]←[RD]+[C] Add Carry bit to specified register contents.
	SLL	RR,(2)	1	X	X			[shift diagram: 15 ← 0, [RR]] Shift logical left one or two bits, clearing bit 0 (and bit 1 if shifting twice).

Table 2-2. CP1600 Instruction Set Summary (Continued)

TYPE	MNEMONIC	OPERAND(S)	WORDS	STATUSES				OPERATION PERFORMED
				S	Z	C	O	
REGISTER OPERATE (CONTINUED)	RLC	RR,(2)	1	X	X	X	2	Rotate left one bit through Carry, or rotate 2 bits left through Overflow and Carry.
	SLLC	RR,(2)	1	X	X	X	2	Shift logical left one bit into Carry, clearing bit 0, or shift left two bits into Overflow and Carry, clearing bits 0 and 1.
	SLR	RR,(2)	1	X	X			Shift logical right one or two bits, clearing bit 15 (and bit 14 if shifting twice).
	SAR	RR,(2)	1	X	X			Shift arithmetic right one or two bits, copying high order bit.
	RRC	RR,(2)	1	X	X	X	2	Rotate right one bit through Carry, or rotate two bits right through Overflow and Carry.
	SARC	RR,(2)	1	X	X	X	2	Shift arithmetic right one bit into Carry, or two bits into Overflow and Carry.
	SWAP	RR,(2)	1	X	X			Swap bytes of register once, or twice.

Table 2-2. CP1600 Instruction Set Summary (Continued)

TYPE	MNEMONIC	OPERAND(S)	WORDS	STATUSES S	Z	C	O	OPERATION PERFORMED
STACK	PSHR	RS	1					Separate mnemonics for MVO@ RS,R6.
	PULR	RD	1					Separate mnemonics for MVI@R6,RD.
INTERRUPT	SIN	(2)	1					$\overline{PCIT} \leftarrow \neg\neg$ Software interrupt.
	EIS		1					Enable interrupt system.
	DIS		1					Disable interrupt system.
	TCI		1					Terminate current interrupt.
	JE	LABEL	3					Jump to given address and enable interrupt system.
	JD	LABEL	3					Jump to given address and disable interrupt system.
	JSRE	RB,LABEL	3					Jump to given address, saving Program Counter in R4, R5 or R6, and enable interrupt system.
	JSRD	RB,LABEL	3					Jump to given address, saving Program Counter in R4, R5 or R6, and disable interrupt system.
STATUS	GSWD	RD	1					[RD<15,12>]←[SW]; [RD<7,4>]←[SW] Place Status Word in upper half of each byte of the specified register. RD may be R0, R1, R2 or R3.
	RSWD	RS	1	X	X	X	X	[SW]←[RS<7,4>] Load Status Word from bits 7 through 4 of the specified register.
	CLRC		1			0		[C]←0 Clear Carry.
	SETC		1			1		[C]←1 Set Carry.
	NOPP	(2)	2					No Operation.
	NOP		1					Halt after executing next instruction.
	HLT		1					Set double byte data mode for next instruction, which must be of one of the following types: Primary or secondary I/O or memory reference Immediate or immediate operate
	SDBD							If implied addressing through R1, R2, or R3 is used, the same byte will be accessed twice; address-ing through R4, R5, or R7 will give bytes from the addressed location and that addressed after auto-increment. Direct addressing and Stack addressing are not allowed in double byte mode.

Table 2-3. CP1600 Branch Conditions and Corresponding Codes

MNEMONIC	BRANCH CONDITION	OBJECT CODE DESIGNATION
C LGT	C = 1 Carry (logical greater than)	0001
NC LLT	C = 0 No Carry (logical less than)	1001
OV	O = 1 Overflow	0010
NOV	O = 0 No overflow	1010
PL	S = 0 Plus	0011
MI	S = 1 Minus	1011
ZE EQ	Z = 1 Zero (equal)	0100
NZE NEQ	Z = 0 Nonzero (not equal)	1100
LT	S⊻O = 1 Less than	0101
GE	S⊻O = 0 Greater than or equal	1101
LE	Z V (S⊻O) = 1 Less than or equal	0110
GT	Z V (S⊻O) = 0 Greater than	1110
USC	C⊻S = 1 Unequal sign and carry	0111
ESC	C⊻S = 0 Equal sign and carry	1111

The following notation is used in Table 2-4:

Where ten digits are shown, they are the ten low-order bits of a 10 to 16-bit word. (Word size depends on the system implementation.) Where four digits are shown, they represent the hexadecimal notation for an entire word (10 to 16 bits).

bb   Two bits indicating one of the first three general purpose registers:
         00 = R0
         01 = R1
         10 = R2

cccc   Four bits giving the branch condition, as shown in Table 2-3.

ddd   Three bits indicating a destination register, RD:
         000 = R0
         001 = R1
         010 = R2
         011 = R3
         100 = R4
         101 = R5
         110 = R6
         111 = R7

eeee   Four bits giving the external branch condition, E. Control signals EBCA0-EBCA3 reflect the state of these four bits.

IIII   One word of immediate data (10 or 16 bits)

mmm　　　Three bits indicating a Data Counter Register RM:
　　　　　　000 = R0
　　　　　　001 = R1
　　　　　　010 = R2
　　　　　　011 = R3
　　　　　　100 = R4
　　　　　　101 = R5
　　　　　　110 = R6
　　　　　　111 = R7

m　　　　One bit indicating the number of rotates or shifts:
　　　　　　0　one bit position
　　　　　　1　two bit positions

p　　　　One bit of immediate address

P　　　　One hexadecimal digit (4 bits) of immediate address

rr　　　　Two bits indicating one of the first four general purpose registers:
　　　　　　00 = R0
　　　　　　01 = R1
　　　　　　10 = R2
　　　　　　11 = R3

sss　　　Three bits indicating a source register, RS:
　　　　　　000 = R0
　　　　　　001 = R1
　　　　　　010 = R2
　　　　　　011 = R3
　　　　　　100 = R4
　　　　　　101 = R5
　　　　　　110 = R6
　　　　　　111 = R7

z　　　　Sign of the displacement:
　　　　　　0 add the displacement to PC contents
　　　　　　1 subtract the displacement from PC contents

In the "Machine Cycles" column, when two numbers are given with one slash between them (e.g., 7/9), execution time depends on whether or not a branch is taken. When two numbers are given, separated by two slashes (such as 8//11), execution time depends on which register contains the implied address.

THE BENCHMARK PROGRAM

For the CP1600 our benchmark program may be illustrated as follows:

```
        MVII    IOBUF,R4    LOAD THE I/O BUFFER STARTING ADDRESS INTO R4
        MVII    TABLE,R1    LOAD THE TABLE STARTING ADDRESS INTO R1
        MVI@    R1,R5       LOAD ADDRESS OF FIRST FREE TABLE WORD INTO R5
        MVII    CNT,R2      LOAD WORD COUNT INTO R2
LOOP    MVI@    R4,R0       LOAD NEXT DATA WORD FROM IOBUF
        MVO@    R0,R5       STORE IN NEXT TABLE WORD
        DECR    R2          DECREMENT WORD COUNT
        BNZE    LOOP        RETURN IF NOT END
        MVO@    R5,R1       RETURN ADDRESS OF NEXT FREE TABLE BYTE
```

This benchmark program makes very few assumptions. The input table IOBUF and the data table TABLE can have any length, and can reside anywhere in memory. The address of the first free word in TABLE is stored in the first word of the TABLE.

Table 2-4. CP1600 Instruction Set Object Codes

INSTRUCTION	OBJECT CODE	WORDS	MACHINE CYCLES
ADCR RD	0000101ddd	1	6
ADD ADDR,RD	1011000ddd PPPP	2	10
ADD@ RM,RD	1011mmmddd	1	8//11
ADDI DATA,RD	1011111ddd IIII	2	8
ADDR RS,RD	0011sssddd	1	6
AND ADDR,RD	1110000ddd PPPP	2	10
AND@ RM,RD	1110mmmddd	1	8//11
ANDI DATA,RD	1110111ddd IIII	2	8
ANDR RS,RD	0110sssddd	1	6
B DISP	1000z00000 PPPP	2	7/9
Bcond DISP	1000z0cccc PPPP	2	7/9
BEXT DISP,E	1000z1eeee PPPP	2	7/9
CLRC	0006	1	4
CLRR RD	0111dddddd	1	6
CMP ADDR,RS	1101000sss PPPP	2	10
CMP@ RM,RS	1101mmmsss	1	8//11
CMPI DATA,RS	1101111sss IIII	2	8
CMPR RS,RD	0101sssddd	1	6
COMR RD	0000011ddd	1	6
DECR RD	0000010ddd	1	6
DIS	0003	1	4
EIS	0002	1	4
GSWD RR	00001100rr	1	6
HLT	0000	1	4
INCR RD	0000001ddd	1	6
J LABEL	0004 11pppppp00 PPPP	3	12
JD LABEL	0004 11pppppp10 PPPP	3	12
JE LABEL	0004 11pppppp01 PPPP	3	12
JR RS	0010sss111	1	7
JSR RB,LABEL	0004 bbpppppp00 PPPP	3	12
JSRD RB,LABEL	0004 bbpppppp10 PPPP	3	12
JSRE RB,LABEL	0004 bbpppppp01 PPPP	3	12
MOVR RS,RD	0010sssddd	1	6//7
MVI ADDR,RD	1010000ddd PPPP	2	10
MVI@ RM,RD	1010mmmddd	1	8//11
MVII DATA,RD	1010111ddd IIII	2	8
MVO RS,ADDR	1001000sss PPPP	2	11
MVO@ RS,RM	1001mmmsss	1	9
MVOI RS,DATA	1001111sss IIII	2	9
NEGR RD	0000100ddd	1	6
NOP (2)	000011010m	1	6
NOPP	1000z01000 PPPP	2	7
PSHR RS	1001110sss	1	9
PULR RD	1010110ddd	1	11
RLC RR(,2)	0001010mrr	1	6/8
RRC RR(,2)	0001110mrr	1	6/8
RSWD RS	0000111sss	1	6
SAR RR(,2)	00011C1mrr	1	6/8
SARC RR(,2)	0001111mrr	1	6/8
SDBD	0001	1	4
SETC	0007	1	4
SIN (2)	000011011m	1	6
SLL RR(,2)	0001001mrr	1	6/8
SLLC RR(,2)	0001011mrr	1	6/8
SLR RR(,2)	0001100mrr	1	6/8
SUB ADDR,RD	1100000ddd PPPP	2	10
SUB@ RM,RD	1100mmmddd	1	8//11
SUBT DATA,RD	1100111ddd IIII	2	8
SUBR RS,RD	0100sssddd	1	6
SWAP RR(,2)	0001000nrr	1	6/8
TCI	0005	1	4
TSTR RS	0010ssssss	1	6//7
XOR ADDR,RD	1111000ddd PPPP	2	10
XOR@ RM,RD	1111mmmddd	1	8//11
XORI DATA,RD	1111111ddd IIII	2	8
XORR RS,RD	0111sssddd	1	6

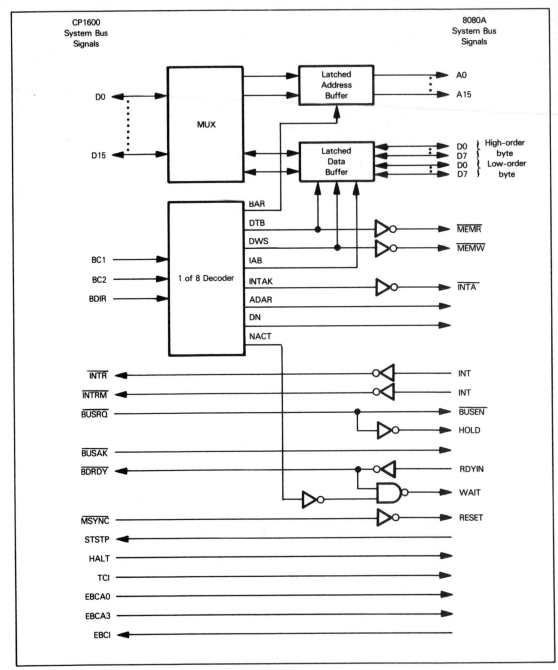

Figure 2-11. CP1600 to 8080A Bus Conversion

SUPPORT DEVICES THAT MAY BE USED WITH THE CP1600

A CP1600 microcomputer system with any significant capabilities will use support devices of some other microprocessor. Parallel I/O capability is available with the CP1680, (described next), but priority interrupt logic, DMA logic, and serial I/O logic, to mention just a few common options, may need additional support devices. Fortunately, **it is quite easy to generate an 8080A-compatible system bus from the CP1600 system bus. Logic is illustrated in Figure 2-11.**

The CP1600A is the fastest version of the CP1600 CPU; it runs with a 500 nanosecond machine cycle. The CP1600 machine cycle is equivalent to an 8080A clock period. Since the standard 8080A clock period is also 500 nanoseconds, no speed conflicts will arise.

The bus-to-bus interface logic illustrated in Figure 2-11 is self-evident, with the exception of bus demultiplexing logic. The CP1600 Data/Address Bus is shown buffered by a demultiplexing buffer that is connected to two latched buffers. One of the latched buffers accepts the demultiplexer outputs only when a valid address is being output, as identified by BAR high. The second latched buffer may be a bidirectional latched buffer, or it may be two unidirectional latched buffers. Three latching strobes are required: DTB, IAB, and DWS.

DTB and IAB are data input strobes. DTB strobes data input that is to be interpreted as data, while IAB stroves data input that is to be interpreted as an address. So far as external logic is concerned, both of these signals are simple data input strobes. We could therefore generate a single data input strobe as the OR of DTB and IAB. When this data input strobe is high, information on the 8080A System Bus side of the latched data buffer must be input to the buffer; this data must simultaneously be transmitted to the multiplexer.

DWS is the data output strobe. When high, this signal must strobe data from the multiplexer to the latched data buffer; this latched data must immediately appear at the 8080A System Bus side of the latched data buffer.

Since the CP1600 uses a 16-bit Data Bus, you will probably have to generate two external device data busses; a high-order byte bus and a low-order byte bus. All external devices that transmit or receive parallel data must be present in duplicate. For example, were 8255 parallel interface devices to be present, the following connections would be required:

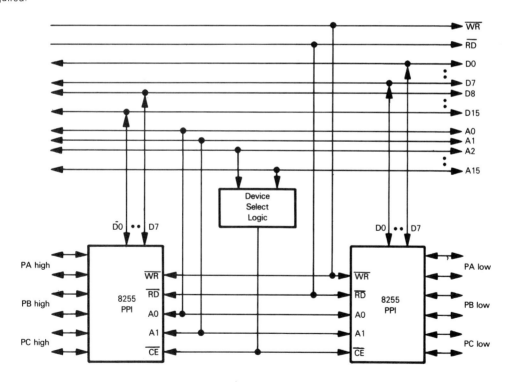

The CP1600 and MC6800 system busses are singularly incompatible. You should not attempt to use MC6800 support devices with the CP1600.

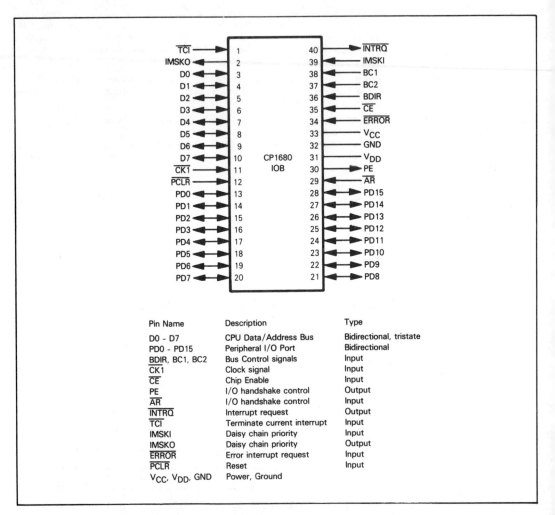

Pin Name	Description	Type
D0 - D7	CPU Data/Address Bus	Bidirectional, tristate
PD0 - PD15	Peripheral I/O Port	Bidirectional
BDIR, BC1, BC2	Bus Control signals	Input
$\overline{CK1}$	Clock signal	Input
$\overline{CE}$	Chip Enable	Input
PE	I/O handshake control	Output
$\overline{AR}$	I/O handshake control	Input
$\overline{INTRQ}$	Interrupt request	Output
$\overline{TCI}$	Terminate current interrupt	Input
IMSKI	Daisy chain priority	Input
IMSKO	Daisy chain priority	Output
$\overline{ERROR}$	Error interrupt request	Input
$\overline{PCLR}$	Reset	Input
V_{CC}, V_{DD}, GND	Power, Ground	

Figure 2-12. CP1680 IOB Signals and Pin Assignments

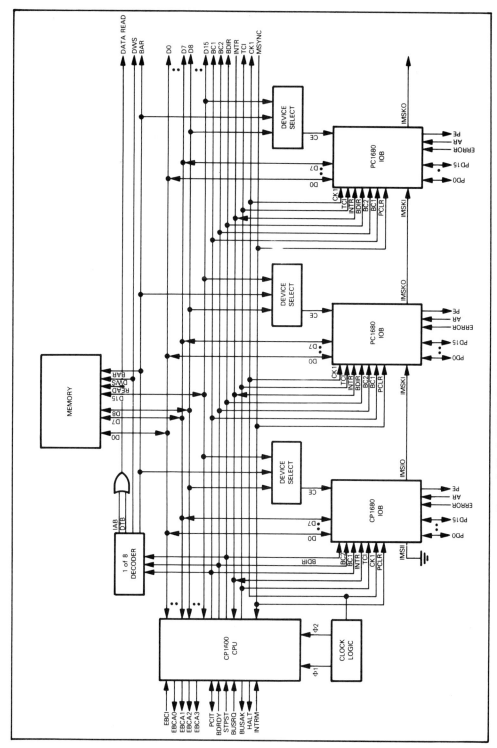

Figure 2-13. A CP1600-CP1680 Microcomputer Configuration

THE CP1680 INPUT/OUTPUT BUFFER (IOB)

The CP1680 IOB is a parallel I/O device designed specifically for the CP1600 CPU. This device provides a single 16-bit parallel I/O port, which may optionally be configured as two 8-bit I/O ports. Primitive handshaking control signals are available with the parallel I/O logic. Elementary interval timer and prioritized interrupt logic is also provided.

Figure 2-1 also illustrates that part of our general microcomputer system logic which has been implemented on the CP1680 IOB.

The CP1600 IOB is packaged as a 40-pin DIP. It requires two power supplies, +5V and +12V. All inputs are TTL compatible. The device is implemented using N-channel MOS technology.

Figure 2-13 illustrates a CP1600 microcomputer system with three CP1680 IOB devices in the configuration.

CP1680 IOB PINS AND SIGNALS

The CP1680 IOB pins and signals are illustrated in Figure 2-12. We will summarize these signals and the functions they serve before examining device operations in detail.

Let us begin by looking at the interface between the CP1680 IOB and the CP1600 CPU.

D0 - D7 provide an 8-bit parallel Data/Address Bus via which all communications between the CPU and IOB occur. This bus must connect to the low-order eight bits of the 16-bit CPU Data/Address Bus.

The three bus control signals, BC1, BC2, and BDIR, connect the CP1680 to the CP1600 as illustrated in Figure 2-13. The CP1680 IOB decodes these three bus control signals internally.

A clock input is required by the CP1680. This **clock input (CK1) is used by internal logic to determine when BC1, BC2, and BDIR are valid.** CK1 must have the following wave form:

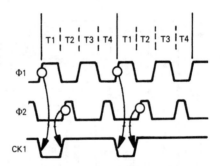

CK1 must be derived from the CP1600 clock signals by external logic.

Let us now look at the interface between external logic and the CP1680 IOB.

PD0 - PD15 provide a 16-bit parallel I/O port which can optionally be configured as two 8-bit I/O ports. While **PD0 - PD15** are in theory bidirectional, these pins **are** more accurately described as **pseudo-bidirectional**. This is because when a zero has been written to one of these pins, the output can sink 1.6 mA for an output voltage of +0.5V. External

> CP1600 I/O
> PORT PIN
> CHARACTERISTICS

logic will have a hard time overcoming this sink in order to pull the pin high. In contrast, when a 1 is written to one of these pins, the output sources just 100μA at +5V. External logic will have little problem sinking 100μA in order to pull a pin low. Therefore, you should output a 1 to any pin that is subsequently to receive input data. External logic will then leave the pin high when inputting 1, while pulling the pin low to input 0.

The handshaking control signals which link the CP1680 IOB with external logic are PE and $\overline{\text{AR}}$. PE is a control signal which is output by the CP1680, and $\overline{\text{AR}}$ is a control signal which is input to the CP1680.

Now consider CP1680 interrupt signals.

An interrupt request is transmitted to the CP1600 CPU via $\overline{\text{INTRQ}}$. The CPU acknowledges the interrupt via the INTAK combination of BDIR, BC1, and BC2. $\overline{\text{TCI}}$ must be output low by the CPU at the end of the interrupt service routine. This signal is required by CP1680 interrupt logic, which uses the low $\overline{\text{TCI}}$ pulse in its priority arbitration, as described later in this chapter.

Interrupts may be generated by conditions internal to the CP1680, or by **a low input at ERROR**. The $\overline{\text{ERROR}}$ input is reserved for error conditions detected by external logic.

IMSKI and IMSKO are interrupt priority input and interrupt priority output signals, respectively. These signals are used to generate daisy chain interrupt priorities between CP1680 IOB devices, as illustrated in Figure 2-13. We will describe CP1680 interrupt priorities in more detail later in this chapter.

$\overline{\text{MCLR}}$ is the master reset control input for the CP1680. This signal must be input low for at least 10 milliseconds in order to reset the CP1680 IOB.

CP1680 ADDRESSABLE REGISTERS

The CP1680 has eight addressable locations, which may be illustrated as follows:

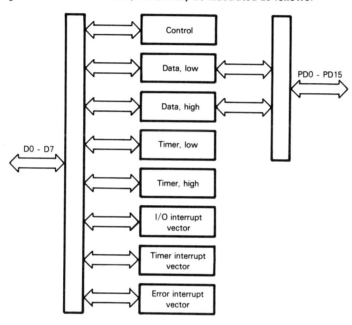

These eight addressable locations are all 8-bit registers; they are addressed using the first eight addresses in a 256-address block, as follows:

Register	Address
Control	0
Data buffer, low-order byte	1
Data buffer, high-order byte	2
Timer, low-order byte	3
Timer, high-order byte	4
I/O interrupt vector	5
Timer interrupt vector	6
Error interrupt vector	7

The actual 256 addresses will be identified by the eight high-order CP1600 Data/Address Bus lines, which will be used to create CP1680 device select logic. This device select logic creates $\overline{CE}$ (the chip enable signal); it may be illustrated as follows:

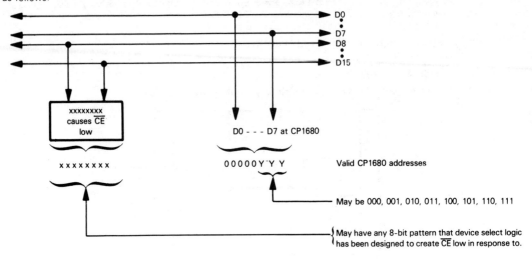

THE CP1680 CONTROL REGISTER

We will summarize the individual bits of the CP1680 control register before describing the operations they control.

Here are CP1680 Control register bit assignments:

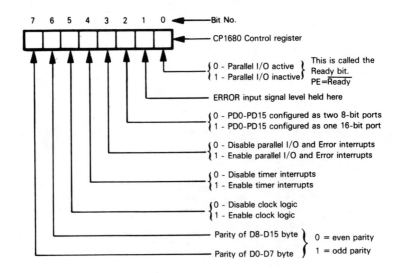

Bit 0 is always the complement of the PE control output. This bit may be interrogated by the CPU. If parallel data transfer interrupts are disabled, this allows the CPU to poll on status when monitoring parallel data transfers. PE signal levels are illustrated in Figures 2-14 and 2-15.

Bit 1 reflects the level of the $\overline{\text{ERROR}}$ input. If parallel data transfer interrupt logic is disabled, then the Error interrupt logic is also disabled. Thus, the CPU must also examine the Error status bit when polling the CP1680.

Bit 2 determines whether PD0 - PD15 will act as a single 16-bit I/O port, or as two 8-bit I/O ports. This is only important when outputting data.

Control register bits 3 and 4 are used to enable and disable parallel data transfer and Error interrupt logic, and timer interrupt logic.

Control register bit 5 is used to enable and disable CP1680 interval timer logic. If this bit is 0, the interval timer will not decrement.

Bits 6 and 7 report the parity of the high-order byte and low-order byte for data that is input or output via PD0 - PD15. 0 indicates even parity while 1 indicates odd parity.

All Control register bits may be written into or read. You should be very careful when setting or resetting individual bits not to simultaneously modify other Control register bits. This means you should use a three-instruction sequence with an AND or OR mask to set or reset any Control register bit. For details see Volume 1, Basic Concepts.

CP1680 DATA TRANSFER OPERATIONS

The CPU inputs and outputs data via the CP1680 IOB by executing MVI and MVO instructions, respectively.

The CPU must access the CP1680 in byte mode, since an 8-bit Data/Address Bus (D0 - D7) connects the CPU and the CP1680 IOB. Whether the I/O port PD0 - PD15 is configured as a single 16-bit port or as two 8-bit ports has no bearing on the fact that the CPU must access the CP1680 in byte mode.

The most efficient way of accessing the CP1680 is by using the SDBD instruction with implied memory addressing. Consider data input. If PD0 - PD15 is configured as two 8-bit I/O ports and you wish to access just one of these I/O ports, then you can use implied memory addressing via R1, R2, or R3. We may illustrate input from the high-order byte of I/O Port PD8 - PD15 as follows:

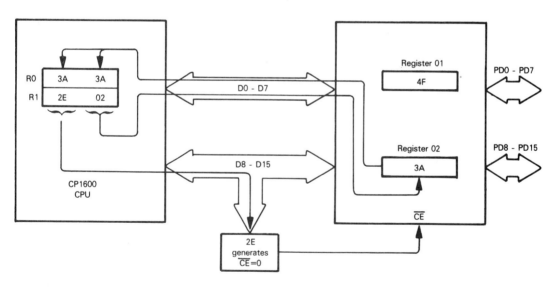

If PD0 - PD15 are configured as two 8-bit I/O ports or as a single 16-bit I/O port, and you want to read both I/O ports, then you should use the SDBD instruction with implied memory addressing via R4 or R5. This may be illustrated as follows:

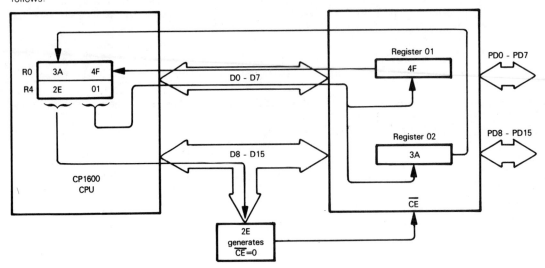

Control register bit 2 configures PD0 - PD15 as a single 16-bit I/O port or as two 8-bit I/O ports.

Given the fact that MVI and MVO instructions (in byte mode) should be used to access the CP1680, when should these accesses occur?

The answer is that the PE and $\overline{AR}$ signals control event sequences.

Consider parallel data input, as illustrated in Figure 2-14.

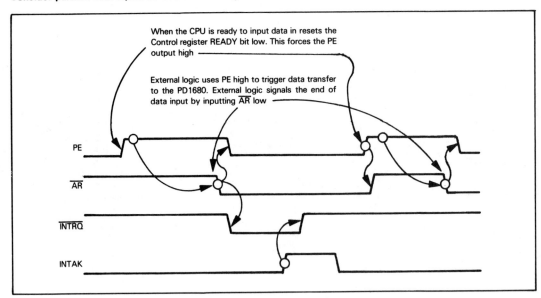

Figure 2-14. PD1680 Handshaking with Data Input

When the CPU is ready to receive data, it resets Control register bit 0 to 0; this forces the PE control signal high.

When external logic senses PE high, it must transmit data to the PD0 - PD15 I/O port. At this point it makes no difference whether pins have been configured as two 8-bit ports or as a single 16-bit port. External logic will pull to ground selected high pins, while leaving other high pins alone. When external logic has completed data input, it signals the fact by inputting $\overline{AR}$ low. It is the high-to-low transition of the $\overline{AR}$ control input which indicates the presence of new data for the CPU to read. When $\overline{AR}$ makes its high-to-low transition, PE also makes a high-to-low transition, and Control register bit 0 is set to 1. If interrupts have been enabled, then an interrupt is requested via $\overline{INTRQ}$. Figure 2-14 assumes that interrupts have been enabled; therefore $\overline{INTRQ}$ is shown making a high-to-low transition.

The CPU will acknowledge the interrupt request, as described earlier in this chapter, by outputting INTAK via BC1, BC2, and BDIR. Logic internal to the CP1680 uses INTAK to reset INTRQ high again.

There are many ways in which external logic can determine when to set $\overline{AR}$ high again. In Figure 2-14 we show external logic using PE to set $\overline{AR}$ high. Clearly, when PE makes a low-to-high transition, the CPU must have acknowledged $\overline{AR}$ low; therefore external logic can now set $\overline{AR}$ high. Now that $\overline{AR}$ is high again, external logic can input new data. An alternative scheme would be for external logic to constantly hold $\overline{AR}$ low, using the level of the PE output to determine when new data could be transmitted. When PE is high, external logic will transmit new data to the CP1680 once. As soon as it transmits new data, external logic will strobe the data with a short, high $\overline{AR}$ pulse, then wait for PE to go low and high again before inputting more data. This may be illustrated as follows:

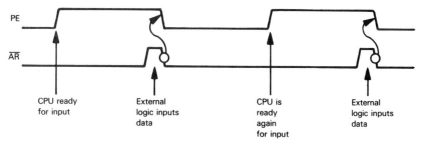

Data output handshaking is illustrated in Figure 2-15.

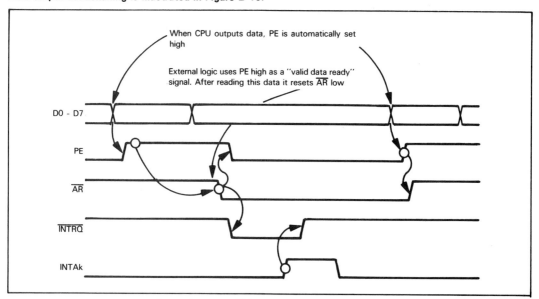

Figure 2-15. PD1680 Handshaking for Data Output

The most important point to note is that there is no control bit which specifies data input mode or data output mode. Thus, the signal sequences we described for data input and those we are about to describe for data output occur automatically; the input or output mode is purely a function of CPU and external logic interpretation.

Whenever the CPU outputs data to the PD1680, the arrival of data forces PE output high. If PD0 - PD15 has been configured as two 8-bit ports, then the arrival of a single data byte to either port will cause PE to be output high. If PD0 - PD15 is configured as a single 16-bit I/O port, then PD will not be output high until two bytes of data have been received from the CPU by the PD1680.

Once PE is output high, nothing more happens until external logic responds. External logic cannot tell by the simple inspection of any control signals whether a data input operation or a data output operation is in progress. It is up to you, when designing your system, to dedicate CP1680 devices to input or output; or you must generate your own identification logic in the event that a CP1680 IOB is bidirectional. In Figure 2-15 we simply assume that external logic knows data is to be read, and knows whether the data is 16 bits or 8 bits wide. Furthermore, if the data is 8 bits wide, external logic must know which 8 bits to read. In any event, when external logic has completed its undefined operations, it must input $\overline{AR}$ low. The high-to-low transition of $\overline{AR}$ forces PE low again, and if interrupts are enabled, an interrupt will be requested via $\overline{INTRQ}$. When the CPU acknowledges the interrupt by outputting INTAK via BC1, BC2, and BDIR, the PD1680 uses the INTAK pulse to reset $\overline{INTRQ}$ high.

The method used by external logic to reset $\overline{AR}$ high again is undefined. In Figure 2-15, we show PE going high as the trigger which external logic uses to reset $\overline{AR}$ high. This is clearly a viable scheme; PE will not go high again until fresh data has been output, at which point it is safe to assume that the CPU knows prior data has been read by external logic. It would be equally viable for external logic to hold $\overline{AR}$ continuously low, transmitting a short, high pulse whenever it reads data. This may be illustrated as follows:

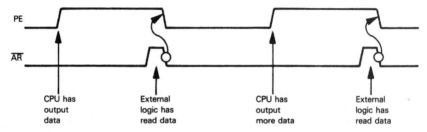

| CPU has output data | External logic has read data | CPU has output more data | External logic has read data |

Because there are no control signals which identify the PD1680 operating in input mode or output mode, there is no straightforward scheme for handling bidirectional data transfers with a single PD1680 device.

THE CP1680 INTERVAL TIMER

The CP1680 has very elementary interval timer logic. A 16-bit Timer register, addressed as two separate 8-bit locations, decrements once every eight CK1 pulses, providing the timer has been enabled. You enable and disable timer logic via Control register bit 5. As a separate event, timer interrupts may be disabled via Control register bit 4. If timer interrupts are enabled, then when the timer decrements to 0, an interrupt request will occur. (Timer interrupt logic is described with other CP1680 interrupt logic later in this chapter.) If timer interrupts are not enabled, then the timer itself is effectively disabled, since you cannot test any timer status flag to see if the timer timed out; nor can you accurately read the contents of the Timer registers on the fly, since there is no protection against reading timer contents while it is in the process of being decremented.

The only timer programmable option you have is to load an initial value before the timer is enabled. The timer has no buffer; therefore, once it times out it begins decrementing again, if still enabled, beginning with the value $FFFF_{16}$. This may be illustrated as follows:

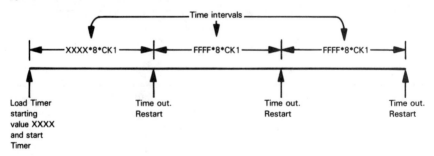

The only accurate long time intervals you can compute are exact multiples of FFFF$_{16}$ • 8 • CK1.

The CP1600A uses a 4MHz two-phase clock, which generates a 500 nanosecond cycle time. Thus, CK1 equals 500 nanoseconds, and long CP1600A time intervals must be an exact multiple of 262.144 milliseconds — the time it will take for the counter to decrement from FFFF$_{16}$ to 0000.

The CP1600 uses a 3.3MHz two-phase clock, which generates a 600 nanosecond cycle time; therefore, long time intervals must be exact multiples of 314.572 milliseconds.

The CP1610, which runs on a 2MHz two-phase clock and has a one microsecond cycle time, will compute long time intervals that are exact multiples of 524.288 milliseconds.

You cannot attempt to generate clock periods that are multiples of shorter time intervals by loading some initial value into the timer following each time out; an unknown amount of time will elapse between the interval timer interrupt occurring and being acknowledged. The length of this unknown period of time will depend on the number of non-interruptable instructions which may be executing in sequence when the interrupt request first occurs, plus any higher priority interrupts which may exist. Therefore, if you load an initial value into the timer, it should be to compute an isolated time interval only. Here is an appropriate instruction sequence:

```
MVI     IOB,R0      ;INPUT CONTROL REGISTER CONTENTS
ANDI    CFH,R0      ;ZERO BITS 4 AND 5
MVO     R0,IOB      ;RETURN TO CONTROL REGISTER
MVII    2AH,R0      ;TRANSMIT LOW-ORDER TIMER
MVO     R0,IOB+3    ;INITIAL BYTE
MVII    34H,R0      ;TRANSMIT HIGH-ORDER TIMER
MVO     R0,JOB+4    ;INITIAL BYTE
MVI     IOB,R0      ;LOAD PRIOR CONTROL REGISTER CONTENTS
ADDI    30H,R0      ;SET BITS 4 AND 5
MVO     R0,IOB      ;START TIMER
```

The instruction sequence above begins with three instructions that load the CP1680 Control register contents into Register R0. Bits 4 and 5 are zeroed, then the result is returned to the Control register. Thus, the timer and timer interrupts are disabled. We do not bother with an SDBD instruction. Since the data source is eight bits wide, only the low-order byte of Register R0 will be significant. This being the case, we can use an 8-bit immediate AND mask to modify Register R0 contents before returning the low-order byte to the Control register.

Next, we load the initial timer value, one byte at a time, into Register R0. Each byte is written out to the appropriate half of the Control register. Once again we do not need to use the SDBD instruction. Since an 8-bit data path connects the CPU to the 1680 IOB, only the low-order byte of Register R0 will be significant during the data output.

Finally, we start the timer by loading Control register contents into Register R0, setting bits 4 and 5 to 1 and writing back the result.

When you write into the Timer registers, you clear any timer interrupt requests which may at that time be pending.

CP1680 INTERRUPT LOGIC

A CP1680 IOB will generate an interrupt request by outputting a low signal at $\overline{INTRQ}$ if any one of these three conditions occurs:

1) A low input at $\overline{ERROR}$. External logic can request an interrupt via the CP1680 using the $\overline{ERROR}$ input.

2) The $\overline{AR}$ handshaking control input makes a high-to-low transition. This is illustrated in Figures 2-14 and 2-15.

3) The Interval Timer decrements from 1 to 0.

Recall that there are two separate interrupt enable/disable control bits in the Control register. One control bit applies to the Interval Timer, while the other control bit applies to both the $\overline{AR}$ handshaking and $\overline{ERROR}$ interrupts.

Interrupt priorities among the three sources within a single CP1680 IOB are as follows:

$\overline{ERROR}$ highest
$\overline{AR}$ handshaking
Timer lowest

When more than one CP1680 IOB is present in a CP1600 microcomputer system, then daisy chain priority is implemented using the MSKI input signal and the MSKO output signal. Signal connections are illustrated in Figure 2-13. **The manner in which interrupt priorities are handled by the CP1680 is a little unusual.**

Two or more CP1680 devices may combine their interrupt request signals, which are wired ORed and input to the CP1600 via $\overline{INTRQ}$. The CP1600 acknowledges an interrupt via the INTAK combination of BC1, BC2, and BDIR. We described this process earlier in the chapter. All CP1680 devices simultaneously receive the INTAK combination; however, a CP1680 which is acknowledged raises its IMSKO signal high, causing it to become the IMSKI input to the next CP1680 in the daisy chain. Any device that receives a high IMSKI input ignores the interrupt acknowledge. Thus, only the highest priority, interrupt requesting CP1680 device in the daisy chain will process the interrupt acknowledge. However, it takes a finite amount of time for IMSKO high signals to propagate as IMSKI signals, and thus ripple through the daisy chain. Consequently, a maximum of eight CP1680 devices may be present in the daisy chain. A ninth device will receive its IMSKI high signal too late and will respond to an interrupt acknowledge.

CP1680 IOB devices maintain their interrupt priority status until they receive a high TCI pulse. At that time, prior interrupt priorities are reset at all devices, and new priority arbitration begins. Thus, **when using CP1680 IOB devices, you are required to end all interrupt service routines by executing a $\overline{\text{TCI}}$ instruction.**

Note that if one CP1680 IOB has more than one active interrupt request (for example, an ERROR interrupt request and a timer interrupt request), then this internal interrupt priority will take precedence over the daisy chain interrupt priority. That is to say, the ERROR interrupt request will be acknowledged and serviced first. After the next TCI instruction is executed, the timer interrupt request will be serviced before any interrupt request from a lower priority CP1680 device is acknowledged.

Every CP1680 device has three 8-bit Interrupt Vector registers, one dedicated to each of the three interrupt sources. These three Interrupt Vector registers were illustrated earlier in the chapter. **Following an interrupt acknowledge, when the IAB combination appears at BC1, BC2, and BDIR, the contents of the Interrupt Vector register for the highest priority active interrupt will be returned to the CPU.** Interrupt acknowledge timing is illustrated in Figure 2-9. At the interrupt service location a Jump-to-Subroutine instruction will probably be stored. Since the Jump-to-Subroutine object code is three words long, a maximum of 85 interrupts can be origined in the first 256 words of memory. This is more than sufficient, since only eight CP1680 devices with 24 interrupts can be supported in a single daisy chain.

DATA SHEETS

This section contains specific electrical and timing data for the following devices:

- CP1600 CPU
- CP1600A CPU
- CP1610 CPU
- IOB1680 I/O Buffer

CP1600·CP1600A·CP1610

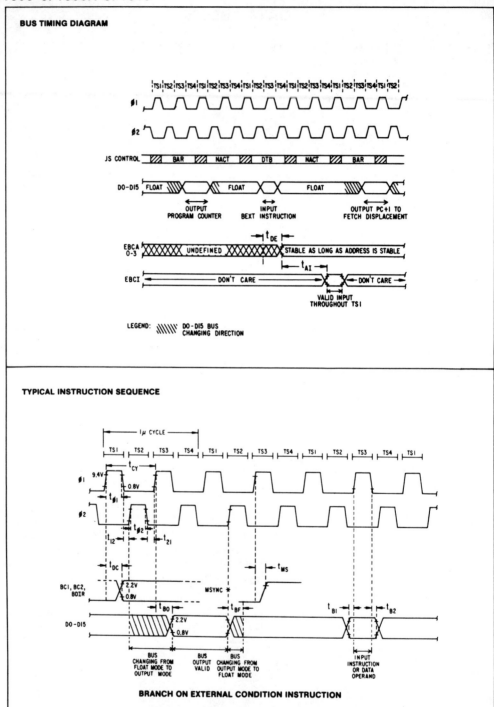

BUS TIMING DIAGRAM

LEGEND: \\\\\\ DO-DI5 BUS
                CHANGING DIRECTION

TYPICAL INSTRUCTION SEQUENCE

BRANCH ON EXTERNAL CONDITION INSTRUCTION

Data sheets on pages 2-D2 through 2-D6 reprinted by permission of General Instrument Corporation.

CP1600

ELECTRICAL CHARACTERISTICS (CP1600)

Maximum Ratings*

V_{DD}, V_{CC}, GND and all other input/output voltages
with respect to V_{BB} . . . . −0.3V to +18.0V
Storage Temperature . . . . −55°C to +150°C
Operating Temperature . . . . .0°C to +70°C

*Exceeding these ratings could cause permanent damage to these devices. Functional operation at these conditions is not implied—operating conditions are specified below.

Standard Conditions: (unless otherwise noted)

V_{DD}=+12V±5%, 70mA(typ), 110mA(max.) V_{BB}= −3V±10%, 0.2mA(typ), 2mA(max.)
V_{CC}=+5V±5%, 12mA(typ), 25mA(max.)   Operating Temperature (T_A)=0°C to +70°C

Characteristic	Sym	Min	Typ**	Max	Units	Conditions
DC CHARACTERISTICS						
Clock Inputs						
High	V_{IHC}	10.4	—	V_{DD}	V	
Low	V_{ILC}	0	—	0.6	V	
Logic Inputs						
Low	V_{IL}	0	—	0.65	V	
High (All Lines except BDRDY)	V_{IH}	2.4	—	V_{CC}	V	
High (Bus Data Ready Line See Note)	V_{IHB}	3.0	—	V_{CC}	V	
Logic Outputs						
High	V_{OH}	2.4	V_{CC}	—	V	I_{OH} = 100μA
Low (Data Bus Lines DO-D15)	V_{OL}	—	—	0.5	V	I_{OL} = 1.6mA
Low (Bus Control Lines, BC1,BC2,BDIR)	V_{OL}	—	—	0.45	V	I_{OL} = 2.0mA
Low (All Others)	V_{OL}	—	—	0.45	V	I_{OL} = 1.6mA
AC CHARACTERISTICS						
Clock Pulse Inputs, φ1 or φ2						
Pulse Width	$t_{φ2}$, $t_{φ2}$	120		—	ns	
Skew (φ1, φ2 delay)	t_{12}, t_{21}	0	—	—	ns	
Clock Period	t_{cy}	0.3	—	2.0	μs	
Rise & Fall Times	tr, tf	—	—	15	ns	
Master SYNC:						
Delay from φ	tms	—	—	30	ns	
DO-D15 Bus Signals						
Output delay from φ1 (float to output)	t_{BO}	—	—	120	ns	1 TTL Load & 25 pF
Output delay from φ2 (output to float)	t_{BF}	—	50	—	ns	
Input setup time before φ1	t_{B1}	0	—	—	ns	
Input hold time after φ1	t_{B2}	10	—	—	ns	
Bus Control Signals BC1,BC2,BDIR						
Output delay from φ1	t_{DC}	—	—	120	ns	
BUSAK Output delay from φ1	t_{BU}	—	150	—	ns	
TCI Output delay from φ1	t_{TO}	—	200	—	ns	
TCI Pulse Width	t_{TW}	—	300	—	ns	
EBCA output delay from BEXT input	t_{DE}	—	—	150	ns	
EBCA wait time for EBCI input	t_{AI}	—	—	400	ns	
CAPACITANCE						T_A = +25°C; V_{DD} = +12V; V_{CC} = +5V; V_{BB} = −3V; tφ1 tφ2 = 120ns
φ1, φ2 Clock Input capacitance	Cφ1, Cφ2	—	20	30	pF	
Input Capacitance						
DO-D15	CIN	—	6	12	pF	
All Other	—	—	5	10	pF	
Output Capacitance						
DO-D15 in high impedance state	C_D	—	8	15	pF	

**Typical values are at +25°C and nominal voltages.

NOTE:
The Bus Data ReaDY(BDRDY) line is sampled during time period TSI after a BAR or ADAR bus control signal. BDRDY must go low requesting a wait state 50 ns before the end of TS1 and remain low for 50 ns minimum. BDRDY may go high asynchronously. In response to BDRDY, the CPU will extend bus cycles by adding additional microcycles up to a maximum of 40 μsec duration.

CP1600A

ELECTRICAL CHARACTERISTICS (CP1600A)

Maximum Ratings*

V_{DD}, V_{CC}, GND and all other input/output voltages
   with respect to V_{BB} . . . . −0.3V to +18.0V
Storage Temperature . . . . −55°C to +150°C
Operating Temperature . . . . .0°C to +70°C

*Exceeding these ratings could cause permanent damage to these devices. Functional operation at these conditions is not implied—operating conditions are specified below.

Standard Conditions: (unless otherwise noted)

V_{DD}=+12V±5%, 70mA(typ) , 140mA(max.) V_{BB}= −3V±10%, 0.2mA(typ) , 2mA(max.)
V_{CC}=+5V±5%, 12mA(typ) , 25mA(max.)   Operating Temperature (T_A)=0°C to +70°C

Characteristic	Sym	Min	Typ**	Max	Units	Conditions
DC CHARACTERISTICS						
Clock Inputs						
High	V_{IHC}	10.4	—	V_{DD}	V	
Low	V_{ILC}	0	—	0.6	V	
Logic Inputs						
Low	V_{IL}	0	—	0.65	V	
High (All Lines except BDRDY)	V_{IH}	2.4	—	V_{CC}	V	
High (Bus Data Ready Line See Note)	V_{IHB}	3.0	—	V_{CC}	V	
Logic Outputs						
High	V_{OH}	2.4	V_{CC}		V	I_{OH} = 100μA
Low (Data Bus Lines DO-D15)	V_{OL}	—	—	0.5	V	I_{OL} = 1.6mA
Low (Bus Control Lines, BC1,BC2,BDIR)	V_{OL}	—	—	0.45	V	I_{OL} = 2.0mA
Low (All Others)	V_{OL}	—	—	0.45	V	I_{OL} = 1.6mA
AC CHARACTERISTICS						
Clock Pulse Inputs, φ1 or φ2						
Pulse Width	$t_{\phi 2}$, $t_{\phi 2}$	95		—	ns	
Skew (φ1, φ2 delay)	t_{12}, t_{21}	0	—	—	ns	
Clock Period	t_{cy}	0.25	—	2.0	μs	
Rise & Fall Times	tr, tf	—	—	15	ns	
Master SYNC:						
Delay from φ	tms	—	—	30	ns	
DO-D15 Bus Signals						
Output delay from φ1 (float to output)	t_{BO}	—	—	95	ns	1 TTL Load & 25 pF
Output delay from φ2 (output to float)	t_{BF}	—	50	—	ns	
Input setup time before φ1	t_{B1}	0	—	—	ns	
Input hold time after φ1	t_{B2}	10	—	—	ns	
Bus Control Signals BC1,BC2,BDIR						
Output delay from φ1	t_{DC}	—	—	200	ns	
BUSAK Output delay from φ1	t_{BU}	—	150	—	ns	
TCI Output delay from φ1	t_{TO}	—	200	—	ns	
TCI Pulse Width	t_{TW}	—	300	—	ns	
EBCA output delay from BEXT input	t_{DE}	—	—	150	ns	
EBCA wait time for EBCI input	t_{AI}	—	—	400	ns	
CAPACITANCE						TA = +25°C; V_{DD} = +12V; V_{CC} = +5V; V_{BB} = −3V; t φ1 t φ2 = 120ns
φ1, φ2 Clock Input capacitance	Cφ1, Cφ2	—	20	30	pF	
Input Capacitance						
DO-D15	CIN	—	6	12	pF	
All Other	—	—	5	10	pF	
Output Capacitance						
DO-D15 in high impedance state	C_D	—	8	15	pF	

**Typical values are at +25°C and nominal voltages.

NOTE:
   The Bus Data ReaDY(BDRDY) line is sampled during time period TSI after a BAR or ADAR bus control signal. BDRDY must go low requesting a wait state 50 ns before the end of TS1 and remain low for 50 ns minimum. BDRDY may go high asynchronously. In response to BDRDY, the CPU will extend bus cycles by adding additional microcycles up to a maximum of 40 μsec duration.

CP1610

ELECTRICAL CHARACTERISTICS (CP1610)

Maximum Ratings*

V$_{DD}$, V$_{CC}$, GND and all other input/output voltages	
with respect to V$_{BB}$	−0.3V to +18.0V
Storage Temperature	−55°C to +150°C
Operating Temperature	.0°C to +70°C

*Exceeding these ratings could cause permanent damage to these devices. Functional operation at these conditions is not implied—operating conditions are specified below.

Standard Conditions: (unless otherwise noted)

V$_{DD}$=+11V±5%, 70mA(typ) , 110mA(max.)   V$_{BB}$= −3V±10%, 0.2mA(typ) , 2mA(max.)

V$_{CC}$=+5V±5%, 12mA(typ) , 25mA(max.)   Operating Temperature (T$_A$)=0°C to +70°C

Characteristic	Sym	Min	Typ**	Max	Units	Conditions
DC CHARACTERISTICS						
Clock Inputs						
High	V$_{IHC}$	10.0	−	V$_{DD}$	V	
Low	V$_{ILC}$	0	−	0.6	V	
Input current	−	−	−	15	mA	V$_{IHC}$ = V$_{DD}$ −1
Logic Inputs						
Low	V$_{IL}$	0	−	0.65	V	
High (All Lines except BDRDY)	V$_{IH}$	2.4	−	V$_{CC}$	V	
High (Bus Data Ready Line See Note)	V$_{IHB}$	3.0	−	V$_{CC}$	V	
Logic Outputs						
High	V$_{OH}$	2.4	V$_{CC}$	−	V	I$_{OH}$ = 100μA
Low (Data Bus Lines DO-D15)	V$_{OL}$	−	−	0.5	V	I$_{OL}$ = 1.6mA
Low (Bus Control Lines, BC1,BC2,BDIR)	V$_{OL}$	−	−	0.45	V	I$_{OL}$ = 2.0mA
Low (All Others)	V$_{OL}$	−	−	0.45	V	I$_{OL}$ = 1.6mA
AC CHARACTERISTICS						
Clock Pulse Inputs, φ1 or φ2						
Pulse Width	t$_{φ2}$, t$_{φ2}$	250		−	ns	
Skew (φ1, φ2 delay)	t$_{12}$, t$_{21}$	0	−	−	ns	
Clock Period	t$_{cy}$	0.5	−	2.0	μs	
Rise & Fall Times	tr, tf	−	−	15	ns	
Master SYNC:						
Delay from φ	tms	−	−	30	ns	
DO-D15 Bus Signals						
Output delay from φ1 (float to output)	t$_{BO}$	−	−	200	ns	1 TTL Load & 25 pF
Output delay from φ2 (output to float)	t$_{BF}$	−	50	−	ns	
Input setup time before φ1	t$_{B1}$	0	−	−	ns	
Input hold time after φ1	t$_{B2}$	10	−	−	ns	
Bus Control Signals BC1,BC2,BDIR						
Output delay from φ1	t$_{DC}$	−	−	200	ns	
BUSAK Output delay from φ1	t$_{BU}$	−	150	−	ns	
TCI Output delay from φ1	t$_{TO}$	−	200	−	ns	
TCI Pulse Width	t$_{TW}$	−	300	−	ns	
EBCA output delay from BEXT input	t$_{DE}$	−	−	150	ns	
EBCA wait time for EBCI input	t$_{AI}$	−	−	400	ns	
CAPACITANCE						TA = +25°C; V$_{DD}$ = +12V; V$_{CC}$ = +5V; V$_{BB}$ = −3V; t φ1 t φ2 = 120ns
φ1, φ2 Clock Input capacitance	Cφ1, Cφ2	−	20	30	pF	
Input Capacitance						
DO-D15	CIN	−	6	12	pF	
All Other	−	−	5	10	pF	
Output Capacitance						
DO-D15 in high impedance state	C$_D$	−	8	15	pF	

**Typical values are at +25°C and nominal voltages.

NOTE:

The Bus Data ReaDY(BDRDY) line is sampled during time period TSI after a BAR or ADAR bus control signal. BDRDY must go low requesting a wait state 50 ns before the end of TS1 and remain low for 50 ns minimum. BDRDY may go high asynchronously. In response to BDRDY, the CPU will extend bus cycles by adding additional microcycles up to a maximum of 40 μsec duration.

IOB1680

ELECTRICAL CHARACTERISTICS

Maximum Ratings*

V_{DD} and V_{CC} and all other input/output voltages
with respect to GND . . . . –0.3V to +18V
Storage Temperature . . . . –55°C to +150°C
Operating Temperature . . . . 0°C to +70°C

*Exceeding these ratings could cause permanent damage. Functional operation of this device at these conditions is not implied—operating ranges are specified below.

Standard Conditions (unless otherwise noted)

All voltages referenced to GND
V_{DD} = +12V ± 5%
V_{CC} = +5V ± 5%
Operating Temperature (T_A) = 0°C to +70°C

Characteristic		Symbol	Min	Typ**	Max	Unit	Condition
DC CHARACTERISTICS							
Clock Input:	High	V_{ihc}	2.4	—	V_{DD}	V	
	Low	V_{ilc}	0	—	.5	V	
Logic Inputs:	High	V_{ih}	2.4	—	V_{CC}	V	
	Low	V_{il}	0	—	.65	V	
Logic Outputs:	High	V_{oh}	2.4	V_{CC}	—	V	I_{oh} = 100µA
	Low	V_{ol}	—	—	.5	V	I_{ol} = 1.6mA
AC CHARACTERISTICS							
Clock Inputs							
$\overline{CK1}$ Clock period		$t_{µc}$	0.4	—	4.0	µs	
Clock width		tcl	70	—	—	ns	
Rise & Fall times		tcr,tcf	—	—	10	ns	
CAPACITANCE (T_A = 25°C, V_{DD} = +12V, V_{CC} = +5V)							
Input Capacitance: D0-D7		C_{in}	—	6	12	pF	V_{in} = 0V
All others			—	5	10	pF	V_{in} = 0V
Output Capacitance:		C_{out}	—	8	15	pF	

**Typical values are at +25°C and nominal voltages.

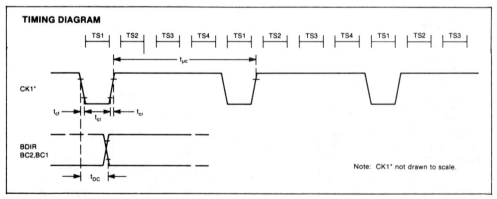

TIMING DIAGRAM

Note: CK1* not drawn to scale.

CIRCUIT DESCRIPTION

This circuit is designed to provide all the data buffering and control functions required when interfacing the Series 1600 Microprocessor System to a simple peripheral device. Data is transferred to and from the peripheral on 16 bidirectional lines, each of which can be considered to be an input or output. The transfer of information with the CP1600 is accomplished via an 8-bit highway, the 16-bits being transferred as two 8-bit bytes. the register addresses are assigned CP1600 memory locations, as follows (N is an arbitrary starting address):

Register Address Description

N	Control Register
N + 1	Data Register Low Order 8-bits
N + 2	Data Register High Order 8-bits
N + 3	Timer Low Order 8-bits
N + 4	Timer High Order 8-bits
N + 5	Peripheral Interrupt Address Vector
N + 6	Timer Interrupt Address Vector
N + 7	Error Interrupt Address Vector

Chapter 3
THE TEXAS INSTRUMENTS TMS 9900, TMS 9980, AND TMS 9940 PRODUCTS

The TMS 9900 was the first 16-bit microprocessor that could compete effectively in the minicomputer market. In fact, **the TMS 9900 is a one-chip implementation of the TM 990 series minicomputer Central Processing Units.**

The TMS 9900 is packaged as a 64-pin DIP; it generates signals for a 15-bit Address Bus and a separate 16-bit Data Bus, whereas other 16-bit microprocessors multiplex their Data and Address Busses. **The TMS 9980 series microprocessors are 40-pin DIP versions of the TMS 9900;** in order to reduce pin counts, the TMS 9980 series microprocessors access external memory via an 8-bit Data Bus and 14-bit Address Bus. **The TMS 9940 is a one-chip microcomputer** containing a subset of the TMS 9900 Central Processing Unit, together with on-chip memory and real-time clock logic.

The TMS 9900 product line has for some time been one of the enigmas of the microprocessor industry. Even a casual examination of the TMS 9900 instruction set shows that from the programmer's viewpoint, this microprocessor was at least two years ahead of its time. While it may have had problems competing in high-volume, simple applications, it was certainly the microprocessor of choice for data processing-type, program-intensive applications, yet it was not widely used in these markets.

The reason for this lack of acceptance has been poor support from Texas Instruments.

Texas Instruments initially offered little support for the TMS 9900 because this microprocessor was designed as a low-end product of the TM 990 minicomputer series. That is to say, customers were expected to develop products around the TM 990 minicomputers; then, if they chose to, they could build production models around the TMS 9900 microprocessor. This development path did not call for extensive TMS 9900 support. In all probability, Texas Instruments was caught by surprise by the buoyancy of the microprocessor market — as a market in its own right. Certainly, if Texas Instruments had given the TMS 9900 the same level of support that Intel gave the 8080A, we would see entirely different microprocessor product distributions today. But the TMS 9900 and its derivative products are powerful enough that the belated support they are now receiving from Texas Instruments will give the product line a reasonable share of future markets.

Texas Instruments now provides full support for the TMS 9900 microprocessor line.

TMS 9900 support devices are designed specifically for the TMS 9900 and can be used with the TMS 9900, TMS 9980, or TMS 9940 products. The following devices are described:

      The TIM 9904 Clock Generator
      The TMS 9901 Programmable System Interface
      The TMS 9902 Asynchronous Communications Controller
      The TMS 9903 Synchronous Communications Controller

Texas Instruments is the primary manufacturer for all of the TMS 9900 series products. TMS 9900 series products are handled out of the following Texas Instruments office:

      TEXAS INSTRUMENTS, INC.
      P.O. Box 1443
      Houston, Texas 77001

Second sources for the TMS 9900 family are:

      AMERICAN MICROSYSTEMS, INC.
      3800 Homestead Road
      Santa Clara, California 95051

      SMC MICROSYSTEMS CORP. (TMS 9980 series only)
      35 Marcus Blvd.
      Hauppage, N.Y. 11787

THE TMS 9900 MICROPROCESSOR

The TMS 9900 is manufactured using N-channel silicon gate MOS technology. It is packaged as a 64-pin DIP. Three power supplies are required: -5V, +5V, and +12V.

Using a 3 MHz clock, instruction execution times range between 3 and 10 microseconds.

A TMS 9900 FUNCTIONAL OVERVIEW

Figure 3-1 illustrates that part of our general microcomputer system logic which is implemented by the TMS 9900 CPU.

The most important features of Figure 3-1 are:

- The absence of programmable registers
- The presence of significant interrupt handling logic
- The presence of serial-to-parallel data conversion logic
- The absence of I/O port interface logic

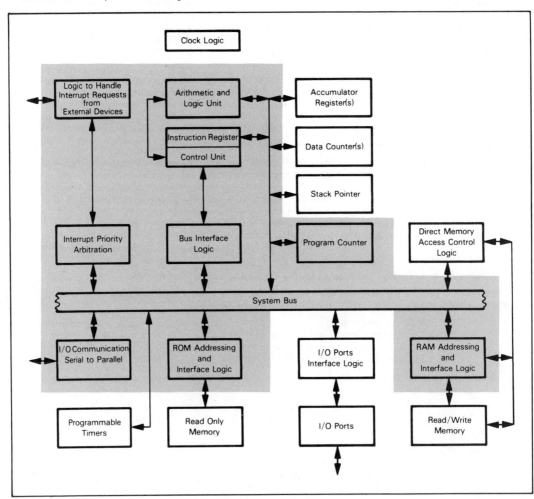

Figure 3-1. Logic of the TMS 9900 CPU

Let us first consider the manner in which the TMS 9900 handles programmable registers.

TMS 9900 PROGRAMMABLE REGISTERS

Within the logic of the TMS 9900 itself, there are just three 16-bit programmable registers: a Program Counter, a Workspace register, and a Status register.

The Program Counter and Status register are straightforward. The Program Counter contains the address of the next instruction to be executed. The Status register maintains various statuses, which we describe later in this chapter.

The Workspace register is a unique and powerful programming feature of the TMS 9900. This register identifies the first of sixteen 16-bit memory locations which act as 16 General Purpose registers. This may be illustrated as follows:

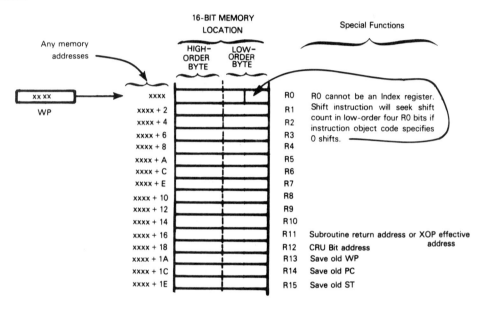

Some of the 16 registers serve special functions, as defined by the text on the right-hand side of the illustration above. For the moment, do not attempt to understand these special functions. They are described later in the chapter.

In TMS 9900 microcomputer systems, external memory consists of 16-bit memory words. Each 16-bit memory word has its own memory address. Within the TMS 9900 CPU, however, memory is addressed as a sequence of 8-bit locations. For this to occur, the CPU

TMS 9900
MEMORY
ADDRESSES

generates an internal 16-bit memory address; the high-order 15 bits of the internal memory address create the external memory addresses. **This may be illustrated as follows:**

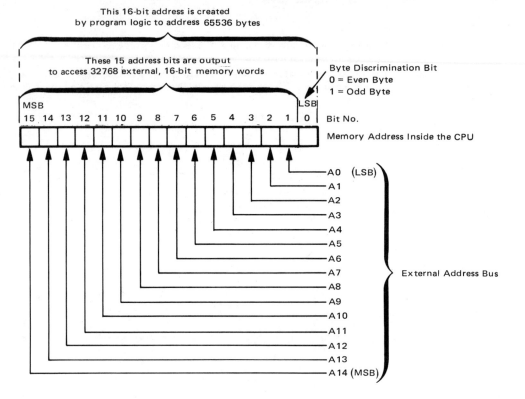

When designing hardware around the TMS 9900, you will implement external memory as 16-bit words, which are addressed by a 15-line Address Bus. That is to say, 32.768 16-bit words may be addressed.

But when you are programming the TMS 9900 you will visualize memory as 65.536 bytes, addressed by a 16-bit address. **An even byte address will access the low-order byte of an external 16-bit memory word, while an odd memory address will access the high-order byte of an external 16-bit memory word.**

Any 16 contiguous words of read/write memory may serve as the current 16 general purpose registers for the TMS 9900.

You may have as many sets of 16-bit registers as you wish, limited only by the size of implemented memory.

If you are using more than one set of 16-bit registers, then at any time just one set of 16-bit registers can be selected. The WP register identifies the first of the 16 contiguous memory locations serving as the current 16 general purpose registers.

Each of the 16 general purpose registers may be used to store data or addresses. Thus, **each general purpose register may serve as an Accumulator or as a Data Counter.**

Registers R11 through R15 are used as special Pointer storage buffers; we will be describing the way in which these registers are used as the chapter proceeds.

Having 16 general purpose registers in read/write memory, rather than in the CPU, is the single most important feature of TMS 9900 architecture. The advantage of having 16 general purpose registers located anywhere in read/write memory is that you can have many sets of 16 general purpose registers. For example, following an interrupt acknowledge, you no longer need to save the contents of general purpose registers — all you need to do is save the contents of the Program Counter, the Workspace register and the Status register, and that is done automatically by TMS 9900 interrupt handling logic. By loading new values into the Program Counter and the Workspace register, you can begin executing a new program. accessing 16 new memory words — which will be treated as a new set of 16 general purpose registers.

The disadvantage of having 16 general purpose registers in read/write memory is that no TMS 9900 microcomputer system can be configured without read/write memory; and if you are going to use many different sets of 16-bit registers. then you are going to require a significant amount of read/write memory. Furthermore. you lose the speed associated with executing register-to-register operations; there are no source and destination locations left in the CPU. Every register access becomes a memory access.

TMS 9900 literature refers to the process of switching from one set of general purpose registers to another as a context switch. This terminology reflects the complete change of program environment that results from the switch.

| TMS 9900 |
| CONTEXT |
| SWITCH |

Special instructions allow you to perform a forward context switch or a backward context switch.

During a forward context switch. you load new values into the Workspace register and Program Counter. while simultaneously saving the old Workspace register. Program Counter. and Status register contents in the new General Purpose Registers R13. R14. and R15.

A backward, or reverse context switch loads the current contents of General Purpose Registers R13. R14. and R15 into the Workspace register. Program Counter. and Status register. respectively. thus returning you to your previous set of general purpose registers.

You can perform context switches as often as you like and whenever you like. For example. a very effective way of using context switching is to group data into contiguous memory words which you can identify as a register set. Upon entering a subroutine. you can perform a context switch which automatically creates all necessary initial data and address values in appropriate general purpose registers. This may be illustrated as follows:

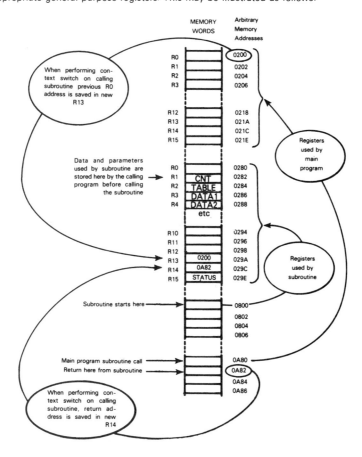

As illustrated above. **when you perform a forward context switch,** the current Program Counter contents. Status register contents. and WP register contents are saved in what will become the new Registers R13. R14 and R15.. respectively. **Here is the exact sequence in which events occur:**

1) The new WP register contents are loaded into the CPU and held in temporary storage.

2) The current Status register contents are written out to the memory location which will become the new Register R15.

3) The current Program Counter contents are written out to the memory location which will become the new Register R14.

4) The current WP register contents are written out to the memory location which will become the new Register R13.

5) The new WP register contents. which were held in temporary storage. are moved into the WP register.

6) The new value is loaded into the Program Counter.

Thus. when a forward context switch is performed. an audit trail ensures that program logic knows the exact machine state at the instant of the forward context switch.

When a backward context switch occurs, the contents of the current General Purpose registers R13, R14, and R15 are loaded into the WP register, the Program Counter, and the Status register, respectively. Thus. program logic returns to the location of the forward context switch.

TMS 9900 MEMORY ADDRESSING MODES

The TMS 9900 provides these four methods of addressing memory:

1) **Direct memory addressing**

2) **Direct, indexed memory addressing**

3) **Implied memory addressing**

4) **Implied memory addressing with auto-increment**

The way in which the TMS 9900 implements these four memory addressing modes is exactly as described in Volume 1. Chapter 6. The important point to note is that the TMS 9900 looks upon its address space as consisting of 32.768 16-bit memory words which are addressed using 15. rather than 16. Address Bus lines; yet programs compute all addresses as 16-bit words. This logic was described earlier.

Direct memory addressing instructions provide the memory address in the second word of an instruction's object code:

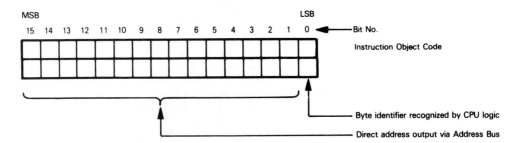

Direct, indexed memory addressing instructions provide a base address in the second object code word, but they also identify a general purpose register whose contents are to be added, as a signed binary number, to the base address. Again. the low-order bit of the computed address is not output via the Address Bus. but is interpreted by CPU logic as a byte identifier.

General Purpose Register R0 cannot be specified as an index register.

Direct. indexed addressing is very useful in a TMS 9900 microcomputer system. It allows you to address the previous set of general purpose registers. following a context switch. without knowing where the previous registers were. Suppose you want to access the contents of the memory word which was being used as General Purpose Register R5 before you switched to your current set of general purpose registers. Recall that the previous Workspace register contents are stored in your current General Purpose Register R13. You could thus address the previous General Purpose Register R5. without knowing where this general purpose register may have been. by using direct. indexed addressing as follows:

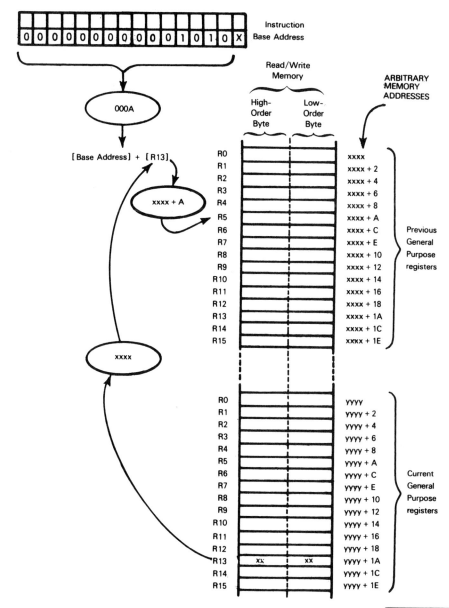

An implied memory addressing instruction will specify one of the 16 current general purpose registers as providing the effective memory address.

If you specify implied memory addressing with auto-increment, then the contents of the identified general purpose register will be incremented after the memory access has been performed. If the instruction specifies a byte operation. the register contents will be incremented by one. the register contents will be incremented by two after a full-word operation.

TMS 9900
IMPLIED
ADDRESSING

Six object code bits identify the data memory addressing option selected by any TMS 9900 instruction that accesses data memory. The six object code bits are interpreted as follows:

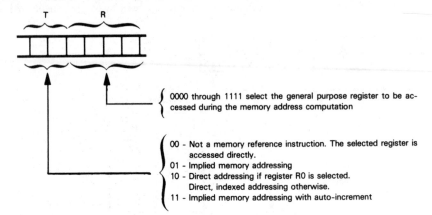

0000 through 1111 select the general purpose register to be accessed during the memory address computation

00 - Not a memory reference instruction. The selected register is accessed directly.
01 - Implied memory addressing
10 - Direct addressing if register R0 is selected. Direct, indexed addressing otherwise.
11 - Implied memory addressing with auto-increment

Two-address instructions will include 12 memory addressing option bits:

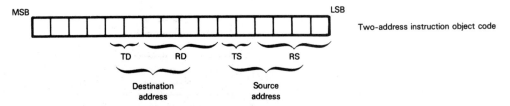

Two-address instruction object code

TD   RD   TS   RS

Destination address   Source address

Some instructions allow a source to be anywhere in memory, but the destination must be a general purpose register. These object codes include TS, RS, and RD, but not TD.

TMS 9900 Jump instructions use program relative, direct addressing. These are one-word instructions, where the low-order byte of the instruction object code provides an 8-bit, signed binary value, which is added to the incremented contents of the Program Counter. This is straightforward program relative, direct addressing.

> TMS 9900
> PROGRAM
> MEMORY
> ADDRESSING

TMS 9900 I/O ADDRESSING

As compared to other microcomputers described in this book, the TMS 9900 has unusual I/O logic. **In addition to addressing I/O devices as memory locations, you can address a separate I/O field of up to 4096 bits. Texas Instruments' literature refers to this field as the "Communications Register Unit" (CRU).** If you are programming a TMS 9900 microcomputer system that has already been configured by Texas Instruments, then it is justifiable to look upon the Communications Register Unit as a form of I/O port. If you are building your own interface to a TMS 9900 CPU, then instructions that are supposed to access the Communications Register Unit in reality simply make alternative use of part of the Address Bus in conjunction with three control signals: CRUCLK, CRUIN, and CRUOUT.

There are two classes of TMS 9900 CRU instructions. The first class accesses individual bits (or signals), while the second class accesses bit fields that may be between 1 and 16 bits wide.

There are three single-bit CRU instructions; they set, reset, or test the identified CRU bit. This is equivalent to setting, resetting, or testing an external signal or single I/O port bit. When a bit is to be set or reset, the new level is output via CRUOUT, and a CRUCLK pulse indicates that valid data is on the CRUOUT line. When the condition of a bit is to be input or tested, then external logic is required to return the level of the tested bit via CRUIN.

A CRU bit instruction outputs a 12-bit address which is computed as follows:

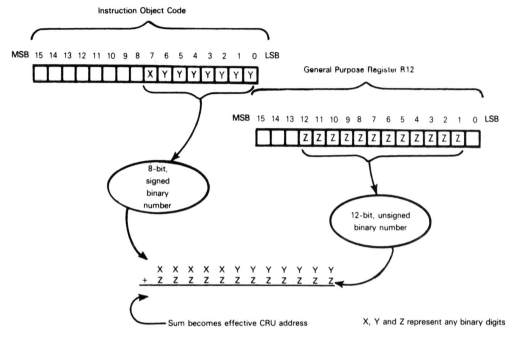

The 12-bit address is output on the 12 lower-order address lines; the three higher-order address lines are all 0 to designate a CRU address.

Now during the execution of a CRU bit instruction. the address which is output is supposed to be a bit address — that is. an address identifying one bit in a possible 4096-bit field. So far as external interface logic is concerned. the address can be interpreted in any way. However. **data output will occur via CRUOUT only; data is input via CRUIN, and stored in the Equal bit of the Status register.**

There are two multi-bit CRU instructions: one. LDCR. transfers data from an addressed memory location to any addressed CRU bit field. The other. STCR. transfers data from an addressed CRU bit field to any addressed memory location. Anywhere from 1 to 16 bits of data may be transferred by the LDCR and STCR instructions. **Instruction object codes are interpreted as follows:**

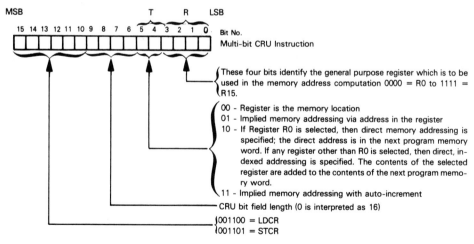

The source/destination memory location is identified as it would be for any memory reference instruction.

The address of the first CRU bit is specified by Register R12. For a multi-bit CRU instruction, the CRU bit address is incremented for each succeeding bit access, but the incremented address is held in a temporary storage location. The contents of Register R12 are not incremented.

Thus, multi-bit CRU instructions may transfer anywhere from 1 to 16 bits between any memory location and any CRU bit field. **Note that memory must be divided into 16-bit words, each of which has identified bit boundaries, but there are no equivalent bit boundaries in the CRU bit field.** That is to say, any CRU bit may be identified via Register R12 as the first bit in a multi-bit field, while the length of the multi-bit field is identified by the instruction object code. This may be illustrated as follows:

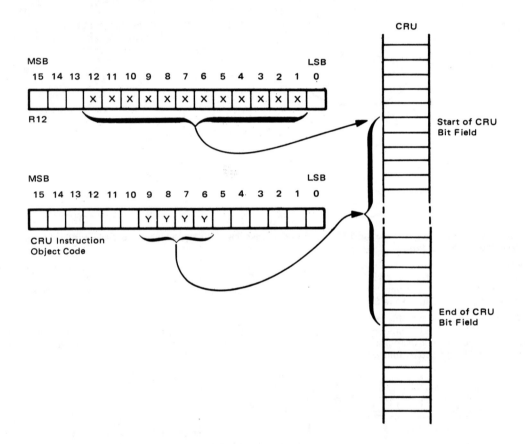

If YYYY is 0000, the CRU bit field is assumed to be 16 bits in length.

When bits are transferred from a memory location to a CRU bit field, the contents of the memory location are not actually modified, but **the transfer occurs as though bits had been right shifted out of the memory location.** Bits arriving within the addressed CRU bit field are stored in sequential CRU bit locations with ascending addresses. This may be illustrated as follows:

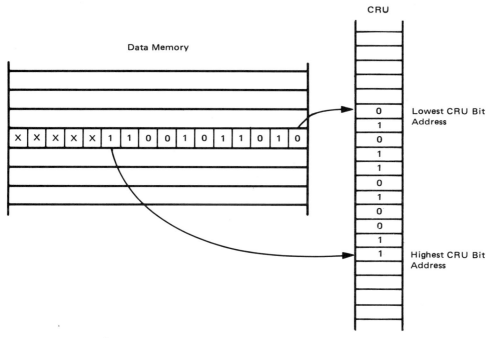

Eleven bits have been transferred in the illustration above. If eight or fewer bits are transferred from a general purpose register, only the more significant byte is accessed:

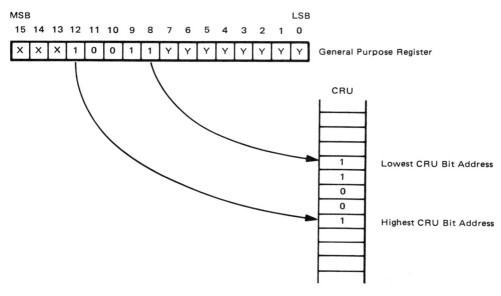

Our illustration shows a transfer of five bits.

If eight or fewer bits are transferred from a memory location, then the memory address will be considered a byte address rather than a word address; that is, the transfer will be from the low-order bits of the addressed byte, which may be either the upper or lower byte of a 16-bit memory word. Thus you can access the lower byte of a general purpose register by addressing it as a memory location.

A data transfer from the CRU to data memory occurs as the exact logical reverse of the illustration above, except that high-order bits of the destination data memory word are zeroed if unfilled. This **may be illustrated as follows:**

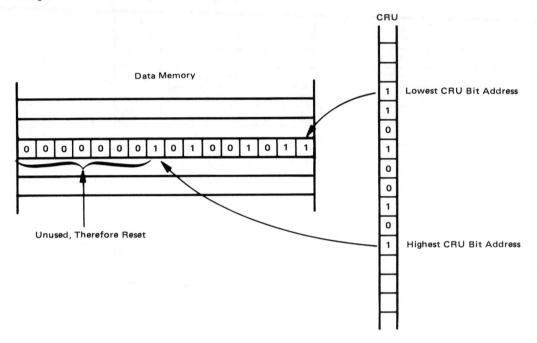

As with data transfers from memory to the CRU, if eight or fewer bits are transferred, only a byte will be affected. This will be either the addressed memory byte:

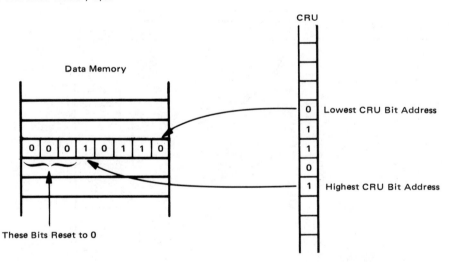

or the high-order byte of a general purpose register:

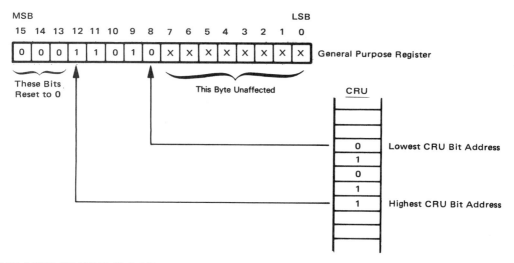

TMS 9900 STATUS FLAGS

The TMS 9900 CPU has a 16-bit Status register which may be illustrated as follows:

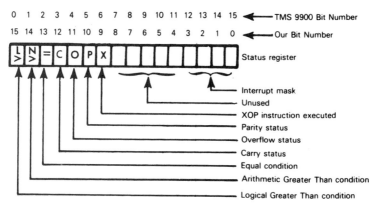

The low-order four bits of the Status register represent an interrrupt mask which identifies the level of interrupt which is currently enabled. As the 4-bit interrupt mask would imply. 16 levels of interrupt are allowed. We will describe interrupt processing later in this chapter.

The X status is set to 1 while an XOP instruction is being executed. This instruction allows you to perform a software interrupt — as described later in this chapter.

The P, O, and C are standard Parity, Overflow and Carry statuses.

The Equal status (=) identifies a condition that currently exists, as the result of the execution of a previous instruction, that will cause a Branch-if-Equal instruction to branch. A CRU bit to be tested also gets stored in the Equal status.

The Logical Greater Than and Arithmetic Greater Than statuses are set or reset following arithmetic. logical. or data move operations. **A Logical Greater Than treats the source data as simple, unsigned binary numbers. An Arithmetic Greater Than interprets the operand as signed binary numbers.**

TMS 9900 CPU PINS AND SIGNALS

Figure 3-2 illustrates the pins and signals of the TMS 9900 CPU.

Being a 64-pin DIP. the TMS 9900 can afford to have separate Address and Data Busses.

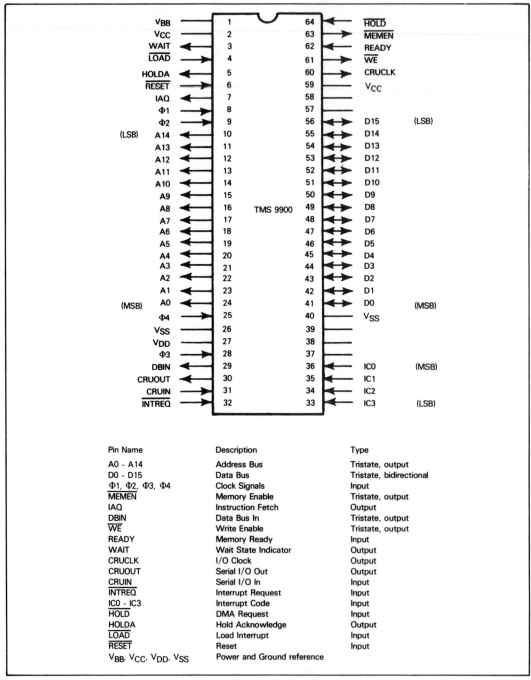

Pin Name	Description	Type
A0 - A14	Address Bus	Tristate, output
D0 - D15	Data Bus	Tristate, bidirectional
Φ1, Φ2, Φ3, Φ4	Clock Signals	Input
MEMEN	Memory Enable	Tristate, output
IAQ	Instruction Fetch	Output
DBIN	Data Bus In	Tristate, output
WE	Write Enable	Tristate, output
READY	Memory Ready	Input
WAIT	Wait State Indicator	Output
CRUCLK	I/O Clock	Output
CRUOUT	Serial I/O Out	Output
CRUIN	Serial I/O In	Input
INTREQ	Interrupt Request	Input
IC0 - IC3	Interrupt Code	Input
HOLD	DMA Request	Input
HOLDA	Hold Acknowledge	Output
LOAD	Load Interrupt	Input
RESET	Reset	Input
VBB, VCC, VDD, VSS	Power and Ground reference	

Figure 3-2. TMS 9900 Signals and Pin Assignments

Pins A0 - A14 provide the 15-bit Address Bus. Note that Texas Instruments' literature numbers bits and pins from left to right; therefore, address line A0 represents the most significant address bit, where as address line A14 represents the least significant address bit.

D0 - D15 provide a 16-bit bidirectional Data Bus. Once again, D0 represents the most significant data bit in Texas Instruments' literature.

Remaining signals may be divided into bus control, interrupt control, and timing.

External logic must provide four clock signals, Φ1, Φ2, Φ3, and Φ4. These are provided by the TIM 9904, described later in this chapter.

Any memory access operation begins with an address being output via the Address Bus. The TMS 9900 CPU identifies a stable address on the Address Bus by outputting MEMEN low.

If the memory access operation is an instruction fetch, the IAQ is output high.

If the memory access is a read, then the TMS 9900 outputs a high level via DBIN. Memory interface logic must interpret the high DBIN level as a signal to place data on the Data Bus.

If the memory access is a memory write, then the TMS 9900 CPU outputs a low pulse via WE. Memory interface logic must use the low WE pulse to signal that valid data is on the Data Bus, and to store it in the addressed memory location. WE low does not last as long as DBIN high.

When external logic cannot respond to a memory access in the available time, it requests a Wait state by inputting READY low. The CPU acknowledges by outputting WAIT high.

CRUCLK, CRUIN, and CRUOUT are three signals used to implement single-bit or serial data transfers via the CRU interface.

CRUOUT is used to output bits of data to the I/O devices, and CRUIN is used to retrieve input data from the I/O devices. CRUCLK is active during output operations only, and defines when data bits on CRUOUT are valid.

Let us now look at interrupt control signals.

There is a single interrupt request input, INTREQ, which must be held low by any external device requesting an interrupt. External devices identify themselves via control signals IC0 - IC3. Thus, an interrupt request must be accompanied by the appropriate input at IC0 - IC3.

Observe that there is no interrupt acknowledge signal.

For DMA operations, external logic requests access to the System Bus by inputting HOLD low. The CPU acknowledges the Hold request by outputting HOLDA high.

LOAD is a nonmaskable interrupt.

RESET is a typical system Reset signal. However, TMS 9900 Reset logic uses the device's interrupt capabilities; therefore, we will describe the Reset operation in detail when discussing TMS 9900 interrupt capabilities in general.

TMS 9900 TIMING AND INSTRUCTION EXECUTION

TMS instructions execute as a sequence of machine cycles, each of which contains two clock periods. Clock periods are timed by four clock signals, Φ1, Φ2, Φ3, and Φ4, as illustrated in Figure 3-3. Note that Φ2 is the first phase of each clock period, and that Φ1 is the last phase.

The simplest instruction execution machine cycle is an internal operations cycle. No external bus signals are active during this machine cycle, and no memory or I/O access occurs. Timing for an internal operations machine cycle will consist of two clock periods, as illustrated in Figure 3-3.

TMS 9900 INTERNAL OPERATIONS MACHINE CYCLE

MEMORY ACCESS OPERATIONS

TMS 9900 memory access operations may consist of a memory read or a memory write. An instruction fetch is a minor variation of a memory read.

Figure 3-4 illustrates memory read machine cycle timing.

MEMEN goes low at the beginning of any memory access machine cycle and stays low for the entire machine cycle.

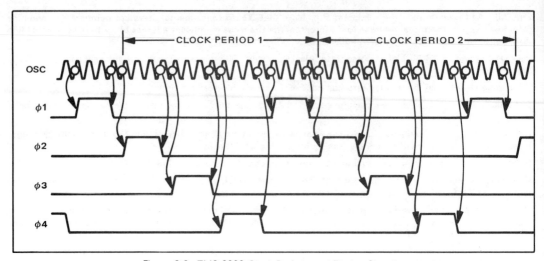

Figure 3-3. TMS 9900 Clock Periods and Timing Signals as
Generated by the TIM 9904

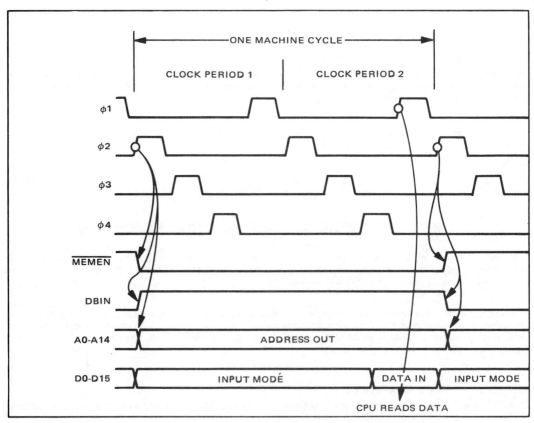

Figure 3-4. A TMS 9900 Memory Read Machine Cycle

DBIN goes high at the beginning of the memory read machine cycle and stays high for the entire machine cycle. External logic can therefore use $\overline{\text{MEMEN}}$ low as a memory address indicator while DBIN high identifies the read operation.

A memory address is output stable on the Address Bus for the entire machine cycle.

The Data Bus operations during a memory read machine cycle represent the only unusual characteristics of the machine cycle. Input data needs to be stable during the Φ1 high pulse of the second clock period. However, the Data Bus is connected to input logic for the entire memory read machine cycle and for a portion of the next machine cycle. Thus, during a memory read machine cycle, external logic cannot access the Data Bus to perform direct memory access, or any other operations, on the assumption that the Data Bus is free until Data In becomes stable. Moreover, since the Data Bus is held by data input logic of the CPU during the next machine cycle, a memory read machine cycle cannot be followed by a memory write machine cycle. **A memory read machine cycle must be followed by an internal operations machine cycle, or by another memory read machine cycle.**

The only difference between an instruction fetch machine cycle and a memory read machine cycle is the fact that **during an instruction fetch machine cycle, IAQ is output high,** along with DBIN, for the duration of the machine cycle.

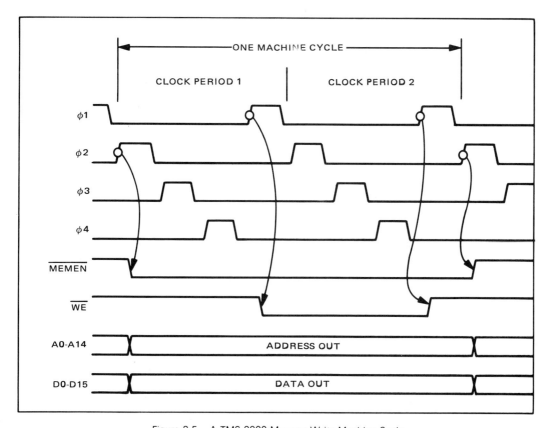

Figure 3-5. A TMS 9900 Memory Write Machine Cycle

Memory write machine cycle timing is illustrated in Figure 3-5. In this illustration, we see that data is output stable on the Data Bus for the entire duration of the memory write machine cycle. The Data Bus is not held by output logic beyond this single machine cycle. Thus, no restrictions are placed on the type of machine cycle which can follow a memory write machine cycle. Even though data output is stable for the entire memory write machine cycle, the write enable strobe $\overline{WE}$ does not go low until close to the end of the first clock period. In many cases it is easier to use NOT DBIN as a write control signal. Here is the necessary logic:

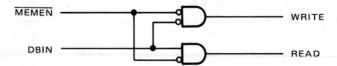

TMS 9900 instruction execution machine cycle sequences are not always self-evident; therefore, let us look at some memory reference examples.

Memory address computations make machine cycle sequences quite complex, particularly for two-operand instructions. Fortunately, the exact machine cycle sequences are rarely of any consequence to you as a programmer or logic designer. The eventual number of machine cycles required to execute an instruction (and therefore its execution time) is important.

Generally stated, **instruction execution proceeds as follows:**

| TMS 9900 |
| **INSTRUCTION** |
| **EXECUTION** |
| **SEQUENCES** |

1) The instruction object code is fetched.

2) The first operand address is computed.

3) The second operand address (if there is one) is computed.

4) Any operation that may be required is performed.

5) If a result is generated, it is returned to the second operand address.

Let us look at operand address computations using the ADD instruction (A) as a general example. First consider the instruction in its simplest form — where the contents of one register are added to the contents of another register:

A   R1,R2

Cycle	Type	Figure	Function
1	MEMORY READ	3-4	Fetch instruction object code
2	ALU	3-3	Decode instruction
3	MEMORY READ	3-4	Fetch R1 contents
4	ALU	3-3	
5	MEMORY READ	3-4	Fetch R2 contents
6	ALU	3-3	Add R1 and R2 contents
7	MEMORY WRITE	3-5	Store sum in R2

Now consider the same instruction's execution. but using implied memory addressing for the first operand:

A   *R1,R2

Cycle	Type	Figure	Function
1	MEMORY READ	3-4	Fetch instruction object code
2	ALU	3-3	Decode instruction
3	MEMORY READ	3-4	Fetch R1 contents
4	ALU	3-3	Use R1 contents as a memory address (implied addressing)
5	MEMORY READ	3-4	Fetch contents of implied address location
6	ALU	3-3	
7	MEMORY READ	3-4	Fetch R2 contents
8	ALU	3-3	Add data fetched in cycles 5 and 7
9	MEMORY WRITE	3-5	Store sum in R2

If the second (destination) operand uses direct addressing, here is the machine cycle sequence:

A   *R1,@LABEL

Cycle	Type	Figure	Function
1	MEMORY READ	3-4	Fetch instruction object code
2	ALU	3-3	Decode instruction
3	MEMORY READ	3-4	Fetch R1 contents
4	ALU	3-3	Use R1 contents as a memory address
5	MEMORY READ	3-4	Fetch contents of implied address location
6,7,8	ALU	3-3	
9	MEMORY READ	3-4	Fetch the second instruction object code word; it holds the direct address
10	ALU	3-3	
11	MEMORY READ	3-4	Fetch contents of directly addressed memory word
12	ALU	3-3	Add words fetched in cycles 5 and 11
13	MEMORY WRITE	3-5	Store sum in directly addressed memory word

Indexed, direct addressing results in the following sequence:

A   *R1,@LABEL(5)

Cycle	Type	Figure	Function
1	MEMORY READ	3-4	Fetch instruction object code
2	ALU	3-3	Decode instruction
3	MEMORY READ	3-4	Fetch R1 contents
4	ALU	3-3	Use R1 contents as a memory address
5	MEMORY READ	3-4	Fetch contents of implied address location
6	ALU	3-3	
7	MEMORY READ	3-4	Fetch the second instruction object code word; it holds the direct address
8	ALU	3-3	
9	MEMORY READ	3-4	Fetch R5, the Index register contents
10	ALU	3-3	Add direct address and index
11	MEMORY READ	3-4	Fetch contents of memory word addressed by cycle 10 addition
12	ALU	3-3	Add memory words fetched in cycles 5 and 11
13	MEMORY WRITE	3-5	Store sum in memory word addressed by cycle 10 addition

If the first operand-implied address specified an auto-increment, we must add one more machine cycle:

A   *R1+,@LABEL(5)

Cycle	Type	Figure	Function
1	MEMORY READ	3-4	Fetch instruction object code
2	ALU	3-3	Decode instruction
3	MEMORY READ	3-4	Fetch R1 contents
4	ALU	3-3	Increment fetched R1 contents
5	MEMORY WRITE	3-5	Write incremented R1 contents back to R1
6	MEMORY READ	3-4	Fetch contents of implied address location
7	ALU	3-3	
8	MEMORY READ	3-4	Fetch the second instruction object code word; it holds the direct address
9	ALU	3-3	
10	MEMORY READ	3-4	Fetch R5, the Index register contents
11	ALU	3-3	Add direct address and index
12	MEMORY READ	3-4	Fetch contents of memory word addressed by cycle 11 addition
13	ALU	3-3	Add memory words fetched in cycles 5 and 12
14	MEMORY WRITE	3-5	Store sum in memory word addressed by cycle 11 addition

MEMORY SELECT LOGIC

$\overline{\text{MEMEN}}$ discriminates between memory and I/O accesses. It is therefore very important that $\overline{\text{MEMEN}}$ low be a necessary component for any memory select.

You can map I/O into the memory space of the TMS 9900. This is true of any microprocessor. Memory addresses that select I/O devices will, of course, also require $\overline{\text{MEMEN}}$ low as a contributor to I/O device select logic.

$\overline{\text{MEMEN}}$ as a contributor to select logic may be illustrated as follows:

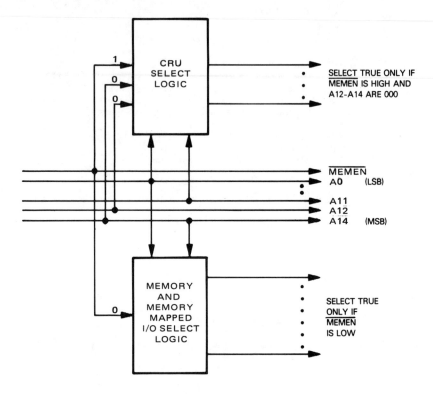

The three high-order address lines, A12, A13, and A14, are not used to address CRU bits. When addressing a CRU bit, these lines are all low. They are not low during execution of externally defined I/O instructions; therefore, A12, A13, and A14 low must be a prerequisite for any CRU bit select.

TMS 9900 I/O INSTRUCTION TIMING

All TMS 9900 I/O instructions transfer serial data via the Communication Register Unit (CRU). (This excludes I/O which is addressed as TMS 9900 memory space.)

There are four types of TMS 9900 I/O instructions. They are:

1) **Data input.** Anywhere from 1 to 16 bits of data may be transferred from the CRU bit field to memory.

2) **Data output.** This is the simple reverse of data input. Anywhere from 1 to 16 bits of data may be output from memory to the CRU bit field.

3) **Bit test.** Any bit in the CRU bit field may be tested. The tested bit is input and stored in the Equal bit of the Status register. Thence, condition branch instructions can be used to test the bit level.

4) **Externally defined I/O instructions.** These instructions generate I/O control signals, but they transfer no data.

Timing for CRU output and input machine cycles is illustrated in Figures 3-6 and 3-7, respectively. Each of these figures shows two bits of data being transferred. (You should not attach any special significance to this fact; depending on the instruction being executed, anywhere from 1 to 16 bits may be transferred.) CRU machine cycles are executed contiguously, one per bit.

Every CRU I/O instruction will require a memory reference machine cycle, together with one or more CRU machine cycles. For example, **when an STCR instruction is executed to input data from the CRU to the CPU, the following machine cycle sequence will occur:**

Cycle	Type	Figure	Function
1	MEMORY READ	3-4	Fetch Instruction Code
2	ALU	3-3	Decode Instruction
a Cycles, where $0 \leqslant a \leqslant 4$			Obtain Destination Address
$3 + a$	MEMORY READ	3-4	Fetch Destination Memory Word Contents
$4 + a$	ALU	3-3	
$5 + a$	MEMORY READ	3-4	Fetch R12
$6 + a$	ALU	3-3	Compute CRU Starting Address and Prepare Control Signals
$7 + a$	ALU		
i Cycles	CRU IN	3-7	Input i CRU Bits
$8 + a + i$	ALU	3-3	Load CRU Bits in Temporary Register
$9 + a + i$	ALU		
r Cycles			Fill Upper Bits of Byte or Word With Zeroes If $i > 8, r = 15 - i$; if $i \leqslant 8, r = 7 - i$
$10 + a + i + r$ to $12 + a + i + r$	ALU	3-3	Prepare to Store Memory Word
$13 + a + i + r$	MEMORY WRITE	3-5	Output Assembled Word to Memory Location Whose Contents Were Fetched in Machine Cycle $3 + a$

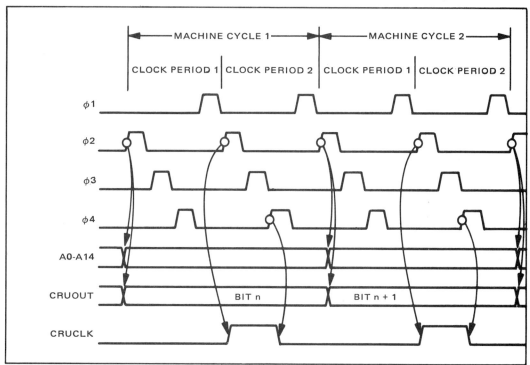

Figure 3-6. Two TMS 9900 Output-to-CRU Machine Cycles

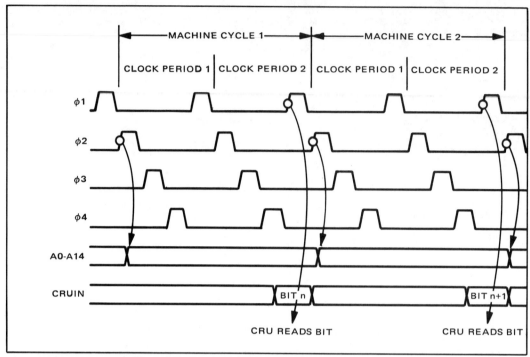

Figure 3-7. Two TMS 9900 Input-from-CRU Machine Cycles

An LDCR instruction outputs a sequence of 1 to 16 data bits to a CRU bit field. Here is the LDCR instruction machine cycle sequence:

Cycle	Type	Figure	Function
1	MEMORY READ	3-4	Fetch instruction object code
2	ALU	3-3	Decode instruction
a Cycles where $0 \leq a \leq 4$		}	Obtain source address
3+a	MEMORY READ	3-4	Fetch source memory word contents
4+a to 7+a	ALU	3-3	Prepare for data transmission
8+a	MEMORY READ	3-4	Fetch R12
9+a	ALU	3-3	Compute CRU starting address
i Cycles	CRU OUT	3-6 }	Output i bits to CRU
10+a+i	ALU	3-3	Machine cycle to conclude instruction

The SBO and SBZ instructions set or reset an addressed CRU bit; in essence, these instructions output one data bit. Here is the machine cycle sequence via which the bit output occurs:

Cycle	Type	Figure	Function
1	MEMORY READ	3-4	Fetch instruction object code
2	ALU	3-3	Decode instruction
3	ALU	3-3	Decode instruction
4	MEMORY READ	3-4	Fetch R12
5	ALU	3-3	Compute CRU address
6	CRU OUT	3-6	Output to addressed CRU bit

The TB instruction inputs one CRU bit; its timing is identical to the SBO and SBZ instructions, except that machine cycle 6 is a CRU IN machine cycle.

The Address Bus is used in an unusual way during a CRU machine cycle. As we have already stated, the CRU bit field is 4096 bits wide — addressed by 12 of the 15 Address Bus lines. **The three high-order Address Bus lines are used to identify I/O control instructions, as defined in Table 3-1.** We can conclude from Table 3-1 that when MEMEN is high and the three high-order Address Bus lines are all low, an I/O transfer is occurring. Otherwise, one of five externally defined I/O control instructions is being executed. There are dedicated functions for these five I/O controls in TM 990 minicomputer systems; these are shown in Table 3-1. But to anyone who is simply building a microcomputer system around a TMS 9900, these five I/O states are undefined. **Thus, Figure 3-8 illustrates TMS 9900 systems' bus utilization during both CRU operations and externally defined I/O operations. If CRU SEL and MEMEN are high, CRU Select logic will be active.**

Externally defined instructions output 0 on the 12 low-order Address Bus lines, A0 - A11; in addition, CRUCLK pulses are output as part of the instruction executions.

CRUCLK is an active CRU output strobe only. This signal pulses high whenever a valid level is present on the CRUOUT signal line. **There is no pulse for CRUIN.** External logic must generate its own strobe if it is needed, by combining MEMEN high with a valid bit pattern on the Address Bus.

CRU instructions that test the level of a bit are, to external logic, no different from CRU input instructions. External logic is required to return, via CRUIN the level of the selected bit. The fact that the CPU interprets this input as status, rather than data, is immaterial to external logic.

THE WAIT STATE

Additional Wait State clock periods may be inserted between clock periods 1 and 2 of any memory access machine cycle. Timing is illustrated in Figure 3-9. At the rising edge of $\Phi1$ of clock period 1, the CPU samples the READY input signal. If this signal is low, then the next clock period is a Wait clock period. During a Wait cycle, the WAIT output signal is high; all other output signals hold the levels they had during clock period 1.

A Wait State can last for any number of clock periods. During the $\Phi1$ high pulse of every Wait clock period, the CPU samples the level of the READY input. As soon as READY is sampled high, the Wait State ends. The next clock period becomes clock period 2 of the machine cycle, and the memory operation is completed.

Table 3-1. High-Order Address Bus Line Used by TMS 9900 I/O Instructions

Instruction Mnemonic	Instruction Type	(MSB) A14	A13	A12	Function
LDCR	Output	0	0	0	Output data to CRU
SBO	Output	0	0	0	Set CRU bit to 1
SBZ	Output	0	0	0	Reset CRU bit to 0
STCR	Input	0	0	0	Input data from CRU
TB	Test (Input)	0	0	0	Input CRU bit to Equal status bit
IDLE	Control	0	1	0	Enter HALT condition
RSET	Control	0	1	1	Reset the Interrupt mask
CKOF	Control	1	0	1	Real time clock on ⎫ These are
CKON	Control	1	1	0	Real time clock off ⎬ TM 990 uses.
LREX	Control	1	1	1	Execute bootstrap ⎭ Instructions are undefined in a TMS 9900 system.

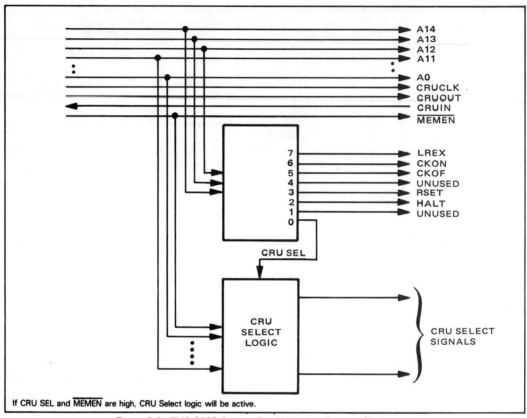

Figure 3-8. TMS 9900 System Bus Utilization During I/O Operations

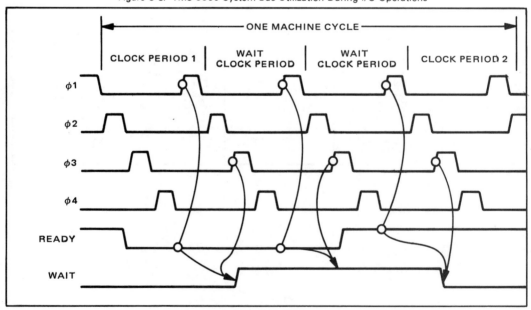

Figure 3-9. The TMS 9900 Wait State

THE HOLD STATE

The TMS 9900 has a typical microcomputer Hold State, used to enable direct memory access operations. External logic initiates a Hold State by inputting $\overline{\text{HOLD}}$ low. At the beginning of the next non-memory reference machine cycle, the CPU floats its Address and Data Busses, together with the DBIN, $\overline{\text{MEMEN}}$ and $\overline{\text{WE}}$ control signals. HOLDA is output high as a Hold Acknowledge. **Timing is illustrated in Figure 3-10.**

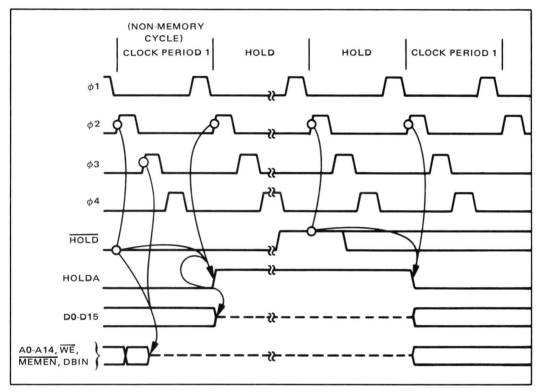

Figure 3-10. TMS 9900 Hold State Timing

The Hold State lasts until external logic raises $\overline{\text{HOLD}}$ high again.

It is up to external logic to perform all operations associated with a DMA transfer. The CPU simply floats the System Bus in response to a Hold request.

The only nonobvious aspect of Figure 3-10 is the fact that Data Bus timing, during normal instruction execution, **differs from other System Bus signal timing.** Figure 3-10 highlights this fact by showing the Data Bus floating at the beginning of the first HOLD clock period, while other signals float earlier in the preceding clock period. This is not a particularly significant event. The entire System Bus is floating once the HOLD clock period has begun. However, the actual tristate condition for any signal begins at that point in the preceding clock period when the signal is no longer being driven by current operations.

THE HALT STATE

The TMS 9900 IDLE I/O instruction generates a Halt State. When this instruction is executed, the CPU suspends all program execution and internal operations. You must terminate the Idle condition with an interrupt request or a low $\overline{\text{LOAD}}$ or $\overline{\text{RESET}}$ input. ($\overline{\text{LOAD}}$ and $\overline{\text{RESET}}$ are treated as interrupts as we will describe soon.)

The TMS 9900 CPU does not relinquish the System Bus while halted. That is to say, after an IDLE instruction has been executed, no System Bus lines are floated.

The IDLE instruction is usually executed when program logic requires that the CPU wait for an interrupt, or when external logic is computing a real-time interval — which will be terminated with an interrupt request.

You can, if you wish, initiate a DMA transfer by executing an IDLE instruction. In order to do this, you must create a HOLD request from the Address Bus output characteristic of the IDLE instruction's execution. This may be illustrated as follows:

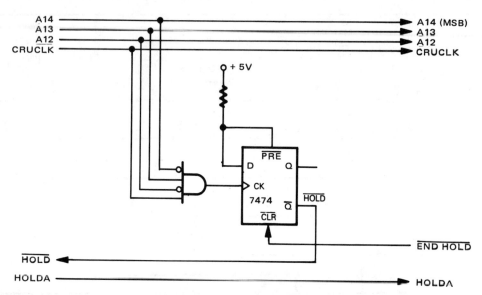

As illustrated above, the combination of 010 on the three high-order Address Bus lines, along with the CRUCLK pulse, identifies the IDLE instruction. Since the process of floating the System Bus will remove the conditions which generated a Hold request, these conditions are used to clock a flip-flop. Thus, external logic which receives the Hold acknowledge signal and takes control of the System Bus must subsequently reset the Hold request flip-flop in order to remove the Hold condition. That is to say, **program logic can begin a Hold state within a Halt state, but it cannot end this combination. Two steps are needed to terminate a Hold within a Halt. The Hold request must be removed, then an interrupt request must follow to terminate the Halt.**

TMS 9900 INTERRUPT PROCESSING LOGIC

The TMS 9900 has complex and capable interrupt processing logic. Sixteen levels of external interrupt are available. Sixteen software interrupts are also available. Fifteen of the sixteen external interrupts are maskable; the nonmaskable interrupt has highest priority and is the system Reset interrupt. There is, in addition, a non-maskable Load interrupt. External interrupts may be summarized as follows:

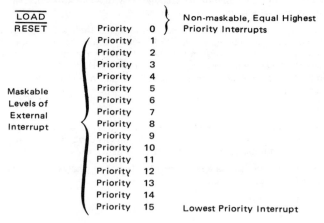

External logic identifies the priority of its interrupt request via the IC0. IC1. IC2. and IC3 inputs. as follows:

IC0	IC1	IC2	IC3	Priority
0	0	0	0	Should not be input by external logic - highest external
0	0	0	1	1
0	0	1	0	2
0	0	1	1	3
0	1	0	0	4
0	1	0	1	5
0	1	1	0	6
0	1	1	1	7
1	0	0	0	8
1	0	0	1	9
1	0	1	0	10
1	0	1	1	11
1	1	0	0	12
1	1	0	1	13
1	1	1	0	14
1	1	1	1	15 lowest external

Software interrupts are executed via the XOP instruction. There are, in addition, instructions that parallel the RESET and LOAD interrupts. We will describe these instructions in due course.

Each one of the external interrupts has two dedicated memory words via which vectoring is enabled following an interrupt acknowledge. Figure 3-11 illustrates the memory map associated with interrupt vectoring. The memory addresses in Figure 3-11 are byte addresses as seen by the programmer. Remember. the low-order bit of the address shown in Figure 3-11 is not output on the Address Bus; therefore. you must divide the memory addresses shown in Figure 3-11 by 2 in order to generate the address which will be seen by external memory.

| TMS 9900 |
| INTERRUPT |
| VECTOR MAP |

The memory words dedicated to interrupt vectoring. as illustrated in Figure 3-11 . can be read-only memory. read/write memory, or any combination of the two. Obviously, read-only memory will be used in applications that have dedicated interrupt service routines for specific interrupt requests. Read/write memory might be used in minicomputer-type applications where the interrupt response will depend on the application being serviced.

Interrupt masking and priorities apply only to external interrupt requests. Interrupt masking priorities cannot be applied to software interrupts (the XOP instruction). Since program logic must generate the software interrupt. program logic can equally be relied on to know which software interrupt is to be executed. and whether the software interrupt is allowed by current program logic. That is to say. from the programmer's viewpoint. a software interrupt is simply the consequence of an XOP instruction's execution; you, as a programmer. can include an XOP instruction anywhere in a program, within or outside an interrupt service routine. XOP instructions might be used in response to error conditions, or to call any frequently used subroutines.

Let us begin by looking at the way in which external interrupts are processed.

Any external device wishing to request an interrupt must pull the INTREQ input low while simultaneously placing a 4-bit code at the IC0 - IC3 inputs. The CPU will acknowledge the interrupt, provided that its priority, as identified by the IC0 - IC3 inputs, is enabled. The interrupt will be acknowledged at the conclusion of the currently executing instruction. The BLWP and XOP instructions are exceptions; for the integrity of program logic. they demand that the next sequential instruction be executed. Therefore. if an interrupt request occurs while either of these two instructions is being executed. the interrupt will not be acknowledged until this instruction and the next instruction have been executed.

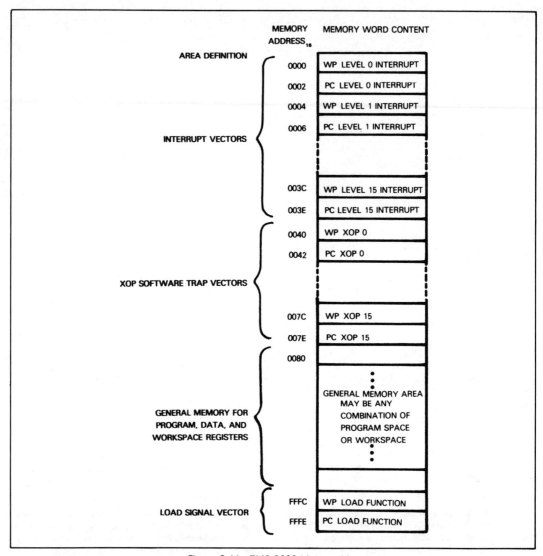

MEMORY
ADDRESS₁₆   MEMORY WORD CONTENT

AREA DEFINITION

0000	WP LEVEL 0 INTERRUPT
0002	PC LEVEL 0 INTERRUPT
0004	WP LEVEL 1 INTERRUPT
0006	PC LEVEL 1 INTERRUPT

INTERRUPT VECTORS

003C	WP LEVEL 15 INTERRUPT
003E	PC LEVEL 15 INTERRUPT
0040	WP XOP 0
0042	PC XOP 0

XOP SOFTWARE TRAP VECTORS

007C	WP XOP 15
007E	PC XOP 15
0080	

GENERAL MEMORY FOR PROGRAM, DATA, AND WORKSPACE REGISTERS

GENERAL MEMORY AREA MAY BE ANY COMBINATION OF PROGRAM SPACE OR WORKSPACE

LOAD SIGNAL VECTOR

FFFC	WP LOAD FUNCTION
FFFE	PC LOAD FUNCTION

Figure 3-11. TMS 9900 Memory Map

When an interrupt is acknowledged, the following machine cycles are executed:

Cycle	Type	Figure	Function
1	ALU	3-3	
2	MEMORY READ	3-4	Move new WP register contents from vector word to temporary storage
3	ALU	3-3	
4	MEMORY WRITE	3-5	Store status in new R15
5	ALU	3-3	Store IC0 - IC3 levels in four low-order Status bits
6	MEMORY WRITE	3-5	Store incremented PC in new R14
7	ALU	3-3	
8	MEMORY WRITE	3-5	Store old WP register contents in new R13
9	ALU	3-3	
10	MEMORY READ	3-4	Fetch new PC contents from vector word
11	ALU	3-3	Fetch new WP contents from temporary storage

Vector words are illustrated in Figure 3-11.

At the conclusion of the interrupt acknowledge sequence listed above, the priority of the acknowledged interrupt request, less one, is recorded in the four low-order Status register bits. Thus, subsequent interrupt requests will be acknowledged only if their priority is higher than that of the interrupt being serviced. That is to say, whenever an interrupt request occurs, CPU logic compares the levels input at IC0 - IC3 with the levels present in the four low-order Status register bits. If IC0 - IC3 is not greater than the mask, then the interrupt request will be acknowledged. If IC0 - IC3 is higher, then the interrupt request will not be acknowledged. Thus, **in the normal course of events, TMS 9900 interrupt priority logio disables all interrupts of equal or lower priority than an acknowledged interrupt,** while leaving higher priority interrupts enabled. **Priorities are maintained for the duration of the interrupt service routine.** This is illustrated in the following figure, which you should read in the sequence Ⓐ - Ⓑ - Ⓒ - Ⓓ - Ⓔ - Ⓕ - Ⓖ :

TMS 9900
NESTED
INTERRUPT
PRIORITIES

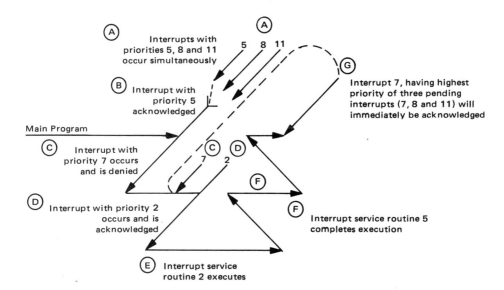

The interrupt priority arbitration logic of the TMS 9900 is exceptional among microcomputers. Most microcomputers arbitrate priorities at the instant interrupts are being acknowledged, and once an interrupt has been acknowledged, all interrupts are disabled. That is to say, interrupt priorities apply only during the acknowledge process. In contrast, the TMS 9900 maintains interrupt priorities for the duration of the interrupt service routine, as illustrated above.

The net effect of the interrupt response steps illustrated above is to perform a context switch while disabling all interrupts that have the same priority as the acknowledged interrupt, or that have a lower priority.

There are some very important and nonobvious advantages to initiating an interrupt service routine with a context switch.

Since the 16 new memory locations that will be used as general purpose registers may lie anywhere in read/write memory, you can store parameters that will be used by the interrupt service routine, in advance of the interrupt, in those memory locations that are ultimately to serve as general purpose registers for the duration of the interrupt service routine.

You can, if you wish, modify the interrupt priority scheme that will control nested interrupts. As we have already stated, if you do nothing about interrupt priorities, then any interrupt service routine may be interrupted by a higher priority external interrupt, but not by an external interrupt that has the same priority or a lower priority.

If you wish to eliminate nested interrupts entirely, then the first instruction executed within an interrupt service routine must be an LIMI 0 instruction (Load Interrupt Mask Immediate), which clears the four low-order Status register bits, thus disabling all maskable interrupts. A $\overline{\text{RESET}}$ or $\overline{\text{LOAD}}$ interrupt — or a level 0 external interrupt request — will still be acknowledged; these should be alarm conditions and not part of the normal interrupt logic of any microcomputer. You can execute variations of the LIMI instruction to increase or decrease the levels of priority that will be masked for the duration of any interrupt service routine (or for that matter, any subsequent instruction within the interrupt service routine) can load appropriate data into the four low-order bits of the Status register, thus changing the priority level at which all subsequent interrupt requests will be disabled.

All interrupt service routines should end with an RTWP (Return Workspace Pointer) instruction. The RTWP instruction performs a reverse context switch, which puts the central processing unit back to the logical environment which was interrupted. Observe that since the Status register is also saved during a forward context switch, the return instruction will restore whatever level of interrupt priorities existed at the instant the interrupt was acknowledged. You can, of course, modify the contents of General Purpose Registers R13, R14, and R15 in the course of an interrupt service routine's execution. This allows program logic to alter the conditions that will be restored when the return instruction executes a reverse context switch.

The TMS 9901 PSI, which we describe later in this chapter, provides multiple interrupt handling for TMS 9900 series CPUs. If your system does not include a TMS 9901, then external hardware required to support multiple interrupts in a TMS 9900 microcomputer system will not be as straightforward as the software response.

First of all, we must cope with the fact that if more than one interrupt request occurs simultaneously, then there will be competition on the $\overline{\text{INTREQ}}$ input, but there will also be competition at the four priority inputs, IC0 - IC3. Resolving competition on the $\overline{\text{INTREQ}}$ input is no problem; you can wire-OR interrupt requests from many devices to create the CPU input. But your external logic must make sure that only the highest priority combination of IC0 - IC3 appears at the TMS 9900 inputs. One method of doing this is to use latched decoders that create a 4-bit output corresponding to the highest level input, provided that the decoder is enabled by a latching signal. This may be illustrated functionally as follows:

**TMS 9900
MULTIPLE
INTERRUPT
HARDWARE
CONSIDERATIONS**

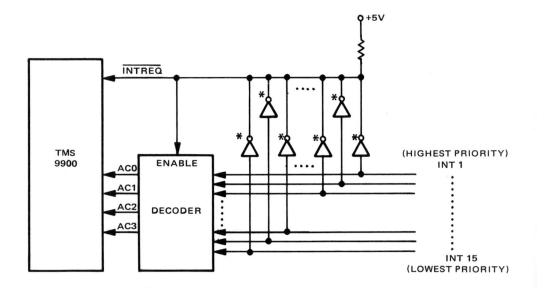

In the illustration above, 15 external interrupt requests are input to a decoder. These interrupt requests are high true. The 15 interrupt requests are buffered, inverted, and wire-ORed to create the master interrupt request $\overline{\text{INTREQ}}$, which is input to the CPU. This master interrupt request also enables the decoder. That is to say, when the enable input to the decoder is high, the four outputs, IC0 - IC3 will be low. When the enable input to the decoder is low, IC0 - IC3 will output a 4-bit value as follows:

IC0	IC1	IC2	IC3	INT 1	INT 2	INT 3	INT 4	INT 5	INT 6	INT 7	INT 8	INT 9	INT 10	INT 11	INT 12	INT 13	INT 14	INT 15
0	0	0	0	0	0	0	0	0	0	0	0	0	0	0	0	0	0	0
0	0	0	1	1	*	*	*	*	*	*	*	*	*	*	*	*	*	
0	0	1	0	0	1	*	*	*	*	*	*	*	*	*	*	*	*	
0	0	1	1	0	0	1	*	*	*	*	*	*	*	*	*	*	*	
0	1	0	0	0	0	0	1	*	*	*	*	*	*	*	*	*	*	
0	1	0	1	0	0	0	0	1	*	*	*	*	*	*	*	*	*	
0	1	1	0	0	0	0	0	0	1	*	*	*	*	*	*	*	*	
0	1	1	1	0	0	0	0	0	0	1	*	*	*	*	*	*	*	
1	0	0	0	0	0	0	0	0	0	0	1	*	*	*	*	*	*	
1	0	0	1	0	0	0	0	0	0	0	0	1	*	*	*	*	*	
1	0	1	0	0	0	0	0	0	0	0	0	0	1	*	*	*	*	
1	0	1	1	0	0	0	0	0	0	0	0	0	0	1	*	*	*	
1	1	0	0	0	0	0	0	0	0	0	0	0	0	0	1	*	*	
1	1	0	1	0	0	0	0	0	0	0	0	0	0	0	0	1	*	
1	1	1	0	0	0	0	0	0	0	0	0	0	0	0	0	0	1	*
1	1	1	1	0	0	0	0	0	0	0	0	0	0	0	0	0	0	1

* REPRESENTS A "DON'T CARE" BIT

If you do not use the TMS 9901, Texas Instruments suggests the following circuit to accomplish priority encoding:

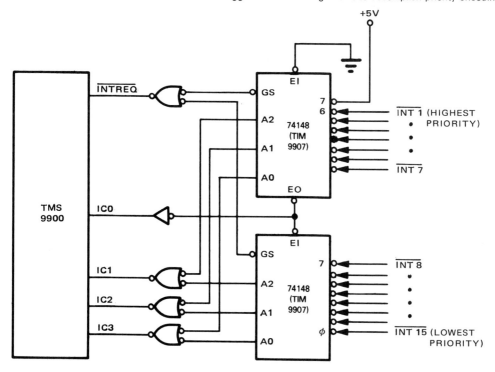

3-31

External logic must maintain its interrupt request until it receives its own specific interrupt acknowledge. This need is obvious. since an interrupt request may be denied for a long time while higher priority interrupts are being serviced.

The problem is that the TMS 9900 has no interrupt acknowledge signals.

Interrupt acknowledge signals can be generated in one of two ways:

1) By using CRU bit instructions to set and reset external flip-flops that create interrupt acknowledge signals.

2) By decoding appropriate addresses on the Address Bus.

Figure 3-12 illustrates two possible configurations that will allow CRU bit set and reset instructions to generate interrupt acknowledge signals. The logic in Figure 3-12A generates a short interrupt acknowledge pulse. CRUOUT becomes the input to a flip-flop which is decoded to generate CRU select signals. The CRU bit select and $\overline{MEMEN}$ are gated to the flip-flop's Clear input. Therefore. when CRU bit "n" is selected. $\overline{CLR}$ is removed and CRUOUT can be clocked through. A set bit (SBO) instruction switches the flip-flop on. As soon as the flip-flop address is removed at the end of the CRU I/O machine cycle. the flip-flop is cleared. thus terminating the interrupt acknowledge pulse.

The logic illustrated in Figure 3-12A requires that you execute an SBO instruction at the beginning of every interrupt service routine in order to generate an interrupt acknowledge. You could require every interrupt service routine to control the length of the interrupt acknowledge pulse by executing an SBZ instruction to terminate the pulse. Figure 3-12B shows logic to implement this scheme. When the flip-flop is selected by the appropriate CRU address, CRUCLK will clock CRUOUT to INT ACK n. At other times. CRUCLK will merely clock the flip-flop's output through. thus making no change. In this way. only SBO and SBZ instructions which address INT ACK n can set or reset the flip-flop.

Figure 3-13 illustrates generation of an interrupt acknowledge signal by identifying specific addresses on the Address Bus. Following any interrupt acknowledge. specific memory locations will be accessed. as identified in Figure 3-11 . in order to fetch the new values for the Program Counter and WP register. Figure 3-13 shows a very simple scheme whereby Address Bus lines are combined with $\overline{MEMEN}$ low to generate high pulses for the duration of a valid address. That is to say. the interrupt acknowledge signal will last for one machine cycle — the time that the valid address exists on the Address Bus.

External logic which requested an interrupt removes its interrupt request and priority signals upon receiving an interrupt acknowledge.

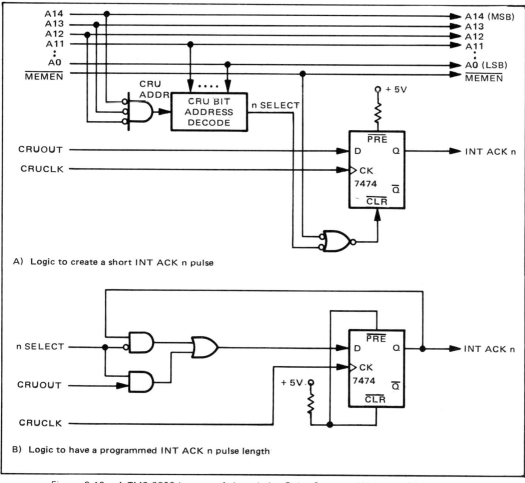

A) Logic to create a short INT ACK n pulse

B) Logic to have a programmed INT ACK n pulse length

Figure 3-12. A TMS 9900 Interrupt Acknowledge Pulse Generated Using an SBO Instruction

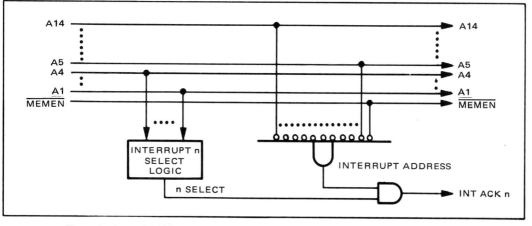

Figure 3-13. TMS 9900 Interrupt Acknowledge Generated by Decoding Valid Addresses

THE TMS 9900 RESET

You reset the 9900 microcomputer system by inputting a low $\overline{\text{RESET}}$ signal. This signal must remain low for at least 3 clock periods. When the low $\overline{\text{RESET}}$ signal is removed, the following machine cycle sequence is executed:

Cycle	Type	Figure	Function
1	ALU	3-3	Prepare for Level 0 interrupt
2	ALU	3-3	
3	ALU	3-3	
4	MEMORY READ	3-4	Fetch new WP register contents from memory word 0000_{16} to temporary storage
5	ALU	3-3	
6	MEMORY WRITE	3-5	Store Status register contents in new R15
7	ALU	3-3	
8	MEMORY WRITE	3-5	Store Program Counter contents in new R14
9	ALU	3-3	
10	MEMORY WRITE	3-5	Store old WP register contents in new R13
11	ALU	3-3	
12	MEMORY READ	3-4	Fetch new Program Counter contents from memory word 0001_{16}
13	ALU	3-3	Load WP register from temporary storage

Thus. program execution begins with a program whose starting address is stored in memory word 1. The starting address for the 16 general purpose registers is stored in memory word 0.

The TMS 9900 has a Reset instruction (RSET). In reality. this instruction resets only the interrupt mask in the Status register; it also outputs a code on the Address Bus. as identified in Table 3-1 and illustrated in Figure 3-8. TM 990 minicomputer systems use this signal to generate a program-initiated Reset. If you are designing your own TMS 9900-based microcomputer system. you are free to use the RSET instruction in any way.

THE TMS 9900 LOAD OPERATION

The $\overline{\text{LOAD}}$ input to the TMS 9900 is a non-maskable, highest priority interrupt. Load must be input low for at least one instruction's duration. Since the length of an instruction can vary, you must use the IAQ signal to control the $\overline{\text{LOAD}}$ input pulse width. Texas Instruments' literature recommends the following circuit:

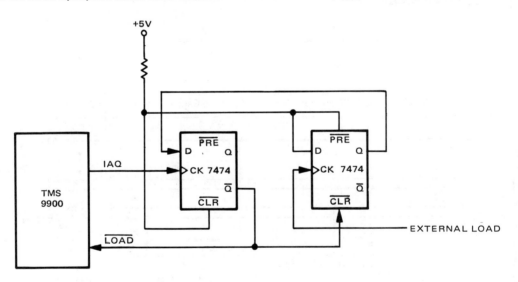

The CPU checks $\overline{\text{LOAD}}$ at the end of each instruction's execution.

After a valid $\overline{\text{LOAD}}$ input has been acknowledged, the following machine cycle sequence is executed:

Cycle	Type	Figure	Function
1	ALU	3-3	
2	MEMORY READ	3-4	Input new WP register contents from memory word $7FFE_{16}$ to temporary storage
3	ALU	3-3	
4	MEMORY WRITE	3-5	Store in new R15
5	ALU	3-3	
6	MEMORY WRITE	3-5	Store incremented Program Counter contents in new R14
7	ALU	3-3	
8	MEMORY WRITE	3-5	Store old WP register contents in new R13
9	ALU	3-3	
10	MEMORY READ	3-4	Input new Program Counter contents from word $7FFF_{16}$
11	ALU	3-3	Load WP register from temporary storage

There are two differences between Reset and Load. First, the $\overline{\text{RESET}}$ input provides a true hardware reset, synchronizing internal operations, as well as a level 0 interrupt; $\overline{\text{LOAD}}$ provides only a non-maskable interrupt. Second, the Reset vector in bytes 0 through 3, while the Load vector is in bytes $FFFC_{16}$ through $FFFF_{16}$.

In TM 990 minicomputer systems, the LREX instruction is frequently used as a software load. Output due to LREX is identified in Table 3-1 and Figure 3-8. In a TMS 9900 microcomputer system, you can use the LREX signal in any way.

THE TMS 9900 INSTRUCTION SET

The TMS 9900 instruction set is extremely powerful when compared to any 16-bit microprocessor described in this book. When you consider that the TMS 9900 was first manufactured in 1976, the power of this instruction set becomes more impressive.

With regard to instructions described in Table 3-2, some explanations are required.

The ABS instruction converts the contents of a memory location to their absolute value. That is to say, this instruction assumes that the memory location contains a signed binary number. If the number is positive, nothing happens. If the number is negative, the twos complement of the number is taken.

A number of instructions act on specific bits within source and destination memory words. These include **the SOC, SOCB, SZC, SZCB, COC, and CZC instructions.** In the OPERATION PERFORMED column of Table 3-2, the word "corresponding" means that the source word bits are affected only if selected by the destination word bit pattern. For example, the SOC instruction will be interpreted as follows:

```
Source:       1 0 1 1 1 0 1 0 0 1 1 0 1 1 0 1
Destination:  1 0 1 1 0 0 1 0 1 0 1 0 0 0 1 0
After SOC:    1 0 1 1 1 0 1 0 1 1 1 0 1 1 1 1     Here are the new destina-
                                                  tion contents.
```

This is equivalent to an OR operation.

The SOCB instruction is identical to the SOC instruction, except that only one byte is affected. This may be any memory byte or the high-order byte of a general purpose register.

The SZC instruction may be illustrated as follows:

```
Source:       1 0 1 0 0 1 1 0 1 0 1 1 1 0 0 1
Destination:  0 1 0 1 1 0 1 1 0 1 0 1 1 0 1 1
After SZC:    0 1 0 1 1 0 0 1 0 0 0 0 1 0 0 1
```

This is equivalent to complementing the source operand and then ANDing the two operands. The SZCB instruction is identical to the SZC instruction, except that only one byte is affected.

The COC instruction compares Source Register 1 bits with general purpose register bits that happen to be in the same bit positions. If all corresponding general purpose register bits are also 1, then the Equal status is set. Matches are not significant in bit positions if the source register bit is 0.

The CZC instruction operates in the same fashion as the COC instruction, except that those source memory word bits that are 0 become significant. That is to say, if every source memory word 0 bit has a corresponding Workspace register 0 bit, then the Equal status is set. Matches are not significant in bit positions if the source register bit is 1.

The BLWP instruction is a subroutine call accompanied by a context switch. The operand memory address identifies the first of two memory words within which the new WP register and Program Counter contents will be stored.

The BLWP instruction is remarkably powerful. The subroutine call and passing parameters to the subroutine become a single operation. The memory words that are to serve as subroutine general purpose registers can be used as general data memory locations prior to the subroutine call. Thus, the subroutine finds its registers pre-loaded with data when it starts executing.

The RTWP instruction should be used to return from a subroutine that is called by the BLWP instruction.

One-bit position arithmetic shifts may be illustrated as follows:

Right Shift   Left Shift

1 0 1 1 0 1 0 1 1 0 1 0 0 1 1 0   1 0 1 1 0 1 0 1 1 0 1 0 0 1 1 0

1 1 0 1 1 0 1 0 1 1 0 1 0 0 1 1 Lost   Lost 0 1 1 0 1 0 1 1 0 1 0 0 1 1 0 0
                                                                                    Inserted

A one-bit-position logical right shift may be illustrated as follows:

1 0 1 1 0 1 0 1 1 0 1 0 0 1 1 0

0 1 0 1 1 0 1 0 1 1 0 1 0 0 1 1 Lost

Inserted

A one-bit right rotate (Shift Right Circular) may be illustrated as follows:

You can specify any number of bits, from 1 to 15, as the number of bit positions for any TMS 9900 shift or rotate instruction. If you specify 0 for the bit count, then the actual bit count is taken from the four low-order bits of general purpose Register R0. If these four low-order bits are 0000, then the bit count is assumed to be 16.

The following symbols are used in Table 3-2:

AG	Arithmetic Greater Than status
C	Carry status
CNT	4-bit count field
CRUA	CRU base address from R12
d	Destination memory word. There are five possible options for the destination memory word. They are represented by these combinations of addressing modes: Workspace Register D Implied through Workspace Register D Direct address Direct, indexed address Implied through Workspace Register D, auto-increment Workspace Register D
DATA4	4-bit data unit
DATA16	16-bit data unit
DISP	8-bit signed displacement
EQ	Equal status bit of Status register
G	Both the AG and LG statuses
LG	Logical Greater Than status
OP	Odd Parity status
OV	Overflow status
PC	Program Counter
R	Any of the 16 Workspace registers
Rxx	Workspace register. For example, R15 is Workspace Register 15
S	Source memory location. Addressing options identical to destination memory location
ST	Status register
WP	Workspace Pointer register
x<y,z>	Bits y through z of the quantity x. For example, ([S] * [R])<31,16> represents the high-order word of the product of the contents of the Source Register S and the Workspace Register R.
[ ]	Contents of location enclosed within brackets. If a register designation is enclosed within the brackets, then the designated register's contents are specified. If a memory address is enclosed within the brackets, then the contents of the addressed memory location are specified.
*	Multiplication
/	Division
Λ	Logical AND
V	Logical OR
∀	Logical Exclusive-OR
←	Data is transferred in the direction of the arrow

Under the heading of STATUSES in Table 3 -2, an X indicates statuses which are modified in the course of the instruction's execution. If there is no X, it means that the status maintains the value it had before the instruction was executed.

Byte-operand instructions will affect half of a 16-bit memory word. If the word is accessed as a general purpose register, then only the high-order byte will be affected. If the word is accessed as non-register memory, then the byte affected is determined by the least significant bit of the 16-bit address: 0 selects the high-order byte; 1 selects the low-order byte.

Table 3-2. TMS 9900 Instruction Set Summary

TYPE	MNEMONIC	OPERAND(S)	BYTES	G	EQ	C	OV	OP	OPERATION PERFORMED
I/O	LDCR	S,CNT	2	X	X			X*	[CRUA]←[S<CNT-1,0>] Transfer the specified number of bits from source memory word to the CRU.
	STCR	D,CNT	2	X	X			X*	[D<CNT-1,0>]←[CRUA] Transfer the specified number of bits from the CRU to destination memory word.
	SBO	DISP	2						[CRUA+DISP]←1 Set bit in CRU to 1.
	SBZ	DISP	2						[CRUA+DISP]←0 Set bit in CRU to 0.
	TB	DISP	2		X				If [CRUA+DISP]=0, then [EQ]=1; or else [EQ]=0 Test bit in CRU.
PRIMARY MEMORY REFERENCE	MOV	S,D	2	X	X				[D]←[S] 16-bit move contents of source memory word to destination memory word.
	MOVB	S,D	2	X	X			X	[D]←[S] 8-bit move contents of source memory byte to destination memory byte.
SECONDARY MEMORY REFERENCE (MEMORY OPERATE)	A	S,D	2	X	X	X	X		[D]←[S]+[D] 16-bit add contents of source memory word to contents of destination memory word.
	AB	S,D	2	X	X	X	X	X	[D]←[S]+[D] 8-bit add contents of source memory byte to contents of destination memory byte.
	S	S,D	2	X	X	X	X		[D]←[D]-[S] 16-bit subtract contents of source memory word from contents of destination memory word.
	SB	S,D	2	X	X	X	X	X	[D]←[D]-[S] 8-bit subtract contents of source memory byte from contents of destination memory byte.
	C	S,D	2	X	X				Set status flags based on 16-bit comparison of source and destination memory word contents.
	CB	S,D	2	X	X			X	Set status flags based on 8-bit comparison of source memory byte contents and destination memory byte contents.
	XOR	S,R	2	X	X				[R]←[S]∀[R] Exclusive-OR contents of source memory word with Workspace Register R.
	MPY	S,R	2						[R]←[((S)·(R))<31,16>] [R+1]←[((S)·(R))<15,0>] Multiply the contents of source memory word by contents of Workspace Register R. Store most significant word of result in R. Store least significant word of result in Workspace Register R+1.
	DIV	S,R	2				X		[R]←((R,R+1)/[S])quotient) [R+1]←((R,R+1)/[S])remainder) Divide the 32-bit quantity represented by R (high-order word) concatenated with R+1 (low order) by the contents of the source memory word. Store the quotient in R, the remainder in R+1 and set overflow if quotient will exceed 16 bits.
	INC	D	2	X	X	X	X		[D]←[D]+1 Increment contents of memory word by 1.
	INCT	D	2	X	X	X	X		[D]←[D]+2 Increment contents of memory word by 2.
	DEC	D	2	X	X	X	X		[D]←[D]-1 Decrement contents of memory word by 1.

The STATUSES columns are grouped as: G, EQ, C, OV, OP.

*OP status is affected only if between 1 and 8 bits are transferred.

Table 3-2. TMS 9900 Instruction Set Summary (Continued)

TYPE	MNEMONIC	OPERAND(S)	BYTES	G	EQ	C	OV	OP	OPERATION PERFORMED
SECONDARY MEMORY REFERENCE (MEMORY OPERATE) (CONTINUED)	DECT	D	2	x	x	x	x		$[D] \leftarrow [D] - 2.$ Decrement contents of memory word by 2.
	CLR	D	2						$[D] \leftarrow 0000_{16}.$ Clear the destination memory word.
	SETO	D	2						$[D] \leftarrow FFFF_{16}.$ Set all bits of memory word.
	INV	D	2	x	x				$[D] \leftarrow [\overline{D}].$ Ones complement the destination memory word.
	NEG	D	2	x	x	x	x		$[D] \leftarrow [\overline{D}] + 1.$ Twos complement the destination memory word.
	ABS	D	2	x	x	x	x		$[D] \leftarrow |[D]|.$ Take the absolute (unsigned) value of the destination memory word's contents.
	SWPB	D	2						$[D<15,8>] \longleftrightarrow [D<7,0>]$ Exchange the high and low bytes of the memory word.
	SOC	S,D	2	x	x				If $[S<i>]=1,$ then $[D<i>] \leftarrow 1$ for all 16 bits. Set the bits in the destination memory word that correspond to 1s in the source memory word for all 16 bits.
	SOCB	S,D	2	x	x			x	If $[S<i>]=1,$ then $[D<i>] \leftarrow 1$ for 8 bits. Set the bits in the destination memory word that correspond to 1s in the source memory word for 8 bits.
	SZC	S,D	2	x	x				If $[S<i>]=1,$ then $[D<i>] \leftarrow 0.$ Clear the bits in the destination memory word that correspond to 1s in the source memory word for all 16 bits.
	SZCB	S,D	2	x	x			x	If $[S<i>]=1,$ then $[D<i>] \leftarrow 0$ for 8 bits. Clear the bits in the destination memory word that correspond to 1s in the source memory word for 8 bits.
	COC	S,R			x				If for all $[S<i>]=1,$ $[R<i>]=1,$ then $[EQ]=1.$ If the bits in the Workspace Register R that correspond to the set bits in the source memory word are all 1s, set the EQUAL status.
	CZC	S,R	2		x				If for all $[S<i>]=1,$ $[R<i>]=0,$ then $[EQ]=1$ If the bits in the Workspace Register R that correspond to set bits in the source memory word are all 0s, set the EQUAL status.
IMMEDIATE	LI	R,DATA16	4	x	x				$[R] \leftarrow DATA16.$ Load immediate to Workspace Register R.
	LWPI	DATA16	4						$[WR] \leftarrow DATA16.$ Load immediate to Workspace Pointer Register, WR.

Table 3-2. TMS 9900 Instruction Set Summary (Continued)

TYPE	MNEMONIC	OPERAND(S)	BYTES	G	EQ	C	OV	OP	OPERATION PERFORMED
IMMEDIATE OPERATE	CI	R,DATA16	4	x	x				Set the status flags based on 16-bit comparison between contents of Workspace Register R and immediate data.
	AI	R,DATA16	4	x	x	x	x		[R]←[R]+DATA16. Add immediate to Workspace Register R contents.
	ANDI	R,DATA16	4	x	x				[R]←[R]∧DATA16. AND immediate with Workspace Register R contents.
	ORI	R,DATA16	4	x	x				[R]←[R]∨DATA16. OR immediate with Workspace Register R contents.
JUMP	B	S	2						[PC]←[S] Branch unconditional to address in Source memory word.
	JMP	DISP	2						[PC]←[PC]+DISP Branch unconditional.
SUBROUTINE CALL AND RETURN	BL	S	2						[R11]←[PC]+1 [PC]←[S] Branch to subroutine at address in source memory word.
	BLWP	S	2						[R13]←[WP] [R14]←[PC] [R15]←[ST] [WP]←[S] [PC]←[S+2] Branch to subroutine whose address is stored in source memory word + 1. Perform context switch to R0 address contained in source memory word.
	RTWP		2	x	x	x	x	x	[WP]←[R13] [PC]←[R14] [ST]←[R15] Perform a backward context switch.
BRANCH ON CONDITION	JEQ	DISP	2						If [EQ]=1; then [PC]←[PC]+DISP Branch if equal.
	JNE	DISP	2						If [EQ]=0; then [PC]←[PC]+DISP Branch if not equal.
	JGT	DISP	2						If [AG]=1; then [PC]←[PC]+DISP Branch on arithmetic greater than.
	JLT	DISP	2						If [AG]=0 and [EQ]=0; then [PC]←[PC]+DISP Branch on arithmetic less than.
	JHE	DISP	2						If [LG]=1 or [EQ]=1; then [PC]←[PC]+DISP Branch on logical greater than or equal.
	JH	DISP	2						If [LG]=1 and [EQ]=0; then [PC]←[PC]+DISP Branch on logical greater than.
	JL	DISP	2						If [LG]=0 and [EQ]=0; then [PC]←[PC]+DISP Branch on logical less than.
	JLE	DISP	2						If [EQ]=1 or [LG]=0; then [PC]←[PC]+DISP Branch on less than or equal.

Table 3-2. TMS 9900 Instruction Set Summary (Continued)

TYPE	MNEMONIC	OPERAND(S)	BYTES	STATUSES					OPERATION PERFORMED
				G	EQ	C	OV	OP	
BRANCH ON CONDITION (CONTINUED)	JNC	DISP	2						If [C]=0; then [PC]←[PC]+DISP Branch on carry reset.
	JNO	DISP	2						If [OV]=0; then [PC]←[PC]+DISP Branch on overflow reset.
	JOC	DISP	2						If [C]=1; then [PC]←[PC]+DISP Branch on carry set.
	JOP	DISP	2						If [OP]=1; then [PC]←[PC]+DISP Branch on odd parity set.
REGISTER OPERATE	SLA	R,CNT	2	X	X	X	X		Arithmetic shift the Workspace Register R left the specified number of bits.
	SRA	R,CNT	2	X	X	X			Arithmetic shift the Workspace Register R right the specified number of bits.
	SRL	R,CNT	2	X	X	X			Logical shift the Workspace Register R right the specified number of bits.
	SRC	R,CNT	2	X	X	X			Rotate the Workspace Register R right the specified number of bits.
STATUS AND INTERRUPT	STST	R	2						[R]←[ST] Store the Status register into Workspace Register R.
	STWP	R	2						[R]←[WP] Store the Workspace Pointer into Workspace Register R.
	LIMI	DATA4	4						[SR$\langle$3,0$\rangle$]←DATA4 Load immediate data into the interrupt mask bits of the Status register.
	XOP	S,R	2					X	[R13]←[WP] [R14]←[PC] [R15]←[ST] [R11]←[S] [WP]←[40_{16}+(4*[R])] [PC]←[41_{16}+(4*[R])] Perform a context switch. This is the software interrupt.
EXECUTE	X	S	2						Execute the instruction represented by the data in the source location. If that instruction has immediate operand words, those words must be located directly after the X instruction. The instruction [S] will affect the status flags but its fetch will not cause IAQ to go high.
EXTERNALLY DEFINED	IDLE		2						CPU enters Halt state.
	RSET								CPU clears interrupt mask and outputs 001 on three high-order Address Bus lines.
	CKOF								011 on three high-order Address Bus lines.
	CKON								110 out on three high-order Address Bus lines.
	LREX								101 out on three high-order Address Bus lines. 111 out on three high-order Address Bus lines.

THE BENCHMARK PROGRAM

For the TMS 9900, our benchmark program may be illustrated as follows:

```
        BLWP    MOVE            CONTEXT SWITCH TO APPROPRIATE REGISTERS
          -
          -
          -
LOOP    MOV     @IOBUF(R1),*R2+ LOAD NEXT INPUT WORD IN NEXT TABLE WORD
        DEC     R1              DECREMENT COUNT
        JNE     LOOP            RETURN FOR MORE
        RTWP                    RETURN FROM SUBROUTINE
```

Let us look at how our benchmark program can collapse to just five instructions.

We assume that there is some set of 16 General Purpose registers within which we store the word count and the address of the first free word in TABLE. We illustrated this idea when describing context switching earlier in the chapter.

Observe that Register R1 contains the word count, and is therefore used as an Index register, while Register R2 addresses the first free word in TABLE. Note that the contents of Register R2 are incremented automatically when the next byte is loaded into the table.

The BLWP instruction will branch to the program which performs the required data move, but simultaneously it loads the Workspace register with the appropriate initial address. We do not need to load any initial addresses or word counts into registers, since we have adopted the memory space where this data is stored to serve as our General Purpose registers.

After the move has been completed, we do not have to update any counters or pointers, because they were updated "in situ". All we have to do upon completing the move is store the contents of the current General Purpose Registers 13 and 14 to the Workspace register and Program Counter.

The following notation is used in Table 3-3:

aa   Two bits determining the addressing mode for the destination memory word

bb   Two bits determining the addressing mode for the source memory word

cccccccc   8-bit signed address displacement

dddd   Four bits used with aa to determine the destination memory word

eeee   4-bit count field

rrrr   Four bits choosing the Workspace register

ssss   Four bits used with bb to determine the source memory word

xx   16 bits of immediate data

If either aa or bb is 10_2, and the corresponding register specified is 0_2, then an additional 16-bit direct memory address word, used in computing the effective memory address of the operand, will follow the instruction.

If aa and bb are 10_2, and both corresponding register specifications are 0, then two additional 16-bit direct memory addressing words will follow the instruction: the first will be used in computing the source address; the second will be used in computing the destination address.

Table 3-3. TMS 9900 Instruction Set Object Codes

INSTRUCTION		OBJECT CODE	BYTES	CLOCK PERIODS*	INSTRUCTION		OBJECT CODE	BYTES	CLOCK PERIODS*
A	S,D	1010aaddddbbssss	2	14-30 (1)	JOP	DISP	00011100cccccccc	2	8/10(15)
AB	S,D	1011aaddddbbssss	2	14-30 (1)	LDCR	S,CNT	001100eeeebbssss	2	22-52 (11)
ABS	D	0000011101aadddd	2	12-20 (6)	LI	R,DATA16	000000100000rrrr	4	12 (19)
AI	R,DATA16	000000100010rrrr	4	14 (17)			XX		
		XX			LIMI	DATA4	0000001100000000	4	16 (21)
ANDI	R,DATA16	000000100100rrrr	4	14 (17)			XX		
		XX			LREX		0000001111100000	2	6 (14)
B	S	0000010001bbssss	2	8-16 (7)	LWPI	DATA16	0000001011100000	4	10 (20)
BL	S	0000011010bbssss	2	12-20 (9)			XX		
BLWP	S	0000010000bbssss	2	26-34 (10)	MOV	S,D	1100aaddddbbssss	2	14-30 (1)
C	S,D	1000aaddddbbssss	2	14-30 (1)	MOVB	S,D	1101aaddddbbssss	2	14-30 (1)
CB	S,D	1001aaddddbbssss	2	14-30 (1)	MPY	S,R	001110rrrrbbssss	2	52-60 (2)
CI	S,D	000000101000rrrr	4	14 (18)	NEG	D	0000010100aadddd	2	12-20 (5)
		XX			ORI	R,DATA16	000000100110rrrr		14 (17)
CKON		0000011111000000	2	6 (14)			XX		
CKOF		0000011110100000	2	6 (14)	RSET		0000001101100000	2	6 (14)
CLR	D	0000010011aadddd	2	10-18 (5)	RTWP		0000001110000000	2	14 (8)
COC	S,R	001000rrrrbbssss	2	10-18 (1)	S	S,D	0110aaddddbbssss	2	14-30 (1)
CZC	S,R	001001rrrrbbssss	2	14-22 (1)	SB	S,D	0111aaddddbbssss	2	14-30 (1)
DEC	D	0000011000aadddd	2	14-22 (5)	SBO	DISP	00011101cccccccc	2	12 (13)
DECT	D	0000011001aadddd	2	10-18 (5)	SBZ	DISP	00011110cccccccc	2	12 (13)
DIV	S,R	001111rrrrbbssss	2	10-18 (3)	SETO	D	0000011100aadddd	2	10-18 (5)
IDLE		0000011101000000	2	6 (14)	SLA	R,CNT	00001010eeeerrrr	2	14-52 (16)
INC	D	0000010110aadddd		16-124 (5)	SOC	S,D	1110aaddddbbssss	2	14-30 (1)
INCT	D	0000010111aadddd	2	10-18 (5)	SOCB	S,D	1111aaddddbbssss	2	14-30 (1)
INV	D	0000010101aadddd	2	10-18 (5)	SRA	R,CNT	00001000eeeerrrr	2	14-52 (16)
JEQ	DISP	00010011cccccccc	2	10-18 (15)	SRC	R,CNT	00001011eeeerrrr	2	14-52 (16)
JGT	DISP	00010101cccccccc	2	8/10 (15)	SRL	R,CNT	00001001eeeerrrr	2	14-52 (16)
JH	DISP	00011011cccccccc	2	8/10 (15)	STCR	D,CNT	001101eeeeaadddd	2	42-60 (12)
JHE	DISP	00010100cccccccc	2	8/10 (15)	STST	R	000000101110rrrr	2	8 (23)
JL	DISP	00011010cccccccc	2	8/10 (15)	STWP	R	000000101010rrrr	2	8 (22)
JLE	DISP	00010010cccccccc	2	8/10 (15)	SWPB	D	0000011011aadddd	2	10-18 (23)
JLT	DISP	00010001cccccccc	2	8/10 (15)	SZC	S,D	0100aaddddbbssss	2	14-30 (1)
JMP	DISP	00010000cccccccc	2	10 (15)	SZCB	S,D	0101aaddddbbssss	2	14-30 (1)
JNC	DISP	00010111cccccccc	2	8/10 (15)	TB	DISP	00011111cccccccc	2	12 (8)
JNE	DISP	00010110cccccccc	2	8/10 (15)	X	S	0000010010bbssss	2	8-16 (7)
JNO	DISP	00011001cccccccc	2	8/10 (15)	XOP	S,R	001011rrrrbbssss	2	44-52 (4)
JOC	DISP	00011000cccccccc	2	8/10 (15)	XOR	S,R	001010rrrrbbssss	2	14-22 (1)

* The number in brackets identifies the instruction's machine cycle sequence, as defined in the preceding text.

The minimum and maximum number of clock periods for the execution of each instruction are shown in the CLOCK PERIODS column of Table 3-3. Remember that a machine cycle consists of two clock periods. The bracketed number after the number of clock periods identifies the machine cycle sequence. Machine cycle sequences associated with each bracketed number are listed below. In the machine cycle list below, the following abbreviations are used:

R represents a memory read machine cycle as identified in Figure 3-4.

A represents an ALU machine cycle as illustrated in Figure 3-3.

W represents a memory write machine cycle as illustrated in Figure 3-5.

C represents a CRU machine cycle as illustrated in Figures 3-6 and 3-7.

A subscript associated with any machine cycle notation identifies that machine cycle repeated a number of times. Thus A_3 is equivalent to -A-A-A-.

M represents memory address computation machine cycles. Memory address computations were described earlier in this chapter. In summary, here are the various possibilities for M:

Register addressing: R

Implied memory addressing: R-A-R

Implied memory addressing with auto-increment (for byte operand):   R-A-W-R

Implied memory addressing with auto-increment (for word operand):   R-A-A-W-R

Direct addressing: A-A-R-A-R

Direct, indexed addressing: R-A-R-A-R

(1)	R-A-M-A-M-A-W
(2)	R-A-M-A-R-A_{18}-W-A-W
(3)	R-A-M-A-R-A-A-R-A_x-W-A-W ($51 \leqslant x \leqslant 35$)
(4)	R-A-M-A_3-R-A-W-A-W-A-W-A-W-A-R-A
(5)	R-A-M-A-W
(6)	R-A-M-A_3-W-A
(7)	R-A-M-A
(8)	R-A-A-R-R-R-A
(9)	R-A-M-A-A-W
(10)	R-A-M-A-A-W-A-W-A-W-A-R-A
(11)	R-A-M-A_4-R-A-C_x-A ($16 \leqslant x \leqslant 1$)
(12)	R-A-M-A-R-A-A-C_x-A_y-W ($16 \leqslant x \leqslant 1$, $11 \leqslant y \leqslant 5$)
(13)	R-A-A-R-A-C
(14)	R-A-A-C-A-A
(15)	R-A_x ($x=3$ or 4)
(16)	R-A-R-A-A-R-A_x-W-A ($18 \leqslant x \leqslant 3$)
(17)	R-A-A-R-R-A-W
(18)	R-A-R-A-R-A-A
(19)	R-A-A-R-A-W
(20)	R-A-A-R-A
(21)	R-A-A-R-A_3
(22)	R-A-A-W
(23)	R-A-M-A-R-A_4-W

THE TMS 9980A AND THE TMS 9981 MICROPROCESSORS

The TMS 9980A and the TMS 9981 are low-cost variations of the TMS 9900. The principal differences between the TMS 9900 series and TMS 9980 series microprocessors are summarized in Table 3-4. Differences between the TMS 9980A and the TMS 9981 are summarized in Table 3-5.

This discussion of the TMS 9980 series microprocessors covers only differences as compared to the TMS 9900.

The TMS 9980 series microprocessors are manufactured using N-channel silicon gate MOS technology. They are packaged as 40-pin DIPs. The TMS 9980A uses three power supplies: -5V, +5V, and +12V. The TMS 9981 uses two power supplies: +5V and +12V.

Typically, a clock cycle time of 400 nanoseconds will be used with TMS 9980 series microprocessors. This generates instruction execution times ranging between 4 and 14 microseconds.

Figure 3-14 illustrates that part of general microcomputer system logic which is implemented by the TMS 9980 series microprocessors. This figure is identical to Figure 3-1, with the exception of clock logic, which is now shown present.

Programmable registers are implemented and used in exactly the same way the TMS 9900 and TMS 9980 series microprocessors. Note, however, that the **TMS 9980 series microprocessors address a 2048-bit CRU;** therefore, bits 1 through 11 of Register R12 identify the origin of any CRU bit field. The TMS 9900 uses bits 1 through 12 of Register R12 to identify the CRU origin within a 4096-bit CRU.

Table 3-4. A Summary of Differences Between the TMS 9900 and TMS 9980 Series Microprocessors

FUNCTION	TMS 9900	TMS 9980A/TMS 9981
Addressable external memory	32.768 x 16-bit words	16.384 x 8-bit words
DIP pins	64	40
Data Bus	16 bits	8 bits
Address Bus	15 bits	13 bits
External interrupt priorities	15	4
CRU field width	4096 bits	2048 bits
Clock logic	Four external inputs	One external input or internal (TMS 9981 only)

Table 3-5. A Summary of Differences Between the TMS 9980A and TMS 9981 Microprocessors

FUNCTION	TMS 9980A	TMS 9981
Power supplies	-5V. +5V. +12V	+5V. +12V
Clock logic	One external input	One external input or crystal only
Pin incompatibility ties	D0 - D7. INT0 - INT2. $\overline{\Phi3}$	

The TMS 9980 series microprocessors have a 14-line Address Bus, used to address up to 16,384 bytes of memory. In contrast, the TMS 9900 addresses up to 32,768 16-bit words of external memory. Thus, TMS 9980 programs address memory as bytes, while externally generated addresses also select bytes. The TMS 9900, by way of contrast, addresses memory as bytes within the CPU, but as 16-bit words externally.

The TMS 9980 series microprocessors use exactly the same memory and CRU addressing techniques as the TMS 9900. General-purpose registers are used in the same way, and instruction object codes are identical.

The Status register and Status flags used by the TMS 9980 series microprocessors are identical to those which we have already described for the TMS 9900.

TMS 9980 SERIES MICROPROCESSOR PINS AND SIGNALS

Figure 3-15 illustrates pins and signals for the TMS 9980A. Figure 3-16 provides the same information for the TMS 9981. In both of these illustrations, signal names conform to Texas Instruments nomenclature. For the Data and Address Busses, our notation is given in brackets. Differences result from the fact that we number bits from right to left (0 being the low-order bit), while Texas Instruments numbers bits from left to right (0 becomes the high-order bit). **TMS 9980A/TMS 9981 pin-out differences are shaded in Figures 3-15 and 3-16 so that you can identify them quickly.**

For descriptions of the individual signals, refer to the earlier TMS 9900 discussion.

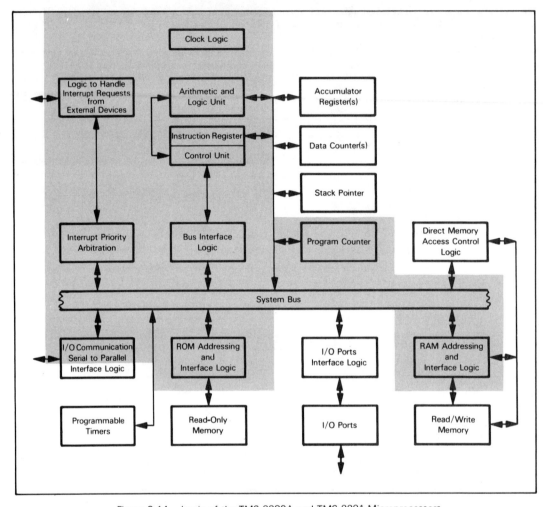

Figure 3-14. Logic of the TMS 9980A and TMS 9981 Microprocessors

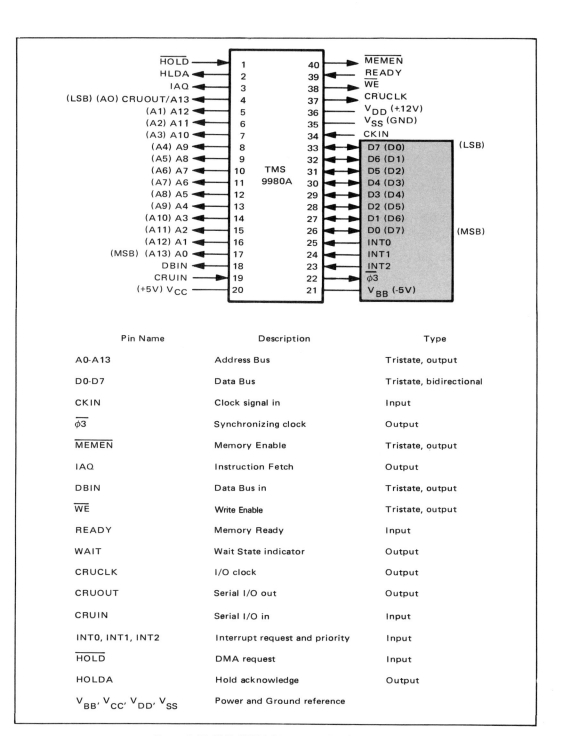

Pin Name	Description	Type
A0-A13	Address Bus	Tristate, output
D0-D7	Data Bus	Tristate, bidirectional
CKIN	Clock signal in	Input
$\overline{\phi 3}$	Synchronizing clock	Output
$\overline{\text{MEMEN}}$	Memory Enable	Tristate, output
IAQ	Instruction Fetch	Output
DBIN	Data Bus in	Tristate, output
$\overline{\text{WE}}$	Write Enable	Tristate, output
READY	Memory Ready	Input
WAIT	Wait State indicator	Output
CRUCLK	I/O clock	Output
CRUOUT	Serial I/O out	Output
CRUIN	Serial I/O in	Input
INT0, INT1, INT2	Interrupt request and priority	Input
$\overline{\text{HOLD}}$	DMA request	Input
HOLDA	Hold acknowledge	Output
$V_{BB}, V_{CC}, V_{DD}, V_{SS}$	Power and Ground reference	

Figure 3-15. TMS 9980A Signals and Pin Assignments

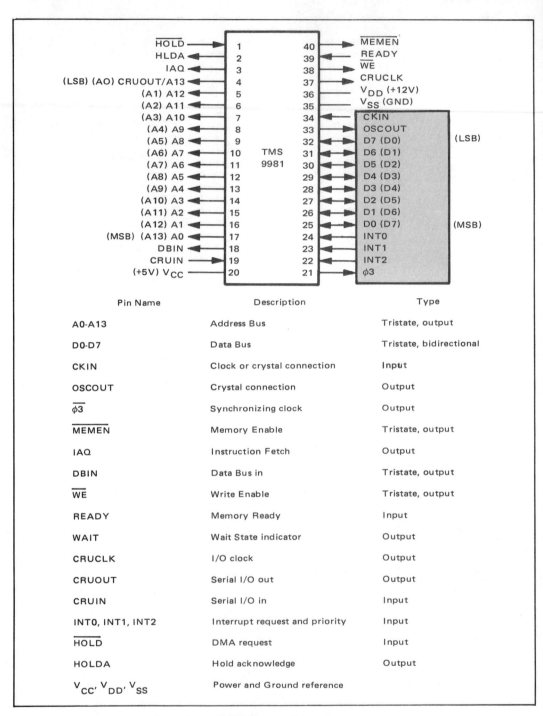

Pin Name	Description	Type
A0-A13	Address Bus	Tristate, output
D0-D7	Data Bus	Tristate, bidirectional
CKIN	Clock or crystal connection	Input
OSCOUT	Crystal connection	Output
$\overline{\phi 3}$	Synchronizing clock	Output
$\overline{\text{MEMEN}}$	Memory Enable	Tristate, output
IAQ	Instruction Fetch	Output
DBIN	Data Bus in	Tristate, output
$\overline{\text{WE}}$	Write Enable	Tristate, output
READY	Memory Ready	Input
WAIT	Wait State indicator	Output
CRUCLK	I/O clock	Output
CRUOUT	Serial I/O out	Output
CRUIN	Serial I/O in	Input
INT0, INT1, INT2	Interrupt request and priority	Input
$\overline{\text{HOLD}}$	DMA request	Input
HOLDA	Hold acknowledge	Output
V_{CC}, V_{DD}, V_{SS}	Power and Ground reference	

Figure 3-16. TMS 9981 Signals and Pin Assignments

TMS 9980 SERIES MICROPROCESSOR TIMING AND INSTRUCTION EXECUTION

The TMS 9980A and TMS 9981 microprocessors have the same signal relationships and instruction execution sequences as the TMS 9900. The few minor waveform differences are identified in the data sheets at the end of this chapter.

The only significant difference between the TMS 9900 and TMS 9980 series is in clock logic. The TMS 9900 requires four clock inputs, as identified in Figure 3-3.

The IMS 9980A requires a single clock signal, input via CKIN. The frequency of this clock input must be four times the desired clock frequency. That is to say, CKIN will be divided by four in order to create one clock period. The TMS 9981 can operate with the same CKIN input as the TMS 9980A; however, you can also connect a crystal across CKIN and OSCOUT. This may be illustrated as follows:

TMS 9980
SERIES
CLOCK
LOGIC

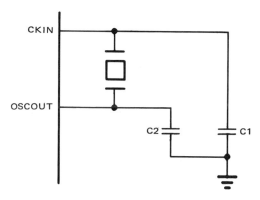

C1 and C2 must have values between 10pf and 25pf, typically 15pf.

The crystal must be of the fundamental frequency type. The frequency will be divided by four in order to create the internal clock frequency.

Both the TMS 9980A and the TMS 9981 output $\overline{\Phi 3}$, a synchronizing clock signal. $\overline{\Phi 3}$ is the inverse of the $\Phi 3$ clock signal shown in Figure 3-3 and in subsequent timing diagrams for the TMS 9900.

Thus you can create the timing diagram for any TMS 9980 operation by looking at the equivalent timing diagram for the TMS 9900 and replacing the four TMS 9900 clock signals by a single timing pulse which will be the complement of $\Phi 3$.

The following operations are identical within TMS 9900 and TMS 9980 systems:

• Memory references. However, note that memory reference will consist of two memory access cycles, as a 16-bit word is handled as two bytes.
• CRU I/O operations (remember that the TMS 9980 series CRU is only 2048 bits wide).
• CRU control operations
• The Wait state
• The Hold state and direct memory access operations
• The Halt state
• The interaction of Hold and Halt states

Refer to the TMS 9900 discussion for any of the above topics.

TMS 9980 SERIES INTERRUPT LOGIC

The TMS 9980A and TMS 9981 microprocessors support four levels of external interrupt, together with a Reset and a Load. Reset and Load are non-maskable interrupts. In contrast, the TMS 9900 supports 15 levels of external interrupt, along with Reset.

The TMS 9980 series microprocessors identify external interrupts via the INT0, INT1, and INT2 inputs as shown in Table 3-6. Figure 3-17 shows the interrupt vector map.

Table 3-6. TMS 9980 Interrupts

INT0	INT1	INT2	Interrupt Decoded
0	0	0	Reset
0	0	1	Reset
0	1	0	Load
0	1	1	Level 1 (Highest Priority)
1	0	0	Level 2
1	0	1	Level 3
1	1	0	Level 4 (Lowest Priority)
1	1	1	No Interrupts

Observe that the TMS 9980A and the TMS 9981 have no $\overline{INTREQ}$ input. Also, the Reset and Load non-maskable interrupts are decoded from the INT0 - INT2 inputs.

Figure 3-18 shows some pin connections for various levels of interrupt complexity in a TMS 9980 series microcomputer system. The three illustrations shown are self-evident; they simply implement the INT0 - INT2 codes defined above.

The TMS 9980 series microprocessors provide all 16 XOP software interrupts available with a TMS 9900.

Observe that Figure 3-17 shows memory as 8-bit units in contrast to Figure 3-11, which shows memory as 16-bit units. This reflects the fact that external memory is addressed as bytes by the TMS 9980A and the TMS 9981.

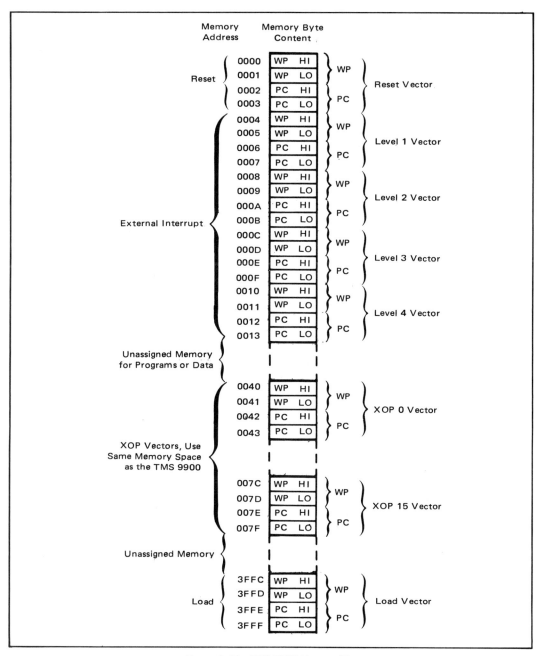

Figure 3-17. TMS 9980 Memory Map

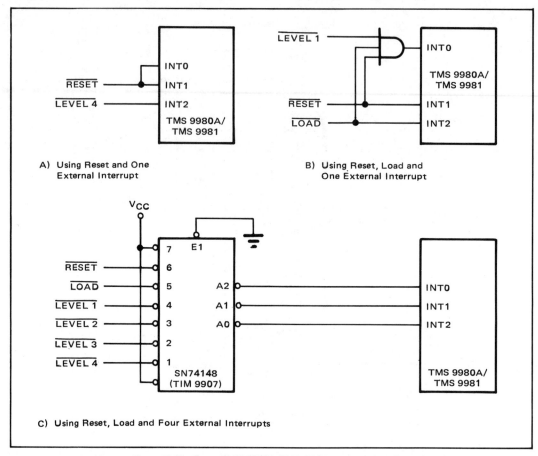

Figure 3-18. Some TMS 9980A/TMS 9981 Interrupt Interfaces

The interrupt acknowledge process and interrupt priority arbitration logic are identical in TMS 9900 and TMS 9980 series microprocessors. For a discussion of these subjects, refer to the earlier TMS 9900 description.

THE TMS 9980 SERIES INSTRUCTION SET

The TMS 9900 and TMS 9980 series microprocessors have identical instruction sets. Instructions execute in almost the same sequences of machine cycles — the only difference is that each memory reference will have twice as many memory access cycles. Refer to Tables 3-2 and 3-3, together with their accompanying text, for details. Remember to substitute two memory cycles for each TMS 9900 memory cycle.

THE TMS 9940 SINGLE-CHIP MICROCOMPUTERS

The TMS 9940 is a single-chip microcomputer based on the TMS 9900 microprocessor. Figure 3-19 illustrates that part of our general microcomputer system logic provided by the TMS 9940 series microcomputer.

Specifically, this is the logic provided by the TMS 9940 series microcomputers:

- A Central Processing Unit, essentially equivalent to **the TMS 9900 Central Processing Unit**

- **2048 bytes of read-only memory.** Erasable Programmable Read-Only Memory (EPROM) is provided by the TMS 9940OE. Normal mask programmable Read-Only Memory (ROM) is available with the TMS 9940M.

- **128 bytes of read/write memory.** This read-write memory is frequently organized as four sets of sixteen 16-bit registers.

- **Two levels of external interrupt**
- **An on-chip timer/event counter with its own interrupt logic**
- **32 I/O pins accessed as 32 CRU bits**
- **A single +5V power supply**
- **On-chip clock logic**

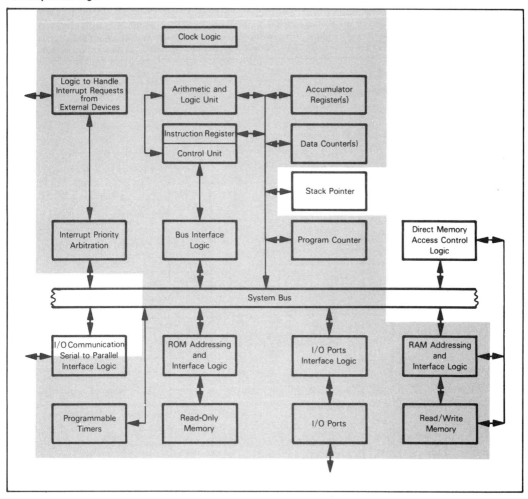

Figure 3-19. Logic of the TMS 9940 Single-Chip Microcomputers

The TMS 9940 microcomputer has very little expansion logic; 256 external CRU bits can be addressed, but there is no provision for executing programs directly from external memory.

But the TMS 9940 is easily included in multiprocessor configurations. For multiprocessor configurations, the TMS 9940 has internal Hold request/acknowledge logic, together with a serial I/O path via which data can be transferred between processors.

The TMS 9940 has two +5V power supplies: a standard operating power supply and a standby power supply. Under program control, it is possible to shut down the TMS 9940, in which case only the standby power supply is active. An external interrupt can subsequently restart the TMS 9940.

The TMS 9940 is manufactured using N-channel silicon gate MOS technology. It is packaged as a 40-pin DIP.

Using a 3 MHz clock, instruction execution times range between 3 and 10 microseconds.

This description of the TMS 9940 microcomputer relies on the preceding detailed description of the TMS 9900. This description of the TMS 9940 does not stand alone, and you should not read it until you understand the TMS 9900 in detail.

TMS 9940 REGISTERS AND READ/WRITE MEMORY

There are some important conceptual differences between the read/write memory/registers of the TMS 9940 and those of the TMS 9900.

The TMS 9940 has only 128 bytes of read/write memory, with all the read/write on the chip itself, and you cannot create an external Data/Address Bus. Therefore, it makes no difference whether memory is addressed as bytes or words. The only remaining restriction is that 16-bit words must be origined on even byte address boundaries.

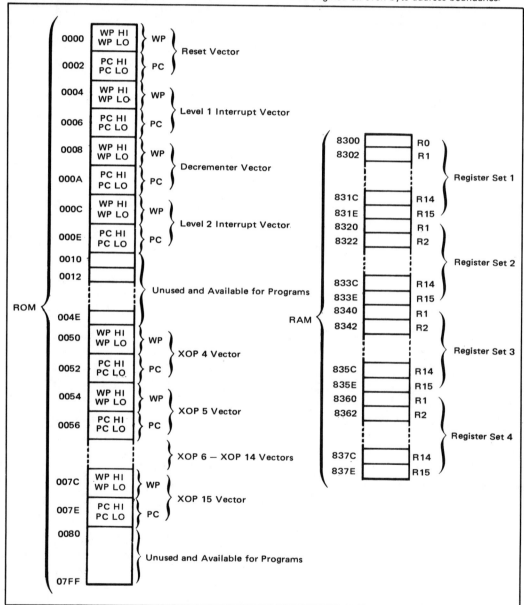

Figure 3-20. TMS 9940 Memory Map

3-54

The TMS 9940 does introduce one additional read/write memory restriction: the **128 bytes of read/write memory are divided into four non-overlapping sets of sixteen 16-bit registers, as illustrated in Figure 3-20.** Note that the 128 bytes of read/write memory have specifically defined addresses. Both the TMS 9900 and the TMS 9980 series microprocessors allow any sixteen 16-bit words of memory to serve as a set of general purpose registers, whether or not they overlap with another set.

The TMS 9940 has the same three CPU registers as the TMS 9900: the Program Counter, the Workspace register, and the Status register. The TMS 9940 sets aside general-purpose registers to serve specific functions, as does the TMS 9900.

Given the configuration of the TMS 9940, many register designations can be justified only as a means of preserving TMS 9900 series compatibility. For example, a 16-bit TMS 9940 Workspace register makes no sense when there are only 64 locations that the Workspace register can possibly address. Moreover, the whole idea of context switching — and tying up three 16-bit registers in order to execute a context switch — is ridiculous, given the few places to which you can context switch.

But there is long-range sense in the TMS 9940 design. Over the next few years, enhancements of the TMS 9940 will appear with substantially more memory — both read-only memory and read/write memory. Since it is absolutely imperative that TMS 9940 programs be compatible with new, enhanced one-chip microcomputers that are likely to appear, it is necessary that addressing modes and architectural features that influence the instruction set be included in the TMS 9940 if they will be useful in later enhancements.

Despite the fact that the TMS 9940 has only 128 bytes of read/write memory and 2048 bytes of read-only memory, the TMS 9940 has all of the TMS 9900 memory addressing modes. Note carefully that so far as memory addressing is concerned, there is no difference between read-only memory and read/write memory. Many one-chip microcomputers have a scratchpad read/write memory which can only be accessed as data memory, while a separate program memory can only store instruction sequences; the TMS 9940 makes no such distinction between its read-only memory and read/write memory. Data and instructions can be stored in read-only memory or in read/write memory.

The TMS 9940 and TMS 9900 CRU addressing techniques are identical; however, the TMS 9940 has just 32 external CRU bits, each with its own dedicated pin. By configuring 11 of these pins as address lines and CRU controls, you can expand external CRU to 256 bits.

There are some small differences between the TMS 9930 Status register as compared to the TMS 9900 Status register. The TMS 9940 Status register may be illustrated as follows:

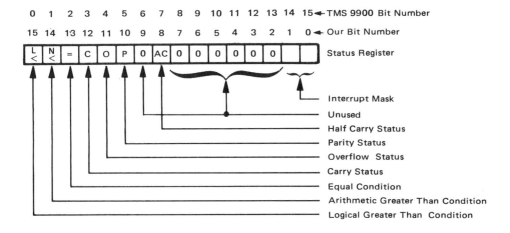

TMS 9940 L, N, =, C, O, and P statuses are the same as those of the TMS 9900.

The TMS 9940 has no XOP instruction executed status, which the TMS 9900 holds in Status register bit 9.

The TMS 9940 has an AC status in bit 8. This is a half-carry status. For byte-oriented instructions, AC represents the carry from the low four bits to the higher four:

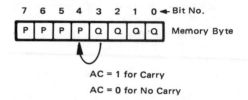

AC = 1 for Carry
AC = 0 for No Carry

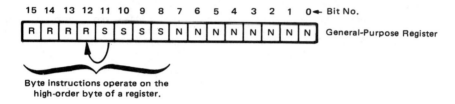

Byte instructions operate on the
high-order byte of a register.

For 16-bit instructions, the AC status represents a carry from bit 11 to bit 12:

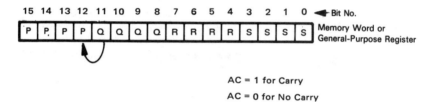

AC = 1 for Carry
AC = 0 for No Carry

Since there are just four levels of external interrupt, the TMS 9940 uses Status register bits 0 and 1 for its interrupt mask. In contrast, the TMS 9900 uses Status register bits 0, 1, 2, and 3 for its interrupt mask.

TMS 9940 CPU PINS AND SIGNAL ASSIGNMENTS

Figure 3-21 illustrates the pins and signals of the TMS 9940 microcomputer.

PO - P31 and 32 I/O pins addressed as 32 CRU bits. Some of these pins serve additional functions which can be selected under program control.

The TMS 9940 can, in fact. use standard TMS 9900 CRU instructions to **address up to 512 CRU bits.** But 512 is the maximum number of CRU bits that the TMS 9940 can address. Therefore. the TMS 9940 uses just 9 bits of General Purpose Register R12 to create CRU bit addresses. For a single-bit CRU instruction. this may be illustrated as follows:

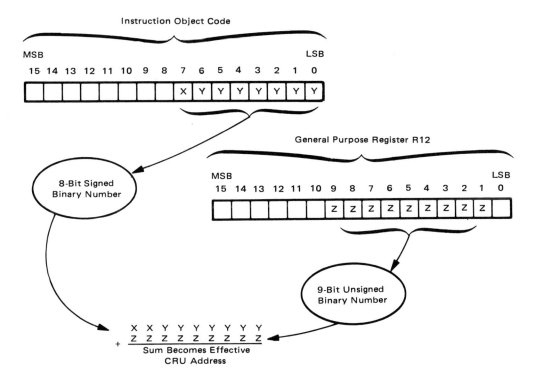

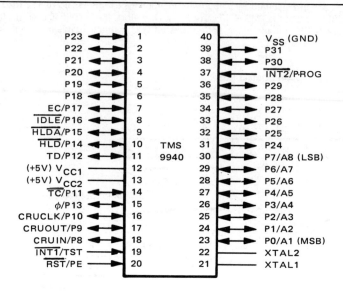

Pin Name	Description	Type
P0 - P31	CRU I/O pins	Bidirectional
INT1/TST	External interrupt and Test select	Input
INT2/PROG	External interrupt and EPROM programmer	Input
RST/PE	System reset and EPROM programmer enable	Input
A0 - A7	External CRU bit address	Output
CRUCLK	External CRU clock	Output
CRUOUT	External serial I/O output	Output
CRUIN	External serial I/O input	Input
TC	Multiprocessor data I/O clock	Bidirectional
TD	Multiprocessor data I/O	Bidirectional
EC	Event counter input	Input
IDLE	Idle state indicator	Output
HLD	Hold request	Input
HLDA	Hold acknowledge	Output
Φ	Synchronizing clock	Output
XTAL2, XTAL1	External crystal connections	
V_{CC1}	Standby +5V power	
V_{CC2}	Normal +5V power	
V_{SS}	Ground reference	

(In this figure, Pn and An numbering conforms to Texas Instruments' policy of beginning with N=0 for the high-order bit. We use N=0 for the low-order bit.)

Figure 3-21. TMS 9940 Microcomputer Signals and Pin Assignments

Table 3-7 shows how the TMS 9940 interprets its 512 available bit addresses.

Table 3-7. TMS 9940 CRU Bit Address Assignments

CRU Address	Read Function	Write Function
000 to 0FF	External CRU bits; the address is output via A1-A8. Data is transferred via CRUIN, CRUOUT and CRUCLK	
100 to 17F	Unused	Unused
180	INT1 state	Unused
181	Decrementer interrupt level	Clear decrementer interrupt
182	INT2 state	Unused
183	Unused	Configuration bit 0 (CB0)
184	Unused	Configuration bit 1 (CB1)
185	Unused	Configuration bit 2 (CB2)
186	Unused	Configuration bit 3 (CB3)
190 to 19D	Decrementer register. 190 is the least significant bit and 19D is the most significant bit	
19E	Unused	Timer (high) or Counter (low) select
19F	Unused	Unused
1A0 to 1AF	Multiprocessor System Interface buffer register 1A0 is the least significant bit and 1AF is the most significant bit	
1B0 to 1BF	General purpose flag bits	
1C0 to 1DF	Unused	Identify direction for P0 (via 1C0) through P31 (via 1DF). 1 specifies output. 0 specifies input
1E0 to 1FF	Local CRU pins (P0 = 1E0, P31 = 1FF)	

The place to begin looking at Table 3-7 is at CRU bits 183, 184, 185, and 186. These four CRU bits represent write-only locations which determine how the 32 CRU pins illustrated in Figure 3-21 will be used.

> **TMS 9940 CRU BIT UTILIZATION**

If you look again at Figure 3-21, you will see that P0 through P17 have shared functions. P18 through P31 are simple I/O pins without other programmable options.

CRU addresses 183, 184, 185 and 186 control the functions of P0 through P16, as illustrated in Table 3-8. P17 options depend on real-time clock logic, which we will describe later.

Let us look at the programmable options available with CRU pins P0 through P31.

It does not matter what options you have selected; **you will actually access the 32 CRU pins P0 - P31 via CRU addresses $1E0_{16}$ through $1FF_{16}$.**

In the simplest case, all 32 pins, P0 - P31, will be used for input or output. We call this Simple I/O mode. In order to use all 32 pins for data input or output. (that is. in Simple I/O mode). all four of the configuration bits. CB0, CB1, CB2. and CB3. must be 0. At any time. a CRU bit can either input data or output data. but it cannot be used for bidirectional data transfer. **You must identify the direction for each pin by outputting appropriate data to CRU addresses $1C0_{16}$ through $1DF_{16}$.** As shown in Table 3-7. each pin has a dedicated CRU address. beginning with pin P0 controlled by

> **TMS 9940 SIMPLE CRU I/O MODE**

$1C0_{16}$ and ending with pin P31 controlled by CRU address $1DF_{16}$. A 1 written to any Direction CRU bit causes the associated pin to output data only. A 0 written to any CRU Direction bit causes the associated pin to input data only. Of course, you can at any time change a pin from input to output or from output to input, under program control, by rewriting control information to Direction CRU bits $1C0_{16}$ through $1DF_{16}$.

Table 3-8. TMS 9940 CRU Bits Whose Functions are Determined Under Program Control

CRU			Function as Configured		
Bit	Address	Pin	CB0 = 0	CB0 = 1	CB1, CB2, CB3
0-7	1E0-1E7	23-30	P0-P7	A1-A8	No Effect
8	1E8	18	P8	CRUIN	No Effect
9	1E9	17	P9	CRUOUT	No Effect
10	1EA	16	P10	CRUCLK	No Effect
			CB1 = 0	CB1 = 1	CB0, CB2, CB3
11	1EB	14	P11	$\overline{TC}$	No Effect
12	1EC	11	P12	TD	No Effect
			CB2 = 0	CB2 = 1	CB0, CB1, CB3
13	1ED	15	P13	ϕ	No Effect
			CB3 = 0	CB3 = 1	CB0, CB1, CB2
14	1EE	10	P14	$\overline{HLD}$	No Effect
15	1EF	9	P15	$\overline{HLDA}$	No Effect
16	1F0	8	P16	$\overline{IDLE}$	No Effect

You will always have to define the direction of data transfer for pins P18 through P31 — assuming that you are using these pins. When pins P0 through P17 are being used in any of the special ways which we are about to describe, then the data direction associated with the special operation will apply, and it makes no difference what you output to the associated Direction CRU bit.

If you wish to use 256 external CRU bits, then you must set CRU bit 183 (CB0) to 1. This is called I/O expansion mode. I/O expansion mode modifies the functions of pins P0 through P10. When you use CRU addresses 00 through FF_{16} in I/O expansion mode, the address is output via pins P0 - P7, which now function as CRU address lines A1 - A8. P8, P9, and P10 serve as the standard CRU data transfer lines: CRUIN, CRUOUT, and CRUCLK. Timing for data input and output via | **TMS 9940 CRU I/O EXPANSION MODE** |

these three lines has been described for the TMS 9900. Refer to the TMS 9900 description for details. **In order to illustrate the use of external CRU, consider execution of the instructions:**

```
LI      R3,>00      LOAD 1010 BINARY INTO UPPER BYTE OF R3
LI      R12,>140    LOAD A BASE ADDRESS OF 82 HEX INTO R12
LDCR    R3,4        OUTPUT FOUR LOW-ORDER BITS OF R3 TO CRU
```

Note that R12 contains 0140_{16} to represent the address 0082_{16}, since R12 bit 0 is unused; therefore the internal address is, in effect, doubled.

This instruction outputs 1010 to CRU bit 082_{16} (0), 083_{16} (1), 084_{16} (0), and 085_{16}(1). Since fewer than eight bits will be transferred, they will come from the upper byte of the general purpose register. This is the event sequence which occurs:

1) The address 82_{16} is output via A1 - A8. Remember, Texas Instruments' literature uses 0 to represent the high-order bit; therefore A1 represents the high-order address bit, and A8 represents the low-order address bit. CRUIN is inactive, but CRUOUT is low to represent 0 while CRUCLK is pulsed high to time the 0 bit on CRUOUT.

2) The address output on A1 - A8 increments to 83_{16}, and CRUOUT goes high, then CRUCLK pulses high.

3) The address on A1 - A8 increments to 84_{16}, CRUOUT goes low again, and CRUCLK pulses high.

4) The address on A1 - A8 increments to 85_{16}, and CRUOUT goes high, and CRUCLK pulses high.

1010 has now been transmitted to four external CRU bits.

Note that it is up to external logic to decode the CRU address output; however, the Parallel System interface (which we will describe in later editions) will connect directly to the TMS 9940 Address and CRU outputs that we have just described.

When you write 1 to CRU bit 184_{16} (CB1), pins P11 and P12 function as serial data **TMS 9940**
transfer pins. The purpose of this logic is to allow the TMS 9940 to operate in multi-CPU **MULTIPROCESSOR**
configurations. This logic is very simple. You output data by writing the data to CRU bits **SYSTEM**
$1A0_{16}$ through $1AF_{16}$. This data is immediately transmitted via TD (P12) as a serial data **INTERFACE**
stream which is clocked by $\overline{TC}$ (P11). In keeping with normal bit sequence protocol, data is
transmitted low-order bit first. Thus, 16 bits of data being output may be illustrated as follows:

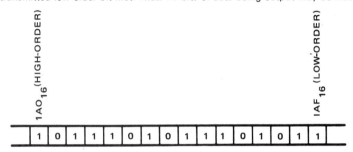

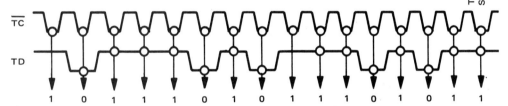

When a TMS 9940 has a 1 written to CB1, it can also receive data via TD. Data input is again clocked by $\overline{TC}$. Input logic is the reverse of the output logic illustrated above; that is say, as a data stream is input, the first input bit is loaded into CRU bit $1AF_{16}$, and the sixteenth input bit is loaded into CRU bit $1A0_{16}$.

TMS 9940 multiprocessor system interface logic is used to transfer data from a memory location in one TMS 9940 to a memory location in another TMS 9940. You will not normally use this logic to transfer data between a TMS 9940 and external logic; the CRU serves that purpose better. There are three reasons why you may want to use the TMS 9940 multiprocessor system interface; they are:

1) **To transmit status information.** For example, one TMS 9940 could tell another how far it has progressed through various phases of a task by transmitting a status word whose bits have some predefined interpretation.

2) **To transmit data.** One TMS 9940 may generate data which another TMS 9940 needs in order to execute its programs.

3) **To transmit instruction sequences.** Instructions could be transmitted from the read-only memory (or the read/write memory) of one TMS 9940 to the read/write memory of another TMS 9940. The receiving TMS 9940 could then execute the instruction sequence out of its read/write memory.

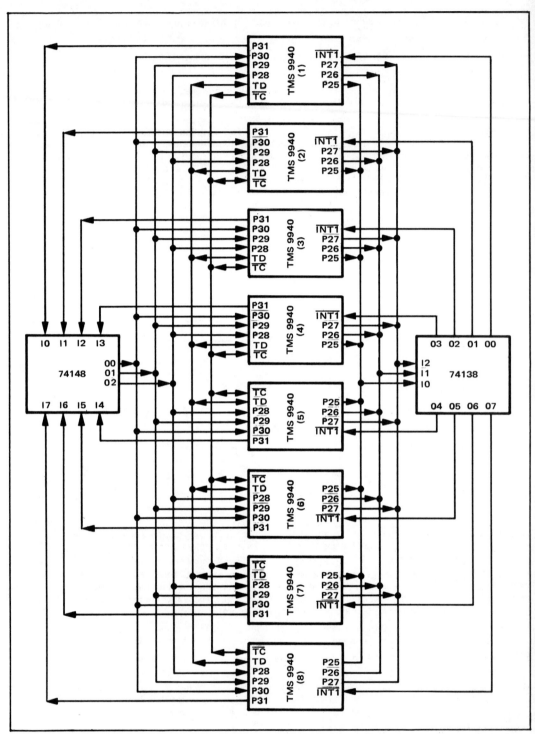

Figure 3-22. Handshaking Logic in a TMS 9940 Multi-Microcomputer Network Communicating via the TD Data Line

You could use the CRU to perform any of the three data transfers described above, but the multiprocessor system interface is somewhat easier to use. We say that data transfer via the multiprocessor system interface is "somewhat" easier to use because many problems still remain when you use the multiprocessor system interface. These problems arise from the fact that **there is absolutely no handshaking protocol associated with the multiprocessor system interface.** For example, there is absolutely no protection against two TMS 9940s simultaneously trying to output data via TD and $\overline{TC}$. There is no predefined protocol whereby a transmitting TMS 9940 identifies the receiving TMS 9940 or the instant data has been transmitted and should be read. Any protocol is your responsibility — to be provided by logic external to the TMS 9940s. Fortunately, **this protocol is easy to implement. Figure 3-22 shows how eight TMS 9940s can communicate with each other, such that each TMS 9940 may transmit data to, or receive data from, any other TMS 9940.** The logic illustrated in Figure 3-22 is more complex than the logic you would need for a small system — for example, a two-microcomputer system, or a system where there are dedicated transmitters and receivers.

While Figure 3-22 shows TMS 9940s communicating with each other, you will in fact use TMS 9940s just as frequently with other microprocessors — such as a TMS 9900. Nevertheless, the concepts embodied in Figure 3-22 would apply, from the viewpoint of the TMS 9940, in any other configuration.

Let us look at how the logic in Figure 3-22 works.

The first problem we must resolve is the problem of transmission contentions. How will we make sure that one TMS 9940 does not try to transmit data while another TMS 9940 is already transmitting data? A simple scheme would be to set aside a particular CRU pin to serve as a "Busy" line. For example, every TMS 9940 could use P31 as a "Busy" output pin and P30 as a "Sense" input pin. We could wire-OR together all P31 Busy outputs and input this wire-OR to all P30 Sense inputs. Now any TMS 9940 that wishes to transmit data will read its P30 CRU bit. If this bit is 0, then it will output 1 to P31. Outputting 1 to P31 causes all other TMS 9940s to receive 1 at their P30 inputs. Thus, no other TMS 9940 will begin transmitting data if another TMS 9940 was in the process of transmitting data. This logic may be illustrated as follows:

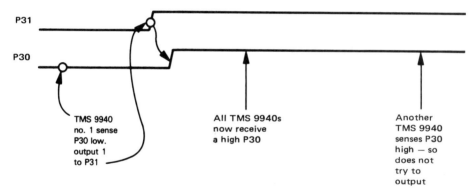

The problem with the logic illustrated above is that two TMS 9940s could simultaneously read P30, find it was 0, output 1 to P31, then output competing data on TD. While the chances of two microcomputers executing identical instructions at exactly the same time are very small, a well-designed microcomputer system must account for every potential error. In Figure 3-22 we resolve our problem by using a 74148 8-to-3 decoder. The P31 output from every TMS 9940 is connected to a different 74148 input. The 74148 outputs, via O0, O1, and O2, the line number for the highest priority active input. This three-line output is connected to the P28, P29, and P30 pins of every TMS 9940; we assume that these three pins are inputs at every TMS 9940. Now every TMS 9940 that wishes to transmit data via TD must output a 1 to P31. It must then input the contents of P30, P29, and P28. Upon detecting its own ID on these three inputs, it begins data transmission. If a TMS 9940 outputs 1 via P31 and then reads in some other ID via P30, P29, and P28, then it must wait. Here is an appropriate instruction sequence:

```
        LI      R12,>3F8      LOAD P28 ADDRESS, X2, INTO R12
        SBO     3             SET P31 ON
LOOP    STCR    R2,3          INPUT P28, P29, AND P30
        CI      R2,ID         COMPARE INPUT WITH DEVICE ID
        JNE     LOOP          RETURN AND RE-ENTER CODE IF NOT CORRECT ID
        LI      R12,>340      LOAD MPSI OUTPUT DATA BASE ADDRESS X2
        LDCR    R3,16         OUTPUT CONTENTS OF R3 VIA TD
```

Assuming that a TMS 9940 has output 1 to P31 and has received back its own ID via P28, P29, and P30, the TMS 9940 is ready to transmit data. However, in addition to simply transmitting the data, the TMS 9940 must tell the intended recipient that the data has been transmitted. In Figure 3-22 we use a 74138 3-to-8 demultiplexer for this purpose. Pins P25, P26, and P27 of every TMS 9940 are outputs that connect to the I0, I1, and I2 inputs of the 74138. The transmitting TMS 9940 outputs data which will be received by every other TMS 9940; however, the transmitting TMS 9940 follows up by outputting a 3-bit code via P25, P26, and P27; this 3-bit code identifies the intended recipient. The 3-bit code is input to the 74138, which generates one of eight possible outputs. These eight outputs become external interrupt request inputs to the eight TMS 9940s. Only the single TMS 9940 will receive the data which was transmitted by the eighth TMS 9940, only one TMS 9940 will receive an interrupt request signal; this is the TMS 9940 for which the transmitted data was intended. The TMS 9940 which receives data simply executes an STRCR instruction to move the data from CRU bits $1A0_{16}$ through $1AF_{16}$ to the appropriate general purpose register.

CRU bit 185_{16}, the CB2 bit, serves the very limited purpose of outputting a synchronizing signal. When you output 1 to CB2, P13 ceases to be an I/O pin and instead outputs the internal TMS 9940 clock signal.

> TMS 9940
> SYNC MODE

CRU bit 186_{16} (CB3) controls idle and hold logic for the TMS 9940. When you write a 1 to CRU bit 186_{16}, pins P14 and P15 act as hold request input ($\overline{\text{HLD}}$) and hold acknowledge output ($\overline{\text{HLDA}}$) signals, respectively. P16 generates an $\overline{\text{IDLE}}$ output.

The Hold request/acknowledge logic of the TMS 9940 is quite standard. The purpose of this logic is to remove the TMS 9940 from any shared busses when some other microprocessor or microcomputer is bus master. If CB3 is 1, then a low signal arriving at the TMS 9940 $\overline{\text{HLD}}$ input will cause the TMS 9940 to enter a Hold state at the conclusion of the current instruction's execution. A low $\overline{\text{HLDA}}$ output marks the beginning of the Hold state.

> TMS 9940
> HOLD LOGIC

The $\overline{\text{IDLE}}$ signal is output low when an IDLE instruction is executed and CB3 is 1. The only way in which you can terminate an Idle state is by requesting an interrupt via $\overline{\text{INT1}}$ or $\overline{\text{INT2}}$. The TMS 9940 three-state signals are not floated in the Idle state. You must additionally enter the Hold state for this.

> TMS 9940
> IDLE LOGIC

The purpose of the IDLE instruction and signal is to enable standby power logic. This may be illustrated as follows:

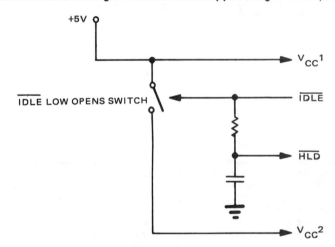

Under normal circumstances, the power supply will input power to $V_{CC}1$ and $V_{CC}2$. When $\overline{\text{IDLE}}$ goes low, the power input to $V_{CC}2$ is switched off. While $V_{CC}1$ only is receiving power, the TMS 9940 read/write memory and interrupt logic is active, but all other logic is inactive. since the interrupt logic is active, any arriving interrupt request will be acknowledged. The process of acknowledging an interrupt request sets $\overline{\text{IDLE}}$ high again. This closes the switch and restores power to $V_{CC}2$, which allows the TMS 9940 to resume normal execution.

In the illustration above, note that $\overline{\text{IDLE}}$ is connected to $\overline{\text{HLD}}$.

TMS 9940 GENERAL PURPOSE FLAGS

If you look again at Table 3-7 , you will see that CRU addresses $1B0_{16}$ through $1BF_{16}$ address 16 general purpose flags. These general purpose flags have no special hardware functions. They are programming aids and that is all. You can write data out to these flags, and you can read back the data. How you use this data is entirely up to program logic.

TMS 9940 TIMER/EVENT COUNTER LOGIC

The TMS 9940 has a timer which can also be used as an event counter. CRU bit $19E_{16}$ determines whether this logic will function as a timer or as an event counter. If CRU bit $19E_{16}$ is high, then this logic serves as a Timer. If CRU bit $19E_{16}$ is low, then this logic serves as an event counter.

Timer and Event Counter logic both use CRU bits 190_{16} through $19D_{16}$ as a 14-bit register whose contents are decremented by Timer or Event Counter logic. This 14-bit register is buffered. That is to say, the initial value which you output to CRU bits 190_{16} through $19D_{16}$ is stored in a buffer, in addition to being loaded into CRU bits 190_{16} through $19D_{16}$. Subsequently, CRU bits 190_{16} through $19D_{16}$ are decremented, but the buffer contents remain unaltered. When CRU bits 190_{16} through $19D_{16}$ decrement to 0, they are reloaded from the buffer. Thus Timer/Event Counter logic runs continuously. An interrupt request is generated internally when CRU bits 190_{16} through $19D_{16}$ decrement to 0.

Remember, CRU bit 190_{16} is the low-order bit, and CRU $19D_{16}$ is the high-order bit. This is the reverse of normal Texas Instruments bit numbering, where the high-order bit has the lowest bit number. However, this is consistent with the fact that Texas Instruments outputs data to the CRU low-order bit first, and addresses CRU bits in numerically ascending address sequence.

When you write 0 to CRU bits 190_{16} through $19D_{16}$, you disable Timer/Event Counter logic.

When the Timer/Event Counter is operating as a timer, the 14-bit register represented by CRU bits 190_{16} through $19D_{16}$ are decremented once every 30 internal clock oscillations. The crystal connected across XTAL1 and XTAL2 determines clock oscillation frequency. When CRU bits 190_{16} through $19D_{16}$ time out to zero, an interrupt request is generated.

When Timer/Event Counter logic is operating as an event counter, pin P17 serves as an input, receiving the event sequence to be counted. Every low-to-high transition of the signal input at P17 decrements the counter. Once again, when the counter counts out to 0, an interrupt request occurs and the counter is reloaded from its buffer register.

TMS 9940 INTERRUPT LOGIC

The TMS 9940 has four external interrupts and twelve internal software interrupts.

These are the four external interrupts:

1) Reset. This has highest priority.

2) A level 1 interrupt occurring at the $\overline{INT1}$ pin. This has second highest priority.

3) A Decrementer/Event Counter interrupt. This has third highest priority.

4) A level 2 interrupt occurring at the $\overline{INT2}$ pin. This has lowest priority.

As described for the TMS 9900, you execute XOP instructions to generate software interrupts. XOP4 through XOP15 are active. XOP0 through XOP3 do not exist on the TMS 9940.

TMS 9940 interrupt vectors, together with a complete TMS 9940 memory map, are illustrated in Figure 3-20.

The actual interrupt acknowledge sequence for a TMS 9940 is identical to that which we have described for the TMS 9900.

TMS 9940 RESET

You Reset the TMS 9940 by inputting a low signal at $\overline{RST}$/PE (pin 20). This low signal must last for at least five clock cycles. A Reset resets to 0 the contents of all pointer registers and all CRU configuration bits. Following a Reset, level 0 interrupt response begins — which means that read-only memory bytes 0 through 3 provide the initial Program Counter and Word Pointer register contents, and therefore the address of the program which will be executed following the Reset.

Note that the TMS 9940, being a smaller and simpler system than the TMS 9900, can use elementary logic to generate an interrupt acknowledge. For the TMS 9900 we suggested an Address Bus decoding technique in order to create an interrupt acknowledge signal. For the TMS 9940 a CRU bit will do just fine. The following circuit is recommended by Texas Instruments:

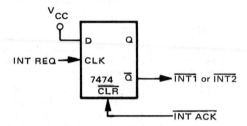

A simple D-type flip-flop has its D input connected to +5V. Every time an interrupt request pulse is input to the clock pin, the $\overline{Q}$ output will go low — generating a valid interrupt request at the TMS 9940. In order to acknowledge the interrupt and remove the interrupt request signal, you can output a low pulse via any of the P pins. This low pulse clears the D-type flip-flop and forces $\overline{Q}$ high again.

PROGRAMMING A TMS 9940E ERASABLE, PROGRAMMABLE READ-ONLY MEMORY

The TMS 9940E has a transparent quartz lid over the device in its dual in-line package. **In order to erase the TMS 9940E EPROM, you should expose it to a high-intensity ultraviolet light with a wavelength of 2537 angstroms.** An intensity of 10 watt-seconds per square centimeter is recommended.

After the TMS 9940E EPROM has been erased, all EPROM memory bits will be 0.

These are the steps required in order to program a TMS 9940E EPROM:

1) Reset the device.

2) Apply the first data byte — to be stored in memory location 0000 to pins P24 through P31. Remember, P24 represents the most significant bit of the byte, and P31 represents the least significant bit of the byte.

3) Apply a 26-volt level to pin 20, the $\overline{RST}$/PE pin. This being the first programming pulse, it resets the internal program memory address point at 0000 and writes the data byte at P24 through P31 into memory location 0.

4) After at least 80 clock cycles, apply 26 volts to pin 37, $\overline{INT2}$/PROG, for 50 milliseconds while changing the data byte (step 5).

5) Apply the next data byte to P24 through P31. At the high-to-low transition of PROG, the data will be written into the next location.

6) Remove the 26 volts from pin 37 for a minimum of 50 clock cycles. Then apply 26V to pin 37 for 50 milliseconds.

7) Return to Step 5 until all of program memory has been programmed.

LOADING A PROGRAM INTO TMS 9940 READ/WRITE MEMORY

You can load a program directly into TMS 9940 read/write memory via pins P24 (MSB) through P31 (LSB) for either the TMS 9940E or the TMS 9940M. Typically, this is done in order to load a small test program. The procedure for loading data into the TMS 9940 read/write memory is exactly as described in the previous section for loading data into EPROM, except: the 26-volt level is applied to pin 19, the TST pin, after the device has been reset by inputting a low signal to pin 20, the $\overline{RST}$/PE pin; and the high pulses at PROG are logic '1' level rather than 26 volts.

When you input data to a TMS 9940 read/write memory using the TEST pin and P24 through P31, the address pointer is initialized to address 8300_{16}. The address keeps incrementing the high-to-low transition of each 50 millisecond programming pulse applied at pin 37. When you finally stop applying programming pulses, the last 16 bits of data input are interpreted as the beginning address for the program to be executed. This address may point to a read/write memory location, or to a read/write memory location. That is to say, the test program may be in read/write memory, in read-only memory, or in both areas.

THE TMS 9940 INSTRUCTION SET

The TMS 9940 instruction set is identical to the TMS 9900 instruction set, with these exceptions:

1) **The RSET, CKOF, CKON and LREX instructions have been deleted.** That is, all the external instructions except IDLE.

2) The XOP instructions will not work with operands 0, 1, 2, or 3.

3) There are new DCA and DCS instructions that enable 8-bit binary-coded decimal arithmetic.

Assuming that you start with two valid 8-bit binary-coded decimal operands, you can add these two 8-bit operands using normal binary addition. The result will be a meaningless 8-bit number; however, if you immediately execute the DCA instruction, this meaningless 8-bit number will be converted to a meaningful 8-bit, 2-BCD-digit number.

DCS, likewise, allows you to perform 8-bit binary-coded decimal subtraction. Assuming that the subtrahend and minuend are both valid 8-bit binary-coded decimal numbers, you perform a subtraction using binary arithmetic and you generate a meaningless 8-bit result. By executing the DCS instruction, you convert this meaningless 8-bit result into a valid 8-bit, 2-BCD-digit binary-coded decimal difference.

The DCA and DCS instructions both generate in the low-order eight bits of the 16-bit word.

For a discussion of decimal adjust logic in BCD addition or subtraction, see Volume 1, Chapter 3.

The LIIM instruction loads a 2-bit interrupt mask into the two low-order bits of the Status register.

Here are the instruction object codes used by the DCA, DCS, and LIIM instructions:

Instruction	Object Code	Bytes	Clock Periods
DCA r	0010110000bbssss	2	7
DCS r	0010110001bbssss	2	7
LIIM n	001011001xxxxxnn	2	10

The object code notation above conforms to that which we have described for Table 3-3. For the LIIM instruction, x represents "don't care" bits and n represents the two binary digits that get loaded into the two low-order Status register bits.

THE TIM 9904 FOUR-PHASE CLOCK GENERATOR/DRIVER

This part is also given the generic TTL name: the SN74LS362. The TIM 9904 provides TMS 9900 microprocessors with the four clock signals: Φ1, Φ2, Φ3, and Φ4. These are +12V MOS driver signals. In addition, four complementary +5V clock signals, $\overline{Φ1}$, $\overline{Φ2}$, $\overline{Φ3}$, and $\overline{Φ4}$, are generated for use elsewhere in a TMS 9900 microcomputer system.

The TIM 9904 device may be driven by an external crystal, an external LC circuit, or a single external clock signal.

The TIM 9904 is manufactured using low-power Schottky technology; hence the 74LS part number. It is packaged as a 20-pin DIP. All signals, other than the four MOS level clocks, are TTL-compatible.

The TIM 9904 allows one asynchronous input signal to be synchronized, via a D flip-flop, with the Φ3 signal. The synchronized signal is output, frequently to be used as a $\overline{RESET}$ input to the TMS 9900.

Figure 3-23 illustrates TIM 9904 pins and signal assignments.

The four clock signals, Φ1, Φ2, Φ3, and Φ4, conform to Figure 3-3. Φ1, Φ2, Φ3, and Φ4 are complements of $\overline{Φ1}$, $\overline{Φ2}$, $\overline{Φ3}$, and $\overline{Φ4}$.

A logic level input at D will be output at Q on the high-to-low transition of Φ3:

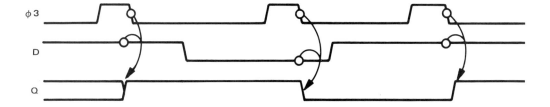

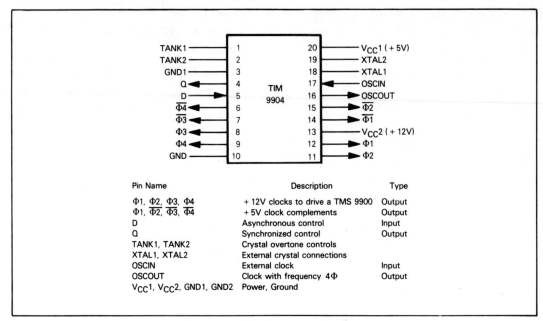

Figure 3-23. TIM 9904 Signals and Pin Assignments

OSCOUT provides a clock frequency four times that of the Φ clocks. Its phase relationship to the Φ clocks may be illustrated as follows:

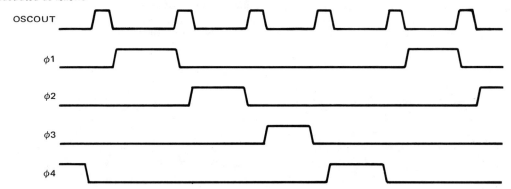

When an external quartz crystal is used to drive the TIM 9904, the following connections are required:

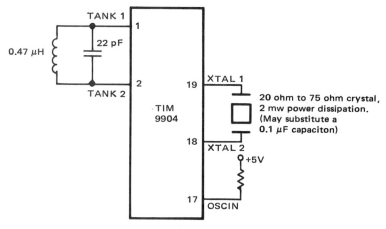

OSCIN must be tied to a high logic level for the internal clock logic to work properly.

Required capacitor and inductance values are shown in the illustration above for a TMS 9900 microprocessor operating with its standard 3 MHz frequency. The crystal must have a resonant frequency of 48 MHz. For 48 MHz operation, a third overtone crystal is used.

For less precise timing, the quartz crystal may be replaced with a 0.1 μf capacitor. The LC-tuned circuit now establishes the clock frequency according to the following equation:

$$f_{osc} = 1/(2\pi\sqrt{LC})$$

where L is the inductance, with units of Henries, and C is the capacitance with units of Farads. This includes the capacitance of the circuit into which the components are mounted.

If an external clock signal is input, it must occur at OSCIN. The crystal connections XTAL1 and XTAL2 should be connected to V_{CC} as follows:

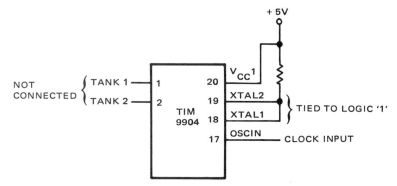

The clock input OSCIN must have a frequency which is four times the clock period frequency and has a 25% duty cycle. Thus, for a 3 MHz frequency, a 12 MHz signal must be input via OSCIN:

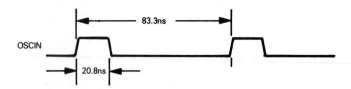

In TMS 9900 microcomputer systems, the D input is used for an asynchronous reset; Q is output as a synchronous reset. This may be illustrated as follows:

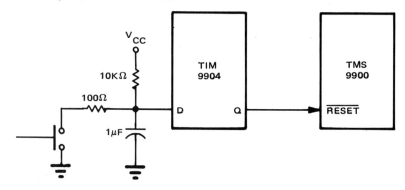

The illustration above shows recommended resistor and capacitor values.

THE TMS 9901 PROGRAMMABLE SYSTEM INTERFACE (PSI)

The TMS 9901 Programmable System Interface (PSI) is a special support part designed for the TMS 9900 series of microprocessors. This relatively primitive device uses 32 bits of the TMS 9900 CRU bit field to support parallel I/O and interrupt request logic. Programmable timer logic is also available.

Figure 3-24 illustrates that part of general microcomputer system logic which has been implemented on the TMS 9901 PSI.

The TMS 9901 PSI is packaged as a 40-pin DIP. It uses a single +5V power supply. All inputs and outputs are TTL-compatible. The device is implemented using N-channel silicon gate MOS technology.

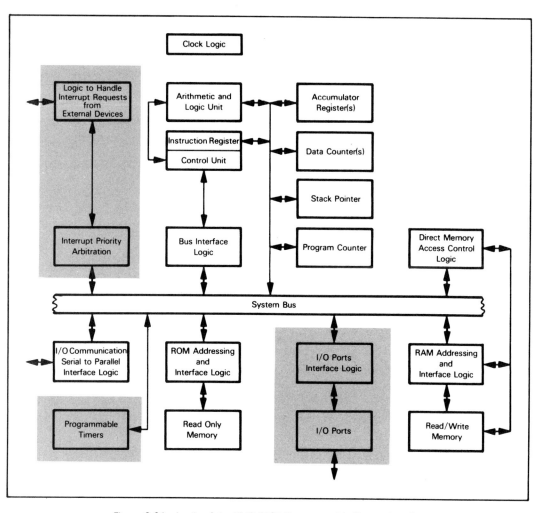

Figure 3-24. Logic of the TMS 9901 Programmable System Interface

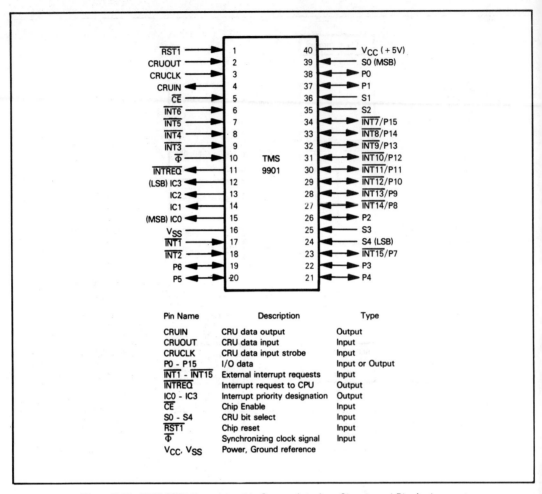

Pin Name	Description	Type
CRUIN	CRU data output	Output
CRUOUT	CRU data input	Input
CRUCLK	CRU data input strobe	Input
P0 - P15	I/O data	Input or Output
$\overline{INT1}$ - $\overline{INT15}$	External interrupt requests	Input
$\overline{INTREQ}$	Interrupt request to CPU	Output
IC0 - IC3	Interrupt priority designation	Output
$\overline{CE}$	Chip Enable	Input
S0 - S4	CRU bit select	Input
$\overline{RST1}$	Chip reset	Input
$\overline{\Phi}$	Synchronizing clock signal	Input
V_{CC}, V_{SS}	Power, Ground reference	

Figure 3-25. TMS 9901 Programmable System Interface Signals and Pin Assignments

In the illustration above, Address lines have been numbered using our standard notation, whereby A14 is the highest-order address line and A0 is the lowest-order address line. This is the opposite of Texas Instruments' notation. The CRU select lines are numbered according to Texas Instruments' notation and Figure 3-25. Therefore, S4 is connected to A0, and S0 is connected to A4.

TMS 9901 PSI PINS AND SIGNALS

The TMS 9901 pins and signals are illustrated in Figure 3-25. The signals which connect the TMS 9901 to a TMS 9900 series microprocessor are quite straightforward; they **consist of the CRU and interrupt signals.**

The CRU signals include CRUIN, CRUOUT, and CRUCLK.

The interrupt signals consist of $\overline{\text{INTREQ}}$, IC0, IC1, IC2, and IC3.

For a description of CRU and interrupt signals, refer back to our TMS 9900 discussion.

Device select logic includes a chip enable input, $\overline{\text{CE}}$, together with five CRU bit select pins, S0 - S4. $\overline{\text{CE}}$ and S0 - S4 will connect to the Address Bus as follows:

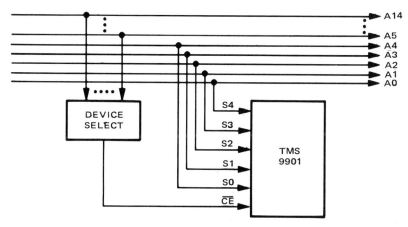

In the illustration above, Address lines have been numbered using our standard notation, whereby A14 is the highest-order address line and A0 is the lowest-order address line. This is the opposite of Texas Instruments' notation. The CRU select lines are numbered according to Texas Instruments' notation and Figure 3-25. Therefore, S4 is connected to A0, and S0 is connected to A4.

Device select logic determines the CRU address space that will be reserved for the TMS 9901 PSI. This may be illustrated as follows:

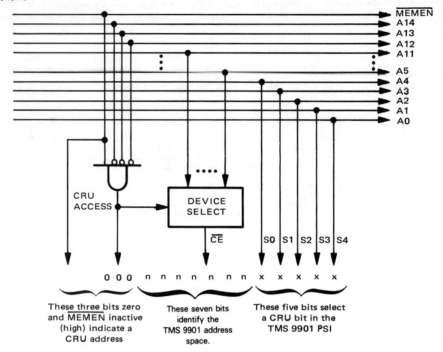

These three bits zero and MEMEN inactive (high) indicate a CRU address

These seven bits identify the TMS 9901 address space.

These five bits select a CRU bit in the TMS 9901 PSI

The high-order three address lines, which we call A14, A13, and A12, are all zero during a CRU access, at which time MEMEN is inactive (high). Thus we decode address lines A11 through A5 to select a particular TMS 9901 device.

Since the TMS 9980 uses the Address Bus differently during a CRU operation, TMS 9901 device select logic would connect to the Address Bus in a different way. The CRU bit select lines S0 - S4 would be tied to lines A5 - A1; device select logic would decode lines A11 - A6; and lines A13 and A12, along with MEMEN, would indicate a CRU access. We illustrate this as follows:

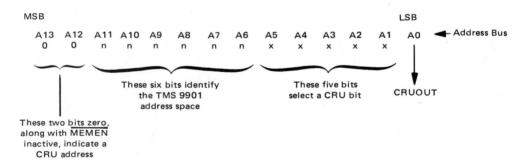

$\overline{\Phi}$ is a synchronizing clock signal used to time data output and to sample interrupts. **$\overline{\Phi}$ is the complement of $\Phi 3$. For the TMS 9900, $\overline{\Phi 3}$ is generated by the TMS 9904. The TMS 9980 outputs $\overline{\Phi 3}$ directly.**

The best way of understanding the interface between a TMS 9901 and external logic is to look at functions performed, as illustrated in Figure 3-26.

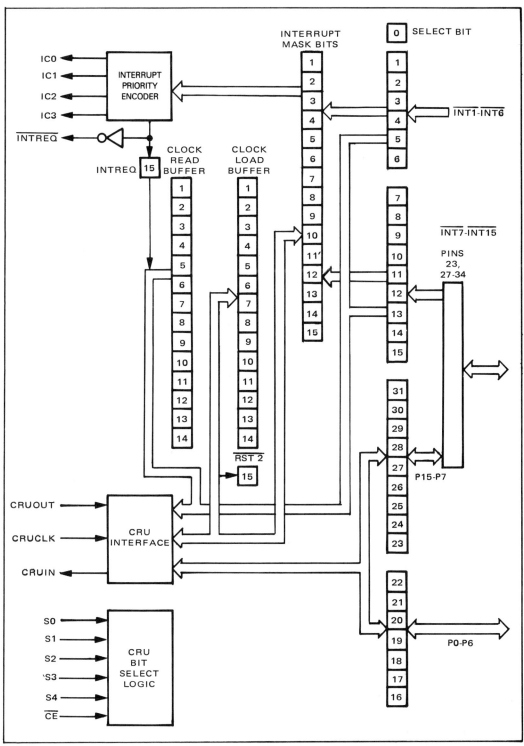

Figure 3-26. TMS 9901 PSI General Data Flows and CRU Bit Assignments

From the programmer's viewpoint, a TMS 9901 looks like 32 contiguous CRU bits. Thus, you will access any part of a TMS 9901 device's logic using CRU input and output instructions.

As you read through the TMS 9901 description that follows, you should bear in mind the power of multi-bit CRU load and store instructions as they apply to TMS 9901 architecture. A single instruction transferring an appropriate bit pattern can frequently perform multiple control and data transfer operations.

The manner in which CRU bits are used by the TMS 9901 is not straightforward. This is because CRU bits share functions and pins. Functions and pins are shared in different ways.

Let us first look at pin connections. CRU bits 1-6 connect to pins $\overline{INT1}$ - $\overline{INT6}$; thus, in interrupt mode each of these CRU bits has its own dedicated input pin.

CRU bits 7-15 share nine input or output pins with CRU bits 23-31. CRU bits share pins as follows:

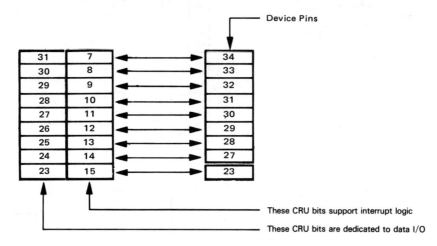

Each of the CRU bits shown above shares a pin with another CRU bit. That is to say, within the illustrated CRU address range, there are two CRU bits which will access the same pin, although each CRU bit performs a different operation. Thus you use the same pin in one of two different ways, using a bit address to select one operation. This may be illustrated as follows:

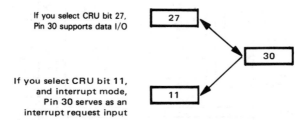

CRU bits 16-22 connect to parallel I/O pins. These bit addresses are not shared with any other TMS 9901 functions.

CRU bit 0 is a select bit that is not connected to any pin. A 1 written into this bit causes bits 1-15 to support real-time clock logic. A 0 written into CRU bit 0 selects interrupt logic. When CRU clock logic is selected, bits 1-14 function as two 14-bit real-time Clock Buffer registers — one a read-only register, the other write-only. Real-time clock logic is separate from, and operates simultaneously with, and/or parallel I/O logic. That is to say, the process of selecting real-time clock logic does not disable any other logic. The select bit merely chooses which registers CRU addresses will access, rather than enabling or disabling any operations.

TMS 9901 PSI INTERRUPT LOGIC

The easiest place to start understanding the TMS 9901 is at its interrupt logic.

External logic can input data to CRU bits 1-15 via their connected pins. These input data signals will be interpreted as interrupt requests if interrupts are enabled. If interrupts are disabled, then these CRU bits act simply as data input.

You access interrupt logic through the CRU when the select bit, CRU bit 0, contains a 0.

CRU bit addresses 1-15 each access separate read-only and write-only locations. The read-only location stores the signal level input at the attached pin. The write-only location accesses an interrupt mask bit. This may be illustrated as follows:

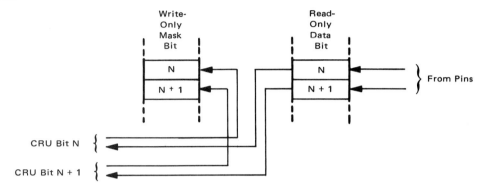

Signals arriving at pins connected to CRU bits 1-15 are immediately reflected by CRU bit contents:

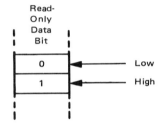

A low level (that is, a 0 bit) is interpreted as an interrupt request. The interrupt request is passed on to the mask bit. If the mask bit contains 1, the interrupt is enabled and the interrupt request is passed on:

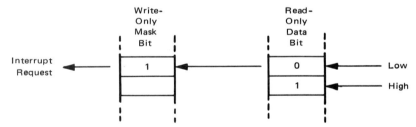

If the mask bit is 0, the interrupt request is disabled and therefore denied:

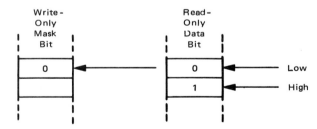

Quite apart from interrupt logic, the CPU can at any time read the contents of one or more CRU bits in the address range 1-15. Here are some instructions that may access CRU bits 1-15 in various ways:

```
LI      R12,PSI+1    LOAD CRU BASE ADDRESS INTO R12
LI      R1,MASK      LOAD INTERRUPT MASK BITS INTO R1
LDCR    R1,15        OUTPUT TO WRITE-ONLY MASK LOCATIONS
-
-
-

STCR    R2,15        INPUT CRU BITS 1 THROUGH 15 AS DATA TO R2
-
-
-
```

For some randomly selected data levels, CRU bits 1-15 may be illustrated as follows:

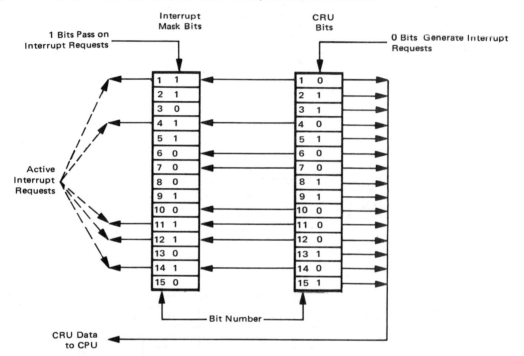

If one or more CRU bit's interrupt requests are low, and the corresponding mask bit is 1, then interrupt priority encoder logic outputs INTREQ low. Simultaneously, the level of the active interrupt request which has highest priority is identified via IC0 - IC3.

INT1, input to CRU bit 1, has highest priority;
INT15, input to CRU bit 15, has lowest priority.

The levels at IC0 - IC3 are maintained until the interrupt request signal is removed at the external pin, or the interrupt mask bit for the level is reset to 0.

TMS 9901 PSI DATA INPUT AND OUTPUT

You can use CRU I/O instructions to input, output, or test external data at CRU bits 16-31. Data is output from the CPU to the TMS 9901 via CRUOUT; it is input from the TMS 9901 to the CPU via CRUIN. Bits are addressed via S0 - S4, as we have already described.

Following a reset, pins connected to CRU bits 16-31 are in input mode. In this mode, external logic can assert high or low levels at connected pins, in which case one or two CRU bits will be affected: a signal input to P0 - P6 will generate data in CRU bits 16-22; if interrupt mode is selected (by a 0 in CRU bit 0), a signal input to INT7/P15-INT15/P7 will generate data in two CRU bits, one in the CRU bit range 7-15, the other in CRU bit range 31-23. **In interrupt mode, if the CPU inputs data from CRU bits 7-15 or 31-23, then it will input the same data, but in reverse order.** This may be illustrated as follows:

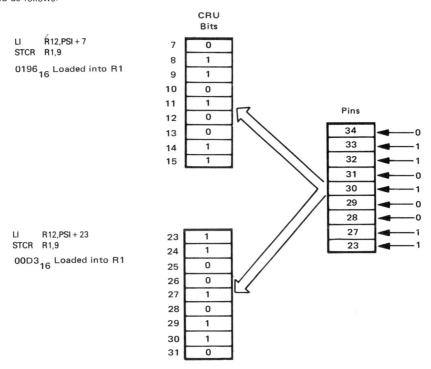

Note that, as in all CRU transfers, the first CRU bit transferred goes to the least significant bit position of the destination register.

As soon as the CPU outputs data to any bit capable of supporting data output, the I/O logic associated with this bit is put into output mode. In this mode, a pin will output a voltage level reflecting data in the corresponding CRU bit. External logic cannot input data to a CRU bit that is in output mode; in fact, driving input currents into an output pin may damage the TMS 9901.

Once a CRU bit has been placed in output mode, it remains in output mode until the TMS 9901 is reset. That is to say, you cannot selectively return CRU bits from output mode to input mode. However, you can always read output bits back to the CPU; that is, **although external logic must never attempt to input to a pin that is in output mode, the CPU can always read the contents of any I/O bit, whether it is an input or an output.**

You cannot output data via CRU bits 7-15, even though these bits are connected to the same pins as CRU bits 31-23. When you output data to CRU bits 7-15, the data is routed to one of two write-only locations, depending on the contents of CRU bit 0: if the select bit is 0, the data goes to interrupt mask bits 7-15; if clock mode is selected (CRU bit 0 contains 1), the data goes to the Clock Load Buffer register (bits 7-14) and $\overline{RST2}$ (bit 15).

In interrupt mode you can input external data from CRU bits 1-6. Once again, you cannot output data via these CRU bit addresses, since any data output will be routed to corresponding interrupt mask bits or Clock Load Buffer bits.

TMS 9901 REAL-TIME CLOCK LOGIC

If you write a 1 into CRU bit 0 of a TMS 9901 device, then CRU bits 1-14 are used as two 14-bit Clock buffers, which may be illustrated as follows:

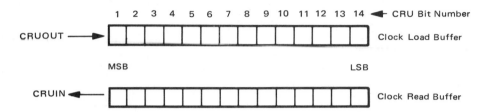

Besides these two buffers, **real-time Clock logic contains a decrementing register which we call the Clock Counter register.** The CPU loads the Clock Counter register via the Clock Load Buffer, and reads the Counter contents via the Clock Read Buffer. We illustrate this in the following way:

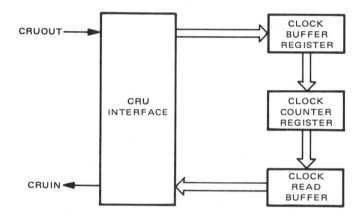

The Clock Counter register decrements continuously as long as the TMS 9901 is powered up. This will cause no problems as long as the clock interrupt is disabled.

When you write any non-zero value into the Clock Load Buffer (CRU bits 1-14), the Clock Counter register starts decrementing from that value. A decrement occurs once every 64 Φ clock pulses. Thus, with a 3 MHz clock, a decrement occurs once every 21.3 microseconds. **When the CRU Clock Counter register decrements to 0, an interrupt request is generated, the previously output starting value is reloaded, and the clock starts to decrement again.** Thus, with a 21.3-microsecond time interval between decrements, the maximum time interval between interrupt requests will be 249 milliseconds.

An enabled clock interrupt request causes $\overline{\text{INTREQ}}$ to be output low, together with a level 3 interrupt identified via IC0 - IC3. That is to say, the $\overline{\text{INT3}}$ external interrupt and the Clock logic share the same interrupt level and interrupt mask bit. In clock mode, CRU bit 15 is used to record the state of the $\overline{\text{INTREQ}}$ signal. Thus, if interrupt requests are disabled, the CPU program can check for a time-out by testing the level at CRU bit 15. This bit will be low if no time-out has occurred, and it will be high if a time-out has occurred; thus this bit is the complement of $\overline{\text{INTREQ}}$.

Following a CRU real-time clock interrupt request, you must write into interrupt mask bit 3 in order to clear the interrupt request. You can write a 0 or a 1 into the interrupt mask bit. Normally, you will write a 1 in order to keep interrupts enabled. Writing a 0 will clear any active real-time clock interrupt request, and will simultaneously disable further real-time clock interrupt requests.

The Clock Read Buffer register contents do not change as long as the TMS 9901 is in clock mode. This characteristic insures that the Clock Read Buffer will hold a stable value while the CPU is reading it — even though the Clock Counter may decrement during the read operation.

Either of the following two events will cause the Clock Counter contents to transfer to the Clock Read Buffer:

• The $\overline{\Phi}$ pulse which causes the Clock Counter to decrement.

• An exit from clock mode.

Thus, the Clock Read Buffer register is updated whenever the TMS 9901 leaves clock mode, and every time the Clock Counter decrements outside of clock mode.

Beware — even if CRU bit 0 contains a 1, the TMS 9901 will exit clock mode for as long as it sees a 1 on select line S0; this will happen whether or not $\overline{CE}$ is active. Thus **the Clock Read Buffer will not hold the same value indefinitely just because the TMS 9901 select bit is set.** The PSI will leave clock mode whenever the CPU reads to or writes from CRU bits 16-31, or if any device accesses a memory address with a 1 on the address line connected to S0 (A4 in a TMS 9900 system).

The logic controlling clock mode and the Clock Read Buffer may be illustrated as follows:

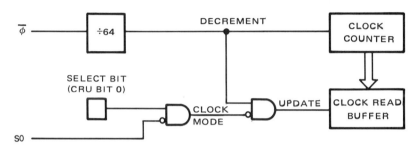

This logic summarizes our discussion above. There are two important things to note about clock mode and Clock Read Buffer update. First, you cannot inadvertently exit clock mode while you are reading the Clock Read Buffer, since you access it as CRU bits 1-14. Second, you cannot enter clock mode solely by accessing CRU bits 0-15; S0 changes clock mode only when the select bit is 1 (clock mode selected).

In order to read the most recent Clock Counter value, you must do two things:

• **Exit clock mode** so the Clock Read Buffer will receive the current Clock Counter contents.

• **Enter clock mode** so the Clock Read Buffer will be stable during the read itself.

Here is the appropriate instruction sequence:

```
LI      R12,PSI+1   LOAD PSI CRU BASE ADDRESS
SBZ     -1          EXIT CLOCK MODE TO UPDATE READ BUFFER
SBO     -1          ENTER CLOCK MODE TO STABILIZE READ BUFFER
STCR    R1,14       READ 14-BIT CLOCK READ BUFFER
```

TMS 9901 RESET LOGIC

You can reset a TMS 9901 in one of two ways:

1) By inputting a low signal at $\overline{RST1}$.

2) By using a programmed reset via $\overline{RST2}$, a CRU bit.

In order to use $\overline{RST1}$, a low level must be input at this pin for at least two clock periods.

You can reset the TMS 9901 under program control only when clock mode is selected (CRU bit 0 is 0). At this time, writing a 0 to CRU bit 15 ($\overline{RST2}$) causes the device to be reset. Thus, the following instruction sequence causes a TMS 9901 device reset:

```
LI      R12,PSI     LOAD PSI CRU BASE ADDRESS
SBO     0           ENTER CLOCK MODE
SBZ     15          RESET PSI
```

When the TMS 9901 is reset, the $\overline{INTREQ}$ signal is output high, IC0 through IC3 are output low, all interrupt requests are disabled, and all I/O CRU bits are placed in input mode.

THE TMS9902 ASYNCHRONOUS COMMUNICATIONS CONTROLLER

The TMS9902 microprocessor family includes two serial I/O parts. The TMS9902 is a simple, asynchronous communications device; the TMS9903 is a more powerful, recently introduced multifunction device. Both of these parts are peculiar to the TMS9900 since they communicate with the CPU via its CRU logic. The two parts are also pin-compatible; that is, the same 20-pin socket can hold either the TMS9902 (an 18-pin part) or the TMS9903.

The TMS9902, which we are about to describe, **offers asynchronous I/O capabilities comparable with those of parts which we describe in Volume 3. The TMS9902 lacks some features which other parts offer:**

1) There are no external clocking signals for received or transmitted data. Receive and transmit rates are computed by logic internal to the TMS9902.

2) There is a single interrupt request which has no accompanying status output lines. Thus interrupt service routines must interrogate status in order to correctly service the interrupt.

3) The TMS9902 has only three Modem control lines and no other lines for handshaking with peripheral logic.

One advantage of the TMS9902 is that it occupies very little board space. It is an 18-pin part, the smallest serial I/O controller on the market. It requires less surrounding logic because it uses the system clock for its time base, and because it provides almost no external status or handshake lines.

Another advantage of the TMS9902, when compared to other serial I/O parts, is the presence of real-time clock logic. Anyone who has worked with serial I/O logic will appreciate the ability to generate interrupt requests at fixed time intervals.

The TMS9902 is fabricated using NMOS technology. It is packaged as an 18-pin DIP and requires a single +5V power supply. All signals are TTL-level compatible.

TMS9902 ACC PINS AND SIGNAL ASSIGNMENTS

TMS9902 pins and signal assignments are illustrated in Figure 3-27. These signal assignments are the same as those of pins 1 through 9 and 12 through 20 of the TMS9903.

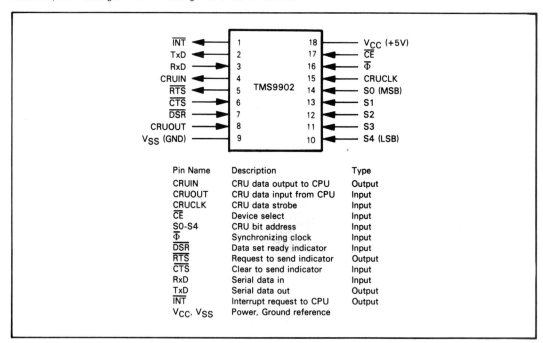

Pin Name	Description	Type
CRUIN	CRU data output to CPU	Output
CRUOUT	CRU data input from CPU	Input
CRUCLK	CRU data strobe	Input
$\overline{CE}$	Device select	Input
S0-S4	CRU bit address	Input
$\overline{\Phi}$	Synchronizing clock	Input
$\overline{DSR}$	Data set ready indicator	Input
$\overline{RTS}$	Request to send indicator	Output
$\overline{CTS}$	Clear to send indicator	Input
RxD	Serial data in	Input
TxD	Serial data out	Output
$\overline{INT}$	Interrupt request to CPU	Output
V_{CC}, V_{SS}	Power, Ground reference	

Figure 3-27. TMS9902 Asynchronous Communications Controller Pins and Signal Assignments

Table 3-9. TMS9902 Control and Status Register Bit Interpretations

CONTROL REGISTER (WRITE)		CRU/REGISTER BIT NUMBER	STATUS REGISTER (READ)
Device Reset (write 1 or 0)		31	Any interrupt pending*
-		30	One or more of control bits 17, 14, 13, 12, or 11 set to 1*
-		29	$\overline{DSR}$ or $\overline{CTS}$ input level change detected. Reset by writing 1 or 0 to CRU bit 21.
-		28	Complement of $\overline{CTS}$ input level
-		27	Complement of $\overline{DSR}$ input level
-		26	Complement of $\overline{RTS}$ output level
-		25	Timer time out*. Reset by writing 1 or 0 to CRU bit 20.
-		24	Timer overrun error*. Reset by writing 1 or 0 to CRU bit 20.
-		23	Transmit Shift register empty*. Automatic reset.
-		22	Transmit buffer empty*. Reset by writing to high-order Transmit buffer bit.
Enable interrupts on $\overline{DSR}$ or $\overline{CTS}$ input level change (1 = enable, 0 = disable)		21	Receive buffer loaded*. Reset by writing 1 or 0 to CRU bit 18.
Enable timer interrupts (1 = enable, 0 = disable)		20	$\overline{DSR}$ or $\overline{CTS}$ input level change interrupt pending*. Reset by writing 1 or 0 to CRU bit 21.
Enable transmitter interrupts (1 = enable, 0 = disable)		19	Timer interrupt pending*. Reset by writing 1 or 0 to CRU bit 20.
Enable receive interrupts (1 = enable, 0 = disable)		18	—
Transmit Break (1 = enable, 0 = disable)		17	Transmit interrupt pending*. Reset either by writing 0 to CRU bit 19 or by writing to high-order Transmit buffer bit.
Enable transmit logic (Complement of $\overline{RTS}$ output)		16	Receive interrupt pending*. Reset by writing 1 or 0 to CRU bit 18.
Test mode select (1 = Test mode, 0 = normal operation)		15	RxD input level
Write to Parameter register		14	Receive start bit detected*. Reset automatically at end of received character.
Write to Timer register		13	Receive first data bit detected*. Reset automatically at end of received character.
Write to Receive Data Rate register		12	Receive framing error detected*. Reset automatically by error free received character.
Write to Transmit Data Rate register		11	Receive overrun error detected*. Reset automatically by error-free received character.
		10	Receive parity error detected.* Reset automatically by error-free received character.
		9	Any receive error detected.* Reset automatically when Status register bits 12, 11, and 10 are all 0.
Receive Data Rate register or Transmit Data Rate register	Parameter register, Timer register, or Transmit buffer	8	
		7	
		6	
		5	
		4	
		3	
		2	
		1	
		0	

*1 = "true" condition. 0 = "false" condition.

Signals that connect the TMS9902 to a TMS9900 series microprocessor include the three CRU signals CRUIN, CRUOUT, and CRUCLK, together with device select logic signals $\overline{CE}$ and S0-S4. The TMS9902 uses these signals exactly as described for the TMS9901. $\overline{CE}$ must be low for the TMS9902 to be selected; if the TMS9902 is selected, then data transfers occur via the CRUIN or CRUOUT lines. S0-S4 identify the CRU bit within the selected TMS9902. Table 3-9 summarizes the way in which the TMS9902 assigns its 32 CRU bit addresses for read and write operations.

$\overline{DSR}$, $\overline{RTS}$, and $\overline{CTS}$ are standard handshaking control signals for communications devices.

$\overline{DSR}$ is a general purpose input signal; its level is reported in Status register bit 27. You can program $\overline{DSR}$ to generate an interrupt request when it makes a high-to-low or low-to-high transition. However, $\overline{DSR}$ plays no part in enabling either transmit or receive logic.

The TMS9902 outputs $\overline{RTS}$ low while transmit logic is enabled. But the transmitter will not actually start transmitting data until $\overline{CTS}$ is input low.

In a standard asynchronous protocol system, TMS9902 transmit logic will output $\overline{RTS}$ low and sometime later receive a low $\overline{CTS}$ input — at which time it will actually start transmitting data. But if TMS9902 transmit logic finds $\overline{CTS}$ low when it outputs $\overline{RTS}$ low, it will start transmitting immediately.

For a discussion of Modem handshaking control signals, see Volume 1, Chapter 5.

Serial data is input via RxD and output via TxD. External logic does not provide signals that clock the serial input or output data. Instead, the $\overline{\Phi}$ synchronizing clock input signal is used to derive data transmit or receive rates. Usually, $\overline{\Phi}$ will be the TIM9904 clock output $\overline{\Phi 3}$ (the complement of CPU clock $\Phi 3$). However, you may use any clock signal that satisfies the timing requirements given in the TMS9902 data sheet at the end of this chapter.

TMS9902 DATA TRANSFER AND CONTROL

The various addressable locations within the TMS9902 are summarized in Figure 3-28.

When you write to CRU bits 31 through 11 you will always access the Control register; when you read these bits you will access the Status register. CRU bits 10 and 9 are also read-only status flags.

CRU bits 0 through 7, on a read, always access the Receive buffer; but via CRU bits 0 through 10 you can send data to a variety of write-only locations.

The Control register contains four address bits, each of which corresponds to one of the write-only locations. When an address bit is set to 1, the associated write-only register will receive data output via CRU bits 0 through 10. If more than one write-only location is selected, then the select priorities shown in Table 3-10 apply. The Transmit Buffer is selected when all four address bits contain 0. If any address bit is set to 1, Status register bit 30 will also contain 1.

TMS9902
REGISTER
ADDRESSING

When you write to the high-order (highest numbered) bit of the Parameter register, the Timer register, or the Receive Rate register, you automatically reset that location's address bit in the Control register.

Table 3-10. TMS9902 Write-Only Register Select Scheme

CRU Output Bit				Addressed Location	CRU Bits in Location
14	13	12	11		
1	X	X	X	Parameter register	7-0
0	1	X	X	Timer register	7-0
0	0	1	X*	Receive Rate register	10-0
0	0	X*	1	Transmit Rate register	10-0
0	0	0	0	Transmit buffer	7-0

"X" means "does not matter"
* If both bits 11 and 12 are set to 1, data will be written to both Rate registers at the same time.

Following a device reset, all write-only location address bits in the Control register are set to 1. This allows you to write data to registers in the priority order shown in Table 3-10 during the device initialization process, without having to reset individual address bits. Thus the initialization process will consist of these steps:

TMS9902 DEVICE
INITIALIZATION

1) Reset the TMS9902 by writing to Control register bit 31.

2) Write to the Parameter register.

3) Write to the Interval Timer register.

4) Write to the Receive Data Rate and Transmit Data Rate registers.

5) Write to the Control register and Transmit buffer.

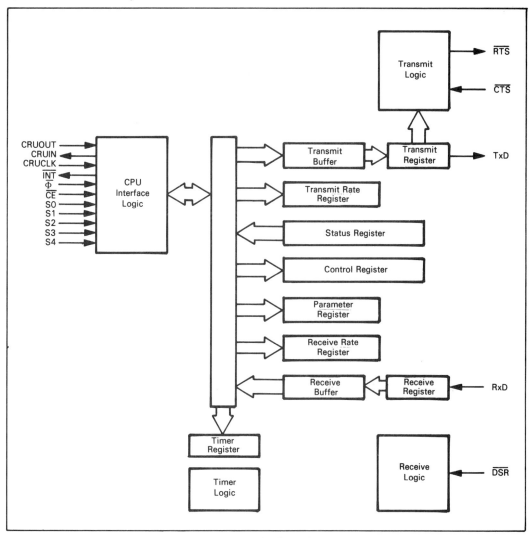

Figure 3-28. TMS9902 Functional Logic

Texas Instruments' literature suggests an initialization instruction sequence such as the following:

```
LI      R12,CRUBS    INITIALIZE CRU BASE ADDRESS IN R12
SBO     31           RESET COMMAND
LDCR    @CNTRL,8     LOAD PARAMETER AND RESET BIT 14
LDCR    @INTVL,8     LOAD INTERVAL AND RESET BIT 13
LDCR    @RDR,11      LOAD RECEIVE RATE AND RESET BIT 12
LDCR    @XDR,12      LOAD TRANSMIT RATE AND RESET BIT 11
-
-
-
```

In the sequence above, CRUBS represents the base address for the 32 CRU bits in the TMS9902. Four memory locations — labeled CNTRL, INTVL, RDR, and XDR — hold the values to be loaded into the write-only locations. Since CRU bit 11 is not reset automatically, the instruction which writes to the Transmit Data Rate register writes 12 bits, the high-order bit being a 0 for CRU bit 11.

Let us now examine Control register bits in detail.

Control register bits may be divided into interrupt enable/disable bits, write-only location address bits, the reset control, and the test mode control.

TMS9902
CONTROL
REGISTER

The test mode control (bit 15) is usually left at 0; this causes normal operations to occur. **When you set the test mode control bit to 1, $\overline{RTS}$ is internally connected to $\overline{CTS}$ and RxD is internally connected to TxD.** Also, $\overline{DSR}$ is held low internally and the interval timer operates at 32 times its normal rate. You will operate the TMS9902 in this condition only when testing its logic.

TMS9902
TEST MODE

You reset the TMS9902 by writing either a 0 or a 1 to Control register bit 31.

You will usually begin every event sequence with a Reset. The following instructions constitute TMS9902 resets:

TMS9902
RESET

```
    LI      R12,ACC          LI      R12,ACC
    SBO     31        or     SBZ     31
```

ACC is a label identifying CRU bit 0 (the CRU base address) for the TMS9902.

When the TMS9902 is reset, the following events occur:

1) All interrupts are disabled.

2) $\overline{RTS}$ is output high; this is the inactive state for $\overline{RTS}$.

3) Control register bits 11, 12, 13, and 14 are set to 1. All other Control register bits are reset to 0.

The TMS9902 should not be accessed for a minimum of eleven $\overline{\Phi}$ clock cycles following the reset command.

There are four interrupt enable control bits. They enable interrupts when set to 1 and disable interrupts when reset to 0.

TMS9902
INTERRUPT
ENABLE

Control bit 21 enables $\overline{CTS}$ and $\overline{DSR}$ input signal level change interrupt requests.

Control bit 20 enables timer time out interrupt requests.

Control bit 19 enables Transmit buffer empty interrupt requests.

Control bit 18 enables Receive buffer full interrupt requests.

In each case a Status register bit is set to identify the condition that can generate an interrupt request. But the interrupt will not actually be requested unless the associated interrupt enable control bit has been set to 1.

You acknowledge any interrupt other than a transmitter interrupt by writing to the interrupt's enable control bit. To acknowledge an interrupt and leave it enabled, rewrite a 1 to the interrupt enable control bit. To acknowledge an interrupt and then disable it, write a 0 to the interrupt enable control bit. But remember, you must write either a 0 or a 1 to the interrupt enable control bit, since this is the mechanism used to reset the status flags that identify the interrupting condition.

TMS9902
INTERRUPT
ACKNOWLEDGE

You acknowledge a transmitter interrupt by writing to bit 7 of the Transmit buffer. If you write a 0 to CRU bit 19, you will disable the interrupt, but you will not reset the status flag which was set by the emptying of the Transmit buffer.

Control register bits 16 and 17 directly control two TMS9902 operations.

Control register bit 16 is the complement of the $\overline{RTS}$ output. You must write a 1 to this bit in order to set $\overline{RTS}$ low. In order to enable transmit logic, $\overline{RTS}$ must be output low while $\overline{CTS}$ is being input low. You must leave $\overline{RTS}$ low while the transmitter is active. To disable the transmitter you raise $\overline{RTS}$ high again by writing 0 to Control register bit 16; if transmit logic is part way through transmitting a character when you write a 0 to Control register bit 16, then it will complete transmitting the character — and the character in the Transmit buffer, if the buffer is full — before outputting $\overline{RTS}$ high.

Transmit break logic is controlled via Control register bit 17. When you set this bit to 1, a break (continuous low output) will be transmitted following the next underrun (that is, when both the Transmit register and Transmit buffer are empty). You must end the break by writing a 0 to Control register bit 17 before you can restart transmitting by writing new data to the Transmit buffer. If you leave Control register bit 17 reset to 0, then following an underrun the transmitter will mark (output a continuously high signal). You can end the mark at any time, and start transmitting a new message, by writing fresh data to the Transmit buffer.

TMS9902
BREAK
LOGIC

When the break control bit is set to 1, Status register bit 30 will also contain a 1.

Let us now examine Status register bits; they may be grouped as follows:

1) Signal level indicators
2) Transmit operation status
3) Receive operation status
4) Timer logic
5) Interrupt logic

TMS9902 STATUS REGISTER

Status register bits 27 and 28 report the complement of the $\overline{\text{DSR}}$ and $\overline{\text{CTS}}$ input signal levels. Bit 26 reports the complement of the $\overline{\text{RTS}}$ output signal level.

When the $\overline{\text{DSR}}$ or $\overline{\text{CTS}}$ input changes level, bit 29 is set. You reset bit 29 by writing to Control register bit 21.

There are three transmit logic status bits. **Bit 22 is set when the Transmit buffer is empty.** The bit is reset when you next write data to the Transmit buffer. **Bit 23 is set when the Transmit Shift register is empty;** this is an underrun condition. Following an underrun, a break or a mark will be transmitted, depending on the level of Control register bit 17. Bit 30 of the Status register contains a 1 if any of the following Control register bits are set to 1:

TMS9902 TRANSMITTER STATUS

• Bit 17, the break control bit
• Bits 14, 13, 12, and 11, the write-only location address bits

Thus Status register bit 30 will be set to 1 whenever Transmit buffer loading is disabled.

For receive logic, bit 21 is set when the Receive buffer is full. The CPU resets this bit by writing to bit 18 of the Control register; usually the program will read the contents of the Receive buffer before resetting the flag bit.

TMS9902 RECEIVER STATUS

RxD, the serial data input line level, **is reported at Status register bit 15.**

The start of each received character is identified by Status register bits 14 and 13. **When the start bit has been detected, Status register bit 14 is set. One bit time later, when the first data bit is being detected, Status register bit 13 is set.** These two bits remain set until the end of the character. They are reset when the last stop bit has been detected.

Framing, overrun, and parity errors are reported by Status register bits 12, 11, and 10, respectively. These error status bits, once set, remain set until an error-free character is loaded into the Receive buffer.

If one or more of the three receive error conditions exist, then Status register bit 9 is set.

There are two timer status bits. **Whenever the timer times out, Status register bit 25 is set to 1.** This bit must be reset by writing 0 or 1 to Control register bit 20. If you do not do so before the next time out, then **Status register bit 24 will be set, indicating a timer error.** The timer error is also cleared by writing 0 or 1 to Control register bit 20.

TMS9902 TIMER STATUS

The four interrupt generating conditions have associated status bits which are set following an interrupt request.

If the $\overline{\text{DSR}}$ or $\overline{\text{CTS}}$ input signal changes level, and the interrupt logic has been enabled, then Status register bit 20 is set at the time that an interrupt request is generated.

TMS9902 INTERRUPT STATUS

If a time out occurs and timer interrupts have been enabled, then Status register bit 19 is set at the time an interrupt request occurs.

When the Transmit buffer becomes empty, if transmitter interrupts have been enabled, then Status register bit 17 is set at the time an interrupt request occurs.

When the Receive buffer is full, if receive interrupts have been enabled, then Status register bit 16 is set at the time a receiver interrupt request is generated.

If one or more of these interrupt requests are active, then Status register bit 31 is set.

Interrupt status bits remain set until you reset either the status bit for the interrupting condition, or its interrupt enable bit in the Control register. In most cases, writing to the enable bit resets the status bit.

For a Modem signal interrupt you must write to Control register bit 21 in order to acknowledge the interrupt, thus resetting the two Status register bits.

For a timer interrupt you must write to Control register bit 20 to reset the interrupt.

For a Transmit buffer empty interrupt you must write new data to the Transmit buffer in order to acknowledge the interrupt; specifically, you must write to bit 7 of the Transmit buffer.

For a Receive buffer full interrupt, you must write to Control register bit 18 in order to acknowledge the interrupt.

Let us now examine Parameter register contents.

After resetting the TMS9902, the next step is to identify subsequent operations by loading appropriate data into the Parameter register. Parameter register bits are interpreted as follows:

TMS9902
PARAMETER
REGISTER

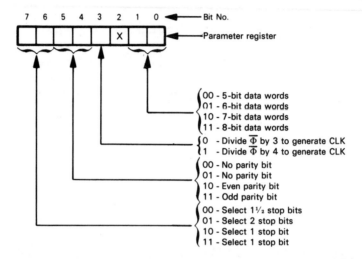

The options presented by the Parameter register, as illustrated above, are self-evident, with the exception of Parameter register bit 3. This bit is used to generate an internal clock signal, CLK. Depending on the setting of Parameter register bit 3, the CLK frequency will be $\overline{\Phi}/3$ or $\overline{\Phi}/4$. CLK is then used to specify the time interval between bit sampling for serial data input or output, as well as the interval timer rate. The frequency of CLK should not be greater than 1.1 MHz; therefore if $\overline{\Phi}$ is faster than 3.3 MHz, Parameter register bit 3 should be set to 1.

TMS9902 INTERNAL
CLOCK SIGNAL

TRANSMIT AND
RECEIVE DATA
RATE REGISTERS

After loading appropriate data into the Parameter register, you must load the Transmit and Receive Data Rate registers in order to specify the time interval that will separate bit sampling. Data Rate register contents are interpreted as follows:

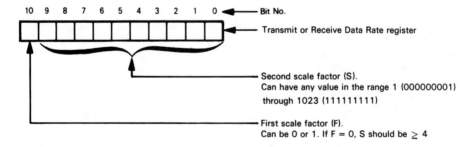

The time interval separating serial bits transmitted or received is given by the equation:

$$t_{CLK} \times 2 \times 8^F \times S$$

For example, suppose the Receive Data Rate register contains 11000111000. $S = 568_{10}$ and $F = 1$:

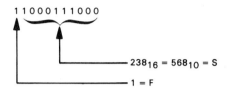

$$238_{16} = 568_{10} = S$$
$$1 = F$$

If $CLK = \overline{\Phi}/3$, and $\overline{\Phi} = 3$ MHz, then the serial data transfer rate will be:

$$(1 \times 10^6) \div (2 \times 8 \times 568) = 110.04 \text{ bits per second}$$

If $F = 0$, then the serial data transfer rate becomes:

$$(1 \times 10^6) \div (2 \times 8 \times 568) = 880.28 \text{ bits per second}$$

Table 3-11 shows sample Data Rate register values for standard Baud rates. The assumed $\overline{\Phi}$ frequency produces very precise Baud rates; it is also within the recommended operating range of TMS9900 series parts.

Table 3-11. Example of Data Rate Register Contents
for Standard Baud Rates

Frequency $\overline{\Phi}$ = 3.168 MHz Frequency CLK = $\overline{\Phi}$ ÷ 3 = 1.056 MHz			
Data Rate Register Contents			Data Rate in Bits per Second
Decimal		Hexadecimal	
F	S		
0	55	037	9600
0	110	06E	4800
0	220	0DC	2400
0	440	1B8	1200
0	880	370	600
1	220	4DC	300
1	440	5B8	150
1	600	658	110
1	880	770	75
Date Rate = CLK ÷ (2 x 8^F x S)			

It is not strictly necessary to have data rates as precise as those we have shown in Table 3-11.

The devices which receive data from the TMS9902 will determine how precise the transmit rate must be.

TMS9902 Receive Logic resynchronizes itself with the beginning of each incoming character. It does this by starting its bit-time count at a high-to-low transition of RxD. When the TMS9902 has counted half a bit-time, it samples RxD; if the line is still low, Receive logic assumes a valid start bit is present. It then samples the line at single-bit-time intervals after the first sample point, until a full character has been received:

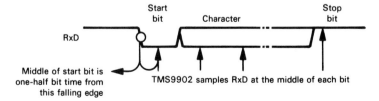

3-89

Because of this resynchronization, no skew errors will occur as long as the transmitted bit rate is within 4% of the TMS9902 Receive data rate.

TMS9902 TRANSMIT OPERATIONS

Let us now examine a serial data transmit event sequence as illustrated in Figure 3-29.

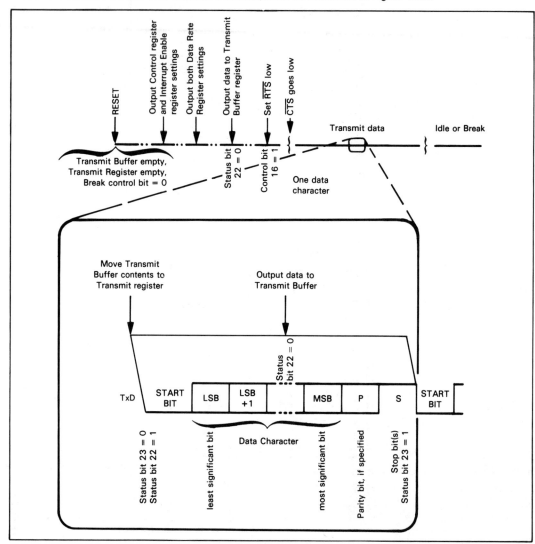

Figure 3-29. TMS9902 Character Transmit Event Sequence

TMS9902
SERIAL
TRANSMIT
EVENT
SEQUENCE

In this example, all operations will begin with a Reset. Remember, you reset the TMS9902 by writing a 0 or 1 to CRU bit 31.

Next, output appropriate codes to the Control and Parameter registers and enable appropriate interrupts.

Output Data Rate register settings.

Output the first character to the Transmit Buffer register.

Transmit logic has now been initialized. You begin actual data transmission by setting $\overline{RTS}$ low. An appropriate initialization instruction sequence was given earlier.

Setting $\overline{RTS}$ low enables transmit logic within the TMS9902, but actual data transmission does not begin until external logic inputs $\overline{CTS}$ low. If $\overline{CTS}$ is already low when $\overline{RTS}$ is reset low, then data transmission will begin as soon as $\overline{RTS}$ is output low.

When a character is transmitted, the Transmit buffer contents are moved to the Transmit register, at which time Status register bit 22 is set. If transmit interrupt logic has been enabled, an interrupt request will occur at this time and Status register bit 17 will be set.

The character is transmitted as illustrated in Figure 3-29; options are specified in the Parameter register. As soon as the character's stop bit (or bits) has been transmitted, transmission of the next data character begins, provided the CPU has by this time loaded the next data character into the Transmit buffer. The CPU will normally have plenty of time to reload the Transmit buffer, since it takes a long time, in terms of instruction execution times, to transmit a character.

Note that you must write to bit 7 of the Transmit buffer in order to reset the Transmit buffer empty flag. Thus even though the character length is less than 8 bits, you will always write 8 bits to the Transmit buffer. You right-adjust Transmit buffer characters; that is, bit 0 of the Transmit buffer is always the least significant bit of the character.

If transmit interrupts have been enabled, an interrupt request will occur when Status register bit 22 is set. The CPU will respond to the interrupt request by interrogating Status register bits to identify the nature of the interrupt. Upon detecting a 1 in bit 17, the CPU will output another data character. If transmit interrupt logic has not been enabled, then the CPU must periodically poll the Status register and output the next data character upon detecting bit 22 set to 1.

If the Transmit buffer is empty at the end of a data character transfer, then the TMS9902 may transmit a Break (if Control register bit 17 is 1), or it may terminate operations and go into an idle state (if Control register bit 17 is 0).	**TMS9902 BREAK**

The TMS9902 will transmit a Break if $\overline{CTS}$ is still low and Control register bit 17 is high. **A Break is a continuous low level output via TxD.** External logic interprets a Break as a signal indicating temporary suspension of data transfer.

Break logic inhibits data transfers to the Transmit buffer. You must terminate a Break by resetting Control register bit 17 to 0, then loading the next data character into the Transmit buffer.

TMS9902 transmit logic will enter an idle state if $\overline{CTS}$ is input high by external logic or if $\overline{CTS}$ is input low, but no new data is ready to transmit and break logic is off. During this idle state TxD will be held high (marking).

The level of the $\overline{RTS}$ output is not affected by a change in the $\overline{CTS}$ input level.

If $\overline{CTS}$ goes high during a transmit operation and you leave $\overline{RTS}$ output low, then as soon as $\overline{CTS}$ goes low again the transmitter will be re-enabled; but if you output $\overline{RTS}$ high by writing 0 to Control register bit 16, then the $\overline{CTS}$ input will be ignored. In order to re-enable transmit logic you must output 1 to Control register bit 16, again setting $\overline{RTS}$ low. If $\overline{CTS}$ is low at this time, transmission will begin immediately; otherwise, transmission will begin as soon as $\overline{CTS}$ is input low — after $\overline{RTS}$ has again been output low. This may be illustrated as follows:

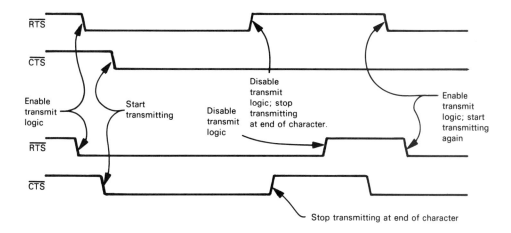

Let us now look at receive logic. Figure 3-30 illustrates the receive event sequence.

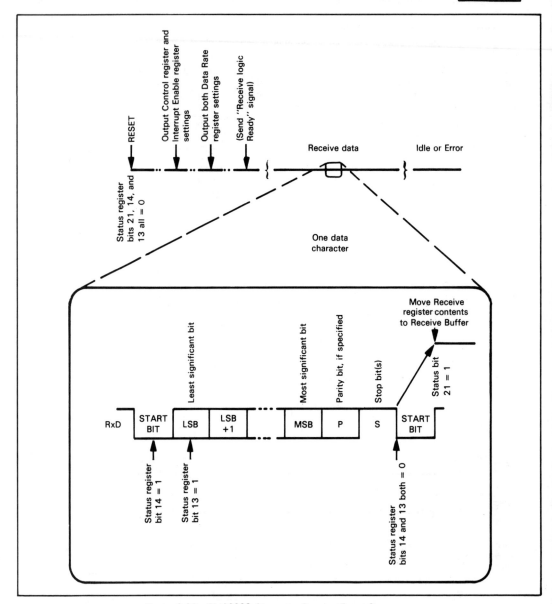

Figure 3-30. TMS9902 Character Receive Event Sequence

TMS9902 RECEIVE OPERATIONS

As soon as the TMS9902 is reset, receive logic is enabled.

The TMS9902 outputs no "ready to receive" signal to external logic telling it when to start transmitting data to the TMS9902. You must create some such signal, since the Parameter register, interrupt flags, and Data Rate register must be initialized before external logic starts to input data; otherwise, the TMS9902 will not know how to interpret the serial data input. **You have three options:**

1) You could use a CRU data bit (perhaps via a TMS9901 pin) for this purpose.
2) You could use the $\overline{RTS}$ output for this purpose, provided transmit logic is not active.
3) External logic could decode a TMS9902 Reset from the $\overline{CE}$ and S0-S4 pins, then, after some standard delay time, external logic could begin transmitting data to the TMS9902. For example, Reset could be used to trigger a one-shot whose output initialized data transfer to the TMS9902.

It does not matter whether you do or do not create a "ready to receive" signal, **receive logic within the TMS9902 will begin operating as soon as it detects a high-to-low transition on the RxD input.** One half of a bit-time after the RxD transition, Status register bit 14 is set to 1. If RxD is high at this time, then Status register bit 14 is reset to 0 and receive logic waits for the next high-to-low transition of RxD. If a true Start bit is present, however, then one bit-time after the setting of bit 14, Status register bit 13 is set to 1 and receive logic assumes that valid data is being input.

Status register bits 14 and 13 are useful only for testing TMS9902 operations. For example, you can use them to verify the Receive data rate. These bits are not particularly useful in normal operation.

As soon as a valid data character has been input, it is transmitted to the Receive buffer, and Status register bit 21 is set to 1. If receive interrupt logic has been enabled, Status register bit 16 is set, and an interrupt request is generated. If interrupts have not been enabled, the CPU will poll the Status register in order to detect a data character which must be read.

There are a number of error conditions that can occur during a receive operation.

If a valid Stop bit is not detected, the receive framing error status (bit 12) is set.

If parity has been specified but incorrect parity is detected, then Status register bit 10 is set.

If the CPU does not read a character in time (that is, before the next character is loaded into the Receive Buffer register), then a receive overrun error occurs and Status register bit 11 is set.

Status register bit 9 is set when any receive error occurs.

A receive error does not generate an interrupt request. The CPU must check the receive error status flags in order to find out if any error has occurred. This is normally a routine part of reading received data.

TMS9902 ERROR FLAGS

TMS9902 INTERVAL TIMER OPERATIONS

TMS9902 interval timer logic is quite straightforward.

You must initialize the interval timer by loading a value into the Interval Timer register. You subsequently start the interval timer by resetting Control register bit 13 to 0. (Remember, this occurs automatically when you write into the high-order Timer register bit.) At this time the contents of the Interval Timer register are moved to interval timer logic, where they are decremented once every 64 internal clock cycles (CLK). Remember, a CLK cycle may be three or four times as long as a Φ cycle. When the interval timer decrements to 0, Status register bit 25 is set and an interrupt request is generated if interval timer interrupt logic has been enabled. Immediately, the contents of the Interval Timer register are moved to interval timer logic and decrementing begins again.

The CPU must reset Status register bit 25 before the next time out occurs; otherwise, when the next time out occurs, an error will be indicated. Status register bit 24 is set to indicate this error.

The CPU can at any time reset the value in the Interval Timer register. However, it is impossible to read the contents of the interval timer on the fly; that is to say, there is no way in which the CPU can read the current decrementing value held within interval timer logic.

TMS9902 TEST MODE

In order to diagnose the TMS9902 on line you can put it into a test mode by writing 1 to Control register bit 15. In Test mode, the following occurs:

1) $\overline{CTS}$ is connected internally to $\overline{RTS}$; therefore, $\overline{CTS}$ will become true internally whenever $\overline{RTS}$ is output low, regardless of the level at the $\overline{CTS}$ input pin.
2) RxD is connected internally to TxD; therefore, whatever is transmitted and output via TxD will be received by receive logic, regardless of the level at the RxD input pin.

3) $\overline{\text{DSR}}$ is held low.

4) The interval timer decrements at 32 times its normal rate.

You can use the Test mode in order to check the TMS9902 when a TMS9900 microcomputer system would otherwise be idle. For example, during times of inactivity, you will frequently execute a "no operation" loop, waiting for an external interrupt. Instead of executing a "no operation" loop, you could execute a short program which puts the TMS9902 into Test mode, sends data to the device, and then checks received data to see if it is the same.

TxD and $\overline{\text{RTS}}$ act as normal outputs during Test mode. Therefore, you might wish to disconnect these lines from external logic during the execution of the test program. One way to do this would be to use an external CRU bit to disable TxD and $\overline{\text{RTS}}$ out; this bit would be set at the beginning of the Test mode program and reset before normal operations resumed. Disconnect logic would be basic AND logic:

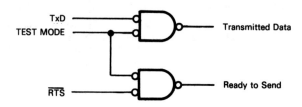

THE TMS9903 SYNCHRONOUS COMMUNICATIONS CONTROLLER

The TMS9903 Synchronous Communications Controller is equivalent to the TMS9902 Asynchronous Communications Controller, which we have just described, with synchronous and SDLC capabilities added. Although the TMS9903 is referred to in Texas Instruments literature as a Synchronous Communications Controller, it also has asynchronous communications capabilities.

Compared to devices described in Section C of Volume 3, you will find that the TMS9903 is a general purpose device of average capabilities.

It is worth comparing the TMS9903 to serial I/O devices described in Section C of Volume 3, since these general purpose serial I/O devices can easily be included in a TMS9900 series microcomputer system in the place of a TMS9903.

This description of the TMS9903 assumes that you understand synchronous, asynchronous, and SDLC protocols. If you do not understand these protocols then see Volume 1, Chapter 5 for a description of synchronous and asynchronous protocols. For a description of SDLC protocol see Volume 3, Chapter C1.

We describe the TMS9903 in this chapter, rather than Section C of Volume 3, because the TMS9903 CPU interface uses the TMS9900 series Communications Register Unit (CRU) logic.

The TMS9903 is manufactured using N-channel silicon gate MOS technology. It is packaged as a 20-pin DIP, making it the smallest synchronous controller chip on the market. All signals are TTL-level compatible. A single +5V power supply is required.

A TMS9903 FUNCTIONAL OVERVIEW

Logic of the TMS9903 is illustrated functionally in Figure 3-31.

On the CPU interface the TMS9903 occupies 32 CRU bits. High numbered CRU bits write to the Control register, and are read from the Status register. Low numbered CRU bits form an internal Data Bus that is bidirectional and has variable width. Via this Data Bus the CPU may read data from the Receive buffer, or it may read one of three cyclical redundancy characters. The CPU may write to the Transmit buffer, the Parameter register, or one of the two Sync registers; it may also output data to be included in either of two cyclical redundancy characters. Thus, **when programming a TMS9900 series microprocessor, you can visualize the TMS9903 32-bit CRU field as follows:**

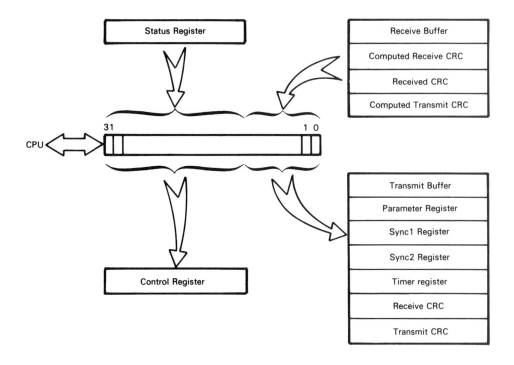

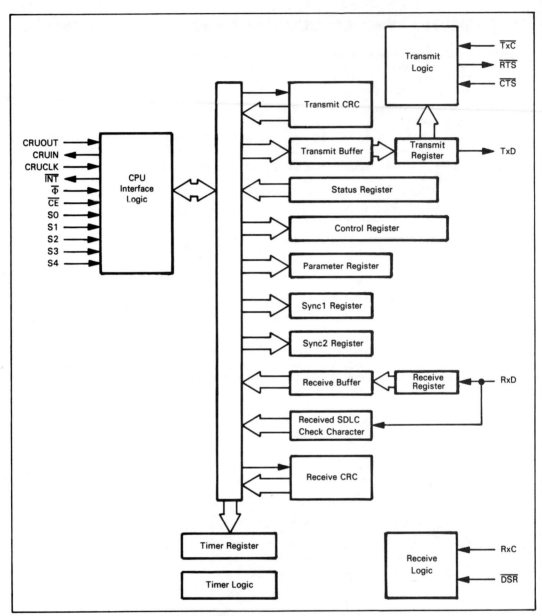

Figure 3-31. TMS9903 Synchronous Communications Controller
Functional Logic

As illustrated above, there are three cyclical redundancy check characters which can be read from the TMS9903.

Transmit and receive logic each compute a cyclical redundancy character (under program control) for transmitted and received messages.

In SDLC mode only, the cyclical redundancy character for a received frame is isolated by receive logic and held in a register out of which it can be read.

We will describe programming aspects of cyclical redundancy characters in more detail as the discussion of the TMS9903 proceeds.

Transmit and receive logic are each buffered. Data is moved from the Transmit buffer to the Transmit Shift register, whence it is output serially via TxD. You have one character transmit time within which to write another character to the Transmit buffer, otherwise an underrun will occur.

Characters are assembled by receive logic in the Receive Shift register; when assembled, they are transferred to the Receive buffer. You have one character receive time within which to read the contents of the Receive buffer, or else a receive overrun will occur.

Data buffers within the TMS9903 are all nine bits wide; this gives you the option of appending a parity bit to any 8-bit character. The Status register is 23 bits wide, the Control register is 20 bits wide, and the Parameter register is 12 bits wide; these odd bit lengths cause no problems due to the nature of the CRU interface between the TMS9903 and the TMS9900 series microprocessor.

The Sync1 and Sync2 registers hold Sync characters; in certain protocols these two registers may hold special control characters. Transmit logic may output the contents of one or both of these registers at the beginning of a message and following an underrun. Receive logic uses the contents of the Sync1 register to detect Sync characters in a received data stream.

You specify the number of data bits per character for received data via Parameter register bit settings.

When receive logic is assembling characters in the Receive Shift register, it uses the bits-per-character specification that was in effect when the current character started to be assembled. If you change the bits-per-character specification, the change will be recognized on the next receive character boundary.

The bits-per-character specification that you make in the Parameter register does not apply to transmit logic or the Sync1 and Sync2 registers. For these three registers the number of data bits you write into the register defines the number of data bits which will be transmitted. The most recently loaded Sync register determines the character length for transmission of both Sync characters.

For example, if you output 6-bit characters to these three registers, then 6-bit characters are assumed by transmit logic. Likewise, if you output 9-bit characters, then transmit logic will subsequently assume 9-bit Sync1 and Sync2 characters.

Sync1 and Sync2 registers should have the same bits-per-character specifications. However, you could, for example, output a 7-bit character to Sync1 and then a 5-bit character to Sync2. If you did, the device would transmit just the lower five bits of Sync1 and Sync2. You could still specify 7-bit characters to receive logic; each received character would be compared to all seven bits of Sync1. The Sync character bit length need not be the same as the bits-per-character specification in the Parameter register or even the number of bits specified by loading the Transmit buffer.

As with the Receiver, you can change the Transmit character length from character to character. As each character is shifted from the Transmit buffer to the Transmit Shift register, transmit logic attaches the bits-per-character specification to the data in the Transmit Shift register. Therefore if you subsequently change the number of bits per transmit character — namely, by loading a different-sized word into the Transmit buffer — it has no effect on the character already in the Transmit Shift register.

Although Texas Instruments literature describes the TMS9903 as supporting six different modes, in fact it supports three: Asynchronous, Synchronous, and SDLC/HDLC.

TMS9903 MODES

Asynchronous and Synchronous mode capabilities are quite standard.

In Synchronous mode you can approximate IBM standard Monosync or Bisync protocols.

Asynchronous mode is well suited to RS-232C and RS-449 EIA standard protocols.

The TMS9903 can be operated in a point-to-point SDLC or HDLC system; also, SDLC loop mode is supported.

The TMS9903, like the TMS9902, has on-chip timer logic.

TMS9903 PINS AND SIGNALS

TMS9903 pins and signals are illustrated in Figure 3-32. Pins 1 through 9 and 12 through 20 are functionally equivalent to TMS9902 pins 1 through 18.

On its CPU interface the TMS9903 has the same standard TMS9900 signals as the TMS9901 and the TMS9902. These include:

TMS9903 CPU INTERFACE SIGNALS

1) The three standard CRU signals: CRUIN, CRUOUT, and CRUCLK.

2) Five select lines (S0-S4) that address a 32-bit CRU field.

3) $\overline{CE}$, an enable signal which must be low for the CPU interface to be enabled.

4) An input clock signal, normally connected to the TIM9904 $\overline{\Phi 3}$ clock.

Refer to our earlier discussion of the TMS9901 for a description of CPU interfacing logic.

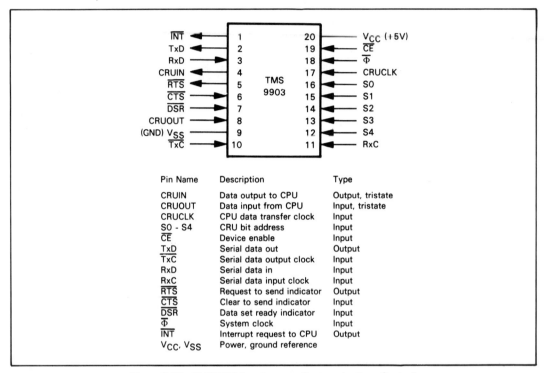

Pin Name	Description	Type
CRUIN	Data output to CPU	Output, tristate
CRUOUT	Data input from CPU	Input, tristate
CRUCLK	CPU data transfer clock	Input
S0 - S4	CRU bit address	Input
$\overline{CE}$	Device enable	Input
TxD	Serial data out	Output
$\overline{TxC}$	Serial data output clock	Input
RxD	Serial data in	Input
RxC	Serial data input clock	Input
$\overline{RTS}$	Request to send indicator	Output
$\overline{CTS}$	Clear to send indicator	Input
$\overline{DSR}$	Data set ready indicator	Input
$\overline{\Phi}$	System clock	Input
$\overline{INT}$	Interrupt request to CPU	Output
V_{CC}, V_{SS}	Power, ground reference	

Figure 3-32. TMS9903 Synchronous Communications Controller
Pins and Signal Assignments

Let us now examine transmit and receive logic signals.

Serial data is output by transmit logic via TxD, as clocked by $\overline{TxC}$. Data is transmitted on high-to-low transitions of $\overline{TxC}$.

> TMS9903
> SERIAL I/O
> SIGNALS

$\overline{RTS}$ and $\overline{CTS}$ are two Modem control signals associated with transmit logic. In order to transmit data you must input $\overline{CTS}$ low while transmit logic is enabled. You have the option of connecting $\overline{RTS}$ to transmit enable logic. If you do, $\overline{RTS}$ will be output low while transmit logic is enabled and it will be output high while transmit logic is disabled. You also have the option of selecting the $\overline{RTS}$ output level under program control, in which case $\overline{RTS}$ is disconnected from transmit enable logic.

Receive logic receives data via RxD as clocked by RxC. Data is sampled on low-to-high transitions of RxC.

$\overline{DSR}$ is shown in Figure 3-31 as a receive logic Modem input signal; in reality it is **an unassigned input control signal.** The $\overline{DSR}$ signal level is reported in a Status register bit, and can generate an interrupt whenever it changes state. $\overline{DSR}$ does not contribute to receive enable logic.

TMS9903 PROGRAMMABLE REGISTERS

The two principal programmable registers of the TMS9903 are the Control and Status registers. We refer to these as "principal" registers because they are automatically accessed by high numbered CRU bits on any CRU access. Low numbered CRU bits transfer data to or from a variety of addressable locations, as specified by Control register bit settings.

Table 3-12. TMS9903 Synchronous Communications Controller CRU Bit Assignments
When Writing to the TMS9903

CRU BIT NUMBER	ASYNC	SYNC	SDLC	FUNCTION
31	X	X	X	1 or 0 = Reset device.
30	X	X	X	1 = Clear transmitter. 0 = Clear receiver. (In each case interrupts are disabled).
29	X	X	X	1 = Clear transmit CRC register. 0 = Clear receive CRC register. (CRC register is reset to 0).
28		X	X	1 = Delete received Sync1 characters (in Bisync mode only).
27	X	X	X	1 = Inhibit transmit logic's zero bit insertion.
26	X	X		1 = Load data at CRU bits 0 - 9 into Sync2 register.
			X	1 = Load data at CRU bits 0 - 9 into Sync1 register (only for versions of Synchronous mode that use Sync1 register).
25	X	X	X	0 = Read received check character via CRU bits 0 - 15.
				1 = Load data output to CRU bits 0 - 8 into Transmit buffer, and update the transmit CRC. Select the transmit CRC to be read via CRU bits 0 - 15.
24	X	X	X	0 = Reset Status register bits 22 and 17.
				1 = Update the transmit CRC with the next word output to CRU bits 0 - 9. Read transmit CRC at CRU bits 0 - 15.
23	X	X	X	1 = Transmit break (low level output) during underrun. Reset this bit to 0 before loading new data into Transmit buffer to end underrun.
				Specify synchronous modes' underrun options. (See text)(General and Bisync only).
22	X	X	X	1 = Transmit Sync2 register contents following an underrun. (Typically $7F_{16}$ for an HDLC abort).
				0 = Abort transmit following an underrun and set Status register bit 23. (General only).
			X	1 = Enable abort interrupt and reset Status register bits 23 and 18. (General only).
				0 = Disable abort interrupt and reset Status register bits 23 and 18. (General only).
21	X	X	X	1 = Enable data set change interrupts and reset Status register bits 29 and 20.
				0 = Disable data set change interrupts and reset Status register bits 29 and 20.
20	X	X	X	1 = Enable timer interrupts and reset Status register bits 25, 24 and 19.
				0 = Disable timer interrupts and reset Status register bits 25, 24 and 19.
19	X	X	X	1 = Enable Transmit buffer empty interrupts.
				0 = Disable Transmit buffer empty interrupts.
18	X	X	X	1 = Enable Receive buffer full interrupts and reset Status register bits 21 and 11.
				0 = Disable Receive buffer full interrupts and reset Status register bits 21 and 11.
			X	1 = Enable Receive buffer full. Received Check Character buffer full and received abort interrupts. Reset Status register bits 21, 14, 11 and 9.
				0 = Disable interrupts listed above. Reset Status register bits 21, 14, 11 and 9.
17	X	X	X	0 or 1 = Output complement via $\overline{RTS}$ and disable automatic $\overline{RTS}$ control logic.
16	X	X	X	1 = Enable transmitter logic.
				0 = Disable transmitter logic after transmitting available data.
15	X	X	X	1 = Test mode. 0 = Normal operation.
14	X	X	X	1 = Load data at CRU bits 0 - 11 into Control register.
13	X	X	X	1 = Load data at CRU bits 0 - 7 into Timer register.
				0 = Move Timer register contents to timer and start timer.
12	X	X	X	1 = Update the Receive CRC with the next word output to CRU bits 0 - 9. Read Receive CRC at CRU bits 0 - 15.

Let us begin by examining the Control register; bit interpretations are defined in Table 3-12.

TMS9903
CONTROL
REGISTER

When you write to a TMS9903, CRU bits 31 through 12 will always access the Control register.

Control register bits may be divided into the following groups:

- Device reset
- Register select
- Variations within mode specifications — which are made in the Parameter register
- Interrupt enable/disable
- Direct device control

In most cases, when you set or reset a TMS9903 Control register bit, this bit setting — and its associated logic — remains in effect until you specifically change the bit setting. When setting a bit to select a data register, be sure to reset any select bits that were previously set. If two or more register select bits are set simultaneously, you will receive no error message, but the device will probably malfunction.

TMS9903
REGISTER
SELECT

Let us now examine Control register bits by group.

There are three device reset CPU bits: 31, 30, and 29.

When you write a 0 or a 1 to CRU bit 31, the entire device is reset; all interrupts are disabled and all flags and register select bits are reset to 0 (with the exception of **Control register bit 14 and Status register bit 22, which are set to 1).** This causes the first data to be loaded into the Parameter register, while a transmit buffer empty condition is reported in the Status register.

TMS9903
DEVICE
RESET

After resetting the TMS9903 by writing a 1 or 0 to CRU bit 31 and loading the Parameter register (CRU bits 0 to 11), you must next clear the transmitter and receiver by writing a 1 and then a 0 to CRU bit 30. (It does not matter whether you clear transmitter or receiver logic first, so long as you do clear each set of logic before attempting to use it.) **You must also initialize CRC accumulation logic at the transmitter and the receiver by writing 1 and then 0 to CRU bit 29.**

TMS9903
INITIALIZE
TRANSMIT/
RECEIVE

INITIALIZE
CRC

In summary, the following steps are required to reset and initialize a TMS9903:

1) Write 1 or 0 to CRU bit 31. This resets the entire device and enables loading of the Parameter register.
2) Load the Parameter register (CRU bits 0-11), establishing the operating mode and configuration.
3) Write 11 to CRU bits 30 and 29. This initializes the transmitter and transmitter CRC logic.
4) Write 00 to CRU bits 30 and 29. This resets the receiver and receive CRC logic.

(Note that when you write to CRU bits 31, 30, and 29, you will always access Control register bits 30, 31, and 29; only CRU bits 0-11 have multiple destinations within the TMS9903.)

After resetting the TMS9903 and initializing transmit/receive logic, you will next select addressable locations to read from or write to.

Selecting the data location from which you will read is straightforward. Normally, CRU bits 0-8 will contain the Receive buffer contents, while CRU bits 9-31 are taken from the Status register. But you can also read one of three 16-bit CRC characters. We may illustrate TMS9903 register addressing during a CPU read as follows:

TMS9903
READ
REGISTER
ADDRESSING

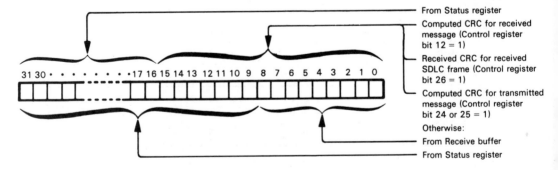

Note carefully that in SDLC mode you can read two receive cyclical redundancy check characters: the first is computed under program control by receive logic for the received frame; the second is received at the end of the frame.

The final 16 bits of the information field are the received cyclical redundancy character. To read the received cyclical redundancy character, set Control register bit 26 to 1. To read the cyclical redundancy character computed by receive logic for the received frame, set Control register bit 12 to 1. These two cyclical redundancy characters will be identical if a valid message was received.

In Synchronous and Asynchronous modes there is no defined end-of-message. Rather, a control character in the received data stream is interpreted as an end-of-message indicator, in which case two previously received data characters are interpreted as the received cyclical redundancy character. Your program logic must compare the two data characters which are being interpreted as the received CRC character with the computed check character, read from receive logic after setting Control register bit 12 to 1.

When the CPU reads from the TMS9903, if Control register bits 12, 24, 25, and 26 are all reset to 0, then as the default case CRU bits 0-8 are taken from the Receive buffer; higher numbered CRU bits are taken from the Status register, as always.

When writing to the TMS9903, Control register address bits used to select a data location for the low numbered CRU bits may be illustrated as follows:

TMS9903 WRITE REGISTER ADDRESSING

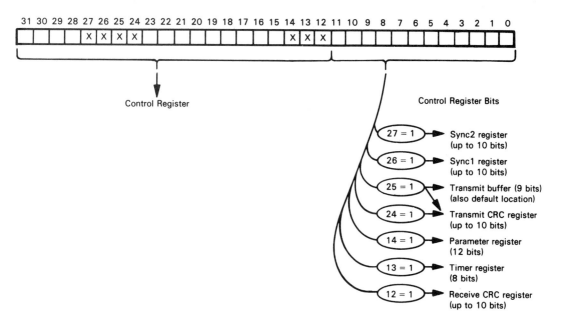

High numbered CRU bits always go to the Control register. Low numbered bits go to the write location whose register select bit within the Control register is 1.

Following a reset, Control register bit 14 is set to 1, therefore data written to CRU bits 0-11 loads the Parameter register. **When you write into the high-order Parameter register bit (bit 11), Control register bit 14 is automatically reset.** But this is an exception. When you set any other register select bit in the Control register it remains set until you specifically reset it.

If the Parameter register select bit (Control register bit 14) is set and you want to write to another addressable location, then you must reset Control register bit 14 to 0 when setting another select bit to 1.

If all select bits in the Control register are 0, then as a default case data will be written to the Transmit buffer.

You can only write into the Sync2 register in Synchronous or SDLC modes.

You can only write into the Sync1 register in Synchronous mode — and only in those variations of Synchronous mode that use the Sync1 register. Variations of Synchronous mode are described later.

There are two Control register bits, 28 and 23, which you use to specify variations of mode specifications. We will describe these two bits together with Parameter register bit settings, since Control register bits 23 and 28 are logically extensions of the Parameter register.

Five conditions capable of requesting interrupts have separate enable bits; these are Control register bits 22 through 18. When you write a 1 to any of these Control register bits, the associated interrupt logic is enabled; when you write a 0 to that Control register bit, interrupt logic is disabled. In most cases, when you write a 0 or a 1 to an enable/disable bit, you reset any associated Status register bits. Exceptions are the Transmit buffer empty status and the Received CRC register full.

> **TMS9903**
> **INTERRUPT**
> **ENABLE/DISABLE**

We will discuss individual interrupts in more detail later when looking at TMS9903 interrupt logic in general.

Direct device control bits consist of transmitter control and receiver controls.

Looking first at the transmitter, **you must enable transmit logic, after clearing it, by setting Control register bit 16 to 1;** transmit logic remains enabled until you reset this bit to 0. Transmit logic will not disable itself in the middle of transmitting a character; if you write a 0 to Control register bit 16 part way through a character's transmission, the character will be transmitted and transmit logic will then be disabled.

> **TMS9903**
> **TRANSMIT**
> **CONTROLS**

If you never write to Control register bit 17 following a reset, then the $\overline{\text{RTS}}$ output signal level is automatically controlled by transmitter logic. As soon as you enable transmitter logic by writing a 1 to Control register bit 16, $\overline{\text{RTS}}$ is output low; $\overline{\text{RTS}}$ remains low until you disable transmitter logic by writing a 0 to Control register bit 16. But **if you ever write to Control register bit 17,** you immediately disable the automatic control of the $\overline{\text{RTS}}$ output level. Now **the $\overline{\text{RTS}}$ output level becomes the reciprocal of Control register bit 17.**

There are two ways in which you can include transmitted characters in any cyclical redundancy character computation.

If you select the Transmit buffer by setting Control register bit 25 to 1, then the character which you write to the Transmit buffer is also included in the transmit cyclical redundancy character computation.

If you select the Transmit buffer as the default write location (i.e., no address bits in the Control register are set to 1), then the character which you write to the Transmit buffer will not be included in the transmit cyclical redundancy character computation unless you set Control register bit 24 to 1 and then output the character to Transmit CRC logic. That is, using bit 24 of the Control register you can write to either the Transmit buffer or to Transmit CRC logic, but not to both at the same time.

When a large sequence of contiguous characters is to be included in the transmit cyclical redundancy character computation, use Control register bit 25.

When characters are to be selectively included and excluded in the transmit cyclical redundancy character computation, use Control register bit 24.

There is no receiver enable control equivalent to the transmitter enable (Control register bit 16). As soon as you clear receive logic, it is enabled and will begin to sample data arriving via RxD. As each character is assembled, it is transferred to the Receive buffer. If a received character is to be included in the computed receive cyclical redundancy character, program logic must output that character to Receive CRC logic after reading it from the Receive buffer. When you set Control register bit 12, data output to CRU bits 0-9 will go to Receive CRC logic.

> **TMS9903**
> **RECEIVE CRC**

Note that CRC logic is not necessarily connected to the transmitter or receiver. The cyclical redundancy calculation registers may be used independently of transmit or receive logic.

The Test mode bit (Control register bit 15) is normally left reset to 0. When you set this bit to 1 the following connections occur:

> **TMS9903**
> **TEST MODE**

1) TxD is connected to RxD.
2) $\overline{\text{RTS}}$ is connected to $\overline{\text{CTS}}$, and $\overline{\text{DSR}}$ is held low.
3) $\overline{\text{TxC}}$ and RxC are both connected to the timer logic clock, which operates at 32 times its normal rate.

This is similar to TMS9902 Test mode, with the exception that, in the TMS9903, the timer determines Receive and Transmit data rates in Test mode.

We will next describe the Parameter register. You will normally write into this register once during any operation in order to define operating modes and options within these modes.

After resetting the TMS9903 by writing to CRU bit 31, you simply output the parameter code to CRU bits 0-11. Resetting the device automatically selects the Parameter register as the write location for the data at CRU bits 0-11. You could also select the Parameter register by writing 0s to CRU bits 27, 26, 25, 24, 13, and 12, and writing a 1 to CRU bit 14. Parameter register contents are interpreted as follows:

TMS9903 PARAMETER REGISTER

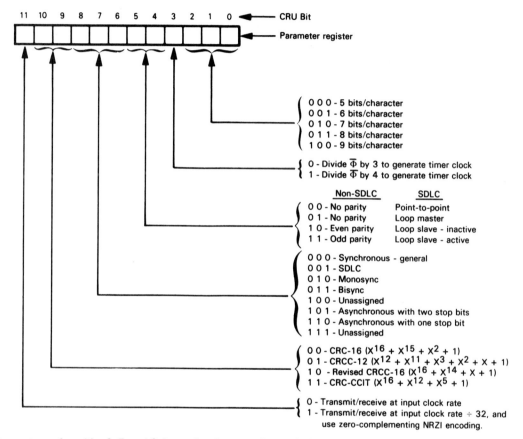

```
0 0 0 - 5 bits/character
0 0 1 - 6 bits/character
0 1 0 - 7 bits/character
0 1 1 - 8 bits/character
1 0 0 - 9 bits/character
```

```
0 - Divide Φ by 3 to generate timer clock
1 - Divide Φ by 4 to generate timer clock
```

	Non-SDLC	SDLC
0 0 -	No parity	Point-to-point
0 1 -	No parity	Loop master
1 0 -	Even parity	Loop slave - inactive
1 1 -	Odd parity	Loop slave - active

```
0 0 0 - Synchronous - general
0 0 1 - SDLC
0 1 0 - Monosync
0 1 1 - Bisync
1 0 0 - Unassigned
1 0 1 - Asynchronous with two stop bits
1 1 0 - Asynchronous with one stop bit
1 1 1 - Unassigned
```

```
0 0 - CRC-16 (X^16 + X^15 + X^2 + 1)
0 1 - CRCC-12 (X^12 + X^11 + X^3 + X^2 + X + 1)
1 0 - Revised CRCC-16 (X^16 + X^14 + X + 1)
1 1 - CRC-CCIT (X^16 + X^12 + X^5 + 1)
```

```
0 - Transmit/receive at input clock rate
1 - Transmit/receive at input clock rate ÷ 32, and
    use zero-complementing NRZI encoding.
```

Parameter register bits 6, 7, and 8 determine the operating mode for transmit and receive logic, and some options within the selected mode.

When you select Asynchronous mode, you also select either one or two stop bits.

In Asynchronous mode, when you set Control register bit 23 to 1, then as soon as an underrun occurs transmit logic will output a continuous low level (break) on TxD. But note carefully that setting Control register bit 23 to 1 does nothing until an underrun occurs. Once an underrun does occur, you cannot load new data into the Transmit buffer until you reset Control register bit 23 to 0 to end the break.

TMS9903 ASYNCHRONOUS BREAK LOGIC

If Control register bit 23 is reset to 0, then following an underrun a continuous high signal is output via TxD. You can at any time restart transmission by loading data into the Transmit buffer — in which case the high level output at TxD ends and the next character is transmitted according to the Asynchronous protocol options specified in the Parameter register.

There are three Synchronous mode options and one SDLC mode option. These four options share Sync character logic, as shown in Table 3-13. This table applies to transmit and receive logic.

Let us first consider SDLC transmit logic.

Table 3-13. TMS9903 Synchronous and SDLC Mode Sync
Character and Underrun Options

Parameter Register CRU Bit			MODE	SYNC Character	Underrun Fill Character	
8	7	6			Control Register CRU Bit 23 = 0	Control Register CRU Bit 23 = 1
0	0	0	Synchronous-General	None	Abort	[SYNC2]
0	0	1	SDLC	$7E_{16}$	Abort	[SYNC2]
0	1	0	Synchronous-Monosync	[SYNC1]	[SYNC2]	[SYNC2]
0	1	1	Synchronous-Bisync	[SYNC1] - [SYNC2]	[SYNC1] - [SYNC1]	[SYNC2] - [SYNC1]

[ ] Means: "contents of register named within brackets"

Every frame must begin with a flag character, therefore $7E_{16}$ is always output as the leading Sync character. You will subsequently reset Control register bit 23 to 0, since underruns are not allowed within an SDLC frame. Should an underrun occur, the transmitter will abort, outputting a continuous high signal and setting appropriate status bits. In order to transmit a valid end-of-message, you must read the computed transmit check character (selected via Control register bit 24 or 25), set Control register bit 23 to 1, load a flag ($7E_{16}$) character into the Sync2 register, and output the computed transmit check character as two data bytes. Now allow an underrun to occur; the contents will be output when the underrun occurs. Since Sync2 contains a flag character, you will have terminated the frame by transmitting the message check character and closing flag, as required by SDLC protocol.

TMS9903 SDLC TRANSMIT OPERATION

There is another way of ending a frame's transmission.

Instead of allowing an underrun and outputting the frame's closing flag from the Sync2 register, you can suppress SDLC 0 insertion by writing a 1 to Control register bit 28, then outputting the closing flag (or flags) as a simple sequence of 8-bit data characters.

If you are operating the TMS9903 using HDLC protocol, then you must output $7F_{16}$ as your abort character. To obtain a valid HDLC abort following a transmit underrun you should write the HDLC abort character to the Sync2 register, then leave Control register bit 23 set to 1 while the frame is being transmitted. Now if an underrun occurs, an HDLC abort character will be output from the Sync2 register.

TMS9903 HDLC ABORT

When detecting a new frame, SDLC receive logic synchronizes itself on flag character $7E_{16}$, which is also the specified Sync character. Consequently the setting of Control register bit 23 and the underrun fill character options shown in Table 3-13 do not apply. When receive logic detects another flag character, it assumes it has received the frame's closing flag. SDLC receive logic can also detect an abort. SDLC receive logic sets appropriate status flags and generates an interrupt request, if enabled.

TMS9903 SDLC RECEIVE LOGIC

The three Synchronous modes shown in Table 3-13, together with their underrun fill character options, allow you (under program control) to emulate any of the synchronous protocol options commonly encountered.

External synchronization uses no leading Sync characters at the head of a message. You can emulate this protocol by choosing the general synchronous option.

TMS9903 EXTERNAL SYNC LOGIC

For TMS9903 transmit logic, make sure that $\overline{CTS}$ is low before you enable the transmitter; then as soon as $\overline{RTS}$ goes low, message transmission begins. A station that receives this transmitted message can use the low $\overline{RTS}$ output as its external Sync input.

TMS9903 receive logic will use the $\overline{DSR}$ Modem input as its external synchronization signal. The station which transmits the signal to the TMS9903 must generate a low $\overline{DSR}$ input just before it starts transmitting a message. The program controlling TMS9903 receive logic must detect the low $\overline{DSR}$ input by interrogating the appropriate Status register bit, and upon detecting $\overline{DSR}$ active should start receiving.

In Monosync mode a single Sync character occurs at the head of a new message. In Bisync mode two Sync characters occur at the head of a new message. Both of these options are allowed.

The Monosync mode outputs the contents of the Sync1 register at the head of a transmitted message and synchronizes on a received message by matching received characters against the contents of the Sync1 register.

TMS9903 MONOSYNC LOGIC
BISYNC LOGIC

In Bisync mode Sync1 contents are output twice at the head of a transmitted message. Receive logic assumes that a new message has been detected when two contiguous characters match the contents of the Sync1 register.

By loading appropriate data into the Sync1 and Sync2 registers you can transmit and detect ASCII, EBCDIC, or any other Sync characters.

When an underrun occurs in Monosync mode, a single Sync character is output. By loading the appropriate character into the Sync2 register you can transmit and detect any underrun fill character.

In the Bisync option greater underrun flexibility is needed. In some cases, following any underrun two Sync characters are transmitted; but in standard Bisync protocol DLE-SYN character combinations are output following an underrun. When Control register bit 23 equals 0 the TMS9903 will output two Sync characters from the Sync1 register. To meet the requirements of Bisync protocol you load the DLE character into the Sync2 register, load the SYN character into the Sync1 register, and leave Control register bit 23 set to 1. Other bisync logic (in particular, the generation and detection of special control character combinations) must be handled by a supervisory program.

Control register bit 28 adds some flexibility to the options shown in Table 3-13. However, this control bit applies only to SDLC and Bisync modes. In SDLC mode, when Control register bit 28 is reset to 0, TMS9903 transmitter logic will insert a 0 after every five consecutive 1s transmitted. Setting Control bit 28 to 1 inhibits this zero bit insertion in SDLC mode.

In Bisync mode, when Control register bit 28 is set to 1 any received character that matches the contents of the Sync1 register is discarded. This allows you to strip received underrun Sync characters.

TMS9903 SYNC STRIP

Parameter register bits 5 and 4 serve different functions in Synchronous and SDLC modes.

In Synchronous and Asynchronous modes Parameter register bits 5 and 4 are used to specify odd parity, even parity, or no parity. When parity is specified, parity bits will automatically be generated for data characters that are transmitted and will be tested for data characters received. **But parity does not apply to the contents of the Sync1 or Sync2 registers.** You must

TMS9903 PARITY OPTIONS

add your own parity bit to the contents of these registers if you want to transmit Sync characters with parity. The Sync registers are each ten bits wide so that you can add one parity bit to the longest specifiable character (nine bits). Receive logic will automatically check the parity of received Sync characters, since received logic treats all receive characters as data.

In SDLC mode, Parameter register bits 5 and 4 specify Loop or Non-loop mode; in fact, they **specify the way in which an EOP character ($7F_{16}$) is handled.**

TMS9903 SDLC CONFIGURATIONS

In a point-to-point configuration the EOP character has no significance, and is ignored.

As a loop master, transmit logic pays no attention to the EOP character; however, receive logic treats the EOP character as a frame's closing flag. This is necessary, since the polling EOP character which a loop master transmits around the loop will eventually be received as the closing flag for the last frame transmitted by a loop secondary.

The loop slave inactive mode is selected for an SDLC loop secondary that is not transmitting data, but may be receiving data. The loop slave active mode, in contrast, is selected for a secondary station in the SDLC loop that wishes to transmit to the primary station.

In **loop slave inactive mode,** a TMS9903 will initially retransmit received data without delay. But, upon detecting an EOP character in the received stream, the TMS9903 will introduce one bit delay before retransmitting received data. So long as you never electrically disconnect a secondary station in an SDLC loop, the inactive slave mode will take care of timing and protocol requirements of a secondary loop station coming on-line. But if you wish to electrically disconnect a TMS9903 secondary station in an SDLC loop, you will require external logic which detours upstream data around the electrically disconnected secondary, while breaking the detour and including the secondary when it is electrically connected. Here is the appropriate logic:

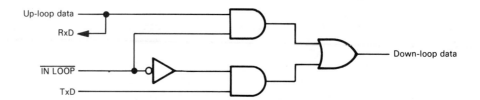

You will normally leave a TMS9903 operating in loop slave active mode if it is functioning as a secondary station in an SDLC loop. **You will only switch to loop slave inactive mode when the secondary station has just entered the loop and is not yet synchronized (has not received EOP).** In the loop slave active mode, TMS9903 receive logic will seek the next EOP character. Upon receiving an EOP character it will convert this character to a flag, which becomes the opening flag for the frame which the station wishes to transmit to the primary. **So long as a TMS9903 is left operating in loop slave active mode, it will continue to trap receive EOP characters and transmit frames behind them.** When a TMS9903 has no further frames to transmit, you should leave it in loop slave active mode, but turn off the transmitter by resetting Control register bit 16 to 0.

For a discussion of SDLC loop secondary station logic see Chapter C1 in Volume 3.

Parameter register bits 0, 1, and 2 allow you to specify 5, 6, 7, 8, or 9 data bits per received character. Note that if parity is enabled, the parity bit is not counted in this specification.

> **TMS9903 RECEIVED CHARACTER SIZE**

If Sync and control characters are eight bits wide, then you cannot specify less than 8-bit characters in Synchronous mode. This is because receive logic does not automatically switch from the specified bits per character to eight bits per character when receiving Sync or control characters. Moreover, a program controlling receive logic cannot make this switch, since it does not know it has received a Sync or special control character until the character is in the Receive buffer — by which time it is too late to make a change.

Parameter register bit 11 allows you to transmit and receive data at the transmit and receive clock rates, or at these clock rates divided by 32. This is normally a standard Synchronous mode option. With the TMS9903 it is available in all modes: Synchronous, SDLC, and Asynchronous. **This bit should be reset to 0 during operation as an SDLC loop slave.**

> **TMS9903 CLOCK RATE OPTION**
>
> **NRZI SELECT**

During synchronous or SDLC operation, if data is being sampled on every 32nd clock pulse (Parameter register bit 11 is 1) then NRZI encoding and decoding of serial data is assumed; that is, the data signal changes state to transmit a 0 or remains in the same state to represent a 1.

Parameter register bits 9 and 10 are used to specify the cyclical redundancy character algorithm which will be used by transmit and receive logic.

> **TMS9903 CRC OPTIONS**

CRC-16 is the normal algorithm used by synchronous and asynchronous protocols.

CRCC-12 is the algorithm used in synchronous and asynchronous protocols with 6-bit characters.

Revised CRCC-16 is the protocol frequently used in standard Bisync protocol.

CRC-CCIT is the standard SDLC algorithm.

Parameter register bit 3 is used by interval timer logic. This bit will be discussed later when we describe the interval timer.

We will now examine TMS9903 Status register bit settings, which are summarized in Table 3-14. Status register bits may be divided into the following groups:

> **TMS9903 STATUS REGISTER**

- interrupt status
- Input signal levels
- Transmit logic status
- Receive logic status
- Timer logic status

Table 3-14. TMS9903 Synchronous Communications Controller CRU Bit Assignments when Reading from the TMS9903

CRU BIT NUMBER	ASYNC	SYNC	SDLC	Function	Reset Condition
31	X	X	X	1 = Any interrupt pending	No interrupt pending
30	X	X	X	1 = One or more Register Load Control flags set.	No Control flag set
29	X	X	X	1 = DSR or CTS or automatic RTS signal level change occurred	Output to CRU bit 21
28	X	X	X	Complement of CTS input	
27	X	X	X	Complement of DSR input	
26	X	X	X	RTS level under automatic control. Transmitter active state if RTS is under program control	
25	X	X	X	1 = Timer decremented to 0	Output to CRU bit 20
24	X	X	X	1 = Timer error. Bit 25 was already 1 when timer decremented to 0	Output to CRU bit 20
23		X	X	1 = Abort followed an underrun (General only)	Output to CRU bit 22
22	X	X	X	1 = Transmit buffer empty	Output 0 to CRU bit 25
21	X	X	X	1 = Receiver buffer full	Output 0 to CRU bit 18
20	X	X	X	1 = Interrupt request accompanying RTS, DSR, or CTS signal level change (Bit 29 = 1)	Bit 29 = 0 or Output to bit 21
19	X	X	X	1 = Interrupt request accompanying timer time out (Bit 25 = 1)	Bit 25 = 0 or Output to bit 20
18		X	X	1 = Interrupt request accompanying an abort (Bit 23 = 1)(General only)	Bit 23 = 0 or Output to bit 22
17	X	X	X	1 = Interrupt request accompanying a Transmit buffer empty	Output 0 to CRU bit 25
16	X			1 = Interrupt request accompanying Receiver buffer full (Bit 21 = 1) only	No active interrupting condition
16		X		1 = Interrupt request accompanying Receiver buffer full (Bit 21 = 1)	No active interrupting condition
16			X	1 = Interrupt request accompanying Receiver buffer full (Bit 21 = 1) or abort received (Bit 14 = 1) or Closing flag received and received check character ready to be read (Bit 13 = 1)	No active interrupting condition
15	X	X		RxD input level	Stop bit(s) received
14	X			1 = Start bit detected	Output to CRU bit 18
14			X	1 = Abort received	Stop bit(s) received
13	X			1 = First character data bit received	Output 0 to bit 26
12			X	1 = Closing flag has been received and check character may be read	Error free character received
11	X	X		1 = Receive framing error detected	Output 0 to bit 26
11			X	1 = Overrun error detected - receive data overrunning previous frame's check character	Output 0 to bit 18
10	X	X		1 = Receive overrun error detected	Output 0 to bit 26
10	X	X		1 = Receive parity error detected	Output 0 to bit 26
9			X	1 = Zero insert error detected	Valid character received
9		X		1 = Any receive error in most recently received character	Valid character received
9			X	1 = Flag detected	Output to bit 18

The interrupt status bits include CRU bit 31, which reports any active interrupt request, and CRU bits 20 through 16, which identify individual interrupts. These status bits are self-evident. In non-vectored interrupt configurations you will test CRU bit 31 to find out if this particular TMS9903 has any active interrupt requests. In a vectored interrupt configuration you can ignore CRU bit 31, since the interrupt acknowledge process will identify the TMS9903 as the device with the active interrupt request. In each case, the interrupt service routine must examine CRU bits 20 through 16 in order to determine which interrupt requests are active. The interrupt service routine must resolve its own interrupt priorities.

Input Modem signals $\overline{DSR}$ and $\overline{CTS}$ modify Status register bits 27 and 28, respectively. The complement of the input signal level is reported. Status bit 29 is set to 1 when either $\overline{DSR}$, $\overline{CTS}$, or automatic $\overline{RTS}$ signal level changes. This signal level change can cause an interrupt request, in which case Status register bit 20 is set. In many serial I/O devices, $\overline{CTS}$ going high in the middle of a transmit operation forces a transmit abort, while $\overline{DSR}$ going high in the middle of a receive operation disables receive logic. The TMS9903 does not make such critical decisions; the supervisory program must respond appropriately.

When $\overline{RTS}$ output level is being controlled automatically, the complement of $\overline{RTS}$ is reported in Status register bit 26. But as soon as you start controlling $\overline{RTS}$ level by writing to Control register bit 17, Status register bit 26 reports the active state of the transmitter.

The serial data input signal RxD has its level reported in Status register bit 15.

There are two status bits associated with transmitter logic: bit 22 reports Transmit buffer empty and bit 23 reports a transmitter abort (in those modes that can generate an abort). If interrupt logic for these conditions has been enabled, then Status register bits 18 and/or 17 will also be set.

There are a number of Status register bit settings associated with receive logic, but there is only one interrupt status bit associated with receive logic — bit 16. Therefore you must use the various receive status bits in order to identify active error or non-error conditions within receive logic.

In all modes Status register bit 21 is set when the Receive buffer is full — and should be read within one character time.

In Synchronous mode, Status register bit 11 reports a receive overrun error, while Status register bit 10 reports a receive parity error. Either of these errors causes Status register bit 9 to be set.

In Asynchronous mode, a receive framing error, overrun error, or parity error is reported in status bits 12, 11, and 10, respectively. Status bit 9 reports one or more of these error conditions. In Asynchronous mode, two status bits are also set at the beginning of each received character. Status bit 14 is set when a valid start bit has been detected for the character, while status bit 13 is set when the first valid data bit has been detected.

In SDLC mode, a receive overrun is reported in status bit 11 and a receive zero insert error is reported in status bit 10. The receive zero insert error means that five contiguous 1 bits were received, followed by a flag character, without the expected zero inserted between them. Thus, status bit 10 will be set when the sequence 0111111011111_2 is received. While a frame is being received, Status register bit 14 is set when an abort is detected and Status register bit 9 is set when any flag character is detected.

An unusual and interesting error reported in SDLC mode is the receive CRC overrun error. If a new frame's data is received before you read the previous frame's cyclical redundancy check character, then status bit 12 is set.

There are two timer logic status bits; bit 25 is set to 1 whenever the timer decrements to zero. If timer interrupts have been enabled, then status bit 19 is also set. You must acknowledge a time-out before another time-out occurs. You acknowledge a time-out by outputting to Control register bit 20. If you do not do so, then on the next time-out Status register bit 24 is set.

You can examine Status register bit 30 at any time to see if one or more write location select bits are set in the Control register.

TMS9903 INTERRUPT LOGIC

There are seven conditions that can generate interrupt requests within the TMS9903. Three of the seven conditions combine to generate a single interrupt request status. Therefore, there are five interrupt request statuses for the seven interrupt generating conditions. **This may be illustrated as follows:**

```
                            Control
                 Status     Register   Status
                 Register   Interrupt  Register
                 Condition  Enable     Interrupt
                 Bit No.    Bit No.    Bit No.                Interrupt

                 29 ——————— 21 ——————— 20 — DSR, CTS, or automatic RTS level change
                 25 ——————— 20 ——————— 19 — Timer time out
                 22 ——————— 19 ——————— 17 — Transmit buffer empty
                 23 ——————— 22 ——————— 18 — Transmit abort
Receive buffer full   21 ⌐
End of SDLC frame     13 ——————— 18 ——————— 16 — Receive interrupt
Receive abort         14 ⌐
```

The TMS9903 has no internal interrupt priority arbitration logic. When one or more conditions capable of requesting an interrupt occur, if the interrupt has been enabled, then INT is output low and Status register bit 31 is set to 1. An interrupt service routine responding to the TMS9903 interrupt request must now interrogate Status register bits in order to determine which interrupt requests are active. **Program logic is responsible for all interrupt priority arbitration. These are the interrupt priorities which normally apply in serial I/O devices:**

1) HIGHEST PRIORITY. Receive buffer full (Status register bits 16 and 21 set)

2) Transmit buffer empty (Status register bits 17 and 22 set)

3) Modem signal level change (Status register bits 20 and 29 set)

4) Receive abort detected (Status register bits 16 and 14 set)

5) Transmitter abort (Status register bits 18 and 23 set)

6) End of SDLC frame detected (Status register bits 16 and 13 set)

7) LOWEST PRIORITY. Timer interrupt (Status register bits 19 and 25 set)

TMS9903 INITIALIZATION PROGRAM LOGIC

The first step in any TMS9903 operation is usually to initialize the device. Here are the necessary steps:

1) Reset the device by writing 0 or 1 to Control register bit 31.

TMS9903 DEVICE INITIALIZATION

2) Now output appropriate Parameter register settings.

3) Output data to Control register bits 18 through 22 to enable appropriate interrupts.

4) In Synchronous and SDLC modes, load appropriate codes into the Sync2 and/or Sync1 registers. These two registers are not used in Asynchronous mode.

5) To initialize receive logic, write 0 to Control register bit 30. If cyclical redundancy is being used, initialize receive CRC logic by writing 0 to Control register bit 29. As soon as this step is complete, receive logic becomes active and starts to assemble received data.

6) To initialize transmit logic, write 1 to Control register bit 30. If cyclical redundancy is being used, initialize transmit CRC logic by writing 1 to Control register bit 29. Transmit logic is now initialized, but it is not yet enabled.

7) Transmit logic will not become active until you enable the transmitter by writing 1 to Control register bit 16. When you enable the transmitter, you should also load data into the Transmit buffer. Refer to our earlier discussion of Control register bits 25 and 24, where data output to the Transmit buffer is described, with or without associated CRC accumulation.

TMS9903 ASYNCHRONOUS OPERATIONS

When you select Asynchronous mode, data will be transmitted with a parity bit if selected, plus one or two stop bits, as specified by the Parameter register. Whenever the Transmit buffer becomes empty, an interrupt request will be generated if the Transmit buffer empty interrupt has been enabled, and appropriate status bits will be set — as described earlier. You have one character time within which to respond by outputting another character, or else an underrun will occur. Following an

TMS9903 ASYNCHRONOUS TRANSMIT

underrun, a continuous high (marking) signal or a continuous low (break) signal will be output, depending on the setting of Control register bit 23. See the break discussion given earlier for details.

When beginning a receive operation, sample the start bit detected status (Status register bit 14) to identify the beginning of a new received message. This status cannot generate an interrupt request. To process received characters, use Receive buffer full interrupt request logic. As characters are received, program logic must read characters out of the Receive buffer within one character time, and check for any of the asynchronous receive error conditions by reading error Status register bits at the same time. Received data and status can be read together by reading CRU bits 0 through 15 from the TMS9903.

There are no other special programming considerations associated with asynchronous operation of the TMS9903. Conversely, any other protocol requirements must be met by the supervisory program's logic.

TMS9903 SYNCHRONOUS OPERATIONS

Most of the logic associated with Monosync and Bisync protocols must be provided by the supervisory program that controls TMS9903 transmit and receive operations. The only logic capabilities provided by the TMS9903 itself are the various Sync register programmable options, the error and normal operation statuses reported, and the character length definition.

For a discussion of the Sync character options, refer to our earlier description of the Parameter register.

For a description of the statuses reported, see the Status register discussion and interrupt logic summary.

TMS9903 SDLC OPERATIONS

When discussing the Parameter register we explained how you will use the Sync2 register in order to transmit and receive frames; but there are additional SDLC protocol requirements and some common protocol variations which need to be discussed.

SDLC and HDLC protocols are described in Chapter C1 of Volume 3. In SDLC protocol, the first byte of every frame is the address field, while the second byte is a control field. In HDLC protocol the address field can have any length, while the control field can be either one or two bytes long. Some variations of SDLC protocol insert a logical control field after the control field; the logical control field can have any length. **Address field, control field, and logical control field characters are all eight bits wide. Information field characters can have any data bit width.** The number of bytes in a multibyte address or logical control field is determined by examining a specific character bit. For example, a protocol may specify that the last byte of an address field will have a 1 in the low-order bit, while all prior bytes have a 0 in the low-order bit.

The TMS9903 has no on-chip logic designed to handle address, control, or logical control fields. Device programming can specify the number of bits per character — and this specification may change from character to character — and that is all. Moreover, **the supervisory program must take into account primary or secondary station logic.**

A supervisory program at a primary station must transmit secondary station addresses and must interpret received addresses as identifying a frame's source.

At a secondary station, the supervisory program must always transmit its own address at the head of a frame and must examine the address at the head of a received frame to see if the rest of the frame should be read or ignored.

When the last byte of the control field (or logical control field) has been received, **program logic must change the bits-per-character specification** in the Parameter register before processing the first character of the information field — should the information field use a different character length. Remember, the bits-per-character specification in the Parameter register applies only to receiver logic; you specify transmit character size by the number of bits you output to the Transmit buffer. Thus it is a simple matter to change character size from character to character as protocol may require. It is also possible for a received character to have a different number of bits than a simultaneously transmitted character.

TMS9903 receive logic in SDLC mode does have one very useful end-of-frame capability: **the received check character** (which must be the 16 data bits preceding the frame's closing flag) **is automatically loaded into a received CRC register.** The microprocessor can read this received check character and compare it with a computed check character.

But there are some additional uses for this received CRC logic.

A valid SDLC frame must have at least 32 bits between the beginning and closing flags; these bits include an 8-bit control field, and a 16-bit cyclical redundancy check character. Frequently, 32-bit frames are transmitted and received to pass a command or response with no associated data. An error occurring within such a short frame can cause complex logic problems; it may be difficult to identify beginning and ending flags for subsequent frames, since the ending flag for the short frame may go undetected. But **you can use the TMS9903 receive CRC logic to identify short received frames.** If you do not get a valid status indicator telling you that the received check character is available, then you know you have received a short frame.

SDLC protocols allow frames to be separated by a single flag character, which serves as the closing flag for one frame and the opening flag for the next frame. Alternatively, a number of flag characters may separate two frames. Either case can be handled by the TMS9903.

When describing the Parameter register, we explained how you can generate a frame's closing flag out of the Sync2 register, after allowing an underrun, or inhibit zero insertion and transmit flag characters as data. Since you can individually specify characters that will or will not be included in cyclical redundancy check accumulations, processing non-data characters as though they are data characters presents no difficulties to a TMS9903. You can use either method of ending a frame to separate frames with one or more flag characters.

If you have generated an end-of-frame using underrun logic, then loading the next frame's first address field byte while a single flag character is being transmitted will cause a single flag to separate the two frames. If you let the underrun last longer, then flag characters will continue to be output until you begin the next frame by writing the frame's first address field byte as data to the Transmit buffer. If you are transmitting flags as data without zero insertion, then the number of flags separating frames is strictly a function of program control — but you must make certain that an underrun does not occur.

Let us now examine programming requirements within an SDLC loop.

> **TMS9903**
> **SDLC LOOP**

There are no special programming requirements for the primary station in an SDLC loop. If you generate an abort at the end of a transmitted frame's closing flag, then the flag's trailing 0 bit, together with the first seven 1 bits of the abort, constitute an EOP character — which is transmitted around the loop in order to poll secondaries. When this EOP character returns to the primary station's receive logic, it is treated as a closing flag. (Refer to our discussion of the TMS9903 Parameter register for details.)

Secondary stations within the SDLC loop should be run in the SDLC loop slave inactive mode until the secondary station has become synchronized with the loop — that is, has received the EOP character and begun retransmitting with a one-bit delay. At this time, change the secondary station mode to SDLC loop slave active. In the active condition, the secondary station will seek the next EOP character arriving at RxD. If the transmitter has been enabled, the TMS9903 will convert this received EOP character to the opening flag character for the frame which it wishes to transmit. The program controlling the secondary SDLC can end the transmission with a closing flag and then an abort, or with an EOP character. The closing flag and following abort generate an EOP character for the next downstream secondary — and multiple flags between frames. A closing EOP character will be converted by the next downstream secondary to a flag or will be passed on to the primary, which interprets EOP characters at receive logic as closing flags. A closing EOP character, therefore, generates a single flag separating two transmitted frames.

For a discussion of normal status and error status that may occur during transmit and receive operations, refer to our earlier description of the Status register. Also, refer to our earlier description of the Parameter register for logic which you will use to abort a mistransmitted frame, or to detect an abort in a received frame. But remember, it is entirely up to the supervisory program to interpret status bits and to handle aborts as required by the local system logic.

TMS9903 INTERVAL TIMER LOGIC

The TMS9903 has an interval timer. You initialize the interval timer by loading a timer count into the Timer register. Remember, you set Control register bit 13 to 1 in order to select the Timer register as the destination for data output via CRU bits 0 through 7. As soon as you reset Control register bit 13 to 0 you enable the timer, which starts to decrement. The rate at which the timer decrements depends on Parameter register bit 3 and Control register bit 15.

Parameter register bit 3 allows you to divide the $\overline{\Phi}$ clock by either 3 (Parameter register bit 3 = 0) **or 4** (Parameter register bit 3 = 1) **in order to create a timer clock. The timer decrements once every 64 timer clock pulses.** For example, if $\overline{\Phi}$ is a 3 MHz clock and Parameter register bit 3 is 0, then the timer clock will be 3 MHz divided by 3, or 1 MHz. Therefore, the timer will decrement once every 64 microseconds.

The contents of the Timer register itself are never altered. Rather, the Timer register contents are shifted into timer logic, where they are decremented. **When a time-out occurs, Status register bit 25 is set; if timer interrupts have been enabled, Status register bit 19 is also set when the interrupt request occurs.** As soon as the timer decrements to 0 it reloads Timer register contents and starts decrementing again. Thus the value you load into the Timer register defines the interval between time-outs, which will apply until you load another value into the Timer register.

You must acknowledge a time-out by writing a 1 to Control register bit 20. If this does not occur before another time-out, then a timer error will be reported and Status register bit 24 will be set.

Timer logic is most frequently used with serial I/O in order to create default interrupts that alert a supervisory program to hangup or any error condition which is not identifying itself.

When you select the Test mode by writing 1 to Control register bit 15, the timer operates at 32 times its normal speed. This allows you to speed up timer testing. In addition, the timer acts as both transmit clock and receive clock in Test mode; therefore you can specify automatic baud rates for testing the transmitter and receiver.

DATA SHEETS

The following pages contain specific electrical and timing data for the following devices:

- TMS9900 CPU
- TMS9940 Microcomputer
- TIM9940 Clock Generator/Driver
- TMS9901 Programmable Systems Interface
- TMS9902 Asynchronous Communications Controller
- TMS9903 Synchronous Communications Controller

TMS 9900 ELECTRICAL AND MECHANICAL SPECIFICATIONS

ABSOLUTE MAXIMUM RATINGS OVER OPERATING FREE-AIR TEMPERATURE RANGE (UNLESS OTHERWISE NOTED)*

Supply voltage, V_{CC} (see Note 1)	-0.3 to 20 V
Supply voltage, V_{DD} (see Note 1)	-0.3 to 20 V
Supply voltage, V_{SS} (see Note 1)	-0.3 to 20 V
All input voltages (see Note 1)	-0.3 to 20 V
Output voltage (with respect to V_{SS})	-2 V to 7 V
Continuous power dissipation	1.2 W
Operating free-air temperature range	0°C to 70°C
Storage temperature range	-55°C to 150°C

*Stresses beyond those listed under "Absolute Maximum Ratings" may cause permanent damage to the device. This is a stress rating only and functional operation of the device at these or any other conditions beyond those indicated in the "Recommended Operating Conditions" section of this specification is not implied. Exposure to absolute-maximum-rated conditions for extended periods may affect device reliability.

NOTE 1: Under absolute maximum ratings voltage values are with respect to the most negative supply, V_{BB} (substrate), unless otherwise noted. Throughout the remainder of this section, voltage values are with respect to V_{SS}.

RECOMMENDED OPERATING CONDITIONS

	MIN	NOM	MAX	UNIT
Supply voltage, V_{BB}	-5.25	-5	-4.75	V
Supply voltage, V_{CC}	4.75	5	5.25	V
Supply voltage, V_{DD}	11.4	12	12.6	V
Supply voltage, V_{SS}		0		V
High-level input voltage, V_{IH} (all inputs except clocks)	2.2	2.4	V_{CC}+1	V
High-level clock input voltage, $V_{IH(\phi)}$	V_{DD}−2		V_{DD}	V
Low-level input voltage, V_{IL} (all inputs except clocks)	-1	0.4	0.8	V
Low-level clock input voltage, $V_{IL(\phi)}$	-0.3	0.3	0.6	V
Operating free-air temperature, T_A	0		70	$^\circ$C

ELECTRICAL CHARACTERISTICS OVER FULL RANGE OF RECOMMENDED OPERATING CONDITIONS (UNLESS OTHERWISE NOTED)

PARAMETER		TEST CONDITIONS	MIN	TYP[†]	MAX	UNIT
I_I Input current	Data bus during DBIN	$V_I = V_{SS}$ to V_{CC}		±50	±100	μA
	WE, MEMEN, DBIN, Address bus, Data bus during HOLDA	$V_I = V_{SS}$ to V_{CC}		±50	±100	
	Clock	$V_I = -0.3$ to 12.6 V		±25	±75	
	Any other inputs	$V_I = V_{SS}$ to V_{CC}		±1	±10	
V_{OH}	High-level output voltage	$I_O = -0.4$ mA	2.4		V_{CC}	V
V_{OL}	Low-level output voltage	$I_O = 3.2$ mA			0.65	V
		$I_O = 2$ mA			0.50	
$I_{BB(av)}$	Supply current from V_{BB}			0.1	1	mA*
$I_{CC(av)}$	Supply current from V_{CC}			50	75	mA*
$I_{DD(av)}$	Supply current from V_{DD}			25	45	mA*
C_i	Input capacitance (any inputs except clock and data bus)	$V_{BB} = -5$, f = 1MHz, unmeasured pins at V_{SS}		10	15	pF
$C_{i(\phi1)}$	Clock-1 input capacitance	$V_{BB} = -5$, f = 1MHz, unmeasured pins at V_{SS}		100	150	pF
$C_{i(\phi2)}$	Clock-2 input capacitance	$V_{BB} = -5$, f = 1MHz, unmeasured pins at V_{SS}		150	200	pF
$C_{i(\phi3)}$	Clock-3 input capacitance	$V_{BB} = -5$, f = 1MHz, unmeasured pins at V_{SS}		100	150	pF
$C_{i(\phi4)}$	Clock-4 input capacitance	$V_{BB} = -5$, f = 1MHz, unmeasured pins at V_{SS}		100	150	pF
C_{DB}	Data bus capacitance	$V_{BB} = -5$, f = 1MHz, unmeasured pins at V_{SS}		15	25	pF

[†] All typical values are at $T_A = 25^\circ$C and nominal voltages.
*D.C. Component of Operating Clock

Data sheets on pages 3-D2 through 3-D17 are reprinted by permission of Texas Instruments Incorporated.

TMS9900

TIMING REQUIREMENTS OVER FULL RANGE OF RECOMMENDED OPERATING CONDITIONS

PARAMETER		MIN	NOM	MAX	UNIT
$t_{c(\phi)}$	Clock cycle time	300	333	500	ns
$t_{r(\phi)}$	Clock rise time	5	12		ns
$t_{f(\phi)}$	Clock fall time	10	12		ns
$t_{w(\phi)}$	Clock pulse width, high level	40	45	100	ns
$t_{s(\phi)}$	Clock spacing, time between any two adjacent clock pulses	0	5		ns
$t_{d(\phi)}$	Time between rising edge valid any two adjacent clock pulses	73	83		ns
t_{su}	Data or control setup time before clock 1	30			ns
t_h	Data hold time after clock 1	10			ns

SWITCHING CHARACTERISTICS OVER FULL RANGE OF RECOMMENDED OPERATING CONDITIONS

PARAMETER		TEST CONDITIONS	MIN	TYP	MAX	UNIT
$t_{PLH (B)}$ or $t_{PHL (B)}$	All other outputs	$C_L = 200$ pF		20	40	ns
$t_{PLH (C)}$ or $t_{PHL (C)}$	Propagation delay CRUCLK, WE, MEMEN, WAIT, DBIN				30	ns

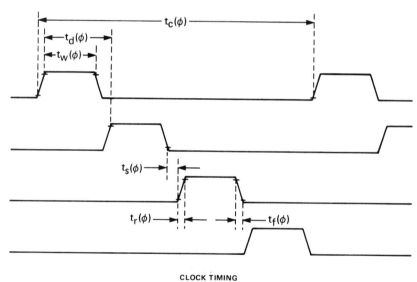

CLOCK TIMING

TMS9900

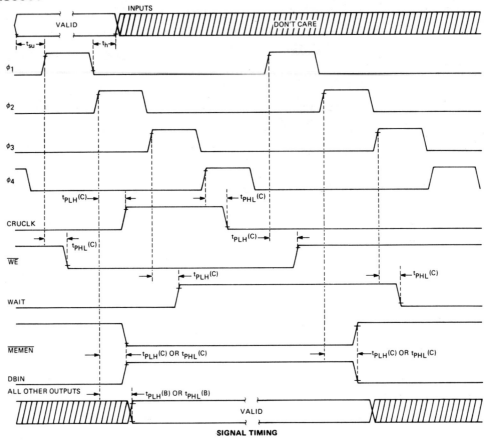

SIGNAL TIMING

TMS9940

TMS 9940E EPROM PROGRAMMING

ERASURE

Before programming, the TMS 9940E is erased by exposing the chip through the transparent lid to high-intensity ultraviolet light (wavelength:253.7 nanometers). The recommended exposure is 10 watt · seconds per square centimeter. This can be obtained by, for instance, 20 to 30 minutes exposure of a filterless Model S52 shortwave UV lamp about 2.5 centimeters above the EPROM. After exposure all bits are in the "0" state.

PROGRAMMING

The TMS 9940E should be initialized by $\overline{\text{RESET}}$ before the programming sequence begins. The EPROM consists of 16K bits of program memory organized as 2K bytes (8 bits each) located at (starting) address 0000_{16}. Data is transferred into the CPU for programming through P24(MSB)—P31 (LSB). Taking the PE signal active high (to V_{IP}) initializes the internal address pointer of 0000_{16} and inputs the first byte of data (see Figure 8). After a minimum delay of 40 clock cycles, PROG can be applied (V_{IP}, 50 ms) and the data present on P24–P31 updated to the next byte. The falling edge of PROG inputs the new byte of data to the next location and after a minimum delay of 25 clock cycles the PROG pulse can be applied again. This sequence is continued until the entire 2K bytes have been programmed. Note that the memory is programmed in sequence starting at 0000_{16}; and the input data must be valid at the rising edge of PE or falling edge of PROG.

TMS9940

RECOMMENDED PROGRAMMING/TEST FUNCTION CONDITIONS

	PARAMETER	MIN	NOM	MAX	UNIT
t_r	TST, PE, PROG input rise time		100		ns
t_f	TST, PE, PROG input fall time		100		ns
t_{su}	Input data setup time to rising edge of PE, TST or to falling edge of PROG		0		ns
t_h	Input data hold time past rising edge of PE, TST		$80\,t_{c(\phi)}$		ns
$t_{h(P-da)}$	Input data hold time past falling edge of PROG		$50\,t_{c(\phi)}$		ns
$t_{h(P-PE,T)}$	PE, TST input hold time past falling edge of PROG		0		ns
$t_{su(P-PE,T)}$	PROG input setup time to rising edge of PE, TST		0		ns
$t_{h(T-PL)}$	PROG input pulse low past rising edge of TST, PE		$80\,t_{c(\phi)}$		ns
$t_{w(PL)}$	PROG input pulse width low		$50\,t_{c(\phi)}$		ns
$t_{w(PHP)}$	PROG input pulse width high in the programming mode		50		ms
$t_{w(PHT)}$	PROG input pulse width high in the test mode		$4\,t_{c(\phi)}$		ns

NOTE: Timing diagrams in Figure 8.

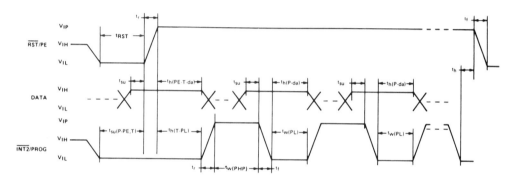

FIGURE 8 – EPROM PROGRAMMING TIMING DIAGRAM

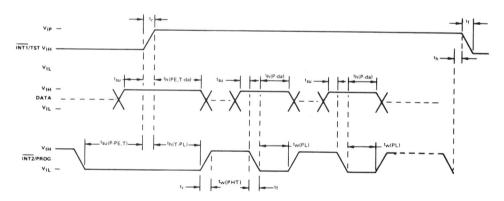

FIGURE 9 – TEST FUNCTION TIMING DIAGRAM

TMS9940

TEST FUNCTION

This test function allows loading a program into the RAM area of the TMS 9940 through pins P24 through P31. This program can then be executed, and the results of this execution used to verify operation of the TMS 9940. The program could include error messages as well as a successful completion message sent to a peripheral device accessed through the CRU.

The processor should be initialized by $\overline{\text{RESET}}$ before any test sequence begins. Data is directly loaded in sequence into the RAM through P24 (MSB)—P31 (LSB). Taking the TST signal high (to V_{IP}) initializes the internal address pointer to 8300_{16} (starting address of RAM) and inputs the first byte of data (see Figure 9). After a minimum delay of 40 clock cycles PROG can be applied (V_{IH}, 4 clock cycles minimum) and the data present on P24—P31 updated to the next byte. The falling edge of PROG inputs the new byte of data to the next location and, after a minimum delay of 25 clock cycles, PROG can be applied again. This sequence is continued until the desired data has been loaded into the RAM. Taking TST inactive will then jump the processor to the address specified by the last 16 bits loaded. Note that the RAM is loaded in sequence starting at 8300_{16}, and the input data must be valid at the rising edge of TST or on the falling edge of PROG.

TMS 9940 ELECTRICAL SPECIFICATIONS

ABSOLUTE MAXIMUM RATINGS OVER OPERATING FREE-AIR TEMPERATURE RANGE (UNLESS OTHERWISE NOTED)*

Supply Voltage, V_{CC1}†	−0.3 to 20 V
Supply Voltage, V_{CC2}	−0.3 to 20 V
Programming Voltage, PE	−0.3 to 35 V
All Input Voltages	−0.3 to 20 V
Output Voltage	−2 to 7 V
Continuous Power Dissipation	1.5 W
Operating Free-Air Temperature Range	0°C to 70°C
Storage Temperature Range	−55°C to 150°C

* Stresses beyond those listed under "Absolute Maximum Ratings" may cause permanent damage to the device. This is a stress rating only and functional operation of the device at these or any other conditions beyond those indicated in the "Recommended Operating Conditions" section of this specification is not implied. Exposure to absolute-maximum-rated conditions for extended periods may affect device reliability.

†All voltage values are with respect to V_{SS}.

RECOMMENDED OPERATING CONDITIONS

PARAMETER	MIN	NOM	MAX	UNIT
Supply voltage, V_{CC1}		5		V
Supply voltage, V_{CC2}		5		V
Supply voltage, V_{SS}		0		V
High-level input voltage, V_{IH}	2			V
Low-level input voltage, V_{IL}			0.8	V
Program/test input voltage, V_{IP}		26		V
Operating free-air temperature, T_A	0		70	°C

ELECTRICAL CHARACTERISTICS

	PARAMETER	TEST CONDITIONS	MIN	TYP	MAX	UNITS
I_I	Input current, any inputs	$V_I = V_{SS}$ to V_{CC}		±10		μA
V_{OH},	High-level output voltage, any outputs	$I_O = 0.4$ mA		2.4		V
V_{OL},	Low-level output voltage, any outputs	$I_O = 2$ mA		0.4		V
I_{CC1},	Supply current from V_{CC1}			10		mA
I_{CC2},	Supply current from V_{CC2}			150		mA
C_i,	Input capacitance, any inputs	f = 1 MHz, unmeasured pins at V_{SS}		15		pF
C_o,	Output capacitance, any outputs	f = 1 MHz, unmeasured pins at V_{SS}		15		pF

TMS9940

CLOCK CHARACTERISTICS

The TMS 9940 has an internal oscillator and a two-phase clock generator controlled by an external or crystal. The user may also disable the oscillator and directly inject a frequency source into the XTAL2 input. The crystal frequency and the external frequency source must be double the desired system CLOCK frequency.

Internal Oscillator

The internal oscillator is enabled by connecting a crystal across XTAL1 and XTAL2. The system CLOCK frequency $1/t_{c(\phi)}$, is one-half the crystal oscillator frequency, f_{osc}.

PARAMETER	PART NUMBER	TEST CONDITIONS	MIN	NOM	MAX	UNITS
f_{osc}	TMS 9940E, TMS 9940M		0.5	5	5.12	MHz
f_{osc}	TMS 9940E-40, TMS 9940M-40		0.5	4	4.10	MHz
f_{osc}	TMS 9940E-30, TMS 9940M-30	$T_A = 0°C$ to $70°C$	0.5	3	3.07	MHz
f_{osc}	TMS 9940E-20, TMS 9940M-20		0.5	2	2.05	MHz
f_{osc}	TMS 9490E-10, TMS 9940M-10		0.5	1	1.02	MHz

Note: $t_{cv} = 1/f_{osc}$
$t_{c(\phi)} = 2 \cdot t_{cy}$

TIM9904

ELECTRICAL SPECIFICATIONS

Absolute Maximum Ratings Over Operating Free-Air Temperature Range (Unless Otherwise Noted)

Supply voltage: V_{CC} (see Note 1) .... 7 V
V_{DD} (see Note 1) .... 13 V
Input voltage: OSCIN .... 5.5 V
FFD .... −0.5 V to 7 V
Operating free-air temperature range .... 0°C to 70°C
Storage temperature range .... −65°C to 150°C

NOTE 1: Voltage values are with respect to the network ground terminals connected together.

Recommended Operating Conditions

		MIN	NOM	MAX	UNIT
Supply voltages	V_{CC}	4.75	5	5.25	V
	V_{DD}	11.4	12	12.6	V
High-level output current, I_{OH}	$\phi1, \phi2, \phi3, \phi4$			−100	μA
	All others			−400	μA
Low-level output current, I_{OL}	$\phi1, \phi2, \phi3, \phi4$			4	mA
	All others			8	mA
Internal oscillator frequency, f_{osc}			48	54	MHz
External oscillator pulse width, $t_{w(osc)}$		25			ns
Setup time, FFD input (with respect to falling edge of $\phi3$), t_{su}		50			ns
Hold time, FFD input (with respect to falling edge of $\phi3$), t_h		−30			ns
Operating free-air temperature, T_A		0		70	°C

TIM9904

Electrical Characteristics Over Recommended Operating Free-Air Temperature Range (Unless Otherwise Noted)

PARAMETER			TEST CONDITIONS		MIN	TYP‡	MAX	UNIT
V_{IH}	High-level input voltage				2			V
V_{IL}	Low-level input voltage	FFD					0.5	V
		OSCIN					0.8	
$V_{T+} - V_{T-}$	Hysteresis	FFD			0.4	0.8		V
V_{IK}	Input clamp voltage		V_{CC} = 4.75 V, V_{DD} = 11.4 V, I_I = −18 mA				−1.5	V
V_{OH}	High-level output voltage	$\phi1, \phi2, \phi3, \phi4$	V_{CC} = 4.75 V, V_{DD} = 11.4 V to 12.6 V	I_{OH} = −100 μA	$V_{DD}-2$	$V_{DD}-1.5$	V_{DD}	V
		Other outputs		I_{OH} = −400 μA	2.7	3.4		
V_{OL}	Low-level output voltage	$\phi1, \phi2, \phi3, \phi4$	V_{CC} = 4.75 V, V_{DD} = 11.4 V	I_{OL} = 4 mA		0.25	0.4	mA
		Other outputs		I_{OL} = 4 mA		0.25	0.4	
				I_{OL} = 8 mA		0.35	0.5	
I_I	Input current at maximum input voltage	FFD	V_{CC} = 5.25 V, V_{DD} = 12.6 V	V_I = 7 V			0.1	mA
		OSCIN		V_I = 5.5 V			0.3	
I_{IH}	High-level input current	FFD	V_{CC} = 5.25 V, V_{DD} = 12.6 V, V_I = 2.7 V				20	μA
		OSCIN					60	
I_{IL}	Low-level input current	FFD	V_{CC} = 5.25 V, V_{DD} = 12.6 V, V_I = 0.4 V				−0.4	mA
		OSCIN					−3.2	
I_{OS}	Short-circuit output current‡	All except $\phi1, \phi2, \phi3, \phi4$	V_{CC} = 5.25 V		−20		−100	mA
I_{CC}	Supply current from V_{CC}		V_{CC} = 5.25 V, FFD and OSCIN at GND, Outputs open			105	175	mA
I_{DD}	Supply current from V_{DD}		V_{CC} = 5.25 V, V_{DD} = 12.6 V, FFD and OSCIN at GND, Outputs open			12	20	mA

† All typical values are at V_{CC} = 5 V, V_{DD} = 12 V, T_A = 25°C.

‡ Not more than one output should be shorted at a time, and duration of the short-circuit should not exceed one second. Outputs $\phi1$, $\phi2$, $\phi3$, and $\phi4$ do not have short-circuit protection.

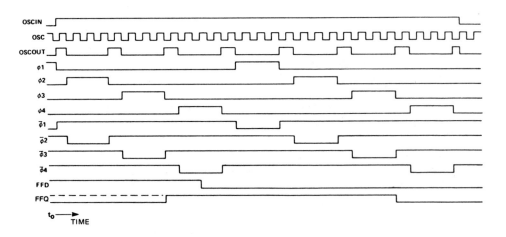

TYPICAL PHASE RELATIONSHIPS OF INPUTS AND OUTPUTS (INTERNAL OSC)

TIM9904

Switching Characteristics, $T_A = 25°C$, $V_{CC1} = 5 V$, $V_{CC2} = 12 V$, $f_{osc} = 48 MHz$

	PARAMETER	TEST CONDITIONS	MIN	TYP	MAX	UNIT
f_{out}	Output frequency, any ϕ or $\bar{\phi}$ TTL			3		MHz
f_{out}	Output frequency, OSCOUT			12		MHz
$t_{c(\phi)}$	Cycle time, any ϕ output		330	333	340	ns
$t_{r(\phi)}$	Rise time, any ϕ output		5		20	ns
$t_{f(\phi)}$	Fall time, any ϕ output		10	14	20	ns
$t_{w(\phi)}$	Pulse width, any ϕ output high		40	55	70	ns
$t_{\phi1L, \phi2H}$	Delay time, ϕ1 low to ϕ2 high		0	5	15	ns
$t_{\phi2L, \phi3H}$	Delay time, ϕ2 low to ϕ3 high		0	5	15	ns
$t_{\phi3L, \phi4H}$	Delay time, ϕ3 low to ϕ4 high		0	5	15	ns
$t_{\phi4L, \phi1H}$	Delay time, ϕ4 low to ϕ1 high	Output loads:	0	5	15	ns
$t_{\phi1H, \phi2H}$	Delay time, ϕ1 high to ϕ2 high	ϕ1, ϕ3, ϕ4: 100 pF to GND	73	83	96	ns
$t_{\phi2H, \phi3H}$	Delay time, ϕ2 high to ϕ3 high	ϕ2: 200 pF to GND	73	83	96	ns
$t_{\phi3H, \phi4H}$	Delay time, ϕ3 high to ϕ4 high	Others: $R_L = 2 k\Omega$,	73	83	96	ns
$t_{\phi4H, \phi1H}$	Delay time, ϕ4 high to ϕ1 high	$C_L = 15 pF$	73	83	96	ns
$t_{\phi H, \phi TL}$	Delay time, ϕ_n high to $\bar{\phi}_n$ TTL low		−14	−4	6	ns
$t_{\phi L, \phi TH}$	Delay time, ϕ_n low to $\bar{\phi}_n$ TTL high		−29	−19	−9	ns
$t_{\phi3L, QH}$	Delay time, ϕ3 low to FFQ output high		−18	−8	2	ns
$t_{\phi3L, QL}$	Delay time, ϕ3 low to FFQ output low		−19	−9	1	ns
$t_{\phi L, OSOH}$	Delay time, ϕ low to OSCOUT high		−30	−20	−10	ns
$t_{\phi H, OSOL}$	Delay time, FFQ high to OSCOUT low		−27	−17	−7	ns

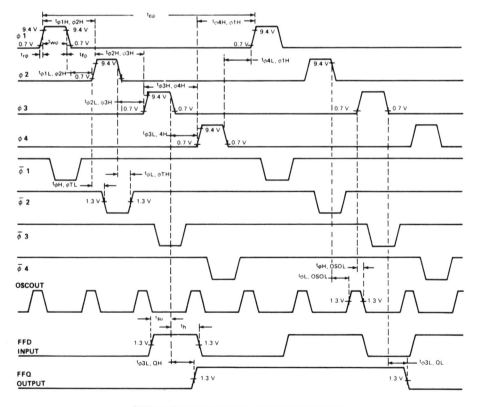

SWITCHING CHARACTERISTICS, VOLTAGE WAVEFORMS

TIM9904

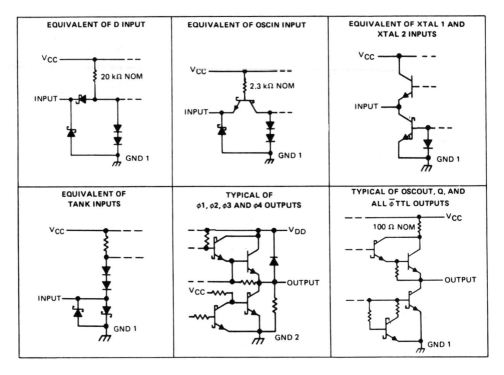

SCHEMATICS OF INPUTS AND OUTPUTS

TMS9901

TMS 9901 ELECTRICAL SPECIFICATIONS

Absolute Maximum Ratings Over Operating Free Air Temperature Range (Unless Otherwise Noted) *

Supply voltage, V_{CC}	-0.3 V to 10 V
All inputs and output voltages	-0.3 V to 10 V
Continuous power dissipation	0.85 W
Operating free-air temperature range	0°C to 70°C
Storage temperature range	$-65°C$ to 150°C

*Stresses beyond those listed under "Absolute Maximum Ratings" may cause permanent damage to the device. This is a stress rating only and functional operation of the device at these or any other conditions beyond those indicated in the "Recommended Operating Conditions" section of this specification is not implied. Exposure to absolute maximum rated conditions for extended periods may affect device reliability.

Recommended Operating Conditions *

PARAMETER	MIN	NOM	MAX	UNIT
Supply voltage, V_{CC}	4.75	5.0	5.25	V
Supply voltage, V_{SS}		0		V
High-level input voltage, V_{IH}	2.0		V_{CC}	V
Low-level input voltage, V_{IL}	$V_{SS}-.3$		0.8	V
Operating free-air temperature, T_A	0		70	°C

TMS9901

Electrical Characteristics Over Full Range of Recommended Operating Conditions (Unless Otherwise Noted) *

PARAMETER		TEST CONDITIONS	MIN	TYP	MAX	UNIT
V_{OH}	High level output voltage	$I_{OH} = -100\ \mu A$	2.4		V_{CC}	V
		$I_{OH} = -200\ \mu A$	2.2		V_{CC}	V
V_{OL}	Low level output voltage	$I_{OL} = 3.2\ mA$	V_{SS}		0.4	V
I_I	Input current (any input)	$V_I = 0\ V$ to V_{CC}			±100	μA
$I_{CC(av)}$	Average supply current from V_{CC}	$t_{c(\phi)} = 330\ ns$, $T_A = 70°C$			150	mA
C_I	Small signal input capacitance, any input	$f = 1\ MHz$			15	pF

Timing Requirements Over Full Range of Operating Conditions

PARAMETER		MIN	TYP	MAX	UNIT
$t_{c(\phi)}$	Clock cycle time	300	333	2000	ns
$t_{r(\phi)}$	Clock rise time	5		40	ns
$t_{f(\phi)}$	Clock fall time	10		40	ns
$t_{w(\phi H)}$	Clock pulse width (high level)	225			ns
$t_{w(\phi L)}$	Clock pulse width (low level)	45		300	ns
$t_{w(CC)}$	CRUCLK pulse width	100	185		ns
t_{su1}	Setup time for CE, S0-S4, or CRUOUT before CRUCLK	100			ns
t_{su2}	Setup time for interrupt before ϕ low	60			ns
t_{su3}	Setup time for inputs before valid CRUIN	200			ns
t_h	Hold time for CE, S0-S4, or CRUOUT after CRUCLK	60			ns

*NOTE: All voltage values are referenced to V_{SS}.

Switching Characteristics Over Full Range of Recommended Operating Conditions

PARAMETER		TEST CONDITION	MIN	TYP	MAX	UNIT
t_{pd1}	Propagation delay, CE to valid CRUIN	$C_L = 100\ pF$			300	ns
t_{pd2}	Propagation delay, S0-S4 to valid CRUIN	$C_L = 100\ pF$			320	ns
t_{pd3}	Propagation delay, ϕ low to valid INTREQ, IC0-IC3	$C_L = 100\ pF$			110	ns
t_{pd}	Propagation delay, CRUCLK to valid data out (P0-P15)	$C_L = 100\ pF$			300	ns

TMS9901

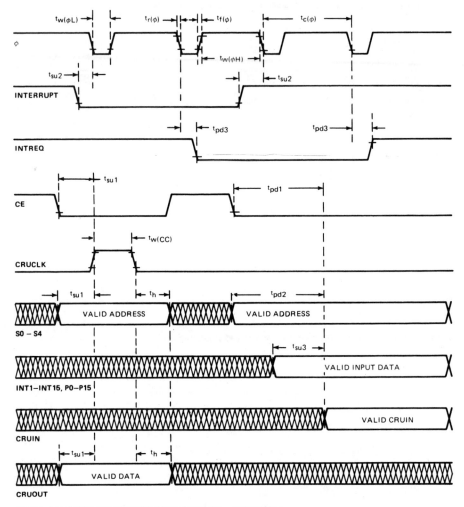

NOTE 1: ALL TIMING MEASUREMENTS ARE FROM 10% and 90% POINTS.

SWITCHING CHARACTERISTICS

TMS9902

TMS 9902 ELECTRICAL SPECIFICATIONS

Absolute Maximum Ratings Over Operating Free Air Temperature Range (Unless Otherwise Noted) *

Supply voltage, V_{CC}	-0.3 V to 10 V
All inputs and output voltages	-0.3 V to 10 V
Continuous power dissipation	0.55 W
Operating free-air temperature range	0°C to 70°C
Storage temperature range	-65°C to 150°C

*Stresses beyond those listed under "Absolute Maximum Ratings" may cause permanent damage to the device. This is a stress rating only and functional operation of the device at these or any other conditions beyond those indicated in the "Recommended Operating Conditions" section of this specification is not implied. Exposure to absolute maximum rated conditions for extended periods may affect device reliability.

Recommended Operating Conditions *

PARAMETER	MIN	NOM	MAX	UNIT
Supply voltage, V_{CC}	4.75	5.0	5.25	V
Supply voltage, V_{SS}		0		V
High-level input voltage, V_{IH}	2.0		V_{CC}	V
Low-level input voltage, V_{IL}	$V_{SS}-.3$		0.8	V
Operating free-air temperature, T_A	0		70	°C

Electrical Characteristics Over Full Range of Recommended Operating Conditions (Unless Otherwise Noted) *

PARAMETER		TEST CONDITIONS	MIN	TYP	MAX	UNIT
V_{OH}	High level output voltage	$I_{OH} = -100\,\mu A$	2.4		V_{CC}	V
		$I_{OH} = -200\,\mu A$	2.2		V_{CC}	V
V_{OL}	Low level output voltage	$I_{OL} = 3.2$ mA	V_{SS}		0.4	V
I_I	Input current (any input)	$V_I = 0$ V to V_{CC}			± 10	μA
$I_{CC(av)}$	Average supply current from V_{CC}	$t_{c(\phi)} = 330$ ns, $T_A = 70$°C			100	mA
C_i	Small signal input capacitance, any input	$f = 1$ MHz			15	pF

Timing Requirements Over Full Range of Operating Conditions

PARAMETER		MIN	TYP	MAX	UNIT
$t_{c(\phi)}$	Clock cycle time	300	333	667	ns
$t_{r(\phi)}$	Clock rise time	5		40	ns
$t_{f(\phi)}$	Clock fall time	10		40	ns
$t_{w(\phi H)}$	Clock pulse width (high level)	225			ns
$t_{w(\phi L)}$	Clock pulse width (low level)	45			ns
$t_{w(CC)}$	CRUCLK pulse width	100	185		ns
t_{su1}	Setup time for $\overline{CE}$ before CRUCLK	150			ns
t_{su2}	Setup time for S0-S4, or CRUOUT before CRUCLK	180			ns
t_h	Hold time for $\overline{CE}$, S0-S4, or CRUOUT after CRUCLK	60			ns

*NOTE: All voltage values are referenced to V_{SS}.

Switching Characteristics Over Full Range of Recommended Operating Conditions

PARAMETER		TEST CONDITION	MIN	TYP	MAX	UNIT
t_{pd1}	Propagation delay, $\overline{CE}$ to valid CRUIN	$CL = 100$pF			300	ns
t_{pd2}	Propagation delay, S0-S4 to valid CRUIN	$CL = 100$pF			320	ns

TMS9902

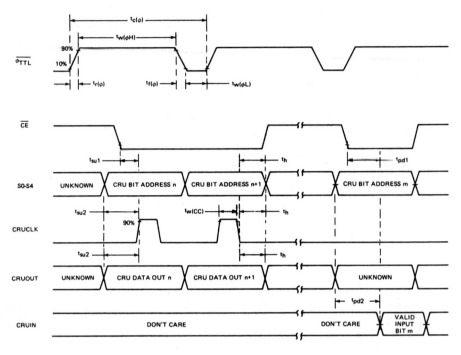

SWITCHING CHARACTERISTICS

NOTE: ALL SWITCHING TIMES ARE ASSUMED TO BE AT 10% OR 90% VALUES.

EQUIVALENT OF I/O INPUTS

EQUIVALENT OF I/O OUTPUTS

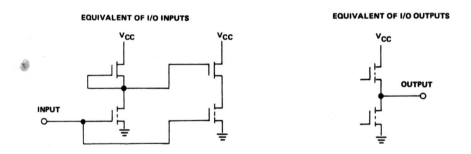

INPUT AND OUTPUT EQUIVALENTS

EQUIVALENT OF OUTPUTS	EQUIVALENT OF INPUTS
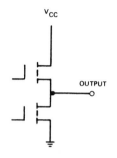	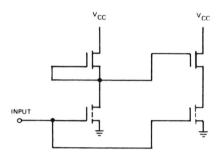

TMS 9903 ELECTRICAL SPECIFICATIONS

ABSOLUTE MAXIMUM RATING OVER OPERATING FREE AIR TEMPERATURE RANGE (UNLESS OTHERWISE NOTED)*

Supply voltage, V_{CC} (Note) .... −0.3 V to 10 V
All inputs and output voltages .... −0.3 V to 20 V
Continuous power dissipation .... 0.7 W
Operating free-air temperature range .... 0°C to 70°C
Storage temperature range .... −65°C to 150°C

*Stresses beyond those listed under "Absolute Maximum Ratings" may cause permanent damage to the device. This is a stress rating only and functional operation of the device at these or any other conditions beyond those indicated in the "Recommended Operating Conditions" section of this specification is not implied. Exposure to absolute maximum rated conditions for extended periods may affect device reliability.

RECOMMENDED OPERATING CONDITIONS

PARAMETER	MIN	NOM	MAX	UNIT
Supply voltage, V_{CC}	4.75	5.0	5.25	V
Supply voltage, V_{SS}		0		V
High-level input voltage, V_{IH}	2.0	2.4	V_{CC}	V
Low-level input voltage, V_{IL}	$V_{SS} - .3$	0.4	0.8	V
Operating free-air temperature, T_A	0		70	°C

ELECTRICAL CHARACTERISTICS OVER FULL RANGE OF RECOMMENDED OPERATING CONDITIONS (UNLESS OTHERWISE NOTED)

	PARAMETER	TEST CONDITIONS	MIN	TYP	MAX	UNIT
V_{OH}	High-level output voltage	$I_{OH} = -100 \mu A$	2.4		V_{CC}	V
		$I_{OH} = -200 \mu A$	2.2			
V_{OL}	Low-level output voltage	$I_{OL} = 3.2$ mA	V_{SS}		0.4	V
I_I	Input current (any input)	$V_I = 0$ V to V_{CC}		±10		μA
$I_{CC(av)}$	Average supply current from V_{CC}	$t_{c(\phi)} = 330$ ns, $t_A = 70°C$		150		mA
C_i	Capacitance, any input	$f = 1$ MHz, all other pins at 0 V		15		pF

NOTE: All voltages are in reference to V_{SS}.

TMS9903

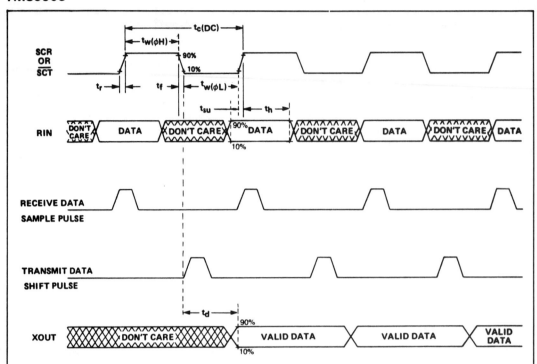

	PARAMETER	MIN	TYP	MAX	UNIT
$t_{c(DC)}$	Receiver/transmit data clock cycle time		4		μS
$t_{w(\phi H)}$	Clock pulse width (high level)		2		μS
$t_{w(\phi L)}$	Clock pulse width (low level)		2		μS
t_r	Rise time		12		ns
t_f	Fall time		12		ns
t_{su}	Setup time for RIN before SCR (DRCK32 = 0)*		250		ns
t_h	Hold time for RIN after SCR (DRCK32 = 0)*		50		ns
t_d	Delay time, SCT to valid XOUT		400		ns

*No setup, hold, or data synchronization is required for pin in the divide-by-32 mode (DRCK32 = 1).

RECEIVE/TRANSMIT DATA CLOCK TIMING DIAGRAM

TMS9903

SWITCHING CHARACTERISTICS OVER FULL RANGE OF RECOMMENDED OPERATING
CONDITIONS

	PARAMETER	TEST CONDITION	MIN	TYP	MAX	UNIT
t_{pD1}	Propagation delay, CE to valid CRUIN	$C_L = 100$ pF		300		ns
t_{pD2}	Propagation delay, S0-S4 to valid CRUIN	$C_L = 100$ pF		320		ns

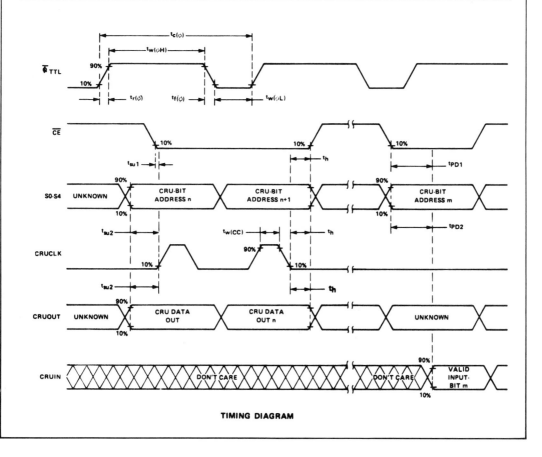

TIMING DIAGRAM

Chapter 4
SINGLE CHIP NOVA MINICOMPUTER
CENTRAL PROCESSING UNITS

In this chapter we are going to look at two microprocessors which are the world's first single chip reproductions of established 16-bit minicomputers. We are going to describe two products which reproduce, on a single chip, the logic of a Nova Central Processing Unit.

Nova minicomputers are built by Data General Corporation.

Data General Corporation offer a set of LSI chips centered on the MicroNova microprocessor. These chips are described quite superficially in this chapter since Data General is not actively marketing them as LSI devices. Rather, Data General favor the sale of MicroNova microcomputer systems.

Fairchild manufacture the 9440 microprocessor, which is sold primarily as an LSI device. The 9440 is therefore described in some detail, together with standard Nova I/O bus and typical memory bus interface bus logic.

The Nova minicomputer was designed as a next generation enhancement of the PDP-8. The IM6100, which is described in Chapter 13 of the Osborne 4 & 8-Bit Microprocessor Handbook is a single chip implementation of the PDP-8 Central Processing Unit.

If you compare the Nova architectures, which we describe in this chapter, with the IM1600, the two products will indeed look very different. But conceptually they are similar. Both the Nova and the PDP-8 Central Processing Units have few addressable registers; for computing power they rely upon instructions which may perform complex sequences of operations. Similarities between the Nova and the PDP-8 will become more apparent if you compare these two devices with the CP1600 and the TMS990 — which we have described in Chapters 2 and 3, respectively.

What is interesting about the Nova minicomputer is that it is one of the most popular in the world; and Data General Corporation is the second largest minicomputer manufacturer in the world, despite the fact that many aspects of the Nova Central Processing Unit may, on first inspection, appear to be very restricting.

The MicroNova is manufactured by:

> DATA GENERAL CORPORATION
> Mail Stop 6-58
> Southborough, MA 01772

The 9440 is manufactured by:

> FAIRCHILD SEMICONDUCTOR
> 464 Ellis Street
> Mountain View, CA 94040

The MicroNova and the 9440 are not the same; differences, however, are small.

The MicroNova is equivalent to the Nova 3 minicomputer. The Nova 3 is a low-end minicomputer recently introduced by Data General. Although it is a low-end product, it includes a number of features not found in the basic Nova architecture.

The 9440 reproduces basic Nova architecture — that is, the lowest common denominator of architectural features found in any Nova Central Processing Unit. As such, the 9440 lacks a number of logic features provided by the MicroNova. The 9440, however, has higher instruction execution speeds.

Because the MicroNova and the 9440 are very similar, we are going to describe them together in this chapter.

The MicroNova is manufactured using NMOS LSI technology. The 9440 is manufactured using Isoplanar integrated injection logic (I^3L) technology.

Both products are packaged as 40-pin DIPs.

The MicroNova requires four power supplies: -4.25V, +5V, +10V and +14V. The 9440 requires two power supplies: +5V and +350 mA.

Using a 240 nanosecond clock, the MicroNova executes instructions in 2.4 to 10 microseconds. Using a 100 nanosecond clock, 9440 instructions will execute in 1 to 2.5 microseconds.

A PRODUCT OVERVIEW

Figure 4-1 illustrates that part of our general microcomputer system logic which has been implemented by the MicroNova and the 9440.

Note that only the MicroNova has a Stack Pointer, and DMA logic.

Most Nova minicomputers do not have a Stack; the 9440 is a reproduction of the basic Nova architecture, which is why the 9440 lacks a Stack.

The MicroNova and Nova 3 do contain Stacks, because the addition of the Stack is technologically straightforward, while the lack of a Stack had been one of the most distressing features of earlier Nova minicomputers.

Both the 9440 and the MicroNova have DMA request and DMA acknowledge signals; however, in response to a DMA request, the 9440 does nothing except float the System Bus. It is up to you to provide any and all external logic needed to actually perform a data transfer via direct memory access. The MicroNova, on the other hand, executes the required sequence of I/O operations to actually perform the DMA transfer. That is why in Figure 4-1 DMA logic is shown as being present on the MicroNova but not the 9440.

What about I/O ports? I/O ports interface logic is shown as absent in Figure 4-1. The I/O port is a microcomputer concept.

In any microcomputer configuration, you will look upon I/O ports as the ultimate interface between the microcomputer system and external logic. You need a conduit via which data bits or signals can be transferred to, or received from logic beyond the microcomputer system. Each conduit becomes an I/O port and an I/O port becomes a set of pins, which can be addressed as a unit on a support device. Minicomputers take a conceptually different approach to I/O operations. To begin with, data is generally transferred to or from the CPU — not signals. The data finishes up on a System Bus. Therefore a minicomputer's interface with the outside world consists of an I/O System Bus and a memory System Bus. In some cases the two busses are one; in other cases, such as the Nova minicomputers, these two are separate and distinct busses. Conceptually, what is important is the fact that the minicomputer anticipates transferring data via its I/O System Bus to line printers, disk units, or other substantial devices each of which is capable of having a significant amount of local logic. Thus the System Bus is as far as the minicomputer attempts to go when defining its interface to the outside world.

Figure 4-1, including bus interface logic within the logic of the Central Processing Unit, needs some clarification. As we have just stated, the Nova minicomputer creates two separate System Busses: one for memory, the other for I/O devices. All the signals of these two busses originate at card edge pins. There is nothing very expensive about adding more pins to the edge of a card, as there is to adding more pins to a DIP. Therefore the Nova System Bus has 47 signals. Since neither the MicroNova nor the 9440 can have 47 signals, neither of these two devices creates standard Nova System Busses; but each device creates its own System Bus which could be used to drive external logic. That is why interface logic is shown as being present in Figure 4-1.

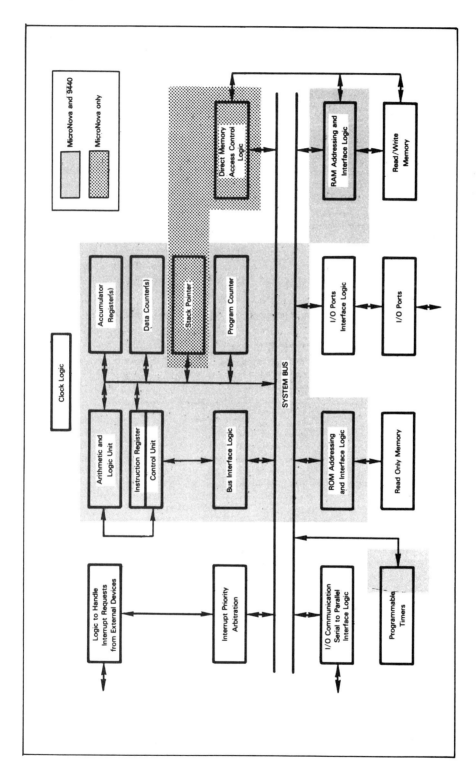

Figure 4-1. Logic of the Data General MicroNova and the Fairchild 9440

There is one further major difference between the MicroNova and the 9440 which is not evident from Figure 4-1. The MicroNova provides transparent dynamic memory refresh logic. The 9440 has no dynamic memory refresh logic.

The MicroNova, but not the 9440, contains an elementary interval timer capability. Providing interrupt timer logic is enabled, the MicroNova will generate an interrupt request every 20,000 instruction cycles. Using a standard 8.333 MHz clock, this translates to an interrupt request occurring every 2.4 msec.

Note that the MicroNova and the Nova 3 interval timer logic differ. The Nova 3 provides four programmable interval timer options; the MicroNova provides just one.

NOVA PROGRAMMABLE REGISTERS

These are the programmable registers of the MicroNova and the 9440:

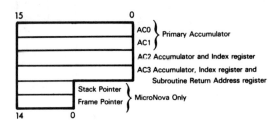

Data General literature numbers registers and memory words from left to right, rather than as illustrated above, from right to left. Also Data General is one of the few minicomputer manufacturers that uses octal numbering. In order to remain consistent with the rest of this book, we will use hexadecimal numbers, and we will number registers from right to left; where confusions may arise, we will show both our standard numbers and Data General equivalents.

AC0 and AC1 are typical primary Accumulators. AC2 and AC3 may be used as Accumulators or as Index registers. The Jump-to-Subroutine instruction automatically stores the return address in AC3. If one subroutine is going to call another (i.e., you are nesting subroutines), then the calling subroutine must save the contents of AC3 before itself calling another subroutine.

Only the MicroNova has a Stack Pointer. The only instructions that access the Stack Pointer are "Push" and "Pop" instructions.

The MicroNova, but not the 9440, also contains a Frame Pointer register. The Frame Pointer register is an address buffer used to access the Stack. This may be illustrated as follows:

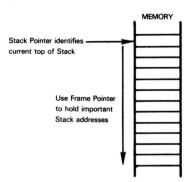

The Frame Pointer is a buffer register; it is not a Data Counter. There are no instructions that access the memory location addressed by the Frame Pointer.

Observe that we show no programmable registers identified as Data Counters, even though in Figure 4-1 we show Data Counter logic as being present. This is because the Data Counter is another microcomputer concept — in effect, a subset of the Index register. If a memory reference instruction specifies direct, indexed addressing with a zero displacement, then Index Registers AC2 and AC3 are equivalent to Data Counters.

NOVA MEMORY ADDRESSING MODES

Both the MicroNova and the 9440 offer the following standard Nova memory addressing modes:

1) **Base page, direct addressing**
2) **Program relative, paged, direct addressing**
3) **Indirect addressing**
4) **Indirect addressing with auto-increment**
5) **Indirect addressing with auto-decrement**
6) **Direct, indexed addressing**
7) **Pre-indexed, indirect addressing**

These addressing modes have been described in Volume 1, Chapter 6.

Nova memory addressing modes are heavily influenced by the fact that every Nova instruction generates a single 16-bit object code — just as the predecessor PDP-8 instructions each generated a single 12-bit object code. Even memory reference instructions are confined to 16 bits of object code; therefore the memory reference instruction can only provide a short address displacement. Whereas PDP-8 memory reference instructions provide a 7-bit address displacement, the Nova provides an 8-bit address displacement, which is handled in a much more intelligent fashion.

Nova instructions that use simple, direct addressing treat the 8-bit displacements as a direct, page zero address, or as a signed binary, program relative displacement. Thus you can directly address the first 256 words of memory, or you can address any location within +127 to -128 words of the memory reference instruction itself:

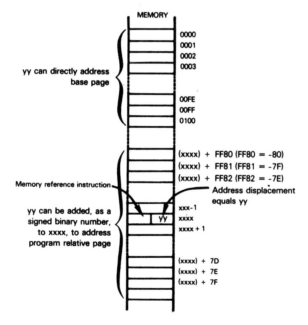

Remember, in microcomputer applications, program relative direct addressing is fine for Jump instructions, but is of limited value when accessing data memory. When a microcomputer program is stored in read-only memory, program relative, direct addressing can be used to read constant data only.

Nova instructions that specify direct, indexed addressing, compute the effective memory address as the contents of either AC2 or AC3, plus the 8-bit displacement provided by the instruction object code. The 8-bit displacement is treated as a signed binary number. Since the Index registers are 16 bits wide, direct indexed addressing allows you to address any memory word. This may be illustrated as follows:

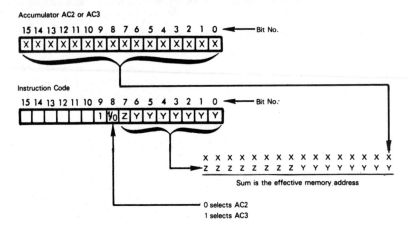

Indirect addressing may be superimposed on any of the memory addressing options described thus far. Indirect addressing is identified by a "1" in bit 10 of the Memory Reference instruction's object code. When indirect addressing is specified, the effective memory address is the contents of the directly addressed memory word.

Let us examine the various indirect addressing options. First there is page zero indirect addressing:

NOVA
DIRECT
MEMORY
ADDRESSING

NOVA
INDIRECT
PAGE ZERO
ADDRESSING

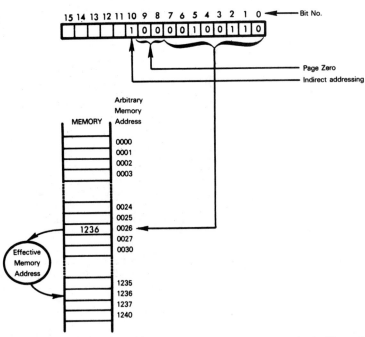

In the illustration above, arbitrary, real memory addresses have been selected to make the illustration easier to understand.

Program relative. indirect addressing may be illustrated as follows:

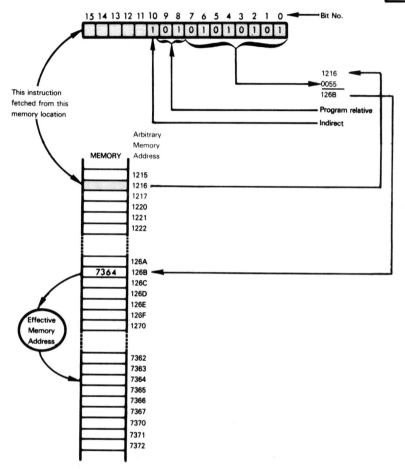

Indirect. indexed addressing may be illustrated as follows:

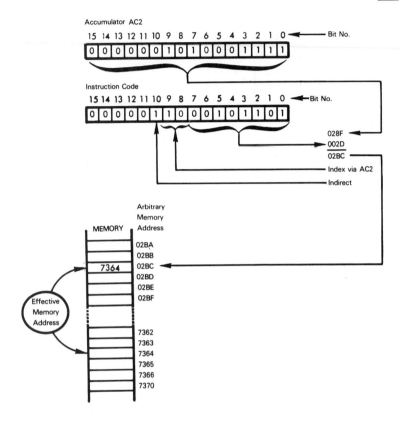

The illustration above arbitrarily uses indexed addressing via Accumulator AC2. Also the computed effective memory address is identical to that which was obtained in the indirect. program relative addressing illustration.

Observe that Nova indirect addressing logic results in pre-indexed indirect addressing. As described in Volume 1. Chapter 6. this is less desirable than post-indexed indirect addressing.

If, and only if indirect addressing has been specified by a "1" in bit 10 of a Memory Reference instruction's object code, then the contents of the data fetched from memory are treated as a direct address, providing the high-order bit of the direct address is 0. If the high-order bit of the address is 1, then the address is treated as another indirect address pointer. This may be illustrated as follows:

NOVA MULTIPLE INDIRECT ADDRESSING

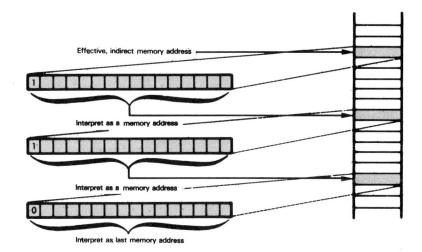

Effective, indirect memory address

Interpret as a memory address

Interpret as a memory address

Interpret as last memory address

Note carefully that multilevel indirect addressing will occur only when indirect addressing is specified in the first place. If you execute a direct memory reference instruction, data will never be interpreted as an address.

The Nova indirect addressing logic means that, given a 16-bit indirect address, only 15 bits actually address memory; therefore you are limited to a 32,768 word memory address space:

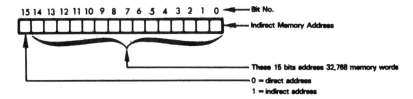

15 14 13 12 11 10 9 8 7 6 5 4 3 2 1 0 ◄— Bit No.

◄— Indirect Memory Address

— These 15 bits address 32,768 memory words
0 = direct address
1 = indirect address

The Nova minicomputers and microcomputers also provide indirect addressing with auto-increment and auto-decrement addressing. If you indirectly address one of the eight memory locations, 0010_{16} through 0017_{16}, then the contents of the addressed memory location are incremented at the beginning of the memory access. Thus you have indirect addressing with auto-increment.

If you indirectly address any one of the locations, 0018_{16} through $001F_{16}$ then the contents of the addressed memory location will be decremented at the beginning of the memory access. Thus you have indirect addressing with auto-decrement.

Neither the MicroNova nor the 9440 provide memory mapping logic. Memory mapping is a technique whereby more than 32,768 words of addressable memory may be accessed. The Nova 3 minicomputer is capable of supporting memory mapping as an option.

Nova minicomputers have separate memory and I/O device spaces. I/O instructions include six bits which identify one of 64 I/O devices. Because Nova minicomputers and microcomputers treat I/O devices in a manner that differs significantly from the typical microcomputer, we will defer our discussion of I/O addressing until we have looked at pins, signals and System Busses.

NOVA I/O DEVICE ADDRESSING

NOVA STATUS FLAGS

Nova minicomputers contain just one status flag, as we would define it, and that is the Carry status. Instructions are able to test for a zero or nonzero condition occurring at the conclusion of an instruction's execution, but no permanent zero status flag exists.

MicroNova also has these interrupt related status flags:

- Interrupt Enable
- Real Time Clock Enable
- Real Time Clock Request
- Stack Overflow Request

} MicroNova Only

The interrupt related status flags do not occur as addressable locations in any Status register; rather they represent flip-flops which are set or reset during the course of interrupt handling.

The interrupt enable bit is a master enable which is set to 1 in order to enable all interrupts. Specific instructions allow all interrupts to be enabled or disabled.

The MicroNova has a Real Time Clock interrupt enable bit and a Real Time Clock request bit. The Real Time Clock enable bit must be set to 1 in order to enable Real Time Clock interrupts; as soon as a Real Time Clock interrupt occurs, the Real Time Clock enable bit and the Real Time Clock request bit are reset to 0.

The Stack Overflow request bit is only present in the MicroNova, since only the MicroNova has a Stack. A Stack overflow condition occurs if, following a push operation, the incremented contents of the Stack register have zeros in the eight low-order bits. What this implies is that the Stack must reside within a 256-word memory page:

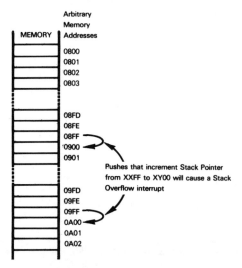

When a Stack overflow occurs, the Stack Overflow request bit is set to 1 and an interrupt is requested.

MICRONOVA AND 9440 CPU PINS AND SIGNALS

As we stated earlier in this chapter, minicomputer Central Processing Units are implemented on cards, not DIPs; therefore they usually have System Busses containing more than 40 signals. The standard Nova System I/O Bus contains 47 signals; furthermore, the Nova System Bus is, in effect, two busses: one communicating with memory, while a separate and distinct bus communicates with I/O devices:

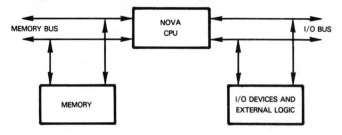

Table 4-1 briefly defines the functions of bus signals. The I/O Bus is standard for all Nova line computers, while the Memory Bus is different for each model. We give the Memory Bus signals of the Nova 2 in Table 4-1.

Table 4-1. Nova System Bus Signals

STANDARD NOVA SYSTEM I/O BUS

SIGNAL	DIRECTION	FUNCTION OR INDICATION
DS0 - DS5	To Device	Device selection
DATA0 - DATA15	Bidirectional	Data and address lines
DATOA	To Device	Data out to device's A buffer
DATIA	To Device	Data in from device's A buffer
DATOB	To Device	Data out to device's B buffer
DATIB	To Device	Data in from device's B buffer
DATOC	To Device	Data out to device's C buffer
DATIC	To Device	Data in from device's C buffer
STRT	To Device	Start device — clear Done flag, set Busy flag and clear device's INT REQ flip-flop
CLR	To Device	Clear device's Busy and Done flags and INT REQ flip-flop
IOPLS	To Device	I/O Pulse — user-defined function
SELB	To Processor	Selected device's Busy flag is set
SELD	To Processor	Selected device's Done flag is set
RQENB	To Device	Enable interrupt or DMA requests
INTR	To Processor	Interrupt request
INTP	To Device	Interrupt priority
INTA	To Device	Interrupt acknowledge
MSKO	To Device	Interrupt mask out
DCHR	To Processor	Data channel request (DMA request)
DCHP	To Device	Data channel priority
DCHA	To Device	Data channel acknowledge
DCHM0, DCHM1	To Processor	Data channel mode:

			DCHM0	DCHM1	
			H	H	Data out
			H	L	Increment memory
			L	H	Data in
			L	L	Add to memory

SIGNAL	DIRECTION	FUNCTION OR INDICATION
DCHI	To Device	Data channel in
DCHO	To Device	Data channel out
OVFLO	To Device	Overflow: result of memory increment or add exceeds $FFFF_{16}$
IORST	To Device	Clear all I/O devices

THE NOVA 2 MEMORY BUS

SIGNAL	DIRECTION	FUNCTION OR INDICATION
A0 - A14	To Memory	Memory address lines
DATA0 - DATA15	Bidirectional	Memory data lines
INHIBIT SELECT	To Memory	Inhibits selection of memory module
BMEMEN	To Memory	Starts memory cycle
WRITE	To Memory	Memory write
BRMW	To Memory	Causes pause between read and write
WE	To Memory	Enable write after pause in read-pause-write cycle
SYNC ENABLE	To Processor	CPU hold control
RELOAD DISABLE	To Memory	Inhibits loading of memory buffer
WAIT	To CPU	Disables other memory modules during write portion of memory cycle
MEM CLOCK	To Memory	Memory Clock
EXTERNAL SELECT	To Memory	Allows module to be selected despite contents of address lines
EXTERNAL MBLD	To Memory	Allows data to be stored in memory buffer without starting a memory cycle

If you are using the MicroNova or 9440 in a new product, then there is no reason why you should create the standard Nova System Busses. Providing the signals generated by the MicroNova or the 9440 are adequate for your needs, you can interface external logic directly to these two devices.

Let us first look at the MicroNova pins and signals, which are illustrated in Figure 4-2.

Two clock signals, Φ1 and Φ2, must be input to synchronize all MicroNova logic.

The Memory Bus consists of a 16-bit Address/Data Bus, plus three control signals: SAE, P and WE.

The Address/Data Bus connects to pins $\overline{MB0}$ - $\overline{MB15}$. P is a synchronization signal, SAE is a read enable and WE is a write enable.

The I/O Bus consists of just four signals:

I/O CLOCK synchronizes I/O transfers.

$\overline{I/O\ DATA1}$ and $\overline{I/O\ DATA2}$ are bidirectional data and control signals.

$\overline{I/O\ INPUT}$ identifies the direction of data transfers occurring via $\overline{I/O\ DATA1}$ and $\overline{I/O\ DATA2}$.

As compared to other microcomputers described in this book, the MicroNova I/O interface is very unusual. Only the TMS 9900 I/O logic is at all similar. A 16-bit I/O data transfer occurs as two 8-bit serial units. This may be illustrated as follows:

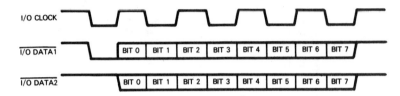

Eight serial bits are input in less than one microsecond; therefore this method of handling I/O is as fast as the parallel data input operations described for other microcomputers.

Each data transfer is preceded by one of four codes generated by levels output via $\overline{I/O\ DATA1}$ and $\overline{I/O\ DATA2}$. These are the four codes:

$\overline{I/O\ DATA1}$	$\overline{I/O\ DATA2}$	INTERPRETATION
1	1	Accompanying I/O low pulse may be used to synchronize interrupt requests and DMA requests.
1	0	DMA request acknowledge.
0	1	I/O data transfer. The transfer direction is specified by $\overline{I/O\ INPUT}$.
0	0	I/O command out.

Thus every I/O operation will begin with $\overline{I/O\ DATA1}$ and $\overline{I/O\ DATA2}$ being output during a low I/O CLOCK pulse. $\overline{I/O\ INPUT}$ will be low at this time since data is being output via $\overline{I/O\ DATA1}$ and $\overline{I/O\ DATA2}$. Providing $\overline{I/O\ DATA1}$ and $\overline{I/O\ DATA2}$ specify a data transfer to follow, the actual data transfer will occur via $\overline{I/O\ DATA1}$ and $\overline{I/O\ DATA2}$ with $\overline{I/O\ INPUT}$ identifying the data transfer direction.

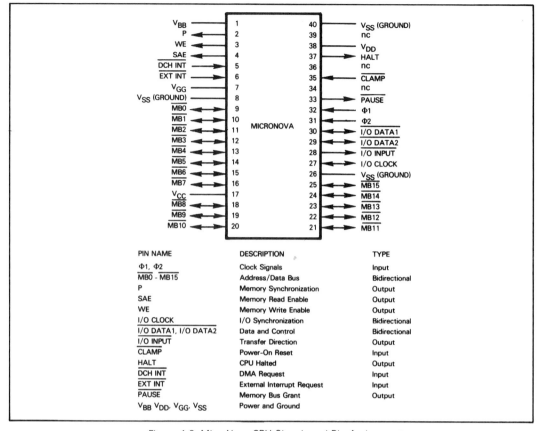

PIN NAME	DESCRIPTION	TYPE
Φ1, Φ2	Clock Signals	Input
MB0 - MB15	Address/Data Bus	Bidirectional
P	Memory Synchronization	Output
SAE	Memory Read Enable	Output
WE	Memory Write Enable	Output
I/O CLOCK	I/O Synchronization	Bidirectional
I/O DATA1, I/O DATA2	Data and Control	Bidirectional
I/O INPUT	Transfer Direction	Output
CLAMP	Power-On Reset	Input
HALT	CPU Halted	Output
DCH INT	DMA Request	Input
EXT INT	External Interrupt Request	Input
PAUSE	Memory Bus Grant	Output
$V_{BB} V_{DD}, V_{GG}, V_{SS}$	Power and Ground	

Figure 4-2. MicroNova CPU Signals and Pin Assignments

There are two CPU control signals which are not part of either the Memory Bus or the I/O Bus.

Following power-up, the MicroNova CPU will not perform any operation until a high input occurs at CLAMP. When CLAMP goes high, interrupts are enabled, Real Time Clock and Stack Overflow interrupt requests are cleared, and the CPU is halted. Once CLAMP has been input high, it is ignored until the MicroNova is powered down and then powered up again.

The HALT signal is output by the MicroNova as a high pulse while the MicroNova CPU has been halted — either in response to execution of a Halt instruction, or following CLAMP going high.

There are two MicroNova signals associated with interrupt logic. DMA requests are made via DCH INT while any external interrupt is requested via EXT INT. Both the DMA request and the interrupt request must be synchronized with instruction execution timing. This synchronization is provided by I/O DATA1 and I/O DATA2, as we have already described. The DMA acknowledge occurs via I/O DATA1 and I/O DATA2. There is no external interrupt acknowledge signal; however, such a signal can be derived from the Memory Bus, as we will describe later in this chapter.

PAUSE is output low by the CPU when devices other than the CPU are permitted to access memory.

Now look at 9440 pins and signals, which are illustrated in Figure 4-3.

These pins and signals create a single System Bus. No attempt is made to create separate Memory and I/O Busses.

You may connect a crystal across CP and XTL in order to create a master clock signal, or you may input a clock signal via CP.

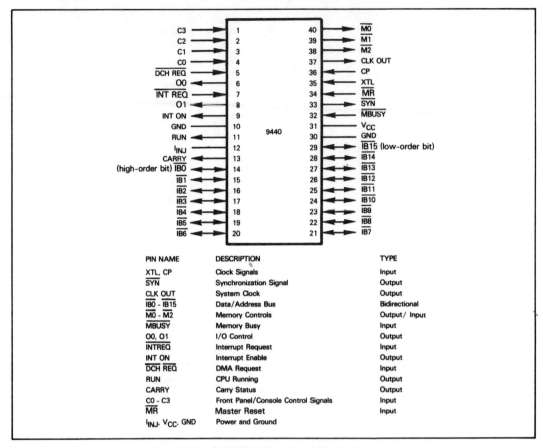

	PIN NAME	DESCRIPTION	TYPE
	XTL, CP	Clock Signals	Input
	$\overline{SYN}$	Synchronization Signal	Output
	CLK OUT	System Clock	Output
	$\overline{IB0}$ - $\overline{IB15}$	Data/Address Bus	Bidirectional
	$\overline{M0}$ - $\overline{M2}$	Memory Controls	Output/ Input
	$\overline{MBUSY}$	Memory Busy	Input
	O0, O1	I/O Control	Output
	$\overline{INTREQ}$	Interrupt Request	Input
	INT ON	Interrupt Enable	Output
	$\overline{DCH\ REQ}$	DMA Request	Input
	RUN	CPU Running	Output
	CARRY	Carry Status	Output
	C0 - C3	Front Panel/Console Control Signals	Input
	$\overline{MR}$	Master Reset	Input
	I_{INJ}, V_{CC}, GND	Power and Ground	

Figure 4-3. 9440 CPU Signals and Pin Assignments

The 9440 generates a single synchronizing output ($\overline{SYN}$). The CPU clock is output to the system via CLK OUT.

9440 SYSTEM BUS

$\overline{IB0}$ - $\overline{IB15}$ provides the 9440 with a multiplexed 16-bit Data and Address Bus. This bus carries addresses to memory and I/O devices, and it carries bidirectional data between the CPU and memory or I/O devices. $\overline{IB0}$ - $\overline{IB15}$ are low true; a low signal level represents a 1 bit.

$\overline{IB0}$ is the high-order bus line while $\overline{IB15}$ is the low-order bus line. This agrees with Nova conventions. This chapter, and this whole book describe the low-order bit as bit 0 — exactly the reverse of $\overline{IB0}$ - $\overline{IB15}$.

There are three control signals on the 9440 CPU-memory interface.

$\overline{M0}$ is output low to identify a memory read.
$\overline{M1}$ is output low to identify a memory write.
$\overline{M2}$ is output low to identify a memory address being output.

$\overline{M0}$ - $\overline{M2}$ have open-collector outputs; you can use these lines as inputs to make the timing of a non-memory machine cycle conform to the timing of a memory cycle. We will discuss this further when we discuss 9440 timing and instruction execution.

External memory interface logic inputs $\overline{MBUSY}$ low while it is responding to any memory access. $\overline{MBUSY}$ is similar to the WAIT signals that we have described for other microcomputers; it can be used to make the CPU wait for slow memory to respond to a CPU access request.

The 9440 has two I/O control signals O0 and O1. These two control signals define I/O and memory accesses as follows:

O1 = 0 O0 = 0 Instruction Fetch
O1 = 0 O0 = 1 Data Channel Access
O1 = 1 O0 = 0 Execute I/O Operation
O1 = 1 O0 = 1 No I/O

There are two signals associated with 9440 interrupt logic.

An external interrupt is requested by inputting $\overline{\text{INT REQ}}$ low.

INT ON indicates whether or not interrupts are enabled. This signal is high when interrupts are enabled; if this signal is low, interrupts are disabled.

A DMA request is made by inputting $\overline{\text{DCH REQ}}$ low. The DMA request is acknowledged by O1 and O0 being output low and high, respectively.

There are seven signals provided by the 9440 specifically to support a front panel or console.

Two of the front panel or console signals are outputs; these are the RUN and CARRY signals.

RUN is output high while the CPU is executing programs; it is output low while the CPU is halted. RUN is used to generate an appropriate front-panel display light; it is also equivalent to a Halt acknowledge, as described in this book for many other microcomputers.

CARRY represents the condition of the Carry status. This signal output specifically to drive a front-panel light.

Five input control signals are provided for switches on a front-panel. Four of these signals are C0, C1, C2 and C3; they perform the following operations:

C3	C2	C1	C0	FUNCTION
0	0	0	0	Display AC0 contents at console
0	0	0	1	Display AC1 contents at console
0	0	1	0	Display AC2 contents at console
0	0	1	1	Display AC3 contents at console
0	1	0	0	Increment Program Counter and then display contents of addressed memory word
0	1	0	1	Display contents of addressed memory word
0	1	1	0	Load memory from console switches
0	1	1	1	Halt
1	0	0	0	Deposit switches into AC0
1	0	0	1	Deposit switches into AC1
1	0	1	0	Deposit switches into AC2
1	0	1	1	Deposit switches into AC3
1	1	0	0	Load Program Counter from console switches
1	1	0	1	Continue/Run
1	1	1	0	Increment Program Counter and then load memory from console switches
1	1	1	1	No Operation

The first 9440 devices decoded the C lines in a slightly different manner. The following combinations were different operations:

C3	C2	C1	C0	FUNCTION
0	1	0	0	Load Program Counter from console switches
0	1	1	0	Not used
1	1	0	1	Load memory from console switches
1	1	1	0	Continue/Run

$\overline{\text{MR}}$ is the Reset input to the 9440. When this line is pulled low; the 9440 halts immediately and clears the Interrupt Enable flip-flop. Once $\overline{\text{MR}}$ goes high, the CPU will remain in the Halt state until it receives the "Run" command from lines C3 - C0. Reset has no further effect on the 9440. **It is up to your hardware to load the Program Counter by manipulating lines C3- C0 and the Information Bus.**

The following sequence is sufficient to start operation of a 9440 system with a "bootstrap" program in non-volatile memory:

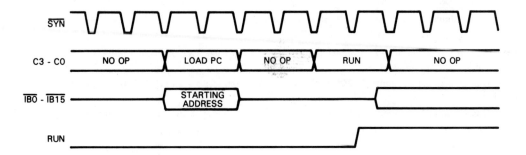

The hardware must provide the program starting address while issuing the "Load Program Counter" command via the C lines. C line codes other than "No Operation" are held for two machine cycles to ensure that the CPU reads them. The "No Operation" code between "Load PC" and "Run" gives the CPU time to finish executing the C line command. See the data sheets at the end of this chapter for more detailed timing information.

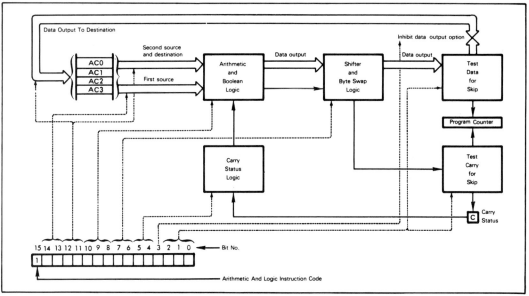

Figure 4-4. The Nova Arithmetic and Logic Unit

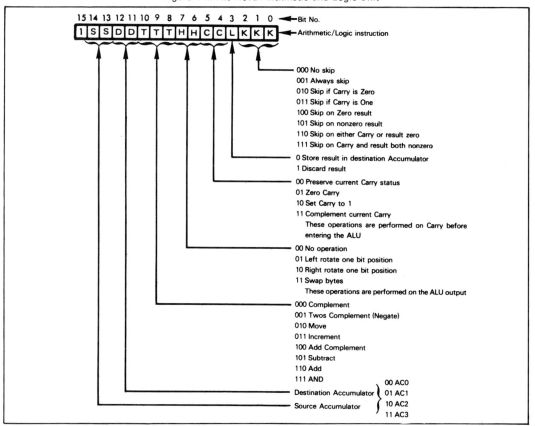

Figure 4-5. Arithmetic/Logic Instruction Object Code Interpretation

CPU LOGIC AND INSTRUCTION EXECUTION

The manner in which the Nova CPU executes instructions differs markedly from microcomputers described earlier in this book. We will therefore begin our discussion of CPU operations by looking at overall CPU architecture.

Our discussion of Nova CPU logic is tied to instruction object code bit patterns; this happens to be the simplest way of describing the Nova CPU. We will look at instructions from a programmer's perspective when we examine the Nova instruction set.

Nova instructions may be divided into these three groups:

1) Arithmetic, Boolean and logical operations which are essentially internal to the CPU.
2) Memory reference instructions which offer a variety of memory addressing modes and very little else.
3) I/O instructions which are designed to allow a considerable amount of intelligence in I/O devices.

Let us examine each group of instructions and associated CPU logic.

ARITHMETIC/LOGIC INSTRUCTIONS

The power of the Nova CPU lies in the fact that many logic functions are implemented sequentially along a single data path through the CPU. This is illustrated in Figure 4-4. This figure shows how individual bits of arithmetic and logic instruction object codes directly identify the many options available as data makes a single tour through the CPU. **Figure 4-5 provides specific arithmetic and logic instruction object code interpretations.**

Data to be operated on is always fetched from the Accumulators. Results are always returned to an Accumulator. For two-operand instructions, such as binary addition, the Destination Accumulator also serves as the second Source Accumulator. For one-operand instructions, such as a complement, there will be one Source Accumulator and one Destination Accumulator; the same Accumulator may serve as source and destination.

As the source and destination definitions would imply, the Nova has no Secondary Memory Reference (or Memory Operate) instructions as we define them; for example, you cannot directly add the contents of a memory word to the contents of an Accumulator.

In addition to one or two 16-bit data words, the Carry status is input to the Arithmetic and Boolean logic unit. You may input the Carry status as is, or you may complement it, reset it to 0 or set it to 1. If you modify the Carry status, then the modified Carry status becomes the new input to the Arithmetic and Boolean logic.

You may specify one of eight Arithmetic and Logic operations. The Move operation serves both as a Move and a No Operation. By specifying the same Accumulator as the source and destination for a Move, Arithmetic and Boolean logic is bypassed. Notice that only one Boolean operation, the AND, is provided. This is an inconvenience rather than a problem. As discussed in Volume 1, Chapter 2, you can combine the AND and complement operations to generate an OR or an Exclusive-OR. The following Nova instruction sequences substitute for the OR and Exclusive-OR:

```
;OR the contents of ACX with ACY. Leave the result in ACY
      COM      ACX,ACX      Complement ACX
      AND      ACX,ACY      AND ACX with ACY. Result to ACY
      ADC      ACX,ACY      Add original ACX. Result to ACY
;Exclusive-OR ACX with ACY. Leave the result in ACY.
;ACZ is needed for temporary data storage
      MOV      ACY,ACZ      Save ACY in ACZ
      ANDZL    ACX,ACZ      Store twice ACX AND ACY in ACZ
      ADD      ACX,ACY      Add ACX to ACY
      SUB      ACZ,ACY      Subtract twice ACX AND ACY
```

The 16-bit output from the Arithmetic and Boolean logic, together with the Carry status, passes to the Shifter and Byte Swap logic; here the 17-bit data unit may be rotated left or right, high and low-order bytes of the 16-bit data unit may be swapped, or this logic may be bypassed.

The Shifter and Byte Swap logic outputs 16 bits of data, plus the Carry status. The data and the Carry status may be tested separately, and based on one of eight identifiable conditions, the Program Counter contents may be incremented; this provides conditional skip logic. Figure 4-5 defines the eight conditions that may cause a skip.

Finally you have the option of preventing results from being stored in the Destination register; this enables conditional branch logic without modifying the contents of any Accumulator.

In summary, the five operations that can be specified by a single arithmetic/logic instruction may be illustrated as follows:

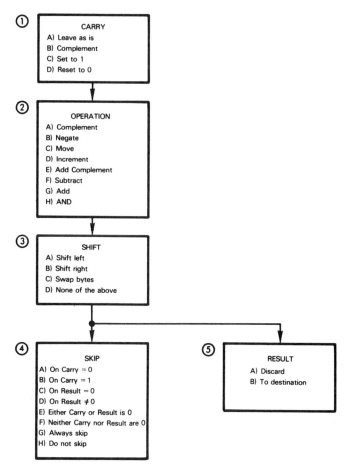

It would take four or five typical microprocessor instructions to perform the same operations that a single Nova instruction can perform.

Arithmetic/logic instruction options are specified in the source program using compound mnemonics. The mnemonics are created as follows:

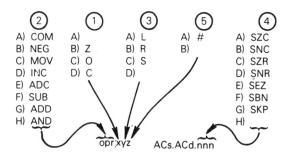

The numbers (1) , (2) , (3) , (4) and (5) and the letters A), B), C), D), E), F), G) and H) are keyed to the previous illustration. ACs represents "Source Accumulator" while ACd represents "Destination Accumulator". Thus the instruction "set carry to 0, then add AC1 contents to AC2, shift the result left one bit, keep the result, but skip on carry set "will create the mnemonic:

ADDZL   AC1,AC2,SNC

All logic associated with the execution of arithmetic/logic instructions is provided by the MicroNova and the 9440 chips.

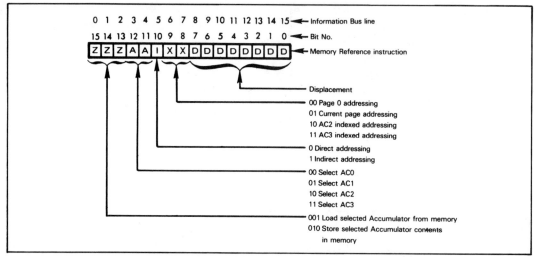

Figure 4-6. Load and Store Instruction Object Codes

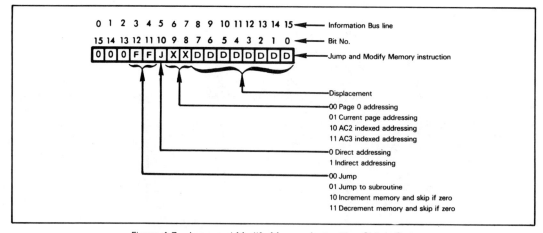

Figure 4-7. Jump and Modify Memory Instruction Object Codes

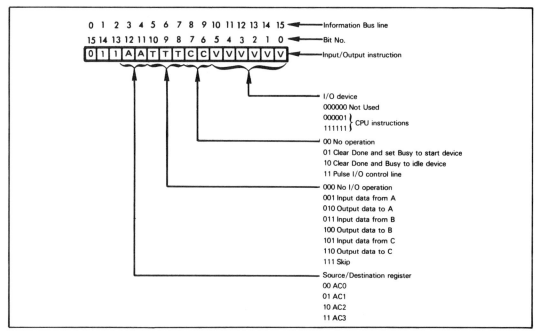

Figure 4-8. General Input/Output Instruction Object Code Interpretation

MEMORY REFERENCE INSTRUCTIONS

Since the four Accumulators of the Nova CPU must provide data sources and destinations for all arithmetic and logic instructions, you will constantly move data between memory and one of the four Accumulators. We have already described the Nova addressing modes. **Figure 4-6 illustrates memory reference instruction object codes and addressing mode specifications.** You can load data into any Accumulator, or you can store the contents of any Accumulator in memory.

There are four Jump and Modify Memory instructions. Object codes are given in Figure 4-7. The memory addressing options described earlier in the chapter apply also to the Jump and Modify Memory instructions.

The Jump-to-Subroutine instruction requires special mention; this instruction **stores the subroutine return address in Accumulator AC3.** If you are going to nest subroutines then **you must write your own subroutine to create a software stack.** Note that **even the MicroNova, which has a stack, does not use it when a Jump-to-Subroutine instruction is executed.**

MicroNova and 9440 chips provide all effective memory address computation logic and reduce memory reference instructions, as external logic sees them, to typical address and data transmissions with accompanying control strobe signals.

But remember, there is no such thing as a "standard" Nova memory bus.

INPUT/OUTPUT INSTRUCTIONS

Figure 4-8 illustrates input/output instruction object code interpretations.

Every I/O device that communicates with a Nova minicomputer must have a Busy status and Done status. These are bidirectional statuses; they are modified by the CPU to control the I/O device and they are modified by the I/O device to indicate the status of the I/O operation.

NOVA I/O
DEVICE
BUSY AND
DONE STATUS

4-21

This is how the Busy and Done statuses are interpreted:

BUSY	DONE	
0	0	Device Idle
1	0	CPU "starts" device by setting Busy to 1.
0	1	Device resets Busy to 0 and sets Done to 1 when device operation is complete.
1	0	CPU resets Done to idle device, or sets Busy for next device operation.
1	1	Illegal

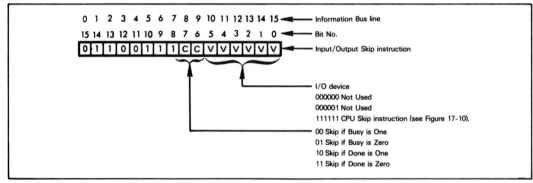

Figure 4-9. Input/Output Skip Instruction Object Code Interpretation

You start and stop I/O devices by manipulating device Busy and Done statuses.

Every I/O device may optionally have up to three individually addressable registers, referred to as Registers A, B and C.

NOVA
I/O DEVICE
REGISTERS

You transfer data between one of the four CPU Accumulators and one of the three I/O device registers.

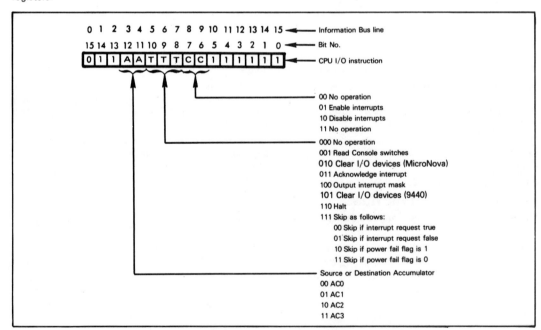

Figure 4-10. CPU Device 3F$_{16}$ Input/Output Instruction Object Code Interpretation

4-22

Both a status manipulation and a data transfer may be specified by a single I/O instruction; these two operations occur in parallel and are supported by appropriate control signals on the I/O bus.

The Nova CPU must be able to poll the Busy and Done statuses of an I/O device, just as most microprocessors read the contents of an I/O device Status register. The Nova CPU responds to status condition tests by optionally performing a Skip (which means the Program Counter contents are incremented). **This variation of I/O instructions is illustrated in Figure 4-9.**

Six bits of every I/O instruction object code are used to identify the I/O device being addressed. This gives you a total of 64 devices in the I/O device address space. But in order to enhance its instruction set, the Nova uses selected I/O device numbers to encode instructions internal to the CPU. I/O device numbers 0, 1 and $3F_{16}$ are reserved for this purpose. **I/O device $3F_{16}$ selects a number of interrupt related instructions whose object codes are defined in Figure 4-10. I/O device numbers 0 and 1 implement instructions illustrated in Figure 4-11.**

> NOVA I/O
> DEVICE
> ADDRESS
> SPACE

You will have to add considerable logic beyond the 9440, or the MicroNova, if you are going to execute all I/O instructions described in Figures 4-8, 4-9, 4-10 and 4-11. The only logic provided by the CPU chips themselves supports that part of the I/O operation which is exclusively internal to the CPU — and that is not much. The CPU will route data to or from the selected Accumulator, if needed, and it will increment the Program Counter in response to a Skip true condition. Everything else is the responsibility of logic beyond the CPU chip.

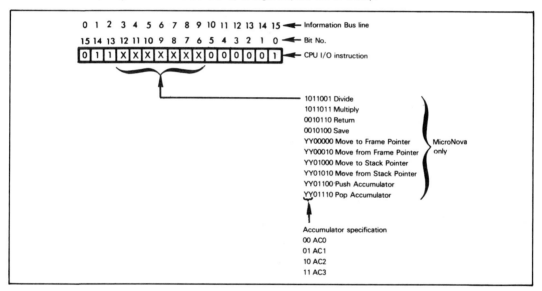

Figure 4-11. CPU Device 1 Input/Output Instruction Object Code Interpretation

A NOVA CPU SUMMARY

If you compare Nova CPU logic with microprocessors described earlier in this book, a number of minicomputer characteristics become self-evident. These characteristics have important implications when we look at bus signals, interfaces and timing; therefore they must be clearly defined.

Minicomputer Central Processing Units are more complex than their microprocessor counterparts. Look at the number of operations which may be performed during execution of a single Nova instruction; only the 8X300 makes any attempt to provide such serial logic. The microprocessor CPU architect has been severely restricted by the fact that only a limited amount of logic can be put on a chip without drastically affecting chip yield — and therefore the price of the microprocessor. When minicomputers were designed, making CPU logic more complex increased the size of the CPU card, or cards, which had some effect on eventual product price, but nothing like the microprocessor price escalations that result from low chip yields.

Thus unconstrained by logic limitations, minicomputer CPU architects also designed complex system busses, requiring equivalently complex logic within I/O devices attached to the system busses. For example, consider the fact that Figure 4-5 defines 32,768 different Register-Register Operate instructions, while the instruction format in Figure 4-8 assumes an I/O System Bus that can simultaneously manipulate I/O device status while transferring data.

These are formidable burdens placed on the designer of a chip which is supposed to reproduce the Nova CPU — with the result that chip designers have elected to tackle only part of the task. Both the MicroNova and the 9440 terminate at 40-pin DIPs; their busses are, in consequence, less than the standard Nova System Busses.

9440 TIMING AND INSTRUCTION EXECUTION

We will now examine 9440 instruction timing in detail.

9440 instructions and internal logic are timed by a master 10 MHz clock signal. Instructions are executed in machine cycles. This is the number of clock periods per machine cycle:

Memory read/instruction fetch	-	15 clock periods ⎫ Depends on actual
Memory write	-	15 clock periods ⎭ memory timing
I/O data in	-	10 clock periods
I/O data out	-	10 clock periods

Let us begin by looking at timing for an instruction fetch or a memory read; these two machine cycles have the timing illustrated in Figure 4-12.

At the end of clock period 2, the three memory control signals $\overline{M0}$, $\overline{M1}$ and $\overline{M2}$ are output with levels that identify the memory access which will be performed during the current machine cycle. For a memory read or instruction fetch, $\overline{M0}$ and $\overline{M2}$ are output low while $\overline{M1}$ remains high.

9440 INSTRUCTION FETCH
9440 MEMORY READ

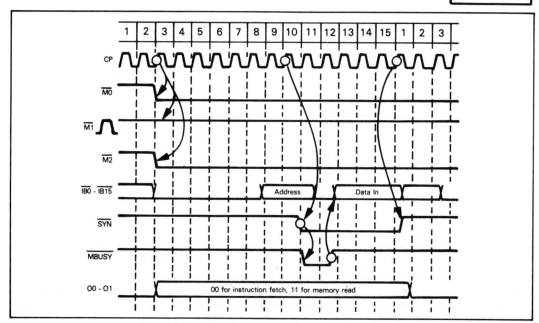

Figure 4-12. 9440 Memory Read/Instruction Fetch Timing

An instruction fetch and a memory read are differentiated by signals O0 and O1; these signals are both low for an instruction fetch and both high for a memory read. The address of the memory location to be accessed is output on the Information Bus ($\overline{IB0}$ - $\overline{IB15}$) beginning at the end of clock period 8. At the end of clock period 9 $\overline{SYN}$ is output low; external logic must use the high-to-low transition of $\overline{SYN}$ as a strobe to latch an address off the Information Bus. External logic must also use the high-to-low transition of $\overline{SYN}$ as a trigger to input $\overline{MBUSY}$ low to the 9440. $\overline{MBUSY}$ must be input low until addressed data has been read from memory and is stable on the Information Bus. At that time $\overline{MBUSY}$ goes high again. When $\overline{MBUSY}$ goes high, the 9440 will read data off the Information Bus. If the Memory Read machine cycle is to execute in the minimum 15 clock periods, then $\overline{MBUSY}$ must be low for one clock period only.

Figure 4-12 shows the CPU driving the Information Bus during the first two clock periods of the machine cycle following the Read or Instruction Fetch cycle. Following an Instruction Fetch, the 9440 will output the instruction address; after any other memory read, the CPU will output the data just read.

During a memory read that is not an Instruction Fetch, data should be available slightly beyond the ending transition (low-to-high) of $\overline{\text{SYN}}$. During an Instruction Fetch, the CPU reads the instruction one clock period after it detects $\overline{\text{MBUSY}}$ high; however, during any other memory read, the 9440 reads the data two clock periods later, on the same clock edge that generates the low-to-high transition of $\overline{\text{SYN}}$. This may be illustrated as follows:

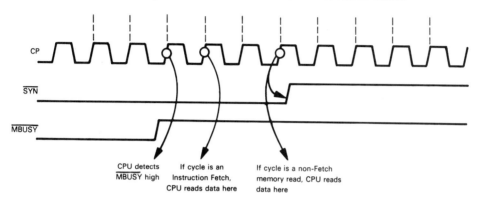

Thus, **on a non-Instruction Fetch memory read, data should be available 15 to 20 nanoseconds beyond the low-to-high transition of $\overline{\text{SYN}}$.**

$\overline{MBUSY}$ is a signal used by external memory interface logic to synchronize itself with the CPU. If $\overline{MBUSY}$ is low while $\overline{SYN}$ is high early in any memory access machine cycle, then the high-to-low transition of $\overline{SYN}$ will be delayed until $\overline{MBUSY}$ goes high. For a Memory Read or Instruction Fetch machine cycle, the trailing edge of the low $\overline{MBUSY}$ pulse also acts as an end-of-machine-cycle trigger. Three clock periods after $\overline{MBUSY}$'s low-to-high transition, the machine cycle ends and $\overline{SYN}$ goes high again. Here is an example of $\overline{MBUSY}$ and $\overline{SYN}$ interaction during termination of a Memory Read or Instruction Fetch machine cycle:

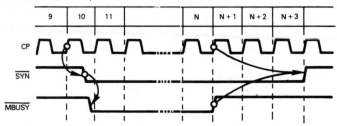

$\overline{MBUSY}$ and $\overline{SYN}$ interaction at the high-to-low $\overline{SYN}$ transition may be illustrated as follows:

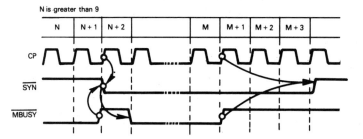

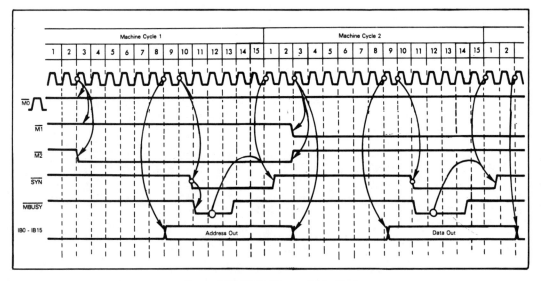

Figure 4-13. 9440 Memory Write Timing

Every instruction's execution will begin with an instruction fetch machine cycle. This machine cycle will be followed by internal operations, another memory read, a memory write, an I/O read, or an I/O write.

If the instruction to be executed requires internal operations only, that is, it is an arithmetic/logic instruction, then **internal operations are executed during clock periods 1 through 8 of the next machine cycle** — which must be another instruction fetch machine cycle.

If a memory read operation is to be performed, then another machine cycle is executed, exactly equivalent to Figure 4-12.

If a memory write is to be performed, then two machine cycles must follow the instruction fetch. During the first machine cycle the external memory address is output. During the second machine cycle data to be written to memory is output. Timing is illustrated in Figure 4-13. This figure is self-evident. During the first machine cycle only $\overline{M2}$ is low since a memory address is being output without a read or a write operation occurring during the same machine cycle. During the second machine cycle only $\overline{M1}$ is output low since a memory write operation alone will occur.

During both machine cycles of a Memory Write operation, $\overline{MBUSY}$ acts as a synchronizing signal, however only the high-to-low transition of $\overline{MBUSY}$ can modify instruction execution time. If $\overline{MBUSY}$ is low prior to $\overline{SYN}$ making its high-to-low transition, then the $\overline{SYN}$ high-to-low transition will be delayed until $\overline{MBUSY}$ goes high. Once $\overline{SYN}$ goes low, the processor waits for $\overline{MBUSY}$ to go low; three clock periods after the $\overline{MBUSY}$ high-to-low transition, the memory write machine cycle will end. The subsequent low-to-high transition of $\overline{MBUSY}$ has no effect on the $\overline{SYN}$ signal, or on internal CPU operations.

The only memory addressing modes that change instruction execution time are indirect addressing and indirect addressing with auto-increment or auto-decrement.

Each level of indirect addressing is equivalent to an additional memory read and an additional memory write. In order to compute instruction execution times for memory references with indirect addressing, therefore, add one memory read machine cycle and one memory write machine cycle for each level of indirection.

Recall that memory locations 10_{16} through $1F_{16}$ are used to store addresses which, when accessed indirectly, will be incremented or decremented. When you use indirect addressing and specify a memory location from 10_{16} through 17_{16}, the address fetched from the specified location will be incremented. An indirect address fetched from locations 18_{16} through $1F_{16}$ will be decremented. The increment or decrement operation requires the memory address to be loaded into the CPU, incremented or decremented, then written back out. Loading the address into the CPU is a routine part of any indirect addressing sequence; however, writing the address back out represents an additional step requiring an additional memory write machine cycle. This may be illustrated as follows:

Machine Cycle 1	Machine Cycle 2	Machine Cycle 3	Machine Cycle 4
Instruction fetch	Fetch address from location $10_{16} - 1F_{16}$	Increment or decrement address and write address back	Perform memory access (read or write)

Memory Write (bracket under Machine Cycle 3)

The increment or decrement and Skip-if-Zero instructions require an instruction fetch, a memory read and a memory write machine cycle. Timing may be illustrated for direct memory addressing as follows:

Machine Cycle 1	Machine Cycle 2	Machine Cycle 3	Machine Cycle 4
Instruction fetch	Fetch data from memory	Increment or decrement data and write data back	Increment Program Counter if needed

Memory Write (bracket under Machine Cycle 3)

Let us now look at I/O instruction execution.

There are no special I/O device select or control signals output by the 9440, rather external I/O devices must have select logic which is created by decoding instruction object codes on the Information Bus. This is done by decoding the three high-order Information Bus lines during an instruction fetch, as characterized by O0 and O1 both low. The three high-order Information Bus lines will at this time be 011 if the instruction to be executed is an I/O instruction. If these conditions are met, then the six low-order Information Bus lines must be decoded by device select logic. If the device code is $3F_{16}$, then all I/O devices must be selected simultaneously; for this to occur a special overriding device select signal must be created in response to device code 3F. If device code 00_{16} occurs, then no device should be selected; this requires no special select logic, rather it means that no external device should have the address 00_{16}. If any device code other than 00_{16}, or $3F_{16}$ appears on the six low-order Information Bus lines, then one external device's select logic should go true.

An actual example of I/O device logic is given later in this chapter.

If device code $3F_{16}$ has been output, then one of the operations defined by Figure 4-10 is about to occur. A significant amount of external logic associated with execution of these instructions may be required. A specific implementation consistent with standard Nova 1200 I/O interface logic is given later in this chapter. Alternatively, you may create a variety of individual control signals unrelated to the standard Nova I/O bus by suitably decoding I/O instruction object code bits 10 through 6.

An I/O instruction which identifies a specific device further identifies the I/O operations which are to occur, via bits 10 through 6 of the instruction object code (Information Bus lines IB5 through IB9). Figures 4-8 and 4-9 show the I/O operations which may be specified. **If data is to be input or output, then timing will conform to Figures 4-14 and 4-15.** But a significant amount of parallel control logic will accompany any I/O data transfer. We will shortly describe logic which implements a typcial I/O device interface.

If you wish to slow down 9440 I/O machine cycles, you can do so by using any one of the lines $\overline{M0}$ - $\overline{M2}$. Normally, the CPU outputs a high level on these three lines during an I/O machine cycle. However, if external logic pulls one of these lines low early enough in the I/O cycle, the 9440 will require the interaction of $\overline{SYN}$ and $\overline{MBUSY}$ to complete the machine cycle, just as if it were a memory cycle. You must pull the M line low before the sixth clock period of the I/O machine cycle.

> **9440 I/O WAIT STATES**

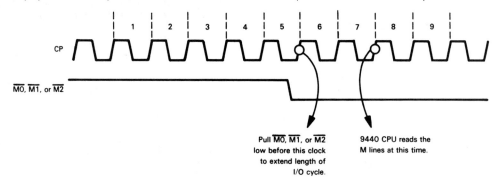

You can complete the machine cycle by manipulating $\overline{MBUSY}$ or by releasing the M line.

An I/O Skip on Busy or Done instruction, as illustrated in Figure 4-9, requires the addressed I/O device to return Busy and Done statuses to the CPU. The addressed I/O device returns these statuses on the two high-order Information Bus lines $\overline{IB0}$ and $\overline{IB1}$, respectively, with timing conforming to Figure 4-14.

See Table 4-4 for the sequences of machine cycles involved in 9440 command execution.

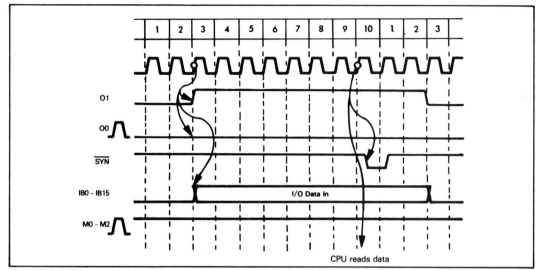

Figure 4-14. 9440 I/O Data Input Timing

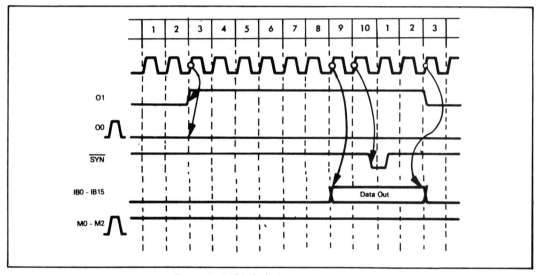

Figure 4-15. 9440 I/O Data Output Timing

MICRONOVA AND 9440 INTERRUPT PROCESSING

At the most elementary level, the MicroNova and the 9440 respond to interrupts in a very simple way.

External logic requests an interrupt by inputting a low signal via INT REQ.

Providing interrupts are enabled, the CPU acknowledges the interrupt upon completing execution of the current instruction; the CPU disables its own interrupt logic, saves the Program Counter contents in memory location 0000, then jumps indirect via location 0001. Thus memory location 0001 must contain the address of the first interrupt service routine instruction.

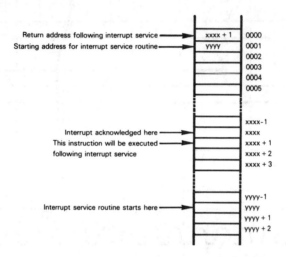

A single interrupt service routine will be executed in response to any external interrupt. In order to discriminate between interrupts, the interrupt service routine must identify the source of the interrupt, then jump to an appropriate individual program. This may be illustrated as follows:

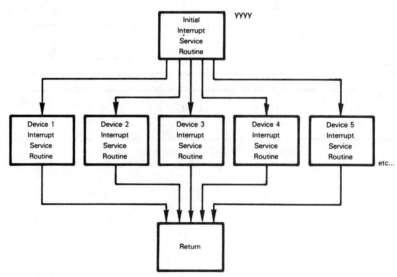

There will be a separate device interrupt service routine for every I/O device capable of representing an interrupt.

There are many ways in which the initial interrupt service routine may identify the interrupting I/O device in a multiple interrupt configuration.

The most primitive method used to identify an interrupting I/O device **is to test the device's Done status.** Standard Nova protocol requires an I/O device to request an interrupt when it sets its Done status. This may be illustrated as follows:

Interrupt Request	Busy	Done	
False	0	0	Device idle
False	1	0	Start I/O operation
True	0	1	End I/O operation

Primitive I/O device interface logic will request an interrupt by applying a low signal at $\overline{\text{INT REQ}}$ when it sets its Done status high. Now the initial interrupt service routine will execute a sequence of "Skip on Done False" instructions in order to identify the highest priority interrupting device. This may be illustrated as follows:

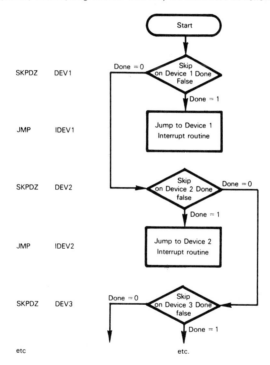

The order in which the initial interrupt service routine program logic tests device Done statuses becomes interrupt priority. You can modify this priority sequence at any time simply by changing the program.

A faster method of identifying an interrupting device is to daisy chain the interrupting devices. Daisy chain logic has been described in Volume 1, and again in Chapter 6 of the Osborne 4 & 8-Bit Microprocessor Handbook (in conjunction with the 8048). Daisy chains are resolved by an interrupt acknowledge signal; but there is no interrupt acknowledge signal output by the MicroNova or the 9440; rather an interrupt acknowledge instruction is executed. This is an I/O instruction addressing device 3F$_{16}$; bits 10, 9, and 8 ($\overline{IB5}$, $\overline{IB6}$, and $\overline{IB7}$) of the instruction object code must be decoded in order to create an interrupt acknowledge signal. Here is appropriate logic:

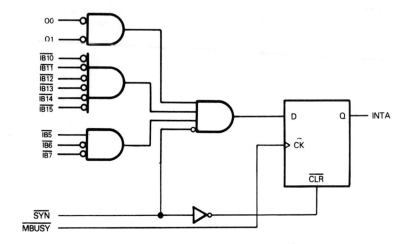

Recall that the Information Bus is low true; that is, a low logic level represents a bit value of 1. To ensure that INTA is generated only when a valid instruction code is on the Information Bus, it should be qualified by $\overline{SYN}$ low and $\overline{MBUSY}$ low-to-high transition. This is illustrated in Figure 4-16.

The highest priority interrupting device identifies itself by placing its device code on the Information Bus lines. The CPU stores the device number in one of the four Accumulators. Thus the interrupt acknowledge instruction is an I/O Data In instruction. Interrupt acknowledge timing is illustrated in Figure 4-16.

Interrupt enable and disable logic exists separately at the CPU and at external I/O devices.

At the CPU all interrupts are disabled as soon as an interrupt is detected. You can disable interrupts at any other time by executing a disable interrupt instruction (NIOC CPU).

In order to enable interrupts you must execute an interrupt enable instruction (NIOS CPU); when an NIOS CPU instruction is executed, interrupts are enabled following execution of the next instruction. This next instruction will usually be a Return instruction:

```
     -
     -
     -
NIOS    CPU    ;Enable interrupts
JMP     @0     ;Return from interrupt service routine
               ;Interrupts are now enabled
```

When nested interrupts are not allowed, all interrupts are disabled following the interrupt detection; interrupts remain disabled until the end of the interrupt service routine. You terminate the interrupt service routine with the two instructions illustrated above; one re-enables interrupts, the other returns from the interrupt service routine. Interrupts are not actually re-enabled until after the Return instruction has been executed; this prevents pending interrupts from being acknowledged before you have finally exited the current interrupt service routine.

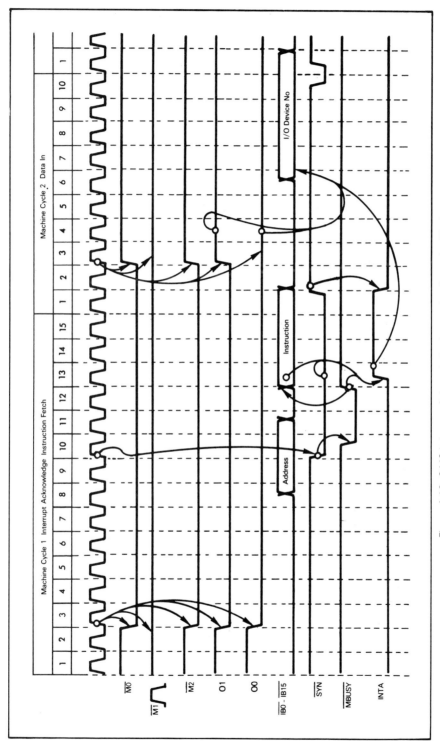

Figure 4-16. 9440 Interrupt Acknowledge Instruction Execution Timing

If you want to nest interrupts then you must execute an interrupt enable instruction within the interruptable interrupt service routine. But make sure that you do not re-enable interrupts until the initial interrupt service routine has executed; remember, the initial interrupt service routine is determining the source of the interrupt — and it makes no sense to allow another interrupt to occur until this determination has been completed.

You can disable interrupts selectively at external devices that have local interrupt disable logic. This is done using the Mask Out instruction (MSKO); MSKO is another I/O instruction addressing device $3F_{16}$. The MSKO instruction outputs data from one of the CPU Accumulators onto the Information Bus. Every I/O device capable of having its interrupt logic disabled must be connected to one of the Information Bus lines. When the MSKO instruction is executed, the I/O device must first decode the MSKO instruction in order to activate its interrupt disable logic; subsequently, if the Information Bus line to which device interrupt disable logic is connected is low, then interrupt request logic must be disabled locally. Timing is illustrated in Figure 4-17.

In order to re-enable interrupts at any external device you output a new mask with a high level on the Information Bus line to which the device's interrupt disable logic is connected.

Interrupt logic again demonstrates the minicomputer emphasis of the Nova. We have assumed that an external device capable of requesting interrupts can decode I/O instruction object codes on the Information Bus and have a considerable amount of logic associated with Busy, Done and Interrupt request flags.

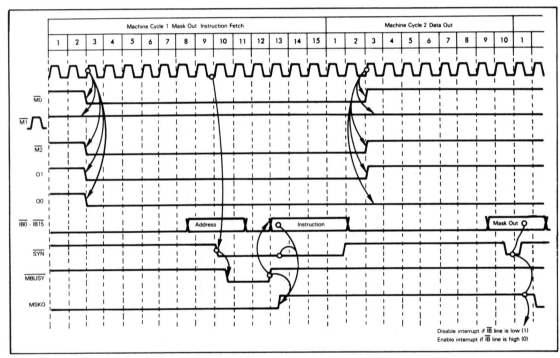

Figure 4-17. 9440 Mask Out Instruction Execution Timing

MICRONOVA AND 9440 DIRECT
MEMORY ACCESS LOGIC

MicroNova and 9440 direct memory access logic differ markedly.

In both cases external logic represents a DMA access by inputting a low signal via $\overline{\text{DCH REQ}}$.

The MicroNova responds by acknowledging the DMA request. This is done by outputting a high $\overline{\text{I/O DATA1}}$ with a low $\overline{\text{I/O DATA2}}$ signal. External logic then identifies the direction of the data transfer via the $\overline{\text{I/O INPUT}}$ control signal. Subsequently, MicroNova logic performs the entire DMA transfer by creating appropriate I/O Bus and Memory Bus signal sequences — but only data may be transferred in only one direction.

The 9440 has a more primitive DMA capability. It responds to $\overline{\text{DCH INT}}$ by outputting lines O1 and O0 low and high, respectively, and floating the Data Bus. External logic must implement the actual DMA transfer.

Standard Nova protocol allows four DMA operations to be defined by external logic via the DCHM0 and DCHM1 I/O bus signals. These are the four DMA operations that may be defined:

$\overline{\text{DCHM0}}$	$\overline{\text{DCHM1}}$	
0	0	Add to memory
0	1	Data in
1	0	Increment memory
1	1	Data out

The MicroNova, as we have already stated, handles data in and data out only; increment memory and add to memory are not available.

The 9440 on the other hand, **does nothing in response to a DMA request other than float the Information Bus. All external logic associated with DMA operations must exist outside the 9440 chip. We will describe suitable logic later in this chapter.**

THE MICRONOVA AND 9440 INSTRUCTION SETS

Table 4-2 summarizes the instruction sets for the MicroNova and the 9440. Observe that there are some instructions available with MicroNova that the 9440 lacks.

The power of the Nova instruction set is derived from the fact that many instructions perform multiple operations. Register Operate instructions, for example, allow you to set, or reset or complement a Carry status before the specified operation is performed. Primary Memory Reference and Register Operate instructions allow you to also perform data shifts, or to swap the high and low-order bytes of the data word being moved or generated.

Primary Memory Reference and Register Operate instructions also allow you to perform a conditional skip based on the results of the operation.

It is the ability of the Nova instruction set to perform a combination of operations, during a single instruction's execution, that makes the instruction set so effective.

THE BENCHMARK PROGRAM

Our benchmark program may be illustrated as follows for the MicroNova and the 9440:

```
        LDA     2,CNT        LOAD WORD COUNT COMPLEMENT INTO AC2
        LDA     0,IOBUF      LOAD IOBUF BASE ADDRESS INTO AUTO-
        STA     0,10         INCREMENT LOCATION
        LDA     0,@TABLE     LOAD ADDRESS OF FIRST FREE TABLE WORD
        STA     0,11         INTO AUTO-INCREMENT LOCATION
LOOP    LDA     0,@10        LOAD NEXT BYTE FROM IOBUF
        STA     0,@11        STORE IN NEXT TABLE WORD
        INC     2,2,SZR      INCREMENT WORD COUNT SKIP IF ZERO
        JMP     LOOP         RETURN FOR MORE
        LDA     0,21         RETURN NEW ADDRESS OF FIRST FREE TABLE
        STA     0,@TABLE     WORD
```

This benchmark program uses indirect addressing with auto-incrementing in order to sequentially access IOBUF and TABLE. We begin the program by loading the word count (CNT) into Accumulator 2, and table base addresses into memory words 10_{16} and 11_{16}. We assume that the address of the first free word in TABLE is stored in the first word of TABLE; thus we can fetch the address of the first free TABLE word by executing a load to Register 0 with indirect addressing.

Data is moved by a four-instruction loop. Two instructions load data from IOBUF and store data in TABLE using indirect addressing with auto-increment. Next we increment the counter stored in Register 2 and skip the following instruction upon detecting a zero count. The following instruction is a jump back to the beginning of the loop.

The final two instructions simply restore the new address for the first free TABLE word into the first word of the TABLE.

The benchmark program makes no assumptions. The source and destination tables may be any size and any number of data words may be transferred, limited only by the available memory space.

The following notation is used in Table 4-2.

An "X" in the column labeled "9440" indicates that the instruction is available on the 9440 CPU.

AC   Any of the four Accumulators.

ACX   A specific Accumulator. For example, AC1 is Accumulator 1.

C   Carry status

D   An Accumulator which serves as the destination for the results of an operation.

DEV   A 6-bit device code.

DEVX   A specific device register. For example, DEVA is Device Register A.

DEVBD   Device Busy-Done flags.

EA   Effective address determined by @DISP (,IX).

FP   Frame Pointer (not present in 9440).

ION   Interrupt ON flag

PC   Program Counter

PM   Priority Mask

S   An Accumulator which serves as the source of an operand.

SP   Stack Pointer (not present in 9440).

(CS#)   Represents three options which are used by the Register-Register operations.

C is a 2-bit field which determines the carry state prior to the ALU operation.

Coded Character	Result Bits	Operation
option omitted	00	No operation
Z	01	Set carry to 0
O	10	Set carry to 1
C	11	Complement carry

For example, ADDO 2,2 would set carry to 1 before adding AC2 to AC2.

S is a 2-bit field which determines how the result of the ALU will be shifted.

Coded Character	Result Bits	Operation
option omitted	00	No shift
L	01	Shift result and carry left one bit
R	10	Shift result and carry right one bit
S	11	Swap result bytes

For example, MOVS 1,2 would swap the bytes of AC1 and store into AC2.

is a 1-bit field which determines whether the result is stored in ACD.

Coded Character	Result Bits	Operation
option omitted	0	Load result into ACD
#	1	Do not load result into ACD

For example, NEGOL# 1,2 would set carry to 1 then negate AC1, shift the result and carry left one bit, but would not store into AC2.

(f)   A 2-bit I/O command whose meaning depends on whether the CPU or another device is being referenced.

CPU	f	Device
No operation	00	No operation
Set Interrupt On to 1	01	Start device by setting Busy to 1 and Done to 0
Set Interrupt On to 0	10	Idle device by setting Busy to 0 and Done to 0
No operation	11	Pulse a special device dependent line

(,SKCND)	A 3-bit skip-on-condition field which is used by the Register-Register Operate instructions.		

Coded Character	Result Bits	Operation
option omitted	000	No operation
SKP	001	Always skip
SZC	010	Skip if Carry = 0
SNZ	011	Skip if Carry = 1
SZR	100	Skip if result = 0
SNR	101	Skip if result ≠ 0
SEZ	110	Skip if either carry or result = 0
SBN	111	Skip if both carry and result ≠ 0

(@) DISP (,IX) Generates the address EA

@ is the indirect bit. If @=1 then indirection is specified.

DISP is an 8-bit address value.

(IX) is a 2-bit field which indicates the addressing Mode:

Bits are Mode

00 Zero page addressing. DISP is an unsigned address between 0 and 256.
EA = DISP

01 PC relative addressing. DISP is a signed two's complement address displacement.
EA = DISP+[PC]

10 Indexed addressing via AC2. DISP is a signed two's complement address displacement.
EA = DISP+[AC2]

11 Indexed addressing via AC3. DISP is a signed two's complement address displacement.
EA = DISP+[AC3]

(t) A 2-bit I/O test field whose meaning depends on whether the CPU or another device is referenced.

CPU	t	Device
Test for Interrupt On=1	00	Test for Busy=1
Test for Interrupt On=0	01	Test for Busy=0
Never skip	10	Test for Done=1
Always skip	11	Test for Done=0

x<y,z> Bits y through z of the quantity x. [AC]<5,0> is the low six bits of the specified Accumulator.

[ ] Contents of location enclosed within brackets. If a register designation is enclosed within the brackets, then the designated register's contents are specified. If a memory address is enclosed within the brackets, then the contents of the addressed memory location are specified.

[[ ]] Implied memory addressing; the contents of the memory location designated by the contents of a register.

Λ Logical AND

← Data is transferred in the direction of the arrow.

Under the heading of STATUS in Table 4-2, an X indicates statuses which are modified in the course of the instruction's execution. If there is no X, it means that the status maintains the value it had before the instruction was executed.

Table 4-2. MicroNova and 9440 Instruction Set Summary

TYPE	MNEMONIC	OPERAND(S)	BYTES	STATUS C	9440	OPERATION PERFORMED
O/I	NIO (f)	DEV	2		X	[DEVBD] — f Set the device's Busy and Done flags according to I/O command.
	DIA (f)	AC,DEV	2		X	[AC] — [DEVA] [DEVBD] — f Read device's A buffer into Accumulator. Set the device Busy and Done flags.
	DIB (f)	AC,DEV	2		X	[AC] — [DEVB] [DEVBD] — f Read device's B buffer into Accumulator. Set the device Busy and Done flags.
	DIC (f)	AC,DEV	2		X	[AC] — [DEVC] [DEVBD] — f Read device's C buffer into Accumulator. Set the device Busy and Done flags.
	DOA (f)	AC,DEV	2		X	[DEVA] — [AC] [DEVBD] — f Write Accumulator into device's A buffer. Set the device Busy and Done flags.
	DOB (f)	AC,DEV	2		X	[DEVB] — [AC] [DEVBD] — f Write Accumulator into device's B buffer. Set the device Busy and Done flags.
	DOC (f)	AC,DEV	2		X	[DEVC] — [AC] [DEVBD] — f Write the Accumulator into device's C buffer. Set the Busy and Done flags.
	SKP (t)	DEV	2		X	If T is true for DEV, [PC] — [PC] + 1 Skip if I/O test true.
	IORST				X	[PM] — 0 [ION] — 10_2 The Busy and Done flags in all I/O devices are set to 0. The Priority Mask is set to 0 and interrupts are turned on.

Table 4-2. MicroNova and 9440 Instruction Set Summary (Continued)

TYPE	MNEMONIC	OPERAND(S)	BYTES	STATUS C	9440	OPERATION PERFORMED
PRIMARY MEMORY REFERENCE	LDA	AC,(∽)DISP,(,IX)	2		X	[AC] ← [EA] Load contents of memory to Accumulator.
	STA	AC,(∽)DISP,(,IX)	2		X	[EA] ← [AC] Store contents of Accumulator into memory.
REGISTER-REGISTER OPERATE	ADD (CS#)	S,D (SKCND)	2	X	X	[D] ← [D]+[S] Add contents of Source register to contents of Destination register. Perform the specified options.
	SUB (CS#)	S,D (,SKCND)	2	X	X	[D] ← [D] - [S] Subtract contents of Source register from contents of Destination register. Perform the specified options.
	NEG (CS#)	S,D (,SKCND)	2	X	X	[D] ← [S] + 1 (twos complement) Place twos complement of the Source register contents in the Destination register. Perform the specified options.
	ADC (CS#)	S,D (,SKCND)	2	X	X	[D] ← [D] + [S̄] Add the ones complement of the Source register contents to contents of Destination register. Perform the specified option.
	MOV (CS#)	S,D (,SKCND)	2	X	X	[D] ← [S] Move contents of Source register to Destination register. Perform the specified options.
	INC (CS#)	S,D (,SKCND)	2	X	X	[D] ← [S] + 1 Place incremented Source register contents into Destination register. Perform specified options.
	COM (CS#)	S,D (,SKCND)	2	X	X	[D] ← [S̄] Complement the Source register contents, then move to Destination register Perform specified options.
	AND (CS#)	S,D (,SKCND)	2	X	X	[D] ← [D] ∧ [S] AND the Source register contents with the Destination register contents. Perform specified options.

Table 4-2. MicroNova and 9440 Instruction Set Summary (Continued)

TYPE	MNEMONIC	OPERAND(S)	BYTES	STATUS C	9440	OPERATION PERFORMED
REGISTER-REGISTER OPERATE (CONTINUED)	MUL		2			[AC0] ← (([AC1] * [AC2]) + [AC0]) <31,16> [AC1] ← (([AC1] * [AC2]) + [AC0]) <15,0> Multiply contents of AC1 by contents of AC2 and add contents of AC0 to result.
	DIV		2	X		[AC1] ← ([AC0],[AC1])/[AC2] (quotient) [AC0] ← ([AC0],[AC1])/[AC2] (remainder) Divide the 32-bit quantity contained in AC0 (high order) and AC1 (low order) by the contents of AC2.
STACK	PSHA	AC	2			[SP] ← [SP] + 1; [[SP]] ← [AC] Push the Accumulator onto the Stack.
	POPA	AC	2			[AC] ← [[SP]; [SP] ← [SP] - 1 Pop the top of the Stack to the Accumulator.
	SAV		2			[[SP]+1] ← [AC0] [[SP]+2] ← [AC1] [[SP]+3] ← [AC2] [[SP]+4] ← [AC3] [[SP]+5] <14,0> ← [PC] [[SP]+5] <15> ← [C] [SP] ← [SP]+5 [FP] ← [SP] Save a return block in the Stack.
	MTSP	AC	2			[SP] ← [AC] <14,0> Move the low 15 bits of the Accumulator to the Stack Pointer.
	MTFP	AC	2			[FP] ← [AC] <14,0> Move the low 15 bits of the Accumulator to the Frame Pointer.

Table 4-2. MicroNova and 9440 Instruction Set Summary (Continued)

TYPE	MNEMONIC	OPERAND(S)	BYTES	STATUS C	9440	OPERATION PERFORMED
STACK (CONTINUED)	MFSP	AC	2			[AC] <14,0> ← [SP] [AC] <15> ← 0 **Move the Stack Pointer to low 15 bits of Accumulator.**
	MFFP	AC	2			[AC] <14,0> ← [FP] [AC] <15> ← 0 **Move the Frame Pointer to the Accumulator.**
JUMP	JMP	(@) DISP (,IX)	2		X	[PC] ← [EA] **Branch unconditional.**
	JSR	(@) DISP (,IX)	2		X	[AC3] ← [PC]+1 [PC] ← [EA] **Branch to subroutine.**
	RET		2	X		[SP] ← [FP] [C] ← [[SP]] <15> [PC] ← [[SP]] <14,0> [AC3] ← [[SP]]-1 [AC2] ← [[SP]]-2 [AC1] ← [[SP]]-3 [AC2] ← [[SP]]-4 [SP] ← [SP]-5 **Return from subroutine and pop a return block off the Stack.**
REAL TIME CLOCK	RTCEN (f)		2		X	[ION] ← f **Enable Real Time Clock then set ION via I/O command.**
	RTCDS (f)		2		X	[ION] ← f **Disable Real Time Clock then set ION via I/O command.**

Table 4-2. MicroNova and 9440 Instruction Set Summary (Continued)

TYPE	MNEMONIC	OPERAND(S)	BYTES	STATUS C	9440	OPERATION PERFORMED
MEMORY OPERATE AND SKIP-ON-CONDITION	ISZ	(•) DISP (,IX)	2		x	[EA] → [EA]+1 / If [EA]=0 then [PC] → [PC]+1 / Increment memory contents and skip if zero.
	DSZ	(•) DISP (,IX)	2		x	[EA] → [EA]-1 / If [EA]=0 then [PC] → [PC]+1 / Decrement memory contents and skip if zero.
INTERRUPT	INTEN		2		x	[ION] → 1 / Enable interrupts. Same as NIOS CPU.
	INTDS		2		x	[ION] → 0 / Disable interrupts. Same as NIOC CPU.
	INTA (f)	AC	2		x	[AC] $<5,0>$ → DEV / [ION] → f / The 6-bit device code of the device closest to the CPU that is requesting an interrupt is loaded into the low six bits of the Accumulator. Set ION via I/O command.
	MSKO (f)	AC			x	[PM] → [AC] / [ION] → f / Move contents of Accumulator to Priority Mask. Set ION via I/O command.
	TRAP		2			[26_{16}] → [PC] / [PC] → [27_{16}] / Performs a software interrupt.
	SKP (t)	CPU	2		x	If t is true, [PC] → [PC]+1 / If interrupt or power fail condition satisfied, skip next instruction.
	HALT (f)		2		x	[ION] → f / Set ION via I/O command, then halt.

Table 4-3. MicroNova and 9440 Instruction Set Object Codes

INSTRUCTION		OBJECT CODE	BYTES	CLOCK PERIODS	9440
ADC(CS #)	S,D (,SKCND)	1ssdd100rrccnwwww	2	5/7	X
ADD(CS #)	S,D (,SKCND)	1ssdd110rrccnwwww	2	5/7	X
AND(CS #)	S,D (,SKCND)	1ssdd111rrccnwwww	2	5/7	X
COM(CS #)	S,D (,SKCND)	1ssdd000rrccnwwww	2	5/7	X
DIAf	AC,DEV	011aa001ffpppppp	2	15	X
DIBf	AC,DEV	011aa011ffpppppp	2	15	X
DICf	AC,DEV	011aa101ffpppppp	2	15	X
DIV		7641	2	123	
DOAf	AC,DEV	011aa010ffpppppp	2	10	X
DOBf	AC,DEV	011aa100ffpppppp	2	10	X
DOCf	AC,DEV	011aa110ffpppppp	2	10	X
DSZ	(*n*) DISP (,IX)	00011ixxbbbbbbbb	2	8/10*	X
HALTf		011aa110ff111111	2	10	X
INC(CS #)	S,D (,SKCND)	1ssdd011rrccnwwww	2	5/7	X
INTAf	AC	011aa011ff111111	2	15	X
INTDS		60BF	2	10	X
INTEN		607F	2	10	X
IORST		011aa010ff111111	2	10	X
ISZ	(*n*) DISP (,IX)	00010ixxbbbbbbbb	2	8/10*	X
JMP	(*n*) DISP (,IX)	00000ixxbbbbbbbb	2	6/8*	X
JSR	(*n*) DISP (,IX)	00001ixxbbbbbbbb	2	7/9*	X
LDA	AC (*n*),DISP (,IX)	011aaixxbbbbbbbb	2	6/8*	X
MFFP	AC	011aa0010000001	2	8	
MFSP	AC	011aa01010000001	2	7	
MOV(CS #)	S,D (,SKCND)	1ssdd010rrccnwwww	2	5/7	X
MSKOf	AC	011aa100ff111111	2	10	X
MTFP	AC	011aa00000000001	2	6	
MTSP	AC	011aa01000000001	2	6	
MUL		76C1	2	86	
NEG(CS #)	S,D (,SKCND)	1ssdd001rrccnwwww	2	5/7	X
NIOf	DEV	01100000ffpppppp	2	10	X
POPA	AC	011aa01110000001	2	7	
PSHA	AC	011aa01100000001	2	7	
RET		6581	2	15	
RTCDSf		01101010ff111111	2	10	X
RTCENf		01110010ff111111	2	10	X
SAV		6501	2	16	
SKPt		01100111ttpppppp	2	15/17	X
SKPT	DEV	01100111tt111111	2	15/17	X
STA	CPU	010aaixxbbbbbbbb	2	6/8*	X
SUB(CS #)	AC,(*n*) DISP (,IX)	1ssdd101rrccnwwww	2	5/7	X
TRAP	S,D (,SKCND)	1ssddqqqqqqq1000	2	9	

*Direct addressing. For indirect addressing, add two clock periods for each level of indirection. For auto-increment or auto-decrement locations, add three clock periods, plus two for each level of indirection.

The following symbols are used in Table 4-3:

aa	Two bits selecting an Accumulator
bbbbbbbb	8-bit signed two's complement address displacement
cc	Two bits selecting the carry option
dd	Two bits selecting the destination Accumulator
ff	Two bits selecting the I/O command
i	One bit selecting indirect addressing
n	One bit choosing the no load option
pppppp	Six-bit device number
rr	Two bits determining the shift option
ss	Two bits choosing the source Accumulator

tt	Two bits choosing the I/O test
www	Three bits selecting the skip-on-condition option
xx	Two bits selecting the index option

Execution times shown are for MicroNova. Where two execution times are shown (for example, 5/7), the second is the instruction time if the skip or branch is taken. See Table 4-4 for 9440 execution times.

Table 4-4 shows the sequences of machine cycles by which the 9440 executes instructions, interrupt and data channel requests, and commands received via lines C3 - C0.

Table 4-4. 9440 Instruction Execution

NO. INSTRUCTION OR OPERATION	CYCLE TYPE AND SEQUENCE**								EXECUTION TIME* (µs)
	FETCH	READ	WRITE	LD MAR	I/O OUT	I/O IN	WAIT	DCH	
1 Jump	1								1.5
2 Jump Indirect	3	1	2						4.5
3 Jump to Subroutine	1								1.5
4 JSR Indirect	3	1	2						4.5
5 Increment and Skip if Zero	3	1	2						4.5
6 ISZ Indirect	5	1, 3	2, 4						7.5
7 Decrement and Skip if Zero	3	1	2						4.5
8 DSZ Indirect	5	1, 3	2, 4						7.5
9 Load Accumulator	2	1							3.0
10 LDA Indirect	4	1, 3	2						6.0
11 Store Accumulator	3	1	2						4.5
12 STA Indirect	5	1, 3	2, 4						7.5
13 Complement	1								1.5
14 Negate	1								1.5
15 Move	1								1.5
16 Increment	1								1.5
17 Add Complement	1								1.5
18 Subtract	1								1.5
19 Add	1								1.5
20 AND	1								1.5
21 ALU with Skip	1, 2								3.0
22 I/O Data In	2					1			2.5
23 I O Data Out	2				1				2.5
24 Skip on Busy or Done	2					1			2.5
25 Interrupt	5	3	2, 4	1					7.5
26 Data Channel								1	1.0
27 Wait							1		1.0
28 Examine Accumulator					2	1			2.0
29 Deposit Accumulator					2	1			2.0
30 Load PC		2				1			2.5
31 Examine Memory		2				1			2.5
32 Examine Next		2				1			2.5
33 Deposit Memory			3	2		1			4.0
34 Deposit Next			3	2		1			4.0
35 Continue	2					1			2.5

*For 9440 System using a 10 MHz oscillator.

**e.g., No. 6, ISZ Indirect: 1st cycle — READ   2nd cycle — WRITE   3rd cycle — READ   4th cycle — WRITE   5th cycle — FETCH

Reprinted by permission of Fairchild Camera and Instrument Corporation.

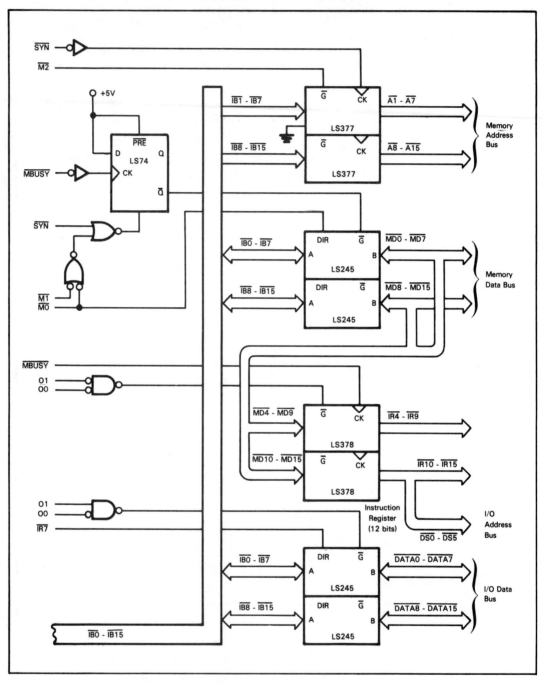

Figure 4-18. 9440 Information Bus Demultiplexing Logic

9440 - NOVA BUS INTERFACE

We will now examine logic which expands the 9440 pins and signals to the standard Nova I/O bus and to a typical microcomputer memory bus. Table 4-1 identifies the Nova I/O bus that is created.

We will also illustrate that part of I/O device interface logic which is common to any I/O device — that is, logic associated with Busy, Done and Interrupt flags.

Our discussion of logic needed to create a memory bus is quite general, reflecting the fact that there is no standard Nova memory bus. We will therefore limit ourselves to demonstrating, in general, how typical memory bus signals may be created from 9440 signals. But we will be specific in describing logic that expands the 9440 interface to a standard Nova I/O bus.

The 9440-Nova bus interface description is divided into three parts:

1) Expansion of the Information Bus into various Address and Data Busses required by the I/O and memory references.

2) Creation of I/O interface control signals.

3) Creation of memory interface control signals.

We will examine each of the three logic expansions in turn.

9440 INFORMATION BUS EXPANSION

These four busses must be created out of the bidirectional 16-bit Information Bus:

1) A bidirectional, 16-bit Memory Data Bus.

2) An output only, 15-bit Memory Address Bus.

3) A bidirectional, 16-bit I/O Data Bus.

4) An output only, 6-bit I/O Device Address Bus.

We must also latch I/O instruction object codes into a buffer out of which I/O instruction code bits can be read by I/O control signal logic.

The 9440 Information Bus is low true; this means a low signal level represents a binary 1, while a high signal level represents a binary 0. Standard Nova I/O Data and Address Busses are also low true; we therefore do not need to invert signals during multiplexing and demultiplexing.

There are many ways in which the 9440 Information Bus may be multiplexed to create the four required busses. We illustrate one possibility in Figure 4-18. This logic uses LS245 8-bit bidirectional tristate buffers to generate the two bidirectional Data Busses, while 8-bit and 6-bit gated, edge-triggered flip-flops create the Address Busses and the Instruction Object Code register.

The Data Bus buffers each have a gate (output enable) input and a data direction input. The gate inputs are low true. Logic shown in Figure 4-18 selects the LS245 buffers while valid memory data or valid I/O data can exist. Within these select periods a data direction control signal is created to ensure that data flows in the correct direction.

For the Memory Data Bus, $\overline{MD0}$ - $\overline{MD15}$, the LS245 buffers must be selected either during a read or a write operation, as identified by $\overline{M0}$ or $\overline{M1}$. But these two signals span addresses and data occurring on the Information Bus. Valid data exists on the Information Bus when $\overline{MBUSY}$ is high while $\overline{SYN}$ is low:

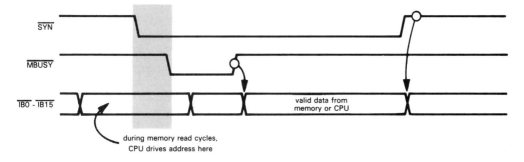

This timing is also illustrated in Figures 4-12 and 4-13. The logic of Figure 4-18 uses an LS74 flip-flop clocked by the low-to-high transition of $\overline{\text{MBUSY}}$. This ensures that data is not driven in the time shaded in the preceding illustration — between the high-to-low transition of $\overline{\text{SYN}}$ and the high-to-low transition of $\overline{\text{MBUSY}}$.

$\overline{\text{M0}}$ is used as the Memory Data Bus data direction control.

The I/O Data Bus buffer logic is somewhat simpler. The Information Bus is dedicated to transferring I/O data for the entire duration of a data input or data output machine cycle, as defined by O1 high and O0 low; these two signals are therefore used to create gate (output enable) logic. The direction of the I/O data transfer is taken from IR7; this bit of the I/O instruction object code defines the direction of an I/O data transfer, as illustrated in Figure 4-18.

For the Address Busses we do not use buffers; rather, we use gated-clock, edge-triggered flip-flops. This allows the address being output to be held stable on the Memory Address Bus, or the I/O Address Bus, after it is no longer on the Information Bus.

In the case of the Memory Address Bus, the gate inputs are tied to $\overline{\text{M2}}$, which will be low whenever a memory address is being output on the Information Bus. The high-to-low transition of $\overline{\text{SYN}}$ is intended to act as a memory address strobe; therefore it is inverted to clock the Memory Address Bus flip-flops when $\overline{\text{M2}}$ is low. Observe that there are only fifteen lines on the Memory Address Bus; the high-order bit of a 16-bit memory address is reserved to indicated an indirect address. Note also that the LS377 outputs are not tristate; therefore the Memory Address Bus will always hold the address of the most recently accessed memory location.

Two LS378 6-bit gated-clock flip-flops are used to latch the lower 12 bits of instruction object codes off the Memory Data Bus, creating the I/O Address Bus and the Instruction register. The six low-order output lines provide the I/O Address Bus, $\overline{\text{S0}}$ - $\overline{\text{S5}}$. As you can see in Figure 19-8, only the low-order 11 bits of the I/O instruction need to be decoded by I/O logic; therefore we use the 16-pin LS378 parts, rather than the 20-pin LS377s which we used for the Memory Address Bus. Like the Memory Address Bus, the Instruction register and I/O Address Bus will always hold the most recently latched data. The Instruction register flip-flops are clocked by the low-to-high transition of $\overline{\text{MBUSY}}$ whenever an instruction object code is on the Memory Data Bus. This condition is guaranteed by logic which enables the clock only when O1 and O0 are both low, signifying an Instruction Fetch machine cycle. If we wished to latch only I/O instructions, we could change the gate logic as follows:

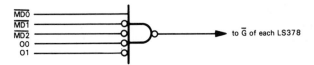

Latching the instruction object code only when its upper three bits are 011 ($\overline{\text{MD0}}$ high, $\overline{\text{MD1}}$ and $\overline{\text{MD2}}$ low) means that the Instruction register will only hold I/O instructions. Latching all instructions is sufficient, since an I/O execution machine cycle (O1 high and O0 low) follows the fetch of an I/O instruction. Our logic will use lines O1 and O0 to indicate execution of an I/O instruction.

Let us now examine I/O bus control signal logic.

9440-NOVA I/O BUS INTERRUPT SIGNALS

Three signals on the standard Nova I/O bus are used by interrupt logic: $\overline{\text{INTR}}$, INTA and $\overline{\text{INTP}}$.

$\overline{\text{INTR}}$ is the standard interrupt request signal. This signal can be tied directly to the 9440 $\overline{\text{INT REQ}}$ input.

The interrupt acknowledge signal INTA is created in response to execution of the interrupt acknowledge instruction. We will describe logic which creates INTA along with other I/O bus control signals when we discuss Figure 4-19.

$\overline{\text{INTP}}$ is the initial input to the highest priority device in an interrupt daisy chain. This may be illustrated as follows:

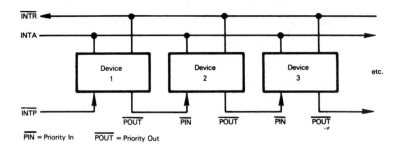

$\overline{INTP}$ may be connected to the complement of the 9440 output INT ON, in which case priorities within a daisy chain will not be resolved while interrupts are disabled. Frequently the initial $\overline{PIN}$ input to a daisy chain will be tied to ground and $\overline{INTP}$ will not be used. Now interrupt priorities will be arbitrated whether or not interrupts have been enabled.

As you will see, it takes very little logic to expand the 9440 interrupt signals to standard Nova I/O bus interrupt lines. But a considerable amount of interrupt-related logic must be present at external device controllers — logic which we will describe later in this chapter.

9440-NOVA DMA CONTROL SIGNALS

The only DMA logic provided by the 9440 consists of a DMA request signal, $\overline{DCH\ REQ}$. When input low, this signal causes the 9440 to complete the instruction currently being executed, then to disable interrupts and wait. The DMA request is acknowledged by outputting O1 low and O0 high.

All logic which actually implements any DMA transfer must be implemented external to the 9440. **We will discuss briefly what logic would be required.**

The Request Enable line, $\overline{RQENB}$, goes true to permit both interrupt and DMA requests. Central DMA control logic would contain an Enable flip-flop, analogous to the CPU's Interrupt Enable flip-flop. The output of this flip-flop, ANDed with INT ON from the 9440, would provide $\overline{RQENB}$ as follows:

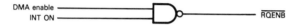

The DMA request line $\overline{DCHR}$ may be connected to the 9440 $\overline{DCH\ REQ}$ input. Thus requests will be accepted and granted by the 9440 CPU. $\overline{DCHA}$, the acknowledgment signal, is simply decoded from lines O1 and O0:

$\overline{DCHP}$ is a priority line just like $\overline{INTP}$. DMA daisy chain priorities would be implemented similarly to interrupt priorities.

The 9440 surrenders control of the System Bus when it acknowledges a DMA request; therefore external logic must perform all signal manipulations and data transfers. DCHI and DCHO, which indicate the direction of data transfer, are signals output by external DMA control logic.

The DMA control logic will input DCHM0 and DCHM1 from the device requesting memory access. Of the four encoded modes shown in Table 4-1, "Data Out" and "Data In" can be handled with relative ease, especially if you use an LSI chip designed for DMA control. Implementing the other two functions, "Increment Memory" and "Add to Memory", requires much more logic since some arithmetic is required. Indeed, a one-chip microcomputer might supply this logic.

Since OVFLO is true when an "Increment Memory" or an "Add to Memory" operation produces a result greater than $FFFF_{16}$, this signal would be produced by the logic which performs those operations.

Figure 4-19 shows 3-to-8 and 2-to-4 decoders creating Nova I/O Bus control signals. The signal logic directly interprets I/O instruction object code bits illustrated in Figures 4-8, 4-9, and 4-10. Note that the Instruction register bits from Figure 4-18 are low true, and that Instruction register lines are numbered according to Nova convention, where the low-order line is $\overline{IR15}$.

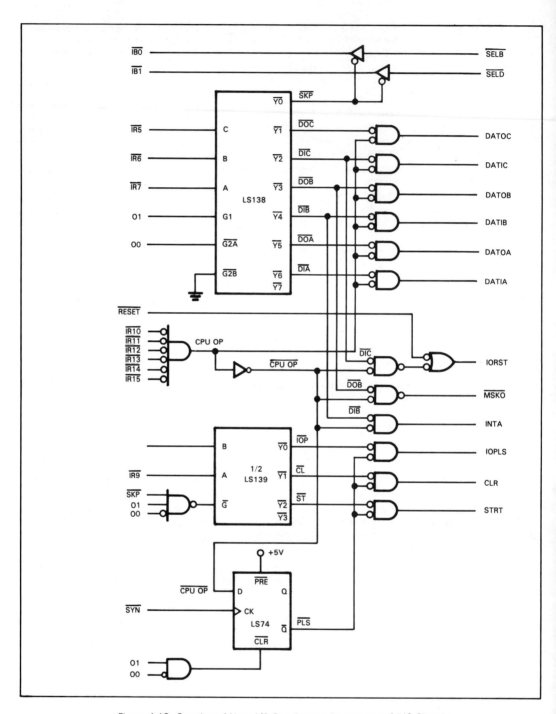

Figure 4-19. Creation of Nova I/O Bus Control Signals from 9440 Signals

Instruction object code bits are continuously read out of the Instruction register ($\overline{IR4}$ - $\overline{IR15}$), but I/O control signals are created only during an I/O Execute machine cycle (when O1 is high and O0 is low).

The logic of Figure 4-19 may be divided into these four sections:

1) Creation of simple data transfer control signals

2) Creation of I/O skip logic.

3) Creation of interrupt control signals.

4) Creation of control signals STRT, CLR and IOPLS.

Let us first consider simple data transfer control signals. There are six signals: DATIA, DATIB, DATIC, DATOA, DATOB, and DATOC. These are created by the LS138 3-to-8 decoder in Figure 4-19, and enabled when the I/O device address is other than $3F_{16}$.

If you look at Figure 4-8 you will see that instruction bits 10 and 9 ($\overline{IR5}$ and $\overline{IR6}$) select one of the three registers that may exist at an I/O device, while bit 8 ($\overline{IR7}$) differentiates between I/O data input and I/O data output. These three bits are input to the LS138 decoder so that the six data transfer signals and the Skip signal are decoded at the outputs. The decoder is enabled only during an I/O Execute machine cycle — that is, when O1 is high and O0 is low. However, if the I/O device address is $3F_{16}$, then CPU OP will be true and no data transfer signal will go true. It is not strictly necessary to disable the signals with CPU OP; since none of the I/O devices will be assigned the address $3F_{16}$, none of them will respond to I/O instructions with that address.

The Skip control, $\overline{SKP}$, output from the LS138 decoder, is used to enable $\overline{SELB}$ and $\overline{SELD}$ onto Information Bus lines $\overline{IB0}$ and $\overline{IB1}$. This is done using three-state buffers enabled by $\overline{SKP}$ low; the buffers in Figure 4-19 might be part of an LS125 or an LS367 chip. $\overline{SELB}$ and $\overline{SELD}$ are inputs to the buffers, while the outputs are connected to Information Bus lines $\overline{IB0}$ and $\overline{IB1}$. We assume that as soon as any I/O device is selected, it immediately connects its Busy and Done statuses to the $\overline{SELB}$ and $\overline{SELD}$ control lines of the I/O bus. However, $\overline{SELB}$ and $\overline{SELD}$ will not appear on Information Bus lines $\overline{IB0}$ and $\overline{IB1}$ unless a Skip I/O instruction has been executed.

When an I/O instruction is executed specifying device $3F_{16}$, a set of interrupt-related I/O instructions is executed, as illustrated in Figure 4-10. Most of the instructions illustrated in this figure specify events internal to the CPU. For example, "enable interrupts" and "disable interrupts" apply to CPU interrupt logic; moreover, the Skip instructions interrogate interrupt request status and power fail status within the CPU. **"Acknowledge Interrupt" (INTA), "Output Interrupt Mask" ($\overline{MSKO}$) and "Clear All I/O Devices" (IORST) are the only instructions which require control signals to be generated on the I/O bus. These control signals are generated by qualifying the decoder of the instruction bits with a device $3F_{16}$ select code.** The device $3F_{16}$ select code, $\overline{CPU\ OP}$, is created by ANDing the low-order six instruction bits ($\overline{IR10}$ through $\overline{IR15}$). Thus the gates producing INTA, $\overline{MSKO}$, and IORST are effectively switched on and off by $\overline{CPU\ OP}$. Note that IORST is generated either by execution of a "Clear I/O Devices" instruction, or by the master system Reset signal, $\overline{RESET}$.

Let us next consider logic needed to create STRT, CLR, and IOPLS.

These control signals should be activated after the appropriate I/O transfer has taken place. Thus the logic in Figure 4-19 provides a gating signal, $\overline{PLS}$, which goes low on the low-to-high transition of $\overline{SYN}$. $\overline{PLS}$ is the $\overline{Q}$ output of the LS74 flip-flop in Figure 4-19. The timing for STRT, CLR, or IOPLS results as follows:

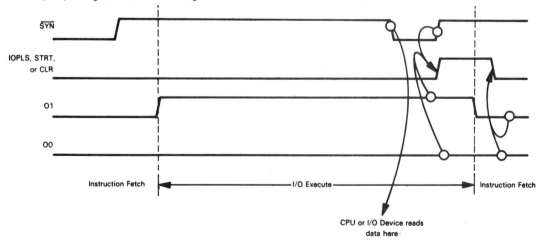

The LS139 2-to-4 decoder decodes instruction object code bits 7 and 6 ($\overline{IR8}$ and $\overline{IR9}$), providing that the I/O instruction being executed is not an I/O Skip instruction. (The other half of the LS139 chip could be used to decode lines O1 and O0, instead of the gating logic shown in Figures 4-18 and 4-19.)

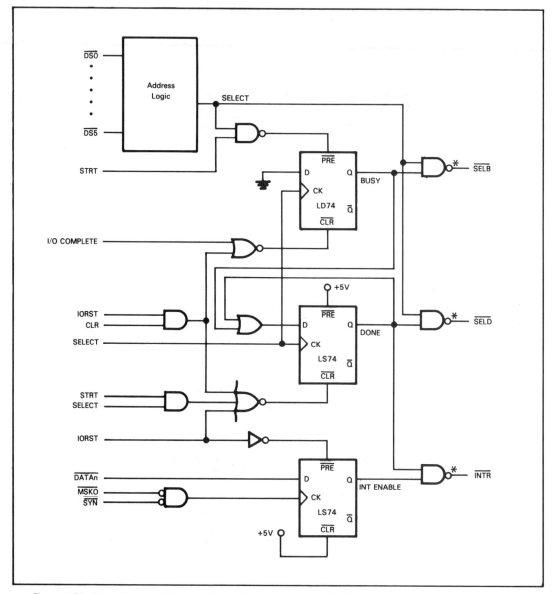

Figure 4-20. Busy, Done, and Interrupt Status Logic Required by I/O Device Controllers on the Nova I/O Bus

NOVA I/O DEVICE CONTROLLER LOGIC

Interface logic which an external device needs in order to connect to the standard Nova I/O bus depends on the nature of the external device. A minicomputer device controller may be very complex, even costing more than the minicomputer itself; that is because minicomputer devices that connect to the I/O bus are peripherals, such as printers, disks, etc. When we reduce the Nova to microprocessor terms, however, external devices connected to the I/O bus reduce to such primitive elements as parallel I/O ports or serial data lines. Within this

reduced context we can synthesize the minimum necessary elements of an I/O interface as consisting of three status flags: Busy, Done, and an Interrupt request. We can implement these three status flags using three LS74 flip-flops, as illustrated in Figure 4-20. Device select logic in this figure is limited to showing a select signal which will be generated true when the appropriate device code appears on the I/O device Address Bus. We have discussed I/O device select logic at various points earlier in this chapter.

Let us look at the BUSY and the DONE status logic. These are the operations which may affect the condition of the BUSY and DONE statuses:

1) At the start of an I/O operation BUSY must be set while DONE is clear. This condition is identified by 01 in bits 7 and 6 ($\overline{IR8}$ and $\overline{IR9}$) of the I/O instruction object code, which generates the STRT control signal of the I/O bus.

2) At the completion of an operation BUSY is cleared and DONE is set. This change in status setting must be implemented automatically by I/O device interface logic; it alone knows when the I/O operation has been completed.

3) BUSY and DONE may be cleared by the CPU. This is specified by 10 in bits 7 and 6 ($\overline{IR8}$ and $\overline{IR9}$) of the I/O instruction, which generates the CLR control signal on the I/O bus.

4) There is a "Clear All I/O Devices" instruction. This instruction generates IORST on the I/O bus; it clears BUSY and DONE statuses at all I/O devices.

5) A Master Reset must also clear the BUSY and DONE statuses. This Master Reset signal can also create IORST, as illustrated in Figure 4-19.

Two D-type flip-flops implement the BUSY and DONE status logic. These two D-type flip-flops are clocked by an "I/O Complete" signal which local device logic must generate. The BUSY and DONE statuses are generated by the flip-flop Q outputs which must connect to $\overline{SELB}$ and $\overline{SELD}$, as required by I/O skip logic, which we have already described.

The BUSY flip-flop uses its Set and Clear logic to control the BUSY status. The BUSY status is set by STRT and SELECT both true. This combination of STRT and SELECT sets the device BUSY status while it resets the DONE status.

Either CLR and SELECT both true or IORST true will activate the Clear input of the BUSY flip-flop. Neither of these conditions will be present when BUSY is set by the STRT pulse. Subsequently, when STRT or SELECT goes false, BUSY will stay true until it is reset by "I/O Complete" or by an active Clear input, which will occur when either IORST or both CLR and SELECT are true.

| IORST |
| CLR |
| STRT |

The DONE status is set by the "I/O Complete" pulse after BUSY has been set. Once DONE is set, it will remain true until the flip-flop is cleared. These conditions are provided by OR logic at the D input to the DONE flip-flop. The Clear input is activated by any one of the following conditions being true:

1) STRT and SELECT both true; thus the DONE status is reset at the same time as the BUSY status is set.

2) The master Reset, IORST.

3) CLR and SELECT both true.

The device interrupt may be individually disabled by a Mask Out instruction's execution; this creates the $\overline{MSKO}$ control signal used to permit the clocking of the interrupt mask flip-flops. Accompanying execution of the Mask Out instruction, a 16-bit data value is output on the I/O Data Bus. An I/O Device's interrupt logic is controlled by one bit of this mask, the bit transmitted via I/O Data Bus line $\overline{DATAn}$. Therefore $\overline{DATAn}$ becomes the D input to the interrupt mask flip-flop. A 1 in the mask bit ($\overline{DATAn}$ low) disables interrupts from the I/O device. In Figure 4-20, the Q output of the flip-flop becomes the interrupt enable signal, INT ENABLE, which gates the device's interrupt request onto $\overline{INTR}$.

The bottom flip-flop in Figure 4-20 implements interrupt logic for the I/O interface. Let us summarize the conditions that can affect I/O interface interrupt logic. Providing interrupts are enabled at the I/O interface, an interrupt will be requested whenever an I/O operation is completed, as identified by the DONE status going true. If INT ENABLE is true, $\overline{INTR}$ will go low as soon as the DONE status is set.

Interrupt logic may be enabled by a master I/O reset; therefore IORST is connected to the flip-flop Preset input.

9440 MEMORY BUS

There being no standard Nova Memory Bus, we will look at the signals available to you when you interface memory to the 9440.

First return to Figure 4-18. This figure shows how stable Data and Memory Busses may be demultiplexed off the 9440 Information Bus. In order to create a Memory Bus of any type, all you need is control signals to accompany the Memory Data Bus and the Memory Address Bus.

Figure 4-21 presents an example of memory control signals derived from 9440 signals, and Figure 4-22 shows the timing for these signals. The four D-type flip-flops of an S175 chip, along with some combinatorial logic, constitute a state machine to generate signals required by memory and the 9440 CPU. The four flip-flops are triggered by MEMORY CLOCK. In order that all worst-case delay times be satisfied, the frequency of MEMORY CLOCK should not exceed 23.8 MHz; if LS parts are used, the maximum worst-case MEMORY CLOCK frequency is 10.8 MHz. The common clear of the four flip-flops will be activated if none of the lines $\overline{M0}$, $\overline{M1}$, or $\overline{M2}$ is true.

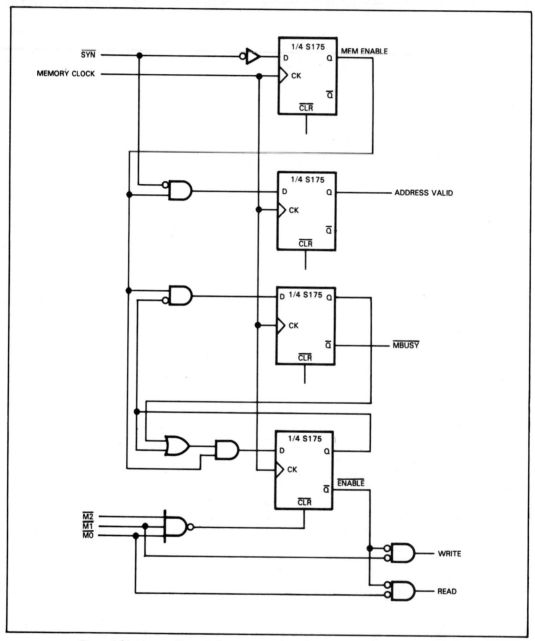

Figure 4-21. Memory Controls Derived from 9440 Signals Using State Machine Logic

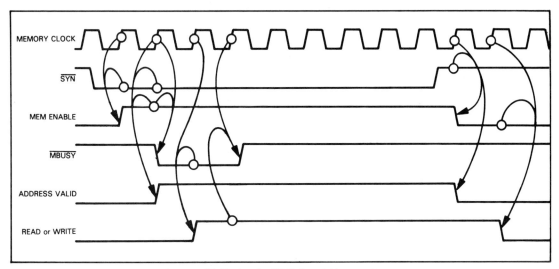

Figure 4-22. Timing for 9440-Based Memory Controls

Provided that either M2, M1 or M0 is low (signifying a memory access machine cycle) **the MEM ENABLE signals will go true on the first MEMORY CLOCK after SYN goes low. MEM ENABLE will stay on until the first MEMORY CLOCK after SYN goes high again.**

On the rising edge of MEMORY CLOCK after MEM ENABLE goes on, MBUSY and ADDRESS VALID will go true.

Memory control logic must return MBUSY to the CPU, since the 9440 requires interaction of the MBUSY and SYN signals in order to complete memory access cycles. We discussed this earlier in this chapter, in the text accompanying Figures 4-12 and 4-13. A more complex memory interface could use MBUSY to lock out CPU memory accesses while the memory is busy — for example, while memory is responding to a direct memory access.

The memory logic itself may require some signal to be true as long as a valid address is on the Memory Address Bus. Thus, our logic provides the signal ADDRESS VALID, which goes on after the contents of the Memory Address register (shown in Figure 4-18) have had time to settle, and remains until the end of the memory cycle. In Figure 4-18, the Memory Address register is clocked by the high-to-low transition of SYN, but a system might use the leading edge of ADDRESS VALID to clock the Memory Address register.

On the MEMORY CLOCK after MBUSY goes on, the ENABLE flip-flop clocks on. If M0 or M1 is low at this time, then READ or WRITE will go on and stay on until the MEMORY CLOCK after MEM ENABLE goes off. The signals READ and WRITE tell the memory chips the direction of the data transfer.

Of course, different system signal and timing specifications would require different implementations of memory signals. A memory system might use one-shots or delay lines to create pulsed signals, and simple combinatorial logic for signal levels. A state machine implementation could use a Counter or Shift register, or perhaps a field-programmable logic sequencer such as the Signetics 82S105.

DATA SHEETS

This section contains specific electrical and timing data for the following devices:

- MicroNova
- 9440

⌐ ABSOLUTE MAXIMUM RATINGS* ⌐

Supply Voltage Range V_{BB}	-2 to -7	Volts
Supply Voltage Range V_{CC}	-0.3 to +7	Volts
Supply Voltage Range V_{DD}	-0.3 to +13	Volts
Supply Voltage Range V_{GG}	-0.3 to +17	Volts
Input Voltage Range V_I	-0.3 to +7	Volts
Input Current Range I_I	0 to 6	mAmps
Operating Temperature Range T_A	0 to +70	°C
Storage Temperature Range T_{stg}	-55 to +125	°C
Average Power Dissipation	1	Watt

NOTES *All voltages in this document are referenced to V_{ss} (ground).*

*Subjecting a circuit to conditions either outside these limits or at these limits for an extended period of time may cause irreparable damage to the circuit. As such, these ratings are not intended to be used during the operation of the circuit. Operating specifications are given in the DC (STATIC) CHARACTERISTICS TABLE.

D. C. (STATIC) CHARACTERISTICS
mN601

OPERATING SPECIFICATIONS

T_A range __0__ to __70__ °C V_{GG} = 14 ± 1.0 Volts I_{CC} = __20__ mAmps Average I_{BB} = __-.1__ mAmps Average

V_{CC} 5 ± 0.25 Volts V_{BB} = -4.25 ± .25 Volts I_{DD} = __50__ mAmps Average I_{SS} = __-150__ mAmps Average

V_{DD} = 10 ± 1.0 Volts V_{SS} = 0 - 0.0 Volts I_{GG} = __20__ mAmps Average

CHARACTERISTIC	SYMBOL	UNITS	PINS	LIMITS MIN.	LIMITS MAX.
INPUT LOW VOLTAGE	V_{IL}	Volts	ɑ1, 3 and ɑ2, 4	-2.0	+0.5
			MB 0-15 , CLAMP EXTINT. DCH INT	-1.0	+1.0
			I O CLOCK. I O DATA 1, I O DATA 2	-1.0	+0.5
INPUT CURRENT FOR LOW STATE	I_{IL}	mAmps	ɑ1, 3 and ɑ2, 4	-	+.01
			MB 0-15	0	-2.0
			EXTINT, DCH INT, CLAMP	-2.0	-4.0
			I O CLOCK, I O DATA 1, I O DATA 2	-2.0	-4.0
INPUT HIGH VOLTAGE	V_{IH}	Volts	ɑ1, 3 and ɑ2, 4	+13.0	+15.0
			MB 0-15 , CLAMP EXTINT, DCH INT	+4.25	+5.8
			I O CLOCK. I O DATA 1, I O DATA 2	+2.5	+5.8
INPUT CURRENT FOR HIGH STATE	I_{IH}	mAmps	ɑ1, 3 and ɑ2, 4	-	-.01
			MB 0-15	-	-.06
			I O CLOCK, I O DATA 1, I O DATA 2	-	-1.0
			EXTINT, DCH INT	-	-.02
			CLAMP	-	+.001
OUTPUT LOW VOLTAGE	V_{OL}	Volts	HALT	-	+3.0
			MB 0-15 , I O INPUT. PAUSE, SAEG. WEG. PG	-	+0.4
			I/O CLOCK, I/O DATA 1, I/O DATA 2		+0.5
OUTPUT CURRENT FOR LOW STATE	I_{OL}	mAmps	PG. I O INPUT	+4.0	
			MB 0-15 , I O CLOCK I O DATA 1, . O DATA 2 PAUSE. SAEG. PG. HALT	+2.0	-
OUTPUT HIGH VOLTAGE	V_{OH}	Volts	MB 0-15 I O CLOCK, I O DATA 1, I O DATA 2 I O INPUT, PAUSE. SAEG. WEG. PG	+4.25	-
			HALT	V_{CC}-0.5	
OUTPUT CURRENT FOR HIGH STATE	I_{OH}	mAmps	HALT-	-	-.01
			MB 0-15	-	-.06
			I O INPUT, PG	-	-.02
			I O CLOCK, I O DATA 1, I O DATA 2, PAUSE SAEG, WEG	-	-.01
INPUT CAPACITANCE	C_I	pF	ɑ1, 3 and ɑ2, 4	-	100
			CLAMP MB 0-15 , I O CLOCK I O DATA 1, I O DATA 2 EXTINT. DCH INT	-	10

NOTE

Logic "1" is defined as the more positive voltage as are the maximum figures given under voltage limits. Logic "0" is defined as the more negative voltage as are the minimum figures given under voltage limits.

Positive current, in the conventional sense, is defined as flowing into the pin.

On power-up, V_{BB} must be within its specified operating range (with respect to V_{SS}) before any of the other power supply voltages are applied to the circuit.

ABSOLUTE MAXIMUM RATINGS (beyond which the useful life of the device may be impaired)

Storage Temperature	$-65°$ to $150°C$
Ambient Temperature Under Bias	-55 to $+125°C$
V_{CC} Pin Potential to Ground Pin	-0.5 to $+6.0$ V
Input Voltage (dc)	-0.5 to $+5.5$ V
Input Current (dc)	-20 to $+5$ mA
Output Voltage (Output HIGH)	-0.5 to $+5.5$ V
Output Current (dc) (Output LOW)	$+20$ mA
Injector Current (I_{INJ})	$+500$ mA
Injector Voltage (V_{INJ})	-0.5 to $+1.5$ V

DC CHARACTERISTICS OVER OPERATING TEMPERATURE RANGE (0 to 75°C)

$I_{INJ(min)}$ = 300 mA, $I_{IN.I(max)}$ = 400 mA, $V_{CC(min)}$ = 4.75 V, $V_{CC(max)}$ = 5.25 V

SYMBOL	CHARACTERISTIC	LIMITS			UNITS	TEST CONDITIONS
		MIN	TYP	MAX		
V_{IH}	Input HIGH Voltage	2.0			V	Guaranteed Input HIGH Voltage
V_{IL}	Input LOW Voltage			0.8	V	Guaranteed Input LOW Voltage
V_{CD}	Input Clamp Diode Voltage		-0.9	-1.5	V	V_{CC} = 4.75 V, I_{IN} = -18 mA I_{INJ} = 300 mA
V_{OH}	Output HIGH Voltage $\overline{RUN}$, CARRY, $\overline{INT\ ON}$, $\overline{SYN}$, CLK OUT, O_0, O_1	2.4	3.4		V	V_{CC} = 4.75 V, I_{OH} = $-400\ \mu A$ I_{INJ} = 300 mA
	Output HIGH Voltage $\overline{IB}_0 - \overline{IB}_{15}$	2.4	3.4		V	V_{CC} = 4.75 V, I_{OH} = -1.0 mA I_{INJ} = 300 mA
I_{CEX}	Output Leakage $\overline{M}_0$, $\overline{M}_1$, $\overline{M}_2$			1.0	mA	V_{CC} = 4.75 V, V_{OH} = 5.25 V I_{INJ} = 300 mA
V_{OL}	Output LOW Voltage		0.25	0.5	V	V_{CC} = 4.75 V, I_{OL} = 8.0 mA I_{INJ} = 300 mA
I_{IH}	Input HIGH Current $C_0 - C_3$, $\overline{DCH\ REQ}$, $\overline{INT\ REQ}$, $\overline{MBSY}$, $\overline{MR}$		1.0	20	μA	V_{CC} = 5.25 V, V_{IN} = 2.7 V I_{INJ} = 300 mA
	Input HIGH Current CP		2.0	40	μA	V_{CC} = 5.25 V, V_{IN} = 2.7 V I_{INJ} = 300 mA
	Input HIGH Current $\overline{IB}_0 - \overline{IB}_{15}$ (3-State)		5.0	100	μA	V_{CC} = 4.75 V, V_{IN} = 2.7 V I_{INJ} = 300 mA
	Input HIGH Current All Inputs			1.0	mA	V_{CC} = 4.75 V, V_{IN} = 5.5 V I_{INJ} = 300 mA
I_{IL}	Input LOW Current All inputs except CP		-0.21	-0.36	mA	V_{CC} = 5.25V, V_{IN} = 0.4 V I_{INJ} = 300 mA
	Input LOW Current CP		-0.42	-0.72	mA	V_{CC} = 5.25 V, V_{IN} = 0.4 V I_{INJ} = 300 mA
I_{OZH}	OFF State (High Impedance) Output Current $\overline{IB}_0 - \overline{IB}_{15}$			100	μA	V_{CC} = 5.25 V, V_{OUT} = 2.4 V I_{INJ} = 300 mA
I_{OZL}	OFF State (High Impedance) Output Current $\overline{IB}_0 - \overline{IB}_{15}$		-0.21	-0.36	mA	V_{CC} = 5.25 V, V_{OUT} = 0.4 V I_{INJ} = 300 mA
I_{OS}	Output Short Circuit Current All Outputs Except $\overline{M}_0$, $\overline{M}_1$, $\overline{M}_2$	-15		-100	mA	V_{CC} = 5.25 V, V_{OUT} = 0.0 V I_{INJ} = 300 mA
I_{CC}	Supply Current		150	200	mA	V_{CC} = 5.25 V
V_{INJ}	Injector Voltage		1.0		V	I_{INJ} = 300 mA

Data sheets on pages 4-D4 through 4-D10 reprinted by permission of Fairchild Camera and Instrument Corporation.

AC CHARACTERISTICS: T_A = 0 to 75°C — Figures 8 & 9

SYMBOL	CHARACTERISTIC	LIMITS-ns			NOTE
		MIN	TYP	MAX	
t_{CPSYL}	Propagation Delay, CLOCK to $\overline{SYN}$ going LOW		150		
t_{CPSYH}	Propagation Delay, CLOCK to $\overline{SYN}$ going HIGH		160		
t_{MBSYL}	Propagation Delay, $\overline{MBSY}$ going HIGH to $\overline{SYN}$ going LOW		70		
t_{MBW}	$\overline{MBSY}$ Min Pulse Width (HIGH)		30		
t_{MBS}	Set-up Time, $\overline{MBSY}$ HIGH to CLOCK		−40		
t_{MBHD}	Hold Time, $\overline{MBSY}$ HIGH after CLOCK		60		
t_{CPMH}	Propagation Delay, CLOCK to $\overline{M}_2$, $\overline{M}_1$, $\overline{M}_0$ going HIGH		160		
t_{CPML}	Propagation Delay, CLOCK to $\overline{M}_2$, $\overline{M}_1$, $\overline{M}_0$ going LOW		170		
t_{CPOH}	Propagation Delay, CLOCK to O_1, O_0 going HIGH		160		Fig. 9 Only
t_{CPOL}	Propagation Delay, CLOCK to O_1, O_0 going LOW		170		Fig. 8 Only
t_{CPAH}	Propagation Delay, CLOCK to ADDRESS $\overline{IB}_{0-15}$ going HIGH		170		
t_{CPAL}	Propagation Delay, CLOCK to ADDRESS $\overline{IB}_{0-15}$ going LOW		180		
t_{MBAF}	Propagation Delay, CLOCK to ADDRESS $\overline{IB}_{0-15}$ going 3-state		110		
t_{DS}	Set-up Time, DATA $\overline{IB}_{0-15}$ to CLOCK		−110		
t_{DHD}	Hold Time, DATA $\overline{IB}_{0-15}$ after CLOCK		130		
t_{CS}	Set-up Time, C_3, C_2, C_1, C_0 to CLOCK		−110		
t_{CHD}	Hold Time, C_3, C_2, C_1, C_0 after CLOCK		130		
t_{CPRH}	Propagation Delay, CLOCK to RUN HIGH		160		
t_{CPRL}	Propagation Delay, CLOCK to RUN LOW		170		
t_{DCS}	Set-up Time, $\overline{DCH\ REQ}$ to CLOCK		−110		
t_{DCHD}	Hold Time, $\overline{DCH\ REQ}$ after CLOCK		130		
t_{IS}	Set-up Time, $\overline{INT\ REQ}$ to CLOCK		−100		
t_{IHD}	Hold Time, $\overline{INT\ REQ}$ after CLOCK		120		Fig. 8 Only
t_{CPCYH}	Propagation Delay, CLOCK to CARRY HIGH		160		
t_{CPCYL}	Propagation Delay, CLOCK to CARRY LOW		150		
t_{CPIOH}	Propagation Delay, CLOCK to INT ON HIGH		200		
t_{CPIOL}	Propagation Delay, CLOCK to INT ON LOW		190		

NOTES:
1. The Information Bus is driven as a result of the previous cycle.
2. The Fetch and Read cycles will be stretched out for slower memories.
3. Applies to console operation using this cycle type.

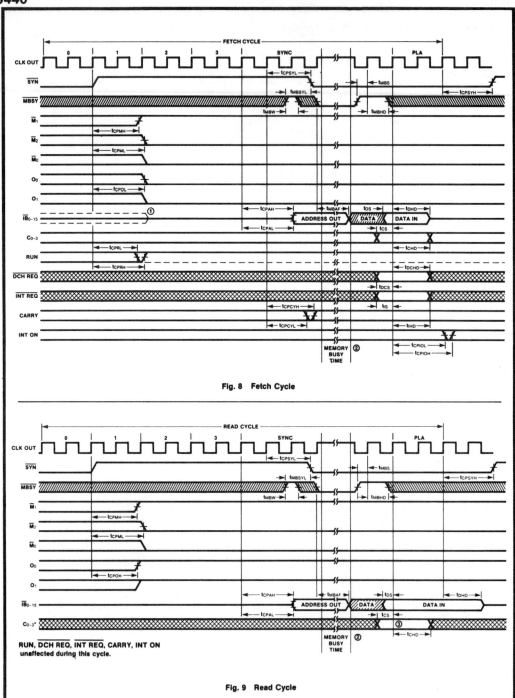

Fig. 8 Fetch Cycle

Fig. 9 Read Cycle

9440

AC CHARACTERISTICS: T_A = 0 to 75°C — Figures 10 & 11

SYMBOL	CHARACTERISTIC	LIMITS-ns			NOTE
		MIN	TYP	MAX	
t_{CPSYL}	Propagation Delay, CLOCK to $\overline{SYN}$ going LOW		150		
t_{CPSYH}	Propagation Delay, CLOCK to $\overline{SYN}$ going HIGH		160		
t_{MBSYL}	Propagation Delay, $\overline{MBSY}$ going HIGH to $\overline{SYN}$ going LOW		70		
t_{MBW}	$\overline{MBSY}$ Min Pulse Width (HIGH)		30		
t_{MBS}	Set-up Time, $\overline{MBSY}$ LOW to CLOCK		−40		
t_{MBHD}	Hold Time, $\overline{MBSY}$ LOW after CLOCK		60		
t_{CPMH}	Propagation Delay, CLOCK to $\overline{M}_2$, $\overline{M}_1$, $\overline{M}_0$ going HIGH		160		
t_{CPML}	Propagation Delay, CLOCK to $\overline{M}_2$, $\overline{M}_1$, $\overline{M}_0$ going LOW		170		
t_{CPOH}	Propagation Delay, CLOCK to O_1, O_0 going HIGH		160		
t_{CPOL}	Propagation Delay, CLOCK to O_1, O_0 going LOW		170		
t_{CPDH}	Propagation Delay, CLOCK to DATA $\overline{IB}_{0-15}$ going HIGH		170		
t_{CPDL}	Propagation Delay, CLOCK to DATA $\overline{IB}_{0-15}$ going LOW		180		Fig. 10 Only
t_{CPDF}	Propagation Delay, CLOCK to DATA $\overline{IB}_{0-15}$ going 3-state		110		
t_{CPAH}	Propagation Delay, CLOCK to ADDRESS $\overline{IB}_{0-15}$ going HIGH		170		
t_{CPAL}	Propagation Delay, CLOCK to ADDRESS $\overline{IB}_{0-15}$ going LOW		180		Fig. 11 Only
t_{CPAF}	Propagation Delay, CLOCK to ADDRESS $\overline{IB}_{0-15}$ going 3-state		160		
t_{CS}	Set-up Time, C_3, C_2, C_1, C_0 to CLOCK		−110		
t_{CHD}	Hold Time, C_3, C_2, C_1, C_0 after CLOCK		130		

NOTES:
3. Applies to console operation using this cycle type.
4. The Information Bus is driven as a result of the previous cycle.
5. The 9440 waits for $\overline{MBSY}$ to go LOW. By holding $\overline{MBSY}$ HIGH, the user may idle the processor.

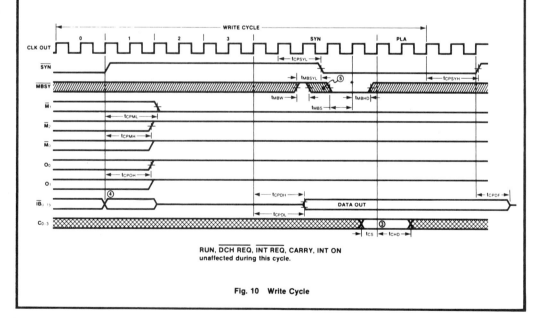

RUN, $\overline{DCH\ REQ}$, $\overline{INT\ REQ}$, CARRY, INT ON
unaffected during this cycle.

Fig. 10   Write Cycle

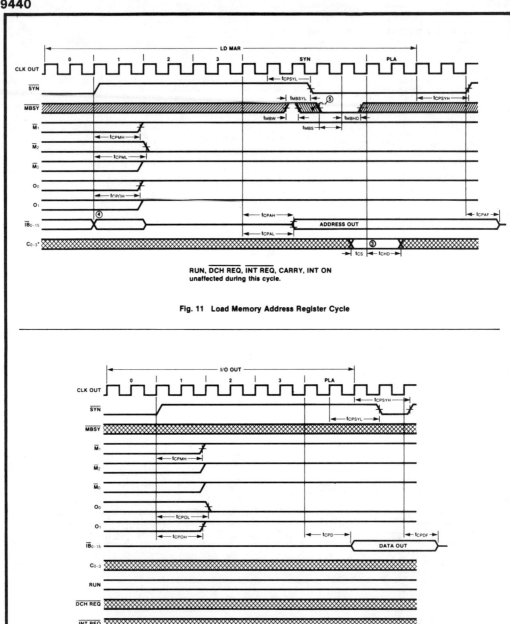

Fig. 11 Load Memory Address Register Cycle

Fig. 12 I/O Out Cycle

9440

AC CHARACTERISTICS: T_A = 0 to 75°C — Figures 12, 13, 14, 15

SYMBOL	CHARACTERISTIC	LIMITS-ns			NOTE
		MIN	TYP	MAX	
t_{CPSYL}	Propagation Delay, CLOCK to $\overline{SYN}$ going LOW		150		
t_{CPSYH}	Propagation Delay, CLOCK to $\overline{SYN}$ going HIGH		160		
t_{CPMH}	Propagation Delay, CLOCK to $\overline{M}_2$, $\overline{M}_1$, $\overline{M}_0$ going HIGH		160		
t_{CPML}	Propagation Delay, CLOCK to $\overline{M}_2$, $\overline{M}_1$, $\overline{M}_0$ going LOW		170		
t_{CPOH}	Propagation Delay, CLOCK to O_1, O_0 going HIGH		160		
t_{CPOL}	Propagation Delay, CLOCK to O_1, O_0 going LOW		170		
t_{CPDH}	Propagation Delay, CLOCK to DATA $\overline{IB}_{0-15}$ going HIGH		170		
t_{CPDL}	Propagation Delay, CLOCK to DATA $\overline{IB}_{0-15}$ going LOW		180		Fig. 12 Only
t_{CPDF}	Propagation Delay, CLOCK to DATA $\overline{IB}_{0-15}$ going 3-state		110		
t_{DS}	Set-up Time, DATA $\overline{IB}_{0-15}$ to CLOCK		−110		
t_{DHD}	Hold Time, DATA $\overline{IB}_{0-15}$ after CLOCK		130		Fig. 13 Only
t_{CS}	Set-up Time, C_3, C_2, C_1, C_0 to CLOCK		−110		
t_{CHD}	Hold Time, C_3, C_2, C_1, C_0 after CLOCK		130		Fig. 14 Only

NOTES:
6. During $\overline{DCH}$, the 9440 is not driving the $\overline{M}$ lines. An external device can control the memory when a LOW is applied to the appropriate $\overline{M}$ line.
7. The 9440 floats the $\overline{IB}_{0-15}$. The Information Bus is available to the I/O devices and the memory as needed.

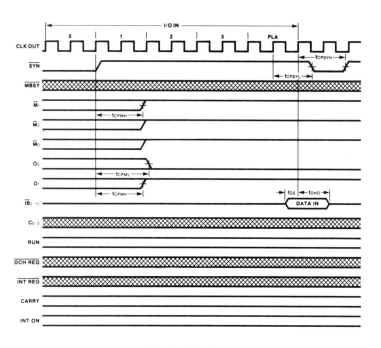

Fig. 13 I/O In Cycle

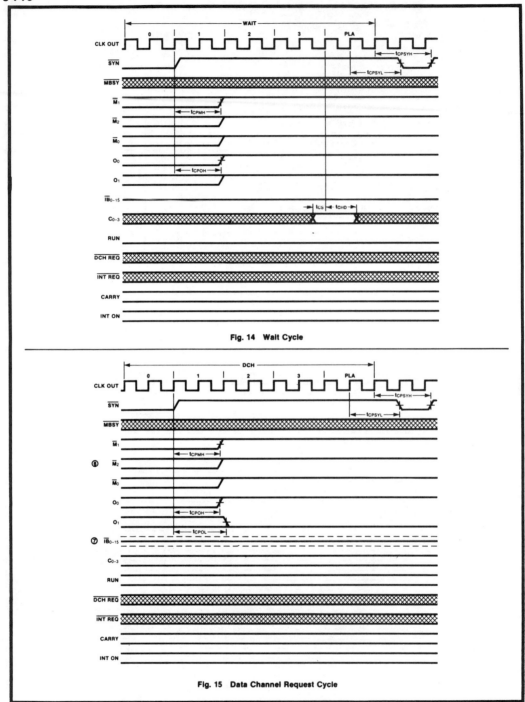

Fig. 14   Wait Cycle

Fig. 15   Data Channel Request Cycle

Chapter 5
THE INTEL 8086

The 8086 is Intel's first 16-bit microprocessor. It is significantly more powerful than any prior microprocessor.

The 8086 assembly language instruction set is upward compatible with 8080A — but at the source program level only. That is to say, every 8080A assembly language instruction can be converted into one or more 8086 assembly language instructions. There is no reason why anyone would try to convert 8086 assembly language instructions, one at a time, into one or more 8080A assembly language instructions, but if you did, you would soon become hopelessly tangled in conflicting memory allocations and special translation rules. That is why we say that the 8086 and 8080A assembly language instruction sets are "upward" compatible.

The 8086 and 8080A assembly language instruction sets are not compatible at the object code level, which means that 8080A programs stored in read-only memory are useless in an 8086 system.

The 8085 and 8080A assembly language instruction sets are identical, with the exception of the 8085 RIM and SIM instructions. The 8085 RIM and SIM instructions cannot be translated into 8086 instructions. This is because the RIM and SIM instructions use the serial I/O logic of the 8085, which has no 8086 counterpart. Without the RIM and SIM instructions, the 8085 and 8080A assembly language instruction sets are identical; therefore **the 8086 assembly language instruction set must also be upward compatible with the 8085 assembly language instruction set — apart from the RIM and SIM instructions.**

The 8085 and 8080A assembly language instruction sets are object code compatible — with the exception of the 8085 RIM and SIM instructions. That is to say, a program existing in read-only memory could be used with one microprocessor or the other.

The 8080A assembly language instruction set is a subset of the Z80 assembly language instruction set. That is to say, the Z80 will execute an 8080A object program — but the reverse is not true. The 8080A cannot execute Z80 programs when the full Z80 instruction set is used. **The 8086 assembly language instruction set is not upward compatible with the Z80 assembly language instruction set.**

As a historical note, it is worth mentioning that the 8008 microprocessor, which preceded the 8080A, was also compatible only at the source program level. That is to say, there is an 8080A assembly language instruction for every 8008 assembly language instruction, but the two microprocessor object code sets are not the same.

The various instruction set compatibilities that we have described may be illustrated as follows:

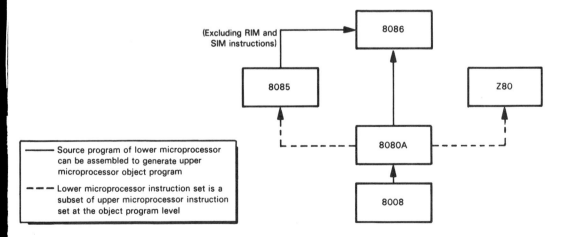

5-1

These are the most interesting innovations to be found in 8086 hardware design:

1) 8086 Central Processing Unit logic has been divided into an Execution Unit (EU) and a Bus Interface Unit (BIU). These two halves operate asynchronously. The Bus Interface Unit handles all interfaces with the external bus; it generates external memory and I/O addresses and has a 6-byte instruction object code queue. Whenever the EU needs to access memory or an I/O device, it makes a bus access request to the Bus Interface Unit. Providing the Bus Interface Unit is not currently busy, it acknowledges the bus access request from the EU. When the Bus Interface Unit has no active pending bus access requests from the EU, it performs instruction fetch machine cycles to fill the 6-byte instruction object code queue. The CPU takes its instruction object codes from the front of the queue. Thus instruction fetch time is largely eliminated.

2) The 8086 has been designed to work in a wide range of microcomputer system configurations, ranging from a simple one-CPU system to a multiple-CPU network. To support this wide flexibility, a number of 8086 pins output alternate signals. This may be illustrated as follows:

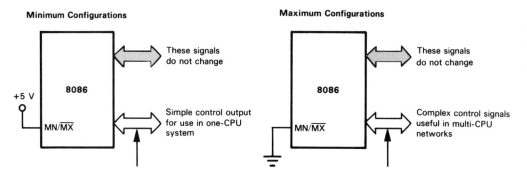

The same pins output these two sets of signals, based on a level of MN/$\overline{\text{MX}}$. This wholesale re-allocation of signals is a highly imaginative and innovative first for the microprocessor industry.

3) The 8086 has built-in logic to handle bus access priorities in multi-CPU configurations. (This is not a new concept; National Semiconductor's SC/MP has had it for years.)

4) In multi-CPU configurations, each 8086 CPU can have its own local memory, while simultaneously sharing common memory. The common memory may be shared by all CPUs, or by selected CPUs.

5) The 8086 has been designed to compete effectively in program intensive applications that have been the domain of the minicomputer. Up to a million bytes of external memory can be addressed directly. All memory addressing is base relative; this memory addressing technique naturally generates relocatable object programs. (Relocatable object programs can be moved from one memory address space to another and re-executed without modification.) Also, since the 8086 utilizes stack-relative addressing, re-entrant programs are easily written. (Re-entrant programs can be interrupted in mid-execution and re-executed. For example, a subroutine which calls itself is re-entrant; a program which can be interrupted in mid-execution by an external interrupt, and then re-executed within the interrupt service routine, is also re-entrant.)

6) The 8086 uses prefix instructions that modify the interpretation of the next instruction's object code.

The 8086, like its predecessor, the 8080A, is really one component of a multiple-chip microprocessor configuration.
In addition to the 8086 microprocessor itself, you must have an 8284 Clock Generator/Driver. You could create the required clock signal using alternative logic, but it would be neither practical nor economical to do so.

The third device necessary in some 8086 microprocessor configurations is the 8288 Bus Controller.

You will usually have an 8288 Bus Controller between an 8086 and its System Bus (or busses), just as you will usually have an 8288 System Bus controller between an 8080A and its System Bus. In the case of the 8086, however, you can dispense with the 8288 Bus Controller in single-bus configurations — and pay no penalty for it.

The 8086 has a large family of support devices. In this chapter we describe the following support devices:

- The 8284 Clock Generator/Driver
- The 8288 Bus Controller
- The 8282/8283 8-bit input/output latches
- The 8286/8287 8-bit parallel bidirectional bus drivers

The 8088, an 8-bit version of the 8086, is also described.

The primary manufacturer of the 8086 is:

INTEL CORPORATION
3065 Bowers Avenue
Santa Clara, California 95051

Second sources are:

MOSTEK CORPORATION
1215 West Crosby Road
Carrollton, TX 75006

NEC MICROCOMPUTERS INC.
Five Militia Drive
Lexington, MA 02173

SIEMENS AG
Components Group
Balanstrasse 73, D8000
Munich-80, West Germany

The 8086 is manufactured using N-channel depletion load, silicon gate technology. It is packaged in a 40-pin DIP. A single +5 V power supply is required. All signals, with the exception of the clock input, are TTL-level compatible. The clock input must be an MOS level signal; it is generated by the 8284 Clock Generator/Driver device, which is described later in this chapter.

Instruction execution times will vary depending on how effectively instruction queuing is used. Typically, between 2 and 30 clock cycles are required to execute an instruction. Multiplication and division instructions require more execution time. Clock cycles may be as short as 125 nanoseconds.

An 8 MHz version of the 8086 has been announced; it is identified as the 8086-2. The 4 MHz version is called the 8086-4. The standard 5 MHz 8086 is referred to without a suffix. There is no difference between the three versions other than maximum allowed clock speeds.

| 8086 |
| 8086-2 |
| 8086-4 |

THE 8086 CPU

Functions implemented on the 8086 microprocessor chip are illustrated in Figure 5-1.

Interrupt priority arbitration logic is shown as only half present; external logic, such as an 8259A, must provide a device code identifying an interrupt, but all arbitration and vectoring logic is subsequently handled by logic within the CPU.

It is worth noting that bus interface logic, which is shown as present in Figure 5-1, is much more extensive than other microprocessors provide. One could rightfully demand that bus interface logic therefore be shown as absent in equivalent figures for other microprocessors.

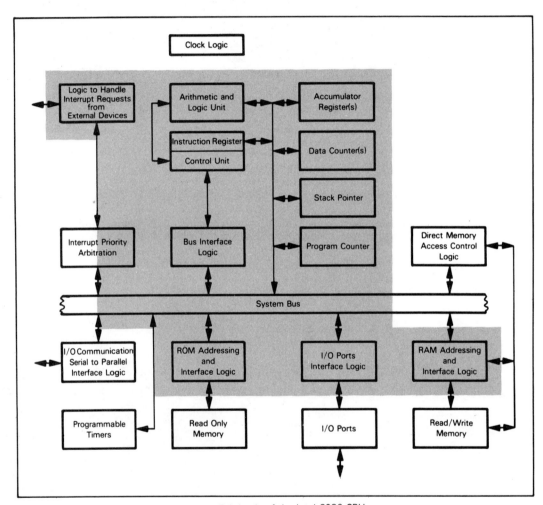

Figure 5-1. Logic of the Intel 8086 CPU

8086 PROGRAMMABLE REGISTERS AND ADDRESSING MODES

We describe 8086 programmable registers in conjunction with 8086 addressing modes, since many 8086 programmable registers are there only to support memory addressing logic. 8086 programmable registers are illustrated in Figure 5-2.

Shaded registers are 8086 equivalents for 8080A registers. 8080A register names are shown in the left margin.

Let us first examine the general purpose registers, AX, BX, CX, and DX. These locations are treated as four 16-bit registers or eight 8-bit registers; they also reproduce the 8080A general purpose registers as follows:

| 8086 AND 8080A REGISTERS' COMPATIBILITY |

AH has no 8080A equivalent. Do not confuse it with the 8080A PSW.

AL is equivalent to the 8080A A register.
BH is equivalent to the 8080A H register.
BL is equivalent to the 8080A L register.
CH is equivalent to the 8080A B register.
CL is equivalent to the 8080A C register.
DH is equivalent to the 8080A D register.
DL is equivalent to the 8080A E register.

Consistent with 8080A register utilization, **register AX serves as a primary Accumulator.** Input and output instructions pass data through AX (or AL) in preference to other general purpose registers; also, selected instruction access AX (or AL) contents only.

| 8086 AX REGISTER |

In addition to serving as a general purpose Accumulator, register BX can serve as a base register when computing data memory addresses.

| 8086 BX REGISTER |

Register CX serves as an Accumulator; it **is also used as a counter** by multi-iteration instructions; these instructions terminate execution when register CX contents increment or decrement to 0.

| 8086 CX REGISTER |

Some I/O instructions move data between an identified I/O port and the memory location addressed by Register DX. Register DX may also serve as an Accumulator.

| 8086 DX REGISTER |

When looking at general purpose registers AX, BX, CX, and DX, there is plenty of opportunity to be confused by terminology.

Intel literature identifies the four 16-bit registers via the labels AX, BX, CX, and DX. Each of these 16-bit registers is subdivided by Intel literature into two 8-bit registers, as follows:

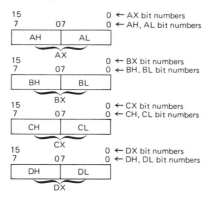

The 8080A Accumulator must be reproduced by AL, since selected 8080A and 8086 instructions access this register and none other.

BH and BL must reproduce the 8080A H and L registers, since only BX can contribute to an 8086 data memory address. On the surface this would appear to present a problem, since the 8080A has a limited number of instructions that use the BC and DE registers to provide 16-bit memory addresses. When 8080A source programs are reassembled to execute on an 8086 microprocessor, 8080A instructions that seek memory addresses out of the BC or DE registers become 8086 instructions that use Index registers.

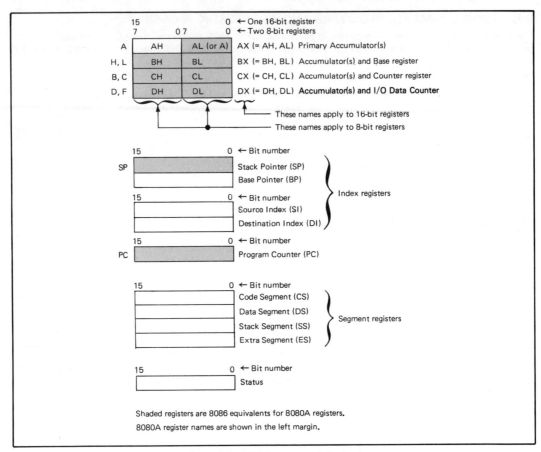

Figure 5-2. 8086 Programmable Registers

All 8086 memory addresses are computed by summing the contents of a Segment register and an effective memory address. The effective memory address is computed via a variety of addressing modes, as it would be for any other microprocessor. The selected Segment register contents are left-shifted four bits, then added to the effective memory address to generate the actual address output as follows:

Segment Register contents:	X X X X X X X X X X X X X X X X 0 0 0 0
Effective memory address:	+ 0 0 0 0 Y Y Y Y Y Y Y Y Y Y Y Y Y Y Y Y
Actual address output:	X X X Z Z Z Z Z Z Z Z Z Z Z Z Z Z Y Y Y Y

X, Y and Z represent any binary digits.

Thus **a 20-bit memory address is computed — which allows 1,048,576 bytes of external memory to be addressed directly.**

The Segment registers of the 8086 are unlike any other microprocessor registers described in this book. They act as base registers which can point to any memory location that lies on an address boundary that is an even multiple of 16 bytes. Using arbitrary memory addresses, this may be illustrated as follows:

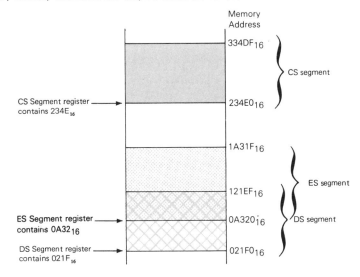

As illustrated above, each Segment register identifies the beginning of a 65,536-byte memory segment. Since the 8086 has four Segment registers, there will at any time be four selected 65,536-byte memory segments. The actual address output will always select a memory location within one of these four segments. For example, if an actual address output is the sum of the DS Segment register and an effective memory address, then the actual address output must select a memory location within the DS segment; that is to say, within the address range $021F0_{16}$ through $121EF_{16}$ in the illustration above. Likewise, an actual address output, which is the sum of the CS Segment register and an effective memory address, must select a memory location within the CS segment, which in the illustration above will lie in the address range $234E0_{16}$ through $334DF_{16}$.

No restrictions are placed on the contents of Segment registers. Therefore, 8086 memory is not divided into 65,536-byte pages, nor do the four Segment registers have to specify non-overlapping memory spaces. Each Segment register identifies the origin of a 65,536-byte memory segment that may lie anywhere within addressable memory and may or may not overlap with one or more other segments.

Even though Segment registers can create overlapping or non-overlapping segments, they do have dedicated addressing functions. That is to say, **different types of memory accesses compute memory address within specific segments.**

During an instruction fetch, the Program Counter contents are added to the Code Segment register (CS) contents in order to compute the memory address for the instruction to be fetched. This may be illustrated as follows:

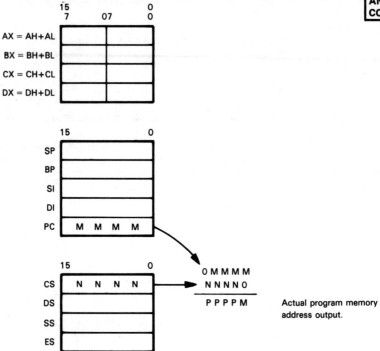

M, N, and P represent any hexadecimal digits.

Any Stack instruction such as a Push, Pop, Call, or Return **adds the Stack Pointer contents to the Stack Segment register (SS) contents** in order to compute the address of the Stack location to be accessed. This may be illustrated as follows:

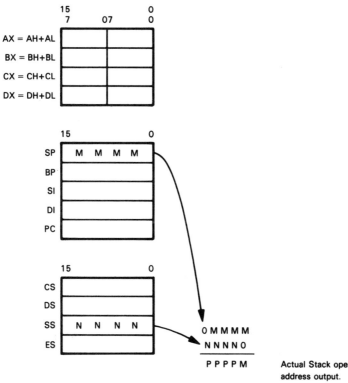

Actual Stack operation address output.

Once again, M, N, and P represent any hexadecimal digits.

Instructions that process data strings use the SI and DI Index registers, together with the Data Segment register (DS) and the Extra Segment register (ES), in order to identify string source and destination addresses. This may be illustrated as follows:

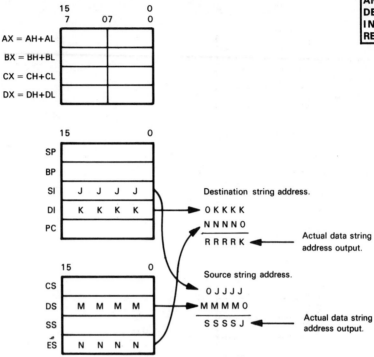

J, K, M, R, and S all represent any hexadecimal digits.

As the above illustration would imply, instructions that process strings require that the source and destination strings reside within a single 65,536-byte address range but not necessarily the same 65,536-byte range.

Instructions that access data memory add an effective memory address to the Data Segment register (DS) or the Stack Segment register (SS). This may be illustrated as follows:

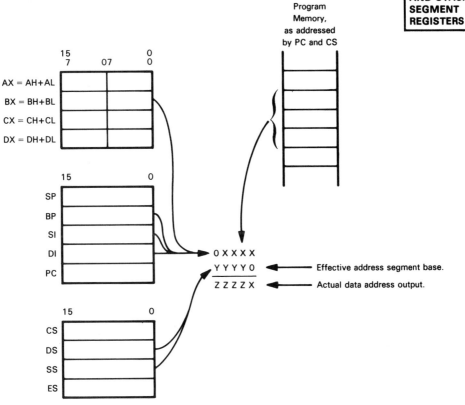

X, Y, and Z represent any hexadecimal digits.

When a data memory address is created, as illustrated above, the BX, BP, SI, and DI registers' contents, plus a displacement coming from the instruction object code, may contribute to the effective memory address. There are, however, very specific register and displacement combinations that can create an active memory address, as summarized in Table 5-1. Each case specifies either the DS or SS register as the default source for the segment base address.

Table 5-1. A Summary of Intel 8086 Memory Addressing Options

Memory Reference	Segment Register	Base Register	Index Register	Possible Displacements		
				16-Bit Unsigned	8-Bit High-Order Bit Extended	None
Normal Data Memory Reference	DS (Alternate*: CS, SS or ES)	None	SI	X	X	X
			DI	X	X	X
		BX	SI	X	X	X
			DI	X	X	X
			None	X	X	X
	DS	None	None	X		
	SS (Alternate*: CS, DS, or ES)	BP	SI	X	X	X
			DI	X	X	X
			None	X	X	
Stack	SS	SP	None			
String Data	DS	None	SI			
	ES	None	DI			
Instruction Fetch	CS	PC	None			
Branch	CS	PC	None		X	
I/O Data	DS	DX	None			

* The segment override allows DS or SS to be replaced by one of the other segment registers
X These are displacements that can be used to compute memory addresses.

When creating any data memory address, you can add a prefix to an instruction to select a Segment register other than the default Segment register. You can only select a Segment register other than the default Segment register when addressing data memory. You must live with the default Segment register when creating program memory addresses, Stack addresses, or string instruction addresses.

It is very important to note that the 8086 has a whole set of data memory addressing options aimed at accessing the Stack as though it were a data area. That is to say, in addition to the normal "Push" and "Pop" type Stack instructions, the 8086 allows normal data memory access instructions to address the Stack. Many assembly language programmers use the Stack to store addresses, and as a general depository for data that must be transmitted between program modules. Anyone favoring this assembly language programming philosophy will be delighted with 8086 data memory addressing options.

Let us now examine the various data memory addressing options in detail. Refer to Table 5-1.

In the simplest case, **we have straightforward direct memory addressing.** A 16-bit displacement provided by two instruction object code bytes is added to the Data Segment register in order to create the actual memory address. This may be illustrated as follows:

8086 DIRECT
MEMORY
ADDRESSING

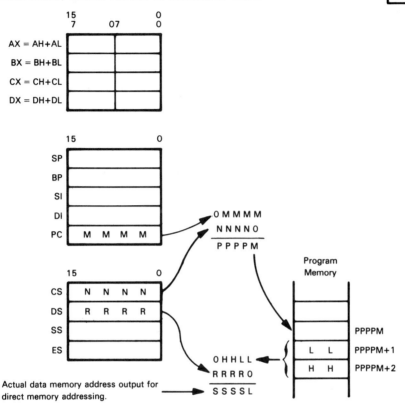

Actual data memory address output for direct memory addressing.

H, L, M, N, P, R, and S all represent any hexadecimal digits.

Note that a 16-bit address displacement, when stored in program memory, has the low-order byte preceding the high-order byte. This is consistent with the way the 8080A stores addresses in program memory.

DS must provide the Segment base address when addressing data memory directly, as illustrated above.

Direct, indexed addressing is also provided. The SI or DI register may be selected as the Index register. You have the option of adding a displacement to the contents of the selected Index register in order to generate the effective address. **If you do not add a displacement, then you have, in effect, implied memory addressing via the SI or DI register.** This may be illustrated as follows:

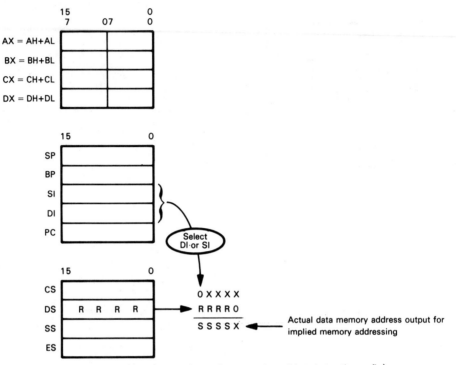

(You may substitute CS, SS or ES for DS by executing a 1-byte instruction prefix.)

X, R, and S represent any hexadecimal digits.

If a displacement is added to the contents of the selected Index register, then you may specify an 8-bit displacement or a 16-bit displacement. A 16-bit displacement is stored in two object code bytes; the low-order byte of the displacement precedes the high-order byte of the displacement, as illustrated for direct memory addressing. If an 8-bit displacement is specified, then the high-order bit of the low-order byte is propagated into the high-order byte to create a 16-bit displacement. This may be illustrated as follows:

Displacements:		1 0 1 1 0 1 0 1	0 1 1 0 1 0 1 1
Sign extended:	1 1 1 1 1 1 1 1	0 1 1 0 1 0 1	0 0 0 0 0 0 0 0	1 1 0 1 0 1 1

We may now illustrate direct, indexed addressing as follows:

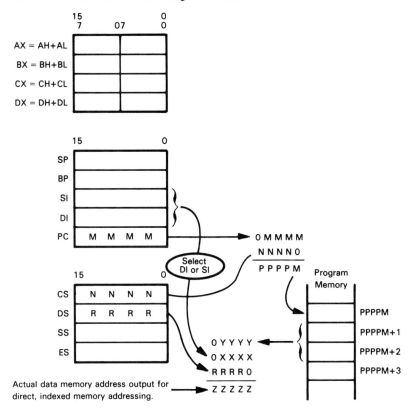

(You may substitute CS, SS or ES for DS by executing a 1-byte instruction prefix.)

M, N, P, R, X, Y, and Z all represent any hexadecimal digits.

YYYY is the 16-bit or 8-bit displacement taken from program memory.

XXXX is the index taken from either the DI or the SI register.

The effective memory address can be computed using base relative addressing. You have two sets of base relative addressing options:

1) Data memory base relative addressing, which is within the DS segment (data memory).

2) Stack base relative addressing, which is in the SS segment (Stack memory).

8086 BASE RELATIVE, INDEXED ADDRESSING

Data memory base relative addressing uses the BX register contents to provide the base for the effective address. All of the data memory addressing options thus far described are available with base relative data memory addressing. In effect, base relative data memory addressing merely adds the contents of the BX register to the effective memory address which could otherwise have been generated. Here, for example, is an illustration of base relative direct addressing:

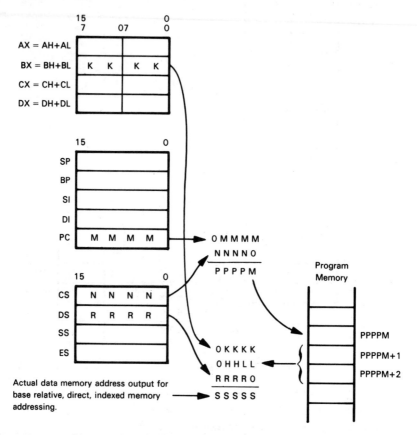

Actual data memory address output for base relative, direct, indexed memory addressing.

(You may substitute CS, ES or SS for DS by executing a 1-byte instruction prefix.)

Simple, direct addressing, which we described earlier, always generated a 16-bit displacement. Base relative, direct addressing allows the displacement, illustrated above as HHLL, to be a 16-bit displacement, an 8-bit displacement with sign extended, or no displacement at all.

Base relative implied data memory addressing simply adds the contents of the BX register to the selected Index register in order to compute the effective memory address. This may be illustrated as follows:

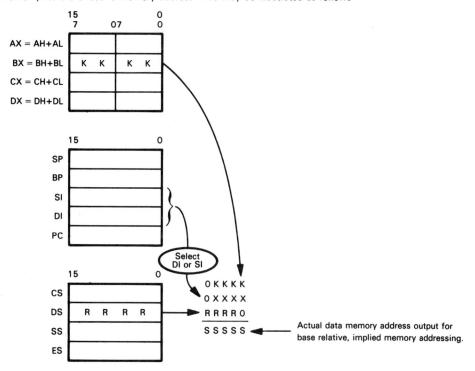

(You may substitute CS, SS or ES for DS by executing a 1-byte instruction prefix.)

Base relative, direct, indexed data memory addressing may appear to be complicated, but in fact it is not. We simply add the contents of the BX register to the effective memory address, as computed for normal direct, indexed addressing. Thus, base relative, direct, indexed data memory addressing may be illustrated as follows:

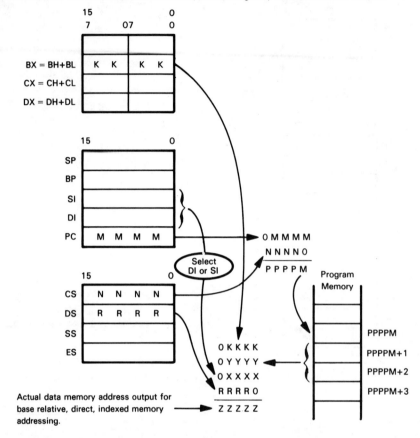

(You may substitute CS, SS or ES for DS by executing a 1-byte instruction prefix.)

The 8086 also has Stack memory addressing variations of the base relative, data memory addressing options just described. Here, for example, is base relative, direct Stack memory addressing:

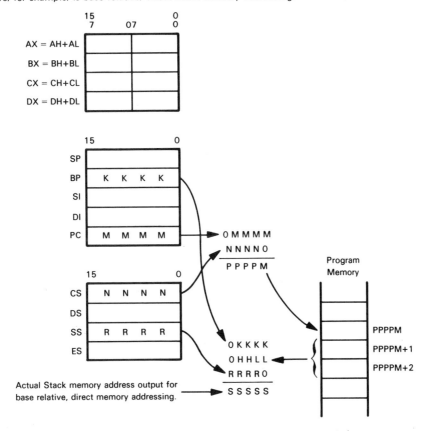

Actual Stack memory address output for base relative, direct memory addressing.

(You may substitute CS, ES or SS for DS by executing a 1-byte instruction prefix.)

In the illustration above, the displacement HHLL must be present, either as a 16-bit displacement, or as an 8-bit displacement with sign extended. Remember, base relative, direct data memory addressing also allows no displacement. However, base relative, direct Stack memory addressing requires a displacement. These options are summarized in Table 5-1.

Here is an illustration of base relative, implied Stack memory addressing:

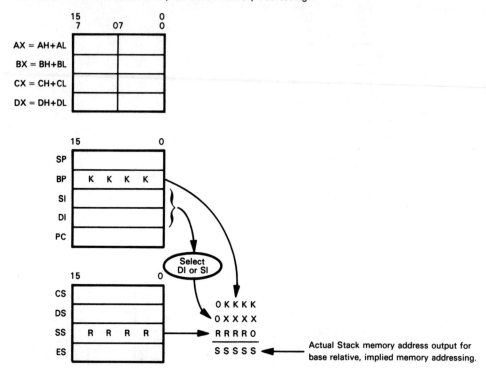

(You may substitute CS, DS or ES for SS by executing a 1-byte instruction prefix.)

X, R, and S represent any hexadecimal digits.

Here is an illustration of base relative, direct, indexed Stack memory addressing:

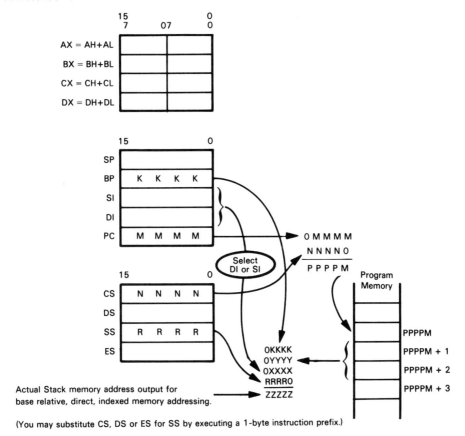

Actual Stack memory address output for base relative, direct, indexed memory addressing.

(You may substitute CS, DS or ES for SS by executing a 1-byte instruction prefix.)

There is one anomolous 8086 addressing mode that can cause confusion. **One variation of I/O instructions addresses an I/O port via the DX register.** The DX register contents are output on the Address Bus, to be interpreted as an I/O port address. This means you can have up to 65,536 I/O port addresses. Since the DX register contents are being output as an I/O port address, it is not

| 8086 I/O |
| PORT |
| ADDRESSING |

added to any Segment register contents. Thus, the DX register outputs an address in the range 0000_{16} through $FFFF_{16}$. This is the only case in which a register's contents are output directly as an address on the Address Bus, without first passing through segmentation logic.

All 8086 Branch-on-Condition instructions use program relative addressing. This feature allows dynamically relocatable code. The Branch-on-Condition instruction provides an 8-bit, signed binary displacement that is added to the contents of the Program Counter. Thus, Branch-on-Condition instructions have an addressing range of -128 through $+127$ bytes from the location of the Branch-on-Condition. **The queuing of instruction object codes has no impact on Branch-on-Condition logic,** or the branch addressing range.

| 8086 |
| PROGRAM |
| RELATIVE |
| ADDRESSING |

8086 Jump and Subroutine Call instructions offer these addressing options:

1) **Program relative addressing.** An 8-bit or 16-bit displacement is added to the contents of the Program Counter.

2) **Direct addressing.** New 16-bit addresses provided by the instruction are loaded into the Program Counter and the CS Segment register.

3) **Indirect addressing.** Any of the data memory addressing options may be used to read data from data memory. However, the data input is interpreted as a memory address. You have two indirect addressing options. A single 16-bit data word may be read, in which case it is loaded into the Program Counter and the Jump or Call references a memory location within the current CS segment. You can also read two 16-bit data words; the first is loaded into the Program Counter and the second is loaded into the CS Segment register. Thus you can Jump or Call indirectly any addressable memory location.

**8086
INDIRECT
ADDRESSING**

8086 STATUS

The 8086 has a 16-bit Stack register with the following satus bit assignments:

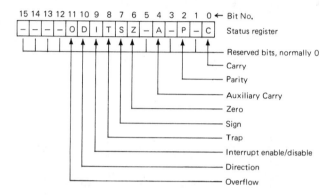

The Carry, Auxiliary Carry, Overflow, and Sign statuses are quite standard; see Volume 1 for a description of these statuses. The Auxiliary Carry status is identical to the 8080A status with the same name. It represents carries out of bit 3 in an 8-bit data unit as described in Volume 1, Chapter 2.

Subtract instructions use twos complement arithmetic in order to subtract the minuend from the subtrahend. However, the Carry status is inverted. That is to say, following a subtract operation, the Carry status is set to 1 if there was no carry out of the high-order bit, and the Carry status is reset to 0 if there was a carry out of the high-order bit. The Carry Status therefore indicates a borrow.

The Parity status is set to 1 when there is an even number of 1 bits in the result of a data operation; an odd number of 1 bits causes the Parity status to be reset to 0.

The Zero status is completely standard. It is set to 1 when the result of a data operation is zero; it is set to 0 when the result of a data operation is not zero.

The Direction status determines whether string operations will auto-increment or auto-decrement the contents of Index registers. If the Direction status is 1, then the SI and DI Index registers' contents will be decremented; that is to say, strings will be accessed from the highest memory address down to the lowest memory address. If the Direction status is 0, then the SI and DI Index register contents will be incremented; that is to say, strings will be accessed beginning with the lowest memory address.

The Interrupt status is a master interrupt enable/disable. This status must be 1 in order to enable interrupts within the 8086. If this status is 0, then all interrupts except the NMI (Non-Maskable Interrupt) will be disabled.

The Trap status is a special debugging aid that puts the 8086 into a "single step" mode. The single step mode is described in detail together with 8086 interrupt logic, since it depends on this interrupt logic for its existence.

The Carry, Auxiliary Carry, Parity, Sign, and Zero statuses are also found in the 8080A. The Overflow, Direction, Interrupt, and Trap statuses are new in the 8086.

8086 CPU PINS AND SIGNALS

8086 CPU pins and signals are illustrated in Figure 5-3.

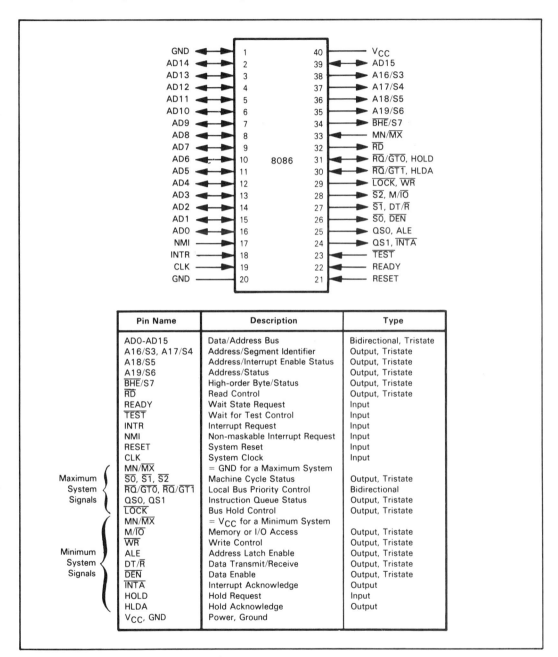

Figure 5-3. 8086 Pins and Signal Assignments

The 8086 outputs a 20-bit memory address. Data is accessed as 16-bit words, subdivided into a low-order byte and a high-order byte. Therefore **the 8086 needs a 20-line Address Bus and a 16-line Data Bus.** In order to have a 40-pin package, **the low-order 16 Address Bus lines are multiplexed with the Data Bus.**

BHE may be looked upon as an additional Address Bus line, since it is used to identify the high-order byte of a memory word, while AD0 identifies the low-order byte of the memory word.

The four high-order Address Bus lines, together with $\overline{BHE}$, are multiplexed with five status lines, thus, we can illustrate Address Bus line multiplexing as follows:

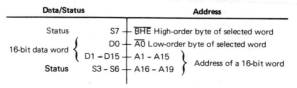

Data/Status		Address
Status	S7	$\overline{BHE}$ High-order byte of selected word
16-bit data word {	D0	$\overline{A0}$ Low-order byte of selected word
	D1 – D15	A1 – A15 } Address of a 16-bit word
Status	S3 – S6	A16 – A19

It is easy to become confused when looking at how the **Address Bus, together with $\overline{BHE}$,** is used to access memory. As seen by external memory, Address Bus lines **are interpreted as follows:**

> **8086 EXTERNAL MEMORY ADDRESSING**

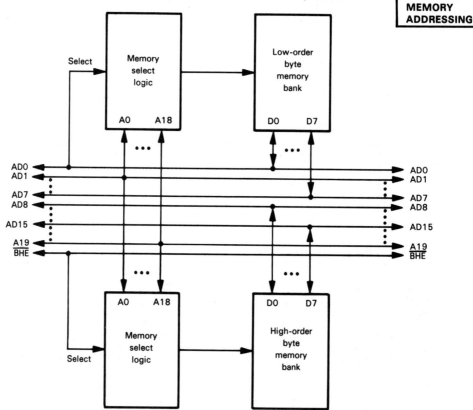

In the previous illustration you will see that memory is indeed organized as bytes.

The data pins of the low-order byte memory bank connect to AD0-AD7. The high-order byte memory bank data pins connect to AD8-AD15.

The low-order and high-order byte memory banks each have memory select logic that decodes AD1-A19. These 19 address lines become inputs A0-A18 at the illustrated memory select logic. Since each memory bank receives 19 address lines, select logic can address up to 524,288 (512K) bytes of memory. These two memory banks, taken together, constitute the advertised one million bytes of directly addressable memory.

Now, you may well ask why one should bother dividing memory into separate low-order and high-order byte banks. If a sixteen-bit word lies on an even-byte address boundary, then we could ignore the memory select logic connections to AD0 and $\overline{BHE}$. The address on AD1-A19 becomes an address identifying a 16-bit word, which just happens to be implemented as two separate 8-bit memory banks.

If an 8086 16-bit memory word does lie on an even-byte address boundary, then the low-order byte address is, in fact, the only address output. $\overline{BHE}$ is pulsed low while the low-order byte address is being output, and both memory banks consider themselves selected even though (in theory) the high-order memory bank's address has not been output.

To illustrate what happens, consider the memory addresses $02A40_{16}$ and $02A41_{16}$. One would normally expect the two addresses to be output sequentially in order to access the low-order byte and then the high-order byte of the 16-bit word. This may be illustrated as follows:

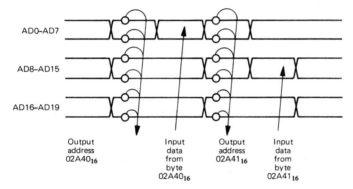

But we could just as easily output the low-order byte address only, using $\overline{BHE}$ as an extra address line to substitute for the odd-byte address — which is never output. This may be illustrated as follows:

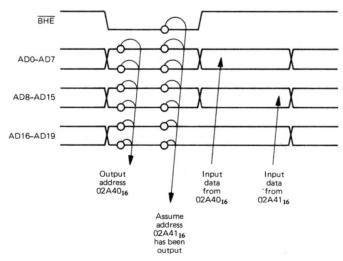

If a word lies on an odd-byte address boundary, then two byte addresses must be output to access the two halves of the 16-bit word. This may be illustrated as follows:

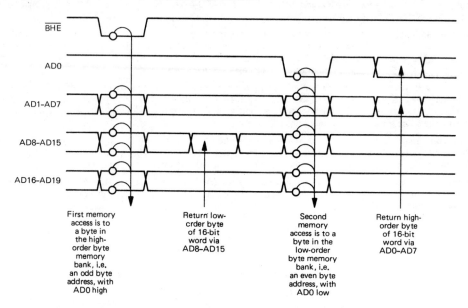

| First memory access is to a byte in the high-order byte memory bank, i.e. an odd byte address, with AD0 high | Return low-order byte of 16-bit word via AD8–AD15 | Second memory access is to a byte in the low-order byte memory bank, i.e. an even byte address, with AD0 low | Return high-order byte of 16-bit word via AD0–AD7 |

When a 16-bit word lies on an odd-byte address boundary, as illustrated above, the low-order byte is input first via AD8-AD15, then the high-order byte is input via AD0-AD7. Logic internal to the 8086 switches the data bytes into their correction locations.

Intel could have elected to implement external memory as 16-bit words, which would eliminate BHE along with the Address Bus complexities we have just described. But this would have forced all instruction object codes, and data, to be accessed as 16-bit units. Why not do it?

One of the most interesting hindsight discoveries that 8080A users have made is the fact that the 8080A is extremely efficient in its use of memory. By having a large number of 8-bit object codes, the 8080A generates object programs as compact as the most powerful minicomputers on the market.

But if the 8086 is to keep 8-bit object codes, and therefore the efficient memory utilization of the 8080A, then it can no longer guarantee that data will lie on even-byte address boundaries. The first 8-bit object code will force the next instruction or data entity to begin on an odd-byte boundary.

By including BHE and the extra logic needed to access 16-bit data units origined at odd-byte boundaries, the 8086 has allowed instructions to generate 1-byte, 3-byte or other odd-byte object codes, rather than 2-byte, 4-byte, and even-byte object codes only.

Simply stated, this is the trade-off: simplify memory addressing so that external memory is accessed only as 16-bit data units and you will use memory less efficiently. Intel elected to make memory addressing logic more complex and memory utilization more efficient.

Moving on from the Data/Address Bus, 8086 signals may be grouped into those that do not change with system complexity, and those that do. Let us first look at the unchanging signals.

CLK is the single clock signal output by the 8284 clock generator to synchronize all 8086 logic.

READY is the Wait state request which slow external logic inputs if it requires more time to respond to an access. A high READY input occurring at the proper time early in a machine cycle causes the 8086 to extend the machine cycle by inserting Wait state clock periods.

$\overline{\text{RD}}$ is a single bus control signal that does not change with system configuration. This signal **is output low when the CPU is inputting data from any external source.**

Even though $\overline{\text{RD}}$ is output by the same physical pin under all circumstances, this signal is functionally part of the group that changes its nature depending on signal complexity. We will therefore refer again to $\overline{\text{RD}}$ when describing the signals that are a function of system complexity.

There are four interrupt and interrupt-related signals.

INTR is a normal interrupt request input.

NMI is a non-maskable interrupt request input.

RESET is a system reset signal; it must be input high to the 8284 clock generator for at least four CLK clock periods. The 8284 transmits a synchronized RESET signal to the CPU. When the 8086 is reset, the following events occur:

```
8086
RESET
```

1) The Status register is cleared. This disables external interrupts.

2) The Program Counter and the three Segment registers, DS, SS, and ES, are cleared.

3) The CS Segment register is set to $FFFF_{16}$. Following a Reset, program execution therefore restarts with the instruction located at memory byte $FFFF0_{16}$.

These reset operations take approximately 10 clock periods to occur — during which time no other operations should occur.

Following power-up, at least 60 microseconds should elapse before the 8086 is reset.

An interrupt request via INTR should not occur sooner than 9 clock periods after the end of the 8086 device reset. An earlier interrupt request will cause one entire instruction to be executed before the interrupt request is recognized or acknowledged.

A nonmaskable interrupt request should not be made during the first clock period following the end of a reset.

$\overline{\text{TEST}}$ is not really an interrupt input, but it is used by program logic that otherwise would rely upon an interrupt. **The 8086 has a special "Wait-for-Test" instruction that puts the CPU into an Idle state; this Idle state ends when the $\overline{\text{TEST}}$ input goes low.**

An 8080A (and other microprocessors) will duplicate the logic of the 8086 "Wait-for-Test" instruction by executing a "no operation" loop, which is terminated by an interrupt request:

```
          ENI              Enable interrupts
   SELF   JMP SELF         Only an interrupt will terminate loop execution
```

There are eight pins that can output one of two signals, depending on whether MN/$\overline{\text{MX}}$ is tied to power or ground. By having two sets of signals, the 8086 can be used in simple configurations, best served by elementary control signals, or in complex configurations, where control signals must provide sufficient information to resolve the contentions and access conflicts that complex microcomputer systems may encounter.

The two sets of signals may be illustrated as follows:

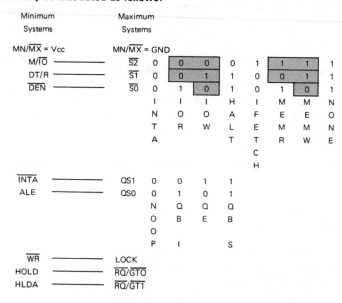

Let us first look at the simple set of control signals that are output when MN/$\overline{\text{MX}}$ is connected to +5 V. These are completely standard microprocessor control signals.

Since data and addresses are multiplexed on a single bus, **ALE is output high to identify a valid memory address.**

When data are being transmitted or received via the Data/Address Bus, **$\overline{\text{WR}}$ is pulsed low to identify data output, while $\overline{\text{RD}}$ is pulsed low as a request for external logic to place data on the Data/Address Bus.** We have already described $\overline{\text{RD}}$. It is not one of the changing signals; nevertheless, it is used by both simple and complex system busses.

For a read or write operation, **M/$\overline{\text{IO}}$ indicates whether memory (M/$\overline{\text{IO}}$ high) or an I/O port (M/$\overline{\text{IO}}$ low) is being accessed.**

DT/$\overline{\text{R}}$ and DEN are two new control signals not found in earlier Intel microprocessors. These two control signals **have been designed** specifically **to control 8286/8287-type bidirectional** transceivers. DT/$\overline{\text{R}}$ identifies the data direction, while DEN is the output enable. The 8286 and 8287 transceivers are described later in this chapter.

HOLD and HLDA are standard hold request/acknowledge signals. When external logic inputs HOLD high, the 8086 CPU enters a Hold state upon completing the current instruction's execution; the 8086 acknowledges the Hold State by outputting HLDA high. We will describe the Hold state in more detail later in the chapter.

Let us now look at the complex System Bus that is generated when MN/$\overline{\text{MX}}$ is tied to ground. Control signals are output as a three-signal combination, decoded by a 3-to-8 decoder, and a two-signal combination, decoded by a 2-to-4 decoder. **Complex System Bus signals have been designed to act as inputs to an 8288 Bus Controller.**

$\overline{\text{S2}}$, $\overline{\text{S1}}$, and $\overline{\text{S0}}$ are decoded to provide eight separate control signals. However, the simple system signals M/$\overline{\text{IO}}$, DT/$\overline{\text{R}}$ and DEN represent a subset of the eight $\overline{\text{S2}}$, $\overline{\text{S1}}$, and $\overline{\text{S0}}$ combinations. In our earlier illustration, we identify this simple system subset by shading the applicable complex system $\overline{\text{S2}}$, $\overline{\text{S1}}$, and $\overline{\text{S0}}$ levels.

The eight combinations of $\overline{S2}$, $\overline{S1}$, and $\overline{S0}$ generate the following control signals:

$\overline{S2}$	$\overline{S1}$	$\overline{S0}$		
0	0	0	INTA	Interrupt acknowledge
0	0	1	IOR	I/O device read
0	1	0	IOW	I/O device write
0	1	1	HALT	CPU has executed a HALT instruction and is in the Halt state
1	0	0	IFETCH	The CPU is fetching an instruction object code byte
1	0	1	MEMR	Memory read
1	1	0	MEMW	Memory write
1	1	1	NONE	The System Bus is inactive

The control signal descriptions above use the words "read" and "write" as seen by the CPU. That is to say, a "read" operation moves data from a memory device or I/O port to the CPU, while a "write" operation moves data from the CPU to a memory location or I/O port.

QS0 and QS1 combine to identify conditions within the 8086 instruction object code queue — which we will describe soon. **The QS0 and QS1 combinations are interpreted as follows:**

QS0	QS1		
0	0	NOOP	No operation. This is the default case
0	1	QB1	The first instruction object code in the queue is being executed
1	0	QE	The queue is empty
1	1	QBS	An instruction object code other than the first one in the queue is being executed

Observe that the simple bus signals INTA and ALE do not correspond to any combination of QS0 and QS1. This is in contrast to M/IO, DT/R and DEN, which constitute a subset of $\overline{S2}$, $\overline{S1}$, and $\overline{S0}$.

$\overline{LOCK}$, $\overline{RQ}/\overline{GT0}$, and $\overline{RQ}/\overline{GT1}$ are not related to their simple system equivalent signals: $\overline{WR}$, HOLD, and HLDA. **$\overline{LOCK}$, $\overline{RQ}/\overline{GT0}$, and $\overline{RQ}/\overline{GT1}$ provide the 8086 with its System Bus priority and control logic in complex configurations.**

$\overline{LOCK}$ is output high to prevent the 8086 from losing bus control while executing a sequence of machine cycles that must not be interrupted. Typically these will be a memory access combination of read-modify-write machine cycles, where an error could result if the CPU lost bus control after the read and before the write.

$\overline{RQ}/\overline{GT0}$ and $\overline{RQ}/\overline{GT1}$ are two-bus priority, bidirectional type signals. They are used to determine which CPU in a multi-CPU configuration will at any time have control of a shared bus. We will discuss these signals in more detail later in the chapter when looking at the capabilities of the 8086 in multi-CPU shared bus configurations.

8086 TIMING AND INSTRUCTION EXECUTION

The most important concept to understand when looking at 8086 instruction execution timing is the fact the 8086 bus control logic has been separated from the 8086 instruction execution logic. That is to say, the 8086 has an Execution Unit (EU), and a Bus Interface Unit (BIU).

8086 EXECUTION UNIT (EU)

The Execution Unit (EU) contains Data and Address registers, the Arithmetic and Logic Unit, plus the Control Unit. The Bus Interface Unit (BIU) contains bus interface logic, Segment registers, memory addressing logic, and a six-byte instruction object code queue. This may be illustrated as follows:

8086 BUS INTERFACE UNIT (BIU)

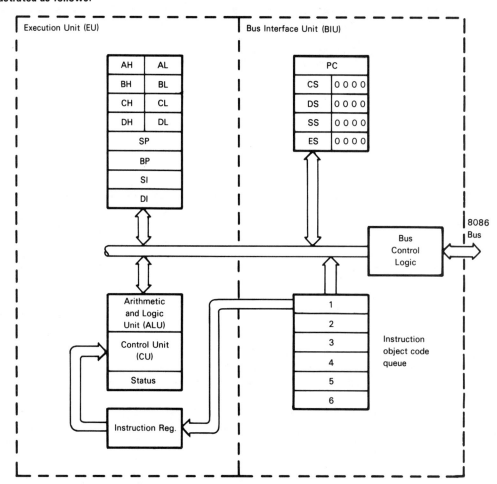

The Execution Unit (EU) and the Bus Interface Unit (BIU) operate asynchronously. Whenever the Execution Unit is ready to execute a new instruction, it fetches the instruction object code from the front of the Bus Interface Unit instruction queue, then it executes the instruction in some number of clock periods that have nothing to do with machine cycles. If the instruction object code queue is empty, then the Bus Interface Unit (BIU) executes an instruction fetch machine cycle — and the CPU waits for the instruction object code to be fetched. But the queue will rarely be empty, for reasons that will soon become apparent; therefore, the EU will usually not have to wait while an instruction fetch is executed.

8086 INSTRUCTION QUEUE

If memory or an I/O device must be accessed in the course of executing an instruction, then the EU informs the BIU of its needs. The BIU executes an appropriate external access machine cycle in response to the EU demand.

The Bus Interface Unit (BIU), for its part, is independent of the Execution Unit (EU), and attempts to keep the six-byte queue filled with instruction object codes. If two or more of these six bytes are empty, then the Bus Interface Unit (BIU) executes instruction fetch machine cycles — providing the EU does not have an active request for bus access pending. If the EU issues a request for bus access while the BIU is in the middle of an instruction fetch machine cycle, then the BIU will complete the instruction fetch machine cycle before honoring the EU bus access request.

> **8086
> INSTRUCTION
> QUEUE**

8086 BUS CYCLES

If we look at the way clock logic is used by the 8086, the term "machine cycle" no longer applies. The EU does not use machine cycles; it executes instructions in some number of clock periods that are not subject to any type of machine cycle grouping. **The only time clock periods are grouped is when the bus control logic wishes to access memory or I/O devices.** Each access requires four clock periods. This is the minimum amount of time required to handle the normal bus protocol that accompanies any transfer of information between a microprocessor and logic beyond the microprocessor. **Since this is the only time the 8086 groups clock periods, it is more accurate to talk about 8086 bus cycles, rather than machine cycles.**

Figure 5-4 illustrates two 8086 bus cycles executed back-to-back. In common with machine cycles, 8086 bus cycles, as illustrated in Figure 5-4 assign individual clock periods to time specific events.

Memory and I/O device addresses are output on the Data/Address Bus during T_1.

Data is transferred between the 8086 and memory or I/O devices during T_3 and T_4. If these two clock periods provide external logic with insufficient time to respond to an access, then Wait state clock periods (T_W) may be inserted between T_3 and T_4.

T_2 is a buffer clock period during which the Data/Address Bus stops outputting an address and starts outputting or inputting data.

During T_4 the CPU identifies the status of the next bus cycle or clock period. In simple configurations when MN/$\overline{MX}$ is tied to +5 V, DT/$\overline{R}$ is the only external signal that changes state during T_4. When MN/$\overline{MX}$ is tied to ground, $\overline{S0}$, $\overline{S1}$, and $\overline{S2}$ change state during T_4. Thus, by examining these three status outputs, external logic knows whether to expect another bus cycle, and, if so, what type of bus cycle.

Now if you look at Figure 5-4, there is very little about it that differentiates an 8086 bus cycle from any other microprocessor's machine cycle. The characteristic of the bus cycle that differentiates it from standard machine cycles is the fact that bus cycles occur only on demand.

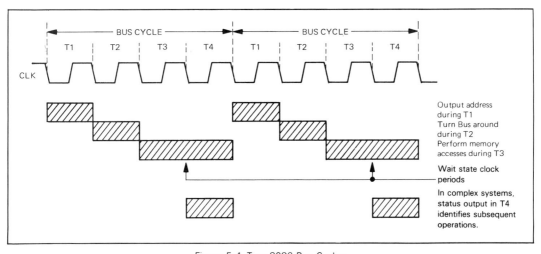

Figure 5-4. Two 8086 Bus Cycles

8086 INSTRUCTION QUEUE

Consider what happens when an instruction is executed. Beginning with the simplest case, the instruction object code queue within the Bus Interface Unit will be empty. When the EU requests an object code byte there is none, so the BIU executes a bus cycle that fetches the first byte of the instruction object code:

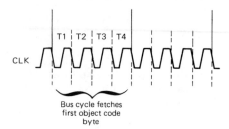

Let us assume that this particular instruction requires two bytes of object code; keeping things simple, we will illustrate another instruction cycle executed immediately to fetch the next instruction byte:

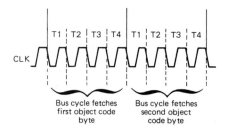

Let us suppose that this instruction reads a word of data from memory, then performs an arithmetic operation using this data. The instruction is going to require some number of clock periods to compute the effective address for the data memory location to be accessed (we will assume seven clock periods are needed). Some additional number of clock periods will also be needed to perform the arithmetic operation (we will assume nine clock periods). In a normal microprocessor, this instruction might be executed as the following sequence of machine cycles:

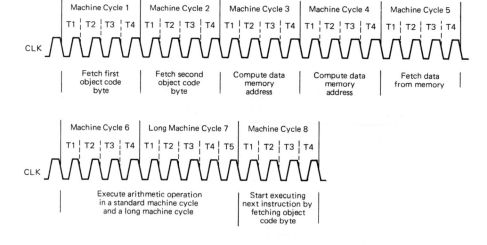

But the 8086, having asynchronous CPU and Bus Control Unit logic, will use clock periods to execute the instruction illustrated above as follows:

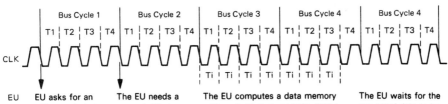

	Bus Cycle 1	Bus Cycle 2	Bus Cycle 3	Bus Cycle 4	Bus Cycle 4
EU	EU asks for an object code byte. There is none, so the BIU fetches one.	The EU needs a second object code byte.	The EU computes a data memory address in 7 clock periods. At the end of the 7th clock period the CPU requests bus access.	The EU waits for the requested data to be fetched by the BIU	
BIU	BIU fetches a byte of object code in one bus cycle.	BIU fetches a second byte of object code in one bus cycle.	Since the EU is not demanding bus access, the BIU fetches the next two object code bytes and stores them in the queue. At the end of bus cycle 4 the EU is requesting bus access, so the BIU services the EU.	BIU fetches data from memory location addressed by the CPU.	

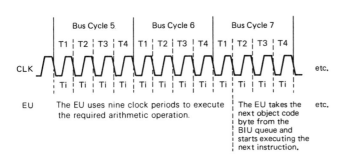

	Bus Cycle 5	Bus Cycle 6	Bus Cycle 7	
EU	The EU uses nine clock periods to execute the required arithmetic operation.		The EU takes the next object code byte from the BIU queue and starts executing the next instruction.	etc.
BIU	The BIU continues executing bus cycles to fill the instruction object code queue.			etc.

Now, the illustration above is not accurate because, you will recall, the 8086 fetches data in 16-bit increments, provided the data address lies on an even-byte boundary. Also, the BIU fetches instruction bytes and loads them into the queue only when there are at least two free bytes in the queue. Let us assume that all data does lie on even-byte boundaries. This is how our timing will now look:

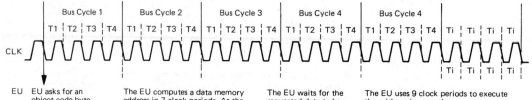

EU	EU asks for an object code byte. There are none, so the BIU executes a bus cycle.	The EU computes a data memory address in 7 clock periods. At the end of the 7th clock period the EU requests bus access.	The EU waits for the requested data to be fetched by the BIU.	The EU uses 9 clock periods to execute the arithmetic operation.
BIU	BIU fetches two bytes of object code in one bus cycle. The CPU takes both of them, so the queue is immediately emptied.	BIU fetches four bytes of object code in two bus cycles and stores them in the queue, which has two empty bytes left.	BIU fetches data from memory location addressed by the EU.	The BIU fetches two more bytes of object code and stores them in the queue which is now full. The BIU is idle.

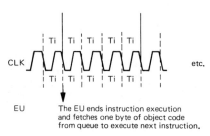

etc.

EU	The EU ends instruction execution and fetches one byte of object code from queue to execute next instruction.
BIU	The BIU remains idle since only one byte of queue is empty.

There are some important points to note regarding 8086 bus cycle timing.

Bus cycles are a Bus Interface Unit (BIU) phenomenon.

So far as the EU logic is concerned, bus cycles do not exist. The EU experiences periods of activity while executing instructions, and periods of inactivity while waiting for instruction object codes or data that the BIU must process via bus cycles. Periods of EU activity are timed by a sequence of clock periods. The EU makes no attempt to group clock periods into machine cycles, nor do EU clock periods have to occur in any special numeric combinations.

The EU asks for memory operands before it needs them, so unless the BIU cannot get immediate bus access the **maximum EU wait time is one clock cycle** for bus access.

So far as the BIU is concerned, clock periods are grouped into bus cycles only when data must be transferred to or from the 8086. First priority is given to a bus access request coming from the EU. If the EU is not requesting bus access, then the BIU executes instruction fetch bus cycles until the queue is full. **These are the prerequisites for the BIU to execute an instruction fetch bus cycle:**

1) The clock period that initiates the bus cycle would otherwise be an idle clock period.

2) The EU does not have an active bus access request pending.

3) There are at least two bytes empty in the queue.

If the queue is full, then the BIU ceases to execute bus cycles; as illustrated above, a sequence of idle clock periods occurs.

Note that **the CPU may have to wait for bus access.** In the illustrations above, the EU requires seven clock periods in order to compute a data memory address. At the end of the seventh clock period, the EU issues a bus access request to the BIU. But at this time the BIU is part way through executing an instruction fetch bus cycle. The BIU completes the instruction fetch bus cycle, then honors the EU bus access request.

In the final illustration above, no bus cycle accompanies the beginning of a new instruction's execution. We are assuming that the next instruction executed has one byte of object code. This object code byte is fetched from the front of the queue — which then has just one empty byte. No bus cycle is executed to fetch the instruction object code, since it is taken out of the queue. Subsequently, the BIU does not execute an instruction fetch bus cycle since there is only one empty byte; there must be at least two empty bytes in the queue before the BIU will execute an instruction fetch bus cycle.

Based on the foregoing discussion of 8086 instruction fetch queuing, we can see that the 8086 has essentially eliminated instruction fetch time. The only time the EU will have to wait while the BIU fetches instruction object codes is when a Branch-on-Condition instruction causes execution to branch out of the queue sequence, or when (for any reason) the memory accesses accompanying an instruction's execution are so dense that the BIU has insufficient idle clock periods within which to insert instruction fetch bus cycles.

8086 MEMORY AND I/O DEVICE READ BUS CYCLE FOR MINIMUM MODE

Figure 5-5 shows timing for an 8086 memory read bus cycle when MN/$\overline{MX}$ equals +5 V; that is to say, for the minimum mode bus configuration.

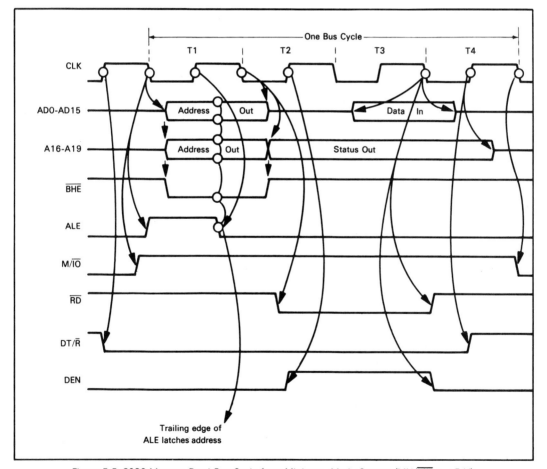

Figure 5-5. 8086 Memory Read Bus Cycle for a Minimum Mode System (MN/$\overline{MX}$ = +5 V)

The memory or I/O device address is output via the Address Bus $\overline{BHE}$ during clock period T_1. AD0-AD15 starts floating in T_2 while turning around internal pin logic so that data can be input during T_3 and T_4. Address lines A16 through A19 are all low when an I/O device address is being output. These address lines output status during T_2, T_3, and T_4. Close to the end of T_4, A16 through A19 start to float.

$\overline{BHE}$ timing follows Address lines A16-A19; that is to say, $\overline{BHE}$ is output low for the time that A16 through A19 is outputting an address.

The trailing edge of the high ALE pulse should be used as the "valid address" strobe. If your 8086 configuration demultiplexes the Data and Address Busses, then the Address Bus demultiplexing buffers should be the "pass through" type and use the high-to-low transition of ALE as their latching strobe.

Remaining control signals consist of M/$\overline{IO}$ and $\overline{RD}$, which are directed at external memory or I/O devices, plus DT/$\overline{R}$ and DEN, which are directed at bus buffers.

M/$\overline{IO}$ differentiates between a memory access and an I/O device access. M/$\overline{IO}$ will be high for a memory access bus cycle; it will be low for an I/O device access bus cycle. M/$\overline{IO}$ will contribute to memory and I/O device select logic when memory and I/O devices have similar addresses.

$\overline{RD}$ is pulsed low as a memory or I/O device read strobe. The addressed memory device must use this low signal to place data on AD0 - AD15.

DT/$\overline{R}$ and DEN are control signals designed to control bidirectional latched buffers on the Data Bus. DT/$\overline{R}$ is output low for the entire memory or I/O device read bus cycle; it should be used to turn the latched buffers around so that they will transmit data to the CPU. DEN subsequently acts as a latching strobe. These two signals have been designed specifically to work with the 8286 and 8287 Data Bus transceivers; however, their logic is quite general.

There is no difference between external timing for an instruction fetch or memory read bus cycle. Given the pipelining instruction fetch logic of the 8086, this makes sense.

The only timing difference between a memory read bus cycle and an I/O device input bus cycle occurs at the M/$\overline{IO}$ signal. This signal will be low for the duration of an I/O input bus cycle, whereas in Figure 5-5 it is shown high for the duration of a memory read bus cycle.

Except for this difference, Figure 5-5 also illustrates I/O input bus cycle timing for a simple 8086 configuration.

During any simple configuration memory access operation, the following status is output on address lines A16 through A19:

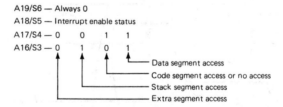

The interrupt enable status appearing on A18 may be used to illuminate an indicator on a control panel, should there be one. This indicator will show whether interrupts are enabled or disabled at any time. This status has no other value.

S3 and S4 together identify the memory segment which is being accessed. This is not very useful information. Even a code segment access cannot be interpreted as an instruction fetch, since data can be addressed out of the program segment.

8086 MEMORY OR I/O DEVICE WRITE BUS CYCLE FOR MINIMUM MODE

Figure 5-6 illustrates timing for an 8086 memory or I/O device write bus cycle when the 8086 is operating in a minimum mode with MN/$\overline{MX}$ tied to +5 V.

Address output logic is identical in read and write bus cycles. As was the case for a read bus cycle, the address is output on the Address Bus, together with $\overline{BHE}$, during T_1. External logic should use the high-to-low transition of the ALE pulse in order to latch a valid address. During T_2, AD0 - AD15 switches to outputting data, while A16 - A19 outputs status. The same status is output in read and write bus cycles.

M/$\overline{IO}$ is output high for the duration of a memory write bus cycle; it is output low for the duration of an I/O device write bus cycle.

$\overline{WR}$ is output low beginning early in T_2 and ending shortly after T_3. Note that $\overline{RD}$ does not go low for a read bus cycle until halfway through T_2.

For an 8286 or 8287 Bus Transceiver, or any similar device, DT/$\overline{R}$ is output high for the entire duration of the write bus cycle. This conditions the device to transmit data from the CPU to external logic. DEN is the chip enable signal provided for the bus transceiver. DEN is output high from the end of T$_1$ until the end of T$_4$. Note that this high pulse is longer than the DEN pulse accompanying a read bus cycle.

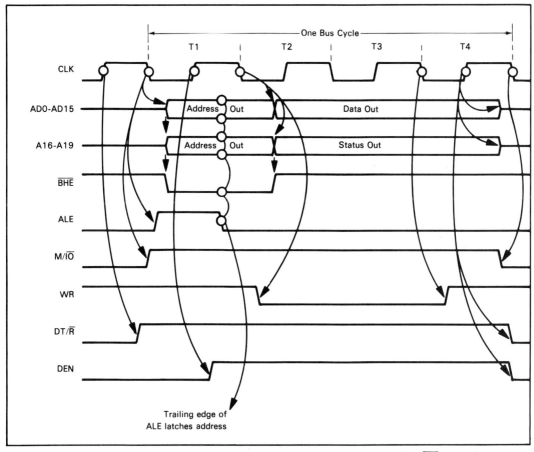

Figure 5-6. 8086 Memory Write Bus Cycle for a Minimum Mode System (MN/$\overline{MX}$ = +5 V)

An I/O write bus cycle has timing identical to Figure 5-6, except that the M/$\overline{IO}$ signal will be low for the duration of the bus cycle, rather than high as shown in Figure 5-6. Wherever a memory word and an I/O port may have the same address, M/$\overline{IO}$ must contribute to device select logic in order to discriminate between memory and I/O devices.

The status output on A16-A19 is no more useful in a write bus cycle than it is in a read bus cycle.

8086 READ AND WRITE BUS CYCLES FOR MAXIMUM MODE

It is not very rewarding looking at maximum mode memory or I/O access bus cycle timing, if we look at timing for an 8086 device on its own. This is because in maximum mode, with MN/$\overline{MX}$ tied to ground, the 8086 has been designed to operate with the 8288 Bus Controller.

Figure 5-7 and 5-8 provide maximum mode timing for the 8086 on its own when executing read or write bus cycles. Only the status signal levels differentiate memory or I/O access bus cycles.

Timing for the Address/Data Bus is identical in minimum and maximum modes. The read strobe $\overline{RD}$ does not change. However, remaining control signals become control inputs to the 8288 Bus Controller.

Observe that QS0 and QS1 change levels on a clock period by clock period basis in order to identify events for individual clock periods. $\overline{S0}$, $\overline{S1}$, and $\overline{S2}$ hold their levels from shortly before T_1 until shortly after the end of T_2.

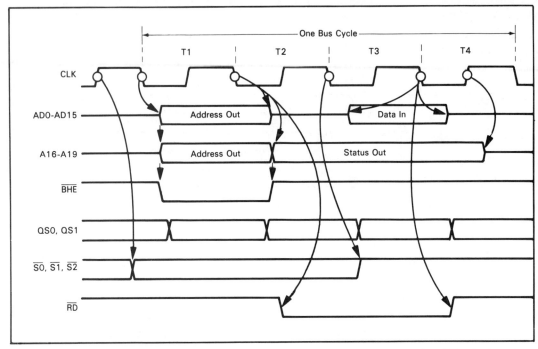

Figure 5-7. 8086 Memory or I/O Read Bus Cycle for a Maximum Mode System (MN/$\overline{MX}$ = 0 V)

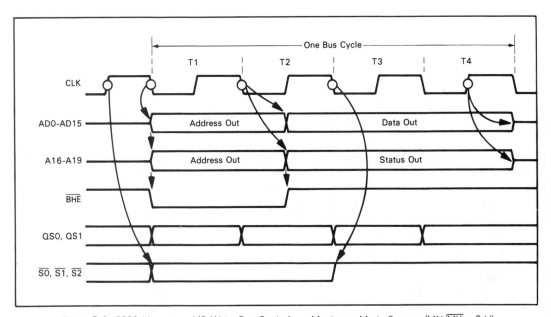

Figure 5-8. 8086 Memory or I/O Write Bus Cycle for a Maximum Mode System (MN/$\overline{MX}$ = 0 V)

The 8288 Bus Controller, described later in this chapter, decodes $\overline{S0}$, $\overline{S1}$, and $\overline{S2}$ in order to generate control signals that are comparable to those illustrated in Figures 5-5 and 5-6. For a complete discussion of bus cycle timing in complex 8086 microcomputer configurations, see the discussion of 8288 Bus Controller.

THE 8086 WAIT STATE

8086 Wait state logic is independent of the MN/$\overline{\text{MX}}$ pin connection and the external access bus cycle being executed. In any bus cycle it is possible to insert one or more Wait clock periods (T_W) between T_3 and T_4. In order to extend a bus cycle with Wait clock periods, external logic must input a low READY signal during T_2 of the bus cycle which is to be extended. The READY input to the 8086 must be synchronized with the falling edge of CLK at the end of T_2; this synchronized READY input is created by the 8284 clock generator. External logic will normally input an asynchronous READY to the 8284 clock device, which outputs a synchronous READY for the 8086. Wait clock periods will continue to be inserted to the bus cycle until READY goes high again. **Timing is illustrated in Figure 5-9.** All output signal levels are maintained for the duration of the Wait state.

THE 8086 HOLD STATE

The 8086 can be forced into a Hold state, at which time all three-state signals are floated. The 8086 Hold state is used to enable direct memory access logic, and in addition to disable inactive 8086 devices when more than one CPU accesses the same System Bus in a multi-CPU configuration.

In a minimum mode configuration, when MN/$\overline{\text{MX}}$ is tied to +5 V, the 8086 has a traditional Hold request input (HOLD) and a Hold Acknowledge output (HLDA). Upon receiving a high HOLD input, the 8086 will complete execution of its current instruction bus cycle before entering the Hold sate and outputting HLDA high. **Timing may be illustrated as follows:**

8086 HOLD IN MINIMUM MODE SYSTEM

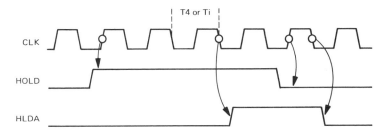

The 8086 samples the HOLD input on the low-to-high transition of CLK. Therefore, HOLD must make its transitions away from this sampling point; that is to say, HOLD must be stable when CLK is making its low-to-high transition.

The 8086 will acknowledge the Hold request by making HLDA high during any idle clock period, or at the end of a bus cycle. If a bus cycle is being executed when a Hold request occurs, the Hold request will not be acknowledged until the end of T_4 for the currently executing bus cycle.

The Hold state will last until the HOLD input goes low again. The 8086 continues to sample the HOLD input on all low-to-high transitions of CLK; therefore, HOLD must make its high-to-low transition away from the rising edge of CLK. When HOLD goes low, the Hold state will immediately end and HLDA will be forced low again.

In 8086 maximum mode configurations where MN/$\overline{\text{MX}}$ is tied to ground, the HOLD and HLDA pins convert to bidirectional type control signals. There are two bidirectional signals; $\overline{\text{RQ}}$/$\overline{\text{GT0}}$ and $\overline{\text{RQ}}$/$\overline{\text{GT1}}$. $\overline{\text{RQ}}$/$\overline{\text{GT0}}$ has higher priority than $\overline{\text{RQ}}$/$\overline{\text{GT1}}$.

8086 HOLD IN MAXIMUM MODE SYSTEM

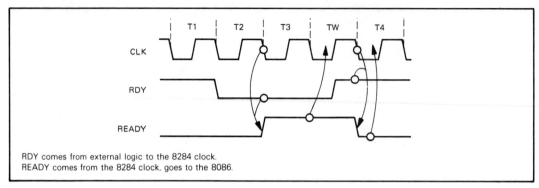

RDY comes from external logic to the 8284 clock.
READY comes from the 8284 clock, goes to the 8086.

Figure 5-9. The 8086 READY Input and Wait States

Any external logic that wishes to put an 8086 CPU into the Hold state transmits a low pulse to $\overline{RQ}/\overline{GT0}$ or $\overline{RQ}/\overline{GT1}$. The 8086 CPU will acknowledge this Hold request immediately, if a bus cycle is not being executed, or at the conclusion of a currently executing bus cycle. The 8086 acknowledges the Hold request transmitting by a low pulse via the same $\overline{RQ}/\overline{GT}$ line; simultaneously the 8086 floats its three-state bus lines. External logic must allow at least one clock period to elpase following the Hold Acknowledge pulse, before attempting to input via the same pin. External logic terminates the Hold state by inputting another low pulse. Timing may be illustrated as follows:

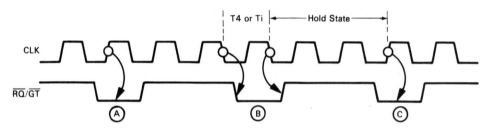

In the illustration above, Ⓐ identifies the instant at which external logic requests a Hold state by transmitting a low pulse via either $\overline{RQ}/\overline{GT}$ line. The 8086 samples $\overline{RQ}/\overline{GT}$ on the rising edge of CLK; therefore, all signal transitions on $\overline{RQ}/\overline{GT}$ must occur away from the CLK low-to-high transitions.

The 8086 will now acknowledge a Hold request during a bus cycle. If a bus cycle is in progress, then the Hold acknowledge will occur at the end of the bus cycle — that is to say, at the end of T_4. If a bus cycle is not in progress, then the Hold request will be acknowledged immediately. In the illustration above, Ⓑ identifies the low pulse the 8086 will output as its Hold acknowledge. The Hold state will last until external logic again transmits a low pulse via $\overline{RQ}/\overline{GT}$. This is identified above as Ⓒ Once again the 8086 samples $\overline{RQ}/\overline{GT}$ on the rising edge of CLK; therefore, $\overline{RQ}/\overline{GT}$ should be stable at this time.

When the 8086 enters the Hold state, it continues executing instructions it takes out of the pipeline, until a bus access is required. When the EU requires a bus access, it stops operating until the end of the Hold state — at which time its bus access request will be honored by the Bus Interface Unit.

In the event that Hold requests occur simultaneously on $\overline{RQ}/\overline{GT0}$ and $\overline{RQ}/\overline{GT1}$, the acknowledge pulse will be output on $\overline{RQ}/\overline{GT0}$. $\overline{RQ}/\overline{GT1}$ will not be acknowledged until the Hold state initiated via $\overline{RQ}/\overline{GT0}$ has ended.

When one Hold state ends, another Hold state can begin immediately for either of these reasons:

1) $\overline{RQ}/\overline{GT1}$ was active when $\overline{RQ}/\overline{GT0}$ was acknowledged; the $\overline{RQ}/\overline{GT1}$ Hold request, being of lower priority, was denied and is pending.

2) While the 8086 was in a Hold state, a new hold request occurs on the other $\overline{RQ}/\overline{GT}$ line.

If a new hold request occurs while the 8086 is in Hold state, priorities no longer apply. For example, if the CPU has acknowledged a Hold request occurring at $\overline{RQ}/\overline{GT1}$ and is in a Hold state, then it will deny a new Hold request arriving via $\overline{RQ}/\overline{GT0}$ until the current Hold state has ended.

If there is an active Hold request when the CPU ends a Hold state, then the CPU will immediately acknowledge the pending Hold request. This may be illustrated as follows:

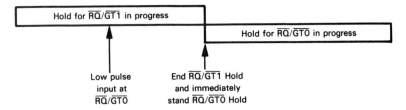

When a Hold state ends, if the CPU has a bus access request pending, then the CPU bus access request will be denied until all active Hold requests have been acknowledged.

Note that there are no 8086 instructions that specifically affect the level of $\overline{RQ}/\overline{GT0}$ or $\overline{RQ}/\overline{GT1}$. That is to say, external logic is entirely responsible for the interfaces to these two signals.

We will discuss $\overline{RQ}/\overline{GT0}$ and $\overline{RQ}/\overline{GT1}$ in more detail later in this chapter when we look at some multiple CPU 8086 configurations.

THE 8086 HALT STATE

The 8086 enters a Halt state after a HALT instruction is executed. In the Halt state no signals are floated, and undefined data is output on the Data/Address Bus. No bus cycles can be executed while the 8086 is in the Halt state.

When a Halt instruction is executed, a bus cycle initiates the Halt state. This Halt state initializing bus cycle has nothing to do with instruction fetch logic. If the Halt instruction object code is fetched by the CPU from the queue, then there will be no preceding instruction fetch bus cycle. If the Halt instruction must be fetched from memory because the queue is empty, or is at the conditional end of a Branch-on-Condition, then the Halt initializing bus cycle will be preceded by an instruction fetch bus cycle.

For a simple system, the HALT initialization bus cycle is given by Figure 5-5, except that $\overline{RD}$, M/$\overline{IO}$, DT/$\overline{R}$ and DEN are not active. ALE is active, although the address output has no meaning.

For a complex system, the HALT initializing bus cycle is illustrated in Figure 5-10. The Halt state combination occurring at $\overline{S0}$, $\overline{S1}$, and $\overline{S2}$ causes the 8288 Bus Controller to issue an ALE pulse before entering the Halt state; however, the occurrence of ALE could not be deduced simply by looking at 8086 timing.

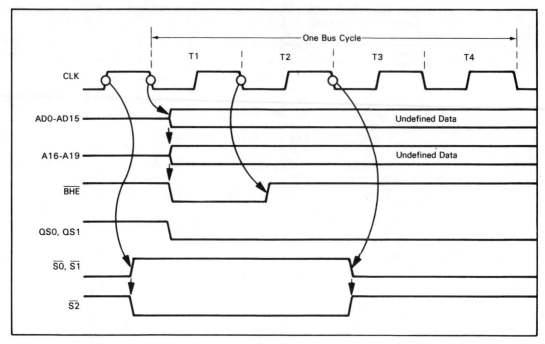

Figure 5-10. 8086 HALT Instruction and Bus Cycle Timing for a Complex Bus Configuration

The Halt state is terminated by an interrupt request or a Reset.

You can freely enter and leave a Hold state within an 8086 Halt state via any of the means that we have just described. The fact that the 8086 is in the Halt state in no way modifies Hold logic.

THE 8086 LOCK

A potential for serious error exists in the Hold request/acknowledge logic of the 8086.

The 8086 will acknowledge a Hold request occurring on the $\overline{RQ}/\overline{GT0}$ or $\overline{RQ}/\overline{GT1}$ lines at the end of the current bus cycle, if one is being executed, or at the next idle clock period, if a bus cycle is not being executed. The 8086 does not wait until the conclusion of the current instruction's execution before acknowledging the Hold request. Therefore, if an instruction reads the contents of a memory location (or I/O port), modifies these contents, then writes it back, a Hold state may separate the read bus cycle from the write bus cycle:

This can cause unexpected errors. If the 8086 enters a Hold state after reading memory location X contents and before writing these contents back, then it is possible for external logic — either direct memory access logic or another Central Processing Unit — to modify the contents of memory location X while the 8086 is in the Hold state. Now when the 8086 writes back the modified word, it may destroy data that should have been preserved.

If a 16-bit data word lies on an odd-byte boundary, it will require two bus cycles to access the data word. Under normal circumstances, a Hold request could be acknowledged between the first and second memory access bus cycles. But what if the word being accessed gets modified during the Hold state? If the Hold state splits two memory read bus cycles, this is what the CPU is going to read:

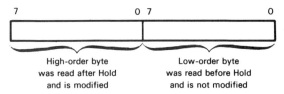

High-order byte was read after Hold and is modified

Low-order byte was read before Hold and is not modified

If a Hold state splits two memory write bus cycles, this is what ultimately gets written:

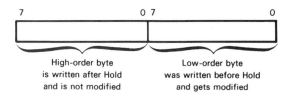

High-order byte is written after Hold and is not modified

Low-order byte was written before Hold and gets modified

You use the 8086 LOCK instruction in order to prevent the types of errors described above.

When a LOCK instruction is executed, the LOCK signal is low for the duration of the next sequential instruction's execution. Also, while the next sequential instruction is being executed, a Hold request will not be acknowledged.

You cannot extend protection against a Hold acknowledge beyond a single instruction's execution. For example, suppose you have two instructions, each of which is preceded by a Lock:

```
LOCK
AND     MEMX, AX
LOCK
OR      MEMX, BX
```

In the instruction sequence above, MEMX is a label which represents the address of a memory location. The contents of this memory location are ANDed with a mask stored in AX, then ORed with a mask stored in BX. The contents of MEMX are read, modified, and written back at each step.

Now, you may wish to inhibit Hold logic for both the AND and the OR operation. You cannot do so using the LOCK instruction. The first LOCK instruction will protect the following AND instruction from being interrupted by a Hold state; however, any pending Hold state will be acknowledged before the second LOCK instruction is executed.

Each LOCK instruction extends protection against a Hold Acknowledge for the duration of the next sequential instruction only. The fact that the following instruction is also a LOCK is irrelevant. The second LOCK instruction will be the first instruction executed following the Hold state, and it will guarantee that no new Hold state begins until it, and the OR instruction, have both been executed.

You can use the LOCK instruction and signal to identify individual instruction execution times. If for any reason external logic needs to know the execution time for certain instructions, then by preceding these instructions with a LOCK instruction you will generate a high pulse on the LOCK output. The width of this high pulse exactly equals the execution time of the instruction which follows the LOCK.

8086 SINGLE INSTRUCTION TIME IDENTIFIED

THE 8086 PROCESSOR WAIT FOR TEST STATE

The 8086 has a program-initiated Wait state that external logic must terminate via the TEST input signal. The WAIT instruction initiates this Wait state. After the WAIT instruction is executed, the 8086 generates an endless sequence of idle clock periods. This sequence lasts until external logic inputs a low signal at the TEST input. TEST must be high for at least four clock periods.

While the endless sequence of idle clock pulses is being executed, the System Bus is not floated and the Bus Interface Unit may execute memory read bus cycles in order to fill up the instruction object code queue.

The processor Wait state can be used to synchronize an 8086 with any external time sequence. For example, you could start two programs, executing in two separate 8086 systems, at exactly the same time, by preceding each program with a Wait instruction. If both 8086's receive low $\overline{\text{TEST}}$ inputs simultaneously, then both microprocessors will start executing their programs at the same instant.

THE 8086 PROCESSOR ESCAPE

The 8086 has a special escape instruction (ESC) intended for use in multi-CPU configurations. **When the ESC instruction is executed, the contents of an addressed memory location are input to the CPU, but the input data is not stored anywhere.** The purpose of the ESC instruction is to place the addressed data on the Data/Address Bus so that any other microprocessor (or external logic) connected to the Data/Address Bus can receive the data.

We will examine the value of the ESC instruction later in the chapter when looking at the 8086 in multiple CPU configurations.

THE 8086 RESET OPERATION

The 8086 has an asynchronous RESET input. This signal can be forced high at any time in order to reset the 8086. The high RESET must be at least four clock cycles long.

The 8086 terminates all current operations as soon as the RESET input makes a low-to-high transition. Nothing more happens until the RESET signal subsequently makes a high-to-low transition. It then takes approximately ten clock periods in order to execute the following operations:

1) The Status register is cleared. Among other things, this resets the interrupt enable flag to 0, thus disabling interrupts.

2) The CS Segment register is set to FFFF_{16}.

3) The DS, SS, and ES Segment registers and the Program Counter are all reset to 0.

4) Program execution begins. Since the CS Segment register contains FFFF_{16} and the Program Counter contains 0, the first instruction executed is taken from memory location FFFF0_{16}.

8086 INTERRUPT PROCESSING

The 8086 allows interrupts to originate in one of three ways:

1) **From software or within program logic.**

2) **From external logic as a nonmaskable interrupt.**

3) **From external logic as a maskable interrupt.**

There is, in addition, a special "single step" condition that makes use of interrupt logic. We will describe single stepping after our discussion of interrupt logic.

In the event that two or more of the three interrupt types occur simultaneously, software generated interrupts have the highest priority and maskable interrupts have the lowest priority.

These are the ways in which a software interrupt request may occur:

> **8086 SOFTWARE INTERRUPTS**

1) Following an attempt to divide by 0. A special divide by 0 interrupt request will occur any time the divide instruction is executed with a 0 dividend.

2) Following execution of an Interrupt instruction (INT).

3) Following execution of an Interrupt-on-Overflow instruction (INTO) — if the Overflow status is set.

A nonmaskable interrupt request is initiated when external logic transmits a low-to-high transition to the NMI pin. This is an edge-triggered signal. A nonmaskable interrupt has lower priority than a software interrupt, but higher priority than a maskable interrupt.

> **8086 NON-MASKABLE INTERRUPT**

A maskable interrupt request will be generated when external logic transmits a high level to the INTR pin. This input is level sensitive; it is the high level at INTR that causes the interrupt requests to occur.

> **8086 MASKABLE INTERRUPT**

Central to all 8086 interrupt processing is a Vector table that can be up to 1024 bytes in length, occupying absolute memory addresses 00000 through 003FF_{16}. This Vector table consists of up to 256 four-byte entries. Each entry contains two 16-bit addresses that get loaded into the CS Segment register and the Program Counter.

> **8086 INTERRUPT VECTOR TABLE**

Figure 5-11 illustrates the 8086 Interrupt Vector table.

A number of the Vector table entries serve specific interrupts. Other entries are reserved by Intel and should be avoided if compatibility with Intel software is desired. These entries are identified in Figure 5-11. As illustrated in Figure 5-11, 32 of the 256 interrupt vectors are not available to external logic; that leaves 224 vectors available to maskable external interrupts — which is plenty.

Taking each of the three interrupt types in turn, let us examine the interrupt acknowledge process.

When any of the software interrupts are acknowledged, the following steps occur:

> **8086**
> **SOFTWARE**
> **INTERRUPT**

1) The Status register contents are pushed onto the Stack; Stack Pointer contents, in consequence, are decremented by two.

2) The Interrupt and Test status flags are cleared; this disables maskable interrupts and single step logic (which we describe after our discussion of interrupt logic).

3) The CS Segment register contents are pushed onto the Stack; Stack Pointer contents, in consequence, are decremented by two.

4) The new CS Segment register contents are taken from the appropriate interrupt vector location. With the exception of the INT instruction, software-generated interrupts have dedicated vector locations as illustrated in Figure 5-11. The INT instruction allows any one of the 256 vector locations to be selected; a default option selects Vector 3.

5) The Program Counter contents are pushed onto the Stack. Stack Pointer contents are decremented by two.

6) The new Program Counter contents are taken from the interrupt vector.

When a nonmaskable interrupt is acknowledged, the following events occur:

> **8086**
> **NONMASKABLE**
> **INTERRUPT**

1) The Status register contents are pushed onto the Stack. The Stack Pointer contents are decremented by two.

2) The Interrupt and Test statuses are reset to 0; this disables nonmaskable interrupts and single stepping mode.

3) The CS Segment register and Program Counter are reloaded from Interrupt Vector 2. See Figure 5-11.

When a maskable interrupt is acknowledged, the following steps occur:

> **8086**
> **MASKABLE**
> **INTERRUPT**

1) Two interrupt acknowledge bus cycles are executed by the Bus Interface Unit of the 8086. An interrupt acknowledge bus cycle is identical to the memory read bus cycles, as illustrated in Figures 5-5 and 5-7, with the exception that an interrupt acknowledge low pulse replaces the memory read low pulse. For a minimum mode system, $\overline{INTA}$ will provide the low $\overline{RD}$ pulse shown in Figure 5-5. Figure 5-7 accurately illustrates timing for an interrupt acknowledge bus cycle in a maximum mode system; however, $\overline{S0}$, $\overline{S1}$, and $\overline{S2}$ will all be low, identifying an interrupt acknowledge, whereas a read I/O port or read memory status combination would be output otherwise. $\overline{LOCK}$ is low beginning at T2 of the first interrupt acknowledge bus cycle and ending at T2 of the second interrupt acknowledge bus cycle. This may be illustrated as follows:

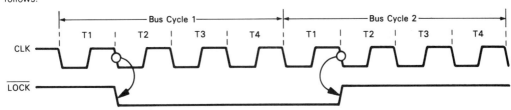

2) The acknowledged external device must send back a byte of data on lines AD0-AD7 in response to the second interrupt acknowledge bus cycle. This data byte is interpreted as a pointer into the interrupt vector. Multiplying this 8-bit value by 4 creates the correct beginning address for the interrupt vector.

3) The Status register contents are pushed onto the Stack.

4) The Interrupt and Test flags in the Status register are cleared. This disables further maskable interrupts and single step logic.

5) The CS Segment register contents are pushed onto the Stack.

6) The next CS Segment register contents are taken from the interrupt vector location identified in Step 2.

7) The Program Counter contents are pushed onto the Stack.

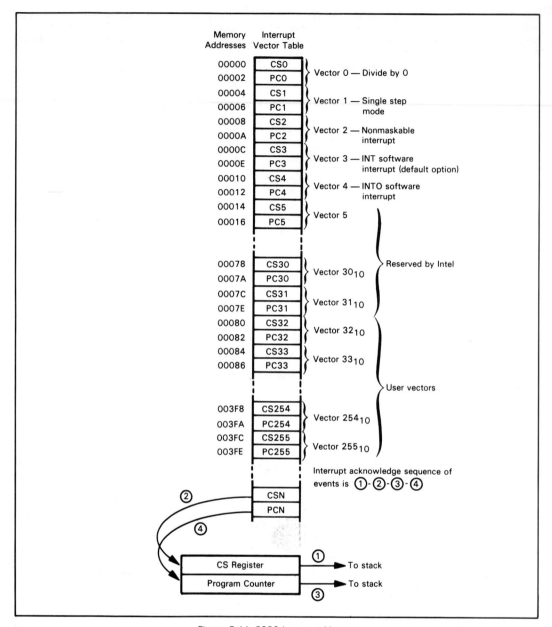

Figure 5-11. 8086 Interrupt Vector

8) The new Program Counter contents are taken from the interrupt vector location identified in Step 2.

9) The first instruction of the interrupt routine is fetched using the new PC and CS.

It takes 60 clock periods to complete the nine interrupt acknowledge steps listed above.

You should use the IRET instruction to exit any interrupt service routine. This instruction restores Program Counter, CS Segment register, and Status register contents from the Stack.

> 8086
> INTERRUPT
> RETURN

SINGLE STEPPING MODE

When the T status bit is set to 1, the 8086 operates in single stepping mode. In the single stepping mode the 8086 executes a software interrupt after each instruction's execution. The software interrupt vectors through Location 1 of the interrupt vector table, as illustrated in Figure 5-11.

Since the process of acknowledging an interrupt resets the TF flag, the single stepping mode will cease to exist once the interrupt service routine identified by Vector 1 is executed. But since the Status register contents prior to the interrupt acknowledge are saved on the Stack and are restored when a return from interrupt instruction is executed, single stepping mode will be restored as soon as the interrupt service routine corresponding to Interrupt Vector 1 concludes execution. Interrupt Vector 1 should therefore vector to a debug routine. Any user program executed in the single step mode will now execute instructions one at a time, branching to the debug program following execution of each instruction.

A particularly pleasing aspect of the 8086 single step mode is the fact that it can cope with interrupt logic. Frequently, microprocessor programs cannot be debugged once interrupt logic is introduced. In the case of the 8086, the interrupt acknowledge process automatically takes the 8086 out of the single step mode. You can insert instructions into any interrupt service routine in order to restore single stepping mode for that particular interrupt service routine. Thus, you have the option of executing any program or interrupt service routine in single step mode, without impacting any other program or interrupt service routine.

THE 8086 INSTRUCTION SET

The 8086 instruction set is summarized in Table 5-4. When compared to other microprocessor instruction sets, the 8086 instruction set might appear quite large. If you look at Table 5-4, you will see that a single instruction mnemonic may appear many times. In reality, these are variations of the same instruction. We show the variations of a single instruction as though they were separable instructions in order to make this description of the 8086 instruction set consistent with similar tables for other microprocessors.

The two I/O instructions, IN and OUT, become eight instructions because each has two sets of options.

Each I/O instruction can access 16-bit words or 8-bit bytes. In each case, the instruction may have a short addressing range or a long addressing range. The short addressing range instruction requires two bytes of object code and can access one of the first 256 I/O port addresses. The I/O address is specified in the second object code byte. The long-range I/O instructions occupy only one byte of object code; however, register DX provides the I/O port address — which can therefore range between 0 and $65,535_{10}$.

Primary memory reference instructions, and memory reference instructions in general, all have byte and word versions. In Table 5-4, the data memory location accessed is identified by the operand label DADDR. Because data memory reference instructions may or may not include a displacement, the object code may be two, three, or four bytes long, as defined in Table 5-5.

By preceding any data memory reference instruction with the SEG prefix, you can force the data memory reference to access a segment other than the data segment. Here, for example, are the two instructions that load a byte of data from the extra segment to Register AL, using direct, indexed addressing:

```
SEG   ES          Select extra segment
MOV   AL, (DI) ADDR   Load data word from extra segment
```

The LEA and LES instructions are unusual in that they load a memory address, rather than the contents of a memory location, into an identified 16-bit register. For the LEA instruction, this may be illustrated as follows:

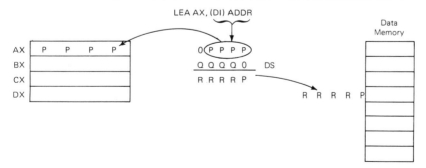

In the illustration above, RRRRP represents a five hexadecimal digit data memory address — the actual location that is addressed. This address is the sum of QQQQ0, the DS Segment register contents, and PPPP, the operand address. The LEA instruction loads the operand address PPPP into the identified 16-bit register.

The LES instruction serves primarily to initialize the address register for string operations. As discussed earlier in this chapter, string instructions access the extra segment via the DI and SI Index registers.

The XLAT instruction is designed for table look-ups. An obvious application for an XLAT instruction would be to convert between ASCII and EBCDIC character codes. EBCDIC character codes being input could be translated into ASCII character codes, prior to being stored in memory, via the following instruction sequence:

```
LABEL  IN    PORT5   Input an EBCDIC code
       XLAT          Convert to ASCII
       STOB  AL      Store in memory
       LOOP  LABEL   Return for next byte if there is one
```

The instruction sequence above inputs character codes from I/O Port 5. These are assumed to be EBCDIC codes which arrive at the AL register. The XLAT instruction uses each EBCDIC code as an index into a conversion table whose base address is assumed held in the BX register. Part of this conversion table may be illustrated as follows:

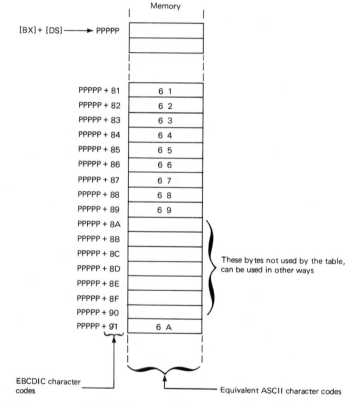

After the XLAT instruction has executed, the ASCII version of the input EBCDIC code will be in the AL register. The STOB instruction stores this ASCII code in the Extra Segment memory location addressed by the DI register; the DI register contents are then incremented so that on the next pass of the iterative loop it addresses the next free memory byte in the Extra Segment table.

The LOOP instruction decrements the CX register and branches back to the IN instruction if the CX register contents are not zero.

Secondary memory reference instructions occur in four versions. Each instruction may access a memory byte or a memory word; in either case, the result of the operation may be returned to a register, or to the memory word from which one operand was fetched.

Note carefully that the Subtract instruction inverts the Carry status.

The following numeric options are available with Add, Subtract, Multiply, and Divide instructions:

Operation	Unsigned Binary		Signed Binary		Packed Decimal		Unpacked Decimal	
	8-bit	16-bit	8-bit	16-bit	2 digit	4 digit	1 digit	2 digit
Add	X	X	X	X	X		X	
Subtract	X	X	X	X	X		X	
Multiply	X	X	X	X			X	
Divide	X	X	X	X			X	

Let us first look at addition and subtraction.

Little needs to be said about **signed and unsigned binary addition or subtraction; these are standard operations** described in Volume 1. The only point to note is that the 8086 Subtract instructions invert the Carry status.

Packed binary coded decimal (BCD) addition and subtraction are also quite standard in that they closely follow the logic described in Volume 1. However, like the 8080A, the 8086 uses Decimal Adjust instructions to handle packed binary coded decimal data.

8086 BCD
ADDITION

When you add two packed binary coded decimal numbers, it is assumed that the two numbers are indeed valid packed binary coded decimal data. The sum, which will not initially be a valid packed binary coded decimal number, is converted into one by the DAA instruction. This may be illustrated as follows:

```
ADD   AL, BL       Add BCD data in BL to AL
DAA                Decimal adjust result
```

Note that you can only add bytes, and AL must be the destination when adding packed BCD data.

Using abbreviations of Table 5-4. **DAA instruction logic may be summarized as follows:**

If (AL) AND $0F_{16}$ is greater than 09_{16}, or if $(AF) = 1$, then:
$(AL) \leftarrow (AL) + 06_{16}$
$(AF) \leftarrow 1$
If (AL) is greater than $9F_{16}$ or if $(CF) = 1$, then:
$(AL) \leftarrow (AL) + 60_{16}$
$(CF) \leftarrow 1$

If one of the numbers being added is not a valid packed binary coded decimal number, then no error indication is given, but the answer will be wrong. For example, there is nothing to stop you from adding $1F_{16}$ to $A3_{16}$ and then executing the DAA instruction to modify the sum; however, the result will be meaningless.

8086 BCD
SUBTRACT

When you subtract packed binary coded decimal numbers, once again it is assumed that the subtrahend and minuend are both valid packed binary coded decimal numbers. The difference will initially be meaningless; however, executing the DAS instruction generates a valid packed binary coded decimal result. This may be illustrated as follows:

```
SBB   AL, BL
DAS
```

Once again you must subtract bytes, and the difference must be returned to the AL register.

Using abbreviations of Table 5-4. DAS instruction logic may be summarized as follows:

If (AL) AND $0F_{16}$ is greater than 09_{16}, or (AF) = 1, then:
(AL) ← (AL) -06_{16}
(AF) ← 1
If (AL) is greater than $9F_{16}$, or (CF) = 1, then:
(AL) ← (AL) -60_{16}
(CF) ← 1

When you subtract packed binary coded decimal numbers and generate a negative result, the Carry status will be 0 (as is the case for binary subtraction) but the numeric negative difference will be a tens complement number rather than a twos complement number. Refer to Volume 1 for details.

You can also add and subtract unpacked binary coded decimal numbers. These numbers may occupy the low-order four bits of a byte, leaving the high-order four bits empty:

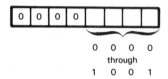

0   0   0   0
through
1   0   0   1

Or you may add and subtract ASCII characters. An ASCII character contains the binary coded decimal digit in low-order four bits and 0011 in the high-order four bits.

When you add unpacked binary coded decimal (BCD) digits, it is assumed that the two numbers being added are indeed valid ASCII characters or unpacked BCD digits. **The sum is initially meaningless; however, after executing the AAA instruction it is converted into one or two valid unpacked binary coded decimal digits.** Note carefully that the AAA instruction does not generate ASCII characters; it generates one binary coded decimal digit per byte — which the four high-order bits zero. **AAA instruction operations may be illustrated as follows:**

If (AL) AND $0F_{16}$ is greater than 09_{16} or (AF) = 1, then:
(AL) ← (AL) + 06_{16}
(AH) ← (AH) + 1
(AF) ← 1

Unconditionally:
(AL) ← (AL) AND $0F_{16}$
(CF) ← (AF)

Note that AH is incremented if the sum in AX is more than 09_{16}, since 09_{16} is the highest one-byte unpacked BCD value that is legal.

When you subtract unpacked binary coded decimal numbers, you can subtract ASCII characters or bytes which have the four high-order bits blank. It makes no difference which option you choose; if you subtract two ASCII characters you will cancel out the four high-order bits — which are identical anyway.

Assuming that the subtrahend and minuend are initially valid unpacked binary coded decimal numbers, the difference, which initially is meaningless, will be converted into one or two valid unpacked binary coded decimal digits by executing the AAS instruction. This may be illustrated as follows:

SUB   AL, BL
AAS

AAS instruction operations may be summarized as follows:

If (AL) AND $0F_{16}$ is greater than 09_{16} or (AF) = 1 then:
(AL) ← (AL) − 6
(AH) ← (AH) − 1
(AF) ← 1

Unconditionally:
(CF) ← (AF)
(AL) ← (AL) AND $0F_{16}$

If you generate a negative result when subtracting unpacked binary coded decimal numbers, the Carry status will be zero and the answer will be in its tens complement form.

You can multiply unpacked binary coded decimal numbers, but not packed binary coded decimal numbers. The multiplier and multiplicand must each be one byte long, with a single binary coded decimal digit in the low-order four bits and 0000 in the high-order four bits. Consider the multiplication $7 \times 8 = 56_{10}$. The instruction sequence:

> 8086 BCD
> MULTIPLICATION

```
MUL    AL, BL
AAM
```

results in these register contents' changes:

	Before					After			
AX	0	0	0	7	AL	AX	0	5	0	6	AL
			0	8	BL				0	8	BL

Assuming that the multiplier and multiplicand are valid, as illustrated above, the product will initially be meaningless. However, after executing the AAM instruction, a valid two-digit product will be generated, with the high-order digit in the AH register and the low-order digit in the AL register.

AAM instruction logic is, in fact, quite simple. It may be illustrated as follows:

(AH) ← (AL) $0A_{16}$ (/ means "divided by")
(AL) ← (AL) modulo $0A_{16}$

Consider again $7 \times 8 = 56_{10}$. This is initially computed as $7 \times 8 = 38_{16}$; therefore, AH contains 00 and AL contains 38 — before the AAM instruction is executed.

(AL)/$0A_{16}$ = 5

Therefore, 05 is loaded into AH. "Modulo" is the remainder after division; therefore (AL) modulo $0A_{16}$ is the remainder following (AL)/$0A_{16}$; it is 6, which is loaded into AL.

Binary coded decimal multiplication does not take sign into account. It is up to your program logic to keep track of the sign.

Binary coded decimal division, like multiplication, works only with unpacked binary coded decimal data. However, you must execute the AAD instruction before the DIV instruction in order to generate a valid unpacked binary coded decimal answer. This may be illustrated as follows:

> 8086 BCD
> DIVISION

```
ADD
DIV    AX, BL
```

The AAD instruction takes the dividend, which we assume to be a valid unpacked binary coded decimal number in the AX register, and **packs it into the AL register as follows:**

(AL) ← (AH) * $0A_{16}$ + (AL)
(AH) ← 0

Consider the reverse of our multiplication examples:

56/8 = 7

Initially, AH contains 05 and AL contains 06. After the AAD instruction is executed, AL contains:

$$05_{16} \cdot 0A_{16} + 06_{16}$$

which is 38_{16}. Now the DIV instruction can perform a pure binary division.

The 8086 allows you to shift and rotate the contents of memory bytes or words. This is very useful since it allows counters and masks to be held in memory, rather than in CPU registers as is the usual case.

Immediate instructions allow immediate data to be loaded into registers or memory locations. When loading immediate data into memory locations, you can generate 3, 4, 5, or 6 byte instruction object codes, depending on the length of the immediate data and the addressing options. See Table 5-5 for details.

The Loop instructions are, in fact, variations of the multi-byte, string-handling 8086 capability. These instructions allow you to set up a counter in the CX register, which is decremented in order to identify the number of iterations for an instruction loop. This may be illustrated as follows for the 8080A and the 8086:

```
       8080A                      8086

       MVI  C, COUNT              MOV  CX, DATA      ← Initialize counter
NEXT   –                   NEXT   –              ⎫
       –                          –              ⎪
       –                          –              ⎬  Repeated instructions
       –                          –              ⎪
       –                          –              ⎭
       DCR  C                     LOOP  NEXT         ← Count and loop logic
       JNZ  NEXT
```

Jump-on-Condition instructions are limited in that they all provide an 8-bit signed binary displacement. Thus, you are limited to jumping within a 256-byte program relative memory page.

Jump-on-Condition instructions are confusing at the best of times, because status combinations determine whether a jump will or will not occur. This is not very interesting information to you as a programmer. It is much easier to jump based on signed and unsigned binary numbers being less than, greater than, or equal to each other. **Table 5-2** therefore **summarizes the way in which you should use 8086 Jump-on-Condition instructions.** This table is similar to the table on page 7-32 of Volume 1; however, the Carry status is inverted, since the 8086 Subtract instruction inverts the Carry status.

The way the 8086 creates Block Transfer and Search instructions is interesting. You begin with a set of instructions, each of which performs a single operation. Each of these instructions can be made to repeat some number of times by preceding the instruction with a repeat (REP).

Table 5-2. 8086 Branch-on-Condition Instructions

Branch Condition	Status Conditions	8086 Instruction	
Unsigned branch on less than or equal	C = 1 or Z = 1	JBE, JNA	
Unsigned branch on less	C = 1	JB, JNAE	
Unsigned branch on equal	Z = 1	JE, JZ	
Unsigned branch on not equal	Z = 0	JNE, JNZ	
Unsigned branch on greater	C = 0 or Z = 0	JA, JNBE	
Unsigned branch on greater than or equal	C = 0	JAE, JNB	These are general status test branch instructions
Signed branch on less than or equal	Z = 1 or S XOR O = 1	JLE, JNG	
Signed branch on less	S XOR O = 1	JL, JNGE	
Signed branch on equal	Z = 1	JE, JZ	
Signed branch on not equal	Z = 0	JNE, JNZ	
Signed branch on greater	Z = 0 or S XOR O = 0	JG, JNLE	
Signed branch on greater than or equal	S XOR O = 0	JGE, JNL	
Branch on counter decrement to zero		JCXZ	
Branch on no overflow	O = 0	JNO	
Branch on overflow	O = 1	JO	
Branch on even parity	P = 1	JP, JPE	These instructions to be used after a subtract or compare
Branch on odd parity	P = 0	JNP, JPO	
Branch on positive	S = 0	JNS	
Branch on negative	S = 1	JS	

The way the 8086 creates Block Transfer and Search instructions is interesting. You begin with a set of instructions, each of which performs a single operation. Each of these instructions can be made to repeat some number of times by preceding the instruction with a repeat (REP). For example, the MOVW instruction, executed on its own, will move one 16-bit word of data from a source memory location to a destination memory location, using Data Segment and Extra Segment addressing as follows:

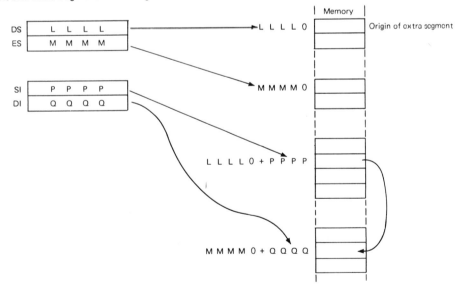

But, precede this instruction with a repeat and you move an entire block of data. This may be illustrated as follows:

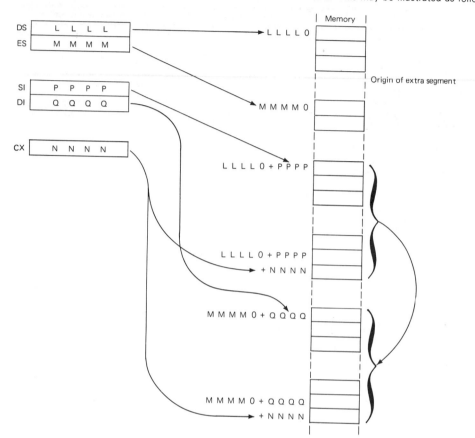

When a Block Transfer or Search instruction is executed, the Program Counter contains the address of the prior instruction until it and the Block Transfer or Search instruction has completed executing. For example, when the REP and MOVS instruction pair executes, the Program Counter keeps pointing to the REP instruction as follows:

```
REP ← PC points here until end of block move
MOVS
```

Only after the MOVS instruction has executed the number of times specified by the repeat will the Program Counter advance to the instruction following MOVS. **This** little piece of **logic is designed to protect repeat instructions during interrupts.** Interrupts are not locked out for the duration of a repeat instruction's execution; that would create intolerable delays between an interrupt request and acknowledge. Providing interrupts are enabled, an interrupt request can be acknowledged at any time during a repeat loop. Within the interrupt service routine, it is only necessary that you save the contents of the SI, DI, and CX registers in order to preserve the repeat loop logic. When you return from the interrupt, the Program Counter is pointing the REP instruction that picks up where it left off, using the restored contents of the SI, DI, and CX registers.

A problem arises if you precede a Block Transfer or Search instruction with more than one prefix. Suppose, for example, you have a LOCK and a REP instruction preceding a MOV:

```
REP
LOCK
MOVS
```

The LOCK must directly precede MOVS; otherwise, it would protect REP against a Hold.

The Program Counter points to the LOCK instruction, not the REP instruction, while the MOVS repeatedly executes the specified number of times. **If at some point an interrupt request is acknowledged,** then after the interrupt service routine completes execution you will return to the LOCK instruction, not the REP. **This will cause the MOVS instruction to be executed once more, rather than the number of times remaining in the repeat loop, as specified by the CX register contents and the REP instruction.** Thus, if both prefixes must be used, interrupts should be disabled. However, you could still run into trouble with a nonmaskable interrupt.

8086 — 8080A INSTRUCTION COMPATIBILITY

As we have already stated, the 8086 instruction set is upward compatible with the 8080A at the source program level. That is, every 8080A instruction can be converted to one or more 8086 instructions. Table 5-6 identifies the source program conversions recommended by Intel. These are by no means the only conversions which are possible, but they are the ones you should use, since they are the ones that Intel plans to support.

THE BENCHMARK PROGRAM

The 8086 makes short work of our Benchmark program, which is well suited to the 8086 block transfer instruction. We assume that the I/O buffer and the table being filled both lie within single 65,536-byte program segments. The displacement to the beginning of the I/O buffer is loaded into the SI Index register, while the displacement to the first free byte of the data table is loaded into the DI Index register. **Our Benchmark program now consists of these few instructions:**

```
LDS     SI,IOBUF     Load I/O Buffer base address displacement in SI
LES     DI,ADDR      Load Data table starting address in ES and displacement to first free byte in DI
MOV     CX, COUNT    Load word count into CX
REP
MOVSW                Move the data block
MOV     ADDR, DI     Return new address of first free table byte
```

Table 5-3. 8086 Memory Addressing Options Identified by the EA Abbreviations in Tables 5-4, 5-5, and 5-6

Memory Reference	Segment Register	Base Register	Index Register	Possible Displacements			Assembly Language Operand Mnemonic
				16-Bit Unsigned	8-Bit High-order Bit Extended	None	
Normal Data Memory Reference	DS (Alternate* CS, SS or ES)	None	SI	X	X	X	
			DI	X	X	X	
		BX	SI	X	X	X	
			DI	X	X	X	
			None	X	X	X	
	DS	None	None	X			
	SS (Alternate* CS, DS or ES)	BP	SI	X	X	X	
			DI	X	X	X	
			None	X	X		
Stack	SS	SP	None				
String Data	DS	None	SI				
	ES	None	DI				
Instruction Fetch	CS	PC	None				
Branch	CS	PC	None		X		
I/O Data	DS	DX	None				

These columns contribute to OEA.

These columns contribute to EA.

This column to be provided

Shaded rows apply to EA and DADDR.

Shaded row applies to EA and LABEL.

* The segment override allows DS or SS to be replaced by one of the other segment registers

X These are displacements that can be used to compute memory addresses.

The following abbreviations are used in Tables 5-4 and 5-5:

AH	Accumulator, high-order byte
AL	Accumulator, low-order byte
AL7	The value of register AL high-order bit (0 or 1) extended to a byte (00_{16} or FF_{16})
AX	Accumulator, both bytes
AX15	The value of register AH high-order bit (0 or 1) extended to a 16-bit word (0000_{16} or $FFFF_{16}$)
BD	The destination is a byte operand (used only by the Assembler)
BH	B register, high-order byte
BL	B register, low-order byte
BRANCH	Program memory direct address, used in Branch addressing option shown in Tables 5-1 and 5-2
BS	The source is a byte operand (used only by the Assembler)
BX	B register, both bytes
C	Carry status
CH	C register, high-order byte
CL	C register, low-order byte
CS	Code Segment register
CX	C register, both bytes
DADDR	Data memory address operands identified in Table 5-3
DATA8	Eight bits of immediate data
DATA16	16 bits of immediate data
DH	D register, high-order byte
DI	Destination Index register
DISP	An 8-bit or 16-bit signed displacement
DISP8	An 8-bit signed displacement
DL	D register, low-order byte
DS	Data Segment register
DX	D register, both bytes
EA	Effective data memory address using any of the memory addressing options identified in Table 5-2
ES	Extra Segment register
I	Status flag set to 1
I/D	Increment/decrement selector for string operations; increment if D is 0, decrement if D is 1
LABEL	Direct data memory address, as identified in Table 5-2
N	A number between 0 and 7
O	Status flag reset to 0
OEA	Offset data memory address used to compute EA: $$EA = OEA + [DS] \cdot 16$$
PC	Program Counter
PDX	I/O port addressed by DX register contents; port number can range from 0 through 65,536
PORT	A label identifying an I/O port number in the range 0 through 255_{10}
RB	Any one of the eight byte registers: AH, AL, BH, BL, CH, CL, DH, or DL
RBD	Any RB register as a destination
RBS	Any RB register as a source
RW	Any one of the eight 16-bit registers: AX, BX, CX, DX, SP, BP, SI, or DI
RWD	Any RW register as a destination
RWS	Any RW register as a source
SEGM	Label identifying a 16-bit value loaded into the CS Segment register to execute a segment jump
SFR	Status Flags register
SI	Source Index register
SP	Stack Pointer
SR	Any one of the Segment registers CS, DS, ES, or SS
SS	Stack Segment register

U	Status flag modified, but undefined
V	Any number in the range 0 through 255_{10}
X	Status flag modified to reflect result
WD	The destination is a word operand (used only by the Assembler)
WS	The source is a word operand (used only by the Assembler)
[[ ]]	Contents of the memory location addressed by the contents of the location enclosed in the double brackets
[ ]	The contents of the location enclosed in the brackets
←	Data on the right-hand side of the arrow is moved to the location on the left-hand side of the arrow
⟷	Contents of locations on each side of ⟷ are exchanged
—	The twos complement of the value under the —
≠	Not equal to

INSTRUCTION EXECUTION TIMES AND CODES

Table 5-5 lists instructions in alphabetical order, showing object codes and execution times, for the 8086 and the 8088, expressed in whole clock cycles. Execution time is the time required from beginning execution of an instruction that is in the queue to beginning execution of the next instruction in the queue. The time required to place an instruction from memory into the queue (instruction fetch time) is not shown in the table; because of queuing, instruction fetch time occurs concurrently with instruction execution time and thus has no effect on overall timing, except as specifically noted in the table.

Instruction object codes are represented as two hexadecimal digits for instruction bytes without variations.

Instruction object codes are represented as eight binary digits for instruction bytes with variations for the instruction.

The following notation is used in Tables 5-4 and 5-5:

[ ]	indicate an optional object code byte

a	one bit choosing length:
	    in bit position 0 a=0 specifies 1 data byte; a=1 specifies 2 data bytes
	    in bit position 1 a=0 specifies 2 data bytes; a=1 specifies 1 data byte

aa	two bits choosing address length:
	        no DISP = 00
	     one DISP byte = 01
	    two DISP bytes = 10, or 00 with bbb = 110
	                        11 causes bbb to select a register, using the 3-bit code given below for reg.

bbb	three bits choosing addressing mode:
	    000 EA = (BX) + (SI) + DISP
	    001 EA = (BX) + (DI) + DISP
	    010 EA = (BP) + (SI) + DISP
	    011 EA = (BP) + (DI) + DISP
	    100 EA = (SI) + DISP
	    101 EA = (DI) + DISP
	    110 EA = (BP) + DISP
	    111 EA = (BX) + DISP

DISP	represents two hexadecimal digit memory displacement
ddd	represents three binary digits identifying a destination register (see reg.)

rr	two binary digits identifying a segment register:
	    00 = ES
	    01 = CS
	    10 = SS
	    11 = DS

reg	three binary digits identifying a register:

	16-bit	8-bit
000 =	AX	AL
001 =	CX	CL
010 =	DX	DL
011 =	BX	BL
100 =	SP	AH
101 =	BP	CH
110 =	SI	DH
111 =	DI	BH

sss	represents three binary digits identifying a source register (see reg)	
PPQQ	represents four hexadecimal digit memory address	
v	one bit choosing shift length:	
	0 count = 1	
	1 count = (CL)	
x	"don't care" bit	
YY	represents two hexadecimal data digits	
YYYY	represents four hexadecimal data digits	
z	one bit where z XOR (ZF) = 1 terminates loop	
*	Execution time is less than or equal to instruction fetch time.	
**	Includes up to eight clock cycles of overhead on each transfer due to queue maintenance. For conditional jumps, the lesser figure is when the test fails (no jump taken).	

Effective Address calculation and extra clock cycles:

Extra Clock Periods			
bbb	EA	8086(1)	8088(2)
000	(BX) + (SI)	7	7
000	(BX) + (SI) + DISP8	11	11
000	(BX) + (SI) + DISP16	11	15
001	(BX) + (DI)	8	8
001	(BX) + (DI) + DISP8	12	12
001	(BX) + (DI) + DISP16	12	16
010	(BP) + (SI)	8	8
010	(BP) + (SI) + DISP8	12	12
010	(BP) + (SI) + DISP16	12	16
011	(BP) + (DI)	7	7
011	(BP) + (DI) + DISP8	11	11
011	(BP) + (DI) + DISP16	11	15
100	(SI) ir (DI) or (BD)	5	5
101	or (BX)		
110	+ DISP8	9	9
111	+ DISP16	9	13
	8-bit immediate	6	6
	16-bit immediate	6	10

(1) Add another 4 clock cycles for each
16-bit operand or an odd address boundary.

(2) Add anoter 4 clock cycles for each
16-bit operand.

Substitute the clock cycles shown above wherever EA appears in Tables 5-4 and 5-5.

Table 5-4. A Summary of 8086 and 8088 Instructions

Type	Mnemonic	Operand(s)	Object Code	Clock Cycles	Statuses O	D	I	T	S	Z	A	P	C	Operation Performed
I/O	IN	AL,PORT	E4 YY	10										[AL] ← [PORT] Load one byte of data from I/O port PORT into AL
	IN	AL,[DX]	EC 1	8										[AL] ← [PDX] Load into AL one byte of data from I/O port whose address is held in the DX register
	IN	AX,PORT	E5 YY	10										[AL] ← [PORT], [AH] ← [PORT+1] Load 16 bits of data into AX, AL receives data from I/O port PORT, AH receives data from I/O port PORT+1
	IN	AX,[DX]	ED	8										[AL] ← [PDX], [AH] ← [PDX+1] Load 16 bits of data into AX, AL receives data from I/O port whose address is held in the DX register. AH receives data from the I/O port whose address is one higher
	OUT	AL,PORT	E6 YY	10										[PORT] ← [AL] Output one byte of data from register AL to I/O port PORT
	OUT	AL,[DX]	EE 1	8										[PDX] ← [AL] Output one byte of data from register AL to the I/O port whose address is held in the DX register
	OUT	AX,PORT	E7 YY	10										[PORT] ← [AL], [PORT+1] ← [AH] Output 16 bits of data. The AL register contents are output to I/O port PORT. The AH register contents are output to I/O port PORT+1
	OUT	AX,[DX]	EF	8										[PORT] ← [PDX], [PORT+1] ← [PDX+1] Output 16 bits of data. The AL register contents are output to the I/O port whose address is held in the DX register. The AH register contents is output to the I/O port whose address is one higher
Primary Memory Reference	LDS	RW,DADDR	C5 aasssbbb [DISP][DISP]	16+EA										[RW] ← [EA], [DS] ← [EA+2] Load 16 bits of data from the memory word addressed by DADDR into register RW. Load 16 bits of data from the next sequential memory word into the DS register
	LEA	RW,DADDR	8D aasssbbb [DISP][DISP]	2+EA										[RW] ← OEA Load into RW the 16-bit address displacement which, when added to the segment register contents, creates the effective data memory address
	LES	RW,DADDR	C4 aasssbbb [DISP][DISP]	16+EA										[RW] ← [EA], [ES] ← [EA+2] Load 16 bits of data from the memory word addressed by DADDR into register RW. Load 16 bits of data from the next sequential memory word into the ES register
	MOV	RB,DADDR	8A aadddbbb [DISP][DISP]	8+EA										[RB] ← [EA] Load one byte of data from the data memory location addressed by DADDR to register RB

Table 5-4. A Summary of 8086 and 8088 Instructions (Continued)

Type	Mnemonic	Operand(s)	Object Code	Clock Cycles	O	D	I	T	S	Z	A	P	C	Operation Performed
Primary Memory Reference (Continued)	MOV	RW,DADDR	8B aadddbbb [DISP][DISP]	8+EA										[RW] ← [EA] Load 16 bits of data from the data memory word addressed by DADDR to register RW
	MOV	DADDR,RB	88 aasssbbb [DISP][DISP]	9+EA										[EA] ← [RB] Store the data byte from register RB in the memory byte addressed by DADDR
	MOV	DADDR,RW	89 aasssbbb [DISP][DISP]	9+EA										[EA] ← [RW] Store the 16-bit data word from register RW in the memory word addressed by DADDR
	MOV	AL,LABEL	A0 PPQQ	10										[AL] ← [EA] Load the data memory byte directly addressed by LABEL into register AL
	MOV	AX,LABEL	A1 PPQQ	10										[AX] ← [EA] Load the 16-bit data memory word directly addressed by LABEL into register AX
	MOV	LABEL,AL	A2 PPQQ	10										[EA] ← [AL] Store the 8-bit contents of register AL into the data memory byte directly addressed by LABEL
	MOV	LABEL,AX	A3 PPQQ	10										[EA] ← [AX] Store the 16-bit contents of register AX into the data memory word directly addressed by LABEL
	MOV	SR,DADDR	8E aa0rrbbb [DISP][DISP]	8+EA										[SR] ← [EA] Load into Segment register SR the contents of the 16-bit memory word addressed by DADDR
	MOV	DADDR,SR	8C aa0rrbbb [DISP][DISP]	9+EA										[EA] ← [SR] Store the contents of Segment register SR in the 16-bit memory location addressed by DADDR
	XCHG	RB,DADDR	86 aaregbbb [DISP][DISP]	17+EA										[RB] ⟷ [EA] Exchange a byte of data between register RB and the data memory location addressed by DADDR
	XCHG	RW,DADDR	87 aaregbbb [DISP][DISP]	17+EA										[RW] ⟷ [EA] Exchange 16 bits of data between register RW and the data memory location addressed by DADDR
	XLAT		D7	11										[AL] ← [[AL] + [BX]] Load into AL the data byte stored in the memory location addressed by summing initial AL contents with BX contents

Table 5-4. A Summary of 8086 and 8088 Instructions (Continued)

Type	Mnemonic	Operand(s)	Object Code	Clock Cycles	O	D	I	T	S	Z	A	P	C	Operation Performed
Secondary Memory Reference (Memory Operate)	ADC	RB,DADDR	12 aadddbbb [DISP][DISP]	9+EA	X				X	X	X	X	X	[RB] ← [EA] + [RB] + [C] Add the contents of the data byte addressed by DADDR, plus the Carry status, to register RB
	ADC	RW,DADDR	13 aadddbbb [DISP][DISP]	9+EA	X				X	X	X	X	X	[RW] ← [EA] + [RW] + [C] Add the contents of the 16-bit data word addressed by DADDR, plus the Carry status, to register RW
	ADC	DADDR,RB	10 aasssbbb [DISP][DISP]	16+EA	X				X	X	X	X	X	[EA] ← [EA] + [RB] + [C] Add the 8-bit contents of register RB, plus the Carry status, to the data memory byte addressed by DADDR
	ADC	DADDR,RW	11 aasssbbb [DISP][DISP]	16+EA	X				X	X	X	X	X	[EA] ← [EA] + [RW] + [C] Add the 16-bit contents of register RW, plus the Carry status, to the data word addressed by DADDR
	ADD	RB,DADDR	02 aadddbbb [DISP][DISP]	9+EA	X				X	X	X	X	X	[RB] ← [EA] + [RB] Add the contents of the data byte addressed by DADDR to register RB
	ADD	RW,DADDR	03 aadddbbb [DISP][DISP]	9+EA	X				X	X	X	X	X	[RW] ← [EA] + [RW] Add the contents of the 16-bit word addressed by DADDR to register RW
	ADD	DADDR,RB	00 aasssbbb [DISP][DISP]	16+EA	X				X	X	X	X	X	[EA] ← [EA] + [RB] Add the 8-bit contents of register RB to the data memory byte addressed by DADDR
	ADD	DADDR,RW	01 aasssbbb [DISP][DISP]	16+EA	X				X	X	X	X	X	[EA] ← [EA] + [RW] Add the 16-bit contents of register RW to the data memory word addressed by DADDR
	AND	RB,DADDR	22 aadddbbb [DISP][DISP]	9+EA	0				X	X	U	X	0	[RB] ← [EA] AND [RB] AND the 8-bit contents of register RB with the data memory byte addressed by DADDR. Store the result in RB
	AND	RW,DADDR	23 aadddbbb [DISP][DISP]	16+EA	0				X	X	U	X	0	[RW] ← [EA] AND [RW] AND the 16-bit contents of register RW with the data memory word addressed by DADDR. Store the result in RW
	AND	DADDR,RB	20 aasssbbb [DISP][DISP]	16+EA	0				X	X	U	X	0	[EA] ← [EA] AND [RB] AND the 8-bit contents of register RB with the addressed data memory byte
	AND	DADDR,RW	21 aasssbbb [DISP][DISP]	16+EA	0				X	X	U	X	0	[EA] ← [EA] AND [RW] AND the 16-bit contents of register RW with the data memory word addressed by DADDR. Store the result in the addressed data memory word
	CMP	RB,DADDR	3A aadddbbb [DISP][DISP]	9+EA	X				X	X	X	X	X	[RB] - [EA] Subtract the contents of the data memory byte addressed by DADDR from the contents of register RB. Discard the result, but adjust status flags
	CMP	RW,DADDR	3B aadddbbb [DISP][DISP]	9+EA	X				X	X	X	X	X	[RW] - [EA] Subtract the 16-bit contents of the data memory word addressed by DADDR from the contents of register RW. Discard the result, but adjust status flags

Table 5-4. A Summary of 8086 and 8088 Instructions (Continued)

Type	Mnemonic	Operand(s)	Object Code	Clock Cycles	O	D	I	T	S	Z	A	P	C	Operation Performed
Secondary Memory Reference (Memory Operate) (Continued)	CMP	DADDR,RB	38 aasssbbb [DISP][DISP]	9+EA	X				X	X	X	X	X	Subtract the 8-bit contents of register RB from the data memory byte addressed by DADDR. Discard the result, but adjust status flags [EA] ← [RB]
	CMP	DADDR,RW	39 aasssbbb [DISP][DISP]	9+EA	X				X	X	X	X	X	Subtract the 16-bit contents of register RW from the data memory word addressed by DADDR. Discard the result, but adjust status flags [EA] ← [RW]
	DEC	DADDR	1111111a aa001bbb [DISP][DISP]	15+EA	X.				X	X	X	X		Decrement the contents of the memory location addressed by DADDR. Depending on the prior definition of DADDR, an 8-bit or a 16-bit memory location may be decremented [EA] ← [EA] − 1
	DIV	AX,DADDR	F6 aa110bbb [DISP][DISP]	(86-96)+EA	U				U	U	U	U	U	Divide the 16-bit contents of register AX by the 8-bit contents of the memory byte addressed by DADDR. Store the integer quotient in AL and the remainder in AH. If the quotient is greater than FF_{16}, execute a "divide by 0" interrupt [AX] ← [AX]/[EA]
	DIV	DX,DADDR	F7 aa110bbb [DISP][DISP]	(150-168)+EA	U				U	U	U	U	U	Divide the 32-bit contents of registers DX (high-order) and AX (low-order) by the 16-bit contents of the memory word addressed by DADDR. Store the integer quotient in AX and the remainder in DX. If the quotient is greater than $FFFF_{16}$, execute a "divide by 0" interrupt [AX] ← [AX]/[EA]
	IDIV	AX,DADDR	F6 aa111bbb [DISP][DISP]	(107-118|8+EA)	U				U	U	U	U	U	Divide the 16-bit contents of register AX by the 8-bit contents of the memory byte addressed by DADDR, treating both contents as signed binary numbers. Store the quotient, as a signed binary number, in AL. Store the remainder, as an unsigned binary number, in AH. If the quotient is greater than $7F_{16}$ or less than -80_{16} execute a "divide by 0" interrupt [AX] ← [AX]/[EA]
	IDIV	DX,DADDR	F7 aa111bbb [DISP][DISP]	(171)-190)+EA	U				U	U	U	U	U	Divide the 32-bit contents of register DX (high-order) and AX (low-order) by the 16-bit contents of the memory word addressed by DADDR. Treat both contents as signed binary numbers. Store the quotient, as a signed binary number, in AX. Store the remainder, as an unsigned binary number, in AH. If the quotient is greater than $7FFF_{16}$ or less than -8000_{16} execute a "divide by 0" interrupt [DX][AX] ← [DX][AX]/[EA]
	IMUL	AL,DADDR	F6 aa101bbb [DISP][DISP]	(86-104)+EA	X				U	U	U	U	X	Multiply the 8-bit contents of register AL by the contents of the memory byte addressed by DADDR. Treat both numbers as signed binary numbers. Store the 16-bit product in AX [AX] ← [AL] • [EA]
	IMUL	AX,DADDR	F7 aa101bbb [DISP][DISP]	(134-160)+EA	X				U	U	U	U	X	Multiply the 16-bit contents of register AX by the 16-bit contents of the memory word addressed by DADDR. Treat both numbers as signed binary numbers. Store the 32-bit product in DX (high-order word) and AX (low-order word) [DX][AX] ← [AX] • [EA]

Table 5-4. A Summary of 8086 and 8088 Instructions (Continued)

Type	Mnemonic	Operand(s)	Object Code	Clock Cycles	O	D	I	T	S	Z	A	P	C	Operation Performed
Secondary Memory Reference (Memory Operate) (Continued)	INC	DADDR	1111111a aaO0Obb [DISP][DISP]	15+EA	X				X	X	X	X		[EA] ← [EA] + 1. Increment the contents of the memory location addressed by DADDR. Depending on the prior definition of DADDR, an 8-bit or a 16-bit memory location may be incremented
	MUL	AL,DADDR	F6 aa100bbb [DISP][DISP]	(76-83)+EA	X				U	U	U	U	X	[AX] ← [AL] • [EA]. Multiply the 8-bit contents of register AL by the contents of the memory byte addressed by DADDR. Treat both numbers as unsigned binary numbers. Store the 16-bit product in AX
	MUL	F7	F7 aa100bbb [DISP][DISP]	(124-139)+EA	X				U	U	U	U	X	[DX][AX] ← [AX] • [EA]. Multiply the 16-bit contents of register AX by the 15-bit contents of the memory word addressed by DADDR. Treat both numbers as unsigned binary numbers. Store the 32-bit product in DX (high-order word) and AX (low-order word)
	NEG	DADDR	1111011a aa011bb [DISP][DISP]	16+EA	X				X	X	X	X	X	[EA] ← $\overline{[EA]}$. Twos complement the contents of the addressed memory location. Depending on the prior definition of DADDR, an 8-bit or 16-bit memory location may be twos complemented
	NOT	DADDR	1111011a aa010bbb [DISP][DISP]	16+EA	X									[EA] ← NOT [EA]. Ones complement the contents of the addressed memory location. Depending on the prior definition of DADDR, an 8-bit or 16-bit memory location may be ones complemented
	OR	RB,DADDR	0A aadddbbb [DISP][DISP]	9+EA	X				X	X	U	X	X	[RB] ← [EA] OR [RB]. OR the 8-bit contents of register RB with the data memory byte addressed by DADDR. Store the result in RB
	OR	RW,DADDR	0B aadddbbb [DISP][DISP]	9+EA	X				X	X	U	X	X	[RW] ← [EA] OR [RW]. OR the 16-bit contents of register RW with the data memory word addressed by DADDR. Store the result in RW
	OR	DADDR,RB	08 aasssbbb [DISP][DISP]	16+EA	X				X	X	U	X	X	[EA] ← [EA] OR [RB]. OR the 8-bit contents of register RB with the data memory byte addressed by DADDR. Store the result in the data memory byte
	OR	DADDR,RW	09 aasssbbb [DISP][DISP]	16+EA	X				X	X	U	X	X	[EA] ← [EA] OR [RW]. OR the 16-bit contents of register RW with the data memory word addressed by DADDR. Store the result in the data memory word

5-64

Table 5-4. A Summary of 8086 and 8088 Instructions (Continued)

Type	Mnemonic	Operand(s)	Object Code	Clock Cycles	O	D	I	T	S	Z	A	P	C	Operation Performed
Secondary Memory Reference (Memory Operate) (Continued)	RCL	DADDR,N	110100va aa011bbb [DISP][DISP]	N=1 15+EA; N>1 4N+20+EA	X								X	Rotate the contents of the data memory location addressed by DADDR left through the Carry status. If N = 1, then rotate one bit position. If N = CL, then register CL contents provide the number of bit positions. Depending on prior definition, DADDR may address a byte: (C ← [EA]) or DADDR may address a word: (C [EA] [EA+1])
	ROL	DADDR,N	110100va aa000bbb											
	RCR	DADDR,N	110100va aa001bbb [DISP][DISP]	N=1 15+EA	X								X	As RCL, but rotate right
	ROL	DADDR,N	110100va aa000bbb [DISP][DISP]	N>1 4N+20+EA	X								X	Rotate the contents of the data memory location addressed by DADDR left. Move the left most bit into the Carry status. If N = 1, then rotate one bit position. If N = CL, then register CL contents provides the number of bit positions. Depending on prior definition, DADDR may address a byte: (C → [EA]) or DADDR may address a word: (C [EA] [EA+1])

5-65

Table 5-4. A Summary of 8086 and 8088 Instructions (Continued)

Type	Mnemonic	Operand(s)	Object Code	Clock Cycles	O	D	I	T	S	Z	A	P	C	Operation Performed
Secondary Memory Reference (Memory Operate) (Continued)	SAL	DADDR,N	110100va aa001bbb [DISP][DISP]	N=1 15+EA	X								X	As ROL, but rotate right. Shift the contents of the data memory location addressed by DADDR left. Move the left most bit into the Carry status. If N = 1, then shift one bit position. If N = CL, then register CL contents provides the number of bit positions. Depending on prior definition, DADDR may address a byte: C ← [EA] ← 0 ; or DADDR may address a word: C ← [EA] [EA+1] ← 0
	SAR	DADDR,N	110100va aa111bbb [DISP][DISP]	N=1 15+EA; N>1 4N+20+EA	X				X	X	U	X	X	As SAL, but shift right and propagate sign: [EA] → C ; or [EA] [EA+1] → C
	SBB	RB,DADDR	1A aaddd bbb [DISP][DISP]	9+EA	X				X	X	X	X	X	[RB] ← [RB] − [EA] − [C] Subtract the contents of the data byte addressed by DADDR from the contents of 8-bit register RB, using twos complement arithmetic. Decrement the result in RB if the Carry status was initially set
	SBB	RW,DADDR	1B aadddbbb [DISP][DISP]	9+EA	X				X	X	X	X	X	[RW] ← [RW] − [EA] − [C] Subtract the contents of the 16-bit data word addressed by DADDR from the contents of the 16-bit register RW, using twos complement arithmetic. Decrement the result in RW if the Carry status was initially set

Table 5-4. A Summary of 8086 and 8088 Instructions (Continued)

Type	Mnemonic	Operand(s)	Object Code	Clock Cycles	O	D	I	T	S	Z	A	P	C	Operation Performed
Secondary Memory Reference (Memory Operate) (Continued)	SBB	DADDR,RB	18 aasssbbb [DISP][DISP]	16+EA	X				X	X	X	X	X	[EA] ← [EA] − [RB] − [C] Subtract the contents of 8-bit register RB from the data byte addressed by DADDR, using twos complement arithmetic. Decrement the result in data memory if the Carry status was initially set
	SBB	DADDR,RW	19 aasssbbb [DISP][DISP]	16+EA	X				X	X	X	X	X	[EA] ← [EA] − [RW] − [C] Subtract the contents of 16-bit register RW from the 16-bit data word addressed by DADDR, using twos complement arithmetic. Decrement the result in data memory if the Carry status was initially set
	SHL	DADDR,N	110100va aa101bb [DISP][DISP]						X	X	U	X	X	This is an alternate mnemonic for SAL
	SHR	DADDR,N		N=1 15+EA; N>1 4N+20+EA	X				X	X	U	X	X	As SAL, but shift right: 0 → [EA] → C or 0 → [EA] [EA+1] → C
	SUB	RB,DADDR	2A aadddbbb [DISP][DISP]	9+EA	X				X	X	X	X	X	[RB] ← [RB] − [EA] Subtract the contents of the data memory byte addressed by DADDR from the contents of 8-bit register RB, using twos complement arithmetic
	SUB	RW,DADDR	2B aadddbbb [DISP][DISP]	9+EA	X				X	X	X	X	X	[RW] ← [RW] − [EA] Subtract the contents of the 16-bit data memory word addressed by DADDR from the contents of 16-bit register RW, using twos complement arithmetic
	SUB	DADDR,RB	28 aasssbbb [DISP][DISP]	16+EA	X				X	X	X	X	X	[EA] ← [EA] − [RB] Subtract the contents of 8-bit register RB from the data memory byte addressed by DADDR, using twos complement arithmetic
	SUB	DADDR,RW	29 aasssbbb [DISP][DISP]	16+EA	X				X	X	X	X	X	[EA] ← [EA] − [RW] Subtract the contents of 16-bit register RW from the 16-bit data memory word addressed by DADDR, using twos complement arithmetic
	TEST	DADDR,RB	84 aaregbbb [DISP][DISP]	9+EA	0				X	X	U	X	0	[EA] AND [RB] AND the 8-bit contents of the data memory location addressed by DADDR with the contents of 8-bit register RB. Discard the result, but adjust status flags appropriately

Table 5-4. A Summary of 8086 and 8088 Instructions (Continued)

Type	Mnemonic	Operand(s)	Object Code	Clock Cycles	O	D	I	T	S	Z	A	P	C	Operation Performed
Secondary Memory Reference (Memory Operate) (Continued)	TEST	DADDR,RW	85 aareg bbb [DISP][DISP]	9+EA	0				X	X	U	X	0	[EA] AND [RW] AND the 16-bit contents of the data memory word addressed by DADDR with the contents of 16-bit register RW. Discard the result, but adjust status flags appropriately
	XOR	RB,DADDR	32 aadddbbb [DISP][DISP]	9+EA	0				X	X	U	X	0	[RB] ← [RB] XOR [EA] Exclusive OR the 8-bit contents of register RB with the data memory byte addressed by DADDR. Store the result in RB
	XOR	RW,DADDR	33 aadddbbb [DISP][DISP]	9+EA	0				X	X	U	X	0	[RW] ← [RW] XOR [EA] Exclusive OR the 16-bit contents of register RW with the 16-bit data memory word addressed by DADDR. Store the result in RW
	XOR	DADDR,RB	30 aasssbbb [DISP][DISP]	16+EA	0				X	X	U	X	0	[EA] ← [RB] XOR [EA] Exclusive OR the 8-bit contents of register RB with the data memory byte addressed by DADDR. Store the result in the addressed data memory byte
	XOR	DADDR,RW	31 aasssbbb [DISP][DISP]	16+EA	0				X	X	U	X	0	[EA] ← [RW] XOR [EA] Exclusive OR the 16-bit contents of register RW with the data memory word addressed by DADDR. Store the result in the addressed data memory word
Immediate	MOV	DADDR, DATA8	C6 aa000bbb [DISP][DISP] YY	10+EA										[EA] ← DATA8 Load the immediate data byte DATA8 into the data memory byte addressed by DADDR
	MOV	DADDR, DATA16	C7 aa000bbb [DISP][DISP] YYYY	10+EA										[EA] ← DATA16 Load the immediate 16-bit data word DATA16 into the data memory word addressed by DADDR
	MOV	RB,DATA8	10110ddd YY	4*										[RB] ← DATA8 Load the immediate data byte DATA8 into 8-bit register RB
	MOV	RW,DATA16	10111ddd YYYY	4*										[RW] ← DATA16 Load the immediate 16-bit data word DATA16 into 16-bit register RW
Jump	JMP	BRANCH	11101a1 DISP [DISP]	15**										[PC] ← [PC] + DISP Jump direct to program memory location identified by label BRANCH. The displacement DISP which must be added to the Program Counter will be computed as an 8-bit or 16-bit signed binary number, as needed, by the assembler
	JMP	BRANCH, SEGM	EA PPQQ PPQQ	15**										[PC] ← DATA16, [CS] ← DATA16 Jump direct into a new segment. BRANCH is a label which becomes a 16-bit unsigned data value which is loaded into PC. SEGM is a label which becomes another 16-bit unsigned data value that is loaded into the CS segment register
	JMP	DADDR	FF aa100bbb [DISP][DISP]	18+EA**										[PC] ← [EA] Jump indirect in current segment. The 16-bit contents of the data memory word addressed by DADDR is loaded into PC

Table 5-4. A Summary of 8086 and 8088 Instructions (Continued)

Type	Mnemonic	Operand(s)	Object Code	Clock Cycles	O	D	I	T	S	Z	A	P	C	Operation Performed
Jump (Cont.)	JMP	DADDR,CS	FF aa101bbb [DISP][DISP]	24+EA**										[PC] ← [EA], [CS] ← [EA+2] Jump indirect into a new segment. The 16-bit contents of the data memory word addressed by DADDR is loaded into PC. The next sequential 16-bit data memory word's contents is loaded into the CS segment register
	JMP	RW	FF 11100reg	11										[PC] ← [RW] Jump to memory location whose address is contained in register RW.
Subroutine Call and Return	CALL	BRANCH	E8 DISP DISP	19**										[[SP]] ← [PC], [SP] ← [SP] −2, [PC] ← [PC] + DISP Call a subroutine in the current program segment using direct addressing
	CALL	BRANCH, SEGM	9A PPQQ PPQQ	28**										[[SP]] ← [CS], [SP] ← [SP] −2, [[SP]] ← [PC], [SP] ← [SP] −2, [PC] ← DATA16, [CS] ← DATA 16 Call a subroutine in another program segment using direct addressing. BRANCH and SEGM are labels that become different 16-bit data words; they are loaded into PC and CS, respectively
	CALL	DADDR	FF aa010bbb [DISP][DISP]	21+EA**										[[SP]] ← [PC], [SP] ← [SP] −2, [PC] ← [EA] Call a subroutine in the current program segment using indirect addressing. The address of the subroutine called is stored in the 16-bit data memory word addressed by DADDR
	CALL	DADDR,CS	FF aa011bbb [DISP][DISP]	37+EA**										[[SP]] ← [CS], [SP] ← [S2] −2, [[SP]] ← [PC], [SP] ← [SP] −2, [PC] ← [EA], [CS] ← [EA+2] Call a subroutine in a different program segment using indirect addressing. The address of the subroutine called is stored in the 16-bit data memory word addressed by DADDR. The new CS register contents is stored in the next sequential program memory word
	CALL	RW	FF 11010reg	16**										[SP] ← [PC],[SP] ← [SP−2], [PC] ← [RW] Call a subroutine whose address is contained in register P.V.
	RET		C3	8**										[PC] ← [[SP]], [SP] ← [SP] + 2 Return from a subroutine in the current segment
	RET	CS	CB	12**										[PC] ← [[SP]], [SP] ← [SP] +2, [CS] ← [[SP]], [SP] ← [SP] +2 Return from a subroutine in another segment
	RET	DATA16	C2 YYYY	17**										[PC] ← [[SP]], [SP] ← [SP] +2 +DATA16 Return from a subroutine in the current segment and add an immediate displacement to SP
	RET	CS,DATA16	CA YYYY	18**										[PC] ← [[SP]], [SP] ← [SP] +2, [CS] ← [[SP]], [SP] ← [SP] +2 +DATA16 Return from a subroutine in another segment and add an immediate displacement to SP

Table 5-4. A Summary of 8086 and 8088 Instructions (Continued)

Type	Mnemonic	Operand(s)	Object Code	Clock Cycles	Statuses O	D	I	T	S	Z	A	P	C	Operation Performed
Immediate Operate	ADD	AL,DATA8	04 YY	4*	X				X	X	X	X	X	[AL] ← [AL] + DATA8 Add 8-bit immediate data to the AL register
	ADD	AX,DATA16	05 YYYY	4*	X				X	X	X	X	X	[AX] ← [AX] + DATA16 Add 16-bit immediate data to the AX register
	ADD	RB,DATA8	80 11000ddd YY	4*	X				X	X	X	X	X	[RB] ← [RB] + DATA8 Add 8-bit immediate data to the RB register
	ADD	RW,DATA16	81 11000ddd YYYY	4*	X				X	X	X	X	X	[RW] ← [RW] + DATA16 Add 16-bit immediate data to the RW register
	ADD	DADDR, DATA8	80 aa000bbb [DISP][DISP] YY	17+EA	X				X	X	X	X	X	[EA] ← [EA] + DATA8 Add 8-bit immediate data to the data memory byte addressed by DADDR
	ADD	DADDR, DATA16	81 aa000bbb [DISP][DISP] YYYY	17+EA	X				X	X	X	X	X	[EA] ← [EA] + DATA16 Add 16-bit immediate data to the data memory word addressed by DADDR
	ADC	AL,DATA8	14 YY	4*	X				X	X	X	X	X	[AL] ← [AL] + DATA8 + [C] Add 8-bit immediate data, plus carry, to the AL register
	ADC	AX,DATA16	15 YYYY	4*	X				X	X	X	X	X	[AX] ← [AX] + DATA16 + [C] Add 16-bit immediate data plus carry, to the AX register
	ADC	B,DATA8	80 11010ddd YY	4*	X				X	X	X	X	X	[RB] ← [RB] + DATA8 + [C] Add 8-bit immediate data, plus carry, to the RB register
	ADC	RW,DATA16	81 11010ddd YYYY	4*	X				X	X	X	X	X	[RW] ← [RW] + DATA16 + [C] Add 16-bit immediate data, plus carry, to the RW register
	ADC	DADDR, DATA8	80 aa010bbb [DISP][DISP] YY	17+EA	X				X	X	X	X	X	[EA] ← [EA] + DATA8 + [C] Add 8-bit immediate data, plus carry, to the data memory byte addressed by DADDR
	ADC	DADDR, DATA16	81 aa010bbb [DISP][DISP]YYYY	17+EA	X				X	X	X	X	X	[EA] ← [EA] + DATA16 + [C] Add 16-bit immediate data, plus carry, to the data memory word addressed by DADDR
	AND	AL,DATA8	24 YY	4*	0				X	X	U	X	0	[AL] ← [AL] AND DATA8 AND 8-bit immediate data with AL register contents
	AND	AX,DATA16	25 YYYY	4*	0				X	X	U	X	0	[AX] ← [AX] AND DATA16 AND 16-bit immediate data with AX register contents
	AND	RB,DATA8	80 11100ddd YY	4*	0				X	X	U	X	0	[RB] ← [RB] AND DATA8 AND 8-bit immediate data with RB register contents
	AND	RW,DATA16	81 11100ddd YYYY	4*	0				X	X	U	X	0	[RW] ← [RW] AND DATA16 AND 16-bit immediate data with RW register contents
	AND	DADDR,8	80 aa100bbb [DISP][DISP] YY	17+EA	0				X	X	U	X	0	[EA] ← [EA] AND DATA8 AND 8-bit immediate data with contents of data memory byte addressed by DADDR
	AND	DADDR, DATA16	81 aa100bbb [DISP][DISP] YYYY	17+EA	0				X	X	U	X	0	[EA] ← [EA] AND DATA16 AND 16-bit immediate data with contents of 16-bit data memory word addressed by DADDR

Table 5-4. A Summary of 8086 and 8088 Instructions (Continued)

Type	Mnemonic	Operand(s)	Object Code	Clock Cycles	O	D	I	T	S	Z	A	P	C	Operation Performed
									Statuses					
Immediate Operate (Continued)	CMP	AL,DATA8	3C YY	4*	X				X	X	X	X	X	[AL] − DATA8 Subtract 8-bit immediate data from AL register contents. Discard result, but adjust status flags
	CMP	AX,DATA16	3D YYYY	4*	X				X	X	X	X	X	[AX] − DATA16 Subtract 16-bit immediate data from AX register contents. Discard result, but adjust status flags
	CMP	RB,DATA8	80 11111ddd YY	4*	X				X	X	X	X	X	[RB] − DATA8 Subtract 8-bit immediate data from RB register contents. Discard result, but adjust status flags
	CMP	RW,DATA16	100000a1 1111ddd YY [YY]	4*	X				X	X	X	X	X	[RW] − DATA16 Subtract 16-bit immediate data from RW register contents. Discard result, but adjust status flags
	CMP	DADDR, DATA8	80 aa111bbb [DISP][DISP] YY	10+EA	X				X	X	X	X	X	[EA] − DATA8 Subtract 8-bit immediate data from contents of data memory byte addressed by DADDR. Discard result, but adjust status flags
	CMP	DADDR, DATA16	100000a1 aa111bbb [DISP][DISP]YY[YY]	10+EA	X				X	X	X	X	X	[EA] − DATA16 Subtract 16-bit immediate data from contents of 16-bit data memory word addressed by DADDR. Discard result, but adjust status flags
	OR	AL,DATA8	0C YY	4*	0				X	X	U	X	0	[AL] ← [AL] OR DATA8 OR 8-bit immediate data with AL register contents
	OR	AX,DATA16	0D YYYY	4*	0				X	X	U	X	0	[AX] ← [AX] OR DATA16 OR 16-bit immediate data with AX register contents
	OR	RB,DATA8	80 11001ddd YY	4*	0				X	X	U	X	0	[RB] ← [RB] OR DATA8 OR 8-bit immediate data with RB register contents
	OR	RW,DATA16	81 11001ddd YYYY	4*	0				X	X	U	X	0	[RW] ← [RW] OR DATA 16 OR 16-bit immediate data with RW register contents
	OR	DADDR, DATA8	80 aa001bbb [DISP][DISP] YY	17+EA	0				X	X	U	X	0	[EA] ← [EA] OR DATA8 OR 8-bit immediate ata with contents of data memory byte addressed by DADDR
	OR	DADDR, DATA16	81 aa001bbb [DISP][DISP] YYYY	17+EA	0				X	X	U	X	0	[EA] ← [EA] OR DATA16 OR 16-bit immediate data with contents of 16-bit data memory word addressed by DADDR
	SBB	AL,DATA8	1C YY	4*	X				X	X	X	X	X	[AL] ← [AL] − DATA8 − [C] Subtract 8-bit immediate signed binary data from AL register contents using twos complement arithmetic. If the Carry status was originally 1 decrement the result
	SBB	AX,DATA16	1D YYYY	4*	X				X	X	X	X	X	[AX] ← [AX] − DATA16 − [C] Subtract 16-bit immediate signed binary data from AX register contents using twos complement arithmetic. If the Carry status was originally 1 decrement the result

Table 5-4. A Summary of 8086 and 8088 Instructions (Continued)

Type	Mnemonic	Operand(s)	Object Code	Clock Cycles	O	D	I	T	S	Z	A	P	C	Operation Performed
Immediate Operate (Continued)	SBB	RB,DATA8	80 11011ddd YY	4*	X				X	X	X	X	X	[RB] ← [RB] – DATA8 – [C] Subtract 8-bit immediate signed binary data from RB register contents using twos complement arithmetic. If the Carry status was originally 1 decrement the result
	SBB	RW,DATA16	100000a1 11011ddd YY [YY]	4*	X				X	X	X	X	X	[RW] ← [RW] – DATA16 – [C] Subtract 16-bit immediate signed binary data from RW register contents using twos complement arithmetic. If the Carry status was originally 1 decrement the result
	SBB	DADDR, DATA8	80 aa011bbb [DISP][DISP] YY	17+EA	X				X	X	X	X	X	[EA] ← [EA] – DATA8 – [C] Subtract 8-bit immediate signed binary data from contents of data memory byte addressed by DADDR using twos complement arithmetic. If the Carry status was originally 1 decrement the result
	SBB	DADDR, DATA16	100000a1 aa011bbb [DISP][DISP]YY [YY]	17+EA	X				X	X	X	X	X	[EA] ← [EA] – DATA16 – [C] Subtract 16-bit immediate signed binary data from contents of 16-bit data memory word addressed by DADDR using twos complement arithmetic. If the Carry status was originally 1 decrement the result
	SUB	AL,DATA8	2C YY	4*	X				X	X	X	X	X	[AL] ← [AL] – DATA8 Subtract the 8-bit immediate signed binary data from AL register contents using twos complement arithmetic
	SUB	AX,DATA16	2D YYYY	4*	X				X	X	X	X	X	[AX] ← [AX] – DATA16 Subtract the 16-bit immediate signed binary data from AX register contents using twos complement arithmetic
	SUB	RB,DATA8	80 11101ddd YY	4*	X				X	X	X	X	X	[RB] ← [RB] – DATA8 Subtract the 8-bit immediate signed binary data from RB register contents using twos complement arithmetic
	SUB	RW,DATA16	81 11101ddd YYYY	4*	X				X	X	X	X	X	[RW] ← [RW] – DATA16 Subtract the 16-bit immediate signed binary data from RW register contents using twos complement arithmetic
	SUB	DADDR, DATA8	80 aa101bbb [DISP][DISP] YY	17+EA	X				X	X	X	X	X	[EA] ← [EA] – DATA8 Subtract the 8-bit immediate signed binary data from the contents of the data memory byte addressed by DADDR using twos complement arithmetic
	SUB	DADDR, DATA16	100000a1 aa101bbb [DISP][DISP]YY [YY]	17+EA	X				X	X	X	X	X	[EA] ← [EA] – DATA16 Subtract the 16-bit immediate signed binary data from the contents of the 16-bit data memory word addressed by DADDR using twos complement arithmetic
	TEST	AL,DATA8	A8 YY	4*	0				X	X	U	X	0	[AL] AND DATA8 AND the 8-bit immediate data and AL register contents. Discard the result but adjust status s

Table 5-4. A Summary of 8086 and 8088 Instructions (Continued)

Type	Mnemonic	Operand(s)	Object Code	Clock Cycles	O	D	I	T	S	Z	A	P	C	Operation Performed
Immediate Operate (Continued)	TEST	AX,DATA16	A9 YYYY	4*	0				X	X	U	X	0	[AX] AND DATA16 AND the 16-bit immediate data and AX register contents. Discard the result but adjust status flags
	TEST	RB,DATA8	F6 11000ddd YY	5*	0				X	X	U	X	0	[RB] AND DATA8 AND the 8-bit immediate data and RB register contents. Discard the result but adjust status flags
	TEST	RW,DATA16	F7 11000ddd YYYY	5*	0				X	X	U	X	0	[RW] AND DATA16 AND the 16-bit immediate data and RW register contents. Discard the result but adjust status flags
	TEST	DADDR, DATA8	F6 aa000bbb [DISP][DISP] YY	11+EA	0				X	X	U	X	0	[EA] AND DATA8 AND the 8-bit immediate data and the contents of the data memory location addressed by DADDR. Discard the result but adjust status flags
	TEST	DADDR, DATA16	F7 aa000bbb [DISP][DISP] YYYY	11+EA	0				X	X	U	X	0	[EA] AND DATA16 AND the 16-bit immediate data and the contents of the 16-bit data memory word addressed by DADDR. Discard the result but adjust status flags
	XOR	AL,DATA8	34 YY	4*	0				X	X	U	X	0	[AL] ← [AL] XOR DATA8 Exclusive OR 8-bit immediate data with AL register contents
	XOR	AX,DATA16	35 YYYY	4*	0				X	X	U	X	0	[AX] ← [AX] XOR DATA16 Exclusive OR 16-bit immediate data with AX register contents
	XOR	RB,DATA8	80 11110ddd YY	4*	0				X	X	U	X	0	[RB] ← [RB] XOR DATA8 Exclusive OR 8-bit immediate data with RB register cortents
	XOR	RW,DATA16	81 11110ddd YYYY	4*	0				X	X	U	X	0	[RW] ← [RW] XOR DATA16 Exclusive OR 16-bit immediate data with RW register contents
	XOR	DADDR, DATA8	80 aa010bbb [DISP][DISP] YY	17+EA	0				X	X	U	X	0	[EA] ← [EA] XOR DATA8 Exclusive OR 8-bit immediate data with contents of the data memory byte addressed by DADDR
	XOR	DADDR, DATA16	81 aa010bbb [DISP][DISP] YYYY	17+EA	0				X	X	U	X	0	[EA] ← [EA] XOR DATA16 Exclusive OR 16-bit immediate data with contents of the 16-bit data memory word addressed by DADDR
Branch On Condition	LOOP	DISP8	E2 DISP	5 or 17**										[CX] ← [CX] −1 If [CX] ≠ 0 then [PC] ← [PC] + DISP8 Decrement CX register and branch if CX contents are not 0
	LOOPE	DISP8	E1 DISP	6 or 18**										[CX] ← [CX] −1 If [CX] ≠ 0 and [Z] = 1 then [PC] + DISP8 Decrement CX register and branch if CX contents is not 0 and Z status is 1
	LOOPNE	DISP8	E0 DISP	5 or 19**										[CX] ← [CX] −1 If [CX] ≠ 0 and [Z] = 0 then [PC] ← [PC] + DISP8 Decrement CX register and branch if CX contents is not 0 and Z status is 0
	LOOPNZ LOOPZ	DISP8 DISP8												See LOOPNE See LOOPE
	JA	DISP8	77 DISP	4 or 16**										[PC] ← [PC] + DISP8 Branch if C or Z is 0

Table 5-4. A Summary of 8086 and 8088 Instructions (Continued)

Type	Mnemonic	Operand(s)	Object Code	Clock Cycles	O	D	I	T	S	Z	A	P	C	Operation Performed
Branch On Condition (Continued)	JAE	DISP8	73 DISP	4 or 16**										[PC] ← [PC] + DISP8 Branch if C is 0
	JB	DISP8	72 DISP	4 or 16**										[PC] ← [PC] + DISP8 Branch if C is 1
	JBE	DISP8	76 DISP	4 or 16**										[PC] ← [PC] + DISP8 Branch if C or Z is 1
	JCXZ	DISP8	E3 DISP	6 or 18**										[PC] ← [PC] + DISP8 Branch if the CX register contents is 0
	JE	DISP8	74 DISP	4 or 16**										[PC] ← [PC] + DISP8 Branch if Z is 1
	JG	DISP8	7F DISP	4 or 16**										[PC] ← [PC] + DISP8 Branch if Z is 0 or the S and O statuses are the same
	JGE	DISP8	7D DISP	4 or 16**										[PC] ← [PC] + DISP8 Branch if the S and O statuses are the same
	JL	DISP8	7C DISP	4 or 16**										[PC] ← [PC] + DISP8 Branch if the S and O statuses differ
	JLE	DISP8	7E DISP	4 or 16**										[PC] ← [PC] + DISP8 Branch if Z is 1 or the S and O statuses differ
	JNA	DISP8												See JBE
	JNAE	DISP8												See JB
	JNB	DISP8												See JAE
	JNBE	DISP8												See JA
	JNE	DISP8	75 DISP	4 or 16**										[PC] ← [PC] + DISP8 Branch if Z is 0
	JNG	DISP8												See JLE
	JNGE	DISP8												See JL
	JNL	DISP8												See JGE
	jnle	disp8												See JG
	JNO	DISP8	71 DISP	4 or 16**										[PC] ← [PC] + DISP8 Branch if O is 0
	JNP	DISP8	7B DISP	4 or 16**										[PC] ← [PC] + DISP8 Branch if P is 0
	JNS	DISP8	79 DISP	4 or 16**										[PC] ← [PC] + DISP8 Branch if S is 0
	JNZ	DISP8												See JNE
	JO	DISP8	70 DISP	4 or 16**										[PC] ← [PC] + DISP8 Branch if O is 1
	JP	DISP8	7A DISP	4 or 16**										[PC] ← [PC] + DISP8 Branch if P is 1
	JPE	DISP8												See JP

Table 5-4. A Summary of 8086 and 8088 Instructions (Continued)

Type	Mnemonic	Operand(s)	Object Code	Clock Cycles	O	D	I	T	S	Z	A	P	C	Operation Performed
BOC (Cont.)	JPO	DISP8												See JNP
	JS	DISP8	78DISP	4 or 16**										[PC] ← [PC] + DISP8 Branch if S is 1
	JZ	DISP8												See JE
Register — Register Move	MOV	RBD,RBS	8A11dddsss	2*										[RBD] ← [RBS] Move the contents of any RB register to any RB register
	MOV	RWD,RWS	8B 11dddsss	2*										[RWD] ← [RWS] Move the contents of any RW register to any RW register
	MOV	SR,RW	8E 110rrsss	2*										[SR] ← [RWS] Move the contents of any RW register to any Segment register
	MOV	RW,SR	8C 110rrddd	2*										[RWD] ← [SR] Move the contents of any Segment register to any RW register
	XCHG	AX,RW	10010reg	3*										[AX] ←→ [RW] Exchange the contents of AX and any RW register
	XCHG	RB,RB	86 11regreg	4*										[RB] ←→ [RB] Exchange the contents of any two RB registers
	XCHG	RW,RW	87 11regreg	4*										[RW] ←→ [RW] Exchange the contents of any two RW registers
Block Transfer and Search	CMPS	BD,BS	A6	22	X	I/D			X	X	X	X	X	[[SI]] − [[DI]], [SI] ← [SI] ± 1, [DI] ← [DI] ± 1 Compare the data bytes addressed by the SI and DI Index registers using string data addressing*
	CMPS	WD,WS	A7	22	X	I/D			X	X	X	X	X	[[SI]] − [[DI]], [SI] ← [SI] ± 2, [DI] ← [DI] ± 2 Compare the 16-bit data words addressed by the SI and DI Index registers using string data addressing*
	LODS	BD,BS	AC	12		I/D								[AL] ← [[SI]], [SI] ← [SI] ± 1 Move a data byte from the location addressed by the SI Index register to the AL register using string data addressing
	LODS	WD,WS	AD	12		I/D								[AX] ← [[SI]], [SI] ← [SI] ± 1 Move a data word from the 16-bit location addressed by the SI Index register to the AX register using string data addressing
	MOVS	BD,BS	A4	18		I/D								[[DI]] ← [[SI]], [SI] ← [SI] ± 1, [DI] ← [DI] ± 1 Move a data byte from the location addressed by the SI Index register to the extra segment location addressed by the DI register using string data addressing*
	MOVS	WD,WS	A5	18		I/D								[[DI]] ← [[SI]], [SI] ← [SI] ± 2, [DI] ← [DI] ± 2 Move a 16-bit data word from the location addressed by the SI Index register to the extra segment location addressed by the DI register using string data addressing*

* For these instructions, the default destination segment register cannot be overriden.

5-75

Table 5-4. A Summary of 8086 and 8088 Instructions (Continued)

Type	Mnemonic	Operand(s)	Object Code	Clock Cycles	O	D	I	T	S	Z	A	P	C	Operation Performed
Block Transfer and Search (Continued)	REP	N	1111001z	+2 per loop		I/D								Repeat the next sequential instruction (which must be a Block Transfer and Search instruction) until CX contents decrements to 0. Decrement CX contents on each repeat. If the next instruction is CMPB, CMPW, SCAB, or SCAW then repeat until CX contents decrements to 0 or Z status does not equal N
	SCAS	BD,BS	AE	15	X	I/D			X	X	X	X	X	[AL] − [[DI]], [DI] ← [DI] ± 1 Compare AL register contents with the extra segment data byte addressed by the DI Index register using string data addressing
	SCAS	WD,WS	AF	15	X	I/D			X	X	X	X	X	[AX] − [[DI]], [DI] ← [DI] ± 2 Compare AX register contents with the extra segment 16-bit data ord addressed by the DI Index register using string data addressing
	STOS	BD,BS	AA	11	X	I/D								[[DI]] ← [AL], [DI] ← [DI] ± 1 Store the AL register contents in the extra segment data memory byte addressed by the DI Index register using string data addressing
	STOS	WD,WS	AB	11	X	I/D								[[DI]] ← [AX], [DI] ← [DI] ± 2 Store the AX register contents in the extra segment 16-bit data memory word addressed by the DI Index register using string data addressing
Register - Register Operate	ADC	RBD,RBS	12 11dddsss	3*	X				X	X	X	X	X	[RBD] ← [RBD] + [RBS] + [C] Add the 8-bit contents of register RBS, plus the Carry status, to register RBD
	ADC	RWD,RWS	13 11dddsss	3*	X				X	X	X	X	X	[RWD] ← [RWD] + [RWS] + [C] Add the 16-bit contents of register RWS, plus the Carry status, to register RWD
	ADD	RBD,RBS	02 11dddsss	3*	X				X	X	X	X	X	[RBD] ← [RBD] + [RBS] Add the 8-bit contents of register RBS to register RBD
	ADD	RWD,RWS	03 11dddsss	3*	X				X	X	X	X	X	[RWD] ← [RWD] + [RWS] Add the 16-bit contents of register RWS to register RWD
	AND	RBD,RBS	22 11dddsss	3*	0				X	X	U	X	0	[RBD] ← [RBD] AND [RBS] AND the 8-bit contents of register RBS with register RBD
	AND	RWD,RWS	23 11dddsss	3*	0				X	X	U	X	0	[RWD] ← [RWD] AND [RWS] AND the 16-bit contents of register RWS with register RWD
	CBW		98	2*										[AH] ← [AL7] Extend AL sign bit into AH
	CMP	RBD,RBS	3A 11dddsss	3*	X				X	X	X	X	X	[RBD] − [RBS] Subtract the contents of register RBD from register RBS. Discard the result, but adjust status flags
	CMP	RWD,RWS	3B 11dddsss	3*	X				X	X	X	X	X	[RWD] − [RWS] Subtract the contents of register RWD from register RWS. Discard the result, but adjust status flags
	CWD		99	5										[DX] ← [AX15] Extend AX sign bit into DX

Table 5-4. A Summary of 8086 and 8088 Instructions (Continued)

Type	Mnemonic	Operand(s)	Object Code	Clock Cycles	O	D	I	T	S	Z	A	P	C	Operation Performed
Register — Register Operate (Continued)	DIV	RBS	F6 11110sss	80-90	U				U	U	U	U	U	[AX] ← [AX]/[RBS] Divide the 16-bit contents of AX by the 8-bit contents of RBS. Store the integer quotient in AL and the remainder in AH. If the quotient is greater than FF_{16}, execute a "divide by 0" interrupt
	DIV	RWS	F7 11110sss	144-162	U				U	U	U	U	U	[DX] [AX] ← [DX] [AX]/[RWS] Divide the 32-bit contents of registers DX (high-order) and AX (low-order) by the 16-bit contents of RWS. Store the integer quotient in AX and the remainder in DX. If the quotient is greater than $FFFF_{16}$, execute a "divide by 0" interrupt
	IDIV	RBS	F6 11111sss	101-112	U				U	U	U	U	U	[AX] ← [AX]/[RBS] Divide the 16-bit contents of register AX by the 8-bit contents of RBS, treating both contents as signed binary numbers. Store the quotient, as a signed binary number, in AL. Store the remainder, as an unsigned binary number, in AH. If the quotient is greater than $7F_{16}$, or less than -80_{16}, execute a "divide by 0" interrupt
	IDIV	RWS	F7 11111sss	165-184	U				U	U	U	U	U	[DX] [AX] ← [DX] [AX]/[RWS] Divide the 32-bit contents of register DX (high-order) and AX (low-order) by the 16-bit contents of RWS. Treat both contents as signed binary numbers. Store the quotient, as a signed binary number, in AX. Store the remainder, as an unsigned binary number, in AH. If the quotient is greater than $7FFF_{16}$, or less than -8000_{16}, execute a "divide by 0" interrupt
	IMUL	RBS	F6 11101sss	80-98	X				U	U	U	U	X	[AX] ← [AL] • [RBS] Multiply the 8-bit contents of register AL by the contents of RBS. Treat both numbers as signed binary numbers. Store the 16-bit product in AX
	IMUL	RWS	F7 11101sss	128-154	X				U	U	U	U	X	[DX] [AX] ← [AX] • [RWS] Multiply the 16-bit contents of register AX by the 16-bit contents of RWS. Treat both numbers as signed binary numbers. Store the 32-bit product in DX (high-order word) and AX (low-order word)
	MUL	RBS	F6 11100sss	70-77	X				U	U	U	U	X	[AX] ← [AL] • [RBS] Multiply the 8-bit contents of register AL by the contents of RBS. Treat both numbers as unsigned binary numbers. Store the 16-bit product in AX
	MUL	RWS	F7 11100sss	118-133	X				U	U	U	U	X	[DX] [AX] ← [AX] • [RWS] Multiply the 16-bit contents of register AX by the 16-bit contents of RWS. Treat both numbers as unsigned binary numbers. Store the 32-bit product in DX (high-order word) and AX (low-order word)
	OR	RBD,RBS	0A 11dddsss	3*	0				X	X	U	X	0	[RBD] ← [RBD] OR [RBS] OR the 8-bit contents of register RBS with register RBD
	OR	RWD,RWS	0B 11dddsss	3*	0				X	X	U	X	0	[RWD] ← [RWD] OR [RWS] OR the 16-bit contents of register RWS with register RWD

Table 5-4. A Summary of 8086 and 8088 Instructions (Continued)

Type	Mnemonic	Operand(s)	Object Code	Clock Cycles	O	D	I	T	S	Z	A	P	C	Operation Performed
Register – Register Operate (Continued)	SBB	RBD,RBS	1A 11dddsss	3*	X				X	X	X	X	X	[RBD] ← [RBD] – [RBS] – [C] Subtract the 8-bit contents of register RBS from RBD using twos complement arithmetic. If the Carry status was originally 1 decrement the result
	SBB	RWD,RWS	1B 11dddsss	3*	X				X	X	X	X	X	[RWD] ← [RWD] – [RWS] – [C] Subtract the 16-bit contents of register RWS from RWD using twos complement arithmetic. If the Carry status was originally 1 decrement the result
	SUB	RBD,RBS	2A 11dddsss	3*	X				X	X	X	X	X	[RBD] ← [RBD] – [RBS] Subtract the 8-bit contents of register RBS from RBD using twos complement arithmetic
	SUB	RWD,RWS	2B 11dddsss	3*	X				X	X	X	X	X	[RWD] ← [RWD] – [RWS] Subtract the 16-bit contents of register RWS from RWD using twos complement arithmetic
	TEST	RBD,RBS	84 11regreg	3*	0				X	X	U	X	0	[RBD] AND [RBS] AND the 8-bit contents of register d and register RBS. Discard the result, but adjust status flags
	TEST	RWD,RWS	85 11regreg	3*	0				X	X	U	X	0	[RWD] AND [RWS] AND the 16-bit contents of register RWD and register RWS. Discard the result, but adjust status flags
	XOR	RBD,RBS	30 11dddsss	3*	0				X	X	U	X	0	[RBD] ← [RBD] XOR [RBS] Exclusive OR the 8-bit contents of register RBS with register RBD
	XOR	RWD,RWS	31 11dddsss	3*	0				X	X	U	X	0	[RWD] ← [RWD] XOR [RWS] Exclusive OR the 16-bit contents of register RWS with register RWD
Register Operate	AAA		37	4*	U				U	U	X	U	X	ASCII adjust Al register contents for addition (as described in accompanying text)
	AAD		D5 0A	60	U				X	X	U	X	U	Decimal adjust dividend in AL prior to dividing an unpacked decimal divisor, to generate an unpacked decimal quotient. (See accompanying text for details)
	AAM		D4 0A	83	U				X	X	U	X	U	After multiplying o unpacked decimal operands, adjust product in AX to become an unpacked decimal result. (See accompanying text for details)
	AAS		3F	4*	U				U	U	X	U	X	After subtracting two unpacked decimal numbers, adjust the difference in AL so that it too is an unpacked decimal number. (See accompanying text for details)
	DAA		27	4*	U				X	X	X	X	X	After adding two packed decimal numbers, adjust the sum in AL so that it too is a packed decimal number. (See accompanying text for details)
	DAS		2F	4*	U				X	X	X	X	X	After subtracting two packed decimal numbers, adjust the difference in AL so that it too is a packed decimal number. (See accompanying text for details)
	DEC	RB	FE 11001ddd	3*	X				X	X	X	X		[RB] ← [RB] –1 Decrement the 8-bit contents of register RB
	DEC	RW	01001ddd	2*	X				X	X	X	X		[RW] ← [RW] –1 Decrement the 16-bit contents of register RW

Table 5-4. A Summary of 8086 and 8088 Instructions (Continued)

Type	Mnemonic	Operand(s)	Object Code	Clock Cycles	O	D	I	T	S	Z	A	P	C	Operation Performed
Register Operate (Continued)	INC	RB	FE 11000ddd	3*	X				X	X	X	X		[RB] ← [RB] + 1 Increment the 8-bit contents of register RB
	INC	RW	01000ddd	2*	X				X	X	X	X		[RW] ← [RW] + 1 Increment the 16-bit contents of register RW
	NEG	RB	F6 11011ddd	3*	X				X	X	X	X	X	[RB] ← [RB] + 1 Twos complement the 8-bit contents of register RB
	NEG	RW	F7 11011ddd	3*	X				X	X	X	X	X	[RW] ← [RW] + 1 Twos complement the 16-bit contents of register RW
	NOT	RB	F6 11010ddd	3*										[RB] ← [RB] Ones complement the 8-bit contents of register RB
	NOT	RW	F7 11010ddd	3*										[RW] ← [RW] Ones complement the 16-bit contents of register RW
	RCL	RB,N	110100v0 11010ddd		X								X	Rotate left through Carry the 8-bit contents of RB register, or the 16-bit contents of RW register, as illustrated for memory operate
	RCL	RW,N	110100v1 11010ddd		X								X	
	RCR	RBN	110100v0 11011ddd		X								X	Rotate right through Carry the 8-bit contents of RB register, or the 16-bit contents of RW register, as illustrated for memory operate
	RCR	RW,N	110100v1 11011ddd		X								X	
	ROL	RB,N	110100v0 11000ddd	N=1 2* N>1 4N+8	X								X	Rotate left the 8-bit contents of RB register, or the 16-bit contents of RW register as illustrated for memory operate
	ROL	RW,N	110100v1 11000ddd		X								X	
	ROR	RB,N	110100v0 11001ddd		X								X	Rotate right the 8-bit contents of RB register, or the 16-bit contents of RW register, as illustrated for memory operate
	ROR	RW,N	110100v1 11001ddd		X								X	
	SAL	RB,N	110100v0 11100ddd		X				X	U	U	X	X	Shift left the 8-bit contents of RB register, or the 16-bit contents of RW register, as illustrated for memory operate
	SAL	RW,N	110100v1 11100ddd		X				X	U	U	X	X	
	SAR	RB,N	110100v0 11111ddd		X				X	U	U	X	X	Shift right the 8-bit contents of register RB, or the 16-bit contents of register RW, as illustrated for memory operate
	SAR	RW,N	110100v1 11111ddd		X				X	U	U	X	X	
	SHL	RB,N			X				X	U	U	X	X	See SAL
	SHL	RW,N			X				X	U	U	X	X	See SAL
	SHR	RB,N	110100v0 11101ddd	N=1 2* N>1 4N+8	X				X	U	U	X	X	Shift right the 8-bit contents of register RB, or the 16-bit contents of register RW, as illustrated for memory operate
	SHR	RW,N	110100v1 11101ddd		X				X	U	U	X	X	
Stack	POP	DADDR	8F aa000bbb [DISP][DISP]	17+EA										[EA] ← [[SP]], [SP] ← [SP] + 2 Load the 16-bit Stack word, addressed using Stack addressing, into the 16-bit data memory word addressed by DADDR. Increment SP by 2
	POP	RW	01011ddd	8										[RW or SR] ← [[SP]], [SP] ← [SP] + 2 Load the 16-bit Stack word, addressed using Stack addressing, into the specified 16-bit register. Increment SP by 2.
	POP	SR	000rr111	8										
	POPF		9D	8	X	X	X	X	X	X	X	X	X	[SFR] ← [[SP]], [SP] ← [SP] + 2 Load the 16-bit Stack word, addressed using Stack addressing, into the Status Flags register
	PUSH	DADDR	FF aa110bbb [DISP][DISP]	16+EA										[SP] ← [SP] − 2, [[SP]] ← [EA] Store the 16-bit contents of the data memory word addressed by DADDR in the 16-bit Stack word addressed using Stack addressing. Decrement SP by 2

Table 5-4. A Summary of 8086 and 8088 Instructions (Continued)

Type	Mnemonic	Operand(s)	Object Code	Clock Cycles	O	D	I	T	S	Z	A	P	C	Operation Performed
Stack (Cont.)	PUSH	RW	01010rrr	11										[SP] ← [SP] −2, [[SP]] ← [RW or SR] Store the contents of the specified 16-bit register in the 16-bit Stack word addressed using Stack addressing. Decrement SP by 2
	PUSH	SR	000rr110	10										
	PUSHF	9C	10											[SP] ← [SP] +2, [[SP]] ← [SFR] Store the Status flags register contents in the 16-bit Stack word addressed using Stack addressing. Decrement SP by 2
Interrupts	INT	3	CC	52		0	0							Execute a software interrupt and vector through table entry 3
	INT	V	CD YY	51		0	0							Execute a software interrupt and vector through table entry V
	INTO		CE	4 or 53		0	0							If the O status is 1, execute a software interrupt and vector through table entry 10_{16}
	IRET		CF	24										Return from interrupt service routine
Status	CLC		F8	2*									0	[C] ← 0 Clear Carry status
	CLD		FC	2*		0								[D] ← 0 Clear Decrement/Increment select
	CLI		FA	2*			0							[I] ← 0 Clear Interrupt enable status, disabling all interrupts
	CMC		F5	2*									X	Complement Carry status [C] ← [C̄]
	LAHF		9F	4*										Transfer flags to AH register as follows: Bit no. 7 6 5 4 3 2 1 0 / AH register / S Z O A O P I C
	SAHF		9E	4*					X	X	X	X	X	Transfer AH register contents to status flags as follows: Bit no. 7 6 5 4 3 2 1 0 / AH register / S Z A P C
	STC		F9	2*									1	[C] ← 1 Set Carry status to 1
	STD		FD	2*		1								[D] ← 1 Set Decrement/Increment status to 1
	STI		FB	2*			1							[I] ← 1 Set interrupt enable status to 1, enabling all interrupts

Table 5-4. A Summary of 8086 and 8088 Instructions (Continued)

Type	Mnemonic	Operand(s)	Object Code	Clock Cycles	Statuses									Operation Performed
					O	D	I	T	S	Z	A	P	C	
Other	ESC	DADDR	11011xxx aaxxbbb [DISP][DISP]	8+EA										? ← [EA] The contents of the data memory location addressed by DADDR is read out of memory and placed on the data bus; however, it is not input to the CPU
	HLT		F4	2*										CPU Halt
	LOCK		F0	2*										Guarantee the CPU bus control during execution of the next sequential instruction
	SEG	SR	001reg110	+ 2										The next sequential allowed memory reference instruction accesses the segment identified by Segment register SR. See Table 20-1 for allowed memory reference instructions
	WAIT		9B	3+5n										CPU enters the WAIT state until TEST pin receives a high input signal
	NOP		90	3*										No operation (This is the same object code as XCHG, AX, AX.)

Table 5-5. 8086 and 8088 Instruction Mnemonics

Instruction		Object Code	Bytes	Clock Periods
AAA		37	1	4*
AAD		D5 0A	2	60
AAM		D4 0A	2	83
AAS		3F	1	4*
ADC	AL,DATA8	14 YY	2	4*
ADC	AX,DATA16	15 YYYY	3	4*
ADC	DADDR,DATA8	80 aa010bbb [DISP] [DISP] YY	3, 4 or 5	17+EA
ADC	DADDR,DATA16	100000a1 aa010bbb [DISP] [DISP] YY[YY]	3, 4, 5 or 6	17+EA
ADC	DADDR,RB	10 aasssbbb [DISP] [DISP]	2, 3, or 4	16+EA
ADC	DADDR,RW	11 aasssbbb [DISP] [DISP]	2, 3 or 4	16+EA
ADC	RB,DADDR	12 aadddbbb [DISP] [DISP]	2, 3 or 4	9+EA
ADC	RB,DATA8	80 11010ddd YY	3	4*
ADC	RBD,RBS	12 11dddsss	2	3*
ADC	RW,DADDR	13 aadddbbb [DISP] [DISP]	2, 3 or 4	9+EA
ADC	RW,DATA16	100000a1 11010ddd YY[YY]	3 or 4	4*
ADC	RWD,RWS	13 11dddsss	2	3*
ADD	AL,DATA8	04 YY	2	4*
ADD	AX,DATA16	05 YYYY	3	4*
ADD	DADDR,DATA8	80 aa000bbb [DISP] [DISP] YY	3, 4 or 5	17+EA
ADD	DADDR,DATA16	100000a1 aa000bbb [DISP] [DISP] YY[YY]	3, 4, 5 or 6	17+EA
ADD	DADDR,RB	00 aasssbbb [DISP] [DISP]	2, 3 or 4	16+EA
ADD	DADDR,RW	01 aasssbbb [DISP] [DISP]	2, 3 or 4	16+EA
ADD	RB,DADDR	02 aadddbbb [DISP] [DISP]	2, 3 or 4	9+EA
ADD	RB,DATA8	80 11000ddd YY	3	4*
ADD	RBD,RBS	02 11dddsss	2	3*
ADD	RW,DADDR	03 aadddbbb [DISP] [DISP]	2, 3 or 4	9+EA
ADD	RW,DATA16	100000a1 11000ddd YY[YY]	3 or 4	4*
ADD	RWD,RWS	03 11dddsss	2	3*
AND	AL,DATA8	24 YY	2	4*
AND	AX,DATA16	25 YYYY	3	4*
AND	DADDR,DATA8	80 aa100bbb [DISP] [DISP] YY	3, 4 or 5	17+EA
AND	DADDR,DATA16	81 aa100bbb [DISP] [DISP] YYYY]	4, 5 or 6	17+EA
AND	DADDR,RB	20 aasssbbb [DISP] [DISP]	2, 3 or 4	16+EA
AND	DADDR,RW	21 aasssbbb [DISP] [DISP]	2, 3 or 4	16+EA
AND	RB,DADDR	22 aadddbbb [DISP] [DISP]	2, 3 or 4	9+EA
AND	RB,DATA8	80 111000dddYY	3	4*
AND	RBD,RBS	22 11dddsss	23*	

Table 5-5. 8086 and 8088 Instruction Mnemonics (Continued)

Instruction		Object Code	Bytes	Clock Periods
AND	RW,DADDR	23 aadddbbb [DISP] [DISP]	2, 3 or 4	9+EA
AND	RW,DATA16	81 11100sss YYYY	4	4*
AND	RWD,RWS	23 11dddsss	2	3*
CALL	BRANCH	E8 DISP DISP	3	19**
CALL	BRANCH,SEGM	9A PPQQPPQQ	5	28**
CALL	DADDR	FF aa010bbb [DISP] [DISP]	2, 3 or 4	21+EA
CALL	DADDR,CS	FF aa011bbb [DISP] [DISP]	2, 3 or 4	37+EA**
CALL	RW	FF 11010reg	2	16**
CBW		98	1	2
CLC		F8	1	2*
CLD		FC	1	2*
CLI		FA	1	2*
CMC		F5	1	2*
CMP	AL,DATA8	3C YY	2	4*
CMP	AX,DATA16	3D YYYY	3	4*
CMP	DADDR,DATA8	80 aa111bbb [DISP] [DISP] YY	3, 4 or 5	10+EA
CMP	DADDR,DATA16	100000a1 aa11bbb [DISP] [DISP] YY[YY]	3, 4, 5 or 6	10+EA
CMP	DADDR,RB	38 aasssbbb [DISP] [DISP]	2, 3 or 4	9+EA
CMP	DADDR,RW	39 aasssbbb [DISP] [DISP]	2, 3 or 4	9+EA
CMP	RB,DADDR	3A aadddbbb [DISP] [DISP]	2, 3 or 4	9+EA
CMP	RB,DATA8	80 11111ddd YY	3	4*
CMP	RBD,RBS	3A 11dddsss	2	3*
CMP	RW,DADDR	3B aadddbbb [DISP] [DISP]	2, 3 or 4	9+EA
CMP	RW,DATA16	100000a1 11111ddd YY[YY]	3 or 4	4*
CMP	RWD,RWS	3B 11dddsss	2	3*
CMPS	BD,BS	A6	1	22
CMPS	WD,WS	A7	1	22
CWD		99	1	5
DAA		27	1	4*
DAS		2F	1	4*
DEC	DADDR	1111 111aa aa001bbb [DISP] [DISP]	2, 3 or 4	15+EA
DEC	RB	FE 11001ddd	2	3*
DEC	RW	01001ddd	1	2*
DIV (8-bit)	AX,DADDR	F6 aa110bbb [DISP] [DISP]	2, 3 or 4	(86-96)+EA
DIV (16-bit)	DX,DADDR	F7 aa110bbb [DISP] [DISP]	2, 3 or 4	(150-168)+EA
DIV	RBS	F6 11110sss	2	80-90
DIV	RWS	F7 11110sss	2	144-162
ESC	DADDR	11011xxx aaxxxbbb [DISP] [DISP]	2, 3 or 4	8+EA
ESC	RW	11011xxx 11xxxreg	2	2
HLT		F4	1	2*

Table 5-5. 8086 and 8088 Instruction Mnemonics (Continued)

Instruction		Object Code	Bytes	Clock Periods
IDIV	AX,DADDR	F6 aa111bbb [DISP] [DISP]	2, 3 or 4	(107-118)+EA
IDIV	DX,DADDR	F7 aa111bbb [DISP] [DISP]	2, 3 or 4	(171-190)+EA
IDIV	RBS	F6 11111sss	2	101-112
IDIV	RWS	F7 11111sss	2	165-184
IMUL	AL,DADDR	F6 aa101bbb [DISP] [DISP]	2, 3 or 4	(86-104)+EA
IMUL	AX,DADDR	F7 aa101bbb [DISP] [DISP]	2, 3 or 4	(134-160)+EA
IMUL	RBS	F6 11101sss	2	80-98
IMUL	RWS	F7 11101sss	2	128-154
IN	AL[DX]	EC	1	8
IN	AL,PORT	E4 YY	2	10
IN	AX,[DX]	ED	1	8
IN	AX,PORT	E5 YY	2	10
INC	DADDR	1111111a aa000bbb [DISP] [DISP]	2, 3 or 4	15+EA
INC	RB	FE 11000ddd	2	3*
INC	RW	01000ddd	1	2*
INT	3	CC	1	52
INT	V	CD YY	2	51
INTO		CE	1	4 or 53
IRET		CF	1	24
JA/JNBE	DISP8	77 DISP	2	4 or 16**
JAE/JNB	DISP8	73 DISP	2	4 or 16**
JB/JNAE	DISP8	72 DISP	2	4 or 16**
JBE/JNA	DISP8	76 DISP	2	4 or 16**
JCXZ	DISP8	63 DISP	2	6 or 18**
JE/JZ	DISP8	74 DISP	2	4 or 16**
JG/JNLE	DISP8	7F DISP	2	4 or 16**
JGE/JNL	DISP8	7D DISP	2	4 or 16**
JL/JNGE	DISP8	7C DISP	2	4 or 16**
JLE/JNG	DISP8	7E DISP	2	4 or 16**
JMP	BRANCH	111010a 1 DISP [DISP]	2 or 3	15**
JMP	BRANCH,SEGM	EA PPQQ PPQQ	5	15**
JMP	DADDR	FF aa100bbb [DISP] [DISP]	2, 3 or 4	18+EA
JMP	DADDR,CS	FF aa101bbb [DISP] [DISP]	2 3 or 4	24+EA
JMP	RW	FF 11100reg	2	11
JNE/JNZ	DISP8	75 DISP	2	4 or 16**
JNO	DISP8	71 DISP	2	4 or 16**
JNP/JPO	DISP8	68 DISP	2	4 or 16**
JNS	DISP8	79 DISP	2	4 or 16**
JO	DISP8	70 DISP	2	4 or 16**
JP/JPE	DISP8	7A DISP	2	4 or 16**
JS	DISP8	78 DISP	2	4 or 16**
LAHF		9F	1	4*
LDS	RW,DADDR	C5 aadddbbb [DISP] [DISP]	2, 3 or 4	16+EA
LEA	RW,DADDR	8D aadddbbb [DISP] [DISP]	2, 3 or 4	2+EA
LES	RW,DADDR	C4 aadddbbb [DISP] [DISP]	2, 3 or 4	4 or 16**
LOCK		F0	1	2*

Table 5-5. 8086 and 8088 Instruction Mnemonics (Continued)

Instruction		Object Code	Bytes	Clock Periods
LODS	BS	AC	1	12
LODS	WS	AD	1	12
LOOP	DISP8	E2 DISP	2	5 or 17**
LOOPE/LOOPZ	DISP8	E1 DISP	2	6 or 18**
LOOPNE/LOOPNZ	DISP8	E0 DISP	2	5 or 19**
MOV	AL,LABEL	A0 PPQQ	3	10
MOV	AX,LABEL	A1 PPQQ	3	10
MOV	DADDR,DATA8	C6 aa000bbb [DISP] [DISP] YY	3, 4 or 5	10+EA
MOV	DADDR,DATA16	C7 aa000bbb [DISP] [DISP] YYYY	4, 5 or 6	10+EA
MOV	DADDR,RB	88 aasssbbb [DISP] [DISP]	2, 3 or 4	9+EA
MOV	DADDR,RW	89 aasssbbb [DISP] [DISP]	2, 3 or 4	9+EA
MOV	DADDR,SR	8C aa0rrbbb [DISP] [DISP]	2, 3 or 4	9+EA
MOV	LABEL,AL	A2 PPQQ	3	10
MOV	LABEL,AX	A 3 PPQQ	3	10
MOV	RB,DADDR	8A aadddbbb [DISP] [DISP]	2, 3 or 4	8+EA
MOV	RB,DATA8	10110ddd YY	2	4*
MOV	RBD,RBS	8A 11dddsss	2	2*
MOV	RW,DADDR	8B aadddbbb [DISP] [DISP]	2, 3 or 4	8+EA
MOV	RW,DATA16	10111ddd YYYY	3	4*
MOV	RW,SR	8C 110rrsss	2	*
MOV	RWD,RWS	8B 11dddsss	2	*
MOV	SR,DADDR	8E aa0rrbbb [DISP] [DISP]	2, 3 or 4	8+EA
MOV	SR,RW	8E 110rrsss	2	*
MOVS	BD,BS	A4	1	18
MOVS	WD,WS	A5	1	18
MUL (8-bit)	AL,DADDR	F6 aa100bbb [DISP] [DISP]	2, 3 or 4	(76-83)+EA
MUL (16-bit)	AX,DADDR	F7 aa100bbb [DISP] [DISP]	2, 3 or 4	(124-139)+EA
MUL	RBS	F6 11100sss	2	70-77
MUL	RWS	F7 11100	2	118-133
NEG	DADDR	1111011a aa011bbb [DISP] [DISP]	2, 3 or 4	16+EA
NEG	RB	F5 11011ddd	2	3*
NEG	RW	F7 11011ddd	2	3*
NOP		90	1	3*
NOT	DADDR	1111011a aa010bbb [DISP] [DISP]	2, 3 or 4	16+EA
NOT	RB	F6 11010sss	2	3*
NOT	RW	F7 11010sss	2	3*
OR	AL,DATA8	0C YY	2	4*
OR	AX,DATA16	0D YYYY	3	4*
OR	DADDR,DATA8	80 aa001bbb [DISP] [DISP] YY	3, 4 or 5	17+EA
OR	DADDR,DATA16	81 aa001bbb [DISP] [DISP] YYYY	4, 5 or 6	17+EA

Table 5-5. 8086 and 8088 Instruction Mnemonics (Continued)

Instruction		Object Code	Bytes	Clock Periods
OR	DADDR,RB	08 aasssbbb [DISP] [DISP]	2, 3 or 4	16+EA
OR	DADDR,RW	09 aasssbbb	2, 3 or 4	16+EA
OR	RB,DADDR	0A aadddbbb [DISP] [DISP]	2, 3 or 4	9+EA
OR	RB,DATA8	80 11001ddd YY	3	4*
OR	RBD,RBS	0A 11dddsss	2	3*
OR	RW,DADDR	0B aadddbbb [DISP] [DISP]	2, 3 or 4	9+EA
OR	RW,DATA16	81 11001ddd YYYY	4	4*
OR	RWD,RWS	0B 11dddsss	2	3*
OUT	AL,[DX]	EE	1	8
OUT	AL,PORT	E6 YY	2	10
OUT	AX,[DX]	EF	1	8
OUT	AX,PORT	E7 YY	2	10
POP	DADDR	8F aa000bbb [DISP] [DISP]	2, 3 or 4	17+EA
POP	RW	01011ddd	1	8
POP	SR	000rr111	1	8
POPF		9D	1	8
PUSH	DADDR	FF aa110bbb [DISP] [DISP]	2, 3 or 4	16+EA
PUSH	RW	01010sss	1	11
PUSH	SR	000rr110	1	10
PUSHF		9C	1	10
RCL	DADDR,N	110100va aa010bbb [DISP] [DISP]	2, 3 or 4	N=1 15+EA N> 4N+20+EA
RCL	RB,N	110100v0 11010sss	2	N=1 2* N>1 4N+8
RCL	RW,N	110100v1 11010sss	2	
RCR	DADDR,N	110100va aa011bbb [DISP] [DISP]	2, 3 or 4	N=1 15+EA N> 4N+20+EA
RCR	RB,N	110100v0 11011sss	2	N=1 2* N>1 4N+8
REP	N	1111001z	1	+2
RET		C3	1	8**
RET	CS	CB	1	12**
RET	CS,DATA16	CA YYYY	3	18**
RET	DATA16	C2 YYYY	3	17**
ROL	DADDR,N	110100va aa000bbb [DISP] [DISP]	2, 3 or 4	N=1 15+EA N>1 4N+20+EA
ROL	RB,N	110100v0 11000ddd	2	N=1 2* N>4N + 8
ROL	RW,N	110100v1 11000ddd	2	
ROR	DADDR,N	110100va aa001bbb [DISP] [DISP]	2, 3 or 4	N=1 15+EA N>1 4N+20+EA
ROR	RB,N	110100v0 11001ddd	2	N=1 2* N>1 4N+8
ROR	RW,N	110100v1 11001ddd	2	
SAHF		9E	1	4*
SAL/SHL	DADDR,N	110100va aa100bbb [DISP] [DISP]	2, 3 or 4	N=1 15+EA N>1 4N+20+EA
SAL/SHL	RB,N	110100v0 11100ddd	2	N=1 2* N>1 4N+8
SAL/SHL	RW,N	110100v1 11100ddd	2	

Table 5-5. 8086 and 8088 Instruction Mnemonics (Continued)

Instruction		Object Code	Bytes	Clock Periods
SAR	DADDR,N	110100va aa111bbb [DISP] [DISP]	2, 3 or 4	N=1 15+EA N>1 4N+20+EA
SAR	RB,N	110100v0 11111ddd	2	N=1 2* N>1 4N+8
SAR	RW,N	110100v1 11111ddd	2	
SBB	AL,DATA8	1C YY	2	4*
SBB	AX,DATA16	1D YYYY	3	4*
SBB	DADDR,DATA8	80 aa011bbb [DISP] [DISP] YY	3, 4 or 5	17+EA
SBB	DADDR,DATA16	100000a1 aa011bbb [DISP] [DISP] YY[YY]	3, 4, 5 or 6	17+EA
SBB	DADDR,RB	18 aasssbbb [DISP] [DISP]	2, 3 or 4	16+EA
SBB	DADDR,RW	19 aasssbbb [DISP] [DISP]	2, 3 or 4	16+EA
SBB	RB,DADDR	1A aadddbbb [DISP] [DISP]	2, 3 or 4	9+EA
SBB	RB,DATA8	80 11011ddd YY	3	4*
SBB	RBD,RBS	1A 11dddsss	2	3*
SBB	RW,DADDR	1B aadddbbb [DISP] [DISP]	2, 3 or 4	9+EA
SBB	RW,DATA16	100000a1 11011ddd YY[YY]	3 or 4	4*
SBB	RWD,RWS	1B 11dddsss	2	3*
SCAS	BD	AE	1	15
SCAS	WD	AF	1	15
SEG Prefix	SR	001rr101	1	+2
SHR	DADDR,N	110100va aa101bbb [DISP] [DISP]	2, 3 or 4	N=1 15+EA N>1 4N+20+EA
SHR	RB,N	110100v0 11101ddd	2	N=1 2* N>1 4N+8
SHR	RW,N	110100v1 11101ddd	2	
STC		F9	1	2*
STD		FD	1	2*
STI		FB	1	2*
STOS	BD	AA	1	11
STOS	WD	AB	1	11
SUB	AL,DATA8	2C YY	2	4*
SUB	AX,DATA16	2D YYYY	3	4*
SUB	DADDR,DATA8	80 aa101bbb [DISP] [DISP] YY	3, 4 or 5	17+EA
SUB	DADDR,DATA16	100000a1 aa101bbb [DISP] [DISP] YY[YY]	3, 4, 5 or 6	17+EA
SUB	DADDR,RB	28 aasssbbb [DISP] [DISP]	2, 3 or 4	16+EA
SUB	DADDR,RW	29 aasssbbb [DISP] [DISP]	2, 3 or 4	16+EA
SUB	RB,DADDR	2A aadddbbb [DISP] [DISP]	2, 3 or 4	9+EA
SUB	RB,DATA8	80 11101ddd YY	3	4*
SUB	RBD,RBS	2A 11dddsss	2	3*
SUB	RW,DADDR	2B aadddbbb [DISP] [DISP]	2, 3 or 4	9+EA
SUB	RW,DATA16	100000a1 11101ddd YY[YY]	3 or 4	4*
SUB	RWD,RWS	2B 11dddsss	2	3*

Table 5-5. 8086 and 8088 Instruction Mnemonics (Continued)

Instruction		Object Code	Bytes	Clock Periods
TEST	AL,DATA8	A8 YY	2	4*
TEST	AX,DATA16	A9 YYYY	3	4*
TEST	DADDR,DATA8	F6 aa000bbb [DISP] [DISP] YY	3, 4 or 5	11+EA
TEST	DADDR,DATA16	F7 aa000bbb [DISP] [DISP] YYYY	4, 5 or 6	11+EA
TEST	DADDR,RB	84 aaregbbb [DISP] [DISP]	2, 3 or 4	9+EA
TEST	DADDR,RW	85 aaregbbb [DISP] [DISP]	2, 3 or 4	9+EA
TEST	RB,DATA8	F6 1000reg YY	3	5*
TEST	RBD,RBS	84 11regreg	2	3*
TEST	RW,DATA16	F7 11000reg YYYY	4	5*
TEST	RWD,RWS	85 11regreg	2	3*
WAIT		9B	1	3+5n
XCHG	AX,RW	10010reg	1	3*
XCHG	RB,DADDR	86 aaregbbb [DISP] [DISP]	2, 3 or 4	17+EA
XCHG	RB,RB	86 11regreg	2	4*
XCHG	RW,DADDR	87 aaregbbb [DISP] [DISP]	2, 3 or 4	17+EA
XCHG	RW,RW	87 11regreg	2	4*
XLAT		D7	1	11
XOR	AL,DATA8	34 YY	2	4*
XOR	AX,DATA16	36 YYYY	3	4*
XOR	DADDR,DATA8	80 aa010bbb [DISP] [DISP] YY	3, 4 or 5	17+EA
XOR	DADDR,DATA16	81 aa010bbb [DISP] [DISP] YYYY	4, 5 or 6	17+EA
XOR	DADDR,RB	30 aasssbbb [DISP] [DISP]	2, 3 or 4	16+EA
XOR	DADDR,RW	31 aasssbbb [DISP] [DISP]	2, 3 or 4	16+EA
XOR	RB,DADDR	32 aadddbbb [DISP] [DISP]	2, 3 or 4	9+EA
XOR	RB,DATA8	80 11110ddd YY	3	4*
XOR	RBD,RBS	32 11dddsss	2	3*
XOR	RW,DADDR	33 aadddbbb [DISP] [DISP]	2, 3 or 4	16+EA
XOR	RW,DATA16	81 11110ddd YYYY	4	4*
XOR	RWD,RWS	33 11dddsss	2	3*

Table 5-6. 8086 and 8088 Instruction Object Codes

Object Code			Mnemonic	
Byte 1	Byte 2	Other Bytes		
00	aasssbbb	[DISP][DISP]	ADD	RBD/DADDR,RBS
01	aasssbbb	[DISP][DISP]	ADD	RWD/DADDR,RWS
02	aadddbbb	[DISP][DISP]	ADD	RBD,DADDR/RBS
03	aadddbbb	[DISP][DISP]	ADD	RWD,DADDR/RWS
04	YY		ADD	AL,DATA8
05	YY	YY	ADD	AX,DATA16
06			PUSH	ES
07			POP	ES
08	aasssbbb	[DISP][DISP]	OR	RBD/DADDR,RBS
09	aasssbbb	[DISP][DISP]	OR	RWD/DADDR,RWS
0A	aadddbbb	[DISP][DISP]	OR	RBD,DADDR/RBS
0B	aadddbbb	[DISP][DISP]	OR	RWD,DADDR/RWS
0C	YY		OR	AL,DATA8
0D	YY	YY	OR	AX,DATA16
0E			PUSH	CS
0F			Not used	(POP CS)
10	aasssbbb	[DISP][DISP]	ADC	RBD/DADDR,RBS
11	aasssbbb	[DISP][DISP]	ADC	RWD/DADDR,RWS
12	aadddbbb	[DISP][DISP]	ADC	RBD,DADDR/RBS
13	aadddbbb	[DISP][DISP]	ADC	RWD,DADDR/RWS
14	YY		ADC	AL,DATA8
15	YY	YY	ADC	AL,DATA16
16			PUSH	SS
17			POP	SS
18	aasssbbb	[DISP][DISP]	SBB	RBD/DADDR,RBS
19	aasssbbb	[DISP][DISP]	SBB	RWD/DADDR,RWS
1A	aadddbbb	[DISP][DISP]	SBB	RBD,DADDR/RBS
1B	aadddbbb	[DISP][DISP]	SBB	RWD,DADDR/RWS
1C	YY		SBB	AL,DATA8
1D	YY	YY	SBB	AX,DATA16
1E			PUSH	DS
1F			POP	DS
20	aasssbbb	[DISP][DISP]	AND	RBD/DADDR,RBS
21	aasssbbb	[DISP][DISP]	AND	RWD/DADDR,RWS
22	aadddbbb	[DISP][DISP]	AND	RBD,DADDR/RBS
23	aadddbbb	[DISP][DISP]	AND	RWD,DADDR/RWS
24	YY		AND	AL,DATA8
25	YY	YY	AND	AX,DATA16
26			SEG	ES
27			DAA	
28	aasssbbb	[DISP][DISP]	SUB	RBD/DADDR,RBS
29	aasssbbb	[DISP][DISP]	SUB	RWD/DADDR,RWS
2A	aadddbbb	[DISP]!DISP]	SUB	RBD,DADDR/RBS
2B	aadddbbb	[DISP][DISP]	SUB	RWD,DADDR/RWS
2C	YY		SUB	AL,DATA8
2D	YY	YY	SUB	AX,DATA16
2E			SEG	CS
2F			DAS	
30	aasssbbb	[DISP][DISP]	XOR	RBD/DADDR,RBS
31	aasssbbb	[DISP][DISP]	XOR	RWD/DADDR,RWS
32	aadddbbb	[DISP][DISP]	XOR	RBD,DADDR/RBS
33	aadddbbb	[DISP][DISP]	XOR	RWD,DADDR/RWS
34	YY		XOR	AL,DATA8
35	YY	YY	XOR	AX,DATA16
36			SEG	SS

Table 5-6. 8086 and 8088 Instruction Object Codes (Continued)

Object Code			Mnemonic	
Byte 1	Byte 2	Other Bytes		
37			AAA	
38	aasssbbb	[DISP][DISP]	CMP	RBD/DADDR,RBS
39	aasssbbb	[DISP][DISP]	CMP	RWD/DADDR,RWS
3A	aadddbbb	[DISP][DISP]	CMP	RBD,DADDR/RBS
3B	aadddbbb	[DISP][DISP]	CMP	RWD,DADDR/RWS
3C	YY		CMP	AL,DATA8
3D	YY	YY	CMP	AX,DATA16
3E			SEG	DS
3F			AAS	
40			INC	AX
41			INC	CX
42			INC	DX
43			INC	BX
44			INC	SP
45			INC	BP
46			INC	SI
47			INC	DI
48			DEC	AX
49			DEC	CX
4A			DEC	DX
4B			DEC	BX
4C			DEC	SP
4D			DEC	BP
4E			DEC	SI
4F			DEC	DI
50			PUSH	AX
51			PUSH	CX
52			PUSH	DX
53			PUSH	BX
54			PUSH	SP
55			PUSH	BP
56			PUSH	SI
57			PUSH	DI
58			POP	AX
59			POP	CX
5A			POP	DX
5B			POP	BX
5C			POP	SP
5D			POP	BP
5E			POP	SI
5F			POP	DI
60-6F			Not used	
70	DISP		JO	DISP8
71	DISP		JNO	DISP8
72	DISP		JB or JNAE or JC	DISP8
73	DISP		JNB or JAE or JNC	DISP8
74	DISP		JE or JZ	DISP8
75	DISP		JNE or JNZ	DISP8
76	DISP		JBE or JNA	DISP8
77	DISP		JNBE or JA	DISP8
78	DISP		JS	DISP8
79	DISP		JNS	DISP8
7A	DISP		JP or JPE	DISP8
7B	DISP		JNP or JPO	DISP8
7C	DISP		JL or JNGE	DISP8

Table 5-6. 8086 and 8088 Instruction Object Codes (Continued)

Object Code			Mnemonic	
Byte 1	Byte 2	Other Bytes		
7D	DISP		JLE or JGE	DISP8
7E	DISP		JLE or JNG	DISP8
7F	DISP		JNLE or JG	DISP8
80	aa000bbb	[DISP][DISP] YY	ADD	RBD/DADDR,DATA8
80	aa001bbb	[DISP][DISP] YY	OR	RBD/DADDR,DATA8
80	aa010bbb	[DISP][DISP] YY	ADC	RBD/DADDR,DATA8
80	aa011bbb	[DISP][DISP] YY	SBB	RBD/DADDR,DATA8
80	aa100bbb	[DISP][DISP] YY	AND	RBD/DADDR,DATA8
80	aa101bbb	[DISP][DISP] YY	SUB	RBD/DADDR,DATA8
80	aa110bbb	[DISP][DISP] YY	XOR	RBD/DADDR,DATA8
80	aa111bbb	[DISP][DISP] YY	CMP	RBD/DADDR,DATA8
81	aa000bbb	[DISP][DISP] YYYY	ADD	RWD/DADDR,DATA16
81	aa001bbb	[DISP][DISP] YYYY	OR	RWD/DADDR,DATA16
81	aa010bbb	[DISP][DISP] YYYY	ADC	RWD/DADDR,DATA16
81	aa011bbb	[DISP][DISP] YYYY	SBB	RWD/DADDR,DATA16
81	aa100bbb	[DISP][DISP] YYYY	AND	RWD/DADDR,DATA16
81	aa101bbb	[DISP][DISP] YYYY	SUB	RWD/DADDR,DATA16
81	aa110bbb	[DISP][DISP] YYYY	XOR	RWD/DADDR,DATA16
81	aa111bbb	[DISP][DISP] YYYY	CMP	RWD/DADDR,DATA16
82	aa000bbb	[DISP][DISP] YY	ADD	RBD/DADDR,DATA8
82	xx001xxx		Not used	
82	aa010bbb	[DISP][DISP] YY	ADC	RBD/DADDR,DATA8
82	aa011bbb	[DISP][DISP] YY	SBB	RBD/DADDR,DATA8
82	xx100xxx		Not used	
82	aa101bbb	[DISP][DISP] YY	SUB	RBD/DADDR,DATA8
82	xx110xxx		Not used	
82	aa111bbb	[DISP][DISP] YY	CMP	RBD/DADDR,DATA8
83	aa000bbb	[DISP][DISP] YYYY	ADD	RWD/DADDR,DATA16
83	xx001xxx		Not used	
83	aa010bbb	[DISP][DISP] YYYY	ADC	RWD/DADDR,DATA16
83	aa011bbb	[DISP][DISP] YYYY	SBB	RWD/DADDR,DATA16
83	xx100xxx		Not used	
83	aa101bbb	[DISP][DISP] YYYY	SUB	RWD/DADDR,DATA16
83	xx110xxx		Not used	
83	aa111bbb	[DISP][DISP] YYYY	CMP	RWD/DADDR,DATA16
84	aasssbbb	[DISP][DISP]	TEST	RBD/DADDR,RBS
85	aasssbbb	[DISP][DISP]	TEST	RWD/DADDR,RWS
86	aadddbbb	[DISP][DISP]	XCHG	RBD/DADDR,RBS
87	aadddbbb	[DISP][DISP]	XCHG	RWD/DADDR,RWS
88	aasssbbb	[DISP][DISP]	MOV	RBD/DADDR,RBS
89	aasssbbb	[DISP][DISP]	MOV	RWD/DADDR,RWS
8A	aadddbbb	[DISP][DISP]	MOV	RBD,DADDR/RBS
8B	aadddbbb	[DISP][DISP]	MOV	RWD,DADDR/RWS
8C	aa0rrbbb	[DISP][DISP]	MOV	RWD/DADDR,SR
8C	xx1xxxxx		Not used	
8D	aadddbbb	[DISP][DISP]	LEA	RWD,DADDR
8E	aa0rrbbb	[DISP][DISP]	MOV	SR,RWD/DADDR
8E	xx1xxxxx		Not used	
8F	aa000bbb	[DISP][DISP]	POP	RWD/DADDR
8F	xx001xxx		Not used	
to 8F	xx111xxx		Not used	
90			XCHG	AX,AX (NOP)
91			XCHG	AX,CX
92			XCHG	AX,DX
93			XCHG	AX,BX
94			XCHG	AX,SP

Table 5-6. 8086 and 8088 Instruction Object Codes (Continued)

Object Code			Mnemonic	
Byte 1	Byte 2	Other Bytes		
95			XCGH	AX,BP
96			XCHG	AX,SI
97			XCHG	AX,DI
98			CBW	
99			CWD	
9A	PP	QQPPQQ	CALL	BRANCH,SEGM
9B			WAIT	
9C			PUSHF	
9D			POPF	
9E			SAHF	
9F			LAHF	
A0	PP	QQ	MOV	AL,LABEL
A1	PP	QQ	MOV	AX,LABEL
A2	PP	QQ	MOV	LABEL,AL
A3	PP	QQ	MOV	LABEL,AX
A4			MOVS	BD,BS
A5			MOVS	WD,WS
A6			CMPS	BD,BS
A7			CMPS	WD,WS
A8	YY		TEST	AL,DATA8
A9	YY	YY	TEST	AX,DATA16
AA			STOS	BD
AB			STOS	WD
AC			LODS	BS
AD			LODS	WS
AE			SCAS	BD
AF			SCAS	WD
B0	YY		MOV	AL,DATA8
B1	YY		MOV	CL,DATA8
B2	YY		MOV	DL,DATA8
B3	YY		MOV	BL,DATA8
B4	YY		MOV	AH,DATA8
B5	YY		MOV	CH,DATA8
B6	YY		MOV	DH,DATA8
B7	YY		MOV	BH,DATA8
B8	YY	YY	MOV	AX,DATA16
B9	YY	YY	MOV	CX,DATA16
BA	YY	YY	MOV	DX,DATA16
BB	YY	YY	MOV	BX,DATA16
BC	YY	YY	MOV	SP,DATA16
BD	YY	YY	MOV	BP,DATA16
BE	YY	YY	MOV	SI,DATA16
BF	YY	YY	MOV	DI,DATA16
C0-C1			Not used	
C2	YY	YY	RET	CS,DATA16
C3			RET	
C4	aadddbbb	[DISP][DISP]	LES	RWD,DADDR
C5	aadddbbb	[DISP][DISP]	LEA	RWD,DADDR
C6	aa000bbb	[DISP][DISP] YY	MOV	DADDR,DATA8
C6	xx001xxx		Not used	
to C6	xx111xxx		Not used	
C7	aa000bbb	[DISP][DISP] YYYY	MOV	DADDR,DATA16
C7	xx001xxx		Not used	
to C7	xx111xxx		Not used	
C8-C9			Not used	

Table 5-6. 8086 and 8088 Instruction Object Codes (Continued)

Object Code			Mnemonic	
Byte 1	Byte 2	Other Bytes		
CA	YY	YY	RET	CS,DATA16
CB			RET	
CC			INT	3
CD	YY		INT	V
CE			INTO	
CF			IRET	
D0	aa000bbb	[DISP][DISP]	ROL	RBD/DADDR,1
D0	aa001bbb	[DISP][DISP]	ROR	RBD/DADDR,1
D0	aa010bbb	[DISP][DISP]	RCL	RBD/DADDR,1
D0	aa011bbb	[DISP][DISP]	RCR	RBD/DADDR,1
D0	aa100bbb	[DISP][DISP]	SAL or SHL	RBD/DADDR,1
D0	aa101bb1	[DISP][DISP]	SHR	RBD/DADDR,1
D0	xx110xxx		Not used	
D0	aa111bbb	[DISP][DISP]	SAR	RBD/DADDR,1
D1	aa000bbb	[DISP][DISP]	ROL	RWD/DADDR,1
D1	aa001bbb	[DISP][DISP]	ROR	RWD/DADDR,1
D1	aa010bbb	[DISP][DISP]	RCL	RWD/DADDR,1
D1	aa011bbb	[DISP][DISP]	RCR	RWD/DADDR,1
D1	aa100bbb	[DISP][DISP]	SAL or SHL	RWD/DADDR,1
D1	aa101bbb	[DISP][DISP]	SHR	RWD/DADDR,1
D1	xx110xxx		Not used	
D1	aa111bbb	[DISP][DISP]	SAR	RWD/DADDR,1
D2	aa000bbb	[DISP][DISP]	ROL	RBD/DADDR,N
D2	aa001bbb	[DISP][DISP]	ROR	RBD/DADDR,N
D2	aa010bbb	[DISP][DISP]	RCL	RBD/DADDR,N
D2	aa011bbb	[DISP][DISP]	RCR	RBD/DADDR,N
D2	aa100bbb	[DISP][DISP]	SAL or SHL	RBD/DADDR,N
D2	aa101bbb	[DISP][DISP]	SHR	RBD/DADDR,N
D2	xx110xxx			
D2	aa111bbb	[DISP][DISP]	SAR	RBD/DADDR,N
D3	aa000bbb	[DISP][DISP]	ROL	RWD/DADDR,N
D3	aa001bbb	[DISP][DISP]	ROR	RWD/DADDR,N
D3	aa010bbb	[DISP][DISP]	RCL	RWD/DADDR,N
D3	aa011bbb	[DISP][DISP]	RCR	RWD/DADDR,N
D3	aa100bbb	[DISP][DISP]	SAL or SHL	RWD/DADDR,N
D3	aa101bbb	[DISP][DISP]	SHR	RWD/DADDR,N
D3	xx110xxx		Not used	
D3	aa111bbb	[DISP][DISP]	SAR	RWD/DADDR,N
D4	0A		AAM	
D5	0A		AAD	
D6			Not used	
D7			XLAT	
D8-DF	aaxxxbbb	[DISP][DISP]	ESC	DADDR
E0	DISP		LOOPNE or LOOPNZ	DISP8
E1	DISP		LOOPE or LOOPZ	DISP8
E2	DISP		LOOP	DISP8
E3	DISP		JCXZ	DISP8
E4	YY		IN	AL,PORT
E5	YY		IN	AX,PORT
E6	YY		OUT	AL,PORT
E7	YY		OUT	AX,PORT
E8	DISP	DISP	CALL	BRANCH
E9	DISP	DISP	JMP	BRANCH
EA	PP	QQ PPQQ	JMP	BRANCH,SEGM
EB	DISP		JMP	BRANCH

Table 5-6. 8086 and 8088 Instruction Object Codes (Continued)

Object Code			Mnemonic	
Byte 1	Byte 2	Other Bytes		
EC			IN	AL,DX
ED			IN	AX,DX
EE			OUT	AL,DX
EF			OUT	AX,DX
F0			LOCK	
F1			Not used	
F2			REPNE or REPNZ	
F3			REP or REPE or REPZ	
F4			HLT	
F5			CMC	
F6	aa000bbb	[DISP][DISP] YY	TEST	RBD/DADDR,DATA8
F6	xx001xxx		Not used	
F6	aa010bbb	[DISP][DISP]	NOT	RBD/DADDR
F6	aa011bbb	[DISP][DISP]	NEG	RBD/DADDR
F6	aa100bbb	[DISP][DISP]	MUL	RBD/DADDR
F6	aa101bbb	[DISP][DISP]	IMUL	RBD/DADDR
F6	aa110bbb	[DISP][DISP]	DIV	RBD/DADDR
F6	aa111bbb	[DISP][DISP]	IDIV	RBD/DADDR
F7	aa000bbb	[DISP][DISP] YYYY	TEST	RWD/DADDR,DATA16
F7	xx001xxx		Not used	
F7	aa010bbb	[DISP][DISP]	NOT	RWD/DADDR
F7	aa011bbb	[DISP][DISP]	NEG	RWD/DADDR
F7	aa100bbb	[DISP][DISP]	MUL	RWD/DADDR
F7	aa101bbb	[DISP][DISP]	IMUL	RWD/DADDR
F7	aa110bbb	[DISP][DISP]	DIV	RWD/DADDR
F7	aa111bbb	[DISP][DISP]	IDIV	RWD/DADDR
F8			CLC	
F9			STC	
FA			CLI	
FB			SII	
FC			CLD	
FD			STD	
FE	aa000bbb	[DISP][DISP]	INC	RBD/DADDR
FE	aa001bbb	[DISP][DISP]	DEC	RBD/DADDR
FE	xx001xxx		Not used	
to FE	xx111xxx		Not used	
FF	aa000bbb	[DISP][DISP]	INC	DADDR
FF	aa001bbb	[DISP][DISP]	DEC	DADDR
FF	aa010bbb	[DISP][DISP]	CALL	RW/DADDR
FF	aa011bbb	[DISP][DISP]	CALL	DADDR,CS
FF	aa100bbb	[DISP][DISP]	JMP	RW/DADDR
FF	aa101bbb	[DISP][DISP]	JMP	DADDR,CS
FF	aa110bbb	[DISP][DISP]	PUSH	DADDR
FF	xx111xxx		Not used	

Table 5-7. 8080A to 8086 Instruction Mapping

8080A Instruction		Equivalent 8086 Instruction(s)		8080A Instruction		Equivalent 8086 Instruction(s)	
IN	DEV	IN	PORT	RC		JNB	next-inst
OUT	DEV	OUT	PORT			RET	
				RNC		JB	next-inst
LDAX	B*	MOV	SI,CX			RET	
		LODB		RZ		JNZ	next-inst
LDAX	D	MOV	SI,DX			RET	
		LODB		RNZ		JZ	next-inst
STAX	B	MOV	DI,CX			RET	
		STOB		RM		JNS	next-inst
STAX	D	MOV	DI,DX			RET	
		STOB		RP		JS	next-inst
MOV	REG,M	MOV	RB,DADDR			RET	
MOV	M,REG	MOV	DADDR,RB	RPE		JPO	next-inst
LDA	ADDR	MOV	AL,LABEL			RET	
STA	ADDR	MOV	LABEL,AL	RPO		JPE	next-inst
LHLD	ADDR	MOV	BX,DADDR			RET	
SHLD	ADDR	MOV	DADDR,BX				
				ADI	DATA	ADD	AL,DATA8
ADD	M	ADD	AL,DADDR	ACI	DATA	ADC	AL,DATA8
ADC	M	ADC	AL,DADDR	SUI	DATA	SUB	AL,DATA8
SUB	M	SUB	AL,DADDR	SBI	DATA	SBB	AL,DATA8
SBB	M	SBB	AL,DADDR	ANI	DATA	AND	AL,DATA8
ANA	M	AND	AL,DADDR	XRI	DATA	XOR	AL,DATA8
XRA	M	XOR	AL,DADDR	ORI	DATA	OR	AL,DATA8
ORA	M	OR	AL,DADDR	CPI	DATA	CMP	AL,DATA8
CMP	M	CMP	AL,DADDR				
INR	M	INC	DADDR	JC	ADDR	JB	DISP8***
DCR	M	DEC	DADDR	JNC	ADDR	JNB	DISP8
				JZ	ADDR	JZ	DISP8
LXI	RP,DATA16	MOV	RW,DATA16	JNZ	ADDR	JNZ	DISP8
				JP	ADDR	JNS	DISP8
MVI	M,DATA	MOV	DADDR,DATA8	JM	ADDR	JS	DISP8
MVI	REG,DATA	MOV	RB,DATA8	JPE	ADDR	JPE	DISP8
JMP	ADDR	JMP	BRANCH**	JPO	ADDR	JPO	DISP8
PCHL		JMP	BX				
				MOV	d,s	MOV	RBD,RBS
CALL	ADDR	CALL	BRANCH	XCHG		XCHG	DX,BX
CC	ADDR	JNB	next-inst	SPHL		MOV	SP,BX
		CALL	BRANCH				
CNC	ADDR	JB	next-inst	ADD	REG	ADD	AL,RBS
		CALL	BRANCH	ADC	REG	ADC	AL,RBS
CZ	ADDR	JNZ	next-inst	SUB	REG	SUB	AL,RBS
		CALL	BRANCH	SBB	REG	SBB	AL,RBS
CNZ	ADDR	JZ	next-inst	ANA	REG	AND	AL,RBS
		CALL	BRANCH	XRA	REG	XOR	AL,RBS
CP	ADDR	JS	next-inst	ORA	REG	OR	AL,RBS
		CALL	BRANCH	CMP	REG	CMP	AL,RBS
CM	ADDR	JNS	next-inst	DAD	RP	LAHF	
		CALL	BRANCH			ADD	BX,RW
CPE	ADDR	JPO	next-inst			RCR	AL
		CALL	BRANCH			SAHF	
CPO	ADDR	JPE	next-inst			RCL	AL
		CALL	BRANCH			or ADD BX,RW (unlike DAD	
RET		RET				will affect AF,PF,SF, and ZF)	

Table 5-7. 8080A to 8086 Instruction Mapping (Continued)

8080A Instruction		Equivalent 8086 Instruction(s)		8080A Instruction		Equivalent 8086 Instruction(s)	
INR	REG	INC	RB	PUSH	RP	PUSH	RW
DCR	REG	DEC	RB	PUSH	PSW	LAHF	
CMA		NOT	AL			PUSH	AX
DAA		DAA		POP	RP	POP	RW
RLC		ROL	AL	POP	PSW	POP	AX
RRC		ROR	AL			SAHF	
RAL		RCL	AL	XTHL		POP	SI
RAR		RCR	AL			XCHG	BX,SI
INX	RP	LAHF				PUSH	SI
		SAHF		EI		STI	
		or INC RW (unlike INX - will		DI		CLI	
		affect AF, PF, SF, and ZF)		RST	N	CALL	8*N
DCX	RP	LAHF					
		DEC	RW	STC		STC	
		SAHF		CMC		CMC	
		or DEC RW (unlike DCX - will					
		affect AF, PF, SF, and ZF)		NOP		XCHG	AX,AX
				HLT		HLT	

*8080A registers map into 8086 registers as follows:

8080A	8086	8080A	8086
A	AL	L	BL
B	CH	BC	CX
C	CL	DE	DX
D	DH	HL	BX
E	DL	SP	SP
H	BH	PC	IP

**Addresses on 8086 jumps and calls are adjusted to be self-relative.

***Conditional jumps to a location out of the short self-relative range must be implemented by using a reversed-sense conditional jump around a normal jump to the location, e.g.:

JC	ADDR	becomes	JNB	next-inst
			JMP	BRANCH

Refer to Table 4-4 for a complete description of 808A mnemonics shown above.

Refer to Table 20-4 for a complete description of 8086 mnemonics shown above.

THE 8088 CPU

The 8088 is an 8086 microprocessor with an 8-bit Data Bus. The two parts are otherwise identical. Therefore we will describe differences between the 8088 and the 8086 in the text which follows.

If you are going to use the 8088, first read the description of the 8086 given at the beginning of this chapter, then note differences as described below.

8088 PROGRAMMABLE REGISTERS AND ADDRESSING MODES

8088 programmable registers and addressing modes are identical to the 8086 in every way.

8088 CPU PINS AND SIGNALS

8088 CPU pins and signals are illustrated in Figure 5-12. As compared to the 8086 pins and signals illustrated in Figure 5-3, only pin 34 differs.

For the 8086, pin 34 outputs $\overline{BHE}$. This signal discriminates between the high-order byte and the low-order byte on the 16-bit 8086 Data Bus. Since the 8088 has an 8-bit Data Bus, $\overline{BHE}$ and associated logic is irrelevant. **The 8088 outputs maximum mode $\overline{SSO}$ status at pin 34.**

The IO/$\overline{M}$ signal has opposite polarity for the 8088, as compared to the 8086. This makes the 8088 compatible with the 8085.

Combining IO/$\overline{M}$, DT/$\overline{R}$, and $\overline{SSO}$, 8088 bus cycles can be decoded as follows:

IO/$\overline{M}$	DT/$\overline{R}$	$\overline{SSO}$	
0	0	0	Code segment access
0	0	1	Memory read
0	1	0	Memory write
0	1	1	No operations
1	0	0	Interrupt acknowledge
1	0	1	I/O read
1	1	0	I/O write
1	1	1	Halt

Since the 8088 has no $\overline{BHE}$ signal, nor need for any such signal, the discussion of external memory addressing and $\overline{BHE}$ given for the 8086 will not apply to the 8088.

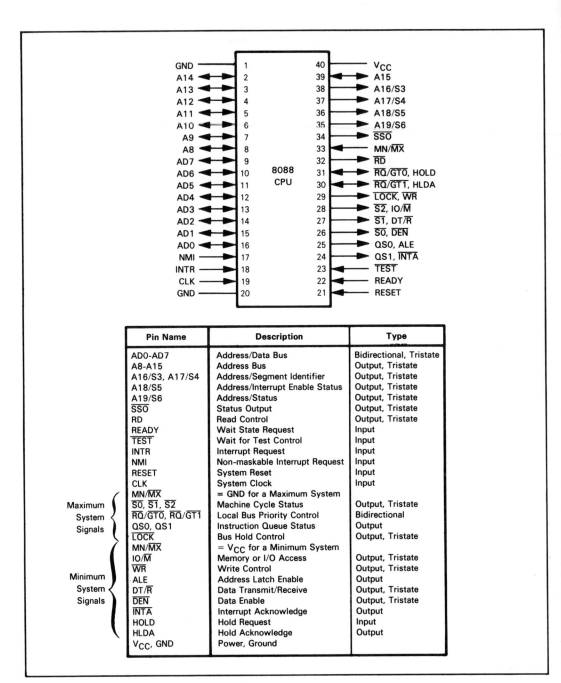

Figure 5-12. 8088 Pins and Signal Assignments

8088 TIMING AND INSTRUCTION EXECUTION

The 8088 has a 4 byte instruction object code queue; the 8086, in contrast, has a 6 byte instruction object code queue. **The 8088 will start executing instruction fetch bus cycles to fill its 4 byte queue as soon as one or more queue bytes are empty.** The 8086, in contrast, will not start pre-fetching instruction object code bytes until two or more of its 6 queue bytes are empty. The description of bus cycles and queue logic given for the 8086 otherwise applies directly to the 8088.

8088
INSTRUCTION
QUEUE

8088 MEMORY AND I/O DEVICE ACCESS BUS CYCLES

Bus cycle timing for the 8088 and the 8086 differ only at the multiplexed Data/Address Bus lines. Timing differences are confined to the eight Address Bus lines A8-A15 and may be illustrated as follows:

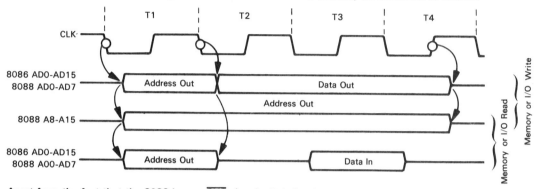

Apart from the fact that the 8088 has no $\overline{\text{BHE}}$ signal, all timing for signals other than the Data/Address Bus is identical for the 8086 and the 8088.

5-99

THE 8088 HALT STATE

When operating in minimum mode, the 8088 delays the ALE pulse by one clock period as compared to 8086 timing. This may be illustrated as follows:

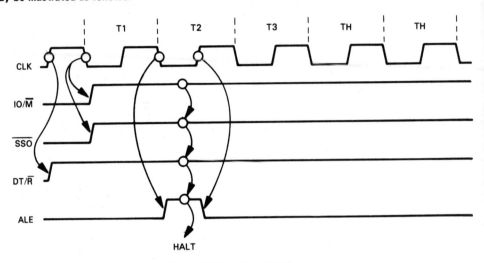

Halt state logic and timing is otherwise identical for the 8086 and the 8088.

OTHER 8086 COMPATIBLE 8088 LOGIC

8086 and 8088 logic is absolutely identical for the following states and logic:

- The Wait state
- The Hold state
- RQ/GT logic
- Lock logic
- Wait for test state
- Processor escape
- Device reset
- Interrupt processing
- Single stepping mode

THE 8088 INSTRUCTION SET

The 8086 and 8088 instruction sets, listed in Table 5-4, are identical with the exception of execution times. Since the 8088 has an 8-bit bus, two bus cycles will have to be executed wherever the 8086 would have executed a single bus cycle to fetch 16 bits of data. Table 5-5 provides execution times for the 8086 and the 8088.

THE INTEL 8284 CLOCK GENERATOR/DRIVER

The 8284 Clock Generator/Driver is a standard component that will be present in every 8086 microcomputer system. In a multimicroprocessor system, each 8086 microprocessor will have its own 8284 Clock Generator/Driver. While one could conceivably have a single 8284 servicing more than one 8086 microprocessor, it will rarely make any economic sense to design a system in this fashion.

Logic implemented on the 8284 Clock Generator/Driver corresponds generally to the block labeled clock logic in Figure 5-1. To be completely accurate, however, a small portion of the bus interface logic should also be illustrated as provided by the 8284 device.

Figure 5-13 illustrates 8284 device internal logic.

The 8284 is manufactured using bipolar technology. It is packaged as an 18-pin DIP. All signals are TTL-level compatible.

8284 CLOCK GENERATOR/DRIVER PINS AND SIGNALS

8284 device pins and signals are illustrated in Figure 5-14. Figure 5-20 illustrates the 8284 device in a single 8086 microprocessor configuration.

Signals may be divided between timing and control logic.

Clock frequency is controlled by a crystal connected across the X1 and X2 pins. Clock frequency must be exactly three times the required clock period. Since the standard 8086 clock period is 200 nanoseconds, a 15 MHz crystal frequency is required.

If an overtone mode crystal is employed, then it must be supported by an external LC network connected to TANK to insure oscillation of the overtone frequency. This is standard clock logic practice; for the 8284 it is illustrated along with other normal connections in Figure 5-15.

You have the option of connecting a crystal across X1 and X2 in order to generate a fundamental frequency, or you can input the fundamental frequency via EFI. The level of F/$\overline{C}$ determines whether an external crystal or a signal input will provide the fundamental frequency. If F/$\overline{C}$ is high, then the fundamental frequency is taken from the EFI input. If F/$\overline{C}$ is low, then the crystal connected across X1 and X2 provides the fundamental frequency.

Three clock outputs are generated:

1) CLK is an MOS level signal designed to meet the requirements of the 8086.

2) PCLK Is a TTL level clock signal, output for support circuits. PCLK runs at half the frequency of CLK.

3) OSC is an oscillator output running at the crystal or EFI input frequency.

These timing signals may be illustrated as follows:

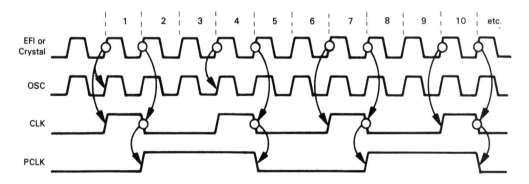

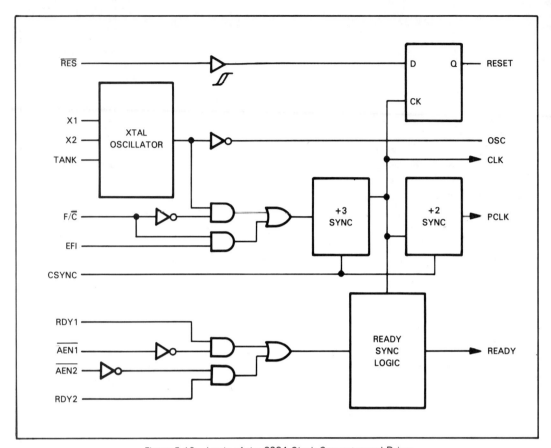

Figure 5-13. Logic of the 8284 Clock Generator and Driver

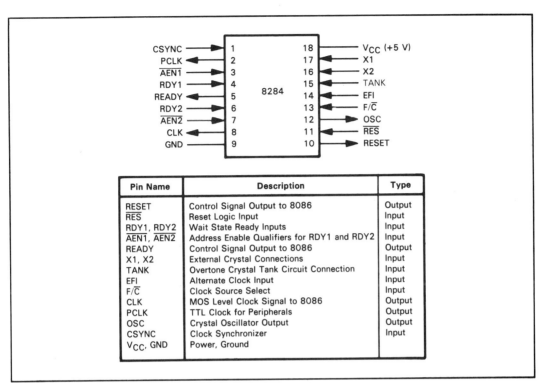

Pin Name	Description	Type
RESET	Control Signal Output to 8086	Output
RES	Reset Logic Input	Input
RDY1, RDY2	Wait State Ready Inputs	Input
AEN1, AEN2	Address Enable Qualifiers for RDY1 and RDY2	Input
READY	Control Signal Output to 8086	Output
X1, X2	External Crystal Connections	Input
TANK	Overtone Crystal Tank Circuit Connection	Input
EFI	Alternate Clock Input	Input
F/$\overline{C}$	Clock Source Select	Input
CLK	MOS Level Clock Signal to 8086	Output
PCLK	TTL Clock for Peripherals	Output
OSC	Crystal Oscillator Output	Output
CSYNC	Clock Synchronizer	Input
V_{CC}, GND	Power, Ground	

Figure 5-14.　8284 Clock Generator and Driver Pins and Signal Assignments

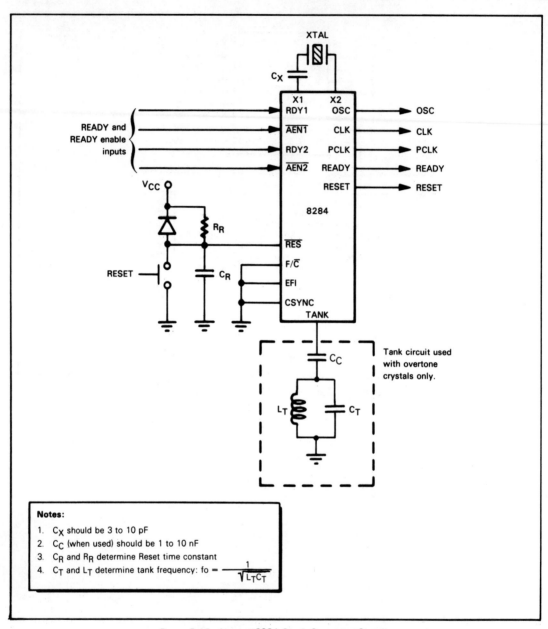

Notes:

1. C_X should be 3 to 10 pF
2. C_C (when used) should be 1 to 10 nF
3. C_R and R_R determine Reset time constant
4. C_T and L_T determine tank frequency: $fo = \dfrac{1}{\sqrt{L_T C_T}}$

Figure 5-15. Normal 8284 Clock Generator Circuit

In multi-CPU configurations you will probably need to synchronize all 8086 clock signals. You use the CSYNC signal for this purpose. When CSYNC is input high, logic internal to the 8284 Clock Generator/Driver is stopped. When CSYNC subsequently goes low, clock outputs restart. If the same CSYNC signal is input to a number of 8284 devices that receive the same EFI input, then all microprocessors in a multi-CPU configuration will be exactly synchronized. Appropriate **logic is illustrated in Figure 5-16.**

SYNCHRONIZING
MULTI-8086
CLOCK
SIGNALS

Note that you cannot use individual crystals for 8284 Clock Generator/Drivers that are supposed to be synchronized with each; minor variations in crystal frequency, which must occur, will quickly distort clock signal synchronization. You can use a crystal to generate the fundamental frequency for one 8284 Clock Generator/Driver, then use the OSC output of this Clock Generator/Driver as the EFI input to other 8284 Clock Generator/Drivers.

The 8086 requires its RESET input to be synchronized with clock logic. The 8284 will receive an asynchronous Reset input at $\overline{\text{RES}}$ and will generate synchronized RESET output, which the 8086 requires. Appropriate logic is illustrated in Figure 5-15. Timing is illustrated in the data sheets at the end of the chapter.

8086
RESET

The 8284 $\overline{\text{RES}}$ input need not make a sharp transition. The 8284 inputs $\overline{\text{RES}}$ to a Schmit trigger that generates the RESET output. $\overline{\text{RES}}$ can make a slow low-to-high transition.

We have described earlier in this chapter how external logic can extend a bus cycle by inserting Wait clock periods between T3 and T4. Figure 5-9 illustrates the READY input that controls Wait states within the 8086 bus controller. As illustrated in Figure 5-9, the 8086 READY input must be synchronized with the clock signal. The 8284 Clock Generator/Driver outputs an appropriately synchronized READY signal to the 8086. **The 8284 creates its READY output from one of two inputs: RDY1 or RDY2.** The 8284 has two READY inputs to support MULTIBUS configurations. A single 8086 may connect to two separate System Busses. Memory or I/O devices attached to either bus may wish to create a Wait state within a bus cycle. Each System Bus may therefore have its own READY line. In order to arbitrate bus priorities, RDY1 and RDY2 have companion enable signals $\overline{\text{AEN1}}$ and $\overline{\text{AEN2}}$, respectively. The 8284 will respond to RDY1 only when $\overline{\text{AEN1}}$ is low. Similarly, the 8284 will respond to RDY2 only when AEN2 is low.

8284
WAIT STATE
LOGIC

$\overline{\text{AEN1}}$ and $\overline{\text{AEN2}}$ are general bus priority signals you must generate through your own bus priority arbitration logic. We will describe these two signals, and methods of generating them, later in this chapter.

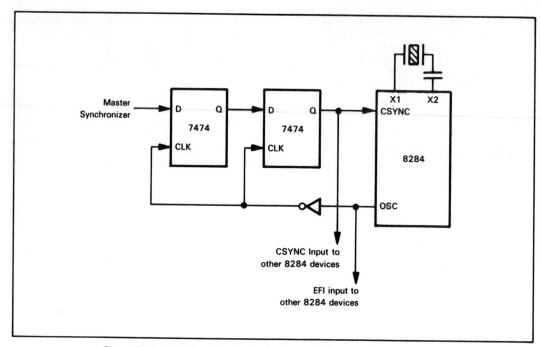

Figure 5-16. Clock Synchronization Logic in a Multi-CPU 8086 Configuration

THE INTEL 8288 BUS CONTROLLER

In configurations where the MN/$\overline{\text{MX}}$ signal is low, you must use an 8288 Bus Controller in order to decode the $\overline{S0}$, $\overline{S1}$, and $\overline{S2}$ status lines, and thus create System Bus control signals. You can also use the 8288 Bus Controller in order to connect more than one processor to a single System Bus, or in order to create more than one System Bus for a single 8086.

Although the primary purpose of the 8288 Bus Controller is to decode the three status signals $\overline{S0}$, $\overline{S1}$, and $\overline{S2}$, a simple 1-of-8 decoder could accomplish this limited task. The 8288 has these additional capabilities:

1) The 8288 can generate control signals for a System Bus or an I/O device only bus.

2) You can float a System Bus's control signals to enable direct memory access, or to arbitrate bus priorities.

3) The two Write control lines have alternate advanced outputs designed for slow memories or I/O devices.

4) You can suppress control signals as a means of implementing memory protect logic in multi-bus or multimicroprocessor configurations.

5) The 8288 generates control signals needed by line drivers.

6) The 8288 generates control signals needed by simple or complex interrupt logic.

The 8288 Bus Controller is manufactured using bipolar technology. It is packaged as a 20-pin DIP. All signals are TTL-level compatible.

8288 BUS CONTROLLER SIGNALS AND PIN ASSIGNMENTS

Figure 5-17 illustrates 8288 Bus Controller signals and pin assignments. Figure 5-21 illustrates an 8288 within an 8086 microcomputer system.

Control signals are generated from $\overline{S0}$, $\overline{S1}$, and $\overline{S2}$ as follows:

$\overline{S0}$	$\overline{S1}$	$\overline{S2}$	8086	8288 Control Output
0	0	0	Interrupt acknowledge	$\overline{\text{INTA}}$ and MCE
0	0	1	I/O read	$\overline{\text{IORC}}$
0	1	0	I/O write	$\overline{\text{IOWC}}$, $\overline{\text{AIOWC}}$
0	1	1	Halt	None
1	0	0	Instruction fetch	$\overline{\text{MRDC}}$
1	0	1	Memory read	$\overline{\text{MRDC}}$
1	1	0	Memory write	$\overline{\text{MWTC}}$, $\overline{\text{AMWC}}$
1	1	1	No operation	None

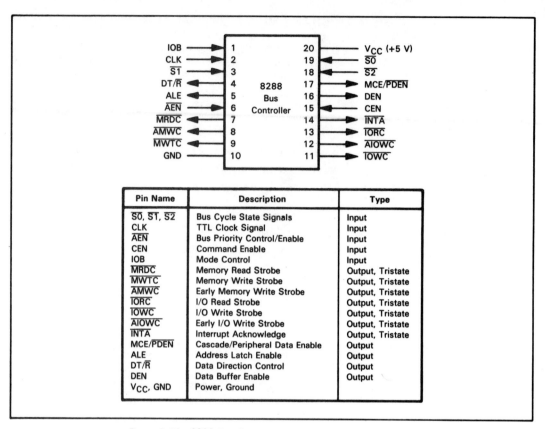

Pin Name	Description	Type
$\overline{S0}$, $\overline{S1}$, $\overline{S2}$	Bus Cycle State Signals	Input
CLK	TTL Clock Signal	Input
$\overline{AEN}$	Bus Priority Control/Enable	Input
CEN	Command Enable	Input
IOB	Mode Control	Input
$\overline{MRDC}$	Memory Read Strobe	Output, Tristate
$\overline{MWTC}$	Memory Write Strobe	Output, Tristate
$\overline{AMWC}$	Early Memory Write Strobe	Output, Tristate
$\overline{IORC}$	I/O Read Strobe	Output, Tristate
$\overline{IOWC}$	I/O Write Strobe	Output, Tristate
$\overline{AIOWC}$	Early I/O Write Strobe	Output, Tristate
$\overline{INTA}$	Interrupt Acknowledge	Output, Tristate
MCE/$\overline{PDEN}$	Cascade/Peripheral Data Enable	Output
ALE	Address Latch Enable	Output
DT/$\overline{R}$	Data Direction Control	Output
DEN	Data Buffer Enable	Output
V_{CC}, GND	Power, Ground	

Figure 5-17. 8288 Bus Controller Pins and Signal Assignments

8288 and 8086 control signal timing is essentially the same. For details, see the data sheets given at the end of this chapter.

If you look again at the Read and Write bus cycle timing descriptions given earlier in this chapter for the 8086 you will see that Read control signals pulse low approximately one clock period earlier than Write control signals. **The 8288 creates two alternate Write control signals whose timing is the same as the Read control signals.** These alternative Write control signals are referred to as advanced Write control signals, because they go low one clock pulse in advance of the standard Write control signals.

8288 ADVANCED WRITE CONTROL SIGNALS

We can thus summarize 8288 System Bus control signals as follows:

$\overline{\text{MRDC}}$ is the memory read control.

$\overline{\text{MWTC}}$ is the memory write control.

$\overline{\text{AMWC}}$ is a memory write control whose timing conforms to MRDC.

$\overline{\text{INTA}}$ is a memory read control signal that is output during the two interrupt acknowledge bus cycles.

$\overline{\text{IORC}}$ is an I/O device read control signal.

$\overline{\text{IOWC}}$ is an I/O device write control signal.

$\overline{\text{AIOWC}}$ is an alternative I/O device write control signal with timing that conforms to $\overline{\text{IORC}}$.

Devices connected to a bus are likely to use $\overline{\text{IOWC}}$ and $\overline{\text{MWTC}}$ o. $\overline{\text{IOWC}}$ and $\overline{\text{AMWC}}$, but not all four signals. That is, you will use either the normal write control signals or you will use the advanced write control signals.

All 8288 control signals are tristate. They can be disabled and thus disconnected from the System Bus.

You have two control options that modify the control signal logic of the 8288 Bus Controller.

Using the IOB pin, you can operate the 8288 device in I/O bus mode or in System Bus mode.

Using the CEN pin, you can suppress control signals.

Let us examine each of these capabilities in turn.

When the IOB pin receives a high input, the 8288 Bus Controller generates an I/O bus. IOB high floats $\overline{\text{MRDC}}$, $\overline{\text{MWTC}}$, and $\overline{\text{AMWC}}$ all of the time but outputs $\overline{\text{INTA}}$, $\overline{\text{IORC}}$, $\overline{\text{IOWC}}$, and $\overline{\text{AIOWC}}$. In I/O bus mode, these four I/O control signals cannot be floated. Since the four I/O control lines will always be active, it is assumed that the I/O bus generated by an 8288 is a logic bus. You cannot share this local I/O bus with another microprocessor.

8288 I/O BUS MODE

The 8288 I/O bus has two control signals, $\overline{\text{PDEN}}$ and DT/$\overline{\text{R}}$, which drive I/O ports and line drivers. DT/$\overline{\text{R}}$, which we have described for the 8086, is used to control a bidirectional bus driver. When high, DT/$\overline{\text{R}}$ puts the bus driver in output mode, while when low, DT/$\overline{\text{R}}$ puts the bus driver in input mode. $\overline{\text{PDEN}}$ pulses low as a data enable signal. $\overline{\text{PDEN}}$ is equivalent to $\overline{\text{DEN}}$, the standard bus data enable signal output by the 8086.

When IOB is low, a normal System Bus is generated. All seven control signals are active; however, $\overline{\text{AEN}}$ is a bus enable control (much as the $\overline{\text{BUSEN}}$ input is used by the 8228 Bus Controller in an 8080A system).

$\overline{\text{AEN}}$ is inactive when IOB is high and an I/O bus is being generated. $\overline{\text{AEN}}$ is active only when IOB is low and a System Bus is generated.

When IOB is low and $\overline{\text{AEN}}$ is high, all control signals are floated. When IOB is low and $\overline{\text{AEN}}$ is low, control signals are connected to the System Bus. You will use $\overline{\text{AEN}}$ to implement bus priority arbitration logic, or direct memory access logic, as described later in this chapter.

CEN is used to disable, but not float, control signals. CEN can be used when an 8288 is generating a System Bus or an I/O bus. CEN will normally be high. When CEN is low, control signals are inactive. CEN does not float signals; it just disables the logic that might otherwise have made a control signal pulse low.

8288 BUS CONTROLLER MEMORY PROTECT

Table 5-8 summarizes the effect of IOB and CEN on control signals generated by the 8288 Bus Controller.

Table 5-8. Effect of IOB, CEN, and $\overline{\text{AEN}}$ on Control Signals Output by the 8288 Bus Controller

Control Unit			Effect on Control Output					
IOB	CEN	$\overline{\text{AEN}}$	INTA, $\overline{\text{IORC}}$, $\overline{\text{IOWC}}$, $\overline{\text{AIOWC}}$			$\overline{\text{MRDC}}$, $\overline{\text{MWTC}}$, $\overline{\text{AMWC}}$		
			Mode	Floated?	Active?	Mode	Floated?	Active?
0	0	0	System	Floated	Active	System	Floated	Active
0	0	1	System	Floated	Inactive	System	Floated	Inactive
0	1	0	System	Connected	Active	System	Connected	Active
0	1	1	System	Connected	Inactive	System	Connected	Inactive
1	0	0	I/O	Floated	Active	Not Used	Floated	Inactive
1	0	1	I/O	Floated	Active	Not Used	Floated	Inactive
1	1	0	I/O	Connected	Active	Not Used	Floated	Inactive
1	1	1	I/O	Connected	Active	Not Used	Floated	Inactive

The CEN control enables memory mapping. Here are some possibilities:

1) In multi-bus configurations, one block of memory addresses may access memory on two or more busses. In order to avoid contentions, you can use the CEN signal to selectively disable busses so that only one bus will actually respond when the 8086 accesses duplicated memory addresses.

2) Privileged memory is frequently present in large microcomputer systems. Privileged memory is likely to become more common in microcomputer systems as they grow larger. Privileged memory is memory that can be accessed only under special circumstances. Frequently, system programs are run out of privileged memory, while application programs are run out of non-privileged memory. This prevents errors in application programs from destroying system programs; it also prevents unauthorized access of reserved memory spaces.

DT/$\overline{\text{R}}$ and DEN, the two standard buffer control signals, are generated by the 8288 when it is creating a normal System Bus. These two control signals, when generated by the 8288 Bus Controller, are identical in form and purpose to the signals that the 8086 creates. DT/$\overline{\text{R}}$ determines the data direction for bidirectional buffers, while DEN is a latching strobe.

The 8288 generates two interrupt control signals: $\overline{\text{INTA}}$ and MCE. $\overline{\text{INTA}}$ is active on a System Bus or an I/O Bus. MCE shares a pin with $\overline{\text{PDEN}}$ and is active only on a System Bus.

8288 BUS CONTROLLER INTERRUPT SIGNALS

As we discussed earlier in this chapter, the 8086 executes two bus cycles when acknowledging an interrupt. During each bus cycle, $\overline{\text{INTA}}$ is output as a low read pulse. On the second low $\overline{\text{INTA}}$ pulse, the acknowledged device must return an 8-bit code, which the 8086 uses as an interrupt vector. The $\overline{\text{INTA}}$ control signal generated by the 8288 Bus Controller is identical to the 8086 $\overline{\text{INTA}}$ control signal and serves the same purpose, on a System Bus or an I/O Bus. The MCE control signal has been added for use in large 8086 microcomputer systems that use a variation of the 8259A Priority Interrupt Control Unit. When you have a master 8259A Priority Interrupt Control Unit and slave 8259A Priority Interrupt Control Units, you will use MCE as a control to the master, while $\overline{\text{INTA}}$ becomes a control to slaves. The 8086 version of the 8259A Priority Interrupt Control Unit is not described in this chapter.

THE 8282/8283 8-BIT INPUT/OUTPUT LATCH

These are simple unidirectional 8-bit latch buffers. The 8283 inverts inputs in order to create outputs; the 8282 does not. That is the only difference between these two devices.

Both devices have three-state outputs. When a device is not selected, its outputs are floated.

These devices are manufactured using bipolar technology. All signals arc TTL-level compatible. Outputs have a high drive capability, as defined in the data sheets at the end of this chapter. The devices are packaged as 20-pin DIPs.

THE 8282/8283 INPUT/OUTPUT LATCH PINS AND SIGNAL ASSIGNMENTS

Figure 5-18 illustrates the pins and signal assignments for the 8282 and 8283 8-bit input/output latches.

Data must be input at DI0-D17.

When STB is high, the internal latches appear transparent and data on the output pins track data on the input pins. The transition from high to low of STB latches the data. The outputs remain stable while STB is low.

Data that is latched internally is output when $\overline{OE}$ is low. The 8282 outputs data unaltered, while the 8283 inverts the data.

Were you to simply ground $\overline{OE}$ and tie STB to +5 V, the 8282 or 8283 I/O ports will function as simple bus drivers. The outputs will continuously track the inputs, but will support heavier signal loads.

If you tie STB high, but use the low $\overline{OE}$ pulse, then input data is constantly available but outputs only become valid while $\overline{OE}$ is low. Timing may be illustrated as follows:

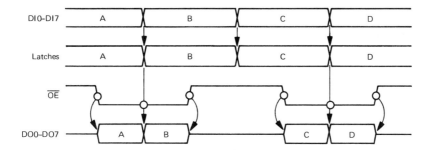

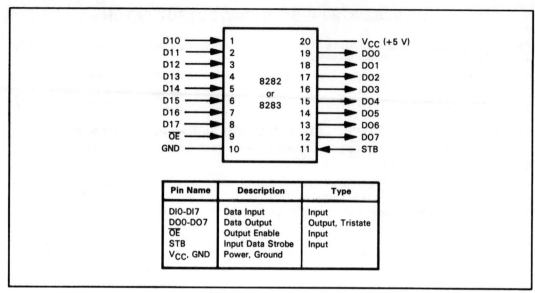

Figure 5-18.   8282 and 8283 Input/Output Latch Pins and Signal Assignments

When the Strobe and Output Enable signal are both active, I/O port logic may be illustrated as follows:

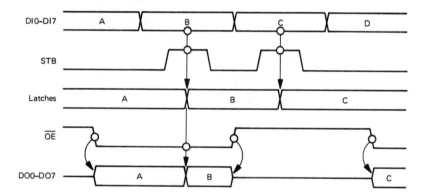

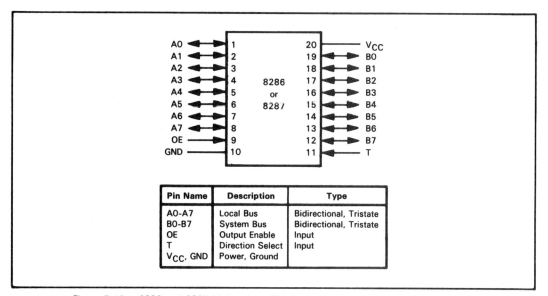

Figure 5-19. 8286 and 8287 Bidirectional Bus Transceiver Pins and Signal Assignments

THE 8286/8287 8-BIT BIDIRECTIONAL BUS TRANSCEIVERS

These two devices are used to buffer bidirectional lines on a System Bus. The 8286 transmits data unaltered, while the 8287 inverts the data. The two devices are otherwise the same.

The 8286 and 8287 bidirectional bus drivers are manufactured using bipolar technology. All pins are TTL-level compatible. The devices are packaged as 20-pin DIPs.

8286 AND 8287 BIDIRECTIONAL BUS TRANSCEIVER PINS AND SIGNAL ASSIGNMENTS

Figure 5-19 illustrates pins and signal assignments for the 8286 and 8287 bidirectional bus drivers.

A0-A7 constitute eight parallel data lines that connect with the microprocessor Data/Address Bus. B0-B7 constitute eight equivalent lines that connect with the System Bus. System Bus outputs have a higher line drive capability (as defined in the data sheets at the end of this chapter); otherwise, there is no difference between the two busses.

When the T input is low, data arriving at the B pins is output via the A pins. When T is high, data arriving at the A pins are output via the B pins. The actual data transfer occurs only while $\overline{OE}$ is low. When used as an 8086 Data Bus transceiver, T should be connected to DT/$\overline{R}$ and $\overline{OE}$ connected to $\overline{DEN}$.

SOME 8086 MICROPROCESSOR BUS CONFIGURATIONS

We are now going to look at some 8086 microprocessor bus configurations.

The flexibility of the 8086 gives rise to such a bewildering array of system configuration possibilities that a whole book could be written on the subject. We are going to fulfill the more limited objective of identifying possibilities.

Figure 5-20 illustrates the simplest case. Here we are using the 8086 to generate a simple microcomputer system. Addresses taken off the bidirectional 8086 Data/Address Bus are unidirectional. We therefore use 8282 I/O ports to latch addresses of the 8086 Data/Address Bus. In Figure 5-20 we show just two 8282 I/O ports generating a 16-line Address Bus. Address lines A16 through A19 are wasted. By adding one more 8282 I/O port to the logic in Figure 5-37, you could include the four missing Address Bus lines.

In Figure 5-20, we ground the Output Enable inputs of the 8282 I/O ports; the Address Bus will therefore never be floated. We use the 8086 ALE pulse to strobe addresses into the 8282 I/O ports.

Since the Data Bus is bidirectional, we use 8286 bidirectional Bus Transceivers in order to create a separate Data Bus from the 8086 Address/Data Bus. Two 8286 bidirectional Bus Transceivers are required to create the 16-line Data Bus. We can use the DT/$\overline{\text{R}}$ and $\overline{\text{DEN}}$ outputs of the 8086 as the 8286 T and $\overline{\text{CS}}$ inputs.

We can now illustrate timing for creation of the Address Bus and Data Bus during a read bus cycle, as follows:

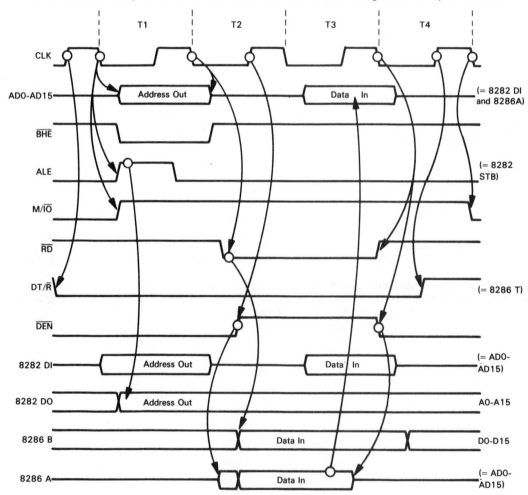

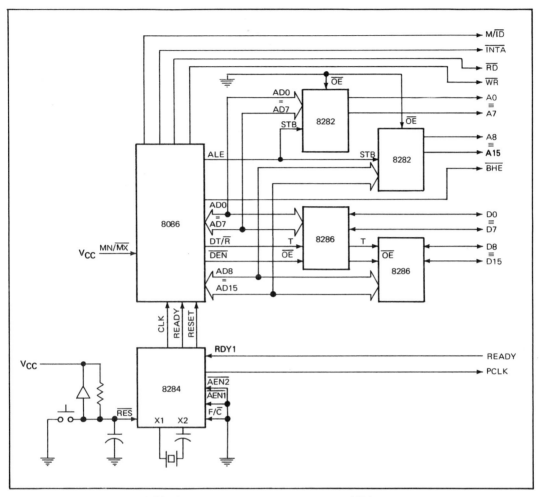

Figure 5-20. Generating a System Bus for a Simple 8086 Configuration

The simple system illustrated in Figure 5-20 will not make use of the dual READY clock logic. A single READY input is connected to RDY1, and both of the READY enables are grounded. Thus, the 8086 READY input will be created directly from the 8284 RDY1 input.

Figure 5-21 illustrates a slightly more complex 8086 microcomputer configuration. Figure 5-21 uses an 8288 Bus Controller to generate System Bus control signals. The DEN, DT/$\overline{R}$, and ALE control outputs, which in Figure 5-20 were generated by the 8086 microprocessor, are now generated by the 8288 Bus Controller.

As a stand-alone microcomputer configuration, Figure 5-21 offers little or no advantage over Figure 5-20. In a single bus, single 8086 microcomputer configuration, there is no compelling reason to use the 8288 Bus Controller. All it does is add an extra component to the system without offering any significant logic enhancement.

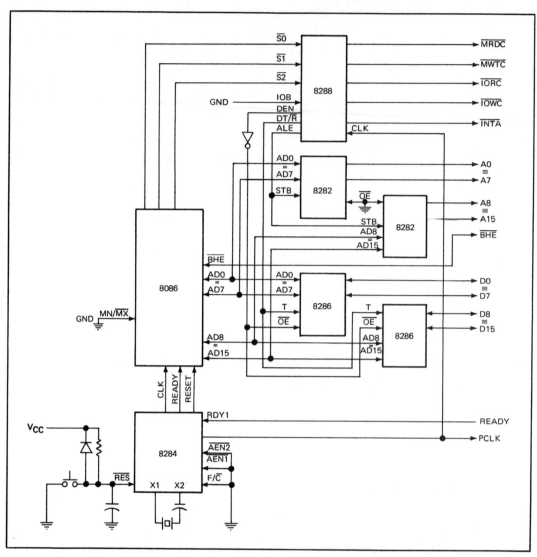

Figure 5-21. Generating a System Bus in an 8086 Microcomputer System Using
an 8288 Bus Controller

DATA SHEETS

This section contains specific electrical and timing data for the following devices:

- 8086 CPU
- 8088 CPU
- 8282/8283 I/O Ports
- 8284 Clock Generator
- 8286/8287 Bidirectional Bus Drivers
- 8288 Bus Controller

ABSOLUTE MAXIMUM RATINGS*

Ambient Temperature Under Bias . . . . 0°C to 70°C
Storage Temperature . . . . −65°C to +150°C
Voltage on Any Pin with
   Respect to Ground . . . . −1.0 to +7V
Power Dissipation . . . . 2.5 Watt

*NOTICE: Stresses above those listed under "Absolute Maximum Ratings" may cause permanent damage to the device. This is a stress rating only and functional operation of the device at these or any other conditions above those indicated in the operational sections of this specification is not implied. Exposure to absolute maximum rating conditions for extended periods may affect device reliability.

D.C. CHARACTERISTICS

    8086: $T_A = 0°C$ to 70°C, $V_{CC} = 5V \pm 10\%$
8086-2/8086-4: $T_A = 0°C$ to 70°C, $V_{CC} = 5V \pm 5\%$

Symbol	Parameter	Min.	Max.	Units	Test Conditions
V_{IL}	Input Low Voltage	−0.5	+0.8	V	
V_{IH}	Input High Voltage	2.0	$V_{CC} + 0.5$	V	
V_{OL}	Output Low Voltage		0.45	V	$I_{OL} = 2.0$ mA
V_{OH}	Output High Voltage	2.4		V	$I_{OH} = -400 \mu A$
I_{CC}	Power Supply Current 8086/8086-4 8086-2		340 350	mA mA	$T_A = 25°C$
I_{LI}	Input Leakage Current		±10	μA	$0V < V_{IN} < V_{CC}$
I_{LO}	Output Leakage Current		±10	μA	$0.45V \leqslant V_{OUT} \leqslant V_{CC}$
V_{CL}	Clock Input Low Voltage	−0.5	+0.6	V	
V_{CH}	Clock Input High Voltage	3.9	$V_{CC} + 1.0$	V	
C_{IN}	Capacitance of Input Buffer (All input except $AD_0 - AD_{15}$, $\overline{RQ}/\overline{GT}$)		15	pF	fc = 1 MHz
C_{IO}	Capacitance of I/O Buffer ($AD_0 - AD_{15}$, $\overline{RQ}/\overline{GT}$)		15	pF	fc = 1 MHz

Data sheets on pages 5-D2 through 5-D29 are reprinted by permission of Intel Corporation.

8086/8086-2/8086-4

A.C. CHARACTERISTICS

8086: $T_A = 0°C$ to $70°C$, $V_{CC} = 5V \pm 10\%$
8086-2/8086-4: $T_A = 0°C$ to $70°C$, $V_{CC} = 5V \pm 5\%$

8086 MINIMUM COMPLEXITY SYSTEM (Figures 8, 9, 12, 15)
TIMING REQUIREMENTS

Symbol	Parameter	8086/8086-4 Min.	8086/8086-4 Max.	8086-2 (Preliminary) Min.	8086-2 (Preliminary) Max.	Units	Test Conditions
TCLCL	CLK Cycle Period — 8086 — 8086-4	200 250	500 500	125	500	ns	
TCLCH	CLK Low Time	$(⅔\ TCLCL) - 15$		$(⅔\ TCLCL) - 15$		ns	
TCHCL	CLK High Time	$(½\ TCLCL) + 2$		$(½\ TCLCL) + 2$		ns	
TCH1CH2	CLK Rise Time		10		10	ns	From 1.0V to 3.5V
TCL2CL1	CLK Fall Time		10		10	ns	From 3.5V to 1.0V
TDVCL	Data In Setup Time	30		20		ns	
TCLDX	Data In Hold Time	10		10		ns	
TR1VCL	RDY Setup Time into 8284 (See Notes 1, 2)	35		35		ns	
TCLR1X	RDY Hold Time into 8284 (See Notes 1, 2)	0		0		ns	
TRYHCH	READY Setup Time into 8086	$(⅔\ TCLCL) - 15$		$(⅔\ TCLCL) - 15$		ns	
TCHRYX	READY Hold Time into 8086	30		20		ns	
TRYLCL	READY Inactive to CLK (See Note 3)	-8		-8		ns	
THVCH	HOLD Setup Time	35		20		ns	
TINVCH	INTR, NMI, TEST Setup Time (See Note 2)	30		15		ns	

TIMING RESPONSES

Symbol	Parameter	8086/8086-4 Min.	8086/8086-4 Max.	8086-2 (Preliminary) Min.	8086-2 (Preliminary) Max.	Units	Test Conditions
TCLAV	Address Valid Delay	10	110	10	60	ns	
TCLAX	Address Hold Time	10		10		ns	
TCLAZ	Address Float Delay	TCLAX	80	TCLAX	50	ns	
TLHLL	ALE Width	TCLCH-20		TCLCH-10		ns	
TCLLH	ALE Active Delay		80		50	ns	
TCHLL	ALE Inactive Delay		85		55	ns	
TLLAX	Address Hold Time to ALE Inactive	TCHCL-10		TCHCL-10		ns	$C_L = 20\text{-}100$ pF for all 8086 Outputs (In addition to 8086 self-load)
TCLDV	Data Valid Delay	10	110	10	60	ns	
TCHDX	Data Hold Time	10		10		ns	
TWHDX	Data Hold Time After WR	TCLCH-30		TCLCH-30		ns	
TCVCTV	Control Active Delay 1	10	110	10	70	ns	
TCHCTV	Control Active Delay 2	10	110	10	60	ns	
TCVCTX	Control Inactive Delay	10	110	10	70	ns	
TAZRL	Address Float to READ Active	0		0		ns	
TCLRL	RD Active Delay	10	165	10	100	ns	
TCLRH	RD Inactive Delay	10	150	10	80	ns	
TRHAV	RD Inactive to Next Address Active	TCLCL-45		TCLCL -40		ns	
TCLHAV	HLDA Valid Delay	10	160	10	100	ns	
TRLRH	RD Width	2TCLCL-75		2TCLCL-50		ns	
TWLWH	WR Width	2TCLCL-60		2TCLCL-40		ns	
TAVAL	Address Valid to ALE Low	TCLCH-60		TCLCH-40		ns	

NOTES: 1. Signal at 8284 shown for reference only.
2. Setup requirement for asynchronous signal only to guarantee recognition at next CLK.
3. Applies only to T2 state. (8 ns into T3)

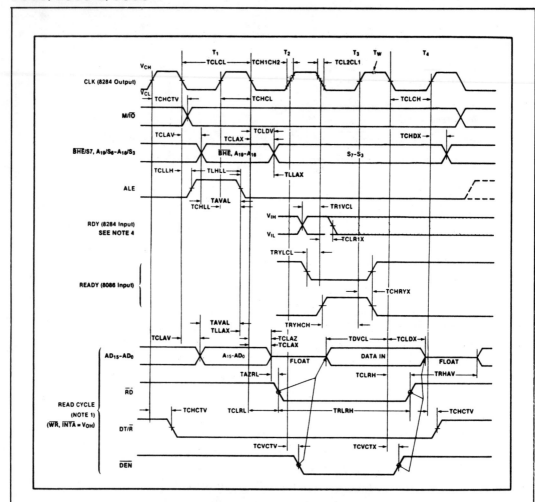

Figure 8. 8086 Bus Timing — Minimum Mode System

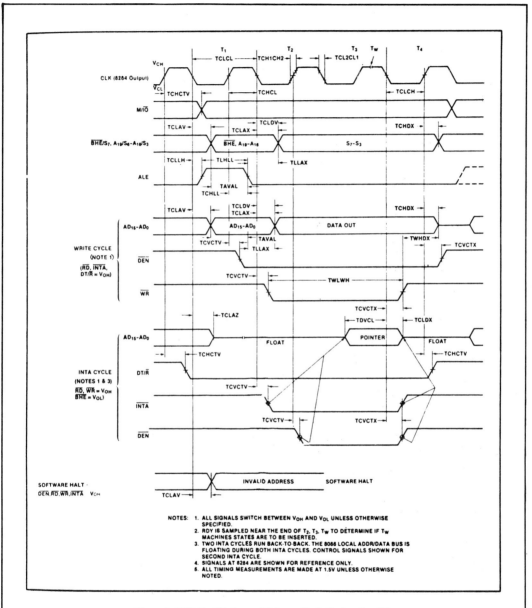

Figure 9. 8086 Bus Timing — Minimum Mode System (cont'd)

8086 MAX MODE SYSTEM (USING 8288 BUS CONTROLLER) (Figures 10-14)

TIMING REQUIREMENTS

Symbol	Parameter	8086/8086-4		8086-2 (Preliminary)		Units	Test Conditions
		Min.	Max.	Min.	Max.		
TCLCL	CLK Cycle Period — 8086	200	500	125	500	ns	
	— 8086-4	250	500				
TCLCH	CLK Low Time	(⅔ TCLCL) – 15		(⅔ TCLCL) – 15		ns	
TCHCL	CLK High Time	(½ TCLCL) + 2		(½ TCLCL) + 2		ns	
TCH1CH2	CLK Rise Time		10		10	ns	From 1.0V to 3.5V
TCL2CL1	CLK Fall Time		10		10	ns	From 3.5V to 1.0V
TDVCL	Data In Setup Time	30		20		ns	
TCLDX	Data In Hold Time	10		10		ns	
TR1VCL	RDY Setup Time into 8284 (See Notes 1, 2)	35		35		ns	
TCLR1X	RDY Hold Time into 8284 (See Notes 1, 2)	0		0		ns	
TRYHCH	READY Setup Time into 8086	(⅔ TCLCL) – 15		(⅔ TCLCL) – 15		ns	
TCHRYX	READY Hold Time into 8086	30		20		ns	
TRYLCL	READY Inactive to CLK (See Note 4)	– 8		– 8		ns	
TINVCH	Setup Time for Recognition (INTR, NMI, TEST) (See Note 2)	30		15		ns	
TGVCH	RQ/GT Setup Time	30		15		ns	
TCHGX	RQ Hold Time into 8086	40		30		ns	

TIMING RESPONSES

Symbol	Parameter	8086/8086-4		8086-2 (Preliminary)		Units	Test Conditions
		Min.	Max.	Min.	Max.		
TCLML	Command Active Delay (See Note 1)	10	35	10	35	ns	
TCLMH	Command Inactive Delay (See Note 1)	10	35	10	35	ns	
TRYHSH	READY Active to Status Passive (See Note 3)		110		65	ns	
TCHSV	Status Active Delay	10	110	10	60	ns	
TCLSH	Status Inactive Delay	10	130	10	70	ns	
TCLAV	Address Valid Delay	10	110	10	60	ns	
TCLAX	Address Hold Time	10		10		ns	
TCLAZ	Address Float Delay	TCLAX	80	TCLAX	50	ns	
TSVLH	Status Valid to ALE High (See Note 1)		15		15	ns	
TSVMCH	Status Valid to MCE High (See Note 1)		15		15	ns	
TCLLH	CLK Low to ALE Valid (See Note 1)		15		15	ns	
TCLMCH	CLK Low to MCE High (See Note 1)		15		15	ns	
TCHLL	ALE Inactive Delay (See Note 1)		15		15	ns	
TCLMCL	MCE Inactive Delay (See Note 1)		15		15	ns	
TCLDV	Data Valid Delay	10	110	10	60	ns	CL = 20-100 pF for all 8086 Outputs (In addition to 8086 self-load)
TCHDX	Data Hold Time	10		10		ns	
TCVNV	Control Active Delay (See Note 1)	5	45	5	45	ns	
TCVNX	Control Inactive Delay (See Note 1)	10	45	10	45	ns	
TAZRL	Address Float to Read Active	0		0		ns	
TCLRL	RD Active Delay	10	165	10	100	ns	
TCLRH	RD Inactive Delay	10	150	10	80	ns	
TRHAV	RD Inactive to Next Address Active	TCLCL–45		TCLCL–40		ns	
TCHDTL	Direction Control Active Delay (See Note 1)		50		50	ns	
TCHDTH	Direction Control Inactive Delay (See Note 1)		30		30	ns	
TCLGL	GT Active Delay	0	85	0	50	ns	
TCLGH	GT Inactive Delay	0	85	0	50	ns	
TRLRH	RD Width	2TCLCL–75		2TCLCL–50		ns	

NOTES: 1. Signal at 8284 or 8288 shown for reference only.
2. Setup requirement for asynchronous signal only to guarantee recognition at next CLK.
3. Applies only to T3 and wait states.
4. Applies only to T2 state (8 ns into T3).

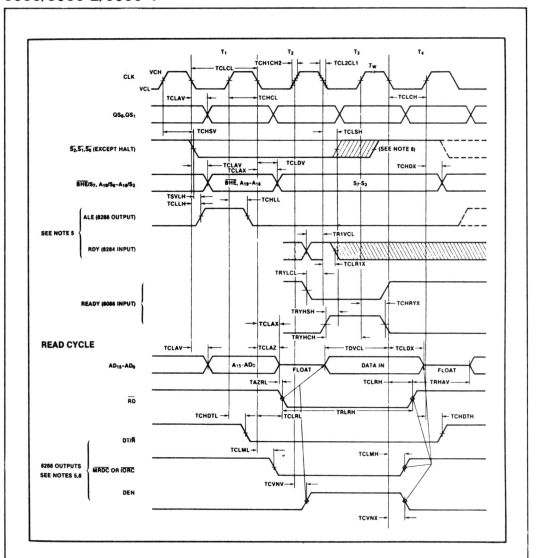

Figure 10. 8086 Bus Timing — Maximum Mode System (Using 8288)

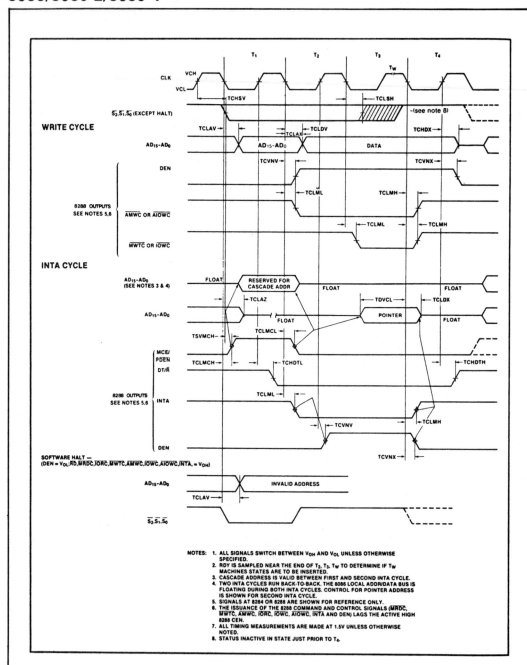

Figure 11. 8086 Bus Timing — Maximum Mode System (Using 8288) (cont.)

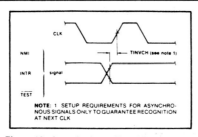

Figure 12. Asynchronous Signal Recognition

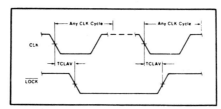

Figure 13. Bus Lock Signal Timing (Maximum Mode Only)

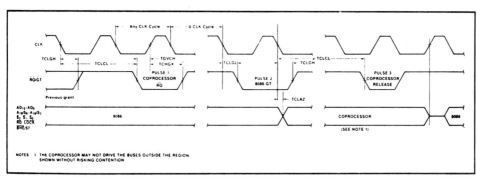

Figure 14. Request/Grant Sequence Timing (Maximum Mode Only)

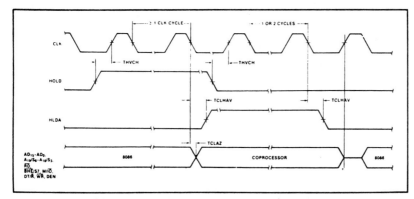

Figure 15. Hold/Hold Acknowledge Timing (Minimum Mode Only)

ABSOLUTE MAXIMUM RATINGS*

Ambient Temperature Under Bias . . . . 0 °C to 70 °C
Storage Temperature . . . . − 65 °C to + 150 °C
Voltage on Any Pin with
   Respect to Ground . . . . − 1.0 to + 7V
Power Dissipation . . . . 2.5 Watt

*NOTICE: Stresses above those listed under "Absolute Maximum Ratings" may cause permanent damage to the device. This is a stress rating only and functional operation of the device at these or any other conditions above those indicated in the operational sections of this specification is not implied. Exposure to absolute maximum rating conditions for extended periods may affect device reliability.

D.C. CHARACTERISTICS

8088: $T_A = 0 °C$ to 70 °C, $V_{CC} = 5V \pm 10\%$

Symbol	Parameter	Min.	Max.	Units	Test Conditions
V_{IL}	Input Low Voltage	− 0.5	+ 0.8	V	
V_{IH}	Input High Voltage	2.0	$V_{CC} + 0.5$	V	
V_{OL}	Output Low Voltage		0.45	V	$I_{OL} = 2.0$ mA
V_{OH}	Output High Voltage	2.4		V	$I_{OH} = 400 \mu A$
I_{CC}	Power Supply Current		340	mA	
I_{LI}	Input Leakage Current		± 10	μA	$0V < VIN < V_{CC}$
I_{LO}	Output Leakage Current		± 10	μA	$0.45V \leq V_{OUT} \leq V_{CC}$
V_{CL}	Clock Input Low Voltage	− 0.5	+ 0.6	V	
V_{CH}	Clock Input High Voltage	3.9	$V_{CC} + 1.0$	V	
C_{IN}	Capacitance of Input Buffer (All input except AD_0-AD_7 RQ/GT)		15	pF	fc = 1 MHz
C_{IO}	Capacitance of I/O Buffer (AD_0-AD_7 RQ/GT)		15	pF	fc = 1 MHz

8088

A.C. CHARACTERISTICS

8088: $T_A = 0\,°C$ to $70\,°C$, $V_{CC} = 5V \pm 10\%$

8088 MINIMUM COMPLEXITY SYSTEM TIMING REQUIREMENTS

Symbol	Parameter	Min.	Max.	Units	Test Conditions
TCLCL	CLK Cycle Period	200	500	ns	
TCLCH	CLK Low Time	$(2/3\,TCLCL)-15$		ns	
TCHCL	CLK High Time	$(1/3\,TCLCL)+2$		ns	
TCH1CH2	CLK Rise Time		10	ns	From 1.0V to 3.5V
TCL2CL1	CLK Fall Time		10	ns	From 3.5V to 1.0V
TDVCL	Data In Setup Time	30		ns	
TCLDX	Data In Hold Time	10		ns	
TR1VCL	RDY Setup Time into 8284 (See Notes 1, 2)	35		ns	
TCLR1X	RDY Hold Time into 8284 (See Notes 1, 2)	0		ns	
TRYHCH	READY Setup Time into 8088	$(2/3\,TCLCL)-15$		ns	
TCHRYX	READY Hold Time into 8088	30		ns	
TRYLCL	READY Inactive to CLK (See Note 3)	-8		ns	
THVCH	HOLD Setup Time	35		ns	
TINVCH	INTR, NMI, $\overline{TEST}$ Setup Time (See Note 2)	30		ns	

TIMING RESPONSES

Symbol	Parameter	Min.	Max.	Units	Test Conditions
TCLAV	Address Valid Delay	15	110	ns	
TCLAX	Address Hold Time	10		ns	
TCLAZ	Address Float Delay	TCLAX	80	ns	
TLHLL	ALE Width	TCLCH-20		ns	
TCLLH	ALE Active Delay		80	ns	
TCHLL	ALE Inactive Delay		85	ns	
TLLAX	Address Hold Time to ALE Inactive	TCHCL-10		ns	
TCLDV	Data Valid Delay	10	110	ns	$C_L = 20\text{-}100$ pF for all 8088 Outputs in addition to internal loads
TCHDX	Data Hold Time	10		ns	
TWHDX	Data Hold Time After $\overline{WR}$	TCLCH-30		ns	
TCVCTV	Control Active Delay 1	10	110	ns	
TCHCTV	Control Active Delay 2	10	110	ns	
TCVCTX	Control Inactive Delay	10	110	ns	
TAZRL	Address Float to READ Active	0		ns	
TCLRL	$\overline{RD}$ Active Delay	10	165	ns	
TCLRH	$\overline{RD}$ Inactive Delay	10	150	ns	
TRHAV	$\overline{RD}$ Inactive to Next Address Active	TCLCL-45		ns	
TCLHAV	HLDA Valid Delay	10	160	ns	
TRLRH	$\overline{RD}$ Width	2TCLCL-75		ns	
TWLWH	$\overline{WR}$ Width	2TCLCL-60		ns	
TAVAL	Address Valid to ALE Low	TCLCH-60		ns	

NOTES: 1. Signal at 8284 shown for reference only.
2. Setup requirement for asynchronous signal only to guarantee recognition at next CLK.
3. Applies only to T2 state (8 ns into T3 state).

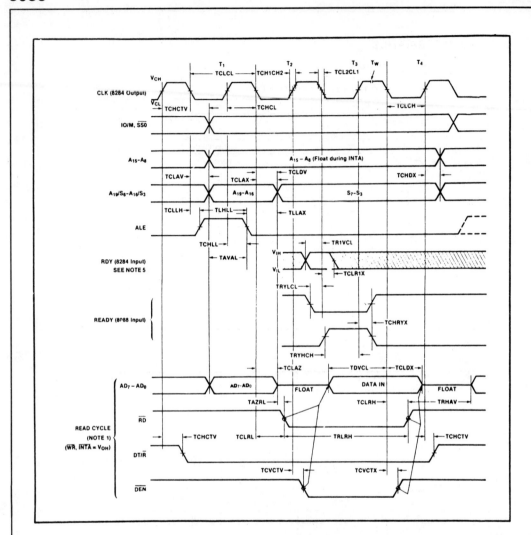

Figure 11: 8088 Bus Timing — Minimum Mode System

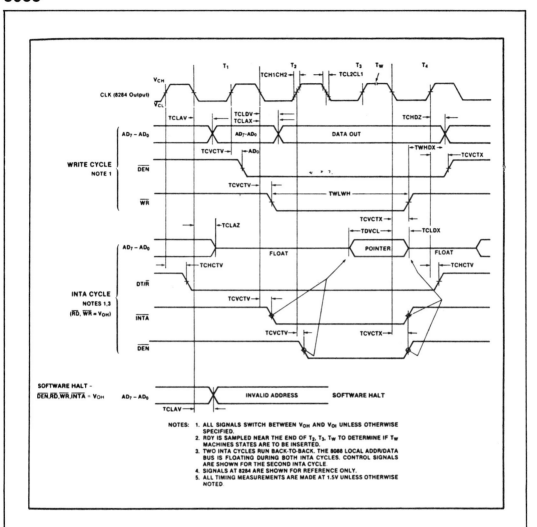

Figure 12. 8088 Bus Timing — Minimum Mode System (cont.)

8088

8088 MAX MODE SYSTEM (USING 8288 BUS CONTROLLER) TIMING REQUIREMENTS

Symbol	Parameter	Min.	Max.	Units	Test Conditions
TCLCL	CLK Cycle Period	200	500	ns	
TCLCH	CLK Low Time	(⅔TCLCL)-15		ns	
TCHCL	CLK High Time	(⅓TCLCL)+2		ns	
TCH1CH2	CLK Rise Time		10	ns	From 1.0V to 3.5V
TCL2CL1	CLK Fall Time		10	ns	From 3.5V to 1.0V
TDVCL	Data In Setup Time	30		ns	
TCLDX	Data In Hold Time	10		ns	
TR1VCL	RDY Setup Time into 8284 (See Notes 1, 2)	35		ns	
TCLR1X	RDY Hold Time into 8284 (See Notes 1, 2)	0		ns	
TRYHCH	READY Setup Time into 8088	(⅔TCLCL)-15		ns	
TCHRYX	READY Hold Time into 8088	30		ns	
TRYLCL	READY Inactive to CLK (See Note 4)	-8		ns	
TINVCH	Setup Time for Recognition (INTR, NMI, $\overline{TEST}$) (See Note 2)	30		ns	
TGVCH	$\overline{RQ}/\overline{GT}$ Setup Time	30		ns	
TCHGX	$\overline{RQ}$ Hold Time into 8086	40		ns	

TIMING RESPONSES

Symbol	Parameter	Min.	Max.	Units	Test Conditions
TCLML	Command Active Delay (See Note 1)	10	35	ns	
TCLMH	Command Inactive Delay (See Note 1)	10	35	ns	
TRYHSH	READY Active to Status Passive (See Note 3)		110	ns	
TCHSV	Status Active Delay	10	110	ns	
TCLSH	Status Inactive Delay	10	130	ns	
TCLAV	Address Valid Delay	15	110	ns	
TCLAX	Address Hold Time	10		ns	
TCLAZ	Address Float Delay	TCLAX	80	ns	
TSVLH	Status Valid to ALE High (See Note 1)		15	ns	
TSVMCH	Status Valid to MCE High (See Note 1)		15	ns	
TCLLH	CLK Low to ALE Valid (See Note 1)		15	ns	
TCLMCH	CLK Low to MCE High (See Note 1)		15	ns	
TCHLL	ALE Inactive Delay (See Note 1)		15	ns	
TCLMCL	MCE Inactive Delay (See Note 1)		15	ns	C_L = 20-100 pF for all 8088 Outputs in addition to internal loads
TCLDV	Data Valid Delay	15	110	ns	
TCHDX	Data Hold Time	10		ns	
TCVNV	Control Active Delay (See Note 1)	5	45	ns	
TCVNX	Control Inactive Delay (See Note 1)	10	45	ns	
TAZRL	Address Float to Read Active	0		ns	
TCLRL	RD Active Delay	10	165	ns	
TCLRH	RD Inactive Delay	10	150	ns	
TRHAV	RD Inactive to Next Address Active	TCLCL-45		ns	
TCHDTL	Direction Control Active Delay (See Note 1)		50	ns	
TCHDTH	Direction Control Inactive Delay (See Note 1)		30	ns	
TCLGL	$\overline{GT}$ Active Delay		110	ns	
TCLGH	$\overline{GT}$ Inactive Delay		85	ns	
TRLRH	$\overline{RD}$ Width	2TCLCL-75		ns	

NOTES: 1. Signal at 8284 or 8288 shown for reference only.
2. Setup requirement for asynchronous signal only to guarantee recognition at next CLK.
3. Applies only to T3 and wait states.
4. Applies only to T2 state (8 ns into T3 state).

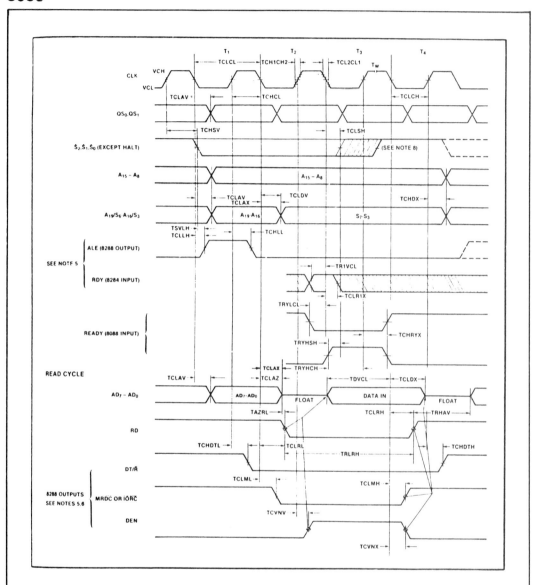

Figure 13. 8088 Bus Timing — Maximum Mode System (Using 8288)

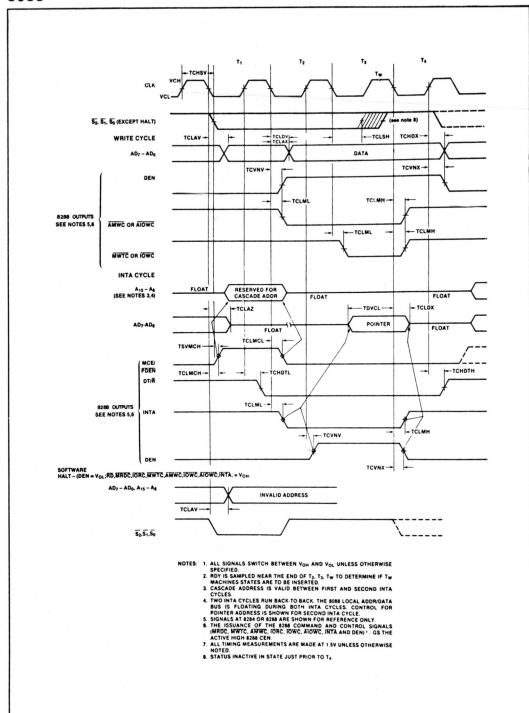

NOTES: 1. ALL SIGNALS SWITCH BETWEEN V_{OH} AND V_{OL} UNLESS OTHERWISE SPECIFIED.
2. RDY IS SAMPLED NEAR THE END OF T_2, T_3, T_W TO DETERMINE IF T_W MACHINES STATES ARE TO BE INSERTED.
3. CASCADE ADDRESS IS VALID BETWEEN FIRST AND SECOND INTA CYCLES.
4. TWO INTA CYCLES RUN BACK-TO-BACK. THE 8088 LOCAL ADDR/DATA BUS IS FLOATING DURING BOTH INTA CYCLES. CONTROL FOR POINTER ADDRESS IS SHOWN FOR SECOND INTA CYCLE.
5. SIGNALS AT 8284 OR 8288 ARE SHOWN FOR REFERENCE ONLY.
6. THE ISSUANCE OF THE 8288 COMMAND AND CONTROL SIGNALS (MRDC, MWTC, AMWC, IORC, IOWC, AIOWC, INTA AND DEN) LAGS THE ACTIVE HIGH 8288 CEN.
7. ALL TIMING MEASUREMENTS ARE MADE AT 1.5V UNLESS OTHERWISE NOTED.
8. STATUS INACTIVE IN STATE JUST PRIOR TO T_4.

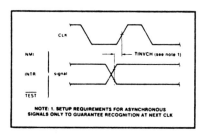

Figure 15. Asynchronous Signal Recognition

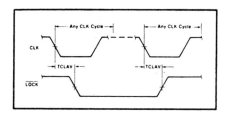

Figure 16. Bus Lock Signal Timing (Maximum Mode Only)

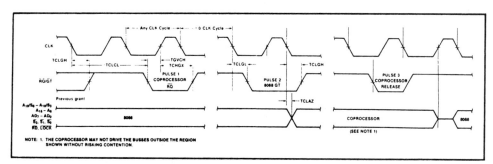

Figure 17. Request/Grant Sequence Timing (Maximum Mode Only)

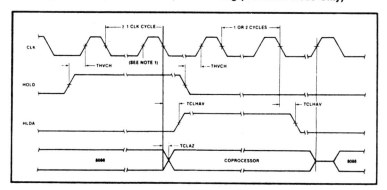

Figure 18. Hold/Hold Acknowledge Timing (Minimum Mode Only)

8282/8283

ABSOLUTE MAXIMUM RATINGS*

Temperature Under Bias.................0°C to 70°C
Storage Temperature............. − 65°C to + 150°C
All Output and Supply Voltages........ − 0.5V to + 7V
All Input Voltages.................. − 1.0V to + 5.5V
Power Dissipation..........................1 Watt

*NOTICE: Stresses above those listed under "Absolute Maximum Ratings" may cause permanent damage to the device. This is a stress rating only and functional operation of the device at these or any other conditions above those indicated in the operational sections of this specification is not implied. Exposure to absolute maximum rating conditions for extended periods may affect device reliability.

D.C. CHARACTERISTICS

Conditions: V_{CC} = 5V ± 10%, T_A = 0°C to 70°C

Symbol	Parameter	Min	Max	Units	Test Conditions
V_C	Input Clamp Voltage		− 1	V	I_C = − 5 mA
I_{CC}	Power Supply Current		160	mA	
I_F	Forward Input Current		− 0.2	mA	V_F = 0.45V
I_R	Reverse Input Current		50	µA	V_R = 5.25V
V_{OL}	Output Low Voltage		.45	V	I_{OL} = 32 mA
V_{OH}	Output High Voltage	2.4		V	I_{OH} = − 5 mA
I_{OFF}	Output Off Current		± 50	µA	V_{OFF} = 0.45 to 5.25V
V_{IL}	Input Low Voltage		0.8	V	V_{CC} = 5.0V See Note 1
V_{IH}	Input High Voltage	2.0		V	V_{CC} = 5.0V See Note 1
C_{IN}	Input Capacitance		12	pF	F = 1 MHz V_{BIAS} = 2.5V, V_{CC} = 5V T_A = 25°C

Notes: 1. Output Loading I_{OL} = 32 mA, I_{OH} = − 5 mA, C_L = 300 pF

A.C. CHARACTERISTICS

Conditions: V_{CC} = 5V ± 10%, T_A = 0°C to 70°C

Loading: Outputs — I_{OL} = 32 mA, I_{OH} = − 5 mA, C_L = 300 pF

Symbol	Parameter	Min	Max	Units	Test Conditions
TIVOV	Input to Output Delay —Inverting —Non-Inverting		22 30	ns ns	(See Note 1)
TSHOV	STB to Output Delay —Inverting —Non-Inverting		40 45	ns ns	
TEHOZ	Output Disable Time		18	ns	
TELOV	Output Enable Time	10	30	ns	
TIVSL	Input to STB Setup Time	0		ns	
TSLIX	Input to STB Hold Time	25		ns	
TSHSL	STB High Time	15		ns	

NOTE: 1. See waveforms and test load circuit on following page.

8282/8283

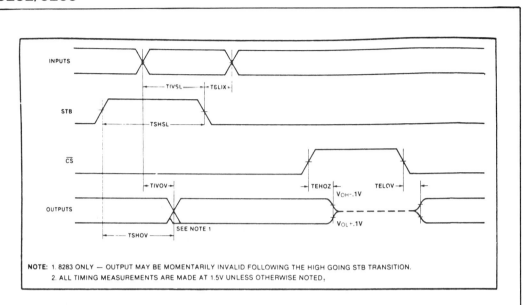

NOTE: 1. 8283 ONLY — OUTPUT MAY BE MOMENTARILY INVALID FOLLOWING THE HIGH GOING STB TRANSITION.
2. ALL TIMING MEASUREMENTS ARE MADE AT 1.5V UNLESS OTHERWISE NOTED.

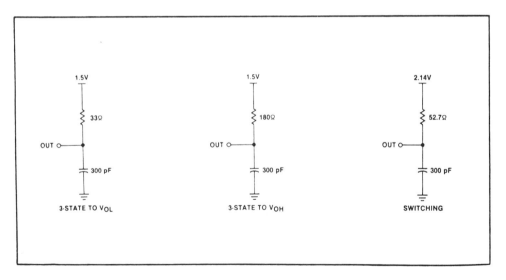

Figure 4. Output Test Load Circuits

OUTPUT DELAY VS. CAPACITANCE

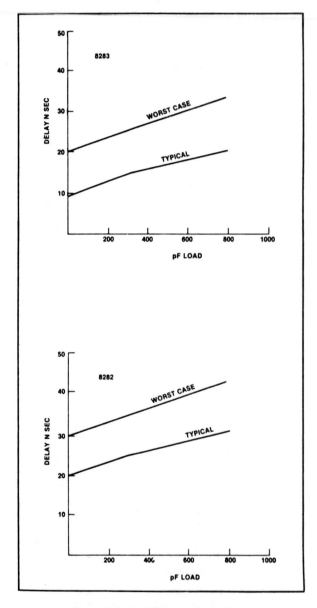

Figure 5. Output Delay vs. Capacitance

8284

ABSOLUTE MAXIMUM RATINGS*

Temperature Under Bias.................0°C to 70°C
Storage Temperature.............−65°C to +150°C
All Output and Supply Voltages........−0.5V to +7V
All Input Voltages..................−1.0V to +5.5V
Power Dissipation.........................1 Watt

*NOTICE: Stresses above those listed under "Absolute Maximum Ratings" may cause permanent damage to the device. This is a stress rating only and functional operation of the device at these or any other conditions above those indicated in the operational sections of this specification is not implied. Exposure to absolute maximum rating conditions for extended periods may affect device reliability.

D.C. CHARACTERISTICS

Conditions: T_A = 0°C to 70°C; V_{CC} = 5V ± 10%

Symbol	Parameter	Min	Max	Units	Test Conditions
I_F	Forward Input Current		−0.5	mA	V_F = 0.45V
I_R	Reverse Input Current		50	μA	V_R = 5.25V
V_C	Input Forward Clamp Voltage		−1.0	V	I_C = −5 mA
I_{CC}	Power Supply Current		140	mA	
V_{IL}	Input LOW Voltage		0.8	V	V_{CC} = 5.0V
V_{IH}	Input HIGH Voltage	2.0		V	V_{CC} = 5.0V
V_{IH_R}	Reset Input HIGH Voltage	2.6		V	V_{CC} = 5.0V
V_{OL}	Output LOW Voltage		0.45	V	5 mA
V_{OH}	Output HIGH Voltage CLK Other Outputs	4 2.4		V V	−1 mA −1 mA
V_{IH_R}−V_{IL_R}	$\overline{RES}$ Input Hysteresis	0.25		V	V_{CC} = 5.0V

A.C. CHARACTERISTICS

Conditions: T_A = 0°C to 70°C; V_{CC} = 5V ± 10%

TIMING REQUIREMENTS

Symbol	Parameter	Min	Max	Units	Test Conditions
TEHEL	External Frequency High Time	13		ns	90% − 90% V_{IN}
TELEH	External Frequency Low Time	13		ns	10% − 10% V_{IN}
TELEL	EFI Period	TEHEL + TELEH ÷ d		ns	(Note 1)
	XTAL Frequency	12	25	MHz	
TR1VCL	RDY1, RDY2 Set-Up to CLK	35		ns	
TCLR1X	RDY1, RDY2 Hold to CLK	0		ns	
TA1VR1V	$\overline{AEN1}$, $\overline{AEN2}$ Set-Up to RDY1, RDY2	15		ns	
TCLA1X	$\overline{AEN1}$, $\overline{AEN2}$ Hold to CLK	0		ns	
TYHEH	CSYNC Set-Up to EFI	20		ns	
TEHYL	CSYNC Hold to EFI	20		ns	
TYHYL	CSYNC Width	2 TELEL		ns	
TI1HCL	$\overline{RES}$ Set-Up to CLK	65		ns	(Note 2)
TCLI1H	$\overline{RES}$ Hold to CLK	20		ns	(Note 2)

8284

TIMING RESPONSES

Symbol	Parameter	Min	Max	Units	Test Conditions
TCLCL	CLK Cycle Period	125		ns	
TCHCL	CLK High Time	($\frac{1}{2}$TCLCL) + 2.0		ns	Fig. 3 & Fig. 4
TCLCH	CLK Low Time	($\frac{2}{3}$TCLCL) – 15.0		ns	Fig. 3 & Fig. 4
TCH1CH2 TCL2CL1	CLK Rise or Fall Time		10	ns	1.0V to 3.5V
TPHPL	PCLK High Time	TCLCL – 20		ns	
TPLPH	PCLK Low Time	TCLCL – 20		ns	
TRYLCL	Ready Inactive to CLK (See Note 4)	–8		ns	Fig. 5 & Fig. 6
TRYHCH	Ready Active to CLK (See Note 3)	($\frac{2}{3}$TCLCL)–15.0		ns	Fig. 5 & Fig. 6
TCLIL	CLK to Reset Delay	40		ns	
TCLPH	CLK to PCLK High Delay		22	ns	
TCLPL	CLK to PCLK Low Delay		22	ns	
TOLCH	OSC to CLK High Delay	–5	12	ns	
TOLCL	OSC to CLK Low Delay	2	20	ns	

Notes: 1. $\frac{1}{2}$ = EFI rise (5 ns max) + EFI fall (5 ns max).
2. Set up and hold only necessary to guarantee recognition at next clock.
3. Applies only to T3 and TW states.
4. Applies only to T2 states.

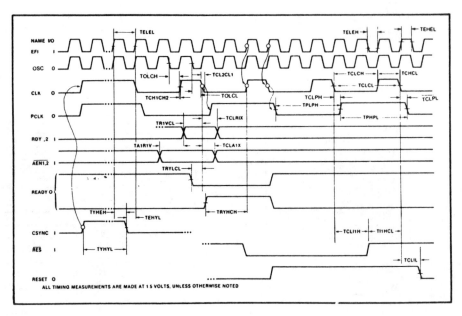

A.C. TEST CIRCUITS

ABSOLUTE MAXIMUM RATINGS*

Temperature Under Bias.................0°C to 70°C
Storage Temperature............. −65°C to +150°C
All Output and Supply Voltages........ −0.5V to +7V
All Input Voltages.................. −1.0V to +5.5V
Power Dissipation..........................1 Watt

*NOTICE: Stresses above those listed under "Absolute Maximum Ratings" may cause permanent damage to the device. This is a stress rating only and functional operation of the device at these or any other conditions above those indicated in the operational sections of this specification is not implied. Exposure to absolute maximum rating conditions for extended periods may affect device reliability.

D.C. CHARACTERISTICS FOR 8286/8287

Conditions: V_{CC} = 5V ±10% T_A = 0°C to 70°C

Symbol	Parameter	Min	Max	Units	Test Conditions
V_C	Input Clamp Voltage		−1	V	I_C = −5 mA
I_{CC}	Power Supply Current —8287		130	mA	
	—8286		160	mA	
I_F	Forward Input Current		−0.2	mA	V_F = 0.45V
I_R	Reverse Input Current		50	μA	V_R = 5.25V
V_{OL}	Output Low Voltage —B Outputs		.45	V	I_{OL} = 32 mA
	—A Outputs		.45	V	I_{OL} = 16 mA
V_{OH}	Output High Voltage —B Outputs	2.4		V	I_{OH} = −5 mA
	—A Outputs	2.4		V	I_{OH} = −1 mA
I_{OFF}	Output Off Current		I_F		V_{OFF} = 0.45V
I_{OFF}	Output Off Current		I_R		V_{OFF} = 5.25V
V_{IL}	Input Low Voltage —A Side		0.8	V	V_{CC} = 5.0V, See Note 1
	—B Side		0.9	V	V_{CC} = 5.0V, See Note 1
V_{IH}	Input High Voltage	2.0		V	V_{CC} = 5.0V, See Note 1
C_{IN}	Input Capacitance		12	pF	F = 1 MHz V_{BIAS} = 2.5V, V_{CC} = 5V T_A = 25°C

Note: 1. B Outputs — I_{OL} = 32 mA, I_{OH} = -5 mA, C_L = 300 pF A Outputs — I_{OL} = 16 mA, I_{OH} = -1 mA, C_L = 100 pF

A.C. CHARACTERISTICS FOR 8286/8287

Conditions: V_{CC} = 5V ±10%, T_A = 0°C to 70°C

Loading: B Outputs — I_{OL} = 32 mA, I_{OH} = −5 mA, C_L = 300 pF
A Outputs — I_{OL} = 16 mA, I_{OH} = −1 mA, C_L = 100 pF

Symbol	Parameter	Min	Max	Units	Test Conditions
TIVOV	Input to Output Delay Inverting		22	ns	(See Note 1)
	Non-Inverting		30	ns	
TEHTV	Transmit/Receive Hold Time	TEHOZ		ns	
TTVEL	Transmit/Receive Setup	30		ns	
TEHOZ	Output Disable Time		18	ns	
TELOV	Output Enable Time	10	30	ns	

Note: 1. See waveforms and test load circuit on following page.

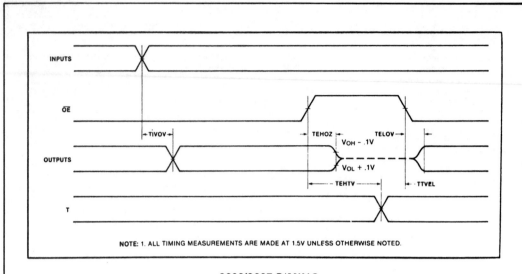

8286/8287 TIMING

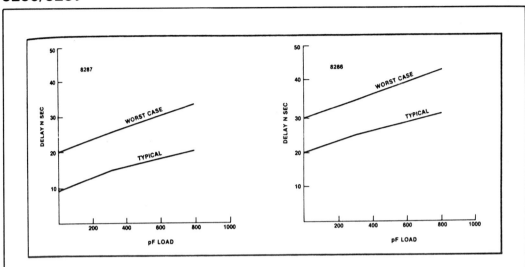

Figure 4. Output Delay vs. Capacitance

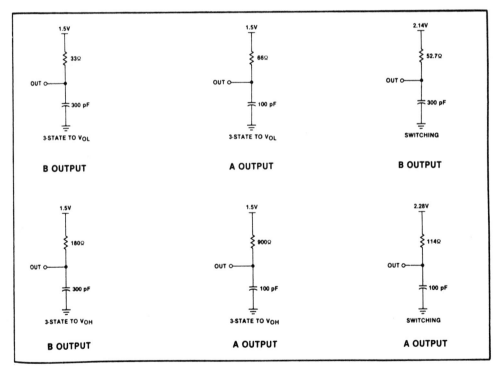

Figure 5. Test Load Circuits

ABSOLUTE MAXIMUM RATINGS*

Temperature Under Bias .... 0°C to 70°C
Storage Temperature .... –65°C to +150°C
All Output and Supply Voltages....................... –0.5V to +7V
All Input Voltages................................. –1.0v to +5.5V
Power Dissipation.................................... 1.5 Watt

*NOTICE: Stresses above those listed under "Absolute Maximum Ratings" may cause permanent damage to the device. This is a stress rating only and functional operation of the device at these or any other conditions above those indicated in the operational sections of this specification is not implied. Exposure to absolute maximum rating conditions for extended periods may affect device reliability.

D.C. CHARACTERISTICS

Conditions: $V_{CC} = 5V \pm 10\%$, $T_A = 0°C$ to $70°C$

Symbol	Parameter	Min	Max	Unit	Test Conditions
V_C	Input Clamp Voltage		–1	V	$I_C = -5$ mA
I_{CC}	Power Supply Current		230	mA	
I_F	Forward Input Current		–0.7	mA	$V_F = 0.45V$
I_R	Reverse Input Current		50	μA	$V_R = V_{CC}$
V_{OL}	Output Low Voltage—Command Outputs		0.5	V	$I_{OL} = 32$ mA
	Control Outputs		0.5	V	$I_{OL} = 16$ mA
V_{OH}	Output High Voltage—Command Outputs	2.4		V	$I_{OH} = -5$ mA
	Control Outputs	2.4		V	$I_{OH} = -1$ mA
V_{IL}	Input Low Voltage		0.8	V	
V_{IH}	Input High Voltage	2.0		V	
I_{OFF}	Output Off Current		100	μA	$V_{OFF} = 0.4$ to $5.25V$

A.C. CHARACTERISTICS

Conditions: $V_{CC} = 5V \pm 10\%$, $T_A = 0°C$ to $70°C$

TIMING REQUIREMENTS

Symbol	Parameter	Min	Max	Unit	Loading
TCLCL	CLK Cycle Period	125		ns	
TCLCH	CLK Low Time	66		ns	
TCHCL	CLK High Time	40		ns	
TSVCH	Status Active Setup Time	65		ns	
TCHSV	Status Active Hold Time	10		ns	
TSHCL	Status Inactive Setup Time	55		ns	
TCLSH	Status Inactive Hold Time	10		ns	

TIMING RESPONSES

Symbol	Parameter	Min	Max	Unit	Loading	
TCVNV	Control Active Delay	5	45	ns		
TCVNX	Control Inactive Delay	10	45	ns		
TCLLH, TCLMCH	ALE MCE Active Delay (from CLK)		15	ns		
TSVLH, TSVMCH	ALE MCE Active Delay (from Status)		15	ns		
TCHLL	ALE Inactive Delay		15	ns	MRDC	
TCLML	Command Active Delay	10	35	ns	IORC	
TCLMH	Command Inactive Delay	10	35	ns	MWTC	$I_{OL} = 32$ mA
TCHDTL	Direction Control Active Delay		50	ns	IOWC	$I_{OH} = -5$ mA
TCHDTH	Direction Control Inactive Delay		30	ns	INTA	$C_L = 300$ pF
TAELCH	Command Enable Time		40	ns	AMWC	
TAEHCZ	Command Disable Time		40	ns	AIOWC	
TAELCV	Enable Delay Time	115	200	ns	Other	$I_{OL} = 16$ mA
TAEVNV	$\overline{AEN}$ to DEN		20	ns		$I_{OH} = -1$ mA
TCEVNV	CEN to DEN, PDEN		20	ns		$C_L = 80$ pF
TCELRH	CEN to Command		TCLML	ns		

8288

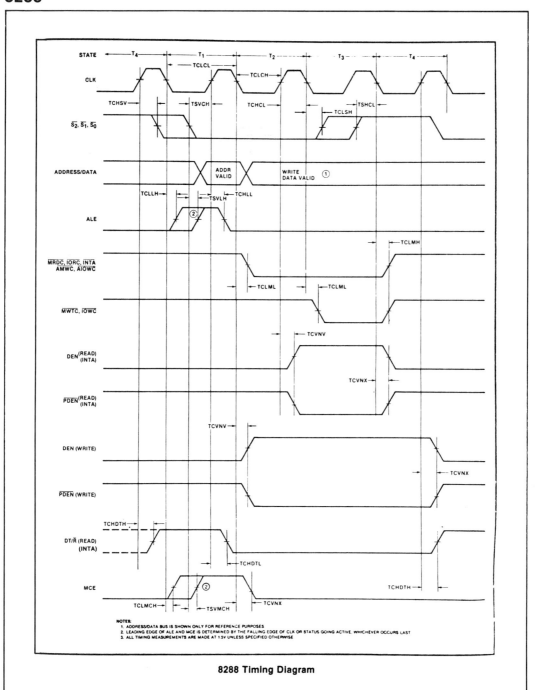

8288 Timing Diagram

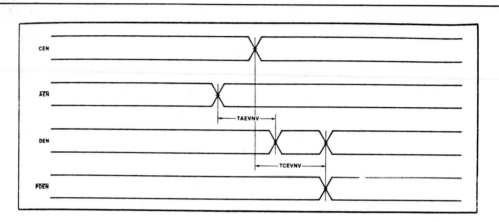

DEN, PDEN Qualification Timing

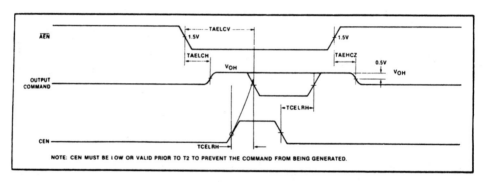

NOTE: CEN MUST BE LOW OR VALID PRIOR TO T2 TO PREVENT THE COMMAND FROM BEING GENERATED.

8288 Address Enable (AEN) Timing (3-State Enable/Disable)

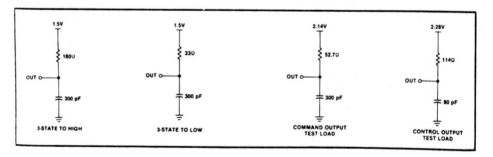

Test Load Circuits - 3 State Command Output Test Load

Chapter 6
THE ZILOG Z8000 SERIES

The Z8000 series of microprocessors represent Zilog's first 16-bit products. The Z8000 is the second of the new 16-bit microprocessor generation. Intel's 8086, described in Chapter 5, was the first product to appear. Motorola's MC68000 will likely be the next.

Two Z8000 series microprocessors have been announced. The Z8002 is a 40-pin package device capable of addressing up to 65,536 bytes of external memory. **The Z8001** is a 48-pin package.device capable of addressing up to eight million bytes of external memory, organized as segments of 65,536 bytes. A third device, the Z8010 Segmentation and Memory Manager, is a companion to the Z8001. The Z8010 allows memory segments to be dynamically allocated under program control anywhere within the eight million bytes of addressable memory.

The Z8000 series microprocessors are upward compatible at the source program level with the 8080A and the Z80.

The following is a comparison of interesting Z8000 and 8086 innovations:

1) Z8000 microprocessors do not pipeline instruction object codes, but under some circumstances they do overlap the next instruction's fetch with the prior instruction's execute. In contrast, the 8086 has a 6-byte object code pipeline, which, with associated instruction fetch overlap timing, effectively eliminates instruction fetch times.

2) The Z8001 and the Z8002 can be visualized as supporting complex and simple microcomputer configurations, respectively. In contrast, a single 8086 can operate either in complex mode, comparable to the Z8001, or in simple mode, comparable to the Z8002.

3) Both the Z8001 and the Z8002 have built-in logic to handle bus access priorities in multi-CPU configurations. The 8086 has equivalent logic.

4) In multi-CPU configurations, each Z8000 series CPU can have its own local memory, while simultaneously sharing common memory. The common memory may be shared by all CPUs or by selected CPUs. In this respect, the 8086 and the Z8000 series are comparable.

5) The Z8001 can address up to eight million bytes of external memory. With the help of the Z8010 Segmentation and Memory Management Device, this large external memory can be accessed as up to 128 relocatable segments, where each segment can have up to 65,536 bytes of external memory. The 8086 offers similar relocatable segments without relying on an additional memory management device; however, the 8086 can directly address only one million bytes of external memory and can only manipulate four segments at a time.

6) Both Z8000 series microprocessors can be operated in separate "System" and "Normal" modes. Certain privileged instructions, including all I/O instructions, can be executed in System mode only. System and Normal modes have separate Stacks, with separate Stack Pointers, Thus, in program-intensive applications, systems software, executed in System mode, can be separated from application programs, executed in Normal mode. The 8086 offers no equivalent logic.

7) The Z8000 has sixteen 16-bit registers that can alternatively be accessed as 8-bit or 32-bit registers. Fifteen of the 16-bit registers can function as index registers. The 8086, in contrast, has four 16-bit registers, plus three separate 16-bit index registers.

The prime source for the Z8000 series is:

ZILOG, INC.
10460 Bubb Road
Cupertino, CA 95014

Second sources include:

ADVANCED MICRO DEVICES
901 Thompson Place
Sunnyvale, CA 94086

SGS-ATES COMPONENTI ELETTRONICI SPA
20019 Castelletto di Settimo
Agrate (Milano)
Italy

The Z8000 series microprocessors are manufactured using N-channel silicon gate MOS technology. The Z8001 is packaged as a 48-pin DIP. The Z8002 is packaged as a 40-pin DIP. Both devices require a single +5 V power supply. All signals are TTL-level compatible.

The Z8000 requires an external clock with up to 4 MHz frequency. Instructions execute in a minimum of three clock periods. The maximum number of clock periods is approximately 20; however, a number of instructions require more time to execute a variety of complex operations.

THE Z8001 AND Z8002 CPU'S

Because these two versions of the Z8000 CPU are so similar, we will describe them together. Functions implemented by Z8000 series microprocessor chips are, in terms of our general illustration, equivalent to those of the 8086, as illustrated in Figure 5-1.

Z8001 AND Z8002 PROGRAMMABLE REGISTERS

Programmable registers for the Z8001 and Z8002 microprocessors are illustrated in Figures 6-1 and 6-2, respectively.

Registers R0 through R15 can be used as general purpose accumulators. Registers R1 through R15 can, in addition, function as index registers. Register R0 is the only general purpose register which cannot function as an index register.

Both the Z8001 and the Z8002 can be operated in System mode or Normal mode. A status flag setting determines the mode of operation. System mode will normally be used by operating system software; Normal mode will be used by application programs. A number of instructions, including all I/O instructions, are privileged, and consequently can be executed in System mode only. **System and Normal modes have separate Stack Pointers.** These are shown in Figures 6-1 and 6-2 by S and N suffixes, which represent "System" and "Normal" modes, respectively.

> **Z8000 SYSTEM AND NORMAL MODES**
>
> **Z8000 STACK POINTERS**

For the Z8002, the single 16-bit register R15 serves as the Stack Pointer.

For the Z8001, two 16-bit registers are needed to implement a Stack Pointer, since memory addresses may be up to 23 bits wide. Registers R14 and R15 are used.

Instructions that access 16-bit registers do not make any special allowance for R15 and/or R14 functioning as Stack Pointers. Thus, **the Stack Pointer can be accessed as a general purpose register/accumulator, or it can be used as the Index register** for indexed memory addressing. The fact that there are separate System and Normal mode Stack Pointers is inconsequential when these registers are being accessed as accumulators or index registers. Depending on the currently selected mode, one or the other Stack Pointer will be accessible. This may be illustrated as follows:

Whenever two 16-bit registers provide a memory address for the Z8001, register bits are utilized as follows:

> **Z8001 32-BIT ADDRESS REPRESENTATION**

| 15 | 14 | 13 | 12 | 11 | 10 | 9 | 8 | 7 | 6 | 5 | 4 | 3 | 2 | 1 | 0 | ◄——Bit No. |

| 0 | Segment No. | | | | | | | 0 | 0 | 0 | 0 | 0 | 0 | 0 | 0 |

Register RN holds the 7-bit segment number in bits 8-14. Other register bits are 0.

| Offset |

Register RN+1 holds the 16-bit offset, or address within the segment identified in Register RN.

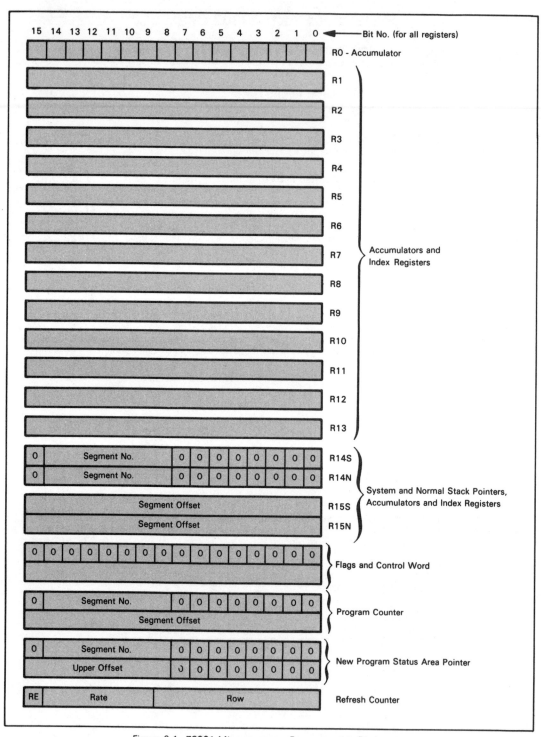

Figure 6-1. Z8001 Microprocessor Programmable Registers

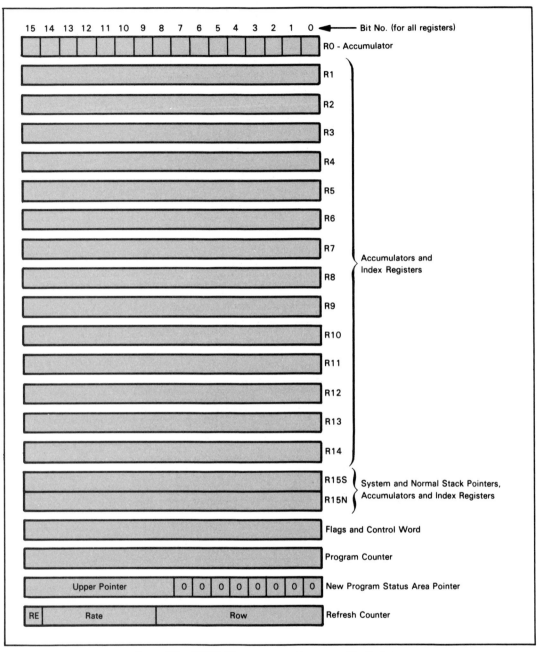

Figure 6-2.   Z8002 Microprocessor Programmable Registers

The segment number and offset translate into a 23-bit memory address as follows:

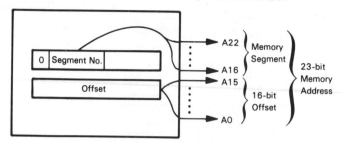

Thus, the Z8001 Stack Pointer is shown in Figure 6-1 with bits 8 through 14 of Register R14 providing the segment number, while the whole of Register R15 provides the segment offset. The Z8002 Stack Pointer, shown in Figure 6-2, is a simple 16-bit address register.

Z8000 STACK POINTER

The Program Counter is a simple 16-bit register for the Z8002, but for the Z8001 two 16-bit words are used, with the 23-bit address divided into a segment number and an offset, as illustrated above.

Z8000 PROGRAM COUNTER

The Z8000 addresses memory as bytes; however 16-bit words must originate on even byte address boundaries. That is why the Z8001 uses two 16-bit words to generate extended memory addresses, even though only 23 bits of address are required. 23-bit addresses could be implemented in three bytes, rather than in two 16-bit words; however, this would complicate pushing and popping memory addresses. Were the addresses implemented as three bytes, all Stack operations would require three byte pushes or three byte pops. By making all addresses occupy two 16-bit words, Stack operations are reduced to two word pushes or two word pops which require no more time than three byte pushes or pops.

The Flags and Control Word provides the Z8001 and the Z8002 with Status and Control bits. Bits are interpreted as follows:

Z8000 STATUS

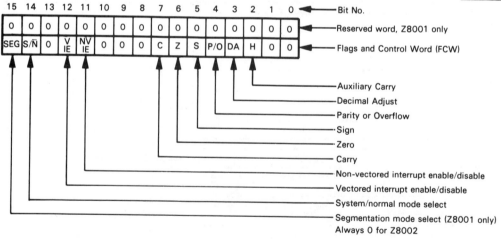

The Parity, Overflow, Sign, Zero, and Carry statuses are absolutely standard.
Parity and Overflow share a status bit.

The Parity status is modified by logical instructions which test the parity of byte data. This status is set to 1 for even parity; it is cleared for odd parity.

The Overflow status is equal to the Exclusive OR of carries out of the high-order and penultimate bits following arithmetic and logical operations.

The Sign status is set to the value of the high-order result bit following arithmetic operations.

The Zero status is set to 1 when the result of an operation is 0; it is reset to 0 otherwise.

The Carry status reports carries out of the high-order bit following arithmetic operations. This status is also used by most shift and rotate instructions.

Most microprocessor instructions routinely modify status bits, whether or not such modifications are relevant to the operation performed. Z8000 status logic generally follows the PDP-11 minicomputer, but the Z8000 has a few anomalies. You should therefore consult Table 6-3, which summarizes the Z8000 instruction set, in order to determine how a particular status is affected by the execution of any specific instruction.

The Auxiliary Carry and Decimal Adjust status flags differ somewhat from normal use. These flags are modified by byte arithmetic instructions in order to make binary coded decimal arithmetic possible. You cannot set or reset these two Status flags using any of the status bit control instructions, and reading the value of these flags provides little useful information. The assembly language programmer should ignore these two flags.

NVIE and VIE are used to enable and disable non-vectored interrupts and vectored interrupts, respectively. You enable interrupts by setting the appropriate status bit to 1, and you disable interrupts by resetting the appropriate status bit to 0.

The S/$\overline{\text{N}}$ status flag is used to switch between System and Normal modes. When this bit is 1, Z8000 microprocessors operate in System mode. When this bit is 0, Z8000 microprocessors operate in Normal mode. Recall that System and Normal modes have their own separate Stack Pointers; also, certain privileged instructions can only be executed in System mode.

The SEG status is used by the Z8001 microprocessor only. When this bit is set to 1, the Z8001 operates in Segmented mode; when this bit is set to 0, the Z8001 operates in Nonsegmented mode.

In Segmented mode, all Z8001 addresses are computed 23 bits wide, using two 16-bit memory words as previously illustrated. Z8001 Nonsegmented, Normal mode is directly equivalent to Z8002 Normal mode operations. Z8001 Nonsegmented System mode is not exactly equivalent to Z8002 System mode; differences occur in interrupt acknowledge stack handling, as explained later in this chapter. Thus Z8002 Normal mode programs can be executed within any single segment of Z8001 memory.

| Z8001 |
| SEGMENTED |
| MODE |

The Z8001 carries an unused word as a companion to the Flag and Control Word, since all Z8001 automatic Stack operations push and pop data in word pairs. Status in the Flag and Control Word must also be pushed and popped as a 32-bit unit — hence the unused companion word.

The New Program Status Area Pointer is used by interrupt logic. It consists of one or two 16-bit words, as illustrated in Figures 6-1 and 6-2.

Following any interrupt acknowledge, a vector address is created using the New Program Status Area Pointer and a 9- or 10-bit displacement provided by interrupt acknowledge logic, as follows:

Z8001

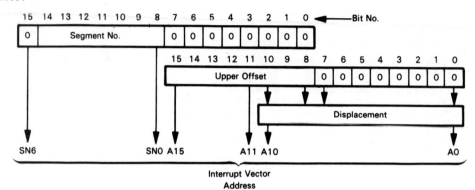

Z8002

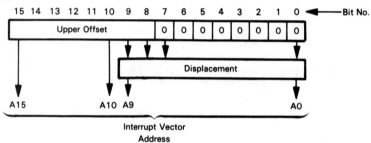

Although the Z8002 uses just one byte of its New Program Status Area Pointer, 16 bits are provided, since all Z8002 automatic Stack operations push and pop 16-bit words. Likewise, the Z8001 New Program Status Area Pointer uses two 16-bit words, where a single 16-bit word would suffice, to accommodate automatic Stack handling logic which pushes and pops data in 32-bit increments.

The Refresh Counter will be described later, along with memory refresh.

Z8000 REGISTER DESIGNATIONS

Z8000 series microprocessor instructions access 8-bit, 16-bit, or 32-bit registers, as illustrated in Figure 6-3.
Register designations used by Zilog assembly language mnemonics are shown in this figure.

Byte instructions access sixteen 8-bit registers, illustrated in Figure 6-3 by **RH0 through RL7.**

Z8000 BYTE REGISTERS

Word instructions access the sixteen 16-bit registers **R0 through R15.**

Z8000 16-BIT REGISTERS

Long word instructions access general purpose registers in pairs. Eight 32-bit registers are therefore available, shown in Figure 6-3 as **RR0 through RR14.**

Z8000 32-BIT REGISTERS

Most Z8000 series instructions that access memory or registers have a word version and a byte version. A limited number of instructions have a long word version.

Multiplication and division instructions sometimes use 64-bit registers, shown in Figure 6-3 as RQ0 through RQ12.

Z8001 AND Z8002 MEMORY ADDRESSING MODES

Most Z8001 memory addressing modes have two forms: one for Nonsegmented mode, the other for Segmented mode.

When operating in Nonsegmented mode, all Z8001 memory reference instructions compute nonsegmented memory addresses; the offset address is modified, but the segment number is not altered.

When operating in Segmented mode, Z8001 memory reference instructions compute segmented memory addresses, provided the instruction also has a segmented memory addressing option. But there are some memory reference instructions that have no segmented option; these instructions compute nonsegmented memory addresses, even for a Z8001 operating in Segmented mode.

A segmented memory reference instruction computes new values for the segment number and offset address.

The Z8002 Program Counter is a single, 16-bit register, equivalent to the Z8001 Program Counter Offset register. Z8002 memory reference instructions therefore compute nonsegmented memory addresses only.

In the discussion which follows, we will illustrate Z8000 memory addressing options for Segmented and Nonsegmented modes.

In Segmented mode the base address always specifies the segment. The base address may occupy two 16-bit words:

Z8001 BASE ADDRESS

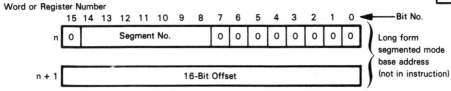

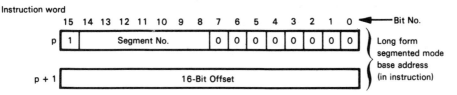

or it may occupy a single 16-bit instruction word:

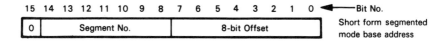

6-9

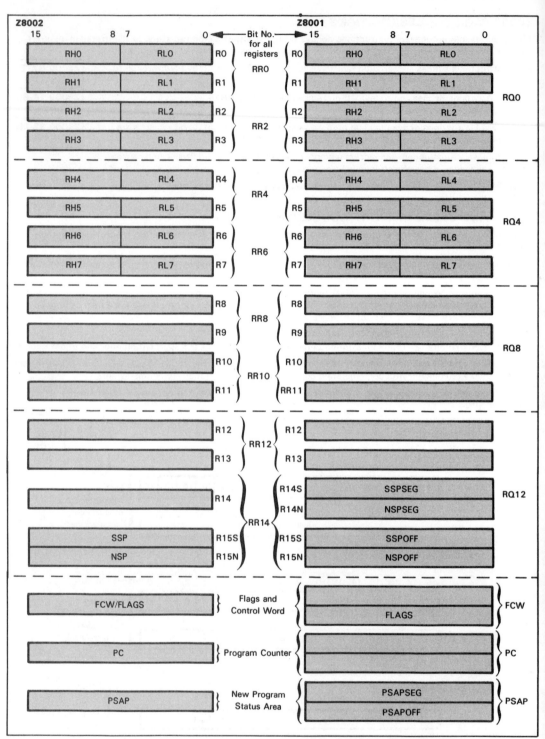

Figure 6-3. Various Register Designations for the Z8001 and Z8002 Microprocessors

The index or displacement portion of a memory address never specifies the memory segment. The index is always a single 16-bit value for any Z8000 microprocessor, operating in any mode. The displacement may be an 8-bit, 12-bit, or 16-bit value; but once again, it is the same for all Z8000 microprocessors, and all modes of operation.

Thus, in Segmented mode, there is a clear difference between a base address and an index or displacement. In Nonsegmented mode, there being no segment number, there is no difference between a base address and an index.

Most Z8000 series memory reference instructions access data memory using implied, direct, or indexed memory addressing.

Z8002 implied memory addressing may be illustrated as follows:

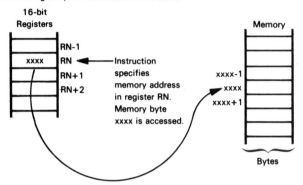

x represents any hexadecimal digit

The Z8001 uses only nonsegmented implied memory reference instructions to access data memory. The Z8001 does not use either short or long segmented implied memory addressing to access data memory. Z8001 implied memory addressing may therefore be illustrated as follows:

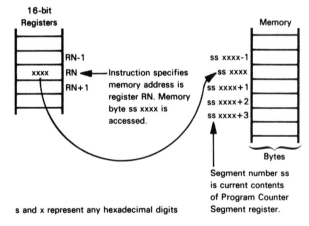

s and x represent any hexadecimal digits

Some Z8001 program memory reference instructions (such as the subroutine call) use long segmented implied memory addressing, which may be illustrated as follows:

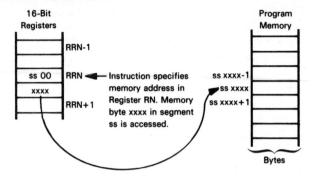

s and x represent any hexadecimal digits.
RRN is a 32-bit register designation.

We will now examine direct memory addressing.

For the Z8002, direct memory addressing may be illustrated as follows:

Z8002
DIRECT
MEMORY
ADDRESSING

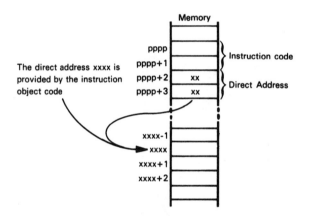

x and p represent any hexadecimal digits

Note that the direct address xxxx, being a 16-bit value, must start at a memory byte with an even address. This requirement is illustrated above by the address pppp+2.

Furthermore, the high-order byte of a 16-bit memory word is at the lower address, preceding the low-order byte:

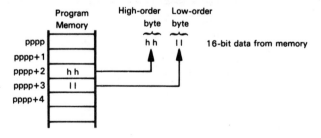

A Z8001 direct memory address may be nonsegmented, short segmented, or long segmented. Nonsegmented Z8001 direct memory address logic is as illustrated above for a Z8002 direct memory address, except that the most recently computed segmented number is output from the Program Counter Segment register via the seven Z8001 segment number lines.

Long segmented Z8001 direct memory addressing may be illustrated as follows:

**Z8001 LONG
SEGMENTED
DIRECT MEMORY
ADDRESSING**

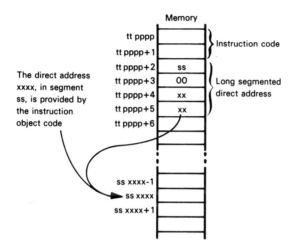

s and t are any hexadecimal digits that specify a segment number in the range 00 through $7F_{16}$.
p and x are any hexadecimal digits that specify a memory address within a segment.

We can illustrate a short segmented Z8001 direct memory addessing as follows:

**Z8002 SHORT
SEGMENTED
DIRECT MEMORY
ADDRESSING**

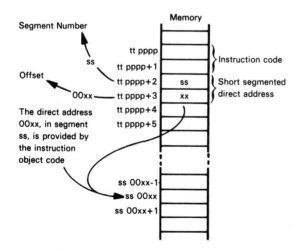

s and t are any hexadecimal digits that specify a segment number in the range 00 through $7F_{16}$.
p and x are any hexadecimal digits that specify an offset, or memory address within the segment.

Z8001 and Z8002 indexed memory addressing adds the contents of an index register to a direct address. 16-bit registers R1 through R15 can function as index registers. Register R0 cannot function as an index register. The direct address provides the base to which an index is added.

Z8002 indexed addressing may be illustrated as follows:

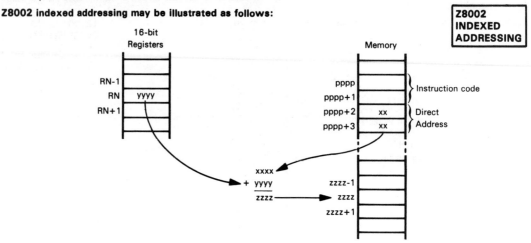

p, x, y and z represent any hexadecimal digits. The selected memory address zzzz is the sum of the direct address xxxx, which is provided by the instruction object code, and the index yyyy.
The instruction code specifies Register RN as the Index register.

The illustration applies also to nonsegmented Z8001 indexed addressing, but for the Z8001 a segment number (ss) would precede the computed address zzzz. Since no segment is computed by the Z8001 in Nonsegmented mode, ss would be the current contents of the Program Counter Segment register.

Here is an illustration of Z8001 short segmented indexed addressing:

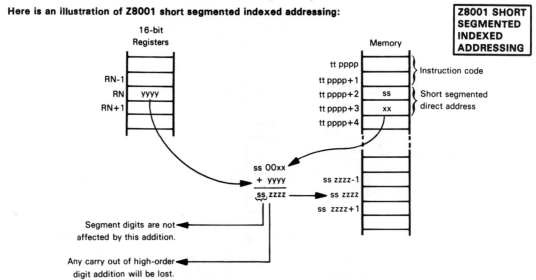

The effective memory address ss zzzz is not the simple sum of ss 00xx and yyyy. The segment number ss is output directly on the segment number pins, bypassing the address addition. 00xx and yyyy are added to create zzzz, the offset, which is output on the Address Bus. In the event that adding 00xx to yyyy generates a carry out of the high-order bit, this carry is lost. Thus the offset addition wraps around from $FFFF_{16}$ to 0000_{16}, without incrementing the segment number.

Long segmented Z8001 indexed addressing uses a four-byte direct address, with a 16-bit offset, as follows:

Memory

ss
00
xx
xx

The computed offset zzzz becomes the sum of xxxx and yyyy.

Note that long segmented indexed addressing offers the same addressing range as short segmented indexed addressing; the index, on its own, can address the entire offset space of 65,536 bytes. Therefore, the one-byte short segmented base address offset is no handicap. Suppose, for example, you use indexed addressing to access a data table in the middle of a segment. Using long segmented indexed addressing, the base of the data table might be provided by the direct address offset, while the Index register provides the displacement into the selected table:

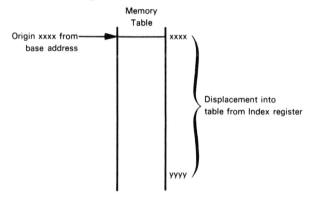

But you could just as easily have the index originate at the base of the segment:

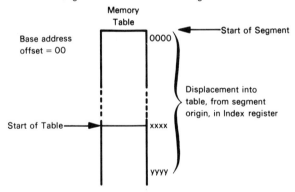

A few Z8001 and Z8002 instructions access data memory using base relative addressing, wherein the contents of an Index register are added to a base address, which is also held in CPU registers. Therefore, Z8000 base relative addressing might also be called "implied, indexed" addressing.

**Z8000 BASE
RELATIVE
ADDRESSING**

**Z8000 IMPLIED
INDEXED
ADDRESSING**

Z8002 base relative addressing may be illustrated as follows:

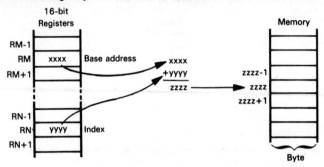

x, y and z represent any hexadecimal digits

The instruction object code must specify the register number from which the base address and the index are taken. In Nonsegmented mode there is no difference between a base address and an index; each is a single 16-bit value. The effective memory address zzzz is simply the sum of any two 16-bit registers' contents.

The illustration above applies also to nonsegmented Z8001 base relative addressing. However, for the Z8001 the memory segment ss, currently in the Program Counter Segment register, is output via the seven Z8001 segment number lines.

Consider next Z8001 segmented base relative addressing. The base address specifies the segment, thus the base address and the index differ. Short segmented base relative addressing may be illustrated as follows:

Z8001 SHORT SEGMENTED BASE RELATIVE ADDRESSING

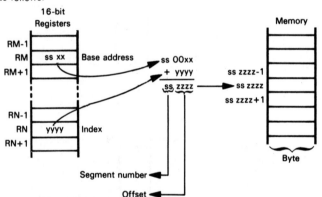

x, y and z represent any hexadecimal digits specifying offsets, or addresses within memory segment ss.
ss can have any value in the range 00 through $7F_{16}$.

The index is added to the base address using the same mechanism described earlier for short segmented indexed addressing. The discussion of addressing range given for short segmented indexed addressing applies also to short segmented base relative addressing.

Long segmented base relative addressing may be illustrated as follows:

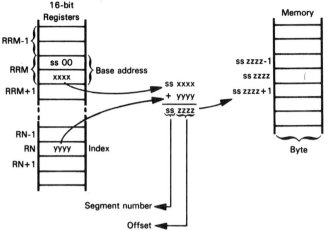

x, y and z represent any hexadecimal digits specifying an offset address within memory segment ss.
RRM designates a 32-bit register, while RN designates a 16-bit register.
These registers are specified by the instruction object code.

Some program memory reference instructions use program relative addressing. A displacement provided by the instruction object code is added, as a signed binary number, to the contents of the Program Counter. For the Z8002 this may be illustrated as follows:

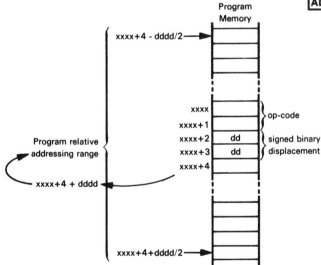

In the illustration above, dddd is divided by 2 to show the addressing range of a program relative address; this is because dddd is a signed binary number. Therefore, half of the possible values will increase the address in the Program Counter (xxxx+4); the other half will decrease this address.

Depending on the instruction, dddd may be an 8, 12, or 16-bit signed binary value. This displacement is added to the contents of the Program Counter after the Program Counter has been incremented to address the first byte of the next sequential instruction. This is illustrated above as location xxxx+4.

Some program relative instructions (such as Jump Relative) have the displacement included in the op-code word, saving memory space and execution time for short displacements. In these instructions the first byte of the next sequential instruction would be xxxx+2, instead of xxxx+4 as illustrated above.

Z8001 program relative addressing, in Segmented or Nonsegmented mode, follows the illustration above; however, the Program Counter also specifies the memory segment. The displacement is added to the Z8001 Program Counter Offset register. The Z8001 Program Counter Segment register is not changed. Thus the displacement for a program relative memory address cannot cross a segment boundary.

A few Z8000 jump instructions use indirect memory addressing. That is to say, the contents of the addressed memory location are loaded into the Program Counter. Very few microprocessors provide indirect addressing. See Volume 1, Chapter 6 for a detailed description of this addressing mode.

The Z8000 instruction set includes a number of memory reference instructions with auto-increment and auto-decrement. An implied memory address held in a 16-bit register is incremented or decremented following an instruction's execution, thus leaving the address pointing to the next sequential memory location in a table or string.

The Z8000 Stack decrements the Stack Pointer before a push and increments the Stack Pointer following a pop. In other words, the beginning of the Stack has the highest memory address, and the current top of Stack has the lowest memory address.

Z8001 AND Z8002 PINS AND SIGNALS

Signals and pin assignments for the two Z8000 series microprocessors are illustrated in Figure 6-4.

AD0-AD15 is a multiplexed 16-bit Data/Address Bus. $\overline{\text{AS}}$ is an address strobe which is pulsed low while an address is being output. $\overline{\text{DS}}$ **is a data strobe** which is pulsed low while data is being output or input.

ST0-ST3 are four machine cycle status signals whose output levels further identify **bus activity,** as summarized in Table 6-1.

Table 6-1. Z8000 Machine Cycle Status Definitions

ST3 - ST0				Machine Cycle
3	2	1	0	
0	0	0	0	Internal operation
0	0	0	1	Memory refresh
0	0	1	0	I/O reference
0	0	1	1	Special I/O reference
0	1	0	0	Segmentation trap acknowledge
0	1	0	1	Non-maskable interrupt acknowledge
0	1	1	0	Non-vectored interrupt acknowledge
0	1	1	1	Vectored interrupt acknowledge
1	0	0	0	Data memory access
1	0	0	1	Stack memory access
1	0	1	0	Reserved
1	0	1	1	Reserved
1	1	0	0	Subsequent instruction fetch
1	1	0	1	First instruction fetch
1	1	1	0	Reserved
1	1	1	1	Reserved

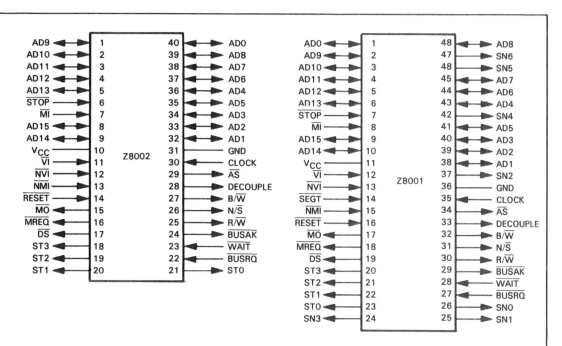

Pin Name	Description	Type
AD0 - AD15	Data/Address Bus	Bidirectional, Tristate
SN0 - SN6*	Segment Number	Output, Tristate
B/$\overline{\text{W}}$	Byte/Word Select	Output, Tristate
R/$\overline{\text{W}}$	Read/Write Select	Output, Tristate
N/$\overline{\text{S}}$	Normal/System Mode Select	Output, Tristate
ST0 - ST3	Machine Cycle Status	Output, Tristate
$\overline{\text{WAIT}}$	Wait State Request	Input
CLOCK	System Clock	Input
$\overline{\text{AS}}$	Address Strobe	Output, Tristate
$\overline{\text{DS}}$	Data Strobe	Output, Tristate
$\overline{\text{MREQ}}$	Memory Request	Output, Tristate
$\overline{\text{VI}}$	Vectored Interrupt Request	Input
$\overline{\text{NVI}}$	Non-vectored Interrupt Request	Input
$\overline{\text{NMI}}$	Non-maskable Interrupt Request	Input
$\overline{\text{RESET}}$	System Reset	Input
$\overline{\text{SEGT}}$*	Segmentation Trap	Input
$\overline{\text{BUSRQ}}$	Bus Request	Input
BUSAK	Bus Acknowledge	Output
$\overline{\text{MI}}$	Multi-micro Input	Input
$\overline{\text{MO}}$	Multi-micro Output	Output
$\overline{\text{STOP}}$	Single-Step Stop	Input
DECOUPLE**	Negative Bias Generator	Output
V$_{CC}$, GND	Power, Ground	

* Z8001 only	**Not presently connected

Figure 6-4. Z8001 and Z8002 Signals and Pin Assignments

MREQ is output low when memory is being addressed. MREQ high, when a valid address is output, therefore selects an I/O port. MREQ indicates codes 7, 8, 9, C or F output via ST0-ST3; but ST0-ST3 also provide additional variations of memory and I/O access machine cycles.

DS and MREQ can generate a rudimentary memory select signal, as follows:

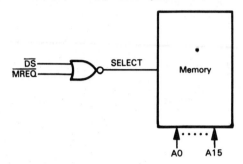

If I/O is being mapped into memory space, you can ignore MREQ.

B/W differentiates between byte and word memory accesses. Z8000 memory is organized and addressed as bytes; however, the 16-bit Data/Address Bus allows 8-bit or 16-bit data accesses within a single machine cycle. **B/W is output high for an 8-bit access; it is output low for a 16-bit access.**

In order to simplify the memory interface logic needed to enable byte and word accesses, **the Z8000 always reads data from even-addressed bytes on the high-order eight Data Bus lines; it reads data from odd-addressed bytes on the low-order eight Data Bus lines.** This may be illustrated as follows:

> **Z8000 MEMORY INTERFACE LOGIC**

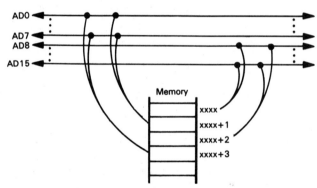

During a one-byte Read instruction, a Z8000 microprocessor will take data from the high-order eight Data Bus lines if the memory address is even; it takes data from the low-order eight Data Bus lines if the memory address is odd. The data is transferred by the CPU to the selected 8-bit register.

In response to a 16-bit read, a Z8000 microprocessor takes data from the 16-bit bus and loads it into the selected register. The high-order byte of the 16-bit word will come from the even-addressed memory byte. The low-order byte of the 16-bit word will come from the odd-addressed memory byte. This may be illustrated as follows:

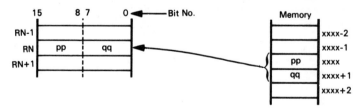

When a Z8000 microprocessor executes a one-byte Write instruction, the same byte of data is output on the eight high-order and low-order Data Bus lines. This may be illustrated as follows:

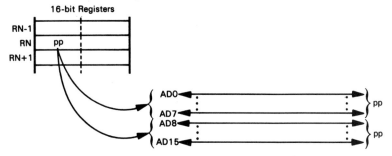

During execution of a 16-bit write instruction, a Z8000 microprocessor will output the selected 16 bits of data in the usual way: across AD0-AD15, the 16-bit Data Bus.

There are a number of ways in which memory interface logic can be designed to comply with Z8000 Data Bus protocols, but **the simplest method** is to divide memory into two halves, with even-addressed bytes in one-half and odd-addressed bytes in the other half. The two halves of memory will in fact have parallel addresses taken from AD1-AD15, with AD0 and B/W̄ combining to generate appropriate select logic. This **may be illustrated as follows:**

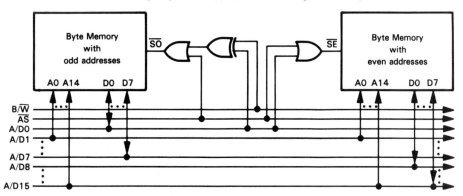

The illustration above shows two blocks of memory with parallel addresses decoded from the same 15 address lines: AD1-AD15. The block of memory labelled "odd addresses" has a Data Bus connection to AD0-AD7. The block of memory labelled "even addresses" has a Data Bus connection to AD8-AD15.

The block of memory with odd addresses is selected when S̄Ō is low; this occurs when B/W̄ and AD0 are both low, or when they are both high. Thus, odd-addressed memory responds to byte accesses with odd addresses, or to word accesses with even addresses.

The block of memory with even addresses is enabled when S̄Ē is low. This occurs for any even address access.

The illustrated memory select logic ensures that no memory is selected by a word access with an odd address. To Z8000 microprocessors this is an illegal condition.

The Z8000 microprocessors also access 32-bit memory "long words." Such accesses occur serially, as two 16-bit words, therefore no special memory interface logic is required.

N/S̄ and various ST0-ST3 combinations can be used to separate memory functionally.

N/S̄ is output low when a Z8000 microprocessor is operating in System mode; it is output high in Normal mode.
Thus, N/S̄ can be used to condition memory select logic so that separate System and Normal mode memory can exist in parallel address spaces. Similarly, if ST0-ST3 is input to a 4-to-16 decoder, statuses 2 and 3 can enable separate I/O spaces, statuses 8 and 9 can select separate Data and Stack memories, while statuses C and D select program memory. Some or all of these status combinations can be used, with or without N/S̄, to implement a variety of special memory spaces. If all external memory exists in a single address space, which is how most microcomputer memory is configured, then you can ignore N/S̄.

For the **Z8001 only,** memory is segmented, and **the currently selected segment is identified by the 7-bit output SN0-SN6.** In the absence of a Z8010 Memory Management Device, SN0-SN6 is directly decoded to select appropriate memory segments. In the presence of a Z8010 Memory Management Device, however, memory select logic can ignore the concept of segmentation, instead deriving addresses from a 24-bit Address Bus which is output by the Z8010 Memory Management Device.

During a memory or I/O access machine cycle, **R/W̄ is output high for a read and low for a write.**

Slow memory or I/O devices can input W̄ĀĪT̄ low in order to extend a machine cycle, thereby gaining more access response time. W̄ĀĪT̄ timing is described later in this chapter.

CLOCK is the single 5 V clock signal required by all Z8000 microprocessors.

There are three interrupt request inputs:

N̄M̄Ī is the highest priority, non-maskable interrupt request.
V̄Ī is the vectored interrupt request.
N̄V̄Ī is the lowest priority, non-vectored interrupt request.

N̄M̄Ī is active on high-to-low transitions. V̄Ī and N̄V̄Ī are active-low signals.

S̄ĒḠT̄ is a segmentation trap interrupt request which is transmitted by the Z8010 Memory Management Device to the Z8001 in response to an illegal segmentation condition.

The response of Z8000 series microprocessors to interrupt requests is described in detail later in this chapter.

When R̄ĒS̄ĒT̄ is input low, Z8000 microprocessors are reinitialized. Reset logic is described later, following descriptions of logic which is affected by a Reset.

The B̄ŪS̄R̄Q̄ and B̄ŪS̄ĀK̄ signals are used by direct memory access logic; they may also be used by CPU priority arbitration logic in multi-CPU configurations. **When B̄ŪS̄R̄Q̄ is input low, a Z8000 series microprocessor will respond by floating its three-state bus lines and outputting B̄ŪS̄ĀK̄ low** at the end of the next machine cycle. Timing for these two signals is given later in this chapter.

M̄Ī and M̄Ō are used by CPU priority arbitration logic in multi-CPU configurations. Under program control, Z8000 series microprocessors can test the level of M̄Ī and control the level of M̄Ō, thus enabling a primitive level of handshaking between CPUs.

S̄T̄Ō̄P̄ allows Z8000 programs to be executed one instruction at a time, thus enabling implementation of typical computer single-stepping debug logic. The S̄T̄Ō̄P̄ signal is described later, together with Z8000 refresh logic.

DECOUPLE is not currently connected. This signal will be used by later versions of the Z8000 microprocessor; it will function as an output from an internal negative bias generator.

Z8001 AND Z8002 TIMING AND INSTRUCTION EXECUTION

Z8000 series microprocessors execute instructions in straightforward sequences of machine cycles. Z8000 machine cycles may vary in length from 3 to 10 clock periods.

Z8000 MEMORY REFERENCE MACHINE CYCLES

Normal memory reference machine cycles have three clock periods. Timing for memory read and memory write machine cycles is illustrated in Figures 6-5 and 6-6, respectively.

Beginning with the memory read machine cycle, note that **the levels output at ST0-ST3 represent the only difference between a memory read or an instruction fetch machine cycle.** A valid 16-bit address is output via AD0-AD15 during the first clock period. $\overline{AS}$ is pulsed low at this time; external logic should use the trailing low-to-high transition of the $\overline{AS}$ pulse as its valid address strobe. For a Z8002 this 16-bit address is the total address information output by the microprocessor. But for the Z8001, this 16-bit address is an offset within the segment specified by SN0-SN7. **The segment is specified during the last clock period of the previous machine cycle** so that the Z8010 Memory Management Device will have one clock period within which to compute an effective address. Timing may be illustrated as follows:

> **Z8000 MEMORY READ MACHINE CYCLE**
>
> **Z8000 INSTRUCTION FETCH MACHINE CYCLE**

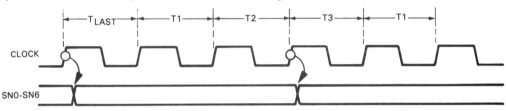

External logic must have stable data on the Data/Address Bus during T3.

During a memory write machine cycle, as illustrated in Figure 6-6, the address is output during the first clock period and is valid on the trailing low-to-high transition of the $\overline{AS}$ pulse, as described for a memory read. Data output appears at AD0-AD15 immediately after the address. Data output is stable during the low $\overline{DS}$ pulse.

> **Z8000 MEMORY WRITE MACHINE CYCLE**

External logic can extend any memory reference machine cycle by inserting Wait state clock periods between T2 and T3. The CPU samples $\overline{WAIT}$ in the middle of T2; if $\overline{WAIT}$ is low, then a Wait state clock period is inserted. Wait state clock periods continue to be inserted until $\overline{WAIT}$ is sampled high in the middle of a Wait clock period. Timing may be illustrated as follows:

> **Z8000 WAIT STATE**

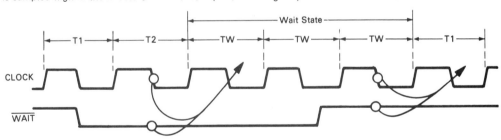

Signal levels and conditions that existed at the end of T2 are maintained for the duration of Wait clock periods.

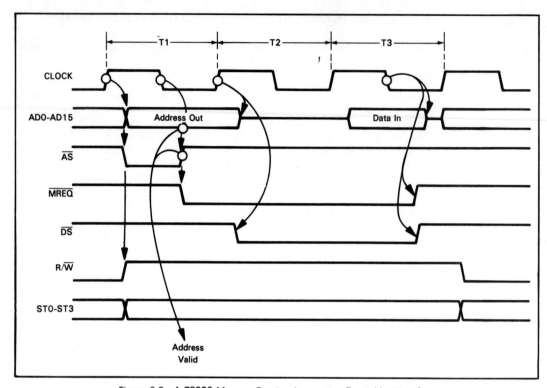

Figure 6-5. A Z8000 Memory Read or Instruction Fetch Machine Cycle

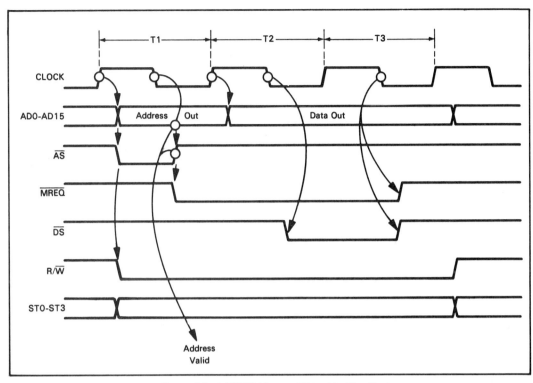

Figure 6-6. A Z8000 Memory Write Machine Cycle

Z8000 INPUT/OUTPUT MACHINE CYCLES

Input and output machine cycles each have a minimum of four clock periods, as illustrated in Figures 6-7 and 6-8.

Input and output machine cycles are very similar to memory read and write machine cycles. These are the significant differences:

1) One Wait clock period is always inserted between T2 and T3 for an I/O machine cycle. Additional Wait clock periods can be inserted using the $\overline{\text{WAIT}}$ control input.

2) $\overline{\text{MREQ}}$ is high during an I/O machine cycle since memory is not being referenced.

3) The status output at ST0-ST3 is 2 or 3, depending on the nature of the I/O instruction.

A 16-bit address is output during all I/O machine cycles. Therefore, up to 65,536 I/O ports may be addressed.

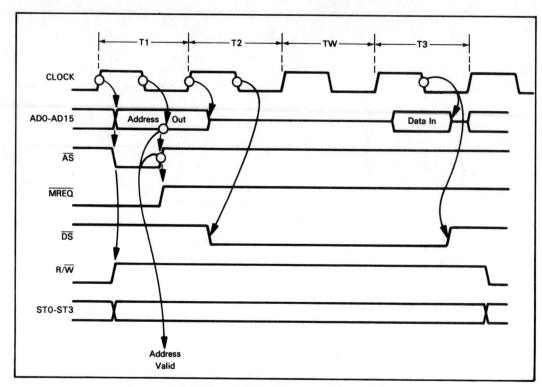

Figure 6-7. A Z8000 I/O Port Input Machine Cycle

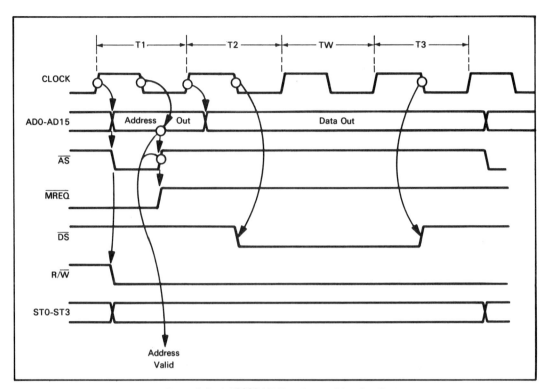

Figure 6-8. A Z8000 I/O Port Output Machine Cycle

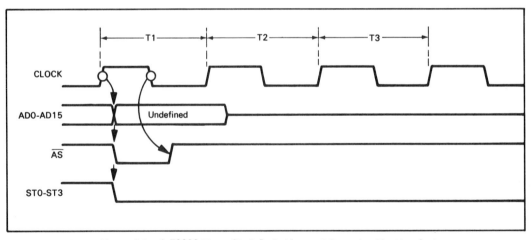

Figure 6-9 A Z8000 Three-Clock-Period Internal Operation Machine Cycle

Z8000 INTERNAL OPERATION MACHINE CYCLES

Internal operation machine cycles may have from 3 to 8 clock periods. During the first clock period an undefined address is output, together with an address strobe; ST0-ST3 are output low to identify the internal operation. $\overline{\text{MREQ}}$, $\overline{\text{DS}}$, and R/$\overline{\text{W}}$ are all high. **Timing for a three-clock-period internal operation machine cycle is illustrated in Figure 6-9.**

Z8000 INSTRUCTION FETCH OVERLAP

The Z8000 has a limited instruction fetch overlap ability. If any instruction concludes with one or more internal operation machine cycles, then the last internal operation machine cycle can overlap the next instruction's first instruction fetch machine cycle. This may be illustrated as follows:

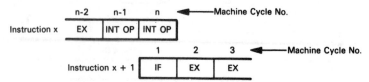

INT OP - Internal operation machine cycle
EX - Any machine cycle
IF - Instruction fetch machine cycle

Note that the next instruction's instruction fetch machine cycle cannot overlap a memory load instruction since there are no trailing internal operation cycles. Also, the last machine cycle of a jump instruction cannot be overlapped since the location of the following instruction has not been determined.

The Z8000 will only overlap a single instruction fetch machine cycle. For example, suppose an instruction concludes with four internal operation machine cycles, and the next instruction has two words of object code; the first object code word will be fetched during the previous instruction's last internal operation machine cycle, even though there are sufficient trailing internal operation machine cycles to fetch both words of the next instruction's object code. This may be illustrated as follows:

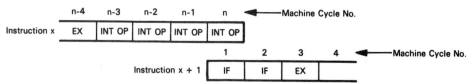

The instruction fetch overlap is constant for a given instruction and addressing mode and is accounted for in computing the number of clock cycles per instruction. The number of clock cycles is counted from the start of the instruction fetch to the start of the next instruction fetch so that the number of clock cycles in an instruction sequence can be computed by simply adding the number of clock cycles given for each instruction without worrying about which instructions overlap and which don't.

Z8000 DYNAMIC MEMORY REFRESH

Z8000 microprocessors have built-in dynamic memory refresh logic. This logic is based on a Refresh Counter that can be accessed by special assembly language instructions. The Refresh Counter is a 16-bit register which may be illustrated as follows:

```
Z8000
REFRESH
COUNTER
```

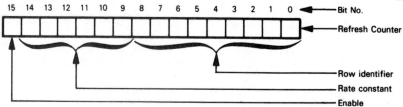

Refresh logic is enabled by setting bit 15 of the Refresh Counter to 1. The refresh rate is determined by the six rate constant bits. The value in these six bits is decremented on every fourth CLOCK pulse. The rate constant initial value is saved and restored when the rate constant decrements to 0. At this time a refresh machine cycle is enabled.

Thus, using a standard 4 MHz clock, the value loaded into the rate constant bits of the refresh counter allows any interval ranging between 1 and 64 microseconds to separate memory refresh machine cycles:

$$\text{Rate} = 4 \times \text{CLOCK} \times (\text{RATE CONSTANT}); \text{RATE CONSTANT} \neq 0$$
$$\text{Rate} = 4 \times \text{CLOCK} \times 64; \text{RATE CONSTANT} = 0$$

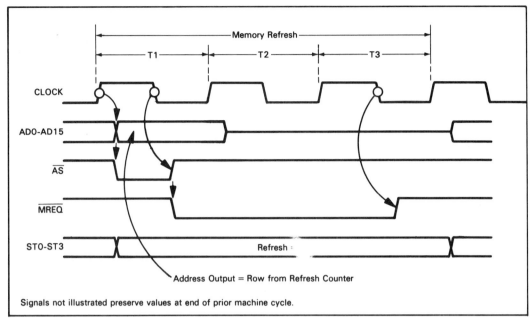

Figure 6-10. A Z8000 Memory Refresh Machine Cycle

When the rate constant bits of the Refresh Counter decrement to 0 and trigger a refresh machine cycle, this machine cycle will in fact occur at the next available refresh access point in the normal sequence of instruction execution machine cycles. These are the available access points:

1) Following the first instruction fetch machine cycle of any instruction's execution.

2) In between repeated sequences of machine cycles for instructions with long execution times. These include MULT, MULTL, DIV, DIVL, HALT, MREQ, all shift instructions, and all block move instructions.

3) During a Stop condition. This is a special case which is described below.

Memory refresh machine cycle timing is illustrated in Figure 6-10. The refresh address which is output is taken from the nine row bits of the Refresh Counter. The Refresh Counter row bits are then incremented by 2. Thus 256 rows may be addressed.

THE Z8000 STOP AND SINGLE-STEPPING LOGIC

The $\overline{\text{STOP}}$ input signal can be used to suspend an instruction's execution. This logic is frequently used to implement single-stepping, whereby a program can be executed one instruction at a time, while being debugged.

The $\overline{\text{STOP}}$ signal, when input low, puts a Z8000 microprocessor into a Stop condition. The Stop condition begins with an instruction fetch machine cycle, and continues with dynamic memory refresh machine cycles. The Stop condition lasts until $\overline{\text{STOP}}$ is input high again. This may be illustrated as follows:

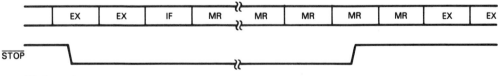

EX - Instruction execute machine cycle.
IF - Instruction fetch machine cycle.
MR - Memory refresh machine cycle.

The signal is sampled in the middle of the last clock period during the last machine cycle of every instruction's execution. This may be illustrated as follows:

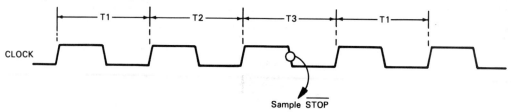

Within the Stop condition, the $\overline{\text{STOP}}$ signal is sampled in the middle of the last clock period of every refresh machine cycle.

The initial instruction fetch machine cycle which begins the Stop condition fetches the next sequential instruction. This instruction is also executed if it happens to be a short instruction that executes within the one instruction fetch machine cycle. But if the fetched instruction requires additional execution machine cycles, then these are suspended until the end of the Stop condition.

Therefore, **the Stop condition may separate two instructions, or it may split a single instruction.**

If a one-machine-cycle instruction follows $\overline{\text{STOP}}$ being detected low, then this entire instruction is executed at the beginning of the Stop condition, and a new instruction is executed at the end of the Stop condition. This may be illustrated as follows:

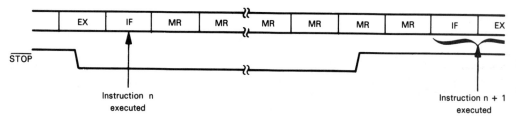

In this case, the $\overline{\text{STOP}}$ signal must be brought low before the end of the next machine cycle in order to stop after the next instruction fetch for single-stepping. This may be illustrated as follows:

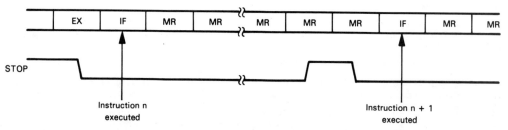

If, on the other hand, a multi-machine cycle instruction is to be executed after $\overline{\text{STOP}}$ is detected low, then the first instruction fetch machine cycle occurs at the beginning of the Stop condition, but remaining machine cycles for the instruction occur at the end of the Stop condition. This may be illustrated as follows:

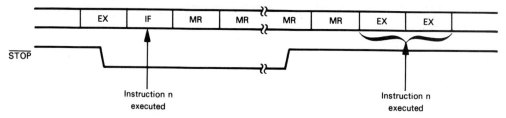

Figure 6-11 summarizes Z8000 Stop condition timing.

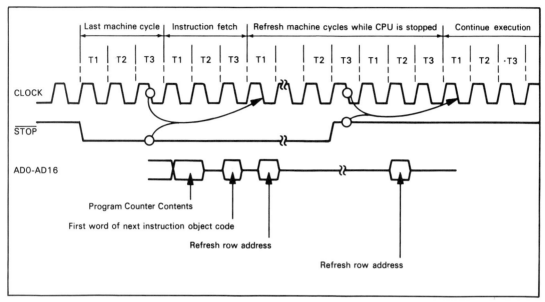

Figure 6-11. Z8000 Stop Condition Timing

While STOP is being input low, refresh logic bypasses the refresh rate constant. The rate constant continues to decrement every fourth clock cycle; however, continuous refresh machine cycles are executed, with the nine row bits of the Refresh Counter being incremented by 2 following each refresh machine cycle.

While STOP is input low, refresh machine cycles are executed, as described above, even if refresh logic has been disabled.

THE Z8000 HOLD STATE

The BUSRQ input and BUSAK output provide Z8000 microprocessors with Hold state logic. External logic that wishes to acquire bus control inputs BUSRQ low to the CPU. The CPU samples BUSRQ at the beginning of any machine cycle. **If BUSRQ is low, then at the conclusion of the current machine cycle, the CPU outputs BUSAK low and floats all three-state signals. This condition lasts until BUSRQ is input high again; three clock periods later, suspended instruction execution resumes** with the machine cycle which would have been executed, had the bus not been floated. **Timing is illustrated in Figure 6-12.**

Note that the MI and MO signals are not comparable to BUSRQ and BUSAK. MI and MO provide program controlled inter-CPU handshaking; alternatively, they can be looked upon as undefined status input and control output signals.

THE Z8000 HALT STATE

Following execution of the Halt instruction, a Z8000 microprocessor will enter a Halt state, during which an endless sequence of internal operation machine cycles will be executed. If memory refresh logic has been enabled, then memory refresh machine cycles will be interspersed among the internal operation machine cycles. The time interval between memory refresh machine cycles will be determined by normal Refresh Counter logic. This is in sharp contrast to the Stop condition, during which an endless sequence of refresh machine cycles are output, bypassing Refresh Counter logic.

No special signal or status is output by a Z8000 microprocessor to identify the Halt state. A Halt state is ended by an interrupt, a segmentation trap, or a Reset. These signals are acknowledged as they would be during any internal operation machine cycle. This logic is described next.

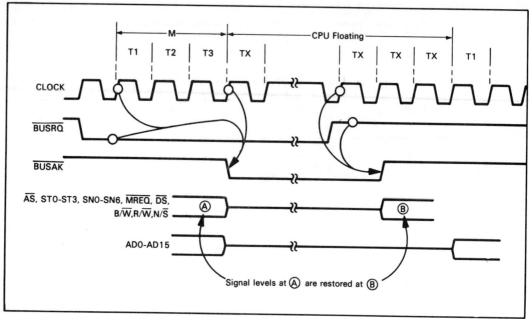

Figure 6-12. Z8000 Hold State

THE Z8000 INTERRUPT ACKNOWLEDGE SEQUENCE

A non-maskable interrupt is requested by a high-to-low transition of $\overline{NMI}$. $\overline{VI}$, $\overline{NVI}$, and $\overline{SEGT}$, on the other hand, are level-sensitive signals; low levels input at these signals request vectored interrupts (for $\overline{VI}$), non-vectored interrupts (for $\overline{NVI}$), or a segmentation trap interrupt (for $\overline{SEGT}$).

The Z8000 microprocessors have three software traps. They are:

1. System Call. This interrupt is initiated by the execution of a System Call instruction. (See Table 21-2.)

Z8000
SOFTWARE
TRAPS

2. Illegal Instruction. This trap is initiated by an attempt to execute an undefined instruction object code.

3. Privileged Instruction. Certain instructions are available for execution in System mode only. An attempt to execute one of these instructions in Normal mode will cause a Privileged Instruction trap.

Z8000 CPU logic checks for interrupt conditions at the beginning of T3, in the last machine cycle of every instruction's execution. A prior high-to-low transition of $\overline{NMI}$ or a low level at $\overline{VI}$, $\overline{NVI}$, or $\overline{SEGT}$ initiates the interrupt acknowledge sequence. In addition, internal traps can generate interrupts. In the event that two or more interrupting conditions exist simultaneously, **priorities are arbitrated as follows:**

> Internal trap (highest)
> Non-maskable interrupt
> Segmentation trap
> Vectored interrupt
> Non-vectored interrupt (lowest)

The interrupt acknowledge sequence, as illustrated in Figure 6-13, begins with an aborted instruction fetch machine cycle. During this machine cycle the next instruction's object code is fetched in the usual way, but this object code is discarded, and the Program Counter is not incremented. The CPU operating mode is automatically switched from Normal to System.

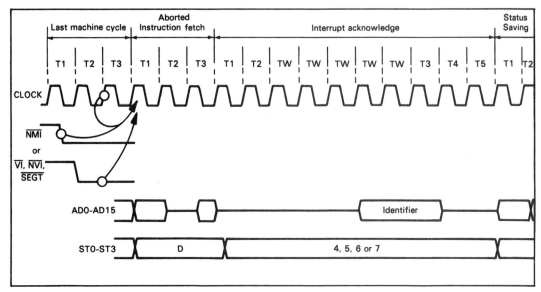

Figure 6-13. Z8000 Interrupt Acknowledge Sequence

Following the aborted instruction fetch, there follows an interrupt acknowledge machine cycle which has five Wait states automatically inserted between T2 and T3. External logic can insert additional Wait states, using the $\overline{WAIT}$ input, as previously described. **During the T3 clock period of the interrupt acknowledge machine cycle, external logic must place an "identifier" on the Data Bus.** The way in which this identifier is used will vary, depending on the nature of the interrupt being acknowledged. **The identifier is used by Z8000 interrupt acknowledge logic, in conjunction with the New Program Status Area Table, illustrated in Figure 6-14.** As shown in Figure 6-14, this table can reside anywhere in memory, providing it originates at the beginning of a 256-byte page. The New Program Status Area Pointer addresses the origin of the New Program Status Area.

Each identifiable interrupt has its own data stored in the new program status area. For a nonsegmented Z8002, two 16-bit words are stored as follows:

New Flag and Control Word Contents
New Program Counter Contents

For a segmented Z8001, four 16-bit words are stored as follows:

Reserved Word (always zero)
New Flag and Control Word Contents
New Program Counter Segment Number
New Program Counter Offset

We described these registers earlier, for the Z8001 and the Z8002, when examining Z8000 programmable registers.

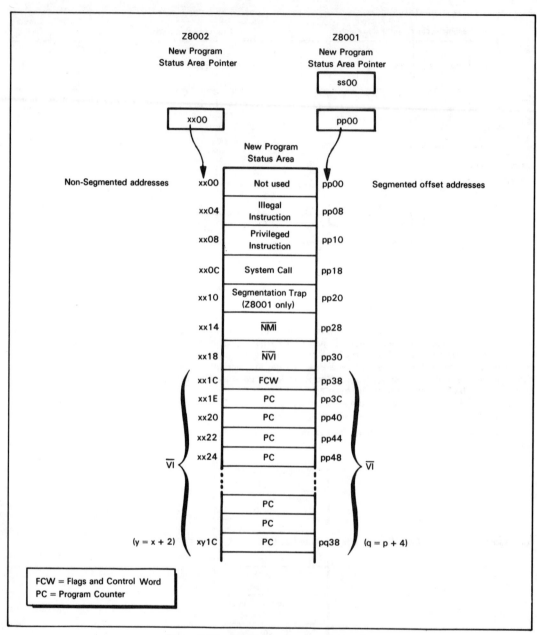

Figure 6-14. Z8000 New Program Status Area

The segmentation trap, internal software traps, non-maskable interrupt, and non-vectored interrupt have dedicated locations in the New Program Status Area. For these interrupts, the identifier which is fetched during the acknowledge cycle can be used in any way. Typically, it will identify the source or nature of the interrupt. For a non-maskable interrupt, a non-vectored interrupt, or segmentation trap, or an internal software trap, all 16 bits of the identifier are available.

For vectored interrupts, the low-order byte of the identifier must provide the offset of the New Program Status Area address for the interrupting device's status area entry. This may be illustrated as follows:

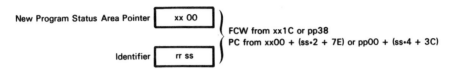

New Program Status Area Pointer | xx 00

FCW from xx1C or pp38
PC from xx00 + (ss•2 + 7E) or pp00 + (ss•4 + 3C)

Identifier | rr ss

We can summarize identifier interpretations as follows:

	Identifier
Segmentation trap:	iiii
System Call:	wwii
Illegal Instruction:	wwww
Privileged Instruction:	wwww
Non-Maskable Interrupt:	iiii
Non-Vectored Interrupt:	iiii
Vectored Interrupt:	iil l

The summary given above lists the identifier contents as a sequence of four hexadecimal digits. Letters are used as follows:

1) i represents any programmer defined identifier information.

2) l represents the offset for the memory address in the New Program Status Area where the new Program Counter contents are stored.

3) w represents the first word (or byte) of the Instruction object code for the instruction which causes a software tap.

Following the interrupt acknowledge machine cycle, data is pushed onto the System Stack, and is loaded into registers, in the following sequence:

Z8002	Z8001
Push PC	Push PC offset
Push FCW	Push PC segment
Push Identifier	Push FCW
Load FCW	Push identifier
Load PC	Load FCW
	Load PC segment
	Load PC offset

A Return-from-Interrupt instruction discards the word at the top of the System Stack — assuming this to be the identifier — then pops the top of the System Stack, restoring the saved Program Counter, and the Flag and Control Word contents. The mode is determined by the saved FCW, thus restoring conditions to those that existed before the interrupt acknowledge.

THE Z8000 RESET

You reset a Z8000 microprocessor by holding the $\overline{\text{RESET}}$ input low for at least five clock periods. This causes signals to be adjusted as follows:

1) AD0-AD15 are floated

2) $\overline{\text{AS}}$, $\overline{\text{DS}}$, $\overline{\text{MREQ}}$, $\overline{\text{BUSAK}}$, and $\overline{\text{MO}}$ are output high

3) ST0-ST3 and SN0-SN6 are output low

4) R/$\overline{\text{W}}$, B/$\overline{\text{W}}$ and N/$\overline{\text{S}}$ are unaffected; they retain whatever signal levels they previously had

5) Dynamic memory refresh logic is disabled

When $\overline{\text{RESET}}$ goes high again, three clock periods elapse, then two consecutive memory read machine cycles are executed. The Flag and Control Word and the Program Counter are reinitialized as follows:

Z8002	Z8001
FCW from 0002	FCW from 0002
PC from 0004	PC segment from 0004
	PC offset from 0006

Program execution then proceeds with the program identified by the new Program Counter contents.

THE Z8000 INSTRUCTION SET

The Z8000 instruction set is summarized in Table 6-3. Instruction object codes and execution times are given alphabetically in Table 6-4. Instruction object codes are given numerically in Table 6-5.

The most striking characteristic of the Z8000 instruction set is its orderliness. Despite its complexity, this instruction set should be relatively easy to learn, since variations are consistent, and therefore predictable. This is in sharp contrast to Zilog's previous offering, the Z80, which was frequently criticized for its complex and disorderly assembly language.

The Z8000 instruction set is also powerful; it at least equals that of any other 16-bit microprocessor, and will rival most 16-bit minicomputers.

Let us examine the Z8000 instruction set by instruction categories, as given in Table 6-3.

All I/O ports are addressed using 16-bit I/O port addresses, which may be specified directly, or via a 16-bit register. Thus 65,536 I/O ports may be addressed.

All I/O instructions have a byte version and a word version. The byte version inputs and outputs 8-bit data. The word version inputs and outputs 16-bit data. 8-bit data is output twice, on both halves of the 16-bit Data/Address Bus. Input data is read off the eight low-order Data/Address Bus lines for input instructions with odd addresses; it is read off the eight high-order Data/Address Bus lines for input instructions with even addresses. Note that this is the same as byte addressing for memory locations.

A general characteristic of Zilog microprocessor components is the extensive use of block transfer logic. Instructions that repeatedly re-execute to move blocks of data occur throughout the Z8000 instruction set, beginning with I/O instructions. **Both the byte and word versions of IN and OUT instructions have auto-increment and auto-decrement variations** that may be illustrated as follows:

Z8000 I/O INSTRUCTIONS

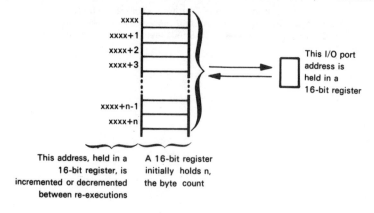

This address, held in a 16-bit register, is incremented or decremented between re-executions

A 16-bit register initially holds n, the byte count

This I/O port address is held in a 16-bit register

Block transfer instructions may transfer a single data byte or word and then stop, leaving counters and pointers ready to handle the next byte; alternatively, instructions may transfer the entire data block within a single execution. In the latter case, interrupt requests are acknowledged between byte or word transfers; also, dynamic memory refresh cycles, if enabled, will be inserted at the proper time.

The entire input and output instruction set is repeated for a set of "special" I/O instructions. (The simple input and output instructions are repeated only for the direct I/O port variation.) The special I/O instructions are intended for use with a Z8010 Memory Management Device or other special system components which may become available in the future. The

> **Z8000
> SPECIAL I/O
> INSTRUCTIONS**

only difference between special I/O instructions and normal I/O instructions is that special I/O instructions output 0011 via the status lines ST0-ST3. Normal I/O instructions output 0010.

Z8000 memory reference instructions generally use one of seven memory addressing modes, all except the first one represented in Tables 6-3, 6-4, and 6-5 by the label adrsx. These seven addressing modes are:

> **Z8000
> PRINICIPAL
> MEMORY
> ADDRESSING
> MODES**

	Mode	Operand
1)	Nonsegmented, implied	@ris
2)	Nonsegmented, direct	addr
3)	Short segmented, direct	addrss
4)	Long segmented, direct	addrls
5)	Nonsegmented, indexed	addr(ri)
6)	Short segmented, indexed	addrss(ri)
7)	Long segmented, indexed	addrls(ri)

The operand abbreviations used above are defined prior to Table 6-3.

Refer to the earlier description of Z8000 memory addressing modes for a more complete description of the seven modes summarized above.

Although Z8000 primary memory reference instructions generally use the seven memory addressing modes listed above, base relative addressing, implied, indexed addressing, and program relative addressing options are also available.

> **Z8000
> PRIMARY
> MEMORY
> REFERENCE
> INSTRUCTIONS**

All primary memory reference instructions have byte and word version; most also have long word versions.

Secondary memory reference instructions use only the seven memory addressing modes. There are byte and word versions for nearly all secondary memory reference instructions, but long word versions are scarce.

> **Z8000
> SECONDARY
> MEMORY
> REFERENCE
> INSTRUCTIONS**

An anomaly of the Z8000 instruction set is the shortage of Add-with-Carry and Subtract-with-Borrow instructions; they are only available as register-register operate instructions. No long word Add-with-Carry or Subtract-with-Borrow is available.

Multiply and divide instructions have register-register and memory-register versions. Both have word and long word options.

The divide instruction holds the dividend in CPU registers; the divisor may reside in memory or in CPU registers, or it may be an immediate operand. Both the divisor and the dividend are treated as signed binary numbers. After the division instruction has been executed, the quotient is returned in the low-order half of the dividend register space, while the remainder is returned in the high-order half of the dividend space. A word division may be illustrated as follows:

Z8000 DIVIDE INSTRUCTION

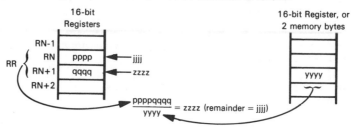

RN is the high-order register
RN+1 is the low-order register
j, p, q, y, and z represent any hexadecimal digits
RN is a 16-bit register
RR represents a 32-bit register pair, as illustrated in Figure 6-3.

Long word division may be illustrated as follows:

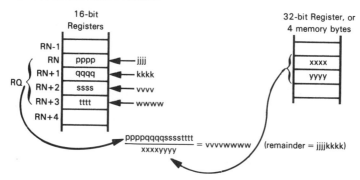

j, k, p, q, s, t, v, w, x, and y represent any hexadecimal digits.
RQ represents a 64-bit register, as illustrated in Figure 6-3.

The sign of the remainder is always the same as the sign of the dividend.

The divisions instruction modifies status flags as follows:

Carry (C). If the quotient overflows or underflows, then C is set. For a word divide, the quotient underflows if it is less than -2^{15}; it overflows if it is 2^{15} or more. For a long word divide, the quotient overflows if it is less than -2^{31}; it overflows if it is 2^{31} or more.

Zero (Z). The Zero status is set to 1 if the quotient or divisor is 0. It is cleared otherwise.

Sign (S). The Sign status reports the sign of the quotient; it is set if the quotient is negative; it is reset if the quotient is positive.

Overflow (O). The Overflow status is set to 1 if the divisor is 0, or if the quotient cannot fit into the low-order half of the dividend space.

The divide instruction's execution is aborted if the dividend high-order half absolute value is larger than the divisor absolute value. This may be illustrated as follows:

$$\text{Abort if } |pppp| > |yyyy|$$
$$\text{Abort if } |ppppqqqq| > |xxxxyyyy|$$

The multiply instruction also has word and long word versions. The multiplicand is held in CPU registers. The multiplier may be held in data memory, in CPU registers, or it may be provided immediately by the multiply instruction. The product is returned in CPU registers. The word option may be illustrated as follows:

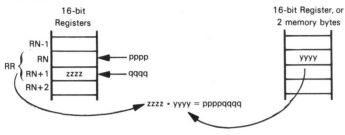

p, q, y, and z represent any hexadecimal digits.

RR represents a 32-bit register pair, as illustrated in Figure 6-3.

Long word multiplication may be illustrated as follows:

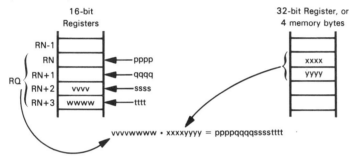

p, q, s, t, v, w, x, and y represent any hexadecimal digts.

RQ represents a 64-bit register, as illustrated in Figure 6-3.

The multiply instruction treats all numbers as signed binary values. Status flags are adjusted as follows:

Carry (C). C is set for overflow or underflow. For word multiplication, underflow occurs if the answer is less than -2^{15}; overflow occurs if the answer is 2^{15} or more. For long word multiplication, underflow occurs if the product is less than -2^{31}; overflow occurs if the product is 2^{31} or more. Carry is cleared if there is no underflow or overflow.

Zero (Z). The Zero status is set if the result is 0; it is cleared otherwise.

Sign (S). The Sign status is set for a negative result; it is reset otherwise.

The Overflow status is always cleared.

The LDPS instruction is somewhat unusual in that it loads both the Program Counter and the Flag and Control Word. Data is taken from memory as follows:

Non-Segmented
(Memory bytes)

FCW (HI)
FCW (LO)
PC (HI)
PC (LO)

Segmented
(Memory bytes)

00
00
FCW (HI)
FCW (LO)
PCSEG(HI)
PCSEG(LO)
PCOFF (HI)
PCOFF(LO)

The LDPS jump instruction uses indirect memory addressing.

A subroutine CALL can use segmented implied memory addressing:

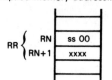

The System Call instruction generates an interrupt acknowledge sequence. You will recall from the discussion of Z8000 interrupt acknowledge logic given earlier in this chapter that an interrupt identifier is pushed onto the Stack during every interrupt acknowledge sequence. For the System Call instruction, this identifier is the System Call instruction object code; the low-order byte is an 8-bit immediate data value which you specify in the instruction operand. This may be illustrated as follows:

$$\underbrace{\text{SC} \quad \text{xx}}_{\text{7F} \quad \text{xx}_{16}}$$

Note that the **JP** conditional jump instruction can use segmented implied memory addressing. **As we might expect from a Zilog high-end microprocessor, the Z8000 has a large number of block transfer and search instructions. These instructions come in groups of eight.** For each type of instruction there are four word versions and four comparable byte versions. The four versions include an increment, an increment and repeat, a decrement, and a decrement and repeat. See our earlier discussion of block transfer I/O instructions for a general description of these four variations.

The LDM block transfer instructions move data between a number of 16-bit registers and memory. You can transfer data from memory words to 16-bit registers or from 16-bit registers to memory words. You can transfer from 1 to 16 words in a single execution. Register addressing is wrap-around. For example, the instruction:

LDM R13,THERE,6

will transfer six words of data from memory to registers, in the following sequence:

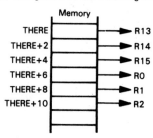

Among the block transfer and search instructions there is a group of translate instructions. These are table look-up instructions; they work as follows:

TRxB   @RM,@RN,RW

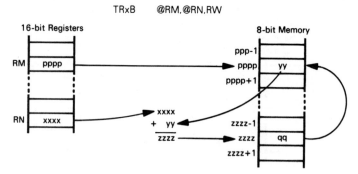

RW is decremented and RM is incremented or decremented, depending on the instruction.

As illustrated above, the contents of the destination memory location serve as an 8-bit index into a memory table. The contents of the addressed table byte replace the index. RH1 is used, and left with an undefined value. Translate instructions are typically used to convert characters from one code to another. For example, a single translate instruction could convert an EBCDIC character to an ASCII character. In this case the EBCDIC character code would constitute an index into a 256-byte ASCII code table. At the location specified by the EBCDIC code, you would store the ASCII equivalent. Executing a translate instruction would then cause the ASCII equivalent of an EBCDIC code to be loaded into the memory location in which the EBCDIC code had been stored.

A variation of the Translate instruction is a Translate-and-Test, which loads the addressed table byte into Register RH1, but leaves it there. The Z flag is set if RH1 is 0, and Overflow is set if the counter decrements to 0.

There are a deceptively large number of shift instructions listed in the register operate group. In fact, the only difference between an arithmetic and a logical left shift lies in the Overflow status. For an arithmetic shift this status is set if the high-order (Sign) bit changes following the shift; the Overflow status is cleared otherwise. Following a logical shift the Overflow status is undefined. For right shifts the Sign bit is replicated for arithmetic shifts, while zeros are filled in for logical shifts.

Z8000 SHIFT INSTRUCTIONS

The only difference between a dynamic shift and a non-dynamic shift is in the location of the shift bit count. A dynamic shift takes its bit count from a CPU register.

A non-dynamic shift takes its bit count from immediate data provided by the instruction operand.

Note from our earlier discussion of the Z8000 Stack that the Stack address is incremented for a pop and decremented for a push. In other words, the bottom of the Stack has the highest memory address, and the top of the Stack has the lowest memory address.

Z8000 STACK INSTRUCTIONS

Four instructions control the $\overline{MI}$ input and $\overline{MO}$ output signals. They are MBIT, MREQ, MRES, and MSET.

Z8000 $\overline{MI}$ AND $\overline{MO}$ INSTRUCTIONS

MBIT simply inverts the level of the $\overline{MI}$ input and returns it in the Sign status.

MRES outputs a high signal via $\overline{MO}$, while MSET outputs a low signal via $\overline{MO}$.

MREQ uses $\overline{MI}$ and $\overline{MO}$ to request external access. This instruction uses Zero and Sign statuses. MREQ execution logic may be illustrated as follows:

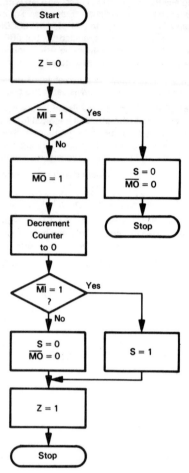

When the MREQ instruction begins execution, the Zero status is cleared; it is set to 1 after MREQ has completed execution if a request was signalled.

The $\overline{MI}$ input is tested to see if the external resource being arbitrated is available. If $\overline{MI}$ is low, then the resource is not available; $\overline{MO}$ is output high and the Sign status is reset to 0.

If $\overline{MI}$ is being input high, then the external resource is available. $\overline{MO}$ is output low, then a time delay is inserted by decrementing the contents of a 16-bit register to 0. This delay gives external logic time to receive and propagate $\overline{MO}$. External logic must acknowledge the resource request by inputting $\overline{MI}$ low. In response to $\overline{MI}$ low, MREQ sets the Sign status and the Zero status to 1. But if $\overline{MI}$ is still high after the counter has decremented to 0, then MREQ outputs $\overline{MO}$ high, resets the Sign status to 0, and sets the Zero status to 1. Therefore, following execution of the MREQ instruction, CPU logic interprets results as follows:

Sign	Zero	$\overline{MO}$	
0	0	0	No request made
0	0	1	Not possible
0	1	0	Request made but not granted
0	1	1	
1	0	0	
1	0	1	Not possible
1	1	0	
1	1	1	Request made and granted

THE BENCHMARK PROGRAM

The Z8000 can execute our benchmark program using just three instructions. We assume the following memory map:

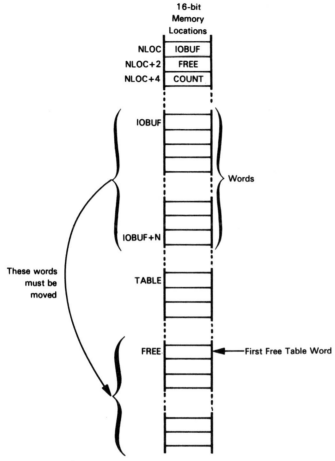

Using the LDM Multiple Register Load instruction, we can initialize the addresses and word count in appropriate registers for an LDIR Block Transfer and Repeat instruction. Finally, we update the address of the first free table word. Here is the necessary instruction sequence:

```
!LOAD IOBUF STARTING ADDRESS INTO R1, TABLE STARTING
!ADDRESS INTO R2, WORD COUNT INTO R3
           LDM      R1, NLOC, 3
           LDIR     @R2, @R1, R3      !MOVE DATA BLOCK
           LD       NLOC+2, R2        !UPDATE ADDRESS OF FIRST FREE WORD IN
                                          TABLE
NLOC       DA       IOBUF             !I/O BUFFER BASE ADDRESS
           DA       FREE              !DATA TABLE FIRST FREE WORD ADDRESS
           DA       COUNT             !WORD COUNT
```

The nomenclature used to identify Z8000 registers is given in Figure 6-3.

The following abbreviations are used in Tables 6-3, 6-4, and 6-5:

addr	any 16-bit nonsegmented address
addrls	any 32-bit long segmented address
addrss	any 16-bit short segmented address
adrsx	one of six standard memory addressing modes
b8	immediate value in the range 0-7
b16	immediate value in the range 0-15
cc	condition codes, as summarized in Table 6-2
data8	8-bit immediate data value
data16	16-bit immediate data value
data32	32-bit immediate data value
disp	address displacement
FCW	the Flags and Control Word
FLAGS	low-order byte of FCW
flag	any or all of C, S, P, O, Z
int	either or both of NVI, VI
ioaddr	an I/O device 16-bit address
(I/O)	an identifier specifying that the prior address is an I/O address
$\overline{\text{MI}}$	the $\overline{\text{MI}}$ signal input level
$\overline{\text{MO}}$	the $\overline{\text{MO}}$ signal output level
MSB	the most significant (high-order) bit of any data value
n16	immediate value in the range 1-16
NSPOFF	Normal Stack Pointer offset
NSPSEG	Normal Stack Pointer segment
PC	Program Counter
PCOFF	Program Counter offset
PCSEG	Program Counter segment
PSAPOFF	Program Status Area Pointer offset
PSAPSEG	Program Status Area Pointer segment
rb	any byte register
rbd	any byte register serving as a destination
rbs	any byte register serving as a source
REFRESH	Refresh Counter
ri	any 16-bit index register
rid	any 16-bit register providing implied destination address
ris	any 16-bit register providing implied source address
rld	any 32-bit register serving as a source
rls	any 32-bit register serving as a source
rqd	any 64-bit register serving as a destination
rw	any 16-bit register
rwd	any 16-bit register serving as a destination
rws	any 16-bit register serving as a source
SP	Stack Pointer (R15 or RR14)

Object Code	b - immediate value corresponding to b8 or b16

Object Code   b - immediate value corresponding to b8 or b16
c - condition code (see Table 6-2)
d - destination register
f - code for flags operated on: CZSP/V
i - index or implied register. If i = 0 no register is specified
n - immediate value corresponding to n16
pppp - 16-bit address word or most significant word of 32-bit address
qqqq - least significant word of 32-bit address
r - register
    0000 = R0, RR0, RQ0, or RH0
    0001 = R1, or RH1
          •
          •
          •
    0111 = R7, or RH7
    1000 = R8, RR8, RQ8, or RL0
          •
          •
          •
    1110 = R14, RR14, or RL6
    1111 = R15 or RL7
s - source register
tttttt - 7-bit unsigned displacement
vv - code for interrupts (VI and/or NVI)
xx - 8-bit address displacement
xxx - 12-bit address displacement
xxxx - 16-bit address displacement
yy - 8-bit immediate data
yyyy - 16-bit immediate data or most significant word of 32-bit data
zzzz - least significant word of 32-bit immediate data

Statuses   The Z8000 has the following status flags:

C - Carry status
Z - Zero status
S - Sign status
P - Parity status
O - Overflow status
D - Decimal-Adjust
H - Half-Carry

The following symbols are used in the Status columns:

x - flag is affected by operation
(blank) - flag is not affected by operation
1 - flag is set by operation
0 - flag is reset by operation
U - flag is unknown after operation

[[ ]]   contents of the memory location or I/O port whose address is contained in the designated register
[ ]   contents of memory location, I/O port, or register
←   data is transferred in the direction of the arrow
←→   data is exchanged between the designated locations on both sides of the arrows
V   logical OR
Λ   logical AND
⊕   logical Exclusive OR

Instruction Mnemonics:

The fixed part of an assembly language instruction is shown in UPPER CASE, the variable part (immediate data, register name, etc.) is shown in lower case.

Instruction Object Codes:

Instruction words are shown as hexadecimal digits with 4-bit variable fields indicated by lower case letters (e.g., 67ib).

Instruction words with variable fields that are not multiples of 4 bits are shown as a pair of hexadecimal digits followed by 8 binary bits (e.g., 7C 000001vv)

Instruction Execution Times:

Tables 6-3 and 6-4 list instruction execution times in clock cycles. Real time is obtained by dividing the number of clock cycles by the clock speed.

When several possible execution times are indicated (i.e., 15-19) the number of clock cycles depends on addressing and segmentation modes. The relationship is as follows:

Clock Cycles = x-y

	Addressing Mode	Clock Cycles
2)	addr	x
3)	addrss	y-3
4)	addrls	y-1
5)	addr(ri)	x+1
6)	addrss(ri)	y-3
7)	addrls(ri)	y

For two execution times (i.e., 10, 15) the first is for Nonsegmented mode, the second for Segmented mode.

Instruction times which depend on condition flags are indicated with a slash (i.e., 10, 15/7) with the first time(s) for condition met and the second for condition not met.

Table 6-2. Condition Codes Used by the Z8000 Assembly Language Instruction Set

Code	CC Value	Meaning	Status Conditions
—	8	Always true	Any
C ULT	7	Carry Unsigned less than	C = 1
EQ Z	6	Equal Zero	Z = 1
GE	9	Signed greater than or equal	S $\oplus$ O = 0
GT	A	Signed greater than	Z V (S $\oplus$ O) = 0
LE	2	Signed less than or equal	Z V (S $\oplus$ O) = 1
LT	1	Signed less than	S $\oplus$ O = 0
MI	5	Minus	S = 1
NC UGE	F	No Carry Unsigned greater than or equal	C = 0
NE NZ	E	Not equal Not zero	Z = 0
NOV PO	C	No overflow Parity is odd	P/O = 0
PE OV	4	Parity is even Overflow	P/O = 1
PL	D	Plus	S = 0
UGT	B	Unsigned greater than	C V Z = 0
ULE	3	Unsigned less than or equal	C V Z = 1

Table 6-3. A Summary of the Z8000 Instruction Set

Type	Mnemonic	Operand(s)	Op Code		Bytes	Clock Cycles	Status H	D	O	P	S	Z	C	Operation Performed
	IN*	rwd,@rw	3Dsd		2	10								[rwd] ← [[rw]](I/O)
	IN*	rwd,ioaddr	3Bd4	pppp	4	12								[rwd] ← [ioaddr](I/O). Input to 16-bit register rwd a data word from the I/O port addressed directly by ioaddr, or implied by rw.
	INB*	rwd,@rw	3Csd		2	10								[rbd] ← [[rw]](I/O)
	INB*	rwd,ioaddr	3Ad4	pppp	4	12								[rbd] ← [ioaddr](I/O). Input to 8-bit register rbd a data byte from the I/O port addressed directly by ioaddr, or implied by rw.
	IND*	@rid,@ris,rw	3Bs8	Ord8	4	21			X					[[rid]] ← [[ris]](I/O). [rid] ← [rid] − 2. [rw] ← [rw] − 1. If [rw] = 0 then O = 1. Otherwise O = 0.
	INDB*	@rid,@ris,rw	3As8	Ord8	4	21			X					[[rid]] ← [[ris]](I/O). [rid] ← [rid] − 1. [rw] ← [rw] − 1. If [rw] = 0 then O = 1. Otherwise O = 0. Input a 16-bit data word (for IND) or a data byte (for INDB) from the I/O port implied by ris to the memory word (for IND) or byte (for INDB) implied by rid. Decrement the implied memory address in rid by 2 (for IND) or by 1 (for INDB). Decrement the 16-bit counter rw by 1. If rw contains 0, set the Overflow status.
	INDR*	@rid,@ris,rw	3Bs8	Ord0	4	21/10**			X					[[rid]] ← [[ris]](I/O). [rid] ← [rid] − 2. [rw] ← [rw] − 1. If [rw] = 0 then O = 1. Otherwise reexecute.
	INDRB*	@rid,@ris,rw	3As8	Ord0	4	21/10**			X					[[rid]] ← [[ris]](I/O). [rid] ← [rid] − 1. [rw] ← [rw] − 1. If [rw] = 0 then O = 1. Otherwise reexecute. INDR and INDRB are identical to IND and INDB, respectively, except that INDR and INDRB are reexecuted until [rw] = 0.
	INI*	@rid,@ris,rw	3Bs8	Ord8	4	21			X					[[rid]] ← [[ris]](I/O). [rid] ← [rid] + 2. [rw] ← [rw] − 1. If [rw] = 0 then O = 1. Otherwise O = 0.
	INIB*	@rid,@ris,rw	3As8	Ord8	4	21			X					[[rid]] ← [[ris]](I/O). [rid] ← [rid] + 1. [rw] ← [rw] − 1. If [rw] = 0 then O = 1. INI and INIB are identical to IND and INDB, respectively, except that rid is incremented.
	INIR*	@rid,@ris,rw	3Bs0	Ord0	4	21/10**			X					[[rid]] ← [[ris]](I/O). [rid] ← [rid] + 2. [rw] ← [rw] − 1. If [rw] = 0 then O = 1. Otherwise reexecute.
	INIRB*	@rid,@ris,rw	3As0	Ord0	4	21/10**			X					[[rid]] ← [[ris]](I/O). [rid] ← [rid] + 1. [rw] ← [rw] − 1. If [rw] = 0 then O = 1. Otherwise reexecute. INIR and INIRB are identical to INI and INIB, respectively, except that rid is incremented; also INIR and INIRB are reexecuted until [rw] = 0.
O/I	OTDR*	@rid,@ris,rw	3BsA	Ord0	4	21/10**			X					[[rid]](I/O) ← [[ris]]. [ris] ← [ris] − 2. [rw] ← [rw] − 1. If [rw] ≠ 0 then reexecute. If [rw] = 0 then O = 1 and end execution.

* Privileged instruction — can be executed only in system mode.

** Number of clock cycles depends on the number of repetitions for n/m**; n = minimum number of clock cycles and m = number of clock cycles added for each additional repetition of operation. The number of clock cycles for an instruction which repeats k times is n + (k-1)•m.

Table 6-3. A Summary of the Z8000 Instruction Set (Continued)

Type	Mnemonic	Operand(s)	Op Code	Bytes	Clock Cycles	H	D	O	P	S	Z	C	Operation Performed
I/O (Continued)	OTDRB*	@rid,@ris,rw	3AsA OrdO	4	21/10**			X					[rid](I/O) ← [ris]. [ris] ← [ris] − 1. [rw] ← [rw] − 1 If [rw] ≠ 0 then reexecute. If [rw] = 0 then O = 1 and end execution. Output a block of 16-bit words (for OTDR) or 8-bit bytes (for OTDRB) from memory to an I/O port. rw specifies the number of words or bytes. Memory is addressed, using implied memory addressing, by 16-bit register ris, which is decremented after each output. 16-bit register rid specifies the I/O port.
	OTIR*	@rid,@ris,rw	3Bs2 OrdO	4	21/10**			X					[rid](I/O) ← [ris]. [ris] ← [ris] + 2. [rw] ← [rw] − 1 If [rw] ≠ 0 then reexecute. If [rw] = 0 then O = 1 and end execution.
	OTIRB*	@rid,@ris,rw	3As2 OrdO	4	21/10**			X					[rid](I/O) ← [ris]. [ris] ← [ris] + 1. [rw] ← [rw] − 1 If [rw] ≠ 0 then reexecute. If [rw] = 0 then O = 1 and end execution. OTIR and OTIRB are identical to OTDR and OTDRB, respectively, except that OTIR and OTIRB increment the memory address in ris.
	OUT*	@rw,rws	3Fds	2	10								[rw](I/O) ← [rws]
	OUT*	ioaddr,rws	3Bs6 pppp	4	12								[ioaddr](I/O) ← [rws] Output the data word from 16-bit register rws to the I/O port addressed directly by ioaddr or implied by rw.
	OUTB*	@rw,rbs	3Eds	2	10								[rw](I/O) ← [rbs]
	OUTB*	ioaddr,rbs	3As6 pppp	4	12								[ioaddr](I/O) ← [rbs] Output the data byte from 8-bit register rbs to the I/O port addressed directly by ioaddr or implied by rw.
	OUTD*	@rid,@ris,rw	3BsA Ord8	4	21			X					[rid](I/O) ← [ris]. [ris] ← [ris] − 2. [rw] ← [rw] − 1 If [rw] = 0 then O = 1; otherwise O = 0.
	OUTDB*	@rid,@ris,rw	3AsA Ord8	4	21			X					[rid](I/O) ← [ris]. [ris] ← [ris] − 1. [rw] ← [rw] − 1 If [rw] = 0 then O = 1; otherwise O = 0. Output a data word (for OUTD) or byte (for OUTDB) from the memory location addressed by 16-bit register ris to the I/O port addressed by 16-bit register rid. Decrement ris by 2 (for OUTD) or 1 (for OUTDB). Decrement the counter 16-bit register rw.
	OUTI*	@rid,@ris,rw	3Bs2 Ord8	4	21			X					[rid](I/O) ← [ris]. [ris] ← [ris] + 2. [rw] ← [rw] − 1. If [rw] = 0 then O = 1; otherwise O = 0.
	OUTIB*	@rid,@ris,rw	3As2 Ord8	4	21			X					[rid](I/O) ← [ris]. [ris] ← [ris] + 1. [rw] ← [rw] − 1. If [rw] = 0then O = 1; otherwise O = 0. OUTI and OUTIB are identical to OUTD and OUTDB, respectively, except that the memory address in ris is incremented.

* Privileged instruction — can be executed only in system mode.

** Number of clock cycles depends on the number of repetitions for n/m**; n = minimum number of clock cycles and m = number of clock cycles added for each additional repetition of operation. The number of clock cycles for an instruction which repeats k times is n + (k-1)•m.

Table 6-3. A Summary of the Z8000 Instruction Set (Continued)

Type	Mnemonic	Operand(s)	Op Code			Bytes	Clock Cycles	H	D	O	P	S	Z	C	Operation Performed
I/O (Continued)	SIN*	rwd,ioaddr	3Bd5	pppp		4	12								These instructions output "special I/O" status via ST0 - ST3; otherwise, they are identical to I/O instructions as follows:
	SINB*	rbd,ioaddr	3Ad5	pppp		4	12								SIN - IN(1) SINB - INB(1)
	SIND*	@rid,@ris,rw	3Bs9	0rd8		4	21			X					SIND - IND SINDB - INDB
	SINDB*	@rid,@ris,rw	3As9	0rd8		4	21			X					SINDR - INDR SINDRB - INDRB
	SINDR*	@rid,@ris,rw	3Bs9	0rd0		4	21/10**			X					SINI - INI SINIB - INIB
	SINDRB*	@rid,@ris,rw	3As9	0rd0		4	21/10**			X					SINIR - INIR SINIRB - INIRB
	SINI*	@rid,@ris,rw	3Bs1	0rd8		4	21			X					SOTDR - OTDR DOTDRB - OTDRB
	SINIB*	@rid,@ris,rw	3As1	0rd8		4	21			X					SOTIR - OTIR SOTIRB - OTIRB(1)
	SINIR*	@rid,@ris,rw	3Bs1	0rd0		4	21/10**			X					SOUT - OUT(1) SOUTB - OUTB(1)
	SINIRB*	@rid,@ris,rw	3As1	0rd0		4	21/10**			X					SOUTD - OUTD SOUTDB - OUTDB
	SOTDR*	@rid,@ris,rw	3BsB	0rd0		4	21/10**			X					SOUTI - OUTI SOUTIB - OUTIB
	SOTDRB*	@rid,@ris,rw	3AsB	0rd0		4	21/10**			X					
	SOTIR*	@rid,@ris,rw	3Bs3	0rd0		4	21/10**			X					(1)Only the direct addressing option exists for the special I/O version of this instruction.
	SOTIRB*	@rid,@ris,rw	3As3	0rd0		4	21/10**			X					
	SOUT*	ioaddr,rws	3Bs7	pppp		4	12								
	SOUTB*	ioaddr,rbs	3As7	pppp		4	12								
	SOUTD*	@rid,@ris,rw	3BsB	0rd8		4	21			X					
	SOUTDB*	@rid,@ris,rw	3AsB	0rd8		4	21			X					
	SOUTI*	@rid,@ris,rw	3Bs3	0rd8		4	21			X					
	SOUTIB	@rid,@ris,rw	3As3	0rd8		4	21			X					
Primary Memory Reference	LD	rwd,adrsx	61id	pppp	qqqq	4/6	9-13								[rwd] ← [adrsx]
	LD	rwd,@ris	21id			2	7								[rwd] ← [[ris]]
															Load data from the 16-bit memory word addressed by adrsx or [ris] into 16-bit register rwd.
	LD	rwd,ris(disp)	31id	xxxx		4	14								[rwd] ← [[ris] + disp]
															Load into 16-bit register rwd the contents of the 16-bit memory word addressed using base relative addressing.
	LD	rwd,ris(rw)	71id	0r00		4	14								[rwd] ← [[ris] + [rw]]
															Load into 16-bit register rwd the contents of the 16-bit memory word addressed using implied, indexed addressing.
	LDB	rbd,adrsx	60id	pppp	qqqq	4/6	9-13								[rbd] ← [adrsx]
	LDB	rbd,@ris	20id			2	7								[rbd] ← [[ris]]
															Load into 8-bit register rbd the contents of the memory byte addressed by adrsx or [ris].

* Privileged instruction — can be executed only in system mode.

** Number of clock cycles depends on the number of repetitions for n/m**; n = minimum number of clock cycles and m = number of clock cycles added for each additional repetition of operation. The number of clock cycles for an instruction which repeats k times is n + (k-1)•m.

Table 6-3. A Summary of the Z8000 Instruction Set (Continued)

Type	Mnemonic	Operand(s)	Op Code		Bytes	Clock Cycles	Status							Operation Performed
							H	D	O	P	S	Z	C	
Primary Memory Reference (Continued)	LDB	rbd,ris(disp)	30id	xxxx	4	14								[rbd] ← [[ris] + disp] Load into 8-bit register rbd the contents of the memory byte addressed using base relative addressing.
	LDB	rbd,ris(rw)	70id	0r00	4	14								[rbd] ← [[ris] + [rw]] Load into 8-bit register rbd the contents of the memory byte addressed using implied, indexed addressing.
	LDL	rld,adrsx	54id pppp	qqqq	4/6	12-16								[rld] ← [adrsx]
	LDL	rld,@ris	14id		2	11								[rld] ← [[ris]] Load into 32-bit register rld the contents of the 32-bit memory location addressed by adrsx or [ris].
	LDL	rld,ris(disp)	35id	xxxx	4	17								[rld] ← [[ris] + disp] Load into 32-bit register rld the contents of the 32-bit memory location addressed using base relative addressing.
	LDL	rld,ris(rw)	75id	0r00	4	17								[rld] ← [[ris] + [rld]] Load into 32-bit register rld the contents of the 32-bit memory location addressed using implied, indexed addressing.
	LD	adrsx,rws	6Fis pppp	qqqq	4/6	11-15								[adrsx] ← [rws]
	LD	@rid,rws	2Fds		2	8								[[rid]] ← [rws] Store data from 16-bit register rws into memory word addressed by adrsx or [rid].
	LD	rid(disp),rws	33is	xxxx	4	14								[[rid] + disp] ← [rws] Store data from 16-bit register rws into memory word addressed using base relative addressing.
	LD	rid(rw),rws	73is	0r00	4	14								[[rid] + [rw]] ← [rws] Store data from 16-bit register rws into memory word addressed using implied, indexed addressing.
	LDB	adrsx,rbs	6Eis pppp	qqqq	4/6	11-15								[adrsx] ← [rbs]
	LDB	@rid,rbs	2Eds		2	8								[[rid]] ← [rbs] Store data from 8-bit register rbs into memory byte addressed by adrsx or [rid].
	LDB	rid(disp),rbs	32is	xxxx	4	14								[[rid] + disp] ← [rbs] Store data from 8-bit register rbs into memory byte addressed using base relative addressing.

*   Privileged instruction — can be executed only in system mode.
** Number of clock cycles depends on the number of repetitions for n/m**; n =minimum number of clock cycles and m = number of clock cycles added for each additional repetition of operation. The number of clock cycles for an instruction which repeats k times is n + (k-1)•m.

Table 6-3. A Summary of the Z8000 Instruction Set (Continued)

Type	Mnemonic	Operand(s)	Op Code	Bytes	Clock Cycles	Status H	D	O	P	S	Z	C	Operation Performed
Primary Memory Reference (Continued)	LDB	rid(rw),rbs	72is 0r00	4	14								[[rid] + [rw]] ← [rbs] Store data from 8-bit register rbs into memory byte addressed using implied, indexed addressing.
	LDL	adrsx,rls	5Dis pppp qqqq	4/6	14-18								[adrsx] ← [rls]
	LDL	@rid,rls	1Dds	2	11								[[rid]] ← [rls] Store data from 32-bit register rls into 32-bit memory long word addressed by adrsx or [rid].
	LDL	rid(disp),rls	37is xxxx	4	17								[[rid] + disp] ← [rls] Store data from 32-bit register rls into 32-bit memory long word addressed using base relative addressing.
	LDL	rid(rw),rls	77is 0r00	4	17								[[rid] + [rw]] ← [rls] Store data from 32-bit register rls into 32-bit memory long word addressed using implied, indexed addressing.
	LDA	rwd,adrsx	76id pppp	4	12-13								[rwd] ← adrsx Load the unsegmented address into 16-bit register rwd.
	LDA	rld,adrsx	76id pppp qqqq	4/6	15-16								[rld] ← adrsx Load the segmented address, in segmented address format, into 32-bit register rld.
	LDA	rwd,ris(disp)	34id xxxx	4	15								[rwd] ← [ris] + disp
	LDA	rld,ris(disp)	34id xxxx	4	15								[rld] ← [ris] + disp Load the base relative address into 16-bit register rwd (nonsegmented mode) or 32-bit register rld (segmented mode).
	LDA	rwd,ris(rw)	74id 0r00	4	15								[rwd] ← [ris] + [rw]
	LDA	rld,ris(rw)	74id 0r00	4	15								[rld] ← [ris] + [rw] Load the implied, indexed memory address into 16-bit register rwd (nonsegmented mode) or 32-bit register rld (segmented mode).
	LDAR	rwd,disp16	340d xxxx	4	15								[rwd] ← [PC] + disp16 Load the program relative memory address into 16-bit register rwd.
	LDAR	rld,disp16	340d xxxx	4	15								[rld] ← [PC] + disp16 Load the program relative segmented memory address, in segmented format, into 32-bit register rld.
	LDR	rwd,disp16	310d xxxx	4	14								[rwd] ← [[PC] + disp16]
	LDRB	rbd,disp16	300d xxxx	4	14								[rbd] ← [[PC] + disp16]

* Privileged instruction — can be executed only in system mode.
** Number of clock cycles depends on the number of repetitions for n/m**; n = minimum number of clock cycles and m = number of clock cycles added for each additional repetition of operation. The number of clock cycles for an instruction which repeats k times is n + (k-1)•m.

Table 6-3. A Summary of the Z8000 Instruction Set (Continued)

Type	Mnemonic	Operand(s)	Op Code	Bytes	Clock Cycles	H	D	P	O	S	Z	C	Operation Performed
Primary Memory Reference (Continued)	LDRL	rld,disp16	350d xxxx	4	17								[rld] ← [[PC] + disp16] Load the memory word (for LDR), byte (for LDRB) or long word (for LDRL) addressed using program relative addressing into the 16-bit, 8-bit or 32-bit register.
	LDR	disp16,rws	330s xxxx	4	14								[[PC] + disp16] ← [rws]
	LDRB	disp16,rbs	320s xxxx	4	14								[[PC] + disp16] ← [rbs]
	LDRL	disp16,rls	370s xxxx	4	17								[[PC] + disp16] ← [rls] Load the register word (for LDR), byte (for LDRB) or long word (for LDRL) into the memory location addressed using program relative addressing.
Secondary Memory Reference	ADD	rwd,@ris	01id	2	7				X	X	X	X	[rwd] ← [rwd] + [[ris]]
	ADD	rwd,adrsx	41id pppp qqqq	4/6	9-13				X	X	X	X	[rwd] ← [rwd] + [adrsx] Add the contents of the addressed memory word to the 16-bit destination register.
	ADDB	rbd,@ris	00id	2	7		0		X	X	X	X	[rbd] ← [rbd] + [[ris]]
	ADDB	rbd,adrsx	40id pppp qqqq	4/6	9-13		0		X	X	X	X	[rbd] ← [rbd] + [adrsx] Add the contents of the addressed memory byte to the 8-bit destination register.
	ADDL	rld,@ris	16id	2	14				X	X	X	X	[rld] ← [rld] + [[ris]]
	ADDL	rld,adrsx	56id pppp qqqq	4/6	15-19				X	X	X	X	[rld] ← [rld] + [adrsx] Add the contents of the addressed memory long word to the 32-bit destination register.
	AND	rwd,@ris	07id	2	7			X		X	X		[rwd] ← [rwd] AND [[ris]]
	AND	rwd,adrsx	47id pppp qqqq	4/6	9-13			X		X	X		[rwd] ← [rwd] AND [adrsx] AND contents of destination 16-bit register with contents of memory word.
	ANDB	rbd,@ris	06id	2	7			X		X	X		[rbd] ← [rbd] AND [[ris]]
	ANDB	rbd,adrsx	46id pppp qqqq	4/6	9-13			X		X	X		[rbd] ← [rbd] AND [adrsx] AND contents of destination 8-bit register with contents of memory byte.
	CLR	@rid	0Dd8	2	8								[[rid]] ← 0
	CLR	adrsx	4Di8 pppp qqqq	4/6	11-15								[adrsx] ← 0 Clear the memory word.
	CLRB	@rid	0Cd8	2	8								[[rid]] ← 0

* Privileged instruction — can be executed only in system mode.

** Number of clock cycles depends on the number of repetitions for n/m**; n = minimum number of clock cycles and m = number of clock cycles added for each additional repetition of operation. The number of clock cycles for an instruction which repeats k times is n + (k-1)·m.

Table 6-3. A Summary of the Z8000 Instruction Set (Continued)

Type	Mnemonic	Operand(s)	Op Code	Bytes	Clock Cycles	H	D	O	P	S	Z	C	Operation Performed
Secondary Memory Reference (Continued)	CLRB	adrsx	4Ci8 pppp qqqq	4/6	11-15								[adrsx] ← 0 / Clear the memory byte.
	COM	@rid	0Dd0 pppp	2	12					X	X		[rid] ← [[rid]] / Ones complement the memory word.
	COM	adrsx	4Di0 pppp qqqq	4/6	15-19					X	X		[adrsx] ← [adrsx]
	COMB	@rid	0Cd0 pppp	2	12				X	X	X		[rid] ← [[rid]] / Ones complement the memory byte.
	COMB	adrsx	4Ci0 pppp qqqq	4/6	15-19				X	X	X		[adrsx] ← [adrsx]
	CP	rwd,@ris	0Bid	2	7			X		X	X	X	[rwd] − [[ris]]
	CP	rwd,adrsx	4Bid pppp qqqq	4/6	9-13			X		X	X	X	[rwd] − [adrsx]
	CPB	rbd,@ris	0Aid	2	7			X	X	X	X	X	[rbd] − [[ris]]
	CPB	rbd,adrsx	4Aid pppp qqqq	4/6	9-13			X	X	X	X	X	[rbd] − [adrsx]
	CPL	rld,@ris	10id	2	14			X		X	X	X	[rld] − [[ris]]
	CPL	rld,adrsx	50id pppp qqqq	4/6	15-19			X		X	X	X	[rld] − [adrsx] / Compare contents of register and memory location. Do not modify contents of register or memory location, but set status flags. Use 16-bit register/memory word for CP, 8-bit register/memory byte for CPB, 32-bit register/memory long word for CPL.
	CP	@rid,data16	0Dd1 yyyy pppp	4	11			X		X	X	X	[rid] − data16
	CP	adrsx,data16	4Di1 yyyy qqqq pppp	6/8	14-18			X		X	X	X	[adrsx] − data16
	CPB	@rid,data8	0Cd1 yy00 pppp	4	11			X		X	X	X	[rid] − data8
	CPB	adrsx,data8	4Ci1 yy00 pppp	6/8	14-18			X		X	X	X	[adrsx] − data8 / Compare contents of memory location with immediate data. Do not modify memory location, but set status flags. Use 16-bit memory word for CP, 8-bit memory byte for CPB.
	DEC	@rid,n16	2Bdn	2	11			X		X	X		[rid] ← [[rid]] − n16
	DEC	adrsx,n16	6Bin pppp qqqq	4/6	13-17			X		X	X		[adrsx] ← [adrsx] − n16
	DECB	@rid,n16	2Adn	2	11			X		X	X		[rid] ← [[rid]] − n16
	DECB	adrsx,n16	6Ain pppp qqqq	4/6	13-17			X		X	X		[adrsx] ← [adrsx] − n16 / Subtract the immediate value n16 from the memory word (for DEC) or memory byte (for DECB) addressed by adrsx or [rid]. Values in the range 1-16 are subtracted.

* Privileged instruction — can be executed only in system mode.
** Number of clock cycles depends on the number of repetitions for n/m**; n = minimum number of clock cycles and m = number of clock cycles added for each additional repetition of operation. The number of clock cycles for an instruction which repeats k times is n + (k-1)•m.

6-53

Table 6-3. A Summary of the Z8000 Instruction Set (Continued)

Type	Mnemonic	Operand(s)	Op Code	Bytes	Clock Cycles	H	D	O	P	S	Z	C	Operation Performed
Secondary Memory Reference (Continued)	DIV	rld,@ris	1Bid pppp	2	note 1			X		X	X	X	Divide
	DIV	rld,adrsx	5Bid pppp qqqq	4/6	note 1			X		X	X	X	Divide
	DIVL	rqd,@ris	1Aid pppp	2	note 1			X		X	X	X	Divide long
	DIVL	rqd,adrsx	5Aid pppp qqqq	4/6	note 1			X		X	X	X	Divide long
	EX	rwd,adrsx	6Did pppp qqqq	4/6	15-19								$[rwd] \longrightarrow [adrsx]$
	EX	rwd,@ris	2Dsd	2	12								$[rwd] \longrightarrow [[ris]]$
	EXB	rbd,adrsx	6Cid pppp qqqq	4/6	15-19								$[rbd] \longrightarrow [adrsx]$
	EXB	rbd,@ris	2Csd	2	12								$[rbd] \longrightarrow [[ris]]$
	INC	@rid,n16	29dn	2	11			X		X	X		$[[rid]] \longleftarrow [[rid]] + n16$
	INC	adrsx,n16	69in pppp qqqq	4/6	13-17			X		X	X		$[adrsx] \longleftarrow [adrsx] + n16$
	INCB	@rid,n16	28dn	2	11			X		X	X		$[[rid]] \longleftarrow [[rid]] + n16$
	INCB	adrsx,n16	68in pppp qqqq	4/6	13-17			X		X	X		$[adrsx] \longleftarrow [adrsx] + n16$
	MULT	rld,@ris	19id	2	note 2			0		X	X	X	Multiply
	MULT	rld,adrsx	59id pppp qqqq	4/6	note 2			0		X	X	X	Multiply
	MULTL	rqd,@ris	18id	2	note 2			0		X	X	X	Multiply long
	MULTL	rqd,adrsx	58id pppp qqqq	4/6	note 2			0		X	X	X	Multiply long
	NEG	@rid	0Dd2	2	12			X		X	X	X	$[[rid]] \longleftarrow - [[rid]].$
	NEG	adrsx	4Di2 pppp qqqq	4/6	15-19			X		X	X	X	$[adrsx] \longleftarrow - [adrsx]$
	NEGB	@rid	0Cd2	2	12			X		X	X	X	$[[rid]] \longleftarrow - [[rid]].$
	NEGB	adrsx	4Ci2 pppp qqqq	4/6	15-19			X		X	X	X	$[adrsx] \longleftarrow - [adrsx]$
	OR	rwd,@ris	05id	2	7				X	X	X		$[rwd] \longleftarrow [rwd] \text{ OR } [[ris]]$
	OR	rwd,adrsx	45id pppp qqqq	4/6	9-13				X	X	X		$[rwd] \longleftarrow [rwd] \text{ OR } [adrsx]$
	ORB	rbd,@ris	04id	2	7				X	X	X		$[rbd] \longleftarrow [rbd] \text{ OR } [[ris]]$

Status / Operation notes for grouped entries:

DIV, DIV, DIVL, DIVL — } see text for a discussion of these instructions

EX/EXB — Exchange contents of the addressed memory location with the selected register. Use 8-bit (for EXB) or 16-bit (for EX) registers and memory locations.

INC/INCB — Add the immediate value n16 to the memory word (for INC) or memory byte (for INCB) addressed by adrsx or [rid]. Values in the range 1 - 16 are added.

MULT, MULT, MULTL, MULTL — } see text for a discussion of these instructions

NEG/NEGB — Replace the contents of the memory word (for NEG) or byte (for NEGB) addressed by adrsx or [rid] with its twos complement.

OR — OR the contents of the specified 16-bit register and memory word. Place the result in the 16-bit register.

* Privileged instruction — can be executed only in system mode.
** Number of clock cycles depends on the number of repetitions for n/m**: n = minimum number of clock cycles and m = number of clock cycles added for each additional repetition of operation. The number of clock cycles for an instruction which repeats k times is n + (k-1)•m.

Table 6-3. A Summary of the Z8000 Instruction Set (Continued)

Type	Mnemonic	Operand(s)	Op Code		Bytes	Clock Cycles	Status							Operation Performed
							H	D	O	P	S	Z	C	
Secondary Memory Reference (Continued)	ORB	rbd,adrsx	44id pppp	qqqq	4/6	9-13					X	X		[rbd] ← [rbd] OR [adrsx] OR the contents of the specified 8-bit register and memory byte. Place the result in the 8-bit register.
	SUB	rwd,@ris	03id	pppp	2	7	X		X		X	X	X	[rwd] ← [rwd] − [[ris]]
	SUB	rwd,adrsx	43id pppp	qqqq	4/6	9-13	X		X		X	X	X	[rwd] ← [rwd] − [adrsx]
	SUBB	rbd,@ris	02id	pppp	2	7			X		X	X	X	[rbd] ← [rbd] − [[ris]]
	SUBB	rbd,adrsx	42id pppp	qqqq	4/6	9-13			X		X	X	X	[rbd] ← [rbd] − [adrsx]
	SUBL	rld,@ris	12id	pppp	2	14			X		X	X	X	[rld] ← [rld] − [[ris]]
	SUBL	rld,adrsx	52id pppp	qqqq	4/6	15-19			X		X	X	X	[rld] ← [rld] − [adrsx] Subtract the contents of the addressed memory location from the selected destination register. Use 8-bit (for SUBB), 16-bit (for SUB) or 32-bit (for SUBL) memory locations and registers.
	TEST	@rid	0Dd4	pppp	2	8					X	X	X	[[rid]] OR 0
	TEST	adrsx	4Di4 pppp	qqqq	4/6	11-15					X	X	X	[adrsx] OR 0
	TESTB	@rid	0Cd4	pppp	2	8				X	X	X	X	[[rid]] OR 0
	TESTB	adrsx	4Ci4 pppp	qqqq	4/6	11-15				X	X	X	X	[adrsx] OR 0
	TESTL	@rid	1Cd0	pppp	2	13					X	X	X	[[rid]] OR 0
	TESTL	adrsx	5Ci0 pppp	qqqq	4/6	16-20					X	X	X	[adrsx] OR 0 OR the specified memory contents with 0. Set status flags. Use a 16-bit location for TEST, an 8-bit location for TESTB, and a 32-bit location for TESTL.
	TSET	@rid	0Dd6	pppp	2	11					X			[s] ← [[rid]].[MSB]. [[rid]] ← FFFF
	TSET	adrsx	4Di6 pppp	qqqq	4/6	14-18					X			[s] ← [adrsx].[MSB]. [adrsx] ← FFFF
	TSETB	@rid	0Cd6	pppp	2	11					X			[s] ← [[rid]].[MSB]. [[rid]] ← FF
	TSETB	adrsx	4Ci6 pppp	qqqq	4/6	14-18					X			[s] ← [adrsx].[MSB]. [adrsx] ← FF Move the most significant bit of the memory word (for TSET) or byte (for TSETB) to the sign status. Then fill the word or byte with 1 bits.
	XOR	rwd,@ris	09id	pppp	2	7					X	X		[rwd] ← [rwd] XOR [[ris]]
	XOR	rwd,adrsx	49id pppp	qqqq	4/6	9-13					X	X		[rwd] ← [rwd] XOR [adrsx]
	XORB	rbd,@ris	08id	pppp	2	7				X	X	X		[rbd] ← [rbd] XOR [[ris]]
	XORB	rbd,adrsx	48id pppp	qqqq	4/6	9-13				X	X	X		[rbd] ← [rbd] XOR [adrsx] Exclusive OR the contents of the addressed memory location and register. Store the result in the register. Use 16-bit memory and registers for XOR. Use 8-bit memory and registers for XORB.

* Privileged instruction — can be executed only in system mode.

** Number of clock cycles depends on the number of repetitions for n/m**; n = minimum number of clock cycles and m = number of clock cycles added for each additional repetition of operation. The number of clock cycles for an instruction which repeats k times is n + (k-1)·m.

Table 6-3. A Summary of the Z8000 Instruction Set (Continued)

Type	Mnemonic	Operand(s)	Op Code	Bytes	Clock Cycles	H	D	O	P	S	Z	C	Operation Performed
Immediate	LD	rwd,data16	210d yyyy	4	7								[rwd] ← data16. Load 16-bit immediate data into 16-bit register rwd.
	LD	@rid,data16	0Dd5 yyyy	4	11								[[rid]] ← data16.
	LD	adrsx,data16	4Di5 yyyy pppp qqqq	6/8	14-18								[adrsx] ← data16. Load 16-bit immediate data into memory word addressed by adrsx or [rid].
	LDB	rbd,data8	Cdyy	2	5								[rbd] ← data8. Load immediate data byte into 8-bit register rbd.
	LDB	@rid,data8	0Cd5 yy00	4	11								[[rid]] ← data8.
	LDB	adrsx,data8	4Ci5 yy00 pppp qqqq	6/8	14-18								[adrsx] ← data8. Load immediate data byte into memory byte addressed by adrsx or [rid].
	LDL	rld,data32	140d yyyy zzzz	6	11								[rld] ← data32. Load 32-bit immediate data into 32-bit register rld.
	LDK	rwd,b16	BDdb	2	5								[rwd] ← b16. Load the immediate 4-bit value b16 into the low-order four bits of rwd. Clear the remaining twelve bits of rwd. (See Stack operations).
	PUSH												
Jump	JP	,@rid	1Ed8	2	10,15								[PC] ← [[rid]]
	JP	,adrsx	5Ei8 pppp qqqq	4/6	7-11								[PC] ← [adrsx]. Jump to the specified memory location. This is the same as a conditional jump with cc = always true.
	JR	,disp	E8xx	2	6								[PC] ← [PC] + (disp•2). Jump program relative. PC is incremented to the next sequential instruction before disp•2 is added as a signed binary number. This is the same as a conditional jump relative with cc = always true (blank).
	LDPS*	@ris	39s0	2	12 / 16	X	X	X	X	X	X	X	[FCW] ← [[ris]]. [PC] ← [[ris] + 1] (nonsegmented) [FCWRES] ← [[ris] + 1]. [PCSEG] ← [[ris] + 2] [PCOFF] ← [[ris] + 3] (segmented)
	LDPS*	adrsx	79i0 pppp qqqq	4/6	16-17 / 20-23	X	X	X	X	X	X	X	[FCW] ← [adrsx]. [PC] ← [adrsx+1] (nonsegmented) [FCWRES] ← [adrsx+1]. [PCSEG] ← [adrsx+2] [PCOFF] ← [adrsx+3] (segmented) Load program status and jump as described in accompanying text.

* Privileged instruction — can be executed only in system mode.
** Number of clock cycles depends on the number of repetitions for n/m**; n =minimum number of repetitions for n/m**; n =minimum number of clock cycles and m = number of clock cycles added for each additional repetition of operation. The number of clock cycles for an instruction which repeats k times is n + (k-1)•m.

6-56

Table 6-3. A Summary of the Z8000 Instruction Set (Continued)

Type	Mnemonic	Operand(s)	Op Code		Bytes	Clock Cycles	H	D	O	P	S	Z	C	Operation Performed
Subroutine Call and Return	CALL	@rid	1Fd0		2	10,15								(1) or (2), [PC] ← [rid]
	CALL	adrsx	5Fi0 pppp	qqqq	4/6	12-21								(1) or (2), [PC] ← [adrsx]
	CALR	disp	Dxxx		2	10,15								(1) or (2), [PC] ← [PC] - disp•2 Program relative memory address. Call the addressed subroutine, saving information on the Stack as follows: (1) [SP] ← [SP] - 2, [[SP]] ← [PC] 16-bit PC (nonsegmented) (2) [SP] ← [SP] - 4, [[SP]] ← [PC] 32-bit PC (segmented)
	RET	cc	9E0c		2	10,13/7								If cc is "true" then [PC] ← [[SP]]. [SP] ← [SP] + 2 (for nonsegmented) or [SP] ← [SP] + 4 (for segmented). If the condition code specified by cc is "true", return from subroutine.
	SC	data8	7Fyy		2	33,39								System subroutine call. See accompanying text for a description of this instruction.
Immediate Operate	ADD	rwd,data16	010d yyyy		4	7	X		X		X	X	X	[rwd] ← [rwd] + data16
	ADDB	rbd,data8	000d yy00		4	7		0	X		X	X	X	[rbd] ← [rbd] + data8
	ADDL	rld,data32	160d yyyy	zzzz	6	14			X		X	X	X	[rld] ← [rld] + data32 Add immediate data to the destination register. Use 32-bit data/register for ADDL, 16-bit data/register for ADD, 8-bit data/register for ADDB.
	AND	rwd,data16	070d yyyy		4	7					X	X		[rwd] ← [rwd] AND data16
	ANDB	rbd,data8	060d yy00		4	7				X	X	X		[rbd] ← [rbd] AND data8 AND immediate data with destination register contents. Use 16-bit data/register for AND, 8-bit data/register for ANDB.
	CP	rwd,data16	0B0d yyyy		4	7			X		X	X	X	[rwd] - data16 Compare 16-bit register contents with immediate 16-bit data. Do not modify register contents, but save Status flags.
	CPB	rbd,data8	0A0d yy00		4	7			X		X	X	X	[rbd] - data8 Compare 8-bit register contents with immediate 8-bit data. Do not modify register contents, but save Status flags.
	CPL	rld,data32	100d yyyy	zzzz	6	14			X		X	X	X	[rld] - data32 Compare 32-bit register contents with immediate 32-bit data. Do not modify register contents, but save Status flags. (See secondary memory reference for memory-immediate compare instructions.)
	DIV	rld,data16	1B0d yyyy		4	note 1			X		X	X	X	Divide
	DIVL	rqd,data32	1A0d yyyy	zzzz	6	note 1			X		X	X	X	Divide long } see accompanying text for a discussion of these instructions

* Privileged instruction — can be executed only in system mode.
** Number of clock cycles depends on the number of repetitions for n/m**; n = minimum number of clock cycles and m = number of clock cycles added for each additional repetition of operation. The number of clock cycles for an instruction which repeats k times is n + (k-1)•m.

Table 6-3. A Summary of the Z8000 Instruction Set (Continued)

Type	Mnemonic	Operand(s)	Op Code	Bytes	Clock Cycles	H	D	O	P	S	Z	C	Operation Performed
Immediate Operate (Continued)	MULT	rld,data16	190d yyyy zzzz	4	note 2			0		X	X	X	Multiply } see accompanying text for a discussion of these instructions
	MULTL	rqd,data32	180d yyyy zzzz	6	note 2			0		X	X	X	Multiply long }
	OR	rwd,data16	050d yyyy	4	7					X	X		[rwd] ← [rwd] OR data16. OR the contents of the specified 16-bit register with the immediate data word.
	ORB	rbd,data8	040d yy00	4	7				X	X	X		[rbd] ← [rbd] OR data8. OR the contents of the specified 8-bit register with the immediate data byte.
	SUB	rwd,data16	030d yyyy	4	7			X		X	X	X	[rwd] ← [rwd] − cata16
	SUBB	rbd,data8	020d yy00	4	7	X		X		X	X	X	[rbd] ← [rbd] − data8
	SUBL	rld,data32	120d yyyy zzzz	6	14		1	X		X	X	X	[rld] ← [rld] − data32. Subtract immediate data from the destination register. Use 32-bit data/register for SUBL, 16-bit data/register for SUB, 8-bit data/register for SUBB.
	XOR	rwd,data16	090d yyyy	4	7					X	X		[rwd] ← [rwd] XOR data16
	XORB	rbd,data8	080d yy00	4	7				X	X	X		[rbd] ← [rbd] XOR data8. Exclusive-OR the contents of the register with immediate data. Store the result in the register. Use 16-bit register and data for XOR. Use 8-bit register and data for XORB.
Branch/Jump on Condition	DJNZ	rw,disp	Fr 1tttttt	2	11								[rw] ← [rw] − 1. [PC] ← [PC] + 2. If [rw] is not 0, then [PC] ← [PC] − [disp•2]
	DBJNZ	rb,disp	Fr 0tttttt	2	11								[rb] ← [rb] − 1. [PC] ← [PC] + 2. If [rb] is not 0, then [PC] ← [PC] − [disp•2]. Decrement a 16-bit register (for DJNZ) or an 8-bit register (for DBJNZ). Increment the Program Counter as per normal operation. If the decremented register contents is not 0, then subtract twice the displacement, as an unsigned binary number, from the incremented Program Counter, causing a branch back to a lower program memory address. If the decremented register contents is 0, continue execution with the next instruction.

* Privileged instruction — can be executed only in system mode.

** Number of clock cycles depends on the number of repetitions for n/m**; n = minimum number of clock cycles and m = number of clock cycles added for each additional repetition of operation. The number of clock cycles for an instruction which repeats k times is n + (k−1)•m.

Table 6-3. A Summary of the Z8000 Instruction Set (Continued)

Type	Mnemonic	Operand(s)	Op Code	Bytes	Clock Cycles	Status							Operation Performed
						H	D	O	P	S	Z	C	
Branch/Jump on Condition (Continued)	JP	cc,@rid	1Edc	2	10,15/7								If cc is true, [PC] — [[rid]]
	JP	cc,adrsx	5Eic pppp qqqq	4/6	7-11								If cc is true, [PC] — [adrsx] / Jump to the memory location specified by adrsx or [rid] if condition code cc is true.
	JR	cc,disp	Ecxx	2	6								If cc is true, [PC] — [PC] + (disp·2) / Jump program relative if condition code is true. PC is incremented to address the next sequential instruction before disp·2 is added as a signed binary number.
Register-Register Move	EX	rwd,rws	ADsd	2	6								[rwd] ⟶ [rws]
	EXB	rbd,rbs	ACsd	2	6								[rbd] ⟶ [rbs] / Exchange registers' contents for 16-bit (EX) or 8-bit (EXB) registers.
	LD	rwd,rws	A1sd	2	3								[rwd] — [rws]
	LDB	rbd,rbs	A0sd	2	3								[rbd] — [rbs]
	LDL	rld,rls	94sd	2	5								[rld] — [rls] / Move data between any two 16-bit registers (for LD), 8-bit registers (for LDB) or 32-bit registers (for LDL).
Block Transfer and Search	CPD	rwd,@ris,rw,cc	BBs8 Ordc	4	20			X		U	X	U	[rwd] – [[ris]]. If cc true, Z = 1. If cc false, Z = 0 / [ris] — [ris] – 2. [rw] — [rw] – 1. If [rw] = 0, O = 1 otherwise O = 0.
	CPDB	rbd,@ris,rw,cc	BAs8 Ordc	4	20			X		U	X	U	[rbd] – [[ris]]. If cc true, Z = 1. If cc false, Z = 0. / [ris] — [ris] – 1. [rw] — [rw] – 1. If [rw] = 0, O = 1 otherwiseO = 0. / Search a string for a condition. Compare a word in rwd (for CPD) or a byte in rbd (for CPDB) with the next word (for CPD) or byte (for CPDB) in a memory string, using implied memory addressing. Register and memory contents are not modified, nor are Status flags changed, but status conditions are compared with cc. If cc is true, Z is set to 1; otherwise Z is reset to 0. Decrement the implied memory address in ris by 2 for CPD, or by 1 for CPDB. Decrement 16-bit counter rw by 1. If rw is 0, set O to 1; otherwise reset O to 0.
	CPDR	rwd,@ris,rw,cc	BBsC Ordc	4	20/9··			X		U	X	U	See CPD.
	CPDRB	rbd,@ris,rw,cc	BAsC Ordc	4	20/9··			X		U	X	U	See CPDB. / CPD and CPDB are identical to CPD and CPDB, respectively, except that instruction execution is repeated until either Z or O status is 1. Interrupts will be acknowledged between reexecutions.

* Privileged instruction — can be executed only in system mode.

** Number of clock cycles depends on the number of repetitions for n/m··; n =minimum number of clock cycles and m = number of clock cycles added for each additional repetition of operation. The number of clock cycles for an instruction which repeats k times is n + (k-1)·m.

Table 6-3. A Summary of the Z8000 Instruction Set (Continued)

Type	Mnemonic	Operand(s)	Op Code	Bytes	Clock Cycles	H	D	O	P	S	Z	C	Operation Performed
								Status					
	CPI	rwd, @ris,rw,cc	BBsO Ordc	4	20			X		U	X	U	[rwd] — [[ris]]. If cc true, Z = 1. If cc false, Z = 0. [ris] ← [ris] + 2. If [rw] — [rw] = 0, O = 1; otherwise O = 0.
	CPIB	rbd, @ris,rw,cc	BAsO Ordc	4	20			X		U	X	U	[rbd] — [[ris]]. If cc true, Z = 1. If cc false, Z = 0. [ris] ← [ris] + 1. If [rw] — [rw] = 0, O = 1; otherwise O = 0. CPI and CPIB are identical to CPD and CPDB, respectively, except that the implied memory address in ris is incremented by 2 for CPI, or by 1 for CPIB.
	CPIR	rwd, @ris,rw,cc	BBs4 Ordc	4	20/9**			X		U	X	U	See CPI.
	CPIRB	rbd, @ris,rw,cc	BAs4 Ordc	4	20/9**			X		U	X	U	See CPIB. CPIR and CPIRB are identical to CPD and CPDB, respectively, except that the implied memory address in ris is incremented by 2 for CPI, or by 1 for CPIB, and instruction execution is repeated until either Z or O status is 1. Interrupts will be acknowleged between reexecutions.
	CPSD	@rid, @ris,rw,cc	BBsA Ordc	4	25			X		U	X	U	[[rid]] — [[ris]]. If cc true, Z = 1. If cc false, Z = 0. [rid] ← [rid] — 2. [ris] ← [rw] — 1. If [rw] = 0, O = 1; otherwise O = 0.
	CPSDB	@rid, @ris,rw,cc	BAsA Ordc	4	25			X		U	X	U	[[rid]] — [[ris]]. If cc true, Z = 1. If cc false, Z = 0. [rid] ← [rid] — 1. [ris] ← [rw] — 1. If [rw] = 0, O = 1; otherwise O = 0. Compare two strings for a condition. Compare the next word (for CPSD) or byte (for CPSDB) in a source string with the next word (for CPSD) or byte (for CPSDB) in a destination string. Both strings are addressed using implied memory addressing. No memory contents are modified, nor are any Status flags changed, but status conditions are compared with cc. If cc is true, Z is set to 1. Otherwise Z is reset to 0. Decrement the implied memory addresses in ris and rid by 2 for CPSD, or by 1 for CPSDB. Decrement 16-bit counter rw by 1. If rw is 0, set O to 1. Otherwise reset O to 0.
	CPSDR	@rid, @ris,rw,cc	BBsE Ordc	4	25/14**			X		U	X	U	See CPSD.
	CPSDRB	@rid, @ris,rw,cc	BAsE Ordc	4	25/14**			X		U	X	U	See CPSDB. CPSDR and CPSDRB are identical to CPSD and CPSDB, respectively, except that the instructions are reexecuted until either Z or O status is 1. Interrupts are acknowleged between reexecutions.

Block Transfer and Search (Continued)

* Privileged instruction — can be executed only in system mode.
** Number of clock cycles depends on the number of repetitions for n/m**; n =minimum number of clock cycles and m = number of clock cycles added for each additional repetition of operation. The number of clock cycles for an instruction which repeats k times is n + (k-1)•m.

Table 6-3. A Summary of the Z8000 Instruction Set (Continued)

Type	Mnemonic	Operand(s)	Op Code		Bytes	Clock Cycles	H	D	O	P	S	Z	C	Operation Performed
Block Transfer and Search (Continued)	CPSI	@rid,@ris,rw,cc	BBs2	Ordc	4	25			X			X	U	[[rid]] — [[ris]]. If cc is true Z = 1. If cc is false, Z = 0. [rid] — [rid] + 2. [ris] — [ris] + 2. [rw] — [rw] — 1. If [rw] = 0, O = 1; otherwise O = 0.
	CPSIB	@rid,@ris,rw,cc	BAs2	Ordc	4	25			X			X	U	[[rid]] — [[ris]]. If cc is true, Z = 1. If cc is false, Z = 0. [rid] — [rid] + 1. [ris] — [ris] + 1. [rw] — [rw] — 1. If [rw] = 0, O = 1; otherwise O = 0. CPSI and CPSIB are identical to CPSD and CPSDB, respectively, except that the implied memory addresses in rid and ris are incremented by 2 (for CPSI) or by 1 (for CPSIB).
	CPSIR	@rid,@ris,rw,cc	BBs6	Ordc	4	25/14**			X		U	X	U	See CPSI.
	CPSIRB	@rid,@ris,rw,cc	BAs6	Ordc	4	25/14**			X		U	X	U	See CPSIB. CPSIR and CPSIRB are identical to CPSD and CPSDB, respectively, except that the implied memory addresses in rid and ris are incremented by 2 (for CPSIR) or by 1 (for CPSIRB) and the instructions are reexecuted until either Z or O status is 1. Interrupts are acknowledged between reexecutions.
	LDD	@rid,@ris,rw	BBs9	Ord8	4	20			X					[[rid]] — [[ris]]. [rid] — [rid] — 2. [ris] — [ris] — 2. [rw] — [rw] — 1. If [rw] = 0, O = 1; otherwise O = 0.
	LDDB	@rid,@ris,rw	BAs9	Ord8	4	20			X					[[rid]] — [[ris]]. [rid] — [rid] — 1. [ris] — [ris] — 1. [rw] — [rw] — 1. If [rw] = 0, O = 1; otherwise O = 0. Transfer a word (for LDD) or a byte (for LDDB) from the memory location addressed by register ris to the memory location addressed by rid. Decrement addresses in rid and ris by 2 (for LDD) or 1 (for LDDB). Decrement the counter rw by 1. If rw contains 0, set the Overflow status to 1.
	LDDR	@rid,@ris,rw	BBs9	Ord0	4	20/9**			1					[[rid]] — [[ris]]. [rid] — [rid] — 2. [ris] — [ris] — 2. [rw] — [rw] — 1. If [rw] ≠ 0, reexecute. If [rw] = 0, O = 1 and end execution.
	LDDRB	@rid,@ris,rw	BAs9	Ord0	4	20/9**			1					[[rid]] — [[ris]]. [rid] — [rid] — 1. [ris] — [ris] — 1. [rw] — [rw] — 1. If [rw] ≠ 0, reexecute. If [rw] = 0, O = 1 and end execution. LDDR and LDDRB are identical to LDD and LDDB, respectively, except that LDDR and LDDRB reexecute until rw has decremented to 0.
	LDI	@rid,@ris,rw	BBs1	Ord8	4	20			X					[[rid]] — [[ris]]. [rid] — [rid] + 2. [ris] — [ris] + 2. [rw] — [rw] — 1. If [rw] = 0 then O = 1; otherwise O = 0.

* Privileged instruction — can be executed only in system mode.
** Number of clock cycles depends on the number of repetitions for n/m**; n = minimum number of clock cycles and m = number of clock cycles added for each additional repetition of operation. The number of clock cycles for an instruction which repeats k times is n + (k-1)·m.

Table 6-3. A Summary of the Z8000 Instruction Set (Continued)

Type	Mnemonic	Operand(s)	Op Code	Bytes	Clock Cycles	Status H	D	O	P	S	Z	C	Operation Performed
Block Transfer and Search (Continued)	LDIB	@rid,@ris,rw	BAs1 0rd8	4	20			X					[[rid]] ← [[ris]]. [rid] ← [rid] + 1. [ris] ← [ris] + 1. [rw] ← [rw] − 1. If [rw] = 0, then O = 0; otherwise O = 0. LDI and LDIB are identical to LDD and LDDB, respectively, except that the source and destination addresses ris and rid are incremented by 2 (for LDI) or 1 (for LDIB).
	LDIR	@rid,@ris,rw	BBs1 0rd0	4	20/9**			1					[[rid]] ← [[ris]]. [rid] ← [rid] + 2. [ris] ← [ris] + 2. [rw] ← [rw] − 1. If [rw] ≠ 0 then reexecute. If [rw] = 0 then O = 1 and end execution.
	LDIRB	@rid,@ris,rw	BAs1 0rd0	4	20/9**			1					[[rid]] ← [[ris]]. [rid] ← [rid] + 1. [ris] ← [ris] + 1. [rw] ← [rw] − 1. If [rw] ≠ 0 then reexecute. If [rw] = 0 then O = 1 and end execution. LDIR and LDIRB are identical to LDD and LDDB, respectively, except that the source and destination addresses ris and rid are incremented; also, LDIR and LDIRB are reexecuted until rw decrements to 0.
	LDM	rwd,@ris,n16	1Cs1 0d0n	4	14/3**								[rwd] ← [[ris]] do n16 times incrementing register and memory addresses
	LDM	rwd,adrsx,n16	5Ci1 0d0n pppp qqqq	6/8	17-21/3**								[rwd] ← [adrsx] do n16 times incrementing register and memory addresses. Move a block of n16 memory words from memory to 16-bit registers. adrsx or @ris addresses the first, lowest addressed memory word. rwd addresses the first 16-bit register. n16 can have any value from 1 to 16. (See accompanying text for more details.)
	LDM	@ris,rws,n16	1Cd9 0s0n	4	14/3**								[[ris]] ← [rws] do n16 times incrementing register and memory addresses
	LDM	adrsx,rws,n16	5Ci9 0s0n pppp qqqq	6/8	17-21/3**								[adrsx] ← [rws] do n16 times incrementing register and memory addresses. This instruction is identical to the one above, except that data moves from registers to memory. Register contents are not affected.
	TRDB	@rid,@ris,rw	B8d8 0rs0	4	25			X			U		[[rid]] ← [[ris] + [[rid]]]. [rid] ← [rid] − 1. [rw] ← [rw] − 1. Translate a memory byte, as described in the accompanying text. Decrement the destination address in rid and the byte counter in rw. If rw = 0, set O to 1. If rw ≠ 0, reset O to 0. Byte register RH1 contents is lost.

*   Privileged instruction — can be executed only in system mode.

** Number of clock cycles depends on the number of repetitions for n/m**; n = minimum number of clock cycles and m = number of clock cycles added for each additional repetition of operation. The number of clock cycles for an instruction which repeats k times is n + (k−1)•m.

Table 6-3. A Summary of the Z8000 Instruction Set (Continued)

Type	Mnemonic	Operand(s)	Op Code	Bytes	Clock Cycles	H	D	O	P	S	Z	C	Operation Performed
Block Transfer and Search (Continued)	TRDRB	@rid,@ris,rw	B8dC OrsO	4	25/14**			1			U	U	[[rid]] ← [[ris] + [[rid]]]. [rw] ← [rw] − 1. [rid] ← [rid] − 1. If [rw] = 0, O = 1 and end execution. If [rw] ≠ 0, reexecute. This instruction is identical to TRDB, except the instruction is reexecuted until [rw] = 0.
	TRIB	@rid,@ris,rw	B8dO OrsO	4	25			X			U	U	[[rid]] ← [[ris] + [[rid]]]. [rw] ← [rw] − 1. [rid] ← [rid] + 1. TRIB is identical to TRDB except that the destination address in rid is incremented.
	TRIRB	@rid,@ris,rw	B8d4 OrsO	4	25/14**			1			U	U	[[rid]] ← [[ris] + [[rid]]]. [rw] ← [rw] − 1. [rid] ← [rid] + 1. If [rw] = 0, O = 1 and end execution. If [rw] ≠ 0, reexecute. TRIRB is identical to TRDB except that the destination address in rid is incremented; also, TRIRB is reexecuted until [rw] = 0.
	TRTDB	@rid,@ris,rw	B8dA OrsO	4	25			X			X	X	[RH1] ← [[ris] + [[rid]]]. [rw] ← [rw] − 1. [rid] ← [rid] − 1. Load a table byte into 8-bit register RH1, as described in the accompanying text. Reset Z status to 0 if [RH1] ≠ 0. Set Z status to 1 if [RH1] = 0. Decrement destination address rid and byte counter rw. If rw = 0, O = 1. If rw ≠ 0, O = 0.
	TRTDRB	@rid,@ris,rw	B8dE OrsE	4	25/14**			X			X	X	[RH1] ← [[ris] + [[rid]]]. [rw] ← [rw] − 1. [rid] ← [rid] − 1. If [rw] = 0, O = 1. If [rw] ≠ 0, O = 0. If [RH1] = 0, Z = 1; otherwise Z = 0. TRTDRB is identical to TRTDB except that TRTDRB is reexecuted until O = 1 or Z = 0.
	TRTIB	@rid,@ris,rw	B8d2 OrsO	4	25			X			X	X	[RH1] ← [[ris] + [[rid]]]. [rw] ← [rw] − 1. [rid] ← [rid] + 1. TRTIB is identical to TRTDB except that TRTIB increments the destination address in rid.
	TRTIRB	@rid,@ris,rw	B8d6 OrsE	4	25/14**			X			X	X	[RH1] ← [[ris] + [[rid]]]. [rw] ← [rw] − 1. [rid] ← [rid] + 1. If [rw] = 0, O = 1. If [rw] ≠ 0, O = 0. If [RH1] = 0, Z = 1; otherwise Z = 0. TRTIRB is identical to TRTDB except that TRTIRB increments the destination address in rid and reexecutes until O = 1 or Z = 0.

* Privileged instruction — can be executed only in system mode.

** Number of clock cycles depends on the number of repetitions for n/m**; n = minimum number of clock cycles and m = number of clock cycles added for each additional repetition of operation. The number of clock cycles for an instruction which repeats k times is n + (k−1)•m.

6-63

Table 6-3. A Summary of the Z8000 Instruction Set (Continued)

Type	Mnemonic	Operand(s)	Op Code	Bytes	Clock Cycles	Status							Operation Performed
						H	D	O	P	S	Z	C	
Register-Register Operate	ADC	rwd,rws	B5sd	2	5			X		X	X	X	[rwd] ← [rwd] + [rws] + C
	ADCB	rbd,rbs	B4sd	2	5	X	0	X		X	X	X	[rbd] ← [rbd] + [rbs] + C Add the source register contents plus the initial Carry to the destination register. Use 16-bit registers for ADC. Use 8-bit registers for ADCB.
	ADD	rwd,rws	81sd	2	4			X		X	X	X	[rwd] ← [rwd] + [rws]
	ADDB	rbd,rbs	80sd	2	4	X	0	X		X	X	X	[rbd] ← [rbd] + [rbs]
	ADDL	rld,rls	96sd	2	8			X		X	X	X	[rld] ← [rld] + [rls] Add the Source register contents to the Destination register. Use 32-bit registers for ADDL, 16-bit registers for ADD and 8-bit registers for ADDB.
	AND	rwd,rws	87sd	2	4					X	X		[rwd] ← [rwd] AND [rws]
	ANDB	rbd,rbs	86sd	2	4				X	X	X		[rbd] ← [rbd] AND [rbs] AND the Source register contents with the Destination register contents. Use 16-bit registers for AND and 8-bit registers for ANDB.
	CP	rwd,rws	8Bsd	2	4			X		X	X	X	[rwd] − [rws] Compare 16-bit register contents by subtracting the Source register from the Destination register values. Do not modify any register contents, but set Status flags.
	CPB	rbd,rbs	8Asd	2	4			X		X	X	X	[rbd] − [rbs] Compare 8-bit register contents by subtracting the Source register from the Destination register values. Do not modify any register contents, but set Status flags.
	CPL	rld,rls	90sd	2	8			X		X	X	X	[rld] − [rls] Compare 32-bit register contents by subtracting the Source register from the Destination register values. Do not modify any register contents, but set Status flags.
	DIV	rld,rws	9Bsd	2	note 1			X		X	X	X	Divide } see text for a discussion of these instructions
	DIVL	rqd,rls	9Asd	2	note 1			X		X	X	X	Divide long }
	MULT	rld,rws	99sd	2	note 2			0		X	X	X	Multiply } see text for a discussion of these instructions
	MULTL	rqd,rls	98sd	2	note 2			0		X	X	X	Multiply long }

* Privileged instruction — can be executed only in system mode.

** Number of clock cycles depends on the number of repetitions for n/m**; n =minimum number of clock cycles and m = number of clock cycles added for each additional repetition of operation. The number of clock cycles for an instruction which repeats k times is n + (k-1)•m.

Table 6-3. A Summary of the Z8000 Instruction Set (Continued)

Type	Mnemonic	Operand(s)	Op Code	Bytes	Clock Cycles	H	D	O	P	S	Z	C	Operation Performed
Register-Register Operate (Continued)	OR	rwd,rws	85sd	2	4				X	X	X		[rwd] ← [rwd] OR [rws] [rbd] ← [rbd] OR [rbs] OR the contents of the Source register with the Destination register contents. Use 16-bit registers for OR and 8-bit register for ORB.
	ORB	rbd,rbs	84sd	2	4				X	X	X		
	RLDB	rbd,rbs	BEsd	2	9			U		X	X		Left rotate BCD digits in two 8-bit registers specified by rbd and rbs. The same register cannot be specified for rbd and rbs. Digits are rotated as follows:
	RRDB	rbd,rbs	BCsd	2	9			U		X	X		Right rotate BCD digits in two 8-bit registers specified by rbd and rbs. The same register cannot be specified for rbd and rbs. Digits are rotated as follows:
	SBC	rwd,rws	B7sd	2	5	X		X		X	X	X	[rwd] ← [rwd] – [rws] – C [rbd] ← [rbd] – [rbs] – C Subtract the Source register contents, plus the initial Carry, from the Destination register contents using twos complement arithmetic. Use 16-bit registers for SBC. Use 8-bit registers for SBCB.
	SBCB	rbd,rbs	B6sd	2	5		1	X		X	X	X	

* Privileged instruction — can be executed only in system mode.
** Number of clock cycles depends on the number of repetitions for n/m**; n = minimum number of clock cycles and m = number of clock cycles added for each additional repetition of operation. The number of clock cycles for an instruction which repeats k times is n + (k-1)•m.

6-65

Table 6-3. A Summary of the Z8000 Instruction Set (Continued)

Type	Mnemonic	Operand(s)	Op Code	Bytes	Clock Cycles	H	D	O	P	S	Z	C	Operation Performed
Register-Register Operate (Continued)	SUB	rwd,rws	83sd	2	4	X	1	X		X	X	X	Subtract the Source register contents from the Destination register. Use 32-bit registers for SUBL, 16-bit registers for SUB, 8-bit registers for SUBB.
	SUBB	rbd,rbs	82sd	2	4			X		X	X	X	
	SUBL	rld,rls	92sd	2	8			X		X	X	X	
	XOR	rwd,rws	89sd	2	4				X	X	X		Exclusive-OR the contents of Source and Destination registers. Store the result in the Destination register. Use 16-bit registers for XOR. Use 8-bit registers for XORB.
	XORB	rbd,rbs	88sd	2	4				X	X	X		[rwd] ← [rwd] XOR [rws] / [rbd] ← [rbd] XOR [rbs]
Register Operate	CLR	rwd	8Dd8	2	7								[rwd] ← 0 Clear the Selected Word register.
	CLRB	rbd	8Cd8	2	7								[rbd] ← 0 Clear the Selected Byte register.
	COM	rwd	8Dd0	2	7								[rwd] ← [rwd] Complement the Selected Word register.
	COMB	rbd	8Cd0	2	7								[rbd] ← [rbd] Complement the Selected Byte register.
	DAB	rbd	B0d0	2	5					X	X	X	Decimal adjust contents of 8-bit register rbd.
	DEC	rwd,n16	ABdn	2	4			X		X	X		[rwd] ← [rwd] − n16 Subtract the immediate value n16 from a 16-bit register (for DEC) or an 8-bit register (for DECB).
	DECB	rbd,n16	AAdn	2	4			X		X	X		[rbd] ← [rbd] − n16
	EXTS	rld	B1dA	2	11								Bits 16 to 31 of [rld] — bit 15 of [rld]. The sign bit of the low-order word of the register pair is copied into all bits of the high-order word of the register pair.
	EXTSB	rwd	B1d0	2	11								Bits 8 to 15 of [rwd] — bit 7 of [rwd] The sign bit of the low-order byte of the register is copied into all bits of the high-order byte of the register.
	EXTSL	rqd	B1d7	2	11								Bits 32 to 63 of [rqd] — bit 31 of [rqd] The sign bit of the low-order register pair of the Quadruple register is copied into all bits of the high-order register pair.

*   Privileged instruction — can be executed only in system mode.
** Number of clock cycles depends on the number of repetitions for n/m**; n =minimum number of clock cycles and m = number of clock cycles added for each additional repetition of operation. The number of clock cycles for an instruction which repeats k times is n + (k-1)•m.

Table 6-3. A Summary of the Z8000 Instruction Set (Continued)

Type	Mnemonic	Operand(s)	Op Code	Bytes	Clock Cycles	H	D	O	P	S	Z	C	Operation Performed
Register Operate (Continued)	INC	rwd,n16	A9dn	2	4			X	X	X	X		$[rwd] \leftarrow [rwd] + n16$
	INCB	rbd,n16	A8dn	2	4			X	X	X	X		$[rbd] \leftarrow [rbd] + n16$ Add the immediate value n16 to a 16-bit register (for INC) or an 8-bit register (for INCB).
	NEG	rwd	8Dd2	2	7			X		X	X	X	$[rwd] \leftarrow - [rwd]$
	NEGB	rbd	8Cd2	2	7			X		X	X	X	$[rbd] \leftarrow - [rbd]$ Replace the contents of the 16-bit register (for NEG) or 8-bit register (for NEGB) with its twos complement.
	RL	rwd,1	B3d8	2	6			X		X	X	X	Left rotate contents of word (for RL) or byte (for RLB) register, n bits (n = 1 or 2), as follows:
	RL	rwd,2	B3dA	2	7			X		X	X	X	
	RLB	rbd,1	B2d8	2	6			X		X	X	X	
	RLB	rbd,2	B2dA	2	7			X		X	X	X	
	RLC	rwd,1	B3d0	2	6					X	X	X	See accompanying text for a discussion of the Overflow status for all Register Operate shift and rotate instructions.
	RLC	rwd,2	B3d2	2	7					X	X	X	Left rotate through Carry contents of word (for RLC) or byte (for RLCB) register, n bits (n = 1 or 2), as follows:
	RLCB	rbd,1	B2d0	2	6					X	X	X	
	RLCB	rbd,2	B2d2	2	7					X	X	X	

* Privileged instruction — can be executed only in system mode.

** Number of clock cycles depends on the number of repetitions for n/m** n = minimum number of clock cycles and m = number of clock cycles added for each additional repetition of operation. The number of clock cycles for an instruction which repeats k times is n + (k-1)·m.

6-67

Table 6-3. A Summary of the Z8000 Instruction Set (Continued)

Type	Mnemonic	Operand(s)	Op Code	Bytes	Clock Cycles	H	D	O	P	S	Z	C	Operation Performed
Register Operate (Continued)	RR	rwd,1	B3dC	2	6			X		X	X	X	Right rotate contents of word (for RR) or byte (for RRB) register, n bits (n = 1 or 2), as follows:
	RR	rwd,2	B3dE	2	7			X		X	X	X	
	RRB	rbd,1	B2dC	2	6			X		X	X	X	
	RRB	rbd,2	B2dE	2	7			X		X	X	X	
	RRC	rwd,1	B3d4	2	6			X		X	X	X	Right rotate through Carry contents of word (for RRC) or byte (for RRCB) register, n bits (n = 1 or 2), as follows:
	RRC	rwd,2	B3d6	2	7			X		X	X	X	
	RRCB	rbd,1	B2d4	2	6			X		X	X	X	
	RRCB	rbd,2	B2d6	2	7			X		X	X	X	
	SDA	rwd,rw	B3dB 0r00	4	18/3**			X		X	X	X	Shift arithmetic the contents of a byte (for SDAB) word (for SDA) or long word (for SDAL) register. [rw] specifies the number of shift bit positions, and the direction (+ for left shift, − for right shift). 0 shift is allowed; it causes no shift, but sets status. [rw] value range is −8 to +8 for SDAB, −16 to +16 for SDA −32 to +32 for SDAL. Bits 0 to 4 of [rw] are active, with bit 15 used for sign. Shifts occur as follows:
	SDAB	rbd,rw	B2dB 0r00	4	18/3**			X		X	X	X	
	SDAL	rld,rw	B3dF 0r00	4	18/3**			X		X	X	X	

Right

7	6		2	1	0	← SDAB →
15	14		2	1	0	← SDA →
31	30		2	1	0	← SDAL →

Bit Numbers

Left

7	6		2	1	0
15	14		2	1	0
31	30		2	1	0

Bit Numbers

* Privileged instruction — can be executed only in system mode.

** Number of clock cycles depends on the number of repetitions for n/m**; n =minimum number of clock cycles and m = number of clock cycles added for each additional repetition of operation. The number of clock cycles for an instruction which repeats k times is n + (k-1)•m.

Table 6-3. A Summary of the Z8000 Instruction Set (Continued)

Type	Mnemonic	Operand(s)	Op Code		Bytes	Clock Cycles	H	D	O	P	S	Z	C	Operation Performed
Register Operate (Continued)	SDL	rwd,rw	B3d3	0r00	4	18/3**			U		X	X	X	SDL, SDLB and SDLL are equivalent to SDA, SDAB and SDAL, respectively, but they perform logical right shifts. Left shifts are identical. Shifts may be illustrated as follows:
	SDLB	rbd,rw	B2d3	0r00	4	18/3**			U		X	X	X	
	SDLL	rld,rw	B3d7	0r00	4	18/3**			U		X	X	X	
	SLA	rwd,data16	B3d9	yyyy	4	16/3**			X		X	X	X	SLA, SLAB and SLAL are identical to SDA, SDAB and SDAL, respectively, when these instructions are performing left shifts, except that SLA, SLAB and SLAL specify the shift bit count immediately.
	SLAB	rbd,data16	B2d9	yyyy	4	16/3**			X		X	X	X	
	SLAL	rld,data16	B3dD	yyyy	4	16/3**			X		X	X	X	
	SLL	rwd,data16	B3d1	yyyy	4	16/3**			U		X	X	X	SLL, SLLB and SLLL are identical to SDL, SDLB and SDLL, respectively, when these instructions are performing left shifts, except that SLL, SLLB and SLLL specify the shift bit count immediately.
	SLLB	rbd,data16	B2d1	yyyy	4	16/3**			U		X	X	X	
	SLLL	rld,data16	B3d5	yyyy	4	16/3**			U		X	X	X	
	SRA	rwd,data16	B3d9	yyyy	4	16/3**			0		X	X	X	SRA, SRAB and SRAL are identical to SDA, SDAB and SDAL, respectively, when these instructions are performing right shifts, except that SRA, SRAB, and SRAL specify the shift bit count immediately.
	SRAB	rbd,data16	B2d9	yyyy	4	16/3**			0		X	X	X	
	SRAL	rld,data16	B3dD	yyyy	4	16/3**			0		X	X	X	
	SRL	rwd,data16	B3d1	yyyy	4	16/3**			U		X	X	X	SRL, SRLB, and SRLL are identical to SDL, SDLB, and SDLL, respectively, when these instructions are performing right shifts, except that SRL, SRLB and SRLL specify the shift bit count immediately.
	SRLB	rbd,data16	B2d1	yyyy	4	16/3**			U		X	X	X	
	SRLL	rld,data16	B3d5	yyyy	4	16/3**			U		X	X	X	
	TSET	rwd	8Dd6		2	7					X			[s] ← [rwd](MSB).[rwd] ← FFFF
	TSETB	rbd	8Cd6		2	7					X			[s] ← [rbd](MSB). [rbd] ← FF Move the most significant bit of the 16-bit register (for TSET) or 8-bit register (TSETB) to the Sign status. Then fill the register with 1 bits.
	TEST	rwd	8Dd4		2	7					X	X	X	[rwd] OR 0
	TESTB	rbd	8Cd4		2	7				X	X	X	X	[rbd] OR 0
	TESTL	rld	9Cd0		2	13					X	X	X	[rld] OR 0 OR the specified register contents with 0. Set Status flags based on the result. Test a 32-bit register for TESTL, a 16-bit register for TEST and an 8-bit register for TESTB.

Shift illustration:

```
          Right                              Left
   ┌──────────────────┐   ┌─C─┐ ┌─C─┐   ┌──────────────────┐  0
0 →│                  │→      ← SDLB →   │                  │→
   7 6      2 1 0          7 6      2 1 0
   15 14    2 1 0    ← SDL → 15 14  2 1 0
   31 30    2 1 0   ← SDLL → 31 30  2 1 0
```

* Privileged instruction — can be executed only in system mode.
** Number of clock cycles depends on the number of repetitions for n/m**: n = minimum number of clock cycles and m = number of clock cycles added for each additional repetition of operation. The number of clock cycles for an instruction which repeats k times is n + (k-1)•m.

Table 6-3. A Summary of the Z8000 Instruction Set (Continued)

Type	Mnemonic	Operand(s)	Op Code	Bytes	Clock Cycles	H	D	O	P	S	Z	C	Operation Performed
Stack	LDCTL*	NSPSEG,rws	7DsE	2	7								[NSPSEG] ← [rws]
	LDCTL*	rwd,NSPSEG	7Dd6	2	7								[rwd] ← [NSPSEG] Transfer data between a 16-bit register and tahe Z8001 normal Stack Pointer Segment Address register (R14N).
	LDCTL*	NSPOFF,rws	7DsF	2	7								[NSPOFF] ← [rws]
	LDCTL*	rwd,NSPOFF	7Dd7	2	7								[rwd] ← [NSPOFF] Transfer data between a 16-bit register and the normal Stack Pointer Address register (R15N).
	POP	rwd,@ris	97sd	2	8								[rwd] ← [[ris]], [ris] ← [ris] + 2
	POP	@rid,@ris	17sd	2	12								[[rid]] ← [[ris]], [ris] ← [ris] + 2
	POP	adrsx,@ris	57si pppp qqqq	4/6	15-19								[adrsx] ← [[ris]], [ris] ← [ris] + 2 Pop the memory word addressed by ris, the designated Stack Pointer. Any register with the exception of R0 (for nonsegmented) or RR0 (for segmented) can be designated as the Stack Pointer. The popped word is loaded into a 16-bit register, or the memory location addressed by adrsx or [rid].
	POPL	rld,@ris	95id	2	12								[rld] ← [[ris]], [ris] ← [ris] + 4
	POPL	@rid,@ris	15id	2	19								[[rid]] ← [[ris]], [ris] ← [ris] + 4
	POPL	adrsx,@ris	55si pppp qqqq	4/6	22-26								[adrsx] ← [[ris]], [ris] ← [ris] + 4 POPL is identical to POP, except that a 32-bit long word is popped.
	PUSH	@rid,rws	93is	2	9								[rid] ← [rid] − 2. [[rid]] ← [rws]
	PUSH	@rid,@ris	13is	2	13								[rid] ← [rid] − 2. [[rid]] ← [[ris]]
	PUSH	@rid,adrsx	53di pppp qqqq	4/6	13-17								[rid] ← [rid] − 2. [[rid]] ← [adrsx]
	PUSH	@rid,data16	0Dd9 yyyy	4	12								[rid] ← [rid] − 2. [[rid]] ← data16 Push a 16-bit word onto a memory stack addressed by rid, the designated Stack Pointer. Any register with the exception of R0 (for nonsegmented) or RR0 (for segmented) can be designated as the Stack Pointer. The pushed word can come from a register, the memory word addressed by adrsx or [ris], or it may be immediate data.
	PUSHL	@rid,rls	91is	2	12								[rid] ← [rid] − 4. [[rid]] ← [rls]
	PUSHL	@rid,@ris	11is	2	20								[rid] ← [rid] − 4. [[rid]] ← [[ris]]
	PUSHL	@rid,adrsx	51di pppp qqqq	4/6	20-24								[rid] ← [rid] − 4. [[rid]] ← [adrsx] PUSHL is identical to PUSH except that a 32-bit long word is pushed, also there is no immediate version of PUSHL.

* Privileged instruction — can be executed only in system mode.

** Number of clock cycles depends on the number of repetitions for n/m**; n = minimum number of clock cycles and m = number of clock cycles added for each additional repetition of operation. The number of clock cycles for an instruction which repeats k times is n + (k-1)•m.

Table 6-3. A Summary of the Z8000 Instruction Set (Continued)

Type	Mnemonic	Operand(s)	Op Code			Bytes	Clock Cycles	H	D	O	P	S	Z	C	Operation Performed
												Status			
Bit Operations	BIT	rwd,b16	A7db			2	4						X	X	Z ← NOT bit b16 of [rwd]
	BIT	@rid,b16	27ib			2	8						X	X	Z ← NOT bit b16 of [[rid]]
	BIT	adrsx,b16	67ib	pppp	qqqq	4/6	10-14						X	X	Z ← NOT bit b16 of [adrsx]
	BIT	rwd,rws	270s	0d00		4	10						X	X	Z ← NOT bit [rws] of [rwd] Set the Z status to the complement of the specified bit, which may be in a 16-bit register or memory word. The bit may be specified immediately, or for a register it may be specified by the low-order four bits of a 16-bit register.
	BITB	rbd,b8	A6db			2	4						X	X	Z ← NOT bit b8 of [rbd]
	BITB	@rid,b8	26ib			2	8						X	X	Z ← NOT bit b8 of [[rid]]
	BITB	adrsx,b8	66ib	pppp	qqqq	4/6	10-14						X	X	Z ← NOT bit b8 of [adrsx]
	BITB	rbd,rws	260s	0d00		4	10						X	X	Z ← NOT bit [rws] of [rbd] Set the Z status to the complement of the specified bit, which may be in an 8-bit register or memory byte. The bit may be specified immediately, or for a register it may be specified by the low-order three bits of one of the registers R0 - R7.
	RES	rwd,b16	A3db			2	4								Bit b16 of [rwd] ← 0
	RES	@rid,b16	23ib			2	11								Bit b16 of [[rid]] ← 0
	RES	adrsx,b16	63ib	pppp	qqqq	4/6	13-17								Bit b16 of [adrsx] ← 0
	RES	rwd,rws	230s	0d00		4	10								Bit [rws] of [rwd] ← 0 Clear the specified bit, which may be in a 16-bit register or memory word. The bit may be specified immediately, or for a register it may be specified by the low-order four bits of a 16-bit register.
	RESB	rbd,b8	A2db			2	4								Bit b8 of [rbd] ← 0
	RESB	@rid,b8	22ib			2	11								Bit b8 of [[rid]] ← 0
	RESB	adrsx,b8	62ib	pppp	qqqq	4/6	13-17								Bit b8 of [adrsx] ← 0
	RESB	rbd,rws	220s	0d00		4	10								Bit [rws] of [rbd] ← 0 Clear the specified bit, which may be in an 8-bit register or memory byte. The bit may be specified immediately, or for a register it may be specified by the low-order three bits of one of the registers R0 - R7.

* Privileged instruction — can be executed only in system mode.

** Number of clock cycles depends on the number of repetitions for n/m**: n =minimum number of clock cycles and m = number of clock cycles added for each additional repetition of operation. The number of clock cycles for an instruction which repeats k times is n + (k-1)•m.

Table 6-3. A Summary of the Z8000 Instruction Set (Continued)

Type	Mnemonic	Operand(s)	Op Code	Bytes	Clock Cycles	H	D	O	P	S	Z	C	Operation Performed
Bit Operations (Continued)	SET	rwd,b16	A5db	2	4								Bit b16 of [rwd] ← 1
	SET	@rid,b16	25ib	2	11								Bit b16 of [[rid]] ← 1
	SET	adrsx,b16	65ib pppp qqqq	4/6	13-17								Bit b16 of [adrsx] ← 1
	SET	rwd,rws	250s 0d00	4	10								Bit [rws] of [rwd] ← 1
	SETB	rbd,b8	A4db	2	4								Bit b8 of [rbd]
	SETB	@rid,b8	24ib	2	11								Bit b8 of [[rid]]
	SETB	adrsx,b8	64ib pppp qqqq	4/6	13-17								Bit b8 of [adrsx]
	SETB	rbd,rws	240s 0d00	4	10								Bit [rws] of [rbd]
													SET and SETB instructions are equivalent to RES and RESB instructions, respectively, except that the selected bit is set.
Interrupt	DI*	int	7C 000000vv	2	6								Disable the indicated interrupt(s). Either or both of VI and NVI may be indicated.
	EI*	int	7C 000001vv	2	6								Enable the indicated interrupt(s). Either or both of VI and NVI may be indicated.
	IRET*		7B00	2	13,16	X	X	X	X	X	X	X	[SP] ← [SP] + 2. [FCW] ← [[SP]]: [SP] + 2. [PC] ← [[SP]] [SP] ← [SP] + 2. (Nonsegmented) [SP] ← [SP] + 2. [FCW] ← [[SP]]. [SP] ← [SP] + 2. [PC] ← [[SP]] [SP] ← [SP] + 4. (Segmented) Return from interrupt. Pop and discard identifier word. Pop flag and control word. Pop Program Counter.
	LDCTL*	PSAPSEG,rws	7DsC	2	7								[PSAPSEG] ← [rws]
	LDCTL*	rwd,PSAPSEG	7Dd4	2	7								[rwd] ← [PSAPSEG]
													These two instructions transfer data between the Z8001 Program Status Area Pointer Segment register, and a 16-bit general purpose register.
	LDCTL*	PSAPOFF,rws	7DsD	2	7								[PSAPOFF] ← [rws]
	LDCTL*	rwd,PSAPOFF	7Dd5	2	7								[rwd] ← [PSAPOFF]
													These two instructions transfer data between the Program Status Area Pointer and a 16-bit general purpose register.

* Privileged instruction — can be executed only in system mode.

** Number of clock cycles depends on the number of repetitions for n/m**; n = minimum number of clock cycles and m = number of clock cycles added for each additional repetition of operation. The number of clock cycles for an instruction which repeats k times is $n + (k-1) \cdot m$.

Table 6-3. A Summary of the Z8000 Instruction Set (Continued)

Type	Mnemonic	Operand(s)	Op Code	Bytes	Clock Cycles	H	D	O	P	S	Z	C	Operation Performed
Status	COMFLG	flag	8Df5	2	7			X	X	X	X	X	Complement each status named in the operand. Any or all of C, Z, S, P, or O may be named in any order.
	LDCTL*	FCW,rws	7DsA	2	7	X	X	X	X	X	X	X	[FCW] ← [rws] Load register contents into FCW. Unassigned bits of FCW are not affected.
	LDCTL*	rwd,FCW	7Dd2	2	7								[rwd] ← [FCW] Load FCW contents into selected register. Unassigned bits of FCW are reset to 0 in rwd.
	LDCTLB	FLAGS,rbs	8Cs9	2	7	X	X	X	X	X	X	X	[FLAGS] ← [rbs] Load byte register contents into low-order byte of FCW. Bits 0 and 1, which are unassigned, are not affected.
	LDCTLB	rbd,FLAGS	8Cd1	2	7								[rbd] ← [FLAGS] Load the low-order byte of FCW into byte register rbd. Bits 0 and 1 of rbd are reset to 0.
	RESFLG	flag	8Df3	2	7			X	X	X	X	X	Reset to 0 each status named in the operand.
	SETFLG	flag	8Df1	2	7			X	X	X	X	X	Set to 1 each status named in the operand.
	TCC	cc,rwd	AFdc	2	5								If cc is "true" then set bit 0 of Register rwd. Otherwise reset bit 0 of Register rwd.
	TCCB	cc,rbd	AEdc	2	5								If cc is "true" then set bit 0 of Register rbd. Otherwise reset bit 0 of Register rbd.

* Privileged instruction — can be executed only in system mode.
** Number of clock cycles depends on the number of repetitions for n/m**. n = minimum number of clock cycles and m = number of clock cycles added for each additional repetition of operation. The number of clock cycles for an instruction which repeats k times is n + (k−1)·m.

Table 6-3. A Summary of the Z8000 Instruction Set (Continued)

Type	Mnemonic	Operand(s)	Op Code	Bytes	Clock Cycles	H	D	O	P	S	Z	C	Operation Performed
Other (CPU and Bus Control)	HALT*		7A00	2	8/3**								Halt CPU until reset or interrupt
	LDCTL*	REFRESH,rws	7DsB	2	7								[REFRESH] ← [rws] Transfer the contents of the specified 16-bit register into the Dynamic Memory Refresh Control register.
	LDCTL*	rwd,REFRESH	7Dd3	2	7								[rwd] ← [REFRESH] Transfer the contents of the Dynamic Memory Refresh Control register to the specified 16-bit register.
	MBIT*		7B0A	2	7					X			[S] ← $\overline{MI}$ Set Sign status to 1 if $\overline{MI}$ is input low (1). Reset Sign status to 0 if $\overline{MI}$ is input high (0).
	MREQ*	rwd	7BdD	2	12/7**					X	X		[Z] ← 0. If $\overline{MI}$ = 1 then [S] ← 0 and [$\overline{MO}$] ← 0. If $\overline{MI}$ = 0 then [$\overline{MO}$] ← 1. Decrement [rwd] to 0. If $\overline{MI}$ is still 0 then [S] ← 0. [$\overline{MO}$] ← 0. If $\overline{MI}$ is now 1 then [S] ← 1. [Z] ← 1. Execute a multi-micro bus request, as described in accompanying text.
	MRES*		7B09	2	5								[$\overline{MO}$] ← 0 Output $\overline{MO}$ high.
	MSET*		7B08	2	5								[$\overline{MO}$] ← 1 Output $\overline{MO}$ low.
	NOP		8D07	2	7								No operation.

* Privileged instruction — can be executed only in system mode.
** Number of clock cycles depends on the number of repetitions for n/m**; n =minimum number of clock cycles and m = number of clock cycles added for each additional repetition of operation. The number of clock cycles for an instruction which repeats k times is n + (k-1)·m.

Table 6-4. Z8000 Instruction Set Object Codes

Mnemonic		Object Code	Bytes	Clock Cycles	Mnemonic		Object Code	Bytes	Clock Cycles
ADC	rwd,rws	B5sd	2	5	CALR	disp	Dxxx	2	10/15
ADCB	rbd,rbs	B4sd	2	5	CLR	adrsx	4Di8	4/6	11-15
ADD	rwd,adrsx	41id	4/6	9-13			pppp		
		pppp					qqqq		
		qqqq				rwd	8Dd8	2	7
	rwd,data16	010d	4	7		@rid	0Dd8	2	8
		yyyy			CLRB	adrsx	4Ci8	4/6	11-15
	rwd,rws	81sd	2	4			pppp		
	rwd,@ris	01id	2	7			qqqq		
ADDB	rbd,adrsx	40id	4/6	9-13		rbd	8Cd8	2	7
		pppp				@rid	0Cd8	2	8
		qqqq			COM	adrsx	4Di0	4/6	15-19
	rbd,data8	000d	4	7			pppp		
		yy00					qqqq		
	rbd,rbs	80sd	2	4		rwd	8Dd0	2	7
	rbd,@ris	00id	2	7		@rid	0Dd0	2	12
ADDL	rld,adrsx	56id	4/6	15-19	COMB	adrsx	4Ci0	4/6	15-19
		pppp					pppp		
		qqqq					qqqq		
	rld,data32	160d	6	14		rbd	8Cd0	2	7
		yyyy				@rid	0Cd0	2	12
		zzzz			COMFLG	flag	8Df5	2	7
	rld,rls	96sd	2	8	CP	adrsx,data16	4Di1	6/8	14-18
	rld,@ris	16id	2	14			yyyy		
AND	rwd,adrsx	47id	4/6	9-13			pppp		
		pppp					qqqq		
		qqqq				rwd,adrsx	4Bid	4/6	9-13
	rwd,data16	070d	4	7			pppp		
		yyyy					qqqq		
	rwd,rws	87sd	2	4		rwd,data16	0B0d	4	7
	rwd,@ris	07id	2	7			yyyy		
ANDB	rbd,adrsx	46id	4/6	9-13		rwd,rws	8Bsd	2	4
		pppp				rwd,@ris	0Bid	2	7
		qqqq				@rid,data16	0Dd1	4	11
	rbd,data8	060d	4	7			yyyy		
		yy00			CPB	adrsx,data8	4Ci1	6/8	14-18
	rbd,rbs	86sd	2	4			yy00		
	rbd,@ris	06id	2	7			pppp		
BIT	adrsx,b16	67ib	4/6	10-14			qqqq		
		pppp				rbd,adrsx	4Aid	4/6	9-13
		qqqq					pppp		
	rwd,b16	A7db	2	4			qqqq		
	@rid,b16	27ib	2	8		rbd,data8	0A0d	4	7
	rwd,rws	270s	4	10			yy00		
		0d00				rbd,rbs	8Asd	2	4
BITB	adrsx,b8	66ib	4/6	10-14		rbd,@ris	0Aid	2	7
		pppp				@rid,data8	0Cd1	4	11
		qqqq					yy00		
	rbd,b8	A6db	2	4	CPL	rld,adrsx	50id	4/6	15-19
	@rid,b8	26ib	2	8			pppp		
	rbd,rws	260s	4	10			qqqq		
		0d00				rld,data32	100d	6	14
CALL	adrsx	5Fi0	4/6	12-21			yyyy		
		pppp					zzzz		
		qqqq				rld,rls	90sd	2	8
	@rid	1Fd0	2	10/15		rld,@ris	10id	2	14

Table 6-4. Z8000 Instruction Set Object Codes (Continued)

Mnemonic		Object Code	Bytes	Clock Cycles
CPD	rwd,@ris,rw,cc	BBs8 Ordc	4	20
CPDB	rbd,@ris,rw,cc	BAs8 Ordc	4	20
CPDR	rwd,@ris,rw,cc	BBsC Ordc	4	20/9**
CPDRB	rbd,@ris,rw,cc	BAsC Ordc	4	20/9**
CPI	rwd,@ris,rw,cc	BBs0 Ordc	4	20
CPIB	rbd,@ris,rw,cc	BAs0 Ordc	4	20
CPIR	rwd,@ris,rw,cc	BBs4 Ordc	4	20/9**
CPIRB	rbd,@ris,rw,cc	BAs4 Ordc	4	20/9**
CPSD	@rid,@ris,rw,cc	BBsA Ordc	4	25
CPSDB	@rid,@ris,rw,cc	BAsA Ordc	4	25
CPSDR	@rid,@ris,rw,cc	BBsE Ordc	4	25/14**
CPSDRB	@rid,@ris,rw,cc	BAsE Ordc	4	25/14**
CPSI	@rid,@ris,rw,cc	BBs2 Ordc	4	25
CPSIB	@rid,@ris,rw,cc	BAs2 Ordc	4	25
CPSIR	@rid,@ris,rw,cc	BBs6 Ordc	4	25/14**
CPSIRB	@rid,@ris,rw,cc	BAs6 Ordc	4	25/14**
DAB	rbd	B0d0	2	5
DEC	adrsx,n16	6Bin pppp qqqq	4/6	13-17
	rwd,n16	ABdn	2	4
	@rid,n16	2Bdn	2	11
DECB	adrsx,n16	6Ain pppp qqqq	4/6	13-17
	rbd,n16	AAdn	2	4
	@rid,n16	2Adn	2	11
*DI	int	7C 000000vv	2	6
DIV	rld,adrsx	5Bid pppp qqqq	4/6	note 1
	rld,data16	1B0d yyyy	4	note 1
	rld,rws	9Bsd	2	note 1
	rld,@ris	1Bid	2	note 1

Mnemonic		Object Code	Bytes	Clock Cycles
DIVL	rqd,adrsx	5Aid pppp qqqq	4/6	note 1
	rqd,data32	1A0d yyyy zzzz	6	note 1
	rqd,rls	9Asd	2	note 1
	rqd,@ris	1Aid	2	note 1
DJNZ	rw,disp	Fr 0ttttttt	2	11
DBJNZ	rb,disp	Fr 1ttttttt	2	11
*EI	int	7C 000001vv	2	6
EX	rwd,adrsx	6Did pppp qqqq	4/6	15-19
	rwd,rws	ADsd	2	6
	rwd,@ris	2Dsd	2	12
EXB	rbd,adrsx	6Cid pppp qqqq	4/6	15-19
	rbd,rbs	ACsd	2	6
	rbd,@ris	2Csd	2	12
EXTS	rld	B1dA	2	11
EXTSB	rwd	B1d0	2	11
EXTSL	rqd	B1d7	2	11
*HALT		7A00	2	8/3**
*IN	rwd,ioaddr	3Bd4 pppp	4	12
	rwd,@rw	3Dsd	2	10
*INB	rbd,ioaddr	3Ad4 pppp	4	12
	rbd,@rw	3Csd	2	10
INC	adrsx,n16	69in pppp qqqq	4/6	13-17
	rwd,n16	A9dn	2	4
	@rid,n16	29dn	2	11
INCB	adrsx,n16	68in pppp qqqq	4/6	13-17
	rbd,n16	A8dn	2	4
	@rid,n16	28dn	2	11
*IND	@rid,@ris,rw	3Bs8 Ord8	4	21
*INDB	@rid,@ris,rw	3As8 Ord8	4	21
*INDR	@rid,@ris,rw	3Bs8 Ord0	4	21/10**
*INDRB	@rid,@ris,rw	3As8 Ord0	4	21/10**
*INI	@rid,@ris,rw	3Bs0 Ord8	4	21

* Privileged instruction — can be executed only in system mode.

** Number of clock cycles depends on the number of repetitions for n/m**; n = minimum number of clock cycles and m = number of clock cycles added for each additional repetition of operation. The number of clock cycles for an instruction which repeats k times is n + (k-1)•m.

Table 6-4. Z8000 Instruction Set Object Codes (Continued)

Mnemonic		Object Code	Bytes	Clock Cycles	Mnemonic		Object Code	Bytes	Clock Cycles
*INIB	@rid,@ris,rw	3As0 0rd8	4	21	LDB (Cont.)	rbd,ris(rw)	70id 0r00	4	14
*INIR	@rid,@ris,rw	3Bs0 0rd0	4	21/10**		rbd,@ris	20id	2	7
*INIRB	@rid,@ris,rw	3As0 0rd0	4	21/10**		rid(disp),rbs	32is xxxx	4	14
*IRET		7B00	2	13,16		rid(rw),rbs	72is 0r00	4	14
JP	cc,adrsx	5Eic pppp qqqq	4/6	7-11		@rid,data8	0Cd5 yy00	4	11
	cc,@rid	1Edc	2	10,15/7		@rid,rbs	2Eds	2	8
JR	cc,disp	Ecxx	2	6	LDL	adrsx,rls	5Dis pppp qqqq	4/6	14-18
LD	adrsx,data16	4Di5 yyyy pppp qqqq	6/8	14-18		rld,adrsx	54id pppp qqqq	4/6	12-16
	adrsx,rws	6Fis pppp qqqq	4/6	11-15		rld,data32	140d yyyy zzzz	6	11
	rwd,adrsx	61id pppp qqqq	4/6	9-13		rld,rls	94sd	2	5
	rwd,data16	210d yyyy	4	7		rld,ris(disp)	35id xxxx	4	17
	rwd,rws	A1sd	2	3		rld,ris(rw)	75id 0r00	4	17
	rwd,ris(disp)	31id xxxx	4	14		rld,@ris	14id	2	11
	rwd,ris(rw)	71id 0r00	4	14		rid(disp),rls	37is xxxx	4	17
	rwd,@ris	21id	2	7		rid(rw),rls	77is 0r00	4	17
	rid(disp),rws	33is xxxx	4	14		@rid,rls	1Dds	2	11
	rid(rw),rws	73is 0r00	4	14	LDA	rld,adrsx	76id pppp qqqq	4/6	13-16
	@rid,data16	0Dd5 yyyy	4	11		rld,ris(disp)	34id xxxx	4	15
	@rid,rws	2Fds	2	8		rld,ris(rw)	74id 0r00	4	15
LDB	adrsx,data8	4Ci5 yy00 pppp qqqq	6/8	14-18		rwd,adrsx	76id pppp qqqq	4	12-13
	adrsx,rbs	6Eis pppp qqqq	4/6	11-15		rwd,ris(disp)	34id xxxx	4	15
	rbd,adrsx	60id pppp qqqq	4/6	9-13		rwd,ris(rw)	74id 0r00	4	15
	rbd,data8	Cdyy	2	5	LDAR	rld,disp	340d xxxx	4	15
	rbd,rbs	A0sd	2	3		rwd,disp	340d xxxx	4	15
	rbd,ris(disp)	30id xxxx	4	14					

*   Privileged instruction — can be executed only in system mode.

** Number of clock cycles depends on the number of repetitions for n/m**; n = minimum number of clock cycles and m = number of clock cycles added for each additional repetition of operation. The number of clock cycles for an instruction which repeats k times is n + (k-1)•m.

Table 6-4. Z8000 Instruction Set Object Codes (Continued)

Mnemonic		Object Code	Bytes	Clock Cycles
*LDCTL	FCW,rws	7DsA	2	7
	NSPOFF,rws	7DsF	2	7
	NSPSEG,rws	7DsE	2	7
	PSAPOFF,rws	7DsD	2	7
	PSAPSEG,rws	7DsC	2	7
	REFRESH,rws	7DsB	2	7
	rwd,FCW	7Dd2	2	7
	rwd,NSPOFF	7Dd7	2	7
	rwd,NSPSEG	7Dd6	2	7
	rwd,PSAPOFF	7Dd5	2	7
	rwd,PSAPSEG	7Dd4	2	7
	rwd,REFRESH	7Dd3	2	7
LDCTLB	FLAGS,rbs	8Cs9	2	7
	rbs,FLAGS	8Cd1	2	7
LDD	@rid,@ris,rw	BBs9 Ord8	4	20
LDDB	@rid,@ris,rw	BAs9 Ord8	4	20
LDDR	@rid,@ris,rw	BBs9 Ord0	4	20/9**
LDDRB	@rid,@ris,rw	BAs9 Ord0	4	20/9**
LDI	@rid,@ris,rw	BBs1 Ord8	4	20
LDIB	@rid,@ris,rw	BAs1 Ord8	4	20
LDIR	@rid,@ris,rw	BBs1 Ord0	4	20/9**
LDIRB	@rid,@ris,rw	BAs1 Ord0	4	20/9**
LDK	rwd,b16	BDdb	2	5
LDM	adrsx,rws,n16	5Ci9 OsOn pppp qqqq	6/8	17-21/3**
	rwd,adrsx,n16	5Ci1 OdOn pppp qqqq	6/8	17-21/3**
	rwd,@ris,n16	1Cs1 OdOn	4	14/3**
	@rid,rws,n16	1Cd9 OsOn	4	14/3**
*LDPS	adrsx	79i0 pppp qqqq	4/6	16-23
	@ris	39s0	2	12,16
LDR	disp,rws	330s xxxx	4	14
	rwd,disp	310d xxxx	4	14

Mnemonic		Object Code	Bytes	Clock Cycles
LDRB	disp,rbs	320d xxxx	4	14
	rbd,disp	300d xxxx	4	14
LDRL	disp,rls	370s xxxx	4	17
	rld,disp	350d xxxx	4	17
*MBIT		7B0A	2	7
*MREQ	rwd	7BdD	2	12/7**
*MRES		7B09	2	5
*MSET		7B08	2	5
MULT	rld,adrsx	59id pppp qqqq	4/6	note 2
	rld,data16	190d yyyy	4	note 2
	rld,rws	99sd	2	note 2
	rld,@ris	19id	2	note 2
MULTL	rqd,adrsx	58id pppp qqqq	4/6	note 2
	rqd,data32	180d yyyy zzzz	6	note 2
	rqd,rls	98sd	2	note 2
	rqd,@ris	18id	2	note 2
NEG	adrsx	4Di2 pppp qqqq	4/6	15-19
	rwd	8Dd2	2	7
	@rid	0Dd2	2	12
NEGB	adrsx	4Ci2 pppp qqqq	4/6	15-19
	rbd	8Cd2	2	7
	@rid	0Cd2	2	12
NOP		8D07	2	7
OR	rwd,adrsx	45id pppp qqqq	4/6	9-13
	rwd,data16	050d yyyy	4	7
	rwd,rws	85sd	2	4
	rwd,@ris	05id	2	7

*   Privileged instruction — can be executed only in system mode.

** Number of clock cycles depends on the number of repetitions for n/m**; n = minimum number of clock cycles and m = number of clock cycles added for each additional repetition of operation. The number of clock cycles for an instruction which repeats k times is n + (k-1)•m.

Table 6-4. Z8000 Instruction Set Object Codes (Continued)

Mnemonic		Object Code	Bytes	Clock Cycles
ORB	rbd,adrsx	44id	4/6	9-13
		pppp		
		qqqq		
	rbd,data8	040d	4	7
		yy00		
	rbd,rbs	84sd	2	4
	rbd,@ris	04id	2	7
*OTDR	@rid,@ris,rw	3BsA	4	21/10**
		0rd0		
*OTDRB	@rid,@ris,rw	3AsA	4	21/10**
		0rd0		
*OTIR	@rid,@ris,rw	3Bs2	4	21/10**
		0rd0		
*OTIRB	@rid,@ris,rw	3As2	4	21/10**
		0rd0		
*OUT	ioaddr,rws	3Bs6	4	12
		pppp		
	@rw,rws	3Fds	2	10
*OUTB	ioaddr,rbs	3As6	4	12
		pppp		
	@rw,rbs	3Eds	2	10
*OUTD	@rid,@ris,rw	3BsA	4	21
		0rd8		
*OUTDB	@rid,@ris,rw	3AsA	4	21
		0rd8		
*OUTI	@rid,@ris,rw	3Bs2	4	21
		0rd8		
*OUTIB	@rid,@ris,rw	3As2	4	21
		0rd8		
POP	adrsx,@ris	57si	4/6	15-19
		pppp		
		qqqq		
	rwd,@ris	97sd	2	8
	@rid,@ris	17sd	2	12
POPL	adrsx,@ris	55si	4/6	22-26
		pppp		
		qqqq		
	rld,@ris	95id	2	12
	@rid,@ris	15id	2	19
PUSH	@rid,adrsx	53di	4/6	13-7
		pppp		
		qqqq		
	@rid,data16	0Dd9	4	12
		yyyy		
	@rid,rws	93is	2	9
	@rid,@ris	13is	2	13
PUSHL	@rid,adrsx	51di	4/6	20-24
		pppp		
		qqqq		
	@rid,rls	91is	2	12
	@rid,@ris	11is	2	20

Mnemonic		Object Code	Bytes	Clock Cycles
RES	adrsx,b16	63ib	4/6	13-17
		pppp		
		qqqq		
	rwd,b16	A3db	2	4
	rwd,rws	230s	4	10
		0d00		
	@rid,b16	23ib	2	11
RESB	adrsx,b8	62ib	4/6	13-17
		pppp		
		qqqq		
	rbd,b8	A2db	2	4
	rbd,rws	220s	4	10
		0d00		
	@rid,b8	22ib	2	11
RESFLG	flag	8Df3	2	7
RET	cc	9E0c	2	10,13/7
RL	rwd,1	B3d8	2	6
	rwd,2	B3dA	2	7
RLB	rbd,1	B2d8	2	6
	rbd,2	B2dA	2	7
RLC	rwd,1	B3d0	2	6
	rwd,2	B3d2	2	7
RLCB	rbd,1	B2d0	2	6
	rbd,2	B2d2	2	7
RLDB	rbd,rbs	BEsd	2	9
RR	rwd,1	B3dC	2	6
	rwd,2	B3dE	2	7
RRB	rbd,1	B2dC	2	6
	rbd,2	B2dE	2	7
RRC	rwd,1	B3d4	2	6
	rwd,2	B3d6	2	7
RRCB	rbd,1	B2d4	2	6
	rbd,2	B2d6	2	7
RRDB	rbd,rbs	BCsd	2	9
SBC	rwd,rws	B7sd	2	5
SBCB	rbd,rbs	B6sd	2	5
SC	data8	7Fyy	2	33,39
SDA	rwd,rw	B3dB	4	18/3**
		0r00		
SDAB	rbd,rw	B2dB	4	18/3**
		0r00		
SDAL	rld,rw	B3dF	4	18/3**
		0r00		
SDL	rwd,rw	B3d3	4	18/3**
		0r00		
SDLB	rbd,rw	B2d3	4	18/3**
		0r00		
SDLL	rld,rw	B3d7	4	18/3**
		0r00		

* Privileged instruction — can be executed only in system mode.

** Number of clock cycles depends on the number of repetitions for n/m**; n = minimum number of clock cycles and m = number of clock cycles added for each additional repetition of operation. The number of clock cycles for an instruction which repeats k times is n + (k-1)•m.

Table 6-4. Z8000 Instruction Set Object Codes (Continued)

Mnemonic		Object Code	Bytes	Clock Cycles	Mnemonic		Object Code	Bytes	Clock Cycles
SET	adrsx,b16	65ib pppp qqqq	4/6	13-17	*SOTIR	@rid,@ris,rw	3Bs3 0rd0	4	21/10**
	rwd,b16	A5db	2	4	*SOTIRB	@rid,@ris,rw	3As3 0rd0	4	21/10**
	rwd,rws	2505 0d00	4	10	*SOUT	ioaddr,rws	3Bs7 pppp	4	12
	@rid,b16	25ib	2	11	*SOUTB	ioaddr,rbs	3As7 pppp	4	12
SETB	adrsx,b8	64ib pppp qqqq	4/6	13-17	*SOUTD	@rid,@ris,rw	3BsB 0rd8	4	21
	rbd,b8	A4db	2	4	*SOUTDB	@rid,@ris,rw	3AsB 0rd8	4	21
	rbd,rws	240s 0d00	4	10	*SOUTI	@rid,@ris,rw	3Bs3 0rd8	4	21
	@rid,b8	24ib	2	11	*SOUTIB	@rid,@ris,rw	3As3 0rd8	4	21
SETFLG	flag	8Df1	2	7	SRA	rwd,data16	B3d9 yyyy	4	16/3**
*SIN	rwd,ioaddr	3Bd5 pppp	4	12	SRAB	rbd,data16	B2d9 yyyy	4	16/3**
*SINB	rbd,ioaddr	3Ad5 pppp	4	12	SRAL	rld,data16	B3dD yyyy	4	16/3**
*SIND	@rid,@ris,rw	3Bs9 0rd8	4	21	SRL	rwd,data16	B3d1 yyyy	4	16/3**
*SINDB	@rid,@ris,rw	3As9 0rd8	4	21	SRLB	rbd,data16	B2d1 yyyy	4	16/3**
*SINDR	@rid,@ris,rw	3Bs9 0rd0	4	21/10**	SRLL	rld,data16	B3d5 yyyy	4	16/3**
*SINDRB	@rid,@ris,rw	3As9 0rd0	4	21/10**	SUB	rwd,adrsx	43id pppp qqqq	4/6	9-13
*SINI	@rid,@ris,rw	3Bs1 0rd8	4	21		rwd,data16	030d yyyy	4	7
*SINIB	@rid,@ris,rw	3As1 0rd8	4	21		rwd,rws	83sd	2	4
*SINIR	@rid,@ris,rw	3Bs1 0rd0	4	21/10**		rwd,@ris	03id	2	7
*SINIRB	@rid,@ris,rw	3As1 0rd0	4	21/10**	SUBB	rbd,adrsx	42id pppp qqqq	4/6	9-13
SLA	rwd,data16	B3d9 yyyy	4	16/3**		rbd,data8	020d yy00	4	7
SLAB	rbd,data16	B2d9 yyyy	4	16/3**		rbd,rbs	82sd	2	4
SLAL	rld,data16	B3dC yyyy	4	16/3**		rbd,@ris	02id	2	7
SLL	rwd,data16	B3d1 yyyy	4	16/3**	SUBL	rld,adrsx	52id pppp qqqq	4/6	15-19
SLLB	rbd,data16	B2d1 yyyy	4	16/3**		rld,data32	120d yyyy zzzz	6	14
SLLL	rld,data16	B3d5 yyyy	4	16/3**		rld,rls	92sd	2	8
*SOTDR	@rid,@ris,rw	3BsB 0rd0	4	21/10**		rld,@ris	12id	2	14
*SOTDRB	@rid,@ris,rw	3AsB 0rd0	4	21/10**	TCC	cc,rwd	AFdc	2	5

* Privileged instruction — can be executed only in system mode.

** Number of clock cycles depends on the number of repetitions for n/m**; n = minimum number of clock cycles and m = number of clock cycles added for each additional repetition of operation. The number of clock cycles for an instruction which repeats k times is n + (k-1)•m.

Table 6-4. Z8000 Instruction Set Object Codes (Continued)

Mnemonic		Object Code	Bytes	Clock Cycles	Mnemonic		Object Code	Bytes	Clock Cycles
TCCB	cc,rbd	AEdc	2	5	TRTIB	@rid,@ris,rw	B8d2	4	25
TEST	adrsx	4Di4	4/6	11-15			OrsO		
		pppp			TRTIRB	@rid,@ris,rw	B8d6	4	25/14**
		qqqq					OrsE		
	rwd	8Dd4	2	7	TSET	adrsx	4Di6	4/6	14-18
	@rid	0Dd4	2	8			pppp		
TESTB	adrsx	4Ci4	4/6	11-15			qqqq		
		pppp				rwd	8Dd6	2	7
		qqqq				@rid	0Dd6	2	11
	rbd	8Cd4	2	7	TSETB	adrsx	4Ci6	4/6	14-18
	@rid	0Cd4	2	8			pppp		
TESTL	adrsx	5CiO	4/6	16-20			qqqq		
		pppp				rbd	8Cd6	2	7
		qqqq				@rid	0Cd6	2	11
	rld	9Cd0	2	13	XOR	rwd,adrsx	49id	4/6	9-13
	@rid	1Cd0	2	13			pppp		
TRDB	@rid,@ris,rw	B8d8	4	25			qqqq		
		OrsO				rwd,data16	090d	4	7
TRDRB	@rid,@ris,rw	B8dC	4	25/14**			yyyy		
		OrsO				rwd,rws	89sd	2	4
TRIB	@rid,@ris,rw	B8d0	4	25		rwd,@ris	09id	2	7
		OrsO			XORB	rbd,adrsx	48id	4/6	9-13
TRIRB	@rid,@ris,rw	B8d4	4	25/14**			pppp		
		OrsO					qqqq		
TRTDB	@rid,@ris,rw	B8dA	4	25		rbd,data8	080d	4	7
		OrsO					yy00		
TRTDRB	@rid,@ris,rw	B8dE	4	25/14**		rbd,rbs	88sd	2	4
		OrsE				rbd,@ris	08id	2	7

* Privileged instruction — can be executed only in system mode.

** Number of clock cycles depends on the number of repetitions for n/m**; n = minimum number of clock cycles and m = number of clock cycles added for each additional repetition of operation. The number of clock cycles for an instruction which repeats k times is n + (k-1)•m.

Note 1

Divisor	DIV			DIVL		
	Not Aborted	Divisor is Zero	Dividend Too Large	Not Aborted	Divisor is Zero	Dividend Too Large
adrsx	96-100	14-18	26-29	724-728	31-35	52-56
All Others	95	13	25	723	30	51

Note 2

Multiplier	MULT		MULTL	
	Normal	Multiplier is Zero	Normal	Multiplier is Zero
adrsx	71-75	19-22	283 + 7•m - 287 + 7•m	31-35
All Others	70	18	282 + 7•m	30

Table 6-5. Z8000 Object Codes

Object Code	Instruction		Object Code	Instruction	
000d yy00	ADDB	rbd,data8	1Aid	DIVL	rqd,@ris
00id	ADDB	rbd,@ris	1B0d yyyy	DIV	rld,data16
010d yyyy	ADD	rwd,data16	1Bid	DIV	rld,@ris
01id	ADD	rwd,@ris	1Cd0	TESTL	@rid
020d yy00	SUBB	rbd,data8	1Cs1 0d0n	LDM	rwd,@ris,n16
02id	SUBB	rbd,@ris	1Cd9 0s0n	LDM	@rid,rws,n16
030d yyyy	SUB	rwd,data16	1Dds	LDL	@rid,rls
03id	SUB	rwd,@ris	1Edc	JP	cc,@rid
040d yy00	ORB	rbd,data8	1Fd0	CALL	@rid
04id	ORB	rbd,@ris	20id	LDB	rbd,@ris
050d yyyy	OR	rwd,data16	210d yyyy	LD	rwd,data16
05id	OR	rwd,@ris	21id	LD	rwd,@ris
060d yy00	ANDB	rbd,data8	220s 0d00	RESB	rbd,rws
06id	ANDB	rbd,@ris	22ib	RESB	@rid,b8
070d yyyy	AND	rwd,data16	230s 0d00	RES	rwd,rws
07id	AND	rwd,@ris	23ib	RES	@rid,b16
080d yy00	XORB	rbd,data8	240s 0d00	SETB	rbd,rws
08id	XORB	rbd,@ris	24ib	SETB	@rid,b8
090d yyyy	XOR	rwd,data16	250s 0d00	SET	rwd,rws
09id	XOR	rwd,@ris	25ib	SET	@rid,b16
0A0d yy00	CPB	rbd,data8	260s 0d00	BITB	rbd,rws
0Aid	CPB	rbd,@ris	26ib	BITB	@rid,b8
0B0d yyyy	CP	rwd,data16	270s 0d00	BIT	rwd,rws
0Bid	CP	rwd,@ris	27ib	BIT	@rid,b16
0Cd0	COMB	@rid	28dn	INCB	@rid,n16
0Cd1 yy00	CPB	@rid,data8	29dn	INC	@rid,n16
0Cd2	NEGB	@rid	2Adn	DECB	@rid,n16
0Cd4	TESTB	@rid	2Bdn	DEC	@rid,n16
0Cd5 yy00	LDB	@rid,data8	2Csd	EXB	rbd,@ris
0Cd6	TSETB	@rid	2Dsd	EX	rwd,@ris
0Cd8	CLRB	@rid	2Eds	LDB	@rid,rbs
0Dd0	COM	@rid	2Fds	LD	@rid,rws
0Dd1 yyyy	CP	@rid,data16	300d xxxx	LDRB	rbd,disp
0Dd2	NEG	@rid	30id xxxx	LDB	rbd,ris(disp)
0Dd4	TEST	@rid	310d xxxx	LDR	rwd,disp
0Dd5 yyyy	LD	@rid,data16	31id xxxx	LD	rwd,ris(disp)
0Dd6	TSET	@rid	320s xxxx	LDRB	disp,rbs
0Dd8	CLR	@rid	32is xxxx	LDB	rid(disp),rbs
0Dd9 yyyy	PUSH	@rid,data16	330s xxxx	LDR	disp,rws
100d yyyy zzzz	CPL	rld,data32	33is xxxx	LD	rid(disp),rws
10id	CPL	rld,@ris	340d xxxx	LDAR	rld,disp
11is	PUSHL	@rid,@ris			rwd,disp
120d yyyy zzzz	SUBL	rld,data32	34id xxxx	LDA	rld,ris(disp)
12id	SUBL	rld,@ris			rwd,ris(disp)
13is	PUSH	@rid,@ris	350d xxxx	LDRL	rld,disp
140d yyyy zzzz	LDL	rld,data32	35id xxxx	LDL	rld,ris(disp)
14id	LDL	rld,@ris	370s xxxx	LDRL	disp,rls
15id	POPL	@rid,@ris	37is xxxx	LDL	rid(disp),rls
160d yyyy zzzz	ADDL	rld,data32	39s0	LDPS	@ris
16id	ADDL	rld,@ris	3As0 0rd0	INIRB	@rid,@ris,rw
17sd	POP	@rid,@ris	3As0 0rd8	INIB	@rid,@ris,rw
180d yyyy zzzz	MULTL	rqd,data32	3As1 0rd0	SINIRB	@rid,@ris,rw
18id	MULTL	rqd,@ris	3As1 0rd8	SINIB	@rid,@ris,rw
190d yyyy	MULT	rld,data16	3As2 0rd0	OTIRB	@rid,@ris,rw
19id	MULT	rld,@ris	3As2 0rd8	OUTIB	@rid,@ris,rw
1A0d yyyy zzzz	DIVL	rqd,data32	3As3 0rd0	SOTIRB	@rid,@ris,rw

Table 6-5. Z8000 Object Codes (Continued)

Object Code	Instruction		Object Code	Instruction	
3As3 0rd8	SOUTIB	@rid,@ris,rw	4Ci6 pppp qqqq	TSETB	adrsx
3Ad4 pppp	INB	rbd,ioaddr	4Ci8 pppp qqqq	CLRB	adrsx
3Ad5 pppp	SINB	rbd,ioaddr	4Di0 pppp qqqq	COM	adrsx
3As6 pppp	OUTB	ioaddr,rbs	4Di1 yyyy	CP	adrsx,data16
3As7 pppp	SOUTB	ioaddr,rbs	pppp qqqq		
3As8 0rd0	INDRB	@rid,@ris,rw	4Di2 pppp qqqq	NEG	adrsx
3As8 0rd8	INDB	@rid,@ris,rw	4Di4 pppp qqqq	TEST	adrsx
3As9 0rd0	SINDRB	@rid,@ris,rw	4Di5 yyyy	LD	adrsx,data16
3As9 0rd8	SINDB	@rid,@ris,rw	pppp qqqq		
3AsA 0rd0	OTDRB	@rid,@ris,rw	4Di6 pppp qqqq	TSET	adrsx
3AsA 0rd8	OUTDB	@rid,@ris,rw	4Di8 pppp qqqq	CLR	adrsx
3AsB 0rd0	SOTDRB	@rid,@ris,rw	50id pppp qqqq	CPL	rld,adrsx
3AsB 0rd8	SOUTDB	@rid,@ris,rw	51di pppp qqqq	PUSHL	@rid,adrsx
3Bs0 0rd0	INIR	@rid,@ris,rw	52id pppp qqqq	SUBL	rld,adrsx
3Bs0 0rd8	INI	@rid,@ris,rw	53di pppp qqqq	PUSH	@rid,adrsx
3Bs1 0rd0	SINIR	@rid,@ris,rw	54id pppp qqqq	LDL	rld,adrsx
3Bs1 0rd8	SINI	@rid,@ris,rw	55si pppp qqqq	POPL	adrsx,@ris
3Bs2 0rd0	OTIR	@rid,@ris,rw	56id pppp qqqq	ADDL	rld,adrsx
3Bs2 0rd8	OUTI	@rid,@ris,rw	57si pppp qqqq	POP	adrsx,@ris
3Bs3 0rd0	SOTIR	@rid,@ris,rw	58id pppp qqqq	MULTL	rqd,adrsx
3Bs3 0rd8	SOUTI	@rid,@ris,rw	59id pppp qqqq	MULT	rld,adrsx
3Bd4 pppp	IN	rwd,ioaddr	5Aid pppp qqqq	DIVL	rqd,adrsx
3Bd5 pppp	SIN	rwd,ioaddr	5Bid pppp qqqq	DIV	rld,adrsx
3Bs6 pppp	OUT	ioaddr,rws	5Ci0 pppp qqqq	TESTL	adrsx
3Bs7 pppp	SOUT	ioaddr,rws	5Ci1 0d0n	LDM	rwd,adrsx,n16
3Bs8 0rd0	INDR	@rid,@ris,rw	pppp qqqq		
3Bs8 0rd8	IND	@rid,@ris,rw	5Ci9 0s0n	LDM	adrsx,rws,n16
3Bs9 0rd0	SINDR	@rid,@ris,rw	pppp qqqq		
3Bs9 0rd8	SIND	@rid,@ris,rw	5Dis pppp qqqq	LDL	adrsx,rls
3BsA 0rd0	OTDR	@rid,@ris,rw	5Eic pppp qqqq	JP	cc,adrsx
3BsA 0rd8	OUTD	@rid,@ris,rw	5Fi0 pppp qqqq	CALL	adrsx
3BsB 0rd0	SOTDR	@rid,@ris,rw	60id pppp qqqq	LDB	rbd,adrsx
3BsB 0rd8	SOUTD	@rid,@ris,rw	61id pppp qqqq	LD	rwd,adrsx
3Csd	INB	rbd,@rw	62ib pppp qqqq	RESB	adrsx,b8
3Dsd	IN	rwd,@rw	63ib pppp qqqq	RES	adrsx,b16
3Eds	OUTB	@rw,rbs	64ib pppp qqqq	SETB	adrsx,b8
3Fds	OUT	@rw,rws	65ib pppp qqqq	SET	adrsx,b16
40id pppp qqqq	ADDB	rbd,adrsx	66ib pppp qqqq	BITB	adrsx,b8
41id pppp qqqq	ADD	rwd,adrsx	67ib pppp qqqq	BIT	adrsx,b16
42id pppp qqqq	SUBB	rbd,adrsx	68in pppp qqqq	INCB	adrsx,n16
43id pppp qqqq	SUB	rwd,adrsx	69in pppp qqqq	INC	adrsx,n16
44id pppp qqqq	ORB	rbd,adrsx	6Ain pppp qqqq	DECB	adrsx,n16
45id pppp qqqq	OR	rwd,adrsx	6Bin pppp qqqq	DEC	adrsx,n16
46id pppp qqqq	ANDB	rbd,adrsx	6Cid pppp qqqq	EXB	rbd,adrsx
47id pppp qqqq	AND	rwd,adrsx	6Did pppp qqqq	EX	rwd,adrsx
48id pppp qqqq	XORB	rbd,adrsx	6Eis pppp qqqq	LDB	adrsx,rbs
49id pppp qqqq	XOR	rwd,adrsx	6Fis pppp qqqq	LD	adrsx,rws
4Aid pppp qqqq	CPB	rbd,adrsx	70id 0r00	LDB	rbd,ris(rw)
4Bid pppp qqqq	CP	rwd,adrsx	71id 0r00	LD	rwd,ris(rw)
4Ci0 pppp qqqq	COMB	adrsx	72is 0r00	LDB	rid(rw),rbs
4Ci1 yy00	CPB	adrsx,data8	73is 0r00	LD	rid(rw),rws
pppp qqqq			74id 0r00	LDA	rld,ris(rw)
4Ci2 pppp qqqq	NEGB	adrsx			rwd,ris(rw)
4Ci4 pppp qqqq	TESTB	adrsx	75id 0r00	LDL	rld,ris(rw)
4Ci5 yy00	LDB	adrsx,data8	76id pppp qqqq	LDA	rld,adrsx
pppp qqqq					rwd,adrsx

Table 6-5. Z8000 Object Codes (Continued)

Object Code	Instruction		Object Code	Instruction	
77is 0r00	LDL	rid(rw),rls	96sd	ADDL	rld,rls
79i0 pppp qqqq	LDPS	adrsx	97sd	POP	rwd,@ris
7A00	HALT		98sd	MULTL	rqd,rls
7B00	IRET		99sd	MULT	rld,rws
7B08	MSET		9Asd	DIVL	rqd,rls
7B09	MRES		9Bsd	DIV	rld,rws
7B0A	MBIT		9Cd0	TESTL	rld
7BdD	MREQ	rwd	9E0c	RET	cc
7C 000000vv	DI	int	A0sd	LDB	rbd,rbs
7C 000001vv	EI	int	A1sd	LD	rwd,rws
7Dd2	LDCTL	rwd,FCW	A2db	RESB	rbd,b8
7Dd3	LDCTL	rwd,REFRESH	A3db	RES	rwd,b16
7Dd4	LDCTL	rwd,PSAPSEG	A4db	SETB	rwd,b8
7Dd5	LDCTL	rwd,PSAPOFF	A5db	SET	rwd,b16
7Dd6	LDCTL	rwd,NSPSEG	A6db	BITB	rbd,b8
7Dd7	LDCTL	rwd,NSPOFF	A7db	BIT	rwd,b16
7DsA	LDCTL	FCW,rws	A8dn	INCB	rbd,n16
7DsB	LDCTL	REFRESH,rws	A9dn	INC	rwd,n16
7DsC	LDCTL	PSAPSEG,rws	AAdn	DECB	rbd,n16
7DsD	LDCTL	PSAPOFF,rws	ABdn	DEC	rwd,n16
7DsE	LDCTL	NSPSEG,rws	ACsd	EXB	rbd,rbs
7DsF	LDCTL	NSPOFF,rws	ADsd	EX	rwd,rws
7Fyy	SC	data8	AEdc	TCCB	cc,rbd
80sd	ADDB	rbd,rbs	AFdc	TCC	cc,rwd
81sd	ADD	rwd,rws	B0d0	DAB	rbd
82sd	SUBB	rbd,rbs	B1d0	EXTSB	rwd
83sd	SUB	rwd,rws	B1d7	EXTSL	rqd
84sd	ORB	rbd,rbs	B1dA	EXTS	rld
85sd	OR	rwd,rws	B2d0	RLCB	rbd,1
86sd	ANDB	rbd,rbs	B2d1 yyyy	SLLB	rbd,data16
87sd	AND	rwd,rws	B2d1 yyyy	SRLB	rbd,data16
88sd	XORB	rbd,rbs	B2d2	RLCB	rbd,2
89sd	XOR	rwd,rws	B2d3 0r00	SDLB	rbd,rw
8Asd	CPB	rbd,rbs	B2d4	RRCB	rbd,1
8Bsd	CP	rwd,rws	B2d6	RRCB	rbd,2
8Cd0	COMB	rbd	B2d8	RLB	rbd,1
8Cd1	LDCTLB	rbd,FLAGS	B2d9 yyyy	SLAB	rbd,data16
8Cd2	NEGB	rbd	B2d9 yyyy	SRAB	rbd,data16
8Cd4	TESTB	rbd	B2dA	RLB	rbd,2
8Cd6	TSETB	rbd	B2dB 0r00	SDAB	rbd,rw
8Cd8	CLRB	rbd	B2dC	RRB	rbd,1
8Cs9	LDCTLB	FLAGS,rbs	B2dE	RRB	rbd,2
8D07	NOP		B3d0	RLC	rwd,1
8Dd0	COM	rwd	B3d1 yyyy	SLL	rwd,data16
8Df1	SETFLG	flag	B3d1 yyyy	SRL	rwd,data16
8Dd2	NEG	rwd	B3d2	RLC	rwd,2
8Df3	RESFLG	flag	B3d3 0r00	SDL	rwd,rw
8Dd4	TEST	rwd	B3d4	RRC	rwd,1
8Df5	COMFLG	flag	B3d5 yyyy	SLLL	rld,data16
8Dd6	TSET	rwd	B3d5 yyyy	SRLL	rld,data16
8Dd8	CLR	rwd	B3d6	RRC	rwd,2
90sd	CPL	rld,rls	B3d7 0r00	SDLL	rld,rw
91is	PUSHL	@rid,rls	B3d8	RL	rwd,1
92sd	SUBL	rld,rls	B3d9 yyyy	SLA	rwd,data16
93is	PUSH	@rid,rws	B3d9 yyyy	SRA	rwd,data16
94sd	LDL	rld,rls	B3dA	RL	rwd,2
95id	POPL	rld,@ris	B3dB 0r00	SDA	rwd,rw

Table 6-5. Z8000 Object Codes (Continued)

Object Code	Instruction	
B3dC	RR	rwd,1
B3dD yyyy	SLAL	rld,data16
B3dD yyyy	SRAL	rld,data16
B3dE	RR	rwd,2
B3dF 0r00	SDAL	rld,rw
B4sd	ADCB	rbd,rbs
B5sd	ADC	rwd,rws
B6sd	SBCB	rbd,rbs
B7sd	SBC	rwd,rws
B8d0 0rs0	TRIB	@rd,@ris,rw
B8d2 0rs0	TRTIB	@rid,@ris,rw
B8d4 0rs0	TRIRB	@rid,@ris,rw
B8d6 0rsE	TRTIRB	@rid,@ris,rw
B8d8 0rs0	TRDB	@rid,@ris,rw
B8dA 0rs0	TRTDB	@rid,@ris,rw
B8dC 0rs0	TRDRB	@rid,@ris,rw
B8dE 0rsE	TRTDRB	@rid,@ris,rw
BAs0 0rdc	CPIB	rbd,@ris,rw,cc
BAs1 0rd0	LDIRB	@rid,@ris,rw
BAs1 0rd8	LDIB	@rid,@ris,rw
BAs2 0rdc	CPSIB	@rid,@ris,rw,cc
BAs4 0rdc	CPIRB	rbd,@ris,rw,cc
BAs6 0rdc	CPSIRB	@rid,@ris,rw,cc
BAs8 0rdc	CPDB	rbd,@ris,rw,cc
BAs9 0rd0	LDDRB	@rid,@ris,rw

Object Code	Instruction	
BAs9 0rd8	LDDB	@rid,@ris,rw
BAsA 0rdc	CPSDB	@rid,@ris,rw,cc
BAsC 0rdc	CPDRB	rbd,@ris,rw,cc
BAsE 0rdc	CPSDRB	@rid,@ris,rw,cc
BBs0 0rdc	CPI	rwd,@ris,rw,cc
BBs1 0rd0	LDIR	@rid,@ris,rw
BBs1 0rd8	LDI	@rid,@ris,rw
BBs2 0rdc	CPSI	@rid,@ris,rw,cc
BBs4 0rdc	CPIR	rwd,@ris,rw,cc
BBs6 0rdc	CPSIR	@rid,@ris,rw,cc
BBs8 0rdc	CPD	rwd,@ris,rw,cc
BBs9 0rd0	LDDR	@rid,@ris,rw
BBs9 0rd8	LDD	@rid,@ris,rw
BBsA 0rdc	CPSD	@rid,@ris,rw,cc
BBsC 0rdc	CPDR	rwd,@ris,rw,cc
BBsE 0rdc	CPSDR	@rid,@ris,rw,cc
BCsd	RRDB	rbd,rbs
BDdb	LDK	rwd,b16
BEsd	RLDB	rbd,rbs
Cdyy	LDB	rbd,data8
Dxxx	CALR	disp
Ecxx	JR	cc,disp
Fr 0ttttttt	DBJNZ	rb,disp
Fr 1ttttttt	DJNZ	rw,disp

DATA SHEETS

This section contains specific electrical and timing data for the following devices:

- Z8001 CPU
- Z8002 CPU

Z8001, Z8002

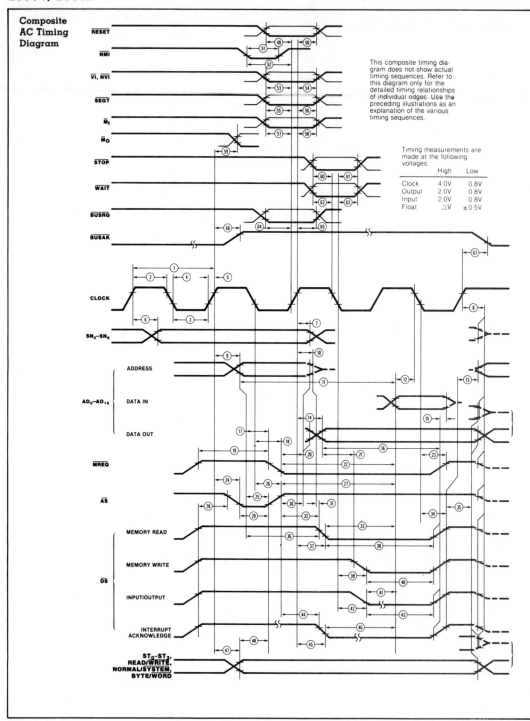

Composite AC Timing Diagram

This composite timing diagram does not show actual timing sequences. Refer to this diagram only for the detailed timing relationships of individual edges. Use the preceding illustrations as an explanation of the various timing sequences.

Timing measurements are made at the following voltages:

	High	Low
Clock	4.0V	0.8V
Output	2.0V	0.8V
Input	2.0V	0.8V
Float	∆V	±0.5V

Data sheets on pages 21-D2 through 21-D4 are reprinted by permission of Zilog, Incorporated.

AC	Number	Symbol	Parameter	Min	Max	Unit
Electrical	1	TcC	Clock Cycle Time	250	2000	ns
Characteristics	2	TwCh	Clock Width (High)	105	2000	ns
	3	TwCl	Clock Width (Low)	105	2000	ns
	4	TfC	Clock Fall Time		20	ns
	5	TrC	Clock Rise Time		20	ns
	6	TdC(SNv)	Clock ↑ to Segment Number Valid (50 pF load)		130	ns
	7	TdC(SNn)	Clock ↑ to Segment Number Not Valid	20		ns
	8	TdC(Bz)	Clock ↑ to Bus Float		65	ns
	9	TdC(A)	Clock ↑ to Address Valid		100	ns
	10	TdC(Az)	Clock ↑ to Address Float		65	ns
	11	TdA(DI)	Address Valid to Data In Required Valid	400		ns
	12	TsDI(C)	Data In to Clock ↓ Setup Time	70		ns
	13	TdDS(A)	DS ↑ to Address Active	80		ns
	14	TdC(DO)	Clock ↑ to Data Out Valid		100	ns
	15	ThDI(DS)	Data In to DS ↑ Hold Time	0		ns
	16	TdDO(DS)	Data Out Valid to DS ↑ Delay	230		ns
	17	TdA(MR)	Address Valid to MREQ ↓ Delay	55		ns
	18	TdC(MR)	Clock ↑ to MREQ ↓ Delay		80	ns
	19	TwMRh	MREQ Width (High)	190		ns
	20	TdMR(A)	MREQ ↓ to Address Not Active	70		ns
	21	TdDO(DSW)	Data Out Valid to DS ↓ (Write) Delay	55		ns
	22	TdMR(DI)	MREQ ↓ to Data In Required Valid	330		ns
	23	TdC(MR)	Clock ↓ to MREQ ↑ Delay		80	ns
	24	TdC(ASf)	Clock ↑ to AS ↓ Delay		80	ns
	25	TdA(AS)	Address Valid to AS ↑ Delay	55		ns
	26	TdC(ASr)	Clock ↓ to AS ↑ Delay		90	ns
	27	TdAS(DI)	AS ↑ to Data In Required Valid	290		ns
	28	TdDS(AS)	DS ↑ to AS ↓ Delay	70		ns
	29	TwAS	AS Width (Low)	80		ns
	30	TdAS(A)	AS ↑ to Address Not Active Delay	60		ns
	31	TdAz(DSR)	Address Float to DS (Read) ↓ Delay	0		ns
	32	TdAS(DSR)	AS ↑ to DS (Read) ↓ Delay	70		ns
	33	TdDSR(DI)	DS (Read) ↓ to Data In Required Valid	155		ns
	34	TdC(DSr)	Clock ↑ to DS ↑ Delay		70	ns
	35	TdDS(DO)	DS ↑ to Data Out and STATUS Not Valid	80		ns
	36	TdA(DSR)	Address Valid to DS (Read) ↓ Delay	120		ns
	37	TdC(DSR)	Clock ↑ to DS (Read) ↓ Delay		120	ns
	38	TwDSR	DS (Read) Width (Low)	275		ns
	39	TdC(DSW)	Clock ↓ to DS (Write) ↓ Delay		95	ns
	40	TwDSW	DS (Write) Width (Low)	160		ns
	41	TdDSI(DI)	DS (Input) ↓ to Data In Required Valid	315		ns
	42	TdC(DSf)	Clock ↓ to DS (I/O) ↓ Delay		120	ns
	43	TwDS	DS (I/O) Width (Low)	400		ns
	44	TdAS(DSA)	AS ↑ to DS (Acknowledge) ↓ Delay	960		ns
	45	TdC(DSA)	Clock ↓ to DS (Acknowledge) ↓ Delay		120	ns
	46	TdDSA(DI)	DS (Ack.) ↓ to Data In Required Delay	420		ns
	47	TdC(S)	Clock ↑ to Status Valid Delay		110	ns
	48	TdS(AS)	Status Valid to AS ↑ Delay	40		ns
	49	TsR(C)	RESET to Clock ↑ Setup Time	180		ns
	50	ThR(C)	RESET to Clock ↑ Hold Time	0		ns
	51	TwNMI	NMI Width (Low)	100		ns
	52	TsNMI(C)	NMI to Clock ↑ Setup Time	140		ns
	53	TsVI(C)	VI, NVI to Clock ↑ Setup Time	110		ns
	54	ThVI(C)	VI, NVI to Clock ↑ Hold Time	0		ns
	55	TsSGT(C)	SEGT to Clock ↑ Setup Time	70		ns
	56	ThSGT(C)	SEGT to Clock ↑ Hold Time	0		ns
	57	TsMI(C)	MI to Clock ↑ Setup Time	180		ns
	58	ThMI(C)	MI to Clock ↑ Hold Time	0		ns
	59	TdC(MO)	Clock ↑ to MO Delay		120	ns
	60	TsSTP(C)	STOP to Clock ↓ Setup Time	140		ns
	61	ThSTP(C)	STOP to Clock ↓ Hold Time	0		ns
	62	TsWT(C)	WAIT to Clock ↓ Setup Time	70		ns
	63	ThWT(C)	WAIT to Clock ↓ Hold Time	0		ns
	64	TsBRQ(C)	BUSRQ to Clock ↑ Setup Time	90		ns
	65	ThBRQ(C)	BUSRQ to Clock ↑ Hold Time	0		ns
	66	TdC(BAKr)	Clock ↑ to BUSAK ↑ Delay		100	ns
	67	TdC(BAKf)	Clock ↑ to BUSAK ↓ Delay		100	ns

Z8001, Z8002

<table>
<tr><td>**Absolute Maximum Ratings**</td><td>Voltages on all inputs and outputs with respect to GND . . . . -0.3 V to +7.0 V

Operating Ambient Temperature . . . . 0°C to +70°C

Storage Temperature . . . . -65°C to +150°C</td><td>Stresses greater than those listed under Absolute Maximum Ratings may cause permanent damage to the device. This is a stress rating only; operation of the device at any condition above those indicated in the operational sections of these specifications is not implied. Exposure to absolute maximum rating conditions for extended periods may affect device reliability.</td></tr>
</table>

<table>
<tr><td>**Standard Test Conditions**</td><td>The characteristics below apply for the following standard test conditions, unless otherwise noted. All voltages are referenced to GND. Positive current flows into the referenced pin. Standard conditions are as follows:

☐ +4.75 V ≤ V_{CC} ≤ +5.25 V

☐ GND = 0 V

☐ 0°C ≤ T_A ≤ +70°C</td><td>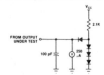

All ac parameters assume a load capacitance of 100 pF max, except for parameter 6 (50 pF max). Timing references between two output signals assume a load difference of 50 pF max.</td></tr>
</table>

DC Characteristics

Symbol	Parameter	Min	Max	Unit	Condition
V_{CH}	Clock Input High Voltage	V_{CC}-0.4	V_{CC}+0.3	V	Driven by External Clock Generator
V_{CL}	Clock Input Low Voltage	-0.3	0.45	V	Driven by External Clock Generator
V_{IH}	Input High Voltage	2.0	V_{CC}+0.3	V	
V_{IL}	Input Low Voltage	-0.3	0.8	V	
V_{OH}	Output High Voltage	2.4		V	I_{OH} = -250 µA
V_{OL}	Output Low Voltage		0.4	V	I_{OL} = +2.0 mA
I_{IL}	Input Leakage		±10	µA	0.4 ≤ V_{IN} ≤ +2.4 V
I_{OL}	Output Leakage		±10	µA	0.4 ≤ V_{OUT} ≤ +2.4 V
I_{CC}	V_{CC} Supply Current		300	mA	

Ordering Information

Part Number	Temperature Range	Number of Pins	Package	Description
Z8001 CPU	0°C to +70°C	48	Ceramic	Segmented 16-Bit Microprocessor
Z8002 CPU	0°C to +70°C	40	Ceramic	Non-Segmented 16-Bit Microprocessor

Chapter 7
THE MOTOROLA MC68000

The MC68000 microprocessor is Motorola's first 16-bit microprocessor. It is the third of the new generation of these devices, having been preceded by Intel's 8086 and Zilog's Z8000.

The MC68000 is not program compatible with Motorola's family of 8-bit microprocessors. Motorola has opted for designing an instruction set which provides maximum power and simplicity rather than compatibility.

The following is a discussion of interesting MC68000 features as compared to similar capabilities of the Z8000 and 8086:

.1) The MC68000 overlaps the fetching of each instruction's object code with the decoding and execution at the two prior instructions to obtain a pipeline effect. The Z8000 uses this approach, but only under certain circumstances. On the other hand, the 8086 performs extensive pipelining using a 6-byte object code pipeline.

2) Both the 8086 and the Z8000 family of microprocessors provide methods of operating the devices in a "simple" system configuration or "complex" system configuration. The 8086 accomplishes this within a single device by having a number of dual-function pins which serve one function in simple systems and another function in complex systems. The Z8000, on the other hand, is supplied in two versions: the Z8001 for complex configurations and the Z8002 for simple configurations. The MC68000 is contained in a 64-pin package and therefore need not attempt to accommodate different complexities of system configurations; it is always capable of operating in what is, effectively, a "maximum" or "complex" system configuration mode.

3) The MC68000 has built-in logic to handle bus access arbitration in multi-CPU configurations. The 8086 and the Z8000 have equivalent logic.

4) The MC68000 can directly access up to 16 million (16M) bytes of memory with its 24-bit Address Bus. This memory space may be expanded to 64M bytes by using the Function Code lines. In comparison, the 8086 can directly address only 64K bytes of memory but can address up to one million bytes using segment registers. The Z8000 is also limited to 64K bytes of directly addressable memory; however, the Z8001 version can address as many as 48M bytes of memory using internal segment registers and external segmentation in a memory management device.

5) The MC68000 can be operated in either a "Supervisor" or a "User" mode. Certain privileged instructions can be executed in Supervisor mode only. Supervisor and User modes also have separate stack pointers. Thus, in program-intensive applications, systems software (executed in Supervisor mode) can be separated from applications programs (executed in User mode). The Z8000 series microprocessors provide similar capabilities. The Supervisor mode of the MC68000 is equivalent to the System mode of the Z8000, while the User mode of the MC68000 is equivalent to the Normal mode of the Z8000. The 8086 offers no similar operating modes.

6) The MC68000 has seventeen 32-bit registers. Eight of the registers are designated as Data registers and can be accessed as either 8, 16, or 32-bit registers. The remaining nine registers are designated as Address registers, with two of these being reserved for use as the stack pointers (Supervisor and User). The Address registers can be accessed as 16 or 32-bit registers. All of the registers can also function as Index registers. In contrast, all of the Z8000 registers are 16-bit registers, although they can be paired to operate as 32-bit registers. The 8086 has only four 16-bit registers plus three separate 16-bit Index registers.

7) The MC68000 provides separate pins for every data line and address output line. This is possible since the MC68000 is contained in a 64-pin package and as a result there is no shortage of pin connections. The Z8000 microprocessors and the 8086 are housed in smaller packages and therefore their data and address lines must share some pins. Thus the Z8000 and 8086 devices multiplex some of the data and address signals on the same pins, and you must provide external logic to demultiplex these signals.

The primary source for the MC68000 is:

MOTOROLA SEMICONDUCTOR, INC.
3501 Ed Bluestein Blvd.
Austin, Texas 78721

The MC68000 is manufactured using N-channel HMOS process technology. The device is contained in a dual inline 64-pin package. A single +5V power supply is required and all signals are TTL-level compatible.

The MC68000 requires an external clock which can be run at a maximum frequency of 8 MHz. The minimum instruction execution time is four clock periods. The maximum number of clock periods for instruction execution is 158 for signed division and multiplication.

THE MC68000 PROGRAMMABLE REGISTERS

Figure 7-1 illustrates the registers provided by the MC68000. There are seventeen 32-bit Data and Address registers, a 32-bit Program Counter (of which only 24 bits are used) **and a 16-bit Status register.** The most significant difference between the registers provided by the MC68000 and those of other 16-bit microprocessors is that the Data and Address registers are all 32 bits wide. By comparison, the 8086 and Z8000 microprocessors use 16-bit wide registers.

The Data registers can be used to handle 8-bit bytes, 16-bit words, or 32-bit long words. The following illustration shows how the various sized operands are positioned within the Data registers.

```
MC68000
DATA
REGISTERS
```

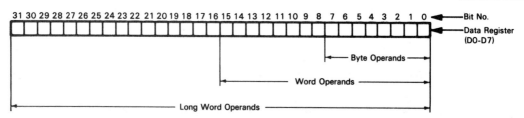

8-bit byte operands occupy bits 0 through 7 of a Data register, while a word operand occupies bits 0 through 15 of a Data register. A long word operand uses all 32 bits of a Data register. When a Data register is used as a source or destination operand, only the appropriate low order portion of the register will be altered by the specified operation; the more significant bits will be unaffected. For example, if you have specified an arithmetic shift left (ASL) instruction with an operand size of eight bits, then only the least significant eight bits (bits 0-7) of the data register will be shifted; bits 8 through 31 will be unchanged by the instruction execution:

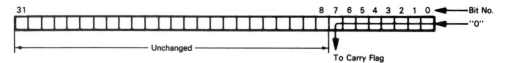

In addition to being used as the source or destination for instructions the Data registers can also be used as index registers or data counters.

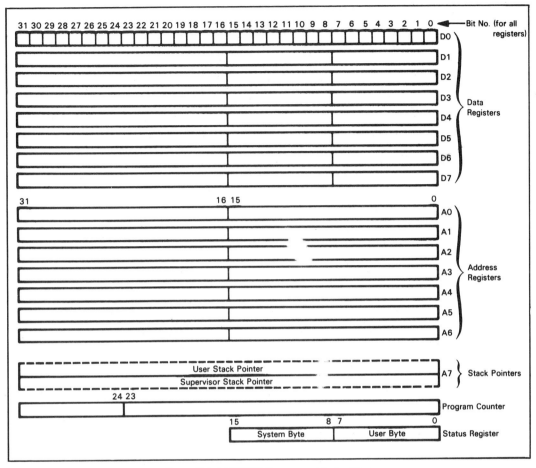

Figure 7-1. MC68000 Programmable Registers

There are seven general purpose Address registers (A0-A6). These registers can handle either 16-bit word or 32-bit long word operands. When you use one of these address registers to provide a source operand, either the low order 16 bits will be used (if a word operand has been specified) or the entire 32 bits will be used (if a long word operand has been specified). If the Address register is used as the source for a word operand, then the more significant 16 bits (bits 16-31) will not be affected. If an Address register is used as the destination operand, however, the contents of the entire register will be affected, regardless of whether a word or long word operand is specified. If you specify a word destination operand for an Address register, that word will be automatically sign-extended to 32 bits before it is loaded into the Address register.

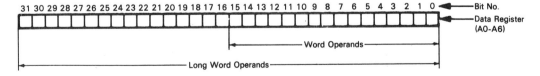

As we have already pointed out, all of the MC68000 Data and Address registers are 32 bits wide versus the 16-bit wide registers of the Z8000 and 8086. Another significant difference between the MC68000 registers and those of the 8086 is the general purpose nature of the MC68000 registers. This is similar to the approach taken in the Z8000 and provides the programmer with increased flexibility. Although there are minor differences between the way the Data and Address (A0-A6) registers handle various data widths, each register type may be used in similar ways. The only dedicated registers are the Stack Pointer registers (A7, Supervisor and User), the Program Counter and the Status register. Let us now examine these dedicated registers.

The MC68000 can be operated in a Supervisor (or system) mode, or in a User (or normal) mode. The state of the S-bit in the Status register determines the mode of operation for the MC68000. Supervisor mode will normally be used by operating system software; User mode will typically be used by application programs. A number of instructions are designated as privileged and can only be executed when the processor is in Supervisor mode. **The Supervisor and User modes also have separate stack pointers as mentioned earlier. As you can see in Figure 7-1, both stack pointers are addressed as Address register A7.** When the MC68000 is operating in the Supervisor state, the User Stack Pointer cannot be referenced. Conversely, when the MC68000 is in the User state, the Supervisor Stack Pointer cannot be referenced.

MC68000 STACK POINTERS

Both the User and Supervisor Stack Pointers operate in the same way: the system stacks are filled from high memory to low memory. On subroutine calls the Program Counter contents are pushed onto the appropriate system stack (Supervisor or User). The Program Counter contents will be pulled from the Stack and restored to the Program Counter on return from subroutines. **Since the Program Counter is a 32-bit register, four bytes (two words) of memory will be required to save the contents of the Program Counter on the Stack. The organization of the Program Counter contents on the System Stack after a subroutine call is illustrated as follows:**

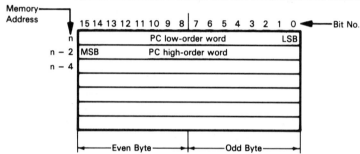

Data that is pushed onto the Stack is always written to a word boundary in memory; that is, to a memory location with an even address. Therefore, when bytes of data must be pushed onto the stack they are written into the high-order half of the memory word, and the low-order half of that word (corresponding to an odd memory address) will be unchanged.

The MC68000 addresses memory as either 8-bit bytes or as a 16-bit word comprised of two bytes. All words must be referenced at even address locations. Otherwise, misalignment could occur when the microprocessor attempts to perform a word operation at an odd-memory address. This same problem exists with any of the 16-bit microprocessors, but the MC68000 is the only microprocessor which automatically checks to ensure that all word references are done at even memory addresses. If a word reference is made to an odd memory address, the MC68000 begins an exception processing sequence, which will be described later.

The following illustration shows how bytes are organized in memory:

```
15 14 13 12 11 10 9 8  7  6  5  4  3  2  1  0  ◀──── Bit No.
┌────────────────────┬────────────────────┐
│     Byte FFFFFE     │     Byte FFFFFF     │  High Memory
├────────────────────┼────────────────────┤
│     Byte FFFFFC     │     Byte FFFFFD     │
├────────────────────┼────────────────────┤
│     Byte FFFFFA     │     Byte FFFFFB     │
├────────────────────┼────────────────────┤
│     Byte FFFFF8     │     Byte FFFFF9     │
├────────────────────┼────────────────────┤
│     Byte FFFFF6     │     Byte FFFFF7     │
├────────────────────┼────────────────────┤
│     Byte FFFFF4     │     Byte FFFFF5     │
└────────────────────┴────────────────────┘
┌────────────────────┬────────────────────┐
│     Byte 000006     │     Byte 000007     │
├────────────────────┼────────────────────┤
│     Byte 000004     │     Byte 000005     │
├────────────────────┼────────────────────┤
│     Byte 000002     │     Byte 000003     │
├────────────────────┼────────────────────┤
│     Byte 000000     │     Byte 000001     │  Low Memory
└────────────────────┴────────────────────┘
```

You will note that the first byte in memory (address 000000) occupies the most significant byte half of a memory word. When words are stored in memory, they are only addressable at even memory addresses, as we have discussed. This can be illustrated as follows:

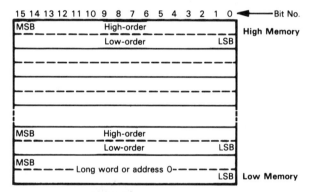

When 32-bit long words (such as 32-bit addresses) are stored in memory, they occupy two adjacent 16-bit memory locations or four bytes. The high-order word of the long words is stored at the higher memory location, as illustrated below:

The MC68000 provides a 16-bit Status register which is divided into two 8-bit bytes: the System byte and the User byte. Figure 7-2 shows the bit assignments for the Status register. The Carry, Overflow, Zero, and Negative bits are the standard ones provided by most microprocessors.

MC68000 STATUS REGISTER

The Carry (C) bit is set if there is a carry out of the most significant bit following an addition operation, or if a borrow is required from the most significant bit during a subtraction. This status bit is also modified by certain shift and rotate instructions.

The Overflow (V) bit is the exclusive-OR of the carries out of the most significant and next higher-order bits of the operand following arithmetic operations. The setting of the overflow bit signifies a magnitude overflow since the result cannot be represented in the specified operand size.

The Zero (Z) bit is set whenever the result of an operation is zero; it is reset otherwise.

The Negative (N) bit is the equivalent of the Sign status bit provided in most microprocessors. The Negative bit is equal to the value of the most significant result bit following arithmetic operations. If a signed binary arithmetic operation is being performed, a Negative status of 0 specifies a positive or zero result, whereas a Negative status of 1 specifies a negative result.

The Extend (X) bit is used in multiprecision arithmetic operations. When it is affected by an instruction, it is set to the same state as the Carry bit.

The three most significant bits (bits 5, 6, and 7) of the User byte of the Status register are not currently assigned and will always be zero.

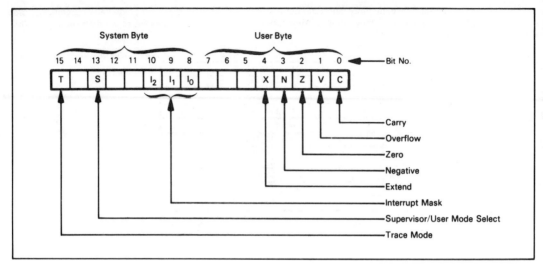

Figure 7-2. MC68000 Status Register Bit Assignments

The System byte of the Status register contains status information that is system-related. The User byte, on the other hand, contains the Condition Code status bits (X, N, Z, V, and C) that are instruction or program related. Bits in the System byte of the Status register can only be altered when the MC68000 is in the Supervisor mode.

The three least significant bits (bits 8, 9, and 10) of the Status register's System byte form the interrupt mask. The MC68000 provides seven levels of interrupts. The level of any given interrupt is decoded from the signal's three interrupt pins, which we will describe later. The interrupt priorities are numbered from 1 to 7, with level 7 having the highest priority, as shown in the following illustration:

Interrupt Level	Interrupt Mask		
	I_2	I_1	I_0
Level 7	1	1	1
Level 6	1	1	0
Level 5	1	0	1
Level 4	1	0	0
Level 3	0	1	1
Level 2	0	1	0
Level 1	0	0	1
Level 0	0	0	0

Highest priority (Non-maskable) ← Level 7

Lowest Priority ← Level 1
No Interrupt Request ← Level 0

The level 7 interrupt is nonmaskable and thus cannot be disabled. Level 0 represents a "no interrupt request" condition. Levels 1 through 6 are the mask-enabled levels. For example, if you set the mask to 100 then only levels 5, 6, and 7 will be enabled; interrupt levels 1 through 4 are disabled and interrupt requests of those levels will be ignored.

Bit 13 of the Status register is the S-bit which specifies whether the MC68000 is in the Supervisor or User mode of operation. When this bit is 1, the MC68000 is in the Supervisor mode, and when it is 0 the microprocessor is in the User mode. Recall that the Supervisor and User modes have their own separate stack pointers; also, certain privileged instructions can only be executed in the Supervisor mode.

The most significant bit of the Status register is the Trace mode (T) flag. If this bit is 0 then the MC68000 operates normally. If this bit is 1, however, the microprocessor is in the trace mode of operation. The trace mode is the approximate software equivalent of a hardware implemented single-step mode. After each instruction is executed in the trace mode, a trap is forced so that a debugging program can monitor the results of that instruction's execution.

Table 7-1. MC68000 Addressing Mode Summary

Mode	Address Formation
Register Direct Addressing Data Register Direct Address Register Direct	EA = DREGn EA = AREGn
Register Indirect Addressing Register Indirect Postincrement Register Indirect Predecrement Register Indirect Register Indirect with Offset Indexed Register Indirect with Offset	EA = (AREGn) EA = (AREGn); Increment (AREGn) Decrement (AREGn); EA = (AREGn) EA = (AREGn) + data16 EA = (AREGn) + (XREGn) + data8
Implied Register Addressing	EA = SR, SP, PC
Absolute Addressing Absolute Short Absolute Long	EA = (Next word) EA = (Next 2 words)
Program Counter Relative Addressing Relative with Offset Relative with Index and Offset	EA = (PC) + data16 EA = (PC) + (XREG) + data8
Immediate Data Addressing Immediate Quick Immediate	Data = Next word or words Data inherent in instruction word
EA = Effective Address DREGn = Any Data Register AREGn = Any Address Register XREGn = Any Data or Address Register used as an Index Register ( ) = Contents of	data8 = 8-bit offset (displacement) data16 = 16-bit offset (displacement) SR = Status Register SP = Stack Pointer (User or Supervisor) PC = Program Counter

MC68000 ADDRESSING MODE SUMMARY

The MC68000 provides six basic types of addressing modes. Variations within these types allow a total of fourteen different modes, as summarized in Table 7-1. At this point, we will look only briefly at the addressing modes and how they utilize the registers of the MC68000. We will discuss each of the addressing modes in detail later, just prior to our description of the instruction set.

Most of the addressing modes use the 32-bit Address registers either directly or indirectly to generate the effective address. The Data registers can be used as sources for addresses in the direct addressing mode, and they can also be used as Index registers in some of the indirect addressing modes. The indirect addressing modes include post-incrementing or pre-decrementing of an Address register; this capability makes it easy to implement stacks and queues in memory.

A number of MC68000 instructions use the implied addressing mode; that is, they make implicit reference to either the Program Counter (PC), Stack Pointer (SP) or Status Register (SR). For example, Branch, Jump, and Return instructions will all reference the Program Counter and Stack Pointer during their execution.

Absolute addressing modes do not utilize the Data or Address registers, but instead form the effective address using data that follows the instruction word in the program. Program Counter relative addressing can use either a displacement or a displacement plus the contents of an Index register to form the effective address. The Index register can be any of the Data or Address registers.

Most instructions can utilize any of the addressing modes, and address formation is always the same regardless of the instruction operation itself. These factors do much to enhance the flexibility and power of the instruction set without making the instruction set difficult to understand.

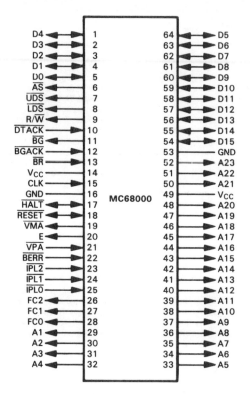

Pin Name	Description	Type
D0-D15	Data Bus	Bidirectional, Tristate
A1-A23	Address Bus	Output, Tristate
$\overline{AS}$	Address Strobe	Output, Tristate
R/$\overline{W}$	Read/Write Control	Output, Tristate
$\overline{UDS}$, $\overline{LDS}$	Upper, Lower Data Strobes	Output, Tristate
$\overline{DTACK}$	Data Transfer Acknowledge	Input
FC0, FC1, FC2	Function Code (status) Outputs	Output, Tristate
$\overline{IPL0}$, $\overline{IPL1}$, $\overline{IPL2}$	Interrupt Requests	Input
$\overline{BERR}$	Bus Error	Input
$\overline{HALT}$	Halt Processor Operation	Input/Output
$\overline{RESET}$	Reset Processor or Reset External Devices	Input/Output
CLK	System Clock	Input
$\overline{BR}$	Bus Request	Input
$\overline{BG}$	Bus Grant	Output
$\overline{BGACK}$	Bus Grant Acknowledge	Input
E	Enable (Clock) Output	Output
$\overline{VMA}$	Valid Memory Address	Output, Tristate
$\overline{VPA}$	Valid Peripheral Address	Input
V$_{CC}$, GND	Power (+5 V) and Ground	

Figure 7-3. MC68000 Pins and Signal Assignments

MC68000 PINS AND SIGNALS

Figure 7-3 illustrates the signals and pin assignments for the MC68000. At this point, we will briefly discuss each of these signals to provide an overview of how the MC68000 operates. We will defer a detailed discussion of signal and timing interactions until later in this chapter.

D0-D15 is the bidirectional 16-bit Data Bus. A1-A23 is the output 24-bit address bus. Because the MC68000 is contained in a 64-pin package, the data and address lines need not be multiplexed onto the same pins, as is the case with the 8086 and Z8000 microprocessors. Note that **A0, the least significant bit of the Address Bus, is not output;** this bit is used internal to the MC68000, in conjunction with the data size specification of each instruction, to generate the $\overline{\text{UDS}}$ and $\overline{\text{LDS}}$ signals.

The $\overline{\text{UDS}}$ **(Upper Data Strobe) and** $\overline{\text{LDS}}$ **(Lower Data Strobe) signals determine whether data is being transferred on either the upper (most significant) byte, the lower (least significant) byte or both bytes of the 16-bit data bus.** Table 7-2 **defines the significance of the** $\overline{\text{UDS}}$**,** $\overline{\text{LDS}}$**, and Read/Write (R/W) signals in relation to the data bus.** When $\overline{\text{UDS}}$ is low, data from memory with an even address is accessed and the byte of data is transferred on D8-D15. When $\overline{\text{LDS}}$ is low, a byte of data located at an odd address is accessed and the transfer occurs on D0-D7. When the MC68000 is transferring a word of data (for example, when fetching an instruction) then both $\overline{\text{UDS}}$ and $\overline{\text{LDS}}$ will be low and all 16 of the data lines (D0-D15) will be used for the transfer.

Table 7-2. MC68000 Data Bus Control Signal Summary

$\overline{\text{UDS}}$	$\overline{\text{LDS}}$	R/$\overline{\text{W}}$	D8-D15	D0-D7	Operation
High	High	—			—
Low	Low	High	Data bits 8-15	Data bits 0-7	Word Read
High	Low	High		Data bits 0-7	Byte Read
Low	High	High	Data bits 8-15		Byte Read
Low	Low	Low	Data bits 8-15	Data bits 0-7	Word Write
High	Low	Low	Data bits 0-7	Data bits 0-7	Byte Write
Low	High	Low	Data bits 8-15	Data bits 8-15	Byte Write

☐ No valid data output or input

Table 7-3. MC68000 Function Code Summary

FC2	FC1	FC0	Machine Cycle Type
0	0	0	
0	0	1	User data memory access
0	1	0	User program memory access
0	1	1	
1	0	0	
1	0	1	Supervisor data memory access
1	1	0	Supervisor program memory access
1	1	1	Interrupt acknowledge

☐ Reserved, currently undefined

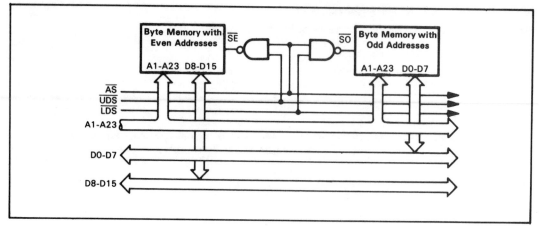

Figure 7-4. MC68000 Interface to Memory

The memory interface implied by the $\overline{\text{UDS}}$ and $\overline{\text{LDS}}$ signals is illustrated in Figure 7-4. Byte-oriented memory with even addresses will be selected by $\overline{\text{UDS}}$, and that memory's data lines are connected to D8-D15. $\overline{\text{LDS}}$ references byte memory with odd addresses, and its data will be applied to D0-D7 of the Data Bus. The $\overline{\text{AS}}$ line, shown in Figure 7-4, is the Address Strobe which is pulsed low to indicate that a valid data address is being output on the Address Bus (A1-A23).

MC68000
MEMORY
INTERFACE

$\overline{\text{DTACK}}$ is the Data Transfer Acknowledge input signal. This signal must be asserted by external logic during every read or write cycle. When the MC68000 is performing a read or write cycle, it will automatically insert wait states in the cycle until the $\overline{\text{DTACK}}$ signal is received. This approach is thus the inverse of the logic used by most other microprocessors: for example, both the Z8000 and 8086 have a "wait" input which external logic can use to extend a read or write cycle — if the wait input is not asserted, the read/write cycle will finish normally. The MC68000 approach provides for completely asynchronous bus operations that can interface to any type of device regardless of that device's speed. This approach specifies, however, that **all devices in the system must include sufficient logic to generate the $\overline{\text{DTACK}}$ signal.**

FC0, FC1, and FC2 are the Function Code or processor cycle status outputs. These outputs identify the type of bus activity currently being performed by the MC68000, as summarized in Table 7-3. The Function Code outputs are valid whenever $\overline{\text{AS}}$ is true. **Five different types of cycles are currently defined: access to either supervisor data memory, supervisor program memory, user data memory, or user program memory, and interrupt acknowledge cycles.** Whenever the MC68000 is involved in fetching instructions, it is considered as accessing program memory. All other memory accesses are identified as data memory accesses. The Function Code outputs could be used to separate memory into the four different categories — user versus supervisor and program versus data. Thus, by using the FC outputs an MC68000 system could directly address up to 64 megabytes of memory, with 16 megabytes devoted to each of the four defined memory categories.

IPL0, IPL1, and IPL2 are the interrupt request inputs. These three inputs are decoded internally by the MC68000 to determine the priority level of the interrupt request. You will recall from our earlier discussion of the Status register that there is a 3-bit interrupt mask which determines what level of interrupt request will be permitted. When all three interrupt inputs are low, a non-maskable interrupt (level 7, which is the highest priority) is present. This level is always recognized by the MC68000. When all three of the interrupt inputs are high, it indicates that no interrupt is being requested.

$\overline{\text{BERR}}$ is the Bus Error input. When this signal is low the MC68000 performs a sequence (exception processing sequence) similar to that which it executes in response to an interrupt request. The purpose of the $\overline{\text{BERR}}$ signal is to inform the MC68000 when an external device has not responded (using the $\overline{\text{DTACK}}$ input) within an expected amount of time during a read or write operation. Since the data transfer handshaking approach used by the MC68000 requires all external devices to actively respond to every data transfer, the system should include a mechanism to ensure that the processor is not hung up indefinitely by a device that fails to respond. Thus external logic should be provided to monitor bus activity and which would utilize the $\overline{\text{BERR}}$ signal to inform the MC68000 of a "failure to respond" condition. This logic would separate the preceding cause of a bus error from other causes, such as might be generated with a Memory Management Unit (MMU). The MMU would generate BERR if an attempt was made to access protected memory.

As we have already mentioned, the reaction of the MC68000 to the Bus Error input is similar to the interrupt request response. We will describe this response, termed "exception processing," in detail later in this chapter. Essentially, exception processing causes processor status information to be saved, and then allows the processor to execute a program to analyze the cause of the error. The MC68000 also provides a hardware-oriented response to a bus error: **if the HALT signal is asserted in conjunction with the BERR signal, the MC68000 will automatically retry the bus cycle that produced the error.**

The HALT signal performs several functions. As we mentioned in the preceding paragraph, **it can be used in conjunction with the BERR signal to initiate rerunning of bus cycles** that produced bus errors. When used alone, it places the MC68000 in a Halt state where the processor is essentially inactive until the HALT signal is negated. This is the familiar Halt function provided by most microprocessors.

The HALT signal is also used in conjunction with the RESET signal to intialize the MC68000. One unusual aspect of the RESET signal is the fact that it is also an ouput signal; **the MC68000 provides a RESET instruction which, when executed, causes a low-going pulse to be output on the RESET pin.** Thus, you can execute a RESET instruction and use it to initialize other devices in the system without resetting the processor.

HALT, like RESET, is an output signal. If the processor ceases executing instructions — for example, if a double bus fault condition occurs — the MC68000 will output HALT low. External logic can be then used to detect this potentially catastrophic condition.

CLK is the single TTL-level compatible clock from which all MC68000 internal timing is derived.

BR (Bus Request), **BG** (Bus Grant), and **BGACK** (Bus Grant Acknowledge) are all bus arbitration signals. These signals are used in systems where other devices, such as DMA controllers on other processors, require control of the System Busses. **External devices request access to the System Bus by asserting the BR input. The MC68000** will then always relinquish the bus after it has completed the current bus cycle. It **will also output Bus Grant (BG) low to let the requesting device know that the bus will become available at the end of the current cycle.** However, as we will see when we discuss the bus arbitration timing in detail, external devices or logic must monitor more than just the Bus Grant signal to determine when the bus will actually be available. **The Bus Grant Acknowledge (BGACK) signal must be input to the MC68000 by the device requesting the bus once that device takes control of the bus.** BGACK must be held low until the device has completed its bus access operations. Thus BGACK is essentially a "bus busy" signal that lets the MC68000 (and other devices in the system) know that the bus is unavailable.

The next three signals — E, VPA, and VMA — are provided so that the MC68000 can be easily interfaced to the standard and widely available 6800 family devices. 6800-based systems use a synchronous method of effecting transfers of data throughout the system. To accomplish this a system clock Enable (E) signal must be distributed to all 6800 devices in the system so that all relevant data transfers may be synchronized to this clock signal. **Thus the Enable (E) signal provided by the MC68000 is the equivalent of the 6800 E signal.** The frequency of E is equal to one-tenth that of the CLK input to the MC68000: the period for E is equal to 10 CLK periods — E is low for six CLK cycles and is high for four CLK cycles.

The Valid Peripheral Address (VPA) signal is used by 6800-type devices in the system to inform the MC68000 that a 6800-type data transfer is required. You must provide address decoding logic in the system that determines when a 6800-type device is being accessed and that generates the VPA signal. **When the MC68000 receives the VPA signal, it alters the data transfer timing so that it is synchronous with the Enable (E) signal. The MC68000 will then output the Valid Memory Address (VMA) signal at the appropriate time.** VMA is another 6800-type signal and will only be output if the VPA input signal has been asserted at the beginning of a data transfer operation. We will defer a detailed discussion of these three signals until later when we describe interfacing between the MC68000 and the 6800-family devices.

MC68000 TIMING AND BUS OPERATION

The basic timing for the MC68000 is quite straightforward: instruction execution consists of a combination of internal cycles and bus access cycles. The total number of clock cycles required for each instruction is defined in the instruction set summary tables later in this chapter. The number of clock cycles required to perform operations internal to the MC68000 are of little interest to other devices in the system since these operations are transparent to external logic. It is only when the MC68000 requires access to the system bus for such operations as instruction fetching, operand fetching, and operand storing that external devices become involved with MC68000 timing.

The MC68000 uses memory mapped I/O. Therefore, bus accesses for data transfers between the MC68000 and

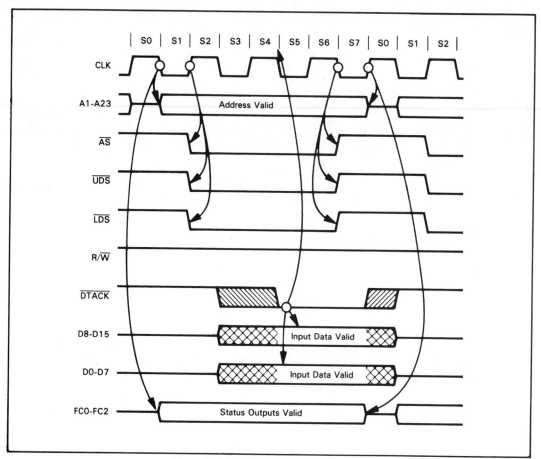

Figure 7-5. MC68000 Read Word Timing

memory are the same as for those between the MC68000 and I/O devices. **Data transfers are defined as either read or write operations,** with the transfer of data into the MC68000 defined as a "read" and the transfer of data from the MC68000 to external logic defined as a "write."

Figure 7-5 illustrates the timing for a read word operation. For purposes of the following timing discussions, each clock period is sub-divided into two states.

MC68000 READ TIMING

During state 0 (S0) of the read word cycle, the address and data busses are in the high impedence state — the MC68000 is not using the System Bus at this point. Address information for the memory or I/O location is output at the beginning of state 1 (S1) on the Address Bus (A1-A23). Processor cycle status information is also output at this point on the FC0-FC2 pins. The Address Strobe (AS) signal is asserted at the beginning of state 2 and can be used by external logic to latch the information on the Address Bus. Simultaneously, the Upper Data Strobe (UDS) and Lower Data Strobe (LDS) signals are asserted to enable selection of both the most significant byte and least significant byte of a 16-bit word. You will note that these signals are not actually data "strobes" since there is no data ready to be input or output at this point; it is more accurate to think of them as memory select signals selecting the upper and/or lower byte of a 16-bit memory word. R/W is normally asserted, so this output does not change during a read cycle.

The MC68000 now waits for the addressed memory or I/O device to present its data on the Data Bus. When the data is ready, the external device must assert Data Acknowledge (DTACK) to the MC68000. The MC68000 expects DTACK and the requested data to be present by state 5 (S5). If DTACK is not present by S5, Wait states (SW) will be automatically inserted into the read timing cycle as illustrated in Figure 7-6. Once $\overline{DTACK}$ is true, the read cycle continues with S5. At the end of state 6 (S6), the $\overline{AS}$, $\overline{UDS}$, and $\overline{LDS}$ signals are negated. At this point the incoming data on D0-D15 is latched into an internal MC68000 register. External devices can use the negative-to-positive transition of $\overline{AS}$, $\overline{UDS}$, or $\overline{LDS}$ as the indication that they can remove data from the Data Bus. The MC68000 maintains the address information and function code information through the end of state 7 (S7) to allow for signal skew within the system. Note that when the external device senses that the MC68000 has captured the data from the Data Bus (by sensing the high-going transition of $\overline{AS}$, $\overline{UDS}$, or $\overline{LDS}$) that device must return $\overline{DTACK}$ high immediately so that it does not interfere with the beginning of the next bus cycle.

If you refer to the Wait state insertion that can occur during read operations, as illustrated in Figure 7-6, you will see that the Wait states occur between state 4 and state 5. The MC68000 will maintain valid address output on the address Bus and will hold $\overline{AS}$, $\overline{UDS}$, and $\overline{LDS}$ low during any Wait states for as long as necessary until $\overline{DTACK}$ is asserted. You should note that there will always be an even number of Wait states inserted; all MC68000 operations are based on a complete CLK cycle and there are two "states" per CLK cycle.

| MC68000 |
| WAIT STATE |

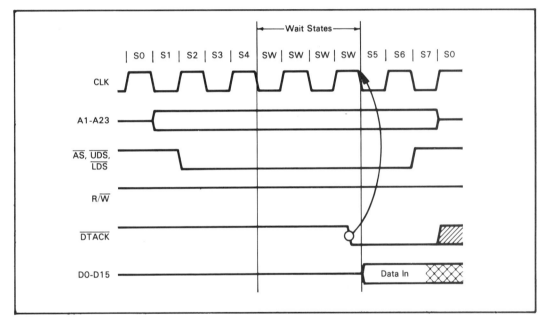

Figure 7-6. MC68000 Wait States During Read Operations

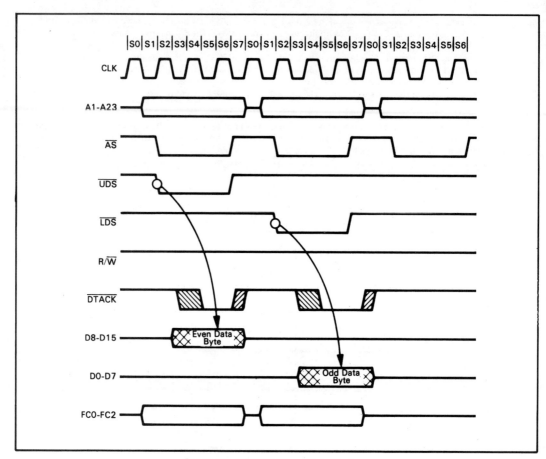

Figure 7-7. MC68000 Read Byte Timing

Timing for a read byte operation is illustrated in Figure 7-7. This figure shows first an even data byte and then an odd data byte being read by the MC68000. As you can see, the only difference between this timing and that illustrated for a read word operation in Figure 7-5 is that only $\overline{\text{UDS}}$ or $\overline{\text{LDS}}$ is asserted and only eight lines of the data bus are utilized when you are reading a byte: $\overline{\text{UDS}}$ is asserted and data is on lines D8-D15 when reading a byte located at an even address and $\overline{\text{LDS}}$ is asserted and data is on lines D0-D7 when reading a byte located at an odd address. You should not be misled by Figure 7-7 into thinking that the MC68000 always reads two consecutive bytes — an even byte and an odd byte. We have simply shown these two read operations consecutively to illustrate timing for both. Again, if the MC68000 requires a word of data, it will utilize the entire 16-bit Data Bus and read the full word in one operation.

Timing for a write word operation is illustrated in Figure 7-8. As was the case with read operations, the address for the memory location or I/O device is output at the beginning of S1 along with the appropriate function code indicating the current type of processor bus cycle. If the Data Bus was utilized by the MC68000 in the preceding cycle, the processor returns all of the data outputs to the high impedence state during S1 and then asserts the Address Strobe (AS) signal and outputs the Read/Write (R/W) signal low. Once again, AS can be used to latch the address externally, and the R/W signal indicates to memory or I/O devices that the MC68000 will be placing data onto the Data Bus. No further signal activity occurs until the MC68000 outputs the data on D0-D15 at the beginning of state 3 (S3). The Upper and Lower Data Strobe signals (UDS, LDS) are asserted at the beginning of state 4 (S4). During write operations, these two signals can be used as "strobe" signals since they indicate that the data on the Data Bus is valid. If the write operation is to proceed unimpeded, external logic must respond to the data strobe signals by asserting the Data Acknowledge (DTACK) signal by the beginning of state 7 (S7). **If DTACK is not true by the beginning of S7, Wait states are automatically inserted by the MC68000, as illustrated in Figure 7-9. This "slow write" operation is the same as was illustrated for read operations except that the Wait states are inserted at a different point in the cycle.**

The MC68000 outputs the data on D0-D15 through the entire write operation. The Address Strobe (AS) and data strobes (UDS, LDS) are negated at the beginning of state 9 (S9) and the Read/Write (R/W) signal is returned high at the end of S9. At that point, the Address Bus, Data Bus, and Function Code outputs are all returned to their high impedance state to free the System Bus for other uses. The external memory or I/O device that was accessed by the write operation

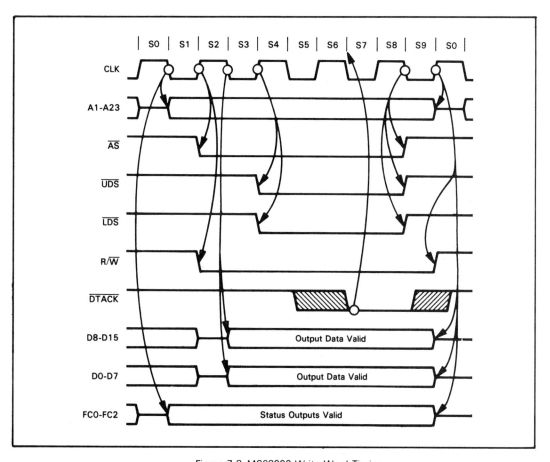

Figure 7-8. MC68000 Write Word Timing

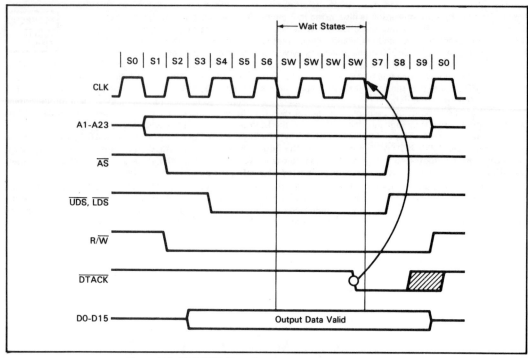

Figure 7-9. MC68000 Wait States During Write Operations

must release the Data Acknowledge (DTACK) signal after it has detected the positive-to-negative transition of the address or data strobe signals. This ensures that a subsequent bus cycle will not be impeded.

Timing for write byte operation is illustrated in Figure 7-10. As you can see, the only difference between this operation and the write word timing illustrated in Figure 7-8 is the fact that only UDS or LDS is output while a byte is being written.

MC68000 READ-MODIFY-WRITE TIMING

The read-modify-write cycle provided by the MC68000 is unusual among microprocessors, although it is frequently provided by minicomputers. The MC68000 uses the read-modify-write cycle only during the execution of the Test and Set (TAS) instruction. This instruction reads a byte of data, sets condition codes according to the contents of that byte, sets bit 7 of the byte, and then writes it back into memory. The TAS instruction is intended to be used as a means of providing "safe" communication between microprocessors in a multi-processor system. Safe communication is ensured with the TAS instruction since the read-modify-write cycle is non-interruptable.

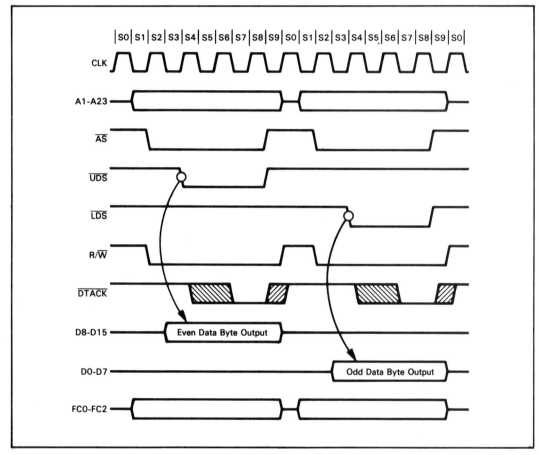

Figure 7-10. MC68000 Write Byte Timing

Figure 7-11 illustrates the timing for a read-modify-write cycle. As you can see, it simply consists of the read-byte cycle followed by a standard write-byte cycle. There is one intervening clock period (S8, S9) between the read and write cycles and it is during this interval that the byte of data is modified internally for the subsequent write. Just as was the case with standard read and write, external logic must reply with DTACK at the proper time or else Wait states will automatically be inserted to lengthen the read or write operations.

Note that in Figure 7-11 we have shown that either UDS or LDS will be asserted during the read-modify-write operation. This is because the TAS instruction always operates on a byte of data, never on a word of data.

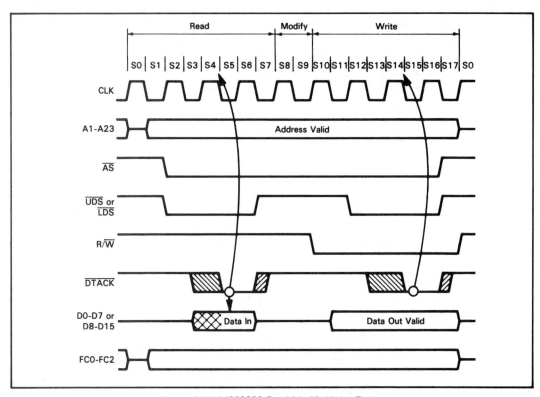

Figure 7-11. MC68000 Read-Modify-Write Timing

The MC68000 RESET OPERATION

The MC68000 has an asynchronous reset input. You reset the microprocessor by holding the RESET and HALT signals low for at least 100 milliseconds. After the RESET and HALT signals are returned high, the MC68000 executes the following operations:

1) The MC68000 reads the first four words from memory (bytes 000000 through 000007) and uses the contents of these locations to load the System Stack Pointer (SSP) and Program Counter (PC). The contents of these eight bytes from the beginning of memory are used as follows:

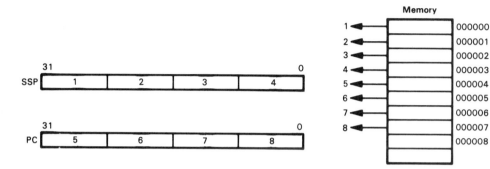

2) The interrupt mask in the Status register is set to all ones so that only level 7 interrupts will be enabled. No other registers are affected by the reset operation: therefore, when a reset is performed after applying power to the MC68000, all registers except SSP, PC, and the Status register will contain indeterminate values.

3) Program execution begins, with the first instruction being fetched from the location indicated by the value loaded into the Program Counter.

The sequence we just described is the typical externally-initiated reset operation similar to that provided by most microprocessors. You will recall, however, that the RESET pin is bidirectional; when the MC68000 executes a Reset instruction, a low-going pulse is sent out on the RESET pin. This software RESET pulse is low for 124 CLK cycles. This instruction has no effect on the internal state of the MC68000, therefore none of its internal registers are affected. In this case, the RESET signal is being used to reset all other devices within the system under the control of the MC68000.

THE MC68000 HALT STATE

The MC68000 can be forced into a Halt state, at which time its Address Bus, Data Bus, and Function Code outputs (FC0-FC2) are placed in the high-impedance state. This state is similar to the Hold state of the 8086 and the Stop state of the Z8000. The Halt state can be used to disable the MC68000 and thus free the System Busses for such activities as direct memory access or multi-processor operations. However, since the MC68000 includes an efficient bus arbitration system, it is more likely that the Halt state will be used to implement a hardware single-step mode.

Figure 7-12 illustrates the timing for the Halt operation. If the MC68000 is in the middle of a bus cycle when the HALT signal is input low, the bus cycle continues to its normal completion. At the end of the cycle the Address Bus, Data Bus, and FC0-FC2 signals are all placed in the high impedance state and the MC68000 halts. While it is in this halted condition, the processor does nothing — it merely waits for the HALT signal to return high. Note that the MC68000 provides no halt acknowledge indication to external logic.

However, while the MC68000 is in the Halt state, its bus arbitration circuitry still operates. Since the MC68000 will not be using the bus while it is halted, any bus request made to the MC68000 will be granted immediately. We will defer a detailed discussion of the bus arbitration circuitry until later.

When the HALT signal is returned high, the MC68000 exits the Halt state within two clock cycles and can then begin another bus cycle.

The execution of most MC68000 instructions requires multiple bus cycles to fetch the instruction and operands and, possibly, to store results of the instruction. **Since the MC68000 will respond to the HALT input upon completion of any bus cycle, the halt sequence can occur between two instructions or in the middle of a single instruction. Therefore, if you are using the HALT input to implement a single-step mode of operation, you will be single-stepping by bus cycles rather than single-stepping by instructions.** If you want to single-step by instructions, you

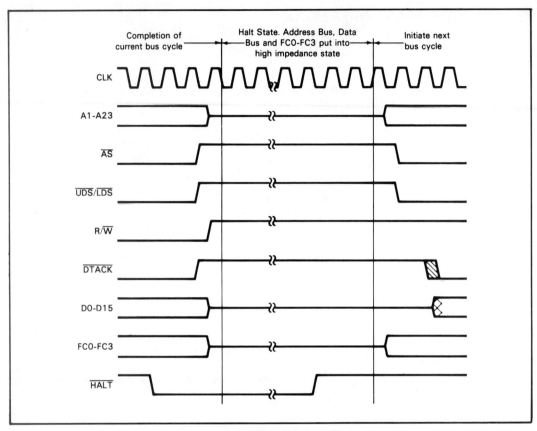

Completion of
current bus cycle

Halt State. Address Bus, Data
Bus and FC0-FC3 put into
high impedance state

Initiate next
bus cycle

CLK

A1-A23

$\overline{AS}$

$\overline{UDS}/\overline{LDS}$

R/$\overline{W}$

$\overline{DTACK}$

D0-D15

FC0-FC3

$\overline{HALT}$

Figure 7-12. MC68000 Halt State Timing

must use the Trace function of the MC68000. This function is implemented by setting the T-bit in the Supervisor byte of the Status register. We will describe the Trace operation in detail later.

The $\overline{HALT}$ signal is bidirectional and will be asserted by the MC68000 if it initiates a Halt state rather than having external logic cause the Halt. The MC68000 will automatically enter the Halt state if there is a double-bus fault (we will discuss bus errors and double-bus faults in detail later). If the MC68000 has automatically entered the Halt state, the processor will output $\overline{HALT}$ low and remain in this halted condition until an externally initiated reset operation is performed using $\overline{RESET}$. Thus, when $\overline{HALT}$ is output low by the MC68000, it indicates a catastrophic failure.

THE MC68000 STOP STATE

Following execution of the STOP instruction, the MC68000 microprocessor will enter a Stop state. The STOP instruction is permitted only when the MC68000 is operating in the Supervisor mode as indicated by the S-bit in the Status register. The Stop state is similar to the HALT state which we just discussed, since the microprocessor essentially does nothing while in this state. When the STOP instruction is executed, the Status register is loaded with a new value contained in the instruction. Next, the Program Counter is advanced to point to the next instruction and the MC68000 stops.

No special signal or status is output by the MC68000 to identify that it is in the Stop state. The Stop state is ended by one of the exception conditions such as an interrupt request or a $\overline{RESET}$. When an exception condition is detected by the MC68000, it leaves the Stop state and will process the exception condition.

THE MC68000 BUS CYCLE RERUN TIMING

As we mentioned earlier, the MC68000 can respond in two ways to a System Bus error, indicated by the assertion of BERR. It can perform exception processing (which we will describe later), or it can attempt to rerun the bus cycle which caused the bus error indication. If BERR is asserted by itself, then the exception processing (or software) method of handling the bus error is taken. **However, if the BERR signal is accompanied by the HALT signal then the MC68000 recognizes this as a request to rerun the bus cycle.**

Figure 7-13 illustrates the timing for the bus cycle rerun operation. In this figure, we have shown a write cycle in progress, with the MC68000 waiting for the external device to respond with DTACK so that the cycle can be completed. Instead of the expected acknowledge signal, external logic forces both the BERR and HALT signals low to indicate that the cycle was not successfully completed and that the MC68000 should rerun the cycle.

The MC68000 proceeds to complete the cycle that was in progress and then enters the HALT state. The Address Bus, Data Bus, and Function Code outputs are all placed in the high impedance state and the microprocessor remains halted until both BERR and HALT are negated. Note that BERR should be negated before HALT is negated to prevent the MC68000 from interpreting the isolated BERR signal as another bus error — one that is expected to be handled in software. After HALT returns high, the MC68000 will proceed to repeat the cycle that was in progress when the rerun request was received; i.e., the same address, data, and function code information that was used in the previous bus cycle will be repeated.

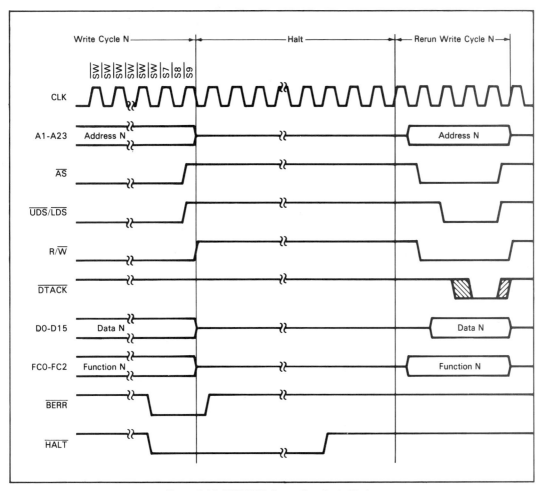

Figure 7-13. MC68000 Rerun Bus Cycle Timing

Figure 7-13 shows the successful completion of the rerun cycle with $\overline{\text{DTACK}}$ being received in the expected interval. Of course, this will not always be the case — the attempt to rerun the bus cycle might also result in a bus error. **External logic can continue to request that the cycle be rerun an unlimited number of times, using the combination of $\overline{\text{BERR}}$ and $\overline{\text{HALT}}$.** You should note, however, that if you are using the software exception processing method of handling the bus error ($\overline{\text{BERR}}$ asserted alone without $\overline{\text{HALT}}$), then two successive bus errors are treated as a catastrophic error and the MC68000 will automatically enter the Halt state and remain there until reset.

If the MC68000 is performing a read-modify-write cycle and a bus error is encountered, it will not rerun the cycle. This is done because the read-modify-write is only used during the Test and Set ($\overline{\text{TAS}}$) instruction. The nature of this instruction demands complete execution cycle integrity, which might be violated if any of the bus cycles were repeated. If external logic requests a rerun of the read-modify-write cycle, the MC68000 will instead perform the bus error exception processing routine, which we will describe later.

MC68000 BUS ARBITRATION LOGIC

The bus arbitration logic provided by the MC68000 is straightforward. The MC68000 does not prioritize requests for bus accesses by external devices. The processor assumes that it is the lowest priority device in the system since it always grants bus access to any requesting device so long as the processor is not currently using the bus itself. Thus the MC68000 allows other devices to utilize the bus between instructions and between bus cycles of a single instruction. Since there is no built-in arbitration there should be some external bus arbitration logic in a system of any complexity to prioritize requests for the System Bus so that a high priority device is not superseded by low priority devices.

There are three signals associated with the bus arbitration logic: Bus Request ($\overline{\text{BR}}$), Bus Grant ($\overline{\text{BG}}$), and Bus Grant Acknowledge ($\overline{\text{BGACK}}$). When the MC68000 is using the System Bus without competition, the input signals — $\overline{\text{BR}}$ and $\overline{\text{BGACK}}$ — will be inactive and the $\overline{\text{BG}}$ output will be negated.

Figure 7-14 illustrates the timing for the bus arbitration performed by the MC68000. Bus arbitration commences when an external device pulls the $\overline{\text{BR}}$ input low. When the MC68000 receives a bus request, it will respond by asserting $\overline{\text{BG}}$ one CLK period later. The only exception to this immediate response is when the MC68000 is in the initial stages of a bus cycle but has not yet asserted $\overline{\text{AS}}$. In this case the MC68000 waits until one CLK period after $\overline{\text{AS}}$ has been asserted before it asserts $\overline{\text{BG}}$; the response time in this case will be a maximum of three CLK periods.

Obviously, **the Bus Grant signal does not indicate that the bus is available for use by the requesting device at that point — the MC68000 may still be using the bus to complete its current bus cycle. Therefore the device requesting the bus must monitor several other signals to determine when the bus is actually available for its use.** First, the external device must wait until $\overline{\text{AS}}$ is negated, indicating that the MC68000 has completed the current bus cycle. The device requesting the bus must also wait until the $\overline{\text{DTACK}}$ signal is negated, since this indicates that the device involved in the current MC68000 cycle is no longer using the bus. However, in some systems it may not be necessary to monitor the $\overline{\text{DTACK}}$ signal. This is the case when system timing is such that you are always assured that all external devices will be off the bus when $\overline{\text{AS}}$ is negated. Lastly, the requesting device must check the state of the $\overline{\text{BGACK}}$ signal. If this signal is true, it indicates that some other device in the system has already been granted use of the System Bus and has not yet finished with it. Conversely, if $\overline{\text{BGACK}}$ is false, then the System Bus will be available for use at the end of the current cycle.

After all of the signal conditions we have described are met, the device requesting the bus must assert $\overline{\text{BGACK}}$. This informs the MC68000 that the requesting device has taken control of the bus. You will note in Figure 7-14 that the MC68000 does not wait for the $\overline{\text{BGACK}}$ signal before it relinquishes control of the bus: the Address and Data Busses, the Function Code outputs, $\overline{\text{AS}}$, $\overline{\text{UDS}}$, $\overline{\text{LDS}}$, and R/$\overline{\text{W}}$ are all placed in the high impedance state as soon as the MC68000 has completed the bus cycle that was in progress when the bus request was received. The device that is using the bus must hold $\overline{\text{BGACK}}$ low for as long as it requires the bus. While an external device has control of the bus, external logic should prevent bus conflicts by monitoring $\overline{\text{BGACK}}$; at this point the behavior of $\overline{\text{BR}}$ and $\overline{\text{BC}}$ is unimportant. However, the device using the bus should negate its $\overline{\text{BR}}$ before negating $\overline{\text{BGACK}}$ to avoid an incorrect bus request.

The MC68000 will maintain its output lines in the high impedance state until $\overline{\text{BGACK}}$ is negated, indicating that the external device is through with the bus. At that point the MC68000 is free to initiate another bus cycle. Note that if another bus request is pending at that point, the MC68000 will acquiesce to that bus request immediately without performing any bus cycles itself.

MC68000 EXCEPTION PROCESSING LOGIC

All of Motorola's literature on the MC68000 refers to "exception processing" when discussing what we usually describe as the interrupt system in other microprocessors. They have chosen to use this nomenclature since the events that can cause "interrupts" in the MC68000 cover a much broader range than those usually associated with an interrupt request in a typical microprocessor. We will also use the "exception processing" nomenclature.

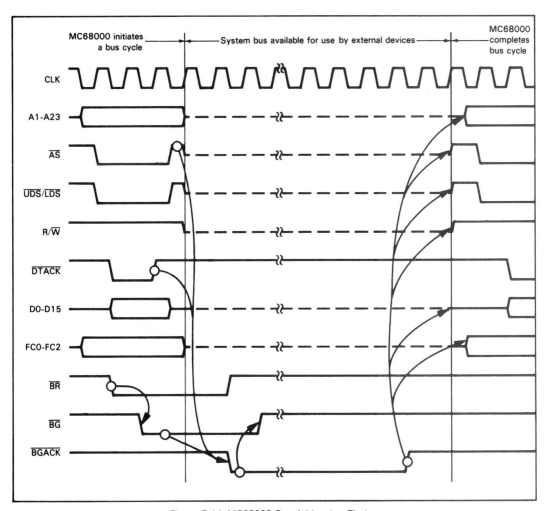

Figure 7-14. MC68000 Bus Arbitration Timing

The MC68000 provides extensive exception processing logic. This logic is similar to that provided by the 8086 and Z8000 in that a jump vector table is used to transfer program control to the appropriate handler program whenever an exception occurs. The biggest difference between the MC68000's logic and that of the Z8000 and 8086 is that the number of events that can generate an exception in the MC68000 is greater than the number of events that cause interrupts in Z8000. In addition, the MC68000 provides a 7-level priority structure for external interrupt requests.

Before proceeding to describe the exception processing system, let us discuss the operating modes of the MC68000, since these affect exception processing. As we mentioned previously, **the MC68000 can operate in either a Supervisor mode or a User mode. When the MC68000 is reset** using the RESET input, it starts operating in the Supervisor mode. The processor remains **in Supervisor mode until one of the following instructions is executed:** Return from Exception **(RTE),** Move to Status Register **(MOVE word to SR),** AND Immediate to Status Register **(ANDI word to SR),** and Exclusive OR Immediate to Status Register (EORI word to SR). None of these instructions automatically causes the transition to User mode of operation — rather, they are capable of changing the state of the S-bit in the Status register. If one of these instructions resets the S-bit, the MC68000 will begin operating in the User mode.

| MC68000 OPERATING MODES |

Once the MC68000 is operating in the User mode, the only thing that can cause a transition back to the Supervisor mode is an exception. All exception processing is performed in Supervisor mode regardless of the current setting of the S-bit of the Status register. When the exception processing has been completed, the Return from Exception (RTE) instruction allows return to the User mode.

A number of instructions, designated as "privileged," are reserved for the Supervisor mode. An attempt to execute one of these instructions in the User mode results in a "privilege violation" which is one type of exception. We will discuss these instructions and the privilege violation response later in this chapter.

MC68000 EXCEPTION TYPES

Exceptions originate in a variety of ways which can be divided into two general categories:

1) **Internally generated exceptions** that result from the execution of certain instructions, or from internally detected errors.

2) **Externally generated exceptions** which include bus errors, reset, and interrupt requests.

The response of the MC68000 to the various types of exceptions is similar. Before we describe this response, let us look at the sources of exceptions since they go well beyond those provided by other microprocessors.

| MC68000 INTERNALLY GENERATED EXCEPTIONS |

The internally generated exceptions to which the MC68000 responds can be further subdivided into three categories: internally detected errors, instruction traps, and the Trace function.

The following are the internally detected errors which will cause the MC68000 to initiate exception processing:

1) **Addressing errors.** Whenever the MC68000 attempts to access word data, long word data, or an instruction at an odd address, this is an address error since all such accesses must be on even address boundaries.

2) **Privilege violations.** Again, some instructions are reserved for use only in the Supervisor mode. Exception processing will be initiated if you attempt to execute any of the following instructions when in the User mode: STOP, RESET, RTE, MOVE to SR, AND (word) Immediate to SR, EOR (word) Immediate to SR, OR (word) Immediate to SR, MOVE USP.

3) **Illegal and unimplemented opcodes.** If an instruction is fetched whose bit pattern is not one of the defined instruction bit patterns for the MC68000, exception processing will be initiated. Two bit patterns are defined as unimplemented rather than illegal; if bits 15-12 are 1010 or 1111, these are treated as unimplemented instruction opcodes. If these opcodes are fetched, special exception processing is initiated which can allow you to use these unimplemented instructions in your own software.

Instruction traps are exceptions which are caused by the execution of instructions in your program. There is a standard TRAP instruction which is similar the Z8000 System Call instruction. **There are four other instructions — TRAPV, CHK, DIVS, and DIVU — which will cause exception processing to be initiated** if certain conditions, such as arithmetic overflows or divide by zero, are detected.

The third type of internally generated exception occurs when the MC68000 is operating with the Trace function. If the T-bit in the supervisor portion of the Status register is set, exception processing will be performed after each instruction. The Trace function is used for program debugging since you can analyze, by stepping through the program, the results of each instruction's execution.

There are three different types of externally generated exceptions:

1) **Bus errors.** When the $\overline{\text{BERR}}$ signal is pulled low by external logic (while $\overline{\text{HALT}}$ is high) exception processing is initiated.

2) **Reset.** When the $\overline{\text{RESET}}$ signal is asserted by external logic, exception processing is initiated.

3) **Interrupt request.** This is the most familiar form of exception processing and is initiated by external logic via the three interrupt request lines ($\overline{\text{IPL0}}$, $\overline{\text{IPL1}}$, and $\overline{\text{IPL2}}$).

The different types of exceptions have different priorities, and processing of an exception depends on its priority. The following table lists the types of exceptions according to their relative priorities, and also defines when processing of each type begins.

Priority	Exception Source	Exception Processing Response
Highest	$\overline{\text{RESET}}$ $\overline{\text{BERR}}$ (Bus Error) Address Error	Abort current cycle, then process exception
	Trace Interrupt Request Illegal/Unimplemented Opcode Privilege Violation	Complete current instruction, then process exception
Lowest	TRAP, TRAPV CHK Divide-by-zero	Instruction execution initiates exception processing

The highest priority types of exceptions are Reset, Bus Error, and Address Error. Any of these exceptions will cause immediate termination of the current instruction, even within a bus cycle. The next group of exceptions — trace, interrupt requests, illegal/unimplemented instructions, and privilege violations — allow completion of the current instruction before initiating exception processing. Note that interrupt requests include an additional prioritization which we discussed earlier. The lowest priority of exceptions are those that are caused by trap-type instructions. These instructions can initiate exception processing as part of their normal execution. All of the instruction trap exceptions have equal priority since it is impossible for two of them to generate exceptions simultaneously.

Central to the MC68000 exception processing sequence is a vector table that occupies 1024 bytes (512 sixteen-bit words) of memory. This table occupies memory addresses 000000_{16} through $0003FF_{16}$. **Figure 7-15 illustrates the exception vector table.** The table is organized as 256 four-byte vectors. Each vector is a 32-bit address which will be loaded into the Program Counter as part of the exception processing sequence.

As you can see, a number of the vector table entries serve the defined types of exceptions which we have discussed. The remaining entries of the vector table are reserved for use by Motorola and should not be used by your program if compatibility with Motorola software is desired. The first 64 exception vectors have predefined uses; this leaves 192 vectors available to external interrupt requests — this should be more than enough for most applications. However, the first 64 vector locations are not protected by the MC68000; thus they can be used by external interrupts if a system requires it.

MC68000 EXCEPTION PROCESSING SEQUENCES

The general sequence of events performed by the MC68000 in response to an exception is the same regardless of the source of the exception. There are, however, some differences. Let us begin by examining the response to internally generated exceptions.

If exception processing is initiated as a result of either the Trace function, a TRAP instruction, an illegal or unimplemented opcode, or a privilege violation, the following steps occur:

1) The Status Register contents are copied into an internal register.

2) The S-bit in the Status Register is set, thus placing the MC68000 in the Supervisor mode of operation.

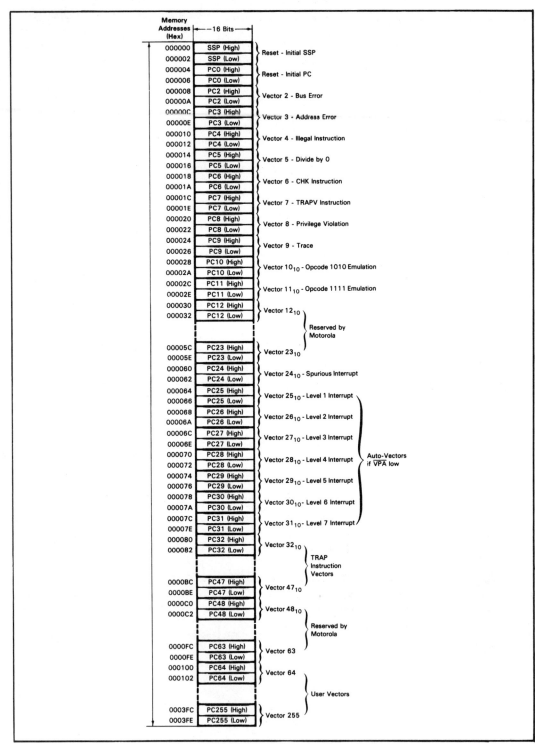

Figure 7-15. MC68000 Exception Vector Table

7-26

3) The T-bit in the Status Register is reset to disable tracing to allow for continuous execution when debugging using TRACE.

4) The Program Counter contents are pushed onto the Supervisor Stack. The contents of SSP will be decremented by four since four bytes are required to store the 32-bit contents of PC.

5) Status register contents are pushed onto the Supervisor stack; SSP contents are decremented by two, since the Status register is a 16-bit register.

6) The new Program Counter contents are taken from the appropriate location in the interrupt vector table.

7) Instruction execution then begins at the location indicated by the new content of the Program Counter; this will be the first instruction of the exception processing program you have provided for that particular type exception.

The way in which the MC68000 responds to an exception caused by a bus error or address error includes several steps in addition to those described in the preceding paragraphs. First, recall that either of these errors causes immediate termination of the bus cycle in progress. The next steps are the following:

MC68000 BUS AND ADDRESS ERROR EXCEPTION PROCESSING

1) The contents of the Status register are copied into an internal register.

2) The S-bit in the Status register is set, placing the MC68000 in the Supervisor mode.

3) The T-bit in the Status register is reset to disable trace operations.

4) The contents of the Program Counter are pushed onto the Supervisor stack and the System Stack Pointer (SSP) is decremented by four.

5) The contents of the Status register are pushed onto the Supervisor stack and the contents of SSP are decremented by two.

6) The contents of the MC68000's instruction register, which constitute the first word of the instruction that was in progress when the bus error occurred, are pushed onto the Supervisor stack and SSP is decremented by two.

7) The 32-bit address that was being used for the bus cycle which was terminated is also pushed onto the Supervisor stack and SSP is decremented by four.

8) A word which provides information as to the type of cycle that was in progress at the time of the error is pushed onto the Supervisor stack and SSP is decremented by two.

9) The Program Counter contents are taken from the appropriate interrupt vector — either the bus error vector or address error vector of the exception vector table.

10) Instruction execution resumes at the location indicated by the new contents of the Program Counter.

Figure 7-16 shows the order in which information is pushed onto the Supervisor stack as part of the exception processing for bus and address errors. The value saved for the Program Counter is advanced two to ten bytes beyond the address of the first word of the instruction where the error occurred according to the length of that instruction and its addressing information, if any.

As you can see in Figure 7-16, **the five least significant bits of the last word pushed onto the Stack provide information as to the type of access that was in progress when the bus error or address error occurred.** The three least significant bits are a copy of the Function Code outputs during the aborted bus cycle. Bit 3 indicates the type of processing that was in progress when the error occurred. This bit is set for Group 0 or 1 exception processing and reset for Group 2 exception and normal instruction processing. Bit 4 indicates whether a read (bit 4 set) or write (bit 4 reset) cycle was in progress when the error occurred. If an error occurs during the exception processing of a preceding bus error, address error, or reset operation, the MC68000 will enter the Halt state and remain there.

All of the information that is pushed onto the Supervisor stack as part of the bus and address error exception processing sequence is intended to aid you in analyzing possible sources of the error. Either of these errors implies a serious system failure and it is not likely that you will be able to return to normal program execution.

An external reset causes a special type of exception processing. After the RESET input has been pulsed low the following steps occur:

MC68000 RESET EXCEPTION PROCESSING

1) The S-bit in the Status register is set, placing the MC68000 in the Supervisor mode.

2) The T-bit in the Status register is reset to disable the trace function.

3) All three interrupt mask bits in the Status register are set, thus specifying the interrupt priority mask at level seven.

4) The Supervisor Stack Pointer (SSP) is loaded with the contents of the first four bytes of memory (addresses 000000-000003).

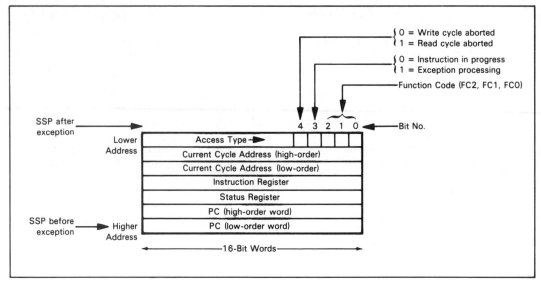

Figure 7-16. MC68000 System Stack After Bus Error or Address Error

5) The Program Counter (PC) is loaded from the next four bytes of memory (addresses 000004-000007).

6) Instruction execution commences at the address indicated by the new contents of the Program Counter, which should reference your power-up/reset initialization program.

The last type of exception processing we will discuss is the sequence initiated by the standard interrupt request. An external device requests an interrupt by encoding an interrupt request level on the IPL0-IPL2 inputs. The MC68000 compares these inputs to the interrupt mask bits in the Status register. If the encoded priority level is less than or equal to the one specified by the three-bit mask, the interrupt request will not be recognized by the MC68000. **If the encoded interrupt level is a higher priority than the level established by the interrupt mask (or if a level seven interrupt request is input) then the interrupt will be processed.** The MC68000 responds to the allowed interrupt request as soon as it completes the instruction execution currently in progress. **Upon completion of the current instruction, the following steps occur:**

> **MC68000 INTERRUPT REQUEST EXCEPTION PROCESSING**

1) The contents of the Status register are saved internally.

2) The S-bit in the Status register is set, placing the MC68000 in the Supervisor mode.

3) The T-bit in the Status register is reset to disable the Trace function.

4) The interrupt mask bits in the Status register are updated to the level of the interrupt request that is encoded on the IPL0-IPL2 inputs. This allows the current interrupt to be processed without being interrupted by lower priority events.

5) The MC68000 then performs an interrupt acknowledge bus cycle. This cycle serves two functions; first, the processor lets the requesting device know that its interrupt request is being serviced, and second, the processor fetches an exception vector byte from the requesting device. **Figure 7-17 shows the timing for this interrupt acknowledge/vector fetch cycle. This cycle is esentially a read cycle with a few minor differences.** First, address lines A1 through A3 will reflect the states of the IPL0-IPL2 inputs so that external logic can determine which interrupt request is being processed. All of the other address outputs are set during the interrupt acknowledge cycle. The requesting device responds to the MC68000 by placing a byte of exception vector data on the lower half of the data bus. The Data Transfer Acknowledge (DTACK) signal is used to effect this transfer of data just as with a normal read cycle. Throughout the interrupt acknowledge cycle, the Function Code outputs (FC0-FC2) will be set high since this represents the interrupt acknowledge function code. After the vector byte has been read from the interrupting device, the MC68000 proceeds with the following exception processing steps.

6) The contents of the Program Counter are pushed onto the Supervisor stack and SSP is decremented by four.

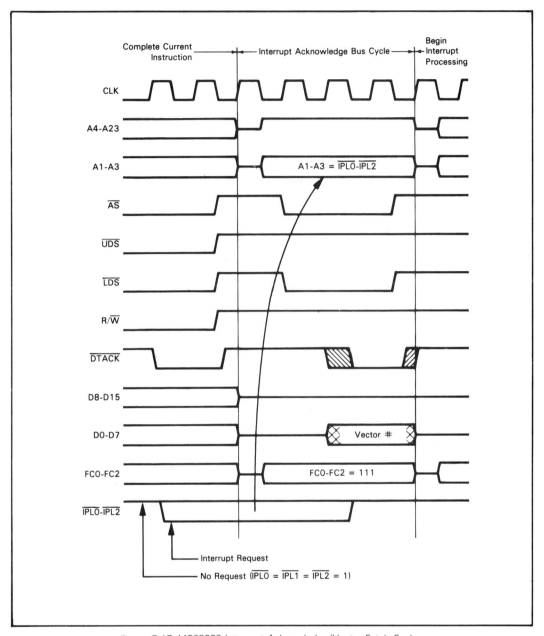

Figure 7-17. MC68000 Interrupt Acknowledge/Vector Fetch Cycle

7) The contents of the Status register are pushed onto the Supervisor stack and SSP is decremented by two.

8) The Program Counter is loaded with four bytes of data from the appropriate location in the exception vector table. The address for this location is derived as shown in the following illustration:

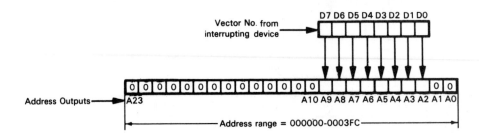

The eight bits of data that were read from the requesting device as part of the interrupt acknowledge cycle are used to form address bits A2 through A9. The two least significant bits and bits A10 through A23 will all be set to zero. Thus, addresses 000000_{16} through $0003FC_{16}$ can be generated. If you refer to Figure 7-15, you will see that these are the upper and lower boundaries of the exception vector table. Under normal circumstances a requesting device should limit itself to producing vectors corresponding to the address range $0000FC_{16}$ through $0003FC_{16}$ since the lower addresses in the vector table have preassigned uses.

After the Program Counter has been loaded with the new value from the exception vector table, instruction execution commences at the location indicated by the new contents of the Program Counter; this will be the first instruction of your interrupt processing routine for the particular device requesting the interrupt.

There are two variations to the interrupt request processing sequence we have just described. First, if during the interrupt acknowledge bus cycle the requesting device responds by asserting BERR instead of DTACK, the MC68000 treats this as an indication that the current interrupt request is a spurious one, and it will use vector 24 in the exception vector table to load the Program Counter.

| MC68000 |
| SPURIOUS |
| INTERRUPT |

The second variation on interrupt request processing is the autovector response. If you refer to Figure 7-15, you will see that seven vector locations are provided in the exception vector table for autovectors, corresponding to the seven interrupt priority levels. These vectors will be used if the device requesting an interrupt responds to the interrupt acknowledge bus cycle by asserting the Valid Peripheral Address (VPA) signal instead of supplying a byte of vector data. If this occurs, the MC68000 will respond by asserting the Valid Memory Address (VMA) signal. The processor will then use the appropriate autovector from the exception vector table to obtain a new Program Counter value. This autovector response was provided specifically to emulate the interrupt timing sequence expected by 6800-family peripheral devices. The VPA/VMA sequence is the standard 6800 microprocessor interrupt sequence. Of course a non-6800-family device in the system could also exploit this autovector capability should it be advantageous.

| MC68000 |
| AUTOVECTOR |
| INTERRUPT |
| RESPONSE |

MC68000 ADDRESSING MODES

The MC68000 utilizes 14 different addressing modes which can be grouped into six basic types. These are:

1) **Direct Register Addressing**
   a) Data Register Direct
   b) Address Register Direct

2) **Direct Memory Addressing**
   a) Absolute Short
   b) Absolute Long

3) **Indirect Memory Addressing**
   a) Register Indirect
   b) Post-increment Register Indirect
   c) Pre-decrement Register Indirect
   d) Register Indirect with Displacement
   e) Register Indirect with Index and Displacement

4) **Implied Register Addressing**

5) Program Counter Relative Addressing
      a) PC-relative with Displacement
      b) PC-relative with Index and Displacement

6) Immediate Data Addressing
      a) Immediate
      b) Quick Immediate

These addressing modes help create a powerful and efficient instruction set. In particular, two useful features of the MC68000 addressing are that any address register may be used for direct or indirect addressing, and any register may be used as an index register.

The general format of a single effective address instruction operation word is shown below. The two least significant 3-bit fields determine the effective address. These fields are the mode field (bits 3-5) and the register field (bits 0-2).

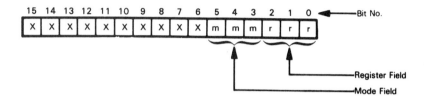

In some cases, the information contained in these two fields may be appended to fully specify the operand. In this case, **one or two additional words are appended onto the instruction**. This additional information is called the effective address extension, and its format is:

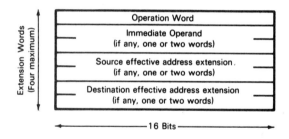

We will now discuss the addressing modes in detail. The following abbreviations are used within this section.

An	Address register n ($0 \leq n \leq 7$)
CCR	Condition code half of the Status register
dddd	displacement value
Dn	Data register n ($0 \leq n \leq 7$)
EA	effective address
N	operand size in bytes (1,2,or 4)
PC	Program Counter
pppp	
qqqq	
xxxx	
yyyy	any four hex digits
zzzz	
Rn	any address or data register n ($0 \leq n \leq 7$)
rrr	the 3-bit value of n
SP	the active Stack Pointer
SR	Status register
SSP	Supervisor Stack Pointer
ssss	sign extension digits
USP	User Stack Pointer

Register Direct Addressing

This addressing mode requires that the operand involved be contained in one of the eight Data registers or one of the eight address registers (Mode = 001_2).

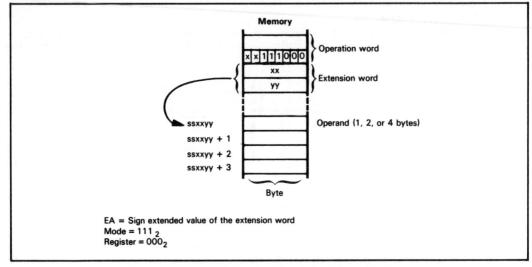

Figure 7-18. MC68000 Absolute Short Direct Memory Addressing

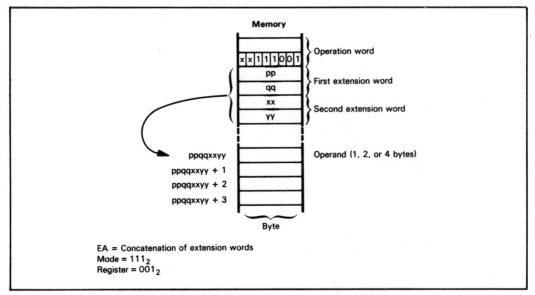

Figure 7-19. MC68000 Absolute Long Direct Memory Addressing

Data Register Direct	Address Register Direct
EA = Dn	EA = An
Mode = 000_2	Mode = 001_2

Absolute Data Addressing

There are two forms of this addressing mode. The short form is called absolute short addressing, while the longer format is called absolute long.

Absolute short. One extension word is necessary for this addressing mode. The address of the operand is the sign extended value of the extension word. Figure 7-18 illustrates the absolute short addressing mode.

Absolute long. Two words of extension are required for this addressing mode. The address of the operand is the concatenation of the two extension words; the first is the high-order portion, the second is the low-order portion. Figure 7-19 illustrates the absolute long addressing mode.

Register Indirect Addressing

The five variations of this addressing mode each reference an operand in memory.

Address register indirect. In this mode, the address of the operand is the contents of the specified Address register. Figure 7-20 illustrates the address register indirect mode.

Address register indirect with postincrement. In this mode, the address of the operand is the contents of the specified Address register. After the instruction using this mode is executed, the contents of this register are incremented by one, two, or four depending on the size of the operand. If the Address register is A7 (SP) then the address is incremented by two regardless of the operand size, because the Stack Pointer must be kept on a word boundary. Figure 7-21 illustrates the Address register indirect with postincrement mode.

Address register indirect with predecrement. This addressing mode is similar to the previous one with the exception that the contents of the specified Address register are decremented before they are used to reference the operand.

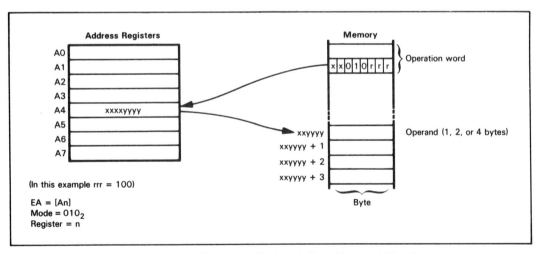

Figure 7-20. MC68000 Address Register Indirect Memory Addressing

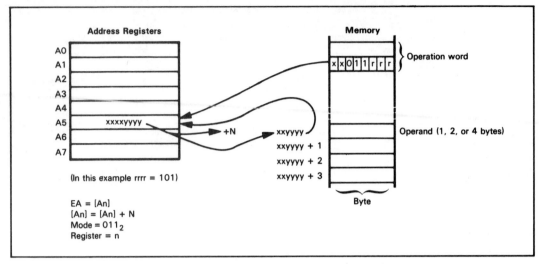

Figure 7-21. MC68000 Address Register Indirect with Postincrement Addressing

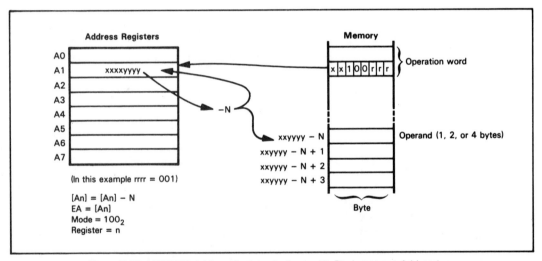

Figure 7-22. MC68000 Address Register Indirect with Predecrement Addressing

Again, if A7 is specified then the address is always decremented by two. Figure 7-22 illustrates the address register indirect with predecrement mode.

Address register indirect with displacement. One word of extension is required with this addressing mode. The address of the operand is the sum of the contents of the specified Address register and the sign-extended 16-bit displacement word contained in the extension word. Figure 7-23 illustrates the address register indirect with displacement mode.

Address register indirect with index and displacement. This addressing mode requires one word of extension which is formatted as shown in Figure 7-24. The operand address is the sum of the specified address register, the sign-extend

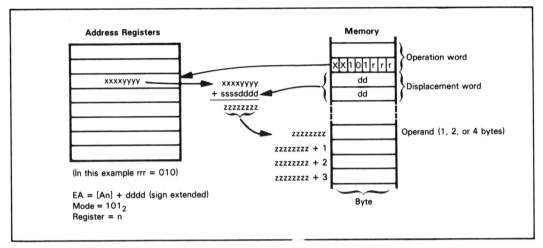

Figure 7-23. MC68000 Address Register Indirect with Displacement Addressing

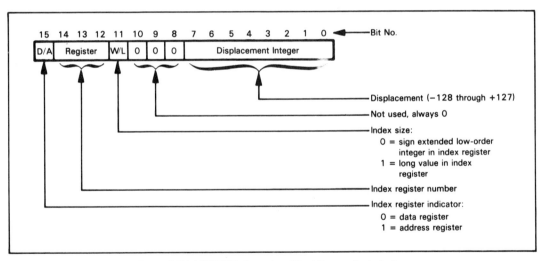

Figure 7-24. MC68000 Extension Word Format for Indexing

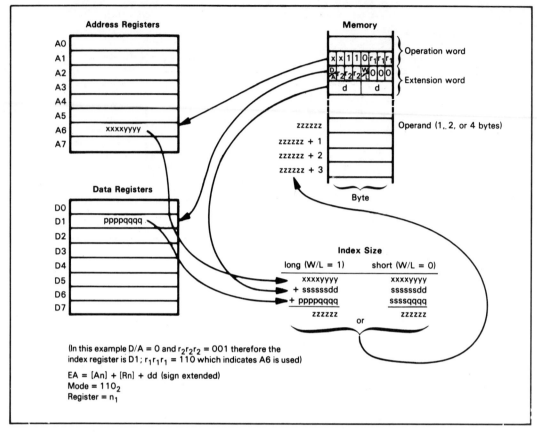

Figure 7-25. MC68000 Address Register Indirect with Index and Displacement Addressing

displacement integer in the least significant byte of the extension word, and the contents of the Index register. Address formation for the Address Register Indirect with Index and Displacement is illustrated in Figure 7-25.

Implied Register Addressing

There are some instructions that implicitly refer to a specific register. These registers are the Program Counter (PC), the Stack Pointer (SP-SSP or USP), and the status register (SR). Table 7-5 shows those instructions in which a register holding the operand is implied.

MC68000
IMPLIED
REGISTER
ADDRESSING

Program Counter Relative Addressing

There are two formats for PC-relative addressing. Both require one word of extension and both provide displacement. The second format includes indexing in additional to displacement.

MC68000
PROGRAM
COUNTER
RELATIVE
ADDRESSING

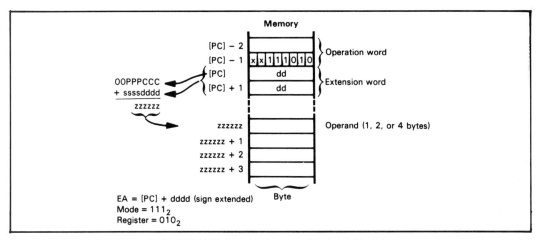

Figure 7-26. MC68000 Program Counter Relative Addressing

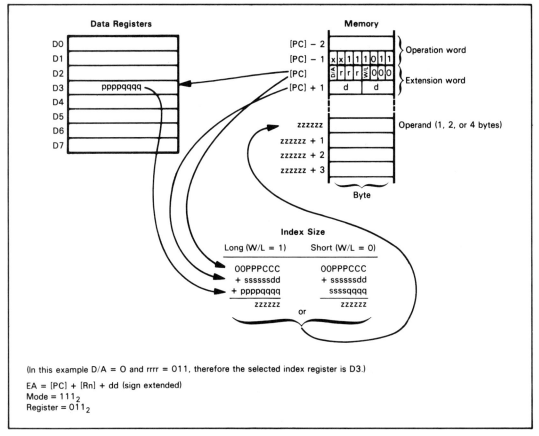

Figure 7-27. MC68000 Program Counter-Relative with Index and Displacement Addressing

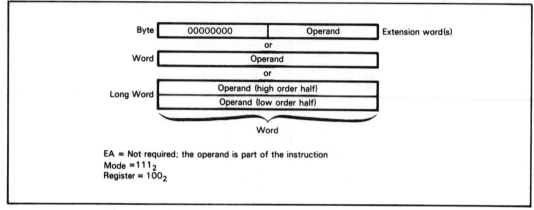

Figure 7-28. MC68000 Immediate Data Addressing Extension Words

The value contained in the Program Counter which is used in address calculation is the address of the extension word.

PC-relative with displacement. This addressing mode generates an effective address by summing together the value of the Program Counter and the sign extended value of the extension word. Figure 7-26 illustrates the PC-relative with displacement mode.

PC-relative with index and displacement. This mode requires an extension word format similar to that required by the address register indirect with index and displacement mode (see Figure 7- 24). The address is calculated as shown in Figure 7-27.

Immediate Data Addressing

The operand for immediate data addressing is the value that immediately follows the instruction word. Thus, depending on the size of the operand, either one or two extension words will be necessary, as illustrated in Figure 7-28.

THE MC68000 INSTRUCTION SET

Table 7-6 summarizes the instruction set of the MC68000. Instruction object codes and execution times are given alphabetically in Table 7-7. Instruction object codes are given numerically in Table 7-8.

When compared to other microprocessor instruction sets, the MC68000 instruction set might seem quite large: over 300 instructions are listed in Table 7-6. However, if you examine this table closely, you will see that slight variations of the same instruction mnemonic may appear several times. These are different forms of the same instruction. **There are actually 56 basic instructions provided in the MC68000.** We have listed all the variations of a single instruction as though they were distinct instructions in order to make our description of the instruction set consistent with similar ones for other microprocessors.

One of the most significant characteristics of the MC68000 instruction set is its orderliness. Despite its apparent complexity, this instruction set should be relatively easy to learn, since the variations are consistent and therefore predictable. These variations are due to the different addressing modes available and to the MC68000's ability to handle five different data types. Since there are really only 56 basic mnemonics that you must learn, it is more likely that you will use all of the instructions in the way that they were intended and thus obtain the full power of the instruction set.

Let us examine the MC68000 instruction set by instruction categories, as given in Table 7-6.

One thing to keep in mind is that the MC68000 uses memory-mapped I/O: therefore there are no separate I/O instructions. The primary memory reference instructions will also be used to accomplish I/O.

The basic format of all instructions is the same. The op-code for every instruction is one word. Additional extension words are required when the addressing modes specified use constants (immediate operands), absolute addresses, or displacements. Accordingly, **an instruction can be anywhere from 2 to 10 bytes in length. The number of bytes for each instruction is listed in Table 7-6.**

All of the primary memory reference instructions have byte, word, and long word versions. Secondary memory reference instructions can use most of the memory addressing modes. There are byte, word, and long word versions of most, but not all, of these instructions.

The Move instruction provided by the MC68000 allows data movement between registers, from register to memory, from memory to register, and directly from one memory location to another. The Move Multiple Registers (MOVEM) instruction allows all of the MC68000 register contents to be quickly saved in memory or restored from memory.

The MC68000 does not provide a block move instruction such as those available with the 8086 and the Z8000 microprocessors. However, since the Move instructions can move data from one memory location to another, **it is simple to move blocks of data by using the Move instruction in conjunction with the Decrement and Branch (DBcc) instruction.**

Both signed and unsigned multiply and divide instructions are included in the instruction set. In comparison, the Z8000 provided only unsigned multiplication and division. However, the Z8000 provides 32-bit multiplication and division while the MC68000 can only multiply two 16-bit operands producing a 32-bit result, or divide a 32-bit dividend by a 16-bit divisor. **The divide instructions reference the dividend in one of the Data registers: the divisor may reside in memory or in another Data register.** Both the divisor and the dividend are treated as signed binary numbers in the DIVS instruction and as unsigned binary numbers in the DIVU instruction. After the division instruction has been executed, the quotient is returned in the low-order half of the dividend register and the remainder is returned in the high-order half of the dividend register.

The multiply instructions also have only a word version: there is no long word version. As with the division, there is a signed (MULS) and unsigned (MULU) version of the multiply instructions. One of the operands must reside in the least significant half of a Data register while the other operand can be either a memory word, the lower half of another Data register, or can consist of immediate data included as part of the instruction. Upon completion of the multiply operation, the 32-bit product is returned in the source operand Data register.

The MC68000 includes standard Jump and Jump to Subroutine instructions (JMP and JSR) which use specific addresses for loading the Program Counter. **There are also the Branch Always and Branch to Subroutine instructions (BRA and BSR)** which cause a transfer of program control relative to the Program Counter's current contents.

The Trap instruction is the MC68000's equivalent of the System Call instruction provided by the Z8000. You will recall from the earlier discussion of the MC68000 exception processing logic that the Trap instruction automatically switches the MC68000 into the Supervisor mode, which utilizes a separate Stack Pointer to isolate the operating system from application programs.

The MC68000 also provides several instructions that are specifically designed to simplify implementation of higher level languages. These instructions are unique to the MC68000. The Link (LINK) and Unlink (UNLK) instructions can be used to maintain a linked list of local data and parameter areas on the Stack and thus simplify operations where there are frequent interrupts of nested subroutines.

The Link instruction uses the System Stack Pointer (SFP), one of the other Address registers, as a "frame pointer" and a displacement value. This instruction will typically be used at the beginning of a subroutine. The Link instruction first pushes the current value of the frame pointer onto the Stack. The current value of the Stack Pointer is then loaded into the frame pointer so that it now points to the top of the current Stack. Finally, the displacement value included with the Link instruction is used to decrement the System Stack Pointer so that it is displaced to clear a space in memory for storage of such things as local variables and parameters. These variables can then be accessed via the frame pointer. The Unlink (UNLK) instruction is used to clean up the Stack at the end of a subroutine and would be executed just prior to returning to a higher level subroutine. The Unlink instruction loads the System Stack Pointer with the contents of the frame pointer. The frame pointer is then loaded with the address pulled off the Stack. Thus, both the frame pointer and the System Stack Pointer will be restored to the values they held before the subroutine was called.

ABBREVIATIONS

Following are the abbreviations used for instruction formats and operation descriptions.

addr	Direct address (16 or 32 bits)
An	Address registers, n = 0-7 (8, 16, or 32 bits, depending on the instruction size)
bitb	Bit number of byte 0-7
bitl	Bit number of long word 0-31
cc	Condition code:

CC	Carry clear	0100
CS	Carry set	0101
EQ	Equal	0111
F	False	0001
GE	Greater than or equal	1100
GT	Greater than	1110
HI	High	0010
LE	Less than or equal	1111
LS	Low or same	0011
LT	Less than	1101
MI	Minus	1011
NE	Not equal	0110
PL	Plus	1010
T	True	0000
VC	No overflow	1000
VS	Overflow	1001

CCR	Condition Code register — the low-order byte of the Status register
count	Shift count (1-8)
dadr	Destination address, which may be any of the following addressing modes:

(An)	Register indirect
(An)+	Register indirect with postincrement
−(An)	Register indirect with predecrement
d16(An)	Register indirect with displacement
d8(An,i)	Register indirect, indexed
addr	Direct address

dAn	Destination Address register. This form is used only when there are two An operands.
aDn	Destination Data register. This form is used only when there are two Dn operands.
data3	3 bits of immediate data
data8	8 bits of immediate data
data16	16 bits of immediate data
data32	32 bits of immediate data
Dn	Data register, n = 0-7 (8, 16, or 32 bits, depending on instruction size)
d8	8-bit address displacement. Required, even if zero on indexed instructions.
d16	16-bit address displacement
i	Index register (An or Dn)
jadr	Jump address — same as sadr except no (An)+ or −(An)
label	Address label
madr	Multiple-instruction address — same as dadr except no (An)+ or −(An)
reg-list	Register list naming one or more registers, each item in the list separated by a comma. Items may have the form:

Dn	Single data register
An	Single address register
rn_1-rn	Range of registers

rd	Destination registers (dDn or dAn)
rs	Source register (sDn or sAn)

sadr   Source address, which may be any of the following address modes:

(An)	Register indirect
(An)+	Register indirect with postincrement
—(An)	Register indirect with predecrement
d16(An)	Register indirect with displacement
d8(An,i)	Register indirect, indexed
addr	Direct address
label	Program relative
label (i)	Program relative, indexed

sAn   Source Address register. This form is used only when there are two An operands.

sDn   Source Data register. This form is used only when there are two Dn operands.

SR   Status register (16 bits)

USP   User Stack Pointer. Note that this is Register A7.

vector   Trap address vector, the memory location containing the address of the Trap routine.

[[ ]]   The contents of the memory location whose address is contained in the designated register (indirect memory addressing, or implied addressing).

[ ]   The contents of a register or memory location (register addressing or direct memory addressing).

For example:

$[Dn] \leftarrow [[An]]$

indicates that the contents of the memory location addressed by Register An are loaded into Dn, whereas:

$[Dn] \leftarrow [An]$

indicates that the contents of Register An itself are loaded into Dn.

$\overrightarrow{x}$ Complement the value of x.

x<y-z>   Bits y through z of x. For example, Dn<0-7> means the low-order byte of Dn. If the z term is omitted, then only the bit selected by y is being referenced. Thus Dn<0> means the least significant bit of Dn.

+	Add
—	Subtract
x	Multiply
÷	Divide
∧	Logical AND
∨	Logical OR
⩛	Logical Exclusive-OR
=	Equals
←	Data moves in the direction of the arrow
←—→	Data are exchanged between two locations

INSTRUCTION MNEMONICS

Table 7-6 summarizes the MC68000 instruction set. The MNEMONIC column lists the instruction mnemonic (e.g., MOVE, ADD, JMP). The OPERAND(s) column lists the operands used with the instruction mnemonic.

The fixed part of an assembly language instruction is shown in UPPER CASE. The variable part (register number, address, immediate data, etc.) is shown in lower case.

The BYTES and CLOCK CYCLES are repeated in this table for reader convenience. Refer to "Instruction Object Code Tables" and the text accompanying Table 7-7 for a description of these entries.

STATUS

The effect of instruction execution on the status bits is listed in Table 7-6. The status bits are:

T — Trace mode
S — Supervisor state
X — Extend bit
N — Negative (or Sign) bit
Z — Zero bit
V — Overflow bit
C — Carry bit

The following symbols are used in the STATUS columns:

X — flag is affected by operation
(blank) — flag is not affected by operation
1 — flag is set by operation
0 — flag is cleared by operation

OPERATION PERFORMED

This column shows the sequence of operations that occurs when the instruction is executed. (Instruction fetches are not shown, nor is the incrementing of the Program Counter for the purpose of instruction fetches.) Each operation is generally shown in the following form:

destination   ←   source

indicating that the source contents moves to the destination, replacing the destination contents. For example, the LEA instruction operation is:

[An]   ←   jadr

The effective address, which may be any of the jadr forms, is loaded into the specified Address register.

Following the arrow sequence is a description of the operation in words.

Alternate Mnemonics

The MC68000 instruction set allows a choice of mnemonics for many operations. An "I" can be appended to the instruction mnemonic for an immediate operation. An "A" can be appended to the instruction mnemonic for an Address register operation. An ".S" can be appended to force a short-form conditional branch instruction.

Mnemonic choices are summarized in Table 7-5 under these headings:

PRIMARY MNEMONIC — Lists the nominal mnemonic form
ALTERNATE MNEMONIC — Lists the alternate choices that can be used in place of the primary mnemonic.
OPERAND — Shows the operand category to which the primary and alternate mnemonics apply. xx is any allowed operand selection.
DESCRIPTION — Identifies the operation.

For simplicity, only the primary mnemonics are shown in the instruction set tables that follow.

Note that there are no mnemonic alternates for the instruction variations X (Extend), M (Multiple), and P (Peripheral Data). These suffixes cannot be omitted from their respective instruction mnemonics.

Bear in mind that the assembler will select the "Quick" version of an instruction (e.g., MOVEQ, ADDQ, SUBQ) whenever possible. Thus you can use the alternates for these mnemonics — the more general MOVE, ADD and SUB — without sacrificing any opportunities for code shortening.

For example: MOVE.L #40,D2
is coded as: MOVEQ #40,D2

Another example: ADD #1, D0
is coded as: ADDQ.W #1,D0

MC68000 INSTRUCTION OBJECT CODE TABLES

The object code for each MC68000 instruction is shown alphabetically by instruction mnemonic in Table 7-6. The object codes are listed in numerical order in Table 7-7.

For instruction words which have no variations, object codes are represented as four hexadecimal digits; for example, 4E71.

For instruction words with variation in one of the two bytes, the object code is shown as a combination of lower case variables, hex digits, and binary digits. Each byte of an instruction word in Tables 7-7 and 7-8 is subdivided into two "nibble" fields (1 nibble = 4 bits). If a single digit appears in a nibble field, it is a hexadecimal digit. If four digits, or a combination of digits and lower-case variables (for example, 1rrr), appear in a nibble field, each digit represents a single bit.

Note that some lower-case variables are used to represent hexadecimal digits rather than binary digits. When four of these hexadecimal variable characters (for example xxxx or yyyy) are used to represent a 16-bit word, they will appear grouped together in the center of the 2-byte column comprising that word.

INSTRUCTION EXECUTION TIMES

Table 7-7 lists the instruction execution time in clock cycles. Each cycle = 125 nanoseconds (when f_{CLK} =8.0 MHz).

The abbreviations and notations used in the "clock cycles" column are defined as follows:

+ea   Effective address overhead. This is the additional time required to execute the instruction for addressing modes that take longer to execute than the nominal register indirect address. The following are the additional clock cycles required:

Addressing Mode	Additional Clock Cycles
(An)	0
(An)+	0
−(An)	2
d16(An)	5
d8(An,i)	7
addr-16-bit	5
addr-32-bit	10
label	5
label(i)	7

N   For shift instructions, the number of shifts. For move multiple instructions, the number of registers being moved.

*   The first value is for branch or trap taken, the second is for branch or trap not taken. In the case of Bcc, the first of the latter numbers is for a two-byte instruction (8-bit displacement), and the second is for a four-byte instruction (16-bit displacement). In the case of DBcc, the first of the latter numbers is for branch not taken due to condition true, and the second is for branch not taken due to counter timeout.

**   Indicates maximum value.

***   The lower value is for condition false (byte set to all ones); the higher value is for condition true (byte cleared to all zeroes).

The following abbreviations are used in Table 7-7:

a   Operand addressing mode (1 bit)
       0 = data register to data register
       1 = memory to memory

bbb   3 bits of immediate data. In bit operations the bit numbers 0 - 7.

bbbbb   Bit numbers 0 - 31.

ccc   Shift count 000 = 8 shifts
       001 = 1 shift
       010 = 2 shifts
       011 = 3 shifts
       100 = 4 shifts
       101 = 5 shifts
       110 = 6 shifts
       111 = 7 shifts

ddd   Destination register — same coding as rrr.

	Address Mode	MODE/REGISTER	[EXT]
eeeee	Source effective address (6 bits)		
	(An)	010rrr	---
	(An)+	011rrr	---
	−(An)	100rrr	---
	d16(An)	101rrr	xxxx
	d8(An,i)	110rrr	a iii w 000 xx
	addr-16-bit	111000	pppp
	addr-32-bit	111001	pppp qqqq
	label	111010	xxxx
	label(i)	111011	a iii w 000 xx

[EXT]   One or two optional words of extension addressing that may or may not appear, depending on the addressing mode (see the Addressing Modes description).

ffffff   Destination effective address — same as eeeee except no label or label(i).

gggggg   Destination effective address but in a format with the MODE and REGISTER fields switched (e.g., (An)=rrr010).

hhhhhh   Multiple-destination effective address — same as ffffff except no (An)+ or −(An).?

iii   Index register — same coding as rrr.

jjjjjj   Jump effective address — same as eeeee except no (An)+ or −(An).

kkkk   Register mask list for predecrement mode, in the following format (a "1" selects the register):

15 14 13 12 11 10 9 8 7 6 5 4 3 2 1 0

D0 D1 D2 D3 D4 D5 D6 D7 A0 A1 A2 A3 A4 A5 A6 A7

mmmm   Register mask list for non-predecrement modes, in the format (a "1" selects the register):

15 14 13 12 11 10 9 8 7 6 5 4 3 2 1 0

A7 A6 A5 A4 A3 A2 A1 A0 D7 D6 D5 D4 D3 D2 D1 D0

pppp   16-bit address word or most significant word of 32-bit address

qqqq   Least significant word of 32-bit address

rrr   Register 000 = D0 or A0
        001 = D1 or A1
        010 = D2 or A2
        011 = D3 or A3
        100 = D4 or A4
        101 = D5 or A5
        110 = D6 or A6
        111 = D7 or A7

sss   Source register — same coding as rrr.

t   Type of register 0 = Dn
        1 = An

vvvv   4-bit vector

w   Index size. 0 = sign extended, low-order integer in index register
        1 = long word value in Index register

xx   8-bit address displacement

xxxx   16-bit address displacement

yy   8-bit immediate data

yyyy   16-bit immediate data or most significant word of 32-bit data

zzzz   Least significant word of 32-bit data

INTERFACING THE MC68000 WITH 6800 PERIPHERALS

Many peripheral components have been developed by Motorola and other manufacturers for the 8-bit 6800 microprocessor. In general, any **asynchronous** peripheral device can be used with the MC68000 with only a small amount of external logic needed to meet the interface requirements (handshaking, etc.). However, **the 6800-family components are based on synchronous read/write operations. This imposes certain constraints when you attempt to use a 6800 peripheral device with** an asynchronous processor such as **the MC68000.** Obviously, it was in Motorola's interest to design the MC68000 so that it would be able to use both conventional asynchronous devices and the family of existing synchronous 6800 devices. Therefore they have included logic to simplify interfacing 6800 peripheral devices.

Again, the MC68000 performs read/write operations asynchronously. The signals involved with these operations are the strobes ($\overline{AS}$, $\overline{UDS}$, $\overline{LDS}$), the R/$\overline{W}$ signal, the Data Transfer Acknowledge signal ($\overline{DTACK}$), and of course the address (A1-A23) and data (D0-D15) signals.

Three additional signals are used to perform the synchronous read/write operations required by 6800 peripheral devices. These signals are Valid Memory Address ($\overline{VMA}$), Valid Peripheral Address ($\overline{VPA}$), and Enable (E). Figure 7-29 illustrates the timing of the synchronous read and write cycles. After the MC68000 has output the address on A1-A23 and has asserted the Address Strobe ($\overline{AS}$), external logic is expected to decode information on the address lines. **If a 6800 peripheral device is being addressed, then the external logic should assert the $\overline{VPA}$ input to the MC68000. This causes the MC68000 to emulate the data transfer timing of the 6800 microprocessor. As a result, the transfer of data is synchronized with the clock signal E.** The MC68000 will keep the address outputs valid throughout this cycle.

During a read cycle, the 6800 peripheral device is expected to place data on the Data Bus when the E signal is high. Note that the Data Transfer Acknowledge ($\overline{DTACK}$) signal is not used since that signal implies an asynchronous transfer of data. Instead, the falling edge of E indicates that the data transfer (either read or write) has been completed. The MC68000 then proceeds to complete the cycle in the normal fashion by negating the strobe signals and returning the Address Bus to the high impedance state.

You will note in Figure 7-29 that there is a difference in the total number of CLK cycles for the read and write operations. You should not infer from this that all 6800-type read operations take four more CLK cycles than write operations. That is only the case in the example shown, and has to do with the phase of E when the read or write operation was begun. In general, the E signal and the current MC68000 cycle state will not be synchronized at the outset of a 6800 reference cycle. This is because the E signal has a duty cycle of 40%: E is high for four CLK periods and low for six CLK periods. The MC68000 instruction cycles, on the other hand, vary in the number of CLK signal periods needed to execute. During the write cycle we have shown in Figure 7-29, the E signal is in synchronization with the instruction execution cycle. Thus this particular write cycle takes the minimum possible number of CLK cycles to execute. Note that the MC68000 automatically inserts wait states after the $\overline{VPA}$ signal is input. The number of wait states inserted will depend on how much time is needed in order to synchronize with the signal.

The $\overline{VMA}$ signal is output by the MC68000 in response to the $\overline{VPA}$ output.

At the end of the read or write cycle, the 6800 peripheral device or the address decoding logic in the system must negate the $\overline{VPA}$ signal within one clock period after the MC68000 negates $\overline{AS}$. Otherwise, the MC68000 will assume that the following cycle is also supposed to be a 6800-type synchronous cycle.

Figure 7-30 summarizes the timing constraints of 6800 peripherals. It includes the 6800 processor signals for reference so you can compare them with those associated with the MC68000.

A SIMPLE MC68000/6800 INTERFACE EXAMPLE

Figure 7-31 illustrates a simple interface of two 6800 peripheral devices in an MC68000-based system. In this example, the address region 000000_{16} through $7FFFFF_{16}$ (the lower eight megabytes) is used for asynchronous devices including memory. The upper eight megabytes is used, albeit inefficiently, for the two synchronous 6800 peripheral devices. The PIA (Peripheral Interface Adaptor) is assigned addresses 800000_{16} through $BFFFFF_{16}$, while the ACIA (Asynchronous Communications Interface Adaptor) is assigned addresses $C00000_{16}$ through $FFFFFF_{16}$.

Interrupt request signals are connected directly to the $\overline{IPL0}$ and $\overline{IPL1}$ input pins of the MC68000. Note that $\overline{IPL2}$ is tied high. In this example, an interrupt from the ACIA causes $\overline{IPL0}$ to become active thus generating an interrupt of level 1 (the lowest priority). Both PIA interrupts are connected to $\overline{IPL1}$. When either of these becomes active, an interrupt of level 2 is generated. If both the ACIA and the PIA request an interrupt simultaneously, an interrupt of level 3 would be generated.

For a detailed description of how the MC68000 responds to interrupt requests, refer to our earlier discussion of MC68000 exception processing.

We have also included logic that will cause the MC68000 to use its autovector capability during response to an interrupt request from one of the 6800 family devices. Recall that if the $\overline{VPA}$ signal is asserted to the MC68000 during an interrupt acknowledge cycle, then no byte of vector data need be supplied by the requesting device; instead, the MC68000 gets the appropriate autovector from the exception processing vector table.

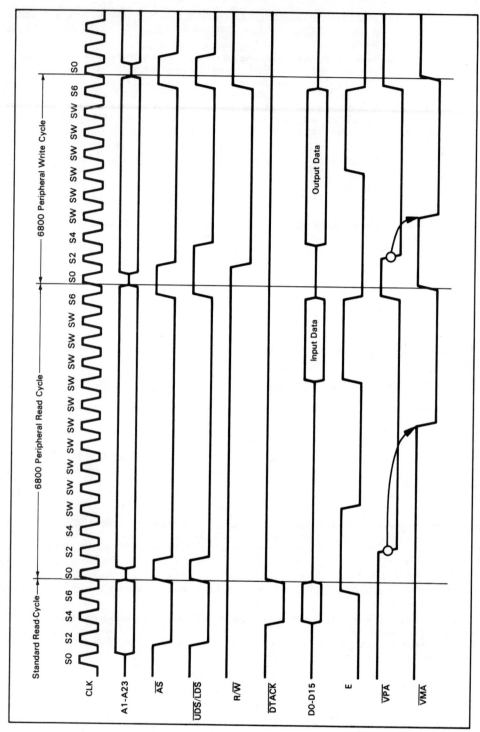

Figure 7-29. MC68000 Synchronous Read/Write Timing for 6800 Peripherals

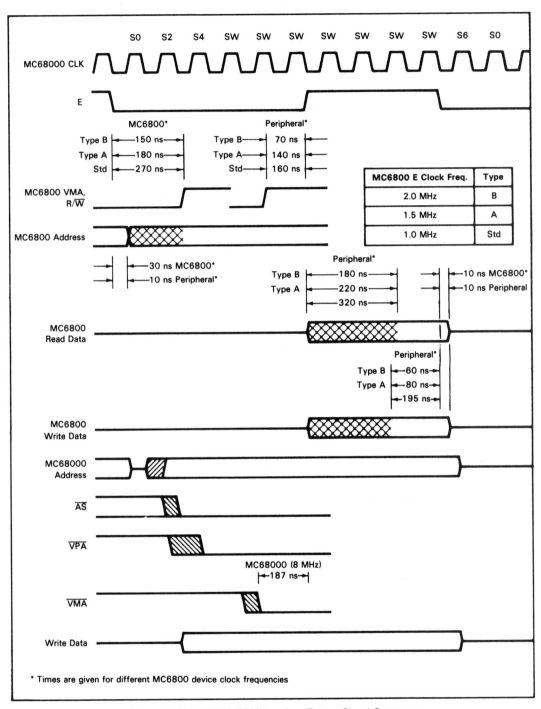

Figure 7-30. MC68000/6800 Interface Timing Signal Summary

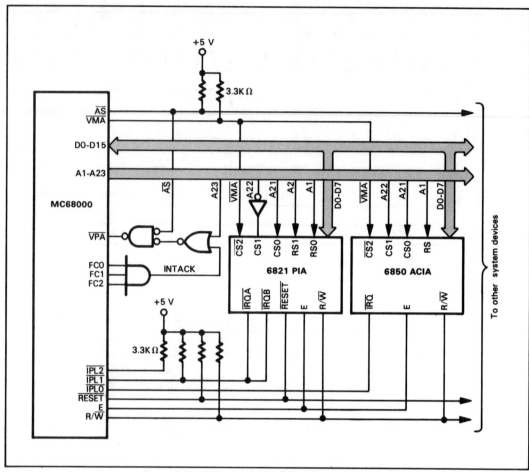

Figure 7-31. A Simple MC68000/6800 Interface Example

Table 7-4. MC68000 Instructions Which Use Implied Registers

Instruction	Implied Register(s)
Branch Conditional (Bcc), Branch Always (BRA)	PC
Branch to Subroutine (BSR)	PC, SP
Check Register against Bounds (CHK)	SSP, SR
Test Condition, Decrement and Branch (DBcc)	PC
Signed Divide (DIVS)	SSP, SR
Unsigned Divide (DIVU)	SSP, SR
Jump (JMP)	PC
Jump to Subroutine (JSR)	PC, SP
Link and Allocate (LINK)	SP
Move Condition Codes (MOVE CCR)	SR
Move Status Register (MOVE SR)	SR
Move User Stack Pointer (MOVE USP)	USP
Push Effective Address (PEA)	SP
Return from Exception (RTE)	PC, SP, SR
Return and Restore Condition Codes (RTR)	PC, SP, SR
Return from Subroutine (RTS)	PC, SP
Trap (TRAP)	SSP, SR
Trap on Overflow (TRAPV)	SSP, SR
Unlink (UNLK)	SP

Table 7-5. MC68000 Instructions Which Use Implied Registers

Primary Mnemonic	Alternate Mnemonic	Operand	Description
ADD. B	ADDI. B	data8,xx	Add Immediate Byte
ADD. W	ADD	xx,xx	Add Word
	ADDA.W	xx,An	Add Address Register Word
	ADDI. W	data16,xx	Add Immediate Word
ADD. L	ADDA.L	xx,An	Add Address Register Long
	ADDI.L	data32,xx	Add Immediate Long
ADDQ.B	ADD.B	data3,xx	Add Quick Byte
ADDQ.W	ADD	data3,xx	Add Quick Word
	ADD. W		
ADDQ.L	ADD. L	data3,xx	Add Quick Long
AND.B	ANDI.B	data8,xx	AND Immediate Byte
AND.W	AND	xx,xx	AND Word
	ANDI.W	data16,xx	AND Immediate Word
AND. L	ANDI.L	data32,xx	AND Immediate Long
Bcc	Bcc.S	xx	Conditional Branch Short
CLR.W	CLR	xx	Clear Word
CMP.B	CMPI.B	data8,xx	Compare Immediate Byte
CMP.W	CMP	xx,xx	Compare Word
	CMPA.W	xx,An	Compare Address Register Word
	CMPI.W	data16,xx	Compare Immediate Word
CMP. L	CMPA.L	xx,An	Compare Address Register Long
	CMPI.L	data32,xx	Compare Immediate Long
EOR.B	EORI. B	data8,xx	Exclusive OR Immediate Byte
EOR. W	EOR	xx,xx	Exclusive OR Word
	EORI. W	data16,xx	Exclusive OR Immediate Word
EOR. L	EORI. L	data32,xx	Exclusive OR Immediate Long
MOVE. W	MOVE	xx,xx	Move Word
	MOVEA. W	xx,An	Move Address Register Word
MOVE. L	MOVEA.L	xx,An	Move Address Register Long
MOVEQ	MOVE. L	data8,xx	Move Quick (always Long)
OR. B	ORI. B	data8,xx	OR Immediate Byte
OR. W	OR	xx,xx	OR Word
	ORI. W	data16,xx	OR Immediate Word
OR. L	ORI. L	data32,xx	OR Immediate Long
SUB. B	SUBI. B	data8,xx	Subtract Immediate Byte
SUB.W	SUB.	xx,xx	Subtract Word
	SUBA. W	xx,An	Subtract Address Register Word
	SUBI.W	data16,xx	Subtract Immediate Word
SUB. L	SUBA. L	xx,An	Subtract Address Register Long
	SUBI. L	data32,xx	Subtract Immediate Long
SUBQ. B	SUB. B	data3,xx	Subtract Quick Byte
SUBQ. W	SUB	data3,xx	Subtract Quick Word
	SUB.W		
SUBQ.L	SUB. L	data3,xx	Subtract Quick Long

Table 7-6. MC68000 Instruction Set Summary

Mnemonic	Operand(s)	Bytes	Clock Cycles	Status T	S	X	N	Z	V	C	Operation Performed
LEA	jadr,An	2,4, or 6	2(0/0)+								[An] — jadr / Load effective address into specified address register. The addressing size is long, although the address loaded may be byte, word, or long, depending on how it is subsequently used.[2]
MOVE.B	(An),Dn	2	8(2/0)				x	x	0	0	[Dn<0-7>] — [[An]] / Register indirect
	(An)+,Dn	2	8(2/0)				x	x	0	0	[Dn<0-7>] — [[An]], [An] — [An] + 1 / Register indirect with postincrement[1]
	−(An),Dn	2	10(2/0)				x	x	0	0	[An] — [An] − 1, [Dn<0-7>] — [[An]] / Register indirect with predecrement[1]
	d16(An),Dn	4	12(3/0)				x	x	0	0	[Dn<0-7>] — [[An] + d16] / Register indirect with displacement
	d8(An,i),Dn (sadr)	4	14(3/0)				x	x	0	0	[Dn<0-7>] — [[An] + d8 + [i]] / Register indirect, indexed
	addr,Dn	4 or 6	4(1/0)+				x	x	0	0	[Dn<0-7>] — [addr] / Direct address
	label,Dn	4	12(3/0)				x	x	0	0	[Dn<0-7>] — [[PC] + d16] / Program relative
	label(i),Dn	4	14(3/0)				x	x	0	0	[Dn<0-7>] — [[PC] + d8 + [i]] / Program relative, indexed / Load byte to data register from memory location specified by any of the addressing modes above. Bits 8-31 of the data register are not affected.
MOVE.B	Dn,(An)	2	9(1/1)				x	x	0	0	[[An]] — [Dn<0-7>] / Register indirect
	Dn,(An)+	2	9(1/1)				x	x	0	0	[[An]] — [Dn<0-7>], [An] — [An] + 1 / Register indirect with postincrement[1]
	Dn,−(An)	2	9(1/1)				x	x	0	0	[An] — [An] − 1, [[An]] — [Dn<0-7>] / Register indirect with predecrement[1]
	Dn,d16(An)	4	13(2/1)				x	x	0	0	[[An] + d16] — [Dn<0-7>] / Register indirect with displacement
	Dn,d8(An, i) (dadr)	4	15(2/1)				x	x	0	0	[[An] + d8 + [i]] — [Dn<0-7>] / Register indirect, indexed
	Dn,addr	4 or 6	5(0/1)+				x	x	0	0	[addr] — [Dn<0-7>] / Direct address / Store byte from data register to memory locat on specified by any of the addressing modes above.
MOVE.B	sadr,dadr	2,4 6,8 or 10	5(1/1)+				x	x	0	0	[dadr] — [sadr] / Store byte from specified source memory location to specified destination memory location.[1]

I/O and Primary Memory Reference

Notes:
1. Postincrement and predecrement change by 1, unless the address register specified is the Stack Pointer (A7), where the address is changed by 2 rather than 1 to keep the Stack Pointer on a word boundary.
2. The effective address must be on an even word boundary (0000, 0002, 0004, etc.).
3. Postincrement and predecrement change by 2.
4. Postincrement and predecrement change by 4.

Table 7-6. MC68000 Instruction Set Summary (Continued)

Mnemonic	Operand(s)	Bytes	Clock Cycles	T	S	X	N	Z	V	C	Operation Performed
MOVE.W	sadr, Dn	2, 4 or 6	4(1/0)+				×		0	0	[Dn<0-15>] ← [sadr] Load word to data register from memory location. Bits 16-31 of the data register are not affected.[2,3]
MOVE.W	sadr,An	2, 4 or 6	4(1/0)+								[An] <0-15>] ← [sadr] [An <16-31>] ← [An<15>] Load word to address register from memory location. The sign is extended to all upper bits of the register.[2,3]
MOVE.W	rs,dadr	2, 4 or 6	5(0/1)+				×	×	0	0	[dadr] ← [rs<0-15>] Store word to memory location from data or address register.[2,3]
MOVE.W	sadr,dadr	2, 4 6, 8 or 10	5(0/1)+				×	×	0	0	[dadr] ← [sadr] Store word from source memory location to destination memory location.[2,3]
MOVE.L	sadr,Dn	2, 4 or 6	4(1/0)+				×	×	0	0	[Dn<0-31>] ← [sadr] Load long word to data register from memory location.[2,3]
MOVE.L	sadr,An	2, 4 or 6	8(2/0)+								[An<0-31>] ← [sadr] Load long word to address register from memory location.[2,4]
MOVE.L	rs,dadr	2, 4 or 6	10(0/2)+				×	×	0	0	[dadr] ← [rs<0-31>] Store long word from data or address register to memory location.[2,4]
MOVE.L	sadr,dadr	2, 4 6, 8 or 10	14(1/2)+				×	×	0	0	[dadr] ← [sadr] Store long word from source memory location to destination memory location.[2,4]
MOVEM.W	jadr,reg-list	4, 6 or 8	8 + 4n(2 + n/0)+								[reg1<0-15>] ← [[An]], [reg1<16-31>] ← [reg1<15>] [reg2<0-15>] ← [[An + 2]],[reg2<16-31>] ← [reg2<15>] [reg3<0-15>] ← [[An + 4]],[reg3<16-31>] ← [reg3<15>] . . . [regn<0-15>] ← [[An + 2n-2]],[regn<16-31>] ← [regn<15>] Load multiple words from sequential memory locations to specified registers, in order D0-D7, A0-A7. The sign is extended to all upper bits of the register.[2]
MOVEM.W	(An)+,reg-list	4	8 + 4n(2 + n/0)+								[reg1<0-15>] ← [[An]],[reg1<16-31>] ← [reg1<15>],[An] ← [An + 2] [reg2<0-15>] ← [[An]],[reg2<16-31>] ← [reg2<15>],[An] ← [An + 2] [reg3<0-15>] ← [[An]],[reg3<16-31>] ← [reg3<15>], [An] ← [An + 2] . . . [regn<0-15>] ← [[An]], [regn<16-31>] ← [regn<15>],[An] ← [An + 2] Same as above except with postincrement.[3]

I/O and Primary Memory Reference (Continued)

Table 7-6. MC68000 Instruction Set Summary (Continued)

Mnemonic	Operand(s)	Bytes	Clock Cycles	T	S	X	N	Z	V	C	Operation Performed
MOVEM.W	reg-list,madr	4, 6 or 8	$4 + 5n(1/n)+$								$[[An]] \leftarrow [reg_1 <0\text{-}15>]$ $[[An + 2]] \leftarrow [reg_2 <0\text{-}15>]$ $[[An + 4]] \leftarrow [reg_3 <0\text{-}15>]$ . . . $[[An + (2n\text{-}2)]] \leftarrow [reg_n <0\text{-}15>]$ Store multiple words to sequential memory locations from specified registers, in order D0-D7, A0-A7.[2]
MOVEM.W	reg-list,−(An)	4	$4 + 5n(1/n)+$								$[An] \leftarrow [An\text{-}2],[[An]] \leftarrow [reg_n <0\text{-}15>]$ . . . $[An] \leftarrow [An\text{-}2],[[An]] \leftarrow [reg_3 <0\text{-}15>]$ $[An] \leftarrow [An\text{-}2],[[An]] \leftarrow [reg_2 <0\text{-}15>]$ $[An] \leftarrow [An\text{-}2],[[An]] \leftarrow [reg_1 <0\text{-}15>]$ Store multiple words to sequential memory locations with predecrement to specified registers, in order A7-A0, D7-D0.[2,3]
MOVEM.L	jadr,reg-list (An)+,reg-list reg-list,madr reg-list,−(An)	4, 6 or 8 4 4, 6 or 8 4	$8 + 8n(2 + 2n/0)$ $8 + 8n(2 + 2n/0)$ $4 + 10n(1/n)+$ $4 + 10n(1/n)$								Same as MOVEM.W except that all 32 bits of the registers are moved.[2,4]
MOVEP.W	d16(An),Dn	4	$16(4/0)$								$[Dn<8\text{-}15>] \leftarrow [[An] + d16],[An] \leftarrow [An] + 2$ $[Dn<0\text{-}7>] \leftarrow [[An] + d16]$ Load peripheral data bytes from alternate memory locations to data register word. The address is a byte address.[3]
MOVEP.W	Dn,d16(An)	4	$18(2/2)$								$[[An] + d16] \leftarrow [Dn <8\text{-}15>],[An] \leftarrow [An] + 2$ $[[An] + d16] \leftarrow [Dn <0\text{-}7>]$ Store peripheral data bytes from data register long to alternate memory locations. The address is a byte address.[3]
MOVEP.L	dos(An),Dn	4	$24(6/0)$								$[Dn<24\text{-}31>] \leftarrow [[An] + d16],[An] \leftarrow [An] + 2$ $[Dn<16\text{-}23>] \leftarrow [[An] + d16],[An] \leftarrow [An] + 2$ $[Dn<8\text{-}15>] \leftarrow [[An] + d16],[An] \leftarrow [An] + 2$ $[Dn<0\text{-}7>] \leftarrow [[An] + d16]$ Load peripheral data bytes from alternate memory locations to data register long. The address is a byte address.[3]
MOVEP.L	Dn,d16(An)	4	$28(2/4)$								$[[An] + d16] \leftarrow [Dn <24\text{-}31>],[An] \leftarrow [An] + 2$ $[[An] + d16] \leftarrow [Dn <16\text{-}23>],[An] \leftarrow [An] + 2$ $[[An] + d16] \leftarrow [Dn <8\text{-}15>],[An] \leftarrow [An] + 2$ $[[An] + d16] \leftarrow [Dn <0\text{-}7>]$ Store peripheral data bytes from data register long to alternate memory locations. The address is a byte address.[3]

I/O and Primary Memory Reference (Continued)

Table 7-6. MC68000 Instruction Set Summary (Continued)

Mnemonic	Operand(s)	Bytes	Clock Cycles	Status							Operation Performed
				T	S	X	N	Z	V	C	
ABCD	-(sAn),-(dAn)	2	19(3/1)			X	U	X	U	X	[sAn] — [sAn] - 1 [dAn] — [dAn]-1 [[dAn]] — [[dAn]] + [[sAn]] + X Add decimal memory byte to memory byte with carry (Extend bit). Both addresses are byte[1].
ADD.B	sadr,Dn	2, 4 or 6	4(1/0)+			X	X	X	X	X	[Dn<0-7>] — [Dn<0-7>] + [sadr] Add byte to data register from memory location. Bits 8-31 of the data register are not affected.[1]
ADD.B	Dn,dadr	2, 4 or 6	9(1/1)+			X	X	X	X	X	[dadr] — [dadr] + [Dn<0-7>] Add byte to memory location from data register.[1]
ADD.W	sadr,Dn	2, 4 or 6	4(1/0)+			X	X	X	X	X	[Dn<0-15>] — [Dn<0-15>] + [sadr] Add word to data register from memory location. Bits 16-31 of the data register are not affected.[2,3]
ADD.W	sadr,An	2, 4 or 6	8(1/0)+								[An<0-31>] — [An<0-31>] + [sadr] (sign extended) Add word to address register from memory location. The sign of the memory word is extended to a full 32 bits for the operation.[2,3]
ADD.W	Dn,Dadr	2, 4 or 6	9(1/1)+			X	X	X	X	X	[dadr] — [dadr] + [Dn<0-15>] Add word to memory location from data register.[2,3]
ADD.L	sadr,Dn	2, 4 or 6	6(1/0)+			X	X	X	X	X	[Dn<0-31>] — [Dn<0-31>] + [sadr] Add long word to data registers from memory location.[2,4]
ADD.L	sadr,An	2, 4 or 6	6(1/0)+								[An<0-31>] — [An<0-31>] + [sadr] Add long word to address register from memory location.[2,4]
ADD.L	Dn,dadr	2, 4 or 6	14(1/2)+			X	X	X	X	X	[dadr] — [dadr] + [Dn<0-31>] Add long word to memory locations from data register.[2,4]
ADDX.B	-(sAn),-dAn)	2	19(3/1)			X	X	X	X	X	[sAn] — [sAn] - 1 [dAn] — [dAn] - 1 [[dAn]] — [[dAn]] + [[sAn]] + X Add memory byte to memory byte with carry (Extend bit). Both addresses are byte.[1]
ADDX.W	-(sAn),-(dAn)	2	19(3/1)			X	X	X	X	X	[sAn] — [sAn] - 2 [dAn] — [dAn] - 2 [[dAn]] — [[dAn]] + [[sAn]] + X Add memory word to memory word with carry (Extend bit). Both address are word.[2,3]
ADDX.L	-(sAn),-(dAn)	2	32(5/2)			X	X	X	X	X	[sAn] — [sAn] - 4 [dAn] — [dAn] - 4 [[dAn]] — [[dAn]] + [[sAn]] + X Add memory long word to memory long word with carry (Extend bit). Both addresses are long word.[2,4]
AND.B	sadr,Dn	2, 4 or 6	4(1/0)+				X	X	0	0	[Dn<0-7>] — [Dn<0-7>] < [sadr] AND byte to data register from memory location. Bits 8-31 of the data register are not affected.[1]
AND.B	Dn,dadr	2, 4 or 6	9(1/1)+				X	X	0	0	[dadr] — [dadr] < [Dn<0-7>] AND byte to memory location from data register.[1]

Secondary Memory Reference (Memory Operate)

7-54

Table 7-6. MC68000 Instruction Set Summary (Continued)

Mnemonic	Operand(s)	Bytes	Clock Cycles	T	S	X	N	Z	V	C	Operation Performed
AND.W	sadr,Dn	2, 4 or 6	4(1/0)+				X	X	0	0	[Dn<0-15>] — [Dn<0-15>] ∧ [sadr] AND word to data register from memory location. Bits 16-31 of the data register are not affected.2, 3
AND.W	Dn,dadr	2, 4 or 6	9(1/1)+				X	X	0	0	[dadr] — [dadr] ∧ [Dn<0-15>] AND word to memory location from data register.2, 3
AND.L	sadr,Dn	2, 4 or 6	6(1/0)+				X	X	0	0	[Dn<0-31>] — [Dn<0-31>] ∧ [sadr] AND long word to data register from memory location.2, 4
AND.L	Dn,dadr	2, 4 or 6	14(1/2)+				X	X	0	0	[dadr] — [dadr] ∧ [Dn<0-31>] AND long word to memory location from data register.2, 4
CLR.B	dadr	2, 4 or 6	9(1/1)+				0	1	0	0	[dadr] — 0 Clear memory byte to zeroes.1
CLR.W	dadr	2, 4 or 6	9(1/1)+				0	1	0	0	[dadr] — 0 Clear memory word to zeroes.2, 3
CLR.L	dadr	2, 4 or 6	14(1/2)+				0	1	0	0	[dadr] — 0 Clear memory long word to zeroes.2, 4
CMP.B	sadr,Dn	2, 4 or 6	4(1/0)+				X	X	X	X	[Dn<0-7>] — [sadr] Compare data register byte with memory byte and set condition codes accordingly. Register/memory data are not changed on any compares.1
CMP.W	sadr,Dn	2, 4 or 6	4(1/0)+				X	X	X	X	[Dn<0-15>] — [sadr] Compare data register word with memory word and set condition codes accordingly.2, 3
CMP.W	sadr,An	2, 4 or 6	6(1/0)+				X	X	X	X	[An<0-15>] — [sadr] Compare address register word with memory word and set condition codes accordingly.2, 3
CMP.L	sadr,Dn	2, 4 or 6	6(1/0)+				X	X	X	X	[Dn<0-31>] — [sadr] Compare data register with memory long word and set condition codes accordingly.2, 4
CMP.L	sadr,An	2, 4 or 6	6(1/0)+				X	X	X	X	[An<0-31>] — [sadr] Compare address register with memory long word and set condition codes accordingly.2, 4
CMPM.B	(sAn)+,(dAn)+	2	12(3/0)				X	X	X	X	[[dAn]] — [[sAn]] [dAn] — [dAn] + 1 [sAn] — [sAn] + 1 Compare memory bytes and set condition codes accordingly. The memory data are not changed on any compares.1
CMPM.W	(sAn)+,(dAn)+	2	12(3/0)				X	X	X	X	[[dAn]] — [[sAn]] [dAn] — [dAn] + 2 [sAn] — [sAn] + 2 Compare memory words and set condition codes accordingly.2, 3
CMPM.L	(sAn)+,(dAn)+	2	20(5/0)				X	X	X	X	[[dAn]] — [[sAn]] [dAn] — [dAn] + 4 [sAn] — [sAn] + 4 Compare memory long words and set condition codes accordingly.2, 4

Secondary Memory Reference (Memory Operate) (Continued)

Table 7-6. MC68000 Instruction Set Summary (Continued)

Mnemonic	Operand(s)	Bytes	Clock Cycles	Status							Operation Performed
				T	S	X	N	Z	V	C	
DIVS	sadr,Dn	2, 4 or 6	<158(1/0)+				X	X	X	0	[Dn<0-15>] ← [Dn<0-31>] ÷ [sadr]; [Dn<16-31>] ← remainder; Divide signed numbers. Division by zero causes a TRAP. The source address is a word address.[2, 3]
DIVU	sadr,Dn	2, 4 or 6	≤140(1/0)+				X	X	X	0	[Dn<0-15>] ← [Dn<0-31>] ÷ [sadr]; [Dn<16-31>] ← remainder; Divide unsigned numbers. Division by zero causes a TRAP. The source address is a word address.[2, 3]
EOR.B	Dn,dadr	2, 4 or 6	9(1/1)+				X	X	0	0	[dadr] ← [dadr] ⊻ [Dn<0-7>]; Exclusive-OR byte to memory location from data register.[1]
EOR.W	Dn,dadr	2, 4 or 6	9(1/1)+				X	X	0	0	[dadr] ← [dadr] ⊻ [Dn<0-15>]; Exclusive-OR word to memory location from data registers.[2, 3]
EOR.L	Dn,dadr	2, 4 or 6	14(1/2)+				X	X	0	0	[dadr] ← [dadr] ⊻ [Dn<0-31>]; Exclusive-OR long word to memory location from data register.[2, 4]
MULS	sadr,Dn	2, 4 or 6	<70(1/0)+				X	X	0	0	[Dn<0-31>] ← [Dn<0-15>] × [sadr]; Multiply two 16-bit signed numbers, yielding a 32-bit signed product. The source address is a word address.[2, 3]
MULU	sadr,Dn	2, 4 or 6	<74(2/0)+				X	X	0	0	[Dn<0-31>] ← [Dn<0-15>] × [sadr]; Multiply two 16-bit unsigned numbers, yielding a 32-bit unsigned product. The source address is a word address.[2, 3]
NBCD	dadr	2, 4 or 6	9(1/1)+			X	U	X	U	X	[dadr] ← 0 - [dadr] - X; Negate decimal memory byte. This operation produces the tens complement if X = 0 or the nines complement if X = 1.
NEG.B	dadr	2, 4 or 6	9(1/1)+			X	X	X	X	X	[dadr] ← 0 - [dadr]; Negate memory byte.[1]
NEG.W	dadr	2, 4 or 6	9(1/1)+			X	X	X	X	X	[dadr] ← 0 - [dadr]; Negate memory word.[2, 3]
NEG.L	dadr	2, 4 or 6	14(1/2)+			X	X	X	X	X	[dadr] ← 0 - [dadr]; Negate memory long word.[2, 4]
NEGX.B	dadr	2, 4 or 6	9(1/1)+			X	X	X	X	X	[dadr] ← 0 - [dadr] - X; Negate memory byte with Extend bit.[1]
NEGX.W	dadr	2, 4 or 6	9(1/1)+			X	X	X	X	X	[dadr] ← 0 - [dadr] - X; Negate memory word with Extend bit.[2, 3]
NEGX.L	dadr	2, 4 or 6	14(1/2)+			X	X	X	X	X	[dadr] ← 0 - [dadr] - X; Negate memory long word with Extend bit.[2, 4]
NOT.B	dadr	2, 4 or 6	9(1/1)+				X	X	0	0	[dadr] ← [dadr]; Ones complement memory byte.[1]
NOT.W	dadr	2, 4 or 6	9(1/1)+				X	X	0	0	[dadr] ← [dadr]; Ones complement memory word.[2, 3]
NOT.L	dadr	2, 4 or 6	14(1/2)+				X	X	0	0	[dadr] ← [dadr]; Ones complement memory long word.[2, 4]
OR.B	sadr,Dn	2, 4 or 6	4(1/0)+				X	X	0	0	[Dn<0-7>] ← [Dn<0-7>] ∨ [sadr]; OR byte to data register from memory location. Bits 8-31 of the data register are not affected.[1]
OR.B	Dn,dadr	2, 4 or 6	9(1/1)+				X	X	0	0	[dadr] ← [dadr] ∨ [Dn<0-7>]; OR byte to memory location from data register.[1]

Secondary Memory Reference (Memory Operate) (Continued)

Table 7-6. MC68000 Instruction Set Summary (Continued)

Mnemonic	Operand(s)	Bytes	Clock Cycles	T	S	X	N	Z	V	C	Operation Performed
OR.W	sadr,Dn	2, 4 or 6	4(1/0)+				X	X	0	0	[Dn<0-15>] ← [Dn<0-15>] ∨ [sadr] OR word to data register from memory location. Bits 16-31 of the data register are not affected.[2,3]
OR.W	Dn,dadr	2, 4 or 6	9(1/1)+				X	X	0	0	[dadr] ← [dadr] ∨ [Dn<0-15>] OR word to memory location from data register.[2,3]
OR.L	sadr,Dn	2, 4 or 6	6(1/0)+				X	X	0	0	[Dn<0-31>] ← [Dn<0-31>] ∨ [sadr] OR long word to data register from memory location.[2,4]
OR.L	Dn,dadr	2, 4 or 6	14(1/2)+				X	X	0	0	[dadr] ← [dadr] ∨ [Dn∨0-31>] OR long word to memory location from data register.[2,4]
SBCD	-(sAn),-(dAn)	2	19(3/1)			X	U	X	U	X	[sAn] ← [sAn] - 1 [dAn] ← [dAn] - 1 [[dAn]] ← [[dAn]] - [[sAn]] - X Subtract decimal memory byte from memory byte with carry (Extend bit). Both addresses are byte.[1]
SCC	dadr	2, 4 or 6	9(1/1)+								[dadr] ← [all 1's if cc = TRUE [dadr] ← [all 0's if cc = FALSE Set status in memory byte.[1]
SUB.B	sadr,Dn	2, 4 or 6	4(1/0)+			X	X	X	X	X	[Dn<0-7>] ← [Dn<0-7>] - [sadr] Subtract memory byte from byte in data register. Bits 8-31 of the data register are not affected.[1]
SUB.B	Dn,dadr	2, 4 or 6	9(1/1)+			X	X	X	X	X	[dadr] ← [dadr] - [Dn<0-7>] Subtract byte in data register from memory byte.[1]
SUB.W	sadr,Dn	2, 4 or 6	4(1/0)+			X	X	X	X	X	[Dn<0-15>] ← [Dn<0-15>] - [sadr] Subtract memory word from word in data register. Bits 16-31 of the data register are not affected.[1]
SUB.W	sadr,An	2, 4 or 6	8(1/0)+								[An<0-31>] ← [An<0-31>] - [sadr] (sign extended) Subtract memory word from address register contents. The sign of the memory word is extended to a full 32 bits for the operation.[2,3]
SUB.W	Dn,dadr	2, 4 or 6	9(1/1)+			X	X	X	X	X	[dadr] ← [dadr] - [Dn<015>] Subtract data register word from memory location word.[2,3]
SUB.L	sadr,Dn	2, 4 or 6	6(1/0)+			X	X	X	X	X	[Dn<0-31>] ← [Dn<0-31>] - [sadr] Subtract memory long word from data register contents.[2,4]
SUB.L	sadr,An	2, 4 or 6	6(1/0)+								[An<0-31>] ← [An<0-31>] - [sadr] Subtract memory long word from address register contents.[2,4]
SUB.L	Dn,dadr	2, 4 or 6	14(1/2)+			X	X	X	X	X	[dadr] ← [dadr] - [Dn<0-31>] Subtract contents of data register from memory long word.[2,4]
SUBX.B	-(sAn),-(dAn)	2	19(3/1)			X	X	X	X	X	[sAn] ← [sAn] - 1 [dAn] ← [dAn] - 1 [[dAn]] ← [[dAn]] - [[sAn]] - X Subtract memory byte from memory byte with borrow (Extend bit). Both addresses are byte.[1]
SUBX.W	-(sAn),-(dAn)	2	19(3/1)			X	X	X	X	X	[sAn] ← [sAn] - 2 [dAn] ← [dAn] - 2 [[dAn]] ← [[dAn]] - [[sAn]] - X Subtract memory word from memory word with borrow (Extend bit). Both addresses are word.[2,3]

Secondary Memory Reference (Memory Operate) (Continued)

Table 7-6. MC68000 Instruction Set Summary (Continued)

Category	Mnemonic	Operand(s)	Bytes	Clock Cycles	T	S	X	N	Z	V	C	Operation Performed
I/O and Primary Memory Reference (Continued)	SUBX.L	-(sAn),-(dAn)	2	32(5/2)			x	x	x	x	x	[sAn] — [sAn] – 4; [dAn] — [dAn] – 4; [[dAn]] — [[dAn]] – [[sAn]] – X; Subtract memory long word from memory long word with borrow (Extend bit). Both addresses are long word.[2, 4]
	TAS	dadr	2, 4 or 6	11(1/1)+				x	x	0	0	[dadr<7>] — 1; Test status of memory byte and set high-order bit to 1.
	TST.B	dadr	2, 4 or 6	4(1/0)+				x	x	0	0	[dadr] — 0; Test status of memory byte. The byte value is not changed.
	TST.W	dadr	2, 4 or 6	4(1/0)+				x	x	0	0	[dadr] — 0; Test status of memory word. The word value is not changed.
	TST.L	dadr	2, 4 or 6	4(1/0)+				x	x	0	0	[dadr] — 0; Test status of memory long word. The long word value is not changed.
Immediate	MOVEQ	data8,Dn	2	4(1/0)				x	x	0	0	[Dn<0-7>] — data8; [Dn<8-32>] — [Dn<7>]; Load immediate data byte to data register. The sign is extended to all upper bits of the data register.
	MOVE.B	data8,Dn	4	8(2/0)				x	x	0	0	[Dn<0-7>] — data8; Load immediate data byte to data register. Bits 8-31 of the data register are not affected.
	MOVE.B	data8,dadr	4, 6 or 8	9(1/1)+				x	x	0	0	[dadr] — [data8]; Load immediate data byte into memory location.[1]
	MOVE.W	data16,Dn	4	8(2/0)				x	x	0	0	[Dn<0-15>] — data16; Load immediate data word to data register. Bits 16-31 of the data register are not affected.
	MOVE.W	data16,An	4	8(2/0)								[An<0-15>] — data16; [An<16-31>] — [An<15>]; Load immediate data word to address register. The sign is extended to all upper bits of the register.
	MOVE.W	data16,dadr	4, 6 or 8	9(1/1)+				x	x	0	0	[dadr] — data16; Load immediate data word into memory location.[2, 3]
	MOVE.L	data32,Dn	6	12(3/0)				x	x	0	0	[Dn<0-31>] — data32; Load immediate data long word into data register.
	MOVE.L	data32,An	6	12(3/0)								[An<0-31>] — data32; Load immediate data long word into address register.
	MOVE.L	data32,dadr	6, 8 or 10	18(2/2)+				x	x	0	0	[dadr] — data32; Load immediate data long word into memory location.[2, 4]
Immediate Operate	ADD.B	data8,Dn	4	8(2/0)			x	x	x	x	x	[Dn<0-7>] — [Dn<0-7>] + data8; Add immediate data byte to data register. Bits 8-31 of the data register are not affected.
	ADD.B	data8,dadr	4, 6 or 8	13(2/1)+			x	x	x	x	x	[dadr] — [dadr] + data8; Add immediate data byte to memory location.[1]
	ADD.W	data16,Dn	4	8(2/0)			x	x	x	x	x	[Dn<0-15>] — [Dn<0-15>] + data16; Add immediate data word to data register. Bits 16-31 of the data register are not affected.

Table 7-6. MC68000 Instruction Set Summary (Continued)

Mnemonic	Operand(s)	Bytes	Clock Cycles	T	S	X	N	Z	V	C	Operation Performed
ADD.W	data16,An	4	8(2/0)								[An<0-31>] ← [An<0-31>] + data 16 (sign extended) Add immediate data word to address register. The sign of the data word is extended to a full 32 bits for the operation.
ADD.W	data16,dadr	4, 6 or 8	13(2/1)+			X	X	X	X	X	[dadr] ← [dadr] + data16 Add immediate data word to memory location.2, 3
ADDL	data32,Dn	6	16(3/0)			X	X	X	X	X	[Dn<0-31>] ← [Dn<0-31>] + data32 Add immediate data long word to data register.
ADDL	data32,An	6	16(3/0)								[An<0-31>] ← [An<0-31>] + data32 Add immediate data long word to address register.
ADDL	data32,dadr	6, 8 or 10	22(3/2)+			X	X	X	X	X	[dadr] ← [dadr] + data32 Add immediate data long word to memory location.2, 4
ADDQ.B	data3,Dn	2	4(1/0)			X	X	X	X	X	[Dn<0-7>] ← [Dn<0-7>] + data3 Add immediate three bits to data register byte. Bits 8-31 of the data register are not affected.
ADDQ.B	data3,dadr	2, 4 or 6	9(1/0)+			X	X	X	X	X	[dadr] ← [dadr] + data3 Add immediate three bits to memory byte.1
ADDQ.W	data3,Dn	2	4(1/0)			X	X	X	X	X	[Dn<0-15>] ← [Dn<0-15>] + data3 Add immediate three bits to data register word. Bits 16-31 of the data register are not affected.
ADDQ.W	data3,An	2	4(1/0)								[An<0-15>] ← [An<0-15>] + data3 Add immediate three bits to address register word. Bits 16-31 of the address register are not affected.
ADDQ.W	data3,dadr	2, 4 or 6	9(1/1)+			X	X	X	X	X	[dadr] ← [dadr] + data3 Add immediate three bits to memory word.2, 3
ADDQL	data3,Dn	2	8(1/0)			X	X	X	X	X	[Dn<0-31>] ← [Dn<0-31>] + data3 Add immediate three bits to data register long word.
ADDQL	data3,An	2	8(1/0)								[An<0-31>] ← [An<0-31>] + data3 Add immediate three bits to address register long word.
ADDQL	data3,dadr	2, 4 or 6	14(1/2)			X	X	X	X	X	[dadr] ← [dadr] + data3 Add immediate three bits to memory long word.2, 4
AND.B	data8,Dn	4	8(2/0)				X	X	0	0	[Dn<0-7>] ← [Dn<0-7>] ∧ data8 AND immediate data byte to data register. Bits 8-31 of the data register are not affected.
AND.B	data8,dadr	4, 6 or 8	13(2/1)+				X	X	0	0	[dadr] ← [dadr] ∧ data8 AND immediate data byte to memory byte.1
AND.W	data16,Dn	4	8(2/0)				X	X	0	0	[Dn<0-15>] ← [Dn<0-15>] ∧ data16 AND immediate data word to data register. Bits 16-31 of the data register are not affected.
AND.W	data16,dadr	4, 6 or 8	13(2/1)				X	X	0	0	[dadr] ← [dadr] ∧ data16 AND immediate data word to memory word.2, 3
ANDL	data32,Dn	6	16(3/0)				X	X	0	0	[Dn<0-31>] ← [Dn<0-31>] ∧ data32 AND immediate data long word to data register.
ANDL	data32,dadr	6, 8 or 10	22(3/2)+				X	X	0	0	[dadr] ← [dadr] ∧ data32 AND immediate data long word to memory word.2, 4

Immediate Operate (Continued)

7-59

Table 7-6. MC68000 Instruction Set Summary (Continued)

Mnemonic	Operand(s)	Bytes	Clock Cycles	T	S	X	N	Z	V	C	Operation Performed
CMP.B	data8,Dn	4	8(2/0)				X	X	X	X	[Dn<0-7>] − data8. Compare data register byte with immediate data byte and set condition codes accordingly. Register data are not changed on any compares.
CMP.B	data8,dadr	4, 6 or 8	8(2/0)+				X	X	X	X	[dadr] − data8. Compare memory byte with immediate data byte and set condition codes accordingly.[1]
CMP.W	data16,Dn	4	8(2/0)				X	X	X	X	[Dn<0-15>] − data16. Compare data register word with immediate data word and set condition codes accordingly.
CMP.W	data16,An	4	8(2/0)				X	X	X	X	[An<0-15>] − data 16. Compare address register word with immediate data word and set condition codes accordingly.
CMP.W	data16,dadr	4, 6 or 8	8(2/0)+				X	X	X	X	[dadr] − data16. Compare memory word with immediate data word and set condition codes accordingly.[2,3]
CMP.L	data32,Dn	6	14(3/0)				X	X	X	X	[Dn<0-31>] − data32. Compare data register with immediate data long word and set condition codes accordingly.
CMP.L	data32,An	6	14(3/0)				X	X	X	X	[An<0-31>] − data32. Compare address register with immediate data long word and set condition codes accordingly.
CMP.L	data32,dadr	6, 8 or 10	12(3/0)+				X	X	X	X	[dadr] − data32. Compare memory long word with immediate data long word and set condition codes accordingly.[2,4]
DIVS	data16,Dn	4	≤162(2/0)				X	X	X	0	[Dn<0-15>] − [Dn<0-31>] ÷ data16; [Dn<16-31>] − remainder. Divide signed numbers. Division by zero causes a TRAP.
DIVU	data16,Dn	4	≤148(2/0)				X	X	X	0	[Dn<0-15>] − [Dn<0-31>] ÷ data16; [Dn<16-31>] − remainder. Divide unsigned numbers. Division by zero causes a TRAP.
EOR.B	data8,Dn	4	8(2/0)				X	X	0	0	[Dn<0-7>] − [Dn<0-7>] ⊻ data8. Exclusive-OR data byte to data register. Bits 8-31 of the data register are not affected.
EOR.B	data8,dadr	4, 6 or 8	13(2/1)+				X	X	0	0	[dadr] − [dadr] ⊻ data8. Exclusive-OR data byte to memory byte.[1]
EOR.W	data16,Dn	4	8(2/0)				X	X	0	0	[Dn<0-15>] − [Dn<0-15>] ⊻ data16. Exclusive-OR data word to data register. Bits 16-31 of the data register are not affected.
EOR.W	data16,dadr	4, 6 or 8	13(2/1)+				X	X	0	0	[dadr] − [dadr] ⊻ data16. Exclusive-OR immediate data word to memory word.[2,3]
EOR.L	data32,Dn	6	16(3/0)				X	X	0	0	[Dn<0-31>] − [Dn>0-31>] ⊻ data32. Exclusive-OR immediate data long word to data register.
EOR.L	data32,dadr	6, 8 or 10	22(3/2)+				X	X	0	0	[dadr] − [dadr] ⊻ data32. Exclusive-OR immediate data long word to memory.[2,4]

Immediate Operate (Continued)

Table 7-6. MC68000 Instruction Set Summary (Continued)

Mnemonic	Operand(s)	Bytes	Clock Cycles	T	S	X	N	Z	V	C	Operation Performed
MULS	data16,Dn	4	≤74(2/0)				X	X	0	0	[Dn<0-311>] — [Dn<0-15>] x data16. Multiply two 16-bit signed numbers, yielding a 32-bit signed product.
MULU	data16,Dn	4	≤74(2/0)				X	X	0	0	[Dn<0-31>] — [Dn<0-15>] x data16. Multiply two 16-bit unsigned numbers, yielding a 32-bit unsigned product.
ORB	data8,Dn	4	8(2/0)				X	X	0	0	[Dn<0-7>] — [Dn<0-7>] V data8. OR immediate data byte to data register. Bits 8-31 of the data register are not affected.
ORB	data8,dadr	4, 6 or 8	13(2/1)+				X	X	0	0	[dadr] — [dadr] V data8. OR immediate data byte to memory byte.[1]
ORW	data16,Dn	4	8(2/0)				X	X	0	0	[Dn<0-15>] — [Dn<0-15>] V data16. OR immediate data word to data register. Bits 16-31 of the data register are not affected.
ORW	data16,dadr	4, 6 or 8	13(2/1)+				X	X	0	0	[dadr] — [dadr] V data16. OR immediate data word to memory word.[2,3]
ORL	data32,Dn	6	16(3/0)				X	X	0	0	[Dn<0-31>] — [Dn<0-31>] V data32. OR immediate data long word to data register.
ORL	data32,dadr	6, 8 or 10	22(3/2)+				X	X	0	0	[dadr] — [dadr] V data32. OR immediate data long word to memory.[2,4]
SUBB	data8,Dn	4	8(2/0)			X	X	X	X	X	[Dn<0-7>] — [Dn<0-7>] - data8. Subtract immediate data byte from data register. Bits 8-31 of the data register are not affected.
SUBB	data8,dadr	4, 6 or 8	13(2/1)+			X	X	X	X	X	[dadr] — [dadr] - data8. Subtract immediate data byte from memory byte.[1]
SUBW	data16,Dn	4	8(2/0)			X	X	X	X	X	[Dn<0-15>] — [Dn<0-15>] - data16. Subtract immediate data word from data register. Bits 16-31 of the data register are not affected.
SUBW	data16,An	4	8(2/0)								[An<0-31>] — [An<0-31>] - data16 (sign extended). Subtract immediate data word from address register. The sign of the data word is extended to a full 32 bits for the operation.
SUBW	data16,dadr	4, 6 or 8	13(2/1)+			X	X	X	X	X	[dadr] — [dadr] - data16. Subtract immediate data word from memory word.[2,3]
SUBL	data32,Dn	6	16(3/0)			X	X	X	X	X	[Dn<0-31>] — [Dn<0-31>] - data32. Subtract immediate long word from data register contents.
SUBL	data32,An	6	16(3/0)								[An<0-31>] — [An<0-31>] - data32. Subtract immediate data long word from address register.
SUBL	data32,dadr	6, 8 or 10	22(3/2)+			X	X	X	X	X	[dadr] — [dadr] - data32. Subtract immediate data long word from memory.[2,4]
SUBQB	data3,Dn	2	4(1/0)			X	X	X	X	X	[Dn<0-7>] — [Dn<0-7>] - data3. Subtract immediate three bits from data register byte. Bits 8-31 of the data register are not affected.
SUBQB	data3,dadr	2, 4 or 6	9(1/1)+			X	X	X	X	X	[dadr] — [dadr] - data3. Subtract immediate three bits from memory byte.[1]

Immediate Operate (Continued)

Table 7-6. MC68000 Instruction Set Summary (Continued)

	Mnemonic	Operand(s)	Bytes	Clock Cycles	T	S	X	N	Z	V	C	Operation Performed
Immediate Operate (Continued)	SUBQW	data3,Dn	2	4(1/0)			X	X	X	X	X	[Dn<0-15>] — [Dn<0>] – data3 / Subtract immediate three bits from data register word. Bits 16-31 of the data register are not affected.
	SUBQW	data3,An	2	4(1/0)								[An<0-15>] — [An<0-15>] – data3 / Subtract immediate three bits from address register word. Bits 16-31 of the address register are not affected.
	SUBQW	data3,dadr	2, 4 or 6	9(1/1)+			X	X	X	X	X	[dadr] — [dadr] – data3 / Subtract immediate three bits from memory word.2, 3
	SUBQL	data3,Dn	2	8(1/0)			X	X	X	X	X	[Dn<0-31>] — [Dn<0-31>] – data3 / Subtract immediate three bits from data register contents.
	SUBQL	data3,An	2	8(1/0)								[An<0-31>] — [An<0-31>] – data3 / Subtract immediate three bits from address register contents.
	SUBQL	data3,dadr	2, 4 or 6	14(1/2)+			X	X	X	X	X	[dadr] — [dadr] – data3 / Subtract immediate three bits from memory long word.2, 4
JUMP, BRANCH	BRA	label	2 or 4	10(2/0)								[PC] — label / Branch unconditionally (short).
	JMP	jadr	2, 4 or 6	4(1/0)+								[PC] — jadr / Jump unconditionally.
Subroutine CALL and RETURN	BSR	label	2 or 4	10, 8(1/0) / 10, 12(2/0)								[A7] — [A7] – 2 / [[A7]] — [PC] / [PC] — label / Branch to subroutine (short).
	JSR	jadr	2, 4 or 6	14(1/2)+								[A7] — [A7] – 2 / [[A7]] — [PC] / [PC] — jadr / Jump to subroutine.
	RTS		2	16(4/0)								[PC] — [[A7]] / [A7] — [A7] + 2 / Return from subroutine
	RTR		2	20(5/0)								[SR<0-4>] — [[A7<0-4>]] / [A7] — [A7] + 2 / [PC] — [[A7]] / [A7] — [A7] + 2 / Restore condition codes and return from subroutine.
Branch on Condition	Bcc	label	2 or 4	10, 8(1/0) / 10, 12(2/0)								[PC] — label / Branch if condition met. / If cc then no further action.
	DBcc	Dn,label	4	12(2/0) / 10(2/0, / 14(3/0)								[Dn<0-15>] — [Dn<0-15>] – 1 / If [Dn<0-15>] = –1 then no further action. / [PC] — label / Test condition, decrement and branch. Loop until the specified condition is true or until the loop count is exhausted.

Table 7-6. MC68000 Instruction Set Summary (Continued)

	Mnemonic	Operand(s)	Bytes	Clock Cycles	T	S	X	N	Z	V	C	Operation Performed
Register-Register Move	MOVE.B	sDn,dDn	2	4(1/0)				X	X	0	0	[dDn<07>] — [sDn<0-7>] Move one byte of any data register to any data register. Bits 8-31 of the destination register are not affected.
	MOVE.W	rs,Dn	2	4(1/0)				X	X	0	0	[Dn<0-15>] — [rs<0-15>] Move one word of any data or address register to any data register. Bits 16-31 of the destination register are not affected.
	MOVE.W	rs,An	2	4(1/0)								[An<015>] — [rs<0-15>] [An<16-31>] — [An<15>] Move one word of any data or address register to any address register. The sign is extended to all upper bits of the address register.
	MOVE.L	rs,Dn	2	4(1/0)				X	X	0	0	[Dn<0-31>] — [rs<0-31>] Move the contents of any data or address register to any data register.
	MOVE.L	rs,An	2	4(1/0)								[An<0-31>] — [rs<0-31>] Move the contents of any data or address register to any address register.
Register-Register Operate	ABCD	sDn,dDn	2	6(1/0)			X	U	X	U	X	[dDn<0-7>] — [dDn<0-7>] + [sDn<0-7>] + X Add decimal source data register byte to destination data register byte with carry (Extend bit). Bits 8-31 of the destination data register are not affected.
	ADD.B	sDn,dDn	2	4(1/0)			X	X	X	X	X	[dDn<0-7>] — [dDn<0-7>] + [sDn<0-7>] Add byte from data registers to data register. Bits 8-31 of the destination data register are not affected.
	ADD.W	rs,Dn	2	4(1/0)			X	X	X	X	X	[Dn<0-15>] — [Dn<0-15>] + [rs<0-15>] Add word from source register to data register. Bits 16-31 of the destination data register are not affected.
	ADD.W	rs,An	2	8(1/0)								[An<0-15>] — [An<0-15>] + [rs<0-15>] (sign extended) Add word from source register to address register. The sign of the source word is extended to a full 32 bits for the operation.
	ADD.L	rs,Dn	2	8(1/0)			X	X	X	X	X	[Dn<0-31>] — [Dn<0-31>] + [rs<0-31>] Add long word from source register to data register.
	ADD.L	rs,An	2	8(1/0)								[An<0-31>] — [An<0-31>] + rs<0-31>] Add long word from source register to address register.
	ADDX.B	sDn,dDn	2	4(1/0)			X	X	X	X	X	[dDn<0-7>] — [dDn<0-7>] + [sDn<0-7>] + X Add source data register byte to destination data register byte with carry (Extend bit). Bits 8-31 of the destination data register are not affected.
	ADDX.W	sDn, dDn	2	4(1/0)			X	X	X	X	X	[dDn<0-15>] — [dDn<0-15>] + [sDn<0-15>] + X Add source data register word to destination data register word with carry (Extend bit). Bits 16-31 of the destination data register are not affected.
	ADDX.L	sDn,dDn	2	8(1/0)			X	X	X	X	X	[dDn<0-31>] — [dDn<0-31>] + [sDn<0-31>] + X Add source data register long word to destination data register long word with carry (Extend bit).
	AND.B	sDn,dDn	2	4(1/0)				X	X	0	0	[dDn<0-7>] — [dDn<0-7>] < [sDn<0-7>] AND byte from data register to data register. Bits 8-31 of the destination data register are not affected.

Table 7-6. MC68000 Instruction Set Summary (Continued)

Mnemonic	Operand(s)	Bytes	Clock Cycles	T	S	X	N	Z	V	C	Operation Performed
AND.W	sDn,dDn	2	4(1/0)				X	X	0	0	[dDn<0-15>] ← [dDn<0-15>] ∧ [sDn<0-15>] AND word from data register to data register. Bits 16-31 of the destination data register are not affected.
AND.L	sDn,dDn	2	8(1/0)				X	X	0	0	[dDn<0-31>] ← [dDn<0-31>] ∧ [sDn<0-31>] AND long word from data register to data register.
CMP.B	sDn,dDn	2	4(1/0)				X	X	X	X	[dDn<0-7>] − [sDn<0-7>] Compare data register bytes and set condition codes accordingly. Register data are not changed on any compares.
CMP.W	rs,Dn	2	4(1/0)				X	X	X	X	[Dn<0-15>] − [rs<0-15>] Compare data register word with register word and set condition codes accordingly.
CMP.W	rs,An	2	6(1/0)				X	X	X	X	[An<0-15>] − [rs<0-15>] Compare address register word with register word and set condition codes accordingly.
CMP.L	rs,Dn	2	6(1/0)				X	X	X	X	[Dn<0-31>] − [rs<0-31>] Compare data register with register and set condition codes accordingly.
CMP.L	rs,An	2	6(1/0)				X	X	X	X	[An<0-31>] − [rs<0-31>] Compare address register with register and set condition codes accordingly.
DIVS	sDn,dDn	2	≤158(1/0)				X	X	X	0	[dDn<0-15>] ← [dDn<0-31>] ÷ [sDn<0-15>] [dDn<016-31>] ← remainder Divide signed numbers. Division by zero causes a TRAP.
DIVU	sDn,dDn	2	≤140(1/0)				X	X	X	0	[dDn<0-15>] ← [dDn<0-31>] ÷ [sDn<0-15>] [dDn<16-31>] ← remainder Divide unsigned numbers. Division by zero causes a TRAP.
EOR.B	sDn,dDn	2	4(1/0)				X	X	0	0	[dDn<0-7>] ← [dDn<0-7>] ⊻ [sDn<0-7>] Exclusive-OR byte from data register to data register. Bits 8-31 of the destination data register are not affected.
EOR.W	sDn,dDn	2	4(1/0)				X	X	0	0	[dDn<0-15>] ← [dDn<0-15>] ⊻ [sDn<0-15>] Exclusive-OR word from data register to data register. Bits 16-31 of the destination data register are not affected.
EOR.L	sDn,dDn	2	8(1/0)				X	X	0	0	[dDn<0-31>] ← [dDn<0-31>] ⊻ [sDn<0-31>] Exclusive-OR long word from data register to data register.
EXG	rs,rd	2	6(1/0)								[rd] ←→ [rs] Exchange the contents of two registers. This is always a long word operation.
MULS	sDn,dDn	2	≤70(1/0)				X	X	0	0	[dDn<0-31>] ← [dDn<0-15>] × [sDn<0-15>] Multiply two 16-bit signed numbers, yielding a 32-bit signed product.
MULU	sDn,dDn	2	≤70(1/0)				X	X	0	0	[dDn<0-31>] ← [dDn<0-15>] × [sDn<0-15>] Multiply two 16-bit unsigned numbers, yielding a 32-bit unsigned product.
OR.B	sDn,dDn	2	4(1/0)				X	X	0	0	[dDn<0-7>] ← [dDn<0-7>] ∨ [sDn<0-7>] OR byte from data register to data register. Bits 8-31 of the destination dat register are not affected.

Register-Register Operate (Continued)

Table 7-6. MC68000 Instruction Set Summary (Continued)

Mnemonic	Operand(s)	Bytes	Clock Cycles	T	S	X	N	Z	V	C	Operation Performed
OR.W	sDn,dDn	2	4(1/0)				X	X	0	0	[dDn<0-15>] ← [dDn<0-15>] ∨ [sDn<0-15>] OR word from data register to data register. Bits 16-31 of the destination data register are not affected.
OR.L	sDn,dDn	2	8(1/0)				X	X	0	0	[dDn<0-31>] ← [dDn<0-31>] ∨ [sDn<0-31>] OR long word from data register to data register.
SBCD	sDn,dDn	2	6(1/0)			X	U	X	U	X	[dDn<0-7>] ← [dDn<0-7>] − [sDn<0-7>] − X Subtract decimal source data register byte from destination data register byte with carry (Extend bit). Bits 8-31 of the destination data register are not affected.
SUB.B	sDn,dDn	2	4(1/0)			X	X	X	X	X	[dDn<0-7>] ← [dDn<0-7>] − [sDn<0-7>] Subtract data register bytes. Bits 8-31 of the destination data register are not affected.
SUB.W	rs,Dn	2	4(1/0)			X	X	X	X	X	[Dn<0-15>] ← [Dn<0-15>] − [rs<0-15>] Subtract register words. Bits 16-31 of the destination data register are not affected.
SUB.W	rs,An	2	8(1/0)								[An<0-15>] ← [An<0-15>] − [rs<0-15>] (sign extended) Subtract source register word from address register. The sign of the source word is extended to a full 32 bits for the operation.
SUB.L	rs,Dn	2	8(1/0)			X	X	X	X	X	[Dn<0-31>] ← [Dn<0-31>] − [rs<0-31>] Subtract source register long word from data register.
SUB.L	rs,An	2	8(1/0)								[An<0-31>] ← [An<0-31>] − [rs<0-31>] Subtract source register long word from address register.
SUBX.B	sDn,dDn	2	4(1/0)			X	X	X	X	X	[dDn<0-7>] ← [dDn<0-7>] − [sDn<0-7>] − X Subtract source data register byte from destination data register byte with borrow (Extend bit). Bits 8-31 of the destination data register are not affected.
SUBX.W	sDn,dDn	2	4(1/0)			X	X	X	X	X	[dDn<0-15>] ← [dDn<0-15>] − [sDn<0-15>] − X Subtract source data register word from destination data register word with borrow (Extend bit). Bits 16-31 of the destination data registers are not affected.
SUBX.L	sDn,dDn	2	8(1/0)			X	X	X	X	X	[dDn<0-31>] ← [dDn<0-31>] − [sDn<0-31>] − X Subtract source data register long word from destination data register long word with borrow (Extend bit).
CLR.B	Dn	2	4(1/0)				0	1	0	0	[Dn<0-7>] ← 0 Clear data register byte to zeroes. Bits 8-31 of the data register are not affected.
CLR.W	Dn	2	4(1/0)				0	1	0	0	[Dn<0-15>] ← 0 Clear data register word to zeroes. Bits 16-31 of the data register are not affected.
CLR.L	Dn	2	6(1/0)				0	1	0	0	[Dn<0-31>] ← 0 Clear data register to zeroes
EXT.W	Dn	2	4(1/0)				X	X	0	0	[Dn<8-15>] ← [Dn<7>] Extend sign bit of data byte to data word size. Bits 16-31 of the data register are not affected.
EXT.L	Dn	2	4(1/0)				X	X	0	0	[Dn<16-31>] ← [Dn<15>] Extend sign bit of data word to long data word size.

Register-Register Operate (Continued) — OR.W through SUBX.L

Register Operate — CLR.B through EXT.L

Table 7-6. MC68000 Instruction Set Summary (Continued)

Mnemonic	Operand(s)	Bytes	Clock Cycles	T	S	X	N	Z	V	C	Operation Performed
NBCD	Dn	2	6(1/0)			X	U	U	U	X	[Dn<0-7>] — [Dn<0-7>] - X Negate decimal register byte. Bits 8-31 of the data register are not affected.
NEG.B	Dn	2	4(1/0)			X	X	X	X	X	[Dn<0>] — 0 - [Dn<0-7>] Negate register byte. Bits 8-31 of the data register are not affected.
NEG.W	Dn	2	4(1/0)			X	X	X	X	X	[Dn<0-15>] — 0 - [Dn<0-15>] Negate register word. Bits 16-31 of the data register are not affected.
NEG.L	Dn	2	6(1/0)			X	X	X	X	X	[Dn<0-31>] — 0 - [Dn<0-31>] Negate register long word.
NEG.B	Dn	2	4(1/0)			X	X	X	X	X	[Dn<0-7>] — 0 - [Dn<0-7>] - X Negate register byte with Extend. Bits 8-31 of the data register are not affected.
NEG.W	Dn	2	4(1/0)			X	X	X	X	X	[Dn<0-15>] — 0 - [Dn<0-15>] - X Negate register word with Extend. Bits 16-31 of the data register are not affected.
NEG.L	Dn	2	6(1/0)			X	X	X	X	X	[Dn<0-31>] — 0 - [Dn<0-31>] - X Negate register long word with Extend.
NOT.B	Dn	2	4(1/0)				X	X	0	0	[Dn<0-7>] — [Dn<0-7>] Ones complement data register byte. Bits 8-31 of the data register are not affected.
NOT.W	Dn	2	6(1/0)				X	X	0	0	[Dn<0-15>] — [Dn<0-15>] Ones complement data register word. Bits 16-31 of the data register are not affected.
NOT.L	Dn	2	6(1/0)				X	X	0	0	[Dn<0-31>] — [Dn<0-31>] Ones complement data register contents.
Scc	Dn	2	9(1/1)								[Dn<0-7>] — all 1's if cc = TRUE [Dn<0-1>] — all 0's if cc = FALSE Set status in data register byte.
SWAP	Dn	2	4(1/0)				X	X	0	0	[Dn<0-15>] ←→ [Dn<16-31>] Exchange the two 16-bit halves of a data register.
TAS	Dn	2	4(1/0)				X	X	0	0	[Dn<7>] — 1 Test status of data register byte and set bit 7 to 1.
TST.B	Dn	2	4(1/0)				X	X	0	0	[Dn<0-7>] - 0 Test status of data register byte. The data register contents are not changed.
TST.W	Dn	2	4(1/0)				X	X	0	0	[Dn<0-15>] - 0 Test status of data register word. The data register contents are not changed.
TST.L	Dn	2	4(1/0)				X	X	0	0	[Dn<0-31>] - 0 Test status of data register long word. The data register contents are not changed.

Register-Register Operate (Continued)

Table 7-6. MC68000 Instruction Set Summary (Continued)

Mnemonic	Operand(s)	Bytes	Clock Cycles	T	S	X	N	Z	V	C	Operation Performed
ASL	dadr	2, 4 or 6	9(1/1)+			X	X	X	X	X	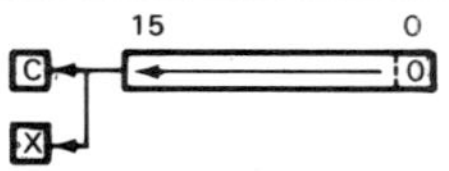 Arithmetic shift left one bit of memory word. A zero is shifted into bit 0. Bit 15 is shifted into both Carry and Extend bits.[2,3]
ASL.B	count,Dn Dn,dDn	2 2	6 + 2N(1/0) 6 + 2N(1/0)			X X	X X	X X	X X	X X	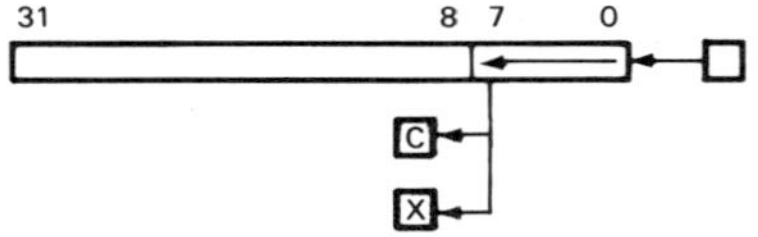 Arithmetic shift left of data register byte. The number of shifts is specified as a direct count (1-8) or in a data register (1-63). Zeroes are shifted into bit 0. Bit 7 is shifted into both Carry and Extend bits.
ASL.W	count,Dn Dn,dDn	2 2	6 + 2N(1/0) 6 + 2N(1/0)			X X	X X	X X	X X	X X	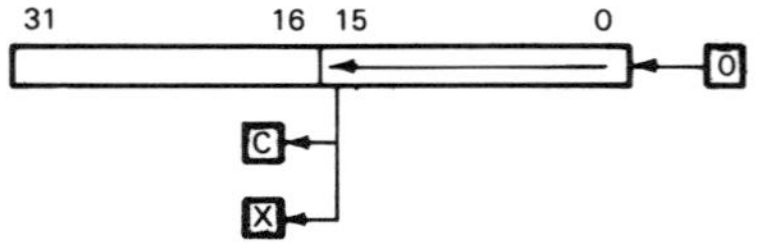 As ASL.B except shifts are for one word.
ASL.L	count,Dn Dn,dDn	2 2	8 + 2N(1/0) 8 + 2N(1/0)			X	X X	X X	X X	X X	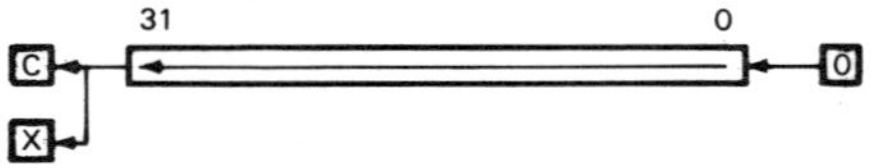 As ASL.B except shifts are for entire register.
ASR	dadr	2, 4 or 6	9(1/1)+			X	X	X	X	X	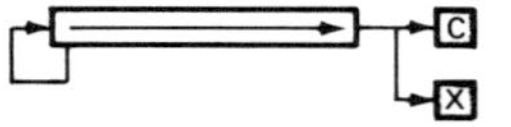 Arithemtic shift right one bit of memory word. Bit 15 is propagated to bit 14. Bit 0 is shifted into both Carry and Extend bits.
ASR.B	count,Dn Dn,dDn	2 2	6 + 2N(1/0) 6 + 2N(1/0)			X X	X X	X X	X X	X X	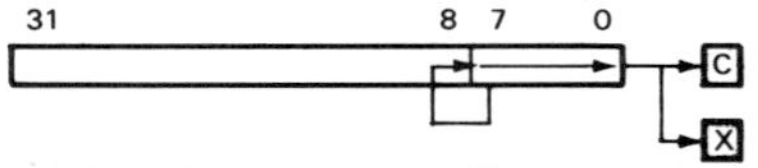 Arithmetic shift right of data register byte. The number of shifts is specified as a direct count (1-8) or in a data register (1-63). Bit 7 is propagated to the right. Bit 0 is shifted into both Carry and Extend bits.

Shift

7-67

Table 7-6. MC68000 Instruction Set Summary (Continued)

Mnemonic	Operand(s)	Bytes	Clock Cycles	T	S	X	N	Z	V	C	Operation Performed
ASR.W	count,Dn Dn,dDn	2 2	6 + 2N(1/0) 6 + 2N(1/0)			× ×	× ×	× ×	× ×	× ×	As ASR.B except shifts are for one word.
ASRL	count,Dn Dn,dDn	2 2	8 + 2N(1/0) 8 + 2N(1/0)			× ×	× ×	× ×	× ×	× ×	As ASR.B except shifts are for entire register.
LSL	dadr	2, 4 or 6	9(1/1)+			×	×	×	0	×	Logical shift left one bit of memory word. A zero is shifted into bit 0. Bit 15 is shifted into both Carry and Extend bits. (Note that LSL is identical to ASL except for the Overflow condition.)[2,3]
LSL.B	count,Dn Dn,dDn	2 2	6 + 2N(1/0) 6 + 2N(1/0)			× ×	× ×	× ×	0 0	× ×	Logical shift left of data register byte. The number of shifts is specified as a direct count (1-8) or in a data register (1-63). Zeroes are shifted into bit 0. Bit 7 is shifted into both Carry and Extend bits.
LSL.W	count,Dn Dn,dDn	2 2	6 + 2N(1/0) 6 + 2N(1/0)			× ×	× ×	× ×	0 0	× ×	As LSL.B except shifts are for one word.
LSL.L	count,Dn Dn,dDn	2	8 + 2N(1/0) 8 + 2N(1/0)			× ×	× ×	× ×	0 0	× ×	As LSL.B except shifts are for entire register.

Shift (Continued)

Table 7-6. MC68000 Instruction Set Summary (Continued)

Mnemonic	Operand(s)	Bytes	Clock Cycles	T	S	X	N	Z	V	C	Operation Performed
LSR	dadr	2, 4 or 6	9(1/1)+			×	×	×	0	×	Logical shift right one bit of memory word. A zero is shifted into bit 15. Bit 0 is shifted into both Carry and Extend bits.
LSR.B	count,Dn Dn,dDn	2 2	6 + 2N(1/0) 6 + 2N(1/0)			× ×	× ×	× ×	0 0	× ×	Logical shift right of data register byte. The number of shifts is specified as a direct count (1-8) or in a data register (1-63). Zeroes are shifted into bit 7. Bit 0 is shifted into both Carry and Extend bits.
LSR.W	count,Dn Dn,dDn	2 2	6 + 2N(1/0) 6 + 2N(1/0)			× ×	× ×	× ×	0 0	× ×	As LSR.B except shifts are for one word.
LSR.L	count,Dn Dn,dDn	2 2	8 + 2N(1/0) 8 + 2N(1/0)			× ×	× ×	× ×	0 0	× ×	As LSR.B except shifts are for entire register.
ROL	dadr	2, 4 or 6	9(1/1)+				×	×	0	×	Rotate left one bit of memory word. Bit 15 is shifted into bit 0 and into the Carry.
ROL.B	count,Dn Dn,dDn	2 2	6 + 2N(1/0) 6 + 2N(1/0)				× ×	× ×	0 0	× ×	Rotate left of data register byte. The number of shifts is specified as a direct count (1-8) or in a data register (1-63). Bit 7 is shifted into bit 0 and into the Carry.

Shift (Continued)

Table 7-6. MC68000 Instruction Set Summary (Continued)

Mnemonic	Operand(s)	Bytes	Clock Cycles	T	S	X	N	Z	V	C	Operation Performed
ROL.W	count,Dn Dn,dDn	2 2	6 + 2N(1/0) 6 + 2N(1/0)				X X	X X	0 0	X X	As ROL.B except shifts are for one word.
ROL.L	count,Dn Dn,dDn	2 2	8 + 2N(1/0) 8 + 2N(1/0)				X X	X X	0 0	X X	As ROL.B except shifts are for entire register.
ROR	oadr	2, 4 or 6	9(1/1)+				X	X	0	X	Rotate right one bit of memory word. Bit 0 is shifted into bit 15 and into the Carry.
ROR.B	count,Dn Dn,dDn	2 2	6 + 2N(1/0) 6 + 2N(1/0)				X X	X X	0 0	X X	Rotate right of data register byte. The number of shifts is specified as a direct count (1-8) or in a data register (1-63). Bit 0 is shifted into bit 7 and into the Carry.
ROR.W	count,Dn Dn,dDn	2 2	6 + 2N(1/0) 6 + 2N(1/0)				X X	X X	0 0	X X	As ROR.B except shifts are for one word.
ROR.L	count,Dn Dn,dDn	2 2	8 + 2N(1/0) 8 + 2N(1/0)				X X	X X	0 0	X X	As ROR.B except shifts are for entire register.
ROXL	dadr	2, 4 or 6	9(1/1)+				X	X	0	X	Rotate left one bit of memory word and Extend one bit. Bit 15 is shifted into both Extend and Carry bits. The Extend bit is shifted into bit 0.

Table 7-6. MC68000 Instruction Set Summary (Continued)

Mnemonic	Operand(s)	Bytes	Clock Cycles	T	S	X	N	Z	V	C	Operation Performed
ROXL.B	count,Dn Dn,dDn	2 2	6 + 2N(1/0) 6 + 2N(1/0)			X X	X X	X X	0 0	X X	Rotate left of data register byte with Extend. The number of shifts is specified as a direct count (1-8) or in a data register (1-63). Bit 15 is shifted into both Extend and Carry bits. The Extend bit is shifted into bit 0.
ROXL.W	count,Dn Dn,dDn	2 2	6 + 2N(1/0) 6 + 2N(1/0)			X X	X X	X X	0 0	X X	As ROXLB except shifts are for one word.
ROXL.L	count,Dn Dn,dDn	2 2	8 + 2N(1/0) 8 + 2N(1/0)			X X	X X	X X	0 0	X X	As ROXLB except shifts are for entire register.
ROXR	dadr	2, 4 or 6	9(1/1)+			X	X	X	0	X	Rotate right one bit of memory word and Extend. Bit 0 is shifted into both Extend and Carry bits. The Extend bit is shifted into bit 15.
ROXR.B	count,Dn Dn,dDn	2 2	6 + 2N(1/0) 6 + 2N(1/0)			X X	X X	X X	0 0	X X	Rotate right of data register byte with Extend. The number of shifts is specified as a direct count (1-8) or in a data register (1-63). Bit 0 is shifted into both Extend and Carry bits. The Extend bit is shifted into bit 7.
ROXR.W	count,Dn Dn,dDn	2 2	6 + 2N(1/0) 6 + 2N(1/0)			X X	X X	X X	0 0	X X	As ROXRB except shifts are for one word.
ROXR.L	count,Dn Dn,dDn	2 2	8 + 2N(1/0) 8 + 2N(1/0)			X X	X X	X X	0 0	X X	As ROXRB except shifts are for entire register.

Shift (Continued)

Table 7-6. MC68000 Instruction Set Summary (Continued)

	Mnemonic	Operand(s)	Bytes	Clock Cycles	T	S	X	N	Z	V	C	Operation Performed
Bit Manipulation	BTST	bitl,Dn	4	10(2/0)					X			$[Z] \leftarrow [Dn<bitl>]$
		Dn,dDn	2	6(1/0)					X			$[Z] \leftarrow [dDn<[Dn]>]$ Test a bit of a data register and reflect status in Zero bit. The bit to be tested may be specified directly or in a data register (bit 0-31 in either case).
	BTST	bitb,dadr	4,6 or 8	8(2/0)+					X			$[Z] \leftarrow [dadr<bitb>]$
		Dn,dadr	2,4 or 6	4(1/0)+					X			$[Z] \leftarrow [dadr<[Dn]>]$ Test a bit of a memory byte and reflect status in Zero bit. The bit to be tested may be specified directly or in a data register (bit 0-7 in either case).[1]
	BSET	bitl,Dn	4	12(2/0)					X			$[Z] \leftarrow [Dn<bitl>], [Dn<bitl>] \leftarrow 1$
		Dn,dDn	2	8(1/0)					X			$[Z] \leftarrow [dDn<[Dn]>], [dDn<[Dn]>] \leftarrow 1$
		bitb,dadr	4,6 or 8	13(2/1)+					X			$[Z] \leftarrow [dadr<bitb>], [dadr<bitb>] \leftarrow 1$
		Dn,dadr	2,4 or 6	9(1/1)+					X			$[Z] \leftarrow [dadr<[Dn]>], [dadr<[Dn]>] \leftarrow 1$ Test a bit as (BTST) and then set the specified bit.
	BCLR	bitl,Dn	4	14(2/0)					X			$[Z] \leftarrow [Dn<bitl>], [Dn<bitl>] \leftarrow 0$
		Dn,dDn	2	8(1/0)					X			$[Z] \leftarrow [dDn<[Dn]>], [dDn<[Dn]>] \leftarrow 0$
		bitb,dadr	4,6 or 8	13(2/1)+					X			$[Z] \leftarrow [dadr<bit\ b>], [dadr<bit\ b>] \leftarrow 0$
		Dn,dadr	2,4 or 6	9(1/1)+					X			$[Z] \leftarrow [dadr<[Dn]>], [dadr<[Dn]>] \leftarrow 0$ Test a bit (as BTST) and then clear the specified bit.
	BCHG	bitl,Dn	4	12(2/0)					X			$[Z] \leftarrow [Dn<bitl>], [Dn<bitl>] \leftarrow \overline{[Dn<bitl>]}$
		Dn,dDn	2	8(1/0)					X			$[Z] \leftarrow [dDn<[Dn]>], [dDn<[Dn]>] \leftarrow \overline{[dDn<[Dn]>]}$
		bitb,dadr	4,6 or 8	13(2/1)					X			$[Z] \leftarrow [dadr<bitb>], [dadr<bitb>] \leftarrow \overline{[dadr<bitb>]}$
		Dn,dadr	2,4 or 6	9(1/1)					X			$[Z] \leftarrow [dadr<[Dn]>], [dadr<[Dn]>] \leftarrow \overline{[dadr<[Dn]>]}$ Test a bit (as BTST) and then complement the specified bit.
Stack	MOVE	An,USP	2	4(1/0)								$[USP] \leftarrow [An]$ Move contents of address register to User Stack Pointer. This is a privileged instruction.
	MOVE	USP,An	2	4(1/0)								$[An] \leftarrow [USP]$ Move contents of User Stack Pointer to address register. This is a privileged instruction.
	LINK	An,d16	4	18(2/2)								$[A7] \leftarrow [A7] - 2$ $[[A7]] \leftarrow [An]$ $[An] \leftarrow [A7]$ $[A7] \leftarrow [A7] + d16$ Save the contents of the specified address register on the Stack, load the current Stack Pointer to the specified address register, and set the Stack Pointer to point beyond the temporary stack storage area.
	PEA	jadr	2,4 or 6	10(1/2)+								$[A7] \leftarrow [A7] - 2$ $[[A7]] \leftarrow jadr$ Compute long word address and push address onto the Stack.[3]

Table 7-6. MC68000 Instruction Set Summary (Continued)

Group	Mnemonic	Operand(s)	Bytes	Clock Cycles	T	S	X	N	Z	V	C	Operation Performed
Stack (Continued)	UWLK	An	2	12(3/0)								[A7] → [An] [An] → [[A7]] [A7] → [A7] + 2 Store the contents of the specified address register to the Stack Pointer (A7) and load the specified address register from the stack.
Interrupt and Trap	CHK	data16,Dn	4	49(6/3) 12(2/0)				x	U	U	U	If [Dn<0-15>] < 0 or [Dn<0-15>] > data16 then [PC] → CHK interrupt vector
	CHK	Dn,dDn	2	45(5/3), 8(1/0)				x	U	U	U	If [dDn<0-15>] < 0 or [dDn<0-15>] > [Dn<0-15>] then [PC] → CHK interrupt vector
	CHK	sadr,Dn	2, 4 or 6	45(5/3), 8(1/0)				x	U	U	U	If [Dn<0-15>] < 0 or [Dn<0-15>] > [sadr] then [PC] → CHK interrupt vector Check register against bounds and initiate Check interrupt processing if register word is out of bounds. The upper bound is a twos complement integer specified as immediate data, in a data register, or in a memory word.[2,3]
	TRAP	vector	2	37(4/3)								[A7] → [A7] − 2 [A7] → [PC] [A7] → [A7] − 2 [A7] → [SR] [PC] → vector Initiate exception processing through specified vector.
	TRAPV		2	37(5/3), 4(1/0)								If Overflow = 1 then TRAP Initiate exception processing through Overflow vector if the Overflow bit is on.
	RTE		2	20(5/0)		x	x	x	x	x	x	[SR] → [[A7]], [A7] → [A7] + 2 [PC] → [[A7]], [A7] → [A7] + 2 Return from exception.
Status	MOVE	Dn,Ccr	2	12(2/0)			x	x	x	x	x	[SR<0-4>] → [Dn<0-4>] Move status data from data register to condition codes.
	MOVE	sadr,CCR	2, 4 or 6	12(2/0)+			x	x	x	x	x	[SR<0-4>] → [sadr<0-4>] Move status data from memory location to condition codes. The source address is a word address.[2,3]
	MOVE	data8,CCR	4	16(3/0)			x	x	x	x	x	[SR<0-4>] → data8<0-4> Move immediate status data to condition codes.
	MOVE	Dn,SR	2	12(2/0)	x	x	x	x	x	x	x	[SR] → [Dn<0-15>] Moves status word from data register to Status register. This is a privileged instruction.
	MOVE	sadr,SR	2, 4 or 6	12(2/0)+	x	x	x	x	x	x	x	[SR] → [sadr] Move status word from memory location to Status register. The source address is a word address.[2,3] privileged instruction.
	MOVE	data16,SR	4	16(3/0)	x	x	x	x	x	x	x	[SR] → data16 Move immediate status word to Status register. This is a privileged instruction.
	MOVE	SR,Dn	2	6(1/0)								[Dn<0-15>] → [SR] Move contents of Status register to data register. Bits 16-31 of the data register are not affected.

Table 7-6. MC68000 Instruction Set Summary (Continued)

	Mnemonic	Operand(s)	Bytes	Clock Cycles	T	S	X	N	Z	V	C	Operation Performed
Status (Continued)	MOVE	SR,dadr	2, 4 or 6	9(1/1)+								[dadr] ← [SR] Move contents of Status register to memory location. The destination address is a word address. 2, 3
	AND.B	data8,SR	4	20(3/0)	x		x	x	x	x	x	[SR<0-7>] ← [SR<0-7>] ∧ data8 AND immediate data byte to low-order Status register byte.
	AND.W	data16,SR	4	20(3/0)		x	x	x	x	x	x	[SR] ← [SR] ∧ data16 AND immediate data with Status register. This is a privileged instruction.
	EOR.B	data8,SR	4	20(3/0)	x		x	x	x	x	x	[SR<0-7>] ← [SR<0-7>] ⊻ data8 Exclusive-OR immediate data byte to low-order Status register byte.
	EOR.W	data16,SR	4	20(3/0)		x	x	x	x	x	x	[SR] ← [SR] ⊻ data16 Exclusive-OR immediate data with Status register. This is a privileged instruction.
	OR.B	data8,SR	4	20(3/0)	x		x	x	x	x	x	[SR<0-7>] ← [SR<0-7>] ∨ data8 OR immediate data byte to low-order Status register byte.
	OR.W	data16,SR	4	20(3/0)		x	x	x	x	x	x	[SR] ← [SR] ∨ data16 OR immediate data with Status register. This is a privileged instruction.
Miscellaneous Control	NOP		2	4(1/0)								No operation.
	RESET		2	132(1/0)								Reset. This is a privileged instruction.
	STOP	data16	4	8(2/0)			x	x	x	x	x	[SR] ← data16 Stop processor. This is a privileged instruction.

Table 7-7. MC68000 Instruction Object Codes

Instruction	Byte 1	Byte 2	Byte 3	Byte 4	Byte 5	Byte 6	Byte 7	Byte 8	Byte 9	Byte 10	Bytes	Clock Cycles
ABCD												
−(SAn),−(dAn)	C dddd1	0 1sss									2	19(3/1)
sDn,dDn	C dddd1	0 Osss									2	6(1/0)
ADD.B												
data8,dadr	O 6	OOff ffff	00	yy	[EXT]		[EXT]				4, 6, or 8	13(2/1)+
data8,Dn	O 6	0 Oddd	00	yy							4	8(2/0)
Dn,dadr	D sss1	OOff ffff	[EXT]		[EXT]						2, 4, or 6	9(1/1)+
sadr,Dn	D ddd0	OOee eeee	[EXT]		[EXT]						2, 4, or 6	4(1/0)+
sDn,dDn	D ddd0	0 Osss									2	4(1/0)
ADD.L												
data32,An	O 6	F C	yyyy		zzzz						6	16(3/0)
data32,dadr	6	10ff ffff	yyyy		zzzz		[EXT]		[EXT]		6, 8, or 10	22(3/2)+
data32,Dn	6	8 Oddd	yyyy		zzzz						6	16(3/0)
Dn,dadr	D ddd1	10ff ffff	[EXT]		[EXT]						2, 4, or 6	14(1/2)+
rs,An	D ddd1	C tsss									2	8(1/0)
rs,Dn	D ddd1	8 tsss									2	8(1/0)
sadr,An	D ddd1	11ee eeee	[EXT]		[EXT]						2, 4, or 6	6(1/0)+
sadr,Dn	D ddd0	10ee eeee	[EXT]		[EXT]						2, 4, or 6	6(1/0)+
ADD.W												
data16,An	O 6	F C	yyyy		[EXT]						4, 6, or 8	13(2/1)
data16,dadr	6	01ff ffff	yyyy		[EXT]						4, 6, or 8	8(2/0)
data16,Dn	6	4 Oddd	yyyy		[EXT]						4	8(1/0)
Dn,dadr	D sss1	01ff ffff	[EXT]		[EXT]						2, 4, or 6	9(1/1)+
rs,An	D ddd0	C tsss									2	8(1/0)
rs,Dn	D ddd0	4 tsss									2	4(1/0)
sadr,An	D ddd1	11ee eeee	[EXT]		[EXT]						2, 4, or 6	8(1/0)+
sadr,Dn	D ddd0	01ee eeee	[EXT]		[EXT]						2, 4, or 6	4(1/0)+
ADDQ.B												
data3,dadr	5 bbb0	Off ffff	[EXT]		[EXT]						2, 4, or 6	9(1/0)+
data3,Dn	5 bbb0	0 Oddd									2	8(1/0)
data3,An	5 bbb0	0 1ddd									2	14(1/2)+
ADDQ.L												
data3,dadr	5 bbb0	10ff ffff	[EXT]		[EXT]						2, 4, or 6	8(1/0)
data3,Dn	5 bbb0	8 Oddd									2	4(1/0)
data3,An	5 bbb0	4 1ddd									2	9(1/1)+
ADDQ.W												
data3,dadr	5 bbb0	01ff ffff	[EXT]		[EXT]						2, 4, or 6	4(1/0)
data3,Dn	D ddd1	0 1sss									2	19(3/1)
data3,An	D ddd1	8 Osss									2	4(1/0)
ADDX.B												
−(SAn),−(dAn)	D ddd1	8 1sss	00	yy							2	32(5/2)
sDn,dDn	D ddd1	4 Osss	00	yy							2	8(1/0)
ADDX.L												
−(SAn),−(dAn)	O 2	OOff ffff			[EXT]		[EXT]				4, 6, or 8	19(3/1)
SDn,dDn	O 2	0 Oddd									4	4(1/0)
ADDX.W												
−(SAn),−(dAn)	O 2	3 C	00	yy							4	20(3/0)
sDn,dDn	C sss1	OOff ffff	[EXT]		[EXT]						2, 4, or 6	9(1/1)+
AND.B												
data8,dadr	C ddd0	OOee eeee	[EXT]		[EXT]						2, 4, or 6	4(1/0)+
data8,Dn	C ddd0	0 Osss									2	4(1/0)
data8,SR	O 2	10ff ffff	yyyy		zzzz		[EXT]		[EXT]		6, 8, or 10	22(3/2)+
Dn,dadr	O 2	8 Oddd	yyyy		zzzz						6	16(3/0)
sadr,Dn	O 2	10ee eeee	[EXT]		[EXT]						2, 4, or 6	14(1/2)+
sDn,dDn	C sss1	10ff ffff	[EXT]		[EXT]						2, 4, or 6	6(1/0)+
AND.L												
data32,dadr	C ddd0	10ee eeee	[EXT]		[EXT]						2, 4, or 6	8(1/0)
data32,Dn	O 2	8 Osss									2	13(2/1)+
Dn,dDn	O 2	01ff ffff	yyyy		[EXT]						4, 6, or 8	8(2/0)
sadr,Dn	O 2	4 Oddd	yyyy		[EXT]						4	20(3/0)
sDn,dDn	O 2	7 C	yyyy		[EXT]						4	9(1/1)
AND.W												
data16,dadr	C sss1	01ff ffff	[EXT]		[EXT]						2, 4, or 6	4(1/0)
data16,Dn	C ddd0	01ee eeee	[EXT]		[EXT]						2, 4, or 6	

Table 7-7. MC68000 Instruction Object Codes (Continued)

Instruction		Byte 1	Byte 2	Byte 3	Byte 4	Byte 5	Byte 6	Byte 7	Byte 8	Byte 9	Byte 10	Bytes	Clock Cycles
ASL	sDn,dDn	C ddd0	4 0sss									2	4(1/0)
ASL.B	dadr	E 1	11ff ffff			[EXT]						2, 4, or 6	9(1/1)+
ASLL	count,Dn	E ccc1	2 0ddd									2	6 + 2N(1/0)
	Dn,dDn	E rrr1	2 0ddd									2	6 + 2N(1/0)
ASLW	count,Dn	E ccc1	8 0ddd									2	8 + 2N(1/0)
	Dn,dDn	E rrr1	A 0ddd									2	8 + 2N(1/0)
ASR	dadr	E 0	11ff ffff			[EXT]						2, 4, or 6	9(1/1)+
ASR.B	count,Dn	E ccc0	0 0ddd									2	6 + 2N(1/0)
	Dn,dDn	E ccc0	2 0ddd									2	6 + 2N(1/0)
ASRL	count,Dn	E rrr0	A 0ddd									2	8 + 2N(1/0)
ASRW	Dn,dDn	E rrr0	6 0ddd									2	8 + 2N(1/0)
BCC	label	6 4	x x			[EXT]						2, 4, or 6	10, 12(2/0)
	label	6 4	x x	xxxx								4	10, 18(1/0)
BCHG	bitb,dadr	0 8	01ff ffff	00	0 Obbb	[EXT]						4, 6, or 8	13(2/1)+
	bit,Dn	0 8	4 0ddd	00	000b bbbb							4	12(2/0)
	Dn,dDn	0 rrr1	01ff ffff	[EXT]								2, 4, or 6	9(1/1)+
	Dn,dDn	0 rrr1	4 0ddd									2	8(1/0)
BCLR	bitb,dadr	0 8	10ff ffff	00	0 Obbb	[EXT]						4, 6, or 8	13(2/1)+
	bit,Dn	0 8	8 0ddd	00	000b bbbb							4	14(2/0)
	Dn,dadr	0 rrr1	10ff ffff	[EXT]								2, 4, or 6	9(1/1)+
	Dn,dDn	0 rrr1	8 0ddd									2	8(1/0)
BCS	label	6 5	x x	xxxx								2	10, 12(2/0)
BEQ	label	6 5	x O	xxxx								4	10, 12(2/0)
BGE	label	6 7	x O	xxxx								2	10, 12(2/0)
BGT	label	6 C	x O	xxxx								4	10, 8(1/0)
BHI	label	6 E	x O	xxxx								2	10, 8(1/0)
BLE	label	6 2	x x	xxxx								4	10, 12(2/0)
	label	6 2	x O	xxxx								2	10, 8(1/0)
BLS	label	6 F	x O	xxxx								4	10, 12(2/0)
BLT	label	6 3	x O	xxxx								2	10, 12(2/0)
BMI	label	6 D	x O	xxxx								4	10, 8(1/0),
	label	6 D	x O	xxxx								2	10, 8(1/0)
BNE	label	6 B	x x	xxxx								4	10, 12(2/0)
BPL	label	6 6	x O	xxxx								4	10, 12(2/0)
BRA	label	6 A	x O	xxxx								2	10, 8(1/0)
	label	6 A	x O	xxxx								4	10, 12(2/0)
	label	6 0	x x	xxxx								2	10(2/0)
BSET	bitb,dadr	0 8	11ff ffff	00	0 Obbb	[EXT]		[EXT]				4, 6, or 8	13(2/1)+
	bit,Dn	0 8	C 0ddd	00	000b bbbb							4	12(2/0)
	Dn,dadr	0 rrr1	11ff ffff	[EXT]		[EXT]						2, 4, or 6	9(1/1)+
	Dn,dDn	0 rrr1	C 0ddd									2	8(1/0)

Table 7-7. MC68000 Instruction Object Codes (Continued)

Instruction		Byte 1	Byte 2	Byte 3	Byte 4	Byte 5	Byte 6	Byte 7	Byte 8	Byte 9	Byte 10	Bytes	Clock Cycles
BSR	label	6 1	0 0	xxxx								4	10, 12(2/0)
BSR	label	6 1	× ×									2	10, 8(1/0)
BTST	bitb,dadr	0 8	00ff ffff	00	0 0bbb	[EXT]		[EXT]				4, 6, or 8	8(2/0)+
BTST	bit,Dn	0 8	0 0ddd	00	000b bbbb							4	10(2/0)
BTST	Dn,dadr	0 rrr1	00ff ffff	[EXT]								2, 4, or 6	4(1/0)
BTST	Dn,dDn	0 rrr1	0 0ddd									2	6(1/0)
BVC	label	6 8	0 0	xxxx								4	10, 12(2/0)
BVC	label	6 8	× ×									2	10, 8(1/0)
BVS	label	6 9	0 0	xxxx								4	10, 12(2/0)
BVS	label	6 9	× ×									2	10, 8(1/0)
CHK	data16,Dn	4 ddd1	B C	yyyy								4	49(6/3), 12(2/0)
CHK	Dn,dDn	4 ddd1	8 0rrr									2	45(5/3), 8(1/0)
CHK	sadr,Dn	4 ddd1	10ee eeee	[EXT]								2, 4, or 6	9(1/1)+
CLR.B	dadr	4 2	00ff ffff	[EXT]								2, 4, or 6	8(1/1)+
CLR.B	Dn	4 2	0 0ddd									2	4(1/0)
CLR.L	dadr	4 2	10ff ffff	[EXT]								2, 4, or 6	12(1/2)+
CLR.L	Dn	4 2	8 0ddd									2	6(1/0)
CLR.W	dadr	4 2	01ff ffff	[EXT]								2, 4, or 6	8(1/1)+
CLR.W	Dn	4 2	4 0ddd									2	4(1/0)
CMP.B	data8,dadr	0 C	00ff ffff	00	yy	[EXT]						4, 6, or 8	8(2/0)+
CMP.B	data8,Dn	0 C	0 0ddd	00	yy							4	8(2/0)
CMP.B	sadr,Dn	B ddd0	00ee eeee	[EXT]								2, 4, or 6	4(1/0)+
CMP.B	sDn,dDn	B ddd0	0 0sss									2	4(1/0)
CMP.L	data32,An	B ddd1	F C	yyyy	yyyy	zzzz	zzzz	[EXT]		[EXT]		6, 8, or 10	14(3/0)
CMP.L	data32,dadr	0 C	10ff ffff	yyyy	yyyy	zzzz	zzzz	[EXT]				6	12(3/0)+
CMP.L	data32,Dn	0 C	8 0ddd	yyyy	yyyy	zzzz	zzzz					6	14(3/0)
CMP.L	rs,An	B ddd1	C 0sss									2	6(1/0)
CMP.L	rs,Dn	B ddd0	8 0sss									2	6(1/0)
CMP.L	sadr,An	B ddd1	11ee eeee	[EXT]								2, 4, or 6	6(1/0)+
CMP.L	sadr,Dn	B ddd0	10ee eeee	[EXT]								2, 4, or 6	6(1/0)+
CMP.W	data16,An	B ddd0	F C	yyyy	yyyy	[EXT]						4, 6, or 8	8(2/0)
CMP.W	data16,dadr	0 C	01ff ffff	yyyy	yyyy	[EXT]						4	8(2/0)
CMP.W	data16,Dn	0 C	4 0ddd	yyyy	yyyy							4	8(2/0)
CMP.W	rs,An	B ddd0	C 0sss									2	6(1/0)
CMP.W	rs,Dn	B ddd0	4 0sss									2	4(1/0)
CMP.W	sadr,An	B ddd0	11ee eeee	[EXT]								2, 4, or 6	6(1/0)+
CMP.W	sadr,Dn	B ddd0	01ee eeee	[EXT]								2, 4, or 6	4(1/0)+
CMPM.B	(sAn)+,(dAn)+	B ddd1	0 1sss									2	12(3/0)
CMPM.L	(sAn)+,(dAn)+	B ddd1	8 1sss									2	20(5/0)
CMPM.W	(sAn)+,(dAn)+	B ddd1	4 1sss									2	12(3/0)
DBCC	Dn,label	5 4	C 1rr	xxxx								4	12(2/0), 10(2/0), 14(3/0)
DBCS	Dn,label	5 5	C 1rr	xxxx								4	12(2/0), 10(2/0), 14(3/0)
DBEQ	Dn,label	5 7	C 1rr	xxxx								4	12(2/0), 10(2/0), 14(3/0)
DBF	Dn,label	5 1	C 1rr	xxxx								4	12(2/0), 10(2/0), 14(3/0)
DBGE	Dn,label	5 C	C 1rr	xxxx								4	12(2/0), 10(2/0), 14(3/0)
DBGT	Dn,label	5 E	C 1rr	xxxx								4	12(2/0), 10(2/0), 14(3/0)
DBHI	Dn,label	5 2	C 1rr	xxxx								4	12(2/0), 10(2/0), 14(3/0)
DBLE	Dn,label	5 F	C 1rr	xxxx								4	12(2/0), 10(2/0), 14(3/0)
DBLS	Dn,label	5 3	C 1rr	xxxx								4	12(2/0), 10(2/0), 14(3/0)
DBLT	Dn,label	5 D	C 1rr	xxxx								4	12(2/0), 10(2/0), 14(3/0)
DBMI	Dn,label	5 B	C 1rr	xxxx								4	12(2/0), 10(2/0), 14(3/0)
DBNE	Dn,label	5 6	C 1rr	xxxx								4	12(2/0), 10(2/0), 14(3/0)
DBPL	Dn,label	5 A	C 1rr	xxxx								4	12(2/0), 10(2/0), 14(3/0)

Table 7-7. MC68000 Instruction Object Codes (Continued)

Instruction		Byte 1	Byte 2	Byte 3	Byte 4	Byte 5	Byte 6	Byte 7	Byte 8	Byte 9	Byte 10	Bytes	Clock Cycles
DBRA	Dn,label	(same as DBF)											
DBT	Dn,label	5 0	C 1rrr									4	12(2/0),10(2/0),14(3/0)
DVC	Dn,label	5 8	C 1rrr									4	12(2/0),10(2/0),14(3/0)
DVS	Dn,label	5 9	C 1rrr									4	12(2/0),10(2/0),14(3/0)
DIVS	data16,Dn	8 ddd1	F C	xxxx	yyyy							4	<162(2/0)
DIVS	sadr,Dn	8 ddd1	11ee eeee	[EXT]								2, 4, or 6	<158(1/0)+
DIVS	sDn,Dn	8 ddd1	C 0sss									2	<158(1/0)
DIVU	data16,Dn	8 ddd0	F C	xxxx	yyyy							4	<148(2/0)
DIVU	sadr,Dn	8 ddd0	11ee eeee	[EXT]								2, 4, or 6	<140(1/0)+
DIVU	sDn,dDn	8 ddd0	C 0sss									2	<140(1/0)
EOR.B	data8,dadr	0 A	00ff ffff	00	yy	[EXT]						4, 6, or 8	13(2/1)+
EOR.B	data8,Dn	0 A	0 0ddd	00	yy							4	8(2/0)
EOR.B	data8,SR	0 A	3 C	00	yy							4	20(3/0)
EOR.B	Dn,dadr	B sss1	00ff ffff	[EXT]								2, 4, or 6	9(1/1)+
EOR.B	sDn,dDn	B sss1	0 0ddd									2	4(1/0)
EOR.L	data32,dadr	0 A	10ff ffff	wwww		zzzz		[EXT]				6, 8, or 10	22(3/2)+
EOR.L	data32,Dn	0 A	8 0ddd	wwww		zzzz						6	16(3/0)
EOR.L	Dn,dadr	B sss1	10ff ffff	[EXT]								2, 4, or 6	14(1/2)+
EOR.L	sDn,dDn	B sss1	8 0ddd									2	8(1/0)
EOR.W	data16,dadr	0 A	01ff ffff	yyyy		[EXT]						4, 6, or 8	13(2/1)+
EOR.W	data16,Dn	0 A	4 0ddd	yyyy								4	8(2/0)
EOR.W	data16,Sr	0 A	7 C	yyyy								4	20(3/0)
EOR.W	Dn,dadr	B sss1	01ff ffff	[EXT]								2, 4, or 6	9(1/1)+
EOR.W	sDn,dDn	B sss1	4 0ddd									2	4(1/0)
EXG	Dn,dDn	C sss1	4 0ddd									2	6(1/0)
EXG	An,An	C sss1	4 1ddd									2	6(1/0)
EXG	An,Dn	C sss1	8 1ddd									2	6(1/0)
EXG	Dn,Dn	(same as An,Dn)										2	6(1/0)
EXT.L	Dn	4 8	C 0ddd									2	4(1/0)
EXT.W	Dn	4 8	8 0ddd									2	4(1/0)
JMP	jadr	4 E	11jjjjjj	[EXT]								2, 4, or 6	4(1/0)+
JSR	jadr	4 E	10jjjjjj	[EXT]								2, 4, or 6	14(1/2)+
LEA	jadr,An	4 ddd1	11jjjjjj	[EXT]								2, 4, or 6	2(0/0)+
LINK	An,d16	4 E	5 0rrr	[EXT]								4	18(2/2)
LSL	dadr	E 3	11ff ffff	[EXT]								2, 4, or 6	9(1/1)+
LSL.B	count,Dn	E ccc1	0 1ddd									2	6 + 2N(1/0)
LSL.B	Dn,dDn	E rrr1	2 1ddd									2	6 + 2N(1/0)
LSL.L	count,Dn	E ccc1	8 1ddd									2	8 + 2N(1/0)
LSL.L	Dn,dDn	E rrr1	A 1ddd									2	6 + 2N(1/0)
LSL.W	count,Dn	E ccc1	4 1ddd									2	6 + 2N(1/0)
LSL.W	Dn,dDn	E rrr1	6 1ddd									2	6 + 2N(1/0)
LSR	dadr	E 2	11ff ffff	[EXT]								2, 4, or 6	9(1/1)+
LSR.B	count,Dn	E ccc0	0 1ddd									2	6 + 2N(1/0)
LSR.B	Dn,dDn	E rrr0	2 1ddd									2	6 + 2N(1/0)
LSR.L	count,Dn	E ccc0	8 1ddd									2	8 + 2N(1/0)
LSR.L	Dn,dDn	E rrr0	A 1ddd									2	6 + 2N(1/0)
LSR.W	count,Dn	E ccc0	4 1ddd									2	6 + 2N(1/0)
LSR.W	Dn,dDn	E rrr0	6 1ddd									2	6 + 2N(1/0)
MOVE	An,USP	4 E	6 0sss									2	4(1/0)
MOVE	data8,CCR	4 4	F C	00	yy							4	16(3/0)
MOVE	data16,SR	4 6	F C	yyyy								4	16(3/0)
MOVE	Dn,CCR	4 4	C 0sss									2	12(2/0)
MOVE	Dn,SR	4 6	C 0sss									2	12(2/0)

Table 7-7. MC68000 Instruction Object Codes (Continued)

Instruction		Byte 1	Byte 2	Byte 3	Byte 4	Byte 5	Byte 6	Byte 7	Byte 8	Byte 9	Byte 10	Bytes	Clock Cycles
MOVE.8	sadr,CCR	4 4	11eeeeee	[EXT]		[EXT]						2, 4, or 6	12(2/0)+
	sadr,SR	4 6	11eeeeee	[EXT]		[EXT]						2, 4, or 6	12(2/0)+
	SR,dadr	4 0	11ffffff	[EXT]		[EXT]						2, 4, or 6	9(1/1)+
	SR,Dn	4 0	C Oddd									2	6(1/0)
	USP,An	4 E	6 1sss									2	4(1/0)
	data8,Dn	1 ddd0	3 C	00	yy							4	8(2/0)
	data8,dadr	1 gggg	gg111100	00	yy	[EXT]		[EXT]				4, 6, or 8	9(1/1)+
	Dn,dadr	1 gggg	gg000sss	[EXT]		[EXT]						2, 4, or 6	5(0/1)+
	sDn,dDn	1 ddd0	O Osss									2	4(1/0)
	sadr,dadr	1 gggg	ggeeeeee	[EXTs]		[EXTs]		[EXTd]		[EXTd]		2, 4, 6, 8, or 10	5(1/1)+
MOVE.L	An,dadr	2 gggg	gg001sss	[EXT]		[EXT]						2, 4, or 6	4(1/0)
	data32,An	2 ddd0	7 C	yyyy		zzzz						6	10(0/2)+
	data32,dadr	2 gggg	gg111100	yyyy		zzzz		[EXT]		[EXT]		6, 8, or 10	12(3/0)
	data32,Dn	2 ddd0	3 C	yyyy		zzzz						6	18(2/2)+
	Dn,dadr	2 gggg	gg000sss	[EXT]		[EXT]						2, 4, or 6	12(3/0)
	rs,An	2 ddd0	4 tsss									2	10(0/2)+
	rs,Dn	2 ddd0	O tsss									2	4(1/0)
	sadr,An	2 ddd0	O1eeeeee	[EXT]		[EXT]						2, 4, or 6	4(1/0)
	sadr,dadr	2 gggg	ggeeeeee	[EXTs]		[EXTs]		[EXTd]		[EXTd]		2, 4, 6, 8, or 10	8(2/0)+
	sadr,Dn	2 ddd0	OOeeeeee	[EXT]		[EXT]						2, 4, or 6	14(1/2)+
MOVE.W	data16,An	3 ddd0	7 C	yyyy		[EXT]						4, 6, or 8	4(1/0)
	data16,dadr	3 gggg	gg111100	yyyy		[EXT]		[EXT]				2, 4, or 6	5(0/1)+
	data16,Dn	3 ddd0	3 C	yyyy								4	8(2/0)
	Dn,dadr	3 gggg	gg000sss	[EXT]		[EXT]						2, 4, or 6	9(1/1)+
	rs,An	3 ddd0	4 tsss									2	8(2/0)
	rs,Dn	3 ddd0	O tsss									2	5(0/1)+
	sadr,An	3 ddd0	O1eeeeee	[EXT]		[EXT]						2, 4, or 6	4(1/0)
	sadr,dadr	3 gggg	ggeeeeee	[EXTs]		[EXTs]		[EXTd]		[EXTd]		2, 4, 6, 8, or 10	4(1/0)
	sadr,Dn	3 ddd0	OOeeeeee	[EXT]		[EXT]						2, 4, or 6	4(1/0)+
MOVEM.L	(An)+,reg-list	4 C	11jjjjjj	mmmm		[EXT]		[EXT]				4	8 + 8n(2 + 2n/0)
	jadr,reg-list	4 C	E Osss	mmmm		[EXT]		[EXT]				4, 6, or 8	8 + 8n(2 + 2n/0)+
	reg-list,-(An)	4 8	E Oddd	kkkk		[EXT]		[EXT]				4	4 + 10n(1/n)
	reg-list,madr	4 8	11hhhhhh	mmmm		[EXT]		[EXT]				4, 6, or 8	4 + 10n(1/n)+
MOVEM.W	jadr,reg-list	4 C	A Osss	mmmm		[EXT]		[EXT]				4	8 + 4n(2 + n/0)
	(An)+,reg-list	4 C	10jjjjjj	kkkk		[EXT]		[EXT]				4, 6, or 8	8 + 4n(2 + n/0)+
	reg-list,-(An)	4 8	A Oddd	mmmm		[EXT]		[EXT]				4	4 + 5n(1/n)
	reg-list,madr	4 8	10hhhhhh	mmmm		[EXT]		[EXT]				4, 6, or 8	4 + 5n(1/n)+
MOVEP.L	d16(An),Dn	0 ddd1	4 1sss	xxxx								4	24(6/0)
	Dn,d16(An)	0 sss1	C 1ddd	xxxx								4	28(2/4)
MOVEP.W	d16(An),Dn	0 ddd1	0 1sss	xxxx								4	16(4/0)
	Dn,d16(An)	0 sss1	8 1ddd	xxxx								4	18(2/2)
MOVEQ	data8,Dn	7 ddd0	yy									2	4(1/0)
MULS	data16,Dn	C ddd1	F C	yyyy		[EXT]						4	<74(2/0)+
	sDn,dDn	C ddd1	C Osss									2	<70(1/0)+
	sadr,Dn	C ddd1	11eeeeee	[EXT]		[EXT]						2, 4, or 6	<70(1/0)+
MULU	data16,Dn	C ddd0	F C	yyyy		[EXT]						4	<74(2/0)+
	sDn,dDn	C ddd0	C Osss									2	<70(1/0)+
	sadr,Dn	C ddd0	11eeeeee	[EXT]		[EXT]						2, 4, or 6	<70(1/0)+
NBCD	dadr	4 8	OOffffff	[EXT]		[EXT]						2, 4, or 6	9(1/1)+
	Dn	4 8	O Oddd									2	6(1/0)
NEG.B	dadr	4 4	OOffffff	[EXT]		[EXT]						2, 4, or 6	9(1/1)+

Table 7-7. MC68000 Instruction Object Codes (Continued)

Instruction		Byte 1	Byte 2	Byte 3	Byte 4	Byte 5	Byte 6	Byte 7	Byte 8	Byte 9	Byte 10	Bytes	Clock Cycles
NEG.L	Dn	44	8 Oddd									2	6(1/0)
	dadr	44	10ff ffff	[EXT]		[EXT]						2, 4, or 6	14(1/2)+
NEG.W	Dn	44	4 Oddd									2	4(1/0)
	dadr	44	01ff ffff	[EXT]		[EXT]						2, 4, or 6	9(1/1)+
NEGX.B	dadr	40	00ff ffff	[EXT]		[EXT]						2, 4, or 6	9(1/1)+
	Dn	40	0 Oddd									2	4(1/0)
NEGX.L	dadr	40	10ff ffff	[EXT]		[EXT]						2, 4, or 6	14(1/2)+
	Dn	40	8 Oddd									2	6(1/0)
NEGX.W	dadr	40	01ff ffff	[EXT]		[EXT]						2, 4, or 6	9(1/1)+
	Dn	40	4 Oddd									2	4(1/0)
NOP		4E	7 1									2	4(1/0)
NOT.B	dadr	46	00ff ffff	[EXT]		[EXT]						2, 4, or 6	9(1/1)+
	Dn	46	0 Oddd									2	4(1/0)
NOT.L	dadr	46	10ff ffff	[EXT]		[EXT]						2, 4, or 6	14(1/2)+
	Dn	46	8 Oddd									2	6(1/0)
NOT.W	dadr	46	01ff ffff	[EXT]		[EXT]						2, 4, or 6	9(1/1)+
	Dn	46	4 Oddd									2	4(1/0)
OR.B	data8,dadr	0	00ff ffff	00	yy	[EXT]		[EXT]				4, 6, or 8	13(2/1)+
	data8,Dn	0	00eeeeee	00	yy							4	8(2/0)
	data8,SR	0	3 C	00	yy							4	20(3/0)
	Dn,dadr	8 sss1	00ff ffff	[EXT]		[EXT]						2, 4, or 6	9(1/1)+
	sadr,Dn	8 ddd0	00eeeeee	[EXT]		[EXT]						2, 4, or 6	4(1/0)+
	sDn,dDn	8 ddd0	0 Osss									2	4(1/0)
OR.L	data32,dadr	0	10ff ffff	yyyy		zzzz		[EXT]		[EXT]		6, 8, or 10	22(3/2)+
	data32,Dn	0	10eeeeee	yyyy		zzzz						6	16(3/0)
	Dn,dadr	8 sss1	10ff ffff	[EXT]		[EXT]						2, 4, or 6	14(1/2)+
	sadr,Dn	8 ddd0	10eeeeee	[EXT]		[EXT]						2, 4, or 6	6(1/0)+
	sDn,dDn	8 ddd0	8 Osss									2	8(1/0)
OR.W	data16,dadr	0	01ff ffff	yyyy		[EXT]		[EXT]				4, 6, or 8	13(2/1)+
	data16,Dn	0	01eeeeee	yyyy								4	8(2/0)
	data16,SR	0	7 C	yyyy								4	20(3/0)
	Dn,dadr	8 sss1	01ff ffff	[EXT]		[EXT]						2, 4, or 6	9(1/1)+
	sadr,Dn	8 ddd0	01eeeeee	[EXT]		[EXT]						2, 4, or 6	4(1/0)+
	sDn,dDn	8 ddd0	4 Osss									2	4(1/0)
PEA	jadr	48	01jj jjjj	[EXT]		[EXT]						2, 4, or 6	10(1/2)+
RESET		4E	7 0									2	132(1/0)
ROL	dadr	E 7	11ff ffff	[EXT]		[EXT]						2, 4, or 6	9(1/1)+
ROL.B	count,Dn	E ccc1	1 1ddd									2	6 + 2N(1/0)
	Dn,dDn	E rrr1	3 1ddd									2	6 + 2N(1/0)
ROL.L	count,Dn	E ccc1	9 1ddd									2	8 + 2N(1/0)
	Dn,dDn	E rrr1	B 1ddd									2	8 + 2N(1/0)
ROL.W	count,Dn	E ccc1	5 1ddd									2	6 + 2N(1/0)
	Dn,dDn	E rrr1	7 1ddd									2	6 + 2N(1/0)
ROR	dadr	E 6	11ff ffff	[EXT]		[EXT]						2, 4, or 6	9(1/1)+
ROR.B	count,Dn	E ccc0	1 1ddd									2	6 + 2N(1/0)
	Dn,dDn	E rrr0	3 1ddd									2	6 + 2N(1/0)
ROR.L	count,Dn	E ccc0	9 1ddd									2	8 + 2N(1/0)
	Dn,dDn	E rrr0	B 1ddd									2	8 + 2N(1/0)
ROR.W	count,Dn	E ccc0	5 1ddd									2	6 + 2N(1/0)
	Dn,dDn	E rrr0	7 1ddd									2	6 + 2N(1/0)
ROXL	dadr	E 5	11ff ffff	[EXT]		[EXT]						2, 4, or 6	9(1/1)+
ROXL.B	count,Dn	E ccc1	1 Oddd									2	6 + 2N(1/0)

Table 7-7. MC68000 Instruction Object Codes (Continued)

Instruction		Byte 1	Byte 2	Byte 3	Byte 4	Byte 5	Byte 6	Byte 7	Byte 8	Byte 9	Byte 10	Bytes	Clock Cycles
ROXL.L	Dn,dDn	E rr1	3 Oddd									2	6 + 2N(1/0)
ROXL.L	count,Dn	E ccc1	9 Oddd									2	8 + 2N(1/0)
ROXL.W	Dn,dDn	E ccc1	B Oddd									2	8 + 2N(1/0)
ROXL.W	count,Dn	E ccc1	5 Oddd									2	6 + 2N(1/0)
	Dn,dDn	E rr1	7 Oddd									2	6 + 2N(1/0)
ROXR	dadr	E 4	11ff ffff	[EXT]								2, 4, or 6	9(1/1)+
ROXR.B	count,Dn	E ccc0	1 Oddd									2	6 + 2N(1/0)
	Dn,dDn	E rr0	3 Oddd									2	6 + 2N(1/0)
ROXR.L	count,Dn	E ccc0	4 Oddd									2	8 + 2N(1/0)
	Dn,dDn	E rr0	B Oddd									2	8 + 2N(1/0)
ROXR.W	count,Dn	E ccc0	5 Oddd									2	6 + 2N(1/0)
	Dn,dDn	E rr0	7 Oddd									2	6 + 2N(1/0)
RTE		4 E	7 3									2	20(5/0)
RTR		4 E	7 7									2	20(5/0)
RTS		4 E	7 5									2	16(4/0)
SBCD	-(sAn),-(dAn)	8 ddd1	0 1sss									2	19(3/1)
	sDn,dDn	8 ddd1	0 Osss									2	6(1/0)
SCC	dadr	5 4	11ff ffff	[EXT]								2, 4, or 6	9(1/1)+
	Dn	5 4	C Oddd									2	6,4(1/0)
SCS	dadr	5 5	11ff ffff	[EXT]								2, 4, or 6	9(1/1)+
	Dn	5 5	C Oddd									2	6,4(1/0)
SEQ	dadr	5 7	11ff ffff	[EXT]								2, 4, or 6	9(1/1)+
	Dn	5 7	C Oddd									2	6, 4, (1/0)
SF	dadr	5 1	1fff ffff	[EXT]								2, 4, or 6	9(1/1)+
	Dn	5 1	C Oddd									2	6,4(1/0)
SGE	dadr	5 C	11ff ffff	[EXT]								2, 4, or 6	9(1/1)
	Dn	5 C	C Oddd									2	6,4(1/0)
SGT	dadr	5 E	11ff ffff	[EXT]								2, 4, or 6	9(1/1)+
	Dn	5 E	C Oddd									2	6,4(1/0)
SHI	dadr	5 2	11ff ffff	[EXT]								2, 4, or 6	9(1/1)+
	Dn	5 2	C Oddd									2	6,4(1/0)
SLE	dadr	5 F	11ff ffff	[EXT]								2, 4, or 6	9(1/1)+
	Dn	5 F	C Oddd									2	6,4(1/0)
SLS	dadr	5 3	11ff ffff	[EXT]								2, 4, or 6	9(1/1)+
	Dn	5 3	C Oddd									2	6,4(1/0)
SLT	dadr	5 D	11ff ffff	[EXT]								2, 4, or 6	9(1/1)+
	Dn	5 D	C Oddd									2	6,4(1/0)
SMI	dadr	5 B	11ff ffff	[EXT]								2, 4, or 6	9(1/1)+
	Dn	5 B	C Oddd									2	6,4(1/0)
SNE	dadr	5 6	11ff ffff	[EXT]								2, 4, or 6	9(1/1)+
	Dn	5 6	C Oddd									2	6,4(1/0)
SPL	dadr	5 A	11ff ffff	[EXT]								2, 4, or 6	9(1/1)+
	Dn	5 A	C Oddd									2	6,4(1/0)
ST	dadr	5 0	11ff ffff	[EXT]								2, 4, or 6	9(1/1)+
	Dn	5 0	C Oddd									2	6,4(1/0)
STOP	data16	4 E	7 2	yyyy								4	8(2/0)
SUB. B	data8,dadr	0 4	OOff ffff	00	yy	[EXT]						4, 6, or 8	13(2/1)+
	data8,Dn	0 4	0 Oddd	00	yy							4	8(2/0)
SUB.	Dn,dadr	9 sss1	1Off ffff	[EXT]		[EXT]						2, 4, or 6	9(1/1)+
	sadr,Dn	9 ddd0	OOee eeee	[EXT]		[EXT]						2, 4, or 6	4(1/0)+
	sDn,dDn	9 ddd0	0 Osss									2	4(1/0)
SUB. L	data32,An	9 ddd1	F C	yyyy		zzzz						6	16(3/0)
	data32,dadr	0 4	10ff ffff	yyyy		zzzz				[EXT]		6, 8, or 10	22(3/2)+

Table 7-7. MC68000 Instruction Object Codes (Continued)

Instruction		Byte 1	Byte 2	Byte 3	Byte 4	Byte 5	Byte 6	Byte 7	Byte 8	Byte 9	Byte 10	Bytes	Clock Cycles
	data32,Dn	0 4	8 0ddd	yyyy	yyyy		zzzz					6	16(3/0)
	Dn,dadr	9 sss1	10ff ffff	[EXT]								2, 4, or 6	14(1/2)+
	rs,An	9 ddd1	C tsss									2	8(1/0)
	rs,Dn	9 ddd0	8 tsss									2	8(1/0)
	sadr,An	9 ddd1	11eeeeee	[EXT]								2, 4, or 6	6(1/0)+
	sadr,Dn	9 ddd0	10eeeeee	[EXT]								2, 4, or 6	6(1/0)+
SUB.W	data16,An	0 4	F C	yyyy								4	8(2/0)
	data16,dadr	0 4	4 0ddd	yyyy	[EXT]			[EXT]				4, 6, or 8	13(2/1)+
	data16,Dn	9 sss1	01ff ffff	yyyy								4	8(2/0)
	Dn,dadr	9 ddd0	C tsss	[EXT]								2, 4, or 6	9(1/1)+
	rs,An	9 ddd1	4 tsss									2	8(1/0)
	rs,Dn	9 ddd0	4 0ddd									2	4(1/0)
	sadr,An	9 ddd1	01eeeeee	[EXT]								2, 4, or 6	8(1/0)+
	sadr,Dn	9 ddd0	01eeeeee	[EXT]								2, 4, or 6	4(1/0)+
SUBQ.B	data3,dadr	5 bbb1	00ff ffff	[EXT]								2, 4, or 6	9(1/1)+
	data3,An	5 bbb1	0 0ddd									2	8(1/0)
	data3,Dn	5 bbb1	8 1ddd									2	8(1/0)+
SUBQ.L	data3,dadr	5 bbb1	10ff ffff	[EXT]								2, 4, or 6	4(1/0)
	data3,An	5 bbb1	8 0ddd									2	4(1/0)
	data3,Dn	5 bbb1	4 1ddd									2	14(1/2)+
SUBQ.W	data3,dadr	5 bbb1	01ff ffff	[EXT]								2, 4, or 6	8(1/0)
	data3,An	5 bbb1	4 0ddd									2	4(1/0)
	data3,Dn	5 bbb1	4 0ddd									2	9(1/1)+
SUBX.B	-(sAn),-(dAn)	9 ddd1	0 1sss									2	19(3/1)
	sDn,dDn	9 ddd1	0 0sss									2	4(1/0)
SUBX.L	-(sAn),-(dAn)	9 ddd1	8 1sss									2	32(5/2)
	sDn,dDn	9 ddd1	8 0sss									2	8(1/0)
SUBX.W	-(sAn),-(dAn)	9 ddd1	4 1sss									2	19(3/1)
	sDn,dDn	9 ddd1	4 0sss									2	4(1/0)
SVC	dadr	5 8	11ff ffff	[EXT]								2, 4, or 6	9(1/1)+
	Dn	5 8	C 0ddd									2	6, 4(1/0)
SVS	dadr	5 9	11ff ffff	[EXT]								2, 4, or 6	9(1/1)+
	Dn	5 9	C 0ddd									2	6, 4(1/0)
SWAP	Dn	4 8	4 0rr									2	4(1/0)
TAS	dadr	4 A	11ff ffff	[EXT]								2, 4, or 6	11(1/1)+
	Dn	4 A	C 0rr									2	4(1/0)
TRAP	vector	4 E	4 0vvv									2	36(4/3)
TRAPV		4 E	7 6									2	37(5/3),4(1/0)
TST.B	dadr	4 A	00ff ffff	[EXT]								2, 4, or 6	4(1/0)+
	Dn	4 A	0 0rrr									2	4(1/0)
TST.L	dadr	4 A	10ff ffff	[EXT]								2, 4, or 6	4(1/0)+
	Dn	4 A	8 0rrr									2	4(1/0)
TST.W	dadr	4 A	01ff ffff	[EXT]								2, 4, or 6	4(1/0)+
	Dn	4 A	4 0rrr									2	4(1/0)
UNLK	An	4 E	5 1rr									2	12(3/0)

Table 7-8. MC68000 Object Codes in Numerical Order

Byte 1	Byte 2	Byte 3	Byte 4	Byte 5	Byte 6	Byte 7	Byte 8	Byte 9	Byte 10	Instruction
00	0 0ddd	00	yy							OR.B data8,Dn
00	00ff ffff	00	yy	[EXT]		[EXT]				OR.B data8,dadr
00	3 c	00	yy							OR.B data8,SR
00	4 0ddd		yyyy							OR.W data16,Dn
00	01ff ffff		yyyy	[EXT]		[EXT]				OR.W data16,dadr
00	7 c		yyyy							OR.W data16,SR
00	8 0ddd		yyyy	zzzz						OR.L data32,Dn
00	10ff ffff		yyyy	zzzz		[EXT]		[EXT]		OR. L data32,dadr
0 rrr1	0 0ddd									BTST Dn,dDn
0 ddd1	0 1sss									MOVEP.W d16(An),Dn
0 rrr1	00ff ffff	[EXT]		[EXT]						BTST Dn,dadr
0 rrr1	A 0ddd									BCHG Dn,dDn
0 ddd1	A 1sss	xxxx								MOVEP.L d16(An),Dn
0 rrr1	01ff ffff	[EXT]		[EXT]						BCHG Dn,dadr
0 rrr1	8 0ddd									BCLR Dn,dDn
0 sss1	8 1ddd	xxxx								MOVEP.W Dn,d16(An)
0 rrr1	10ff ffff	[EXT]		[EXT]						BCLR Dn,dadr
0 rrr1	C 0ddd									BSET Dn,dDn
0 sss1	C 1ddd	xxxx								MOVEP.L Dn,d16(An)
0 rrr1	11ff ffff	[EXT]		[EXT]						BSET Dn,dadr
02	0 0ddd	00	yy							AND.B data8,Dn
02	00ff ffff	00	yy	[EXT]		[EXT]				AND.B data8,dadr
02	3 c	00	yy							AND.B data8,SR
02	4 0ddd		yyyy							AND.W data16,Dn
02	01ff ffff		yyyy	[EXT]		[EXT]				AND.W data16,dadr
02	7 c		yyyy							AND.W data16,SR
02	8 0ddd		yyyy	zzzz						AND.L data32,Dn
02	10ff ffff		yyyy	zzzz		[EXT]		[EXT]		AND.L data32,dadr
04	0 0ddd	00	yy							SUB.B data8,Dn
04	00ff ffff	00	yy	[EXT]		[EXT]				SUB.B data8,dadr
04	4 0ddd		yyyy							SUB.W data16,Dn
04	01ff ffff		yyyy	[EXT]		[EXT]				SUB.W data16,dadr
04	8 0ddd		yyyy	zzzz						SUB.L data32,Dn
04	10ff ffff		yyyy	zzzz		[EXT]		[EXT]		SUB.L data32,dadr
06	0 0ddd	00	yy							ADD.B data8,Dn
06	00ff ffff	00	yy	[EXT]		[EXT]				ADD.B data8,dadr
06	4 0ddd		yyyy							ADD.W data16,Dn
06	01ff ffff		yyyy	[EXT]		[EXT]				ADD.W data16,dadr
06	8 0ddd		yyyy	zzzz						ADD.L data32,Dn
06	10ff ffff		yyyy	zzzz		[EXT]		[EXT]		ADD.L data32,dadr
08	0 0ddd	00	000b bbbb							BTST bitl,Dn
08	00ff ffff	00	0 0bbb	[EXT]		[EXT]				BTST bitb,dadr
08	4 0ddd	00	000b bbbb							BCHG bitl,Dn
08	01ff ffff	00	0 0bbb	[EXT]		[EXT]				BCHG bitb,dadr
08	8 0ddd	00	000b bbbb							BCLR bitl,Dn
08	10ff ffff	00	0 0bbb	[EXT]		[EXT]				BCLR bitb,dadr
08	C 0ddd	00	000b bbbb							BSET bitl,Dn
08	11ff ffff	00	0 0bbb	[EXT]		[EXT]				BSET bitb,dadr
0A	0 0ddd	00	yy							EOR.B data8,Dn
0A	00ff ffff	00	yy	[EXT]		[EXT]				EOR.B data8,dadr
0A	3 C	00	yy							EOR.B data8,SR
0A	4 0ddd		yyyy							EOR.W data16,Dn
0A	01ff ffff		yyyy	[EXT]		[EXT]				EOR.W data16,dadr
0A	7 C		yyyy							EOR.W data16,SR
0A	8 0ddd		yyyy	zzzz						EOR.L data32,Dn
0A	10ff ffff		yyyy	zzzz		[EXT]		[EXT]		EOR.L data32,dadr
0C	0 0ddd	00	yy							CMP.B data8,Dn
0C	00ff ffff	00	yy	[EXT]		[EXT]				CMP.B data8,dadr
0C	4 0ddd		yyyy							CMP.W data16,Dn
0C	01ff ffff		yyyy	[EXT]		[EXT]				CMP.W data16,dadr
0C	8 0ddd		yyyy	zzzz						CMP.L data32,Dn
0C	10ff ffff		yyyy	zzzz		[EXT]		[EXT]		CMP.L data32,dadr
1 ddd0	0 0sss									MOVE.B sDn,dDn
1 ddd0	00ee eeee	[EXT]		[EXT]						MOVE.B sadr,Dn
1 ddd0	3 C	00	yy							MOVE.B data8,Dn
1 gggg	gg00 0sss	[EXT]		[EXT]						MOVE.B Dn,dadr
1 gggg	ggee eeee	[EXTs]	[EXTs]	[EXTd]		[EXTd]				MOVE.B sadr,dadr
1 gggg	gg11 C	00	yy	[EXT]		[EXT]				MOVE.B data8,dadr
2 ddd0	0000 0tsss									MOVE.L rs,Dn
2 ddd0	00ee eeee	[EXT]		[EXT]						MOVE.L sadr,Dn
2 ddd0	3 C		yyyy	zzzz						MOVE.L data32,Dn
2 ddd0	0100 0tsss									MOVE.L rs,An
2 ddd0	01ee eeee	[EXT]		[EXT]						MOVE.L sadr,An

Table 7-8. MC68000 Object Codes in Numerical Order (Continued)

Byte 1	Byte 2	Byte 3	Byte 4	Byte 5	Byte 6	Byte 7	Byte 8	Byte 9	Byte 10	Instruction	
2ddd0	7 C	yyyy		zzzz						MOVE.L	data32,An
2gggg	gg00tss	[EXT]		[EXT]						MOVE.L	rs,dadr
2gggg	ggee eeee	[EXTs]		[EXTs]		[EXTd]		[EXTd]		MOVE.L	sadr,dadr
2gggg	gg11 C	yyyy		zzzz		[EXT]		[EXT]		MOVE.L	data32,dadr
3ddd0	0 tsss									MOVE.W	rs,Dn
3ddd0	00ee eeee	[EXT]		[EXT]						MOVE.W	sadr,Dn
3ddd0	3 C	yyyy								MOVE.W	data16,Dn
3ddd0	4 tsss									MOVE.W	rs,An
3ddd0	01ee eeee	[EXT]		[EXT]						MOVE.W	sadr,An
3ddd0	7 C	yyyy								MOVE.W	data16,An
3gggg	gg00tss	[EXT]		[EXT]						MOVE.W	rs,dadr
3gggg	ggee eeee	[EXTs]		[EXTs]		[EXTd]		[EXTd]		MOVE.W	sadr,dadr
3gggg	gg11 C	yyyy		[EXT]		[EXT]				MOVE.W	data16,dadr
40	0 0ddd									NEGX.B	Dn
40	00ff ffff	[EXT]		[EXT]						NEGX.B	dadr
40	4 0ddd									NEGX.W	Dn
40	01ff ffff	[EXT]		[EXT]						NEGX.W	dadr
40	8 0ddd									NEGX.L	Dn
40	10ff ffff	[EXT]		[EXT]						NEGX.L	dadr
40	C 0ddd									MOVE	SR,Dn
40	11ff ffff	[EXT]		[EXT]						MOVE	SR,dadr
4ddd1	8 0rrr									CHK	Dn,dDn
4ddd1	10ee eeee	[EXT]		[EXT]						CHK	sadr,Dn
4ddd1	B C	yyyy								CHK	data16,Dn
4ddd1	11jj jjjj	[EXT]		[EXT]						LEA	jadr,An
42	0 0ddd									CLR.B	Dn
42	00ff ffff	[EXT]		[EXT]						CLR.B	dadr
42	4 0ddd									CLR.W	Dn
42	01ff ffff	[EXT]		[EXT]						CLR.W	dadr
42	8 0ddd									CLR.L	Dn
42	10ff ffff	[EXT]		[EXT]						CLR.L	dadr
44	0 0ddd									NEG.B	Dn
44	00ff ffff	[EXT]		[EXT]						NEG.B	dadr
44	4 0ddd									NEG.W	Dn
44	01ff ffff	[EXT]		[EXT]						NEG.W	dadr
44	8 0ddd									NEG.L	Dn
44	10ff ffff	[EXT]		[EXT]						NEG.L	dadr
44	C 0sss									MOVE	Dn,CCR
44	11ee eeee	[EXT]		[EXT]						MOVE	sadr,CCR
44	F C	00	yy							MOVE	data8,CCR
46	0 0ddd									NOT.B	Dn
46	00ff ffff	[EXT]		[EXT]						NOT.B	dadr
46	4 0ddd									NOT.W	Dn
46	01ff ffff	[EXT]		[EXT]						NOT.W	dadr
46	8 0ddd									NOT.L	Dn
46	10ff ffff	[EXT]		[EXT]						NOT.L	dadr
46	C 0sss									MOVE	Dn,SR
46	11ee eeee	[EXT]		[EXT]						MOVE	sadr,SR
46	F C	yyyy								MOVE	data16,SR
48	0 0ddd									NBCD	Dn
48	00ff ffff	[EXT]		[EXT]						NBCD	dadr
48	4 0rrr									SWAP	Dn
48	01jj jjjj	[EXT]		[EXT]						PEA	jadr
48	8 0ddd									EXT.W	Dn
48	10hh hhhh	mmmm		[EXT]		[EXT]				MOVEM.W	reg-list,madr
48	A 0ddd	kkkk								MOVEM.W	reg-list,-(An)
48	C 0ddd									EXT.L	Dn
48	11hh hhhh	mmmm		[EXT]		[EXT]				MOVEM.L	reg-list,madr
48	E 0ddd	kkkk								MOVE.L	reg-list,-(An)
4A	0 0rrr									TST.B	Dn
4A	00ff ffff	[EXT]		[EXT]						TST.B	dadr
4A	4 0rrr									TST.W	Dn
4A	01ff ffff	[EXT]		[EXT]						TST.W	dadr
4A	8 0rrr									TST.L	Dn
4A	10ff ffff	[EXT]		[EXT]						TST.L	dadr
4A	C 0rrr									TAS	Dn
4A	11ff ffff	[EXT]		[EXT]						TAS	dadr
4C	10jj jjjj	mmmm		[EXT]						MOVEM.W	jadr,reg-list
4C	A 0sss	mmmm								MOVEM.W	(An)+,reg-list
4C	E 0sss	mmmm								MOVEM.L	(An)+,reg-list
4C	11jj jjjj	mmmm		[EXT]						MOVEM.L	jadr,reg-list
4C	E 0sss	mmmm								MOVEM.L	(An)+,reg-list
4E	4 vvvv									TRAP	vector

Table 7-8. MC68000 Object Codes in Numerical Order (Continued)

Byte 1	Byte 2	Byte 3	Byte 4	Byte 5	Byte 6	Byte 7	Byte 8	Byte 9	Byte 10	Instruction	
4E	5 Orrr	xxxx								LINK	An,d16
4E	5 1rrr									UNLK	An
4E	6 Osss									MOVE	An,USP
4E	6 1sss									MOVE	USP,An
4E	7 0									RESET	
4E	7 1									NOP	
4E	7 2	yyyy								STOP	data16
4E	7 3									RTE	
4E	7 5									RTS	
4E	7 6									TRAPV	
4E	7 7									RTR	
4E	10jj jjjj	[EXT]	[EXT]							JSR	jadr
4E	11jj jjjj	[EXT]	[EXT]							JMP	jadr
5 bbb0	0 Oddd									ADDQ.B	data3,Dn
5 bbb0	00ff ffff	[EXT]	[EXT]							ADDQ.B	data3,dadr
5 bbb0	4 Oddd									ADDQ.W	data3,Dn
5 bbb0	4 1ddd									ADDQ.W	data3,An
5 bbb0	01ff ffff	[EXT]	[EXT]							ADDQ.W	data3,dadr
5 bbb0	8 Oddd									ADDQ.L	data3,Dn
5 bbb0	8 1ddd									ADDQ.L	data3,An
5 bbb0	01ff ffff	[EXT]	[EXT]							ADDQ.L	data3,dadr
50	C Oddd									ST	Dn
50	C 1rrr	xxxx								DBT	Dn,label
50	11ff ffff	[EXT]	[EXT]							ST	dadr
5 bbb1	0 Oddd									SUBQ.B	data3,Dn
5 bbb1	00ff ffff	[EXT]	[EXT]							SUBQ.B	data3,dadr
5 bbb1	4 Oddd									SUBQ.W	data3,Dn
5 bbb1	4 1ddd									SUBQ.W	data3,An
5 bbb1	01ff ffff	[EXT]	[EXT]							SUBQ.W	data3,dadr
5 bbb1	8 Oddd									SUBQ.L	data3,Dn
5 bbb1	8 1ddd									SUBQ.L	data3,An
5 bbb1	01ff ffff	[EXT]	[EXT]							SUBQ.L	data3,dadr
51	C Oddd									SF	Dn
51	C 1rrrr	xxxx								DBF	Dn,label
51	11ff ffff	[EXT]	[EXT]							SF	dadr
52	C Oddd									SHI	Dn
52	C 1rrrr	xxxx								DBHI	Dn,label
52	11ff ffff	[EXT]	[EXT]							SHI	dadr
53	C Oddd									SLS	Dn
53	C 1rrr	xxxx								DBLS	Dn,label
53	11ff ffff	[EXT]	[EXT]							SLS	dadr
54	C Oddd									SCC	Dn
54	D 1rrr	xxxx								DBCC	Dn,label
54	11ff ffff	[EXT]	[EXT]							SCC	dadr
55	C Oddd									SCS	Dn
55	C 1rrr	xxxx								DBCS	Dn,label
55	11ff ffff	[EXT]	[EXT]							SCS	dadr
56	C Oddd									SNE	Dn
56	C 1rrr	xxxx								DBNE	Dn,label
56	11ff ffff	[EXT]	[EXT]							SNE	dadr
57	C Oddd									SEQ	Dn
57	C 1rrrr	xxxx								DBEQ	Dn,label
57	11ff ffff	[EXT]	[EXT]							SEQ	dadr
58	C Oddd									SVC	Dn
58	C 1rrr	xxxx								DVC	Dn,label
58	11ff ffff	[EXT]	[EXT]							SVC	dadr
59	C Oddd									SVS	Dn
59	C 1rrr	xxxx								DVS	Dn,label
59	11ff ffff	[EXT]	[EXT]							SVS	dadr
5A	C Oddd									SPL	Dn
5A	C 1rrr	xxxx								DBPL	Dn,iabel
5A	11ff ffff	[EXT]	[EXT]							SPL	dadr
5B	C Oddd									SMI	Dn
5B	C 1rrr	xxxx								DBMI	Dn,label
5B	11ff ffff	[EXT]	[EXT]							SMI	dadr
5C	C Oddd									SGE	Dn
5C	C 1rrr	xxxx								DBGE	Dn,label
5C	11ff ffff	[EXT]	[EXT]							SGE	dadr
5D	C Oddd									SLT	Dn
5D	C 1rrr	xxxx								DBLT	Dn,label
5D	11ff ffff	[EXT]	[EXT]							SLT	dadr
5E	C Oddd									SGT	Dn
5E	C 1rrr	xxxx								DBGT	Dn,label

Table 7-8. MC68000 Object Codes in Numerical Order (Continued)

Byte 1	Byte 2	Byte 3	Byte 4	Byte 5	Byte 6	Byte 7	Byte 8	Byte 9	Byte 10	Instruction	
5E	11ff ffff	[EXT]		[EXT]						SGT	dadr
5F	C 0ddd									SLE	Dn
5F	C 1rrr	xxxx								DBLE	Dn,label
5F	11ff ffff	[EXT]		[EXT]						SLE	dadr
60	0 0	xxxx								BRA	label
60	xx									BRA	label
61	00	xxxx								BSR	label
61	xx									BSR	label
62	00	xxxx								BHI	label
62	xx									BHI	label
63	00	xxxx								BLS	label
63	xx									BLS	label
64	00	xxxx								BCC	label
64	xx									BCC	label
65	00	xxxx								BCS	label
65	xx									BCS	label
66	00	xxxx								BNE	label
66	xx									BNE	label
67	00	xxxx								BEQ	label
67	xx									BEQ	label
68	00	xxxx								BVC	label
68	xx									BVC	label
69	00	xxxx								BVS	label
69	xx									BVS	label
6A	00	xxxx								BPL	label
6A	xx									BPL	label
6B	00	xxxx								BMI	label
6B	xx									BMI	label
6C	00	xxxx								BGE	label
6C	xx									BGE	label
6D	00	xxxx								BLT	label
6D	xx									BLT	label
6E	00	xxxx								BGT	label
6E	xx									BGT	label
6F	00	xxxx								BLE	label
6F	xx									BLE	label
7ddd0	yy									MOVEQ	data8,Dn
8ddd0	0 0sss									OR.B	sDn,dDn
8ddd0	00eeeeee	[EXT]		[EXT]						OR.B	sadr,Dn
8ddd0	4 0sss									OR.W	sDn,dDn
8ddd0	01eeeeee	[EXT]		[EXT]						OR.W	sadr,Dn
8ddd0	8 0sss									OR.L	sDn,dDn
8ddd0	10eeeeee	[EXT]		[EXT]						OR.L	sadr,Dn
8ddd0	C 0sss									DIVU	sDn,dDn
8ddd0	11eeeee	[EXT]		[EXT]						DIVU	sadr,Dn
8ddd0	F C	yyyy								DIVU	data16,Dn
8ddd1	0 0sss									SBC	sDn,dDn
8ddd1	0 1sss									SBCD	−(sAn),−(dAn)
8sss1	00ff ffff	[EXT]		[EXT]						OR.B	Dn,dadr
8sss1	01ff ffff	[EXT]		[EXT]						OR.W	Dn,dadr
8sss1	10ff ffff	[EXT]		[EXT]						OR.L	Dn,dadr
8ddd1	C 0sss									DIVS	sDn,dDn
8ddd1	11eeeeee	[EXT]		[EXT]						DIVS	sadr,Dn
8ddd1	F C	yyyy								DIVS	data16,Dn
9ddd0	0 0sss									SUB.B	sDn,dDn
9ddd0	00eeeeee	[EXT]		[EXT]						SUB.B	sadr,Dn
9ddd0	4 tsss									SUB.W	rs,Dn
9ddd0	01eeeeee	[EXT]		[EXT]						SUB.W	sadr,Dn

DATA SHEETS

This section contains specific electrical and timing data for the following devices:

- . MC68000L4
- . MC68000L6
- . MC68000L

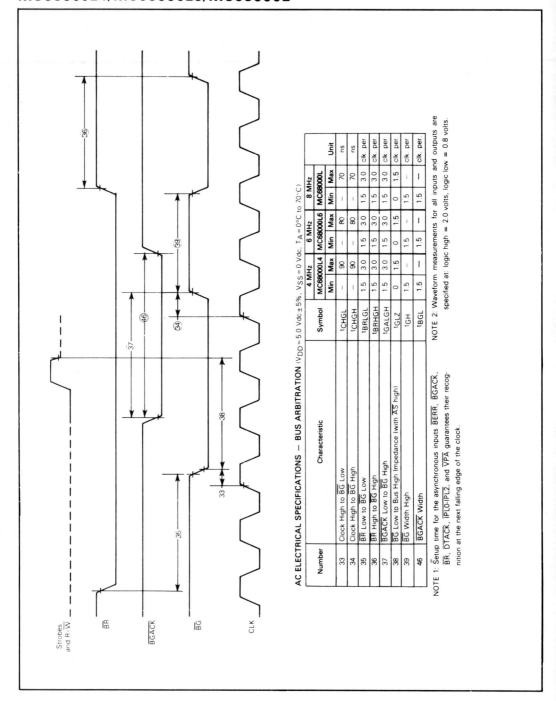

AC ELECTRICAL SPECIFICATIONS — BUS ARBITRATION (V_{DD} = 5.0 Vdc ± 5%, V_{SS} = 0 Vdc, T_A = 0°C to 70°C)

Number	Characteristic	Symbol	MC68000L4 4 MHz		MC68000L6 6 MHz		MC68000L 8 MHz		Unit
			Min	Max	Min	Max	Min	Max	
33	Clock High to $\overline{BG}$ Low	t_{CHGL}	—	90	—	80	—	70	ns
34	Clock High to $\overline{BG}$ High	t_{CHGH}	—	90	—	80	—	70	ns
35	$\overline{BR}$ Low to $\overline{BG}$ Low	t_{BRLGL}	1.5	3.0	1.5	3.0	1.5	3.0	clk per
36	$\overline{BR}$ High to $\overline{BG}$ High	t_{BRHGH}	1.5	3.0	1.5	3.0	1.5	3.0	clk per
37	$\overline{BGACK}$ Low to $\overline{BG}$ High	t_{GALGH}	1.5	3.0	1.5	3.0	1.5	3.0	clk per
38	$\overline{BG}$ Low to Bus High Impedance (with $\overline{AS}$ high)	t_{GLZ}	0	1.5	0	1.5	0	1.5	clk per
39	$\overline{BG}$ Width High	t_{GH}	1.5	—	1.5	—	1.5	—	clk per
46	$\overline{BGACK}$ Width	t_{BGL}	1.5	—	1.5	—	1.5	—	clk per

NOTE 1: Setup time for the asynchronous inputs $\overline{BERR}$, $\overline{BGACK}$, $\overline{BR}$, $\overline{DTACK}$, $\overline{IPL0}$-$\overline{IPL2}$, and $\overline{VPA}$ guarantees their recognition at the next falling edge of the clock.

NOTE 2: Waveform measurements for all inputs and outputs are specified at: logic high = 2.0 volts, logic low = 0.8 volts.

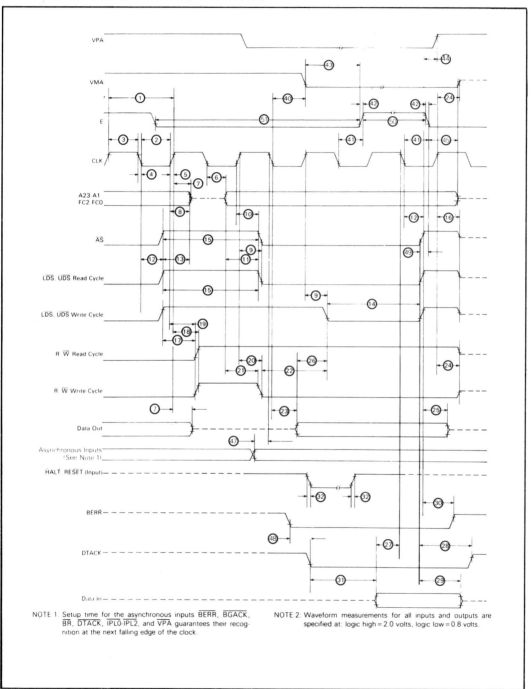

NOTE 1: Setup time for the asynchronous inputs $\overline{BERR}$, $\overline{BGACK}$, $\overline{BR}$, $\overline{DTACK}$, IPL0-IPL2, and $\overline{VPA}$ guarantees their recognition at the next falling edge of the clock.

NOTE 2: Waveform measurements for all inputs and outputs are specified at: logic high = 2.0 volts, logic low = 0.8 volts.

MC68000L4/MC68000L6/MC68000L

ELECTRICAL CHARACTERISTICS (V_{CC} = 5.0 Vdc ± 5%; V_{SS} = 0 Vdc; T_A 0°C to 70°C, Figures 33, 34, 35)

Characteristic		Symbol	Min	Typ	Max	Unit
Input High Voltage		V_{IH}	2.0	–	V_{CC}	Vdc
Input Low Voltage		V_{IL}	V_{SS} – 0.3		0.8	Vdc
Input Leakage Current	$\overline{BERR}$, $\overline{BGACK}$, $\overline{BR}$, $\overline{DTACK}$, $\overline{IPL0}$-$\overline{IPL2}$, $\overline{VPA}$, $\overline{HALT}$, $\overline{RESET}$	I_{in}	–	1.0	–	μAdc
			–	2.0	–	
Three-State (Off State) Input Current	$\overline{AS}$, A1-A23, D0-D15, FC0-FC2, $\overline{LDS}$, R/$\overline{W}$, $\overline{UDS}$, $\overline{VMA}$	I_{TSI}	–	70	–	μAdc
Output High Voltage (I_{OH} = – 400 μAdc)	$\overline{AS}$, A1-A23, $\overline{BG}$, D0-D15, E, FC0-FC2, $\overline{LDS}$, R/$\overline{W}$, $\overline{UDS}$, $\overline{VMA}$	V_{OH}	2.4	–	–	Vdc
Output Low Voltage (I_{OL} = 1.6 mA)	$\overline{HALT}$	V_{OL}	–	–	0.5	Vdc
(I_{OL} = 3.2 mA)	A1-A23, $\overline{BG}$, E, FC0-FC2		–	–	0.5	
(I_{OL} = 5.0 mA)	$\overline{RESET}$		–	–	0.5	
(I_{OL} = 5.3 mA)	$\overline{AS}$, D0-D15, $\overline{LDS}$, R/$\overline{W}$, $\overline{UDS}$, $\overline{VMA}$		–	–	0.5	
Power Dissipation (Clock Frequency = 8 MHz)		P_D	–	1.0	–	W
Capacitance (Package Type Dependent) (V_{in} = 0 Vdc; T_A = 25°C; Frequency = 1 MHz)		C_{in}	–	10.0	–	pF

FIGURE 33 — RESET TEST LOAD   FIGURE 34 — HALT TEST LOAD   FIGURE 35 — TEST LOADS

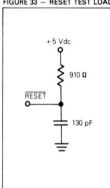

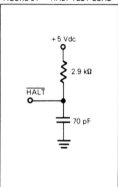

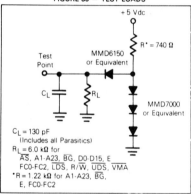

FIGURE 36 — INPUT CLOCK WAVEFORM

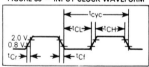

MAXIMUM RATINGS

Rating	Symbol	Value	Unit
Supply Voltage	V_{CC}	– 0.3 to + 7.0	Vdc
Input Voltage	V_{in}	– 0.3 to + 7.0	Vdc
Operating Temperature Range	T_A	0 to 70	°C
Storage Temperature	T_{stg}	– 55 to 150	°C

CLOCK TIMING (Figure 36)

Characteristic	Symbol	4 MHz MC6800L4		6 MHz MC68000L6		8 MHz MC68000L		Unit
		Min	Max	Min	Max	Min	Max	
Frequency of Operation	F	2.0	4.0	2.0	6.0	2.0	8.0	MHz
Cycle Time	t_{cyc}	250	500	167	500	125	500	ns
Clock Pulse Width	t_{CL}	115	250	75	250	55	250	ns
	t_{CH}	115	250	75	250	55	250	
Rise and Fall Times	t_{Cr}	–	10	–	10	–	10	ns
	t_{Cf}	–	10	–	10	–	10	

MC68000L4/MC68000L6/MC68000L

AC ELECTRICAL SPECIFICATIONS ($V_{CC} = 5.0$ Vdc $\pm 5\%$; $V_{SS} = 0$ Vdc, $T_A = 0°C$ to $70°C$)

Number	Characteristic	Symbol	4 MHz MC68000L4		6 MHz MC68000L6		8 MHz MC68000L		Unit
			Min	Max	Min	Max	Min	Max	
1	Clock Period	t_{CYC}	250	500	167	500	125	500	ns
2	Clock Width Low	t_{CL}	115	250	75	250	55	250	ns
3	Clock Width High	t_{CH}	115	250	75	250	55	250	ns
4	Clock Fall Time	t_{Cf}	–	10	–	10	–	10	ns
5	Clock Rise Time	t_{Cr}	–	10	–	10	–	10	ns
6	Clock Low to Address/FC Valid	t_{CLAV}	–	90	–	80	–	70	ns
7	Clock High to Address/FC/Data High Impedance (maximum)	t_{CHAZx}	–	120	–	100	–	80	ns
8	Clock High to Address/FC Invalid (minimum)	t_{CHAZn}	20	–	20	–	20	–	ns
9[1]	Clock High to $\overline{AS}$, $\overline{DS}$ Low (maximum)	t_{CHSLx}	–	80	–	70	–	60	ns
10	Clock High to $\overline{AS}$, $\overline{DS}$ Low (minimum)	t_{CHSLn}	20	–	20	–	20	–	ns
11[2]	Address/FC Valid to $\overline{AS}$, $\overline{DS}$ (read) Low	t_{AVSL}	55	–	35	–	30	–	ns
12[1]	Clock Low to $\overline{AS}$, $\overline{DS}$ High	t_{CLSH}	–	90	–	80	–	70	ns
13[2]	$\overline{AS}$, $\overline{DS}$ High to Address/FC Invalid	t_{SHAZ}	60	–	40	–	30	–	ns
14[2]	$\overline{AS}$, $\overline{DS}$ Width Low	t_{SL}	285	–	170	–	115	–	ns
15[2]	$\overline{AS}$, $\overline{DS}$ Width High	t_{SH}	285	–	180	–	150	–	ns
16	Clock High to $\overline{AS}$, $\overline{DS}$ High Impedance	t_{CHSZ}	–	120	–	100	–	80	ns
17[2]	$\overline{DS}$ High to R/$\overline{W}$ High	t_{SHRH}	60	–	50	–	40	–	ns
18[1]	Clock High to R/$\overline{W}$ High (maximum)	t_{CHRHx}	–	90	–	80	–	70	ns
19	Clock High to R/$\overline{W}$ High (minimum)	t_{CHRHn}	20	–	20	–	20	–	ns
20[1]	Clock High to R/$\overline{W}$ Low	t_{CHRL}	–	90	–	80	–	70	ns
21[2]	Address/FC Valid to R/$\overline{W}$ Low	t_{AVRL}	45	–	25	–	20	–	ns
22[2]	R/$\overline{W}$ Low to $\overline{DS}$ Low (write)	t_{RLSL}	200	–	140	–	80	–	ns
23	Clock Low to Data Out Valid	t_{CLDO}	–	90	–	80	–	70	ns
24	Clock High to R/$\overline{W}$, $\overline{VMA}$ High Impedance	t_{CHRZ}	–	120	–	100	–	80	ns
25[2]	$\overline{DS}$ High to Data Out Invalid	t_{SHDO}	60	–	40	–	30	–	ns
26[2]	Data Out Valid to $\overline{DS}$ Low (write)	t_{DOSL}	55	–	35	–	30	–	ns
27	Data In to Clock Low (set up time)	t_{DICL}	30	–	25	–	15	–	ns
28[2]	$\overline{DS}$ High to $\overline{DTACK}$ High	t_{SHDAH}	0	240	0	160	0	120	ns
29	$\overline{DS}$ High to Data Invalid (hold time)	t_{SHDI}	0	–	0	–	0	–	ns
30	$\overline{AS}$, $\overline{DS}$ High to $\overline{BERR}$ High	t_{SHBEH}	0	–	0	–	0	–	ns
31[2]	$\overline{DTACK}$ Low to Data In (setup time)	t_{DALDI}	–	180	–	120	–	90	ns
32	HALT and $\overline{RESET}$ Input Transition Time	t_{RHrf}	0	200	0	200	0	200	ns
33	Clock High to $\overline{BG}$ Low	t_{CHGL}	–	90	–	80	–	70	ns
34	Clock High to $\overline{BG}$ High	t_{CHGH}	–	90	–	80	–	70	ns
35	$\overline{BR}$ Low to $\overline{BG}$ Low	t_{BRLGL}	1.5	3.0	1.5	3.0	1.5	3.0	clk. per
36	$\overline{BR}$ High to $\overline{BG}$ High	t_{BRHGH}	1.5	3.0	1.5	3.0	1.5	3.0	clk. per
37	$\overline{BGACK}$ Low to $\overline{BG}$ High	t_{GALGH}	1.5	3.0	1.5	3.0	1.5	3.0	clk. per
38	$\overline{BG}$ Low to Bus High Impedance (with $\overline{AS}$ high)	t_{GLZ}	0	1.5	0	1.5	0	1.5	clk. per
39	$\overline{BG}$ Width High	t_{GH}	1.5	–	1.5	–	1.5	–	clk. per
40	Clock Low to $\overline{VMA}$ Low	t_{CLVML}	–	90	–	80	–	70	ns
41	Clock Low to E Transition	t_{CLE}	–	65	–	60	–	55	ns
42	E Output Rise and Fall Time	t_{Erf}	–	25	–	25	–	25	ns
43[2]	$\overline{VMA}$ Low to E High	t_{VMLEH}	325	–	240	–	200	–	ns
44	$\overline{AS}$, $\overline{DS}$ High to $\overline{VPA}$ High	t_{SHVPH}	0	240	0	160	0	120	ns
45	E Low to Address/$\overline{VMA}$/FC Invalid	t_{ELAI}	50	–	35	–	30	–	ns
46	$\overline{BGACK}$ Width	t_{BGL}	1.5	–	1.5	–	1.5	–	clk. per
47	Asynchronous Input Setup Time	t_{ASI}	30	–	25	–	20	–	ns
48	$\overline{BERR}$ Low to $\overline{DTACK}$ Low	t_{BELDAL}	50	–	50	–	50	–	ns
49	E Low to $\overline{AS}$, $\overline{DS}$ Invalid	t_{ELSI}	– 80	–	– 80	–	– 80	–	ns
50	E Width High	t_{EH}	900	–	600	–	450	–	ns
51	E Width Low	t_{EL}	1400	–	900	–	700	–	ns

NOTE 1: For a loading capacitance of less than or equal to 50 picofarads, subtract 5 nanoseconds from the values given in these columns.

NOTE: 2 Actual value depends on actual clock period.

Data Sheets on pages 110 through 113 reprinted by permission of Motorola Semiconductor Products, Inc.

Chapter 8
2900 SERIES CHIP SLICE PRODUCTS

Chip slice products represent a radical departure from the single-chip Central Processing Units that we have described up to this point. Chip slice products are, in fact, the building blocks for many Central Processing Units; they are also used to build intelligent controllers.

There are a variety of chip slice-type products on the market today; however, the 2900 series products are the clear leaders in terms of sales and customer acceptance. The 2900 series is an enhancement of the older 6700 series chip slice products, which are not described since they are now obsolete.

Chip slice products are described conceptually in Chapter 4 of Voume 1 (in fact, the "general case" product described in Volume 1, Chapter 4 is a thinly disguised variation of the 2901 microprocessor slice). Therefoer, the discussion which follows assumes that you have a conceptual understanding of chip slice devices and microprogramming. If you do nto have this background, see Chapter 4 of Volume 1 before reading any further.

In this chapter we will describe the following 2900 series parts:

- The 2901, 2901A, and 2901B microprocessor slices
- The 2902A Look-Ahead Carry Generator
- The 2903 Enhanced Microprocessor Slice
- The 2909A, 2910, and 2911A Microprogram Sequencers
- The 2930 and 2932 Program Control Units

All 2900 series devices use bipolar LSI technology. 2900 series microinstruction execution times vary with manufacturer and device. Consult the data sheets at the end of this chapter for details.

The primary source for the 2900 series chip slice products is:

ADVANCED MICRO DEVICES
901 Thompson Place
Sunnyvale, California 94086

Secondary sources for the 2900 series include:

MOTOROLA SEMICONDUCTOR
Box 20912
Phoenix, Arizona 85036

RAYTHEON SEMICONDUCTOR
350 Ellis Street
Mountain View, California 94042

NATIONAL SEMICONDUCTOR
2900 Semiconductor Drive
Santa Clara, California 95050

FAIRCHILD CAMERA & INSTRUMENT CORPORATION
464 Ellis Street
Mountain View, California 94042

THE 2901, 2901A, AND 2901B MICROPROCESSOR SLICE

The 2901, 2901A, and 2901B are identical except for execution speeds. The 2901A is approximately 30% faster than the 2901; the 2901B is about 25% faster than the 2901A. For details see the data sheets at the end of this chapter.

The 2901 provides a 4-bit slice through the arithmetic and logic unit of a Central Processing Unit. Some or all of the Central Processing Unit's registers may also be generated out of 2901 logic.

Figures 8-1 and 8-2 functionally illustrate 2901 logic.

Figure 8-1 is a variation of Figure 4-3 from Volume 1; it illustrates 2901 logic in terms of the general chip slice description given in Chapter 4 of Volume 1. Figure 8-2 is a more accurate representation of 2901 logic and data paths. Note that all logic and data paths in Figure 8-2 are four bits wide.

2901 logic consists of an arithmetic and logic unit, a local, two-part read/write memory, and shift logic. The arithmetic and logic unit performs addition, subtraction, and the standard Boolean operations. The arithmetic and logic unit receives two inputs and generates one output. The local read/write memory stores data, which may be operands or results. In addition to the local read/write memory there is a "Q register" which is used as a temporary register or for double-length operations. You may compare the 2901's 16 registers to a CPU with 16 accumulators. You will not usually implement a CPU's accumulator in the Q register, and you may or may not implement a CPU's general purpose registers in local RAM (in general, however, you will implement these registers in local RAM).

You will frequently see obvious parallels between 2901 logic and CPU logic. You may use these parallels to help you understand 2901 logic; however, do not assume that these parallels translate into CPU implementation.

The many data paths within the 2901 have been selected to link the ALU, local read/write memory, data input and data output in a functionally efficient manner. Shift logic has been inserted at selected points along data paths so that the combination of data paths with ALU and shift logic minimizes the number of steps needed to create typical Central Processing Unit functions.

The few 2901 enhancements over the prior 6701 were designed specifically to reduce the number of steps required to implement typical CPU operations; and these few enhancements were sufficient to render the 6701 obsolete.

2901 MICROPROCESSOR SLICE PINS AND SIGNALS

Pins and signal assignments for the 2901 are illustrated in Figure 8-3. We will summarize functions performed by each of these signals superficially before examining device operations in detail.

We may divide 2901 signals into these three categories:

1) Control inputs that are generated by a microinstruction
2) Control signals connecting 2901 slices
3) Data and status outputs

First consider microinstruction-generated inputs.

A0-A3 and B0-B3 are two 4-bit addresses which select locations within the 2901 local 16 X 4 bit RAM.

I0-I8 is a 9-bit instruction code which determines data flow and arithmetic/logical operations within the 2901. This 9-bit control code can be divided into three 3-bit fields as follows:

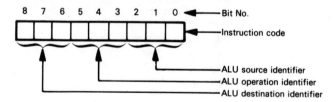

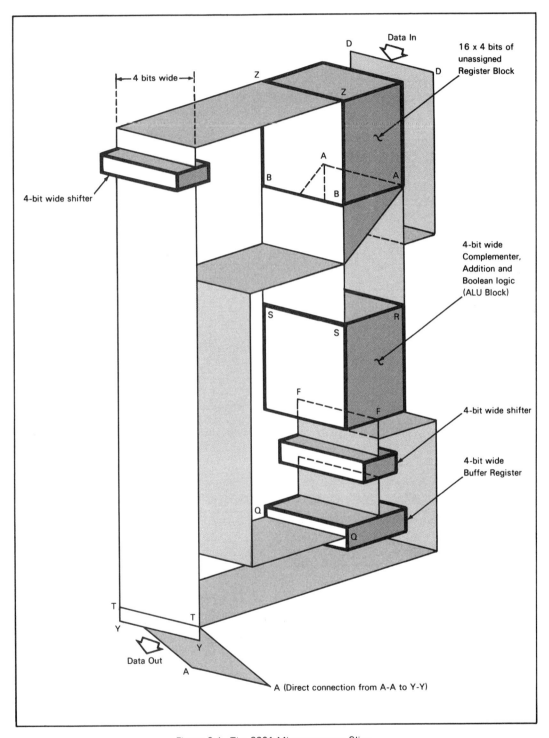

Figure 8-1. The 2901 Microprocessor Slice

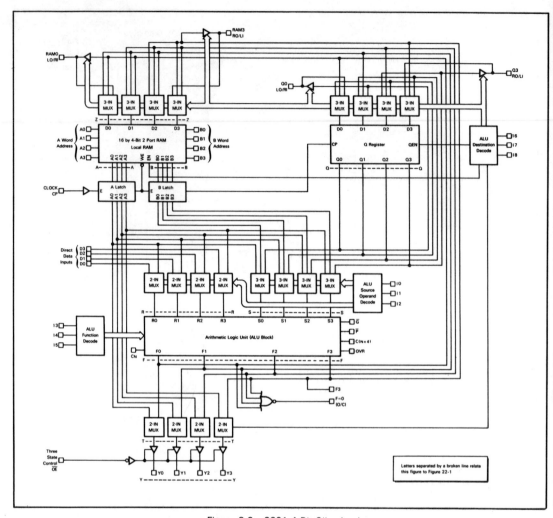

Figure 8-2. 2901 4-Bit Slice Logic

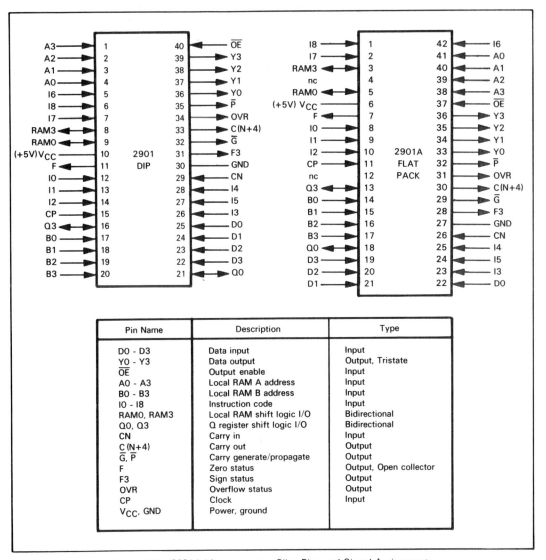

Pin Name	Description	Type
DO - D3	Data input	Input
YO - Y3	Data output	Output, Tristate
$\overline{OE}$	Output enable	Input
A0 - A3	Local RAM A address	Input
B0 - B3	Local RAM B address	Input
I0 - I8	Instruction code	Input
RAM0, RAM3	Local RAM shift logic I/O	Bidirectional
Q0, Q3	Q register shift logic I/O	Bidirectional
CN	Carry in	Input
C (N+4)	Carry out	Output
$\overline{G}$, $\overline{P}$	Carry generate/propagate	Output
F	Zero status	Output, Open collector
F3	Sign status	Output
OVR	Overflow status	Output
CP	Clock	Input
V_{CC}, GND	Power, ground	

Figure 8-3. 2901A Microprocessor Slice Pins and Signal Assignments

D0-D3 is a data input port. All data entering a 2901 must be input via D0-D3. We include these four pins among the microinstruction-generated group since a microinstruction could indeed generate immediate data (in macro assembly language terms) to be input via D0-D3. A more common alternative might be to generate this data out of an external buffer, using microinstruction bits to enable a single output as follows:

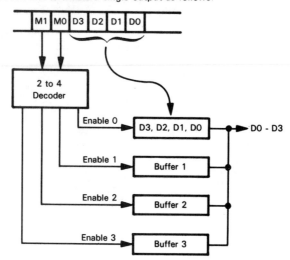

OE is an output enable control. When $\overline{OE}$ is low, the 2901 can output data via Y0-Y3. When $\overline{OE}$ is high, Y0-Y3 is floated. A microinstruction must anticipate microcycles within which data output is to occur and must generate a low $\overline{OE}$ control at this time. When no data output is anticipated Y0-Y3 should be floated.

Let us now examine data and status output signals.

As indicated in the previous paragraph, **a 2901 outputs the results of internal operations via the four pins Y0-Y3. In addition, separate Overflow (OVR) and Zero (F) status indicators are output.** These indicators are used to generate standard Overflow and Zero statuses — as we will describe later.

Carry Status logic and associated signals are not simple status outputs; they are more accurately represented as interslice connecting signals. **CN is the carry in used by addition and subtraction. C(N+4) is the carry out generated by addition and subtraction. Carry Look-Ahead logic uses the $\overline{P}$ and $\overline{G}$ signals,** together with the 2902 Carry Generator, in order to compute the carry for an arithmetic operation occurring in parallel at two or more 2901 slices. This carry logic has been described in Volume 1, Chapter 4; it is summarized later in this chapter when we describe the 2902 Carry Look-Ahead Generator.

The 2901 has two sets of internal shift, logic. For multislice shifts, bits shifted out from one slice must be shifted into the adjacent slice. **Q0 and Q3 are the shift pins used by one set of shift logic; RAM0 and RAM3 are the shift pins used by the other set of shift logic.**

CP is the master clock signal used to control and synchronize event sequences within the 2901.

2901 LOGIC

We will now examine 2901 logic in detail.

The best place to start understanding 2901 logic is at the read/write memory (local RAM):

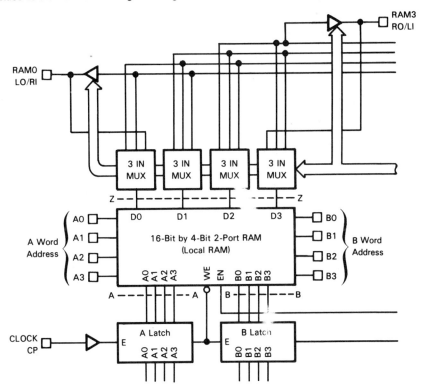

The 2901 local RAM consists of sixteen 4-bit locations.

You use pins A0-A3 to identify the location from which data will be output to the A latch. This may be illustrated as follows:

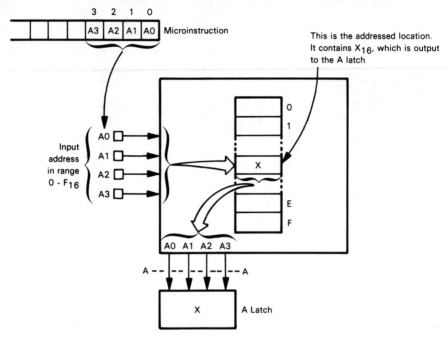

You use pins B0-B3 to identify the 4-bit location from which data will be output to the B latch and into which data from the ALU will be written. This may be illustrated as follows:

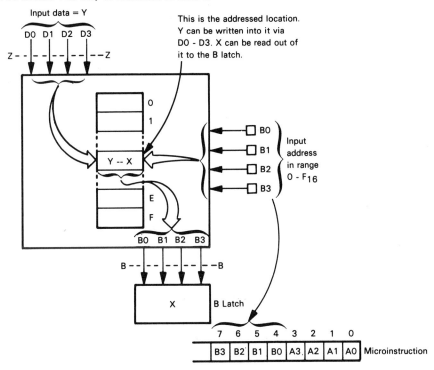

In the two illustrations above we show the A and B pin inputs coming from eight bits of a microinstruction. This data may come from the Instruction register as well. The selected microinstruction bit numbers are not significant.

2901 MICRO-INSTRUCTION

The same address input at A0-A3 and B0-B3 results in the same data out the A and B latches.

In order to avoid race conditions which could result if you attempted to read and write at the same time, the clock signal CP controls event sequences as follows:

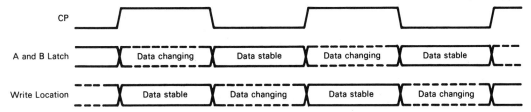

In the timing diagram above, the A and B latch will receive data from the local RAM location addressed by the A and B address inputs. However, the A and B latch will only receive data from its associated RAM location while CP is high. As soon as CP goes low, and A and B latches hold whatever data they contained at the time CP made its high-to-low transition.

Similarly, data at the D0-D3 inputs can be written into the local RAM location addressed by the B address inputs while CP is low. While CP is high, the addressed local RAM location will hold whatever data it contained when CP made its low-to-high transition; thus, the addresses can be changed. These internal RAM latches cause the RAM to appear to the user as a (low-to-high) edge-triggered RAM.

The 2901 local RAM generates a 4-bit word through selected programmable registers of a Central Processing Unit. But these sixteen local RAM locations do not represent the only place where CPU registers can be created; that would limit you to a combined total of sixteen programmable registers — which is frequently insufficient.

Using register terminology from Chapters 6 and 7 of Volume 1, Primary Accumulators will most likely occupy 2901 local RAM locations; this is because Primary Accumulators are frequent sources and destinations for data operated on by the arithmetic and logic unit.

Secondary Accumulators may or may not occupy 2901 local RAM locations. Certainly if there are spare local RAM locations it would make sense to allocate these to Secondary Accumulators, or fixed, "non-programmable" constants. But if there are no spare local RAM locations, then Secondary Accumulators could easily occupy external read/write memory. A 2901 can access external memory to read or write data, but this has some associated restrictions — which are described later in this chapter when we examine the 2903.

Central Processing Unit registers that are normally used to compute memory addresses for the macroprogram may or may not occupy 2901 RAM space. To the 2901 ALU, there is no difference between computing an address, or data. Adding an Index to a base address is the same as adding the contents of two Accumulators; both are simple addition.

For a simple Central Processing Unit, address registers are likely to be located in the 2901 local RAM; then memory address computations and data computations must occur sequentially. In more complex Central Processing Units, you will compute assembly language memory addresses using one of the special memory addressing devices — the 2930 or the 2932. These devices contain their own registers; also, they compute memory addresses while the 2901 is performing ALU operations in parallel. Alternatively, the designer may choose to use a second set of 2901s to build a high-speed memory addressing unit.

In the preceding discussion we used the term "macroprogram memory address" to identify computer memory, in contrast to memory within Central Processing Unit logic, where microinstructions are stored. If you are confused by the difference between a macroinstruction memory address and a microinstruction memory address, refer again to Chapter 4 of Volume 1.

If a memory address register, such as an Index register, is also to serve as a general purpose Accumulator, it will have to be located in the 2901 local RAM, or in the external memory that accommodates Secondary Accumulators.

The Instruction register will almost never be housed in local 2901 RAM. The macroinstruction object code will be held in an external buffer (the Instruction register) whose contents are decoded by logic external to the 2901 in order to trigger execution of appropriate microinstruction sequences. We will describe this logic later.

The D0-D3 inputs to the local RAM come from a 3-IN MUX. The 3-IN MUX receives the arithmetic and logic unit output, which it can shift up or down one bit position. The shift is achieved by connecting each ALU output line to three local RAM inputs. The RAM0 and RAM3 pin connections of the 2901 allow you to cascade 2901 slices so that an up or down shift can be propagated through eight, twelve, sixteen, or more bit positions.

Beginning at the 4-bit level, we can illustrate logic for unshifted local RAM input as follows:

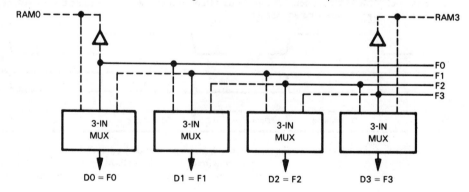

Data shifted up one bit receives a new low-order bit from RAM0 and outputs the high-order ALU product bit via RAM3 as follows:

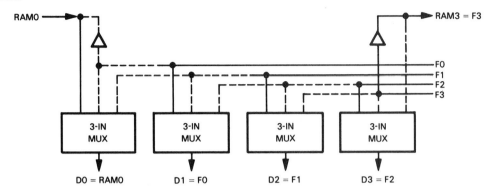

Similarly, a 1-bit downshift receives a new high-order bit from RAM3 and outputs the low-order product bit via RAM0 as follows:

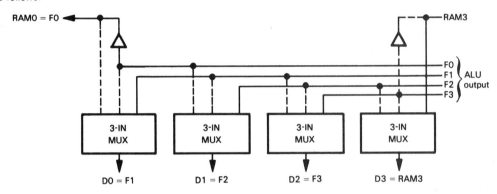

The Q register is a single 4-bit location with 3-IN MUX input logic similar to the local RAM input logic which we have just described. Q register logic may be illustrated as follows:

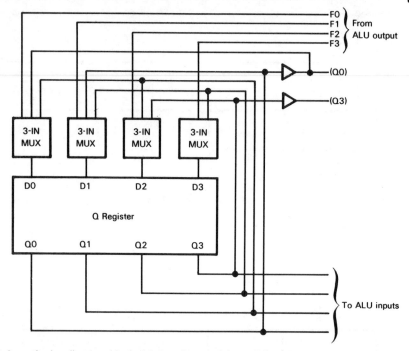

Q register logic is used primarily to enable double length up and down shifts which are needed by binary multiply and divide logic. Accordingly the Q register 3-IN MUX receives these inputs:

- The ALU output
- Its own output - shifted up or down one bit position

Thus fresh data entering the Q register comes from the arithmetic and logic unit output. Subsequently, this data may be shifted up or down any number of bit positions by recycling the Q register output back to the 3-IN MUX input, shifted down one bit position:

or shifted up one bit position:

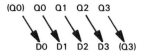

The Q0 and Q3 pin connections serve the same purpose for the Q register shift logic as the RAM0 and RAM3 pin connections serve for local RAM logic.

We will now examine the arithmetic and logic unit, including the following logic from Figure 8-2:

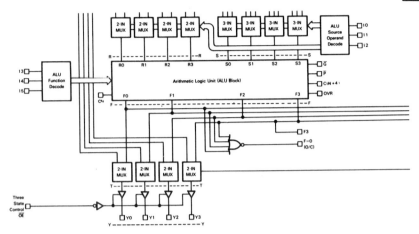

These three aspects of ALU logic are important:

1) The ALU operation which is to be performed.

2) The operands which are input to the ALU.

3) The destination for the ALU output. Shift logic lies in the path of ALU output data, therefore the destination specification includes any shift operation.

Instruction code bits I0, I1, and I2 control the data input to the 2901 ALU; instruction code bits I3, I4, and I5 determine the operations which occur within the arithmetic and logic unit. Table 8-1 summarizes I0, I1, and I2 interpretations, while Table 8-2 summarizes I3, I4, and I5 interpretations. Table 8-3 shows the result of I0-I5 combinations.

The two arithmetic and logic unit inputs are generated by a 2-IN MUX and a 3-IN MUX. The 2-IN MUX (which generates the R inputs) receives external data, or the A latch outputs from the local RAM. The 3-IN MUX (which generates the S inputs) receives the A or B latch outputs from the local RAM, or the Q register output. As an additional option, 0 can be inserted at the R or S inputs of the arithmetic and logic unit. Thus the following twelve R and S input combinations could be generated.

```
R  -  A  A  A  A      D  D  D  D      0  0  0  0
S  -  A  B  Q  0      A  B  Q  0      A  B  Q  0
         •  •         •     •  •      •  •  •              Used by 2901
      •     •            •              •              Not used by 2901
```

A 3-bit input code can specify eight of the twelve input combinations illustrated above.

A,A is eliminated since it is equivalent to A,B with the same address input at A and B.

A,0 is eliminated since it is equivalent to 0,A.

D,B is eliminated since it is equivalent to D,A; remember, the A and B addresses can be the same.

0,0 is eliminated since you cannot perform a useful arithmetic or logic operation on two zero operands.

Table 8-1. ALU Source Operand Control

I2	I1	I0	Hex Code	R	S
0	0	0	0	A	Q
0	0	1	1	A	B
0	1	0	2	0	Q
0	1	1	3	0	B
1	0	0	4	0	A
1	0	1	5	D	A
1	1	0	6	D	Q
1	1	1	-	D	0

Table 8-2. 2901 ALU Function Control

I5	I4	I3	Hex Code	ALU Function	Symbol
0	0	0	0	R Plus S	R + S
0	0	1	1	S Minus R	S - R
0	1	0	2	R Minus S	R - S
0	1	1	3	R OR S	R V S
1	0	0	4	R AND S	R $\wedge$ S
1	0	1	5	$\overline{R}$ AND S	$\overline{R}$ $\wedge$ S
1	1	0	6	R EX-OR S	R $\oplus$ S
1	1	1	7	R EX-NOR	$\overline{R \oplus S}$

Table 8-3. 2901 Source Operand and ALU Function Matrix

I5 4 3 \ ALU Function / I210 ALU Source		0 A,Q	1 A,B	2 O,Q	3 O,B	4 O,A	5 D,A	6 D,Q	7 D,O
0	CN = L R Plus S	A+Q	A+B	Q	B	A	D+A	D+Q	D
	CN = H	A+Q+1	A+B+1	Q+1	B+1	A+1	D+A+1	D+Q+1	D+1
1	CN = L S Minus R	Q-A-1	B-A-1	Q-1	B-1	A-1	A-D-1	Q-D-1	-D-1
	CN = H	Q-A	B-A	Q	B	A	A-D	Q-D	-D
2	CN = L R Minus S	A-Q-1	A-B-1	-Q-1	-B-1	-A-1	D-A-1	D-Q-1	D-1
	CN = H	A-Q	A-B	-Q	-B	-A	D-A	D-Q	D
3	R OR S	A V Q	A V B	Q	B	A	D V A	D V Q	D
4	R AND S	A $\wedge$ Q	A $\wedge$ B	0	0	0	D $\wedge$ A	D $\wedge$ Q	0
5	$\overline{R}$ AND S	$\overline{A}$ $\wedge$ Q	$\overline{A}$ $\wedge$ B	Q	B	A	$\overline{D}$ $\wedge$ A	$\overline{D}$ $\wedge$ Q	0
6	R EX-OR S	A $\oplus$ Q	A $\oplus$ B	Q	B	A	D $\oplus$ A	D $\oplus$ Q	D
7	R EX-NOR S	$\overline{A \oplus Q}$	$\overline{A \oplus B}$	$\overline{Q}$	$\overline{B}$	$\overline{A}$	$\overline{D \oplus A}$	$\overline{D \oplus Q}$	$\overline{D}$

+ = Plus; - = Minus; V = OR; $\wedge$ = AND; $\oplus$ = EX-OR

The eight ALU operations specified by I3, I4, and I5, combined with operand options, generate more than eight effective operations. If you look at Table 8-3 you will see that you can increment, decrement, complement or negate data; you can simply pass data through the ALU, or you can generate a zero ALU output. Any of the functions shown in Table 8-3 can become an ALU output. You have the option of shifting these functions up or down one bit position.

Instruction bits I6, I7, and I8 select the destination for ALU output, plus any shift which will be performed on the ALU output. Table 8-4 summarizes the eight destination options.

Table 8-4. ALU Destination Control

Micro Code				RAM Function		Q Register Function		Y Output	RAM Shifter		Q Shifter	
I8	I7	I6	Hex Code	Shift	Load	Shift	Load		RAM0	RAM3	Q0	Q3
0	0	0	0	X	NONE	NONE	F → Q	F	X	X	X	X
0	0	1	1	X	NONE	X	NONE	F	X	X	X	X
0	1	0	2	NONE	F → B	X	NONE	A	X	X	X	X
0	1	1	3	NONE	F → B	X	NONE	F	X	X	X	X
1	0	0	4	DOWN	F/2 → B	DOWN	Q/2 → Q	F	F0	IN3	Q0	IN3
1	0	1	5	DOWN	F/2 → B	X	NONE	F	F0	IN3	Q0	X
1	1	0	6	UP	2F → B	UP	2Q → Q	F·	IN0	F3	IN0	Q3
1	1	1	7	UP	2F → B	X	NONE	F	IN0	F3	X	Q3

X = Don't care. Electrically, the shift pin is a TTL input internally connected to a three-state output which
  is in the high impedance state.
B = Register addressed by B inputs.
Up is toward MSB, Down is toward LSB.

Because these options are not self-evident, they are illustrated in Figures 8-4 through 8-11.

You will note that most destination codes generate a Y output. In many cases you will not wish to use this output. The $\overline{OE}$ control input, if high, disables the Y output — in which case ALU output does not appear at the Y pins.

The primary purpose of destination code 0, illustrated in Figure 8-4, is to load the Q register.

Destination code 1 generates a Y output only. In this case the $\overline{OE}$ control input will be low.

Destination code 2, illustrated in Figure 8-6, is a little unusual. This code outputs data directly from local RAM to the Y pins; simultaneously the ALU output is loaded into local RAM. If the Program Counter is one of the sixteen general purpose registers, this code is used to load the Memory Address register and simultaneously update the Program Counter to point to the address of the next instruction.

Destination code 3, illustrated in Figure 8-7, loads ALU outputs into local RAM, and transmits ALU outputs to the Y pins.

Destination codes 4, 5, 6, and 7, illustrated in Figures 8-8 through 8-11, are quite similar. These four codes output the ALU product at the Y pins and load this product into local RAM. Codes 4 and 6 also transfer Q register output back as Q register input. Codes 4 and 5 generate downshifts at the local RAM and Q register inputs, while codes 6 and 7 generate upshifts at the local RAM and Q register inputs.

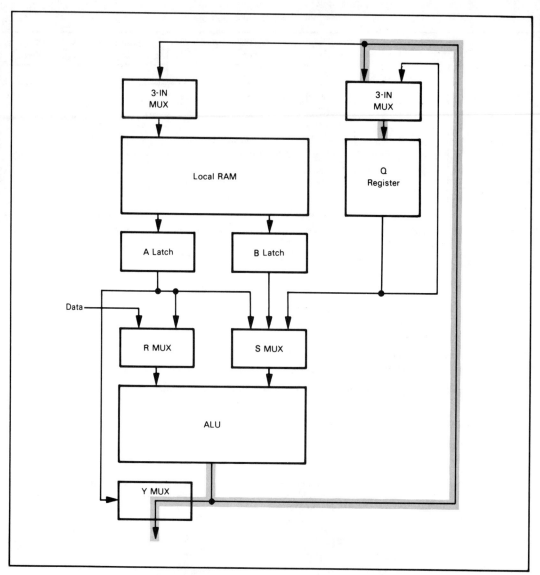

Figure 8-4. 2901 Destination Code 0 Data Paths

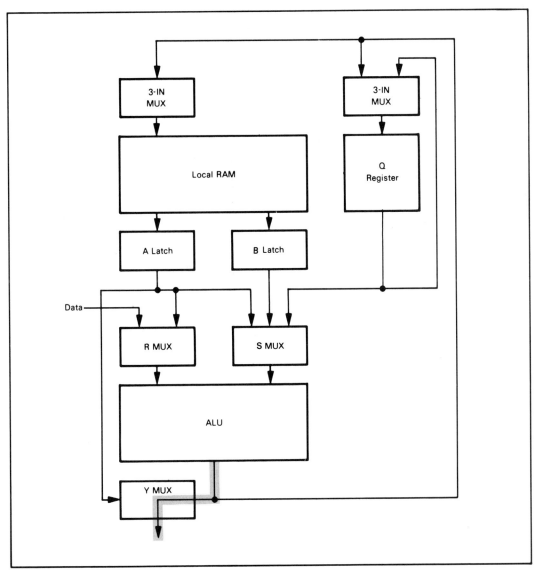

Figure 8-5. 2901 Destination Code 1 Data Paths

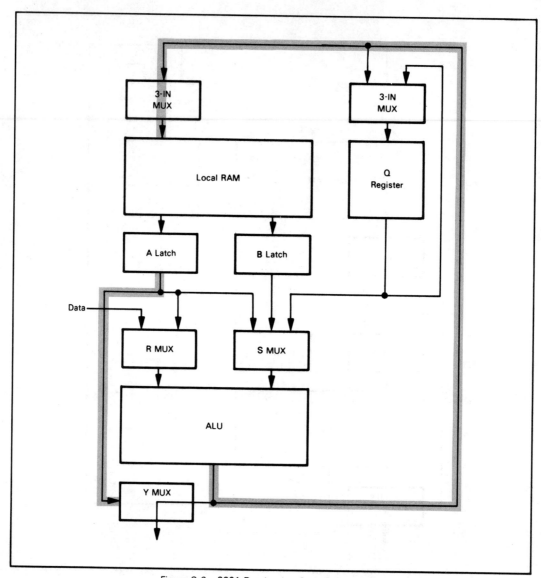

Figure 8-6. 2901 Destination Code 2 Data Paths

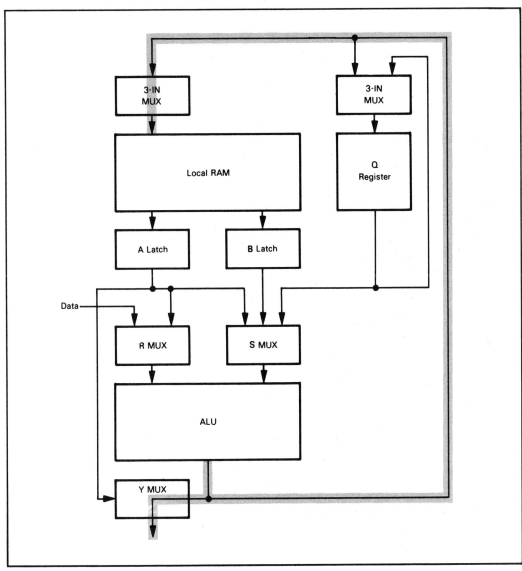

Figure 8-7.   2901 Destination Code 3 Data Paths

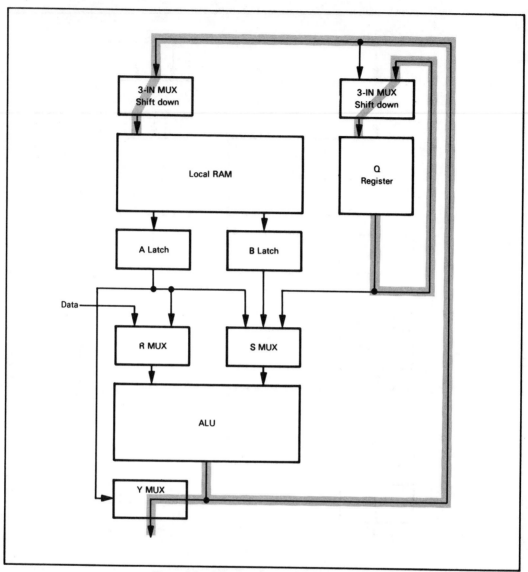

Figure 8-8.   2901 Destination Code 4 Data Paths

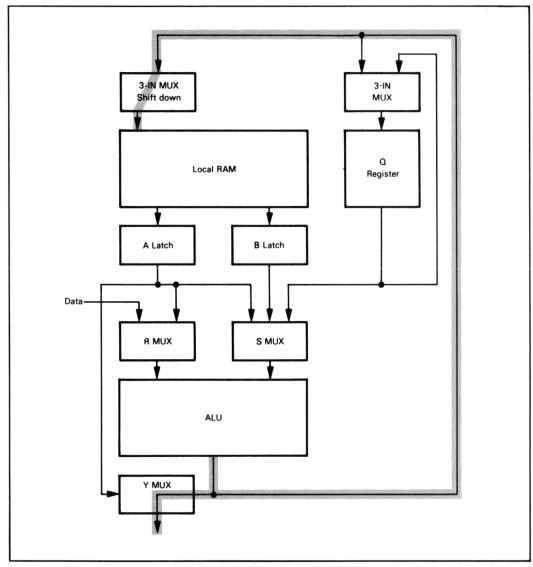

Figure 8-9.   2901 Destination Code 5 Data Paths

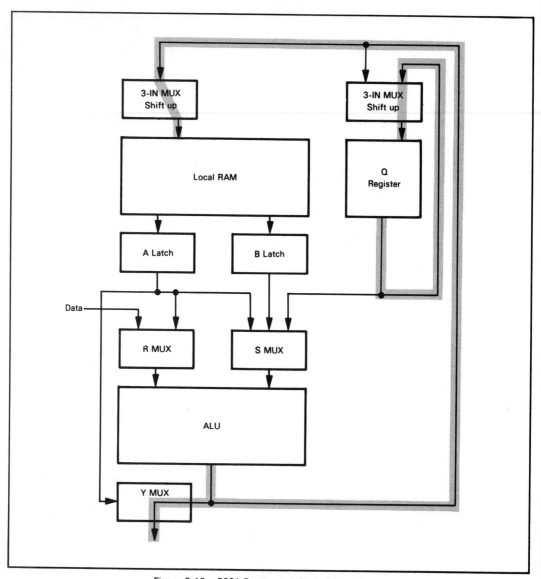

Figure 8-10. 2901 Destination Code 6 Data Paths

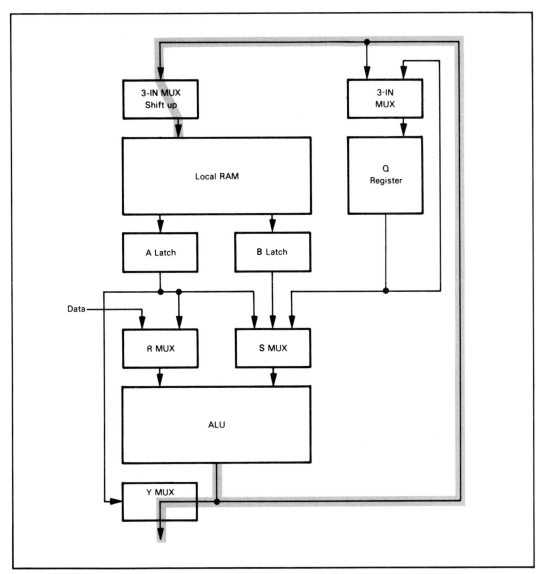

Figure 8-11. 2901 Destination Code 7 Data Paths

Let us now examine status logic of the 2901. You can generate Zero, Sign, Overflow and Carry statuses. The Zero, Sign and Overflow statuses are easy to understand, so we will look at them first.

Every 2901 generates an Overflow status at the OVR pin. This status is the exclusive-OR of carries out of the penultimate bit and the high-order bit. This may be illustrated as follows:

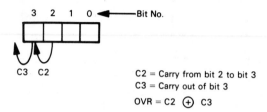

$C2$ = Carry from bit 2 to bit 3
$C3$ = Carry out of bit 3
$OVR = C2 \oplus C3$

Every 2901 generates an Overflow status; however, in a multi-2901 configuration only the high-order (or most significant) 2901 Overflow status is usually used. Lower-order 2901 Overflow status outputs can be ignored. For an 8-bit configuration this may be illustrated as follows:

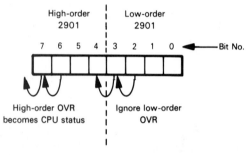

The Sign status which **is output at pin F3** is the level of the high-order ALU output bit. Like the Overflow status, the Sign status is output by every 2901 in a multislice configuration; however, only the high-order 2901 Sign status is significant. For an 8-bit configuration this may be illustrated as follows:

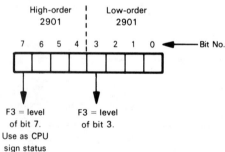

The Zero status is the NOR of the four ALU output lines, F0, F1, F2, and F3. If all four of these outputs are 0, then the Zero status output is 1. The Zero status is an open collector signal; therefore in multislice configurations Zero status outputs can be wire-ANDed. The AND of all Zero status outputs in a multi-2901 configuration generates the Zero status for the CPU (Zero = $\overline{F0} \cdot \overline{F1} \cdot \overline{F2} \cdot$ etc.).

2901 Carry status logic is not straightforward because in a multi-2901 configuration an arithmetic operation (such as addition) should occur in parallel at each slice; but the carry from a low-order slice will not be generated in time to be accounted for by a parallel operation occurring at a higher-order slice. This problem has been described in detail in Chapter 4 of Volume 1, therefore we will not dwell on it at this time. For now it suffices to note that you can use the CN and C(N+4) pins of a 2901 to generate carry if you allow ample time between clock cycles for the carry to ripple up through the slices. But if you want to perform the entire arithmetic operation optimally, you must use the propagate $(\overline{P})$ and generate $(\overline{G})$ signals, in addition to CN and C(N+4). These signals are processed by the 2902 Carry Look-Ahead device, which is described later in this chapter.

Table 8-10, given in the 2902 Carry Look-Ahead device discussion, summarizes the exact logic used by the 2901 to generate $\overline{P}$, $\overline{G}$, CN and C(N+4).

The 2901 can generate a Half-Carry status. The Half-Carry status is needed by microprocessors that use binary arithmetic with decimal adjust to generate binary coded decimal logic. In an 8-bit configuration the C(N+4) output from the low-order 2901 becomes the Half-Carry status.

2901
HALF-
CARRY
STATUS

SOME 2901 OPERATIONS

In order to illustrate 2901 logic in action, we will now show how various operations can be performed for a Central Processing Unit created using two 2901 slices. We will show the microcode for each operation, based on the following 34-bit microinstruction code:

2901
SAMPLE
MICROCODE

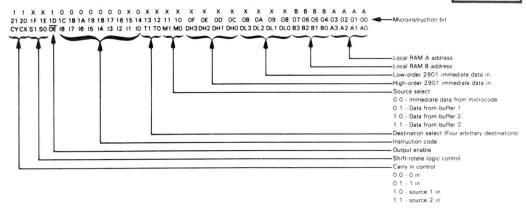

The fields of the illustrated microinstruction are all self-evident, and have been described in the preceding text, with the exception of CY, CX, S1 and S0. These four bits are used by shift and rotate logic, which we are about to describe. Note that all fields, with the exception of the immediate data fields, are shared by the two 2901 devices. This is because 2901 devices operate in parallel and must perform identical operations at any instant. The immediate 4-bit data fields differ since an 8-bit data field is unlike 4-bit halves.

Consider shift and rotate logic (in macroprogram terms) for one or more 2901 slices. Figure 22-12 shows one possibility using 25LS253 Dual 4 Input Multiplexers to select the correct connections for RAM0, RAMN, Q0, and QN. We refer to the high-order pins as "QN" and "RAMN" since one or more slices may be present. For a single slice, RAMN and QN would become RAM3 and Q3, respectively. For two 2901 slices, RAMN and QN would become RAM7 and Q7, respectively.

2901 SHIFT
AND ROTATE
OPERATIONS

The key to Figure 8-16 lies in the I7 signals which are input to the 1G and 2G pins of the 25LS253 device. Recall that I7 is one of three control signals input to the 2901 destination control logic. I7 controls shift logic at the local RAM and Q register 3-IN MUX inputs. I7 is always high when a downshift occurs. I7 is always low when an upshift occurs. Thus in Figure 8-12, I7 conditions one 25LS253 device to output data, while disabling the other device.

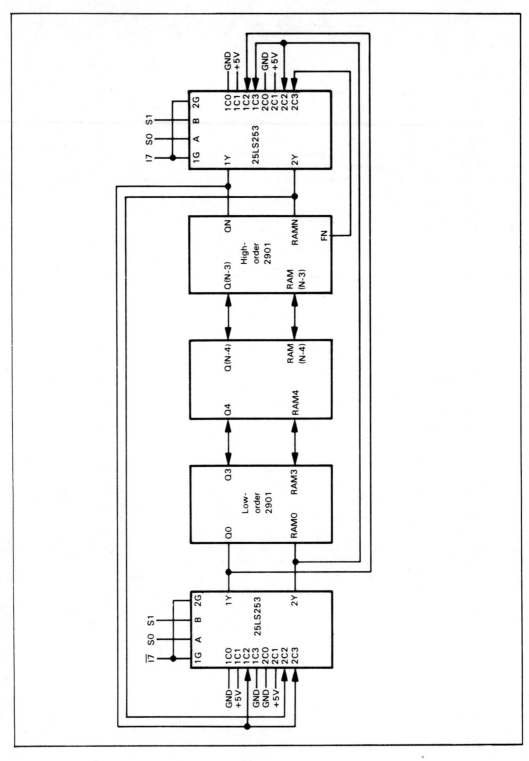

Figure 8-12. 2901 Shift and Rotate Logic

Shifts do not always occur at the 2901 local RAM or Q register inputs (see Figures 8-4 through 8-11). But that is not a problem. If the low-order to high-order 25LS253 device is enabled by I7, but no shift is to occur, then the 2901 will ignore the active 25LS253 output.

When a shift is specified by I6, I7, and I8, then the S0 and S1 inputs control the output of the selected 25LS253 device — which determines the kind of shift or rotate that will occur.

In this discussion of shifts and rotates, the sense of a "left" or "right" shift can cause confusion since all vendor 2900 literature illustrates bit positions from right to left:

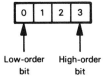

We have elected to make our illustrations compatible with vendor literature so that you will have less trouble connecting descriptions of the same parts. But in macro assembly language terms a left shift normally implies multiplication:

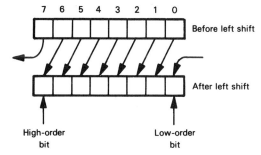

while a right shift implies division:

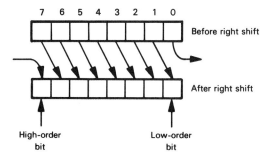

Given the bit numbering system used by 2900 vendor literature, the opposite shift logic would apply. That is to say, a left shift would become a divide:

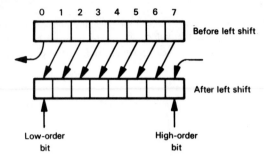

while a right shift becomes a multiply:

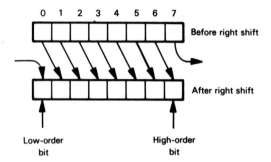

In order to avoid confusion, we shall refer to "upshifts" and "downshifts". An "upshift" causes multiplication, while a "downshift" causes division. An upshift becomes a left shift in macrolanguage terms, but looks like a right shift in 2900 vendor literature, and in the illustrations of this chapter. A downshift becomes a right shift in macrolanguage terms, but looks like a left shift in 2900 vendor literature, and in the illustrations of this chapter. We have elected to live with this confusion since it is smaller than the confusion which would arise if all our 2900 series part descriptions inverted bit numbers and data flows with respect to vendor literature.

Beginning with the simplest case, consider a simple downshift where zero is loaded into the high-order bit and the low-order bit is lost. In effect the number has been divided by two.

Figure 8-13 illustrates a downshift occurring in local RAM only. I7 is low, therefore the right-most 25LS253 device (as illustrated in Figure 8-13) is enabled, while the left-most 25LS253 device is disabled. S0 and S1 are both low, therefore 1C0 is output at 1Y and 2C0 is output at 2Y. Thus 0 is loaded into RAMN — and it is assumed that the three bits I6, I7, and I8 cause the downshift to occur at the local RAM 3-IN MUX logic.

Note that a Q downshift will occur in Figure 8-13 at the same time as the local RAM downshift — if I6, I7, and I8 codes have enabled the Q register 3-IN MUX downshift logic. For clarity we have not shown both downshifts occurring.

Were I7 high, then in Figure 8-13 an upshift would occur with 0 loaded into RAM0, and thence D0.

When executing a down- or upshift, as illustrated in Figure 8-13, you could shift in 1, rather than 0, by inputting S0 high and S1 low. This causes 1C1 to be output at 1Y and 2C1 to be output at 2Y.

Next consider **a down rotate;** this operation **is illustrated in Figure 8-14.**

The only difference between the down rotate illustrated in Figure 8-14 and the downshift illustrated in Figure 8-13 is the source for the Y2 output. A high input at S1 with a low input at S0 causes 1C2 to be output at 1Y and 2C2 to be output at 2Y. 1C2 and 2C2 receive their inputs from Q0 and RAM0 of the low-order 2901, respectively; hence a down rotate is achieved.

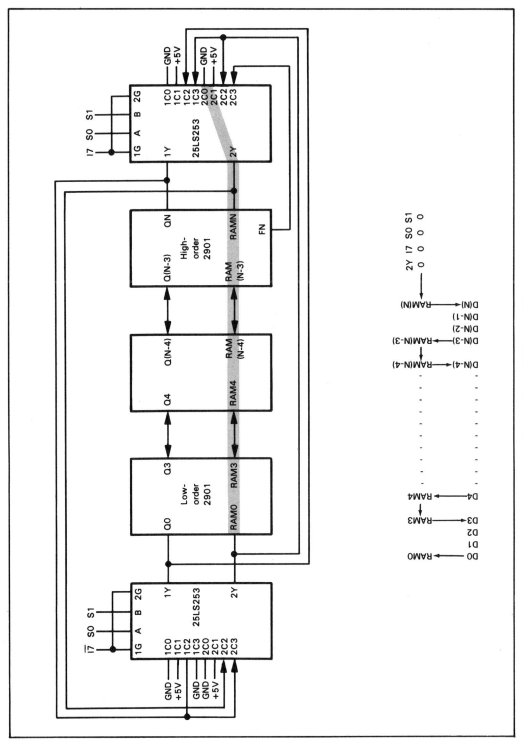

Figure 8-13. A 2901 Downshift

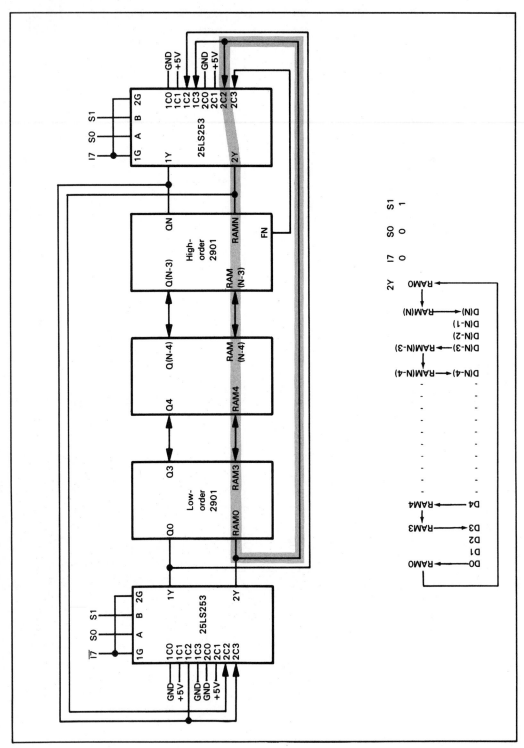

Figure 8-14. A 2901 Down Rotate

You can generate an up rotate by inputting I7 high — which disables the right-most 25LS253 (as illustrated in Figure 8-14) and enables the left-most 25LS253.

We need to stress again the fact that I7 has been chosen to enable the left-most 25LS253 when high, and the right-most 25LS253 when low, because this conforms to the way in which shift logic within the 2901 is controlled.

Let us now examine arithmetic shifts. The difference between an arithmetic shift and a logical shift lies in the high-order bit of a binary number, which arithmetic shift logic treats as a sign bit; the sign bit must be excluded from the shift. For arithmetic shifts the logic illustrated in Figure 8-12 concatenates local RAM with the Q registers to generate a double length number. For two 2901 slices this may be illustrated as follows:

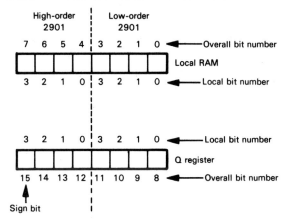

When an **arithmetic downshift** occurs, the high-order ALU output bit — which is the signed bit — is recycled back to RAMN, thus ensuring that it is preserved through the downshift. The remainder of the arithmetic number is shifted down one bit position, with the low-order local RAM bit (output via RAM0) becoming the high-order Q register bit (via QN). This may be illustrated as follows:

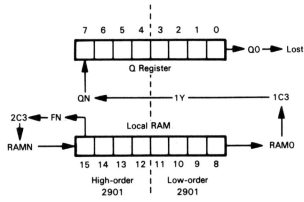

As illustrated in Figure 8-12, an arithmetic downshift is generated by I7=0, S0=1 and S1=1.

An **arithmetic upshift** causes 0 to be shifted into Q0 while QN, the high-order Q register bit, is shifted into RAM0. This may be illustrated as follows:

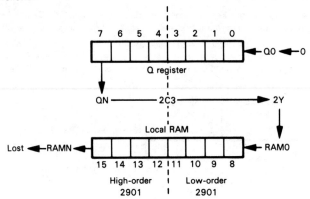

Note that this arithmetic upshift does not preserve the high-order sign bit. Therefore the arithmetic upshift is really a double length logical upshift.

You can easily generate double length down and up logical rotates by concatenating the Q registers with the local RAM. Connect the 1C3 input of the left side 25LS253 device to the RAMN output. Connect the 2C3 input of the left side 25LS253 device to the QN output. Connect the 1C3 input of the right side 25LS253 device to the RAM0 output. Connect the 2C3 input of the right side 25LS253 device to the Q0 output.

All of the shift and rotate logic functions we have just described, as well as the Status register and carry-in multiplexer, are contained in the 2904 Status and Shift Control Unit. This device eliminates most of the MSI, such as the two 25LS253s around the 2901s.

Let us now look at the simple problem of loading data into a local RAM location. If the data is immediate — that is to say, if it is provided by the microinstruction itself — then the following single microinstruction will load eight bits of data into the local RAM location addressed by the B address:

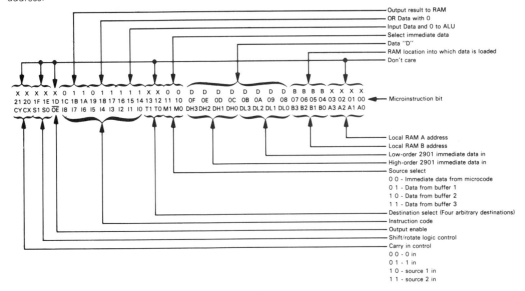

If the data which is to be loaded into local RAM comes from an external buffer, and we arbitrarily assume that it comes from external data buffer number 2, then the following single microinstruction will transfer the data from external buffer 2 to the local RAM location selected by the B address:

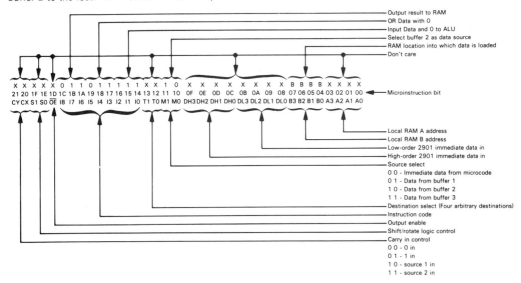

We described logic associated with microinstruction bits M1 and M0 earlier.

An arithmetic or logic operation performed on two sources taken from local RAM, with the result being output via Y to external destination number 1, requires the following single microinstruction:

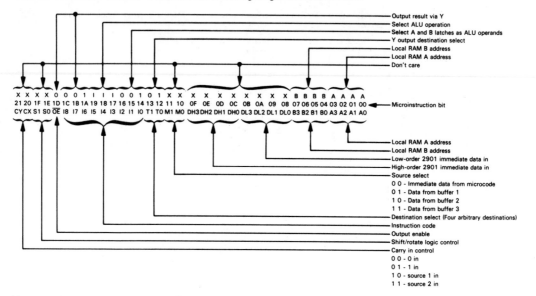

Now consider the same operation performed on one operand taken from local RAM (as addressed by A), while the other operand is provided by the microinstruction as immediate data; the result is returned to the local RAM location addressed by B. Here is the necessary microinstruction:

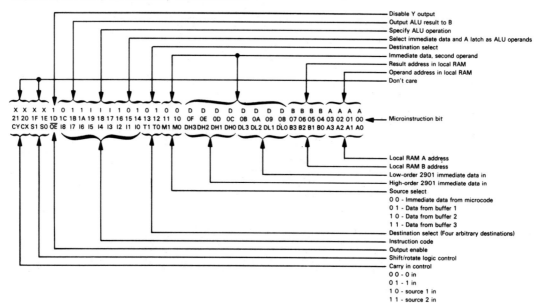

Two microinstructions, with appropriate looping and select logic, is all you need in order to multiply two 8-bit numbers and generate a 16-bit product. The algorithm needed for this multiplication initially stores the multiplier in the low-order eight bits of the product space with the multiplicand in a separate 8-bit storage location as follows:

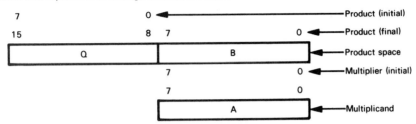

We are going to downshift the contents of the 16-bit product space eight times. After eight shifts, the multiplier will have been shifted out and lost. Therefore the high-order eight bits of the product space will initially be assigned to the low-order eight bits of the product, as shown above.

In the typical "shift" and "add" multiplication routine (which we have described in Volume 1) the multiplicand is upshifted one bit position at a time, and is added to the product whenever there is a 1 in the multiplier bit corresponding to the current upshift. Here is a simple illustration of two 4-bit numbers being multiplied to create an 8-bit product:

$$1\,0\,1\,0 \cdot 0\,1\,0\,1 = 0\,0\,1\,1\,0\,0\,1\,0$$

Step 1:   0 0 0 0 0 0 0 0   1 0 1 **0**
                  0 1 0 1

Step 2:   0 0 0 0 0 0 0 0   1 0 **1** 0
              0 1 0 1 0
        0 0 0 0 1 0 1 0

Step 3:   0 0 0 0 1 0 1 0   1 **0** 1 0
             0 1 0 1 0 0

Step 4:   0 0 0 0 1 0 1 0   **1** 0 1 0
           0 1 0 1 0 0 0
        0 0 1 1 0 0 1 0

The multiplicand initially corresponds to the low-order multiplier bit. The multiplicand is subsequently upshifted three times, corresponding to the three higher-order multiplier bits. Following the first and third upshift, the multiplicand is added to the product, since bits 1 and 3 of the multiplier are 1.

Now instead of upshifting the multiplicand, as illustrated above, we could downshift the product's space. This may be illustrated as follows:

Step 1:   0 0 0 0 0 0 0 0   1 0 1 **0**
               0 1 0 1

Step 2:   0 0 0 0 0 0 0 0   1 0 **1** 0
               0 1 0 1
        0 0 0 0 1 0 1 0

Step 3:   0 0 0 0 1 0 1 0   1 **0** 1 0
               0 1 0 1

Step 4:   0 0 0 0 1 0 1 0   **1** 0 1 0
              0 1 0 1
        0 0 1 1 0 0 1 0

This is the algorithm we are about to use. This algorithm allows the multiplier to be stored in half of the product space, since this space is slowly shifted out.

Returning to our 8-bit X 8-bit multiplication, after the first shift the 16-bit product space will be shared by the low-order nine bits of the product and the high-order seven bits of the multiplier:

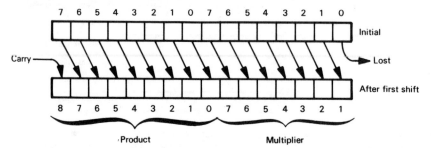

and ultimately the sixteen bits of the product space will be occupied by the 16-bit product — after the entire multiplier has been shifted out. Each time the contents of the product space are shifted down one bit position, the next low-order bit of the multiplier will be shifted out and will appear at output pin RAM0. This output is tested. If it is 1, then the multiplicand is added to the high-order eight bits of the product space (the Q register) before the next shift occurs. The carry from the addition must become the next high-order product bit prior to the next addition. Therefore the carry is shifted into the high-order Q register bit via Q7.

In this fashion, the multiplicand is added to the product in each bit position that corresponds to a 1 in the multiplier. The logic for this operation may be illustrated as follows:

Since we have discussed multiplication algorithms in some detail in Volume 1, we will not spend more time in this chapter describing the theory of this multiplication algorithm. Rather, consider the following example:

```
             2C · A4 = 1C30

Start        0 0 0 0 0 0 0 0 0 0 1 0 1 1 0 0
             1 0 1 0 0 1 0 0

Step 1:      0 0 0 0 0 0 0 0 0 0 1 0 1 1 0 0 ──► 0 0 0 0 0 0 0 0 0 0 0 1 0 1 1 0
Step 2:      0 0 0 0 0 0 0 0 0 0 0 1 0 1 1 0 ──► 0 0 0 0 0 0 0 0 0 0 0 0 1 0 1 1
Step 3:      0 0 0 0 0 0 0 0 0 0 0 0 1 0 1 1 ──► 0 0 0 0 0 0 0 0 0 0 0 0 0 1 0 1
                                                 1 0 1 0 0 1 0 0
                                                 1 0 1 0 0 1 0 0 0 0 0 0 0 1 0 1   C = 0
Step 4:      1 0 1 0 0 1 0 0 0 0 0 0 0 1 0 1 ──► 0 1 0 1 0 0 1 0 0 0 0 0 0 0 1 0
                                                 1 0 1 0 0 1 0 0
                                                 1 1 1 1 0 1 1 0 0 0 0 0 0 0 1 0   C = 0
Step 5:      1 1 1 1 0 1 1 0 0 0 0 0 0 0 1 0 ──► 0 1 1 1 1 0 1 1 0 0 0 0 0 0 0 1
Step 6:      0 1 1 1 1 0 1 1 0 0 0 0 0 0 0 1 ──► 0 0 1 1 1 1 0 1 1 0 0 0 0 0 0 0
                                                 1 0 1 0 0 1 0 0
                                                 1 1 1 0 0 0 0 1 1 0 0 0 0 0 0 0   C = 0
Step 7:      1 1 1 0 0 0 0 1 1 0 0 0 0 0 0 0 ──► 0 1 1 1 0 0 0 0 1 1 0 0 0 0 0 0
Step 8:      0 1 1 1 0 0 0 0 1 1 0 0 0 0 0 0 ──► 0 0 1 1 1 0 0 0 0 1 1 0 0 0 0 0
End          0 0 0 1 1 1 0 0 0 0 1 1 0 0 0 0
```

The algorithm above starts by downshifting Q and B registers' contents as a single 16-bit entity. Carry, which must initially be 0, is shifted into the high-order Q register bit via Q7, while the low-order bit of B appears at RAM0. If RAM0 is 0, then 0 must be added to Q. If RAM0 is 1, then the multiplier in the local RAM location with address A must be added to Q. A second microinstruction accomplishes this addition. If this addition generates a carry, then the carry bit must be loaded into the next high-order product bit. By connecting the carry to Q7 we make sure that any carry is loaded into the next high-order product bit on the next downshift of Q and B registers' contents. Necessary logic is illustrated in Figure 22-15.

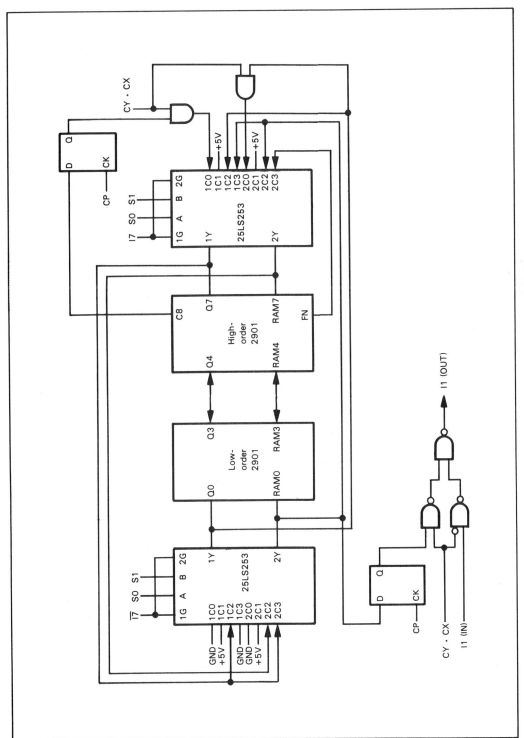

Figure 8-15. 2901 Connections for Binary Multiplication

In Figure 8-15, CX and CY high is the characteristic combination identifying binary multiplication. As compared to Figure 8-12, we have modified the 1C0 and 2C0 inputs to the right-most 25LS253 device so that when CY and CX are both high, a downshift loads the Carry out into the high-order bit of Q7, while Q0 is loaded into RAM7 — and thence into the high-order bit of the local RAM location with address B. Thus a downshift treats the Q and local RAM locations as a single 16-bit register, which, following a downshift, causes a prior carry to be input at Q7 while the low-order multiplier bit is output at RAM0.

Before describing the logic surrounding I1 in Figure 8-15, let us look at the two microinstructions which must be executed sequentially within a loop in order to perform the required multiplication. First we execute a downshift microinstruction, then we execute an add microinstruction, as follows:

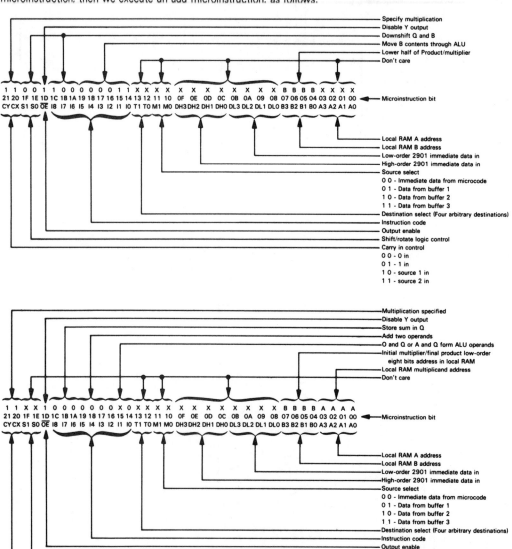

The downshift microinstruction is self-evident. Note, however, that RAM0 must become the I1 instruction bit for the addition so that 0 will be added to Q when RAM0 outputs 0, while the contents of the local RAM location addressed by A are added to Q when RAM0 outputs 1. But when CY and CX are not both high, binary multiplication is not in progress; therefore I1 comes directly from the microinstruction. The three NAND gates shown in Figure 8-15 provide the necessary logic.

The multiplication example we have just described is a useful illustration of 2901 logic, but the 2903, which we describe next, performs binary multiplication and division automatically.

THE 2903 MICROPROCESSOR SLICE

The 2903 is a 4-bit microprocessor slice. The 2903 is conceptually similar to the 2901, which we have already described. The 2903 has more versatile signals than the 2901, and more on-chip functions; however, the 2903 and the 2901 are driven by clocks with approximately equal frequency. But remember, the 2901A and 2901B are faster than the 2901; therefore, they are faster than a 2903 — excluding special 2903 functions. The 2903A is currently in development and, when available, will offer faster operation than the 2903.

The 2903 is not a superset of the 2901. Microprograms written for the 2903 and the 2901 will be completely different; so will external logic supporting the two devices. Nor is the 2903 always the part of choice, as compared to a 2901. If your application uses a lot of complex arithmetic and logic operations, or if your application requires a large number of local registers, then the 2903 is the part of choice. But if your application stresses execution speed, then the 2901A or 2901B may be a better choice.

2901 and 2903 ALU logic also differ sharply. The 2903 performs operations which encompass the simple 2901 ALU functions; the 2903 also performs a separate set of more complex operations. Furthermore, 2903 ALU logic discriminates between a high-order slice, a low-order slice, and an intermediate slice; 2901 logic makes no such high/intermediate/low-order distinctions. By discriminating between high-order, low-order, and intermediate slices, the 2903 is able to perform operations on non-symmetrical data. For example, a twos complement binary number is non-symmetrical since the high-order bit is a sign bit subject to different interpretation from other bits, which are magnitude bits. Also, by discriminating between high-order, low-order, and intermediate slices, the 2903 makes double use of many signals; signals perform secondary functions at slices where the primary function is meaningless. For example, Carry, Generate, and Propagate signals share pins with Overflow and Sign status, since the Carry, Generate, and Propagate signals are meaningless at the most significant slice, while status signals are meaningful only at the most significant slice.

In the description of the 2903 which follows, we will compare and contrast the 2903 with the 2901. We will refer to the 2901 description, together with Chapter 4 of Volume 1 for all conceptual information.

The 2903 is packaged as a 48-pin DIP. It uses bipolar LSI technology.

A 2903 FUNCTIONAL OVERVIEW AND COMPARATIVE ANALYSIS

Figures 8-16 and 8-17 functionally illustrate 2903 logic. Figure 8-16 is a variation of Figure 8-1, given earlier in this chapter, and of Figure 4-3, from Volume 1; it illustrates the 2903 in terms of the general chip slice description given in Chapter 4 of Volume 1. Figure 8-17 is a more accurate representation of 2903 logic and data paths.

Superficially the 2903 and the 2901 look very similar. Both have an arithmetic and logic unit which receives two inputs and generates a single output. Both have a 16 x 4-bit, two output-port RAM, additional local data storage in the 4-bit Q register, and two sets of shift logic.

The 2903 16 x 4-bit local RAM, like the 2901, receives two 4-bit addresses — the A and B addresses. Data can be written into the 2903 local RAM location addressed by B, but only when the separate $\overline{WE}$ control input is low. The 2901 has no signal equivalent to $\overline{WE}$. Data addressed by A and B is output to the 2903 A and B latches; but the 2903 B latch has an output enable control, $\overline{OE}_B$, which must be low for the B latch contents to be passed on. The 2901 has no signal equivalent to $\overline{OE}_B$.

Both 2901 and 2903 A and B latch outputs are transmitted to the R and S ALU input multiplexers; but that is the only similarity between the two sets of ALU input logic. The 2901 uses three instruction code bits to generate eight possible combinations of R and S inputs. The 2903 uses one instruction code bit, together with two new control signals to select substantially different ALU operand combinations. The 2903 then makes up for the lack of operand input options with additional ALU functions.

Both 2901 and 2903 ALU outputs may go to the Q register, the Y port, or the 16 X 4-bit local RAM.

Like the 2901, the 2903 Q register has shift logic at its input. The 2903 also has shift logic on the local RAM data path; but 2903 shift logic precedes the Y outputs, and has a separate output enable control signal $\overline{OE}_Y$ like the 2901.

Perhaps the most obvious difference between the 2901 and the 2903 lies in the data input and output ports. The 2901 has a single data input port, D0-D3, and a single data output port, Y0-Y3. The 2903 has the same data input port, DA0-DA3, but the 2903 has two bidirectional data output ports, DB0-DB3 and Y0-Y3.

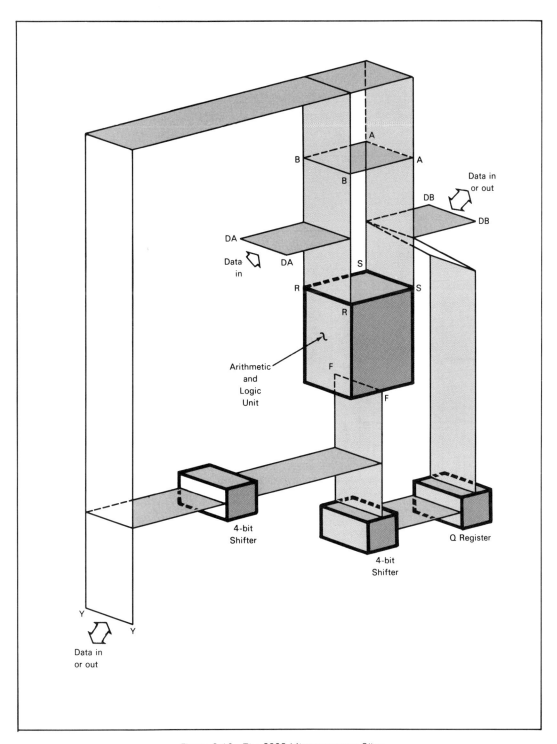

Figure 8-16. The 2903 Microprocessor Slice

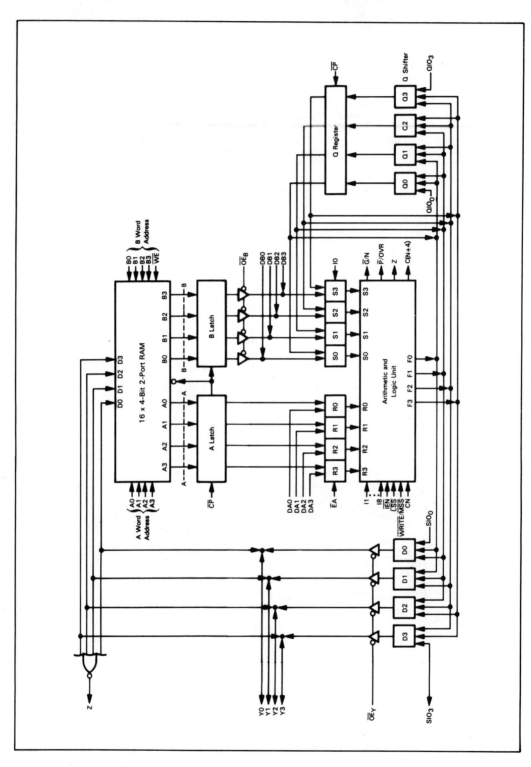

Figure 8-17. 2903 4-Bit Slice Logic

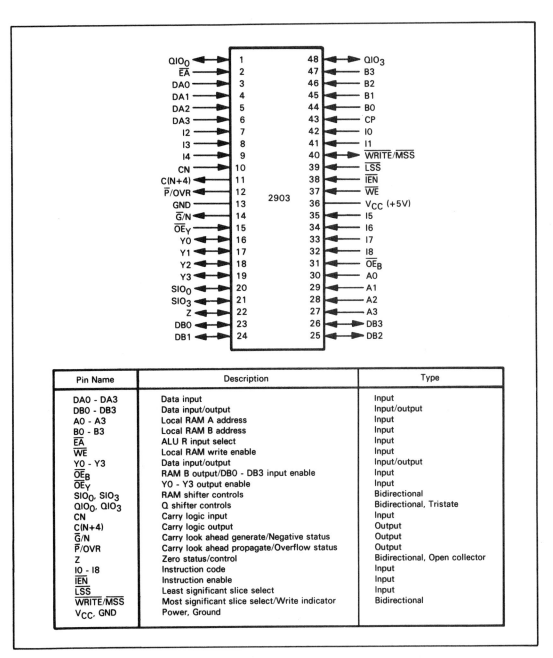

Pin Name	Description	Type
DA0 - DA3	Data input	Input
DB0 - DB3	Data input/output	Input/output
A0 - A3	Local RAM A address	Input
B0 - B3	Local RAM B address	Input
$\overline{\text{EA}}$	ALU R input select	Input
$\overline{\text{WE}}$	Local RAM write enable	Input
Y0 - Y3	Data input/output	Input/output
$\overline{\text{OE}}_B$	RAM B output/DB0 - DB3 input enable	Input
$\overline{\text{OE}}_Y$	Y0 - Y3 output enable	Input
SIO$_0$, SIO$_3$	RAM shifter controls	Bidirectional
QIO$_0$, QIO$_3$	Q shifter controls	Bidirectional, Tristate
CN	Carry logic input	Input
C(N+4)	Carry logic output	Output
$\overline{\text{G}}$/N	Carry look ahead generate/Negative status	Output
$\overline{\text{P}}$/OVR	Carry look ahead propagate/Overflow status	Output
Z	Zero status/control	Bidirectional, Open collector
I0 - I8	Instruction code	Input
$\overline{\text{IEN}}$	Instruction enable	Input
$\overline{\text{LSS}}$	Least significant slice select	Input
$\overline{\text{WRITE}}$/$\overline{\text{MSS}}$	Most significant slice select/Write indicator	Bidirectional
V$_{CC}$, GND	Power, Ground	

Figure 8-18. 2903 Microprocessor Slice Pins and Signal Assignments

2903 MICROPROCESSOR SLICE PINS AND SIGNALS

Pins and signal assignments for the 2903 are illustrated in Figure 8-18. We will summarize functions performed by each of these signals superficially before examining device operations in detail.

2903 signals can be divided into these three categories:

1) Data inputs and outputs

2) Instruction and control inputs that are generated by a microinstruction

3) Control and status signals connecting 2903 slices, and status signals generated by 2903 slices

First consider data inputs, outputs and associated address signals.

A0-A3 and B0-B3 are two 4-bit addresses which select locations within the 2903 local 16 x 4-bit RAM. Data may be written into the local RAM location addressed by B — but only while both WE and the clock signal, CP, are input low.

While CP is high, the contents of the local RAM location addressed by A0-A3 are written into the A latch — which is therefore changing continuously. When CP goes low, the A latch contents are stable, holding whatever data was read from local RAM at the instant that CP made its high-to-low transition. The A latch contents are continuously output to the ALU R input multiplexer.

The B latch output is enabled by the $\overline{OE}_B$ control signal. When this signal is high, the B latch still receives data from the local RAM location addressed by B0-B3, but the B latch output is floated.

If $\overline{OE}_B$ is low and the B output from local RAM is enabled, then **DB0-DB3 becomes a 4-bit output.** The B output appears at DB0-DB3, as illustrated earlier. **When $\overline{OE}_B$ is high** and the B latch output is disabled, **DB0-DB3 becomes a 4-bit data input.** Data input via DB0-DB3 can be selected as the ALU S operand.

DA0-DA3 always functions as a 4-bit data input.

The R input to the ALU may be the A latch output from local RAM, or the DA0-DA3 external data input. If $\overline{EA}$ is high, then DA0-DA3 is selected. If $\overline{EA}$ is low then the local RAM A latch output is selected.

2903 ALU INPUT OPTIONS

The low-order instruction code input (I0) determines the ALU S input. If I0 is high, the Q register output becomes the S input to the ALU. If I0 is low, the B output from the local RAM, or data input via DB0-DB3 becomes the ALU S input. These options are summarized in Table 8-5; logically they may be illustrated as follows:

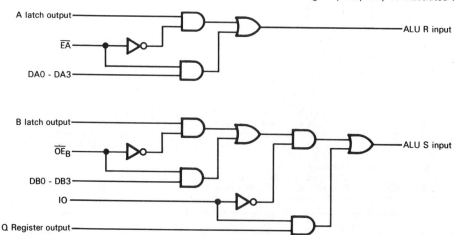

ALU input options are described in more detail later when we look at 2903 logic.

Y0-Y3, which were data output pins of the 2901, are bidirectional 2903 pins (see Figure 8-17).

$\overline{OE}_Y$ **is a control signal which enables or disables the ALU output.** If $\overline{OE}_Y$ is low, then ALU output, after passing through the ALU shifter, appears at the Y0-Y3 pins. But if $\overline{OE}_Y$ is high, ALU output is disabled and Y0-Y3 become input pins. Data input at Y0-Y3 can be written into the local RAM location addressed by B0-B3, provided WE and CP are low.

The 2903 has a 9-bit instruction code which is input via I0-I8. The interpretation of this instruction code differs sharply from the 2901. Without reference to the 2901, **the 2903 instruction code interpretation may be illustrated as follows:**

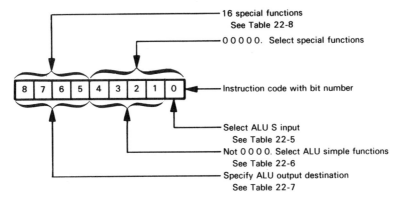

As illustrated above, the 2903 instruction code has two different interpretations.

We can compare 2901 and 2903 instruction codes, but to do so we must include the $\overline{EA}$ and $\overline{OE}_B$ control inputs as instruction code contributors. The two instruction codes may now be compared as follows:

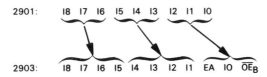

Note that $\overline{OE}_B$ and $\overline{EA}$ do not usually come from the microcode.

2903 instruction code interpretations are quite complex and make use of additional control and status signals. Therefore we will complete our summary of signals before examining instruction code interpretations in detail.

Let us now examine status and control signals of the 2903. We have already described $\overline{WE}$, $\overline{EA}$, $\overline{OE}_B$, and $\overline{OE}_Y$.

The 2903 has logic to discriminate between a most significant slice, a least significant slice, or an intermediate slice.

> **2903 SLICE SIGNIFICANCE SELECT**

When $\overline{LSS}$ is input low, a 2903 acts as a least significant slice. As a least significant slice, the $\overline{WRITE/MSS}$ signal becomes a $\overline{WRITE}$ output. As such, $\overline{WRITE/MSS}$ is output low for every microcycle during which data is written into local RAM. Frequently the $\overline{WE}$ inputs for all 2903 slices will be connected to the $\overline{WRITE}$ output of the least significant 2903 slice. This may be illustrated as follows:

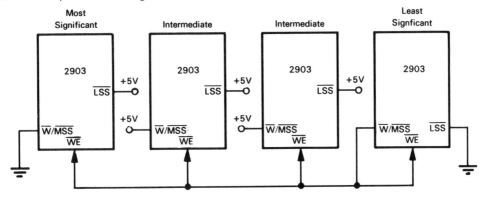

At intermediate and most significant slices, $\overline{LSS}$ is input high. Now the $\overline{WRITE/MSS}$ signal becomes an $\overline{MSS}$ input. A low $\overline{MSS}$ input selects the most significant slice, while a high $\overline{MSS}$ input selects an intermediate slice, as illustrated above.

$\overline{IEN}$ **is described in vendor literature as an "instruction enable" input.** This may lead you to believe that it enables or disables the I0-I8 instruction code inputs, **but in fact the effect of $\overline{IEN}$ is more limited.** When low, $\overline{IEN}$ allows data to be written into the Q register; it also enables the $\overline{WRITE}$ output at the least significant slice. When $\overline{IEN}$ is high, data cannot be written into the Q register, and the $\overline{WRITE}$ output at the least significant slice is constantly output high. If the $\overline{WE}$ inputs for all slices are connected to the $\overline{WRITE}$ output of the least significant slice, then $\overline{IEN}$ high effectively disconnects the instruction code input, since it prevents data from being written into the Q register or local RAM; but it does not prevent an instruction from being decoded and executed by the ALU, and it does allow data to be output via the DB and/or Y pins.

2903 ALU logic has the standard Carry In (CN) and Carry Out (C(N+4)) signals. The 2903 also has the Carry Look-Ahead signals $\overline{G}$ and $\overline{P}$. But if you look at the discussion of Carry Look-Ahead logic given in Chapter 4 of Volume 1 (and later in this chapter for the 2902), you will see that $\overline{G}$ and $\overline{P}$ outputs are not used at the most significant slice. Conversely, the Sign and Overflow status out-puts are meaningful only at the most significant slice. Therefore **2903 pins share $\overline{G}$ with the Sign status (N) and $\overline{P}$ with the Overflow status (OVR).** These pins output Sign (N) and Overflow (OVR) statuses at the most significant slice; they output Carry generate ($\overline{G}$) and propagate ($\overline{P}$) for intermediate and least significant slices.

The 2903 also has an open-collector Zero status output (Z). This signal is output high when all ALU outputs are low.

The 2903 makes additional use of its shifter signals (SI00, SI03, QI00, QI03) and its status signals (CN, C(N+4), N, OVR, and Z). These signals are occasionally used in special ways by ALU operations that do not use the signals for their primary purpose. For a summary see Table 8-8 and associated text.

SI00 and SI03 are ALU shifter connections. QI00 and QI03, likewise, are Q register shifter connections. These signals allow shifts to occur across multiple slices as described for the 2901. These signals will always be connected as follows:

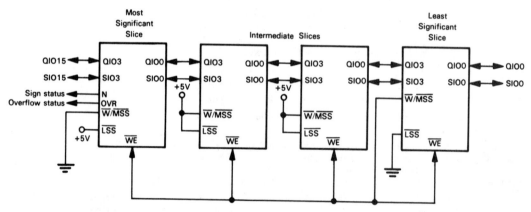

CP is the master clock signal used to control and synchronize events within the 2903.

2903 LOGIC

We will now examine 2903 logic in detail.

The best place to start understanding 2903 logic is at the read/write memory (local RAM):

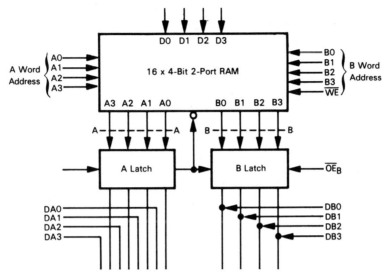

The 2903 local RAM consists of sixteen 4-bit locations. You will use pins A0-A3 to identify the location from which data will be output at the A latch. You use pins B0-B3 to identify the 4-bit location from which data may be output to the B latch or into which data may be written via Y0-Y3.

Data may be written into the local RAM location addressed by B — but only while $\overline{WE}$ and CP are input low. This may be illustrated as follows:

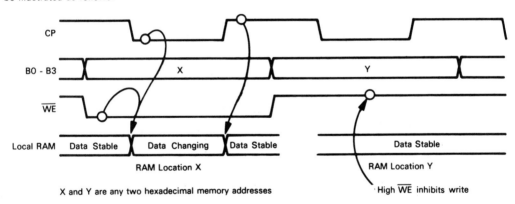

X and Y are any two hexadecimal memory addresses

High $\overline{WE}$ inhibits write

As illustrated above, the contents of the local RAM location addressed by B are changing while $\overline{WE}$ and CP are both low. When CP goes high, contents of the addressed RAM location are stable, holding whatever data was input when CP made its low-to-high transition. If $\overline{WE}$ is high, local RAM is not accessed and its contents remain stable.

Data is output from the local RAM locations addressed by A and B when CP is high. The contents of the local RAM location addressed by A are output to the A latch. The contents of the local RAM location addressed by B are output to the B latch. These outputs occur when CP is high; therefore the A and B latch contents are continuously changing while CP is high, but they are stable while CP is low, holding whatever data was input when CP made its high-to-low transition.

The A latch contents are output continuously. **We can** therefore **illustrate A latch output timing as follows:**

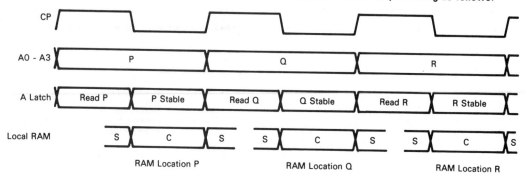

P,Q, and R are any three hexadecimal addresses. S represents stable data, and C represents changing data in the selected RAM location.

In the illustration above, the RAM location addressed by A is shown as stable while CP is high and changing while CP is low. The stable data is output to the A latch while CP is high. The A latch contents subsequently become stable while CP is low — at which time local RAM contents are changing until RAM access time has elapsed. Thus race conditions are avoided.

The A latch outputs are continuously enabled.

B latch timing is a little more complex than A latch timing because the B latch has its own output enable control signal $\overline{OE}_B$. When $\overline{OE}_B$ is high, the B latch output is floated. But when $\overline{OE}_B$ is low, the B latch outputs are enabled. **B latch timing may be illustrated as follows:**

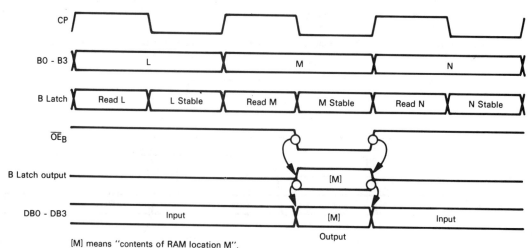

[M] means "contents of RAM location M".

The Y0-Y3 input to local RAM may come from the ALU output, or from the Y0-Y3 pins. Unlike the 2901, there is no shifter at the local RAM input; rather, the shifter has been moved to the ALU output, and the shifter output is itself enabled or disabled by the $\overline{OE}_Y$ control input. If $\overline{OE}_Y$ is low, then the shifter output is enabled; it appears as output at Y0-Y3 and at RAM D0-D3. But if $\overline{OE}_Y$ is high, Y0-Y3 become input pins providing local RAM with its data input.

| 2903 ALU |
| INPUT |

The 2903 local RAM, like the 2901, generates a 4-bit slice through selected programmable registers of a Central Processing Unit. But it is much easier to extend 2903 local RAM using external memory. This is because the 2903 has one data input port and two bidirectional data ports situated between local RAM and the ALU. The 29705 is used as an expansion RAM.

CPU register implementation and ALU operand inputs are logically dependent on each other, since the primary function of CPU registers is to store ALU source or destination data. We will therefore explore the ALU operand options available using a 2903, and see what impact these options have on register implementation.

Turning to the 2903 Arithmetic and Logic Unit, these three aspects of ALU logic are important:

<table><tr><td>**2903 ARITHMETIC AND LOGIC UNIT**</td></tr></table>

1) The operands which are input to the ALU

2) The ALU operation which is to be performed

3) The destination for the ALU output. (The destination specification includes any shift operations.)

Instruction code bit I0, together with $\overline{EA}$ and $\overline{OE}_B$, controls the data input to the 2903 ALU; instruction code bits I1 through I4 specify simple ALU functions, while I5 through I8 specify the destination and shift operation for simple functions. Instruction code bits I5 through I8 may also specify special 2903 functions.

Table 8-5 shows the ALU operand source options that can be specified using I0, $\overline{EA}$, and $\overline{OE}_B$. Let us now explore these options in detail.

<table><tr><td>**2903 ALU OPERAND OPTIONS**</td></tr></table>

Table 8-5. 2903 ALU R and S Operand Selections

Control Signal			R Operand	S Operand
$\overline{EA}$	I0	$\overline{OE}_B$		
0	0	0	A latch output	B latch output
0	0	1	A latch output	DB0 - DB3 input
0	1	0/1	A latch output	Q register output
1	0	0	DA0 - DA3 input	B latch output
1	0	1	DA0 - DA3 input	DB0 - DB3 input
1	1	0/1	DA0 - DA3 input	Q register output

Beginning with the logically simplest case, we will assume that $\overline{EA}$ is low, so the A latch output becomes the ALU R input. Any of the ALU S input options could also accompany $\overline{EA}$ high, in which case DA0-DA3 becomes the ALU R input. Consider Q0-Q3 providing the ALU S input, while DB0-DB3 is idle:

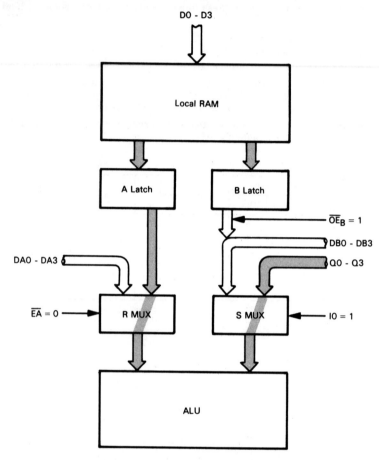

Data paths illustrated above would probably be used by a complex ALU operation involving one source operand. This source operand comes from local RAM via the A latch, while the complex ALU operation acts on temporary data held in the Q register.

Now consider the same data paths illustrated above, but with $\overline{OE}_B$ input low, so that B latch data is output via DB0-DB3:

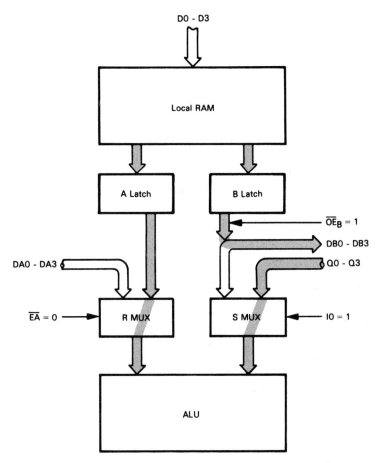

Data being output via DB0-DB3 will probably come from a CPU register implemented in local RAM. DB0-DB3 could be connected to external read/write memory within which additional CPU registers are implemented. The direct data path from local RAM to DB0-DB3 can be used effectively to implement any register-to-register operation within a CPU. If, for example, an Accumulator or other primary register is implemented in local RAM while secondary registers are held in external RAM, then the data path illustrated above lends itself readily to register-register data transfers, which may, or may not, occur in parallel with any other CPU operation.

Now consider the data paths we just illustrated, but with $\overline{EA}$ high, so that the ALU R operand comes from the external data inputs DA0-DA3. This may be illustrated as follows:

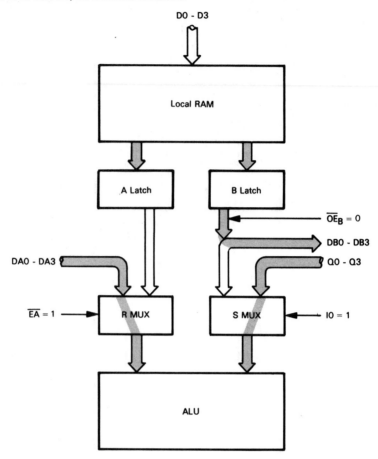

Data input via DA0-DA3 may be immediate data coming from a microinstruction, or non-immediate data taken from any other source. DA0-DA3 may also receive its input from an external RAM within which additional CPU registers are held.

But, moving away from complex operations that may require the ALU S operand to come from the Q register, let us examine some more complex data paths used by simple CPU operations. In the simplest case, the two ALU operands will come from local RAM. This may be illustrated as follows:

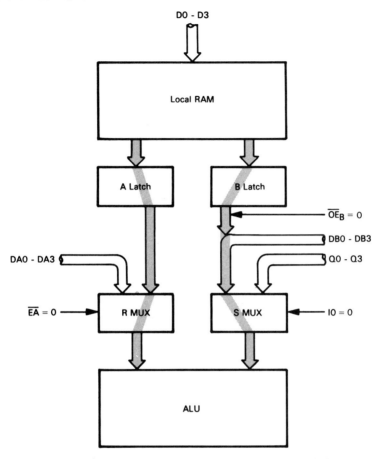

Data paths illustrated above show two ALU operands being taken from local RAM locations — probably CPU registers.

We can take the S ALU input from DB0-DB3 by inputting $\overline{OE}_B$ high, thus enabling the data from the B latch. This may be illustrated as follows:

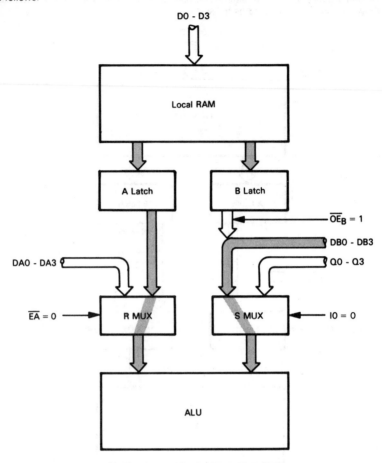

Data entering at DB0-DB3 could be immediate data coming from a microinstruction, or data from an external RAM location being used to implement additional CPU registers. By inputting $\overline{EA}$ high, we can take both the R and S ALU inputs from external RAM:

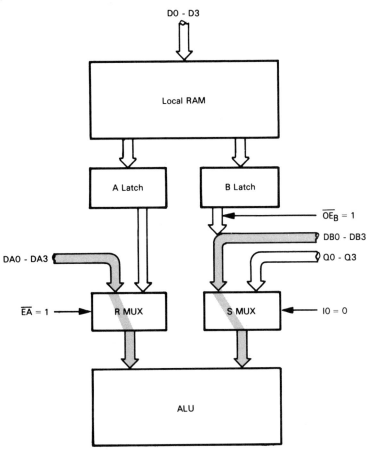

In the illustration above you see one of the more significant 2903 advantages, as compared to the 2901. The 2901 allows a single operand to be taken from external RAM, and that reduces the effectiveness of external RAM as a means of implementing the two-port CPU registers in a 2901 configuration. It limits you to CPU architectures that include a group of secondary registers, only one of which can provide an ALU operand during the execution of any instruction. But the 2903, by allowing external data inputs to the R and S ALU operands, allows you to implement CPU registers in internal local RAM, or in external RAM like the 29705, without compromising register logic associated with either implementation.

The 2903 has local RAM addressing. The 2901 allows you to specify just two local RAM addresses within a single microcycle. The A and B addresses identify the two ALU operands while the B address also identifies the destination address for the ALU product. Thus the ALU operand specified by the B address must be overwritten if the ALU product is to be returned to local RAM. But **the 2903 allows either two or three local RAM addresses to be specified within a single microcycle;** you have the option of creating one, or two B addresses within a single microcycle. **If you create one B address, timing may be illustrated as follows:**

2903 LOCAL RAM ADDRESSING

2903 TWO-ADDRESS TIMING

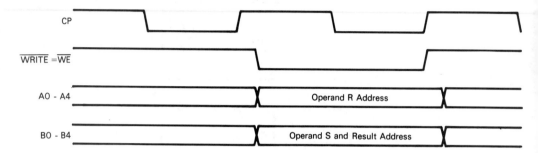

A and B provide the two local RAM addresses. As described earlier, while CP is high the contents of these two local RAM locations are output to the A and B latches. Subsequently, when CP is low, data is written back to the local RAM location addressed by B, since WE is low. In the illustration above, we show WE being driven low at the proper time by the WRITE output. WE will usually be connected to the WRITE output from the least significant 2903 slice.

We generate three local RAM addresses in a single 2903 microcycle by changing the B address after reading an operand, and before writing back the result. Timing may be illustrated as follows:

2903 THREE-ADDRESS MICROCYCLE

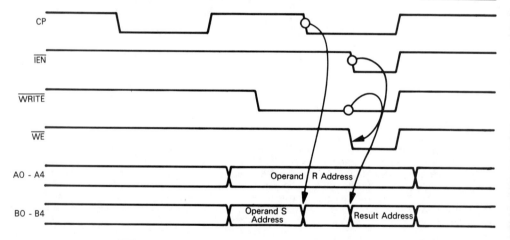

In the illustration above we delay IEN going low until the last quarter of the microcycle. This gives external logic sufficient time to change the B address. While IEN is high, WRITE is held high. Thus, delaying the IEN low pulse delays the WRITE pulse — which in turn delays the WE low input until a new address is stable at B. You can generate three-address timing, as illustrated above, by changing the IEN waveform from its normal two-address shape:

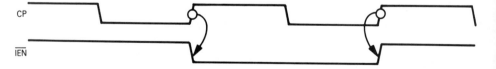

to the following continuous three-address shape:

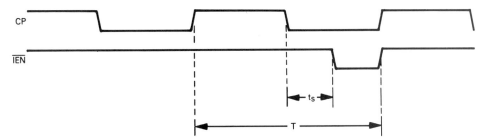

You cannot directly drive $\overline{WE}$ from external logic in order to create a three-address microcycle since external logic may not be able to identify microcycles during which no write operation is to occur — and $\overline{WE}$ should be held high. By using $\overline{IEN}$, and connecting $\overline{WE}$ to $\overline{WRITE}$, you use $\overline{IEN}$ logic to provide $\overline{WE}$ with its correct shape, while you use $\overline{WRITE}$ to discriminate between microcycles within which a write should, or should not, occur.

You use **instruction code bits I0 through I4 to distinguish between simple ALU functions and special 2903 functions.** When the five instruction code inputs I0-I4 are all low, I5 through I8 are interpreted by the 2903 as "special function" identifiers. **If one or more of the five inputs I0-I4 are high, then simple ALU functions are interpreted as summarized in Table 8-6.** These simple functions are all self-evident and need no special discussion.

| 2903 |
| SIMPLE |
| ALU |
| FUNCTIONS |

Table 8-6. 2903 Simple ALU Function Specifications

Instruction Code	ALU Operation and Output	ALU Dependent Output Signals					
		C(N+4)	$\overline{P}$/OVR		$\overline{G}$/N		Z
I4 I3 I2 I1 I0			MSS	Other	MSS	Other	
0 0 0 0 0	See Table 22-8						
0 0 0 0 1	All ALU outputs high	0	0	0	N	$\overline{G}$	0
0 0 0 1 X	S - R - 1 + CN	C(N+4)	OVR	$\overline{P}$	N	$\overline{G}$	Z
0 0 1 0 X	R - S - 1 + CN	C(N+4)	OVR	$\overline{P}$	N	$\overline{G}$	Z
0 0 1 1 X	R + S + CN	C(N+4)	OVR	$\overline{P}$	N	$\overline{G}$	Z
0 1 0 0 X	S + CN	C(N+4)	OVR	$\overline{P}$	N	$\overline{G}$	Z
0 1 0 1 X	$\overline{S}$ + CN	C(N+4)	OVR	$\overline{P}$	N	$\overline{G}$	Z
0 1 1 0 X	R + CN	C(N+4)	OVR	$\overline{P}$	N	$\overline{G}$	Z
0 1 1 1 X	$\overline{R}$ + CN	C(N+4)	OVR	$\overline{P}$	N	$\overline{G}$	Z
1 0 0 0 X	All ALU outputs low	0	0	0	N	$\overline{G}$	1
1 0 0 1 X	$\overline{R}$ AND S	0	0	0	N	$\overline{G}$	Z
1 0 1 0 X	R EXCLUSIVE NOR S	0	0	0	N	$\overline{G}$	Z
1 0 1 1 X	R EXCLUSIVE OR S	0	0	0	N	$\overline{G}$	Z
1 1 0 0 X	R AND S	0	0	0	N	$\overline{G}$	Z
1 1 0 1 X	R NOR S	0	0	0	N	$\overline{G}$	Z
1 1 1 0 X	R NAND S	0	0	0	N	$\overline{G}$	Z
1 1 1 1 X	R OR S	0	0	0	N	$\overline{G}$	Z

R = R operand input
S = S operand input
$\overline{R}$ and $\overline{S}$ are the complements of R and S operand inputs, respectively
CN = Carry in. C(N+4) = Carry out
MSS = Most Significant Slice

Table 8-6 also summarizes output signal levels associated with each ALU operation. Additional signal levels more closely associated with the ALU destination specification are given in Table 8-7.

Table 8-7. 2903 Destination and Shift Specifications for Simple ALU Operations

I8	I7	I6	I5	Hex Code	ALU Output Shift	ALU Output Result (= Y if $\overline{OE}_Y = 0$)	Q Register Shift	Q Register Load	Y3 MSS[1]	Y3 Other	Y2 MSS[1]	Y2 Other	Y0 All	SIO3 MSS[1]	SIO3 Other	SIO0 All	QIO3	QIO3	QIO0	WRITE
0	0	0	0	0	DA[2]	$(F/2)_A$	None	Q	F3	SIO3	SIO3	F3	F2	F1	—	—	F0	Hi-Z	Hi-Z	0
0	0	0	1	1	DL[3]	$(F/2)_L$	None	Q	SIO3	SIO3	F3	F3	F2	F1	—	—	F0	Hi-Z	Hi-Z	0
0	0	1	0	2	DA[2]	$(F/2)_A$	DL[3]	$(Q/2)_L$	F3	SIO3	SIO3	F3	F2	F1	—	—	F0	—	Q0	0
0	0	1	1	3	DL[3]	$(F/2)_L$	DL[3]	$(Q/2)_L$	SIO3	SIO3	F3	F3	F2	F1	—	—	F0	Hi-Z	Q0	0
0	1	0	0	4	None	F	None	Q	F3	F3	F2	F2	F1	F0	—	—	P	Hi-Z	Hi-Z	0
0	1	0	1	5	None	F	DL[3]	$(Q/2)_L$	F3	F3	F2	F2	F1	F0	—	—	P	—	Q0	1
0	1	1	0	6	None	F	None	F	F3	F3	F2	F2	F1	F0	—	—	P	Hi-Z	Hi-Z	1
0	1	1	1	7	None	F	None	F	F3	F3	F2	F2	F1	F0	—	—	P	Hi-Z	Hi-Z	0
1	0	0	0	8	UA[4]	$(2F)_A$	None	Q	F3	F3	F2	F1	F0	SIO0	F2	F3	—	Hi-Z	Hi-Z	0
1	0	0	1	9	UL[5]	$(2F)_L$	None	Q	F2	F2	F2	F1	F0	SIO0	F3	F3	—	Hi-Z	Hi-Z	0
1	0	1	0	A	UA[4]	$(2F)_A$	UL[5]	$(2Q)_L$	F3	F3	F2	F1	F0	SIO0	F2	F3	—	Q3	—	0
1	0	1	1	B	UL[5]	$(2F)_L$	UL[5]	$(2Q)_L$	F2	F2	F2	F1	F0	SIO0	F3	F3	—	Q3	—	0
1	1	0	0	C	None	F	None	Q	F3	F3	F2	F2	F1	F0	F3	F3	Hi-Z	Hi-Z	Hi-Z	1
1	1	0	1	D	None	F	UL[5]	$(2Q)_L$	F3	F3	F2	F2	F1	F0	F3	F3	Hi-Z	Q3	—	1
1	1	1	0	E	None	SIO0	None	Q	SIO0	SIO0	SIO0	SIO0	SIO0	SIO0	SIO0	SIO0	—	Hi-Z	Hi-Z	0
1	1	1	1	F	None	F	None	Q	F3	F3	F2	F2	F1	F0	F3	F3	Hi-Z	Hi-Z	Hi-Z	0

1) MSS = Most Significant Slice   I = Input pin
2) DA = Down Arithmetic   P = Parity of SIO3, F3, F2, F1, F0
3) DL = Down Logical   HI-Z = High impedance
4) UA = Up Arithmetic   F3, F2, F1 and F0 are the four ALU output bits. F3 is the high-order bit. F0 is the low-order bit.
5) UL = Up Logical

With regard to Table 8-6, note that the Carry Out signal, C(N+4), is active for arithmetic operations only.

$\overline{P}$/OVR generates an Overflow status (OVR) at the most significant slice, and a Carry propagate signal ($\overline{P}$) at other slices. Like the Carry Out, $\overline{P}$/OVR is active only for arithmetic operations. Unlike $\overline{P}$/OVR, $\overline{G}$/N is active for all ALU operations — arithmetic and logical. The most significant slice outputs the Sign status (N) which is, in fact, the level of the high-order ALU output bit. Other slices output the Carry generate signal ($\overline{G}$).

For a discussion of the Carry generate and propagate signals ($\overline{G}$ and $\overline{P}$) refer to the 2902 description.

The Zero status is active for all slices, during all simple ALU operations. The Zero status is output high when all four ALU output signals are low. The Zero status output is low otherwise.

Let us now examine 2903 destination options.

Table 8-7 summarizes destination and shift specifications implied by instruction code bits I5 through I8 for the simple ALU operations summarized in Table 8-6. In Table 8-7 **we show the ALU output and Q register operations, together with a detailed summary of associated signal levels.** The detailed signal summary is given since slice significance and shift specifications combined make signal levels less than self-evident. If you look at the signal outputs shown in the signal detail section of Table 8-7, and compare these signal outputs with the illustrations of arithmetic and logic shifts given below, then the table will be easy to understand.

| 2903 |
| DESTINATION |
| OPTIONS |

Note that signals SIO0, QIO0, and QIO3 are frequently in a high impedance state.

Selected destination specifications hold $\overline{\text{WRITE}}$ high. These specifications give you the option of not writing ALU output into local RAM — assuming that the $\overline{\text{WE}}$ inputs are connected to the least significant slice $\overline{\text{WRITE}}$ output.

Destination code E propagates the SIO0 input across all Y outputs. This code is used to extend the sign of a binary number, as we will describe later.

Destination codes 4, 5, 6, and 7 report parity of the ALU output at the SIO0 pin. Parity is reported for the 5-bit binary number given by SIO3, F3, F2, F1, and F0. Odd parity generates a high output at SIO0 while even parity generates a low output at SIO0.

Parity logic of the 2903 is cascadable across chip slices since the SIO0 parity output of each slice becomes the SIO3 input for the adjacent, less significant slice. **The SIO0 output from the least significant slice will always report the parity for the combined ALU output.** We will demonstrate this multislice parity logic for the simple case of 8-bit data generated using two 2903 slices. This may be illustrated as follows:

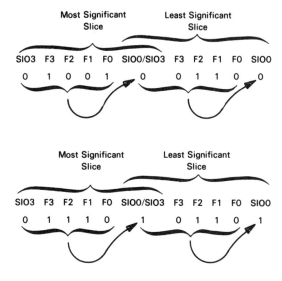

8-59

The ALU shifter, but not the Q shifter, gives you the option of specifying either an arithmetic or a logical shift. The Q shifter allows you to specify logical shifts only.

Logical shifts treat all bits in the same way. Thus, an 8-bit upshift may be illustrated as follows:

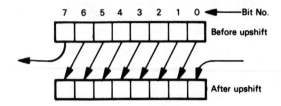

An 8-bit downshift may be illustrated as follows:

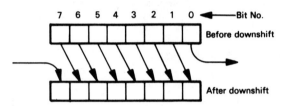

An arithmetic shift assumes that the high-order bit is a sign bit — which must be excluded from any shift. Thus an 8-bit arithmetic upshift may be illustrated as follows:

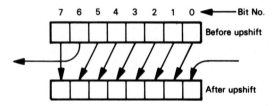

An 8-bit arithmetic downshift may be illustrated as follows:

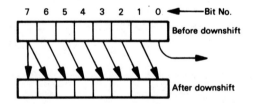

The 2903 can perform arithmetic shifts since you must identify the most significant, least significant, and intermediate 2903 slices in a multislice configuration. Thus, when you specify an arithmetic shift, logic internal to the most significant slice isolates the high-order bit from the shift, while intermediate and least significant slices perform simple logic shifts.

The 2903 ALU shifter is located on the ALU output, in front of the Y data input/output port. In contrast, the 2901 ALU shifter is located at the local RAM input. Also, the 2903 ALU shifter output can be enabled or disabled via the $\overline{OE}_Y$ control signal. Thus **you have a large number of microprogram-selectable options for handling ALU output,** over and above the destination options summarized in Table 8-7. ALU output may be transmitted to local RAM:

> 2903 ALU
> SHIFTER

> 2903 ALU
> OUTPUT
> DESTINATIONS

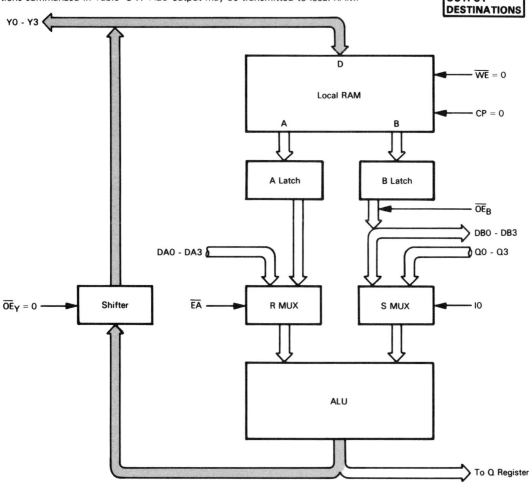

By holding $\overline{WE}$ high you can output data at the Y pins, but not write the output to local RAM:

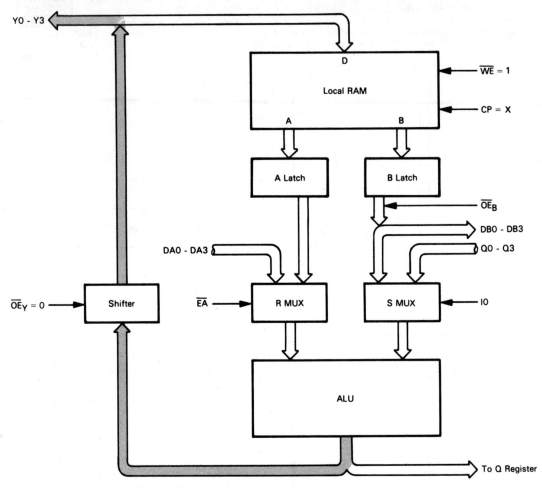

In either of the above cases the data may be shifted up or down, if so specified by instruction code bits I5-I8 (see Table 8-7).

You can also discard the ALU output and use the Y pins as the data input port to local RAM:

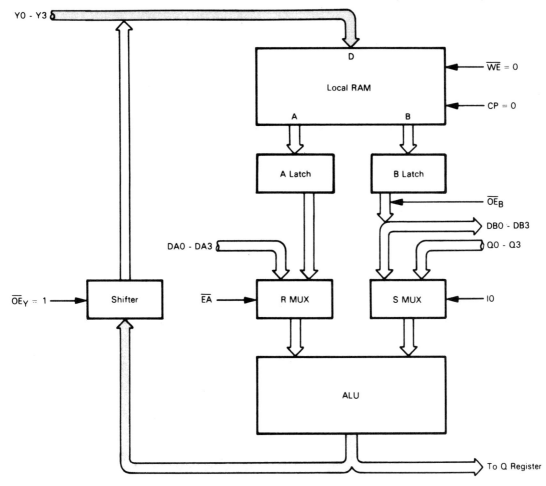

If $\overline{WE}$ and $\overline{OE}_Y$ are both high, ALU output to Y0-Y3 or local RAM is discarded.

You can use the last two ALU destination codes shown in Table 8-7 to extend a sign bit across one or more parallel 2903 devices within a single microcycle. Since the ALU destination code is used to generate sign extend logic, this operation can occur in conjunction with any compatible ALU operation specified by instruction code bits I4, I3, I2, and I1.

> **2903 SIGN EXTEND LOGIC**

ALU destination code F transmits the ALU output to the Y pins, and pulses $\overline{WRITE}$ low. Assuming that $\overline{OE}_Y$ and $\overline{WE}$ are both low, the ALU output will appear at the Y pins, and will be written into local RAM while CP is low.

ALU destination code E transmits the SI00 input across all four ALU output lines. Again, $\overline{WRITE}$ is pulsed low; if $\overline{OE}_Y$ and $\overline{WE}$ are both input low, then the SI00 level is output at all Y pins, and is written into local RAM while CP is low.

You can use this pair of ALU destination codes to extend a sign bit by applying the level of the sign bit to the SIO0 input of those 2903 slices that are to extend the sign. Consider a 16-bit Central Processing Unit where the sign for the low-order byte must be extended across the high-order byte. This may be illustrated conceptually as follows:

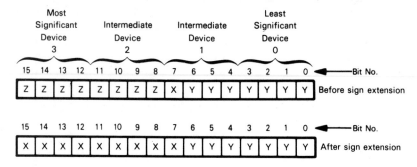

X = sign bit
Y = data bit
Z = irrelevant bit

A Central Processing Unit implemented using 2903 slices will automatically generate a sign extended ALU result for any arithmetic operation. **You use sign extend logic to create data, rather than modify results of any computation.** Suppose, for example, an 8-bit data input is received from an I/O port; if a 16-bit CPU is to interpret this data byte as a signed binary number, then the high-order bit must be propagated through the high-order byte of a 16-bit word as illustrated above.

This is easily done using the E and F ALU destination codes. **This is illustrated in Figure 8-19.**

Let us examine Figure 8-19. The two low-order 2903 slices are generating real data. These two slices therefore receive an F ALU destination code via I8-I5. This destination code causes the ALU output to appear at the Y pins, and the high-order ALU output bit to appear at SIO3. The two high-order 2903 slices generate the high-order byte across which the sign must be extended. These two 2903 slices therefore receive an E destination code via I8-I5. The E destination code causes the SIO0 input to be propagated across the ALU outputs.

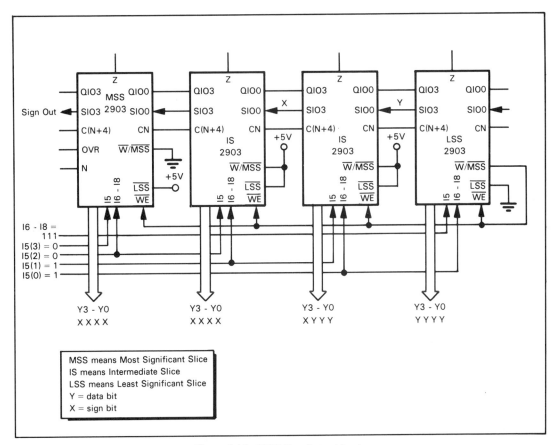

Figure 8-19. 2903 Sign Extend Logic

2903 SPECIAL FUNCTIONS

Let us now examine special 2903 functions. These functions are summarized in Table 8-8.

Special functions are implied by instruction codes bits I5 through I8 when instruction code bits I0 through I4 are all 0. **Nine special functions are provided; seven special function codes are unused. You should be sure not to use any of the unspecified special function codes** since the 2903 device's response to these unspecified function codes is not guaranteed.

Table 8-8 summarizes signal outputs and exact ALU operations associated with each of the special functions. Wherever a signal's primary purpose is meaningful, the signal is so used by a special function. Where a signal's primary purpose is not meaningful, the special function may generate an output to meet its specific needs.

Do not attempt to understand ALU operations or signal utilization merely by inspecting Table 8-8. Many of the ALU operations, although absolutely accurate representations of ALU logic, rely on specific external pin connections to generate the required net effect. Signals, likewise, are used in special ways that depend not only on the special function, but also on the required pin connections which have been arbitrarily selected by the 2903 designers.

ALU logic and signal utilization is described in detail function by function.

We will begin by examining the simpler 2903 special functions, since many of these simple special functions act as accessory commands to the more complex functions.

There are two normalization functions: a single length and a double length normalization. The double length normalization function is also the first twos complement divide instruction.

Table 8-8. 2903 Special Functions Summary

Instruction Code(1) I8 I7 I6 I5	ALU Operation	ALU Function	SIO3 MSS	SIO3 Other	SIO0	QIO3	QIO0	WRITE	CIN+4i	P̄/OVR MSS	P̄/OVR Other	Ḡ/N MSS	Ḡ/N Other	N MSS	N IS	N LSS
0 0 0 0	Unsigned multiply	$F = S + CN$ if $Z = L$ $F = R + S + CN$ if $Z = H$	Hi-Z	1	F0	1	Q0	0	CN+4i	OVR	P̄	N	Ḡ	1	1	Q0
0 0 0 1	Unused															
0 0 1 0	Twos complement multiply	$F = S + CN$ if $Z = L$ $F = R + S + CN$ if $Z = H$	Hi-Z	1	F0	1	Q0	0	CN+4i	OVR	P̄	N	Ḡ	1	1	Q0
0 0 1 1	Unused															
0 1 0 0	Increment	$F = S + 1 + CN$	–	–	P	Hi-Z	Hi-Z	0	CN+4i	OVR	P̄	N	iḠ	N	N	N
0 1 0 1	Sign/Magnitude twos complement	$F = S + CN$ if $Z = L$ $F = \overline{S} + CN$ if $Z = H$	–	–	P	Hi-Z	Hi-Z	0	CN+4	OVR	P̄	(2)	Ḡ	S3	–	–
0 1 1 0	Twos complement multiply, last cycle	$F = S + CN$ if $Z = L$ $F = S - R - 1 + CN$ if $Z = H$	Hi-Z	–	F0	–	Q0	0	CN+4i	OVR	P̄	N	Ḡ	–	–	Q0
0 1 1 1	Unused															
1 0 0 0	Single length normalize	$F = S + CN$	F3	F3	Hi-Z	Q3	–	0	(3)	Q2⊕Q1	P̄	Q3	Ḡ	(4)	(4)	(4)
1 0 0 1	Unused															
1 0 1 0	Double length normalize	$F = S + CN$	R3⊕F3	F3	–	Q3	–	0	(5)	F2⊕F1	P̄	N	Ḡ	(6)	(6)	(6)
1 0 1 1	Unused															
1 1 0 0	Twos complement divide	$F = S + R + CN$ if $Z = L$ $F = S - R - 1 + CN$ if $Z = H$	R3⊕F3	F3	Hi-Z	Q3	–	0	CN+4i	OVR	P̄	N	Ḡ	(7)	–	–
1 1 0 1	Unused															
1 1 1 0	Twos complement divide, final	$F = S + R + CN$ if $Z = L$ $F = S - R - 1 + CN$ if $Z = H$	F3	F3	Hi-Z	Q3	–	0	CN+4i	OVR	P̄	N	Ḡ	(7)	–	–
1 1 1 1	Unused															

Q0, Q1, Q2 and Q3 are the four Q register output bits.
F0, F1, F2 and F3 are the four ALU output bits.
R0, R1, R2 and R3 are the four R operand bits.
S0, S1, S2 and S3 are the four S operand bits.

Bit 3 is the high-order bit.
Bit 0 is the low-order bit.

1) I0 - I4 must all be 0.
2) N if Z = 0. S3 ⊕ F3 if Z = 1.
3) Q3 ⊕ Q2 at MSS. CIN+4i at other slices.
4) Zero status for Q register output.
5) F3 ⊕ F2 at MSS. CIN+4i at other slices.
6) Zero status for combined, 8-bit Q register and ALU outputs.
7) Sign compare output.

Hi-Z = Signal floated
I = Input signal
P = Parity of SIO3, Y3, Y2, Y1, Y0
MSS = Most Significant Slice
IS = Intermediate Slice
LSS = Least Significant Slice
Other = IS or LSS

The normalization operation upshifts the contents of a data word until the two high-order bits have different values. Zeros are shifted into low-order bit positions. Here are some normalization illustrations for 16-bit words:

2903
NORMALIZE
SPECIAL
FUNCTIONS

Initial	Normalized
0 0 0 0 0 0 1 0 1 1 0 0 0 1 1 1	0 1 0 1 1 0 0 0 1 1 1 0 0 0 0 0
1 1 1 0 1 0 1 1 0 1 0 0 0 1 0 1	1 0 1 0 1 1 0 1 0 0 0 1 0 1 0 0
0 1 1 0 1 0 1 1 0 1 0 1 1 0 1 0	0 1 1 0 1 0 1 1 0 1 0 1 1 0 1 0
0 0 0 0 0 0 0 0 0 0 0 0 0 0 0 0	Cannot be normalized
1 1 1 1 1 1 1 1 1 1 1 1 1 1 1 1	1 0 0 0 0 0 0 0 0 0 0 0 0 0 0 0

Each normalize instruction is executed in one microcycle. During this microcycle one upshift occurs if the two high-order bits of the most significant slice S ALU operand are both 0, or both 1. No operation occurs if the two high-order bits differ. In order to complete the normalization process for a multibit word that has many leading 0 or 1 bits, you must re-execute the normalize instruction the required number of times to shift out leading similar bits. If, for example, there are five leading 0 bits, followed by a 1 bit, you will have to execute a normalize instruction four times before the data is normalized. On the fifth execution of the normalize instruction the data will be left unaltered.

Your logic must identify the point at which data has been normalized; the normalize instruction outputs appropriate status signals to identify normalization — as we will describe shortly.

If binary data is being interpreted as a signed binary number, then a positive number, after normalization, will have a 0 in the high-order bit and a 1 in the adjacent bit:

01XXX----

After normalization a negative number will have a 1 in the high-order bit and a 0 in the adjacent bit.

10XXX----

The single length normalization instruction generates a data word out of the Q registers of parallel 2903 slices. Thus, you would generate an 8-bit data word out of two parallel slices as follows:

2903
SINGLE
LENGTH
NORMALIZATION

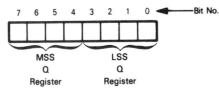

Four 2903 slices generate a 16-bit data word as follows:

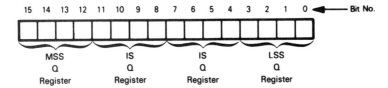

MSS means Most Significant Slice. IS means Intermediate Slice. LSS means Least Significant Slice.

The double length normalization instruction generates a data word out of the Q register and the local RAM location addressed by B. Two 2903 slices would generate a 16-bit word as follows:

2903
DOUBLE
LENGTH
NORMALIZATION

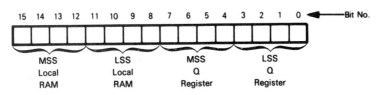

There are some differences between the single and double length normalization instructions resulting from the fact that the double length normalization instruction must use local RAM, and the ALU, while the single length normalization instruction needs Q register logic only. We will therefore look at the single length normalization instruction first.

The single length normalization instruction performs a number of upshifts until the most significant 2903 Q register has different values in its two high-order bits. Each upshift requires one microcycle, therefore the total execution time for the normalization instruction is variable. But the C(N+4) and OVR outputs are used to identify the last, and second to the last microcycles of the single length normalization instruction. On the second to the last cycle the OVR signal is output high; OVR therefore outputs the Exclusive-OR of Q2 and Q1 at the most significant slice. C(N+4), likewise, outputs the Exclusive-OR of Q3 and Q2 at the most significant 2903 slice. This may be illustrated as follows:

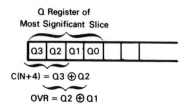

Thus C(N+4) goes high on the last microcycle of the single length normalization instruction, while OVR goes high on the previous microcycle.

You cannot normalize a data word that is initially all 0 bits. Since zeros are shifted into the low-order bit position with each upshift, the normalization operation would never end. The single length normalization instruction therefore outputs a high signal on the 0 status line and terminates in a single microcycle. For this to be possible the single length normalization instruction uses Z status logic to indicate Q register contents, rather than ALU output. That is to say, **Z is output high when all Q register bits are 0,** not when all ALU outputs are 0.

You will now understand the special information output via C(N+4), OVR, and Z signals, as shown in Table 22-8 for the single length normalization instruction.

During each microcycle of a single length normalization instruction the Q register contents are recycled through Q shifter logic. ALU logic, which would otherwise be unused, adds the contents of CN to the S operand input. This logic allows you to count the number of microcycles — and therefore upshifts — performed by the single length normalization instruction. Assuming that $\overline{WE}$, $\overline{OE_Y}$, $\overline{OE_B}$, and I0 are all low and CN is high, then the RAM location addressed by B becomes a microcycle counter. This RAM location becomes the ALU S operand, and the destination for the ALU output. The ALU output is simply the S operand input incremented by 1, assuming that CN is indeed high.

Single length normalization instruction pin connections are illustrated in Figure 8-20.

You can, if you wish, maintain a microcycle counter in external memory by inputting the ALU S operand from DB0-DB3 and outputting the ALU result at Y0-Y3. This requires that $\overline{WE}$ and $\overline{OE_B}$ be input high.

If you execute the single length normalization instruction with I0 high, then the Q register contents also become the ALU S input. Now on each microcycle the Q register contents, before they are upshifted, are output by the ALU to Y0-Y3, and/or local RAM, optionally incremented by 1 if CN is input high.

Let us now examine the double length normalization instruction. The RAM location addressed by B provides the high-order half of the word being normalized. QIO3 from the most significant 2903 slice must therefore be connected to SIO0 at the least significant 2903 slice. Also, **you cannot use ALU logic to count instruction microcycles since ALU logic contributes to the normalization operation. Therefore CN must be input low, and if you wish to count microcycles you must use external logic or an extra microcycle per cycle.**

> **2903 DOUBLE LENGTH NORMALIZATION**

The high-order half of the word being normalized can come from internal or external RAM. If it comes from internal RAM then the RAM location addressed by B must provide the S operand to the ALU, and must receive the ALU output.

But you can also use external RAM to provide the high-order half of the word being normalized; now DB0-DB3 generates the ALU S operand and the ALU output is transmitted to Y0-Y3. For this to occur $\overline{OE_B}$ and $\overline{WE}$ must both be high.

The C(N+4) and OVR statuses identify the last and second to the last microcycles of the double length normalization instruction's execution — just as they do for the single length normalization instruction. The double length normalization instruction also terminates in a single microcycle when you attempt to normalize a word which is initially 0. At this time the Z status is output high. For this to be possible double length normalization logic tests the combined contents of the Q register and ALU output in order to generate a Z status — as indicated in Table 8-8. **Double length normalization pin connections are illustrated in Figure 8-21.**

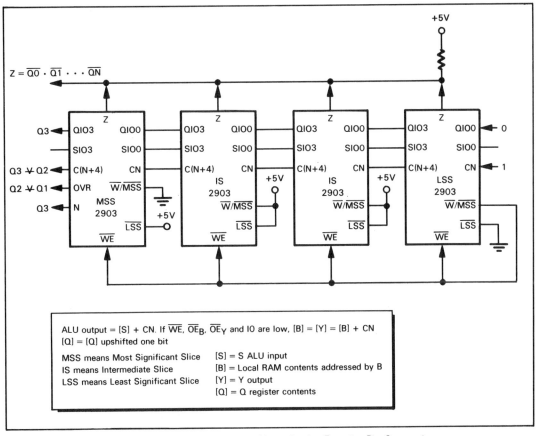

Figure 8-20. 2903 Single Length Normalization Function Pin Connections

Another simple 2903 special function is the Sign/Magnitude Twos Complement. This function converts negative twos complement numbers to this positive form, while leaving positive twos complement numbers alone. This may be illustrated as follows for 16-bit numbers:

<table>
<tr><td colspan="3">**2903 SIGN/ MAGNITUDE TWOS COMPLEMENT FUNCTION**</td></tr>
</table>

	After Sign/Magnitude	
Initial	Twos Complement	
0110010111010010	0110010111010010	Unchanged positive number
1110101111010101	0001010000101011	Twos complement of negative number

The 2903 uses slightly devious logic in order to implement the Sign/Magnitude Twos Complement function. This is the actual ALU algorithm executed:

$$\text{ALU output} = [S] + CN \text{ if Z status is 0}$$
$$\text{ALU output} = [\overline{S}] + CN \text{ if Z status is 1}$$

[S] means ALU S operand. $\overline{S}$ is the complement of the S operand.

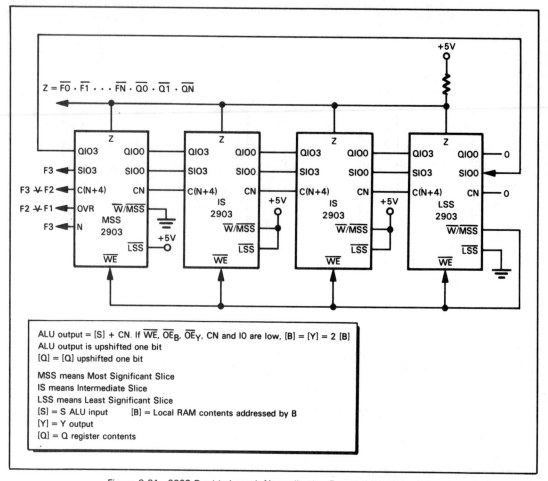

Figure 8-21. 2903 Double Length Normalization Function Pin Connections

During execution of the Sign/Magnitude Twos Complement instruction, the Zero status at the most significant 2903 slice directly outputs the high-order S operand bit — which is the sign bit for a twos complement number. The Zero status becomes an input to intermediate and least significant slices, which therefore receive the sign bit from the most significant slice. For a 16-bit number this may be illustrated as follows:

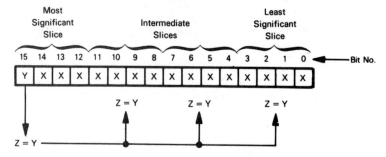

Now you can connect pins of 2903 slices in any way to make use of the Sign/Magnitude Twos Complement ALU logic, but to use it for its intended purpose, the connections illustrated in Figure 8-22 are required.

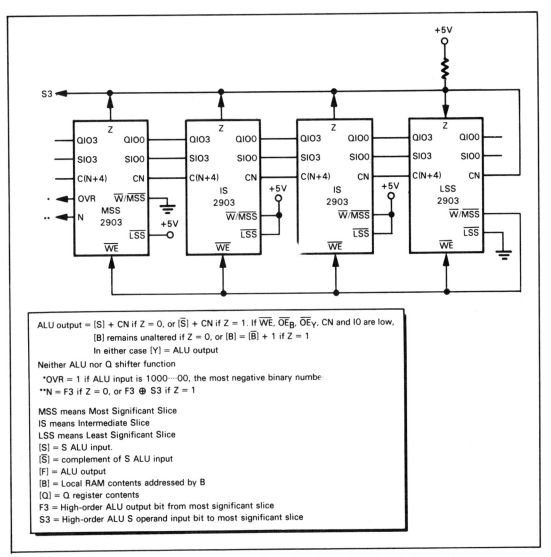

Figure 8-22. 2903 Sign/Magnitude Twos Complement Function Pin Connections

By connecting Z to CN positive, twos complement numbers are passed unaltered through the ALU:

$$[F] = [S] + CN \text{ if } Z = 0$$
$$CN = Z, \text{ therefore } [S] = [S] + 0$$

But a negative twos complement number is complemented and then incremented:

$$[F] = [\overline{S}] + CN \text{ if } Z = 1$$
$$CN = Z, \text{ therefore } [S] = [\overline{S}] + CN$$

In other words, a twos complement number is twos complemented — which generates a positive number. (If you are unclear on this twos complement logic refer to Volume 1, Chapter 2.)

The negative status, N, is output high at the most significant slice if a negative twos complement number was converted to its positive form. This is the actual logic used by the most significant 2903 slice:

If $Z = 0$, $N = F3$
$Z = 0$ when $S3 = 0$, in which case $[F] = [S]$
Therefore $N = F3 = S3 = 0$

If $Z = 1$, $N = F3 \oplus S3$
$Z = 1$ when $S3 = 1$, in which case $[F] = [\bar{S}] + 1$
Therefore $N = F3 \oplus S3 = \overline{S3} \oplus S3 = 1$

The Overflow status indicates the only overflow condition which can occur when a Sign/Magnitude Twos Complement conversion is performed. **There is no twos complement positive representation for the most negative twos complement number which can be represented:**

If $[S] = 1000\cdots0$
$[F] = 0111\cdots1 + 1, = 1000\cdots0$

If this most negative number is received at the S operand, it is passed through unaltered and the Overflow status from the most significant slice is output high.

The Sign/Magnitude Twos Complement instruction places no restrictions on where the S operand may come from. Any of the three options — external memory, local RAM, or the Q register — may provide the S operand to the ALU.

The third and last of the simple 2903 special functions is the Increment. This special function adds 1, plus the Carry In to the S operand. This algorithm may be illustrated as follows:

| 2903 |
| INCREMENT |
| FUNCTION |

$$[F] = [S] + 1 + CN$$

[F] is the ALU output, [S] is the ALU S operand input, and CN is the Carry In. If CN is 0, you increment by 1; if CN is 1, you increment by 2. This is useful in byte/word machines if the Program Counter is kept in local RAM.

Once again the S operand may come from external or local RAM or from the Q register.

The increment special function makes no special use of status logic.

| 2903 |
| UNSIGNED |
| MULTIPLY |

Let us now look at the unsigned multiply special function. The algorithm used by the 2903 to perform an unsigned multiply is exactly the same as the algorithm which we described earlier in this chapter, when showing how to program an unsigned multiply for the 2901. Initially the multiplier must be in the Q register and the multiplicand in the RAM location which provides the ALU R input. This may be external RAM connected to DA0-DA3, or local RAM addressed by A. The product will be generated in the RAM location that receives ALU output, and the Q register. The RAM location connected to ALU output may be external RAM connected to Y0-Y3, or local RAM addressed by B; it ultimately holds the upper half of the product. The Q register holds the lower half of the product. The RAM location that finally holds the upper half of the product must initially contain 0. Thus we can illustrate initial and final data locations as follows:

Multiplicand Multiplier (0)

Initial: | R | | S | Q |

Product
upper lower
Multiplicand

Final: | R | | S | Q |

The 2903 unsigned multiply operation will multiply two 16-bit numbers to generate a 32-bit product. If you wish to multiply larger numbers you must do so in 16-bit increments and add partial products using additional microcycles.

If we compare the register utilization illustrated above with the unsigned multiply description given for the 2901, the local RAM location addressed by B in the illustration above becomes the window into which the multiplicand is added whenever a 1 bit is shifted out of the multiplier; but 2903 logic tests this bit internally, outputting the least significant Q register bit from the least significant 2903 slice via the Z status. The Z status becomes an input to the most significant and intermediate slices, so that these 2903 devices can also tell whether the multiplicand is to be added into the product window. Thus the unsigned multiply consists of 16 microcycles. In each microcycle the low-order bit of the Q register in the least significant slice is tested. If this bit is 1, the multiplicand is added to the partial product. If this bit is 0, no addition is performed. Addition, if it occurs, consists of adding the ALU R and S inputs, which probably means adding the contents of the RAM location addressed by A to the contents of the RAM location addressed by B. If A and B are the R and S ALU inputs, respectively, with the sum returned to the RAM location addressed by B, then $\overline{WE}$, $\overline{OE_B}$, $\overline{OE_Y}$, $\overline{EA}$, and I0 must all be 0.

After the low-order bit of the Q register in the least significant slice has been tested, and a conditional addition has been performed, the product space (local RAM addressed by B, and the Q register) is downshifted one bit position during the same microcycle. The Carry status following the addition is shifted into the high-order bit of the ALU output for the most significant slice. If no addition is performed, then the Carry will equal 0, and 0 will be shifted into the high-order ALU output bit of the most significant 2903 slice. This may be illustrated as follows:

Most Significant Slice

A single microinstruction performs the actual unsigned multiplication; however, preceding instructions must load the multiplier and multiplicand into their appropriate registers, and must zero the RAM location to be used for the running partial product.

Necessary pin connections in a 2903 configuration that uses the unsigned multiply function are illustrated in Figure 8-23.

The use of status by the unsigned multiply function is straightforward — with the exception of **the Zero status** which **propagates the current low-order multiplier bit to all 2903 slices** as we have already described. **The Carry In, CN, must be 0.** If it is 1 you get the wrong answer when the multiplicand is added to the product window. **The Carry Out, C(N+4), the Overflow, and the Sign status are all output by the most significant 2903 slice to reflect the result of each partial product addition.** However, these statuses are useless and should be ignored.

The 2903 will also perform twos complement multiplication on two 16-bit signed binary numbers to generate a 32-bit signed binary result. The algorithm for performing twos complement multiplication is essentially the same as the unsigned multiplication algorithm which we have already described; the same registers are used to hold the multiplier, the multiplicand, and results.

2903 TWOS COMPLEMENT MULTIPLY FUNCTION

There are two differences between signed and unsigned multiplication; they are:

1) We must account for the sign bit of the multiplier, which is not a magnitude bit.

2) Slightly different logic is needed to generate the bit which is shifted into the high-order ALU output from the most significant 2903 slice following each downshift.

The logic of twos complement multiplication using signed binary arithmetic is readily deducible from the unsigned multiplication algorithm which we described for the 2901, together with the discussion of signed binary arithmetic given in Chapters 2 and 3 of Volume 1. Moreover, you the user cannot modify twos complement multiply logic in any way; therefore a detailed understanding of the algorithm is of academic interest only. **The algorithms for signed and unsigned binary multiplication remain the same until the last microcycle** — at which time the sign bit of the multiplier is in the low-order bit of the product space. This may be illustrated as follows:

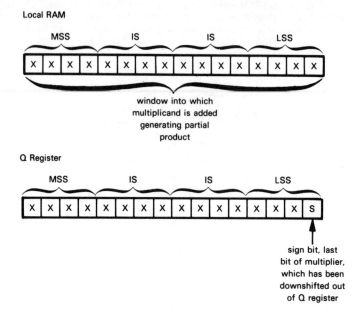

If the sign bit is 0, then the multiplier is positive and the multiplicand need not be added again to the partial product; following the next downshift the multiplication is complete. But if the sign bit is 1, then on the last microcycle the multiplicand must be subtracted from the partial product before the final downshift.

When the Twos Complement Multiply function is executed, **following each downshift, the Exclusive-OR of the Overflow and Sign statuses is moved into the high-order bit position of the most significant 2903 slice.** This ensures that a 1 is shifted into the high-order bit position if addition generated a Carry, or if a negative result must have its sign extended.

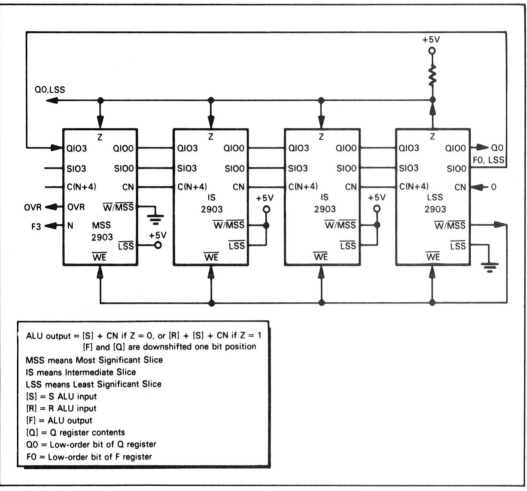

ALU output = [S] + CN if Z = 0, or [R] + [S] + CN if Z = 1
[F] and [Q] are downshifted one bit position
MSS means Most Significant Slice
IS means Intermediate Slice
LSS means Least Significant Slice
[S] = S ALU input
[R] = R ALU input
[F] = ALU output
[Q] = Q register contents
Q0 = Low-order bit of Q register
F0 = Low-order bit of F register

Figure 8-23. 2903 Unsigned Binary Multiply Function Pin Connections

Figure 8-24 illustrates pin connections needed to execute Twos Complement Multiply and Twos Complement Multiply Last Cycle special functions.

The only non-obvious aspect of Figure 8-24 is the generation of the Carry In (CN) to the least significant 2903 slice. This Carry In must be 0 until the last microcycle, at which time it must receive the Zero status. We therefore show the Twos Complement Multiply Last Cycle instruction code uniquely generating an ENABLE signal which conditions an AND gate that generates the CN input. The AND gate passes through the Zero status during the Twos Complement Multiply Last Cycle instruction's execution, but at other times the AND gate does not pass the Zero status, generating a 0 CN input. This function is provided in the 2904 logic.

You must execute twos complement multiply instructions in the proper sequence in order to perform twos complement multiplication using 2903 devices. You execute the Twos Complement Multiply special function fifteen times, then you execute the Twos Complement Multiply Last Cycle special function.

The two microinstructions which perform the twos complement multiply and the last cycle of the twos complement multiply must of course be preceded by microinstructions that correctly load registers and zero the memory word being used for the high-order half of the product.

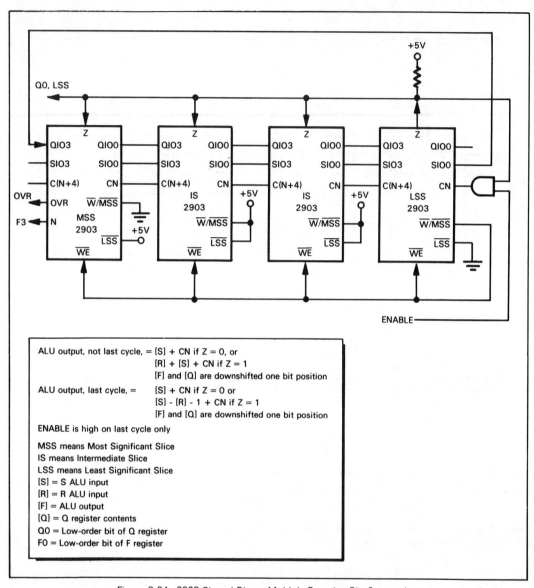

ALU output, not last cycle, = [S] + CN if Z = 0, or
[R] + [S] + CN if Z = 1
[F] and [Q] are downshifted one bit position

ALU output, last cycle, = [S] + CN if Z = 0 or
[S] - [R] - 1 + CN if Z = 1
[F] and [Q] are downshifted one bit position

ENABLE is high on last cycle only

MSS means Most Significant Slice
IS means Intermediate Slice
LSS means Least Significant Slice
[S] = S ALU input
[R] = R ALU input
[F] = ALU output
[Q] = Q register contents
Q0 = Low-order bit of Q register
F0 = Low-order bit of F register

Figure 8-24. 2903 Signed Binary Multiply Function Pin Connections

We will now examine the 2903 Twos Complement divide special function.

2903 TWOS COMPLEMENT DIVIDE FUNCTION

You divide a divisor into a dividend. The answer is called a quotient, and there will be a remainder. This may be illustrated as follows:

$$\text{Divisor } \overline{)\text{Dividend}} \quad \text{Quotient} \quad r = \text{Remainder}$$

Conceptually the algorithm for performing binary division is very straightforward. As for decimal division, you begin at the most significant end of the dividend:

$$1\ 0\ 1 \ldots 1\ 1 \overline{)1\ 0\ 0 \cdots 1\ 1\ 0\ 1 \cdots}$$
$$1\ 1\ 0 \cdots 1\ 1$$

But when you perform binary division the problem reduces to comparing the magnitude of the divisor and the current dividend field:

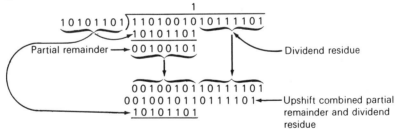

When performing a twos complement divide we begin by subtracting the divisor from the high-order end of the dividend:

$$1$$
$$1\ 0\ 1\ 0\ 1\ 1\ 0\ 1 \overline{)1\ 1\ 0\ 1\ 0\ 0\ 1\ 0\ 1\ 0\ 1\ 1\ 1\ 1\ 0\ 1}$$
$$1\ 0\ 1\ 0\ 1\ 1\ 0\ 1$$
$$0\ 0\ 1\ 0\ 0\ 1\ 0\ 1 \longleftarrow \text{Partial remainder}$$

Dividend most significant field

If the divisor is the smaller number, as it is in the illustration above, then the partial remainder is positive; we add the next dividend bit and subtract again:

$$1$$
$$1\ 0\ 1\ 0\ 1\ 1\ 0\ 1 \overline{)1\ 1\ 0\ 1\ 0\ 0\ 1\ 0\ 1\ 0\ 1\ 1\ 1\ 1\ 0\ 1}$$
$$1\ 0\ 1\ 0\ 1\ 1\ 0\ 1$$
$$0\ 0\ 1\ 0\ 0\ 1\ 0\ 1\ 1$$
$$1\ 0\ 1\ 0\ 1\ 1\ 0\ 1$$

This is equivalent to upshifting the combined partial remainder and dividend residue one bit position, and then subtracting the divisor again:

$$1$$
$$1\ 0\ 1\ 0\ 1\ 1\ 0\ 1 \overline{)1\ 1\ 0\ 1\ 0\ 0\ 1\ 0\ 1\ 0\ 1\ 1\ 1\ 1\ 0\ 1}$$
$$1\ 0\ 1\ 0\ 1\ 1\ 0\ 1$$

Partial remainder → $0\ 0\ 1\ 0\ 0\ 1\ 0\ 1$ ————— Dividend residue

$$0\ 0\ 1\ 0\ 0\ 1\ 0\ 1\ 1\ 0\ 1\ 1\ 1\ 1\ 0\ 1$$
$$0\ 0\ 1\ 0\ 0\ 1\ 0\ 1\ 1\ 0\ 1\ 1\ 1\ 1\ 0\ 1 \longleftarrow \text{Upshift combined partial}$$
$$1\ 0\ 1\ 0\ 1\ 1\ 0\ 1 \qquad\qquad \text{remainder and dividend}$$
$$\text{residue}$$

But what happens if you get a negative result after subtracting the divisor from the current dividend field? The answer is that you must add the divisor back to the partial remainder before upshifting the dividend one bit position; and then subtract the divisor again. But in binary logic this is what happens:

(Partial remainder + Divisor) x 2 - Divisor

this is the equivalent of an upshift

The sequence of operations is equivalent to:

Partial remainder x 2 - Divisor

Therefore when you subtract the divisor and get a negative result, you simply upshift the concatenated Partial remainder and Dividend residue fields one bit position, then subtract the divisor on the next step.

This is, in essence, the algorithm used by the 2903 to perform binary division, and is called "non-restoring" division. It is based on the Twos Complement Divide special function, which performs the following net operations:

$$[F] = [S] + [R] \quad \text{if } Z = 0$$
$$[F] = [S] - [R] \quad \text{if } Z = 1$$

[F], [S], and [R] are the ALU output, S operand and R operand, respectively.

The Zero status is generated by sign compare logic as the complement of the Exclusive-OR of most significant slice high-order ALU output and R operand input bits:

$$Z = \overline{R3 \oplus F3}$$

Additional required conditions are that $\overline{IEN}$ be low and one of the Twos Complement Divide special functions be executed.

The sign compare level is output at the most significant 2903 Zero status and it is input to the Zero status of intermediate and least significant 2903 slices. In effect, the sign compare logic compares the sign of the partial remainder with the sign of the divisor. This generates the following logic sequence:

1) If [F] and [R] signs are the same, the divisor had a smaller absolute magnitude than the dividend field from which it was subtracted. Z is therefore 0, so on the next microcycle we get:

$$[F] = [S] + [R]$$

2) If [F] and [R] signs differ, the divisor had a larger absolute magnitude than the dividend field from which it was subtracted. Z is therefore 1, so on the next microcycle we get:

$$[F] = [S] - [R]$$

The quotient bits are also determined by comparing the sign of the partial remainder with the sign of the divisor. If the signs differ, the current quotient digit is 0 because the divisor has the larger absolute value; but if the signs are the same, the current quotient digit is 1 because the divisor has the smaller absolute value.

Let us now look at the exact 2903 implementation of the binary division. The two steps defined above do not take into account the first step — at which time we have no partial remainder, or ALU output. **2903 division logic** therefore **demands that the absolute magnitude of the divisor be greater than the absolute magnitude of the most significant half of the dividend. To ensure that the divisor does indeed have larger absolute magnitude, the algorithm illustrated in Figure 8-25 is recommended in Advanced Micro Devices' literature.** We will describe this logic, even though other logic could achieve the same desired result.

In order to compare the absolute magnitude of divisor and dividend, we need to work only with the most significant half of the dividend. Comparison instructions destroy the data, therefore we begin by moving the divisor and the most significant half of the dividend to temporary buffers — in all probability additional locations in local RAM.

When moving the divisor to an alternate RAM location we can test the Zero status to see if the divisor is 0. If it is, the division must be aborted.

Next we use the Sign/Magnitude Twos Complement special function (which we have already described) to generate positive magnitudes for the copies of the divisor, and the most significant half of the dividend; now we can compare these magnitudes without bothering about sign.

The Sign/Magnitude Twos Complement function, when executed, generates a positive Overflow status if the data input is the most negative binary number allowed — in our case -2^{16}. We take advantage of this Overflow status when operating on the most significant half of the dividend. If the most significant half of the dividend is -2^{16}, then the divisor cannot possibly be larger, so we downshift the entire dividend one bit position and restart. We also check the

Overflow status when performing the Sign/Magnitude Twos Complement operation on the divisor. If the divisor is -2^{16}, then it must be larger than the dividend, which is not -2^{16}, since the dividend test was made first. We therefore go straight to the division operation.

If neither the divisor nor the most significant half of the dividend is -2^{16}, we upshift both numbers one bit position to remove the sign bit, then subtract the most significant half of the dividend from the divisor. If the dividend is larger, it must be downshifted one bit position — and the test repeated. When the divisor is larger, we are ready to start the division.

If you scale the divisor or the dividend, then the quotient must be scaled in compensation. Divisor, dividend and quotient scaling logic is entirely your responsibility.

Combining the data preparation and division programs, **the sequence of 2903 special functions shown in Table 8-9 is recommended in vendor literature to perform binary division.** Table 8-9 shows a 16-bit divisor divided into a 32-bit dividend to generate a 16-bit quotient and a 16-bit remainder.

The instruction sequence preceding the actual division instructions implement Figure 8-26 logic. These instructions need no special discussion. But **we do need to clarify the manner in which status signals output by the 2903 are handled.** The 2903 outputs status and data at the same time. For timing details refer to the 2903 microcycle description given earlier in this chapter. Some 2903 functions require status output by one 2903 slice to be input to other 2903 slices within the same microcycles; for an example of this look at the way Z is used by the Twos Complement Divide special function. Status is output early enough in the microcycle for an output to become an input to another 2903 slice within the same microcycle. But external logic will not have time to process any 2903 status outputs in the process of generating 2903 inputs for the same microcycle. Status output in one microcycle must be processed by external logic during the next microcycle. In Table 8-9 the comments associated with each microinstruction identify relevant status, if any, which is generated during the microinstruction's execution. Comments make clear the fact that the generated status must be tested during the next microcycle's execution time. Status output by the 2903 is usually tested by microprogram address generation logic. Later in this chapter, when we describe microprogram address generation devices, the consequences of testing status while executing the next microinstruction will become self-evident.

The three divide instructions use 2903 local RAM and Q registers as follows:

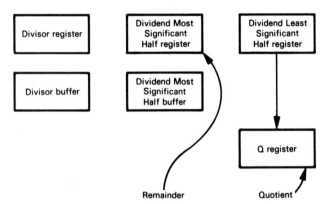

The divisor and dividend require initial memory locations identified as registers in the illustration above. The divisor and the most significant half of the dividend also require temporary buffers. The contents of these buffers are destroyed in the process of comparing the divisor and dividend magnitudes.

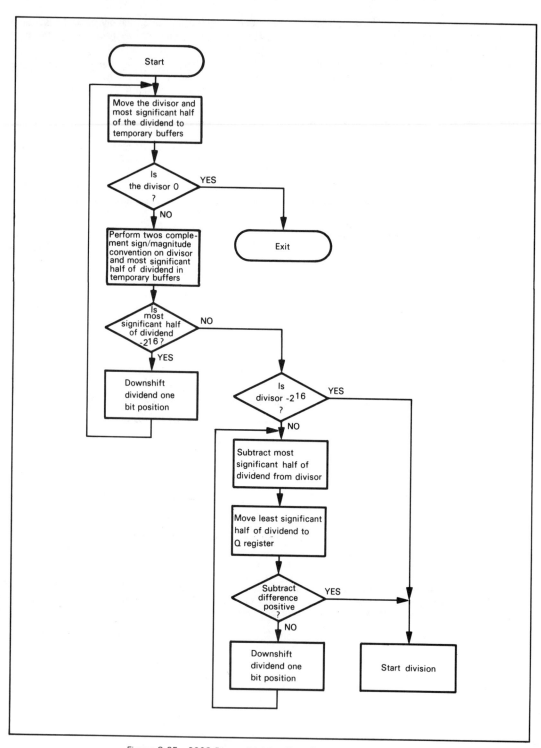

Figure 8-25. 2903 Binary Division Data Preparation Algorithm

8-80

Table 8-9. A Possible 2903 Twos Complement Binary Division Microprogram

No	Microinstruction			$\overline{EA}$	CN	A0 - A3	B0 - B3	Comment
	I8 - I5	I4 - I1	I0					
1	4	6	0	0	0	Divisor register (R0)	Divisor buffer (R3)	Copy divisor to temporary buffer.
2	4	6	0	0	0	Dividend (MS) register (R1)	Dividend (MS) buffer (R2)	Copy dividend most significant half to temporary buffer.
3	5	0	0	X	.0	X	Dividend (MS) buffer (R2)	Convert dividend (MS) from twos complement to sign/magnitude version. Test OVR externally while next microinstruction is being executed. If OVR is 1, branch to subroutine that downshifts dividend.
4	5	0	0	X	0	X	Divisor buffer (R3)	Convert divisor (MS) from twos complement to sign/magnitude version. Test OVR externally. If OVR is 1, branch to microinstruction 9.
5	9	4	0	X	0	X	Dividend (MS) buffer (R2)	Shift out sign bit of dividend (MS) half in temporary buffer.
6	9	4	0	X	0	X	Divisor buffer (R3)	Shift out sign bit of divisor in temporary buffer.
7	F	2	0	0	1	Dividend (MS) buffer (R2)	Divisor buffer (R3)	Subtract sign bit stripped divisor from sign bit stripped dividend (MS) half. If Carry = 1 (dividend larger) branch to subroutine that downshifts dividend or upshifts divisor.
8	6	6	0	0	0	Dividend (LS) register (R4)	X	Copy dividend least significant half to Q register.
9	A*	0	0	0	0	Divisor register (R0)	Dividend (MS) register (R1)	Double length normalize dividend in MS register and Q register.
10	C*	0	0	0	Z	Divisor register (R0)	Dividend (MS) register (R1)	Execute twos complement divide instruction fourteen times.
11	E	0	0	0	Z	Divisor register (R0)	Dividend (MS) register (R1)	Twos complement divide final instruction.

*CN is connected to Z status while these two special functions are being executed.

Before the actual division begins, the least significant half of the dividend is moved to the Q register. The quotient is ultimately returned in the Q register and the remainder in the Dividend Most Significant Half register. Taking a simple case, if local RAM is used to implement Divisor and Dividend registers and buffers, then we can illustrate local RAM and Q registers utilization as follows:

Initial:

R0 - Divisor

R1 - Dividend, most significant half

R2 - Copy of R1, dividend most significant half

R3 - Copy of divisor

R4 - Dividend, least significant half

Q - Dividend, least significant half

Final:

R1 - Remainder

Q - Quotient

The Q register, which initially holds the least significant half of the dividend, ultimately holds the quotient. As the dividend is upshifted out of the Q register and into the Dividend Most Significant Half register, quotient bits get shifted into the Q register via Q0.

If you look again at Table 8-9, you will see that the actual division operation executes three functions:

1) The Double Length Normalize function, which serves as the first divide function.
2) The Twos Complement Divide function; this function is executed N-2 times, where N is the number of divisor and quotient bits.
3) A final Twos Complement Divide Correction function completes the division.

Necessary pin connections for the Double Length Normalize function are given in Figure 8-21. Figure 8-26 shows necessary pin connections for the Twos Complement Divide and Twos Complement Divide Correction functions.

Zero status logic is used to transmit sign compare information from the most significant 2903 slice to intermediate and least significant slices. The level transmitted is the complement of the Exclusive-OR of the most significant bits of the ALU output and R operand input. This may be illustrated as follows:

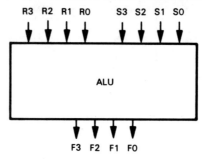

$$Z = \overline{R3 \oplus F3}$$

This Z status logic works only when an A or C special function code is input via I8-I5, and $\overline{IEN}$ is simultaneously low. The Z status also becomes the CN input to the least significant slice in order to neutralize CN within the ALU functions performed. This may be illustrated as follows:

$$[F] = [S] + [R] + CN \text{ if } Z = 0$$
$$\text{so } [F] = [S] + [R] \text{ if } CN = Z$$
$$[F] = [S] - [R] - 1 + CN \text{ if } Z = 1$$
$$\text{so } [F] = [S] - [R] \text{ if } CN = Z$$

The Q register and ALU register are connected so that an upshift causes the high-order bit of the Q register to be input to the low-order ALU bit. The high-order ALU bit is lost, and the next quotient digit is shifted into the least significant bit of the Q register. This may be illustrated as follows:

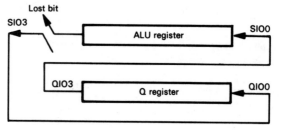

The level actually output at SIO3 is also $\overline{R3 \oplus F3}$. This becomes the next bit shifted into the quotient.

The final Twos Complement Divide Correction function forces a 1 into the low-order quotient bit, leaving the remainder adjusted accordingly.

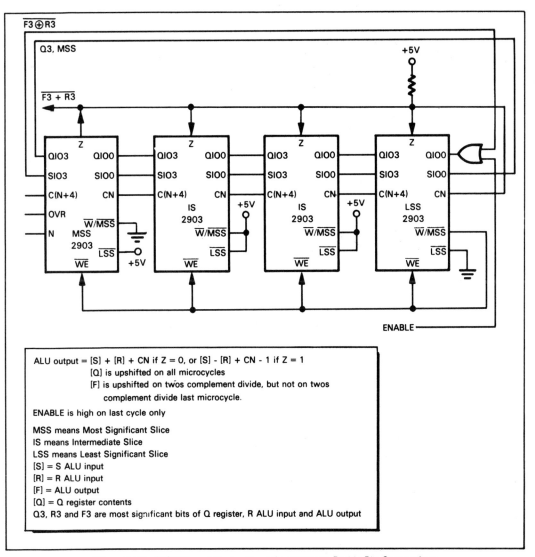

Figure 8-26. 2903 Signed Binary Twos Complement Divide Pin Connections

Merely understanding the pin connections and functions shown in Figure 8-25 is quite straightforward. Understanding how binary division is performed using these pin connections, and the three binary division functions, is not self-evident. Let us therefore take a very simple example and analyze divide logic in conjunction with this example. **Consider the following simple division:**

$$\frac{24_{10}}{7_{10}} = \frac{18_{16}}{7_{16}} = 3 \text{ remainder } 3$$

We have a 4-bit divisor and an 8-bit dividend which generate a 4-bit quotient and a 4-bit remainder. We must therefore execute the Double Length Normalize function, followed by two Twos Complement Divide functions, and a Twos Complement Divide Correction function.

For **Step 1** we execute the Double Length Normalize function. This upshifts the dividend and generates the sign of the quotient at SIO3 of the most significant slice. The quotient sign bit gets shifted into the low-order Q register bit. Logic may be illustrated as follows:

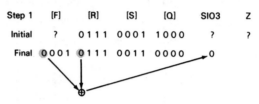

SIO3 is the Exclusive-OR of the most significant slice ALU output and R operand input bits. This may be illustrated as follows:

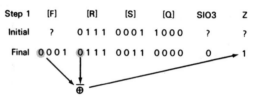

This SIO3 logic says that when the divisor and the dividend have the same sign, the quotient is positive; the quotient is negative when the divisor and the dividend have opposite signs. What is not self-evident is the fact that we have multiplied the dividend by two before starting to work with the divisor. In consequence, we must finally upshift the quotient and the remainder to generate answers that stand numerical comparison.

Moving on to **Step 2**, we execute the Twos Complement Divide function for the first time. The Zero status is 1:

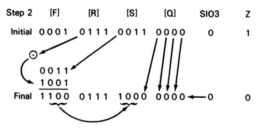

Therefore, we subtract the divisor from the high-order four dividend bits. This may be illustrated as follows:

Step 2	[F]	[R]	[S]	[Q]	SIO3	Z
Initial	0 0 0 1	0 1 1 1	0 0 1 1	0 0 0 0	0	1
		0 0 1 1				
		1 0 0 1				
Final	1 1 0 0	0 1 1 1	1 0 0 0	0 0 0 0 ◄— 0		0

This step is very logical. It is equivalent to initially subtracting the divisor from the dividend in any decimal division:

$$25\overline{)237642} \ldots$$
$$\underline{25}$$
$$-2$$

In our binary example the divisor is larger than the dividend, even though the dividend has been upshifted; therefore the next quotient bit shifted into the Q register is 0. 0 is indeed output by the most significant slice at SIO3:

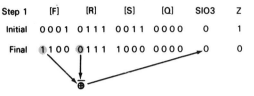

In **Step 3** the Twos Complement Divide function is executed a second time. The Zero status is now 0:

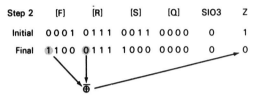

Therefore, during Step 3 we add the divisor to the high-order four bits of the shifted dividend. This addition, and the subsequent upshift, may be illustrated as follows:

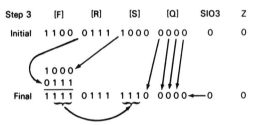

Adding the divisor to the upshifted dividend is also self-evident. We got a negative answer during Step 2, therefore (as described earlier) we must now compensate by adding the divisor to the upshifted dividend. The dividend is still smaller than the divisor, so once again SIO3 outputs 0 at the most significant 2903 slice:

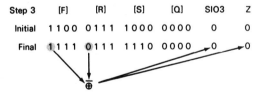

and zero gets shifted into the Q register to become the next quotient bit.

Finally, in **Step 4** we execute a Twos Complement Divide Correction function. Once again we test the Z status, which is 0, therefore we add the divisor to the high-order four bits of the upshifted dividend. Together with the final shift this may be illustrated as follows:

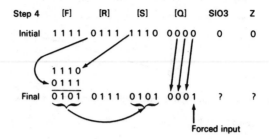

During the final shift a 1 is forced into the quotient to become the quotient low-order bit. The four high-order dividend bits do not change. Thus our final answer is:

$$\text{Quotient} = 0001$$
$$\text{Remainder} = 0101$$

In order to test the numeric accuracy of our answer we must upshift one bit position:

$$\text{Quotient} = 0010$$
$$\text{Remainder} = 1010$$

Thus, the answer is 2 with a remainder of A_{16} — which is not 3 with a remainder of 3, but it is correct.

Your external logic (2904) must upshift the quotient and the remainder, if your algorithm demands it, and must adjust the quotient and the remainder if your algorithm requires the remainder to be less than the divisor.

THE 2902 CARRY LOOK-AHEAD DEVICE

This device serves just one function: when performing binary addition or subtraction using cascaded 2901 or 2903 systems, it creates parallel carry inputs for 4-bit slices beyond the least significant slice. Carry Look-Ahead logic has been described in detail in Volume 1, Chapter 4. We will therefore provide a simple summary of the 2902 device in this chapter, stating its logic functions, but omitting Carry Look-Ahead theory.

The 2902 is packaged as a 16-pin DIP. All signals are TTL-level compatible and a single +5V power supply is required. The 2902A is a faster version of the 2902.

2902 PINS AND SIGNALS

Figure 8-27 illustrates pins and signal assignments for the 2902 Carry Look-Ahead device. Figure 22-28 shows a 2902 device connected to four parallel 2901 devices. If you replace the 2901 devices with 2903 devices, connections between the 2902 and the 2901 or 2903 devices do not change.

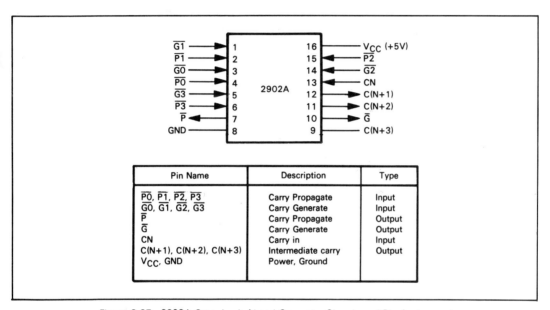

Figure 8-27. 2902A Carry Look-Ahead Generator Signals and Pin Assignments

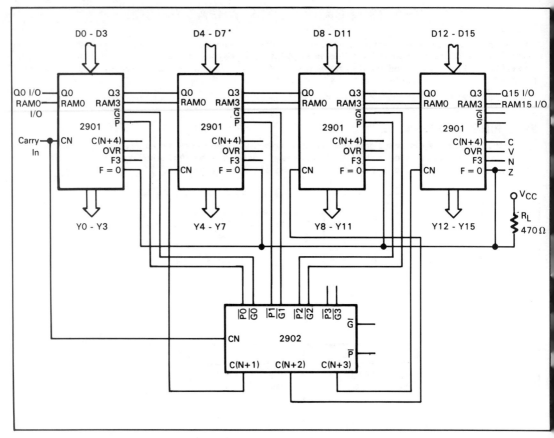

Figure 8-28. Four 2901s in a 16-Bit CPU Using the 2902 for Carry Look-Ahead

$\overline{G0}$, $\overline{G1}$, $\overline{G2}$, and $\overline{G3}$ are Carry Generate inputs received from 2901 or 2903 slices. $\overline{G0}$ is the least significant slice and $\overline{G3}$ is the most significant slice. **These $\overline{G}$ inputs are generated by 2901 and 2903 devices as shown in Table 8-10.**

$\overline{P0}$, $\overline{P1}$, $\overline{P2}$, and $\overline{P3}$ are Carry Propagate signals received from four 2901 or 2903 slices. These signals are generated as shown in Table 8-10.

In a 2901 or 2903 configuration with four slices, $\overline{G3}$ and $\overline{P3}$ are unused, as illustrated in Figure 8-28. This is logical; there are no higher-order devices to receive Carry Look-Aheads, therefore generate and propagate outputs from the most significant 2901 or 2903 slice are not meaningful. In fact, the most significant 2903 slice does not output a Carry Generate or Propagate signal.

If you have fewer than four 2901 or 2903 slices in a configuration, then you leave unconnected the high-order 2902 $\overline{G}$ and $\overline{P}$ inputs. For example, an 8-bit Central Processing Unit configured with two 2901 slices would receive $\overline{P0}$ and $\overline{G0}$ inputs from the least significant slice, and that is all. $\overline{P1}$ and $\overline{G1}$ inputs would not be received from the most significant slice since the most significant slice $\overline{P}$ and $\overline{G}$ outputs are always meaningless.

C(N+1), C(N+2), and C(N+3) are the three Carry levels output by the 2902 device. These signals should be connected to the CN inputs of the 2901 or 2903 slices as illustrated in Figure 8-29.

Table 8-10. P and G Generation Logic for 2901 and 2903 Devices

I_{543}	Function	$\overline{P}$	$\overline{G}$	$C(N+4)$	OVR
0	R + S	$\overline{P_3P_2P_1P_0}$	$\overline{G_3 + P_3G_2 + P_3P_2G_1}$ $\overline{+ P_3P_2P_1G_0}$	C4	C3 $\oplus$ C4
1	S - R		Same as R + S equations, but substitute $\overline{R_i}$ for R_i definitions in definitions		
2	R - S		Same as R + S equations, but substitute $\overline{S_i}$ for S_i in definitions		
3	R V S	Low	$P_3P_2P_1P_0$	$\overline{P_3P_2P_1P_0}$ + CN	$\overline{P_3P_2P_1P_0}$ + $\overline{CN}$
4	R $\wedge$ S	Low	$\overline{G_3 + G_2 + G_1 + G_0}$	$G_3 + G_2 + G_1 + G_0$ + CN	$G_3 + G_2 + G_1 + G_0$ + CN
5	$\overline{R} \wedge S$	Low		Same as R + S equations, but substitute $\overline{R_i}$ for R_i in definitions	
6	R $\oplus$ S		Same as $\overline{R \oplus S}$, but substitute $\overline{R_i}$ for R_i in definitions		
7	$\overline{R \oplus S}$	$G_3 + G_2 + G_1 + G_0$	$G_3 + P_3G_2 + P_3P_2G_1$ $+ P_3P_2P_1G_0$	$\overline{G_3 + P_3G_2 + P_3P_2G_1}$ $\overline{+ P_3P_2P_1P_0 (G_0 + \overline{CN})}$	See note

Note: $[\overline{P_2} + \overline{G_2}\overline{P_1} + \overline{G_2}\overline{G_1}\overline{P_0} + \overline{G_2}\overline{G_1}\overline{G_0}CN] \oplus [\overline{P_3} + \overline{G_3}\overline{P_2} + \overline{G_3}\overline{G_2}\overline{P_1} + \overline{G_3}\overline{G_2}\overline{G_1}\overline{P_0} + \overline{G_3}\overline{G_2}\overline{G_1}\overline{G_0}CN]$

Definitions (+ = OR, $\oplus$ = Exclusive-OR)

$P_0 = R_0 + S_0 \qquad G_0 = R_0S_0$

$P_1 = R_1 + S_1 \qquad G_1 = R_1S_1$

$P_2 = R_2 + S_2 \qquad G_2 = R_2S_2$

$P_3 = R_3 + S_3 \qquad G_3 = R_3S_3$

$C_4 = G_3 + P_3G_2 + P_3P_2G_1 + P_3P_2P_1G_0 + P_3P_2P_1P_0CN$

$C_3 = G_2 + P_2G_1 + P_2P_1G_0 + P_2P_1P_0CN$

CN is an input signal. This is logical, since the least significant 2901 or 2903 slice can receive any Carry In.

The $\overline{P}$ and $\overline{G}$ outputs from the **2902 device allow you to cascade more than one 2902 device, and thus compute look-ahead carries for more than four parallel 2901 or 2903 slices. Figure 8-29 shows pertinent pin connec-**tions for a **48-bit CPU generated using twelve 2901 or 2903 devices.**

Figure 8-30 illustrates the actual logic used by the 2902 device to generate its output signals from its input signals.

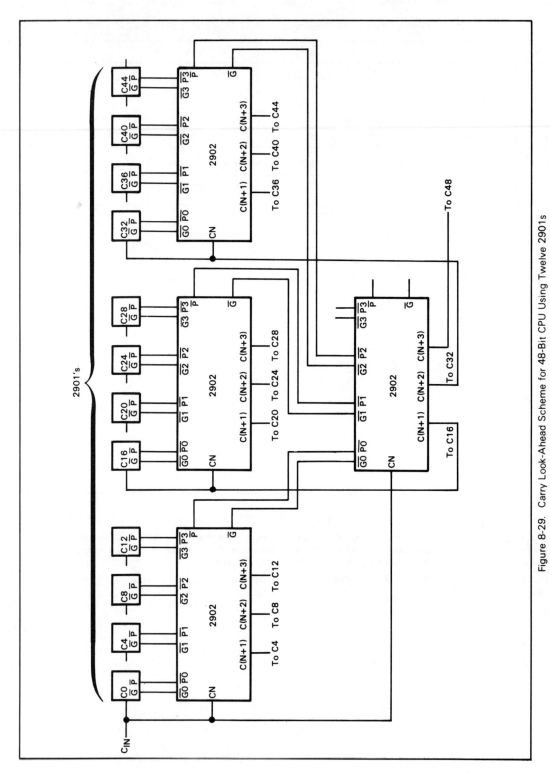

Figure 8-29. Carry Look-Ahead Scheme for 48-Bit CPU Using Twelve 2901s

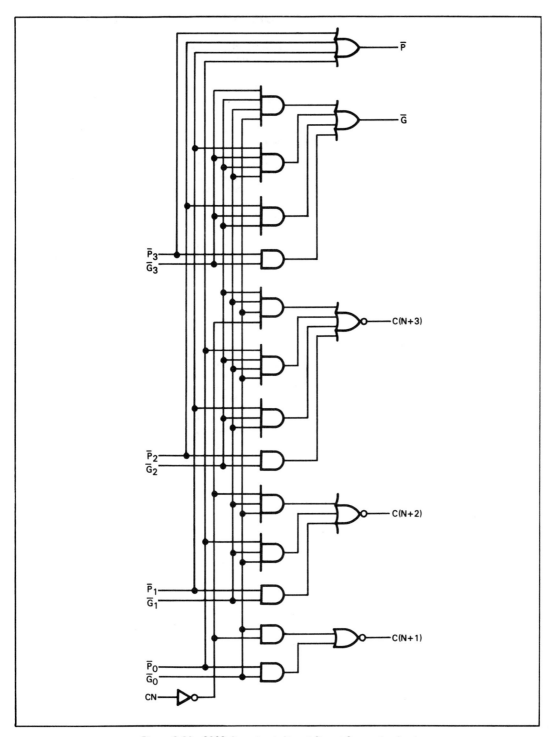

Figure 8-30. 2902 Carry Look-Ahead Signal Generation Logic

THE 2909 AND 2911 MICROPROGRAM SEQUENCERS

These two devices control the sequence in which microinstructions are fetched from memory and transmitted to 2901 or 2903 microprocessor slices. The 2910, a more capable microprogram sequencer, is described later in this chapter.

The 2909 Microprogram Sequencer is packaged as a 28-pin DIP. The 2911 Microprogram Sequencer is packaged as a 20-pin DIP. Both devices use bipolar technology and have TTL-level compatible signals. Both devices use a single +5V power supply.

The 2911 Microprogram Sequencer is a subset of the 2909. The 2911 has one less data input option and no output mask option. The two devices are otherwise identical.

THE PURPOSE OF MICROPROGRAM SEQUENCER LOGIC

Figure 8-31 functionally illustrates microinstruction generation logic that might precede 2901 or 2903 microprocessor slices in a Central Processing Unit, or equivalent system. We will explain the purpose of microprogram sequencer logic before describing the devices themselves. This discussion of microprogram sequencer logic assumes that you understand the relationship between microinstructions, a microprogram, and macroinstructions. If you do not understand these relationships, then refer to Volume 1, Chapter 4.

Beginning at the top of Figure 8-31, a macroinstruction will be received and stored in a Macroinstruction register. When describing microprocessors and Central Processing Units in general, we refer to the Macroinstruction register simply as the "Instruction register". This register holds the assembly language instruction object code that is to be executed.

A macroinstruction object code will normally have two components: an instruction definition, and associated data. The instruction definition, frequently referred to as an operation code (or op-code), identifies the actual CPU operations which are to occur. The additional data may be used in a variety of ways to identify sources and destinations, to contribute external memory addresses, or to be interpreted as immediate data.

Events which are to occur within the CPU in response to a macroinstruction's execution are defined as one or more microinstructions. These microinstructions will be held in a high-speed read-only memory (ROM) or programmable read-only memory (PROM). The op-code portion of a macroinstruction identifies the microinstruction(s) to be executed in response to the macroinstruction. The additional information portion of the macroinstruction is simply held available until required by logic operations resulting from microinstruction execution. This may be illustrated as follows:

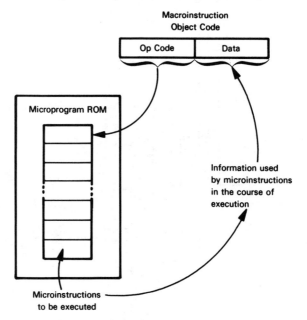

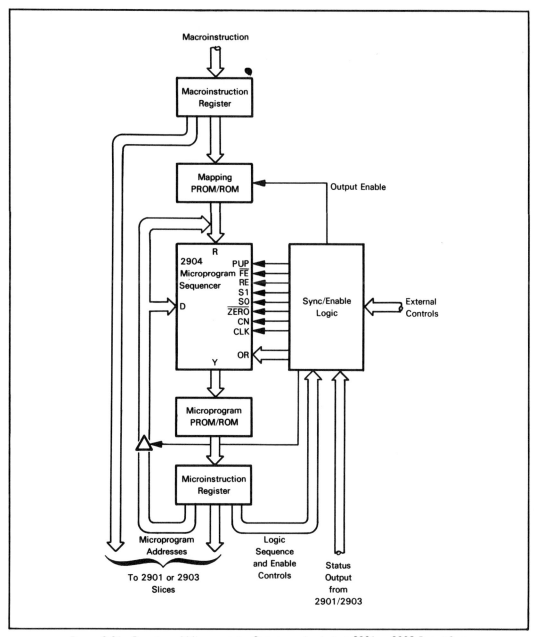

Figure 8-31. Function of Microprogram Sequencer Logic in a 2901 or 2903 Based System

Macroinstruction object codes have been described in considerable detail in Volume 1, Chapter 7. This discussion emphasizes the fact that macroinstruction object codes are selected to optimize Central Processing Unit operations, without regard to microprograms, or how microprograms may be stored in a memory device. This being the case, there is no chance that the op-code portion of any macroinstruction will have a bit pattern that addresses the correct microinstruction, or initial microinstruction that must be executed in response to the macroinstruction's execution. Instead, a mapping read-only memory or a programmable logic array is used as an address translator. The mapping ROM or PLA treats the op-code portion of the macroinstruction as an input. In the ROM, the actual microprogram starting address is stored at the location addressed by the op-code bit pattern. Conceptually, this may be illustrated as follows:

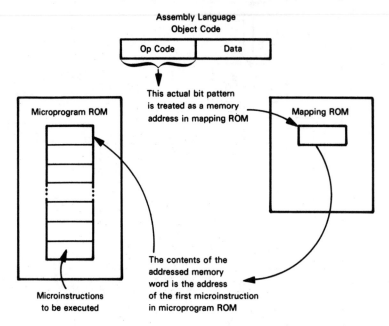

The size of the mapping ROM and the width of the address which it outputs depend on the size of the microprogram — that is to say, the length of the microprogram in terms of the number of microinstructions. This may be illustrated as follows:

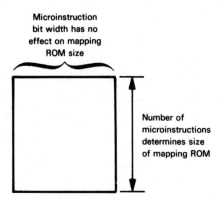

If, for example, 256 or fewer microinstructions constitute the entire microprogram, then an 8-bit address can be output by the mapping ROM, irrespective of whether the microinstructions are 16 bits wide, 64 bits wide or have any other bit width. But, if the total length of the microprogram were 1024 microinstructions, then a 10-bit address would have to be output by the mapping ROM.

If every macroinstruction resulted in the execution of a single microinstruction, then there would be no need for 2909/2911 Microprogram Sequencers. The mapping ROM could output a single address to the microprogram ROM. The contents of the addressed microprogram ROM would be output to the Microinstruction register — to become the microinstruction that enables operations required by the macroinstruction.

But it is most unlikely that the Central Processing Unit's assembly language will consist of instructions that are all primitive enough to be implemented via a single microinstruction. In particular, as Central Processing Units become more complex, an ever larger number of microinstructions may have to be executed in response to a single macroinstruction execution; and the sequence in which these microinstructions are stored may also become more complicated. The 2909 and 2911 Microprogram Sequencers provide the logic which takes you from the initial microinstruction through the microprogram.

There is one very important conceptual aspect of the 2909 and 2911 Microprogram Sequencers which must be clearly understood. These Microprogram Sequencer devices are, like the 2901 and 2903, cascadable 4-bit devices. But there is no relationship between the number of 2909/2911 devices which are cascaded. 2901 or 2903 devices are cascaded to give you the required CPU word width. Two 2901/2903 devices generate an 8-bit word; four 2901/2903 devices generate a 16-bit word; eight 2901/2903 devices generate a 32-bit word, etc. 2909 or 2911 devices are cascaded to address the required length of microprogram memory. The number of 2909 or 2911 devices cascaded together is in no way influenced by the width of the microinstruction, or the width of the CPU word. For example, if the microprogram has 256 or fewer microinstructions, two 2909 or 2911 devices cascaded together are sufficient. This holds true whatever the microinstruction width may be, and whatever the CPU word width may be. Thus the number of parallel 2901 or 2903 slices has no bearing whatsoever on the number of parallel 2909 or 2911 devices. You cannot even generalize by stating that there will be a tendency to require more 2909/2911 devices as the number of parallel 2901/2903 devices increases. Rather, the width of the microinstruction will increase with the number of 2901/2903 devices and, as we have already stated, the width of a microinstruction has no bearing on the length of the microprogram, or the number of parallel Microprogram Sequencer devices that will be needed.

2909/2911 MICROPROGRAM SEQUENCER PINS AND SIGNALS

Pins and signal assignments for the 2909 and 2911 Microprogram Sequencers are illustrated in Figure 8-32. These signals are most easily understood in conjunction with the functional logic illustrations for the two devices which are given in Figures 8-33 and 8-34.

Central to the logic of 2909 and 2911 Microprogram Sequencers is the Output Multiplexer, which receives four inputs. S0 and S1 are two control inputs that select an output as follows:

| 2909/2911 |
| OUTPUT |
| SELECT |

S0	S1	Output Multiplexer Source
0	0	Microprogram Counter
0	1	Address register
1	0	Stack
1	1	Direct inputs (via D0-D3)

We will for the moment ignore the Microprogram Counter and Stack, two data storage areas whose functions will be described shortly.

D0-D3 are four data input lines. Data input via these four lines can be selected by the Output Multiplexer and output immediately (if S0 and S1 are both high).

| 2909/2911 |
| IMMEDIATE |
| DATA INPUT |

Data input via R0-R3 is held in the Address register. Timing for Address register access may be illustrated as follows:

| 2909/2911 |
| ADDRESS |
| REGISTER |

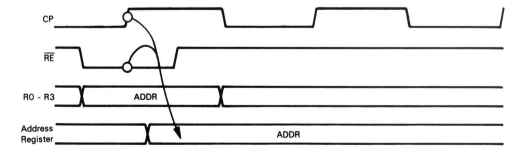

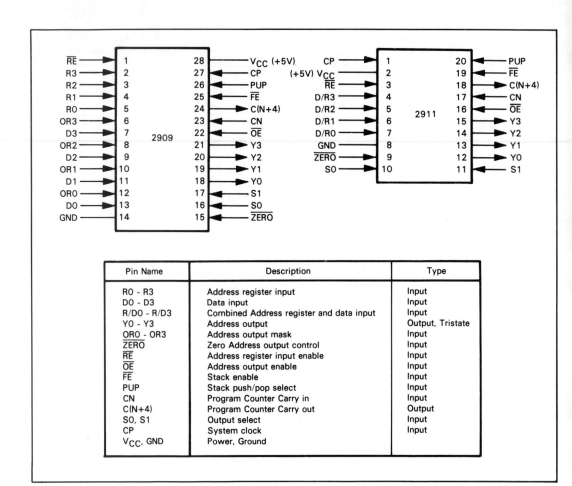

Pin Name	Description	Type
R0 - R3	Address register input	Input
D0 - D3	Data input	Input
R/D0 - R/D3	Combined Address register and data input	Input
Y0 - Y3	Address output	Output, Tristate
OR0 - OR3	Address output mask	Input
$\overline{\text{ZERO}}$	Zero Address output control	Input
$\overline{\text{RE}}$	Address register input enable	Input
$\overline{\text{OE}}$	Address output enable	Input
$\overline{\text{FE}}$	Stack enable	Input
PUP	Stack push/pop select	Input
CN	Program Counter Carry in	Input
C(N+4)	Program Counter Carry out	Output
S0, S1	Output select	Input
CP	System clock	Input
V$_{CC}$, GND	Power, Ground	

Figure 8-32. 2909 and 2911 Microprogram Sequencer Pins and Signal Assignments

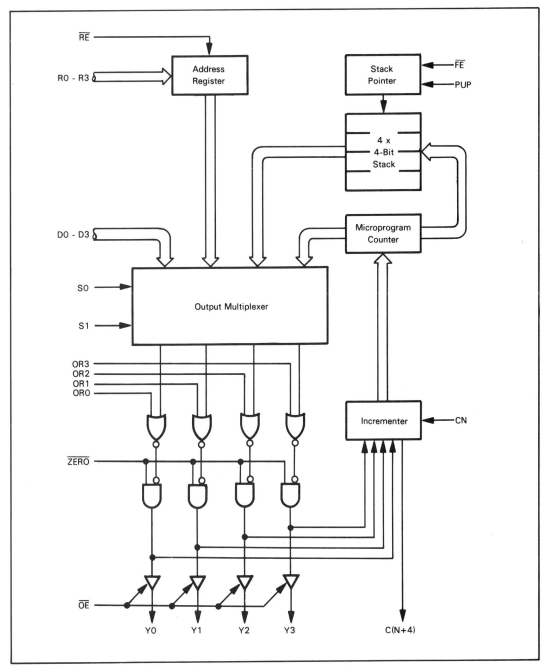

Figure 8-33. 2909 Microprogram Sequencer Functional Logic

8-97

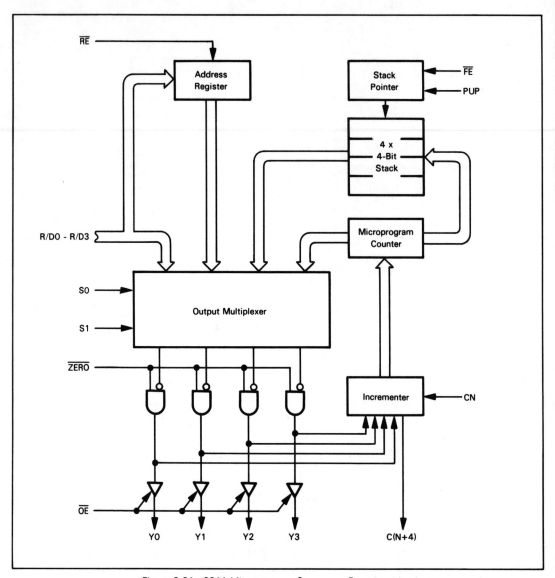

Figure 8-34. 2911 Microprogram Sequencer Functional Logic

As illustrated above, **the Address register enable signal $\overline{RE}$ must be low before data can be written into the Address register via R0-R3.** If $\overline{RE}$ is low, then data is written into the Address register when the clock signal CP makes its high-to-low transition. But $\overline{RE}$ has no effect on Address register output. Whether $\overline{RE}$ is low or high, the Address register contents are transmitted to the Output Multiplexer.

The 2911 shares D and R inputs. Data input at R/D0-R/D3 will be written into the Address register if $\overline{RE}$ is low, and will be output via the Output Multiplexer if S0 and S1 are both high.

Multiplexer output lines Y0-Y3 have their own enable signal $\overline{OE}$. If this signal is high, Y0-Y3 outputs are floated. This allows you to disconnect Microprogram Sequencer devices from the microprogram ROM, something you may do when switching to an external tester.

2909/2911 DATA OUTPUT

The 2911 has one set of conditioning logic on the Y outputs. The 2909 has two sets of conditioning logic on the Y outputs. **Both devices have a $\overline{ZERO}$ input which, when low, unilaterally forces the four lines Y0, Y1, Y2, and Y3 to output 0.** Frequently you will use the $\overline{ZERO}$ line as a restart — with an initialization microinstruction sequence origin at microinstruction number 0 in the microprogram ROM. **The 2909, but not the 2911, has four mask signals, OR0, OR1, OR2, and OR3, which can individually force Y0, Y1, Y2, and Y3, respectively, low.** Typically you will use the mask signals to implement conditional logic. For example, we have already seen how the Overflow status (OVR), output by the most significant 2901 and 2903 slice, signals an overflow or "exceptional" condition. By tying the Overflow status to OR0, you can implement microinstruction pairs. The Output Multiplexer outputs a 0 low-order microinstruction address via Y0, which OR0 can override and convert to 1. For an 8-bit microprogram address this may be illustrated as follows:

2909/2911 OUTPUT ZERO CONTROL

2909 OUTPUT MASK

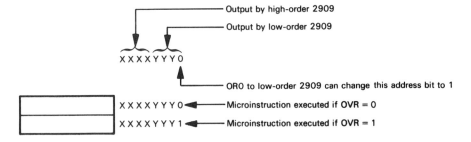

Of course, having a mask line associated with every microinstruction address output line lets you generate more complex conditional logic schemes than the simple illustration above.

There are two internal locations within the 2909 and the 2911 which can hold addresses. These are the Microprogram Counter and the Stack.

Let us first look at the Microprogram Counter. This location is equivalent to the typical Central Processing Unit Program Counter.

2909/2911 MICROPROGRAM COUNTER

When S0 and S1 are both low, Microprogram Counter contents are read by the Output Multiplexer, and are output via Y0-Y3.

New data is written into the Microprogram Counter whenever data is input from the Output Multiplexer, whether or not the Microprogram Counter was selected as the Output Multiplexer input. Data written back to the Microprogram Counter is taken from the Y0-Y3 path following the OR and AND gates. Therefore, if you use either of the output conditioning gates, you will also modify the Microprogram Counter contents. This, of course, is no different to a Central Processing Unit's Program Counter, which is also modified by a restart or jump instruction.

Data being written back to the Microprogram Counter passes through an Incrementer. **The Incrementer adds the CN level to data which is on its way to the Microprogram Counter.** Thus if CN is low, the Incrementer passes data through unmodified; but the data is incremented if CN is high. **An Incrementer overflow generates a high C(N+4) output.**

2909/2911 INCREMENTER

Let us look at the various ways in which you may use Microprogram Counter logic.

In the simplest case, you may wish to sequentially access a number of microinstructions. You can begin the sequence by inputting the first microinstruction address to the Address register via R0-R3, or as immediate data via D0-D3. Remember, 2909 and 2911 devices are cascadable; therefore we are not limited to 4-bit addresses. The initial address, when output by the Output Multiplexer, also gets written to the Microprogram Counter. Assuming that CN is high, the address written into the

2909/2911 SEQUENTIAL ADDRESSES

Microprogram Counter will be one more than the starting address input via R0-R3 or D0-D3. For a number of subsequent microcycles, you will continue to select the Microprogram Counter, leaving CN high, so that Microprogram Counter contents are incremented on each microcycle. Selecting addresses arbitrarily, this sequence may be illustrated as follows:

D0-D3	S0	S1	CN	Y0-Y3	Microprogram Counter Contents
30	1	1	1	30	31
XX	0	0	1	31	32
XX	0	0	1	32	33
XX	0	0	1	33	34
		etc.			etc.

XX represents "don't care" inputs.

There are some non-obvious problems that can occur when you generate sequential microinstruction addresses using Program Counter logic as illustrated above.

The next very simple microprogram counter sequence involves the re-execution of a single microinstruction — as you may do while performing a normalize or twos complement divide operation using the 2903 special functions. If the Output Multiplexer selects the Microprogram Counter contents while CN is input low, then the Microprogram Counter contents will not change on succeeding microcycles — and the same microinstruction will be executed repeatedly.

2909/2911
SINGLE
INSTRUCTION
RE-EXECUTION

You can skip a microinstruction with an even address within an otherwise consecutive instruction sequence. To do this you keep CN high, so that the Microprogram Counter increments on each microcycle, but you input a high OR0 mask bit in order to skip an instruction. This may be illustrated as follows:

2909/2911
INSTRUCTION
SKIP

S0	S1	CN	OR0	Microprogram Counter Contents
0	0	1	0	34
0	0	1	0	35
0	0	1	1	37 OR0 forces low-order
0	0	1	0	38 address bit to 1.
0	0	1	0	39
		etc.		etc.

You can also use mask bits to jump between microprogram pages. For example, within a 256-microinstruction program you can jump in sixteen microinstruction increments by inputting a high signal at the OR0 mask bit of the high-order 2909 slice. This may be illustrated as follows:

2909/2911
JUMP

Address	Both 2909's		Most Significant 2909		Least Significant 2909	
	S0	S1	OR0	Microprogram Counter	CN	OR0	Microprogram Counter
34	0	0	0	0 0 1 0	1	0	0 1 0 0
35	0	0	0	0 0 1 0	1	0	0 1 0 1
46	0	0	1	0 0 1 1	1	0	0 1 1 0
47	0	0	0	0 0 1 1	1	0	0 1 1 1
etc.							

By applying high inputs to other mask bits you can span almost any number of microinstructions in a single jump.

The 2909/2911 Stack has four locations.

2909/2911
STACK

A Stack Pointer identifies the currently selected Stack location. If the Output Multiplexer receives S0 low and S1 high, then it reads the contents of the currently selected Stack location and outputs this data via Y0-Y3. This output address, like all other output addresses, passes through the Incrementer and is loaded into the Program Counter.

You modify the Stack Pointer address using the FE and PUP signals. FE must be low in order to modify the Stack Pointer. FE does not have to be low in order to output data from the Stack to the Output Multiplexer.

When FE and PUP are both low, the Stack Pointer decrements on the low-to-high transition of CP. Timing may be illustrated as follows:

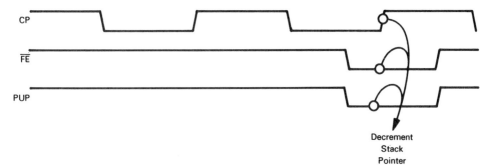

If FE is low and PUP is high, the Stack Pointer is incremented, then the contents of the Microprogram Counter are loaded into the newly addressed Stack register. Timing may be illustrated as follows:

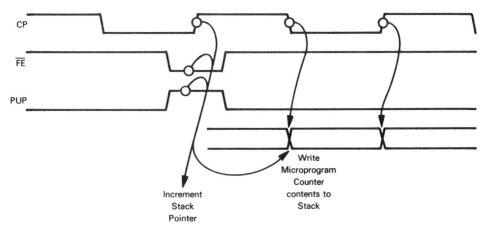

The address in the Program Counter which gets written into the newly addressed Stack register will be the address which was output by the Output Multiplexer — incremented by one, assuming that CN is high. This enables traditional subroutine call and return logic, as we will see soon.

The Stack Pointer is a roll-over counter. That is to say, it will decrement from 0 to 3:

$$\rightarrow 2 \rightarrow 1 \rightarrow 0 \rightarrow 3 \rightarrow 2 \rightarrow 1 \rightarrow 0 \rightarrow 3 \rightarrow$$

and it will increment from 3 to 0:

$$\rightarrow 2 \rightarrow 3 \rightarrow 0 \rightarrow 1 \rightarrow 2 \rightarrow 3 \rightarrow 0 \rightarrow 1 \rightarrow 2 \rightarrow$$

This is normally not advantageous.

Let us look at some of the address sequences which can be generated using the Stack.

Consider first a typical subroutine call — in the classical assembly language sense. The microinstruction which causes the subroutine call increments the Stack Pointer. Assuming that CN is high, the address of the microinstruction which causes the subroutine call is incremented by one, written into the Microprogram Counter, and thence to the newly addressed Stack register, to the address of the microinstruction to which execution will return at the end of the subroutine. This sequence may be illustrated as follows:

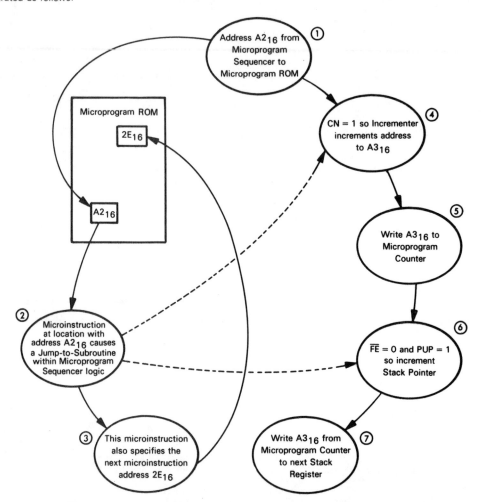

With reference to the illustration above, the microinstruction which causes the subroutine call is arbitrarily assumed to reside in microprogram read-only memory location $A2_{16}$. Therefore the subroutine call begins with the Microprogram Sequencer outputting address $A2_{16}$, as illustrated above by ①

For the microinstruction in location $A2_{16}$, only those bits that affect the Microprogram Sequencer are of interest to us. These bits cause the Microprogram Sequencer to receive high inputs at CN and PUP, with a low input at $\overline{FE}$. This microinstruction will also provide the address for the next microinstruction, arbitrarily assumed to be $2E_{16}$ at ③ in the illustration above. But this address will be output on the next microcycle. On the current microcycle, CN causes the current address ($A2_{16}$) to be incremented to $A3_{16}$. This is shown above at ④. The new incremented address $A3_{16}$ is written to the Microprogram Counter; see ⑤ above. Since $\overline{FE}$ is low and PUP is high, the Stack Pointer is incremented (⑥ above) and the current Microprogram Counter contents, which is $A3_{16}$, is saved in the Stack.

On the next microcycle the address $2E_{16}$ will be output, initiating the subroutine's execution. When the subroutine completes execution, it has the return address $A3_{16}$ stored at the Stack register identified by the Stack Pointer.

The final instruction of the subroutine must execute a Stack PUP and cause the Output Multiplexer to select the Stack as its input. This requires S1 to be high while S0, $\overline{FE}$, and PUP are all low. The Output Multiplexer will read A3$_{16}$ from the Stack and output this address next. A3$_{16}$ is incremented to A4$_{16}$ and returned as the new Microprogram Counter contents. The Stack Pointer decrements. Thus a classical Stack-Oriented Return-from-Subroutine has been executed.

A subroutine can consist of a single microinstruction. If you look again at the subroutine call illustration given earlier, the first instruction of the subroutine, which in our illustration will be the instruction stored at location 2E$_{16}$, has nothing said about its Microprogram Sequencer bits. If this instruction causes a Return-from-Subroutine, then you have created a single-microinstruction subroutine.

Using the Stack you can nest subroutines to a depth of four. In most microprograms, nesting to a depth of four is perfectly adequate.

2909/2911 SUBROUTINE NESTING

A computed multidestination jump is easily implemented using a 2909 or 2911 Microprogram Sequencer. A 16-way jump to individual instructions can be achieved by inputting data via OR0-OR4 to the least significant 2909/2911, while generating more significant portions of the address from some other location, such as the Address register.

2909/2911 MULTIPLE JUMP

2909/2911 SYNC/ENABLE LOGIC

There are innumerable ways in which the Sync/Enable logic portion of Figure 8-31 could be designed. At its most elementary level, 2909/2911 control signals will be generated (possibly from a read-only memory) based on Microinstruction register outputs which become a read only memory address. This may be illustrated as follows:

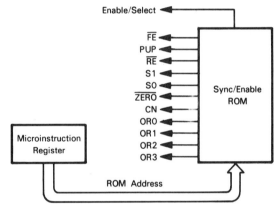

A 12-bit wide read-only memory would be required in the illustration above to generate eleven input signals needed by the 2909/2911, plus an Enable/Select signal for the R input 2-IN MUX. (The clock signal CP could not be generated by a ROM.) It would be possible to generate 4096 different combinations of 12 signals. Very few of these possibilities will ever be encountered. In all probability, a maximum of 32 different signal combinations may be seen, in which case a 32 x 12-bit read-only memory will suffice, with a 5-bit address provided by the Microinstruction register. Each microinstruction stored in the microprogram ROM will then contain a 5-bit address field; the address field selects one of the 32 signal combinations that define the next step of Microprogram Sequencer control inputs. Thus we are able to achieve address continuity within a microprogram. In many applications, the 29811A provides this function.

But in Figure 8-31 three sets of inputs to the Sync/Enable logic section are shown.

The "logic sequence and enable" control emanating from the Microinstruction register becomes the 5-bit address which we have already described.

Table 8-11. The 2903 Twos Complement Binary Division Microprogram Subroutine from Table 8-9, with 2911 Addressing Microinstruction Fields Added

No	Microinstruction			$\overline{EA}$	CN	A0 - A3	B0 - B3	Comment
	I8 - I5	I4 - I1	I0					
1	4	6	0	0	0	Divisor register (R0)	Divisor buffer (R3)	Copy divisor to temporary buffer.
2	4	6	0	0	0	Dividend (MS) register (R1)	Dividend (MS) buffer (R2)	Copy dividend most significant half to temporary buffer.
3	5	0	0	X	0	X	Dividend (MS) buffer (R2)	Convert dividend (MS) from twos complement to sign/magnitude version. Test OVR externally while next microinstruction is being executed. If OVR is 1, branch to subroutine that downshifts dividend.
4	5	0	0	X	0	X	Divisor buffer (R3)	Convert divisor (MS) from twos complement to sign/magnitude version. Test OVR externally. If OVR is 1, branch to microinstruction 9.
5	9	4	0	X	0	X	Dividend (MS) buffer (R2)	Shift out sign bit of dividend (MS) half in temporary buffer.
6	9	4	0	X	0	X	Divisor buffer (R3)	Shift out sign bit of divisor in temporary buffer.
7	F	2	0	0	1	Dividend (MS) buffer (R2)	Divisor buffer (R3)	Subtract sign bit stripped divisor from sign bit stripped dividend (MS) half. If Carry = 1 (dividend larger) branch to subroutine that downshifts dividend or upshifts divisor.
8	6	6	0	0	0	Dividend (LS) register (R4)	X	Copy dividend least significant half to Q register.
9	A*	0	0	0	0	Divisor register (R0)	Dividend (MS) register (R1)	Double length normalize dividend in MS register and Q register.
10	C*	0	0	0	Z	Divisor register (R0)	Dividend (MS) register (R1)	Execute twos complement divide instruction fourteen times.
11	E	0	0	0	Z	Divisor register (R0)	Dividend (MS) register (R1)	Twos complement divide final instruction.

*CN is connected to Z status while these two special functions are being executed.

Table 8-11. The 2903 Twos Complement Binary Division Microprogram Subroutine from Table 8-9, with 2911 Addressing Microinstruction Fields Added (Continued)

Microinstruction Number	Microinstruction bits covering 2903 and two 2911 input (Bit positions are arbitrary and have no significance)		2911 Addressing Operations
	2903 Bits I8 I7 I6 I5 I4 I3 I2 I1 I0 EA CN A3 A2 A1 A0 B3 B2 B1 B0	**2911 Bits** D7 D6 D5 D4 D3 D2 D1 D0 RE S1 S0 ZERO CN FE PUP	
1	0 1 0 0 0 1 1 0 0 0 0 0 0 0 0 0 0 1 1 4 6 0 0 0 R0 R3	A A A A A A A A 0 0 0 1 1 1 X Abort Address 0 0 1 1	Select next sequential instruction. Load abort address into Address register.
2	0 1 0 0 0 1 1 0 0 0 0 0 0 0 1 0 0 1 0 4 6 0 0 0 R1 R2	X X X X X X X X 1 0 Z 1 1 1 X 1 1 1 1	Select next sequential instruction, or abort address if Z = 1 from microinstruction 1.
3	0 1 0 1 0 0 0 0 0 X 0 X X X X 0 0 1 0 5 0 0 0 R2	X X X X X X X X 1 0 0 1 1 1 X 1 0 1 1 1	Select next sequential instruction.
4	0 1 0 1 0 0 0 0 0 X 0 X X X X 0 0 1 1 5 0 0 0 R3	S S S S S S S S 1 0 0 1 1 1 X Scale Dividend 1 1 1 1 0 1 Subroutine	OVR = 0. Select next sequential instruction. OVR = 1. Call "scale dividend" subroutine.
5	1 0 0 1 0 1 0 0 0 X 0 X X X X 0 0 1 0 9 4 0 0 R2	B B B B B B B B 1 0 0 1 1 1 X Microinstruction 1 1 1 1 1 X 8 Address	OVR = 0. Select next sequential address. OVR = 1. Branch to microinstruction 8.
6	1 0 0 1 0 1 0 0 0 X 0 X X X X 0 0 1 1 9 4 0 0 R3	X X X X X X X X 1 0 0 1 1 1 X 0	Select next sequential instruction.
7	1 1 1 1 0 0 1 0 0 0 1 0 0 1 0 0 0 1 1 F 2 0 1 R2 R3	X X X X X X X X 1 0 0 1 1 1 X 0	Select next sequential instruction.
8	0 1 1 0 0 1 1 0 0 0 0 0 1 0 0 X X X X 6 6 0 0 0 R4	T T T T T T T T 1 0 0 1 1 1 X Scale divisor or 1 1 1 1 0 1 Dividend Subroutine	C(N+4) = 0. Select next sequential instruction. C(N+4) = 1. Call "scale divisor or dividend" subroutine.
9	1 0 1 0 0 0 0 0 0 0 0 0 0 0 0 0 0 0 1 A 0 0 0 0 R0 R1	X X X X X X X X 1 0 0 1 1 1 X 0	Select next sequential instruction.
10	1 1 0 0 0 0 0 0 0 X 0 0 0 0 0 0 0 0 1 C 0 0 0 R0 R1	X X X X X X X X 1 0 0 1 0/1 1 X 0	Execute this instruction 14 times, then select next sequential instruction.
11	1 1 1 0 0 0 0 0 0 X 0 0 0 0 0 0 0 0 1 E 0 0 0 R0 R1	X X X X X X X X 1 1 0 1 1 0 0 2	Return from subroutine.

X = "Don't Care" bits

Status outputs from the 2901 or 2903 devices have already been encountered; we have, for example, discussed the way in which the Overflow status may generate one of the OR mask lines. The most effective way of handling status outputs from 2901 or 2903 slices is to use the test input of 29811A. This might be illustrated as follows:

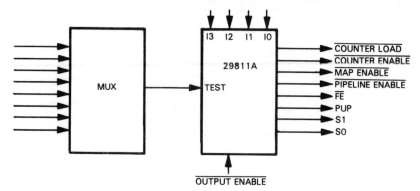

2909/2911 ADDRESSING EXAMPLE

We will now complete our discussion of 2909 and 2911 operations by looking at a specific example — the twos complement binary division microprogram summarized in Table 8-9. Table 8-9 shows only those microinstruction bits required by the 2903 device. In Table 8-11 we add microinstruction bits for two 2911 Microprogram Sequencers. We assume that the two 2911 Microprogram Sequencers address the 2903 twos complement binary division microprogram as a subroutine, within a 256-microinstruction microprogram memory.

In the lower half of Table 8-11, RAM locations used by the twos complement binary division microprogram are identified using register designations "R0" through "R4". These designations represent RAM locations with addresses 0 through 4, respectively.

Additional microinstruction bits added in the lower half of Table 8-11 provide the two 2911 Microprogram Sequencers with their data and control inputs. Eight data input bits are needed, four for each of the two 2911 Microprogram Sequencers. But since both 2911 Microprogram Sequencers will receive exactly the same control inputs, one set of control signals is sufficient. Table 8-11 shows the six control signals $\overline{RE}$, S1, S0, $\overline{ZERO}$, CN, $\overline{FE}$, and PUP being generated by individual microinstruction bits. But earlier we generated these control codes out of a read-only memory. In the discussion which follows we will compare these two methods of generating control inputs.

Microinstruction 1 in Table 8-11 **copies the divisor into a temporary register.** If the divisor is not 0, the next sequential microinstruction must be executed. If the divisor is 0, microprogram execution must be aborted, since you cannot divide by 0. The most significant 2903 slice outputs Z high if the divisor is 0. Z is output low if the divisor is not 0. The Z status is output at the end of the microinstruction 1 microcycle, too late to influence 2911 Microprogram Sequencer logic. Microinstruction 1, therefore, provides the 2911 with data needed to evaluate the Z status while microinstruction 2 is executing. S0 and S1 are both low while CN is high; therefore, while microinstruction 1 is executing, the 2911 Output Multiplexer selects the Microprogram Counter as its source, then increments the Microprogram Counter contents. Thus, the next sequential microinstruction, microinstruction 2, is selected. Simultaneously, microinstruction 1 inputs the abort address to the 2911 Address register. The abort address is input at D0-D7 while $\overline{RE}$ is low.

If logic associated with execution of microinstruction 2 conflicted in any way with testing the Z status, then we would have to insert a dummy microinstruction in front of microinstruction 2, whose sole function would be to test the Z status.

But microinstruction 2 has no such conflicting logic, so we can use its execution time to test the $\overline{ZERO}$ status generated by microinstruction 1. If this $\overline{ZERO}$ status is 1, then the abort address, input to the Address register by microinstruction 1, will be selected; execution of microinstruction 2 becomes redundant insofar as 2903 logic events are concerned, but, providing execution of microinstruction 2 is inconsequential, no harm is done.

The 2911 bits provided by microinstruction 2 can be quite simple. S1 is 0 and S0 is connected to the $\overline{ZERO}$ status; if the $\overline{ZERO}$ status is 0, the Output Multiplexer will select the Microprogram Counter — and thus the next sequential instruction. But if the $\overline{ZERO}$ status is 1, the Address register will be selected by the Output Multiplexer — and thus an abort will occur. In order to connect S0 to a $\overline{ZERO}$ status we would probably include an additional enable bit, not shown in microinstruction 2. This enable bit, when high, will link S0 to the $\overline{ZERO}$ status, but when low will cause S0 to be derived directly from its microinstruction bit. This may be illustrated as follows:

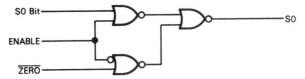

Addressing logic for microinstructions 3 and 4 is similar to that which we have just described for microinstructions 1 and 2.

Microinstruction 3 converts the most significant half of the dividend from twos complement to sign/magnitude form. If the dividend has the largest possible twos complement value, then the Overflow status is set and the dividend must be downshifted. If the dividend has any other twos complement value, the Overflow status is not set and the next sequential instruction must be executed. But as we found when examining microinstruction 1, the Overflow status is generated at the end of the microinstruction 3 microcycle, therefore the 2911 bits shown in Table 8-11 for microinstruction 3 simply select the next sequential microinstruction — microinstruction 4. But while microinstruction 4 is being executed, 2911 logic tests the Overflow status generated by microinstruction 3. Now we can delay testing microinstruction 3 Overflow status until microinstruction 4 has been executed because execution of microinstruction 4 does not conflict with Overflow = 1. If it did, we would have to insert a dummy microinstruction between 3 and 4 which did nothing at the 2903, but gave the 2911 an additional microcycle time within which to test the Overflow status generated by microinstruction 3, and determine subsequent addressing based on Overflow status level. Since this additional dummy instruction is not needed, microinstruction 4 provides the address for the "Scale Dividend" subroutine via data bits D0-D7. Two sets of control inputs are generated. If the Overflow status left over from microinstruction 3 is 0 then the control inputs to the 2911 simply select the next sequential microinstruction — microinstruction 5. But if the Overflow status left over from microinstruction 3 is 1 then control inputs cause the 2911 to push Microprogram Counter contents onto the Stack, then have the Output Multiplexer choose as its source the address input at D0-D7. Thus the scale dividend subroutine is called.

If you look at the 2911 control bits of microinstruction 4 in Table 8-11, you will see that three bits, S0, S1, and $\overline{FE}$, must change, depending on the level of the Overflow status left over from the execution of microinstruction 3. PUP need not change, since its level is not significant when OVR is low. We could control all three bit levels using an enable bit, as described for the $\overline{ZERO}$ status in microinstruction 2. But it is probably simpler and cheaper to use a read-only memory device, as suggested earlier in this chapter. Consider the following possibility:

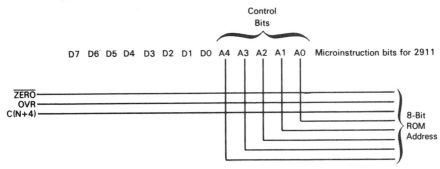

Instead of having seven separate 2911 control bits in every microinstruction, we now have five control bits. Three status bits ($\overline{ZERO}$, OVR, and C(N+4), generated by the 2903) provide the three low-order bits for an 8-bit read-only memory address. The five microinstruction control bits, together with the three status bits generated by the 2903, create an 8-bit read-only memory address. The addressed read-only memory location outputs the seven signal levels required by the 2911. For microinstructions 1 through 4, read-only memory might arbitrarily be mapped as shown in Figure 8-35.

Microinstruction 5 has 2911 addressing bits that are similar to microinstruction 4. Microinstruction 4 not only tests the Overflow status left over from microinstruction 3, but itself generates an Overflow status which must be tested while microinstruction 5 is being executed. In the event that the 2903 Overflow status generated by microinstruction 4 is low, the next sequential microinstruction, microinstruction 6, is selected. But if the Overflow status is high, then a branch to microinstruction 8 occurs. Since this is a simple branch, no push is required; therefore $\overline{FE}$ remains high in both cases. See Figure 8-35.

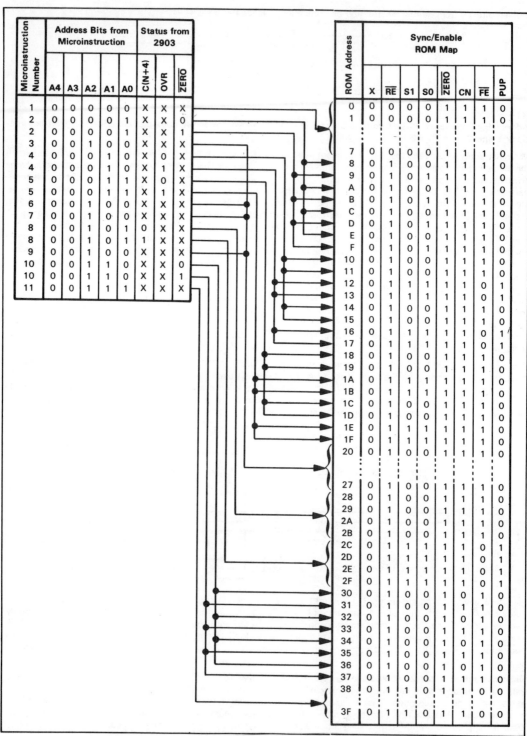

Figure 8-35. 2911 Sync/Enable ROM for the 2903 Twos Complement Binary
Division Microprogram Subroutine

Microinstructions 6 and 7 both have very simple 2911 addressing logic. Each microinstruction chooses the next sequential microinstruction. But the Carry status generated by the 2903 following execution of microinstruction 7 must be tested by address generation logic while microinstruction 8 is being executed. The fact that microinstruction 5 can branch directly to microinstruction 8 causes no problem since microinstruction 5 will always generate a low 2903 Carry status; thereforhe Carry status testing logic which we are about to describe does no harm.

If the Carry status generated by the 2903 during execution of microinstruction 7 is low, then no further divisor or dividend scaling is needed, and the next sequential microinstruction is selected. But if the 2903 generates a high Carry status while executing microinstruction 7, then a subroutine must be called to scale the divisor or dividend. Therefore **microinstruction 8 provides the address of the scaling subroutine at the data inputs D0-D7; it generates the same two sets of 2911 control inputs which we described for microinstruction 4.** However, the level of C(N+4) determines which set of 2911 control inputs are selected by microinstruction 8. See Figure 8-35.

We now come to the last three microinstructions (9, 10, and 11) which together perform the actual twos complement binary division. Microinstruction 9 must be executed once, followed by fourteen executions of microinstruction 10, and one execution of 11. Fourteen executions of microinstruction 10 are required because we are dividing a 16-bit divisor into a 32-bit dividend. From our previous discussion of the twos complement binary division algorithm, recall that microinstruction 10 must be executed N times, where the divisor has N bits and the dividend has 2N bits. Our 2911 addressing logic implements this multiple execution requirement by keeping the CN input low for thirteen executions of microinstruction 10. But this requires an external counter. Here is one possibility:

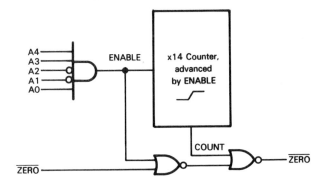

There are innumerable ways (including the use of a 2910) in which the counting logic required to augment microinstruction 10 may be implemented. The one we have shown assigns one set of eight read-only memory addresses to a preloaded counter. This preloaded counter provides the level of the low-order address bit (zero) which must be input to the 2911 select ROM. The preloaded counter decrements once every time ENABLE goes high; it outputs COUNT low until it decrements to 0. Upon decrementing to 0 the counter outputs COUNT high.

Apart from the external counter required by microinstruction 10, microinstructions 9 and 10 generate simple next sequential address controls for the 2911. Microinstruction 11 causes the 2911 to pop its Stack — on the assumption that the entire twos complement binary division microprogram is itself a microprogram subroutine. Thus, if a read-only memory is used to generate 2911 control inputs Figure 8-35 illustrates the final read-only memory map and addressing bits required for the microinstruction sequence given in Table 8-11.

THE 2910 MICROPROGRAM SEQUENCER

This device is an enhancement of the 2909/2911 Microprogram Sequencers which we have just described.

Here is a summary of 2910 enhancements, as compared to the 2909 and 2911:

1) The 2910 is a 12-bit device capable of addressing up to 4096 microinstructions. The 2909 and 2911 are 4-bit devices. Therefore the 2910 is equivalent to three parallel 2909/2911 devices.

2) The 2910 has sixteen address generation sequences, selected individually via four instruction code inputs. Many of these sixteen address generation sequences have alternate forms that depend on the level of a condition code. The 2909/2911 has no such address generation sequences; rather, individual control signal levels (such as output selects S0 and S1, and output masks OR0-OR3) provide more primitive control of addressing logic.

3) The 2910 has three enable signals. One of the three is output low on each microcycle. You can use these enable signals to selectively strobe data out of different sources to meet the specific needs of any microcycle. The 2909 and 2911 have no such enable outputs.

4) The Address register of the 2909/2911 becomes an Address register or a down counter within the 2910. As a down counter, the 2910 Address register controls loop iteration.

5) The 2910 has a five-level Stack, as compared to the 2909/2911 four-level Stack. Also, the 2910 has slightly different Stack Pointer logic.

The fact that the 2910 is an enhancement of the 2909/2911 does not necessarily mean that the 2910 is always the part of choice. The 2910 is more expensive. In most cases, a small microprogram consisting of 256 or fewer microinstructions is more economically served by two 2909 or 2911 devices, rather than a single 2910 device.

The 2910 is packaged as a 40-pin DIP or a 42-pin flat package. The device is manufactured using bipolar technology. A single +5V power supply is required. All signals are TTL-level compatible.

2910 MICROPROGRAM SEQUENCER PINS AND SIGNALS

For an overview of Microprogram Sequencer logic, and how it is used within a 2900-based system, refer to our earlier discussion of this subject given for the 2909/2911 devices. The discussion which follows assumes that you understand how a Microprogram Sequencer fits into a 2900-based configuration.

2910 pins and signal assignments are illustrated in Figure 8-35. Figure 8-37 illustrates 2910 functional logic. We will describe signals in conjunction with functional logic.

The Output Multiplexer is central to logic of the 2910 Microprogram Sequencer. An instruction code input via I0-I3 determines which of the four possible inputs will be selected by the Output Multiplexer. In contrast, the 2909 and 2911 have two control inputs, S0 and S1, that determine the source which the Output Multiplexer selects.

> **2910
> MICROPROGRAM
> COUNTER**

D0-D11 are twelve data input lines which, like the 2911, can input data to the Address register, or to the Output Multiplexer. If $\overline{\text{RLD}}$ is low, then data input at D0-D11 is loaded into the Address register on the low-to-high transition of clock signal CP. Data input via D0-D11 is selected by the Output Multiplexer when an appropriate instruction is input via I0-I3. Timing for an Address register access may be illustrated as follows:

> **2910 DATA
> INPUT**

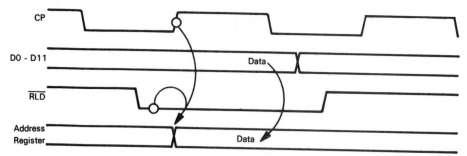

The 2910 outputs the microprogram address via Y0-Y11. These address output lines have their own enable signal $\overline{\text{OE}}$. If this signal is high, Y0-Y11 outputs are floated. This allows you to disconnect Microprogram Sequencer devices from the microprogram ROM, something you will likely do when switching to a test program.

> **2910
> ADDRESS
> OUTPUT**

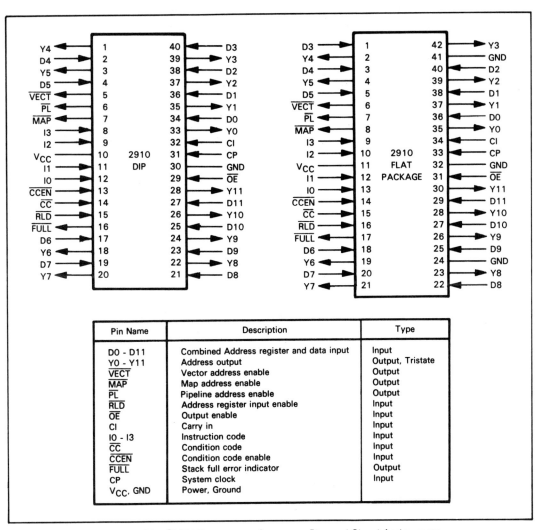

Pin Name	Description	Type
D0 - D11	Combined Address register and data input	Input
Y0 - Y11	Address output	Output, Tristate
$\overline{VECT}$	Vector address enable	Output
$\overline{MAP}$	Map address enable	Output
$\overline{PL}$	Pipeline address enable	Output
$\overline{RLD}$	Address register input enable	Input
$\overline{OE}$	Output enable	Input
CI	Carry in	Input
I0 - I3	Instruction code	Input
$\overline{CC}$	Condition code	Input
$\overline{CCEN}$	Condition code enable	Input
$\overline{FULL}$	Stack full error indicator	Output
CP	System clock	Input
V_{CC}, GND	Power, Ground	

Figure 8-36. 2910 Microprogram Sequencer Pins and Signal Assignments

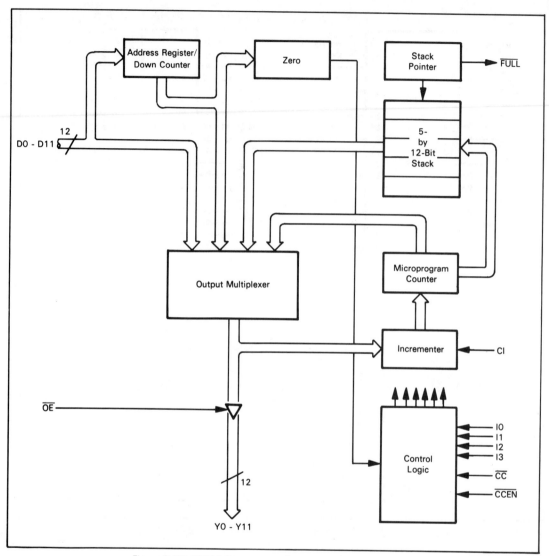

Figure 8-37. 2910 Microprogram Sequencer Functional Logic

Note that the 2910 has no zero input control on the address output lines, nor does it have any OR mask inputs. The 2909 and 2911 have such logic on the address output path. Instead, the 2910 uses its instruction codes to generate equivalent addressing logic.

Like the 2909 and the 2911, the **2910 has two internal locations within which addresses can be held. These are the Microprogram Counter and the Stack.**

The 2910 Microprogram Counter logic is functionally identical to that of the 2909/2911 Microprogram Counter. **Any address output by the output multiplexer also passes through the incrementer, and is then stored in the Microprogram Counter. If CI is input high, then the address output by the multiplexer is incremented** by 1 before being written to the Microprogram Counter. If CI is input low, then the address is written into the Microprogram Counter without being incremented.

| 2910 MICROPROGRAM COUNTER |
| 2910 INCREMENT |

The 2910 incrementer generates no Carry Out. Thus if you connect two 2910 Microprogram Sequencers in parallel, you cannot increment the resultant 24-bit Microprogram Counter contents across the low- and high-order halves of the address. But, given current microprogramming technology, this is unlikely to pose any problem. Few single microprograms have more than 4096 microinstructions, and you can use multiple 2910 Microprogram Sequencers to address large microprograms in discrete 4096-microinstruction blocks.

The 2910 Microprogram Sequencer has a five-level Stack. The Stack is addressed by a Stack Pointer which initially addresses Stack Register 0. Appropriate instruction codes, input via I0-I3, generate Stack pushes or pops. A Stack push writes the Microprogram Counter contents to the currently selected Stack location and then increments the Stack Pointer. The Stack Pointer always points to the last word written. A Stack pop decrements the Stack Pointer. You must select the Stack as the output multiplexer source in order to load the current top-of-stack plus one via the incrementer into the Microprogram Counter.

| 2910 STACK |

If you execute more than five pushes, the Stack Pointer continues to address the last Stack location (number 4); the Microprogram Counter contents are written into this location, overwriting prior data. This will inevitably cause an error. The 2910 Stack Pointer does not wrap around, and will not increment from 4 to 0. Stack full is indicated by the $\overline{FULL}$ signal. When either four words have been pushed and a fifth push is selected via I0-I3 or five words have been pushed, $\overline{FULL}$ goes low. Thus it can be tested to see if the Stack is full.

If you try to pop the Stack when the Stack Pointer is addressing location 0, then the Stack Pointer continues to select location 0. Since no data is written into the Stack following a pop, no prior information will be destroyed; however, in all probability you have a microprogramming error. No error signal is output at this time.

The various addressing operations which the 2910 Microprogram Sequencer can perform are identified using an instruction code input at I0-I3. $\overline{CCEN}$ (condition code enable) and $\overline{CC}$ (condition code) are two additional control inputs that in some cases modify the addressing operations which the 2910 Microprogram Sequencer will perform. These six 2910 signals — I0-I3, $\overline{CC}$, and $\overline{CCEN}$ — together replace the 2909/2911 signals S0, S1, $\overline{ZERO}$, OR0-OR3, $\overline{FE}$, and PUP.

| 2910 INSTRUCTION CODES |

2910 responses to I0-I3 inputs are summarized in Table 8-12. As shown in this table, many of the responses depend on the level of the $\overline{CC}$ and $\overline{CCEN}$ inputs. Vendor literature describes $\overline{CC}$ as a "condition code" and $\overline{CCEN}$ as an enable; however, in effect, **$\overline{CCEN}$ must be low while $\overline{CC}$ is high to select a "fail" condition, while any other combination of $\overline{CC}$ and $\overline{CCEN}$ input levels select a "pass" condition.** Your design logic can use $\overline{CC}$ as a pass/fail selector, with $\overline{CCEN}$ as an override. This logic may be illustrated as follows:

| 2910 CONDITION CODES |

In response to each instruction code input at I0-I3, 2910 logic performs operations which we will describe individually. Also, 2910 logic outputs low one of the three signals $\overline{PL}$, $\overline{MAP}$, or $\overline{VECT}$. You can use these three signals as you see fit, however their intended purpose is to enable one of three possible inputs to D0-D11. Figure 8-38 functionally illustrates timing for $\overline{PL}$, $\overline{MAP}$, and $\overline{VECT}$ as part of the 2910 microcycle response.

$\overline{VECT}$ low will normally select a restart interrupt or other special address.

$\overline{MAP}$ will normally enable the mapping ROM out of which a microprogram starting address is generated in response to a macroinstruction op-code.

$\overline{VECT}$ and $\overline{MAP}$ are the exceptional enable outputs. $\overline{PL}$ is the enable signal which is usually output low. This signal will likely enable the Microinstruction register, or a connected Data register, allowing the microinstruction to determine the next data input to appear at D0-D11. With reference to Figure 8-31, Figure 8-39 identifies how $\overline{VECT}$, $\overline{MAP}$ and $\overline{PL}$ will likely be used.

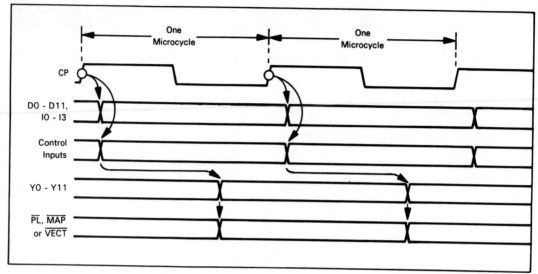

Figure 8-38. 2910 Microcycle Event Sequences

2910 MICROPROGRAM SEQUENCER INSTRUCTIONS

We will now examine 2910 Microprogram Sequencer instructions in detail. First, we will describe each instruction individually, then we will look at the instructions functionally, showing when instructions are likely to be used, and in what combinations.

Instruction 0 (JZ) is a Jump-to-Zero instruction. This instruction forces the address to be output at Y0-Y11; therefore the Microprogram Counter will subsequently hold the address 0 or 1, depending on the level of the CI input. The JZ instruction also resets the Stack Pointer to 0, effectively clearing the Stack. Since this instruction restarts execution with the microinstruction stored at microprogram memory location 0, JZ is frequently used as a power-up, reset, or Restart instruction code.

Instruction 1 (CJS) is a Conditional Jump-to-Subroutine instruction. A "pass" condition pushes the current Microprogram Counter contents onto the Stack and takes the next microinstruction address from the D0-D11 inputs. A "fail" condition causes the next sequential microinstruction to be executed. This may be illustrated as follows:

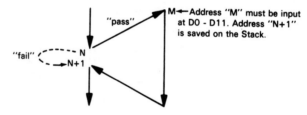

M ← Address "M" must be input at D0 - D11. Address "N+1" is saved on the Stack.

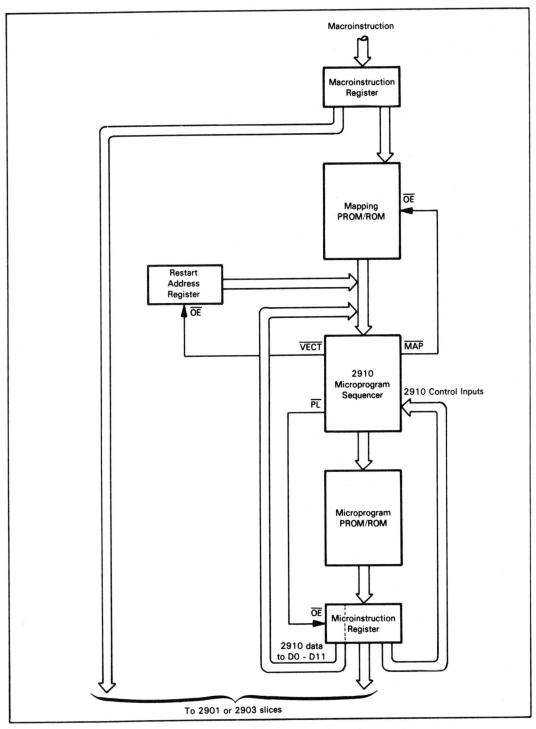

Figure 8-39. 2910 Enable Signal Utilization

Table 8-12. 2910 Microprogram Sequencer Instruction Codes Summary

Instruction Code					Vendor Mnemonic	Y Output	Enable Output	Stack Operation	Address Register/ Counter Operation	Comment
I3	I2	I1	I0	CC [1]						
0	0	0	0	X	JZ	0	PL	SP = 0	—	Reset or restart
0	0	0	1	0	CJS	D0 - D11	PL	PUSH	—	Jump to subroutine if $\overline{CC}$ is "pass"
0	0	0	1	1		[PC]	PL	—	—	Continue otherwise
0	0	1	0	X	JMAP	D0 - D11	MAP	—	—	Start new microprogram
0	0	1	1	0	CJP	D0 - D11	PL	—	—	Jump if $\overline{CC}$ is "pass"
0	0	1	1	1		[PC]	PL	—	—	Continue otherwise
0	1	0	0	0	PUSH	[PC]	PL	PUSH	D0 - D11	Push Stack and load Address register
0	1	0	0	1		[PC]	PL	PUSH	—	Push Stack
0	1	0	1	0	JSRP	D0 - D11	PL	PUSH	—	Jump- to-Subroutine
0	1	0	1	1		[AR]	PL	PUSH	—	
0	1	1	0	0	CJV	D0 - D11	VECT	—	—	Accept vector address if $\overline{CC}$ is "pass"
0	1	1	0	1		[PC]	VECT	—	—	Continue otherwise
0	1	1	1	0	JRP	D0 - D11	PL	—	—	Jump
0	1	1	1	1		[AR]	PL	—	—	
1	0	0	0	X	RFCT	[S]	PL	—	DEC	Counter not 0 } Repeat subroutine until
						[PC]	PL	POP	—	Counter 0 } Counter is 0
1	0	0	1	X	RPCT	D0 - D11	PL	—	DEC	Counter not 0 } Repeat loop until
						[PC]	PL	—	—	Counter 0 } Counter is 0
1	0	1	0	0	CRTN	[S]	PL	POP	—	Return from subroutine if $\overline{CC}$ is "pass"
1	0	1	0	1		[PC]	PL	—	—	Continue otherwise
1	0	1	1	0	CJPP	D0 - D11	PL	POP	—	Jump and return if $\overline{CC}$ is "pass"
1	0	1	1	1		[PC]	PL	—	—	Continue otherwise
1	1	0	0	X	LDCT	[PC]	PL	—	D0 - D11	Load Address register/Counter
1	1	0	1	0	LOOP	[PC]	PL	POP	—	End loop if $\overline{CC}$ is "pass"
1	1	0	1	1		[S]	PL	—	—	Continue otherwise
1	1	1	0	X	CONT	[PC]	PL	—	—	Continue with normal sequence
1	1	1	1	0	TWB	[PC]	PL	POP	DEC	Counter not 0 } If $\overline{CC}$ is "pass"
						[PC]	PL	POP	—	Counter 0 } decrement Counter to 0
1	1	1	1	1		[S]	PL	—	DEC	Counter not 0 } Otherwise decrement Counter
						D0 - D11	PL	POP	—	Counter 0 } to 0 and branch

[1] 0 represents $\overline{CC}$ is "pass" condition. $\overline{CCEN}$ = 1, or $\overline{CCEN}$ = 0 and $\overline{CC}$ = 0.
 1 represents $\overline{CC}$ "fail" condition. $\overline{CCEN}$ = 0 and $\overline{CC}$ = 1.
D0 - D11 = data input at D0 - D11.
[PC] = contents of Microprogram Counter.
[AR] = contents of Address register/Down Counter.
[S] = contents of Stack register currently addressed by the Stack Pointer.
SP = 0 means the Stack Pointer is reset to 0.
PUSH means write [PC] to [S] then increment Stack Pointer.
POP means decrement Stack Pointer.
DEC means decrement [AR].

Instruction 2 (JMAP) is a Jump Map instruction. This instruction outputs the address input at D0-D11, together with a low $\overline{MAP}$ enable. The Microprogram Counter subsequently holds the address which was input at D0-D11, or this address incremented by 1, depending on the CI input. JMAP is usually the first code input to a 2910 Microprogram Sequencer at the start of a new macroinstruction's execution. That is to say, the last microinstruction implementing the Central Processing Unit's instruction fetch sequence will transmit a JMAP code to the 2910 Microprogram Sequencer. The $\overline{MAP}$ output will enable the mapping ROM which receives as its address input the macroinstruction op-code, and generates as its output the address for the first microinstruction to be executed in response to the macroinstruction (see Figure 8-40). We described this sequence in detail when discussing the 2909 and 2911 Microprogram Sequencer. We can illustrate the JMAP instruction code as follows:

Instruction code 3 (CJP) is a Conditional Jump Pipeline instruction. If the condition code "passes", then D0-D11 provides the next address output via Y.

If the condition code "fails", then the next sequential instruction is executed. The address input to D0-D11 will come from the external location enabled by $\overline{PL}$. As illustrated in Figure 8-40, this will probably be the Microinstruction register. This may be illustrated as follows:

Instruction code 4 (PUSH) is a Stack Push instruction which also loads the Address register if the condition code passes. There are many ways in which you can use this instruction. At its most elementary level, it is a Subroutine Call (represented by the push) with an optional simultaneous data load into the Address register. The data loaded into the Address register will probably come from the microinstruction itself, since PL is output low by the push.

Instruction code 5 is a Conditional Jump-to-Subroutine (JSRP). This instruction code pushes the Microprogram Counter contents onto the Stack, and calls one of two subroutines, depending on the condition code. If the condition code "passes", then the subroutine starting address is provided immediately at the D0-D11 inputs. If the condition code "fails", then the subroutine starting address is taken from the Address register. This may be illustrated as follows:

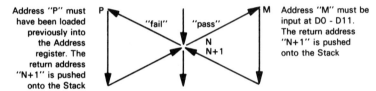

Instruction code 6 is a Conditional Jump Vector (CJV). It is significant principally because it is the only instruction code which generates a low $\overline{VECT}$ output. This low output usually enables a special Address register, out of which a direct memory access or interrupt address is fetched.

If $\overline{CC}$ is in the "pass" condition, then the output multiplexer takes as its source D0-D11. If $\overline{CC}$ is in the "fail" condition, the next sequential instruction is executed.

Instruction code 7 is a Conditional Jump (JRP) which differs from the Conditional Jump-to-Subroutine (instruction code 5) only in that no push occurs. If the condition code "passes", then the microinstruction execution sequence jumps to the address which is input at D0-D11; otherwise, the microinstruction sequence jumps to the address held in the Address register. This may be illustrated as follows:

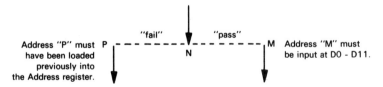

Instruction code 8 is a Repeat-Loop-Until-Counter-Is-Zero (RFCT) instruction. The purpose of this instruction code is to re-execute one or more microinstructions some fixed number of times. The microinstruction loop to be re-executed has its starting address stored in the Stack. The loop count is handled by the Address register, which must be preloaded with a number that is one less than the required count. For example, if the Address register is loaded with an initial value of 8, then the microinstruction loop will be executed 9 times. Thus, you can load into the Address register values ranging between 0 and 4095 to generate counts ranging between 1 and 4096.

When the 2910 receives an RFCT instruction code, it examines the Address register contents. If the Address register does not contain 0, then the output multiplexer takes as its source the currently addressed Stack location; the Address register contents are then decremented. If the Address register contents are 0, then the output multiplexer selects the Microprogram Counter as its source; also the Stack is popped.

We can illustrate the RFCT instruction code as follows:

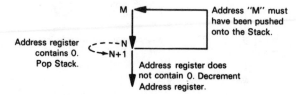

Now the RFCT instruction, as illustrated above, re-executes a loop if the branch address M precedes N, where N is the microprogram location. But you can push any address onto the Stack prior to executing an RFCT code. For example, RFCT could be used to branch some fixed number of times without re-executing a loop. This may be illustrated as follows:

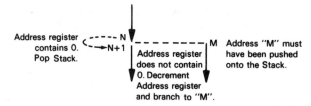

Instruction code 9, the Repeat-Register-Until-Counter-Is-Zero (RPCT) instruction, is almost identical to instruction code 8. RPCT again uses the Address register as a counter. If when RPCT is executed the Address register does not contain 0, then it is decremented and the output multiplexer chooses as its source an immediate address input at D0-D11. If the Address register contents are 0, then the output multiplexer selects as its source the Microprogram Counter. The Stack is not used.

If the microinstruction which generates the RPCT code supplies its own address at D0-D11, then this microinstruction gets re-executed the number of times specified by the Address register contents. This may be illustrated as follows:

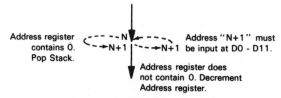

But a microinstruction does not have to supply its own address at D0-D11 when specifying the RPCT instruction code. It can input any address at D0-D11. Thus, RPCT can be used to re-execute an instruction loop, or RPCT can be used to execute any other branch some fixed number of times, as illustrated for the RFCT instruction code.

Instruction code A is a Conditional Return-from-Subroutine (CRTN). If the condition code "passes", then a Return-from-Subroutine occurs. The output multiplexer takes the currently addressed Stack register as its source, then pops the Stack. If the condition code "fails", then the next microinstruction address is taken from the Microprogram Counter. This may be illustrated as follows:

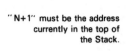 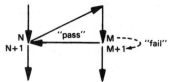

Instruction code B is a Conditional Jump-and-Return instruction (CJPP). If the condition code "passes", then the Stack is popped, but the output multiplexer takes D0-D11 as its source. This is equivalent to a subroutine return where the return address is not taken from the Stack, even though the Stack is popped; rather, the return address is taken from D0-D11. If the condition code "fails", then normal sequential microinstruction execution occurs with the next microinstruction address being taken from the Microprogram Counter.

Instruction code C is a Load Counter instruction (LDCC). When this instruction code is executed, microprogram execution continues sequentially, with the output multiplexer taking the Microprogram Counter as its source; however, data input at D0-D11 is loaded into the Address register.

Instruction code D is a Conditional End-of-Loop (LOOP). As long as the condition code "fails", the output multiplexer selects the currently addressed Stack register as its source. When the condition code "passes", the Microprogram Counter is selected as the output multiplexer source and the Stack is popped. This may be illustrated as follows:

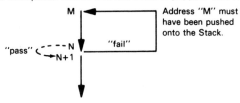

Address "M" must have been pushed onto the Stack.

The LOOP instruction code is equivalent to the RFCT instruction code, with the condition code, rather than the Address register, determining the number of loop iterations.

The LOOP instruction code does not have to be used to re-execute a loop. In the illustration above a loop is re-executed only because the address M is shown preceding N, the microinstruction address where the loop code is generated. If the address M does not precede N, then the LOOP instruction code becomes a simple conditional jump, where the jump address is held at the top of the Stack.

Instruction code E is a Continue instruction (CONT). This is the normal default instruction code. It causes the next sequential microinstruction to be addressed. The output multiplexer selects the Microprogram Counter as its source. No other operations occur.

Instruction code F is a three-way branch (TWB); it uses the condition code and the Address register. Whether the condition code "passes" or "fails", the Address register contents are decremented to 0. If the condition code "passes", then the Stack is popped and the Microprogram Counter is selected as the output multiplexer source. If the condition code "fails", then the Stack is selected by the output multiplexer while the Address register is decrementing, but when the Address register has decremented to 0, the Stack is popped and the output multiplexer selects as its source data input at D0-D11. These options may be illustrated as follows:

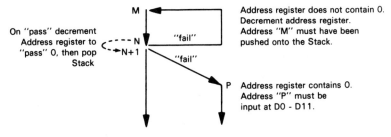

Address register does not contain 0. Decrement address register. Address "M" must have been pushed onto the Stack.

Address register contains 0. Address "P" must be input at D0 - D11.

The TWB instruction code is, in effect, a conditional loop execute. While the condition code is failing, the microinstruction sequence between M and N is re-executed a number of times, as defined by the Address register; microprogram execution then branches to an address input at D0-D11. But any single loop iteration can be bypassed by a "pass" condition code; moreover, when the Address register has decremented to 0, microprogram execution can continue sequentially, or it can branch to the address input at D0-D11.

2910 MICROPROGRAM SEQUENCER ADDRESSING SEQUENCES

Let us now examine some of the more common microprogram address sequences which you are likely to encounter, and how these address sequences will be generated using a 2910 Microprogram Sequencer.

A simple sequence of consecutive microinstructions represents the simplest case:

Address Sequence	2910 Instruction Code Sequence
N	CONT
N+1	CONT
N+2	CONT
N+3	CONT
etc	etc

You generate sequential microinstruction addresses, as required by the sequence above, using instruction code E, with the CI input high.

You will likely initialize your microprogram in one of two ways:

1) Following a restart or special condition, use instruction code 0 (JZ); this forces a 0 output at Y. 0 or 1 can be written to the Microprogram Counter — depending on the level of the CI input.

2) At the end of an instruction fetch, use instruction code 2 (JMAP) to take the microprogram starting address from a mapping ROM. We described this instruction code earlier.

2910 MICROPROGRAM INITIALIZATION

The 2910 Microprogram Sequencer gives you many ways of jumping within a microprogram. Any instruction code that causes the output multiplexer to select D0-D11 or the Address register as its source can be used to generate a microprogram jump. Instruction code 3 (CJP) jumps to the address input at D0-D11 if the condition code passes. So does instruction code 6 (CJV), but instruction code 6 (CJV) outputs $\overline{VECT}$ low — and the $\overline{VECT}$ enable signal is commonly used to select a special DMA or interrupt address. Instruction code 7 (JRP) is a dual, unconditional jump; if the condition code "passes", the jump address is taken from D0-D11, while the jump address is taken from the Address register if the condition code "fails".

2910 MICROPROGRAM JUMP

A microprogram subroutine is called using instruction code 5 (JSRP). This instruction code pushes the Microprogram Counter contents onto the Stack; the subroutine starting address is taken from D0-D11 if the condition code "passes", and from the Address register if the condition code "fails". The Address register must have been preloaded with an appropriate starting address if the condition code "fails". Generally, instruction code C (LDCT) is used to load the Address register.

2910 MICROPROGRAM JUMP-TO-SUBROUTINE

A normal Return-from-Subroutine will use instruction code A (CRTN) with the condition code held "passing".

There are two types of loop you may encounter in a microprogram. You may wish to re-execute a single microinstruction, or a sequence of microinstructions some number of times.

The simplest way of re-executing a single microinstruction some fixed number of times is to load the Address register with a number one less than the required count, then issue instruction code 9 (RPCT). This may be illustrated as follows:

Address Sequence	2910 Instruction Code Sequence
N	LDCT with M-1 to D0-D11
N+1 (M times)	RPCT with N+1 to D0-D11
N+2	CONT

You can alternatively use instruction code 8 (RFCT) to re-execute a single microinstruction, but the microinstruction address must be preloaded onto the Stack.

More frequently, instruction code 8 (RFCT) will be used at the end of a multi-microinstruction loop. This may be illustrated as follows:

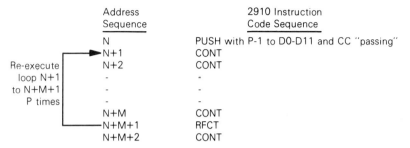

	Address Sequence	2910 Instruction Code Sequence
	N	PUSH with P-1 to D0-D11 and CC "passing"
	N+1	CONT
Re-execute	N+2	CONT
loop N+1	-	-
to N+M+1	-	-
P times	-	-
	N+M	CONT
	N+M+1	RFCT
	N+M+2	CONT

As illustrated above, the microinstruction preceding the loop must input instruction code 4 (PUSH) with the condition code passing. This simultaneously loads the count into the Address register while pushing the next sequential address onto the Stack. Subsequently instruction code 8 (RFCT) decrements the Address register, selecting the address which PUSH saved on the Stack, until the Address register has decremented to 0.

2910 ADDRESSING EXAMPLE

As we did for the 2911 Microprogram Sequencer, we will now look again at the twos complement binary division microprogram given in Table 8-9, adding address generation microinstruction bits needed by the 2910 Microprogram Sequencer. See Table 8-13.

We are going to treat the twos complement binary division microprogram as a subroutine. We assume, therefore, that microinstruction 1 is executed following a Jump-to-Subroutine instruction code input to the 2910 Microprogram Sequencer.

Microinstruction 1 inputs a CONT instruction code to I0-I3 of the 2910 Microprogram Sequencer. This causes the next sequential microinstruction to be executed. Since the 2910 does not sample its D0-D11 inputs, these bits are irrelevant. CI is input high since the 2910 Microprogram Counter contents must increment. $\overline{RLD}$ and $\overline{CCEN}$ are high since no data is to be written into the Address register, and the condition code is not used.

Although microinstruction 1 itself transmits the simplest possible addressing logic to the 2910, the ZERO status output by the 2903 while microinstruction 1 is executed contributes to microinstruction 2 address generation logic. The binary division subroutine must be aborted if the divisor is 0. This abort condition is indicated by a ZERO status output following execution of microinstruction 1. This ZERO status is output too late during microinstruction 1's microcycle to be considered by 2910 addressing logic during execution of microinstruction 1. Therefore, in the event that the subroutine must be aborted, microinstruction 2 gets executed gratuitously, but causes an abort exit from the subroutine after its gratuitous execution. **The CJP instruction code is input to the 2910 Microprogram Sequencer by microinstruction 2** in order to achieve this end. This instruction code causes the next sequential microinstruction to be addressed if the condition code "fails", while the addressing input at D0-D11 is selected if the condition code "passes". The address of the microinstruction to be selected following an abort is therefore input via bits D0-D11. In order to enable the condition code, $\overline{CCEN}$ is low. $\overline{CC}$ must be connected to the complement of Z while microinstruction 2 is being executed. This allows the ZERO status output by the execution of microinstruction 1 to generate the $\overline{CC}$ input during microinstruction 2 — and thus generate an abort, if needed. We do not show the logic which causes $\overline{CC}$ to be connected to the complement of the 2903 Z status. There are many ways in which such "one time" connections can be made. Possibly the simplest technique is to add microinstruction bits which enable a specific NOR gate linking the 2910 $\overline{CC}$ input with the 2903 Z output. This may be illustrated as follows:

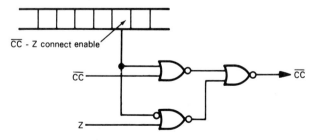

$\overline{CC}$ - Z connect enable

$\overline{CC}$

Z

$\overline{CC}$

Table 8-13. The 2903 Twos Complement Binary Division Microprogram Subroutine from Table 8-9, with 2910 Addressing Microinstruction Fields Added

No	Microinstruction			$\overline{EA}$	CN	A0 - A3	B0 - B3	Comment
	I8 - I5	I4 - I1	I0					
1	4	6	0	0	0	Divisor register (R0)	Divisor buffer (R3)	Copy divisor to temporary buffer.
2	4	6	0	0	0	Dividend (MS) register (R1)	Dividend (MS) buffer (R2)	Copy dividend most significant half to temporary buffer.
3	5	0	0	X	0	X	Dividend (MS) buffer (R2)	Convert dividend (MS) from twos complement to sign/magnitude version. Test OVR externally while next microinstruction is being executed. If OVR is 1, branch to subroutine that downshifts dividend.
4	5	0	0	X	0	X	Divisor buffer (R3)	Convert divisor (MS) from twos complement to sign/magnitude version. Test OVR externally. If OVR is 1, branch to microinstruction 9.
5	9	4	0	X	0	X	Dividend (MS) buffer (R2)	Shift out sign bit of dividend (MS) half in temporary buffer.
6	9	4	0	X	0	X	Divisor buffer (R3)	Shift out sign bit of divisor in temporary buffer.
7	F	2	0	0	1	Dividend (MS) buffer (R2)	Divisor buffer (R3)	Subtract sign bit stripped divisor from sign bit stripped dividend (MS) half. If Carry = 1 (dividend larger) branch to subroutine that downshifts dividend or upshifts divisor.
8	6	6	0	0	0	Dividend (LS) register (R4)	X	Copy dividend least significant half to Q register.
9	A*	0	0	0	0	Divisor register (R0)	Dividend (MS) register (R1)	Double length normalize dividend in MS register and Q register.
10	C*	0	0	0	Z	Divisor register (R0)	Dividend (MS) register (R1)	Execute twos complement divide instruction fourteen times.
11	E	0	0	0	Z	Divisor register (R0)	Dividend (MS) register (R1)	Twos complement divide final instruction.

*CN is connected to Z status while these two special functions are being executed.

Microinstruction Number	2903 Bits: I8 I7 I6 I5 I4 I3 I2 I1 I0 EA CN A3 A2 A1 A0 B3 B2 B1 B0	2910 Bits: I3 I2 I1 I0 D11 D10 D9 D8 D7 D6 D5 D4 D3 D2 D1 D0 / CCEN CI RLD	2910 Addressing Operations
1	0 1 0 0 0 1 1 0 0 0 0 0 0 0 0 0 0 0 1 1 — 4 6 0 0 0 R0 R3	1 1 1 0 X X X X X X X X X X X X — E = CONT / 1 1 1 / 1 1 1	Select next sequential instruction.
2	0 1 0 0 0 1 1 0 0 0 0 0 0 0 1 0 0 1 0 — 4 6 0 0 0 R1 R2	0 0 1 1 A A A A A A A A A A A A — 3 = CJP / Address for abort / 0 1 1 / 0 1 1	$\overline{CC}$ is generated by 2903 Z status ($\overline{CC} = \overline{Z}$). Select next sequential microinstruction unless R0 from microinstruction 1 is 0. Then abort.
3	0 1 0 1 0 0 0 0 0 X 0 X X X X 0 0 1 0 — 5 0 0 0 R2	1 1 1 0 X X X X X X X X X X X X — E = CONT / 1 1 1 / 1 1 1	Select next sequential instruction.
4	0 1 0 1 0 0 0 0 0 X 0 X X X X 0 0 1 1 — 5 0 0 0 R3	0 0 0 1 S S S S S S S S S S S S — 1 = CJS / Scale dividend subroutine / 0 1 1 / 0 1 1	$\overline{CC}$ is generated by $\overline{OVR}$ status. ($\overline{CC} = \overline{OVR}$). Select next sequential instruction unless OVR = 1. Then call "scale dividend" subroutine.
5	1 0 0 1 0 1 0 0 0 X 0 X X X X 0 0 1 0 — 9 4 0 0 R2	0 0 1 1 B B B B B B B B B B B B — 3 = CJP / Microinstruction 8 address / 0 1 1 / 0 1 1	$\overline{CC}$ is generated by OVR status. ($\overline{CC} = \overline{OVR}$). Select next sequential instruction unless OVR = 1. Then branch to microinstruction 8.
6	1 0 0 1 0 1 0 0 0 X 0 X X X X 0 0 1 1 — 9 4 0 0 R3	1 1 1 0 X X X X X X X X X X X X — E = CONT / 1 1 1 / 1 1 1	Select next sequential instruction.
7	1 1 1 1 0 0 1 0 0 0 1 0 0 1 0 0 0 1 1 — F 2 0 0 1 R2 R3	1 1 1 0 X X X X X X X X X X X X — E = CONT / 1 1 1 / 1 1 1	Select next sequential instruction.
8	0 1 1 0 0 1 1 0 0 0 0 0 1 0 0 X X X X — 6 6 0 0 0 R4	0 0 0 1 T T T T T T T T T T T T — 1 = CJS / Scale divisor or dividend subroutine / 0 1 1 / 0 1 1	$\overline{CC}$ is generated by C(N+4). ($\overline{CC} = \overline{C(N+4)}$). Select next sequential instruction unless C(N+4) = 1. Then call "scale divisor or dividend" subroutine.
9	1 0 1 0 0 0 0 0 0 0 0 0 0 0 0 0 0 0 1 — A 0 0 0 0 R0 R1	0 1 0 0 0 0 0 0 0 0 0 0 1 1 0 1 — 4 = PUSH / Count = 13 / 1 1 0 / 1 1 0	Load count into address register, push next sequential instruction address onto Stack and select next sequential instruction.
10	1 1 0 0 0 0 0 0 0 X 0 0 0 0 0 0 0 0 1 — C 0 0 0 0 R0 R1	1 0 0 0 X X X X X X X X X X X X — 8 = RFCT / 1 1 1 / 1 1 1	Re-execute instruction addressed by Stack until count decrements to 0.
11	1 1 1 0 0 0 0 0 0 X 0 0 0 0 0 0 0 0 1 — E 0 0 0 0 R0 R1	1 0 1 0 X X X X X X X X X X X X — A = CRTN / 1 1 1 / 1 1 1	Return from subroutine.

X = "Don't Care" bits

While it may appear wasteful to dedicate a single microinstruction bit to enabling such a connection, perhaps only once in an entire microprogram, in fact the economics of microprogramming often favor wasting a single bit in this way. The alternative is to have additional logic which generates a particular input, from one of a variety of outputs, depending on complex combinations of circumstances. To evaluate this reasoning look at Table 8-13, where $\overline{CC}$ may be connected at different times to a Zero, Overflow or C(N+4) status. You cannot guarantee that the $\overline{CC}$ generation logic will be a known function of any bit field within the microinstruction, since the same bit field may recur somewhere else in the microprogram without having the same $\overline{CC}$ logic requirements. Your only alternative to dedicating a microinstruction bit to each $\overline{CC}$ generation possibility would be to decode the microinstruction address itself; and that would not be simple.

Microinstruction 3 is another example of a microinstruction that **generates a status output which contributes to subsequent addressing logic** — but not until the next microinstruction. Microinstruction 3 itself provides the 2910 with a CONT instruction code, which together with a high CI causes the next sequential microinstruction address to be output by the 2910. The data bits D0-D11 are not used; $\overline{RLD}$ and $\overline{CCEN}$ are both high (i.e., in the "off" state). At the 2903, microinstruction 3 performs a twos complement to sign/magnitude conversion on the contents of RAM location R2. If this operation generates a high Overflow status, then R2, which contains the high-order half of the dividend, must be scaled by shifting down one bit position. The subroutine should be called, if needed, after microinstruction 3 has been executed, and before microinstruction 4 is executed. But microinstruction 3 outputs OVR too late in its microcycle for this status to contribute to the next microinstruction address. Therefore microinstruction 4 provides the 2910 with addressing logic that tests the OVR status from microinstruction 3's execution. CJS, the Conditional Jump-to-Subroutine, is specified by inputting 1 as the 2910 instruction code. The address of microinstruction 1's subroutine is held in data field bits D0-D11. $\overline{CCEN}$ is output low so that $\overline{CC}$ can be tested. $\overline{CC}$ must be connected to the complement of the 2903 OVR status output. If $\overline{CC}$ is low — and OVR is high — then the subroutine addressed by D0-D11 will be called. Otherwise, since CI is high, the 2910 will output the next sequential microinstruction address — which is the address of microinstruction 5. $\overline{RLD}$ is output high since the address at D0-D11 must not be written into the Address register. As we did in instruction 2, again in microinstruction 4 an additional microinstruction bit will likely connect $\overline{CC}$-to-OVR via NOR gates. And once again we will choose to waste this $\overline{CC}$-to-OVR connector bit for the vast majority of microinstructions where such a connection does not apply.

While microinstruction 4 provides the 2910 with addressing inputs that test the Overflow status generated by microinstruction 3, the Overflow status itself is modified by the 2903 while microinstruction 4 is being executed. This presents no timing problems, since the 2910 has stopped sampling its $\overline{CC}$ input by the time microinstruction 4 modifies the Overflow status. See Figure 8-38.

Microinstruction 5 must provide the 2910 with addressing inputs that account for the Overflow status generated by microinstruction 4, just as microinstruction 4 had to provide the 2910 with addressing inputs that took into account the Overflow status generated by microinstruction 3. Microinstruction 5 causes the 2910 to execute a conditional jump, rather than a conditional subroutine call, since a high Overflow status generated by the 2903 while executing microinstruction 4 requires microinstructions 5, 6, and 7 to be bypassed. We do not bypass microinstruction 5, since it is during this microinstruction's execution that the 2910 will test the Overflow status from microinstruction 4 — and determine if a jump is required. This would present a problem if execution of microinstruction 5 upset the 2903 logic sequence; but it does not. If executed unnecessarily no harm is done. But remember, there may be circumstances under which you may have to insert a dummy microinstruction that generates no operation at a 2903, but gives the 2910 time to test 2903 status from the previous microinstruction.

In our present example **microinstruction 5 inputs a CJP instruction code** at I0-I3 of the 2910 and the address of microinstruction 8 at D0-D11. $\overline{CCEN}$ is low so that 2910 condition code logic will sample $\overline{CC}$, which remains connected to the 2903 OVR status, as it was during execution of microinstruction 4. $\overline{RLD}$ is high so that the address input at D0-D11 does not get written into the Address register. CI is high since the next sequential microinstruction must be selected if OVR is low — and the condition code test "fails"

If the condition code test "fails" at the 2910 during execution of microinstruction 5, then **microinstructions 6 and 7 are next executed sequentially.** Each of these microinstructions provides the 2910 with a simple CONT input at I0-I3, no data inputs, and $\overline{CCEN}$ and $\overline{RLD}$ disabled with CI high, so that the Microprogram Counter will increment.

Microinstruction 7 subtracts modified versions of the divisor from the dividend. If the Carry Out generated by the 2903 at C(N+4) is 1, then the divisor must be upshifted (or the dividend must be downshifted) in order to guarantee that the divisor ultimately has the larger absolute value. C(N+4) is generated by the 2903 at the end of the microinstruction 7 microcycle — too late for the 2910 to take this status output into account until the next microcycle, during which microinstruction 8 is executed. **In Table 8-13 we show microinstruction 8 providing a Conditional-Jump-to-Subroutine input to I0-I3, with a subroutine address input to D0-D11.** This 2910 addressing logic is identical to that which we have already described for microinstruction 4, except that the condition code $\overline{CC}$ will now be connected to the 2903 C(N+4) output — again via a special enabling microinstruction bit. The fact that microinstruction 5 might have caused the 2910 to generate a branch to microinstruction 8 is not a problem, since C(N+4) will be low following execution of microinstruction 5; therefore if microinstruction 8 is executed next, the condition code must fail.

Microinstruction 9 is executed after microinstruction 8 — possibly with a scaling subroutine executed in between. **Microinstruction 9 prepares the 2910 for execution of microinstruction 10.** A PUSH instruction code is input at I0-I4, with a count input at D0-D11. $\overline{RLD}$ is low so that the count gets written into the Address register. The 2910 then outputs the address of microinstruction 10 since CI is high — so the Microprogram Counter gets incremented.

Microinstruction 10 outputs an RFCT instruction code to the 2910 via I0-I3. This instruction code causes the 2910 to output the address held at the top of the Stack until the Address register decrements to zero. The push performed by the 2910 while microinstruction 9 was executing loaded microinstruction 10's address onto the Stack, therefore microinstruction 10 gets re-executed 13 times — for a total of 14 executions.

After the Address register has decremented 13 times to 0, the RFCT instruction code causes the 2910 to output the next sequential instruction — that of **microinstruction 11. This is the terminating microinstruction** for the twos complement binary division microprogram subroutine. Therefore a Return-from-Subroutine code, CRTN, is transmitted to the 2910 via I0-I3. In order to force a pass condition, this being a Conditional Subroutine Return instruction, code $\overline{CCEN}$ is output high.

THE 2930 AND 2932 PROGRAM CONTROL UNITS

**These two parts were designed to provide assembly language instructions with their memory address genera-
tion logic. The internal architecture of these two devices approximates a 2901 whose local RAM has been converted into a Stack, while the Q register functions as a local data register.**

In reality, **the 2930 series devices** are hybrid parts that **may substitute for 2909/10/11 Microprogram Sequencers, or they may be used separately to implement assembly language instructions' memory addressing logic.
The 2930 series devices are probably more effective as microprogram sequencers.** In this role you need only make
sure that timing requirements of the 2930 series devices are compatible with the 2901 or 2903 central logic you are
using. But as assembly language memory address generators 2930 series devices leave a great deal to be desired. They
cannot cope with indirect memory addressing, since by its very definition indirect memory addressing requires intermediate access of external memory. Also, most minicomputer and microcomputer assembly languages depend on an
external memory stack which cannot be implemented within the small, local stack provided by 2930 series devices.
Therefore, 2930 series devices do little more than add indexes to base addresses. But the value of 2930 series devices
increases dramatically when you are not building a general purpose central processing unit. If you are building dedicated CPU-based logic that uses both microcode and higher level instructions, then you can probably avoid indirect addressing, and you can work with the limited 2930 series stack.

**The 2930 series devices are both 4-bit slices. The 2930 is the most advanced of the two devices; it is fully
cascadable and packaged as a 28-pin DIP. The 2932 device is packaged as a 20-pin DIP and is also cascadable.**

These two devices differ only in their internal instruction logic.

Both 2930 devices are manufactured using bipolar technology; they use a single +5V power supply and have TTL-level
compatible signals.

2930/32 DEVICE PINS AND SIGNALS

**We will describe pins and signal assignments for these two devices together, and in conjunction with their
functional logic. Device pins and signals are illustrated in Figure 8-40. Functional logic is illustrated in Figure
8-41.**

The Adder is central to 2930 series operations. The Adder accepts one or two operands as inputs, and generates a
single output. The Adder can perform three different operations:

1) It can add (with carry) the two operand inputs. CN determines the level of the carry during addition.

2) It can increment a single operand by adding CN to the operand.

3) It can output a single operand unaltered.

R and S in Figure 8-41 are the two Adder operands. The R operand can have one of three | **2930 SERIES**
sources. The S operand can have one of four sources. An instruction code selects the source for | **INSTRUCTION**
the R and S operands, together with Adder operations. **The 2930 has a 5-bit instruction code,** | **CODES**
input at I0-I4. The 2932 has a 4-bit instruction code, input at I0-I3. These instruction codes do
more than control logic around the Adder and its inputs, they also control the Stack Accumulator and Program
Counter, **as summarized in Table 8-14.**. This table is keyed to the 2930. The set of 2932 instruction codes is a subset
of the 2930 instruction code set, and is so identified.

The 2930 allows you to enable or disable the Adder output using the output enable signal $\overline{OE}$. The 2932 has no
such output enable signal; Adder output from this device is always enabled. But when $\overline{OE}$ is input high to the 2930 the
Y0-Y3 outputs are floated.

Data may be held in three different places within 2930 series devices; these three places are the Accumulator, the Program Counter, and the Stack.

The Accumulator is a single 4-bit location that can receive data input via D0-D3, or it can | **2930 SERIES**
receive output from the Adder. The instruction code determines which of the two inputs, if | **ACCUMULATOR**
either, will be written into the Accumulator. **The 2930,** but not the 2932, **has a separate Ac-**
cumulator enable control signal $\overline{RE}$. This enable control signal is subordinate to the instruction code. The level of $\overline{RE}$ is
unimportant when the instruction code specifies that data will be written into the Accumulator. For other instruction
codes, a low $\overline{RE}$ input causes immediate data at D0-D3 to be written into the Accumulator.

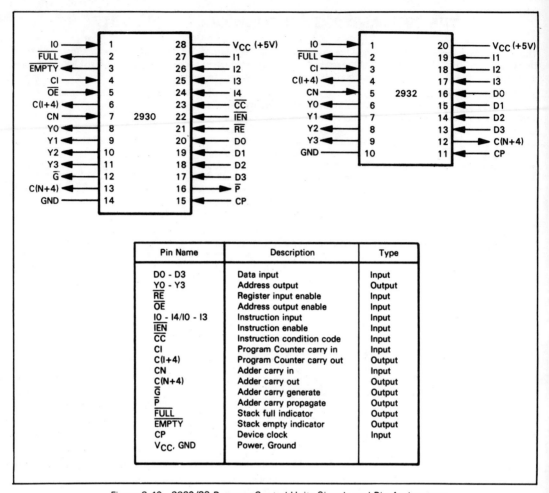

Pin Name	Description	Type
DO - D3	Data input	Input
YO - Y3	Address output	Output
$\overline{RE}$	Register input enable	Input
$\overline{OE}$	Address output enable	Input
IO - I4/IO - I3	Instruction input	Input
$\overline{IEN}$	Instruction enable	Input
$\overline{CC}$	Instruction condition code	Input
CI	Program Counter carry in	Input
C(I+4)	Program Counter carry out	Output
CN	Adder carry in	Input
C(N+4)	Adder carry out	Output
$\overline{G}$	Adder carry generate	Output
$\overline{P}$	Adder carry propagate	Output
$\overline{FULL}$	Stack full indicator	Output
$\overline{EMPTY}$	Stack empty indicator	Output
CP	Device clock	Input
V_{CC}, GND	Power, Ground	

Figure 8-40. 2930/32 Program Control Units Signals and Pin Assignments

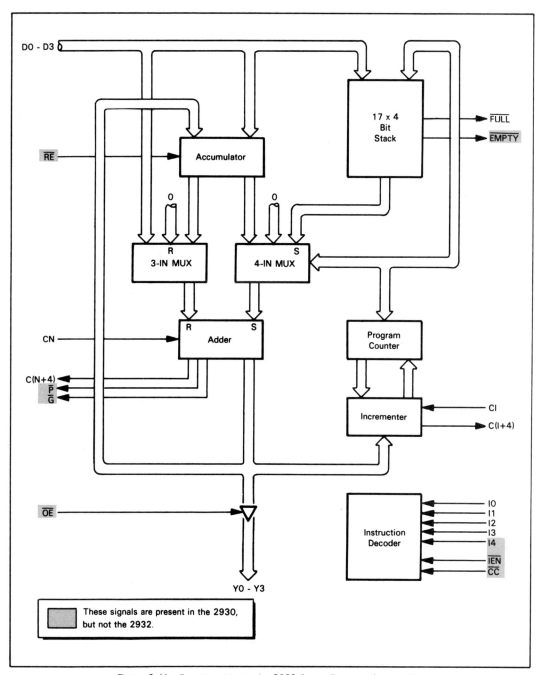

Figure 8-41. Functional Logic for 2930 Series Program Control Units

8-127

Table 8-14. 2930 Series Program Control Unit Instruction Codes Summary

	Instruction Code No.	I4 I3 I2 I1 I0	Output at Y0-Y3	New PC Contents	Accumulator Contents (1)	Stack Operation	2932 (4) Instructions No.	I3 I2 I1 I0	Comment
Unconditional Instructions	0	0 0 0 0 0	0	CI	[D]	0 →[SP]	0	0 0 0 0	Device reset
	1	0 0 0 0 1	[PC]	[PC] + CI	[D]	None	4	0 1 0 0	Output Program Counter contents
	2	0 0 0 1 0	[R]	[PC] + CI	[D]	None	8	1 0 0 0	Output Accumulator contents
	3	0 0 0 1 1	[D]	[PC] + CI	[D]	None			Output immediate data
	4	0 0 1 0 0	[R] + [D] + CN	[PC] + CI	[D]	None			Output sum of Accumulator contents and Immediate data
	5	0 0 1 0 1	[PC] + [D] + CN	[PC] + CI	[D]	None			Output sum of Program Counter and immediate data
	6	0 0 1 1 0	[PC] + [R] + CN	[PC] + CI	[D]	None	9	1 0.,0 1	Output sum of Program Counter and Accumulator
	7	0 0 1 1 1	[S] + [D] + CN	[PC] + CI	[D]	None			Output sum of Stack and immediate data
	8	0 1 0 0 0	[PC]	[PC] + CI	[PC]*	None	A	1 0 1 0	Output Program Counter contents and unconditionally load Accumulator
	9	0 1 0 0 1	[R] + [D] + CN	[PC] + CI	[R] + [D] + CN*	None			Output sum of Accumulator and immediate data, and unconditionally load Accumulator
	A	0 1 0 1 0	[PC]	[PC] + CI	[D]*	None	F	1 1 1 1	Output Program Counter contents. Unconditionally load immediate data into Accumulator
	B	0 1 0 1 1	[PC]	[PC] + CI	[D]	PUSH [PC]	6	0 1 1 0	Output and push Program Counter contents
	C	0 1 1 0 0	[PC]	[PC] + CI	[D]	PUSH [D]	2	0 0 1 0	Output Program Counter contents and push immediate data
	D	0 1 1 0 1	[S]	[PC] + CI	[D]	POP			Pop and output Stack
	E	0 1 1 1 0	[PC]	[PC] + CI	[D]	POP	3	0 0 1 1	Output Program Counter and pop Stack
	F	0 1 1 1 1	[PC]	[PC]	[D]	None			Output and hold Program Counter
Conditional Instructions (3)	10	1 0 0 0 0	[R]	[R + CI	[D]	None	B	1 0 1 1	Jump to address in Accumulator
	11	1 0 0 0 1	[D]	[D] + CI	[D]	None	5	0 1 0 1	Jump to address given by immediate data
	12	1 0 0 1 0	0	CI	[D]	None			Jump to "0"
	13	1 0 0 1 1	[R] + [D] + CN	[R] + [D] + CN + CI	[D]	None			Jump to address given by sum of Accumulator and immeidate data
	14	1 0 1 0 0	[PC] + [D] + CN	[PC] + [D] + CN + CI	[D]	None			Jump to address given by sum of Program Counter contents and immediate data
	15	1 0 1 0 1	[PC] + [R] + CN	[PC] + [R] + CN + CI	[D]	None	C	1 1 0 0	Jump to address given by sum of Program Counter and Accumulator contents
	16	1 0 1 1 0	[R]	[R] + CI	[D]	PUSH [PC]	D	1 1 0 1	Jump to subroutine addressed by Accumulator
	17	1 0 1 1 1	[D]	[D] + CI	[D]	PUSH [PC]			Jump to subroutine addressed by immediate data
	18	1 1 0 0 0	0	CI	[D]	PUSH [PC]			Jump to subroutine origined at 0
	19	1 1 0 0 1	[R] + [D] + CN	[R] + [D] + CN + CI	[D]	PUSH [PC]			Jump to subroutine addressed by sum of Accumulator contents and immediate data
	1A	1 1 0 1 0	[PC] + [D] + CN	[PC] + [D] + CN + CI	[D]	PUSH [PC]			Jump to subroutine addressed by sum of Program Counter and immediate data
	1B	1 1 0 1 1	[PC] + [R] + CN	[PC] + [R] + CN + CI	[D]	PUSH [PC]	E	1 1 1 0	Jump to subroutine addressed by sum of Program Counter and Accumulator contents
	1C	1 1 1 0 0	[S]	[S] + CI	[D]	POP	7	0 1 1 1	Return from subroutine
	1D	1 1 1 0 1	[S] + [D] + CN	[S] + [D] + CN + CI	[D]	None			Return from subroutine to return address plus immediate data
	1E	1 1 1 1 0	[PC]	[PC]	[D]	None			Output and hold Program Counter
	1F	1 1 1 1 1	Off (2)	[PC]	[D]	None	1	0 0 0 1	High impedance output. Hold Program Counter

(1) The Accumulator is loaded only when RL is input low. Exceptions are the three instructions marked *, which cause the Accumulator to be loaded unconditionally.

(2) The Y0 - Y3 outputs are in the high impedance state.

(3) Conditional instructions execute as described only when CC is input low. Otherwise instruction 1 is executed. These instructions are unconditional for the 2932 which has no CC input.

(4) The 2932 has no RL input, therefore only the three instructions marked * load the Accumulator.

The Program Counter normally receives the Adder output as its new input. **The Adder output may or may not be incremented, depending on the level of the CI input.** When the Adder is not outputting the prior Program Counter contents, loading this different output into the Program Counter constitutes a program jump. Many instruction codes bypass this jump logic by recycling the Program Counter contents back through the incrementer while some other output is generated by the Adder. For example, one instruction code causes the Adder to output data input at D0-D3. But the Program Counter contents are held unaltered, or incremented, depending on the level of the CI input.

Both 2930 series devices have a 17-level Stack. Program Counter contents or data input at D0-D3 can be pushed onto the Stack. **The 2930 series push operation is a little unusual.** The Stack Pointer is incremented, then the selected data is written into the newly addressed Stack location. Thus, following a push, the Stack Pointer addresses the data most recently pushed onto the Stack. It is more traditional for the Stack Pointer to address the first free Stack location. **When you pop a 2930 series Stack, you decrement the Stack Pointer contents, and that is all.** Thus, in order to read data off the top of the Stack, you select an instruction code which reads data from the Stack, then you pop the Stack. The more traditional Stack architecture requires that you pop the Stack, then read data from the top of the Stack.

The 2930 series Stack Pointer is not wrap-around. If the number of pushes exceeds the number of pops by more than seventeen, the Stack Pointer continues to address the topmost Stack location. If you attempt to pop the Stack when the Stack Pointer is addressing location 0, then it continues to address location 0.

When the Stack Pointer is addressing either of the two top Stack locations, the $\overline{\text{FULL}}$ signal is output low. When you execute a push while the Stack Pointer is addressing the top Stack location, data is written into this top location, overwriting whatever was there before.

The 2930, but not the 2932, has a Stack Empty indicator. This signal, $\overline{\text{EMPTY}}$, is output low following a reset, or after the lowest level Stack location has been popped.

2930 series devices are cascadable. However, the 2930 has more cascading logic than the 2932. Unlike the 2901 and the 2903, the 2930 series devices do not have Shifters along data paths, therefore the Accumulator, Stack, and Program Counter do not need parallel interconnect signals. Parallel interconnect signals are needed only to cascade the Program Counter as it increments, or the Adder following an increment or addition. For the Program Counter there is a carry input, CI, and a carry output, C(I+4). The delay between CI being input and C(I+4) being output is very short. There is plenty of time for this ripple carry to propagate through four slices, for a 16-bit address, within one microcycle. For timing details see the data sheets at the end of this chapter.

Both 2930 series Adders have a carry input, CN, and a carry output, C(N+4). Only the 2930 has $\overline{P}$ and $\overline{G}$ outputs, the carry propagate and generate. Therefore only the 2930 allows you to use a 2902 carry look-ahead generator. When using the 2932 device, you must rely on ripple carry. For a discussion of carry look-ahead and ripple carry, refer to the 2901 and 2902 device descriptions given earlier in this chapter.

USING 2930 SERIES DEVICES

You must be careful when deciding how to use 2930 device read/write locations. You should not use these locations to implement CPU registers if you are designing any type of general purpose minicomputer or microcomputer. That is because you will have to perform a sequence of pushes and pops, each requiring a single microcycle, in order to select an arbitrary location. Moreover, every time you perform a push in order to increment the address, you will simultaneously write into the newly addressed location — something you may not wish to do. Thus the Stack lets you have 17 levels of subroutine within the program logic that you use to generate addresses.

You can use the 2930 series Accumulator to implement a CPU register. For example, many primitive Central Processing Units have a single Index register whose contents can contribute to address generation logic, but not to CPU arithmetic or logic operations. The 2930 series Accumulator would be an ideal location for such an Index register.

If you are designing a special purpose Central Processing Unit using 2930 series devices, you may well be able to use the 17-level Stack to give you all the CPU registers you require. Knowing in advance the limitations of 2930 series Stack access, you can design your microprogram around these limitations so that addresses are stored in the proper serial sequence within the 2930 series Stack.

DATA SHEETS

This section contains specific electrical and timing data for the following devices:

- Am2901, Am2901A, and Am2901B
- Am2902A Carry Look-Ahead Generator
- Am2903 Enhanced Microprocessor Slice
- Am2910, Am2909, and Am2911 Microprogram Sequencers
- Am2930 Program Control Unit

Am2901/Am2901A

MICRO CODE				ALU SOURCE OPERANDS	
I_2	I_1	I_0	Octal Code	R	S
L	L	L	0	A	Q
L	L	H	1	A	B
L	H	L	2	0	Q
L	H	H	3	0	B
H	L	L	4	0	A
H	L	H	5	D	A
H	H	L	6	D	Q
H	H	H	7	D	0

Figure 2. ALU Source Operand Control.

MICRO CODE				ALU Function	Symbol
I_5	I_4	I_3	Octal Code		
L	L	L	0	R Plus S	$R + S$
L	L	H	1	S Minus R	$S - R$
L	H	L	2	R Minus S	$R - S$
L	H	H	3	R OR S	$R \vee S$
H	L	L	4	R AND S	$R \wedge S$
H	L	H	5	$\bar{R}$ AND S	$\bar{R} \wedge S$
H	H	L	6	R EX-OR S	$R \veebar S$
H	H	H	7	R EX-NOR S	$\overline{R \veebar S}$

Figure 3. ALU Function Control.

MICRO CODE				RAM FUNCTION		Q-REG. FUNCTION		Y OUTPUT	RAM SHIFTER		Q SHIFTER	
I_8	I_7	I_6	Octal Code	Shift	Load	Shift	Load		RAM_0	RAM_3	Q_0	Q_3
L	L	L	0	X	NONE	NONE	$F \rightarrow Q$	F	X	X	X	X
L	L	H	1	X	NONE	X	NONE	F	X	X	X	X
L	H	L	2	NONE	$F \rightarrow B$	X	NONE	A	X	X	X	X
L	H	H	3	NONE	$F \rightarrow B$	X	NONE	F	X	X	X	X
H	L	L	4	DOWN	$F/2 \rightarrow B$	DOWN	$Q/2 \rightarrow Q$	F	F_0	IN_3	Q_0	IN_3
H	L	H	5	DOWN	$F/2 \rightarrow B$	X	NONE	F	F_0	IN_3	Q_0	X
H	H	L	6	UP	$2F \rightarrow B$	UP	$2Q \rightarrow Q$	F	IN_0	F_3	IN_0	Q_3
H	H	H	7	UP	$2F \rightarrow B$	X	NONE	F	IN_0	F_3	X	Q_3

X= Don't care. Electrically, the shift pin is a TTL input internally connected to a three-state output which is in the high-impedance state.
B = Register Addressed by B inputs.
Up is toward MSB, Down is toward LSB.

Figure 4. ALU Destination Control.

I_{210} OCTAL / ALU Source		0 A,Q	1 A,B	2 O,Q	3 O,B	4 O,A	5 D,A	6 D,Q	7 D,O
I_{543} OCTAL / ALU Function									
0 R Plus S	$C_n = L$	A+Q	A+B	Q	B	A	D+A	D+Q	D
	$C_n = H$	A+Q+1	A+B+1	Q+1	B+1	A+1	D+A+1	D+Q+1	D+1
1 S Minus R	$C_n = L$	Q–A–1	B–A–1	Q–1	B–1	A–1	A–D–1	Q–D–1	–D–1
	$C_n = H$	Q–A	B–A	Q	B	A	A–D	Q–D	–D
2 R Minus S	$C_n = L$	A–Q–1	A–B–1	–Q–1	–B–1	–A–1	D–A–1	D–Q–1	D–1
	$C_n = H$	A–Q	A–B	–Q	–B	–A	D–A	D–Q	D
3 R OR S		$A \vee Q$	$A \vee B$	Q	B	A	$D \vee A$	$D \vee Q$	D
4 R AND S		$A \wedge Q$	$A \wedge B$	0	0	0	$D \wedge A$	$D \wedge Q$	0
5 $\bar{R}$ AND S		$\bar{A} \wedge Q$	$\bar{A} \wedge B$	Q	B	A	$\bar{D} \wedge A$	$\bar{D} \wedge Q$	0
6 R EX-OR S		$A \veebar Q$	$A \veebar B$	Q	B	A	$D \veebar A$	$D \veebar Q$	D
7 R EX-NOR S		$\overline{A \veebar Q}$	$\overline{A \veebar B}$	$\bar{Q}$	$\bar{B}$	$\bar{A}$	$\overline{D \veebar A}$	$\overline{D \veebar Q}$	$\bar{D}$

+ = Plus; − = Minus; V = OR; ∧ = AND; ⊻ = EX-OR

Figure 5. Source Operand and ALU Function Matrix.

SOURCE OPERANDS AND ALU FUNCTIONS

There are eight source operand pairs available to the ALU as selected by the I_0, I_1, and I_2 instruction inputs. The ALU can perform eight functions; five logic and three arithmetic. The I_3, I_4, and I_5 instruction inputs control this function selection. The carry input, C_n, also affects the ALU results when in the arithmetic mode. The C_n input has no effect in the logic mode. When I_0 through I_5 and C_n are viewed together, the matrix of

Figure 5 results. This matrix fully defines the ALU/source operand function for each state.

The ALU functions can also be examined on a "task" basis, i.e., add, subtract, AND, OR, etc. In the arithmetic mode, the carry will affect the function performed while in the logic mode, the carry will have no bearing on the ALU output. Figure 6 defines the various logic operations that the Am2901A can perform and Figure 7 shows the arithmetic functions of the device. Both carry-in LOW (C_n = 0) and carry-in HIGH (C_n = 1) are defined in these operations.

Octal I_{543}, I_{210}	Group	Function
4 0	AND	A∧Q
4 1		A∧B
4 5		D∧A
4 6		D∧Q
3 0	OR	A∨Q
3 1		A∨B
3 5		D∨A
3 6		D∨Q
6 0	EX-OR	A∀Q
6 1		A∀B
6 5		D∀A
6 6		D∀Q
7 0	EX-NOR	$\overline{A∀Q}$
7 1		$\overline{A∀B}$
7 5		$\overline{D∀A}$
7 6		$\overline{D∀Q}$
7 2	INVERT	$\overline{Q}$
7 3		$\overline{B}$
7 4		$\overline{A}$
7 7		$\overline{D}$
6 2	PASS	Q
6 3		B
6 4		A
6 7		D
3 2	PASS	Q
3 3		B
3 4		A
3 7		D
4 2	"ZERO"	0
4 3		0
4 4		0
4 7		0
5 0	MASK	$\overline{A}∧Q$
5 1		$\overline{A}∧B$
5 5		$\overline{D}∧A$
5 6		$\overline{D}∧Q$

Figure 6. ALU Logic Mode Functions.

Octal I_{543}, I_{210}	C_n = 0 (Low) Group	C_n = 0 (Low) Function	C_n = 1 (High) Group	C_n = 1 (High) Function
0 0	ADD	A+Q	ADD plus one	A+Q+1
0 1		A+B		A+B+1
0 5		D+A		D+A+1
0 6		D+Q		D+Q+1
0 2	PASS	Q	Increment	Q+1
0 3		B		B+1
0 4		A		A+1
0 7		D		D+1
1 2	Decrement	Q−1	PASS	Q
1 3		B−1		B
1 4		A−1		A
2 7		D−1		D
2 2	1's Comp.	−Q−1	2's Comp. (Negate)	−Q
2 3		−B−1		−B
2 4		−A−1		−A
1 7		−D−1		−D
1 0	Subtract (1's Comp)	Q−A−1	Subtract (2's Comp)	Q−A
1 1		B−A−1		B−A
1 5		A−D−1		A−D
1 6		Q−D−1		Q−D
2 0		A−Q−1		A−Q
2 1		A−B−1		A−B
2 5		D−A−1		D−A
2 6		D−Q−1		D−Q

Figure 7. ALU Arithmetic Mode Functions.

Am2901

MAXIMUM RATINGS (Above which the useful life may be impaired)

Storage Temperature	$-65°C$ to $+150°C$
Temperature (Ambient) Under Bias	$-55°C$ to $+125°C$
Supply Voltage to Ground Potential	-0.5 V to $+6.3$ V
DC Voltage Applied to Outputs for HIGH Output State	-0.5 V to $+V_{CC}$ max.
DC Input Voltage	-0.5 V to $+5.5$ V
DC Output Current, Into Outputs	30 mA
DC Input Current	-30 mA to $+5.0$ mA

OPERATING RANGE

P/N	Ambient Temperature	V_{CC}
Am2901PC, DC	$0°C$ to $+70°C$	4.75 V to 5.25 V
Am2901DM, FM	$-55°C$ to $+125°C$	4.50 V to 5.50 V

STANDARD SCREENING
(Conforms to MIL-STD-883 for Class C Parts)

Step	MIL-STD-883 Method	Conditions	Level Am2901PC, DC	Level Am2901DM, FM
Pre-Seal Visual Inspection	2010	B	100%	100%
Stabilization Bake	1008	C 24-hour 150°C	100%	100%
Temperature Cycle	1010	C $-65°C$ to $+150°C$ 10 cycles	100%	100%
Centrifuge	2001	B 10,000 G	100% *	100%
Fine Leak	1014	A 5×10^{-8} atm-cc/cm^3	100% *	100%
Gross Leak	1014	C2 Fluorocarbon	100% *	100%
Electrical Test Subgroups 1 and 7	5004	See below for definitions of subgroups	100%	100%
Insert Additional Screening here for Class B Parts				
Group A Sample Tests				
Subgroup 1			LTPD = 5	LTPD = 5
Subgroup 2			LTPD = 7	LTPD = 7
Subgroup 3	5005	See below for definitions of subgroups	LTPD = 7	LTPD = 7
Subgroup 7			LTPD = 7	LTPD = 7
Subgroup 8			LTPD = 7	LTPD = 7
Subgroup 9			LTPD = 7	LTPD = 7

*Not applicable for Am2901PC

ADDITIONAL SCREENING FOR CLASS B PARTS

Step	MIL-STD-883 Method	Conditions	Level Am2901DMB, FMB
Burn-In	1015	D 125°C 160 hours min.	100%
Electrical Test Subgroup 1	5004		100%
Subgroup 2			100%
Subgroup 3			100%
Subgroup 7			100%
Subgroup 9			100%
Return to Group A Tests in Standard Screening			

ORDERING INFORMATION

Package Type	Temperature Range	Order Number
Molded DIP	$0°C$ to $+70°C$	AM2901PC
Hermetic DIP	$0°C$ to $+70°C$	AM2901DC
Hermetic DIP	$-55°C$ to $+125°C$	AM2901DM
Hermetic Flat Pack	$-55°C$ to $+125°C$	AM2901FM
Dice	$0°C$ to $+70°C$	AM2901XC

GROUP A SUBGROUPS
(as defined in MIL-STD-883, method 5005)

Subgroup	Parameter	Temperature
1	DC	25°C
2	DC	Maximum rated temperature
3	DC	Minimum rated temperature
7	Function	25°C
8	Function	Maximum and minimum rated temperature
9	Switching	25°C
10	Switching	Maximum Rated Temeperature
11	Switching	Minimum Rated Temperature

Am2901

ELECTRICAL CHARACTERISTICS OVER OPERATING RANGE (Unless Otherwise Noted)
(Group A, Subgroups 1, 2 and 3)

Parameters	Description	Test Conditions (Note 1)		Min.	Typ. (Note 2)	Max.	Units
V_{OH}	Output HIGH Voltage	V_{CC} = MIN. V_{IN} = V_{IH} or V_{IL}	I_{OH} = −1.6mA Y_0, Y_1, Y_2, Y_3	2.4			Volts
			I_{OH} = −1.0mA, C_{n+4}	2.4			
			I_{OH} = −800µA, OVR, $\overline{P}$	2.4			
			I_{OH} = −600µA, F_3	2.4			
			I_{OH} = −600µA $RAM_{0,3}, Q_{0,3}$	2.4			
			I_{OH} = −1.6mA, $\overline{G}$	2.4			
I_{CEX}	Output Leakage Current for F = 0 Output	V_{CC} = MIN., V_{OH} = 5.5V V_{IN} = V_{IH} or V_{IL}				250	µA
V_{OL}	Output LOW Voltage	V_{CC} = MIN., V_{IN} = V_{IH} or V_{IL}	I_{OL} = 16mA $Y_0, Y_1, Y_2, Y_3, \overline{G}$			0.5	Volts
			I_{OL} = 10mA, C_{n+4}, F=0			0.5	
			I_{OL} = 8.0mA, OVR, $\overline{P}$			0.5	
			I_{OL} = 6.0mA, F_3 $RAM_{0,3}, Q_{0,3}$			0.5	
V_{IH}	Input HIGH Level	Guaranteed input logical HIGH voltage for all inputs		2.0			Volts
V_{IL}	Input LOW Level	Guaranteed input logical LOW voltage for all inputs	Military			0.7	Volts
			Commercial			0.8	
V_I	Input Clamp Voltage	V_{CC} = MIN., I_{IN} = −18mA				−1.5	Volts
I_{IL}	Input LOW Current	V_{CC} = MAX. V_{IN} = 0.5V	Clock, $\overline{OE}$			−0.36	mA
			A_0, A_1, A_2, A_3			−0.36	
			B_0, B_1, B_2, B_3			−0.36	
			D_0, D_1, D_2, D_3			−0.72	
			I_0, I_1, I_2, I_6, I_8			−0.36	
			I_3, I_4, I_5, I_7			−0.72	
			$RAM_{0,3}, Q_{0,3}$ (Note 4)			−0.8	
			C_n			−3.6	
I_{IH}	Input HIGH Current	V_{CC} = MAX. V_{IN} = 2.7V	Clock, $\overline{OE}$			20	µA
			A_0, A_1, A_2, A_3			20	
			B_0, B_1, B_2, B_3			20	
			D_0, D_1, D_2, D_3			40	
			I_0, I_1, I_2, I_6, I_8			20	
			I_3, I_4, I_5, I_7			40	
			$RAM_{0,3}, Q_{0,3}$ (Note 4)			100	
			C_n			200	
I_I	Input HIGH Current	V_{CC} = MAX., V_{IN} = 5.5V				1.0	mA
I_{OZH} I_{OZL}	Off State (High Impedance) Output Current	V_{CC} = MAX.	Y_0, Y_1, Y_2, Y_3 V_O = 2.4V			50	µA
			V_O = 0.5V			−50	
			$RAM_{0,3}, Q_{0,3}$ V_O = 2.4V (Note 4)			100	
			V_O = 0.5V (Note 4)			−800	
I_{OS}	Output Short Circuit Current (Note 3)	V_{CC} = 5.75V V_O = 0.5V	$Y_0, Y_1, Y_2, Y_3, \overline{G}$	−15		−40	mA
			C_{n+4}	−15		−40	
			OVR, $\overline{P}$	−15		−40	
			F_3	−15		−40	
			$RAM_{0,3}, Q_{0,3}$	−15		−40	
I_{CC}	Power Supply Current	V_{CC} = MAX.	Military		185	280	mA
			Commercial		185	280	

Notes: 1. For conditions shown as MIN. or MAX., use the appropriate value specified under Electrical Characteristics for the applicable device type.
2. Typical limits are at V_{CC} = 5.0V, 25°C ambient and maximum loading.
3. Not more than one output should be shorted at a time. Duration of the short circuit test should not exceed one second.
4. These are three-state outputs internally connected to TTL inputs. Input characteristics are measured with I_{678} in a state such that the three-state output is OFF.

GUARANTEED OPERATING CONDITIONS OVER TEMPERATURE AND VOLTAGE

Tables I, II, and III below define the timing requirements of the Am2901 in a system. The Am2901 is guaranteed to function correctly over the operating range when used within the delay and set-up time constraints of these tables for the appropriate device type. The tables are divided into three types of parameters; clock characteristics, combinational delays from inputs to outputs, and set-up and hold time requirements. The latter table defines the time prior to the end of the cycle (i.e., clock LOW-to-HIGH transition) that each input must be stable to guarantee that the correct data is written into one of the internal registers.

The performance of the Am2901 within the limits of these tables is guaranteed by the testing defined as "Group A, Subgroup 9" Electrical Testing. For a copy of the tests and limits used for subgroup 9, contact Advanced Micro Devices' Product Marketing.

TABLE I

CYCLE TIME AND CLOCK CHARACTERISTICS

TIME	Am2901DC,PC	Am2901DM,FM
Read-Modify-Write Cycle (time from selection of A, B registers to end of cycle)	105ns	120ns
Maximum Clock Frequency to Shift Q Register (50% duty cycle)	9.5MHz	8.3MHz
Minimum Clock LOW Time	30ns	30ns
Minimum Clock HIGH Time	30ns	30ns
Minimum Clock Period	105ns	120ns

TABLE II

MAXIMUM COMBINATIONAL PROPAGATION DELAYS (all in ns, $C_L \leqslant 15pF$)

From Input \ To Output	Am2901DC, PC (0°C to +70°C; 5V ±5%)								Am2901DM, FM (−55°C to +125°C; 5V ±10%)							
	Y	F_3	C_{n+4}	$\overline{G},\overline{P}$	F=0 R_L=470	OVR	RAM0 RAM3	Q0 Q3	Y	F_3	C_{n+4}	$\overline{G},\overline{P}$	F=0 R_L=470	OVR	RAM0 RAM3	Q0 Q3
A, B	110	85	80	80	110	75	110	—	120	95	90	90	120	85	120	—
D (arithmetic mode)	100	70	70	70	100	60	95	—	110	80	75	75	110	65	105	—
D (I = X37) (Note 5)	60	50	—	—	60	—	60	—	65	55	—	—	65	—	65	—
C_n	55	35	30	—	50	40	55	—	60	40	30	—	55	45	60	—
I_{012}	85	65	65	65	80	65	80	—	90	70	70	70	85	70	85	—
I_{345}	70	55	60	60	70	60	65	—	75	60	65	65	75	65	70	—
I_{678}	55	—	—	—	—	—	45	45	60	—	—	—	—	—	50	50
$\overline{OE}$ Enable/Disable	40/25	—	—	—	—	—	—	—	40/25	—	—	—	—	—	—	—
A bypassing ALU (I = 2xx)	60	—	—	—	—	—	—	—	65	—	—	—	—	—	—	—
Clock ⌐ (Note 6)	115	85	100	100	110	95	105	60	125	95	110	110	120	105	115	65

SET-UP AND HOLD TIMES (all in ns) (Note 1)   **TABLE III**

From Input	Notes	Am2901DC,PC (0°C to +70°C, 5V ±5%)		Am2901DM,FM (−55°C to +125°C, 5V ±10%)	
		Set-Up Time	Hold Time	Set-Up Time	Hold Time
A, B Source	2, 4 3, 5	105 $t_{pw}L + 30$	0	120 $t_{pw}L + 30$	0
B Dest.	2, 4	$t_{pw}L + 15$	0	$t_{pw}L + 15$	0
D (arithmetic mode)		100	0	110	0
D (I = X37) (Note 5)		60	0	65	0
C_n		55	0	60	0
I_{012}		85	0	90	0
I_{345}		70	0	75	0
I_{678}	4	$t_{pw}L + 15$	0	$t_{pw}L + 15$	0
RAM0, 3, Q0, 3		30	0	30	0

Notes: 1. See Figure 11 and 12.
2. If the B address is used as a source operand, allow for the "A, B source" set-up time; if it is used only for the destination address, use the "B dest." set-up time.
3. Where two numbers are shown, both must be met.
4. "$t_{pw}L$" is the clock LOW time.
5. $DV0$ is the fastest way to load the RAM from the D inputs. This function is obtained with I = 337.
6. Using Q register as source operand in arithmetic mode. Clock is not normally in critical speed path when Q is not a source.

Am2901A

ELECTRICAL CHARACTERISTICS OVER OPERATING RANGE (Unless Otherwise Noted)
(Group A, Subgroups 1, 2, and 3) Data in bold face is changed from Am2901

Parameters	Description	Test Conditions (Note 1)			Min.	Typ. (Note 2)	Max.	Units
V_{OH}	Output HIGH Voltage	V_{CC} = MIN. $V_{IN} = V_{IH}$ or V_{IL}	I_{OH} = −1.6mA Y_0, Y_1, Y_2, Y_3		2.4			Volts
			I_{OH} = −1.0mA, C_{n+4}		2.4			
			I_{OH} = −800µA, OVR, $\overline{P}$		2.4			
			I_{OH} = −600µA, F_3		2.4			
			I_{OH} = −600µA $RAM_{0,3}, Q_{0,3}$		2.4			
			I_{OH} = −1.6mA, $\overline{G}$		2.4			
I_{CEX}	Output Leakage Current for F = 0 Output	V_{CC} = MIN., V_{OH} = 5.5V $V_{IN} = V_{IH}$ or V_{IL}					250	µA
V_{OL}	Output LOW Voltage	V_{CC} = MIN., $V_{IN} = V_{IH}$ or V_{IL}	Y_0, Y_1, Y_2, Y_3	**I_{OL} = 20mA (COM'L)**			0.5	Volts
				I_{OL} = 16mA (MIL)			0.5	
			$\overline{G}$, F = 0	I_{OL} = 16mA			0.5	
			C_{n+4}	I_{OL} = 10mA			0.5	
			OVR, $\overline{P}$	I_{OL} = 8.0mA			0.5	
			$F_3, RAM_{0,3}, Q_{0,3}$	I_{OL} = 6.0mA			0.5	
V_{IH}	Input HIGH Level	Guaranteed input logical HIGH voltage for all inputs (Note 7)			2.0			Volts
V_{IL}	Input LOW Level	Guaranteed input logical LOW voltage for all inputs (Note 7)					**0.8**	Volts
V_I	Input Clamp Voltage	V_{CC} = MIN., I_{IN} = −18mA					−1.5	Volts
I_{IL}	Input LOW Current	V_{CC} = MAX., V_{IN} = 0.5V	Clock, $\overline{OE}$				−0.36	mA
			A_0, A_1, A_2, A_3				−0.36	
			B_0, B_1, B_2, B_3				−0.36	
			D_0, D_1, D_2, D_3				−0.72	
			I_0, I_1, I_2, I_6, I_8				−0.36	
			I_3, I_4, I_5, I_7				−0.72	
			$RAM_{0,3}, Q_{0,3}$ (Note 4)				−0.8	
			C_n				−3.6	
I_{IH}	Input HIGH Current	V_{CC} = MAX., V_{IN} = 2.7V	Clock, $\overline{OE}$				20	µA
			A_0, A_1, A_2, A_3				20	
			B_0, B_1, B_2, B_3				20	
			D_0, D_1, D_2, D_3				40	
			I_0, I_1, I_2, I_6, I_8				20	
			I_3, I_4, I_5, I_7				40	
			$RAM_{0,3}, Q_{0,3}$ (Note 4)				100	
			C_n				200	
I_I	Input HIGH Current	V_{CC} = MAX., V_{IN} = 5.5V					1.0	mA
I_{OZH} I_{OZL}	Off State (High Impedance) Output Current	V_{CC} = MAX.	$Y_0, Y_1,$ Y_2, Y_3	V_O = 2.4V			50	µA
				V_O = 0.5V			−50	
			$RAM_{0,3}$	V_O = 2.4V (Note 4)			100	
			$Q_{0,3}$	V_O = 0.5V (Note 4)			−800	
I_{OS}	Output Short Circuit Current (Note 3)	V_{CC} = 5.75V, V_O = 0.5V	$Y_0, Y_1, Y_2, Y_3, \overline{G}$		−30		−85	mA
			C_{n+4}		−30		−85	
			OVR, $\overline{P}$		−30		−85	
			F_3		−30		−85	
			$RAM_{0,3}, Q_{0,3}$		−30		−85	
I_{CC}	Power Supply Current (Note 6)	V_{CC} = MAX. (See graph)		T_A = 25°C		160	250	mA
			Am2901APC, DC	T_A = 0°C to +70°C		160	265	
				T_A = +70°C		160	220	
			Am2901ADM, FM	T_C = −55°C to +125°C		160	280	
				T_C = +125°C		160	190	

Notes: 1. For conditions shown as MIN. or MAX., use the appropriate value specified under Electrical Characteristics for the applicable device type.
2. Typical limits are at V_{CC} = 5.0V, 25°C ambient and maximum loading.
3. Not more than one output should be shorted at a time. Duration of the short circuit test should not exceed one second.
4. These are three-state outputs internally connected to TTL inputs. Input characteristics are measured with I_{678} in a state such that the three-state output is OFF.
5. "MIL" = Am2901AXM, DM, FM. "COM'L" = Am2901AXC, PC, DC.
6. Worst case I_{CC} is at minimum temperature.
7. These input levels provide zero noise immunity and should only be tested in a static, noise-free environment.

Am2901A

SWITCHING CHARACTERISTICS OVER OPERATING RANGE

Tables IV, V, and VI below define the timing characteristics of the Am2901A at 25°C over the operating voltage and temperature range. The tables are divided into three types of parameters; clock characteristics, combinational delays from inputs to outputs, and set-up and hold time requirements. The later table defines the time prior to the end of the cycle (i.e., clock LOW-to-HIGH transition) that each input must be stable to guarantee that the correct data is written into one of the internal registers.

Measurements are made at 1.5V with $V_{IL} = 0V$ and $V_{IH} = 3.0V$. For three-state disable tests, $C_L = 5.0pF$ and measurement is to 0.5V change on output voltage level.

Commercial =	Am2901APC, DC, XC 0°C to +70°C 4.75 to 5.25V
Military =	Am2901ADM, FM, XM −55°C to +125°C 4.50 to 5.50V

TABLE IV
CYCLE TIME AND CLOCK CHARACTERISTICS

TIME	COMMERCIAL	MILITARY
Read-Modify-Write Cycle (time from selection of A, B registers to end of cycle)	100	110
Maximum Clock Frequency to Shift Q Register (50% duty cycle) I = 432 or 632	15MHz	12MHz
Minimum Clock LOW Time	30ns	30ns
Minimum Clock HIGH Time	30ns	30ns
Minimum Clock Period	100ns	110ns

TABLE V
COMBINATIONAL PROPAGATION DELAYS (all in ns, $C_L = 50pF$ (except output disable tests))

From Input \ To Output	COMMERCIAL								MILITARY							
	Y	F3	C_{n+4}	$\overline{G}, \overline{P}$	F=0 R_L=470	OVR	Shift Outputs RAM0 RAM3	Shift Outputs Q0 Q3	Y	F3	C_{n+4}	$\overline{G}, \overline{P}$	F=0 R_L=470	OVR	Shift Outputs RAM0 RAM3	Shift Outputs Q0 Q3
A, B	80	80	75	65	90	85	95	—	85	85	80	70	100	90	100	—
D (arithmetic mode)	45	45	45	35	60	55	65	—	50	50	50	40	65	60	70	—
D (I = X37) (Note 5)	40	40	—	—	55	—	60	—	45	45	—	—	60	—	65	—
C_n	30	30	20	—	50	30	50	—	35	35	25	—	55	35	55	—
I_{012}	55	55	50	45	70	65	75	—	60	60	55	50	75	70	80	—
I_{345}	55	55	55	50	70	65	75	—	60	60	60	55	75	70	80	—
I_{678}	30	—	—	—	—	—	30	30	35	—	—	—	—	—	35	35
$\overline{OE}$ Enable/Disable	35/25	—	—	—	—	—	—	—	40/25	—	—	—	—	—	—	—
A bypassing ALU (I = 2xx)	45	—	—	—	—	—	—	—	50	—	—	—	—	—	—	—
Clock ⌐ (Note 6)	60	60	60	50	75	70	80	30	65	65	65	55	85	75	85	35

SET-UP AND HOLD TIMES (all in ns) (Note 1)   **TABLE VI**

From Input	Notes	COMMERCIAL		MILITARY	
		Set-Up Time	Hold Time	Set-Up Time	Hold Time
A, B Source	2, 4 3, 5	100 $t_{pw}L$+30	0	110 $t_{pw}L$+30	0
B Dest.	2, 4	$t_{pw}L$+15	0	$t_{pw}L$+15	0
D (arithmetic mode)		70	0	75	0
D (I = X37) (Note 5)		60	0	65	0
C_n		55	0	60	0
I_{012}		80	0	85	0
I_{345}		80	0	85	0
I_{678}	4	$t_{pw}L$+30	0	$t_{pw}L$+30	0
RAM0, 3, Q0, 3		25	0	25	0

Notes: 1. See Figure 11.
2. If the B address is used as a source operand, allow for the "A, B source" set-up time; if it is used only for the destination address, use the "B Dest" set-up time.
3. Where two numbers are shown, both must be met.
4. "$t_{pw}L$" is the clock LOW time.
5. D V 0 is the fastest way to load the RAM from the D inputs. This function is obtained with I = 337.
6. Using Q register as source operand in arithmetic mode. Clock is not normally in critical speed path when Q is not a source.

Am2901A

SET-UP AND HOLD TIMES (minimum cycles from each input)

Set-up and hold times are defined relative to the clock LOW-to-HIGH edge. Inputs must be steady at all times from the set-up time prior to the clock until the hold time after the clock. The set-up times allow sufficient time to perform the correct operation on the correct data so that the correct ALU data can be written into one of the registers.

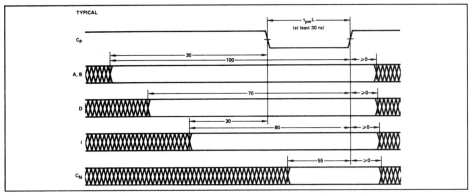

Figure 11. Minimum Cycle Times from Inputs. Numbers Shown are Minimum Data Stable Times for Am2901ADC, in ns. See Table III for Detailed Information.

Typical I_{CC} Versus Temperature

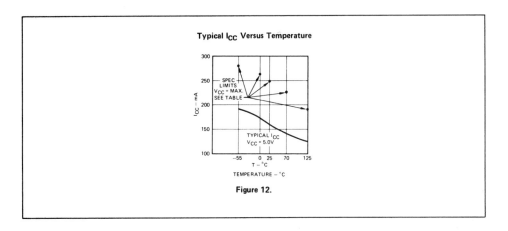

Figure 12.

Am2901B

PRELIMINARY DATA
ELECTRICAL CHARACTERISTICS OVER OPERATING RANGE (Unless Otherwise Noted)
(Group A, Subgroups 1, 2, and 3)

Parameters	Description	Test Conditions (Note 1)			Min	Typ (Note 2)	Max	Units
V_{OH}	Output HIGH Voltage	V_{CC} = MIN. $V_{IN} = V_{IH}$ or V_{IL}	I_{OH} = −1.6mA Y_0, Y_1, Y_2, Y_3		2.4			Volts
			I_{OH} = −1.0mA, C_{n+4}		2.4			
			I_{OH} = −800μA, OVR, $\overline{P}$		2.4			
			I_{OH} = −600μA, F_3		2.4			
			I_{OH} = −600μA RAM$_{0,3}$, Q$_{0,3}$		2.4			
			I_{OH} = −1.6mA, $\overline{G}$		2.4			
I_{CEX}	Output Leakage Current for F = 0 Output	V_{CC} = MIN., V_{OH} = 5.5V $V_{IN} = V_{IH}$ or V_{IL}					250	μA
V_{OL}	Output LOW Voltage	V_{CC} = MIN., $V_{IN} = V_{IH}$ or V_{IL}	Y_0, Y_1, Y_2, Y_3	I_{OL} = 20mA (COM'L)			0.5	Volts
				I_{OL} = 16mA (MIL)			0.5	
			$\overline{G}$, F = 0	I_{OL} = 16mA			0.5	
			C_{n+4}	I_{OL} = 10mA			0.5	
			OVR, $\overline{P}$	I_{OL} = 8.0mA			0.5	
			F_3, RAM$_{0,3}$, Q$_{0,3}$	I_{OL} = 6.0mA			0.5	
V_{IH}	Input HIGH Level	Guaranteed input logical HIGH voltage for all inputs (Note 7)			2.0			Volts
V_{IL}	Input LOW Level	Guaranteed input logical LOW voltage for all inputs (Note 7)					0.8	Volts
V_I	Input Clamp Voltage	V_{CC} = MIN., I_{IN} = −18mA					−1.5	Volts
I_{IL}	Input LOW Current	V_{CC} = MAX., V_{IN} = 0.5V	Clock, $\overline{OE}$				−0.36	mA
			A_0, A_1, A_2, A_3				−0.36	
			B_0, B_1, B_2, B_3				−0.36	
			D_0, D_1, D_2, D_3				−0.72	
			I_0, I_1, I_2, I_6, I_8				−0.36	
			I_3, I_4, I_5, I_7				−0.72	
			RAM$_{0,3}$, Q$_{0,3}$ (Note 4)				−0.8	
			C_n				−3.6	
I_{IH}	Input HIGH Current	V_{CC} = MAX., V_{IN} = 2.7V	Clock, $\overline{OE}$				20	μA
			A_0, A_1, A_2, A_3				20	
			B_0, B_1, B_2, B_3				20	
			D_0, D_1, D_2, D_3				40	
			I_0, I_1, I_2, I_6, I_8				20	
			I_3, I_4, I_5, I_7				40	
			RAM$_{0,3}$, Q$_{0,3}$ (Note 4)				100	
			C_n				200	
I_I	Input HIGH Current	V_{CC} = MAX., V_{IN} = 5.5V					1.0	mA
I_{OZH} I_{OZL}	Off State (High Impedance) Output Current	V_{CC} = MAX.	Y_0, Y_1, Y_2, Y_3	V_O = 2.4V			50	μA
				V_O = 0.5V			−50	
			RAM$_{0,3}$ Q$_{0,3}$	V_O = 2.4V (Note 4)			100	
				V_O = 0.5V (Note 4)			−800	
I_{OS}	Output Short Circuit Current (Note 3)	V_{CC} = MAX. + 0.5V, V_O = 0.5V	$Y_0, Y_1, Y_2, Y_3, \overline{G}$		−30		−85	mA
			C_{n+4}		−30		−85	
			OVR, $\overline{P}$		−30		−85	
			F_3		−30		−85	
			RAM$_{0,3}$, Q$_{0,3}$		−30		−85	
I_{CC}	Power Supply Current (Note 6)	V_{CC} = MAX. (See Fig. 12)	Am2901BPC, DC	T_A = 25°C		160	250	mA
				T_A = 0°C to +70°C			265	
				T_A = +70°C			220	
			Am2901BDM, FM	T_C = −55°C to +125°C			265	
				T_C = +125°C			198	

Notes: 1. For conditions shown as MIN. or MAX., use the appropriate value specified under Electrical Characteristics for the applicable device type.
2. Typical limits are at V_{CC} = 5.0V, 25°C ambient and maximum loading.
3. Not more than one output should be shorted at a time. Duration of the short circuit test should not exceed one second.
4. These are three-state outputs internally connected to TTL inputs. Input characteristics are measured with I_{678} in a state such that the three-state output is OFF.
5. "MIL" = Am2901BXM, DM, FM. "COM'L = Am2901BXC, PC, DC.
6. Worst case I_{CC} is at minimum temperature.
7. These input levels provide zero noise immunity and should only be tested in a static, noise-free environment.

Am2901B

I. Typical Room Temperature Performance

The tables below specify the typical performance of the Am2901B at 25°C and 5.0V. All data are in ns, with inputs changing between 0V and 3V at 1V/ns and measurements made at 1.5V. For guaranteed data, see following pages.

A. Cycle Time and Clock Characteristics.

Read-Modify-Write Cycle (from selection of A, B registers to end of cycle.)	45ns
Maximum Clock Frequency to shift Q (50% duty cycle, I = 432 or 632)	33MHz
Minimum Clock LOW Time	30ns
Minimum Clock HIGH Time	30ns
Minimum Clock Period	60ns

B. Combinational Propagation Delays.
C_L = 50pF

To Output From Input	Y	F3	Cn+4	$\overline{G}, \overline{P}$	F=0	OVR	RAM0 RAM3	Q0 Q3
A, B Address	38	41	39	33	44	44	50	–
D	22	23	24	20	28	29	31	–
Cn	17	19	13	–	22	19	26	–
I012	30	30	29	27	34	34	38	–
I345	32	32	30	25	32	30	34	–
I678	17	–	–	–	–	–	16	16
A Bypass ALU (I = 2XX)	22	–	–	–	–	–	–	–
Clock ⌐	29	31	29	23	33	35	40	19

C. Set-up and Hold Times Relative to Clock (CP) Input.

Input	CP: Set-up Time Before H → L	Hold Time After H → L	Set-up Time Before L → H	Hold Time After L → H
A, B Source Address	8	0 (Note 3)	45 (Note 4)	0
B Destination Address	4	Do Not Change		0
D	–	–	35	0
Cn	–	–	26	0
I012	–	–	37	0
I345	–	–	38	0
I678	0	Do Not Change		0
RAM0, 3, Q0, 3	–	–	9	0

D. Output Enable/Disable Times.
Output disable tests performed with C_L = 5pF and measured to 0.5V change of output voltage level.

Input	Output	Enable	Disable
$\overline{OE}$	Y	12	27

Notes: 1. A dash indicates a propagation delay path or set-up time constraint does not exist.
2. Certain signals must be stable during the entire clock LOW time to avoid erroneous operation. This is indicated by the phrase "do not change".
3. Source addresses must be stable prior to the clock H → L transition to allow time to access the source data before the latches close. The A address may then be changed. The B address could be changed if it is not a destination; i.e. if data is not being written back into the RAM. **Normally A and B are not changed during the clock LOW time.**
4. The set-up time prior to the clock L → H transition is to allow time for data to be accessed, passed through the ALU, and returned to the RAM. It includes **all** the time from stable A and B addresses to the clock L → H transition, regardless of when the clock H → L transition occurs.

Am2901B

I. Guaranteed Commercial Range Performance

The tables below specify the guaranteed performance of the Am2901B over the commercial operating range of 0°C to +70°C, with V_{CC} from 4.75V to 5.25V. All data are in ns, with inputs switching between 0V and 3V at 1V/ns and measurements made at 1.5V. All outputs have maximum DC load.

This data applies to the following part numbers: Am2901BPC
Am2901BDC

A. Cycle Time and Clock Characteristics.

Read-Modify-Write Cycle (from selection of A, B registers to end of cycle.)	69ns
Maximum Clock Frequency to shift Q (50% duty cycle, I = 432 or 632)	16MHz
Minimum Clock LOW Time	30ns
Minimum Clock HIGH Time	30ns
Minimum Clock Period	69ns

B. Combinational Propagation Delays.
C_L = 50pF

To Output From Input	Y	F3	Cn+4	$\overline{G}, \overline{P}$	F=0	OVR	RAM0 RAM3	Q0 Q3
A, B Address	60	61	59	50	70	67	71	–
D	38	36	40	33	48	44	45	–
Cn	30	29	23	–	37	29	38	–
I012	50	47	45	45	56	53	57	–
I345	49	48	44	45	54	49	53	–
I678	28	–	–	–	–	–	27	27
A Bypass ALU (I = 2XX)	37	–	–	–	–	–	–	–
Clock ⌐	49	48	47	37	58	55	59	29

C. Set-up and Hold Times Relative to Clock (CP) Input.

Input	CP: Set-up Time Before H → L	Hold Time After H → L	Set-up Time Before L → H	Hold Time After L → H
A, B Source Address	20	0 (Note 3)	69 (Note 4)	0
B Destination Address	9	Do Not Change		0
D	–	–	51	0
Cn	–	–	39	0
I012	–	–	56	0
I345	–	–	55	0
I678	11	Do Not Change		0
RAM0, 3, Q0, 3	–	–	16	0

D. Output Enable/Disable Times.
Output disable tests performed with C_L = 5pF and measured to 0.5V change of output voltage level.

Input	Output	Enable	Disable
$\overline{OE}$	Y	35	25

Notes: 1. A dash indicates a propagation delay path or set-up time constraint does not exist.
2. Certain signals must be stable during the entire clock LOW time to avoid erroneous operation. This is indicated by the phrase "do not change"
3. Source addresses must be stable prior to the clock H → L transition to allow time to access the source data before the latches close. The A address may then be changed if it is not a destination; i.e. if data is not being written back into the RAM. **Normally A and B are not changed during the clock LOW time.**
4. The set-up time prior to the clock L → H transition is to allow time for data to be accessed, passed through the ALU, and returned to the RAM. It includes **all** the time from stable A and B addresses to the clock L → H transition, regardless of when the clock H → L transition occurs.

Am2901B

II. Am2901B Guaranteed Military Range Performance

The tables below specify the guaranteed performance of the Am2901B over the military operating range of −55°C to +125°C, with V_{CC} from 4.5V to 5.5V. All data are in ns, with inputs switching between 0V and 3V at 1V/ns and measurements made at 1.5V. All outputs have maximum DC load.

This data applies to the following part numbers: Am2901BDM
Am2901BFM

A. Cycle Time and Clock Characteristics.

Read-Modify-Write Cycle (from selection of A, B registers to end of cycle.	88ns
Maximum Clock Frequency to shift Q (50% duty cycle, I = 432 or 632)	15MHz
Minimum Clock LOW Time	30ns
Minimum Clock HIGH Time	30ns
Minimum Clock Period	88ns

B. Combinational Propagation Delays.
$C_L = 50pF$

To Output From Input	Y	F3	Cn+4	$\overline{G}, \overline{P}$	F=0	OVR	RAM0 RAM3	Q0 Q3
A, B Address	82	84	80	70	90	86	94	–
D	44	38	40	34	50	45	48	–
Cn	34	32	24	–	38	31	39	–
I012	53	50	47	46	59	55	58	–
I345	53	50	46	45	58	50	55	–
I678	29	–	–	–	–	–	27	27
A Bypass ALU (I = 2XX)	50	–	–	–	–	–	–	–
Clock ⤒	53	50	49	41	63	58	61	31

C. Set-up and Hold Times Relative to Clock (CP) Input.

Input	CP: Set-up Time Before H → L	Hold Time After H → L	Set-up Time Before L → H	Hold Time After L → H
A, B Source Address	20	0 (Note 3)	88 (Note 4)	0
B Destination Address	9	Do Not Change		0
D	–	–	55	0
Cn	–	–	42	0
I012	–	–	58	0
I345	–	–	58	0
I678	14	Do Not Change		0
RAM0, 3, Q0, 3	–	–	18	3

D. Output Enable/Disable Times.

Output disable tests performed with $C_L = 5pF$ and measured to 0.5V change of output voltage level.

Input	Output	Enable	Disable
$\overline{OE}$	Y	40	35

Notes: 1. A dash indicates a propagation delay path or set-up time constraint does not exist.
2. Certain signals must be stable during the entire clock LOW time to avoid erroneous operation. This is indicated by the phrase "do not change".
3. Source addresses must be stable prior to the clock H → L transition to allow time to access the source data before the latches close. The A address may then be changed. The B address could be changed if it is not a destination; i.e. if data is not being written back into the RAM. **Normally A and B are not changed during the clock LOW time.**
4. The set-up time prior to the clock L → H transition is to allow time for data to be accessed, passed through the ALU, and returned to the RAM. It includes all the time from stable A and B addresses to the clock L → H transition, regardless of when the clock H → L transition occurs.

Am2902A

MAXIMUM RATINGS (Above which the useful life may be impaired)

Storage Temperature	$-65°C$ to $+150°C$
Temperature (Ambient) Under Bias	$-55°C$ to $+125°C$
Supply Voltage to Ground Potential	$-0.5V$ to $+7.0V$
DC Voltage Applied to Outputs for HIGH Output State	$-0.5V$ to $+V_{CC}$ max.
DC Input Voltage	$-0.5V$ to $+5.5V$
DC Output Current, Into Outputs	30 mA
DC Input Current	-30 mA to $+5.0$ mA

ELECTRICAL CHARACTERISTICS OVER OPERATING TEMPERATURE RANGE (Unless Otherwise Noted)

Am2902AXC $T_A = 0°C$ to $+70°C$ $V_{CC} = 5.0V \pm 5\%$ (COM'L) MIN. = 4.75V MAX. = 5.25V

Am2902AXM $T_A = -55°C$ to $+125°C$ $V_{CC} = 5.0V \pm 10\%$ (MIL) MIN. = 4.50V MAX. = 5.50V

Parameters	Description	Test Conditions (Note 1)		Min.	Typ. (Note 2)	Max.	Units
V_{OH}	Output HIGH Voltage	V_{CC} = MIN., $I_{OH} = -1mA$ $V_{IN} = V_{IH}$ or V_{IL}	MIL	2.5	3.4		Volts
			COM	2.7	3.4		
V_{OL}	Output LOW Voltage	V_{CC} = MIN., I_{OL} = 20mA $V_{IN} = V_{IH}$ or V_{IL}				0.5	Volts
V_{IH}	Input HIGH Level	Guaranteed input logical HIGH voltage for all inputs		2.0			Volts
V_{IL}	Input LOW Level	Guaranteed input logical LOW voltage for all inputs				0.8	Volts
V_I	Input Clamp Voltage	V_{CC} = MIN., $I_{IN} = -18mA$				-1.2	Volts
I_{IL}	Input LOW Current	V_{CC} = MAX., V_{IN} = 0.5V	C_n			-2	mA
			$\overline{P}_3$			-4	
			$\overline{P}_2$			-6	
			$\overline{P}_0, \overline{P}_1, \overline{G}_3$			-8	
			$\overline{G}_0, \overline{G}_2$			-14	
			$\overline{G}_1$			-16	
I_{IH}	Input HIGH Current	V_{CC} = MAX., V_{IN} = 2.7V	C_n			50	μA
			$\overline{P}_3$			100	
			$\overline{P}_2$			150	
			$\overline{P}_0, \overline{P}_1, \overline{G}_3$			200	
			$\overline{G}_0, \overline{G}_2$			350	
			$\overline{G}_1$			400	
I_I	Input HIGH Current	V_{CC} = MAX., V_{IN} = 5.5V				1.0	mA
I_{SC}	Output Short Circuit (Note 3)	V_{CC} = MAX., V_{OUT} = 0.0V		-40		-100	mA
I_{CC}	Power Supply Current	V_{CC} = MAX. All Outputs LOW	MIL		69	99	mA
			COM'L		69	109	
		V_{CC} = MAX. All Ouputs HIGH	MIL		35		mA
			COM'L		35		

Notes: 1. For conditions shown as MIN. or MAX., use the appropriate value specified under Electrical Characteristics for the applicable device type.
2. Typical limits are at V_{CC} = 5.0V, 25°C ambient and maximum loading.
3. Not more than one output should be shorted at a time. Duration of the short circuit test should not exceed one second.

SWITCHING CHARACTERISTICS
($T_A = +25°C$, $V_{CC} = 5.0V$)

Parameters	Description	Min.	Typ.	Max.	Units	Test Conditions
t_{PLH}	$\overline{G}_i/\overline{P}_i \rightarrow C_{n+j}$		4.5	7	ns	
t_{PHL}			4.5	7		
t_{PLH}	$\overline{G}_i/\overline{P}_i \rightarrow \overline{G}$		5	7.5	ns	
t_{PHL}			7	10.5		
t_{PLH}	$\overline{P}_i \rightarrow \overline{P}$		4.5	6.5	ns	C_L = 15pF R_L = 280Ω
t_{PHL}			6.5	10		
t_{PLH}	$C_n \rightarrow C_{n+j}$		6.5	10	ns	
t_{PHL}			7	10.5		

Am2903

Am2903
OPERATING RANGE

P/N	Range	Temperature	V_{CC}	
Am2903PC, DC	COM'L	$T_A = 0°C$ to $+70°C$	$V_{CC} = 5.0V \pm 5\%$	(MIN. = 4.75V, MAX. = 5.25V)
Am2903DM, FM	MIL	$T_C = -55°C$ to $+125°C$	$V_{CC} = 5.0V \pm 10\%$	(MIN. = 4.50V, MAX. = 5.50V)

DC CHARACTERISTICS OVER OPERATING RANGE

Parameters	Description	Test Conditions (Note 1)		Min.	Typ. (Note 2)	Max.	Units
V_{OH}	Output HIGH Voltage	$V_{CC} = $ MIN. $V_{IN} = V_{IH}$ or V_{IL}	$I_{OH} = -1.6mA$ Y_0-Y_3, $\overline{G}/N$	2.4			Volts
			$I_{OH} = -800\mu A$ $DB_{0\text{-}3}$, $\overline{P}/OVR$ SIO_0, SIO_3, QIO_0, QIO_3, $\overline{WRITE}$, C_{n+4}	2.4			
I_{CEX}	Output Leakage Current for Z Output (Note 4)	$V_{CC} = $ MIN., $V_{OH} = 5.5V$ $V_{IN} = V_{IH}$ or V_{IL}				250	μA
V_{OL}	Output LOW Voltage	$V_{CC} = $ MIN. $V_{IN} = V_{IH} = $ or V_{IL}	Y_0, Y_1, Y_2 Y_3, Z	$I_{OL} = 20mA$ (COM'L)			0.5	Volts
				$I_{OL} = 16mA$ (MIL)			
			DB_0, DB_1, DB_2, DB_3	$I_{OL} = 12mA$ (COM'L)			0.5	
				$I_{OL} = 8.0mA$ (MIL)			
			$\overline{G}/N$	$I_{OL} = 18mA$			0.5	
			$\overline{P}/OVR$	$I_{OL} = 10mA$			0.5	
			C_{n+4}, SIO_0 SIO_3, QIO_0 QIO_3, $\overline{WRITE}$	$I_{OL} = 8.0mA$			0.5	
V_{IH}	Input HIGH Level	Guaranteed input logical HIGH voltage for all inputs (Note 6)		2.0			Volts
V_{IL}	Input LOW Level	Guaranteed input logical LOW voltage for all inputs (Note 6)				0.8	Volts
V_I	Input Clamp Voltage	$V_{CC} = $ MIN., $I_{IN} = -18mA$				-1.5	Volts
I_{IL}	Input LOW Current	$V_{CC} = $ MAX., $V_{IN} = 0.5V$ (Note 4)	C_n			2.50	mA
			Y_0, Y_1, Y_2, Y_3			1.08	
			I_0, I_1, I_2, I_3, I_4, DA_0, DA_1, DA_2, DA_3, SIO_0 SIO_3, QIO_0, QIO_3, $\overline{MSS}$, DB_0, DB_1, DB_2, DB_3			0.72	
			All other inputs			0.36	
I_{IH}	Input HIGH Current	$V_{CC} = $ MAX., $V_{IN} = 2.7V$ (Note 4)	C_n			120	μA
			Y_0, Y_1, Y_2, Y_3			110	
			I_0-I_4, DA_0-DA_3			40	
			SIO_0, SIO_3, QIO_0, QIO_3, $DB_{0\text{-}3}$, $\overline{MSS}$			90	
			All other inputs			20	
I_I	Input HIGH Current	$V_{CC} = $ MAX., $V_{IN} = 5.5V$				1.0	mA
I_{OZH} I_{OZL}	Off State (HIGH Impedance) Output Current	$V_{CC} = $ MAX., (Note 4)	Y_0-Y_3	$V_O = 2.4V$			110	μA
				$V_O = 0.5V$			-1130	
			$DB_{0\text{-}3}$, QIO_0, QIO_0, SIO_0, SIO_3, $\overline{MSS}$/IS	$V_O = 2.4V$			90	
				$V_O = 0.5V$			-770	
I_{OS}	Output Short Circuit Current (Note 3)	$V_{CC} = $ MAX $+ 0.5V$ $V_O = 0.5V$		-30		-85	mA
I_{CC}	Power Supply Current (Note 5)	$V_{CC} = $ MAX.	$T_A = 25°C$		220	335	mA
			COM'L	$T_A = 0$ to $70°C$			350	
				$T_A = 70°C$			291	
			MIL	$T_C = -55$ to $125°C$			395	
				$T_C = 125°C$			258	

Notes: 1. For conditions shown as MIN. or MAX., use the appropriate value specified under Electrical Characteristics for the applicable device type.
2. Typical limits are at $V_{CC} = 5.0V$, 25°C ambient and maximum loading.
3. Not more than one output should be shorted at a time. Duration of the short circuit test should not exceed one second.
4. Y_{0-3}, DB_{0-3}, $SIO_{0,3}$, $QIO_{0,3}$ and WRITE/MSS are three state outputs internally connected to TTL inputs. Z is an open-collector output internally connected to a TTL input. Input characteristics are measured under conditions such that the outputs are in the OFF state.
5. Worst case I_{CC} is at minimum temperature.
6. These input levels provide zero noise immunity and should only be tested in a static, noise-free environment.

Am2903

SWITCHING CHARACTERISTICS (Typical Room Temperature Performance)

Tables I, II, and III define the nominal timing characteristics of the Am2903 at 25°C and 5.0V. The Tables divide the parameters into three types: pulse characteristics for the clock and write enable, combinational delays from input to output, and set-up and hold times relative to the clock and write pulse.

Measurements are made at 1.5V with $V_{IL} = 0V$ and $V_{IH} = 3.0V$. For three-state disable tests, $C_L = 5.0pF$ and measurement is to 0.5V change on output voltage level.

TABLE I
Write Pulse and Clock Characteristics

Time	
Minimum Time CP and $\overline{WE}$ both LOW to write	30ns
Minimum Clock LOW Time	30ns
Minimum Clock HIGH Time	50ns

TABLE II
Combinational Propagation Delays, All in ns.
Outputs Fully Loaded. CL = 50pf (except output disable tests)

From Input \ To Output	Y	C_{n+4}	$\overline{G}, \overline{P}$	Z	N	OVR	DB	$\overline{WRITE}$	QIO_0, QIO_3	SIO_0	SIO_3	SIO_3 (Parity)
A, B Addresses (Arith. Mode)	65	60	55	75	64	70	33	–	–	61	69	87
A, B Addresses (Logic Mode)	56	–	46	67	56	–	33	–	–	55	64	81
DA, DB Inputs (Logic Mode)	39	–	25	48	38	–	–	–	–	36	47	56
DA, DB Inputs (Arith. Mode)	39	37	26	52	38	51	–	–	–	36	47	60
$\overline{EA}$	44	38	29	54	44	53	–	–	–	42	52	
C_n	25	21	–	39	20	38	–	–	–	21	25	48
I_0	39	35	24	48	37	48	–	*15	–	41	46	
I_{4321}	45	43	32	55	44	55	–	*17	–	45	51	
I_{8765}	25	–	–	37	–	–	–	18	22	24	27	
$\overline{I_{EN}}$	–	–	–	–	–	–	–	10	–	–	–	–
$\overline{OEB}$ Enable/Disable	–	–	–	–	–	–	7	–	–	–	–	–
$\overline{OEY}$ Enable/Disable	10	–	–	–	–	–	–	–	–	–	–	–
SIO_0, SIO_3	13	–	–	–	–	–	–	–	–	–	12	18
Clock	58	52	40	72	56	72	24	–	28	55	63	76

*Applies only when leaving special functions.

TABLE III
Set-Up and Hold Times (All in ns)
CAUTION: READ NOTES TO TABLE III.
NA = Not Applicable; no timing constraint.

Input	With Respect to to this Signal	HIGH-to-LOW Set-up	HIGH-to-LOW Hold	LOW-to-HIGH Set-up	LOW-to-HIGH Hold	Comment
Y	Clock	NA	NA	10	0	To store Y in RAM or Q
$\overline{WE}$ HIGH	Clock	5	Note 2	Note 2	0	To Prevent Writing
$\overline{WE}$ LOW	Clock	NA	NA	30	0	To Write into RAM
A,B as Sources	Clock	20	0	NA	NA	See Note 3
B as a Destination	Clock and $\overline{WE}$ both LOW	0	Note 4	Note 4	0	To Write Data only into the Correct B Address
QIO_0, QIO_3	Clock	NA	NA	10	0	To Shift Q
I_{8765}	Clock	30	Note 5	Note 5	0	
$\overline{IEN}$ HIGH	Clock	10	Note 2	Note 2	0	To Prevent Writing
$\overline{IEN}$ LOW	Clock	NA	NA	10	0	To Write into Q

Am2910

MAXIMUM RATINGS (Above which the useful life may be impaired)

Storage Temperature	−65°C to +150°C
Temperature (Ambient) Under Bias	−55°C to +125°C
Supply Voltage to Ground Potential	−0.5V to +7.0V
DC Voltage Applied to Outputs for High Output State	−0.5V to V_{CC} max.
DC Input Voltage	−0.5V to +5.5V
DC Output Current, Into Outputs	30mA
DC Input Current	−30mA to +5.0mA

ELECTRICAL CHARACTERISTICS The Following Conditions Apply Unless Otherwise Specified:

COM'L T_A = 0°C to +70°C V_{CC} = 5.0V ±5%   MIN. = 4.75V   MAX. = 5.25V

MIL T_C = −55°C to +125°C V_{CC} = 5.0V ±10%   MIN. = 4.50V   MAX. = 5.50V

DC CHARACTERISTICS OVER OPERATING RANGE

Parameters	Description	Test Conditions (Note 1)		Min.	Typ. (Note 2)	Max.	Units
V_{OH}	Output HIGH Voltage	V_{CC} = MIN., I_{OH} = −1.6mA V_{IN} = V_{IH} or V_{IL}		2.4			Volts
V_{OL}	Output LOW Voltage	V_{CC} = MIN. V_{IN} = V_{IH} or V_{IL}	Y_{0-11}, I_{OL} = 12mA			0.5	Volts
			$\overline{PL}$, $\overline{VECT}$, $\overline{MAP}$, $\overline{FULL}$, I_{OL} = 8mA				
V_{IH}	Input HIGH Level (Note 4)	Guaranteed Input Logical HIGH voltage for all inputs		2.0			Volts
V_{IL}	Input LOW Level (Note 4)	Guaranteed input logical LOW voltage for all inputs				0.8	Volts
V_I	Input Clamp Voltage	V_{CC} = MIN., I_{IN} = −18mA				−1.5	Volts
I_{IL}	Input LOW Current	V_{CC} = MAX., V_{IN} = 0.5V	D_{0-11}			−0.87	mA
			CI, $\overline{CCEN}$			−0.54	
			I_{0-3}, $\overline{OE}$, $\overline{RLD}$			−0.72	
			$\overline{CC}$			−1.31	
			CP			−2.14	
I_{IH}	Input HIGH Current	V_{CC} = MAX., V_{IN} = 2.7V	D_{0-11}			80	μA
			CI, $\overline{CCEN}$			30	
			I_{0-3}, $\overline{OE}$, $\overline{RLD}$			40	
			$\overline{CC}$			50	
			CP			100	
I_I	Input HIGH Current	V_{CC} = MAX., V_{IN} = 5.5V				1.0	mA
I_{SC}	Output Short Circuit Current (Note 3)	V_{CC} = MAX.		−30		−85	mA
I_{OZL}	Output OFF Current	V_{CC} = MAX. $\overline{OE}$ = 2.4V	V_{OUT} = 0.5V			−50	μA
I_{OZH}			V_{OUT} = 2.4V			50	
I_{CC}	Power Supply Current	V_{CC} = MAX.	T_A = 25°C		195	320	mA
			Am2910PC, DC T_A = 0°C to +70°C			344	
			T_A = +70°C			280	
			Am2910DM, FM T_C = −55°C to +125°C			340	
			T_C = +125°C			227	

Notes: 1. For conditions shown as MIN. or MAX., use the appropriate value specified under Electrical Characteristics for the applicable device type.
2. Typical limits are at V_{CC} = 5.0V, 25°C ambient and maximum loading.
3. Not more than one output should be shorted at a time. Duration of the short circuit test should not exceed one second.
4. These input levels provide no guaranteed noise immunity and should only be tested in a static-, noise-free environment.

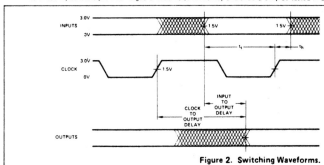

See Tables A for t_s and t_h for various inputs. See Tables B for combinational delays from clock and other inputs to outputs. See Figure 5 for timing of a typical CCU cycle.

Figure 2. Switching Waveforms.

Am2910

SWITCHING CHARACTERISTICS

The tables below define the Am2910 switching characteristics. Tables A are set-up and hold times relative to the clock LOW-to-HIGH transition. Tables B are combinational delays. Tables C are clock requirements. All measurements are made at 1.5V with input levels at 0V or 3V. All values are in ns.

TYPICAL ROOM TEMPERATURE CHARACTERISTICS (T_A = 25°C, V_{CC} = 5.0V, C_L = 50pF)

A. Set-up and Hold Times

Input	t_s	t_h
$D_i \rightarrow R$	9	3
$D_i \rightarrow PC$	34	1
I_0-I_3	64	0
$\overline{CC}$	46	0
$\overline{CCEN}$	49	0
CI	26	2
$\overline{RLD}$	18	2

B. Combinational Delays

Input	Y	PL, $\overline{VECT}$, $\overline{MAP}$	Full
D_0-D_{11}	14	—	—
I_0-I_3	40	27	—
$\overline{CC}$	21	—	—
$\overline{CCEN}$	23	—	—
CP(note) I = 8, 9, 15	54	—	29
CP All other I	26	—	29
$\overline{OE}$		—	—

C. Clock Requirements

Minimum Clock LOW Time	30	ns
Minimum Clock HIGH Time	30	ns
Minimum Clock Period, I=8, 9, 15		ns
Minimum Clock Period, I=14		ns

(Clock periods for other instructions are determined by external conditions.)

Note: These instructions are conditional on the counter. Delays from CP to outputs will be longer if the instruction prior to the clock was 4 or 12 or $\overline{RLD}$ was LOW.

GUARANTEED ROOM TEMPERATURE CHARACTERISTICS (T_A = 25°C, V_{CC} = 5.0V, C_L = 50pF)

A. Set-up and Hold Times

Input	t_s	t_h
$D_i \rightarrow R$		
$D_i \rightarrow PC$		
I_0-I_3		
$\overline{CC}$		
$\overline{CCEN}$		
CI		
$\overline{RLD}$		

B. Combinational Delays

Input	Y	PL, $\overline{VECT}$, $\overline{MAP}$	Full
D_0-D_{11}			
I_0-I_3			
$\overline{CC}$			
$\overline{CCEN}$			
CP(note) I = 8, 9, 15			
CP All other I			
$\overline{OE}$			

C. Clock Requirements

Minimum Clock LOW Time		ns
Minimum Clock HIGH Time		ns
Minimum Clock Period, I=8, 9, 15		ns
Minimum Clock Period, I=14		ns

(Clock periods for other instructions are determined by external conditions.)

Note: These instructions are conditional on the counter. Delays from CP to outputs will be longer if the instruction prior to the clock was 4 or 12 or $\overline{RLD}$ was LOW.

GUARANTEED CHARACTERISTICS OVER COMMERCIAL OPERATING RANGE
Am2910PC, DC (T_A = 0°C to +70°C, V_{CC} = 4.75V to 5.25V, C_L = 50pF)

A. Set-up and Hold Times

Input	t_s	t_h
$D_i \rightarrow R$	15	5
$D_i \rightarrow PC$	58	3
I_0-I_3	100	0
$\overline{CC}$	80	0
$\overline{CCEN}$	85	0
CI	45	5
$\overline{RLD}$	35	3

B. Combinational Delays

Input	Y	PL, $\overline{VECT}$, $\overline{MAP}$	Full
D_0-D_{11}	25	—	—
I_0-I_3	65	48	—
$\overline{CC}$	45	—	—
$\overline{CCEN}$	40	—	—
CP(note) I = 8, 9, 15	92	—	—
CP All other I	65	—	50
$\overline{OE}$		—	—

C. Clock Requirements

Minimum Clock LOW Time	50	ns
Minimum Clock HIGH Time	30	ns
Minimum Clock Period, I=8, 9, 15		ns
Minimum Clock Period, I=14		ns

(Clock periods for other instructions are determined by external conditions.)

Note: These instructions are conditional on the counter. Delays from CP to outputs will be longer if the instruction prior to the clock was 4 or 12 or $\overline{RLD}$ was LOW.

GUARANTEED CHARACTERISTICS OVER MILITARY OPERATING RANGE
Am2910DM, FM (T_C = −55°C to +125°C, V_{CC} = 4.5V to 5.5V, C_L = 50pF)

A. Set-up and Hold Times

Input	t_s	t_h
$D_i \rightarrow R$		
$D_i \rightarrow PC$		
I_0-I_3		
$\overline{CC}$		
$\overline{CCEN}$		
CI		
$\overline{RLD}$		

B. Combinational Delays

Input	Y	PL, $\overline{VECT}$, $\overline{MAP}$	Full
D_0-D_{11}			
I_0-I_3			
$\overline{CC}$			
$\overline{CCEN}$			
CP(note) I = 8, 9, 15			
CP All other I			
$\overline{OE}$			

C. Clock Requirements

Minimum Clock LOW Time		ns
Minimum Clock HIGH Time		ns
Minimum Clock Period, I=8, 9, 15		ns
Minimum Clock Period, I=14		ns

(Clock periods for other instructions are determined by external conditions.)

Note: These instructions are conditional on the counter. Delays from CP to outputs will be longer if the instruction prior to the clock was 4 or 12 or $\overline{RLD}$ was LOW.

Am2909 · Am2911

OPERATION OF THE Am2909/Am2911

Figure 5 lists the select codes for the multiplexer. The two bits applied from the microword register (and additional combinational logic for branching) determine which data source contains the address for the next microinstruction. The contents of the selected source will appear on the Y outputs. Figure 5 also shows the truth table for the output control and for the control of the push/pop stack. Figure 6 shows in detail the effect of S_0, S_1, $\overline{FE}$ and PUP on the Am2909. These four signals define what address appears on the Y outputs and what the state of all the internal registers will be following the clock LOW-to-HIGH edge. In this illustration, the microprogram counter is assumed to contain initially some word J, the address register some word K, and the four words in the push/pop stack contain R_a through R_d.

Address Selection

OCTAL	S_1	S_0	SOURCE FOR Y OUTPUTS	SYMBOL
0	L	L	Microprogram Counter	μPC
1	L	H	Register	REG
2	H	L	Push-Pop stack	STK0
3	H	H	Direct inputs	D_i

Output Control

OR_i	$\overline{ZERO}$	$\overline{OE}$	Y_i
X	X	H	Z
X	L	L	L
H	H	L	H
L	H	L	Source selected by S_0 S_1

Z = High Impedance

Synchronous Stack Control

$\overline{FE}$	PUP	PUSH-POP STACK CHANGE
H	X	No change
L	H	Increment stack pointer, then push current PC onto STK0
L	L	Pop stack (decrement stack pointer)

H = High
L = Low
X = Don't Care

Figure 5.

CYCLE	S_1, S_0, $\overline{FE}$, PUP	μPC	REG	STK0	STK1	STK2	STK3	Y_{OUT}	COMMENT	PRINCIPLE USE
N	0 0 0 0	J	K	Ra	Rb	Rc	Rd	J	Pop Stack	End
N+1	—	J+1	K	Rb	Rc	Rd	Ra	—		Loop
N	0 0 0 1	J	K	Ra	Rb	Rc	Rd	J	Push μPC	Set-up
N+1	—	J+1	K	J	Ra	Rb	Rc	—		Loop
N	0 0 1 X	J	K	Ra	Rb	Rc	Rd	J	Continue	Continue
N+1	—	J+1	K	Ra	Rb	Rc	Rd	—		
N	0 1 0 0	J	K	Ra	Rb	Rc	Rd	K	Pop Stack;	End
N+1	—	K+1	K	Rb	Rc	Rd	Ra	—	Use AR for Address	Loop
N	0 1 0 1	J	K	Ra	Rb	Rc	Rd	K	Push μPC;	JSR AR
N+1	—	K+1	K	J	Ra	Rb	Rc	—	Jump to Address in AR	
N	0 1 1 X	J	K	Ra	Rb	Rc	Rd	K	Jump to Address in AR	JMP AR
N+1	—	K+1	K	Ra	Rb	Rc	Rd	—		
N	1 0 0 0	J	K	Ra	Rb	Rc	Rd	Ra	Jump to Address in STK0;	RTS
N+1	—	Ra+1	K	Rb	Rc	Rd	Ra	—	Pop Stack	
N	1 0 0 1	J	K	Ra	Rb	Rc	Rd	Ra	Jump to Address in STK0;	
N+1	—	Ra+1	K	J	Ra	Rb	Rc	—	Push μPC	
N	1 0 1 X	J	K	Ra	Rb	Rc	Rd	Ra	Jump to Address in STK0	Stack Ref
N+1	—	Ra+1	K	Ra	Rb	Rc	Rd	—		(Loop)
N	1 1 0 0	J	K	Ra	Rb	Rc	Rd	D	Pop Stack;	End
N+1	—	D+1	K	Rb	Rc	Rd	Ra	—	Jump to Address on D	Loop
N	1 1 0 1	J	K	Ra	Rb	Rc	Rd	D	Jump to Address on D;	JSR D
N+1	—	D+1	K	J	Ra	Rb	Rc	—	Push μPC	
N	1 1 1 X	J	K	Ra	Rb	Rc	Rd	D	Jump to Address on D	JMP D
N+1	—	D+1	K	Ra	Rb	Rc	Rd	—		

X = Don't care, 0 = LOW, 1 = HIGH, Assume C_n = HIGH
Note: STK0 is the location addressed by the stack pointer.

Figure 6. Output and Internal Next-Cycle Register States for Am2909/Am2911.

Am2909 · Am2911

Figure 7 illustrates the execution of a subroutine using the Am2909. The configuration of Figure 3 is assumed. The instruction being executed at any given time is the one contained in the microword register (μWR). The contents of the μWR also controls (indirectly, perhaps) the four signals S_0, S_1, $\overline{FE}$, and PUP. The starting address of the subroutine is applied to the D inputs of the Am2909 at the appropriate time.

In the columns on the left is the sequence of microinstructions to be executed. At address J+2, the sequence control portion of the microinstruction contains the command "Jump to sub-

routine at A". At the time T_2, this instruction is in the μWR, and the Am2909 inputs are set-up to execute the jump and save the return address. The subroutine address A is applied to the D inputs from the μWR and appears on the Y outputs. The first instruction of the subroutine, I(A), is accessed and is at the inputs of the μWR. On the next clock transition, I(A) is loaded into the μWR for execution, and the return address J+3 is pushed onto the stack. The return instruction is executed at T_5. Figure 8 is a similar timing chart showing one subroutine linking to a second, the latter consisting of only one microinstruction.

CONTROL MEMORY

Execute Cycle	Microprogram Address	Sequencer Instruction
	J−1	−
T_0	J	−
T_1	J+1	−
T_2	J+2	JSR A
T_6	J+3	−
T_7	J+4	−
	−	−
	−	−
	−	−
	−	−
T_3	A	I(A)
T_4	A+1	−
T_5	A+2	RTS
	−	−
	−	−
	−	−
	−	−
	−	−
	−	−

Execute Cycle		T_0	T_1	T_2	T_3	T_4	T_5	T_6	T_7	T_8	T_9
Clock Signals											
Am2909 Inputs (from μWR)	S_1, S_0	0	0	3	0	0	2	0	0		
	$\overline{FE}$	H	H	L	H	H	L	H	H		
	PUP	X	X	H	X	X	L	X	X		
	D	X	X	A	X	X	X	X	X		
Internal Registers	μPC	J+1	J+2	J+3	A+1	A+2	A+3	J+4	J+5		
	STK0	−	−	−	J+3	J+3	J+3	−	J+5		
	STK1	−	−	−	−	−	−	−	−		
	STK2	−	−	−	−	−	−	−	−		
	STK3	−	−	−	−	−	−	−	−		
Am2909 Output	Y	J+1	J+2	A	A+1	A+2	J+3	J+4	J+5		
ROM Output	(Y)	I(J+1)	JSR A	I(A)	I(A+1)	RTS	I(J+3)	I(J+4)	I(J+5)		
Contents of μWR (Instruction being executed)	μWR	I(J)	I(J+1)	JSR A	I(A)	I(A+1)	RTS	I(J+3)	I(J+4)		

Figure 7. Subroutine Execution. C_n = HIGH

CONTROL MEMORY

Execute Cycle	Microprogram Address	Sequencer Instruction
	J−1	−
T_0	J	−
T_1	J+1	−
T_2	J+2	JSR A
T_9	J+3	−
	−	−
	−	−
	−	−
	−	−
T_3	A	−
T_4	A+1	−
T_5	A+2	JSR B
T_7	A+3	−
T_8	A+4	RTS
	−	−
	−	−
T_6	B	RTS
	−	−
	−	−

Execute Cycle		T_0	T_1	T_2	T_3	T_4	T_5	T_6	T_7	T_8	T_9
Clock Signals											
Am2909 Inputs (from μWR)	S_1, S_0	0	0	3	0	0	3	2	0	2	0
	$\overline{FE}$	H	H	L	H	H	L	L	H	L	H
	PUP	X	X	H	X	X	H	L	X	L	X
	D	X	X	A	X	X	B	X	X	X	X
Internal Registers	μPC	J+1	J+2	J+3	A+1	A+2	A+3	B+1	A+4	A+5	J+4
	STK0	−	−	−	J+3	J+3	J+3	A+3	J+3	J+3	−
	STK1	−	−	−	−	−	−	J+3	−	−	−
	STK2	−	−	−	−	−	−	−	−	−	−
	STK3	−	−	−	−	−	−	−	−	−	−
Am2909 Output	Y	J+1	J+2	A	A+1	A+2	B	A+3	A+4	J+3	J+4
ROM Output	(Y)	I(J+1)	JSR A	I(A)	I(A+1)	JSR B	RTS	I(A+3)	RTS	I(J+3)	I(J+4)
Contents of μWR (Instruction being executed)	μWR	I(J)	I(J+1)	JSR A	I(A)	I(A+1)	JSR B	RTS	I(A+3)	RTS	I(J+3)

Figure 8. Two Nested Subroutines. Routine B is Only One Instruction. C_n = HIGH

Am2909/Am2911

MAXIMUM RATINGS (Above which the useful life may be impaired)

Storage Temperature	-65°C to $+150^\circ$C
Temperature (Ambient) Under Bias	-55°C to $+125^\circ$C
Supply Voltage to Ground Potential	-0.5 V to $+7.0$ V
DC Voltage Applied to Outputs for HIGH Output State	-0.5 V to $+V_{CC}$ max.
DC Input Voltage	-0.5 V to $+7.0$ V
DC Output Current, Into Outputs	30 mA
DC Input Current	-30 mA to $+5.0$ mA

OPERATING RANGE

P/N	Ambient Temperature	V_{CC}
Am2909/2911DC, PC	0°C to $+70^\circ$C	4.75 V to 5.25 V
Am2909/2911DM, FM	-55°C to $+125^\circ$C	4.50 V to 5.50 V

STANDARD SCREENING
(Conforms to MIL-STD-883 for Class C Parts)

Step	MIL-STD-883 Method		Conditions	Level Am2909/Am2911PC, DC	Level Am2909/Am2911DM, FM
Pre-Seal Visual Inspection	2010	B		100%	100%
Stabilization Bake	1008	C	24-hour 150°C	100%	100%
Temperature Cycle	1010	C	-65°C to $+150^\circ$C 10 cycles	100%	100%
Centrifuge	2001	B	10,000 G	100% *	100%
Fine Leak	1014	A	5 x 10^{-8} atm-cc/sec	100% *	100%
Gross Leak	1014	C2	Fluorocarbon	100% *	100%
Electrical Test Subgroups 1 and 7	5004		See below for definitions of subgroups	100%	100%
Insert Additional Screening here for Class B Parts					
Group A Sample Tests Subgroup 1				LTPD = 5	LTPD = 5
Subgroup 2				LTPD = 7	LTPD = 7
Subgroup 3	5005		See below for definitions of subgroups	LTPD = 7	LTPD = 7
Subgroup 7				LTPD = 7	LTPD = 7
Subgroup 8				LTPD = 7	LTPD = 7
Subgroup 9				LTPD = 7	LTPD = 7

*Not applicable for Am2909PC or Am2911PC.

ADDITIONAL SCREENING FOR CLASS B PARTS

Step	MIL-STD-883 Method		Conditions	Level Am2909/Am2911DMB, FMB
Burn-In	1015	D	125°C 160 hours min.	100%
Electrical Test Subgroup 1	5004			100%
Subgroup 2				100%
Subgroup 3				100%
Subgroup 7				100%
Subgroup 9				100%
Return to Group A Tests in Standard Screening				

GROUP A SUBGROUPS
(as defined in MIL-STD-883, method 5005)

Subgroup	Parameter	Temperature
1	DC	25°C
2	DC	Maximum rated temperature
3	DC	Minimum rated temperature
7	Function	25°C
8	Function	Maximum and minimum rated temperature
9	Switching	25°C
10	Switching	Maximum Rated Temperature
11	Switching	Minimum Rated Temperature

Am2909 · Am2911

ELECTRICAL CHARACTERISTICS OVER OPERATING RANGE (Unless Otherwise Noted)

Parameters	Description	Test Conditions (Note 1)			Min.	Typ. (Note 2)	Max.	Units
V_{OH}	Output HIGH Voltage	V_{CC} = MIN., $V_{IN} = V_{IH}$ or V_{IL}	MIL	$I_{OH} = -1.0$mA	2.4			Volts
			COM'L	$I_{OH} = -2.6$mA	2.4			
V_{OL}	Output LOW Voltage	V_{CC} = MIN., $V_{IN} = V_{IH}$ or V_{IL}	$I_{OL} = 4.0$mA				0.4	Volts
			$I_{OL} = 8.0$mA				0.45	
			$I_{OL} = 12$mA (Note 5)				0.5	
V_{IH}	Input HIGH Level	Guaranteed input logical HIGH voltage for all inputs			2.0			Volts
V_{IL}	Input LOW Level	Guaranteed input logical LOW voltage for all inputs	MIL				0.7	Volts
			COM'L				0.8	
V_I	Input Clamp Voltage	V_{CC} = MIN., $I_{IN} = -18$mA					−1.5	Volts
I_{IL}	Input LOW Current	V_{CC} = MAX., $V_{IN} = 0.4$V	C_n				−1.08	mA
			Push/Pop, $\overline{OE}$				−0.72	
			Others (Note 6)				−0.36	
I_{IH}	Input HIGH Current	V_{CC} = MAX., $V_{IN} = 2.7$V	C_n				40	μA
			Push/Pop				40	
			Others (Note 6)				20	
I_I	Input HIGH Current	V_{CC} = MAX., $V_{IN} = 7.0$V	C_n, Push/Pop				0.2	mA
			Others (Note 6)				0.1	
I_{OS}	Output Short Circuit Current (Note 3)	V_{CC} = MAX.	$Y_0 - Y_3$		−30		−100	mA
			C_{n+4}		−30		−85	
I_{CC}	Power Supply Current	V_{CC} = MAX. (Note 4)				80	130	mA
I_{OZL}	Output OFF Current	V_{CC} = MAX., $\overline{OE} = 2.7$V	$V_{OUT} = 0.4$V				−20	μA
I_{OZH}			$V_{OUT} = 2.7$V				20	

Notes: 1. For conditions shown as MIN. or MAX., use the appropriate value specified under Electrical Characteristics for the applicable device type.
    2. Typical limits are at V_{CC} = 5.0V, 25°C ambient and maximum loading.
    3. Not more than one output should be shorted at a time. Duration of the short circuit test should not exceed one second.
    4. Apply GND to C_n, R_0, R_1, R_2, R_3, OR_0, OR_1, OR_2, OR_3, D_0, D_1, D_2, and D_3. Other inputs open. All outputs open. Measured after a LOW-to-HIGH clock transition.
    5. The 12mA guarantee applies only to Y_0, Y_1, Y_2 and Y_3.
    6. For the Am2911, D_i and R_i are internally connected. Loading is doubled (to same values as Push/Pop).

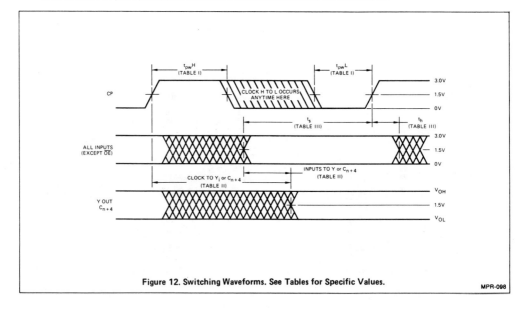

Figure 12. Switching Waveforms. See Tables for Specific Values.

MPR-098

Am2909 · Am2911

SWITCHING CHARACTERISTICS
OVER OPERATING RANGE

Tables I, II, and III below define the timing characteristics of the Am2909 and Am2911 over the operating voltage and temperature range. The tables are divided into three types of parameters; clock characteristics, combinational delays from inputs to outputs, and set-up and hold time requirements. The latter table defines the time prior to the end of the cycle (i.e., clock LOW-to-HIGH transition) that each input must be stable to guarantee that the correct data is written into one of the internal registers.

Measurements are made at 1.5V with $V_{IL} = 0V$ and $V_{IH} = 3.0V$. For three-state disable tests, $C_L = 5.0pF$ and measurement is to 0.5V change on output voltage level.

TABLE I
CYCLE TIME AND CLOCK CHARACTERISTICS

TIME	COMMERCIAL	MILITARY
Minimum Clock LOW Time	30	35
Minimum Clock HIGH Time	30	35

TABLE II

MAXIMUM COMBINATIONAL PROPAGATION DELAYS
(all in ns, $C_L = 50pF$ (except output disable tests))

From Input	COMMERCIAL		MILITARY	
	Y	C_{n+4}	Y	C_{n+4}
D_i	17	30	20	32
S_0, S_1	30	48	40	50
OR_i	17	30	20	32
C_n	–	14	–	16
$\overline{ZERO}$	30	48	40	50
$\overline{OE}$ LOW (enable)	25	–	25	–
$\overline{OE}$ HIGH (disable)	25	–	25	–
Clock ↑ $S_1S_0 = LH$	43	55	50	62
Clock ↑ $S_1S_0 = LL$	43	55	50	62
Clock ↑ $S_1S_0 = HL$	80	95	90	102

Operating Range	Part Numbers	Power Supply	Temperature Range
Commercial	Am2909PC, DC Am2911PC, DC	5.0V ± 5%	$T_A = 0°C$ to +70°C
Military	Am2909DM, FM Am2911DM	5.0V ± 10%	$T_C = -55°C$ to +125°C

TABLE III
GUARANTEED SET-UP AND HOLD TIMES (all in ns) (Note 1)

From Input	Notes	COMMERCIAL		MILITARY	
		Set-Up Time	Hold Time	Set-Up Time	Hold Time
$\overline{RE}$		22	5	22	5
R_i	2	10	5	12	5
PUSH/POP		26	6	30	7
$\overline{FE}$		26	5	30	5
C_n		28	5	30	5
D_i	2	30	0	35	3
OR_i		30	0	35	3
S_0, S_1		45	0	50	0
$\overline{ZERO}$		45	0	50	0

Notes: 1. All times relative to clock LOW-to-HIGH transition.
2. On Am2911, R_i and D_i are internally connected together and labeled D_i. Use R_i set-up and hold times when D inputs are used to load register.

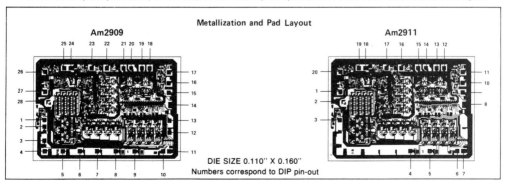

Metallization and Pad Layout
Am2909   Am2911

DIE SIZE 0.110'' X 0.160''
Numbers correspond to DIP pin-out

Am2930

MAXIMUM RATINGS (Above which the useful life may be impaired)

Storage Temperature	−65 to +150°C
Temperature (Ambient) Under Bias	−55 to +125°C
Supply Voltage to Ground Potential	−0.5 to +7.0V
DC Voltage Applied to Outputs for High Output State	−0.5V to V_{CC} max.
DC Input Voltage	−0.5 to +5.5V
DC Output Current, Into Outputs	30mA
DC Input Current	−30 to +5.0mA

OPERATING RANGE

Part Number	Temperature	V_{CC}
Am2930PC, DC	T_A = 0 to 70°C	4.75V to 5.25V
Am2930DM, FM	T_C = −55 to +125°C	4.50V to 5.50V

DC CHARACTERISTICS OVER OPERATING RANGE

Parameters	Description	Test Conditions (Note 1)			Min	Typ (Note 2)	Max	Units
V_{OH}	Output HIGH Voltage	V_{CC} = MIN., V_{IN} = V_{IL} or V_{IH}	Y_0, Y_1, Y_2, Y_3 $\overline{G}$, C_{n+4}, C_{i+4}	I_{OH} = −1.6mA	2.4			Volts
			$\overline{P}$, $\overline{FULL}$, $\overline{EMPTY}$	I_{OH} = −1.2mA	2.4			
V_{OL}	Output LOW Voltage	V_{CC} = MIN. V_{IN} = V_{IL} or V_{IH}	Y_0, Y_1, Y_2, Y_3	I_{OL} = 20mA (COM'L)			0.5	Volts
				I_{OL} = 16mA (MIL)			0.5	
			$\overline{G}$, C_{n+4} C_{i+4}	I_{OL} = 16mA			0.5	
			$\overline{P}$, $\overline{FULL}$, $\overline{EMPTY}$	I_{OL} = 12mA			0.5	
V_{IH}	Input HIGH Level (Note 4)				2.0			Volts
V_{IL}	Input LOW Level (Note 4)						0.8	Volts
V_I	Input Clamp Voltage	V_{CC} = MIN., I_{IN} = −18mA					−1.5	Volts
I_{IL}	Input LOW Current	V_{CC} = MAX., V_{IN} = 0.5V	D_{0-3}				−.360	mA
			I_{0-4}, $\overline{RE}$, $\overline{IEN}$, CP, $\overline{OE}$				−.702	
			$\overline{CC}$				−.657	
			C_i				−2.31	
			C_n				−3.25	
I_{IH}	Input HIGH Current	V_{CC} = MAX., V_{IN} = 2.7V	D_{0-3}				20	μA
			I_{0-4}, $\overline{RE}$, $\overline{IEN}$, CP, $\overline{OE}$				40	
			$\overline{CC}$				50	
			C_i				90	
			C_n				250	
I_I	Input HIGH Current	V_{CC} = MAX., V_{IN} = 5.5V					1.0	mA
I_{SC}	Output Short Circuit Current (Note 3)	V_{CC} = MAX.			−30		−85	mA
I_{OZL}	Output OFF Current	V_{CC} = MAX., $\overline{OE}$ = 2.4V	V_{OUT} = 0.5V				−50	μA
I_{OZH}			V_{OUT} = 2.4V				50	
I_{CC}	Power Supply Current (Note 5)	V_{CC} = 5.0V	T_A = 25°C			150	205	mA
		V_{CC} = MAX.	T_C = −55 to +125°C				239	
			T_C = +125°C				170	
			T_A = 0 to 70°C				220	
			T_A = 70°C				185	

Notes: 1. For conditions shown as MIN. or MAX., use the appropriate value specified under Electrical Characteristics for the applicable device type.
2. Typical limits are at V_{CC} = 5.0V, 25°C ambient and maximum loading.
3. Not more than one output should be shorted at a time. Duration of the short circuit test should not exceed one second.
4. These input levels provide no guaranteed noise immunity and should only be tested in a static-, noise-free environment.
5. Minimum I_{CC} is at maximum temperature.

Am2930 SWITCHING CHARACTERISTICS

Tables A, B, C and D define the timing characteristics of the Am2930. Measurements are made at 1.5V with $V_{IL} = 0V$ and $V_{IH} = 3.0V$. For three-state disable tests, $C_L = 5.0pF$ and measurement is to 0.5V change on output voltage level.

I. Typical Room Temperature Performance.
$V_{CC} = 5.0V$, $T_A = 25°C$

TABLE IA
Clock Characteristics.

Minimum Clock LOW Time	18ns
Minimum Clock HIGH Time	20ns

TABLE IB
Output Enable/Disable Times.
All in ns.
$C_L = 5.0pF$ for output disable tests.

From	To	Enable	Disable
$\overline{OE}$	Y	18	17
$\overline{CC}$ (Note 1)	Y	39	27
I_{4-0} (Note 1)	Y	57	41

TABLE IC
Combinational Propagation Delays.
All in ns.
Outputs fully loaded. $C_L = 50pF$.

From Input	To Output Y	$\overline{G}$, $\overline{P}$	C_{n+4}	C_{i+4} $I_4=L$	C_{i+4} $I_4=H$	$\overline{Full}$	$\overline{Empty}$
I_{4-0}	61	50	57	61	69	52	–
$\overline{CC}$	46	32	39	–	53	29	–
C_n	25	–	17	–	32	–	–
C_i	–	–	–	14	14	–	–
CP	52	40	46	33	58	40	40
D	37	23	30	–	43	–	–
$\overline{IEN}$	–	–	–	–	–	27	–

Note 1: "Suspend" instruction.

TABLE ID
Set-up and Hold Times. All in ns.
All relative to clock
LOW-to-HIGH transition.

Input	CP: Set-up Time	Hold Time
I_{4-0}	68	0
$\overline{CC}$	53	0
$\overline{IEN}$	39	0
C_n	28	0
C_i	18	3
D ($\overline{RE}$ = L, I_{4-0} = 0-8 or 10-15)	14	0
D (All other conditions)	44	0
$\overline{RE}$	13	2

II. Guaranteed Performance Over Commercial Operating Range.
$V_{CC} = 4.75$ to $5.25V$, $T_A = 0$ to $70°C$

TABLE IIA
Clock Characteristics.

Minimum Clock LOW Time	31ns
Minimum Clock HIGH Time	33ns

TABLE IIB
Output Enable/Disable Times.
All in ns.
$C_L = 5.0pF$ for output disable tests.

From	To	Enable	Disable
$\overline{OE}$	Y	27	26
$\overline{CC}$ (Note 1)	Y	55	37
I_{4-0} (Note 1)	Y	80	55

TABLE IIC
Combinational Propagation Delays.
All in ns.
Outputs fully loaded. $C_L = 50pF$.

From Input	To Output Y	$\overline{G}$, $\overline{P}$	C_{n+4}	C_{i+4} $I_4=L$	C_{i+4} $I_4=H$	$\overline{Full}$	$\overline{Empty}$
I_{4-0}	81	67	77	80	91	69	–
$\overline{CC}$	63	45	55	–	72	42	–
C_n	32	–	25	–	45	–	–
C_i	–	–	–	22	22	–	–
CP	69	53	61	43	78	55	55
D	49	33	40	–	59	–	–
$\overline{IEN}$	–	–	–	–	–	40	–

Note 1: "Suspend" instruction.

TABLE IID
Set-up and Hold Times. All in ns.
All relative to clock
LOW-to-HIGH transition.

Input	CP: Set-up Time	Hold Time
I_{4-0}	114	0
$\overline{CC}$	75	0
$\overline{IEN}$	55	0
C_n	43	0
C_i	32	5
D ($\overline{RE}$ = L, I_{4-0} = 0-8 or 10-15)	25	2
D (All other conditions)	66	2
$\overline{RE}$	24	4

III. Guaranteed Performance Over Military Operating Range.
$V_{CC} = 4.5$ to $5.5V$, $T_C = -55$ to $+125°C$

TABLE IIIA
Clock Characteristics.

Minimum Clock LOW Time	35ns
Minimum Clock HIGH Time	35ns

TABLE IIIB
Output Enable/Disable Times.
All in ns.
$C_L = 5.0pF$ for output disable tests.

From	To	Enable	Disable
$\overline{OE}$	Y	32	31
$\overline{CC}$ (Note 1)	Y	60	42
I_{4-0} (Note 1)	Y	85	60

TABLE IIIC
Combinational Propagation Delays.
All in ns.
Outputs fully loaded. $C_L = 50pF$.

From Input	To Output Y	$\overline{G}$, $\overline{P}$	C_{n+4}	C_{i+4} $I_4=L$	C_{i+4} $I_4=H$	$\overline{Full}$	$\overline{Empty}$
I_{4-0}	88	74	82	87	97	78	–
$\overline{CC}$	68	52	60	–	78	47	–
C_n	37	–	30	–	46	–	–
C_i	–	–	–	23	23	–	–
CP	74	58	66	48	84	60	60
D	55	38	45	–	65	–	–
$\overline{IEN}$	–	–	–	–	–	45	–

Note 1: "Suspend" instruction.

TABLE IIID
Set-up and Hold Times. All in ns.
All relative to clock
LOW-to-HIGH transition.

Input	CP: Set-up Time	Hold Time
I_{4-0}	124	0
$\overline{CC}$	80	0
$\overline{IEN}$	69	0
C_n	52	0
C_i	37	5
D ($\overline{RE}$ = L, I_{4-0} = 0-8 or 10-15)	30	2
D (All other conditions)	72	2
$\overline{RE}$	29	4

INDEX

CP1600
  direct addressing, 2-3
  implied addressing, 2-4
  I/O port pin characteristics, 2-30
  stack addressing, 2-5
8086
  AX register, 5-5
  base relative, indexed addressing, 5-15
  BCD addition, 5-49
  BCD division, 5-51
  BCD multiplication, 5-51
  BCD subtraction, 5-49
  Bus Interface Unit (BIU), 5-30
  BX register, 5-5
  Code Segment register, 5-8
  Control signals, simple and complex, 5-28
  CX register, 5-5
  data memory base relative addressing, 5-16
  Data Segment register, 5-11
  Destination Index register, 5-10
  direct memory addressing, 5-13
  dual bus complexity, 5-28
  DX register, 5-5
  −8080A register compatibility, 5-5
  Execution Unit (EU), 5-30
  external memory addressing, 5-24
  Extra Segment register, 5-10
  hold, in min. and max. mode systems, 5-39
  implied memory addressing, 5-14
  indirect addressing, 5-22
  instruction queue, 5-31
  interrupt return, 5-46
  interrupt vector table, 5-44
  I/O port addressing, 5-21
  maskable interrupt, 5-44, 5-45
  non-maskable interrupt, 5-44, 5-45
  program counter, 5-8
  program relative addressing, 5-21
  reset, 5-27
  Segment registers, 5-7
  software interrupts, 5-44, 5-45
  Source Index register, 5-10
  Stack Pointer register, 5-9, 5-11
  Stack Segment register, 5-9
8212, used in INS8900 system
  as input port, 1-39, 1-40
  as output port, 1-41
8251 USART, used in INS8900 system, 1-43
8253 Programmable Counter/Timer,
  used in INS8900 system, 1-43
8288 Bus Controller
  interrupt signals, 5-110
  I/O bus mode, 5-109
  memory protect, 5-109
  write control signals, 5-109

INS8900. *See also* PACE/INS8900
  address/data lines, demultiplexing, 1-38
  control signal polarity considerations, 1-39
  8251 and 8253 used with, 1-43

  8255 PPI devices used with, 1-42, 1-43
  6800 support devices not compatible with, 1-44
INS8900/PACE. *See* PACE/INS8900

MC68000
  absolute data addressing, 7-30
  address registers, 7-3
  autovector interrupt response, 7-27
  bus and address error exception processing, 7-25
  data registers, 7-2
  exception priorities, 7-23
  exception vector table, 7-23
  externally generated exceptions, 7-23
  immediate data addressing, 7-37
  implied register addressing, 7-32
  internally generated exceptions, 7-22, 7-23
  interrupt request exception processing, 7-26
  memory interface, 7-9
  operating modes, 7-22
  program counter relative addressing, 7-32
  read timing, 7-13
  register direct addressing, 7-30
  register indirect address, 7-30
  reset exception processing, 7-25
  spurious interrupt, 7-27
  Stack Pointer, 7-4
  Status register, 7-5
  wait state, 7-14
  write timing, 7-14
MicroNova I/O bus, 4-12

Nova
  addressing, 4-6−9
  address space, 4-23
  busy status, 4-21
  done status, 4-21
  registers, 4-22
9440
  initialization, 4-16
  instruction fetch, 4-24
  I/O wait states, 4-28
  memory read, 4-24
  system bus, 4-14

PACE. *See also* PACE/INS8900
  clock signals, 1-11
  level 0 interrupt problems, 1-24
  stack interrupt problems, 1-22
  substrate bias voltage, generating, 1-35
  TTL-level bus, 1-2
PACE/INS8900
  address latches and decoders, 1-2
  bidirectional transceiver element (BTE), 1-2
  BTE mode control signals, 1-37
  busses, floating, 1-15
  CONTIN signal, 1-15
  CPU-initiated DMA block data transfers, 1-16
  cycle-stealing DMA, 1-17, 1-18
  data input cycle, 1-12
  data output cycles, 1-13
  direct addressing options, 1-24

PACE/INS8900 (Continued)
  direct indexed addressing, 1-7
  DMA block data transfers, 1-16, 1-17
  execution speed, 1-1
  Extend signal for slow I/O operations, 1-13
  Extend used to suspend I/O during DMA operations, 1-17
  Halt state, 1-14
  interrupts, 1-21–23
  logic level, 1-2
  machine cycle, 1-12
  NHALT signal, 1-15
  power supply, 1-1
  processor stall, 1-15
  registers, saving during interrupts, 1-22
  return from interrupt, 1-21
  signal differences, 1-10
  split base page, 1-6, 1-7
  stack interrupts, 1-5
  STE clock frequency, 1-35
  system timing element (STE), 1-2
TMS 9900
  context switch, 3-5, 3-6
  memory addresses, 3-3
  direct addressing, 3-6
  indexed addressing, 3-6
  instruction execution sequences, 3-18
  internal operations machine cycle, 3-15
  interrupt vector map, 3-27
  multiple interrupt hardware considerations, 3-30
  program memory addressing, 3-8
TMS 9902
  break, 3-91
  break logic, 3-86
  Control register, 3-86
  device initialization, 3-84
  error flags, 3-93
  internal clock signal, 3-88
  interrupts, 3-86, 3-87
  receive logic, 3-92
  receiver status, 3-87
  register addressing, 3-84
  reset, 3-86
  Status register, 3-87
  test mode, 3-86
  timer status, 3-87
  Transmit/Receive Data Rate register, 3-88
  transmit event sequence, 3-90
  transmitter status, 3-87
TMS 9903
  asynchronous break logic, 3-103
  asynchronous receive, 3-110
  asynchronous transmit, 3-109
  bisync logic, 3-105
  clock rate option, 3-106
  Control register, 3-100
  CRC options, 3-106
  device intialization, 3-109
  device reset, 3-100
  external sync logic, 3-104
  HDLC abort, 3-104
  initialize CRC, 3-100
  initialize transmit/receive, 3-100
  interface signal, 3-97
  interrupt enable/disable, 3-102
  modes, 3-97
  monosync logic, 3-105
  NRZI select, 3-106
  Parameter register, 3-103

  parity options, 3-105
  Read register addressing, 3-100
  receive CRC, 3-102
  received character size, 3-106
  register select, 3-100
  SDLC configurations, 3-105
  SDLC loop, 3-111
  SDLC receive logic, 3-104
  serial I/O signals, 3-98
  Status register, 3-106
  sync strip, 3-105
  test mode, 3-102
  transmit controls, 3-102
  transmit operation, 3-104
  Write register addressing, 3-101
TMS 9940
  CRU bit utilization, 3-59
  hold logic, 3-64
  idle logic, 3-64
  expansion mode, 3-60
  multiprocessor system interface, 3-61
  simple CRU I/O mode, 3-59
  sync mode, 3-64
TMS 9980 series clock logic, 3-49
2901
  ALU logic, 8-13
  carry status, 8-24
  data input, 8-33
  half-carry status, 8-25
  local RAM, 8-7
  microcode, sample, 8-25
  microinstruction, 8-9
  multiply, 8-35
  overflow status, 8-24
  Q register, 8-12
  RAM and CPU registers, 8-10
  rotate operation, 8-25
  sample microcode, 8-25
  shift operation, 8-25
  sign status, 8-24
  status logic, 8-24
  zero status, 8-24
2903
  ALU functions, 8-57
  ALU input, 8-48
  ALU input options, 8-44
  ALU operand options, 8-49
  ALU output destinations, 8-61
  ALU shifter, 8-61
  Arithmetic and Logic Unit (ALU), 8-49
  destination options, 8-59
  double length normalization, 8-67, 8-68
  increment function, 8-72
  local RAM addressing, 8-56
  normalize special functions, 8-67
  shift logic, 8-60
  sign extend logic, 8-63
  signal/magnitude twos complement function, 8-69
  single length normalization, 8-7
  slice significance select, 8-45
  status signals, 8-46
  three-address microcycle, 8-56
  two-address timing, 8-56
  twos complement divide function, 8-77
  twos complement multiply function, 8-73
  unsigned multiply, 8-72
2909 output mask, 8-99
2909/2911
  Address, 8-95

data output, 8-99
immediate data input, 8-95
incrementer, 8-99
instruction skip, 8-100
jump, 8-100
microprogram counter, 8-99
multiple jump, 8-103
output select, 8-95
output zero control, 8-99
sequential addresses, 8-99
single instruction reexecution, 8-100
stack, 8-100
subroutine call, 8-102
subroutine nesting, 8-103
2910
address output, 8-110
condition codes, 8-113
data input, 8-110
increment, 8-113
instruction codes, 8-113
microprogram counter, 8-110, 8-113
microprogram initialization, 8-120
microprogram jump, 8-120
microprogram jump-to-subroutine, 8-120
stack, 8-113
2930 series
accumulator, 8-125
carry logic, 8-129
Index register, 8-129
instruction codes, 8-125
Program Counter, 8-129
Stack Pointer, 8-129
Stack, Push, Pop, 8-129

Z8000
auto-increment, 6-18
auto-decrement, 6-18
base relative addressing, 6-15
block transfer instructions, 6-40
byte registers, 6-9
conditional jump instructions, 6-40
divide instruction, 6-38
implied indexed addressing, 6-15
implied memory addressing, 6-11

indirect memory addressing, 6-18
instruction fetch machine cycle, 6-23
I/O instructions, 6-36
LDPS instruction, 6-39
M1 and M0 instructions, 6-41
memory interface logic, 6-20
memory read machine cycle, 6-23
memory write machine cycle, 6-23
multiply instruction, 6-39
New Program Status Area pointer, 6-8
normal mode, 6-3
primary memory reference instructions, 6-37
principal memory addressing modes, 6-37
Program Counter 6-6
Refresh Counter, 6-28
secondary memory reference instructions, 6-37
shift instructions, 6-41
sixteen-bit registers, 6-9
software traps, 6-32
Special I/O instructions, 6-37
stack, 6-18
stack instructions, 6-41
Stack Pointer, 6-3
status, 6-6
subroutine call, 6-40
system call, 6-40
system mode, 6-3
thirty-two-bit registers, 6-9
wait state, 6-23
Z8001
address representation, 6-3
base address, 6-9
long segmented base relative addressing, 6-17
long segmented direct memory addressing, 6-13
long segmented indexed addressing, 6-15
program relative addressing, 6-18
segmented mode, 6-7
short segmented base relative addressing, 6-16
short segmented indexed addressing, 6-14
Z8002
direct memory addressing, 6-12
indexed addressing, 6-14
program relative addressing, 6-17
short segmented direct memory addressing, 6-13

OSBORNE/McGraw-Hill Books of Interest

The 8086 Book
 by R. Rector and G. Alexy
8080 Programming for Logic Design
 by Adam Osborne
6800 Programming for Logic Design
 by Adam Osborne
Z80 Programming for Logic Design
 by Adam Osborne

8080A/8085 Assembly Language Programming
 by L. Leventhal
6800 Assembly Language Programming
 by L. Leventhal
Z80 Assembly Language Programming
 by L. Leventhal
6502 Assembly Language Programming
 by L. Leventhal
Z8000 Assembly Language Programming
 by L. Leventhal et al.
Running Wild: The Next Industrial Revolution
 by Adam Osborne
PET/CBM Personal Computer Guide — Second Edition
 by Adam Osborne and Carroll Donahue
PET and the IEEE 488 Bus (GPIB)
 by E. Fisher and C. W. Jensen
Practical Basic Programs
 by L. Poole et al.
Some Common BASIC Programs
 by L. Poole and M. Borchers
Payroll with Cost Accounting — CBASIC
 by Lon Poole et al.
Accounts Payable and Accounts Receivable — CBASIC
 by Lon Poole et al.
General Ledger — CBASIC
 by Lon Poole et al.

Some Common Basic Programs — PET/CBM
 edited by Lon Poole et al.